Encyclopedia of Race and Racism

Encyclopedia of Race and Racism

VOLUME 2

g–r

John Hartwell Moore

EDITOR IN CHIEF

MACMILLAN REFERENCE USA

An imprint of Thomson Gale, a part of The Thomson Corporation

Detroit • New York • San Francisco • New Haven, Conn. • Waterville, Maine • London

Encyclopedia of Race and Racism
John Hartwell Moore, Editor in Chief

For more information, contact
Macmillan Reference USA
An imprint of The Gale Group
27500 Drake Rd.
Farmington Hills, MI 48331-3535
Or you can visit our Internet site at
http://www.gale.com

LIBRARY OF CONGRESS CATALOGING-IN-PUBLICATION DATA

Encyclopedia of race and racism / John H. Moore, editor in chief.
p. cm.
Includes bibliographical references and index.
ISBN 978-0-02-866020-2 (set : alk. paper) — ISBN 978-0-02-866021-9 (vol 1 : alk. paper) — ISBN 978-0-02-866022-6 (vol 2 : alk. paper) — ISBN 978-0-02-866023-3 (vol 3 : alk. paper) — ISBN 978-0-02-866116-2 (ebook)
1. Racism—United States—Encyclopedias. 2. United States—Race relations—Encyclopedias. 3. United States—Ethnic relations—Encyclopedias. 4. Minorities—United States—Social conditions—Encyclopedias. 5. Race relations—Encyclopedias. 6. Racism—Encyclopedias. I. Moore, John H., 1939- II. Title.

E184.A1E584 2008
305.800973—dc22

2007024359

ISBN-13: 978-0-02-866020-2 (set);
ISBN-10: 0-02-866020-X (set);
0-02-866021-8 (vol. 1);
0-02-866022-6 (vol. 2);
0-02-866023-4 (vol. 3)

This title is also available as an e-book.
ISBN-13: 978-0-02-866116-2; ISBN-10: 0-02-866116-8
Contact your Gale representative for ordering information.
Printed in the United States of America

10 9 8 7 6 5 4 3 2 1

Editorial Board

Editorial and Production Staff

PROJECT EDITORS

Rachel Kain
Mark Mikula
Nicole Watkins

CONTRIBUTING EDITORS

Deirdre Blanchfield
Jason M. Everett
Dawn M. Sobraski
Andrew Specht

EDITORIAL TECHNICAL SUPPORT

Mark Drouillard
Mike Weaver

MANUSCRIPT EDITORS

Judith Clinebell
Jessica Hornik Evans
Peter Jaskowiak
Christine Kelley
John Krol
Michael J. O'Neal
Dave Salamie

PROOFREADERS

Stacey Chamberlin
Pamela S. Dear
Melodie Monahan
Kathy Wilson

INDEXER

Laurie Andriot

PRODUCT DESIGN

Pamela A. E. Galbreath

IMAGING

Leitha Etheridge-Sims
Lezlie Light

GRAPHIC ART

Pre-PressPMG

RIGHTS ACQUISITION MANAGEMENT

Sue Rudolph

Mardell Glinski-Schultz

Tracie Richardson

COMPOSITION

Evi Abou-El-Seoud

MANUFACTURING

Wendy Blurton

DIRECTOR, NEW PRODUCT DEVELOPMENT

Hélène Potter

PUBLISHER

Jay Flynn

Contents

G

GALARZA, ERNESTO
1905–1984

Ernesto Galarza was born August 15, 1905, in Jalcocotán, Nayarit, a small state on the central Pacific coast of Mexico. When he was eight years old, his family migrated to the United States. His family, like thousands of others, was motivated to migrate because of the social and economic instability brought about by the Mexican Revolution (1910–1917). These migrants were drawn to the United States by the need for cheap labor in agriculture and other U.S. industries. In his autobiography, *Barrio Boy* (1971), Galarza describes the difficulties on the trek north to California, his cultural assimilation, and his early experiences working in the fields. Despite these difficulties, however, Galarza excelled in school and eventually earned a Ph.D. in history at Columbia University in 1944.

Galarza distinguished himself as an activist and scholar in the areas of labor, community development, and education. Before becoming a labor organizer, he served for eight years as director of the Office of Labor and Education at the Pan American Union (PAU) in Washington, D.C. During that time, he wrote about a dozen short studies on topics ranging from educational conditions to militarism in Latin America. In 1948 he left the PAU to become an organizer in California for the National Farm Labor Union (NFLU), which was later renamed the National Agricultural Workers Union (NAWU). He focused his efforts on organizing agricultural workers and defending their civil rights. After participating in more than a dozen strikes, he came to realize that one of the major obstacles to unionizing farmworkers was the 1942 Mexican Farm Labor Program Agreement. Known as the Bracero Program, this agreement granted Mexican laborers (*braceros*) temporary work contracts in U.S. agriculture. In 1956, after conducting meticulous research on the living and working conditions of braceros, he published *Strangers in Our Fields,* which turned public opinion against the Bracero Program and led to its eventual termination in 1964. His book *Merchants of Labor,* published in 1964, is a seminal study of the bracero labor system; it exposed the collusion between growers and the government in exploiting braceros.

After withdrawing from labor organizing in 1960, Galarza shifted his attention to urban issues confronting the Mexican community. In doing so, he devoted himself to defending the civil rights of Mexicans and played a key role in creating community organizations. He was also involved in a very important mobilization to prevent the destruction of Alviso, a barrio north of San Jose, California. However, although the community struggled to prevent the city of San Jose from annexing Alviso, the city prevailed. In 1968 Galarza established the Southwest Council of La Raza, which he initially envisioned as a grassroots organization for community development. Eventually, it evolved into the National Council of La Raza (NCLR), which in the early twenty-first century is the most important organization advocating civil rights and socioeconomic advancement for Latinos.

In the early 1970s, Galarza founded and directed the Studio Laboratory, a resource center for bilingual education teachers in San Jose. The goals of the center were to change the curriculum, train teachers, and encourage parent involvement. He organized parents to demand quality bilingual education for their children and was a pioneer in the development of bilingual/bicultural materials. He wrote more than a dozen books for bilingual children, emphasizing Mexican cultural values and nature. In 1971, for example, he published *Historia Verdadera de una Gota de Miel* (*The True Story of a Drop of Honey*). Galarza died in San Jose in 1984.

SEE ALSO *Braceros, Repatriation, and Seasonal Workers; Chávez, César Estrada; Day Laborers, Latino; Farmworkers; United Farm Workers Union.*

BIBLIOGRAPHY

Galarza, Ernesto. 1956. *Strangers in Our Fields*. Washington, DC: Joint United States-Mexico Trade Union Committee.

———. 1964. *Merchants of Labor: The Bracero Story*. Santa Barbara, CA: McNally & Loftin.

———. 1970. *Spiders in the House and Workers in the Field*. Notre Dame, IN: University of Notre Dame Press.

———. 1971. *Barrio Boy: The Story of a Boy's Acculturation*. Notre Dame, IN: University of Notre Dame Press.

———. 1971. *Historia Verdadera de Una Gota de Miel*. San Jose, CA: Editorial Almaden.

———. 1974. "Alviso: A Town Besieged by 'Progress.'" In *Action Research: In Defense of the Barrio, Interviews with Ernesto Galarza, Guillermo Flores, and Rosalio Muñoz*, collected by Mario Barrera and Geralda Vialpando. Los Angeles, CA: Aztlan Publications.

———. 1977. *Farm Workers and Agribusiness in California, 1947–1960*. Notre Dame, IN: University of Notre Dame Press.

Roberto M. De Anda

GALTON, FRANCIS
1822–1911

Francis Galton was born in Birmingham, England, on February 16, 1822 and he died in Surrey, England, on January 17, 1911. He was a founding figure in the field of mental testing and intelligence and in the pseudoscience of "proving" class and racial inferiorities. He also helped develop the racist theories of social Darwinism that led to nineteenth and twentieth century eugenics programs in Europe and North America. He is recognized in the discipline of psychology as a pioneer of standardized intelligence testing and of original anthropometric and sociological methods used to demonstrate the importance of heredity in human differences. In this area, he also helped develop an experimental research laboratory that led to the development of the subfield of experimental psychology.

Sir Francis Galton was influenced by his cousin Charles Darwin's evolutionary theories, which led him to explore the relationship between intelligence and the evolution of humans. Following Darwin's ideas about biological evolution of species, he added the social to the biological and developed a hierarchy of ranked races, nations, and classes. Through a simple rendering of evolutionary ideas into a social theory—known as "social Darwinism"—Galton held that biological differences were predestined by genetics, with limited effects possible from environmental influence. Individual differences, he argued, are the result of two principle factors, environment and heredity, with heredity being by far the more important. It was a simple step from Galton's social Darwinist theories to the eugenics movements of the nineteenth and twentieth centuries that advocated the unnatural selection of the "fittest" individuals and groups to reproduce, while social engineering programs were established to discourage or prohibit "inferior" individuals from reproducing. It is an irony of history that Francis Galton—whose racist analysis has since been discredited—was knighted by the English crown in 1909 for his contributions, while Charles Darwin—whose works remain influential in the early twenty-first century—was not.

Galton's *Hereditary Genius* (1869) is his classic work and represents a milestone in the history of racialist scholarship. Like Arthur Gobineau, whose *Essai sur l'inégalité des races humaines* (*Essay on the Inequality of the Human Races*) was published in four volumes from 1853 to 1855, Galton used racism as a major framework in asserting that there are higher and lower races. Galton graded men on a scale of genius from "A" to "G", with "G" being the highest grade. He found the greatest majority of humans were in the "mediocre classes"—represented by the bulge in the "bell curve" he developed in relation to intelligence testing—while there were only a small number of men of great ability and an equally small number of mental defectives. Thus, he posited that the rarity of genius and the vast abundance of mediocrity was no accident, but due to natural, hereditary forces. Further, those at the "genius" level were not found randomly among all humans, but instead concentrated in the upper classes of northern Europeans.

According to Galton, classical Greece and the England of his day possessed the highest percentage of per capita geniuses of the first class, while the Negro race had failed to produce any man of genius in all of history (1869, pp. 325–337). For Galton, genius clustered in families, and no matter how rich the social and cultural environment, a genius could never be created out of a mediocre man. Indeed, he held that the success of some English families over generations proved his hypothesis that intelligence is inherited. Although *Hereditary Genius* represented unsound science with an *a priori* bias that intelligence is hereditary, it was a useful political tool for many, and the book was reprinted many times and was an inspiration to proponents of eugenics and social Darwinism well into the twentieth century.

Added to Galton's testing and analysis of hereditary difference was his fear that the lower races and poorer classes were breeding at a faster rate than the upper classes and higher races. Fearing a "dysgenic" trend of future genetic inferiority, he coined the term *eugenics*, meaning "science of the well-born," and advocated eugenic programs that would limit the number of individuals from "defective," and "inferior" races and classes. Galton's ideas are linked to the origins of the eugenics movement, which sought to improve the racial stock of humans through selective mating. Indeed, some eugenics groups called themselves "Galton Societies." Thus, Galton's *Hereditary Genius* lies at the base of much of the literature that makes a false correlation among race, class, and intelligence.

Galton introduced to science the idea of the "bell curve," around which human intelligence can be measured and interpreted along a "normal distribution." For Galton, human intelligence varied by individuals (from geniuses to the "feebleminded" and retarded) and by groups (from the highest genius [English noblemen] to the dullest [Negroes]) along a predictable bell curve of frequency distribution. It is noteworthy that the controversial 1994 work *The Bell Curve: Intelligence and Class Structure in American Life*, by Richard J. Herrnstein and Charles Murray, was a revival of the theories of Galton. The book opens with a reverent bow to Galton, and the authors restate Galton's idea that some people are smarter, positing the novel racist idea that East Asians (Japanese and Chinese) are more intelligent than whites.

Galton made a number of methodological contributions to the discipline of psychology, including pioneering the development, application, and analysis of tests demonstrating hereditary differences in ability. He assumed that human intelligence is innate and can be objectively measured though the administration of tests. His intelligence tests were mainly devoted to measurement of the acuity of the senses, and they were developed and administered at the anthropometric laboratory at his South Kensington Museum, where he tested his hypotheses regarding the influence of heredity on the characteristics of related persons, particularly parents and children, twins, and brothers and sisters. From his results, he persuaded a number of educational institutions in England to keep systematic anthropometric records on their students, thus establishing the precedent for the public application of racialist data in education. By these methods, Galton created the first systematic body of data on individual differences.

Galton devised simple tests for his anthropometric lab, many of which are still in use, some in their original forms. Examples include the "Galton bar" for measuring visual discrimination of length, the "Galton whistle" for determining the ability to hear the highest audible pitch, and a test measuring muscular strength using graduated weights in order to determine kinesthetic ability. Galton believed that sensory skill is a measure of intellect. He noted, for example, that extreme mental retardates tend to be defective in their ability to discriminate cold, heat, and pain. His association of reaction time with intelligence was established with the g-factor in IQ tests. In the 1890s, Galton's reaction-time test was applied by R. Meade Bache to three groups by race: Caucasians, American Indians, and Negroes. Bache found that Caucasians had the slowest reaction times, American Indians had the fastest, and that Negroes were in between the two. However, with science having become thoroughly racialized, Bache's analysis interpreted that rapid reaction time is inversely related to intelligence, so the slower Caucasians were actually deemed to be smarter.

Galton innovated the study of twins, believing that observing differences between fraternal and identical twins demonstrates the significance of heredity. Biologically identical twins are destined to be alike, even if they are reared apart, whereas fraternal twins are not necessarily similar even if they are reared together. The conclusion from twins and other Galtonian studies was that heredity is more important than environment. In this respect, he influenced the racialist work of Sir Cyril Burt (1883–1971) and Edward Lee Thorndike (1874–1949), both of whom have since been discredited. Challengers of Galton, including Franz Boas (1858–1942), have emphasized the role of environmental factors, focusing the debate about race and intelligence around the relative importance of heredity and environment.

The mental tests that succeeded Galton's reaction-time tests were originally developed by the French psychologist Alfred Binet (1857–1911), whose nonracialist interest in ability testing represented a stark contrast to Galton. Binet was unable to define or accurately measure what he called "general intelligence." His more complex view of intelligence was more in tune with modern psychology, but he died before his view prevailed. His tests were grossly oversimplified by others and made into the first standardized intelligence tests, which were then graded according to an "intelligence quotient," or "IQ." "Mental age" was divided by the chronological age and multiplied by 100, with the net result being the intelligence quotient. This type of testing rested upon two basic premises: (1) intelligence can be measured objectively by tests yielding an Intelligence Quotient, or "IQ," and (2) IQ is largely inherited, (Galton asserted that heredity accounted for 80% of performance; 60% has been alleged by Herrnstein and Murray in *The Bell Curve*).

Galton pioneered the application of the rating-scale and questionnaire methods, as well as "free association tests." He developed statistical methods for the analysis of individual differences, adapting techniques previously used only by mathematicians (such as the correlation coefficient analyzing the relationship between two variables). Thus, Galton was a founder of quantitative methods in psychology. The chair in eugenics at the University of London was first held by his protégé Karl Pearson (1857–1936), who also founded the university's Department of Applied Statistics, reflecting the influence of his mentor.

Galton's role in pioneering tests of ability and intelligence is still highly regarded in the field of educational and psychological testing, while his class-biased and racially motivated interpretations have yet to be thoroughly critiqued. Since the beginning of intelligence testing, calculating and ranking differences by race has been a key feature of this enterprise. It remains so to this day, along with other measures of academic potential, such as the common measure of scholastic achievement in the United States, the SATs.

SEE ALSO *Eugenics, History of.*

BIBLIOGRAPHY

PRIMARY WORKS

1869. *Hereditary Genius: An Inquiry into Its Laws and Consequences.* London: Macmillan. (2nd ed. published in 1892).

1879. "Psychometric Experiments." *Brain* 2: 149–162.

1883. *Inquiries into Human Faculty and Its Development.* London: Macmillan.

1888. "Co-relations and their Measurement, Chiefly from Anthropological Data." *Proceedings of the Royal Society of London,* 45: 135–145.

SECONDARY WORKS

Anastasi, Anne. 1988. *Psychological Testing.* 6th ed. New York: Macmillan.

Fluehr-Lobban, Carolyn. 2006. *Race and Racism: An Introduction.* Lanham, MD: AltaMira Press.

Herrnstein, Richard J., and Charles Murray. 1994. *The Bell Curve: Intelligence and Class Structure in American Life.* New York: Free Press.

Carolyn Fluehr-Lobban

GANDHI, MOHANDAS KARAMCHAND
1869–1948

Born on October 2, 1869, in the coastal town of Porbandar in the Gujarati-speaking Kathiawar region of western India, Mohandas Karamchand Gandhi died in 1948, five and a half months after achieving his goal of India's freedom from British rule. Though less successful in attaining two other aims of his, Hindu-Muslim amity and justice for India's "untouchables," Gandhi (a Hindu, like a majority of his compatriots) saw to it that independent India assured equal rights to its Muslim and other religious minorities, and to "untouchables." He claimed that his efforts in India were relevant for "an aching, storm-tossed and hungry world" (*Collected Works*, vol. 98, pp. 218–220), and the participation of thousands of men and women in the nonviolent campaigns he led, first in South Africa and then in India, inspired nonviolent struggles on different continents.

In the 1960s, Martin Luther King Jr. would acknowledge the debt he and the American civil rights movement owed to Gandhi, and there have been similar expressions from Cesar Chavez (1927–1993), the North American farmworkers' leader; from Abdul Ghaffar Khan (1890–1988), who in the 1930s raised a nonviolent army of Pashtuns not far from the Afghan–Pakistan border; from Benigno Aquino (1932–1983), the chief opponent of Marcos's military regime in the Philippines; from His Holiness the Dalai Lama of Tibet (1935–); and from Aung San Suu Kyi (1945–), the leading fighter for democratic rights in her country of Burma (Myanmar); and others.

Though the Gandhis belonged to the "bania," or trader, caste (third in the hierarchy of Hindu castes, but a "high" caste still), Mohandas's father, Karamchand, was not a trader or businessman. He was a public official, the "first minister" to the ruler of Porbandar state, which included the town of Porbandar. The British governed much of India directly and the rest indirectly, through chieftains or princes. Porbandar was one of over 500 princely states in India. Karamchand's father, Ota Gandhi, had also been Porbandar's "first minister," as were Ota's father and grandfather.

When Mohandas was seven, Karamchand moved to Rajkot, another princely state in Kathiawar, serving there also as first minister. He and his wife, Putlibai, were liberal by the standards of their time, but their children were enjoined not to touch "untouchables" or Muslims or to eat meat. At thirteen Mohandas was married to Kasturbai Kapadia, who was a few months older and from the same bania caste—virtually all marriages occurred within a caste and when the bride and groom were thirteen or younger.

The boy Mohandas had a rebellious side (he secretly ate meat) and also a prickly conscience (he confessed petty thefts in a note he handed to his ailing father). After Karamchand's death, Mohandas persuaded his mother and other relatives to send him to London to study law, but he was required before departure to promise that he would avoid liquor, meat, and women in England.

IDENTITY IN LONDON

Leaving behind his wife and a newborn son, Mohandas arrived in England in the summer of 1888, enrolled at the Inner Temple (one of London's Inns of Court, a law school), and sought to fashion himself as an "English gentleman," wearing "proper" clothes and learning ballroom dancing, elocution, and the violin. But his bid to find a British identity lasted only a few months. Engaged in London with political and religious questions, and evidently keeping to his three pledges, Gandhi learned public campaigning from England's vegetarian movement, of which he became an active member. In 1891 he returned to India as a barrister who sought Indians' equality with whites but not secession from the British Empire, and he believed that all souls had equal worth, irrespective of skin color or religious views.

In Bombay, western India's biggest city, Gandhi formed a friendship with Rajchandra, a jeweler who was also a scholar of the Hindu, Jaina, and Buddhist religions. Success in the law seemed to elude him, however, and in early 1893 he collided in Rajkot against colonial arrogance. Charles Ollivant, the British officer supervising all princely states in Kathiawar and someone Gandhi had met in England, was examining a charge of impropriety against Gandhi's brother Laxmidas, who pressed his younger brother to intercede. Against his better judgment Gandhi called on his acquaintance, who ordered a servant to remove the young barrister from his office. When the ejected Gandhi threatened a lawsuit, Ollivant dared him to do his worst. Told by India's leading lawyer of the day, Pherozeshah Mehta, that he would invite ruin by suing Ollivant, Gandhi pocketed the affront. But the descendant of "first ministers" fumed and looked for a life outside Kathiawar.

FINDING A PURPOSE

Gandhi did not have to wait for long: A South Africa–based firm with origins in Porbandar asked him if he would assist for a year with a legal case in Pretoria, and Gandhi grabbed the opening. He was twenty-three when, in May 1893, he landed in Port Durban. The three weeks that followed saw more incidents of ejection or attempts at ejection: from a courtroom in Durban, from a train at Pietermaritzburg station, from a stagecoach in Pardekoph in the Transvaal, and from a hotel in Johannesburg. During the Pardekoph incident he was soundly thrashed as well. By the time he reached Pretoria in the first week of June, he was a different man: resolute, realistic, and ready to fight for South Africa's persecuted Indian minority, which had come from all parts of India. He had found a purpose, and now realized how India's "untouchables" felt.

In Pretoria he read Leo Tolstoy's *The Kingdom of God Is Within You* and six volumes on an 1857 revolt in India crushed by the British. He conversed with Christians keen to convert him and exchanged letters with Rajchandra. Christianity was not embraced but thoughts of hate and violence were yielded, as well as "pride of birth and education" (Doke 1909, p. 45). The following year (1894), Gandhi founded a political party, the Natal Indian Congress, and in 1906 he felt he had found a special way to fight. Coining a phrase, he called it *satyagraha,* which combined two Indian words, *satya* (truth) and *agraha (*firmness). Gandhi translated the phrase variously as "truth-force," "soul-force," or "love-force," and he insisted on nonviolent fighting. When people opposing an unjust law refuse to kill but are ready to be killed, their *satyagraha* could win, claimed Gandhi.

Gandhi, 1903. *Mohandas Gandhi spent twenty years working as an attorney in South Africa and developing his strategy of nonviolent fighting.* KEYSTONE/GETTY IMAGES.

One year in South Africa turned out to be a period of twenty years, during which Gandhi made money as a lawyer, gave large sums to South Africa's Indian community, simplified his life and the lives of his wife and four sons, took vows of celibacy and poverty for the rest of his life, launched a journal, *Indian Opinion,* and started two centers for community living and training in *satyagraha,* one in Phoenix near Durban in Natal and the other in Lawley near Johannesburg in the Transvaal.

Several whites backed Gandhi in South Africa and worked at his side, including Christians and Jews, clergymen, journalists, secretaries, and housewives. Henry Polak (a Jewish journalist born in Britain), Hermann Kallenbach (a German Jew trained in architecture), and Joseph Doke (a Baptist minister) were among them. While Polak edited *Indian Opinion* for several years, Kallenbach placed at Gandhi's disposal the 1,000 acres that housed the Lawley center, which was named Tolstoy Farm in honor of the Russian novelist and thinker whose views had influenced Gandhi, and who, shortly before dying, expressed great satisfaction at Gandhi's battles in South Africa. In 1909 Joseph Doke published (in England) the first Gandhi biography. Scores of others would follow.

GANDHI AND AFRICANS

Gandhi's interaction with Africans was more limited. His aim of Indian equality with whites in South Africa was different from a fight for African rights. Moreover, for some time Gandhi seemed to share a general Indian sense of superiority vis-à-vis Africans. In 1908, however, he envisioned a day when "all the different races [of South Africa] commingle and produce a civilization that perhaps the world has not yet seen" (*Collected Works*, vol. 8, p. 323). That year Jan Smuts, a future prime minister of South Africa, warned that the Indian defiance initiated by Gandhi could lead one day to African defiance (Nayar 1989, vol. 4, p. 168), a possibility Gandhi recognized and welcomed.

Later, after returning to India, Gandhi would speak in his weekly, *Young India*, of political conversations with Africans in South Africa (March 28, 1929), but the discussions are not recorded. John Dube, a founder of the African National Congress, was one of the leaders Gandhi had met; Dube's Ohlange center in Phoenix predated Gandhi's center in the same place. In 1914 Dube spoke of the impact made on him by the bravery of nonviolent Indians whom Gandhi had inspired but added that he could not see Africans fighting that way; they were likely, Dube thought, to invite a massacre by hitting back at whites (Patel 1990, pp. 216–217). While not joining the Indian defiance, Africans silently applauded and blessed it.

Led by Gandhi, hundreds of Indians of different religions and castes, mostly from the Transvaal, peacefully broke discriminatory laws from 1908 to 1910 and incurred imprisonment; and in 1913 thousands of Indians working in Natal's coal mines, sugar plantations, the railways, hotels, and restaurants disobeyed laws and marched for rights. Many women joined the disobedience. Repression from the South African government was brutal, and over two dozen Indians were killed, but strong reactions in India, Britain, and South Africa forced the government to modify its laws. Claiming victory, a forty-five-year-old Gandhi returned in January 1915 to India, where people called him "Mahatma" (great soul).

STRATEGY FOR INDIA

British control over India seemed permanent in 1915. Peasants, the bulk of the population, appeared grateful for stability; the British policy of divide and rule had separated Hindus from Muslims; leaders of the "untouchables" preferred alien rule to an independence dominated by "high" castes; and India's princes relied on British officials to prevent uprisings by subjects. These facts shaped Gandhi's strategy: He would aim to enlist the peasants, unite Hindus and Muslims, convince caste Hindus of the folly of untouchability, and ask the princes to find safety in their subjects' goodwill. And he would present the weapon of *satyagraha* to his people.

His years in South Africa had familiarized Gandhi with Indians of all kinds and from all regions. Although establishing a base in Ahmedabad, the largest city in Gujarati-speaking India, he traveled to almost every part of the land, sharing his vision, challenging and encouraging his audiences, recruiting allies, and probing issues where *satyagraha* could be employed. In 1917 *satyagraha* was successfully used in defense of indigo-raising peasants in Bihar in eastern India; in 1918 it was conducted on behalf of peasants in rural Gujarat and textile workers in Ahmedabad; and April 1919 saw the first all-India demonstration in the country's entire history, when place after place responded to Gandhi's call for a nonviolent protest against new curbs on free speech.

A massacre occurred on April 13, 1919, in Amritsar, the Sikhs' holy city: At least 389 Indians—Hindus, Muslims, and Sikhs—were gunned down in less than ten minutes by troops commanded by a British general, Reginald Dyer. The following year Gandhi launched a joint Hindu-Muslim struggle for Indian independence and in support of Muslim control over Islam's holy places in the Middle East.

In this program of "nonviolent noncooperation," tens of thousands were arrested, including some women; lawyers quit British-run courtrooms, students left British-run colleges, and a host of distinguished Indians returned British honors and titles. Muslims were invited to Hindu homes, and vice versa; and the removal of untouchability was made a central plank of the Indian National Congress (INC), the country's principal political organization (founded in 1885), which accepted Gandhi as its guide. India was experiencing both a new spirit and a new unity.

Fearing uncontrollable unrest, and also acknowledging his commitment to nonviolence, the British refrained from arresting Gandhi. In February 1922, however, after a demonstrating mob killed twenty-two policemen in

Chauri Chaura in northern India, Gandhi called off the movement, saying he did not want a foundation of murder for a free India. The suspension demoralized the public, and the British felt they could safely arrest Gandhi. He was taken prisoner in March 1922, the first of his six incarcerations in India. In South Africa he had been jailed three times; altogether he spent ten years in prison.

SALT MARCHES

Hindu-Muslim recrimination followed the 1922 suspension. Released after two years, Gandhi gradually rebuilt his nonviolent forces, but it was not until 1930 that he launched another all-India struggle. The issue he chose this time was the British monopoly of the salt trade and the tax on salt. Collecting the salt left by the sea was illegal, as was selling or buying untaxed salt. Gandhi asked Indians on the coast to scoop up their own salt, and Indians elsewhere to buy or sell contraband salt. Since the salt tax hurt every Indian, and the poorest the most, a *satyagraha* against it was an issue on which all united: Hindus and Muslims, caste Hindus, and "untouchables."

Spectacular salt marches made news worldwide, American reporters sent home accounts of police brutalities on violators of salt laws who remained nonviolent, and tens of thousands filled India's jails. A year later, the British viceroy, Lord Irwin, admitted that underestimating a national movement's power was a profound mistake and released Gandhi and his political colleagues of the Indian National Congress. A Gandhi-Irwin accord that followed made coastal salt collection legal, and Gandhi agreed to attend a political conference in London in the fall of 1931, though he did not expect much from it.

Also invited to the London conference, Gandhi's political opponents in India claimed that he did not speak for India's princes, Muslims, or "untouchables." Saying that Indians had to agree among themselves before demanding self-government, British leaders announced the conference's failure, but outside the conference Gandhi made friends with the British people. Based in London's downscale East End, he traveled widely, including to Manchester, where he met textile workers hurt by boycotts in India. The suffering of India's poor was even worse than theirs, Gandhi told them. He was given a warm, understanding response. At England's elite school, Eton, Gandhi told its students: "It can be no pride to you that your nation is ruling over ours. No one chained a slave without chaining himself" (*Collected Works*, vol. 54, p. 82).

AFRICAN AMERICANS

Two years earlier, invited by W. E. B. Du Bois to send a message for African Americans through Du Bois's journal, *The Crisis*, Gandhi had expressed a similar thought: "Let not the twelve million Negroes be ashamed of the fact that they are the grandchildren of slaves. There is no dishonor in being slaves. There is dishonor in being slave-owners." In a note printed next to Gandhi's message, the journal called him "the greatest colored man in the world, and perhaps the greatest man in the world" (*The Crisis*, July 1929).

Gandhi, 1930. *Mohandas Gandhi leads a Salt March in protest of the British monopoly of the salt trade and tax on salt. The spectacular marches made news worldwide.* **CENTRAL PRESS/ GETTY IMAGES.**

In 1936, two African American couples visiting India, Howard and Sue Bailey Thurman and Edward and Phenola Carroll, asked Gandhi why he did not speak of "love" instead of "nonviolence." Admitting his attraction to "love in the Pauline sense," Gandhi added that "love" did not always connote struggle, whereas "nonviolence" did. Mahadev Desai, Gandhi's secretary from 1917, told the Thurmans and the Carrolls that the warmth in Gandhi's welcome to them was unprecedented (Kapur 1992, p. 88). It derived from Gandhi's view that untouchability and slavery were similar evils and that India's fight against imperialism paralleled black America's struggle against racism.

Gandhi asked his visitors "persistent, pragmatic questions about American Negroes, about the course of slavery, and how we had survived it" (Kapur 1992, p. 88). Was color prejudice growing or dying? Did American law recognize marriages between blacks and whites? And so forth. It was during this 1936 conversation (in Bardoli, Gujarat) that Gandhi made the prophetic remark: "Well, if it comes true it may be through the

Negroes that the unadulterated message of non-violence will be delivered to the world" (*Collected Works,* vol. 68, pp. 237–238).

South Africa remained on Gandhi's mind. In 1926 he said in *Young India* (July 22) that he could not imagine "justice being rendered to [South Africa's] Indians, if none is rendered to the natives of the soil." Two years later he reiterated the necessity of African-Indian cooperation: "[Indians] cannot exist in South Africa for any length of time without the active sympathy and friendship of the Africans" (*Young India,* April 5, 1928).

India's natives gained a slice of power in 1937. While the center remained firmly under British control, elected legislatures could form governments in provinces. Following Gandhi's advice, the INC contested elections and formed ministries in a majority of the provinces. But in 1939, when World War II started, the British clipped provincial powers, citing the war's requirements. When London refused to assure Indian independence at the end of the war, the INC broke with the British, its sympathy for the Allied cause notwithstanding, and its ministries resigned.

QUIT INDIA

With popular opinion turning increasingly anti-British, the British encouraging anti-INC elements, especially the Muslim League (ML), which in 1940 demanded secession from India of Muslim-majority areas, and other separatist movements gaining strength, Gandhi asked the INC, in August 1942, to issue a call to the British to quit India. There was a nationwide eruption, which in some places took a violent form. It was the greatest defiance the British had faced in India. It was eventually suppressed, and Gandhi and all INC leaders and tens of thousands of others were quickly put behind bars, yet two outcomes now became certain: India would be free after the war, and the INC would inherit the power left by the departing British.

The INC's leaders—Jawaharlal Nehru (1889–1964), who would be India's prime minister from 1947 to 1964, Vallabhbhai Patel (1875–1950), Abul Kalam Azad (1890–1958), Chakravarti Rajagopalachari (1878–1972), and Rajendra Prasad (1883–1962), among others—were more than political colleagues to Gandhi, and he more than a mentor to them. They had struggled and suffered together.

Released in the summer of 1944, and striving again for a Hindu-Muslim alliance through an agreement between the INC and the ML, Gandhi held fourteen talks in September 1944 with the ML's president, Muhammad Ali Jinnah. But the talks failed. In the summer of 1945 the INC leaders were released. The two years that followed saw intense negotiations involving the British, the INC, and the Muslim League; they also saw the INC leaders separating from Gandhi.

ISOLATION

These leaders felt that agreeing to the division demanded by the ML and Jinnah would put an end to Hindu-Muslim violence. Gandhi thought it would increase the violence. They envisioned India as a militarized, industrial power; Gandhi saw India as a land of peace and he championed rural India. An increasingly isolated Gandhi spent much of 1946 and 1947 in areas that had seen Hindu-Muslim violence, restoring peace and instilling courage in victims.

A London announcement in February 1947 that within months the British would definitely leave India, transferring power to one or more governments, produced a scramble for leverage that heightened the Hindu-Muslim tension, especially in northern India's large Punjab province, which contained areas passionately claimed by both Muslims and non-Muslims (Hindus and Sikhs). As a possible solution, Gandhi asked the INC leaders and Lord Mountbatten, the last British viceroy, to invite Jinnah to head a new government, but the viceroy as well as the INC leaders rejected the proposal.

Gandhi was excluded from the negotiations of April, May, and June 1947 that led to an agreement on independence and India's division into a Hindu-majority India and a Muslim-majority Pakistan. On August 14 Pakistan came into being. The next day independent India emerged. But violence exploded. About half a million were killed, mostly in the Punjab, in August and September 1947. Almost twelve million moved. Half of them, Muslims, trudged westward to Pakistan, and the other half, Hindus and Sikhs, in the opposite direction. On the other hand, Gandhi's 1946–1947 interventions in eastern India probably saved many lives.

EMPOWERING THE WEAK

Close to the day of Indian independence, Gandhi answered, in the city of Calcutta (now Kolkata), a question on coping with doubts:

> I will give you a talisman. Whenever you are in doubt, or when the self becomes too much with you, apply the following test. Recall the face of the poorest and the weakest man whom you may have seen, and ask yourself if the step you contemplate is going to be of any use to him. Will he gain anything by it? Will it restore him to a control over his own life and destiny? . . . Then you will find your doubts and yourself melting away. (Tendulkar 1951–1958, vol. 8, facsimile facing p. 89)

Though INC leaders turned down several of Gandhi's proposals, he supported India's new government led by Nehru and Patel (who became deputy prime minister). Gandhi's view that an "untouchable" should become India's first head of state, occupying the mansion where the British Empire's viceroys had lived, was not endorsed, but, following Gandhi's advice, Nehru and Patel embraced Bhimraro Ramji Ambedkar (1891–1956), the brilliant leader of the "untouchables" who for years had criticized Gandhi and the INC as not being radical enough over caste. Chairing the committee that drafted the Indian constitution, Ambedkar played a crucial role in independent India's evolution.

On January 30, 1948, while walking to a prayer meeting in New Delhi, Gandhi was killed by Nathuram Godse, who planted himself about four feet in front of Gandhi and fired three bullets into his chest and stomach. Godse was part of a group of high-caste Hindus who alleged that Gandhi had emasculated India's Hindus with his nonviolence and friendship with Muslims. Gandhi's wife, Kasturbai, had died four years earlier while the two were prisoners of the British. The Gandhis had four sons, Harilal, Manilal, Ramdas, and Devadas, and fifteen grandchildren.

Gandhi wrote two books (both in the mid-1920s), an autobiography entitled *The Story of My Experiments with Truth*, and *A History of Satyagraha in South Africa*; a tract called *Hind Swaraj* (Indian Home Rule), published in 1910; a translation (in the 1920s) of the Hindu religious text, the *Bhagavad Gita;* and innumerable articles in his journals, *Indian Opinion*, *Young India*, and *Harijan*. The 100 volumes of the *Collected Works of Mahatma Gandhi* contain almost all that he wrote, including letters, and most of his speeches.

SEE ALSO *Anti-Apartheid Movement; Muslims.*

BIBLIOGRAPHY

PRIMARY WORKS

Gandhi, Mohandas Karamchand. 1927–1929. *The Story of My Experiments with Truth*. 2 vols. Translated by Mahadev Desai. Ahmedabad, India: Navajivan.

———. 1951–2000. *Collected Works of Mahatma Gandhi*. 100 vols. New Delhi, India: Publications Division, Ministry of Information and Broadcasting.

SECONDARY WORKS

Ambedkar, B. R. 1945. *What Congress and Gandhi Have Done to the Untouchables*. Bombay, India: Thacker.

Ashe, Geoffrey. 1968. *Gandhi: A Study in Revolution*. Bombay, India: Asia Publishing House.

Brown, Judith. 1990. *Gandhi: Prisoner of Hope*. New Delhi, India: Oxford University Press.

Doke, Joseph J. 1909. *An Indian Patriot in South Africa*. London: Indian Chronicle Press. 1967 edition, New Delhi, India: Publications Division.

Erikson, Erik H. 1969. *Gandhi's Truth: On the Origins of Militant Nonviolence*. New York: Norton.

Fischer, Louis. 1950. *The Life of Mahatma Gandhi*. New York: Harper.

Gandhi, Rajmohan. 2007. *Mohandas: A True Story of the Man, His People, and an Empire*. New Delhi, India: Viking.

Kapur, Sudarshan. 1992. *Raising Up a Prophet: The African-American Encounter with Gandhi*. Boston: Beacon Press.

Nanda, B. R. 1997. *Mahatma Gandhi*. New Delhi, India: Oxford University Press.

Nayar, Sushila. 1989, 1994. *Mahatma Gandhi: India Awakened*, vols. 4 and 5. Ahmedabad, India: Navajivan.

Patel, Ravjibhai. 1990. *The Making of the Mahatma*. Ahmedabad, India: Navajivan.

Pyarelal. 1956–1986. *Mahatma Gandhi*. 5 vols. Ahmedabad, India: Navajivan.

Tendulkar, D. G. 1951–1954. *Mahatma: Life of Mohandas Karamchand Gandhi*. 8 vols. Bombay, India: Times of India Press.

Rajmohan Gandhi

GANGS AND YOUTH VIOLENCE

Gangs are primarily made up of groups of male adolescents and youths who have grown up together as children, usually as cohorts in a low-income neighborhood of a city. Oftentimes, the gang is a multiple-aged peer group, with older members in their late teens or early twenties acting as role models for younger members. According to several researchers (Morales 1982, Short 1996, Vigil 2002), only about 10 percent of the youths in most low-income neighborhoods join gangs. Further, gangs are an outgrowth of the strains and stresses that immigrant and historically marginalized populations experience in urban settings, a phenomenon that can be traced back to the nineteenth century. These populations typically face problems with jobs, living conditions, isolation and segregation from mainstream society, and abrasive interactions with public institutions. These situations and conditions tend to be especially persistent when the immigrants are defined as a distinct race from the dominant society based on physical rather than simply behavioral differences.

THE ROOTS OF URBAN GANGS

There are various factors involved in understanding gangs, such as racism and its repercussions in other realms, including socioeconomic segregation, breakdowns in social control, education difficulties, and antagonistic interactions with law enforcement. Los Angeles is a major city marked by these dynamics, and it will serve as the major multiethnic focus here to highlight broader gang issues. Toward this end, long-term racism and persistent poverty have lingering effects on how life is structured and organized, including basic family dynamics. For example, schooling for minority youth and relations with law enforcement both affect family life, particularly because poor people often receive short shrift from authorities in these major public institutions. Schooling problems, in particular, have plagued the lives and careers of blacks and Latinos (and in some cases, Asians) in the United States. These groups have a long and well-documented history of exclusion from or isolation within public schools, along with other forms of unfair and unequal scholastic treatment, such as the racism that affects testing and "tracked" learning programs. In tandem with institutional racist barriers, this has worked to historically establish an oppositional attitude and lackadaisical approach to the dominant culture's education routines. Remarkably, most families in these communities have been able to weather these conditions and maintain a semblance of stability.

Most of the ethnic (i.e., Chicano, African American, Vietnamese, Puerto Rican, and Salvadoran) communities examined here are made up of members who are, for the most part, physically distinguishable from dominant whites. They have all also faced race-based discrimination, though the impact of race and racism on each group varies. Race, racism, and the attitudes of prejudice that have devalued and disparaged each group, and the groups' subsequent segregation and isolation into ethnic enclaves, are central to understanding the emergence and perpetuation of gangs. Race and class are both heavily implicated in the marginalization of each of these ethnic groups, and in the resultant social and cultural repercussions that have led to street socialization. Nevertheless, each group has unique aspects. Race has been a more overtly dominant issue for African Americans, among whom it is more pervasive and salient in all aspects of life. The dual nature of Chicanos' relationship with dominant society—as natives and immigrants—is similarly distinctive, as is the dual relationship of Puerto Rico's status vis-à-vis the United States.

The entry into the United States of both Salvadorans and Vietnamese entailed global, cold-war political ramifications. Marginalization for many in these communities began before they entered the country. Importantly, similar processes are unfolding in other regions of the globe, as witnessed by the appearance of transnational gangs in places such as Europe and Latin America, where immigration has brought different peoples to urban settings. (In the U.S. context, transnational gangs typically refer to organized networks of peer groups that are connected to one another and operate across national borders.) In addition, the processes of globalization have led to human migration and the marginalization of many families and children.

The street gang dominates the lives of untethered youth in these minority communities because other institutions have become undermined, fragmented, fragile, and largely ineffective. Some of the Los Angeles gangs can be traced as far back as the 1930s, and social neglect, ostracism, economic marginalization, and cultural repression are largely responsible for the endurance of the subculture. Members of these communities have often faced inadequate living conditions, stressful personal and family changes, and racism and cultural repression in schools.

FAMILY LIFE AND GANG MEMBERSHIP

Families do not exist in a vacuum. Even in the oppressive environment generated by the combination of racial prejudice and economic marginalization, most families succeed in raising socially productive children, but a significant number of families cannot. These stressed and overwhelmed families, stripped of their coping skills, often end up in attenuated family arrangements that can include separation, divorce, and single-parent households—which also tend to be low-income households. Home life in poor households or in households undergoing change can be stressful, with parents less able to adequately care for and supervise their children. Street socialization of children emerges in the context of such strained family situations and conditions. Significantly, many of the male children in these situations are raised in a female-centered household, and when they reach adolescence they must learn to contend with the male-dominated street culture. Much of the homophophic nature and organization of the gang stems from the adjustment males make in reconciling these ambivalent experiences and feelings. Most often, they emphasize a hyper-masculinity to compensate for this emotional strain, wiping out any vestige of femininity.

THE GHETTOIZATION OF CHICANO AND AFRICAN-AMERICAN POPULATIONS

Chicanos were initially spread all over the Southwest in little *colonias* (Mexican housing projects or neighborhoods) near where they labored in mining, ranching, and agriculture. In the early twenty-first century they are predominantly found in urban areas, where many work in the low-paid service economy. Historically, their children have been compelled to attend schools where instruction was only in English and where speaking Spanish was punished. While children from the more stable households managed to acquire English and a modicum of the "three R's," despite the handicaps they faced, others could cope only by sitting in the back of the classroom, ignoring their books, ditching school in a show of resistance, and sometimes joining other similarly harassed Chicanos and Chicanas in "race riots" at Anglo-majority schools. Dropping out is the ultimate show of defiance, nurtured by school officials' practice of encouraging their departure or expelling students. Early on, education for Mexicans was referred to as an "Americanization" program—with the aim of providing the children with a more "appropriate culture"—but schools were typically kept separate and unequal.

In the case of African Americans, despite the prevalent racism of the 1920s, the black community in Los Angeles displayed unity and relative economic prosperity—more than one-third of the families owned their own homes. The proliferation of neighborhoods with housing covenants and restrictions, however, was an even more extreme attempt at "keeping them in their place." For this community the problem of street gangs surfaced during the Great Depression and accelerated in the aftermath of World War II, when there was a high rate of immigration from the South. As a result, the problem of ghettoization—of poverty and neighborhood deterioration—soon worsened. Children in overcrowded neighborhoods without sufficient public recreation facilities had no place to play safely. Indeed, only limited opportunities existed for African American youth in organizations such as the Boy Scouts or the YMCA. In the summer, the municipal swimming pools only admitted African Americans and Latinos on special days, after which the pools were drained and then refilled. Knowledge of this historical racism goes a long way in understanding the emergence of gang activity and the state of the African American community in the early 2000s.

Ironically, public housing was introduced to counter the effects of racism by providing decent, affordable housing, but the results only complicated the initial difficulties associated with racism. Living in the "projects" has become a synonym for living in the most destitute, underserved neighborhoods in the city. Most residents are people of color, with only a few public developments of mixed racial groups.

Along with family life being undermined by these patterns of exclusion and isolation, the schools, by incorporating racist assumptions into their teaching and testing procedures, have continually failed to accommodate black and brown youth. The criminal justice system has been an even worse offender, ensuring continued stresses and strains on these communities. Police, courts, and prisons have historically practiced an unofficial type of racism when dealing with racial minority communities, who have harsher treatment, an uneven application of the law, and higher incarceration rates. Los Angeles has been one of the leading centers of this institutionalized legal inequality. This is evident from a recitation of only the best-publicized outbreaks of police-community hostility: the Zoot Suit Riots in 1943, the Watts revolt of 1965, the Black Panther shoot-out in 1968, the Eula Love killing in 1979, and the Rodney King riots of 1992. Statistical data also reveal the disparately high proportion of ethnic minorities arrested, convicted, and imprisoned. Gang members similarly make up a disproportionate number of the imprisoned population. Rather than addressing the roots of gang life, American society has instead attempted to resolve problems associated with gangs by suppression alone. In sum, racism and prejudice in the pre-civil rights decades segregated and isolated most blacks in overcrowded areas of the city, and Mexicans and the new migrants in their neighborhoods all underwent a marginalization process that is still playing out.

NEWER IMMIGRANT POPULATIONS

In contrast, the Salvadoran and Vietnamese populations in Los Angeles (and in the United States) share a more recent migratory background, in both cases from homelands wracked by civil war. Most of the Vietnamese immigrants and a large proportion of those from El Salvador arrived in the United States as political refugees, beginning in the 1970s. The unraveling of social control actually began for both groups in their home countries, where the United States played a prominent role in volatile military situations. Thus, geopolitical considerations are paramount for both groups.

The Central American populations in Los Angeles are relatively new. These groups had to find their way to the United States during a time of economic instability and an intense anti-immigrant social and political climate. The Salvadorans carry the burden of having had to leave their homeland in the midst of a highly charged civil war, with death threats propelling hundreds of thousands out of the country. In Los Angeles, they settled into neighborhoods with high concentrations of Latinos—mostly Chicanos—and pre-existing neighborhood gangs.

Along similar lines, the Vietnamese are best examined within the context of a war-torn homeland and an especially strife-ridden journey to the United States. Most found their way to the United States as members of a second wave of refugees known as the "boat people." What they encountered in the United States was racism from both the white population and racial-ethnic minorities. While many entrepreneurial families prospered in their new community, despite the ethnic hostility that greeted them, many of the youth were drawn into loose-knit gangs formed at school to offer mutual support in the face of racial-ethnic hostility. Like the Chicanos before them, they often encountered language difficulties and racist assumptions in school.

Investigations conducted over several years by graduate students at the University of California, Irvine have shown that relations with police were also difficult. Gang members noted that they received high levels of attention from police. In a recent study of Little Saigon, many informants complained that they have been unjustifiably harassed and even beaten by police on several occasions (Vigil, Yun, and Chang 2004). One twenty-year-old explained: "Sometimes when I drive a fixed-up car, they stop us for nothing. Just because we're young and Vietnamese. We're driving normally, like everybody else is, but they just pull us over. They be searching us, search the car, and we don't have anything. They treated us like shit" (p. 212). African Americans and Chicanos understand this experience all too well, often referring to it as being stopped for DWB, or "driving while black (or brown)."

GANGS AS SOCIAL SUPPORT

Racism and other adjustment issues in the educational context have only fueled the sense of hopelessness and alienation that many children in these minority communities have already experienced. In the face of unpredictable forces and inadequate support structures, the gang comes to be perceived as a bastion of dependability for children with inadequate nurturing in the home and an inability to overcome the barriers they encounter in school. In the eyes of similarly situated children facing an incredible array of challenges, the gang comes to hold appeal as a provider of affiliation, material well-being, protection, and guidance. For many, it is an all-too-scarce source of security and comfort.

The costs that the gang imposes for providing a secure self-identity and sense of belonging, however, can be very high, not only for the individual youth but also for the entire community. While many activities that gang youth engage in together are no different that those pursued by others their age, the alienation to society engendered and nurtured by street socialization also provokes gang activity that has violent consequences for gang members and others. No matter how understandable the motivation for engaging in such "gangbanging" is, the collateral costs to neighborhoods and families are lost on these tough, young gang members. In this self-centered scenario, communities are decaying from the inside out. While larger forces of racism and poverty provide the impetus for such transformations, the gang members themselves unleash great damage on the community, and their violence exacerbates the other problems the community faces.

SEE ALSO *Central Americans; Criminal Justice System; Cultural Deficiency; Latinos.*

BIBLIOGRAPHY

Anderson, Elijah. 1990. *Streetwise: Race, Class, and Change in an Urban Community.* Chicago: University of Chicago Press.

———, and Douglas Massey. 2001. *Problem of the Century: Racial Stratification in the United States.* New York: Russell Sage Foundation.

Bass, Sandra. 2001. "Policing Space, Policing Race: Social Control Imperatives and Police Discretionary Decisions." *Social Justice* 28 (1): 156–173.

Esbensen Finn-Aage, and L. Thomas Winfree Jr. 2001. "Race and Gender Differences Between Gang and Nongang Youths." In *The Modern Gang Reader*, 2nd ed., edited by Jody Miller, Cheryl L. Maxson, and Malcom W. Klein, 106–120. Los Angeles: Roxbury.

Gibbons, Don C. 1997. "Review Essay: Race, Ethnicity, Crime, and Social Policy." *Crime and Delinquency* 43 (2): 358–380.

Matsueda, Ross L., and Karen Heimer. 1987. "Race, Family Structure, and Delinquency: A Test of Differential Association and Social Control Theories." *American Sociological Review* 52 (6): 826–840.

Morales, Armando. 1982. "The Mexican American Gang Member." In *Mental Health and Hispanic Americans*, edited By Rosina Barerra, Marvin Karno, and Javier Escobar, 133–152. New York: Grune and Stratton.

Short, James F. 2002. "Personal, Gang, and Community Career." In *Gangs in America*, 3rd ed., edited by C. Ronald Huff, 3–11. Thousand Oaks, CA: Sage.

Vigil, James Diego. 2002. *A Rainbow of Gangs: Street Cultures in the Mega-City.* Austin: University of Texas Press.

———, Steve Yun, and Jesse Chang. 2004. "A Shortcut to the American Dream? Vietnamese Youth Ganges in Little Saigon." In *Asian American Youth: Culture, Ethnicity, and Identity*, edited by Min Zhou and Jennifer Lee, 207–220. New York: Routledge.

James Diego Vigil

GARNET, HENRY HIGHLAND
1815–1882

Henry Highland Garnet was an orator, preacher, educator, nationalist, and abolitionist. Believed to be a descendant of the Mandingo kings of West Africa, Garnet began life in a slave cabin, and by the time he died in 1882, he had become one of the most significant African American leaders of the nineteenth century. Known for his radical abolitionism, Garnet urged African Americans to resort to militant means to secure their rights.

Garnet was born into slavery in 1815 on the William Spencer plantation near New Market, Maryland. In 1824, Garnet's parents, George and Henrietta Trusty, took their children, escaped through Delaware, and arrived in New York City the following year. Once in New York, George changed the family's surname—a common practice among fugitives—to Garnet. In 1827, when legal slavery ended in New York State, the fugitive Garnets no longer had to fear slave catchers.

Garnet's father believed in education and instilled that value into his son. Shortly after escape from slavery, Garnet immersed himself in schooling. In 1826, he entered New York African Free School. It was here that he began to sharpen the focus of his antislavery struggle. His heart "ached for the children of Africa," he confided, adding that he had nightmares over the "clanking of the chains" and "the voices of the groans." At the school he had the opportunity to reflect on the deeper meaning of freedom. But after graduation, there was little improvement in his life. Racism excluded him from many job opportunities. In 1831, he entered the High School for Colored Youth in New York City. There he studied poetry, Latin, and Greek philosophers. He also met and cultivated lifetime friendships with people such as Alexander Crummell, who was to become famous in his own right as a minister and black leader. In 1835 Garnet enrolled at the Noyes Academy in Canaan, New Hampshire. The Noyes Academy was an awakening for him. Three hundred racists destroyed the school rather than have blacks study there. Even though his stay at the Noyes Academy was short-lived, the impact of Noyes on him was unmistakable. He began to see that violence was needed to fend off racist attacks.

In 1836, Garnet entered Oneida Theological Institute near Utica, New York, a seminary where he studied theology for three years. It was an important move for him, for the seminary had a symbolic significance: It is generally believed that here students had formed the first antislavery society in New York. Garnet studied hard. He graduated in 1840, settled in Troy, New York, married in 1842, and was ordained in 1843 as a Presbyterian minister.

By 1840 Garnet was ready to take the public stage with his abolitionist message. Speaking during the anniversary meeting of the American Anti-slavery Society, Garnet implored Christians to eradicate slavery. He questioned America's commitment to democratic practices, referring to American democracy as a sham. The nation suffered from a deeply rooted moral failure, Garnet intoned. His speech was praised by many, including William Lloyd Garrison, and became a dress rehearsal for the one he gave three years later.

In 1843, speaking at the National Negro Convention in Buffalo, New York, Garnet broke from the tactic of moral suasion to end slavery. Slavery was a cruel and vicious system, he said. Tracing the origins of slavery from Africa, Garnet called on blacks to secure their own freedom. Repeatedly, he invoked the names of nationalists such as Toussaint-Louverture, Nat Turner, and Denmark Vesey to illustrate his point. "Rather die freemen than live life as a slave. Remember that you are FOUR million," he thundered. "Heaven, as with a voice of thunder, calls on you to arise from the dust. Let your motto be RESISTANCE! RESISTANCE! RESISTANCE! No oppressed people have ever secured their Liberty without resistance," he added (Garnet 1848, p. 96). Garnet's speech was in support of a motion that the convention published in David Walker's 1829 *Appeal* calling on slaves physically to revolt. Garnet had made his most important point, but the convention delegates voted 19 to 18 against publishing this document, which had caused consternation throughout the South fourteen years earlier.

In 1850 Garnet was a delegate to the World Peace Congress in Frankfurt, Germany. In 1851 he gave several antislavery speeches in Europe. Between 1853 and 1856, he served as a pastor in Jamaica. Following his return to the United States, he became pastor of the Shiloh Presbyterian Church in New York City.

After the passage of the Fugitive Act in 1850, which placed the nation off limits for runaway slaves, and the announcement of the *Dred Scott* decision declaring that blacks, slave or free, had no legal rights in America, Garnet concluded that racial equality in the United States was never to be. With the silent assistance of the white New York Colonization Society, he cofounded the new African Civilization Society to support black emigration to Africa and other parts of the world. However, colonization did not gain much support among African Americans.

In 1861, when the Civil War broke out, Garnet joined Frederick Douglass and other blacks in actively encouraging black enlistment. In 1864 Garnet moved his ministry to Washington, D.C. On February 12, 1865, he became the first African American to preach in the House of Representatives, encouraging congressional representatives to "to Emancipate, Enfranchise, Educate and give the blessings of the Gospel to every American citizen." On December 18, 1865, the Thirteenth Amendment became part of the U.S. Constitution. While delighted to see slavery outlawed, Garnet was disappointed by the government's failure to redistribute abandoned plantations to ex-slaves whose work made them possible.

Late in life Garnet remained prominent in religious circles. In 1881 President Garfield appointed him as minister to Liberia, but his stay in Africa was short-lived: In February 1882 he died and was buried in Liberia.

SEE ALSO *Abolition Movement.*

BIBLIOGRAPHY

PRIMARY WORKS

Garnet, Henry Highland, ed. 1848. *Walker's Appeal, With a Brief Sketch of His Life.* New York n.p. Available from http://www.gutenberg.org/etext/16516.

SECONDARY WORKS

Asante, Molefi Kete. 2002. *100 Greatest African Americans: A Biographical Encyclopedia.* Amherst, MA, and New York: Prometheus.

Bennett, Lerone, Jr. 1968. *Pioneers in Protest.* Chicago: Johnson.

Glaude, Eddie S., Jr. 2000. *Exodus!: Religion, Race, and Nation in Early Nineteenth-Century Black America.* Chicago: University of Chicago Press.

Harrold, Stanley. 2004. *The Rise of Aggressive Abolitionism: Addresses to the Slaves.* Lexington: University Press of Kentucky.

Litwack, Leon, and August Meier, eds. 1988. *Black Leaders of the Nineteenth Century.* Urbana: University of Illinois Press.

Mitchell, Beverly Eileen. 2005. *Black Abolition: A Quest for Human Dignity.* Maryknoll, NY: Orbis.

Pasternak, Martin B. 1995. *Rise Now and Fly to Arms: The Life of Henry Highland Garnet.* New York: Garland.

Tackach, James, ed. 2005. *The Abolitionist Movement.* Farmington Hills, MI: Greenhaven Press.

Julius Amin

GARRISON, WILLIAM LLOYD
1805–1879

Born in Newburyport, Massachusetts, on December 12, 1805, William Lloyd Garrison would eventually become the leading white radical abolitionist and critic of racial prejudice of the antebellum era. Garrison was the founder and editor of the *Liberator*, an abolitionist newspaper that he published weekly, without fail, from 1831 until the ratification of the Thirteenth Amendment in 1865, which abolished slavery. Garrison also co-founded the American Anti-Slavery Society (AAS) in 1833, which he led for many years. Both the *Liberator* and the AAS were dedicated to the eradication of racial prejudice and the immediate emancipation of slaves.

THE MAKING OF A RADICAL ABOLITIONIST

Born the third and youngest child of a devout evangelical Baptist mother and mariner father, the young Garrison grew up in a region economically devastated by the 1807 Jeffersonian Embargo against trade with Europe. Unable to find work and ultimately turning to drink, Garrison's father abandoned his wife and children, and the family struggled to make ends meet. After receiving a common school education, the young Garrison struggled unsuccessfully with a series of apprenticeships and clerkships in both Massachusetts and Maryland when the editor of the Federalist *Newburyport Herald*, Ephraim Allen, agreed to take him under his wing at the age of thirteen. Garrison discovered that he possessed an insatiable appetite for the books on hand at Allen's press, from the Bible to the works of William Shakespeare, John Milton, Hannah More, Sir Walter Scott, and Lord Byron. Possessed of his mother's evangelical piety, his era's Romantic sensibility, and his newfound skills as a printer, Garrison set out to make his mark.

In 1826 Garrison moved to Boston where he fell in with a group of young evangelical reformers who found meaning above the muck and mire of partisan politics by endeavoring to remake the world through their benevolent and philanthropic enterprises. Steering clear of drink, which had enslaved both his father and elder brother, Garrison began editing the *National Philanthropist,* a temperance newspaper that he infused with the sort of intemperate language and sense of urgency that raised hackles among an older generation of genteel reformers. It was at this point that Garrison met a tireless and unassuming Quaker saddlemaker by the name of Benjamin Lundy who was in Boston to raise money for his Baltimore-based newspaper, the *Genius of Universal Emancipation,* a one-man outfit dedicated to the gradual abolition of slavery. In 1829, upon Lundy's invitation, Garrison left Boston for Baltimore to help edit the Quaker's antislavery paper.

As the new co-editor of the *Genius*, Garrison pushed the newspaper in a more radical direction. While Lundy's editorials continued to endorse the notion of gradual emancipation and financial compensation for slaveholders, Garrison increasingly promoted the "immediatism" most fully articulated by the English Quaker abolitionist Elizabeth Heyrick and shared by many of the young printer's free African American neighbors in Baltimore. Garrison and other radicals demanded an immediate end to slavery and refused to make any deals with slaveholders, whom they considered both unjust and sinful.

In 1830 Garrison's uncompromising stance and unrelenting critique both landed him in prison for libel and threatened the financial stability of the *Genius*, but the month and a half he spent in jail only steeled his resolve and during this time he began to style himself a prophet and martyr for the emerging radical abolitionist cause. While the relationship between Lundy and his younger partner remained cordial, Garrison returned to Boston where he founded his own antislavery newspaper, the *Liberator*, which was dedicated to attacking slavery and racial prejudice, and whose principal financial backer at the time was James Forten, a successful black sailmaker and civic leader in Philadelphia. In his inaugural issue on January 1, 1831, Garrison audaciously proclaimed: "I am in earnest—I will not equivocate—I will not excuse—I will not retreat a single inch—AND I WILL BE HEARD." Most of his subscribers were blacks, but copies were passed from hand to hand among both races throughout the East Coast. True to his word, Garrison never ceased issuing the weekly newspaper until he witnessed the ratification of the Thirteenth Amendment abolishing slavery on December 18, 1865. Eleven days later, Garrison published the final issue of the *Liberator*, number 1820.

CONDEMNING THE RACIAL POLITICS OF COLONIZATION

In order to unleash the transforming power of radical abolitionism, Garrison believed that he first needed to debunk the dominant but misguided black "colonization" program that had won the support of many of the nation's leading politicians, ministers, and philanthropists. Deportation of free blacks was promoted through the American Colonization Society (ACS) with chapters in the North and South. Blacks in Baltimore, the erudite William Watkins among them, convinced Garrison of the impracticality, the immorality, and most significantly, the racial prejudice of colonization. Garrison pointed out that free black emigration would leave the remaining slave population bereft of their closest allies. Most importantly, colonization plans rested upon the premise that America could not absorb free blacks. In short, despite the antislavery motives of some colonizationists, Garrison argued that their program was functionally proslavery. In his lengthy pamphlet, *Thoughts on African Colonization* (1832), Garrison also reprinted the speeches and resolutions of free blacks who had condemned the racial prejudice implicit in the ACS program, thereby providing blacks with a larger audience for their views.

AN ABOLITIONIST CAREER

As a founder of the New England Anti-Slavery Society in 1832, and the larger American Anti-Slavery Society (AAS) the following year, Garrison embraced what might be called a politics of moral suasion. He believed that a radical transformation in public opinion regarding slavery and racial prejudice was necessary before politicians and their parties could be convinced to act justly. Garrison lambasted not only the rabidly anti-black prejudice of most working-class Democrats, but also the racial politics of the members of the Free Soil and Republican Parties, who not only sought to keep the Western territories free of slavery, but of blacks as well.

Garrison advocated not only for equality among the races, but for equality among the sexes as well, a position that ultimately led to a split in the abolitionist movement. Garrison's support of women's rights prompted more cautious abolitionists, including the evangelical New York philanthropists Arthur and Lewis Tappan and the antislavery presidential aspirant James G. Birney, to organize a breakaway organization called the American and Foreign Anti-Slavery Society (AFAS) in 1840.

In the 1840s and 1850s Garrison came to see the U.S. Constitution as profoundly proslavery, going so far as to call it a "covenant with death," and burning the document before a large crowd. Thinking of government as inherently authoritarian, he publicly advocated a philosophy of "non-resistance," or non-participation in the institutional aspects of politics, which also meant a rejection of voting. He also preferred disunion to a continued union with slaveholding Southerners. But as the Civil War came, he worked to transform the bloody conflict between the states into a struggle for the liberation of enslaved African Americans.

POST-EMANCIPATION CAREER

In 1865 Garrison resigned from the presidency of the AAS, and called for the dissolution of the antislavery organization. He parted company with the organization, but continued to devote himself to the promotion of black civil rights, women's suffrage, and temperance. Garrison died in 1879, three years after the death of his wife, and was survived by his five children.

SEE ALSO *Abolition Movement.*

BIBLIOGRAPHY

PRIMARY WORKS

Garrison, William L. 1832. *Thoughts on African Colonization.* Boston: Garrison and Knapp. Reprint, 1968. New York: Arno Press.

SECONDARY WORKS

Laurie, Bruce. 2005. *Beyond Garrison: Antislavery and Social Reform.* Cambridge, U.K.: Cambridge University Press.

Mayer, Henry. 1998. *All on Fire: William Lloyd Garrison and the Abolition of Slavery.* New York: St. Martin's Press.

Stauffer, John. 2002. *The Black Hearts of Men: Radical Abolitionists and the Transformation of Race.* Cambridge, MA: Harvard University Press.

Anthony A. Iaccarino

GARVEY, MARCUS
1887–1940

Marcus Mosiah Garvey was born on August 17, 1887 in St. Ann's Bay, Jamaica. He founded the Universal Negro Improvement Association (UNIA) in Jamaica in 1914, after four years of travel in Latin America, the Caribbean, and Europe. In 1916 Garvey immigrated to the United States, where he quickly reconstituted the UNIA, with new headquarters in Harlem, New York. By the mid-1920s the UNIA had expanded to more than forty countries and almost forty U.S. states, making it the largest Pan-African movement of all time.

As a youth, Garvey excelled in the printing trade and became Jamaica's youngest foreman printer. He studied oratory, became a pioneer trade-union leader, dabbled in journalism, and served on the executive committee of the

National Club, an early Jamaican anticolonial organization. He also became an avid reader, with a special interest in Pan-African history. His travels, beginning in 1910, brought him face to face with the universal suffering of Africans. He published newspapers and became a community agitator in Costa Rica and Panama. In London he worked and wrote for the *Africa Times and Orient Review,* the leading Pan-African journal of the period.

His decision to found a race-uplift organization received its final impetus after he read Booker T. Washington's autobiography, *Up From Slavery,* in 1914. Washington was the principal of the most African-American educational institution, Tuskegee Institute in Alabama. He was politically conservative but a strong advocate of racial uplift and self-reliance, both of which appealed to Garvey. Inspired by the harsh observations of his travels and the promise inherent in Washington's success, Garvey famously asked, in his *Philosophy and Opinions of Marcus Garvey,* "Where is the black man's Government? Where is his King and his Kingdom? Where is his President, his country, and his ambassador, his army, his navy, his men of big affairs?" "I could not find them," Garvey said, "and then I declared, 'I will help to make them.' "

The question of race dominated the UNIA from its beginnings. The initial objects sought "To establish a Universal Confraternity among the race; To promote the spirit of race pride and love; To reclaim the fallen of the race" [and] "To establish Commissionaries or Agencies in the principal countries of the world for the protection of all Negroes, irrespective of nationality." The centrality of race was reflected in the UNIA's slogan, "Africa for the Africans, those at home and those abroad," and in its motto, "One God, One Aim, One Destiny." Its main guiding principles were "race first," self-reliance, and nationhood (political self-determination). Only people of African descent could join the organization, and it mostly eschewed financial help from outside the race. The UNIA was organized around branches called "divisions" and "chapters." There were around 1,200 branches worldwide with more than 700 of them in the United States. Branches existed in Central America and the Caribbean, Canada, South America, Africa, Europe and Australia. The New York City branch had an estimated 35,000 to 40,000 members. Louisiana, with more than seventy (possibly more than eighty) branches, had a heavier UNIA presence than anywhere else in the world. Estimates of world membership range from one million to more than ten million. Financing came mostly from members and the UNIA's business ventures.

By 1918 Garvey had made his decision to remain in the United States, and the UNIA thereafter underwent a rapid expansion. It spawned the *Negro World* (1918), the most widely circulated African newspaper in the world, the Black Star Line Shipping Corporation, and the Negro Factories Corporation, which owned a number of small businesses. It also acquired schools and bought huge amounts of real estate. The *Negro World* employed some of the best journalistic talent in African America, including Thomas Fortune, John Edward Bruce, and Amy Jacques Garvey, Garvey's second wife. It provided wide coverage of African American and Pan-African affairs and doubled as a major literary journal in the era of the cultural movement known as the Harlem Renaissance.

In 1920 Garvey attracted 25,000 people to his First International Convention of the Negro Peoples of the World. Success, however, brought entanglements with a variety of adversaries, including European governments, integrationist organizations such as the NAACP (which was largely led and financed by whites), the Communist International (which espoused "class first" over "race first") and dishonest or disaffected elements within the UNIA. The U.S. government, ever protective of its status quo against any manifestations of radicalism, began plotting his deportation from at least 1919. They infiltrated the UNIA and brought Garvey into court on a variety of charges, culminating in a conviction for alleged mail fraud in connection with the eventual failure of the Black Star Line. Garvey served almost three years of a five-year sentence until President Calvin Coolidge commuted his sentence late in 1927. Immediate deportation to Jamaica followed.

After returning to Jamaica, Garvey published newspapers, founded the Peoples Political Party, was elected to the principal local government body (the Kingston and St. Andrew Corporation Council), and was imprisoned by the British authorities. Garvey spent his last five years (1935–1940) in London, where he continued to lead his now-reduced organization.

Garvey's emphasis on race was due to a careful analysis of the situation around him. "The world has made being black a crime," he said, "and I have felt it in common with men who suffer like me, and instead of making it a crime I hope to make it a virtue" (Martin 1986 [1976]). He was born into a world of pseudo-scientific racism. Nineteenth-century thinkers such as American Thomas Jefferson (1743–1826), American German Georg Hegel (1770–1831) and Englishman James Anthony Froude (1818–1894) all espoused notions of African inferiority, and they were all challenged by Pan-African intellectuals. As early as 1829 African-American David Walker (1785–1830) lambasted Jefferson's allegations of African genetic inferiority in the seminal *David Walker's Appeal.* In 1889, two years after Garvey's birth, his Trinidadian compatriot John Jacob Thomas (1841–1889) challenged Froude's views in his polemic *Froudacity.* Haitian Anténor Firmin (1850-1911) challenged Frenchman Joseph Arthur Comte de Gobineau's (1816–1882) white supremacist treatise *Essai sur l'inégalité des races humaines* (Essay on the inequality of the human race) in his 1885 response *On the Equality of Human Races.*

Garvey was aware of the widely disseminated pseudo-scientific racist ideas. He read such Pan-African challengers to these views as Edward Blyden (1832–1912) of Liberia and W. E. B. Du Bois (1868–1963) of the United States. He said in 1923, "White philosophers, Darwin, Locke, Newton and the rest … forgot that the monkey would change to a man, his tail would drop off and he would demand his share."

Every aspect of the UNIA was therefore ultimately designed to demonstrate that Africans could—self-reliantly and through the power of organization—help themselves to a position of equality with other races. Garveyites sought to uplift the race through an activist literature and through revisionist historical writing. In the process, they helped usher in the period of literary and cultural flowering known as the Harlem Renaissance. Garvey personally took issue with American anthropologists Franz Boas (1858–1942) and Clark Wissler (1870–1947) for their inconsistent definitions of race. "The custom of these anthropologists," Garvey lamented in *The Philosophy and Opinions of Marcus Garvey*, is "whenever a black man … accomplishes anything of importance, he is no longer a negro."

Garveyites portrayed God as black, even while acknowledging that God was a spirit without color. They tried to employ their own and to provide insurance against sickness and death. They hoped to establish a beachhead in Liberia, from where the task of rehabilitating the race might be expedited. Garveyites accepted past miscegenation as an unfortunate *fait accompli* induced by slavery, and they welcomed racially mixed persons who acknowledged their African ancestry. They nevertheless frowned on new miscegenation, which they saw as an acknowledgement of inferiority.

Garvey's ideology of "race first" was, in essence, a reformulation of the perennial ideas of black nationalism that have infused other Pan-African mass movements. His influence was transmitted directly to Malcolm X, Elijah Muhammad of the Nation of Islam, the Rastafarian movement, and nationalist movements of the African diaspora. He died on June 10, 1940, in London.

SEE ALSO *African Diaspora; American Colonization Society and the Founding of Liberia; Boas, Franz; Firmin, Anténor; Pan-Africanism; Walker, David; Washington, Booker T.*

BIBLIOGRAPHY

Garvey, Amy Jacques, ed. 1986 (1925). *The Philosophy and Opinions of Marcus Garvey, Or, Africa for the Africans.* Dover, MA: Majority Press.

Garvey, Marcus. 1986. *Message to the People: The Course of African Philosophy.* Edited by Tony Martin. Dover, MA: The Majority Press.

Hill, Robert A., ed. 1983–1990. *Marcus Garvey and the Universal Negro Improvement Association Papers.* 7 vols. Los Angeles: University of California Press.

Martin, Tony. *Literary Garveyism: Garvey, Black Arts, and the Harlem Renaissance.* Dover, MA: Majority Press, 1983.

———, ed. 1983. *The Poetical Works of Marcus Garvey.* Dover, MA: Majority Press.

———. 1986 (1976). *Race First: The Ideological and Organizational Struggles of Marcus Garvey and the Universal Negro Improvement Association.* Dover, MA: Majority Press.

———, ed. 1991. *African Fundamentalism: A Literary and Cultural Anthology of Garvey's Harlem Renaissance.* Dover, MA: Majority Press.

Tony Martin

GAY MEN

The images, experiences, and histories of gay men are multifaceted. Social-science research has shown that gay men come from all racial and ethnic experiences and include men from all socioeconomic backgrounds. Still, some of the most persistent and dominant conceptions of gay men describe them as being white, middle-class, and well-educated. While these characteristics may very well apply to some gay men, there are others, particularly of different racial and ethnic backgrounds, who continue to challenge these stereotypical constructs. Other social forces besides race also shape our understandings of gay men. These include heterosexism and homophobia, which, in and of themselves, can be detrimental to the existence of gay men in general, but when viewed in conjunction with racial and ethnic stereotyping can also limit the ways in which people come to know and understand gay men.

Because the term *gay* does not always resonate with some racial or ethnic groups, different names have been used to describe same-sex sexual contact between men, reflecting linguistic conventions and offering oppositional, or alternative, forms of self-identification. For instance, in many Latino cultures, men who have sex with men often describe themselves as either *activo* (active) or *pasivo* (passive), highlighting the behavioral aspects of homosexuality. For many blacks, meanwhile, the term *same gender loving* is employed in order to denote same-sex sexuality. Such terms do not necessarily exclude lesbians, bisexuals, or transgender people. For example, the term *two-spirit* is often used in Native American populations to refer to homosexual people in general. This is similar to the use of *queer* for many white and Asian groups.

The study of gay men has a long and vast history, yet its links to other social forces, such as nationality, religion, popular culture, and race, has only recently been explored by researchers, theorists, and others. Twentieth-century investigations of the intersections of race and homosexuality have been fueled by numerous forces, such as feminist inquiry, the U.S. Civil Rights struggles of the 1950s and 1960s, identity politics, and research on HIV and AIDS. Still, forces such as homophobia (the fear of homosexuals and homosexuality, often accompanied by negative thoughts, feelings, and actions against this group) and heterosexism (the belief that heterosexuality is the basis of all social interaction, and that same-sex families, unions, and interactions should not be allowed) continue to shape the ways in which gay men live their lives and are represented by others.

Embedded in discussions and examinations of homosexuality are the arguments that link it to nature and to various social forces. Does nature dictate beliefs about homosexuality (the essentialist view), or is homosexuality a product of socially constructed norms and behaviors (the social constructivist view)? This is one of the most salient dichotomies present in the study of sexuality in general. Throughout history, attempts have been made to link homosexuality to nature, to the environment, to the psyche, to race, and to policy.

In the late nineteenth and early twentieth centuries, Karl Heinrich Ulrichs (1825–1895), Magnus Hirschfeld (1868–1935), and Havelock Ellis (1859–1939) were all influential pioneers in sexology—the scientific study of sexuality—and they argued for the decriminalization of homosexuality by using a nature-based argument. In fact, Ellis defined homosexuals as "inverts"—people who had the body of one sex and the soul of the other sex. One of the main goals for these early sexologists was to document the various kinds of sexualities present in their time.

More recently, social scientists in the United States have attempted to continue the work of early sexologists, but these researchers also acknowledge that sexuality reveals as much about social forces as it does about nature. Two works by researcher Alfred Kinsey (1894–1956) and his research team—*Sexual Behavior in the Human Male* (1948) and the subsequent *Sexual Behavior in the Human Female* (1953)—were influential because they showed how sexuality was fluid. This development was important because it destabilized the categories of "heterosexual" and "homosexual" and introduced fluidity to the understanding of sexuality in general. Similarly, in *The Social Organization of Sexuality: Sexual Practices in the United States* (1994), the sociologist Edward O. Laumann (b. 1938) and his colleagues emphasized that sexuality is largely organized by other social forces, such as the state, gender, race, and place of birth.

In addition, in *The History of Sexuality: An Introduction* (Vol. 1, 1978), the philosopher Michel Foucault (1926–1984) directly challenged the belief that contemporary societies are plagued by the silences of sexuality that dominated the Victorian era. Further, Foucault argued that sexuality has been regulated by the power-knowledge effect—the extent to which those in power and those who possess (or have access to) knowledge use these forces to either reproduce inequality or to sustain the status quo. Clearly, Foucault's theory of sexuality is located in the social constructivist camp, and his work continues to influence much of the research on homosexuality today.

According to historical and personal accounts around the world, gay men have developed various strategies in order to develop a community of like-minded men and in order to combat the stigma attached to being gay or homosexual. Such strategies include specific dress codes and linguistic references, ultimately resulting in the establishment of safe spaces in which to congregate. Many gay men have also achieved worldwide recognition for various successes in the arts, politics, sports, and entertainment. Some examples of these include, but are in no way limited to, the writers Reinaldo Arenas (1943–1990) and James Baldwin (1924–1987); the French politician Bertrand Delanoe (b. 1950), the German politician Klaus Wowereit (b. 1953), and the U.S. politician Barney Frank (b. 1940); the athletes Bill Tilden (1893–1953) and Greg Louganis (b. 1960); and the entertainers Elton John (b. 1947) and Nathan Lane (b. 1956). Still, state-sponsored homophobia and heterosexism—which often take the form of legally sanctioned vice patrols, as well as other forms of legislation that overtly targets gay men specifically and homosexuality in general—often contribute to the ways in which gay men have been oppressed and continue to be punished on the basis of their sexual identities and desires. Globally, gay men have been the targets of legal and extralegal stoning, imprisonment, castration, honor killing, disenfranchisement, and other forms of execution and discrimination.

The work of scholars in the field of sexuality studies has also accounted for the ways in which race continues to be an important factor in the lives of people of color. In fact, intersectionality—a framework used to understand the ways in which multiple forms of oppression affect people differently—has become an important feature in the broad fields of race and sexuality studies. Noted feminist scholars such as Audre Lorde (1934–1992), Kimberle Crenshaw (b. 1959), and Patricia Hill Collins (b. 1948) all helped to develop the concept of intersectionality, which attempts to analyze individual- and group-level dynamics where there is more than one oppressed identity present. Ostensibly, gay men of color often face discrimination based on their sexual and racial identities. This is complicated by other social forces they may face, such as unemployment or insufficient health care. Similarly, researchers interested in racial stigma have called attention to a phenomenon known as secondary

Black Gay Pride Parade, 2002. *Two men participate in Atlanta's second annual Stand Up and Represent National Black Gay Pride march. Gay men of color often face discrimination based on their sexual and racial identities.* AP IMAGES.

marginalization, the process through which a marginalized group is regulated by more privileged members within their very group. Within the larger population of gay men, stereotypical racial hierarchies and dynamics exist, mimicking the presence of racism that many continue to document within the larger society.

In an essay titled "How Gay Stays White and What Kind of White It Stays" (2001), Allan Berube documents how the category *gay* is often assumed to be white, and how this in turn voids all other kinds of racialized, gay existences. Such work is important because it demonstrates how racism and homophobia, while different, coexist and reinforce each other. An examination of one without the other, therefore, would result in lopsided analyses. This is similar to what many feminists of color have written about in terms of employing an intersectionist perspective—which would account for the ways in which multiple forms of oppression affect people differently. Berube's work also underscores how whiteness becomes the default for many socially constructed categories, including *gay.* This becomes complicated when one considers the various political strategies that gay men have employed in order to advocate for rights. For instance, early gay male liberationist battles in the United States rested on a mostly white agenda that included fighting for the end of vice patrols in the bars and clubs where homosexual men came together. On the other hand, race-specific research on gay men in the United States has revealed at least three layers of racism and homophobia: in the general population, in homosexual communities, and in their own respective racial or ethnic communities. Awareness of these levels of discrimination and oppression, coupled with an understanding that same-sex sexuality is present in all racial or ethnic communities, makes for a more accurate picture of gay men.

SEE ALSO *Baldwin, James; Heterosexism and Homophobia; Lesbians; Sexuality.*

BIBLIOGRAPHY

Battle, Juan, and Natalie Bennett. 2005. "Striving for Place: Black Lesbian, Gay, Bisexual, and Transgender (LGBT) People in History and Society." In *A Companion to African American History*, edited by Alton Hornsby. Malden, MA: Blackwell.

Berube, Allan. 2001. "How Gay Stays White and What Kind of White It Stays." In *The Making and Unmaking of Whiteness,* edited by Birgit Brander Rasmussen, Eric Klinenberg, Irene J. Nexica, and Matt Wray. Durham, NC: Duke University Press.

Diaz, Rafael M. 1998. *Latino Gay Men and HIV: Culture, Sexuality, and Risk Behavior.* New York: Routledge.

Eng, David L. 2000. *Racial Castration: Managing Masculinity in Asian America.* Durham, NC: Duke University Press.

Foucault, Michel. 1978. *The History of Sexuality: An Introduction,* Vol. 1. New York: Vintage Books.

Institute for Sex Research. 1953. *Sexual Behavior in the Human Female.* Philadelphia, PA: W.B. Saunders.

Kinsey, Alfred, Wardell Baxter Pomeroy, and Clyde E. Martin. 1948. *Sexual Behavior in the Human Male.* Philadelphia, PA: W.B. Saunders.

Laumann, Edward O., John H. Gagnon, Robert T. Michael, and Stuart Michaels. 1994. *The Social Organization of Sexuality: Sexual Practices in the United States.* Chicago: University of Chicago Press.

Sears, James T., and Walter L. Williams, eds. 1997. *Overcoming Heterosexism and Homophobia: Strategies That Work.* New York: Columbia University Press.

Williams, Walter L. 1986. *The Spirit and the Flesh: Sexual Diversity in American Indian Culture.* Boston: Beacon Press.

Antonio Pastrana Jr.
Juan Battle

GENDER IDEOLOGY

Like race, masculinity and femininity are socially constructed concepts that convey values and social status. Gender ideology works in two ways. First, it prescribes proper behavior and demeanor for boys and girls, men and women. There are different prescriptions for masculinity and femininity in societies that are racially and ethnically diverse, and the gendered behavior and demeanor of some of the members of less valued groups may violate the dominant group's ideas of what is proper. Thus, boys and girls and women and men who adopt different ideas of how to behave, look, walk, dress, and relate to others may be doing what is tabooed by the dominant group's gender ideology, justifying their devaluation and discrimination against them. Second, these negative responses are reinforced by demeaning stereotypes about women and men of different racial and ethnic groups, which usually do not represent the behavior of most of the members of these groups.

The mixture of stereotypes and behavior often produces contradictory racial imagery of masculinity and femininity. In the United States in the nineteenth century, African-American enslaved men were considered sexually dangerous for Southern white women, who were supposedly sexually pure and physically vulnerable. Yet the enslaved men had no status as full-fledged men; they were "boys" and were expected to be deferential to any white person. Enslaved African-American women were all "body"—sexually vulnerable breeders and wet nurses in service of their white masters or physically strong field hands—not "women." The racial and gender contradictions of the time were aptly summed up in Sojourner Truth's famous speech, "Ain't I a Woman?" She was an African-American former slave and preacher who made the speech at a women's rights convention in Akron, Ohio, in 1851. Challenging the stereotypical view of women as helpless and dependent, which was proper behavior for upper- and middle-class white women, she said:

> That man over there says that women need to be helped into carriages, and lifted over ditches, and to have the best place everywhere. Nobody ever helps me into carriages, or over mud-puddles, or gives me any best place! And ain't I a woman? Look at me! Look at my arm! I have ploughed and planted, and gathered into barns, and no man could head me! And ain't I a woman? I could work as much and eat as much as a man—when I could get it—and bear the lash as well! And ain't I a woman? I have borne thirteen children, and seen most all sold off to slavery, and when I cried out with my mother's grief, none but Jesus heard me! And ain't I a woman? (Internet Modern History Sourcebook)

Late twentieth and twenty-first century views of masculinity and femininity in the United States are equally complicated by racial differences and produce similar contradictions of what it is to be a man or woman. In popular views and the mass media, diversity of behavior within the group is often ignored, and a stereotypical imagery of masculinity and femininity predominates. The stereotypes reflect beliefs about the group and justify their oppression and subordinate status, even when only a small percentage of the group has gendered cultural patterns that differ from middle-class whites, the dominant group in the United States. In addition to African Americans, gender ideologies reinforce racial stereotypes for Latinos, Asians, Arabs, and other nondominant groups. The bulk of the research on institutionalized racism, however, is on black-white relations.

BLACK MASCULINITY

Machismo, first used to describe the masculinity of Latinos, has become a generalized term for "doing masculinity." *Black macho* is a phrase that is the essence of the gender ideology surrounding black masculinity. It depicts a young, swaggering, defiant, bold, cool competitor for physical space and the upper hand—for respect, most of all. He is sexually attractive and physically adept, but there is an undertone of repressed violence that can emerge in fights, rapes, and homicides. He is street-smart rather than book-learned, and somewhat contemptuous of black college graduates working in corporations or professions, whose demeanor is likely to mirror white middle-class manners. The physical strengths and aggressive competitiveness are valued by sports recruiters and team owners, especially for football, basketball, and boxing, and may lead to upward mobility and even great wealth and adulation for a few successful professional athletes.

Aspects of the gender ideology of black masculinity include sexual prowess with many women and fathering several children, but not long-term relationships or emotional closeness with children. In actuality, many black men are hard-working, responsible fathers. Leonard Pitts Jr., a *Miami Herald* journalist who interviewed African-American men about their troubled relationships with their fathers, says that for him and others there were always role models: "fathers, black men, *family* men who came up on hard streets, sired by disappointing dads, yet get up every morning and do the hard work of raising and supporting their children" (1999, p. 198).

The machismo or cool pose of young African-American men is a form of defiance against their subordinate position in the U.S. stratification system, which disadvantages them economically and educationally. The pose enables them to establish a confident masculine identity but may also prevent them from full participation in a racist society that sees their swaggering as hostile and dangerous. White boys may admire and adopt their style of dress, music, walk, and attitude, but to adult white men they defy proper middle-class demeanor. Thus the masculinity that may command respect on the street limits the chances for upward mobility in the white-controlled work world, except through the venues of sports and music. Movements such as the Promise Keepers have tried to shift the ideology of black masculine identity from personal aggrandizement to valorizing the husbands and fathers who take on the commitment of life-long emotional and financial support of their children and their children's mothers. Even under slavery, black family life was strong; but gender ideology has not been supportive of family men as an image of black masculinity.

BLACK FEMININITY

Gender ideology depicts black women through a variety of contradictory femininities—sexy Jezebels, nurturant mothers, domestics, welfare recipients, and domineering matriarchs. Each of these is one-dimensional and objectifies and demeans black women who, like black men, are diverse in social class, education, family status, and occupation.

The imagery of the sexually available black woman and the loving mammy, nursemaid, nurse, and general caregiver is both positive and negative. Stereotypes of black beauty place value on elements of sexual attractiveness, especially large breasts and buttocks, but devalue black facial features and hair. The conventional ideal of black feminine beauty is lush curves, thin lips and noses, light skin, and straightened hair or elaborate cornrows. For black women, achieving these standards may mean intensive dieting, cosmetic surgery, and long, painful hours at the beauty salon.

The imagery of sexual attractiveness and availability, with early pregnancy or sex work as a possible outcome, has been countered by black parents who urge daughters to put off sexual activity and concentrate on their schoolwork. Like adolescent girls in many other racial ethnic groups, young black women face an either-or dilemma: either to remain aloof or to seek emotional relationships that will render them vulnerable to sexual pressure. The conventional gender ideology does not offer positive images of educated black women in prestigious occupations and professions; rather, such women are accused of emasculating black men.

The most contradictory racialized gender ideology surrounds motherhood. Under slavery, black women with qualities valued by masters—good health and strength—were encouraged to breed with black men; they were also raped by white owners and their sons and overseers. None of the children they bore belonged to them. After slavery, many black mothers left their children with kin to obtain work in white homes as maids and nannies for white children. Poverty and men's relocation for jobs made it difficult to keep families intact, and many mothers cared for their own and others' children. After a fight to obtain welfare benefits, black women who used that means of support to stay home with their children were condemned as lazy and shiftless, and welfare reforms have mandated work requirements to keep receiving benefits. Black mothers who work and those on welfare are both blamed for sons not doing well in school and getting in trouble with drugs and crime, daughters getting pregnant, and black men's low self-esteem. Yet many of these same mothers join together in grassroots fights for better local social conditions for their families.

The conventional gender ideology of black femininity is blind to black women's successful efforts at raising daughters and sons who stay in school, go on to college, and are upwardly mobile. It does not acknowledge black women who have stable marriages, raise well-adjusted children, and hold middle-class jobs throughout their lives, or competent single mothers who are heads of households for extended families and often are grassroots activists. Yet these women are the Sojourner Truths of the early twenty-first century—strong, self-reliant, political, and assertive role models for their sons and daughters.

SEE ALSO *Feminism and Race; Sexuality.*

BIBLIOGRAPHY

Collins, Patricia Hill. 2000. *Black Feminist Thought: Knowledge, Consciousness, and the Politics of Empowerment*, rev. ed. New York: Routledge.

Connell, R.W. 2005. *Masculinities*, 2nd ed. Berkeley: University of California Press.

Hobson, Janell. 2005. *Venus in the Dark: Blackness and Beauty in Popular Culture*. New York: Routledge.

Kimmel, Michael S. 2006. *Manhood in America: A Cultural History*, 2nd ed. New York: Oxford University Press.

Landry, Bart. 2000. *Black Working Wives: Pioneers of the American Family Revolution*. Berkeley: University of California Press.

Majors, Richard, and Janet Mancini Billson. 1992. *Cool Pose: The Dilemmas of Black Manhood in America*. New York: Lexington Books.

Melhuus, Marit, and Kristi Anne Stølen, eds. 1997. *Machos, Mistresses, Madonnas: Contesting the Power of Latin American Gender Imagery*. New York and London: Verso.

Messner, Michael A. 1992. *Power at Play: Sports and the Problem of Masculinity*. Boston: Beacon Press.

Naples, Nancy A. 1998. *Grassroots Warriors: Activist Mothering, Community Work, and the War on Poverty*. New York: Routledge.

Pitts, Leonard Jr. 1999. *Becoming Dad: Black Men and the Journey to Fatherhood*. Atlanta: Longstreet.

Truth, Sojourner. "Ain't I a Woman?" Internet Modern History Sourcebook. Available from http://www.fordham.edu/halsall/mod/sojtruth-woman.html.

Wallace, Michele. 1990. *Black Macho and the Myth of the Superwoman*. London: Verso.

Judith Lorber

GENE POOL

The division of the human species into races implies that there are separate breeding populations that are genetically differentiated from each other in many inherited traits. It is assumed that while there may be some matings between individuals belonging to different races, the small amount of such cross-racial interbreeding has been insufficient to eliminate the group differences that are said to characterize the races. This view of well-defined separate breeding populations of individuals with an occasional migrant between them is typical of the extremely simplified models of population structure that characterized population genetics in the early and mid-twentieth-century. An element in these models is a metaphor for the collection of genes in a population, the gene pool.

Since the early 1900s, scientists have known that there is a great deal of genetic variation in any assemblage of individuals in any species. More recent work characterizing proteins and DNA from many individuals has shown that essentially every gene has some variation within a population. For some genes, nearly every individual in any species, including humans, is genetically identical, though there are rare variant forms of these genes. For about one-third of the genes in a sexually reproducing population, however, there is considerable variation, with two or more relatively common alternative forms (*alleles*). The "gene pool" of a population is a metaphor for the collection of all the different variants of all the genes in proportion to the relative frequencies of the alleles. Imagine that all the females in a population deposited their eggs in one container and all the males deposited their sperm in another. If the males and females in the population mate with each other at random, the offspring generation that results is equivalent to producing the offspring by drawing, over and over again, one sperm and one egg from the containers. The contents of the containers together constitute the gene pool of the population, from which offspring are said to be drawn. The complete specification of the makeup of that gene pool is then taken as the genetic description of the population.

No description of the complete gene pool of any real population has ever been attempted, but a sample of different genes in a reasonably large sample of individuals from different populations in a variety of species has provided a fairly accurate characterization of the genetic variation within and between populations. In humans, for example, about 85 percent of the genetic variation in the species as a whole can be found within the gene pool of a local population, defined geographically and linguistically.

The concept of a gene pool from which individuals in a population are drawn and which distinguishes one population from another depends on an idealized and simplified model of populations. The model is that of a *Mendelian population*, a collection of individuals clearly bounded off from other such populations, within which offspring are produced by the random pairing of males and females. Matings with individuals from other populations are either nonexistent or sufficiently rare that their effect can be modeled as the introduction into the population of an occasional genetic variant, equivalent to the occurrence of a mutation. The pool, then, is a well-defined collection of genes into which an occasional gene is imported from other pools. The consequence is that different gene pools will be distinguishable by the frequency and kind of genetic variants they contain, and despite an occasional imported variant, each will maintain a genetic distance from other such gene pools.

The reality is more complex, however, making the metaphor of the "pool" inappropriate. First, individuals belonging to a species are not generally broken up into separate geographical populations with clear boundaries between them and random mating within them. The probabilities of an individual mating with other individuals varies continuously with geographical distance, even within a region that is separated from other regions by uninhabited territory. Isolated islands are periodically invaded. In seasonal environments, populations that are more or less continuous during the favorable part of the year (when population densities are high) break up into isolated discontinuous pockets during the unfavorable season. Thus, the history of human populations has been marked by massive migrations and invasions followed by interbreeding.

Second, the probabilities of mating within well-defined geographical limits vary continuously with the characteristics of individuals. In human populations, variables such as social class, religion, and socially defined race and ethnicity do not act as absolute population boundaries, but rather as probabilistic determinants of mating (with historical changes in the probabilities). The realization of these complexities has led to an abandonment of the concept of gene pool as an analytic device in the literature of population genetics.

SEE ALSO *Genetic Variation among Populations.*

BIBLIOGRAPHY

Cavalli-Sforza, Luigi L., Paolo Menozzi, and Alberto Piazza. 1994. *The History and Geography of Human Genes*. Princeton, NJ: Princeton University Press.

Dobzhansky, Theodosius. 1951. *Genetics and the Origin of Species*, 3rd ed. Rev. New York: Columbia University Press.

Lewontin, Richard C. 1972. "The Apportionment of Human Diversity." In *Evolutionary Biology*, Vol. 6, edited by Theodosius Dobzhansky, Max K. Hecht, and William C. Steere. New York: Appleton-Century-Crofts.

R.C. Lewontin

GENES AND GENEALOGIES

When the "one drop rule" was implemented in the United States during the period of slavery to designate all people with African ancestry as "Negroes," the question of descent often became a matter of life or death. People with even one African ancestor and no documents of "manumission," which freed an ancestor from slavery, could be returned to slave status, frequently by means of a public auction. Before the Civil War, free blacks were in constant danger of being kidnapped, deprived of their documents, carried to another city, and sold back into slavery. On one notorious occasion, Black Seminoles on their way to Indian Territory under protection of a treaty were lined up in New Orleans and inspected, with darker-skinned people sold into slavery and the profits going to the U.S. government. Even after the war, the "one drop rule" was directed against people of color—blacks, Native Americans, and Asians—most notably in the 1924 Virginia Racial Integrity Act, the most vicious of the "Jim Crow" laws.

Another aspect of this genealogical approach to ancestry is represented in the idea of blood fraction. As the African slave trade developed in the seventeenth century, there was increased mating between black and white, and one's worth as a slave depended on the fraction of white as opposed to black ancestry. A vocabulary was developed to describe ancestry in a genealogical manner. One could be half white (mulatto), one-fourth white (quadroon), or one-eighth white (octoroon), and other terms were invented to describe a nearly white appearance such as "High Yellow," a designation applied especially to the mistresses of white aristocrats in southern cities, including the Texas woman memorialized in the song "The Yellow Rose of Texas." One's role in slave society, then, depended largely on color, so that lighter-colored slaves were expected to perform household work and skilled trades, while darker-colored slaves were field hands and manual laborers who performed more exhausting and dangerous work.

The genealogical idiom, then, incorporates at least two mistaken ideas: (1) that each person is equally descended from each parent and (2) that a person can retain an indelible marker of racial origin, characterized in this context as "one drop of blood." This idiom becomes even more complicated, and more mistaken, in the calculation of "blood quantum" among Native Americans.

HISTORY OF THE GENEALOGICAL METHOD

Genealogy has been the most traditional method of describing ancestry, with people recounting the identity of their parents, their parents' parents, and so on back in time as far as they could go. Before writing was invented, about 3000 BCE, people had to rely on memory to recall their ancestors, often appointing special persons to remember everyone's ancestry. Native Hawaiian society, for example, is notable for maintaining a class of historians who could recite genealogies reaching hundreds of years into the past. Many societies in Africa and South America supported similar specialists. Without some special effort of this kind, "genealogical amnesia" usually sets in, so that most people even now cannot recall the names of all eight of their great-grandparents without help—and those ancestors are only three generations back.

Within "clan" or "unilineal" societies, which preceded complex societies around the world and are still maintained by hundreds of "tribal" or small-scale societies, these genealogies have been crucial in determining access to property, political office, and religious roles. In some "unilineal" societies, it was necessary to remember only the male or the female line, since property or privileges only passed through one line or the other. But in "bilateral" societies such as existed in Europe, tracing ancestry through both males and females was more common, and much more difficult, since in every ascending generation there were twice as many ancestors to remember. This takes the form of a geometric progression so that in a bilateral society, after five generations there are 2 + 4 + 8 + 16 + 32 = 62 ancestors in the family tree to be remembered. But after 300 years, or twelve generations, a person has an estimated 8,190 ancestors. Inverting the genealogy, and estimating that each person has two children, a single person emigrating to America in 1700, black or white, would have had an estimated 8,190 descendants by the year 2000.

While many people's ancestors have been completely forgotten by history, the descendants of celebrated people often have their names recorded, or they constitute special clubs or societies of some sort, providing some notion of how extensive a person's genealogy might be. For example, the names of Pocahontas's descendants, since about 1614, are presently exhibited in three official volumes, comprising more than 30,000 people. At a more serious, religious level, the descendants of the Prophet Muhammad are said to constitute more than 30 million people, often designated by distinctive dress or title, although these figures are disputed among the various sects of Islam. King Edward of England is said to be the ancestor of 80 percent of living English people, while 90 percent of the people who lived before 1100 are said to be the ancestors of everyone now living, while the other 10 percent have died without issue (Olson 2002).

In the large genealogical picture, then, everyone is descended from everyone in the past thousand years, and applying the "one drop rule" to the human species means that everyone belongs to all races. Everyone has at least one ancestor among every "race" that has ever existed. If all humans are not literally brothers and sisters to one another, they are at least cousins—at least fortieth cousins to be exact. The genealogical method, then, does not provide a very good tool for differentiating among human beings or for tracing their migrations and histories.

GENES

The discovery of genes in the early twentieth century dramatically contradicted these notions of fractional ancestry and what was called at the time "descent by blood." But to consider the advantages of genetic theory, we need to begin with a consideration of the difference between genes and alleles, a distinction that is frequently lost in popular and journalistic descriptions of modern genetics. Simply put, a gene is a location on a chromosome whose DNA transcribes the sequence of amino acids to build proteins that may, for example, relate to eye shape or color. An allele is one of the alternative sequences of DNA that then codes for a different color. That is, to simplify an example, the gene is for eye color, but the allele might be for black, brown, green, or blue eyes. Gene refers to the location; allele refers to the color. One cannot have a gene for blue eyes, but one might have an allele for blue eyes.

All humans have the same set of chromosomes and genes. Surprisingly, most of the alleles (the form of the genes) are also identical. However, each person is slightly unique in his or her alleles. Cavalli-Sforza, Menozzi, and Piazza's (1994) massive survey of research in human genetics shows the worldwide distribution of alleles as known to him and his associates in 1994. Many more examples have been examined since then, but the general conclusion is the same—that all human societies on every continent comprise essentially the same genes, although the alleles of a gene might have a slightly different frequency in different populations.

From the fractional, genealogical perspective, biological information is in different packages, corresponding to one's ancestors. If one is one-fourth from a grandmother, then one should have one-fourth of her biological characteristics. But genetic studies show that this is not the way it works. Although the genes are in different "packages," the packages are chromosomes, each of which contains a string of thousands of genes. All of the genes on one chromosome are inherited together from parent to child, but the number of packages inherited from a single ancestor can be highly variant, beginning in the second generation. In the first generation a child inherits twenty-three chromosomes from each parent. But in the next generation it is possible, although only slightly, that a grandchild could inherit no chromosomes at all from a grandparent, receiving all its chromosomes from the other three grandparents. Although the genealogical method would designate all four grandparents as providing one-quarter ancestry, in fact one grandparent could provide from zero to twenty-three chromosomes. That is, a grandparent could provide from none to half the genetic material represented in a grandchild.

Concerning the "one drop rule," a particular person's genetic contribution to a lineage might be wiped out after only two generations, in defiance of the assertion that a particular ancestor has a permanent biological effect on all descendants. In sum, the one drop rule and the notion of fractional ancestry were both invented for social, economic, and political purposes and are only approximately related to human biology.

SEE ALSO *Blood Quantum.*

BIBLIOGRAPHY

Brown, Stuart E., Lorraine F. Myers, and Eileen M. Chappel. 2003. *Pocahontas' Descendants.* Baltimore, MD: Genealogical Publishing Co.

Cavalli-Sforza, L. L., Paolo Menozzi, and Alberto Piazza. 1994. *The History and Geography of Human Genes.* Princeton, NJ: Princeton University Press.

Malik, Ghulam. 1996. *Muhammad: An Islamic Perspective.* Lanham, MD: University Press of America.

Olson, Steve. 2002. "The Royal We." *Atlantic Monthly,* May: 62–64. Available from http://www.theatlantic.com/doc/200205/olson.

Porter, Kenneth W. 1996. *The Black Seminoles: History of a Freedom-Seeking People,* ed. Alcione M. Amos and Thomas P. Senter. Gainesville: University Press of Florida.

John H. Moore

GENESIS AND POLYGENESIS

For those Europeans who wanted to justify slavery and the colonial system in the sixteenth and seventeenth centuries, nothing was sacred, not even the Bible. Christian ideas about equality under God and the brotherhood of man had to be abandoned, or at least modified, if slavery was to be accommodated to Christian ideology. To accomplish this, leading clerics and other intellectuals selected and distorted particular passages in the Old Testament, and they took an arithmetic approach to Biblical chronology to develop four arguments for racism that were widely disseminated by the end of the eighteenth century.

REVISING BIBLICAL HISTORY

The new, pseudoscientific chronology of Bible history was created by applying the Julian Calendar to the sacred events of the Book of Genesis, so that according to the Venerable Bede, a British cleric of the 8th century AD, the world was created in 710 (by the Julian calendar), or 3952 BC (according to the BC/AD notation invented by Bede himself). In 1650, Bishop James Ussher, another British cleric, revised Bede's date for creation to 4004 BC, adding that it occurred on Sunday, October 23. He also gave the date for the end of the Biblical Flood as Wednesday, May 5, 2348 BC. Both Bede and Ussher used some very questionable demographic assumptions about life span and the age of reproduction to do their calculations, but their opinions soon began to carry the weight of legal authority within the Church.

Bede, Ussher, and their followers went far beyond the actual facts as stated in the Bible, and their elaborations of scriptural accounts at first created significant problems for their colleagues in theology and history who were trying to justify slavery, racism, and even genocide. First of all, their version of creation did not leave much time for the development of diverse languages, tribes, and races for the peopling of the Earth, as described in scripture, and their date of creation was quite close to the beginnings of secular Mediterranean history, which at that time was thought to be about 500 BCE (or BC), the time of Herodotus. Worse than that, as far as the slavery of Africans and American Indians was concerned, their theory of monogenesis—that all humans were descended from Adam and Eve, and descended again from Noah and his sons following the Flood—implied that all humans were kin to one another. Consequently, the slavery of humans by humans was the enslavement of cousins by cousins, a moral dilemma for Christians.

JUSTIFYING SLAVERY

To overcome this dilemma, four solutions were proposed that had the power to excuse the practice of slavery, upon which an increasing portion of the European economy depended in the so-called Age of Discovery.

One solution was to argue that American Indians and Africans were not humans at all, and that they had no souls. Thus, enslaving or killing them was not a mortal sin as far as Christians were concerned. Two other solutions were polygenetic in nature and alleged that although the "primitive races" or "savages" of the Earth were human, they were either "pre-Adamites," meaning they were created long before Adam and Eve, or "post-Adamites," created after Adam and Eve were driven from the Garden of Eden. In either case these were people engendered by "separate creations," and thus were not proper objects for the application of Christian morality.

Another powerful theory offered by Christian apologists for slavery concerned the unequal distribution of sinfulness among the sons of Noah. This involved an ingenious reading of the story of the aftermath of the Flood, during which it was said that Ham, the alleged ancestor of Africans, had abused his drunken father (some interpreters said he raped him, others that he castrated him), while Shem, the ancestor of Asians and American Indians, had watched but did not interfere, and it was only Japheth, the ancestor of Europeans (including Jews), who had the decency to "cover his father's nakedness." According to Genesis 9:24–25 (in the King James version): "Noah awoke from his wine and knew what his younger son had done unto him. And he said, Cursed be Canaan; a servant of servants shall he be unto his brethren." That is, he cursed Ham's son, whose name was Canaan. According to this interpretation (known as the curse of Ham, or the curse of Canaan), Ham and his descendants, exiled to Africa, were to be servants for the descendants of Noah's other sons; that is, they were to be slaves. The various allegations of heinous sexual violations attributed to Ham in the most sacred literature of Christianity thus supplied a convenient rationale for European slave raiders, slave traders, and slave owners even though Genesis says nothing about the pigmentation of Africans.

A subsequent verse of Genesis, which addressed the situations of both Africans and Native Americans (the sons of Shem) seemed exactly appropriate for English colonists in New England and Virginia in the early seventeenth century. Genesis 9:27 states: "God shall enlarge Japheth, and he shall dwell in the tents of Shem; and Canaan shall be his servant." Colonial Virginians took this to mean that God knew they would some day outgrow their homeland (the British Isles), and that they would at that point have divine approval to come to Virginia and take the houses and farmlands of local Indians ("the tents of Shem"), whom they were at liberty to massacre, after which they could import African slaves to do the work. Their importation of Africans came after a period in which they experimented unsuccessfully with Indian slavery. In New England, the preference was to sell Indian captives to Jamaica or exchange them for African slaves.

A bizarre footnote was added to the racist account of the origins of "Hamites" by J. B. Stoner, the editor in the 1960s of the *Thunderbolt*, a publication of the National States' Rights Party, and the man convicted of bombing a black church in Alabama in 1958. Inspired by the French racist Jean-Joseph Virey, Stoner asserted that not only were modern Africans the descendants of Ham's accursed son Canaan, but they were also the result of unions between "Hamites and Great Apes," thereby making them only half human. This assertion served to justify the next episode of moral atrocities against the Bible, the Trial in Valladolid, in Spain, which in the sixteenth century was part of the Holy Roman Empire.

THE DEBATE IN VALLADOLID

For the first twenty years in their "New World" of the Americas, Spanish conquistadores could kill or enslave Indians with impunity, because they were regarded as "black dogs" without souls. But in 1512 the Laws of

Burgos were promulgated, stating that Indians were humans, had souls, and could be converted to Christianity. The Catholic world then became divided on the issue of whether Indians were "natural slaves," born into a naturally servile condition, or whether they had the same rights as other citizens. To settle this issue, Emperor Charles V convened a panel of distinguished scholars in 1550–1551, for the trial in Valladolid. Arguing for the status of Indians as "natural slaves" was Juan Sepúlveda, who took the "colonialist" position, while Bartolomé de Las Casas took the "indigenist" position, defending the Indians. Both sides drew heavily on the writings of Aristotle and St. Thomas Aquinas concerning natural slavery and the notion of the "just war," whereby captured enemies could be enslaved.

Although no "winner" of the debate was ever announced, it resulted in an improvement for the situation of Indians, especially with the General Ordinance of 1573, which specified that before the population of an Indian pueblo could be enslaved, someone had to announce to them that the village was about to be attacked, and that the consequences would be death or enslavement. In practice, this might mean that a soldier could sneak up to the outskirts of a village at night and yell out (or whisper) the prescribed warning in Spanish or Latin, followed quickly by the attack.

The situation of Indians in North America, under assault by French and English colonial forces, was no better, and perhaps worse. The English goal was not so much to enslave Indians, but to kill or expel them and take their land. Both the French and English considered Indians to be cannibals and Satanists who could be killed at will by Europeans. During his 1577 search for a Northwest Passage around North America, Martin Frobisher hiked up the skirts of an Indian woman to see if she had cloven hooves. After the Pequot Massacre of hundreds of Indian women and children in Masssachusetts in 1637, the English leader John Underhill announced: "Sometimes the Scripture declareth women and children must perish with their parents. … We had sufficient light from the word of God for our proceedings." The writings of John Smith and other Virginia colonists express the same sentiments, as did some Canadian priests, such as Paul Le Jeune in his contributions to the *Jesuit Relations*.

POLYGENETIC JUSTIFICATION

Two of the four theories listed above are "polygenetic" in nature, arguing that the "lower races" were created separately, either before or after the creation of white people during the events recounted in the Book of Genesis. Both theories were based on anthropological evidence that had been accumulating in the eighteenth and nineteenth centuries. In Europe, primitive tools called "thunderstones" and ape-like human skulls had begun to accumulate in museums, which indicated that some kind of "ape-man" or "cave-man" had existed in Europe for hundreds of thousands, or perhaps millions, of years. In the meantime, geologists such as Charles Lyell, a Southern Confederacy sympathizer, were arguing persuasively that the Earth was millions of years old.

Proponents of polygenesis accommodated this new evidence by explaining that these bones and tools represented some early experiments in human creation, before God "got it right" with the creation of white people in the events described in Genesis. It was argued further that these early fossils were the ancestors of the "primitive people" discovered around the world by European explorers. That is, modern "primitives" or "savages" were supposed to be the descendants of God's "failed attempts" to create perfect humans "in his own image."

Those polygeneticists who argued that Africans and others were post-Adamites, created after rather than before the events of Genesis, relied more on Biblical texts than on anthropological evidence. They argued that, in the Bible, husbands and wives of the descendants of Adam and Eve came from foreign countries unaccounted for in Biblical narrative. Therefore, there must have been other creations, which they say included those of the "inferior races."

A more modern advocate of polygenesis was Carleton Coon, a Harvard-trained anthropologist who hypothesized in the 1950s that there were five separate lines of human ancestry, corresponding to the five races of humankind, each of which crossed the human "threshold" separately. Thus, European people had been human longer than Africans, and thus were more "advanced." Although Coon admitted that Africa was the "cradle of mankind," he wrote in *The Origin of Races* (1962) that the continent was "only an indifferent kindergarten," as compared to Europe, the "cradle of civilization" (p. 656).

Even in the early twenty-first century, the theory of creation as an instantaneous event leaves the door open for theories of polygenesis, theories that have always operated to the detriment of nonwhites. Darwinian theories, like the fundamentalist monogenetic theories celebrated by most Christians, argue for a common ancestry for all humans, and thus for the "brotherhood of man." All present evidence indicates, contrary to what Carleton Coon argued, that human beings have developed and evolved through history not as separate races, but as a single species, constantly sharing their genes, languages, and cultures as they developed and migrated around the world.

BIBLIOGRAPHY

Coon, Carleton S. 1967. *The Origin of Races*. New York: Alfred A. Knopf.

Frederickson, George M. 2002. *Racism: A Short History*. Princeton, NJ: Princeton University Press.

Goldenberg, David M. 2003. *The Curse of Ham: Race and Slavery in Early Judaism, Christianity, and Islam*. Princeton, NJ: Princeton University Press.

Hanke, Lewis. 1959. *Aristotle and the American Indians*. Chicago: Henry Regnery.

Haynes, Stephen R. 2002. *Noah's Curse: The Biblical Justification of American Slavery*. Oxford: Oxford University Press.

Leach, Edmund. 1969. *Genesis as Myth*. London: Cape Edition, Grossman.

MacLeod, William Christie. 1928. *The American Indian Frontier*. London: Kegan Paul.

Shipmen, Pat. 1994. *The Evolution of Racism: Human Differences and the Use and Abuse of Science*. New York: Simon & Schuster.

Thwaites, Reuben Gold. 1896–1901. *The Jesuit Relations and Allied Documents: Travels and Explorations of the Jesuit Missionaries in New France 1610–1791*. 73 volumes. Cleveland: Burrows Bros.

Winchell, Alexander. 1878. *Adamites and Preadamites*. Syracuse, NY: John T. Roberts.

John H. Moore

GENETIC DISTANCE

Genetic distance refers to the mathematical reduction of multidimensional genetic differences to one-dimensional lengths, which can then be easily compared. While mathematical precedents existed, the use of genetic distance flowered in the 1960s with the conjunction of two biological programs: (1) racial serology, which had been amassing genetic data on differences across populations but was quantitatively unsophisticated; and (2) numerical taxonomy, which was developing a radical post-Linnaean approach to biological systematics and was mathematically sophisticated but philosophically unpersuasive.

Racial serology, the study of human diversity using immunological reactions of the blood, began during World War I. As the collection and analysis expanded, it became clear that different blood markers showed different patterns of diversity across the human gene pool. For example, diverse populations, such as Navajos and Estonians, might have very different allele frequencies for the ABO blood group, but very similar allele frequencies for the MN blood group. With many populations and many blood group markers, these data quickly become unwieldy.

Numerical taxonomy sought to replace the verbal impressionistic taxonomy of earlier generations with a rigorous, mathematical approach to scientific classification. Its focus was on establishing patterns of relationships, based on quantifiable similarity, among groups of objects, which came to be called *operational taxonomic units*, or OTUs. The goal of numerical taxonomy was to create a tree-like structure, or *dendrogram*, a statistical digestion summarizing the similarities of OTUs.

The techniques of numerical taxonomy lent themselves well to the analysis of data from many genetic loci across many human populations. Unfortunately, their formalism tended to obscure layers of subjectivity. At the most fundamental level, different statistical algorithms can produce different trees from the same data. Moreover, the trees are generated regardless of whether or not the OTUs are comparable. Thus, if the African gene pool subsumes the European gene pool, then they cannot be intelligibly contrasted against one another (although the computer programs will mindlessly do so). Likewise, the computer will produce relationships among groups defined geographically, linguistically, politically, ethnically, and racially in the same study, in spite of the fact that such comparisons may be largely meaningless.

Further, the meaning of a relatively small genetic difference may be problematic. Above the species level, it likely indicates a close phylogenetic relationship (a recent divergence time between the species being compared). Below the species level, however, it may indicate both phylogenetic proximity and complex patterns of genetic contact (gene flow).

Consequently, the greatest success of genetic distance studies has come above the species level. In 1967, Vincent Sarich and Allan Wilson were able to show that (1) measurable rates of genetic change appear to be roughly constant; (2) the genetic distance between human and chimpanzee seem to correspond to a divergence time of 3 to 5 million years; and therefore (3) the fossils called *Ramapithecus*, dated to 14 million years ago, could not be on the uniquely human evolutionary line, because that line was not established for nearly another 10 million years.

Meanwhile, direct DNA sequence comparisons were facilitated technologically in the 1980s and 1990s. The most fundamental problem faced by these comparisons is the relationship between the amount of difference observed and the amount of evolution inferred. Where DNA sequence changes are rare, the number of differences observed between two species will approximate the number of evolutionary changes that actually occurred to the DNA. The sample size of those changes is small, however. In contrast, where DNA sequence differences between two species are copious, the sample of evolutionary changes is high. Regardless, the number of observed differences will *underestimate* the actual number of mutations that have occurred, because a single observed difference may represent multiple changes ("hits") at the same nucleotide site.

Thus, rapidly evolving mitochondrial DNA (mtDNA) may be valuable for estimating reliable and precise genetic distances among human populations over a span of thousands of years. It is less valuable for the distances among ape species over millions of years, where unacceptably high levels of homoplasy (parallel mutations in different lineages) may create a disjuncture between the genetic distances measured and the evolutionary patterns inferred from them.

Mitochondrial DNA comparisons do suggest that human beings are about forty to fifty times more similar to each another than any human is to a chimpanzee. The detectable mtDNA distance between human and Neanderthal appears to be comparable to that between chimpanzee subspecies.

BIBLIOGRAPHY

Hull, David L. 1988. *Science as a Process: An Evolutionary Account of the Social and Conceptual Development of Science.* Chicago, University of Chicago Press.

Marks, Jonathan. 1995. *Human Biodiversity: Genes, Race, and History.* New York, Aldine de Gruyter.

Nei, Masatoshi. 1987. *Molecular Evolutionary Genetics.* New York, Columbia University Press.

Sarich, Vincent M., and Allan C. Wilson. 1967. "Immunological Time Scale for Hominid Evolution." *Science* 158: 1200–1203.

Jonathan Marks

GENETIC MARKER

A genetic marker is a trait transmitted from parent to child, thus potentially permitting the reconstruction of patterns of descent on the basis of its distribution among population members. Genetic markers are thus estimators of biological relatedness, and when they are shared by individuals they are interpreted as evidence of a "natural" link between them. Genetic markers have been used to establish paternity, to identify the origin of a biological sample at a crime scene, to create maps of disease-causing genes, and to link people who have never met one another into new networks of kinship relations. The reliability of the inferences derived from any genetic marker is a function of three properties: (1) mode of inheritance, (2) stability, and (3) rarity.

The mode of inheritance of a genetic marker may be quite variable. Surnames in many societies are inherited in a fashion that mimics a Y chromosome (that is, a father and son are very highly correlated), and thus can serve as a noninvasive estimator of relatedness. (The method of tracking genetic inbreeding in a population through surname distribution is called isonymy.) By contrast, chromosomes from the cell's nucleus are transmitted to offspring biologically. However, because each parent passes on only one member of each pair of chromosomes, a child ordinarily has only a 50 percent chance of matching a parent's (or sibling's) corresponding genetic marker. There are exceptions to this rule:. Most of the Y chromosome is transmitted intact from father to son, so that the Y chromosomes of a father and son should be nearly identical. Likewise, the DNA of the mitochondria, which exist in the cell but outside the nucleus, is transmitted intact from mother to offspring, so that there should be a perfect match between a mother and child (and the father is paradoxically unrelated to the child with this marker).

Stable genetic markers are preferred for comparisons because they enable tracking over many generations. Physical features with multifactorial or polygenic causes, such as features of the bones and teeth, may appear to blend away over generations from intermarriage, or they may have their expression altered by the environmental conditions in which the organism grows and develops. Very rapidly mutating segments of DNA may be just as compromised for use as genetic markers, if their rate and mode of change preclude a secure match between related individuals.

A common genetic marker is less valuable than a rare one, for the simple reason that a match between two samples is more likely to be due to chance, rather than to familial descent, if the genetic marker is a common one. Because type O blood is the most ubiquitous blood type among all human populations, two people who are not close relatives are nevertheless very likely to exhibit this genetic marker. It would consequently be a genetic match, but not a very informative one.

Even before the development of the science of genetics, however, similarities of the language, skeleton, and teeth were being understood as crude genetic markers. Certain traits (ranging from diseases or deformities to simple quirks) were recognized to run in families, and thus to attest to close kinship among the bearers of such traits. In the early part of the twentieth century, serologists developed blood tests to detect biochemical differences among people, which were very close to direct products of the genes, if not the genes themselves. The most immediate value of these differences was in paternity exclusion, but they were also quickly adopted to study racial relationships. This proved to be a very frustrating exercise because groups of humans identified serologically corresponded very poorly to common concepts of "races" (see Marks 1995).

In modern forensic contexts, in order to connect a suspect to a sample (and to rule out the possibility of such a match coming at random), genetic markers need to be both highly variable and individually uncommon. Short, localized repetitive DNA sequences, in which the number of tandem repetitions of the specific DNA sequence varies strikingly from person to person, have proven to be most effective for this purpose. In gene-mapping studies, DNA markers are commonly differences of a single base among individuals in a population (such differences are called single nucleotide polymorphisms, or SNPs). A linear series of these genetic markers, usually transmitted as a single block of DNA, is called a haplotype.

Genetic ancestry services principally use markers derived from Y chromosome DNA and mitochondrial DNA to establish matches between samples of presumptive relatives. Others use nuclear DNA markers from small samples of diverse peoples as a baseline to establish a customer's "racial" affiliation, which simply expresses an overall pattern of similarity to one or more of these standard samples.

BIBLIOGRAPHY

Bolnick, Deborah A. Forthcoming 2008. "Individual Ancestry Inference and the Reification of Race as a Biological Phenomenon." In *Revisiting Race in the Age of Genomics*, edited by Barbara Koenig, Sandra Lee, and Sarah Richardson. Piscataway, NJ: Rutgers University Press.

Marks, Jonathan. 1996. "The Legacy of Serological Studies in American Physical Anthropology." *History and Philosophy of the Life Sciences* 18 (3): 345–362.

Jonathan Marks

GENETIC VARIATION AMONG POPULATIONS

Questions regarding the usefulness of the concept of "race" to the study of human genetic diversity must ultimately be answered with reference to the degree and patterning of genetic variation. Specifically, three questions must be addressed. First, how much variation exists among populations, relative to the amount of variation within populations? Second, what is the pattern of genetic variation among populations? That is, are all populations equally related—and if not, what are the geographic and historical factors that have influenced the genetic relationship among populations? Third, do studies of the degree and pattern of human genetic variation provide any answers to questions regarding the utility of the "race" concept?

THE APPORTIONMENT OF VARIATION

One of the main interests in studies of genetic variation is the question of how variation is apportioned both within and among populations. In other words, if a species is considered as made up of a number of different populations, how much of the total variation in the species exists within each population, and how much variation exists among all the populations? Although it is most convenient to define and discuss these concepts in mathematical terms, an intuitive approach is taken here in order to provide an understanding of the basic principles behind the apportionment of diversity.

The amount of variation within a population refers to the differences that exist between the members of that population. If, for example, a population consisted entirely of clones, then everyone in the population would be genetically the same, and there would be no variation within the population. The more different the individuals are from each other genetically, the greater the level of variation within the population. The exact level of this variation can be measured in different ways, depending on the specific measure or estimate of genetic variation at which one is looking. Variation among populations refers to the level of differences between two or more populations. If two populations were genetically the same, then there would be no variation among the populations. The more different the populations are from each other, the greater the level of variation among the populations.

A simple example of how these concepts work uses an analogy based on sorting out shapes. So, if one has ten squares and ten triangles, what are the different ways these twenty objects can be placed into two buckets, with each containing half of the objects? Three different cases are illustrated in Figure 1. In case number one, the first bucket contains ten squares and the second bucket contains ten triangles. Because all of the objects in the first bucket are squares, they are by definition all the same, so there is no variation within that bucket. The same result applies to the second bucket: each of the ten objects is a triangle, so there is no variation within that bucket. In both cases, the amount of variation within buckets is zero. Now, consider the amount of variation that exists among the buckets. This is by considering the frequency of squares and triangles in each bucket. The first bucket is made up of 100 percent squares and 0 percent triangles, whereas the second bucket has 0 percent squares and 100 percent triangles. In other words, the composition of the two buckets is completely different. When apportioning diversity, the amount of within-group variation plus the amount of among-group variation adds up to 100 percent. In this example, all of the variation exists among the two buckets, so that we could state that the amount of variation among groups is 100 percent and the amount of variation within groups is 0 percent.

The second case in Figure 1 shows the opposite pattern. There are still ten squares and ten triangles, but they are apportioned differently between the two buckets. Each bucket contains five squares and five triangles. Thus, there is variation within each bucket, because there are the two different shapes in each. However, there is no difference in the relative frequency of squares and triangles among the two buckets, as each bucket consists of 50 percent squares and 50 percent triangles. Because the two frequencies are the same, there is no difference among the buckets, and therefore the level of among-group variation is zero. In this case, all of the variation is within the buckets, meaning that the among-group variation is 0 percent and the within-group variation is 100 percent.

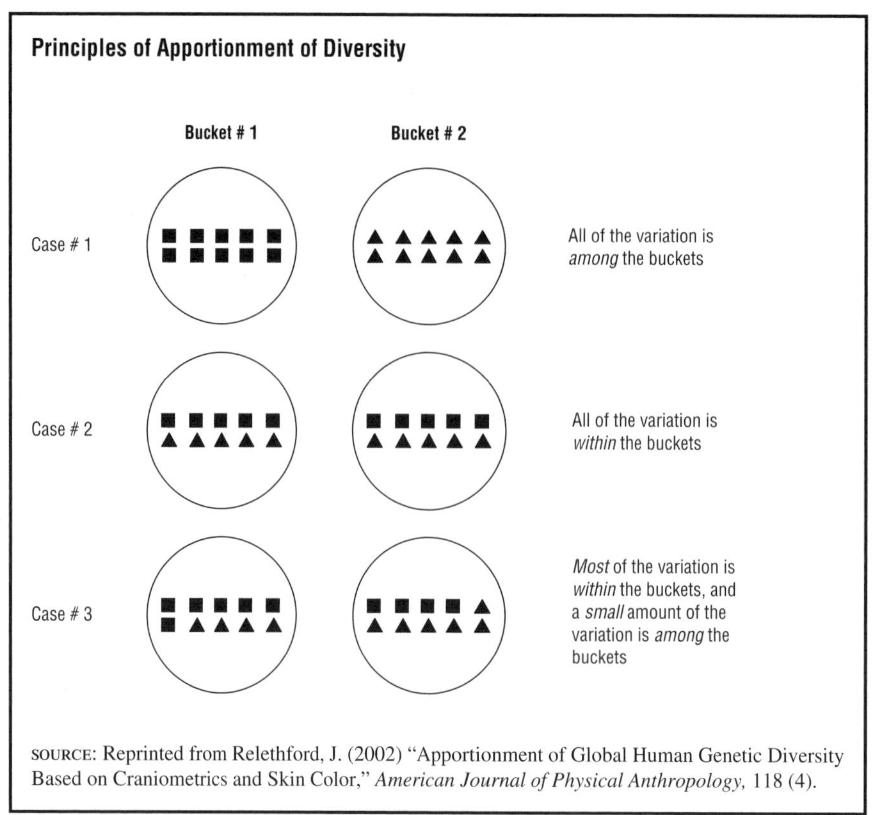
Principles of Apportionment of Diversity
Bucket # 1
Bucket # 2
Case # 1
All of the variation is *among* the buckets
Case # 2
All of the variation is *within* the buckets
Case # 3
Most of the variation is *within* the buckets, and a *small* amount of the variation is *among* the buckets
SOURCE: Reprinted from Relethford, J. (2002) "Apportionment of Global Human Genetic Diversity Based on Craniometrics and Skin Color," *American Journal of Physical Anthropology*, 118 (4).

Figure 1. *An example of the principles of apportionment of diversity. The three cases represent three different ways in which twenty objects (ten squares and ten triangles) can be divided into two buckets.*

The third case in Figure 1 has the first bucket containing six squares and four triangles and the second bucket containing four squares and six triangles. Thus, some variation exists within each bucket and, because the proportions of squares and triangles in the two buckets are not quite the same, some variation exists among the buckets as well.

What does all of this have to do with genetics and populations? The same principles of apportionment of variation apply to genetic data. Completing the analogy, consider the squares and triangles as equivalent to different forms of a gene and the buckets as equivalent to populations. In genetics, we refer to different forms of a gene as *alleles*. When looking at biochemical and molecular data, such as blood groups and DNA markers, there are standard methods for measuring the levels of within-group and among-group variation based on the relative frequency of alleles.

VARIATION AMONG POPULATIONS (F_{ST})

In population genetics, researchers are interested in the relative amount of variation that exists among populations, a term known by a number of symbols and names, but most often labeled F_{ST}. F_{ST} is the proportion of total variation that is due to variation among populations. The value of F_{ST} can range from 0.0 to 1.0 (or, in terms of percentages, from 0 percent to 100 percent). Considering the objects in Figure 1 as equivalent to alleles, the first case would have an F_{ST} equal to 1.0, meaning that the two populations are completely different in their allele frequencies and that everyone within the groups is genetically the same. In the second case in Figure 1, F_{ST} is equal to 0.0, meaning that the two populations have the same allele frequencies and that all of the genetic variation in the species occurs within the populations. The solution for F_{ST} in the third case is not intuitively obvious but can be computed using a standard population genetics formula, which results in F_{ST} being 0.04 in this example. This value means that 4 percent of the total variation exists among the two populations, leaving the remainder (96%) of the variation existing within the populations.

In reality, what is desired is not a reliance on only one gene for these estimates, but instead an average across as many genes as possible. There are several reasons for this. First, using numerous genes where possible minimizes sampling error. Second, natural selection can lead to differences in F_{ST} above or below what would be expected on average. If, for example, one were looking at a gene where different alleles were selected for in different populations, then the genetic difference between the populations would be greater than expected for genes not affected by differences in adaptation (neutral genes). Overall, F_{ST} is affected by the balance between gene flow (and mutation) and genetic drift. Gene flow and mutation lower the average F_{ST} and genetic drift increases average F_{ST}.

ESTIMATES OF F_{ST} FOR GEOGRAPHIC RACES

Given this background, the discussion can now return to the question of the amount of genetic variation that exists between races. This problem was first tackled quantitatively by Richard Lewontin in 1972 by using allele frequencies from across the world for a number of genetic markers based on red blood cells. Lewontin then subdivided the world into seven geographic "races" (although noting the difficulty in doing so): "Caucasians," "Black Africans," "Mongoloids," "South Asian Aborigines," "Amerinds," "Oceanians," and "Australian Aborigines." Within each of the seven races, he collated genetic data for a number of different local populations. For example, within the "Caucasian" race, he collected data on Belgians, Greeks, Italians, Iranians, Indians, and other populations in Europe, the Middle East, and South Asia. By looking at data at the level of race and local population, Lewontin was able to extend the principle of apportionment by breaking down the "within-race" component into: (1) variation among local populations within race, and (2) variation within local populations. He found that 6.3 percent of the total variation existed among races, 8.3 percent existed among local populations within races, and 85.4 percent existed within local populations. Lewontin concluded "human races and populations are remarkably similar to each other, with the largest part by far of human variation being accounted for by the differences between individuals" (Lewontin 1972, p. 397).

Since Lewontin's original work, additional data have been collected for red blood cell and other genetic markers for many more populations. Different researchers, realizing the arbitrary nature of enumerating and categorizing different geographic races, have tried different clusterings of local populations that make up each race. Overall, the results are consistent: approximately 10 percent of the genetic variation in the human species is among races (geographic regions), 5 percent is among local populations within races, and 85 percent is within local populations. The same pattern was also found in a comprehensive analysis of newer DNA markers by Guido Barbujani and colleagues (1997): 11 percent among geographic regions, 5 percent among local populations within geographic regions, and 84 percent within local populations. Another study by Lynn Jorde and colleagues (2000) showed that although some genetic traits, such as mitochondrial DNA, have higher levels of variation among geographic regions, the majority of variation is still within local populations (roughly 70%).

The principles of apportionment of diversity have also been extended to complex physical traits, such as cranial length. Even though such traits are affected by nongenetic as well as genetic factors, it is possible to obtain a rough estimate of the percentage of variation among and within groups. John Relethford (2002) examined a global sample of cranial measures and found results very similar to those from genetic markers: 13 percent among geographic regions, 6 percent among populations within geographic regions, and 81 percent within local populations.

The major inference from these studies is that if the world is divided into a set of races, then the overwhelming amount of human genetic diversity exists within races (and most of that further exists within the local population), and consequently that race explains a relatively small fraction of the species' diversity. This finding runs counter to views on race that emphasize group differences while minimizing variation within races.

To put it another way, the relatively low levels of variation among geographic races means that there is a great deal of overlap in the distributions of most traits, including blood cell markers, DNA markers, and cranial measures. Thus, the idea of discrete races that are easily identifiable from one another based on allele frequencies (or measures of metric traits) does not hold up well. There is certainly variation in most traits, as well as a geographic patterning to such variation, because human populations in different parts of the world tend to differ somewhat from each other. However, the level of these differences, as estimated by F_{ST} and related statistics, is rather low.

SKIN COLOR, RACIAL CLASSIFICATION, AND F_{ST}

Not all traits, genetic or physical, show low levels of among-group variation. In some cases, there is a high level of variation among geographic races. However, these exceptions to the general rule do not provide evidence of the existence of discrete human races, but instead point to the action of natural selection operating on some traits to inflate the level of among-group variation. One example that is particularly relevant to the question of racial classification is skin color, a trait that is measured in human populations using a reflectance spectrophotometer, a device that measures the percentage of light reflected back from the skin at given wavelengths.

John Relethford examined the apportionment of diversity using a global compilation of skin reflectance data and found that skin color showed the opposite pattern from that revealed by genetic markers and cranial measures. For skin color, the vast majority of variation was found to exist among geographic races (88%), with only 3 percent among local populations within geographic races, and 9 percent within local populations. These results are expected and intuitively obvious. For example, even though there is variation in skin color among indigenous Scots or indigenous Ethiopians, it is clear that the former have very light skin and the latter have very dark skin. Indeed, the large and easily noticeable difference in skin color across the globe is a reason that skin color factors into virtually every racial classification scheme that has been proposed.

However, the finding of a large level of among-group variation for skin color does not provide support for the existence of discrete races whose very definition was linked to skin color in the first place. If such discrete groups are so readily identifiable based on one trait, they should also be found based on other traits, but this is not the case. What needs to be explained is why skin color is so atypical when compared to all of the other genetic and physical traits that show low levels of among-group variation.

The answer is that skin color is affected differentially by natural selection across geographic space. Skin color shows a very strong correlation with latitude, so that indigenous populations near or at the equator tend to be the darkest, while populations farther away from the equator (north or south) tend to be lighter. This correlation has been linked to levels of ultraviolet radiation, which also varies by latitude—ultraviolet radiation levels are highest at or near the equator and lower farther away from the equator. A traditional explanation of the evolution of human skin color differences is as follows. In human species' past, darker skin was selected for in populations that lived in areas of high ultraviolet radiation, because the darker skin is less prone to damage such as sunburn, skin cancer, and the photodestruction of folate, a needed nutrient. As human ancestors dispersed out of Africa, they moved into areas of lower ultraviolet radiation. For these groups, the problem of survival changed from danger due to too much ultraviolet radiation to danger from too little, such as lower levels of vitamin-D synthesis (ultraviolet radiation provided the major source of vitamin D in most human populations prior to modern times). It appears that, in this situation, lower levels of ultraviolet radiation selected for lighter skin in human populations. Although there is some debate over the exact factors responsible for changes in human skin color, there is little argument that natural selection has shaped the range of human skin color variation. The result has been the evolution of extreme levels of pigmentation in different environments geographically far apart, thus leading to an increased level of among-group variation.

Even if one ignores data showing low levels of racial differences and focuses on skin color, a closer examination shows that the geographic pattern of human skin-color variation does not fit a model of discrete racial groupings. Quite simply, skin color does not come in a finite number of shades, despite the repeated use of classificatory words such as "black," "white," and "brown." Instead, the distribution of human skin color shows a gradient that is correlated with latitude. To put this in a nonstatistical frame of reference, imagine someone starting at the equator and walking north. As that person starts walking, the indigenous people he or she sees will tend to be very darkly pigmented. With continued walking, the average skin color will tend to become lighter and lighter. In other words, the walker will see one level of pigmentation blend into the next, with no apparent discontinuities, a pattern that is at odds with a discontinuous and discrete definition of race.

GEOGRAPHIC DISTANCE AND THE PATTERN OF GENETIC VARIATION

The majority of genetic variation in the human species exists within local populations, and a smaller fraction (typically about 10 to 15%) is found among geographic races. It is also important to consider the pattern of among-group variation as well as the magnitude. Human genetic variation typically follows a pattern known as "isolation by distance." This means that the farther two populations are from one another geographically, the more genetically different they will be from one another. To test this model, genetic data is used to derive measures of genetic distance between pairs of populations, and these values are plotted as a function of the geographic distance between each pair of populations. Figure 2 shows an example of the relationship between genetic distance and geographic distance on a global scale using the genetic distances given by L. Luca Cavalli-Sforza and colleagues (1994). The figure clearly shows how the genetic differences between human populations are smallest among those populations that live close to each other, and how they increase among populations that are located farther away from each other. Similar results have been found for a variety of genetic data and cranial measures (Relethford 2004).

This pattern of isolation by distance is frequently found among populations in a small region, such as villages within a country, and it typically reflects the limiting effect of geographic distance on the movement of people, and hence on the movement of genes. Throughout human history and prehistory, the highest frequency of mating took place close

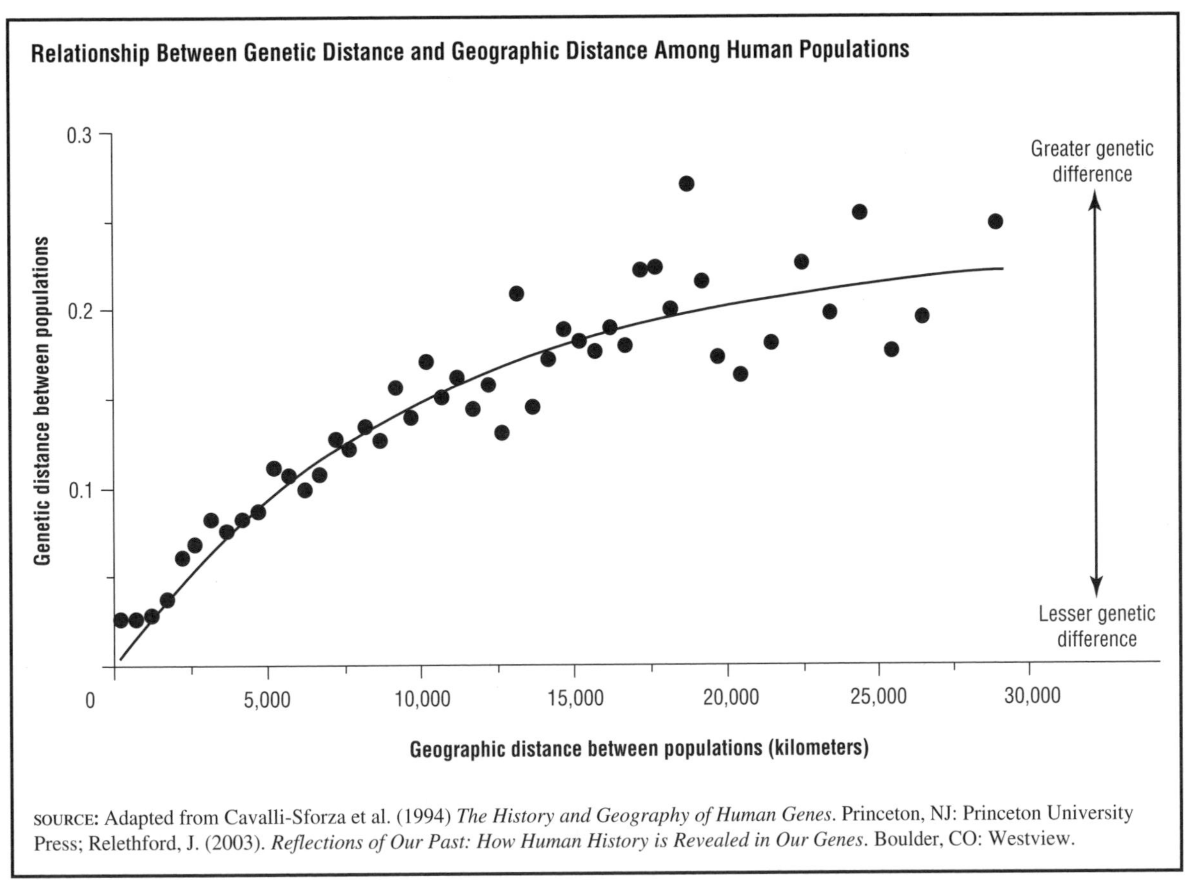

SOURCE: Adapted from Cavalli-Sforza et al. (1994) *The History and Geography of Human Genes.* Princeton, NJ: Princeton University Press; Relethford, J. (2003). *Reflections of Our Past: How Human History is Revealed in Our Genes.* Boulder, CO: Westview.

Figure 2. *The farther human populations are from one another geographically, the greater the genetic difference between them. Genetic distances are from Cavalli-Sforza et al. (1994) and grouped into different geographic distance classes as described by Relethford (2003). The solid line represents the best fitting curve to the observed data.*

to home, such that populations close to each other in space have tended to share more genes, all other things being equal. It is easy to see how geographic distance can limit movement, and this was particularly true in earlier times. It is less clear, however, if the global pattern of isolation by distance is completely due to the limiting impact of geographic distance. It is also quite likely that the human species' origins played a role in structuring the geographic correlation of genetic diversity. Most anthropologists agree that modern human populations appeared first in sub-Saharan Africa somewhere between 130,000 and 195,000 years ago, followed by dispersion throughout the rest of the world. Although there is continuing debate over whether modern humans replaced or mixed with pre-existing humans outside of Africa (such as the Neandertals of Europe), the general finding of an African origin and dispersal is supported by both genetic and fossil evidence. Therefore, the correlation seen in the early twenty-first century between geographic distance and genetic distance may be a reflection of this dispersal.

Regardless of the relative impact of migration and population history, the important point here is that human genetic variation is geographically structured. The genetic differences that exist among human populations in distant parts of the planet have often been considered representative of racial differences, but the actual pattern of geographic variation is continuous and does not fit a model of discrete races.

An analysis of the pattern of genetic variation among living human populations does not provide support for a rigid application of the biological race concept to the human species. First, the amount of variation that exists among geographic races is relatively low, indicating a great deal of overlap in allele frequencies and measures of physical traits. Second, those traits that do show higher levels of racial differences, such as skin color, are atypical in this respect and reflect the evolutionary history of the trait. Third, the pattern of genetic differences among human populations is a reflection of geographic distance and migration history, and thus does not conform to a model of discrete and non-overlapping races.

It is also clear, that denying an application of a strict definition of biological race does not mean that human genetic variation is nonexistent or that all human populations are genetically the same. A refutation of the race concept does not equate to a denial of variation. It is clear that there is genetic variation in the human species and that it is geographically structured. What continues to be debated in the "race question" is the best way to describe this variation and how well the race concept, other than as a first-order approximation, serves a descriptive function. An application of the concept of race is only a crude attempt to describe continuous variation in terms of discrete clusters, much as people attempt to reduce socioeconomic variation into "classes" or political orientation into "liberals" and "conservatives." Imposing discrete labels on continuous variation is not necessarily bad, as long as one is careful not to reify those labels, and as long as there is some justification for its use over analyses that focus on local populations as the unit of evolution and analysis. In terms of analyzing human biological variation, it has long been known that subdividing the human species into races is at best an exercise in classification, but one that obscures the fine details of variation and explains little about the underlying causes of variation.

SEE ALSO *Clines and Continuous Variation; Forensic Anthropology and Race; Gene Pool; Genetic Distance; Genetic Marker; Genetics, History of; Human and Primate Evolution; Human Genetics; "Out of Africa" Hypothesis; Racial Hierarchy; Skin Color; UNESCO Statements on Race.*

BIBLIOGRAPHY

Barbujani, Guido, Arianna Magagni, Eric Minch, and L. Luca Cavalli-Sforza. 1997. "An Apportionment of Human DNA Diversity." *Proceedings of the National Academy of Sciences USA* 94 (9): 4516–4519.

Brown, Ryan A., and George J. Armelagos. 2001. "Apportionment of Racial Diversity: A Review." *Evolutionary Anthropology* 10 (1): 34–40.

Cavalli-Sforza, L. Luca, Paolo Menozzi, and Alberto Piazza. 1994. *The History and Geography of Human Genes.* Princeton, NJ: Princeton University Press.

Jablonski, Nina G., and George Chaplin. 2000. "The Evolution of Human Skin Coloration." *Journal of Human Evolution* 39 (1): 57–106.

Jorde, Lynn B., et al. 2000. "The Distribution of Human Genetic Diversity: A Comparison of Mitochondrial, Autosomal, and Y-Chromosome Data." *American Journal of Human Genetics* 66 (3): 979–988.

Lewontin, Richard C. 1972. "The Apportionment of Human Diversity." *Evolutionary Biology* 6: 381–398.

Relethford, John H. 2002. "Apportionment of Global Human Genetic Diversity Based on Craniometrics and Skin Color." *American Journal of Physical Anthropology* 118 (4): 393–398.

———. 2003. *Reflections of Our Past: How Human History Is Revealed in Our Genes.* Boulder, CO: Westview.

———. 2004. "Global Patterns of Isolation by Distance Based on Genetic and Morphological Data." *Human Biology* 76 (4): 499–513.

Templeton, Alan R. 1998. "Human Races: A Genetic and Evolutionary Perspective." *American Anthropologist* 100 (3): 632–650.

John H. Relethford

GENETICS, HISTORY OF

Genetics is the study of the biological process of heredity. Although human beings have been interested in heredity—of both themselves and domesticated animals and plants—for thousands of years, genetics as a science was only formally born at the beginning of the twentieth century. At this time, the breeding experiments of Gregor Mendel, an Augustinian monk in Brünn, Austria, originally published in 1866, were rediscovered. The term *genetics* was introduced in 1906 by the British biologist William Bateson and was meant to distinguish Mendel's experimental approach from older, speculative theories.

The history of genetics from 1900 onward can be divided conveniently into two periods. During the first, or "classical," period (1900–1950), the focus was on the extension and modification of Mendel's original hypotheses to a wide variety of animals and plants (including humans), and to establishing the physical basis for heredity in cell structures known as *chromosomes.* The second period, that of "molecular" genetics (1950–present), has been dominated by the search for the molecular and biochemical basis of gene structure and function. This period began with experiments showing that the molecule that carried information from parent to offspring is deoxyribonucleic acid (DNA). The working out of DNA's detailed molecular structure as a double helix was accomplished by James D. Watson and Francis Crick in 1953.

A major assumption throughout both periods has been that the hereditary process is basically the same in all organisms, and genetics thus served as a major unifying principle for biology in the twentieth century. By the end of the century, with completion of the Human Genome Project (which sequenced the DNA of all the functional regions of the human chromosomes, and that of five other species for comparison) and the rise of the computer-based field of genomics (which studies DNA sequences among different individuals and groups of organisms) genetics came to dominate biology both conceptually and commercially. In both periods, genetics has also been used in attempts to elucidate human "races" and the biological basis of racial differences.

THE PERIOD OF CLASSICAL GENETICS (1900–1950)

Mendel's hybridization experiments between 1856 and 1865 with the common garden pea, *Pisa sativum*, laid the groundwork for the development of classical genetics. Mendel had crossed pea plants that differed by one or two observable traits, such as height (either tall or dwarf), or pod color (yellow or green), which led him to put forward several hypotheses, particularly those of dominance and recessiveness. Mendel noted that when he crossed a pure-bred tall plant with a pure-bred short (dwarf) plant, all the offspring of the first generation (called the F_1) were tall; thus he proposed that tallness was "dominant" over shortness, and, conversely, that shortness was "recessive" to tallness. However, when he crossed members of the F_1 generation he found that the offspring showed a ratio of roughly three tall plants to one short, and that the one short plant was on average as short as the original short parent.

To explain these results, Mendel hypothesized that each parent contained two "factors" (the term gene was introduced in 1909 by the Danish plant breeder Wilhelm Johannsen) for any trait (in this case height), and that these factors segregated in the formation of the egg or pollen cells (the gametes, or egg and sperm in animals). Using capital letters for dominant traits, and small-case letters for recessives, Mendel represented his original, pure-bred parental plants as *T* (in the early twenty-first century *TT* is used, representing a pure or homozygous tall) and *t* (currently *tt* is used, representing a pure or homozygous dwarf). During segregation, the two *TT*s would be separated from each other and would end up in a separate egg or pollen cell; the same would be true of the two *tt*s. The offspring of the F_1 would thus all be *Tt* and would appear tall. When these were crossed with each other, the second generation (F_2) could have one of three possible gene combinations: *TT, Tt,* and *tt.* Since *T* was dominant over *t*, both *TT* and *Tt* types would appear tall, and only *tt* would appear short. This would explain the 3:1 ratio in the F_2 (one *TT,* two *Tt*s, and one *tt*). Furthermore, when he went on to observe two traits at a time, such as height and pod color, he got all possible combinations—tall-yellow, tall, green, short yellow and short green, and in predictable ratios (9:3:3:1, respectively). These observations suggested to Mendel that various traits in an organism were inherited independently of each other (what became known as the principle of independent assortment).

Mendel's work also showed that there was a clear-cut theoretical basis for the distinction between what came to be known as an organism's *phenotype* (its appearance, as in tall or short) and its *genotype* (what genes it can pass on to its offspring, as in *T* or *t*). Thus Mendel's F_2 tall plants all had the same phenotype, but they did not all have the same genotype. Mendel's experimental and mathematical approach provided the basis for a new research program that included the search for the physical and chemical nature of the gene itself.

Finding a generally applicable theory of heredity was of great importance in the late nineteenth and early twentieth centuries. For centuries, agricultural breeders had been trying to develop some understanding of how to improve their stocks in an efficient and systematic way. Mendel provided some hope that the process could be made more scientific, and thus more predictable. In addition, one of the major problems Darwin had left unsolved in *The Origin of Species* and other evolutionary writings was the nature of heredity: Were the variations on which natural selection acted large and discontinuous, or small and continuous? Which variations were inherited and which were not? How could the reappearance of traits that had skipped one or more generations be explained? And finally, because Mendel's work appeared to apply to humans as well as other organisms (by 1910 a number of human traits, such as eye color, color blindness, hemophilia, the ABO blood groups, and Huntington's disease had been shown to follow basic Mendelian rules), it was hoped that knowledge of the inheritance patterns, especially of pathological traits, would provide an important way to control human reproduction and eliminate inherited diseases.

The Chromosome Theory of Heredity. The hypothetical nature of Mendel's "factors" were a major stumbling block in the general acceptance of Mendelian theory. It was Thomas Hunt Morgan and his group, working with fruit flies (*Drosophila melanogaster*) at Columbia University from 1910 onward, that established the physical basis for Mendelian genetics. Using a combination of breeding experiments and cytological study (microscopical examination of the chromosomes found in the cell nucleus), Morgan and his group were able to establish that genes were discrete units arranged linearly on the chromosomes. Starting from the observation that some traits do not appear to segregate randomly, but are rather inherited together (they are said to be "linked"), Morgan and his group established that in *Drosophilia* there were four linkage groups, corresponding to the four sets of paired chromosomes characteristic for the species. Moreover, Morgan and his group devised a method, using the process of breakage and recombination that occasionally occurs between members of a chromosome pair, to map the position of genes on the chromosomes. It was the combination of Mendelian breeding experiments with cytological observations that led to what became known as the Mendelian chromosome theory of heredity (MCTH). For this work, Morgan received the Nobel Prize for Physiology or Medicine in 1933, the first such award to be given in genetics.

ELABORATION OF THE MENDELIAN CHROMOSOME THEORY OF HEREDITY

Almost as soon as biologists and breeders adopted the MCTH they began to encounter exceptions to Mendel's original formulation. One was linkage, but it was accounted for by the chromosome theory. Another was incomplete dominance, in which the offspring showed a form of the trait intermediate between that of the two parents (as in pink flowers from a cross between white- and red-flowered parents). Another was epistasis, in which genes interact with each other to produce an effect that neither produced on its own. The converse of epistasis was pleiotropy, in which it came to be recognized that every gene has multiple effects, meaning each one influences more than one trait. Still another exception was what became known as quantitative inheritance, in which genes for a trait could exist in different doses, so that a continuous series of phenotypes (from light red to dark red, for example) could be generated simply by breeding for different dosages of a pigment gene. Last of all, it was observed that changes in environmental conditions during development of the organism could alter the expression of genes. *Drosophila* larvae of one genotype, when raised at a slightly higher-than-normal temperature, produced adult flies that looked like another genotype (these were called *phenocopies*). Ironically, most geneticists were so focused on the gene itself that they failed to understand the importance of phenocopies for investigating how genes might function during embryonic development. The few who tried to emphasize the plasticity of the gene, such as Richard Goldschmidt of Germany, were strongly attacked.

EUGENICS

During the classical period, genetics was used as scientific backing for the eugenics movement in many countries of North and South America, Europe, and Asia. The term *eugenics* was coined in 1883 by Darwin's cousin, the geographer and statistician Francis Galton, to refer to the right to be "purely, or truly born" (in a biological sense). In *Inquiries into Human Faculty and Its Development*, Galton wrote that "Eugenics takes cognisance of all the influences that tend in however remote a degree to give the more suitable races or strains of blood a better chance of prevailing over the less suitable than they otherwise would have had" (pp. 24–25). Galton, along with eugenicists in the United States and Europe, thought that a large number of social and mental traits (e.g., alcoholism, feeblemindedness, schizophrenia, criminality, "nomadism," pauperism, even a sense of fair play), were all determined by a few Mendelian genes. Especially in the United States (and later in Germany and Scandinavia), eugenicists wanted to apply genetic theories to the guidance of social policy. Prevention of the "unfit" from reproducing was one of the major goals of the eugenics movement. Eugenicists were convinced that "defectives" had a much higher birth rate than normal or "high-grade" people, and that if various methods to reduce this rate were not undertaken, high quality human lines would be "swamped" by those of low quality, causing the population as a whole to degenerate. By appealing to these fears, eugenicists were able to influence more than thirty states to pass compulsory sterilization laws that could be applied to institutionalized individuals, such as those in prisons or state mental hospitals. The U.S. sterilization laws formed the basis for similar laws passed in the late 1920s in the Scandinavian countries, Canada, and, after the Nazis came to power, in Germany in 1933. Sweden and the United States, for example, each forcibly sterilized more than 65,000 people, while Germany, under the Nazis, sterilized 400,000.

Eugenicists were also concerned about what they considered to be the deleterious effects of race-crossing (which at the time also meant crossing between ethnic groups). It was thought that, in such mixtures, whatever good qualities existed in either group would tend to get lost. One writer, the mammalian geneticist William E. Castle at Harvard argued that crosses between a Negro and a white person could produce individuals that were out of proportion. Another, Madison Grant, a wealthy New York lawyer and self-styled anthropologist, wrote in *The Passing of the Great Race* that race-crossing always produces offspring that revert to the lower type: "Whether we like to admit it or not, the result of the mixture of the two races, in the long run, gives us a race reverting to the more ancient, generalized and lower type. . . . The cross between a white man and a negro is a negro, and a cross between any of the three European races and a Jew is a Jew" (pp. 15–16). Thus, eugenicists supported strengthening existing antimiscegenation laws.

A further area of social concern for eugenicists was immigration, particularly in the United States, where the influx from eastern and southern Europe, the Balkans, and Russia had exploded in the 1880s. Claiming that these non-Aryan groups were genetically inferior to northern and western Europeans, eugenicists lobbied successfully for immigration restriction. The Reed-Johnson Act (Immigration Restriction Act), passed in 1924, limited immigration from the regions eugenicists claimed harbored inferior genes.

BIOCHEMICAL AND MOLECULAR GENETICS

Biochemical genetics deals with the way in which genes act to influence biochemical processes leading to one or another form of a trait, without trying to determine the chemical structure of the gene itself. Molecular genetics, explicitly aims at elucidating the three-dimensional structure of the gene and showing how that structure relates to its function. During much of the classical phase of genetics, it was not even clear what the molecular components of the gene were. The two most likely candidates were proteins and nucleic acids, because chemical analysis of chromosomes had shown they contained both substances.

Proteins versus Nucleic Acid as the Molecule of Heredity. Several lines of evidence initially suggested that proteins might be the genetic material. Proteins are composed of subunits known as *amino acids*, of which there are some twenty known types. These can be strung together in any sequence, giving an infinite number of different possible protein "words." Nucleic acids, on the other hand, are made up of only four kinds of subunits (known as nucleotides), and so they appeared to have less potential for carrying the large amount of genetic information thought to be required to "code" for all the traits in an organism. It was the work of Oswald T. Avery, Maclyn McCarty and Colin MacLeod in 1944, and of A.D. Hershey and Martha Chase in 1952, that showed decisively that nucleic acid, most notably the form known as deoxyribonucleic acid (DNA) was the "stuff" of which genes were made.

James Watson. *Geneticists James Watson (pictured) and Francis Crick determined that the genetic structure of DNA was a double helix.* ANDREAS FEININGER/TIME LIFE PICTURES/GETTY IMAGES.

X-RAY CRYSTALLOGRAPHY AND THE THREE-DIMENSIONAL STRUCTURE OF DNA

In a separate line of work, the newly introduced technology of X-ray crystallography was applied to determining the three-dimensional structure of molecules such as proteins and nucleic acids. Much of this work was carried out in England by John Desmond Bernal, Max Perutz, John Kendrew, Maurice Wilkins, and Rosalind Franklin. When a beam of electrons is passed through a crystal made up of a pure sample of a given molecule, the scattered rays can be recorded on a photographic plate; the position and intensity of the dots provides the means for inferring molecular structure. Perutz and Kendrew had already used X-ray crystallography to devise models of the oxygen-carrying molecules myoglobin and hemoglobin, while Wilkins and Franklin were using it in the early 1950s to study DNA. In 1951 a young postdoctoral student, James D. Watson, from the United States, came to work in the Cambridge Laboratory where another young investigator, Francis Crick, a former physicist, was also working. They teamed up to work out a model for the structure of DNA that would account for its ability to replicate itself and to direct the development of adult phenotypes.

X-ray data suggested the DNA molecule was helical in shape (like a spiral staircase), but it was not clear whether it was one helix (as in parts of some proteins) or multiple intertwined helices. It was only after visiting Rosalind Franklin's laboratory and seeing her outstanding x-ray diffraction photographs that Watson and Crick were able to decide on the correctness of a double-helix model. Their model showed that DNA consisted of two intertwined helices, each composed of a linear sequence of the nucleotide bases, adenine (A), thymine (T), guanine (G) and cytosine (C). Each base on one of the helices was paired by weak chemical bonds (hydrogen bonds) to a base on the other helix, such that A always paired with T, and C always paired with G (these were known as "base pairs").

Watson and Crick recognized that this model had implications for how DNA replicated, and for how it controlled cell reactions to eventually produce the adult phenotype. To replicate, the two helices separate, each one serving as a template to make its partner. It was also clear that DNA could carry genetic information in the sequence of its nucleotides along each helix. What was less clear at first was how that information was translated into phenotypes. However, one line of evidence going back to the early decades of the twentieth century had shown that the direct product of gene action was the production of a specific protein. In 1941, George Beadle and E. L. Tatum had shown that genes produce enzymes (virtually all enzymes are proteins), which in turn catalyze steps in metabolic reactions, such as those leading to a particular eye color. Mutations in the gene resulted in imperfect proteins, and thus altered phenotype. The Watson-Crick model suggested that the helical strands of DNA were read as a linear sequence in such a way as to determine the amino acid sequence of a specific protein. Mutations were alterations in the sequence of bases on DNA, and they could lead to altered amino acid sequences in the protein product. How all this worked was not clear at first, but it quickly became the focus of the molecular genetics research program of the 1960s and 1970s.

The Genetic Code and Protein Synthesis. A major problem for molecular geneticists was how the sequence of bases in DNA was organized to contain information, as well as how that information was "read." The first question was that of the "genetic code," and the second that of translation of that code into specific protein molecules. It was first hypothesized that the minimum number of base sequences on DNA that could code for the twenty-one known amino acids was three (with only four bases, combined into threes there could be sixty-four possible combinations, more than enough for each of the twenty amino acids to have its own code. By a variety of both genetic and biochemical experiments, Crick and his colleagues in England, and Marshall Nirenberg and Severo Ochoa in the United States, determined that the genetic code was indeed composed of three nucleotides (the code was a triplet one, such that TTT coded for the amino acid phenylalanine and AGC for serine). Thus, wherever a specific triplet appeared in the DNA molecule, the amino acid for which it coded would appear at that point in the protein chain. There was thus colinearity between the sequence of triplets in DNA and the amino acids in the corresponding protein for which it coded. Further work showed that the first step in protein synthesis involved transcription of the DNA sequence onto another kind of nucleic acid molecule, called messenger ribonucleic acid (mRNA), which was single-stranded and complementary to the DNA strand that gave rise to it. Further, mRNA met up with other kinds of RNA molecules, known as transfer RNA (tRNA) with each type specific for a given amino acid. The site of this interaction was a small cell structure, the *ribosome*, and the amino acids brought to the ribosome were joined up in the sequence specified by the mRNA to form the protein.

GENETIC TECHNOLOGY, RACE, AND THE HUMAN GENOME INITIATIVE

The new technology associated with molecular genetics had many applications regarding issues of human evolution and the nature of race. One of the earliest applications of the new knowledge of DNA was its use in reconstructing and verifying existing phylogenies of all sorts of organisms, including humans. In the 1980s, DNA from cell organelles known as mitochondria (which have their own DNA inherited strictly from the mother) was used to trace human migrations. Mitochondrial DNA does not undergo a crossing-over and exchange of segments between maternal and paternal genomes (as does nuclear DNA), and it mutates slowly, making it extremely useful for reconstructing lineages and following migration patterns. Applied to human evolution, mitochondrial DNA evidence showed that the human species evolved from ancestors of the twenty-first century's great apes somewhere between 5 and 6 million years ago in Africa, migrated to other major continents such as Europe and Asia, about 100 to 150 thousand years ago, and differentiated in these regions into separate populations.

DNA and Racial Differences. Biologically, the term *race* has come to be synonymous with what taxonomists call subspecies, that is, somewhat separate and distinct populations within a species that are capable of interbreeding. When applied to the human species (*Homo sapiens*), the term has a much less precise biological meaning, because human populations have been so mobile for so long a period of time, and have thus always experienced gene mixing, or gene flow. Most geneticists and anthropologists in the early twenty-first century argue that human racial groups are socially constructed, that racial divisions have been made in particular historical contexts and are based on social, rather than significant biological, distinctions. Thus, when Europeans first came into contact with the people in Africa, Asia, and the Americas, racial classifications arose to support social and political agendas (e.g., the expropriation of land or wealth, or the slave trade). By the later eighteenth and nineteenth centuries, most biologists and anthropologists agreed that the indigenous people of Africa or the New World were the same species as Europeans, but they divided humans into three common subspecies, or "races," arranged in a hierarchical order: Caucasians were at the top, Asians in the middle, and Negroids (Africans) were at the bottom. These divisions, and the exploitation they justified, were based on a few superficial traits, such as skin color, hair form, shape of the nose, and body proportions. To varying degrees, these divisions have persisted in the social sphere down to the present day. Modern genetic evidence, however, does not support any such divisions as having a significant biological reality. For example, one could group fruits by color (green cucumbers and limes; yellow lemons and bananas; and red cherries and peppers), but biologically these groups would share few other common properties. Applied to the human racial groupings the few traits used to make the distinction do not necessarily predict what other genes an individual will have. This does not mean, of course, that skin color and hair form are not genetic traits. For the classification of humans into the three traditional racial groups to be biologically significant, correlations between skin color, hair form, and a wide variety of other traits would be necessary.

There are several reasons why the concept of race in human beings is not biologically meaningful. One of the problems is that the boundaries between the various racial groupings is far more difficult to draw in humans than in many other animal species. In the twentieth century alone, the number of supposed "racial groups" has been as few as three (Caucasian, Negroid, and Asian) or as great as seventeen or eighteen, including such separate "races" as Irish, Mediterranean, Alpine, Nordic, Anglo-Saxon, and Slavic. For such classifications to be meaningful in a genetic sense, it would be necessary to assume that each group maintained a relatively closed inbreeding system, and that it had done so for hundreds or even thousands of generations. But because of extensive gene flow, few populations of humans have remained isolated for very long. This means that mixing of genes from populations of humans has occurred to such a degree over long historical periods, that there has come to be a greater range of variability within any one geographic group (e.g., Africans and Europeans) than there is between them. While some relatively isolated groups (the Australian Aborigines, for example) have maintained more of a common gene pool than others, such inbreeding is quite rare in humans. For "race," in its usual social sense, to have any biological meaning would require that the presence of gene A in the group would also correlate with the presence of gene B, C, D, and a host of others. But such correlations do not in fact exist. For example, people often speak of "Africans" (or "African-Americans") as if all people so identified shared one common genetic background. But North Africans are very different from sub-Saharan or southern Africans, while East Africans are very different from West Africans. For instance, the claim that an African American is more likely to have the gene for sickle-cell anemia (a severe blood disorder in the homozygous mutant state) is an overstatement. It would depend on what part of Africa the individual's ancestry came from (the sickle-cell gene is rare in Ethiopia or southern Africa, but much more common in central and West Africa).

From a biological and genetic point of view, the only meaningful groupings of human beings are geographic populations. Thus, people who come from a given geographic locality are indeed likely to share more genes in common than those who come from more distant localities, but these differences do not make races in the common social use of the term. Genetically differentiated populations, with a profile of certain gene frequencies, can be identified and described, but they do not map onto the conventional notions of race. It has thus been argued that, biologically speaking, humans comprise one large, global species whose local differentiations are minor compared to those found in many other animal species.

It is clear that modern genetics, especially molecular genetics, has seriously undermined the sociological notion of race as it persisted throughout the nineteenth and twentieth centuries. Human "races," as any kind of clearly differentiated, taxonomically significant groups, simply do not exist. This does not mean that the social concept of race has therefore lost its significance. Concepts of racial differences and hierarchies do not disappear simply because biology says they have no meaning, but because people struggle in the social arena to combat the racism and ethnocentrism that has for too long been accepted because of its purported (but nonexistent) biological basis.

SEE ALSO *Eugenics, History of; Galton, Francis; Gene Pool; Genetic Distance; Genetic Variation among Populations; Human and Primate Evolution; Human Genetics.*

BIBLIOGRAPHY

Allen, Garland E. 1978. *Thomas Hunt Morgan: The Man and His Science.* Princeton, NJ: Princeton University Press.

Carlson, Elof A. 1981. *Genes, Radiation and Society: The Life and Work of H.J. Muller.* Ithaca, NY: Cornell University Press.

———. 2004. *Mendel's Legacy: The Origin of Classical Genetics.* Cold Spring Harbor, NY: Cold Spring Harbor Laboratory Press.

De Chadarevian, Soraya, 2002. *Designs for Life: Molecular Biology after World War II.* Cambridge, U.K.: Cambridge University Press.

Dunn, Leslie C. 1965. *A Short History of Genetics. Development of Some of the Main Lines of Thought: 1864–1939.* New York: McGraw-Hill.

Galton, Francis. 1883. *Inquiries into Human Faculty and Its Development.* London: Macmillan.

Grant, Madison. 1916. *The Passing of the Great Race.* New York: Scribners.

Judson, Horace C. 1979. *The Eighth Day of Creation.* New York: Simon & Schuster.

Kay, Lily E. 2000. *Who Wrote the Book of Life? A History of the Genetic Code.* Stanford, CA: Stanford University Press.

Keller, Evelyn Fox. 2000. *The Century of the Gene.* Cambridge, MA: Harvard University Press.

Kevles, Daniel J. 1985. *In the Name of Eugenics.* New York: Knopf.

Kohler, Robert E. 1994. *Lord of the Flies: Drosophila Genetics and the Experimental Life.* Chicago: University of Chicago Press.

Morange, Michel. 1998. *A History of Molecular Biology.* Translated by Matthew Cobb. Cambridge, MA: Harvard University Press.

Olby, Robert C. 1974. *Path to the Double Helix.* Seattle: University of Washington Press.

Paul, Diane B. 1995. *Controlling Human Heredity, 1865 to the Present.* Atlantic Highlands, NJ: Humanities Press.

Witkowski, Jan A. 2000. *Illuminating Life: Selected Papers from Cold Spring Harbor Laboratory, 1903–1969*. Cold Spring Harbor, NY: Cold Spring Harbor Laboratory Press.

Garland E. Allen

GENETICS AND ATHLETIC PERFORMANCE

The correlation between genetics and athletic performance has long been a general topic of discussion among scientists, athletes, coaches, sports fans, and the general public, particularly in light of the success of African and African-American athletes in certain sports. The notion of racial differences in athletic performance has been connected by some scientists to the amount of fast-twitch and slow-twitch muscles possessed by different "racial" groups. This raises the question of whether a specific racial group might be inherently better at certain athletic events. To answer this question in the affirmative would mean that the members of a racial group share some genetically transmitted traits.

Many experts have come to view "race" as a socially constructed phenomenon, with racial categories often based on physical attributes, skin color, and other identifiable physical characteristics, not on genetic differences. This system of categorizing groups is not recognized by social scientists as a valid method of defining humans. Indeed, modern genetic science has found little genetic variation between the so-called races. In addition, in attempting to distinguish groups by race, many tend to ignore important socioeconomic variables, including economic, political, cultural, and social factors.

ATHLETICS AND RACE

The analysis of race as a factor in athletic performance has launched a spate of social and biomedical studies, and several factors have been examined to see if they contribute to the making of an elite athlete. This question takes on a particular fascination when certain ethnic groups show signs of dominating in certain sports. In particular, the success of African Americans in basketball, of East Africans in middle- and long-distance running, and of individuals of West African descent in sprinting have fueled speculation about racial and genetic differences. However, some genetic research scholars have utilized genotype as a founding principle towards the inherited fundamental metabolic racial differences theory.

On one side of the debate is the author Jon Entine. In his book *Taboo* (2000), Entine states that the scientific evidence for black athletic superiority is overwhelming. His theoretical framework is based on the belief that racial populations have evolved functional biomechanical and physiological differences that can and do determine the outcome of elite athletic competition Likewise, John Hoberman, a professor of Germanic studies at the University of Texas at Austin, contends it is possible that there is a population of West African origin that is endowed with an unusual proportion of fast-twitch muscle fibers. He also states that it is "likely that there are East Africans whose resistance to fatigue, for both genetic and cultural reasons, exceeds that of other racial groups" (1997) Attempting to understand the biological and sociological implications associated with these notions could have a major impact on the multiple discourses concerning genetics and athletic performance.

On the other side of the debate is the sociologist Harry Edwards. According to Edwards, "The argument that blacks are physically superior to whites is merely a racist ideology camouflaged to appeal to the ignorant, the unthinking and the unaware" (Burfoot 1992). Dr. Edwards challenged the notion of racial categories by questioning what portion or percentage of being black constitutes or supports the physical superiority debate. The ideology of biological determinism contends that genetic differences can be used to explain complex linked genetic traits associated with athletic success. The publication of Richard Herrnstein and Charles Murray's *The Bell Curve* (1996) signaled an important debate regarding race and IQ and further fueled the discussion regarding race, sport and genetics. Hoberman, Burfoot, and Entine infer that research suggests that different phenotypes are encoded in the genes, conferring genotypic differences that may result in an advantage in certain sports.

RESEARCH ON RACE AND ATHLETIC PERFORMANCE

In the 1990s, Bengt Saltin, the head of the Copenhagen Muscle Research Centre in Denmark, conducted research on the physiology of Kenyan and Swedish distance runners. His findings indicate there are differences in the cross-sectional area of the muscle of the two groups, but no significant differences in the muscle fibers or in physiological variables related to fatigue (Hoberman 1997).

In the years since the Saltin study, other scientists have ruled out most explanations for Kenyans' dominance in long-distance running. Many had speculated that Kenya's altitude was a factor, but no difference has been found between Kenyans and Scandinavians in their capacity to consume oxygen. The speculation that Kenyans have larger lung capacities has also been examined. The fact that many of these runners were training at higher altitude levels may have contributed to the capacity to expend as well as process oxygen. Researchers observed greater percentages of combined effects skeletal muscle oxidative

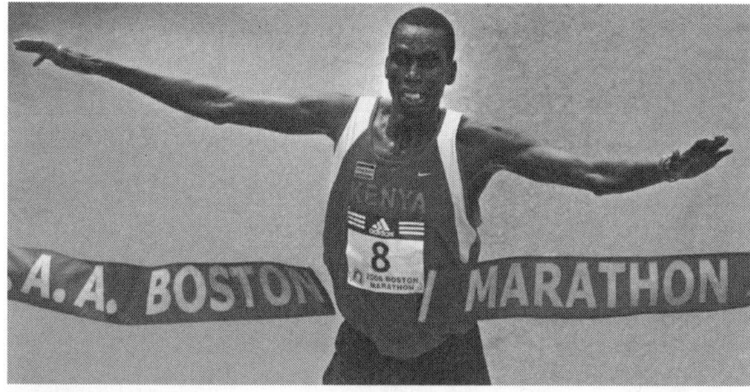

Boston Marathon Winners, 2006. *Robert Cheruiyot and Rita Jeptoo, both of Kenya, won the 2006 Boston Marathon. Several factors have been examined in an effort to determine if race plays a role in athletic performance.* AP IMAGES.

capacity and the percentage of type 1 fibers accounts for 72 percent of the variance in the body oxygen consumption. The final determination was that a range of factors contribute to the dominance of East African runners to include environmental, social, psychological, and physiological variables. One significant finding is that Kenyans can resist fatigue longer than athletes from other nations. Specifically, the lactate generated by tired, oxygen-deprived muscles accumulates more slowly in their blood. Comparisons of lactate levels have suggested that Kenyan runners squeeze about 10 percent more oxygen from the same intake as Europeans. J. E. Lindsay Carter, a professor emeritus in the Department of Exercise and Nutritional Sciences at San Diego State University, has conducted several studies of Olympic athletes, and he has observed that the biomechanical demands of a particular sport limit the range of physiques that can satisfy these demands. Optimal performance in certain activities involving endurance activities are partially dependent on skeletal muscle characteristics. This would include activities such as swimming, long distance running, and long distance cycling. A larger amount of type 1 fibers in the primary muscles of the lower limbs is directly associated with increased performance outcomes in association with aerobic energy. Thus body type and skeletal make up factors into athletic performance and type of activity.

Claude Bouchard, the director of the Pennington Biomedical Research Center at Louisiana State University, is considered one of the world's most renowned researchers and sport geneticists. His research on human obesity shows that the degree of fat deposition in humans is largely determined by heredity. From these findings he has determined the hereditability of some human traits, including some that have a direct relationship to athletic performance. For example, his findings indicate that anaerobic power is from 44 percent to 92 percent inherited. That a trait is inherited does not mean that it is inherent to a "race."

MUSCLE FIBER AND RACE

Bouchard has also examined physiological differences between white French Canadians and black West Africans, particularly comparing muscle-fiber percentages. He found that the West Africans had significantly more fast-twitch fibers and anaerobic enzymes than the whites. Many sport physiologists believe that fast-twitch muscle fibers create explosiveness, which can be channeled into distinct advantages during competition, specifically in sprinting and other short-duration events.

Briefly, skeletal muscles are divided into two groups based on their contractile speed: type I, or slow-twitch muscles, and type II, or fast-twitch muscles. Endurance runners, in general, have more type I fibers, which tend to have denser capillary networks and are packed with more mitochondria. Sprinters, on the other end of the spectrum, have more type II fibers, which tend to hold more significant amounts of sugar and certain enzymes that can burn fuel in lieu of oxygen. It has been suggested that there is a difference in the types of muscle fibers that predominate in certain racial groups. Bouchard's findings seem to support this view. Bouchard took biopsies from the thigh muscles of white Canadians and West African students. He concluded that Africans averaged significantly more fast twitch muscle fibers (67.5) than the Canadians (59). The study suggests that in West Africa there may be a larger pool of people with elevated levels of oxygen uptake. The challenge to this research comes in the form of many sociologists that contend the basic hypothesis of superior athleticism associated with race is fundamentally meaningless. It is the actual social values associated with the discussion of speed, strength and endurance in relationship to race that should be of concern. St. Louis (2003) argues that the appropriation of scientific method constructs racial athleticism through a naïve inductive approach. Davis (1992) contends that white male athletes that compete at elite levels in certain sports are taken as the norm and their performance is not seen as requiring an explanation as to their dominance. However, while some point to the dominance of Kenyan runners, they also question the lack of Africans in other endurance sports, such as cycling. There are certainly multiple sporting events that require very high levels of endurance, yet only within certain sports do certain individual ethnic groups tend to dominate. If a specific group possesses exemplary fast-twitch muscles, why does that group only dominate in certain sports? The only answer seems to be that other factors play an equally important role.

Several debates have stemmed from research on race and athletic performance. The collision of scientific and cultural frameworks is sharply divided. Considering genetic linearity as an absolutism counters the notion of socialized phenotypes, characteristics, and cultures. Many scientists now isolate groups based on genotype patterns, rather than identifying races by facial characteristics or geography (Brownlee 2005).

Georgia Dunston, the founding director of Howard University's National Human Genome Center in Washington, D.C., studies how the human immune system distinguishes between a person's tissues and foreign material, such as a bacterium or transplanted organ. According to Dunston, "We have this thinking in America that there are some deep differences in biology between whites and blacks, that tissue in whites is more similar to tissues in whites than tissue in blacks, but when we look at the genetics, because of the tremendous variations in all groups, and especially in the group called black, it is not uncommon at all to find two blacks who could be very different from each other" (Brownlee 2005). Another perspective is based on research conducted by Rushton (2000). His findings were that genes play a part in IQ, personality, attitudes and other behaviors. Trans-racial adoption studies are where infants of one race are adopted and reared by parents of a different race. Regression analysis contends that genes cause races to differ in personality and that only cultural theory can not fully explain his results.

STEREOTYPE THREAT

The dominance of black athletes in certain sports has also been attributed to factors such as social Darwinism. In this view, black dominance is associated with slavery, genetic selection, and psychological and physiological adaptations to a person's physical and social environment. The theory of stereotype threat is based on the idea that individuals believe what is postulated about their racial and genetic makeup, and that these beliefs are more important than their actual ability. Jeff Stone, a professor of social psychology at the University of Arizona, gave black and white students a laboratory golf task intended to measure natural athletic ability, sport intelligence or sport psychology, depending on which test was given. According to Stone, nothing changed in the test itself, just the perception of what the test measured. Black and white students scored equally well on the controlled psychology test. However, blacks outperformed whites when the test was framed as a measure of natural ability, while the whites outperformed blacks when the test was framed as a measure of sport intelligence. The concept of stereotype threat may provide additional frameworks with which to examine genetic or racial factors in relation to athletic performance as well as performance in other areas. The research suggests that beliefs about one's self-efficacy and ability can have a large impact on both individual and group performances.

Similar research has been conducted in the area of standardized testing. Minorities typically score lower on such tests than non-Hispanic whites. The social psychologist Claude Steele has examined the effect of stereotype threat on standardized intelligence scores. He found that black students scored as well as white students on standardized intelligence tests when the tests were framed as diagnostic tests that did not measure intellectual capacities. His findings concluded that psychological factors may perpetuate perceptions that impact one's self efficacy to accomplish and complete tasks. The test itself was not the variable, but the variables surrounding the test. This included resources available to students, quality of delivered learning objectives, positive reinforcement, and diagnostic tools. If one is consistently reinforced that they are capable of mastering certain skill sets, their psychological approach to the task will impact the results. This finding suggests that situational variables, including cultural, social, and environmental factors, play a role in the lower scores of some groups.

CHALLENGING RACIAL THEORIES OF ATHLETIC PERFORMANCE

Thus, while some research indicates there are distinct differences in the biological make-up of certain ethnic groups, other research indicates that physical superiority is not contingent on physical phenomena, but on demographic and socioeconomic variables. However, theories of racial factors determining athletic superiority have been challenged by the emergence of international athletes competing in events that have traditionally been dominated by African Americans or other groups. For example, athletes from a number of nations have begun to emerge and excel in professional basketball, a sport dominated in recent decades by African Americans. This suggests that environmental factors play a significant role in achieving success in this sport. Likewise, in the 2004 Olympics in Athens, Greece, Jeremy Wariner, a white American from Texas, won the gold medal in the 400-meter sprint, an event previously dominated by individuals of African ancestry.

Persons of color have also begun to make inroads in sports usually dominated by whites. In tennis, a sport in which wealth and class certainly convey a great advantage,

Tiger Woods. Tiger Woods receives the Green Jacket after winning the Masters Golf Tournament, on April 14, 2002. The performance of Tiger Woods in golf, which has been long dominated by whites, may lead to more in-depth analysis of biological versus sociocultural impacts on athletic performances. AP IMAGES.

Venus and Serena Williams have made it to the top of the professional ranks, while James Blake and others have had success in men's tennis. The performance of Tiger Woods in golf, which has also been long dominated by whites, may lead to more in-depth analysis of biological versus sociocultural impacts on athletic performances.

Tiger Woods and James Blake are also of interest here because they are both of mixed descent and ethnicity. They both compete at the elite level among their peers, but both are difficult to label or categorize in terms of racial identification. Indeed, due to the extensive interactions of various cultures, it is becoming more and more difficult to clearly define a person's true ethnicity. Thus, the notion of "race" has taken on multiple dimensions. It is, in fact, difficult to get most scientists to say the word "race" when referring to people. In traditional scientific language, races are synonymous with subspecies, or organisms within the same species that can be interbred but are nevertheless genetically distinctive.

Races are not clearly defined biological categories. Attempts to create racial categorizations tend to intersect ethnically and culturally. Human racial categorization attempts to construct and determine defined structures of racial formations. Many times individuals may be a blend of several ethnicities as well as cultures. This creates challenges to the traditional mode of categorization of race and human subjects.

There have been multiple studies conducted relating to the social, economic, and cultural factors that influence athletic performance. But regardless of the possible existence of physiological findings, or the indications that sociological factors contribute significantly to the performance of athletes, it is likely that there will always be multiple discourses at play when discussing these issues. Research will continue to explore the subject of racial difference in athletic performance, and physiologists, sociologists, and scientists will continue to expand, investigate, and postulate theories concerning this topic.

SEE ALSO *Basketball; Track and Field.*

BIBLIOGRAPHY

Baker, J., and S. Horton. 2003. "East African Running Dominance Revisited: A Role for Stereotype Threat?" *British Journal of Sports Medicine* 37 (6): 553–555.

Brownlee, Christen. 2005. "Code of Many Colors: Can Researchers See Race in the Genome?" *Science News* 167 (15): 232–234.

Burfoot, Ambrose. 1992. "White Men Can't Run." *Runners World* 27 (8): 89–95.

Eitzen, D. Stanley, and Maxine Baca Zinn. 2006. *Social Problems*, 10th ed. Boston: Pearson/Allyn & Bacon.

Entine, Jon. 2000. *Taboo: Why Black Athletes Dominate Sports and Why We Are Afraid to Talk About It.* New York: Public Affairs.

Hoberman, John M. 1997. *Darwin's Athletes: How Sport Has Damaged Black America and Preserved the Myth of Race.* Boston: Houghton Mifflin.

Steele, Claude M., and Joshua Aronson 1995. "Stereotype Threat and the Intellectual Test Performance of African Americans." *Journal of Personality and Social Psychology* 69 (5): 797–811.

Stone, Jeff, Christian I. Lynch, Mike Sjomeling, and John M. Darley. 1999. "Stereotype Threat Effects on Black and White Athletic Performance." *Journal of Personality and Social Psychology* 77 (6): 1213–1227.

Fritz G. Polite

GENOCIDE

The United Nations Convention on the Prevention and Punishment of the Crime of Genocide states that "genocide is a crime under international law," and "that at all periods of history genocide has inflicted great losses on humanity." This contradiction between a specific legal concept defined by an international convention and an eternal political and social phenomena characterizes both the global approach to genocide and the dilemmas it encounters.

DEFINING GENOCIDE

The concept of genocide was first voiced by a Polish Jewish lawyer, Raphael Lemkin, who worked tirelessly during World War II and in its immediate aftermath to achieve public recognition of this hideous crime. The impetus came from the wide recognition of the heinous crimes of the Nazi regime. Indeed, Lemkin quoted the British prime minister Winston Churchill, who described the killing of millions as "a crime without a name." Lemkin responded by formulating the term *genocide*. His activism facilitated not only the recognition of the new concept but also the adoption of the Genocide Convention. Since then, writing about genocide has been divided between those who view it as a new phenomenon, largely an innovation of the Nazis in their extermination of the Jews, and those who view it as permanent phenomena that describes wars of extermination and ethnic cleansing throughout history.

The Genocide Convention (approved on December 9, 1948; came into force on January 12, 1951) states that:

> Genocide means any of the following acts committed with intent to destroy, in whole or in part, a national, ethnical, racial or religious group, as such:
>
> (a) Killing members of the group;
>
> (b) Causing serious bodily or mental harm to members of the group;
>
> (c) Deliberately inflicting on the group conditions of life calculated to bring about its physical destruction in whole or in part;
>
> (d) Imposing measures intended to prevent births within the group;
>
> (e) Forcibly transferring children of the group to another group.

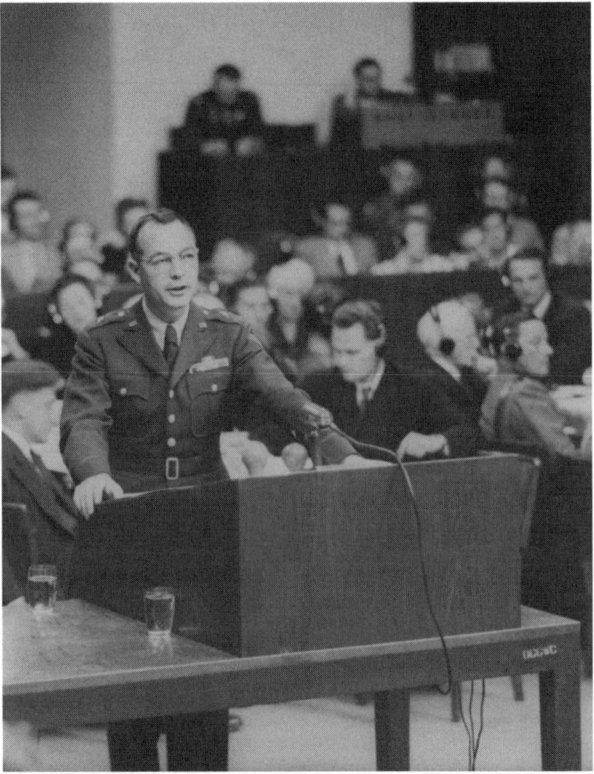

War Crimes Trial, 1947. *Brigadier General Telford Taylor delivers opening statements during the Nuremberg Trials of Nazi war criminals. The trials marked the first time the crime of genocide was introduced into an international proceeding.* AP IMAGES.

This is the only legal definition available, but it is inadequate. It diverges significantly from the daily use of the term, which views it as the ultimate crime and alludes to the Holocaust as the paradigmatic case and as a yardstick. The Nuremberg Trials of Nazi war criminals marked the first time the crime of genocide was introduced into an international proceeding. There was a belief that a new type of crime had been committed by the Germans, and a new term was therefore needed. This obviously contradicts Lemkin's own view that only the term was new, not the crime. This tension remains: Does genocide refer to an exceptional crime, or to a crime that occurs all too frequently, most often during war time? The cry of "Never Again," made in reference to the Holocaust, points in the direction of exceptionalism, but the public discourse points in the other direction.

On the other end of the spectrum, according to the Genocide Convention, genocide can take place without any killing. Indeed, it states that genocide can occur through the removal of children from a particular group, if this is done as a way of destroying the future existence of the group. In Australia, the National Inquiry into the Separation of Aboriginal and Torres Strait Islander Children from Their Families issued a report in 1995 titled *Bringing Them Home* (also known as the "Stolen Children" report). This report accused the Australian government of genocide not for killing Aborigines, but for the removal of their children. While this has been a controversial political issue in Australia, such a definition of genocide diverges from the idea of mass killing that is generally conveyed by the term.

On the other hand, the definition in the Genocide Convention can be viewed as too narrow, for it excludes political motivations as grounds for genocide. In other words, the killing of members of a political group or economic class is not defined as genocide. Both the Soviet and the Chinese regimes killed tens of millions of people as part of political campaigns. Under the Convention, however, mass murder for political reasons is not considered genocide.

This dissonance between the popular and political use of the term and the legal definition of it is important because it obfuscates the demarcation of the concept itself. As a category, genocide describes the ultimate victimization of the group "as such." The expansion of the concepts of "holocaust" and "genocide," together with "ethnic cleansing," to characterize all mass violence has led certain groups of victims to feel that their suffering—both historical and contemporary—has not receive adequate attention if they are not viewed as victims of genocide. Extensive atrocities have also been characterized as "gross violations of human rights" or "war crimes," but these descriptions have not been embraced by the affected groups to describe their own suffering.

The list of those who argue that they are victims of genocide, and prosecutors' efforts to indict offenders with the charge of genocide, make it all the more complicated. When a prosecutor in Mexico indicted a former president for ordering an attack on student demonstrators with charges of genocide, the inclusion in the UN definition of the phrase "intent to destroy, in whole or in part" argued against such a charge (the ex-President was cleared of the charges in 2006). There have been attempts within the United Nations (UN) (in conjunction with the claimed genocide in Darfur, Sudan) to rein in the definition by requiring that it include "the intention to destroy 'a considerable number of individuals' or 'a substantial part,'" but the exact demarcation is further obscured by the introduction of the term *ethnic cleansing,* which was popularized during the 1990s, to describe the war in the former Yugoslavia,

The difficulty with such expansive usage is that it hinders the significance of the concept—intellectually, politically, morally, and in every other way. The force of naming particular crimes and violence as genocide, and its attractiveness to victims as a designation of their own case, is that genocide is perceived as the "crime of crimes." But if the concept comes to designate every case of group violence, is it then cheapened or minimized? And should it therefore carry less severe consequences? In 2004 the UN Secretary General created the office of Special Advisor on Genocide Prevention. There is little doubt that the international community shares a consensus that genocide is a horrific crime that deserves special attention. The world is not as unified, however, on what should be included under the designation of "genocide." In the spirit of Lemkin's definition, which he illustrated by referring to occurrences throughout history, modern writers have listed numerous cases as genocide. Mindful of these extensive claims, and without attempting to arbitrate an agreed definition, several controversial aspects of the use of the term will be discussed here.

THE HOLOCAUST

The Holocaust was the momentous event during World War II when the Nazis almost succeeded in exterminating European Jewry and gypsies. The shock of the extermination and the concentration camps, and the view that the Nazis constituted the ultimate evil, enabled the postwar international community to agree on the Genocide Convention. As such, the Holocaust became the ultimate unique example of this crime. Uniqueness does not work as a comparative tool, and it is difficult to designate an event as both unique and a yardstick. And while there was an agreement that, in principle, there were other genocides, the debate over the uniqueness of the Holocaust and of evilness of the Nazis coincided with the cold war, which meant that no mass murders, whether in a war or otherwise, were designated as genocides over the next four decades. Under the banner of "Never Again," the international community was steadfast in refusing to label the killings in Bangladesh, Biafra, Cambodia, and other places as genocide, and they did little to stop the mass murder itself. Only in the aftermath of the cold war, when the bipolar international community became both plural and unipolar, and in the face of the killings in the former Yugoslavia and Rwanda, did the debate over the designation of genocide become integral to the international discourse.

The uniqueness of the Holocaust stemmed from the German goal of annihilating all Jewish persons because of their race. Because Jewishness was deemed to be a racial category, a Jew could not convert to be saved, and even those with only Jewish grandparents (and whose parents converted) were subject to annihilation. Furthermore, Germany directed significant resources to the destruction, which involved a vast system of government agencies and personnel, all conducted by a modern state. This was done in spite of the fact that the Jews did not present any concrete danger to Germany, even from a German perspective. The struggle was cosmic and mythological, aimed at ruling the world. It was fought between the Nazis and their imagined enemies constructed from anti-Semitic propaganda. But real Jews were killed. The Holocaust shocked the world in part because of these bureaucratic and modern characteristics, but more so because it was directed at those who were, essentially, "people like us." Europeans and Americans were used to stories of mass killings of "inferior" races and to mass murder during war, but the gassing of millions in cold blood was a novelty. The combination of ferocious racism and atrocities perpetrated by the common German created an incomprehensible aura.

In the early twenty-first century, the Holocaust is both unique and more integrated in world history. It is unique as the epitome of evil, and all other catastrophes and mass murders are measured against it. The Holocaust is comparable to other cases, because perpetrators of other genocides also tried to kill all the members of a specific group. That such a mass killing is irrational (e.g., in taking away resources from other goals) is the nature of genocide, not the exception. But more importantly, the growing number of studies comparing genocides teaches that each is different in its own way, and the question of uniqueness creates the appearance of ranking, which is bound to ruffle other groups. So the dilemma remains: While ranking is impossible, the politics of classifying genocide is crucial for the identity of victims.

OTHER INSTANCES OF GENOCIDE

The vast destruction of lives of indigenous peoples around the world as a result of the encounter with modernity is one of the most vexing in the dilemmas of designating a mass killing as genocide. On one side is the incontrovertible fact of the extensive destruction and death that befell the indigenous peoples. Furthermore, there is no doubt that racism motivated many of the policies that led to the devastation, and that the colonists in many places expected and hoped for the disappearance of the indigenous peoples. The "vanishing" indigenous group was a constant trope in descriptions of the frontier on every continent. However, the question remains whether the colonists acted "with intent to destroy," or whether the violence and racism were separate from the expectations that the indigenous peoples would die, as a people, in the future, but not as a result of particular acts. The question becomes more complicated because of the tendency to discuss the destruction of indigenous peoples as a single event, rather than as widely spread phenomena that might have involved numerous genocides. In addition, perhaps the worst demographic destruction of indigenous peoples resulted from epidemics that nobody controlled. Here the tension between activist-historians and the legal definition of genocide is wide. This is an active field of scholarship, and much is changing in evaluating its history.

Armenia. Hitler famously said "Who remembers the Armenians?" when he contemplated the extermination of the Jews. The statement is repeatedly quoted to signal the crucial role of deterrence in avoiding future genocides, but it is also quoted as proof that the genocide of the Armenians in Turkey in 1915 was widely seen as the precedent for (and the first instance of) genocide in the twentieth century. In order to forget, one has to have knowledge that can be forgotten. But if the Armenian massacres were largely forgotten by the 1930s, an even earlier twentieth-century genocide also went unnoticed by the world, and it remained so until recently. This was the genocide perpetrated by German colonialists against the Herero, of South-West Africa (later known as Namibia). In an effort to capture the Herero's land, the German army tried to annihilate the Herero, killing tens of thousands and expelling many others to the desert between 1904 and 1907.

The massacres of Armenians under the Ottoman Empire go back to the second half of the nineteenth century. But it was during World War I, against the background of a disintegrating empire with many Muslim refugees fleeing to Anatolia (the Asian portion of Turkey), primarily from the Balkans, that the massacre of a million Armenians throughout Asia Minor occurred (as well as that of other Christian minorities, such as the Assyrians and Chaldeans, who are rarely mentioned at all). In the days before the word *genocide* was invented, the world press wrote about the massacres, the expulsion, the long marches through the desert, and even the carnage of the war, all of which were singled out as constituting horrific crimes. The survivors attempted to rebuild their lives, many in the United States and France, but after the war, with the new Turkish republic flexing its political muscles, attempted trials of the leaders responsible for the crime were aborted. Mass ethnic cleansing (or "population exchange" between Greece and Turkey) overshadowed any active involvement with the Armenian suffering; the Armenian suffering was set aside and ceased to be a burning issue. Only in the last generation has the memory of the Armenian genocide resurfaced and become a defining political issue for Turkey. Amid the nation's efforts to legitimize itself in Europe as an European Union (EU) member, the killing of the Armenians has become a symbol of the difficulties of domestic democratization. In the early twenty-first century, many around the world accept the designation of the events as genocide, while official Turkey sees this as a manifestation of anti-Turkish policies. The civil society in Turkey, meanwhile, views reconciliation with Armenia and the recognition of historical responsibility for the destruction of the Armenian community as an essential step in the democratization of Turkey.

Rwanda and the Former Yugoslavia. During the 1990s, the genocide in Rwanda and the ethnic cleansing in the former Yugoslavia gripped public attention. The failure of the international community to intervene in a timely fashion enabled the Serbs to perpetrate the first genocide in postwar Europe when seven thousand Muslim males were murdered in July 1995 in Srebrenica. In this case, the International Tribunal designated the murder as genocide, though the war in its totality was not so designated. In Rwanda, the mass killing of the Tutsis by the Hutus was stopped only when the Tutsis defeated the Hutus. The response of the UN was to authorize a tribunal post facto. Both of these cases were fresh on politicians' minds when the Serb expulsion of Kosovars in 1999 was met with a NATO military response that may well have stopped genocidal acts. These precedents had little effect in Africa, and particularly in Sudan's Darfur region, where in 2004 the United States determined that genocide was taking place. The United States did not intervene, however, and a UN investigation avoided the use of the term *genocide* because no "intent" on the part of the perpetrators could be established. The report was very specific in clarifying international law with regard to genocide, and it expanded the groups subject to the Genocide Convention beyond named groups to those with "the self-perception of the members of each group." The report attempted to skirt the primacy of genocide as the "crime of crimes" because, as the Rwanda

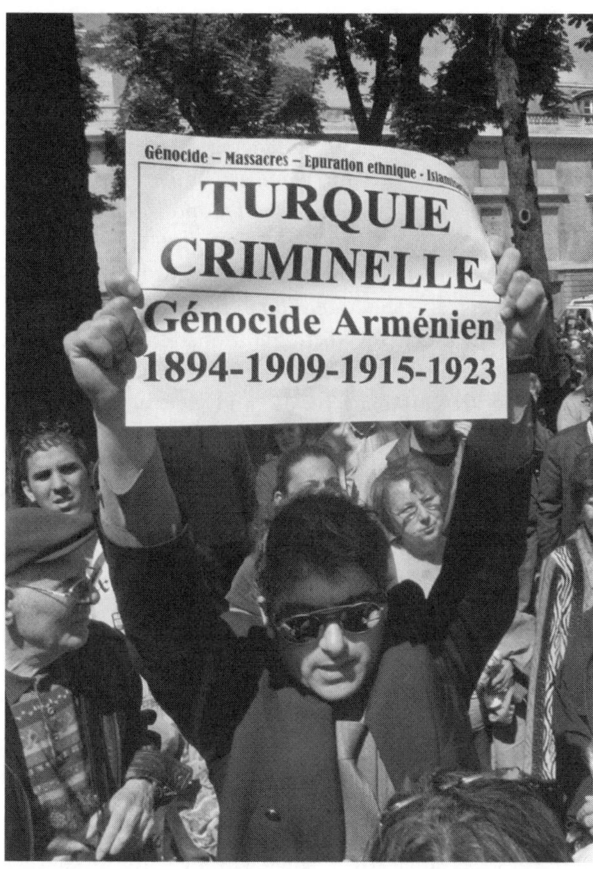

Armenian Genocide. *In 2006 French lawmakers debated a proposal that would make the denial of the Armenian Genocide a crime. In this photograph, an Armenian expresses his support of the proposal.* AP IMAGES.

tribunal determined, "there is no such hierarchical gradation of crimes." The report argued that "some categories of crimes against humanity may be similarly heinous [to genocide] and carry a similarly grave stigma." This form of normalization of genocide, making it comparable to other grave crimes, may be the wave of the future. This would be a shift from the special status accorded to genocide by the UN in the Genocide Convention.

The tribunals for Rwanda and the former Yugoslavia and the new International Criminal Court are all addressing the crime of genocide, and their determinations will define the nature of genocide in international law in the future. The political nature of responding to genocides, and the failure of the international community to address the crisis in Darfur, or even to agree upon whether it is genocide or not, has placed the Genocide Convention under great stress. While the punishment of genocide through the tribunals has been extremely expensive and inefficient—few were brought to justice and a sense of impunity is widespread—the capacity to prevent genocide is even weaker. Not only is the Convention vague about prevention (Article VIII enables any party to bring a case before the UN), the lack of prevention is viewed as indirectly encouraging more atrocities.

Genocide has become a fixture of modernity, both as the ultimate crime against a group and as the identity marker of a group's victimization. One would like to imagine that "Never Again" will someday be transformed from a slogan to a policy. But skepticism is justified. Can memory of genocide lead to reconciliation? The recounting of history has been exploited to provoke conflict, incite war, and inflame genocides, particularly since the end of the Cold War. Can it also be drawn upon to facilitate reconciliation? The narration of genocide may be as important as the policies that governments pursue in determining whether this will be the case.

SEE ALSO *Ethnic Cleansing; Genocide and Ethnocide; Genocide in Rwanda; Genocide in Sudan; Holocaust; Mayan Genocide in Guatemala.*

BIBLIOGRAPHY

Akçam, Taner. 2004. *From Empire to Republic: Turkish Nationalism and the Armenian Genocide.* London and New York: Zed Books.

Andreopoulos, George J., ed. 1994. *Genocide: Conceptual and Historical Dimensions.* Philadelphia: University of Pennsylvania Press.

Bartov, Omer, ed. 2000. *The Holocaust: Origins, Implementation and Aftermath.* London and New York: Routledge.

Courtois, Stéphane, and Mark Kramer. 1999. *The Black Book of Communism: Crimes, Terror, Repression.* Cambridge, MA, and London: Harvard University Press.

Fein, Helen. 1990. *Genocide: A Sociological Perspective.* London and Newbury Park, CA: Sage Publications.

Gellately, Robert, and Ben Kiernan, eds. 2003. *The Specter of Genocide: Mass Murder in Historical Perspective.* Cambridge, U.K. and New York: Cambridge University Press.

Mamdani, Mahmood. 2001. *When Victims Become Killers: Colonialism, Nativism, and the Genocide in Rwanda.* Princeton, NJ: Princeton University Press.

Marrus, Michael Robert. 1987. *The Holocaust in History.* Hanover, NH: Published for Brandeis University Press by University Press of New England, 1987.

Power, Samantha. 2002. *A Problem from Hell: America and the Age of Genocide.* New York: Basic Books.

Schabas, William A. 2000. *Genocide in International Law: The Crimes of Crimes.* Cambridge, U.K. and New York: Cambridge University Press.

United Nations. 2005. *Report of the International Commission of Inquiry on Darfur to the United Nations Secretary-Genera, Geneva, 25 January 2005.* Geneva: United Nations.

Weitz, Eric D. 2003. *A Century of Genocide: Utopias of Race and Nation.* Princeton, NJ: Princeton University Press.

Elazar Barkan

GENOCIDE AND ETHNOCIDE

In its darkest, most virulent form, racism can spark acts of genocide and ethnocide. The colonization of the Americas was accompanied by widespread acts of genocide and ethnocide, creating a holocaust on an unprecedented scale. Such acts persist in Latin America, where the extinction of tribes and disappearance of cultures occurred throughout the twentieth century and continue into the present. In North America, it is primarily ethnocide that stalks surviving Native American communities and endangers their remaining cultures.

GENOCIDE AND ETHNOCIDE IN NATIVE NORTH AMERICA

As used here, the term *Native American* refers to members of the American Indian tribes, nations, and groups who inhabited North America before Europeans arrived. They are part of the world's *indigenous peoples,* who are defined as the non-European populations who resided in lands colonized by Europeans before the colonists arrived. In 1992, Senator Daniel K. Inouye, chairman of the Senate Indian Affairs Committee, observed that "in many newly-established nations that were formerly colonies, while freedom for the majority was achieved, the indigenous population was excluded from the body politic. Widespread cultural and racial genocide was the consequence" (Inouye 1992, p. 6). It is important to confront and better understand acts of genocide and ethnocide, so that these forms of racism can be recognized and arrested.

When Columbus arrived in the New World, North America teemed with diverse native civilizations. The anthropologist Russell Thornton estimates that more than 72 million indigenous people inhabited the Western Hemisphere in 1492. This population declined to only about four million within a few centuries, however, making it one of the largest population collapses ever recorded. In North America, more than five million American Indians inhabited the area now occupied by the continental United States in 1492; by 1900, however, only 250,000 remained, indicating a decline in excess of one million persons per century.

DEFINITIONS OF GENOCIDE AND ETHNOCIDE

Genocide is narrowly defined in the United Nation's Convention on the Prevention of and Punishment of the Crime of Genocide (1948) as the deliberate destruction of members of a national, ethnic, racial, or religious group. Genocidal acts include: (1) killing members of the group; (2) causing serious bodily or mental harm to them; (3) inflicting conditions of life calculated to bring about a group's destruction in whole or part; (4) imposing measures intended to prevent births within the group; and (5) forcibly transferring children of one group to another. In *Century of Genocide* (1997), Robert Hitchcock and Tara Twedt explain that genocidal acts do not usually succeed in killing all members of the targeted group. However, the survivors are sometimes "raped, enslaved, deprived of their property, and forcibly moved to new places" (p. 379). Where indigenous peoples are concerned, some researchers would add to the definition of such acts as the "intentional prevention of ethnic groups from practicing their traditional customs; forced resettlement; denial of access to food relief, health assurance, and development funds; and destruction of the habitats utilized by indigenous peoples" (p. 378). Major causes of genocide among indigenous peoples have been the conquest and colonization of their lands and, more recently, the extraction of their natural resources.

Ethnocide (or cultural genocide) is a related concept that refers to acts that contribute to the disappearance of a culture, even though its bearers are not physically destroyed. Acts of ethnocide include denying a group its right to speak its language, practice its religion, teach its traditions and customs, create art, maintain social institutions, or preserve its memories and histories. "Indigenous populations frequently have been denied the right to practice their own religions and customs and to speak their own languages by nation-states, a process described as 'cultural genocide' or 'ethnocide'" (Hitchcock and Twedt 1997, p. 373).

Genocide and ethnocide against indigenous peoples arise for many reasons, including colonization; greed for gold or other natural resources; nation-building efforts in countries containing a diverse populace; and religious, racial, tribal, or ideological differences. In each case, these crimes against humanity are justified and fueled by racism. Indigenous peoples are victimized by such crimes partly because they have been viewed "as 'primitives,' 'subhuman,' 'savages,' 'vermin,' or 'nuisances' … and other negative stereotypes for generations." These stereotypes "reinforce the tendencies of governments to establish destructive and oppressive racial policies" (Hitchcock and Twedt 1997, p. 382).

Governmental efforts "to vilify indigenous groups are frequently preconditions for genocidal action" (Hitchcock and Twedt 1997). Indeed, racial slurs do accompany acts of genocide and ethnocide against Native Americans. For example, in U.S. Supreme Court decisions between 1823 and 1903 that curtailed native rights, the Court commonly describes American Indians as "inferior," "ignorant," "savages," "heathens," and "uncivilized." In *Lone Wolf v. Hitchcock* (1903), for example, the Court ruled that Congress could abrogate an Indian treaty partly because Indians are "an ignorant and dependent race." Likewise, in *Johnson v. M'Intosh* (1823) the Court ruled that Indian tribes do not own legal title to their land partly because Indians are "heathens" and "fierce savages."

Ethnocide is a central feature of Indian–white race relations in the United States, and the government has at times resorted to genocidal acts. The threat and reality of ethnocide continue to cloud the lives of contemporary Native Americans.

SPANISH GENOCIDE IN THE AMERICAN COLONIES

Colonialism in the New World was filled with acts of genocide. More than 12 million Indians died during the first forty years, as Spaniards killed, tortured, terrorized, and destroyed each group of native people they encountered. The depopulation of the Americas was witnessed by Bartolome de Las Casas (c. 1474–1566), who arrived in Hispaniola in 1502 and spent more than forty years in American colonies. He chronicled the death of millions of Indians killed by the Spaniards and claimed that more than forty million were killed by 1560. In 1542, Las Casas reported to King Charles of Spain that mass murder was being committed throughout the Americas. The report provides horrifying firsthand details, but cautions that "no tongue would suffice, nor word nor human efforts, to narrate the frightful deeds by the Spaniards" (Las Casas 1974, p. 69). The death toll reported by Las Casas is staggering.

In Hispaniola, almost two million Indians were killed. In Puerto Rico and Jamaica, Las Casas reported that more than 600,000 Indians were killed. Between four and five million people were killed in Guatemala. In Venezuela, the Spanish sold one million Indians into slavery. In Nicaragua, they killed between 500,000 and 600,000 Indians and sold more than 500,000 survivors into slavery. In Honduras and the Yucatan, more than 200,000 were killed. In Peru, the Spaniards "wiped out a great portion of the human family" by 1542, killing "more than ten million souls" (Las Casas 1974, p. 129). At least four million were killed in Mexico, not counting victims who died from mistreatment under servitude.

In other places, almost all of the Indians were killed. For example, Cuba was almost "completely depopulated," and in the few months Las Casas was there "more than seventy thousand children, whose fathers and mothers had been sent to the mines, died of hunger" (Las Casas 1974, pp. 39, 53). Las Casas warned that "unless the King orders remedial measures to be taken soon, there will be no Indians left" in Columbia. No one was spared in the Bahama Islands. There, more than 500,000 inhabitants died leaving sixty islands "inhabited by not a single living creature" (p. 40). Similarly, by 1542, thirty islands surrounding Puerto Rico were largely "depopulated."

The extermination of Indians was justified by leading Spanish thinkers. Most notably, the theologian Juan de Sepulveda (1494–1573) argued that killing Indians was "just" because they are inferior. He divided humanity into two groups: (1) civilized men with intelligence, sentiments, emotions, beliefs, and values; and (2) primitive brutes who lacked these essential human and Christian qualities, and who by their inherent nature would find it difficult, if not impossible, to acquire them. Sepulveda reasoned that civilized men were naturally the masters who could conduct "just" wars against non-Christian primitive brutes that were, by their very nature, nothing more than slaves. Las Casas, on the other hand, asked the King to curb the genocide. Unfortunately, the seeds of genocide were too firmly planted in the New World, and the laws that were promulgated in 1542 proved ineffectual.

Spain's legacy continues in Latin America. In Brazil, more than eighty tribes were destroyed between 1900 and 1957. The Indian population dropped from a million to less than 200,000. Spain was not alone. According to the historian Kirkpatrick Sale, "there is not a single European nation which, when the opportunity came, did not engage in practices as vicious and cruel as those of Spain—and in the case of England, worse—with very much the same sort of demographic consequences" (Sale 1990, p. 161).

GENOCIDE AND ETHNOCIDE IN THE UNITED STATES

Scholars have identified various interrelated factors that led to the depopulation of American Indians in the United States and the destruction of their cultures. "All of the reasons stemmed from European contact and colonization: introduced disease, including alcoholism; warfare and genocide; geographical removal and relocation; and destruction of ways of life" (Thornton 1987, pp. 43–44). These factors fall squarely within definitions of genocide and ethnocide.

Warfare. Between 150,000 and 500,000 Native Americans died in forty wars with Americans and Europeans between 1775 and 1894; in intertribal wars prompted by European or American involvement in tribal relations; in warfare between 1492 and 1775; and in conflicts between Indians and settlers (Thornton 1987, pp. 48–49). Colonial governments encouraged colonists to kill Indians by paying bounties. In 1735, for example, the governor of Massachusetts called upon citizens to kill or capture all Penobscot Indians. He proclaimed a bounty of fifty pounds for every male above age twelve (or forty pounds for their scalps) and twenty-five pounds for every female or youth under age twelve (or twenty pounds for their scalps). Blatant acts of genocide occurred in Texas, where Indians were almost completely exterminated by

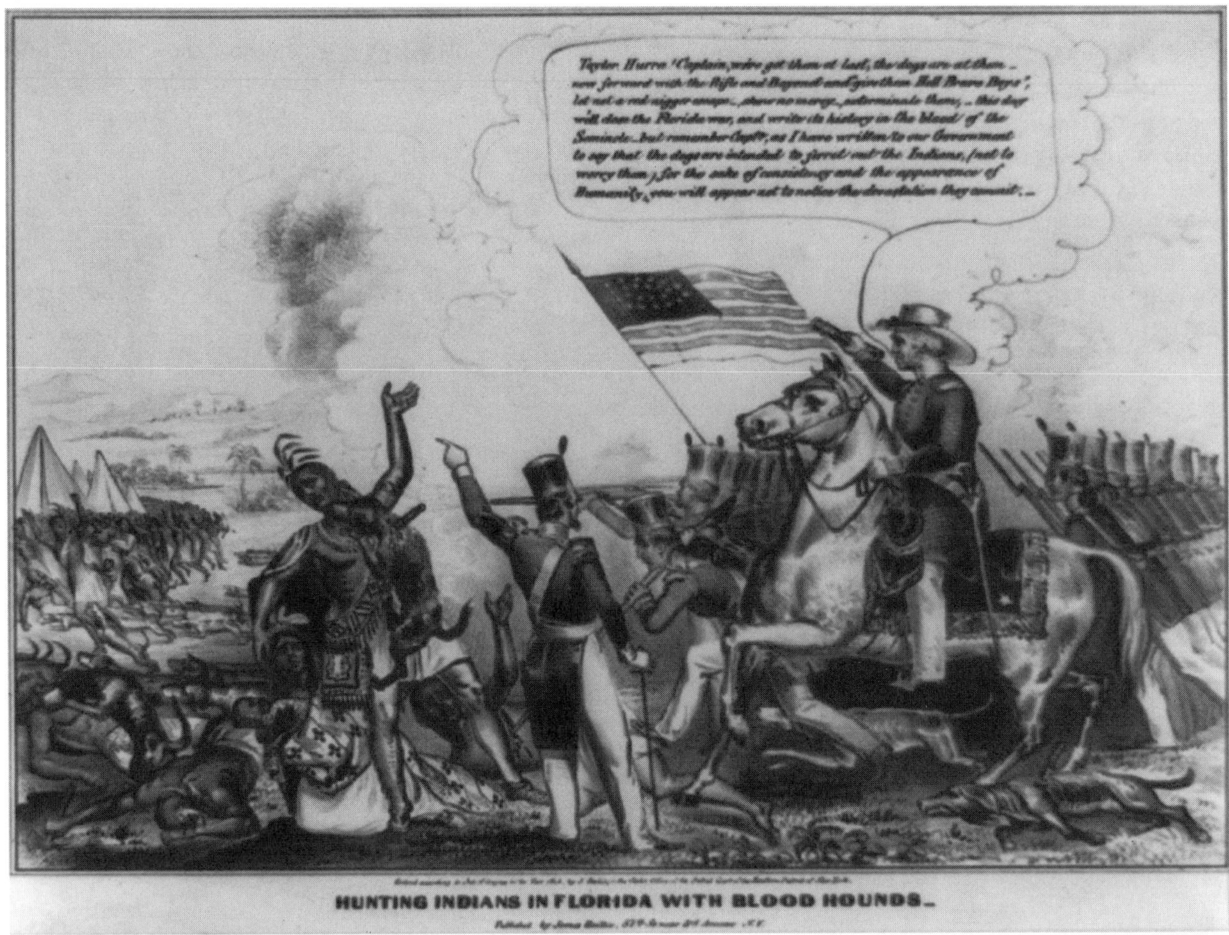

Zachary Taylor's Tactics Against Seminole Indians. *The indigenous people of America faced extensive destruction and death at the hands of whites. As early Americans began to move west, Native Americans were pushed out of their home territories and resistance was harshly put down by the military. Some of the brutal tactics used in the face of Native resistance are seen in this illustration originally published in 1848.* THE LIBRARY OF CONGRESS.

whites, and in California, where miners and early settlers killed 230,000. Thousands more died in places such as Sand Creek, Wounded Knee, Washita River, and Fort Robinson.

Disease. The germ, however, was the primary agent of destruction. Virtually every tribe was decimated by Old World diseases to which Indians had no immunity. Europeans and Africans introduced these diseases, sometimes intentionally through smallpox-infected blankets and other means. The diseases include smallpox, measles, bubonic plague, cholera, typhoid, scarlet fever, diphtheria and whooping cough. From 1520 to 1900, as many as ninety-three epidemics and pandemics spread among the Indians. Thornton states that the destruction of American Indians was initially "a medical conquest, one that paved the way for the more well-known and glorified military conquests and colonizations" (Thornton 1987, p. 47).

Dispossession, Resettlement and Destruction of Indigenous Habitat. From time immemorial, Native Americans developed land-based religions, cultures, economies, and ways of life based upon close relationships with diverse indigenous habitats. Forced removal under President Andrew Jackson began in 1828, when numerous eastern tribes were marched to reservations located west of the Mississippi River. Many died on forced marches or from starvation, disease, and harsh conditions on new reservations. Indians were forced to leave behind holy places, burial grounds, and indigenous habitats where they had developed their ways of life and special relationships with particular plants and animals.

In the 1880s, laws were enacted to break up reservation land owned by tribes, allot it to individual Indians, and allow white settlement on land promised to the tribes. Millions of acres were lost during this process, and some tribes became landless. These laws were justified in the name of assimilation by proponents who "maintained that if Indians adopted the habits of civilized life they would need less land" (Cohen 1982, p. 128).

The appropriation of land was a primary purpose of colonialism in the New World. As early as 1493, Pope Alexander VI conferred upon explorers the inherent power to claim land discovered by them on behalf of their countries of origin. He issued a Papal Bull declaring, "whereas Columbus had come upon lands and peoples undiscovered by others . . . all the lands discovered or to be discovered in the name of the Spanish Crown in the region legally belonged to Ferdinand and Isabella." This doctrine became the legal basis for acquiring all of the land that is now the United States. In *Johnson v. M'Intosh* (1823), the Supreme Court legalized the appropriation of America under the doctrine of discovery and justified it as follows:

> However extravagant the pretension of converting discovery of an inhabited country into conquest may appear, if the principle has been asserted in the first instance, and afterwards sustained; if a country has been acquired and held under it; if the property of a great mass of the community originates under it, it becomes the law of the land and cannot be questioned.

The destruction of American Indians was also furthered through the deliberate destruction of their indigenous habitats, as graphically seen in the near extermination of the immense herds of buffalo upon which the Plains Indian Tribes depended. It also occurred through widespread destruction of native plant life and its replacement with foreign vegetation imported from other places. The ethnobotanist Melvin Gilmore has documented an amazing number of plant uses among Plains Indians and decried their replacement by alien plant life more familiar to American settlers. In addition, the destruction of indigenous habitats occurred during the twentieth century through deforestation in the Pacific Northwest and the destruction of salmon runs upon which the tribes of that region depend for their ways of life.

Prohibition of Religion and Language, Assimilation, and the Taking of Children. In the 1880s, the government turned in earnest to the task of assimilating Indians. Assimilation was a deliberate program to strip Indians of their religions, cultures, languages, ways of life, and identities as native people and turn them into white farmers with Christian values.

The outright government prohibition of tribal religions began in the 1890s. "Federal troops slaughtered Indian practitioners of the Ghost Dance religion at Wounded Knee, and systematically suppressed this tribal religion on other Indian reservations" and in 1892 and 1904, "federal regulations outlawed the practice of tribal religions entirely" (Inouye 1992, pp. 13–14). The government furthered its program by conveying Indian land to Christian groups to establish religious schools and by placing missionaries as federal Indian agents in charge of reservations.

Indian children were taken, sometimes forcibly, and placed into government boarding schools. Separated from their parents, families, and communities, they received haircuts and uniforms and were, in effect, incarcerated for years at a time in authoritarian institutions that systematically stripped their identities. Teachers strictly prohibited native students from speaking their language and taught them to be ashamed of their parents and cultures. For almost one hundred years the government sought to "kill the Indian, and save the man." Several generations of institutionalized youth lost their language, culture, and religion, and hundreds of native languages were lost.

Congress continued its assimilation policy long after Indian citizenship was granted in 1924. Termination laws in the 1950s ended federal relationships with many Indian tribes, sold remaining land on many reservations, and subjected Indians to state jurisdiction.

The Legacy of Genocide and Ethnocide Professor Charles Wilkinson has observed that American Indians hit rock bottom during the 1950s. They lived in abject poverty in a segregated, racist society intent upon terminating their rights as native people and stamping out their cultural identity. The human spirit, however, cannot easily be stamped out. Wilkinson chronicles the rise from that nadir by modern Indian Nations, as Native Americans waged a historic movement over the next fifty years to reclaim their sovereignty, lands, and cultural heritage.

By 2005, the Native American population had recovered to more than two million people. A growing appreciation of their contributions to American heritage and their inherent worth has emerged, as seen in the opening of the National Museum of the American Indian in Washington, D.C., in 2004. Genocide is a sleeping evil, rarely mentioned in schoolbooks. Ethnocide, however, continues to haunt Native Americans. This is seen in the English-only laws of twenty-one states; the ongoing destruction of tribal holy places unprotected by American law; and the derogatory racial stereotypes used in Hollywood and the mass media, or in the sporting world by teams with names such as "Redskins." Native Americans fear the federal court system, which has grown increasingly hostile to protecting their legal rights. In 1992, Senator Inouye warned that as a result of recent Supreme Court decisions denying Native Americans religious freedom, "it appears that we are regressing to a dark period where once again our government is allowing religious discrimination against our indigenous people to go unchecked" (Inouye 1992, p. 14–15). History counsels that society must remain vigilant to safeguard Native Americans against racism, particularly the destructive and harmful acts of genocide and ethnocide.

SEE ALSO *American Indian Movement (AIM); Forced Sterilization of Native Americans; Holocaust.*

BIBLIOGRAPHY

De Las Casas, Bartolome. 1974 (1542). *The Devastation of the Indies: A Brief Account.* Translated by Herma Briffault. New York: Seabury Press.

———. 1974 (1552). *In Defense of the Indians.* Translated by Stafford Poole. DeKalb: Northern Illinois University Press.

Denevan, William, ed. 1976. *The Native Population of the Americas in 1492.* Madison: University of Wisconsin Press.

Echo-Hawk, Walter R. 2005. "Law, Legislation, and Native Religion." In *American Indian Religious Traditions: An Encyclopedia,* Vol. II, edited by Suzanne J. Crawford and Dennis F. Kelly, 455–473. Santa Barbara, CA: ABC-CLIO.

Gilmore, Melvin R. 1991 (1919). *Uses of Plants by the Indians of the Missouri River Region.* Lincoln: University of Nebraska Press.

Hitchcock, Robert K., and Tara M. Twedt. 1997. "Physical and Cultural Genocide of Various Indigenous Peoples." In *Century of Genocide: Eyewitness Accounts and Critical Views,* edited by Samuel Totten, Israel W. Charny, and William S. Parsons, 372–407. New York: Garland.

———. 1999. "Indigenous Peoples, Genocide Of." In *Encyclopedia of Genocide,* Volume II, edited by Israel W. Charny, 349–354. Santa Barbara, CA: ABC-CLIO.

Inouye, Senator Daniel K. 1992. "Discrimination and Native American Religious Rights." *University of West Los Angeles Law Review* 23: 3–19; and *Native American Rights Fund (NARF) Legal Review,* 18 (1993): 1–8.

Sale, Kirkpatrick. 1990. *The Conquest of Paradise: Christopher Columbus and the Columbian Legacy.* New York: Alfred A. Knopf.

Strickland, Rennard, ed. 1982. *Felix S. Cohen's Handbook of Federal Indian Law.* Charlottesville, VA: Michie Bobbs-Merrill.

Thorton, Russell. 1987. *American Indian Holocaust and Survival: A Population History since 1492.* Norman: University of Oklahoma Press.

Wilkinson, Charles. 2005. *Blood Struggle: The Rise of Modern Indian Nations.* New York: Norton.

Walter R. Echo-Hawk

GENOCIDE IN RWANDA

The African nation of Rwanda has become a metaphor for political violence, and more particularly for senseless violence. Two kinds of writings have come to dominate the literature on the Rwandan genocide. The first is preponderant in the academy, the second in the world of journalism.

Academic writing on Rwanda is dominated by authors whose intellectual perspective was shaped by sympathy with the Rwandan Revolution of 1959. They saw the revolution and the political violence that affected it as progressive, as ushering in a more popular political and social order. Unable to see the dark underbelly of the revolution, and thus to grasp the link between it and the 1994 genocide, these authors portray the genocide as exclusively or mainly a state project, engineered and executed by a narrow ruling elite. In doing so, they avoid the question of popular violence in the genocide. The singular failing of this view is its inability to come to terms with the genocide as a social project.

The massacres in the Rwandan genocide were carried out in the open—roughly 800,000 Tutsi were killed in a hundred days. The state organized the killings, but the killers were, by and large, ordinary people. The killing was done mainly by machete-wielding mobs. People were killed by their neighbors and workmates, and even by human rights advocates and spouses.

Unlike Nazi Germany, where the authorities made every attempt to isolate victims from the general population, the Rwandan genocide was both a more public and a more intimate affair. Street corners, living rooms, and churches became places of death. It was carried out by hundreds of thousands of people, and witnessed by millions. In a private conversation with the author in 1997, a Rwandan government minister contrasted the two horrors. "In Germany," he said, "the Jews were taken out of their residences, moved to distant far away locations, and killed there, almost anonymously. In Rwanda, the government did not kill. It prepared the population, enraged it and enticed it. Your neighbors killed you" (Mamdani 2001, p. 6). A few years ago, four Rwandan civilians stood trial for crimes against humanity in Belgium. Among the four were two nuns and a physicist. The challenge for academic writing is to explain the perversely "popular" character of the violence.

In contrast, journalistic writing focuses precisely on this aspect of the genocide. Its peculiar characteristic is a pornography of violence. As in pornography, the nakedness is of others, not us. The exposure of the other goes alongside the unstated claim that we are not like them. This is pornography in which senseless violence is a feature of other people's cultures: they are violent, but we are pacific, and a focus on their debasedness easily turns into another way of celebrating and confirming our exalted status.

The journalistic writing gives a simple moral world, where a group of perpetrators face another group of victims, but where neither history nor motivation are thinkable because both stand outside history and context. Though these writers highlight the genocide as a social project, they fail to understand the forces that shaped the agency of the perpetrator. Instead, they looked for a clear and uncomplicated moral in the story, where the victim was untainted and the perpetrator evil. In a context where victims and perpetrators have traded places, they look to distinguish victim from perpetrator for all times. But because victims have turned into perpetrators, this attempt to find an African replay of the Nazi Holocaust has not worked.

How many perpetrators were victims of yesteryear? What happens when yesterday's victims act out of a determination that they must never again be victimized, and therefore embrace the conviction that power is the only guarantee against victimhood, and that the only dignified alternative to power is death? What happens when they are convinced that the taking of life is really noble because it signifies the willingness to risk one's own life and is thus, in the final analysis, proof of one's own humanity? The German philosopher G. W. F. Hegel (1770–1831) once said that the difference between humans and animals is that humans are willing to give life for a reason considered higher than life. He should have added that humans are also willing to take life for a reason considered higher than life.

To address these questions, it is important to understand the humanity of the perpetrator. This is not to excuse the perpetrator, or the killing, but to make the act thinkable: so that we can learn something about ourselves as humans. Which history framed the agency of the perpetrator, and which institutions reproduced that agency? Who did the Hutu who did the killing think they were? And whom did they think they were killing in the person of the Tutsi?

THE RWANDA GENOCIDE AND THE HOLOCAUST

Before placing the Rwandan genocide in the context of Rwandan history, it is helpful to locate it in the history of modern genocides. In the corpus of Holocaust-writing, Hannah Arendt stood apart in her insistence on locating the Holocaust in the history of genocide. The history she sketched was that of the genocide of native populations by settler colonial nations. It was the history of imperialism, and specifically of racism in South Africa and bureaucracy in India and Algeria.

The Germans first attempted mass extermination in Africa. In 1904, German Southwest Africa—the territory that would ultimately become Namibia—faced a deepening political crisis. The future of the colony seemed suddenly precarious; the Herero, an agricultural people numbering some 80,000, had taken up arms to defend their land and cattle from German settlers. General Lothar von Trotha, the local German military commander, later wrote in stark terms of the options he faced:

> Now I have to ask myself how to end the war with the Herero. The views of the Governor and also a few old Africa hands on the one hand, and my views on the other, differ completely. The first wanted to negotiate for some time already and regard the Herero nation as necessary labour material for the future development of the country. I believe that the nation as such should be annihilated, or, if this was not possible by tactical measures, expelled from the country by operative means and further detailed treatment. This will be possible if the water-holes ... are occupied. The constant movement of our troops will enable us to find the small groups of the nation who have moved back westwards and destroy them gradually. (Gewald, p. 173)

Trotha's arguments carried the day, over the objections of the "Africa hands" who saw the Herero as necessary labor and the missionaries who viewed them as potential converts. As the Herero fled the German assault, every avenue of escape was blocked, save one: the southeast route, through the Kalahari Desert. Denied access to water, their journey across the desert was a death march, and almost 80 percent of the Herero perished. This was not an accident, as a gleeful notice in *Die Kampf*, the official publication of the German General Staff, attested:

> No efforts, no hardships were spared in order to deprive the enemy of his last reserves of resistance; like a half-dead animal he was hunted from water-hole to water-hole until he became a lethargic victim of the nature of his own country. The waterless Omaheke [desert] was to complete the work of the German arms: the annihilation of the Herero people. (Dedering 1999).

General Lothar von Trotha had a distinguished record in the German army and was a veteran of colonial warfare. Involved in suppressing the Boxer Rebellion in China in 1900, he was also a veteran of "pacification campaigns" throughout the colonies that would later become Rwanda, Burundi, and Tanzania.

The surviving Herero were rounded up and placed in camps run by missionaries, in conjunction with the German army. Overworked and hungry, susceptible to diseases such as typhoid and smallpox, many more Herero perished in the camps, and Herero women were taken as sex slaves by German soldiers. When the camps were closed in 1908, the remaining Herero were distributed among settlers as laborers. Henceforth, every Herero over the age of seven was required to wear a metal disc around the neck, bearing his or her labor registration number.

The extermination of the Herero was the first genocide of the twentieth century, and its connection to the

Jewish holocaust is difficult to ignore. When von Trotha sought to diffuse responsibility for the genocide, he accused the missions of inciting the Herero with images "of the bloodcurdling Jewish history of the Old Testament." And it was in the Herero concentration camps that the German geneticist Eugene Fischer first investigated the "science" of race-mixing, experimenting on both the Herero and the half-German children born to Herero women. Fischer deduced that the Herero "mulattos" were physically and mentally inferior to their German parents. Later, Hitler read his book, *The Principle of Human Heredity and Race Hygiene* (1921), while in prison, and he eventually made Fischer rector of the University of Berlin, where he taught medicine. One of Fischer's prominent students was Josef Mengele, who went on to run the gas chambers at Auschwitz.

Hannah Arendt was right to establish a link between the genocide of the Herero and the Nazi Holocaust. That link was "race branding," whereby it is possible not only to set a group apart as an enemy, but also to annihilate it with an easy conscience. To understand the mindset that conceived the Holocaust, one must remember the political identities crafted by modern imperialism, those of the "settler" and the "native." Hannah Arendt focused on the agency of the settler, but not on the agency of the native. The point is that it is not just the settler, but the native, too, who is a product of the imperial imagination. Both identities are framed by a common history. Both remain postcolonial identities, and unless they are sublated together, they will be reproduced together.

Hannah Arendt sketched half a history: that of settler annihilation of the native. To glimpse how this could trigger a countertendency leading to the native annihilating the settler, one has to turn to Frantz Fanon (1925–1961). It is in Fanon that one finds the premonition of the native turned perpetrator, of the native who kills not just to extinguish the humanity of the Other, but to defend his or her own—and of the moral ambivalence this must provoke in other human beings. Although the extermination of colonizers by natives never came to pass, it hovered on the horizon as a historical possibility. No one understood the genocidal impulse better than Frantz Fanon, a Martinican-born psychoanalyst and Algerian freedom fighter. Native violence, he insisted, was the violence of yesterday's victims, the violence of those who had cast aside their victimhood to become masters of their own lives: "He of whom they have never stopped saying that the only language he understands is that of force, decides to give utterance by force. … The argument the native chooses has been furnished by the settler, and by an ironic turning of the tables it is the native who now affirms that the colonialist understands nothing but force" (Fanon 1967, p. 66).

For Fanon, the proof of the native's humanity consisted not in the willingness to kill settlers, but in the willingness to risk his or her own life. "The colonized man," he wrote, "finds his freedom in and through violence." If the outcome was death—natives killing settlers—that was still a derivative outcome. "The settler's work is to make even dreams of liberty impossible for the native. The native's work is to imagine all possible methods for destroying the settler. … For the native, life can only spring up again out of the rotting corpse of the settler. … For the colonized people, this violence, because it constitutes their only work, invests their character with positive and creative qualities" (Fanon 1967, p. 73).

THE HISTORY OF VIOLENCE BETWEEN HUTU AND TUTSI

The significance of "native" and "settler" as political identities, embedded in the history of colonialism, becomes clear in the light of the history of political violence in Rwanda. The most striking fact about this history is that there is no significant violent episode before the 1959 revolution, when battle lines were drawn sharply between Hutu and Tutsi. That year marked the first significant episode where the Hutu were pitted against the Tutsi in a political struggle, so that Hutu and Tutsi became names identifying political adversaries locked in a violent contest for power.

This becomes clearer if one contrasts 1959 with the Nyabingi anticolonial resistance that marked the beginning of the colonial period. *Nyabingi* was the name of a spiritual cult, as well as a political movement, in what became northern Rwanda, a region incorporated into the expanding Kingdom of Rwanda at the beginning of the twentieth century. Two facts about this movement are relevant. First, when the Bakiga fought the alliance of German imperial power and the Tutsi aristocracy of the Rwandan Kingdom, they did not fight as Hutu against Tutsi. They fought the Tutsi who were in power, but in alliance with the Tutsi who were out of power, under the leadership of Muhumuza, a former Tutsi queen.

Second, these mountain people did not call themselves Hutu, but Bakiga (the people of the mountains). Only when they were defeated and incorporated into the Rwanda Kingdom did they cease to be Bakiga and become Hutu. For "Hutu" was not the identity of a discrete ethnic group, but the political identity of all those subjugated to the power of the Rwandan state.

In Rwanda before colonialism, prosperous Hutu became Tutsi over a period of generations. Even if the numbers involved were too few to be statistically significant, this was a process of great social and ideological significance. This process of ritual ennoblement, whereby a Hutu shed his Hutuness, even had a name: *Kwihutura*.

Belgian Congo Soldiers Guard Rwandan Prisoners, 1959. *Conflict between the Tutsis and Hutus goes back many years before the genocide that took place in the 1990s. In this 1959 photo, Belgian Congo soldiers guard a group of prisoners after intervening in a fight between the Tutsis and Hutus.* AP IMAGES.

Its counterpart, whereby an impoverished Tutsi family lost its status, also had a name: *Gucupira*.

Belgian colonialism did not invent Tutsi privilege. What was new with Belgian colonialism was the justification for it. For the first time in the history of Rwanda, the terms "Hutu" and "Tutsi" came to identify two groups, one branded indigenous, the other exalted as alien. For the first time, Tutsi privilege claimed to be the privilege of a group identified as Hamitic, as racially alien. Only with Belgian colonialism did the degradation of the Hutu turn into a native degradation, and Tutsi privilege became a racially alien privilege. As Belgian authorities issued identity cards to Hutu and Tutsi, the Tutsi became sealed off from the Hutu. Legally identified as two biologically distinct races—Tutsi as Hamites and Hutu as Bantu—Hutu and Tutsi became distinct legal identities. The language of race functioned to underline this difference between indigenous and alien groups.

This point becomes clear upon return to the difference between race and ethnicity in twentieth-century colonial thought. Only natives were classified as "tribes" in colonial Africa, and as "ethnic groups" in postcolonial Africa. Nonnatives, those not considered African, were tagged as "races." Tribes were neighbors, but races were aliens. This contrast underlined the difference between ethnic and racial violence. Ethnic violence is between neighbors. It is about transgression across borders, about excess. In the conflict between neighbors, what is at issue is not the legitimacy of the presence of others. At issue is an overflow, a transgression. It is only with "race" that the very presence of a group can come to be considered illegitimate, with its claim for power considered an outright usurpation. Thus, when political violence takes the form of a genocide, it is more likely between races, not between ethnic groups.

Alongside the master race, the law constituted subject races. While full citizenship in the colony was reserved for members of the master race, the subject races were virtual or partial citizens. Though subject to discrimination, they were still considered part of the world of rights, of civil law, and they were integrated into the machinery of colonial rule as agents and administrators in both the public and the private sector. As such, they came to be seen as both instruments and beneficiaries of colonialism, even as civil law codified their second-class citizenship.

The so-called subject races of colonial Africa were many. Besides the Asians of East Africa, there were the Colored of South Africa, the Arabs of Zanzibar, and the Tutsi of Rwanda and Burundi. Historically and culturally, these groups had little in common. The Asians obviously had their origins elsewhere, but the question of what distinguished other subject races from indigenous people was more complex. In Zanzibar, "Arab" was a kind of catchall identity, denoting both those with Arab ancestry and those with ties to Arab culture. South Africa's Coloreds were identified by their mixture, by their ancestral links to Asia, Africa, and Europe. The Tutsi, on the other hand, were wholly indigenous to Africa. So the colonial designation "nonindigenous" needs to be understood as a legal and political fiction, not a historical or cultural reality.

The racialization of the Tutsi, and of the difference between Hutu and Tutsi, is key to understanding the political violence between Hutu and Tutsi. It was the language of race that defined insiders and outsiders, distinguishing "indigenous" from "alien." It set apart neighbors from outsiders and, ultimately, friends from enemies.

Colonial Rwanda was a halfway house, stuck between direct and indirect rule, with features of both in effect. "Customary laws" and "native authorities" were established alongside civic law and civic authorities. But the Hutu were ruled by Tutsi rather than Hutu chiefs. The same reforms established the Tutsi as a distinct race. Unlike indirect rule elsewhere, the colonial state in Rwanda engendered polarized racial identities among indigenous people, rather than plural ethnic identities. The colonized population was split in two, with the majority, the Hutu, opposed to both Belgian and Tutsi.

Why was Rwanda different? The answers lie buried in the recesses of the racist mind. "Africa proper," Hegel said, "has remained—for all purposes of connection with the rest of the world, shut up; it is the gold-land compressed within itself—the land of childhood, which lying beyond the day of conscious history is enveloped in the dark mantle of Night" (Hegel 1966, p. 91).

But the more Europeans got to know Africa, the less tenable was the notion that the Sahara divided barbarism and civilization. Europeans were increasingly confronted with—and had to explain—evidence of organized life on the continent before their arrival. This sometimes came in the form of ruins, such as the Sudanese pyramids or the ruin at Great Zimbabwe. It also came in the form of highly developed African societies such as the Kingdom of Rwanda, whose political history stretched back several hundred years. Rwanda belied the racist conviction that the natives had no civilization of their own.

The colonialists' explanation—the "Hamitic hypothesis"—was ingenious: Every sign of "progress" on the Dark Continent was taken as proof of the civilizing influence of an alien race. Ancient Egypt, Ethiopia, Rwanda—all these were the work of an ancient European race, the children of Ham (Noah's son in the Hebrew Bible). The Hamites were taken to be black-skinned Caucasians who had wandered across the African continent and ruled over their racial inferiors, the black-skinned blacks. In Rwanda, the Europeans identified the ruling Tutsi as Hamitic and the Hutu as Bantu—or "real Africans" who served the Tutsi. In 1870, at the Vatican I council, a group of cardinals called for a mission to Central Africa in order to rescue "hapless Hamites caught amidst Negroes," to alleviate "the antique malediction weighing on the shoulders of the misfortunate Hamites inhabiting the hopeless Nigricy."

Of course, the Hamitic hypothesis failed to resolve some glaring contradictions. While the term was introduced by linguists to describe the languages of the Hamitic peoples, the Tutsi spoke Kinyarwanda, a Bantu language. And although the notion of a Hamitic race implied a shared phenotype—tall, thin, with aquiline noses and coppery skin—most Rwandans were born of mixed Hutu-Tutsi unions and could not be told apart as distinct phenotypes. The greatest difficulty, perhaps, was that the Hamites were supposed to be cattle-herding pastoralists, unlike the agriculturalist Bantu. But by the second half of the nineteenth century, many Tutsi lived just like their Hutu neighbors, without cattle and working the land under feudal overlords, who were also Tutsi. No wonder that official identification of Hutu from Tutsi relied on identity cards that spelled out the racial identity of the holder. It is also why without the involvement of neighbors and intimates, it would have been difficult to tell Tutsi apart from Hutu during the genocide.

While numerous African peoples were identified as Hamites—indeed, three of the precolonial political entities that became part of Uganda were considered Hamitic kingdoms—Rwanda was the only colony where Hamitic ideology came to be the law of the land. The "foreignness" of the Tutsi was institutionalized by a series of reforms that embedded the Hamitic hypothesis in the Belgian colonial state. This set the Tutsi apart from other so-called Hamites in Africa; it also ruptured the link between race and color in Rwanda.

Between 1926 and 1937, the Belgian authorities made Tutsi superiority the basis of changes in political, social, and cultural relations. Key institutions of feudal Rwanda were dismantled; power was centralized; and Western-style schools were opened, with admission largely limited to Tutsi. Tutsis received an assimilationist education: they were taught in French, in preparation for administrative positions in the colonial government. When Hutu were admitted, they received a separate curriculum, taught in Kiswahili. (The graduates of the French language curriculum were called "Hamites.") The underlying message was that Hutu were not destined for citizenship.

In the 1950s, as the struggle for decolonization raged across the African continent, Rwandan society began to splinter. While the Tutsi agitated for independence—and a Tutsi state without Belgian masters—the Hutu made increasingly strident demands for social reform. Having been branded with a subject identity, a new political elite emerged from the ranks of the socially oppressed and made it a badge of pride expressed in the slogan "Hutu Power." The revolution of 1959 was ushered in by violence that targeted Tutsi and dissolved the middle ground between Hutu and Tutsi. When Rwanda became independent in 1960, it was the self-consciously Hutu counter-elite that came to power.

POLITICAL IDENTITIES AND THE NATIONALIST REVOLUTION

Thus, colonialism is the genesis of Hutu-Tutsi violence in Rwanda. But colonialism does not explain why this violence continued after the revolution. If the origin of the Hutu-Tutsi problem lies in the racialized political identities forged by colonialism, then nationalism reproduced that problem. Here is the dilemma that must be confronted: Race-branding was not simply a state ideology, it also became a social ideology, reproduced by some of the same Hutu and Tutsi that had been branded as "native" and "alien."

The Rwandan Revolution of 1959 was heralded as the "Hutu Revolution." As the revolutionaries built Rwanda into a "Hutu nation," they embarked on a program of justice—that is, justice for Hutu, and a reckoning for Tutsi. In so doing, they confirmed Hutu and Tutsi as political identities: Hutu as native, Tutsi as alien.

The irony is that instead of transforming the political world created by colonialism, the world of natives and settlers, the revolutionaries confirmed it. Postcolonial nationalism in Rwanda raises two important questions: (1) In what ways did nationalism build on the colonial political edifice, instead of transforming it? (2) When does the pursuit of justice turn into revenge?

For a political analysis of the genocide in Rwanda, there are three pivotal moments. The first moment is that of colonization and the racialization of the state apparatus by Belgians in the 1920s. The second is that of nationalism and the revolution of 1959, a turning of tables that entrenched colonial political identities in the name of justice. The third moment is that of the civil war of 1990. The civil war was not borne of a strictly internal process; it was an outcome of a regional development, one that joined the crisis in Rwanda with that in Uganda.

The Tutsi exiles of 1959 found refuge in many countries, including Uganda. Living on the margins of society, many joined the guerrilla struggle against the regime of the Ugandan leader Milton Obote from 1981 to 1985. When the victorious National Resistance Army (NRA) entered the capital city of Kampala in January 1986, roughly a quarter of the 16,000 guerrillas were Banyarwanda. (Banyarwanda refers to the people of Rwanda, those who speak Kinyarwanda, whether they be Hutu or Tutsi.) Banyarwanda had immigrated to Uganda throughout the colonial period. In the Luwero Triangle (the theater of the guerrilla struggle) migrants were nearly half the population, and the largest group of migrants was from Rwanda.

Every time the NRA guerrillas liberated a village and organized an assembly, they confronted a challenge: Who could participate in an assembly? Who could vote? Who could run for office? The dilemma sprang from the colonial political legacy, which linked rights to ancestry. By defining migrants as not indigenous, it deprived them of political rights. The NRA's answer was to redefine the basis of rights, from ancestry to residence. Simply put, every adult resident of a village was considered to have the right of participation in the village assembly. This new notion of rights was translated into a nationality law after 1986, so that anyone with a ten-year residence in the country had the right to be a citizen. The big change was that the 1959 refugees of the Rwandan Revolution were now considered Ugandans.

This political inheritance was called into question with the NRA's first major political crisis in 1990, which was triggered by an attempt to honor one of the ten points in the guerrilla program: the pledge to redistribute absentee land to pastoralist squatters. When it came to distributing the land among a population of mobile pastoralists, the question of who should get the land naturally arose. Who, in fact, was a citizen?

The opposition mobilized around this question, aiming to exclude Banyarwanda as noncitizens. The magnitude of the resulting crisis was signified by an extraordinary session of parliament that lasted three days. At the end of its deliberation, parliament changed the citizenship law from a ten-year residence to a requirement that to be recognized as a citizen a person must show an ancestral connection with the land; that is, one had to show that at least one grandparent was born in the territory later demarcated as Uganda. In another month, the Rwandan Patriotic Front (RPF), comprising mainly of Tutsi refugees seeking to overthrow the Hutu government of Rwanda, crossed the border. Thus, 1990 was not

Mass Grave of Rwandans, 1994. *The bodies of Rwandan genocide victims are buried in a mass grave near Goma, Zaire. Over a period of only 100 days, roughly 800,000 people lost their lives in the genocide and war.* AP IMAGES.

simply an armed return to Rwanda; it was also an armed expulsion from Uganda.

The civil war of 1990–1994 hurled Rwanda back into the world of Hutu Power and Tutsi Power. Faced with a possible return of Tutsi Power, it provided Hutu Power, a marginal tendency in the Second Republic that had in 1972 followed the revolutionary First Republic born of the 1959 Revolution, with its first opportunity to return to the political center stage as defenders of the revolution. Without the civil war, there would have been no genocide.

The Rwandan genocide needs to be located in a context shaped by three related moments: the global *imperial* moment defined by Belgian colonialism and its racialization of the state; the *national* moment established by the 1959 revolution that reinforced racialized identities in the name of justice; and the *postcolonial* regional moment, born of a link between the citizenship crisis in postrevolutionary Rwanda and its neighbors. The first lesson of the Rwandan genocide is that it was not a necessary outcome, but rather a contingent outcome in a context where nationalism failed to come to terms with the racialized legacy of colonialism critically.

The dilemma of postgenocide Rwanda lies in the chasm that divides the Hutu majority from the Tutsi minority. The minority demands justice, while the majority calls for democracy. The two demands seem irreconcilable, however, because violence has long been motivated by a mutual fear of victimhood. Every round of perpetrators has justified the use of violence as the only effective guarantee against being victimized yet again. The continuing tragedy of Rwanda is that each round of violence serves only to create yet another set of victims-turned-perpetrators.

Ultimately, the Rwandan government may need to recognize that the central conclusion to be drawn from the history of post-independence Rwanda—that the only possible peace between Tutsi and Hutu is an armed peace—is shortsighted. It is currently an article of faith in Kigali that power is the precondition for survival. But Rwanda's Tutsi leadership may have to consider the opposite possibility: that the prerequisite to cohabitation, to reconciliation, and to a common political future, might be to give up the monopoly of power. Like the Arabs of Zanzibar, or even the whites of South Africa, the Tutsi of Rwanda may also have to learn that—so long as

Hutu and Tutsi remain alive as political identities—relinquishing power may be a surer guarantee of survival than holding on to it. The first concrete step ought to be what the Banyarwanda outside Rwanda sought: equal citizenship rights of all based on a single criterion—residence, not race.

The genocide weighs heavily on the minds of Tutsi survivors. And it is true that neither the Arabs of Zanzibar nor the whites of South Africa have suffered such genocidal violence. To find historical parallels to this situation, where an imperiled minority fears to come under the thumb of a guilty majority yet again—even if the thumbprint reads "democracy"—we must take leave of Africa. For only in the erstwhile settler colonies of the New World is there a comparable history of violence—a history that has rendered the majority guilty in the eyes of victimized minorities. Such, indeed, has been the aftermath of genocide and slavery, particularly the genocide of indigenous populations in the Americas, Australia, and New Zealand, and the slavery of Africans in the Americas. If one is to go by these experiences, one has to admit that the attainment of enlightenment by guilty majorities has been a painfully slow process.

If the Nazi Holocaust was testimony to the crisis of the nation-state in Europe, the Rwandan genocide is testimony to the crisis of citizenship in postcolonial Africa. But if the Nazi Holocaust breathed life into the Zionist demand that Jews too must have a political home, few have argued that the Rwandan genocide warrants the establishment of a Tutsi-land in the region. Indeed, Europe "solved" its political crisis by exporting it to the Middle East, but Africa has no place to export its political crisis. Thus, the Tutsi demand for a state of their own cannot—and should not—be met.

In Rwanda, as elsewhere, a conflict can end only when the victor reaches out to the vanquished. In Rwanda, as elsewhere, this process of reconciliation will begin when both groups relinquish claims to victimhood, embracing their identity as survivors. In this sense, "survivor" does not just refer to surviving victims—as it does in the rhetoric of the Rwandan government. In a Rwanda that has truly transcended the racial divisions of colonialism, "survivor" will refer to all those who continue to be blessed with life in the aftermath of a civil war and a genocide.

SEE ALSO *Genocide and Ethnocide; Holocaust.*

BIBLIOGRAPHY

Arendt, Hannah. 1975. *The Origins of Totalitarianism.* New York: Harcourt Brace.

Dedering, Tilman. 1999. "'A Certain Rigorous Treatment of all Parts of the Nation': The Annihilation of the Herero in German South West Africa, 1904." In *The Massacre in History*, edited by Mark Levine and Penny Roberts, 204–222. New York: Berghahn Books.

Fanon, Frantz. 1967. *The Wretched of the Earth.* London: Penguin.

Gewald, Jan-Bart. 1999. *Herero Heroes: A Socio-Political History of the Herero of Namibia, 1890-1923.* Oxford: James Currey, 1999.

Hegel, Georg Wilhelm Friedrich. 1966. *The Philosophy of History.* Translated by John Sibree, New York: Dover Publications.

Mazimpaka, Patrick, interview, Kigali, 11 July 1997. Cited in Mamdani, Mahmood 2001. *When Victims Become Killers: Colonialism, Nativism and the Genocide in Rwanda*, p. 6. Princeton, NJ: Princeton University Press.

Mahmood Mamdani

GENOCIDE IN SUDAN

In the early twenty-first century, the tragic and discomforting topic of genocide is centered on the grave humanitarian crisis of death, injury, and dislocation in the western Sudanese province of Darfur, adjacent to Chad. The discourse revolves around several questions. Where is the conflict and why there? What factors precipitated the conflict? How should the conflict be measured and characterized? How should the legal and humanitarian issues be addressed? Who is responsible? What can be done?

CAUSES OF THE CONFLICT

Like most cases of human strife, the conflict in Darfur in this African and Arab nation has many causes, with specific turning points that sent the various antagonists to new levels of violence.

Geographical Features. Darfur is physically located on the Sahelian ecological border between desert to the north and savanna to the south, with micro-climatic variation in the central region that creates small streams, and hillside agriculture in Jebel Marra. The micro-ecological variations result in competition among the various African and Arab groups that seek to make their livings in different ways in these different regions. With only seasonal variations, a symbiotic balance can be struck, but when land competition is exacerbated by southward desertification of the Sahara, along with intense demographic pressure, the competition increases.

Another geographical factor is that Darfur straddles a key east-west trade route from central Sudan west to Chad. Central Darfur and Egypt are linked by the famed "forty-day road" (Darb al-Arba'in). Thus, commerce in even southern Darfur is networked to the wider world. Commercial control of these routes is also a factor. The conflict cannot be reduced to solely geographical factors, but decreased rainfall in the last two decades in these trade and ecological zones do contribute.

Historical and Ethnographic Factors. The conflict is also fueled by economic rivalries between the Daju kingdom peoples (controlling trade and resources in southern Darfur), the Tunjur kingdom peoples (controlling east-west trade and the forty-days road trade), and the Keira dynasties that, from the seventeenth to the twentieth centuries, dominated trade through central Darfur. Although seemingly marginal to the modern conflict and often minimized, the divisions between the multiple rebel groups in Darfur stem, in part, from these deeply rooted ethnic rivalries (e.g., Zaghawa, Fur [both non-Arabic-speaking], Camel-Arabs, and Cattle-Arabs).

Beyond the internal struggles to rule Darfur as a sovereign polity or sultanate, Darfur's history contains examples of external competitive relationships and other wider political interests. Depending on the period, the state of Wadai (now in Chad) was interested in economic control over Darfur, as were the Arab powers based in the central Sudan. In medieval times the Funj sultans of Sennar (1504–1821) and the sultans of Darfur clashed or cooperated in the middle lands of Kordofan in the eighteenth century. During the Turkiya (1821–1885) the slave and ivory trader Zubeir Pasha came to control Darfur for himself. During the Mahdiya (1885–1989) Khalifa ʿAbdullahi ruled Sudan and Darfur from Omdurman and he was himself a Ta'isha Baggara Arab from Darfur. In 1916, during the Anglo-Egyptian Condominium (1889–1956), the British assassinated the last sultan of Darfur, ʿAli Dinar, to complete their military colonization of the Sudan. In short, the historical record is replete with precedents of external and internal forces who tried to protect, rule, take over, or otherwise manipulate Darfur. This dynamic history presages many of the present conflicts. Simple polarities are not operable.

Religion. Because virtually all of the present antagonists in Darfur are Sunni Muslims, one might imagine that religion is not a factor in the conflict. Yet religion is involved. One may distinguish four forms of Islamic observance: First, folk and syncretic Islam marries traditional non-Islamic beliefs and practices with those of orthodox Islam. Second, Islam is represented by those who are simply "good" Muslims following their faith as a matter of their cultural upbringing. Third, there are followers of politicized Islam, which substantially defines the government of Sudan, especially during its association with the National Islamic Front; one faction of the Darfur rebels has a similar orientation. Fourth, there are Muslims in Darfur who want to respect Islam on personal status matters but prefer a separation between state and belief in this multi-religious, sectarian, and culturally plural nation. Thus, politico-religious issues are part of this dispute.

Race. Other elements of the conflict revolve around contentious and complex social constructions of racial identity that prevail in Sudan in general and in Darfur in particular. On one level all Sudanese are "black"; indeed that is what the word *sudan* means in Arabic for the entire region of Bilad as-Sudan (Land of the Blacks). Moreover, all Sudanese are Africans, given that their nation is on the African continent. Although these points might seem obvious, they are at the foundation of much miscommunication, misrepresentation, and misunderstanding of the present conflict. Nonetheless there certainly are dimensions of ethnically based conflict between such groups as the Zaghawa and Camel-Arabs for competing for grazing territory under ecological pressure. Some Arabs mobilize their identity around revivalist Islamo-Arabist models and prejudicial terminology such as Zarqa (blue-black people); in parts of Darfur even the term *kufar* (nonbelievers) or *ʿabeed* (slaves) is sometimes heard in violent and disparaging contexts. On the other hand "Africans" such as the Zaghawa, Fur, and Masalit certainly have formulated angry and negative stereotypes about Jellaba Arabs and especially about the *janjaweed* or *fursan* (terrible horsemen). Each side has mobilized and polarized the conflict while "othering" their respective enemies.

Traditional cases of interethnic conflict in Darfur were usually resolved by local governance at low levels (especially over water and grazing rights). During the Jaafar Nimieri regime (1969–1983), there was an effort to "modernize" public administration and abolish or transform the traditional councils. When the current conflict began, in the wider context of marginalized people, Sudanese class stratification, and wide opposition to military rule, there was little to stop or buffer the violence from climbing to new heights.

THE POLITICS OF GENOCIDE

As the violence escalated, beginning in March 2003, the humanitarian crisis itself became politicized. Some international bodies and nations were using the word *genocide* either to dramatize the distressing situation, or to put political pressures on the antagonists to get them to negotiate plans for armed forces separation, peace keeping, and conflict resolution. The majority of African and Arab nations and Amnesty International were concerned with the deepening humanitarian crisis but were broadly reluctant to polarize the situation, and few used the term genocide. Notably, three non-African and non-Arab nations—England, the United States, and Israel—were the most interested in applying this term, perhaps because of

Sudanese Liberation Army Rebels, 2004. *Members of the Sudanese Liberation Army (SLA), one of the factions involved in the terrible conflict in Darfur, on patrol.* DESIREY MINKOH/AFP/GETTY IMAGES.

domestic pressure or as diversionary efforts. Each of these states has at various times been at war with Arab or Islamic states, sometimes acting in concert. The United States does not have ambassadorial relations with Sudan for a variety of reasons; Israel is not recognized by Sudan; and England had formerly conquered the Sudan (1898–1956), not to mention that it overthrew the independent Sultanate of Darfur. Such historical and political facts were not overlooked by Sudanese, whether democrats or military governments. In this context the term genocide itself also became part of the conflict, as each side sought to project the conflict as much worse, or much better, than it actually was to address its own public relations and propaganda concerns.

LEGAL ASPECTS OF GENOCIDE

Aside from these distracting politics of genocide, the December 1948 First Geneva Accords (UN Convention on the Prevention and Punishment of the Crime of Genocide) establishes some real tests and raises valid concerns. The accords call for international action if crimes against humanity are taking place. In the wake of the Nuremberg Trials following World War II, the crime of genocide was specifically defined in article one as murder "committed with the intent to destroy, in whole or in part, a national, ethnical, racial or religious group." Perpetrators could be convicted for conspiracy to commit genocide, to incite genocide, to attempt to commit genocide, or otherwise be complicit in genocide. More than twenty specific crimes and articles were recognized in 1949, and these conventions were further updated and expanded in 1977. Sadly, clear violations took place in such places as Cambodia, Rwanda, and Serbia following the Geneva Accords. Some prosecutions have slowly taken place, but some victimizers could not be apprehended, or died, or were too powerful to be brought before world courts that they refused to recognize.

Within this substantial legal and historical framework, charges and evidence of genocide can be presented at the International Criminal Court (ICC). In the case of Darfur, the United States has identified fifty-one individuals (representing the government, militias, and rebel groups), and extensive evidence and testimony has been collected; but there have been no arrests or prosecutions because of the ongoing dispute. The unilateral military actions of the Sudan Liberation Army (SLA) and the Justice for Equality Movement (JEM) against substantial Sudanese government military targets in Darfur in March 2003 launched the heavy rounds of fighting. Also, many Darfuri people have long been in the Sudanese army, and many refugees from Darfur have actually fled to other cities in Sudan where they might live in poor conditions, but they are not racially persecuted.

On the other hand, among the *janjaweed* and regular government forces, the counterinsurgency strategy has employed extreme and frightful measures to drive the rural populations (supporters of the rebels) to IDP (internally displaced persons) camps, to other Sudanese cities, and across international borders. An internationally brokered effort to reach a peaceful solution between the government of Sudan and the rebels was achieved in Abuja in 2006 with the largest rebel faction, while others kept maneuvering and splintering for more favorable outcomes. The remaining rebels caused some of the subsequent bloodshed. With these attacks the Government of Sudan (GoS) resorts to the right, maintained by any sovereign state, to deploy its military. These circumstances certainly do not diminish the horrors. But perhaps they weaken or cast doubt on the legal case for genocide. In Cambodia, Rwanda, and Serbia, or in Nazi Germany, *all* members of the targeted groups were at risk *any* place under the control of those committing genocide. This is not the case in Sudan.

Likewise, in Darfur the apparent victims of this crime, the rebels, certainly initiated, then escalated, this conflict as an understandable but perhaps misguided political movement seeking a more favorable position vis-à-vis Khartoum that would be parallel to what they saw was achieved in the North-South (CPA) accords. The rebel forces failed to calculate the role of *murahaleen* militias in that dispute and did not adequately account for the probability that Khartoum would likely respond in a similar way in Darfur. In short, it appears that the legal or criminal aspects of this conflict, however horrible, were apparently not built on a plan of extermination or ethnic cleansing of the Darfuri people from the nation of Sudan, but by a counterinsurgency campaign to clear the conflicted zone of civilian support. Moreover, judging from the fact that most of the main Darfur rebel parties attended and participated in the Abuja meetings and that the largest (SLA-Minnawi) signed the accords, it can be seen that most sought a political and peaceful solution of the disputes. Some rebels have supplemental agendas about the political equation in Khartoum or even some interest in secession. Such goals are not the case for genocide in general.

GENDER AND HUMAN RIGHTS ASPECTS

United Nations Security Council resolution 1593 of March 31, 2005, referred this conflict to the International Criminal Court. China abstained, while the United States awkwardly feared that it would itself be judged by this judicial body for alleged war crimes and Geneva Accord abuses in its "war on terrorism." The United States is not a signatory of the ICC, and it was hesitant to charge Sudanese with war crimes, especially while working with Sudan on counterterrorism intelligence and jointly protecting the Comprehensive Peace Agreement that both value. Former president of the African Union (AU), Nigerian President Olasegun Obasanjo bravely proposed creating an African panel for Criminal Justice and Reconciliation for the Darfur situation. To push this point, the normal rotation of the AU presidency was slated to put Sudanese President Omar al-Bashir in this position during the AU summit in Khartoum. This became so problematic that al-Bashir stepped away from this notable appointment. The ICC continued to investigate human rights abuses in Eastern Congo and Uganda.

Meanwhile, the United Nations created an International Commission of Inquiry on Darfur to document the patterns of abuses in that Sudanese province. The commission concluded that the government of Sudan and its *janjaweed* militia were largely responsible for human rights abuses and other legal violations that could reach the level of "war crimes" according to the principles of the Geneva Accords, including rape, gang rape, and other forms of sexual and criminal violence. The SLA and JEM factions that existed at that time were also charged with such violations.

It is clear that, with the breakdown of the civil and legal order, gender-based abuses occurred because women and children are highly vulnerable and their own male kin had often joined with various armed groups. Violence against women, children, and the elderly in a scorched earth approach aimed partly to make "free-fire zones" in the government counterinsurgency strategy for rebel vs. *janjaweed* engagements and partly to deny the human resources base for the rebel groups in Darfur. This rural depopulation tactic to "break the will" of the rebels backfired, only intensifying their anger and resolve to fight on. International anguish and hand-wringing grew as the zone of death, destruction, and displacement steadily widened.

The number of cases of violence against women represented only a small portion of incidents: A larger number of women were discouraged to report incidents of violence given the extreme sanctions imposed on the Sudanese government, the general state of fear of retaliation, cultural patterns relating to shameful acts, and very few prosecutorial measures that might redress their grievances. For these reasons a culture of impunity developed. The economic and practical need for women to move out of the relative protection of refugee camps to seek firewood and tend small herds compelled them to be continually vulnerable to abuse and violence. It now appears that in Darfur and elsewhere, sexual violence was incorporated as a part of a psychological warfare program against the insurgents. If these acts were organized and institutionalized, such a program would be in clear violation of some of the legal principles of the Geneva Accords.

ETHICAL AND MORAL ASPECTS

Certain ethical and moral aspects can be added to the mix of complex issues. The ethical obligation to engage in conflict negotiation and resolution and humanitarian concerns (especially for children and women) are paramount, along with documenting cases of a possible criminal nature. Ethics and morality should drive the global community into

Sudanese Village Following a Raid by Rebels, 2004. *The charred remains of Abu Sheik, a village in Darfur, after a raid by rebels. The inhabitants of this village had either been killed or became refugees.* AP IMAGES.

further education and study, as well as nonpartisan advocacy to bring all combatants to the bargaining table to implement force separation, compel disarmament, begin conflict resolution with adjudication, and restore security and justice. Some of these concerns can be addressed with international and local nongovernmental organizations (NGOs). These are far from utopian concerns, as the peace accords accepted for military conflicts in the Southern and Eastern Sudan were "resolved" during the period of conflict in Darfur. Respect for the sovereignty of Sudan should also be a priority, rather than the internationalization of the conflict and escalation to a greater level that puts even more people at risk relative to global security and development concerns about "failed states" in Africa.

DEMOGRAPHY AND SCALE: THE "NUMBERS DEBATES"

Among the many contentious topics raging around the Darfur conflict is just how many people have been killed, injured, and displaced by the conflicting parties, and who is responsible for what. For the Government of Sudan or the Government of National Unity (GNU), there is a political tendency to deflate the numbers; among the rebels, their supporters, and genocide activists there has been a tendency to inflate the numbers. Serious problems afflict the methodology and motivation of both, and the chain of zeroes usually attached to, or subtracted from, the numbers of casualties suggests the high level of approximation. Without doubt, there are certainly tens of thousands of dead and wounded people, and minimally hundreds of thousands of people are displaced from the contested zones in Darfur. Relatively low or high numbers would serve either to minimize or dramatize the claim of genocide. In fact, the legal aspects of the Geneva Accords set no specific requirement for numbers of victims, because what is central to the charge of genocide is the motivation and coordination of the alleged act and not if the "genocidal mission" was achieved.

Nothing in the numbers game suggests that the humanitarian crisis is in any sense diminished. There is little question from any perspective that the situation is grave and deteriorating. So whether the numbers of dead are 200,000 or 300,000 or 400,000 is not really the legal question. Whether the number of displaced persons is one or two million, it is clear that access, aid, and protection by NGOs are needed immediately.

There is an urgent "do something" need to return to negotiation, stop the attacks by all parties on humanitarian agencies, and start to deescalate the conflict, separate the warring parties, and prepare for criminal prosecutions wherever possible. Only then can reconciliation be based in a just resolution that is already within the present, albeit incomplete and unimplemented, Darfur Peace Accords.

BIBLIOGRAPHY

Ahmed, Abdel Ghaffar M., and Leif Manger, eds. 2006. *Understanding the Crisis in Darfur: Listening to Sudanese Voices.* Bergen, Norway: Global Research at the University of Bergen.

Ali, Hayder Ibrahim. 2006. *Darfur Report.* Cairo: Sudanese Studies Center.

Cox, Philip. 2004. "Inside Sudan's Rebel Army." BBC Focus on Africa, April 5. Available from http://news.bbc.co.uk/1/hi/world/africa/3586217.stm.

De Waal, Alex. 2004. "Tragedy in Darfur." *Boston Review* (October/November). Available from http://www.bostonreview.net/BR29.5/dewaal.html.

———. 2005. "Briefing: Darfur, Sudan: Prospects for Peace." *African Affairs* 104: 127–135.

———. 2005. *Famine that Kills: Darfur, Sudan*, rev. ed. Oxford, U.K., and New York: Oxford University Press.

Iyob, Ruth, and Gilbert M. Khadiagala. 2006. *Sudan: The Elusive Quest for Peace.* Boulder, CO: Lynne Rienner.

McGregor, Andrew. 2005. "Terrorism and Violence in the Sudan: The Islamist Manipulation of Darfur, Part Two." *Terrorism Monitor* 3 (13), July 1. Available from The Jamestown Foundation, Global Terrorism Analysis. Available from http://jamestown.org/terrorism/news/article.php?articleid=2369734.

Nkrumah, Gamal. 2003. "Winning the West." *Al-Ahram Weekly* (Cairo), May 1–7. Available from http://weekly.ahram.org.eg/2003/636/re5.htm. Reprinted in *Damanga: Coalition for Freedom and Democracy*, Representatives of the Massaleit Community in Exile. Available from http://www.damanga.org.

Plaut, Martin. 2004. "Who Are Sudan's Darfur Rebels?" BBC Africa broadcast, 30 September. Available from http://news.bbc.co.uk/2/hi/africa/3702242.stm.

Prunier, Gérard. 2007. *Darfur: The Ambiguous Genocide*, rev. and updated ed. Ithaca, NY: Cornell University Press.

Respini-Irwin, Cyrena. 2005. "Geointelligence Informs Darfur Policy." *Geointelligence Magazine*, 1 September.

Segar, Derk. 2005. "Sudan: UN Official Urges Darfur Rebel Leaders to Unite." *Sudaneseonline/IRIN*, 9 November.

Theobald, A. B. 1965. *'Ali Dinar, Last Sultan of Darfur, 1898–1916.* London: Longmans.

United Nations High Commissioner for Refugees. 2006. *The State of the World's Refugees: Human Displacement in the New Millennium.* New York: Oxford University Press.

United Nations Mission in Sudan. 2006. "UNMIS Media Monitoring Report." 29 January, Khartoum. Available from http://www.unmis.org/english/documents/mmr/MMR2006/MMR-jan18.pdf.

United Nations Security Council Resolutions 1706, 1679, 1665, 1663, 1593, 1591, 1590, 1574, 1564, and 1556.

Young, Helen, et al. 2005. *Darfur: Livelihoods under Siege.* Medford, MA: Feinstein International Famine Center, Tufts University.

Richard A. Lobban Jr.

GLOBAL ENVIRONMENT MOVEMENT

Race and class may be viewed as major predictors of participation in activities and actions associated with local undesirable land uses (LULUs). This growing social problem affects quality of life for many diverse groups, but especially the poor and people of color.

The Environmental Justice Movement (EJM) fights against environmental racism and injustices in the allocation and distribution of environmental contaminants in and around communities of color, the political powerless, and the economically less fortunate. Since the mid-1980s, the EJM has become a multicultural grassroots social movement that aims to seek fairness, and meaningful involvement in the imposition of environmental poisons on disenfranchised communities of color. It seeks to promote environmental justice for people who are most at risk of exposure to toxins. The United States Environmental Protection Agency (EPA; 1998) defines environmental justice as the "fair treatment and meaningful involvement for people of all races, ethnicities, cultures, national origins and incomes, regarding the development, implementation, and enforcement of environmental laws, regulations and policies" (Government Code Section 65040.12 and Public Resources Code Section 72000).

Fair treatment means that no specific population group should bear the brunt of a disproportionate share of environmental problems brought about by industrial facilities, governmental structures, and policies. *Meaningful involvement* means that at-risk communities of color should be participatory agents in the decision-making process that affects their local communities and thus puts them at a higher risk for environmental dangers than other, more affluent segments of our population. Thus, the environmental justice movement is the vehicle environmental justice advocates and grassroots groups use in ameliorating many of the environmental disparities among people of color and the poor communities. The goal is to provide a safe environment free of environmental stressors so people can work, live, play, learn, and pray in a nontoxic environment.

HISTORY OF THE MOVEMENT

Several major forces have contributed to the growth of the environmental justice movement since the 1980s. These include grassroots activism, an active research agenda, the environmental justice leadership summit, establishment of the Office of Environmental Equity, and the signing of Executive Order 12898. Data show that one of the earliest grassroots actions occurred in Memphis, Tennessee, in 1968 when Dr. Martin Luther King Jr. was scheduled to lead a group of African American sanitation workers in a garbage strike. Unfortunately, King was assassinated on April 4, 1968, before he could complete the environmental and economic activism process. Another case can be found in California in 1969, where Ralph Abascal of California Rural Legal Assistance filed a lawsuit on behalf of several migrant farm workers. This resulted in the ban of the pesticide DDT. Following this protest, Linda McLeever Bullard in 1979 filed the *Bean v. Southwestern Waste Management, Inc.* lawsuit on behalf of Houston's Northeast Community Action Group, the first civil rights suit challenging the siting of a waste facility.

Also in 1979, Robert D. Bullard completed his *Houston Waste and Black Community Study* for the *Bean v. Southwestern Waste Management, Inc.* lawsuit. He found that waste dumps were not randomly scattered throughout the city but were disproportionately located in African American neighborhoods. This was the first study to examine the causal factors of environmental racism. Bullard also found that housing discrimination, lack of zoning, and decisions by public officials over fifty years produced the environmentally unequal outcomes (Bullard 2000a, 2005). However, it was not until 1982 that environmental justice received national attention in the United States. In 1982 African American residents in Warren County, North Carolina, protested against a PCB (polychlorinated biphenyl) landfill being placed in their community, which resulted in over 500 activists being arrested. This outcry for environmental justice was the most widely publicized case of collective behavior and social-movement activism. It galvanized the environmental justice movement in the United States, prompting the need for national studies to validate the existence of environmental racism. It also sparked the conceptualization of the concept "environmental racism," a term coined by Benjamin Chavis to refer to "racial discrimination in race-based differential enforcement of environmental rules and regulations; the intentional or unintentional targeting of minority communities for the siting of polluting industries such as toxic waste disposal; and the exclusion of people of color from public and private boards, commissions, and regulatory bodies" (Chavis 1992, pp. 4–5).

Two major landmark studies in the 1980s confirmed the validity of racial differences in the distribution of toxic sites among local communities. These included the U.S. General Accounting Office and the United Church of Christ studies. The U.S. General Accounting Office study (1983) chronicled eight southern states. The goal was to determine the impact and correlation of environmental degradation on communities of color. This study revealed that three out of four off-site commercial hazardous waste landfills in the southeastern United States were located within predominately African American communities. The national study in 1987 by the United Church of Christ Commission for Racial Justice found that race was the most significant factor in determining where waste facilities were located. Some of the study's findings showed that three out of five African Americans and Hispanic Americans lived in communities with one or more uncontrolled toxic waste sites, and that 50 percent of Asian-Pacific Islander Americans and Native Americans lived in such communities. Scholars continue to document environmental concerns faced by minorities and the poor with respect to environmental contaminants—showing that health risks from being exposed to such hazards are higher for minorities than for their white counterparts.

Research by Bobby Emmett Jones and Shirley Rainey on perceptions of environmental justice and awareness and health and justice in the Red River community found that blacks were more concerned about environmental issues than whites and that they perceived environmental exposure as placing them at a higher health risk than whites (Rainey 2005). They also thought that environmental racism was the cause of their environmental situation. Bullard asserts that environmental racism combined with public policies and industry practices provides benefits for whites while shifting industry costs to communities of color. It is reinforced by governmental, legal, economic, political, and military institutions.

Another milestone in the growth of the environmental justice movement was the First National People of Color Environmental Leadership Summit in Washington, DC, in 1991, which led to the identification of seventeen environmental justice principles as a guide to address environmental problems. These environmental justice principles available at www.toxicspot.com, serve as a guide for grassroots groups:

1. Environmental Justice affirms the sacredness of Mother Earth, ecological unity and the

interdependence of all species, and the right to be free from ecological destruction.

2. Environmental Justice demands that public policy be based on mutual respect and justice for all people, free from any form of discrimination and bias.
3. Environmental Justice mandates the right to ethical, balanced and responsible uses of land and renewable resources in the interest of a sustainable planet for humans and other living things.
4. Environmental Justice calls for universal protection from nuclear testing, extraction, production and disposal of toxic/hazardous wastes and poisons and nuclear testing that threaten the fundamental right to clean air, land, water, and food.
5. Environmental Justice affirms the fundamental right to political, economic, cultural and environmental self-determination of all peoples.
6. Environmental Justice demands the cessation of production of all toxins, hazardous wastes and radioactive materials and that all past and current producers be held strictly accountable to the people for detoxification and the containment at the point of production.
7. Environmental Justice demands the right to participate as equal partners at every level of decision-making including needs assessment, planning, implementation, enforcement, and evaluation.
8. Environmental Justice affirms the right of all workers to a safe and healthy work environment, without being forced to choose between an unsafe livelihood and unemployment. It also affirms the right of those who work at home to be free from environmental hazards.
9. Environmental Justice protects the right of victims of environmental injustices to receive full compensation and reparations for damages as well as quality health care.
10. Environmental Justice considers government acts of environmental injustice a violation of international law, the Universal Declaration On Human Rights, and the UN Convention on Genocide.
11. Environmental Justice must recognize a special legal and natural relationship of Native Peoples to the U.S. government through treaties, agreements, compacts, and covenants affirming sovereignty and self-determination.
12. Environmental Justice affirms the need for urban and rural ecological policies to clean up and rebuild our cities and rural areas in balance with nature, honoring the cultural integrity of all our communities, and providing fair access for all to the full range of resources.
13. Environmental Justice calls for the strict enforcement of principles of informed consent, and a halt to the testing of experimental reproductive and medical procedures and vaccinations on people of color.
14. Environmental Justice opposes the destructive operations of multi-national corporations.
15. Environmental Justice opposes military occupation, repression and exploitation of lands, peoples and cultures, and other life forms.
16. Environmental Justice calls for the education of present and future generations which emphasizes social and environmental issues, based on our experience and an appreciation of our diverse cultural perspectives.
17. Environmental Justice requires that we, as individuals, make personal and consumer choices to consume as little of Mother Earth's resources and produce as little waste as possible; and make the conscious decisions to challenge and reprioritize our lifestyles to insure the health of the natural world for present and future generations.

The efforts of the summit led to the establishment in 1992 of the U.S. Environmental Protection Agency's Office of Environmental Equity, later renamed the Office of Environmental Justice (OEJ). The purpose of the OEJ is to serve as the focal point for environmental justice concerns within EPA. It provides coordination and oversight regarding these concerns to all parts of the agency. The OEJ engages in public-outreach activities, provides technical and financial assistance to outside groups investigating environmental justice issues, and serves as a central environmental justice information clearinghouse.

Finally, President Bill Clinton's 1994 signing of Executive Order 12898 was another milestone for the environmental justice movement. This Executive Order required all federal agencies to develop environmental justice strategies and to promote nondiscrimination in federal programs substantially affecting human health and the environment and to provide minority and low-income communities access to public participation in matters relating to human health or the environment. These events have been instrumental in the growth of the environmental justice movement. Environmental justice advocates continue to fight against environmental injustices that plague many people of color and poor communities.

DUMPING GROUND FOR EXPLOITATION

Many communities of color and economically distressed communities have become dumping grounds for community exploitation and environmental racism. This type of environmental injustice can be found throughout the world. In the

United States, for example, "Cancer Alley"—an eighty-five mile industrial corridor in Louisiana stretching from Baton Rouge to New Orleans—is home to 138 of the nation's petrochemical production facilities. This industrial corridor has been described as the "Zone of National Sacrifice" (Wright 1998; Johnson 2005). There are several environmental problems in the United States that have received local, national, and international attention. Affected communities include West Dallas, Texas (lead contamination); Northwood Manor, Texas (municipal landfill); Institute, West Virginia (chemical emission); Alsen, Louisiana (hazardous waste); Tuscon, Arizona (industrial toxic waste site); Emelle, Alabama (hazardous waste site); southside Chicago (waste sites); Oak Ridge, Tennessee (toxic chemical plant exposure); Dickson, Tennessee (well water and landfill); and Nashville, Tennessee (landfill). Exposure to environmental hazards has impacted negatively on residents of these communities' health and quality of life.

GLOBAL ENVIRONMENTAL JUSTICE PROBLEMS

Environmental degradation also poses a threat to economically and socially disadvantaged communities globally. For example, the Bhopal disaster in India in 1984 caused a toxic chemical release of heated methyl isocyanate (MIC) gases from Union Carbide, which catastrophically killed over 20,000 and injured between 150,000 and 600,000 people. Other examples include the Niger Delta, Nigeria, where oil resource exploration and production has taken place and has impacted disastrously on the environment and quality of life of the people of this territory (Douglas et al. 2005; Westra 1998); Puerto Rico has become one of the "world's most heavily polluted places" as a consequence of toxic exposure from oil refineries, petrochemical plants, and pharmaceutical companies (Weintraub 2006); in the Pacific, islands have been used for nuclear and atomic weapons testing. Residents' exposure to radiation from this testing has caused major health problems.

In North America, Native American groups have also been very active in their efforts to protect and reclaim land, resources, culture, religion, and all else that belongs to them from social and environmental exploitation. Environmental activist Winona LaDuke points out that even though Native Americans and other indigenous peoples worldwide have been exploited for economic gain and bear the health risks from industry and public policies, including the danger posed by the high number of radioactive sites on Native American land, they are virulent in their actions to bring about environmental justice (LaDuke 1999, 2005). Native Americans are addressing environmental justice initiatives by producing energy for their communities using green power. The White Earth Reservation is reintroducing sturgeon into the headwaters of the Mississippi and Red Rivers, and the Nez-Perce are returning to the breeding of quality horses (LaDuke 2005).

Finally, a local environmental justice grassroots movement (made up of women) in Plachimada, the southern state of Kerala, India, formed to fight against environmental racism from the Coca-Cola Company. These local residents, along with national and international leaders such as Vandana Shiva, protested the unfair treatment of their water supply and won a victory over the environmental exploitation by Coca-Cola. The Coca-Cola plant in Plachimada is accused of creating severe water shortages and pollution by stealing over 1.5 million liters of water per day to use in production. Pollution is said to come from the company depositing waste material outside the company premises on paddy fields, canals, and wells, causing serious health hazards and deaths. Shiva continues to fight against pollution, diversion through dams, and privatization that is killing rivers and water bodies and affecting the health and quality of life of India's population. These are only a few examples of how economic exploitation, racial oppression, devaluation of human life and the natural environment, and corporate greed are compromising the quality of life of communities and cultures around the globe.

THE ENVIRONMENTAL JUSTICE FUTURE

From its strong civil rights beginnings, the EJM in the United States has grown from a small number of grassroots groups to over 500, not counting grassroots groups that are developing on a global scale to fight environmental racism. This movement has been led mainly by local working-class women of color with the aid of scholars, social activists, and policy makers, who have argued in countless studies, reports, congressional testimonies, theoretical and popular books and journals—in print and broadcast media—that environmental racism is a real problem that must be addressed.

Environmental justice groups started out framing environmental racism issues around civil rights issues but have grown to include land rights and sovereignty, social justice, and sustainable development (Agyeman et al. 2003; Bullard 2005). These groups have expanded their grievances from toxic waste to incinerators, smelters, sewage treatment plants, chemical industries, air pollution, waste disposal, facility siting, wildlife, pesticides, lead, asbestos, landfills, water contamination, urban sprawl, transportation, and sustainability in general. The EJMs goal is for better living in local communities, with safe jobs, urban redevelopment, and clean air and water. The grassroots activism of environmental justice groups is an ongoing process fueled by unresolved environment justice issues.

SEE ALSO *Antiracist Social Movements.*

BIBLIOGRAPHY

Agyeman, J., R. D. Bullard, and B. Evans. 2003. *Just Sustainabilities: Development in an Unequal World.* London: Earthscan/MIT Press.

Bullard, Robert D. 2000a. *Dumping in Dixie: Race, Class, and Environmental Quality.* Boulder, CO: Westview Press.

———. 2000b. "Principles of Environmental Justice." Adopted October 27, 1991, in Washington, D.C. In *People of Color Environmental Groups Directory,* ed. Robert D. Bullard. Atlanta, GA: Clark Atlanta University Environmental Justice Resource Center.

———., ed. 2005. *The Quest for Environmental Justice: Human Rights and the Politics of Pollution.* San Francisco: Sierra Club Books.

Chavis, Benjamin. 1992. "Environmental Racism Defined." In *Race and the Incidence of Environmental Hazards: A Time for Discourse,* ed. Bunyon Bryant and Paul Mohai, 4–5, 163–178. Boulder, CO: Westview Press.

Douglas, Oronto, Von Kemedi, Ike Okonta, and Michael Watts. 2005. "Alienation and Militancy in the Niger Delta: Petroleum, Politics, and Democracy in Nigeria." In *Quest for Environmental Justice: Human Rights and the Politics of Pollution,* edited by Robert D. Bullard. San Francisco, CA: Sierra Club Books

"Environmental Justice: Principles." Available at http://www.toxicspot.com/env_justice/env_principles.html.

Foster, Sheila. 1993. "Race(ial) Matters: The Quest for Environmental Justice." *Ecology Law Quarterly* 20 (4): 721–753.

Johnson, Glenn S. 2005. "Grassroots Activism in Louisiana." *Humanity and Society* 29 (3–4): 285–304.

LaDuke, Winona. 1999. *All Our Relations: Native Struggles for Land and Life.* Cambridge, MA: South End Press.

———. 2005. *Recovering the Sacred: The Power of Naming and Claiming.* Cambridge, MA: South End Press.

Rainey, Shirley. 2005. "Residents Speak Out: Sharing Concerns About Environmental Problems, Public Health, and Justice in Clarksville, Tennessee." *Humanity and Society* 29 (3–4): 270–284.

U.S. Environmental Protection Agency. 1998. *Guidance for Incorporating Environmental Justice in EPA's NEPA Compliance Analysis.* Washington, DC: Author.

U.S. General Accounting Office. 1983. *Siting of Hazardous Waste, Landfills, and Their Correlation with Racial and Economic Status of Surrounding Communities.* Washington, DC: U.S. Government Printing Office.

Weintraub, Irwin. 1994. "Fighting Environmental Racism: A Selected Annotated Bibliography." *Electronic Green Journal* Issue 1, June. Available from http://egj.lib.uidaho.edu.

Westra, Laura. 1998. "Development and Environmental Racism: The Case of Ken Saro-wiwa and the Ogoni." *Race, Gender, and Class* 6 (1): 152–162.

Wright, Beverly. 1998. "Endangered Communities: The Struggle for Environmental Justice in the Louisiana Chemical Corridor." *Journal of Public Management and Social Policy* 4 (2): 181–191.

Shirley Ann Rainey

GREAT CHAIN OF BEING

From the time of the ancient Greeks, it has been commonplace to think and write about animals as if they were part of a linear hierarchy. While this view of the natural world may be related to the basic structure of writing in general, in that it is an essentially linear mode of communication, it backgrounds much of pre-Enlightenment thought, and it became a formal feature of early modern scientific thought on natural history. The medieval cultural conception of such a natural hierarchy is known as the "Great Chain of Being."

The French anthropologists Émile Durkheim (1858–1917) and Marcel Mauss (1872–1950) famously observed that the way people organize nature replicates, in some fashion, their own social relations; that is, the way in which they organize themselves. The Great Chain of Being is an excellent example of this. In a social environment structured as a rigid linear hierarchy—from the king, princes, and various ranks of nobles down through vassals, peasants, and perhaps even slaves, all occupying particular slots in vertical relation to one another—it is certainly reasonable to imagine the animal kingdom as similarly organized.

The Great Chain of Being, then, represented an imposition of medieval European political relations upon the natural world. To the extent that the idea was present in earlier times, it was part of a plurality of speculations on the relations of animals. Aristotle said that man is the most perfect animal, and he suggested ranking animals in terms of their mode of reproduction and body temperature. He did not take this idea very far, however. Pliny the Elder did not even incorporate it into the framework of his first-century *Natural History*. In medieval Christian Europe, however, it developed into the dominant, if not exclusive, way of thinking about nature. In Latin, the Great Chain of Being was called the *scala naturae*; in French, *echelle des êtres*.

COMPONENTS OF THE GREAT CHAIN OF BEING

The Great Chain of Being was conceptualized differently by scholars at different times. The historian Arthur O. Lovejoy (1936) identified three basic intellectual components of the Great Chain of Being, which he called the principles of Plenitude, Continuity, and Gradation.

The Principle of Plenitude is derived from the Christian view of the earth as a vessel for the products of God's creation, and as evidence of his bounty. In this view, God is demonstrating his wisdom and goodness through the diversity of his species. Since omnipotence and humility would seem to be incompatible, God is considered to be showing his creative power by bringing into existence not just a finite sample of life forms, but all possible species. Consequently, there was no line recognized between real animal species and imaginary ones; everything from crows and pigs to mermaids and centaurs must exist somewhere.

The Principle of Continuity held that there were no gaps separating different kinds of living beings. The transcendent line on which various species fell was itself unbroken, and it was an additional manifestation of God's wisdom and power that he created species that blended into one another. Thus, the apes (actually, tailless macaques that are technically monkeys) connected monkeys to people, and the discovery of chimpanzees at the end of the eighteenth century filled in another segment between the "apes" and people (Gould 1983).

Finally, the Principle of Gradation incorporated the assumption about the geometry of the natural order as essentially a line leading from lowest (or simplest, or least like us) up to the highest form of life, the most complex and most intelligent—namely humans. This is the sense in which the linear rankings replicated the social order on earth. In some versions of the Great Chain, the human species was not at the top, but rather in the middle, below a celestial hierarchy of angels, and archangels, leading up to God.

The eighteenth century brought a final component to the Great Chain of Being, the idea of Progress (Bury 1932). In a social universe that saw massive growth in the intellectual arena through developments in science, and unprecedented economic growth through the application of technology, it seemed reasonable to look to the future with anticipation. As the history of life, via the fossil record, began concurrently to be understood, it was an easy step to see progress in the succession of living things through time, or a "temporalizing" of the Great Chain.

EVOLUTIONARY IMPLICATIONS OF THE GREAT CHAIN OF BEING

Eighteenth-century scholars of natural history were increasingly pulled in two directions as they tried to reconcile their inferences about nature to their interpretations of scripture. The leading social issue of the day was slavery, which was increasingly being rationalized by recourse to the supposed inferiority and lesser humanity of the non-European races (Stanton 1960). Abolitionists commonly invoked the Bible in support of the unity of the species, the product of a single creative act by God on the sixth day. The monogenists (believers in a single origin of people) were necessarily struck by the diversity of human form that had been produced from the loins of Adam and Eve. If Adam and Eve looked like Europeans, then obviously the facial features of Africans must have arisen subsequently; or vice-versa. Thus, from the very fact of human variation, coupled with a single origin for the human species as recorded in Genesis, the earliest theories of microevolution were deduced.

However, science seemed to link the other races to apes through measurements of the skull and face, at least according to scholars concerned with justifying the practice of slavery by dehumanizing Africans. Rejecting Biblical literalism, the polygenists (believers in multiple origins of people) separated the human races, but in so doing they drew the entire species closer to the apes and, by implication, to the rest of life on earth in their hierarchical framework. Thus, according to Jordan, "To call the Negro a man and the ape a beast was in effect to shatter the Great Chain" (1968, p. 230). To be sure, the relationships among the Great Chain, slavery, and evolution were somewhat nuanced and idiosyncratic (Haller 1970), but there were nevertheless broad correspondences and rationalizations afforded by relating science and politics to one another.

Two bitter controversies of early modern biology were based on interpretations of the Great Chain of Being and its implications. The first, in the middle of the eighteenth century, was over classification; the second, at the turn of the nineteenth century, was over extinction.

The Swedish botanist-physician Carl (Carolus) Linnaeus revolutionized biology in the eighteenth century with his development of formal principles of classification. In his view, rather than forming a single series, life was hierarchically organized into nested categories of equal rank: On earth there were kingdoms of animals, plants, and minerals; within animals there were classes of fish, reptiles, worms, insects, mollusks, and mammals; within mammals there were orders; within orders there were genera; and within genera there were species. Every species ultimately had its place within a genus, order, class, and kingdom.

This system lent itself to comparison and diagnosis, but not easily to a classically linear conception of nature (see Figure 1). While it took hold quickly and firmly in the academic community, it met opposition among other scholars, chief among them the French naturalist Count de Buffon. Buffon opposed the Linnaean system on three grounds. First, it was fairly obvious that nature was organized into higher and lower forms of life, so the linearity of nature could not be discounted. Second, it seemed to imply common descent, for what else could it mean to say that a donkey and a horse should be grouped together? For that matter, "Once it is admitted that there are families of plants and animals, that the donkey is of the horse family, and that it differs only because it has degenerated, then one could equally say that man and ape have had a common origin like the horse and donkey—that each family among the animals and vegetables have had but a single stem, and that all animals have

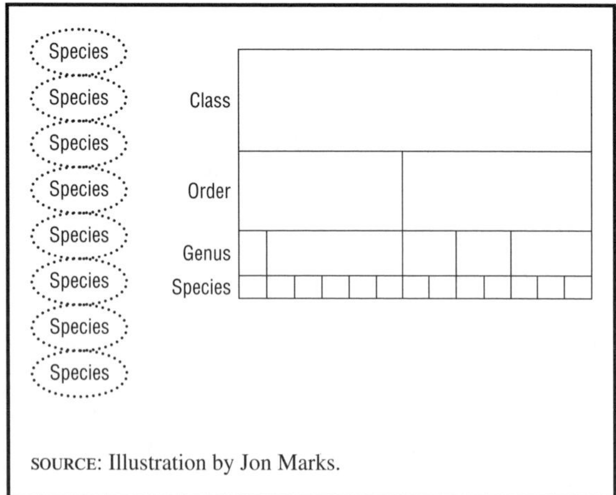

Figure 1. *Left, the Great Chain of Being, a one-dimensional hierarchy in which animals are ranked in relation to humans, placed at the top. Right, the Linnaean system, in which animals are placed in relation to each other, in nested categories of equal rank.*

emerged from but a single animal which, through the succession of time, has produced by improvement and degeneration all the races of animals" (Buffon, *Histoire Naturelle* IV, "The Ass" 1753) which of course could not possibly be true. Lastly, if the Linnaean hierarchy was not a reflection of common descent, then what produced it? Linnaeus was not saying, and a serious (i.e., post-Newtonian) scholar could not merely describe a pattern in nature, so Buffon felt he was obliged to explain it as well.

Linnaeus and Buffon were both monogenists and creationists, although Buffon developed a theory of microevolution to account for the obvious biological diversity to be found within any species. Late in life, Linnaeus backpedaled from his belief that new species could never arise. But Linnaeus's nonlinear approach to nature also involved classifying humans into four color-coded geographical subspecies. Tom Gundling (2005) notes that there is indeed linearity in Linnaeus' treatment of the animal kingdom, which begins with humans and works its way downward; but it may also be noted that he presented his subspecies in an order (American, European, Asian, African) that did not seem intended to express any superiority of Native Americans. Buffon, on the other hand, wrote about human "races" in a very casual and informal sense, and he was struck by their essential identity: "Such differences are not primordial—the dissimilarities are merely external, the alterations of nature but superficial. It is certain that all represent the same human, whether varnished black in the tropics, or tanned and shrunken in the glacial cold of the polar circle" (Buffon, *Histoire Naturelle* XIV "On The Degeneration Of Animals" 1766).

The paradox becomes clearer when Buffon's use of the Great Chain of Being is seen as restricted to macroevolutionary patterns; within a species, such as humans, he saw only undirected variation, or "degeneration." Further, Linnaeus's rejection of the Great Chain as an organizing principle incorporated elements of superiority and inferiority in a human classification, as he listed (in the tenth edition of *System of Nature* [1758]) the attributes of white *Homo sapiens Europaeus* as "vigorous, muscular ... sensitive, very smart, creative, ... governed by law" but those of black *Homo sapiens Afer* as "sluggish, lazy ... sly, slow, careless ... governed by whim." Buffon's descriptions could incorporate unflattering terms, but not in such broad strokes and with such zoological formality that they might imply a transcendent ranking of human kinds (Sloan 1973; Eddy 1984).

EXTINCTION AND THE RISE OF BIOLOGICAL RELATIVISM

The other great controversy faced by the Great Chain of Being was the problem of extinction. The late seventeenth-century English naturalist John Ray had made it clear that his basic view of nature would be undermined if it could be shown that any species had gone extinct. Such a fact would represent a break in the cosmic Chain; it would either show a basic flaw in the design of God's creation or the fragility of God's handiwork in the face of human agency. It would represent, wrote Ray, "a dismemb'ring of the universe," which would presumably be a bad thing.

However, by the middle of the eighteenth century, it was clear that extinction was a fact of life that would have to be accommodated by science. Not only was the large, flightless dodo gone for good from the island of Mauritius, but since that was the only place it had ever been found, it was unlikely to turn up again anywhere else. Moreover, the copious fossil remains of prehistoric life forms, familiar yet distinct from any known species, made it increasingly necessary to incorporate the apparent fact of extinction into any scientific theory of the history of life (Rudwick 1985).

The two principal attempts to do so in the earliest part of the nineteenth century were those of Jean-Baptiste Lamarck and Georges Cuvier. Lamarck developed a theory in which the imminent threat of extinction produced a response on the part of the organism that involved incorporating stable improvements into its organic features; in essence, it climbed a notch up the Great Chain of Being to avoid extermination. Within this framework, he explicitly envisioned the possible transformation of an ape into a human. Cuvier, on the other hand, began with the premise that the Great Chain was false, for (following the Linnaean approach) he saw four noncomparable, and therefore nonrankable, kinds of creatures: vertebrates, mollusks, insects, and radiates. Cuvier's theory incorporated extinction as a real phenomenon—a periodic purging of existing animals, with their replacement by newer forms of life. In this conception, the transformation of species was neither necessary nor likely.

The shift in the eighteenth century from the linear ranking of life forms (in terms of their approximation to the human) to the establishment of their places in a natural order derived from patterns of similarity to one another must be seen as part of a broader set of relativizing discourses. Civilization could be seen as a glorious culmination of history (as per Thomas Hobbes), or as decadent and unnatural (as per Jean-Jacques Rousseau); perhaps, then, civilization merely comprised one set of ways of living, with its own attendant merits and deficiencies. Concurrently, age-old social and political hierarchies were crumbling, as the revolutionary idea of a nation composed of citizens with equal rights began to be implemented in America in 1776 and in France in 1789. Ironically, the institution of slavery would stand in the way of the full implementation of those ideas in America for many decades.

It was clear, however, that the future of biology lay in establishing the relationships of plants and animals to each other, not to a transcendent and arbitrary standard; just as modern political society would be founded on the equal relationships of citizens to each other, not to the ancient standard of hereditary aristocracy.

RACIAL SCIENCE AND THE GREAT CHAIN

The early nineteenth century was a time of considerable intellectual ferment in natural history, particularly in relation to the position of people in the natural order, and in their relation to one another. Cranial studies were undertaken and quickly invoked to differentiate and rank the peoples of the world. These ranged from Morton's studies of cranial volume through Retzius' cranial or cephalic index, a measurement of skull shape. The most powerful measure, however, turned out to be the facial angle, derived by a Dutch anatomist named Pieter (Petrus) Camper, who tried to devise a method that would permit the accurate artistic rendering of the heads of different people for aesthetic purposes. However, Camper's work was seized upon by polygenists to emphasize the differences between Europeans and Africans, for it supposedly showed the intermediacy of Africans in facial form between Europeans and apes.

Indeed, the power of the Great Chain of Being to dehumanize non-Europeans by linking them to lower forms of life proceeded largely unaffected by the emergence of Darwinism. Some pre-Darwinians, such as the French naturalist Julien-Joseph Virey, placed Europeans, Africans, and apes in a series and casually connected the dots. The famous pre-Darwinian evolutionary scheme in *Vestiges of the Natural History of Creation* (1844) ran from amoebas, through other species and other races, to Europeans:

> We have already seen that various leading animal forms represent stages in the embryotic [sic] progress of the highest—the human being. Our brain goes through the various stages of a fish's, a reptile's, and a mammifer's brain, and finally becomes human. There is more than this for, after completing the animal transformations, it passes through the characters in which it appears, in the Negro, Malay, American, and Mongolian nations, and finally is Caucasian.
>
> The leading characters, in short, of the various races of mankind, are simply representations of particular stages in the development of the highest or Caucasian type. The Negro exhibits permanently the imperfect brain, projecting lower jaw, and slender bent limbs, of the Caucasian child, some considerable time before the period of its birth. The aboriginal American represents the same child nearer birth. The Mongolian is an arrested infant newly born. (Chambers 1844, pp. 306, 307)

The Darwinian revolution had little effect upon the racial conception of the Great Chain. Scarcely two decades after the initial publication of the *Vestiges*, Thomas Huxley (who had recently reviewed and excoriated a later edition of the *Vestiges*) would be faced with arguing for Darwinism in the absence of a human fossil record. Fatefully, the first-generation Darwinians would argue that the absence of such evidence for evolution was unnecessary, since (by drawing upon preexisting imagery) Europeans could be linked to the apes via the nonwhite races.

Thus, Thomas Huxley—an abolitionist, monogenist, and evolutionist—explained the position of black people in the natural order in an 1865 essay:

> It may be quite true that some negroes are better than some white men; but no rational man, cognisant of the facts, believes that the average negro is the equal, still less the superior, of the average white man. And, if this be true, it is simply incredible that, when all his disabilities are removed, and our prognathous relative has a fair field and no favour, as well as no oppressor, he will be able to compete successfully with his bigger-brained and smaller-jawed rival, in a contest which is to be carried on by thoughts and not by bites. The highest places in the hierarchy of civilisation will assuredly not be within the reach of our dusky cousins, though it is by no means necessary that they should be restricted to the lowest.

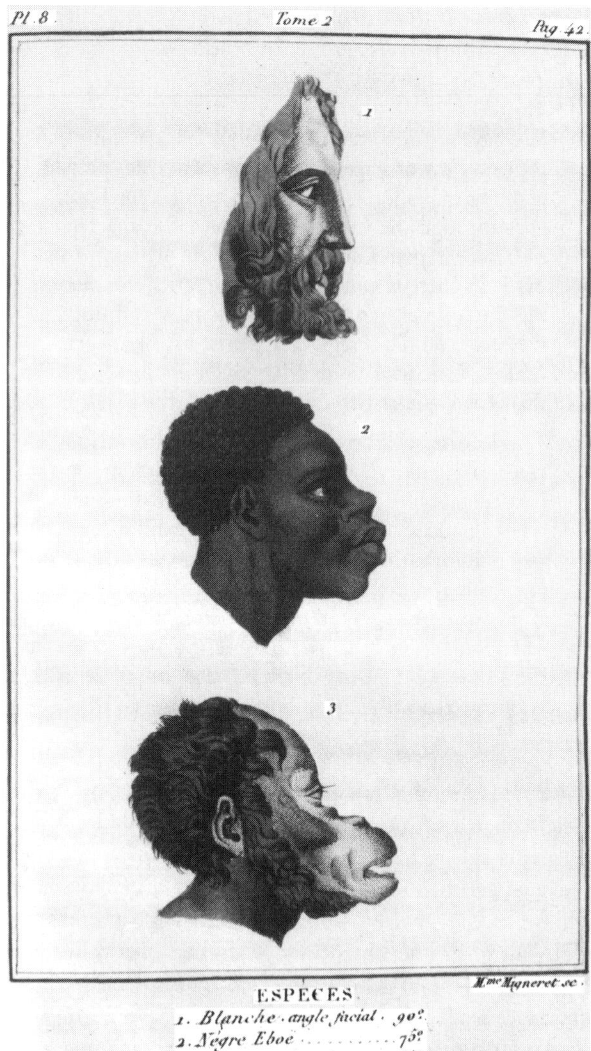

***Histoire naturelle de genre humain* by Julien-Joseph Virey (1824).** *The Great Chain of Being doctrine dehumanized non-Europeans by linking them to lower forms of life. French naturalist Julien-Joseph Virey placed people of African descent between apes and whites in the evolutionary latter, as seen by this illustration.* REPRINTED FROM JEAN-JULIS VIREY, HISTOIRE NATURELLE DE GENRE HUMAIN. PARIS: CHROCARD, 1824.

Darwinism's German apostle, Ernst Haeckel, would go further, constructing a theory of evolution that stretched from the amoeba to the German nation, driven by his "biogenetic law" (that ontogeny recapitulates phylogeny, or that individuals personally pass through developmental stages representing their ancestry). In such a grand view, not only would other races be primitive and inferior, but so would other social institutions and political systems. These primitivizing and dehumanizing aspects of the Great Chain of Being would be invoked to legitimize (by recourse to nature) the most notorious practices of modern technological states in the service of imperial aspirations in the nineteenth and twentieth centuries (Dubow 1995; McMaster 2001).

A considerable effort in evolutionary biology and anthropology since World War II has been devoted to divesting Darwinism of the metaphor of linearity. Some notable examples include the interpretation of human ancestry (Tattersall 1998); primate psychology (Povinelli 2000); life on earth (Simpson 1949; Foley 1987; Ayala 1988) and adaptation (Gould and Lewontin 1979). Likewise, to purge Darwinism of the ideology of racism required considerable effort after World War II (Washburn 1951; Haraway 1988; Barkan 1992), and to some extent continues to do so (Graves 2001; Marks 2002; Brace 2005). Perhaps the last major holdout of the Great Chain in science lies in the idea that intelligence is a singular and innate property, ascertainable through standardized tests, and permitting the establishment of everyone's relative positions by their scores, or IQs.

SEE ALSO *Colonialism, Internal; Genocide; Racial Hierarchy.*

BIBLIOGRAPHY

Ayala, F. J . 1988. "Can 'Progress' Be Defined As a Biological Concept?" In *Evolutionary Progress?*, edited by M. Nitecki. Chicago: University of Chicago Press, pp. 75–96.

Barkan, Elazar A. 1992. *The Retreat of Scientific Racism: Changing Concepts of Race in Britain and the United States between the World Wars.* New York: Cambridge University Press.

Brace, C. Loring. 2005. *"Race" Is a Four-Letter Word: The Genesis of the Concept.* New York: Oxford University Press.

Bury, John B. 1932. *The Idea of Progress: An Inquiry into Its Origin and Growth.* New York: Macmillan.

Chambers, Robert. 1844. *Vestiges of the Natural History of Creation.* London: John Churchill.

Corbey, Raymond. 2005. *The Metaphysics of Apes: Negotiating the Animal-Human Boundary.* New York: Cambridge University Press.

Dubow, Saul. 1995. *Scientific Racism in Modern South Africa.* New York: Cambridge University Press.

Durkheim Émile, and Mauss Marcel. 1903. "De quelques formes primitives de classification." *L'Année Sociologique* 6: 1–72.

Eddy, John H., Jr. 1984. "Buffon, Organic Alterations, and Man." *Studies in the History of Biology* 7: 1–46.

Foley, Robert. 1987. *Another Unique Species: Patterns in Human Evolutionary Ecology.* New York: Wiley.

Gould, Stephen Jay. 1978. "Morton's Ranking of Races by Cranial Capacity." *Science* 200: 503–509.

———. 1983. "Chimp on a Chain." *Natural History* 92 (12): 18–27.

———. 1987. "Petrus Camper's Angle." *Natural History* 96 (7): 12–18.

———, and Richard Lewontin. 1979. "The Spandrels of San Marco and the Panglossian Paradigm: A Critique of the Adaptationist Programme." *Proceedings of the Royal Soceity of London, Series B* 205: 581–598.

Gundling, Tom. 2005. *First in Line: Tracing Our Ape Ancestry.* New Haven, CT: Yale University Press.

Haller, John S., Jr. 1970. "The Species Problem: Nineteenth-Century Concepts of Racial Inferiority in the Origin of Man Controversy. *American Anthropologist* 72: 1319–1329.

Haraway, Donna. 1988. "Remodelling the Human Way of Life: Sherwood Washburn and the New Physical Anthropology, 1950–1980." In *Bones, Bodies, Behavior: Essays on Biological Anthropology. History of Anthropology,* Vol. 5, edited by George W. Stocking. Madison, WI: University of Wisconsin Press.

Huxley, Thomas H. 1865 [1901]. "Emancipation–Black and White." In: *Man's Place in Nature, and Other Anthropological Essays.* New York, Macmillan.

Jahoda, Gustav. 1999. *Images of Savages: Ancient Roots of Modern Prejudice in Western Culture.* New York, Routledge.

Jordan, Winthrop D. 1968. *White Over Black: American Attitudes toward the Negro 1550–1812.* Chapel Hill: University of North Carolina Press.

Lovejoy, Arthur O. 1936. *The Great Chain of Being.* Cambridge, MA: Harvard University Press.

Marks, Jonathan. 2002. *What It Means to Be 98% Chimpanzee: Apes, People, and Their Genes.* Berkeley: University of California Press.

McMaster, Neil. 2001. *Racism in Europe: 1870–2000.* New York: Palgrave.

Povinelli, Daniel. 2000. *Folk Physics for Apes: The Chimpanzee's Theory of How the World Works.* New York: Oxford University Press.

Rudwick, Martin J. S. 1985 (1972). *The Meaning of Fossils: Episodes in the History of Palaeontology.* Chicago: University of Chicago Press.

Ruse, Michael. 1996. *Monad to Man: The Concept of Progress in Evolutionary Biology.* Cambridge, MA: Harvard University Press.

Sloan, Philip R. 1973. "The Idea of Racial Degeneracy in Buffon's Histoire Naturelle." In *Racism in the Eighteenth Century,* Vol. 3, edited by Harold E. Pagliaro, 293–321. Cleveland, OH: Case Western Reserve University Press.

Stanton, William R. 1960. *The Leopard's Spots: Scientific Attitudes toward Race in America, 1815–59.* Chicago: University of Chicago Press.

Tattersall, Ian. 1998. *Becoming Human: Evolution and Human Uniqueness.* New York: Harcourt Brace.

Virey, J.-J. 1824. *Histoire naturelle du genre humain.* Paris: Crochard.

Washburn, Sherwood L. 1951. "The New Physical Anthropology." *Transactions of the New York Academy of Sciences, Series II* 13: 298–304.

Jonathan Marks

GYPSIES

SEE *Roma.*

H

HAITIAN RACIAL FORMATIONS

When it declared its independence from France in 1804, Haiti defined itself as a "black" nation-state. Born out of the only successful slave revolution in world history, Haiti remained diplomatically and culturally isolated throughout the nineteenth century in a Caribbean zone where slavery, colonialism, and racism were the norm. Moreover, the country's colonial experience had generated persistent divisions between Haitians of full African descent and those of mixed European and African ancestry. The terms "black" and "mulatto" described these two groups, but the tension between them was more a matter of social and political conflict than racial prejudice, as it might be defined in the United States. Nevertheless, the "color question" was a major source of internal political conflict into the twentieth century.

MAIN GROUPS AND LABELS

Historically, Haitians have described mulattos and blacks as the two major social or ethnic groups in their country. Haiti is also home to a small number of families of Middle Eastern descent. In the early 1970s, however, the Canadian sociologist Micheline Labelle found that Haitians used as many as 120 different racial terms, and that more than 95 percent of these labels were based on a set of between eight to ten terms. Labelle's Haitian informants agreed that each of these racial terms represented a specific mix of physical characteristics, especially skin color, hair texture, hair color, and facial features. But when she asked individual Haitians to classify drawings of faces, they applied racial labels in ways that did not match their abstract definitions. Labelle's other major finding was that informants used these racial labels in class-specific ways.

Labelle's study confirmed what Haitian intellectuals have long maintained: The terms *mulatto* and *black* are more determined by social class than by physical characteristics. Though the wealthiest members of Haitian society also include people who describe themselves as black, all mulattos are, by definition, members of the elite. In other words, light-skinned Haitians who are poor, without much formal schooling, are unlikely to be described as mulattos, regardless of their physical appearance. Since colonial times, mulattos have been seen as more European in culture, education, and lifestyle. After independence, members of important mixed-race families used these characteristics to justify their political dominance. Haiti's black politicians and intellectuals have historically claimed to represent the majority population, and criticized lighter-skinned Haitians as racist. Yet these tensions were usually confined to the cities. In the 1970s Labelle met many rural Haitians who said they had never seen a mulatto and did not know what one was. Other rural respondents identified mulattos as *blancs,* a term that means both "white" and "foreigner."

Haiti's racial terminology also has a geographic component. The country's southern peninsula has been historically identified with rich mulattos, while after independence the northern region was controlled by black landowning families. Urban areas, especially Port-au-Prince, were historically the seat of mulatto power, because these families dominated foreign trade and the government offices. The countryside, where high mountains kept peasants isolated, was stereotypically black.

Race labels also have a religious and linguistic significance. Although nearly all Haitians participate in the Vodou religion ("voodoo" is seen as a disparaging term), it is strongly associated with black Haitians. Vodou was only recognized as an official religion in Haiti in 2002.

Though 80 percent of Haitians identify themselves as Catholics, the Haitian Catholic Church, administered by white foreign bishops from 1860 to the 1960s, was long identified with the mulatto class. In the 1980s and 1990s, however, politically active priests helped mobilize poor black parishioners. In addition, the ability to speak French is an important marker of mulatto social status. Though French has been the official language of Haiti since independence, only about 10 percent of Haitians can speak it fluently. All Haitians speak Creole, but the government only recognized this as an official language in 1983.

RACISM AND ANTIRACISM IN HAITIAN HISTORY

Haiti's colonial history began when the island was colonized by the Spanish who named it Santo Domingo, but the country's Francophone identity began in the middle of the 1600s, when French-speaking buccaneers settled on the island's western coast. France claimed one-third of Hispaniola, naming its colony Saint-Domingue. Gradually the buccaneers became planters, importing hundreds of thousands of enslaved Africans. By the 1780s, slaves outnumbered French colonists ten to one in Saint-Domingue. The Spanish colony of Santo Domingo, on the eastern side of the island, remained relatively undeveloped, with few whites or enslaved Africans.

By the early 1700s, many of Saint-Domingue's male planters had had children with their slaves. Evidence shows that colonists treated free mixed-race people as white well past the middle of the century. In the 1760s, however, colonial authorities began to worry about colonists' loyalty. French attempts to "civilize" Saint-Domingue included removing free mixed-race people from "respectable" society. The island had as many free people of color as it had whites by 1780, and this included hundreds of wealthy French-educated mixed-race men and women.

In 1789, two such men were in Paris when the French Revolution broke out. One of them, the indigo planter Julien Raimond (1744–1802), worked with French abolitionists to make racism, not slavery, the revolution's main colonial controversy. The other, the merchant and landowner Vincent Ogé (ca. 1768–1791), returned to Saint-Domingue in 1790 and demanded voting rights. Colonists were determined to limit voting to "pure" whites, and they executed Ogé and twenty-three of his supporters. Yet free coloreds continued to demand civil rights, unintentionally opening the way for a slave insurrection.

In August of 1791, hundreds of slaves carried out a massive rebellion in the North Province. As a class, free coloreds sided against the slaves, but many whites resisted granting civil rights to free coloreds until a new revolutionary law was passed in April 1792. Conservative colonists plotted against revolutionary officials, and in June 1793 they rose against them. In exchange for help in fighting these counterrevolutionaries, the revolutionaries offered freedom to slave rebels. On October 31, 1793, they emancipated all the slaves.

Rebels increasingly came to join the revolutionary army, the most notable being Toussaint-Louverture (1743–1803), who had joined the rebels by July 1794. Yet the revolution's new black officers clashed with lighter-skinned leaders, and in 1798 Toussaint accused the mulatto general André Rigaud (1761–1806) of racism and separatism. His army finally defeated Rigaud's forces in 1800.

In 1802, French emperor Napoleon Bonaparte (1769–1821) sent an expedition to Saint-Domingue. Its commander, Charles Leclerc (1772–1802), had orders to remove all nonwhites from power, and when he died from yellow fever, his successor, Donatien Rochambeau (1755–1813), used genocidal techniques against a popular rebellion. His brutality led black and mulatto officers to unite against him. Leclerc had exiled Toussaint, but another black general, Jean-Jacques Dessalines (1758–1806), forced Rochambeau to surrender. On January 1, 1804, Dessalines declared the existence of an independent Haiti, and in 1805 a new constitution proclaimed that all Haitians were black, though more than half the generals who signed it were mulattos.

The following year a coalition of black and mulatto officers assassinated Dessalines and founded two independent states. In the North, Henri Christophe (1767–1820) established a self-consciously "black" kingdom, while in the West and South, Alexandre Pétion (1770–1818) headed a "mulatto" republic. In 1820, Pétion's lieutenant, Jean-Pierre Boyer (1776–1850), united the two territories, but a revolt overthrew Boyer in 1843. Although peasants, led by a charismatic small farmer named Jean-Jacques Acaau (d. 1846) could not force Boyer's successors to respond to their demands, from this point the mulatto class began to rule through a series of black presidents. But not all black leaders, especially military officers, would accept this "government by understudy." By the 1860s, Haitian politics had become a rivalry between the mulatto Liberal Party and the black National Party. From 1879 on, the National Party dominated the presidency, though regional revolts still deposed individual leaders.

In 1915 the United States Marines invaded Haiti after several violent political riots in Port-au-Prince, and the United States ruled the country until 1934. During the long occupation, anger at U.S. racism fostered a new interest in Haiti's African roots among urban intellectuals and the rising black middle class. But mulatto politicians and businessmen were the real beneficiaries of the U.S. occupation, which brought foreign investment and the modernization of Haiti's ports, army, and system of tax collection.

In 1957 a popular reaction against the stronger army and more efficient state created by the United States brought a black country doctor, François "Papa Doc" Duvalier (1907–1971), into the presidency. Under his leadership, racial polarization reached new heights after Duvalier struck out against the mulatto elite. Deeply familiar with Haitian rural culture, Duvalier presented himself as the culmination of a long line of strong black Haitian leaders. He created his own militia, the Tonton Macoutes, to terrorize opponents and overbalance the power of the U.S.-trained army. Thousands of wealthy light-skinned Haitians went into exile. While his racial rhetoric appealed to Haiti's black majority, Duvalier directed foreign aid and government revenues into his own accounts. When Duvalier died in 1971, his son, Jean-Claude (b. 1951), took over the presidency. Far less capable than his father, "Baby Doc" presided over a series of economic crises, including foreign hysteria over AIDS in Haiti, which destroyed the fledgling tourist industry. He was driven into exile in 1986.

The Duvaliers' corruption made it impossible for any Haitian politician to claim to represent the black majority. Instead, a charismatic priest named Jean-Bertrand Aristide (b. 1953) created a political movement called Lavalas, or The Flood, by openly discussing the tensions between rich and poor. Aristide won Haiti's first truly democratic election in 1990, and when the army drove him into exile eight months later, no one used racial labels to describe the event. But Lavalas splintered after U.S. troops returned Aristide to power in 1994. He was re-elected in 2001, but many supporters had lost confidence in him. Refusing to denounce the violence of gangs that claimed to be his supporters, and unable to create a functioning government, Aristide was driven into exile in 2004 by a coalition of opposition groups and private militias, with the support of the United States.

RACE AND RACISM IN CONTEMPORARY SOCIAL ISSUES

Since the fall of the Duvalier regime in 1986, labels such as "black" and "mulatto" have been increasingly replaced in Haitian public discourse by a more frank discussion of the tensions between rich and poor, between urban elites and rural masses. On the other hand, emigration from Haiti has made racism more than ever a problem for Haitians leaving their country. In 1980, approximately 12 percent of Haitians were living abroad, and that number rose dramatically in the following decades.

Since the early 1900s, sugar companies in Cuba and the Dominican Republic recruited Haitians as field workers. Between 1915 and 1929 there were as many as 300,000 Haitian workers in Cuba, and a similar number worked in the Dominican Republic. Reviled and persecuted in these countries, many migrants could not afford to return home, even when the Great Depression closed the plantations. In 1937 the Dominican army massacred between 10,000 and 30,000 Haitians after President Rafael Trujillo (1891–1961) launched a program of "racial cleansing." Nevertheless, Haitians continued to work on Dominican sugar estates into the 1990s. Similarly, there are well over 100,000 Haitians working on other islands throughout the Caribbean, often illegally.

According to the U.S. Census, there were nearly 750,000 Haitians living in the United States in the year 2000, and their experience has also been marked by racism. This is best demonstrated by the explanations some U.S. medical researchers offered in the early 1980s to explain the emerging AIDS epidemic. The presence of Haitians among the earliest victims of the mysterious new disease produced lurid theories that AIDS originated amid the orgiastic rites imagined to be part of Haitian Vodou. Until 1985, "Haitian" was a medically defined "risk group" for AIDS. Throughout the decade, Haitians living in the United States lost jobs and were shunned by their neighbors because of this identification with the dreaded disease.

MAJOR FIGURES IN HAITIAN RACIAL POLITICS

Anténor Firmin (1850–1911) was the most prominent antiracist intellectual in late nineteenth-century Haiti. European writers such as Arthur de Gobineau had used Haitian "savagery" as evidence to support racial theories that Africans were incapable of civilization. In 1885 Firmin published *De l'égalité des races humaines* (*On the Equality of the Human Races*) in response to Gobineau's influential *Essai sur l'inégalité des races humaines* (Essay on the inequality of the human race, 1853–1855). Firmin directly challenged the racist anthropology of the day and suggested that race was a social construction. At the same time, Firmin condemned both Vodou and the Creole language. Because these "backwards" traits were a product of Haiti's environment, he believed they would eventually be eradicated.

The physician, diplomat, and anthropologist Jean Price-Mars (1876–1969) was the founder of Haiti's *Négritude* movement of the 1920s and 1930s, which was begun in recognition and support of African cultures. Price-Mars's book, *Ainsi Parla L'Oncle* (*So Spoke the Uncle*, 1928), written under the racism of the American occupation, led many Haitian intellectuals to reconsider their attitudes about peasant culture. Price-Mars insisted that Haitians recognize that their cultural roots were in Africa as well as France. He described Vodou as a theological system, not a collection of superstitions. In 1941 he helped found the Bureau and Institute of Ethnology in Port-au-Prince, though this did not prevent a state-run "anti-superstition campaign" targeting Vodou practitioners that very year.

SEE ALSO *Caribbean Racial Formations; Children, Racial Disparities and Status of; Firmin, Anténor; HIV and AIDS; Poverty; Racial Formations; Social Welfare States.*

BIBLIOGRAPHY

Dubois, Laurent. 2004. *Avengers of the New World: The Story of the Haitian Revolution.* Cambridge, MA: Harvard University Press.

———, and John D. Garrigus, eds. 2006. *Slave Revolution in the Caribbean, 1789–1804: A Brief History with Documents.* New York: Bedford/St. Martin's.

Farmer, Paul. 1999. *Infections and Inequalities: The Modern Plagues.* Berkeley: University of California Press.

———. 2003. *The Uses of Haiti,* 2nd ed. Monroe, ME: Common Courage Press.

Firmin, Anténor. 2002 (1879). *The Equality of the Human Races.* Translated by Asselin Charles. Urbana: University of Illinois Press.

Garrigus, John D. 1996. "Redrawing the Colour Line: Gender and the Social Construction of Race in Pre-Revolutionary Haiti." *Journal of Caribbean History* 30 (1-2): 28–50.

Geggus, David P. 2002. *Haitian Revolutionary Studies.* Bloomington: Indiana University Press.

Labelle, Micheline. 1978. *Idéologie de couleur et classes sociales en Haïti.* Montréal: Presses de l'Université de Montréal.

Nicholls, David. 1996. *From Dessalines to Duvalier: Race, Colour, and National Independence in Haiti,* rev. ed. New Brunswick, NJ: Rutgers University Press.

Plummer, Brenda Gayle. 1992. *Haiti and the United States: The Psychological Moment.* Athens: University of Georgia.

Price-Mars, Jean. 1983 (1928). *So Spoke the Uncle.* Translated by Magdaline W. Shannon. Washington, D.C.: Three Continents Press.

Trouillot, Michel-Rolph. 1990. *Haiti, State against Nation: The Origins and Legacy of Duvalierism.* New York: Monthly Review Press.

John D. Garrigus

HAMER, FANNIE LOU
1917–1977

Fannie Lou Hamer was born Fannie Lou Townsend on October 6, 1917, in Montgomery County, Mississippi. She was the youngest of twenty children born to sharecroppers Jim and Lou Ella Townsend. At the age of six she began working in the cotton fields of Sunflower County and by age twelve she had dropped out of school. She married Perry "Pap" Hamer in 1944, and the couple settled in Ruleville, Mississippi, to work as sharecroppers.

Hamer did not know that blacks could vote until 1962 when, at age forty-four, she attended a mass meeting of the Student Nonviolent Coordinating Committee (SNCC). She volunteered, along with seventeen others, to attempt to register to vote. She failed the required literacy test, however, and when she returned home she learned that she had also lost the job she had held for eighteen years because of her attempt to register. Thus began a public life dedicated to having America fulfill its democratic promises to all citizens. She became a political, social, and economic activist.

In 1964 Hamer helped to organize the events of Freedom Summer, out of which emerged the Mississippi Freedom Democratic Party (MFDP) to which she was selected as vice chairman. As a delegate to the Democratic National Convention in Atlantic City, she challenged the seating of the all-white party delegation (the "Regulars"). Hamer became a national figure when she provided testimony during televised hearings before the Credentials Committee. She spoke of atrocities faced by blacks in Mississippi when attempting to register and vote and of being severely beaten after she was arrested in Winona, Mississippi, for attending a civil rights meeting. She stated, "If the Freedom Democratic Party is not seated now, I question America, is this America, the land of the free and the home of the brave where we have to sleep with our telephones off the hook because our lives be threatened daily?"(Mills 1993, p. 121). As a compromise, the MFDP was offered two seats, which Hamer rejected, stating, "We didn't come all this way for no two seats 'cause all of us is tired" (Mills 1993, p. 5). The MFDP did not win its political challenge, but this effort paved the way for future delegations to Democratic conventions to be integrated.

In 1968 the Loyalists Democrats of Mississippi, a biracial outgrowth of the MFDP, ousted the Regulars at the Chicago Democratic Convention. Hamer was selected as a delegate, but she argued that the party had lost touch with poor people. In the lawsuit *Hamer v. Campbell,* Hamer sought to block elections in Sunflower County on the grounds that blacks had not had an opportunity to register. A federal appeals court overturned a district court decision against her, and new elections were ordered. Hamer also helped organize the National Women's Political Caucus in 1971.

Hamer dedicated her life to helping the poor, children and working people. In 1963 she formed Delta Ministry, a community development program. In 1968, she founded

Freedom Farms Cooperative, a nonprofit venture designed to help poor farming families. The cooperative purchased forty acres of land and, with help from the National Council of Negro Women, created a pig bank so families could support themselves. (A pig bank loaned adult pigs to local families who would breed them, keep the piglets, and return the mama pig for other families to use.) She also supported efforts of striking members of the Mississippi Farm Labor Union and spoke at rallies to save Head Start programs. A life dedicated to serving others ended March 14, 1977, when Fannie Lou Hamer died of heart failure in Mound Bayou, Mississippi.

BIBLIOGRAPHY

Hamer, Fannie Lou. 1967. *To Praise Our Bridges: An Autobiography*. Jackson, MI: KIPCO.

Locke, Mamie E. 1990. "Is This America? Fannie Lou Hamer and the Mississippi Freedom Democratic Party." In *Women in the Civil Rights Movement: Trailblazers and Torchbearers 1941–1965*, edited by Vicki L. Crawford, Jacqueline Anne Rouse, and Barbara Woods. Bloomington: Indiana University Press.

Mills, Kay. 1993. *This Little Light of Mine: The Life of Fannie Lou Hamer*. New York: Dutton Books.

Reagon, Bernice Johnson. 1990. "Women as Culture Carriers in the Civil Rights Movement." In *Women in the Civil Rights Movement: Trailblazers and Torchbearers 1941–1965*, edited by Vicki L. Crawford, Jacqueline Anne Rouse, and Barbara Woods. Bloomington: Indiana University Press.

Williams, Juan. 1987. *Eyes on the Prize: America's Civil Rights Years, 1954–1964*. New York: Viking-Penguin Press.

Mamie E. Locke

HATE CRIMES

Hate crimes are message crimes. They affect more than the targeted individual; they affect the entire community. When a person of a selected race or ethnicity is attacked simply because of skin color, the entire ethnic community is put in fear.

Hate crime laws have spawned much debate in modern society. They are viewed as essential by some segments of the community as a powerful tool with which to combat violent bigotry, but they are denounced by others as an overextension of governmental power designed to legislate morality. Addressed here are the specifics of hate crime laws, some of the reasons for the controversy that surrounds them, the reliability of statistics, and the different types of hate crime offenders and hate crime victims.

HATE CRIME LAWS

Most states in the early twenty-first century have some form of hate crime legislation. Many such laws create criminal enhancements that increase the level of punishment for crimes with a "hate" component. The wording of hate crime laws often includes numerous protected classes, in addition to race. In California for example, Penal Code Section 422.55(a) defines a hate crime as "a criminal act committed, in whole or in part, because of one or more of the following actual or perceived characteristics of the victim: (1) Disability, (2) Gender, (3) Nationality, (4) Race or ethnicity, (5) Religion, (6) Sexual orientation, (7) Association with a person or group with one or more of these actual or perceived characteristics." Penal Code Section 422.56(d) explains that the phrase "in whole or in part, because of" means that "the bias motivation must be a cause in fact of the offense, whether or not other causes also exist. When multiple concurrent motives exist, the prohibited bias must be a substantial factor in bringing about the particular result. There is no requirement that the bias be a main factor, or that the crime would not have been committed but for the actual or perceived characteristic."

Hate crime laws apply even if the offender mistakenly believes a victim has a characteristic that the person does not in fact have. They criminalize actions committed against a person who belongs to a particular ethnic group, or against a person whom the perpetrator believes is a member of such a group. An assault against an Asian who is mistakenly believed to be a person of Middle Eastern ancestry is no less a hate crime just because the perpetrator's perception of the victim's ethnicity was incorrect.

Opponents of hate crime laws feel that the government should not function as "thought police," and that the motivation of the perpetrator should be irrelevant. This viewpoint often stems from a misunderstanding of the scope of hate crime laws. Citizens are free to hold whatever biases they choose; it is only when they commit a crime because of such biases that hate crime laws apply. This distinction is often frustrating for targeted individuals to hear, but it is important for communities to understand that as sympathetic as law enforcement might be, they can only enforce violations of the criminal law.

The controversy over hate crime laws is also fueled by the misconception that hate crime laws infringe upon constitutionally protected freedom of speech. Racial slurs constitute free speech. Such language, unless it qualifies as a criminal threat, is not criminal. The distribution of racist leaflets or brochures is another exercise of free speech and is not subject to prosecution. Hate crimes are criminal acts committed against someone because of their membership in one of the protected classes. But that does not mean that noncriminal acts of discrimination such as racial slurs or the distribution of leaflets should necessarily go undocumented. Although not criminally actionable on their own, they may be useful in proving the motive behind a criminal act. Law enforcement agencies are thus encouraged to document them for tracking purposes and future use. Individuals who exhibit this kind of blatant bigotry by engaging in such behavior often graduate to committing crimes against people of the targeted race. When they do, evidence of their history of intolerance may establish the motive necessary to prove the commission of a hate crime.

THE PREVALENCE OF HATE CRIMES

Because of underreporting, it is statistically difficult to determine the prevalence of hate crimes. Many hate crime victims do not report their victimization because they are unaware of the existence of such laws. Others do not trust the police or do not feel that anything will be done. In some cases this hopelessness is the result of prior bad experiences with law enforcement agencies who were themselves unfamiliar with hate crime laws and the resources available to victims. Other reasons victims do not report hate crimes include fear of retaliation, fear of deportation, and fear that their status as private members of the gay and lesbian community will be revealed.

On the positive side, increased community education about hate crimes has resulted in an increase in the number of hate crimes that are reported. Someone unfamiliar with this area of the law might look at the statistical increase in reported hate crimes and conclude that there has been an alarming increase in hate crimes. The professional opinion of those involved in the field, however, is that the statistical increase is not due to an actual increase in hate crimes committed, but rather to an increase in hate crimes reported. This increase in reporting is attributed in part to the proactive nature of tolerance-based programs and hate crime law-enforcement teamwork. Partnerships among peace officers, prosecutors, the Anti-Defamation League, and other community groups have resulted in greater public awareness of hate crimes and how communities can report and combat such bias.

For over a decade, the Federal Bureau of Investigation's Uniform Crime Reporting (UCR) Program has been collecting information on hate crimes. The 2003 Hate Crime Statistics report, which was published in November 2004, listed 8,715 offenses, 4,574 of which were motivated by racial bias. With all fifty states reporting, the 2003 report broke down the 8,715 offenses committed by state. California was in the lead, with 1,701 offenses reported; in second place was New Jersey, with 638; third was New York, with 625; and rounding out fourth and fifth place were Michigan and Massachusetts, with 487 and 473, respectively.

Although the numbers reported serve a statistical purpose, the unfortunate reality for victims is that most hate crimes go unsolved. This is because most hate crimes are attacks on strangers without any motive but intolerance and hatred. There is no preexisting relationship to lead police to a suspect; there is no stolen property to trace; and because hate crimes are often impulsive, there is no evidence of prior planning that might generate leads.

Family Visits Hate Crime Victim's Grave. *The parents of James Byrd Jr. visit his grave. Byrd, an African American, had accepted a ride from three white men, who instead beat him and then dragged him from their truck for about three miles. Byrd's assailants were convicted of a hate crime; two were sentenced to death and one life in prison.* AP IMAGES.

PROFILES OF HATE CRIME OFFENDERS

Research and experience show that there are different categories of hate crime offenders and that different factors contribute to a perpetrator's motivation. *Responding to Hate Crime* (2000), by the National Center for Hate Crime Prevention Education Development Center, identifies three common types of hate crime offenders. *Thrill-seeking offenders* are the most common. Usually acting in groups, these are typically young people who seek out victims on the victim's own turf, usually to gain "bragging" rights. These perpetrators, who commit more crimes against property than against persons, are predominantly motivated by a desire for acceptance by their peers, rather than by hatred for the victims. *Reactive offenders* feel a sense of entitlement with respect to rights and privileges they feel they should enjoy, and they are threatened by their victims, usually people of color, whom they perceive as a threat to these rights and privileges. They consequently feel justified in intimidating and committing crimes against these victims, who are often members of the offender's neighborhood, workplace, or school. *Mission offenders* are the most violent type of hate crime offender, though fortunately they are the rarest. They view their victims as "subhuman" and part of a conspiracy, and they are motivated by a psychotic belief that they must rid the world of such people. They seek out their victims where such victims are likely to be found. Some mission offenders conclude their mission with their own suicide.

Hate crime offenders can be identified circumstantially through many different factors, including bigoted remarks, manner of dress, racist tattoos, "White Pride" music playing in their vehicles, and sometimes even the date they choose for their attack. For example, many hate crimes are committed on certain holidays, such as Martin Luther King Day or on the birthday of Adolf Hitler.

Dramatic profiles aside, hate crimes are also committed by ordinary citizens, often in response to a real or perceived threat by a particular group. These retaliatory hate crimes are actually inappropriate expressions of anger or fear. Shortly after the attacks of September 11, 2001, the following "retaliatory" hate crimes were reported: A woman in traditional Muslim dress was almost hit when a car intentionally swerved towards her as she was crossing the street; an Arab-American family arrived to open their grocery store in the morning only to find "Go Home Arabs" spray-painted on the front of their door; an evening prayer service was interrupted by cherry bombs exploding outside on the sidewalk of a mosque. Scores of Arab-Americans, and also those who appeared to be of such ethnicity, were subjected to the wrath of frustrated citizens in the aftermath of the September 11 tragedy. Many of the victims became afraid to go to work, afraid to worship, even afraid to send their children to school because some of their children had been subjected to violence there.

THE VICTIM'S PERSPECTIVE

Many citizens cannot imagine what it is like to be a hate crime victim. Hate crime victims cannot employ traditional means of self-protection because they are targeted by criminals with a unique motivation. Criminals motivated by financial gain commit crimes such as theft and embezzlement. Criminals motivated by a quest for sex or power commit sexual assaults. Physically violent crimes are often the result of arguments, or they are committed for revenge. Awareness of criminal motivations allows society to protect itself to some extent. To avoid a mugging, one does not wear expensive jewelry or walk down dark alleys at night. To prevent car theft, one locks one's car, equips it with an alarm system, and parks it in lighted areas. Hate crime victims, however, cannot take precautionary measures to defend themselves. A person targeted due to the color of their skin cannot eliminate that risk factor.

When a person is attacked based on an immutable characteristic, the fear of revictimization may lead to helplessness and isolation. Victims of hate crimes feel degraded, frustrated, and afraid. These emotions ripple through their community, leading to outrage, blame, and collective fear. Because most hate crimes go unsolved, victims often suffer the additional frustration of knowing that the offender is unlikely to be brought to justice, and is therefore more likely to re-offend. This frustration, like the outrage of the crime itself, spreads throughout the victim's community.

THE FUTURE

Despite the best efforts of law enforcement and human rights groups, hate crimes will probably never be completely eradicated, and an overnight transformation from intolerance to acceptance cannot be expected. Therefore, the debate over hate crime laws will continue. In the meantime, those with first-hand experience in the field understand that although the fight can be difficult, in the balance, the opportunity to help victims regain their dignity outweighs the frustration of unsolved cases.

BIBLIOGRAPHY

Anti-Defamation League. 2001. *Extremism in America: A Guide.* Available from http://www.adl.org/learn/Ext_US/.

Devine, Richard A. 1998. *Hate Crime: A Prosecutor's Guide.* Chicago: Cook County State Attorney's Office.

McLaughlin, Karen A., Stephanie M. Malloy, Kelly J. Brilliant, and Cynthia Lang. 2000. *Responding to Hate Crime: A Multidisciplinary Curriculum for Law Enforcement and Victim Assistance Professionals.* Newton, MA: National Center for Hate Crime Prevention Education Development Center, Inc.

United States Department of Justice, Federal Bureau of Investigation. *Hate Crime Statistics 2003.* Available from http://www.fbi.gov/ucr/ucr.htm#hate.

Wendy Patrick Mazzarella

HEALTH CARE GAP

In the preamble to the constitution of the World Health Organization (WHO) health is defined as "a state of complete physical, mental and social well-being and not merely the absence of disease or infirmity." While this definition has not been amended since 1948, this concept of a "complete state of health" is rarely held by those responsible for delivering medical or public health programs. Rather, utilitarian measures that bring the "greatest good to the greatest number of people" are often adopted, based on the premise that the resources needed to deliver a state of complete health to all persons are not available. Under this model, those most vulnerable to disease and those most needing preventive and curative services are the ones excluded from good health and health care.

Race is an oft-stated correlate of disease. Although some diseases are indeed more common to a particular ethnic group, such as sickle-cell anemia among those of African decent, much of the correlation between race and disease is associated more with social than biological determinants. Racism creates an environment in which the conditions that promote disease and the barriers to health are greatest in communities of color. Mortality statistics in the United States represent a concrete example of the effect of racism on health. In 2002 the life expectancy at birth of a white girl was 80.3 years, while that of an African-American boy was 68.8 years. (National Center for Health Statistics 2004). These differential mortality statistics are due not to racial predilection of disease but rather to differential access to prevention, diagnosis, and treatment of disease, as well as to the impact of racism and oppression on health. The correlation between economic and social marginalization and disease is clearly linked in the Universal Declaration of Human Rights, which mentions health only in the following terms:

> Everyone has the right to a standard of living adequate for the health and well-being of himself and of his family, including food, clothing, housing and medical care and necessary social services, and the right to security in the event of unemployment, sickness, disability, widowhood, old age or other lack of livelihood in circumstances beyond his control.

Recognizing that the disparities in attaining a "complete state of health" are due to social and economic conditions rather than biological determinants, the focus here will be on three aspects of health disparities that are the consequences of racism: (1) the structural factors that result in an increased risk of disease among communities of color, (2) the racial disparities in access to quality health care, and (3) the psychological impact of racism on individual and community health.

STRUCTURAL VIOLENCE AND THE RISK OF DISEASE

One step in achieving the complete state of health described by the WHO is the maintenance of good health and the absence of disease. Health maintenance can be viewed as two interrelated entities: the promotion of health through the behaviors that are known to maintain health (such as a balanced diet, sufficient sleep, and regular exercise) and the prevention of disease—specifically, the mitigation of risk (avoiding drugs, wearing a condom, etc.). Both health promotion and disease prevention are often presented as "lifestyle choices" that are within the control of the individual. Yet among the consequences of racism are unequal access to housing, employment, education, and even quality food and water (Williams 1999). The lack of these basic necessities constrains the choices available to populations marginalized by racism. The systematic exclusion of a group from the resources needed to develop their full human potential has been called "structural violence" (Galtung 1969). The concept of structural violence is useful in understanding the barriers that prevent health maintenance and risk mitigation in a racist society. Because infectious diseases are among the most "preventable" illnesses, and because communities of color bear a disproportion risk of transmissible disease, health promotion and disease prevention will be explored through the examples of tuberculosis (TB) and the human immunodeficiency virus (HIV).

TB is one of the most cogent examples of relationship between poor living conditions and the spread of disease among the poor, particularly African Americans. While the treatment of TB is highly effective, it was not the advent of anti-tuberculosis treatment but the improvement of living conditions that heralded the decline of TB in the United States. The rate of active TB plummeted in New York City in the late 1940s due to the post–World War II economic boom and the migration of people from urban tenements to single-family homes in the suburbs. Thus, the best way to prevent TB is to live in a less crowded environment. However, conditions of urban poverty—particularly overcrowding, poor housing, and inadequate nutrition—continue to propagate the spread of TB worldwide and are largely drawn along socioeconomic lines. The striking reappearance of TB in the United States in the 1990s has been discussed extensively in the medical literature, especially its association with HIV. Yet the underlying causes of the epidemic were structural factors rather than biological susceptibility. The overcrowding in U.S. prisons that has occurred since the 1980s as a result of the "war on drugs" has significantly impacted African Americans, who make up only 12 percent of the U.S. population but constitute more than 40 percent of those incarcerated in state and federal prisons (Human Rights Watch 2001). Additionally, the 1980s saw increased rates of homelessness due to decreased government spending on public housing. The main risk factors for TB in the 1990s outbreak were a history of homelessness and incarceration, and African-American men were disproportionately affected (Brudney and Dobkin 1991).

Some scholars trace the upsurge in TB back even earlier, to policies designed to address what was called "social pathology" in urban neighborhoods (Wallace

2001). An advisor to Mayor John Lindsey of New York developed a policy of "Planned Shrinkage" of poor African-American communities. This policy involved the withdrawal of essential services (particularly fire brigades) to encourage residents to relocate out of certain areas. As fires burned in 1975 and 1976, residents did indeed relocate, often living with several other families in one apartment or becoming homeless, as a consequence of the planned shrinkage of poor communities. Not surprisingly, the beginning of the rise of TB in New York City began in the late 1970s. While an airborne disease would seemingly be as ubiquitous as the air people breathe, the air in corridors created by structural violence considerably increases risk of TB. In the early twenty-first century, TB continues to spread along lines of racial segregation.

Like airborne diseases, sexually transmitted diseases are ubiquitous, though their distribution follows society's racial and economic fault lines. AIDS is arguably the worst epidemic disease of the early 2000s, and it has a strikingly unequal distribution among populations, both worldwide and locally. While prevention programs are often focused on increasing knowledge and resultant behavior change; it is likely that internalized racism and low self-esteem decreases the ability of individuals to act on such knowledge. Moreover, the economic situation of the most marginalized communities may result in the exchange of sex for money, housing, security, or drugs. These situations are worsened not only by racism but by gender inequality. Lastly, the epidemic of incarceration of African-Americans foments the AIDS epidemic by increasing exposure to sexual violence and drug use and by worsening the level of poverty faced by many prisoners upon release.

The AIDS epidemic in the United States now disproportionately affects African Americans. In 2002 the Centers for Disease Control (CDC) reported that 39 percent of all AIDS cases and 54 percent of new cases of HIV infection were among African Americans. Nearly one third of all HIV infections in African-American men are due to intravenous drug use (as compared to 9 percent in white men). Yet white adolescents have been shown to start using drugs at earlier ages than their African-American counterparts. If initial use and experimentation with drugs is less common among African Americans, what would cause the high rate of HIV transmission from drug use among this population? Again, incarceration appears to be a significant risk, with both African-American men and women being incarcerated at rates upward of five times that of whites. Moreover, much of the increase in incarceration has not been for violent crime but for possession of drugs. In a 1999 report by Marc Mauer and the Sentencing Project, the disproportionate punishment meted out against African Americans in the "war on drugs" is clearly depicted: "State prison inmates sentenced for drug offenses increased 306% between 1985 and 1995, the number of African American state prison inmates sentenced for drug offenses increased 707% in the same time period."

Once in prison, HIV risk increases significantly, due to both the high prevalence of rape and the flow of illicit drugs into prison. Additionally, life after incarceration is characterized by a tightening noose of structural violence, including joblessness, homelessness, and poverty—factors that lead to drug use, the selling of drugs, and an increase in the commoditization of sex as a means for survival.

Neither HIV nor TB has a specific racial predilection, but they are both examples of the risk for ill health that is promulgated by institutionalized racism and a lack of social and economic rights. Such structures make the maintenance of health subjugated to the daily want of basic necessities. Much of public health is focused on health promotion and disease prevention, yet such programs never identify the mitigation of racism and its social consequences as a preventive strategy.

ACCESS TO AND QUALITY OF HEALTH CARE

The social and economic consequences of racism put a disproportionate burden of disease on populations of color. Yet this larger burden of disease has not led to an increased provision of diagnosis or treatment of illness. Instead, the same structural barriers that cause ill health also prevent equal access to high-quality health care. Among the most salient examples of the poor state of health care for African Americans in the United States is the gross disparity in infant mortality. Table 1 demonstrates the nearly three-fold difference in infant death rate between infants born to African-American mothers and those born to Asian, Hispanic, or non-Hispanic white mothers. The causes of the striking inequities in health outcomes of both adults and children of color are multidimensional and complex. However, several key factors result in poor health outcomes and higher mortality rates for people of color.

The United States has the largest percentage of people without health insurance of any developed nation. In 2004 more than 45 million people in the United States were without health insurance. Of the uninsured, 11.3 percent were white, 19.7 percent were black, and 32 percent were Hispanic. Lack of health insurance coverage has significant effects on health-seeking behaviors and health outcomes. For example, people without health insurance do not access screening services such as mammography for breast cancer, and they thus often delay seeking treatment until their disease is at an advanced state (Ayanian et al. 1993).

Difference Between Infant Mortality Rates by Race or Hispanic Origin of the Mother: United States, 2000

Race and Hispanic origin of mother	Number of infant deaths	Number of live births	Infant Mortality rate (deaths per 1000)
American Indian	346	41,668	8.3
Asian or Pacific Islander	977	200,544	4.9
Hispanic	4564	815,883	5.6
Non-Hispanic black	8212	604,367	13.6
Non-Hispanic white	13,461	2,362,982	5.7

SOURCE: Adapted from *National Vital Statistics Report*, Vol. 50, No. 12, August 28, 2002.

Table 1.

Yet the difference in mortality is not only due to a lack of insurance and the late detection of disease. Even when these factors are controlled for, African-American women suffer a significantly higher mortality rate from breast cancer than white women (Joslyn et al. 2000). This difference in outcomes along racial lines has been documented in numerous other diseases as well, including heart disease, lung cancer, and colorectal cancer, which are the major killers of Americans. These studies postulate a variety of reasons for higher mortality rates among African Americans, including a lower rate of subspecialty referrals and less aggressive use of medical or surgical therapies. Poor health outcomes—even among people of color who have "access" to the health-care system, as measured by comparable insurance coverage and income—prompted the Institute of Medicine to commission a study in 2003 to examine the causes of this disparate outcomes. This study found:

> Stereotyping, biases, and uncertainty on the part of healthcare providers can all contribute to unequal treatment. The conditions in which many clinical encounters take place—characterized by high time pressure, cognitive complexity, and pressures for cost containment—may enhance the likelihood that these processes will result in care poorly matched to minority patients' needs. Minorities may experience a range of other barriers . . . including barriers of language, geography, and cultural familiarity. (Smedley et al. 2003)

Both access to and quality of health care is affected by racist structures within health insurance and the medical system itself. These factors contribute to a significantly higher mortality rate throughout the spectrum of life in communities of color, and a systematic change in the health system is needed to address this problem.

PSYCHOLOGICAL AND SOCIAL IMPACT OF RACISM ON HEALTH

While racism affects physical health in overt ways, such as promoting health risks and restricting access to and quality of care, the psychological and social results of racism also affect physical and mental health, and these factors may be even more insidious and deadly than the others. One definition of health that is pertinent to racism's impact is the concept of health as freedom or autonomy. The notion of "complete health" requires control of one's destiny, even in the face of a physical condition termed a "disease." A diabetic, for example, who has managed to bring her blood sugar into the normal range long-term may be considered healthy, while a Palestinian in exile from his homeland may find himself in terrible health even when there is no evident diagnosable disease. As Alastair Cambell writes, in *Health as Liberation* (1995), "Provided that I can follow at least some of my basic aspirations in life, I will regard myself as retaining my health, whatever the threats to my bodily or mental well-being. Without such physical and mental freedom, functional ability loses its point" (p.11).

Racism negates or diminishes the autonomy of individuals to participate in society, and this lack of connectedness affects social health. The restriction of employment and educational opportunities; the engineering of challenges to the right to vote; and the relegating of groups into neighborhoods with substandard quality of food and environmental, security, and transportation conditions are all factors that affect the social health of marginalized communities.

Racism is normalized and institutionalized by legal policies such as racial profiling, which can add hours to the transit plans of people of color. For many being stopped by the police while walking or driving and being subjected to body searches when flying or entering a building can become part of the daily routine. At its worst, racial profiling involves lethal forms of police and gang brutality against people of color. Such policies are painful reminders to oppressed groups that society accepts that some persons should be treated differently due to a perceived physical distinction associated with potential communal danger. For whites who witness profiling, the process legitimizes latent racism, while if one of the persons profiled concurs that the process is necessary he or she may internalize the racism into his or her own psyche and persona. Camera Jones defines internalized racism as "acceptance by members of the stigmatized races of negative messages about their own abilities and intrinsic worth" (Jones 2000, p. 1213).

The psychological damage from the internalization of racism includes poor self-esteem and may result in depression and other mental illnesses as well as substance abuse. People from racial minorities may internalize racism by affiliating with entities that promote the status quo such as denouncing affirmative action and promoting racial profiling or by practicing self-marginalization such as making the decision not vote. Usually, such decisions are evidence-based. For example, when racism is widely accepted as a societal norm (such areas can still be found within the United States), such decisions are made to prevent consequences that might immediately endanger the physical or mental health of an individual or community. As Stephen Biko said of the South African apartheid government that eventually killed him, "the greatest weapon in the hands of the oppressor is the mind of the oppressed." Like the many other health effects of racism, marginalization afflicts the health of the entire community, not just the stigmatized.

As long as racist social structures continue, the health of those marginalized and stigmatized by these structures will be seriously and often lethally affected. Complete health must be viewed as a societal challenge, not just a medical one. The root causes of many diseases lie in the architecture of structural violence, which must be considered one of the main enemies of health promotion and disease prevention. Furthermore, improved access to and provision of high quality and equitable health care for individuals from minority groups must be the top priority for a medical system that is failing the most vulnerable. Lastly, the demonstrable nature of racism and its deleterious effect on individual and community health suggests that racism itself should be defined as a diagnosable disease, with its own category in medical literature, education, research, and policy. Based on the grim statistics that the disease of racism brings to society, major institutions, such as the National Institutes of Health, should support formal research on codifying racism's symptoms, signs, and sequelae. Such research should inform the investments needed to address and remediate the unacceptable human cost that racism incurs on individuals and society.

SEE ALSO *Brazilian Racial Formations; Canadian Racial Formations; Caribbean Racial Formations; Cuban Racial Formations; Diseases, Racial; Haitian Racial Formations; Health Disparities between Indians and Non-Indians; Infant Mortality and Birth Weight; Medical Experimentation; Medical Racism; Mental Health and Racism; Social Problems; South African Racial Formations; Transnationalism; United Kingdom Racial Formations.*

BIBLIOGRAPHY

Acevedo-Garcia, D. 2000. "Residential Segregation and the Epidemiology of Infectious Diseases." *Social Science and Medicine* 51: 1143–1161.

Ayanian, J. Z., B. A. Kohler, T. Abe, and A. M. Epstein. 1993. "The Relation between Health Insurance Coverage and Clinical Outcomes among Women with Breast Cancer." *New England Journal of Medicine* 329: 326–331.

Bach, P. B., L. D. Cramer, J. L. Warren, et al. 1999. "Racial Differences in the Treatment of Early-Stage Lung Cancer." *New England Journal of Medicine* 341: 1198–1205.

Biko, Stephen Bantu. "Black Consciousness and the Quest for a True Humanity." *South African History Online*. Available from http://www.sahistory.org.za/pages/specialprojects/black-consciousness/biko/writings-humanity.htm.

Blankenship, K. M., A. B. Smoyer, S. J. Bray, and K. Mattocks. 2005. "Black-White Disparities in HIV/AIDS: The Role of Drug Policy and the Corrections System." *Journal of Health Care for the Poor and Underserved* 16: 140–156.

Brudney, K., and J. Dobkin. 1991. "Resurgent Tuberculosis in New York City: Human Immunodeficiency Virus, Homelessness, and the Decline of Tuberculosis Control Programs." *American Review of Respiratory Disease* 144: 745–9.

Campbell, Alaistair. 1995. *Health as Liberation: Medicine, Theology, and the Quest for Justice*. Cleveland, OH: The Pilgrim Press.

Centers for Disease Control and Prevention (CDC). 2004. *Fact Sheet—HIV/AIDS among African Americans*. Atlanta: CDC, National Center for HIV, STD and TB Prevention, Division of HIV/AIDS Prevention.

Cooper, G. S., Z. Yuan, C. S. Landefeld, et al. 1996. "Surgery for Colorectal Cancer: Race-Related Differences in Rates and Survival among Medicare Beneficiaries." *American Journal of Public Health* 86: 582–586.

DeNavas-Walt, Carmen, Bernadette D. Proctor, and Cheryl Hill-Lee. U.S. Census Bureau. 2005. *Current Population Reports, P60-299: Income, Poverty, and Health Insurance Coverage in the United States: 2004*. Washington, DC: U.S. Government Printing Office.

Ellickson, P. L., and S. C. Morton. 1999. "Identifying Adolescents at Risk for Hard Drug Use: Racial/Ethnic Variations." *Journal of Adolescent Health* 25 (6): 382–95.

Frieden, T. R., L. F. Sherman, K. L. Maw, et al. 1996. "A Multi-Institutional Outbreak of Highly Drug-Resistant Tuberculosis: Epidemiology and Clinical Outcomes." *Journal of the American Medical Association* 276 (15): 1229–1235.

Fuller, C. M., D. Vlahov, D. C. Ompad, et al. 2002. "High-Risk Behaviors Associated with Transition from Illicit Non-Injection to Injection Drug Use among Adolescent and Young Adult Drug Users: A Case Control Study." *Drug and Alcohol Dependency* 66 (2): 189–98.

Galtung, J. 1969. "Violence, Peace, and Peace Research." *Journal of Peace Research* 6 (3), 167–191.

Golub, A., and B. D. Johnson. 2001. "Variation in Youthful Risks of Progression from Alcohol and Tobacco to Marijuana and to Hard Drugs across Generations." *American Journal of Public Health* 91 (2): 225–32.

Human Rights Watch. "World Report, 2001." Available from http://www.hrw.org/wr2k1/.

Jones, C. P. 2000. "Levels of Racism: A Theoretic Framework and a Gardener's Tale." *American Journal of Public Health* 90 (8): 1212–1215.

Joslyn, S. A., and M. M. West. 2000. "Racial Differences in Breast Carcinoma Survival." *Cancer* 88: 114–123.

Mauer, M. 1999. *Race to Incarcerate*. New York: The New Press.

Mukamel, D. B., A. S. Murthy, and D. L. Weimer. 2000. Racial Differences in Access to High-Quality Cardiac Surgeons." *American Journal of Public Health* 90: 1774–1777.

National Center for Health Statistics. 2004. *Health, United States, 2003, with Chartbook on Trends in the Health of Americans*. DHHS Publication No. 2004–1232. Hyattsville, MD: CDC.

Official Records of the World Health Organization, no. 2, p. 100; Adopted by the International Health Conference, New York, 19–22 June 1946; signed on 22 July 1946; Entered into Force on 7 April 1948.

Salazar, L., R. Crosby, R. J. DiClemente, et al. "Self-Esteem and Theoretical Mediators of Safer Sex among African American Female Adolescents: Implications for Sexual Risk Reduction Interventions." *Health Education and Behavior* 32 (3): 413–427.

Smedley, B. D., A. Y. Stith, and A. R. Nelson, eds. 2003. *Unequal Treatment: Confronting Racial and Ethnic Disparities in Health Care*. Washington, DC: National Academies of Science Press.

Universal Declaration of Human Rights, Article 25.

Wallace, D. N. 2001. "Discriminatory Public Policies and the New York City Tuberculosis Epidemic, 1975–1993." *Microbes and Infection*. 515–524.

Williams, D. R. 1999. "Race, Socioeconomic Status, and Health: The Added Effects of Racism and Discrimination." *Annals of the New York Academy of Sciences* 896: 173–188.

Joia S. Mukherjee
Lanny Smith

HEALTH DISPARITIES BETWEEN INDIANS AND NON-INDIANS

BACKGROUND INFORMATION AND POLITICAL CONTEXT

American Indians experience health and disease in a way different from that of any other group of people in the United States. Their life expectancy is the lowest of any group in the United States, and Indians have the highest prevalence of Type 2 diabetes in the world. It is not uncommon to see alarming statistics in the press concerning the health of North American indigenous people. According to the National Congress of American Indians, the most recent statistics recount stunning differences in the infant mortality rate for Native American babies—150 percent higher than that of white infants. Additionally, the suicide rate for American Indians and Alaska Natives is two-and-a-half times greater than the national average. A 2003 report from the U.S. Commission on Civil Rights also indicated that American Indians are 630 percent more likely to die from alcoholism and 650 percent more likely to die from tuberculosis than other persons in the United States. American Indians have high death rates from motor-vehicle crashes, unintentional injuries, alcohol-induced injuries, and malignant neoplasm.

PUBLIC-HEALTH CRISIS

Countless scientific research projects and subsequent reports indicate that Native Americans are in the midst of a public-health crisis concerning diabetes and other health-related problems. While many scientific studies tend to focus on genetic and lifestyle choices and their relationships to Native American health, more often than not, the sociopolitical and sociohistorical aspects of Native American health are not addressed. These aspects, however, are essential to understanding health disparities in Native North America. Traditional health to most Native Americans is a balance of spiritual, physical, mental, and emotional components. This balance is not addressed by Western medicine, and patients are apprehensive about seeking health care because of what they consider to be incomplete care.

Access to health care, poverty, discrimination, cultural differences, low educational attainment, and poor social conditions are often cited as reasons for Native American health disparities. Some policy analysts would argue that access is no longer an issue for Native Americans. However, it is imperative to understand the political nature of American Indian health care when attempting to address the numerous disparities, because funding levels for government-sponsored health care are directly tied into appropriations by politicians and are subject to the political climate of the time. As of mid-2007, the Indian Health Care Improvement Act (Public Law 94–437) had not been renewed, and the Bush administration was attempting to limit the number of Native Americans the act could serve. The Snyder Act of 1921 (Public Law 67–85), the same law that conferred citizenship on all American Indians, authorizes Congress to appropriate funds for "the relief of distress and conservation of health" of American Indians, but it is up to the discretion of the government to determine how much relief is offered.

The federal responsibility to provide health care is carried out by the secretary of the Department of Health and Human Services through the Indian Health Service (IHS). The IHS provides directly or indirectly the majority of funds for the health care of American Indians and Alaska Natives (AI/AN). The U.S. government has been negligent in its responsibility to provide health care to

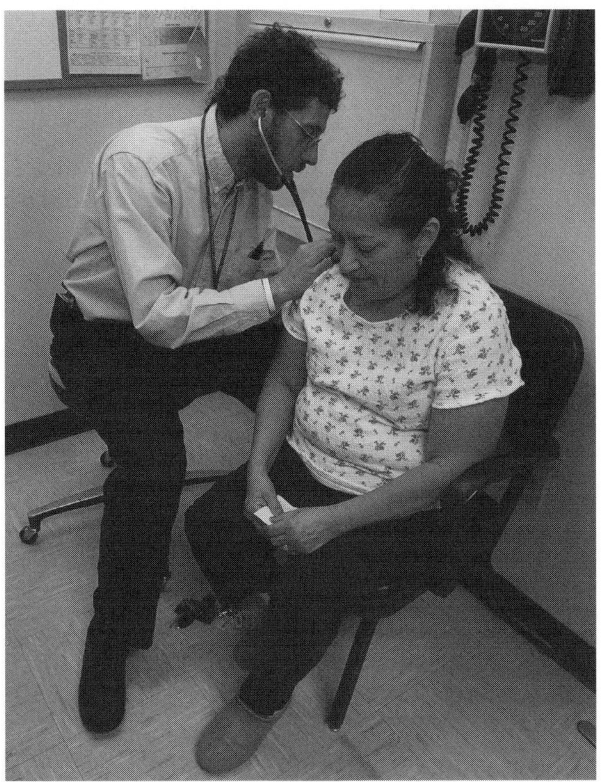

Health Disparities. *A doctor listens to a patient's lungs at a Tohono O'odham reservation hospital. Native Americans have higher rates of chronic and disabling illness, infectious disease, and mortality compared with whites.* AP IMAGES.

AI/ANs. Funding for AI/ANs is neither a congressional nor presidential priority, as the IHS budget lacks funds to provide adequate services. Per capita, the IHS budget ($1,914) is 50 percent that of federal prisoners ($3,803) and is far behind that of Medicare ($5,915), the Department of Veterans Affairs ($5,214), and the U.S. population in general ($5,065). The IHS non-medical budget is $614 per person served.

An important feature of this act is that it sets the programmatic and legal framework for the government in meeting its responsibility to provide health care to American Indians. Another important political feature that impedes access is the uncertainty of services. Most recently, the Bush administration attempted to eliminate clinical health care services that directly serve urban American Indians. Approximately two-thirds of AI/ANs do not reside on reservations because of migration and ethnocidal relocation programs to force assimilation. During the period when the Indian Health Care Improvement Act was in effect, mainstream health care and health care delivery changed dramatically to emphasize prevention and the "whole person" approach, which some say is analogous to the balance recognized by AI/AN. Most recently in mainstream health care, mental health is recognized as a "health threat," and practitioners have begun to incorporate a strong health promotion and preventative emphasis. Another important feature of the Indian Health Care Improvement Act is the ability to create local level health care models that, coupled with the 1975 Indian Self-Determination Act (Public Law 638), allow tribes to run their own health care clinics. These clinics work hard to incorporate traditional models into health care promotion and delivery. But because of the politicized nature of health care services, a common adage in areas with significant Indian populations is that one should not get sick after June because no funding is available. Against this complicated political backdrop, American Indians receive their health care. The availability of clinics has improved over the years, but the highly political nature of health care has not.

DIABETES

Diabetes is a major health threat to American Indians. "Diabetes is a chronic disease that occurs when the pancreas does not produce enough insulin, or alternatively, when the body cannot effectively use the insulin it produces" (World Health Organization, 2006). There are several forms of diabetes, including Type 1 and Type 2. Type 1 is an insulin-dependent type, usually with childhood onset (and hence formerly called juvenile diabetes). This type results from low insulin production in the pancreas. Type 2 is generally an adult onset type, but Native American children as young as ten years old have been diagnosed with this type. Type 2 results primarily from insulin resistance, or the inability of cells to absorb insulin, along with other factors, and until recently was attributed to the combination of poor diet and lack of exercise. Once a person is diagnosed with Type 2 diabetes, the first-line treatment is generally diet and exercise. If these fail to bring down blood glucose, the next step is oral medication, then combined oral medications and insulin. If the first regime is not effective, then different medications are introduced.

As of 2007, the National Institutes of Health recognized that stress is a contributor to uncontrolled Type 2 diabetes. Stress, especially from trauma, including physical and sexual abuse, or witnessing abuse, is now considered a contributor to an increase in blood glucose. Many of the ethnocidal federal policies—manifested as day-to-day stress on Native American people—have contributed to the high levels of Type 2 diabetes among Native American communities. Some of the historical stressors were and are (1) removal of people from their homelands, disrupting their indigenous diet, and subsequently making many of them dependent upon government food programs (which are inherently political); (2) imposing a new religion; (3) forced removal of children from their families and their subjection to abuse for being "Indian" at federal American Indian boarding schools, and subsequent loss of culture and traditional child-rearing practices through forced assimilation.

Diabetes also creates comorbidities associated with the disease, including diabetic retinopathy, renal failure, heart disease and stroke, diabetic neuropathy, and peripheral vascular disease, to name a few. The Web site for the Centers for Disease Control and Prevention (CDC) lists heart disease, diabetes, and stroke as, respectively, the first, fourth, and fifth leading causes of death among AI/ANs. Even though a person may die of heart disease or stroke, a person with diabetes likely developed these conditions as a result of the disease.

Until American Indian health care is depoliticalized and American Indians are allowed to exercise their sovereign rights as outlined in law and treaty, they are more vulnerable to experience disease and public-health-related issues than other populations in the United States.

SEE ALSO *Diabetes; Diseases, Racial; Infant Mortality and Birth Weight; Medical Racism.*

BIBLIOGRAPHY

Centers for Disease Control and Prevention. 2007. "American Indian and Alaska Native (AI/AN) Populations." Office of Minority Health. Available from http://www.cdc.gov/omh/populations/aian/aian.htm.

Stempel, Thomas K. 2007. "Indian Health Service: Providing Care to Native Americans and Alaska Natives." *Bulletin of the American College of Surgeons* 92 (6).

World Health Organization. 2006. "Diabetes." Available from http://www.who.int/mediacentre/factsheets/fs312/en.

Zhang, Y., E. T. Lee, R. B. Devereux, J. Yeh, L. G. Best, R. R. Fabsitz, and B. V. Howard. 2006. "Prehypertension, Diabetes, and Cardiovascular Disease Risk in a Population-Based Sample: The Strong Heart Study." *Hypertension* 47 (3): 410–414.

L. Marie Wallace
Isaac F. Parr

HERITABILITY

An often repeated claim of those who analyze the social status of blacks and whites is that differences between the groups in average IQ test scores is a result of genes that directly cause that difference in mental ability. This claim is said to be validated by observations that point to the *heritability* of IQ test performance. For example, the IQ scores of adopted children are correlated with the IQ scores of their biological parents, even though the children were adopted at an early age. That is, the higher the IQ scores of the biological parents, the higher the IQ scores of their children raised by adopting parents, indicating an effect of heredity. What this observation, however, does not take into account is that the average IQ score of the adopted children as a group is much higher than the average score of the biological parents and is equal to the average IQ score of the adopting parents as a group. That is, being raised by the adopting parents, who, in fact, have higher IQ scores as a group than do their biological parents, results in an increase in the IQ scores of the children over those of their biological parents.

Differences between individual organisms in measurable characteristics such as weight, growth rate, susceptibility to physical disorders, or behavior are a consequence of three interacting causes: genetic differences, environmental differences, and random developmental events. In the absence of detailed experimental modifications of the developmental process by controlled genetic and environmental manipulations, it is impossible to provide an accurate description of the causal pathways leading to a mature organism. Plant and animal breeders, however, need to choose breeding stocks and techniques of artificial selection that enable them to produce, as quickly and efficiently as possible, higher-yielding and more disease-resistant agricultural varieties. For this purpose, they developed, in the first half of the twentieth century, techniques for estimating the "heritability" of observed differences. The heritability of a trait in a particular variety estimates what proportion of the difference between the measurement of the trait in a population and the measurement of it in a specially selected group from that population would be preserved in the next generation if only the selected group were used as parents for that next generation. If the selected group of parents is three inches taller than the average of the population, how much taller than average will their offspring be? The proportion of selection difference that appears in the next generation is the *realized heritability* of the trait. If the next generation is only 1.5 inches taller, on average, then the realized heritability is 50 percent.

Such a measure is only useful for breeding experiments if the environment is kept the same in the two generations. If the environment is not the same, it cannot be known whether the selection really worked or whether it was the result of an environmental improvement.

A more sophisticated experimental approach to this same problem is to vary the environment and the genetic parentage of the organisms in a controlled way and to then analyze the variation in the offspring to estimate what proportion of that variation can be attributed to genetic differences, what proportion to environmental differences, and how much specific interaction there is between the genetic and environmental variations. A common technique is observing the amount of similarity between relatives of various degrees while keeping the distribution of environments the same for all of the relatives. Such an analysis, however, is not an analysis of causal pathways, and it is a serious error to confuse such an analysis of variation with an analysis of causation (Lewontin 1976). The same set of genetic lines, when tested in a different average environment but with the same amount of environmental variation, will give a different estimate of heritability, and the lines may be in a different relative order in their performance.

Despite this meaning of heritability, human geneticists and psychologists have repeatedly estimated heritability of human traits, especially traits of mental performance, in the process making serious methodological and conceptual errors. First, because they cannot control human developmental environments, many studies have either ignored the problem or made a variety of convenient but untestable assumptions about environmental similarities. Identical twins raised apart, for example, may be separated at various times after birth or may be raised by close relatives in the same locality. Second, interpretation may confuse the analysis of the variation with a separation of genetic and environmental causes, arguing, for example, that because the estimate of heritability of IQ was 70 percent, then only 30 percent of the observed differences in IQ could be eliminated by environmental interventions.

Finally, there is a confusion of the heritability of a trait within a population and the heritability of differences between populations. This is important in analyzing claims about differences between races. Differences within a population can be entirely genetic, while differences between populations can be entirely environmental. As an example, suppose a handful of seed from a genetically variable population of maize is planted in a chemically controlled, uniform environment. All the differences in growth among individuals will then be the consequence of their genetic differences. Suppose a second sample of seed from the same variety is grown in a uniform environment like the first, except it is deficient in an important nutrient, leading to all the seeds growing poorly. Again, the variation among plants within that environment will be entirely genetic, but the difference between the two groups of seed will be entirely environmental. In like manner, the differences in mental performance among individual children within a racial group may be strongly influenced by genetic differences, yet the differences between the groups may be the result of the different social and educational environments in which the groups find themselves.

SEE ALSO *Genetic Variation Among Populations; Genetics, History of; IQ and Testing.*

BIBLIOGRAPHY

Bodmer, Walter F., and Luigi L. Cavalli-Sforza. 1970. "Intelligence and Race" *Scientific American* 223 (October): 19–29.

Lewontin, Richard C. 1974. "Annotation: The Analysis of Variance and the Analysis of Causes." *American Journal of Human Genetics* 26 (3): 401–411.

———, Steven Rose, and Leon J. Kamin. 1984. *Not in Our Genes*. New York: Pantheon.

R.C. Lewontin

HERRNSTEIN, RICHARD J.
1930–1994

The child of Hungarian immigrants, Richard J. Herrnstein was born on May 20, 1930. He received his undergraduate degree at City College of New York before going on to Harvard University, where he studied with the famed psychologist B. F. Skinner. He obtained his Ph.D. in psychology in 1955. After three years in the U. S. Army, during which he worked at the Walter Reed Army Medical Center laboratories in Washington, D.C., he accepted a faculty position at Harvard. He spent the rest of his life at this institution, eventually becoming the Edgar Pierce Professor of Psychology.

Herrnstein initially specialized in animal learning behavior, and he quickly produced a dramatic change in the field by developing a mathematical structure for relating behavior to reinforcement, resulting in what came to be called the "matching law." Taking over the Harvard pigeon lab, which Skinner had made famous, Herrnstein soon established a reputation as one of the leading researchers in the world on the behavior of these birds, and he looked forward to his work having a wide range of applications. He expected, for example, that pigeons would eventually replace—and even outperform—human workers in numerous perfunctory tasks in both industry and military security. By the late 1960s, however, the study of animal behavior had lost the cachet it once enjoyed, and it became relegated to a backwater within the discipline. Herrnstein then turned to the opposite end of the behavioral spectrum, relinquishing the Skinnerian environmentalism that had informed his work with animals in favor of an emphasis on the predominant influence of genes in shaping human intelligence.

In September 1971, Herrnstein published his first contribution to his new interest, a highly controversial article that appeared not in a scientific journal but in a popular magazine, the *Atlantic Monthly*. He did not report any new research, and most of this article was merely a straightforward discussion of the psychometric definition of intelligence and the evidence for its high heritability. In the last couple of pages, however, Herrnstein outlined what he saw as the social implications of the science. He speculated that as equality of opportunity steadily increased, arbitrary advantages would play less and less of a role in determining life outcomes, leaving genetic differences in intelligence as the principal cause of individual differences in earnings and prestige. This would result in a new sort of class stratification, one in which those at the top would deserve their privileged position by virtue of their innate intellectual superiority. At the other end of the economic spectrum, he predicted that "the tendency to be unemployed may run in the genes of a family about as certainly as bad teeth do now" (Herrnstein 1971, p. 63).

Although Herrnstein made no mention of race, the issue of racial differences in intelligence was clearly lurking in the background. Arthur Jensen, an educational psychologist at the University of California, Berkeley, had published his own inflammatory analysis of heredity and intelligence in 1969, concluding that racial differences were in part genetic and that as a consequence current programs of compensatory education were destined to fail. Coming on the heels of Jensen's article, Herrnstein's was perceived as support for the embattled Berkeley professor. In addition, the editors' introductory comments to the article strengthened this impression by presenting Herrnstein's article as a continuation of the discussion on race and intelligence.

Twenty-three years later, the argument that originated in the *Atlantic* was elaborated into *The Bell Curve*, an 845-page tome coauthored by Herrnstein and his collaborator Charles Murray, a policy analyst at the conservative American Enterprise Institute. Much of the book was dedicated to demonstrating that intelligence test scores show a stronger correlation than socioeconomic background to a wide variety of variables indicative of social and occupational success. In other words, the authors held that intelligence exerted greater influence on each of these variables than did class background. This time, however, Herrnstein and Murray included a chapter on "Ethnic Differences in Cognitive Ability," in which they found it "highly likely" that genes were involved in the differences in test scores between blacks and whites, although they were "resolutely agnostic" on the relative strength of the genetic and environmental influences: "As far as we can determine," they wrote, "the evidence does not yet justify an estimate."

Although these comments on racial differences were controversial, what turned the book into a cause célèbre was its discussion of the social policy consequences of genetic differences in intelligence, both among individuals and between races. Insisting that affirmative action had been based on the explicit assumption that there were no genetic differences in intelligence between the races, Herrnstein and Murray called for radical modifications in the policy, both in university admissions and employment decisions. Indeed, they blamed the rash of criminal behavior by police in some cities on the changes in hiring standards introduced by affirmative action measures.

The Bell Curve concluded with a cautionary tale about the risks of ignoring genetic differences in intelligence, and it offered two visions of the future. A failure to face the scientific facts about intelligence, and especially the innate cognitive disadvantage of the underclass, the book predicted, would lead inevitably to a "custodial state." This would essentially be a "high-tech and more lavish version of the Indian reservation," the inhabitants of which, most of them residents of the "inner city," would be segregated from the more capable citizenry and subjected to various forms of surveillance and control. The alternative to this dismal prospect, Herrnstein and Murray argued, was a society that offered "a place for everyone," even the less intelligent, by ensuring that society's rules were simple and direct. Someone caught committing a crime, for example, should have to face consequences that are swift and clear. Likewise, a woman who bore a child out of wedlock should not be able legally to demand support from the father. Thus, the policy implications of genetic intellectual differences turned out to be synonymous with the initiatives promoted by Murray in his capacity as a scholar at a conservative think tank.

Herrnstein died of lung cancer on September 13, 1994, only a week or two before the publication of this hugely controversial book, and he thus did not participate in what one collection of reviews aptly called "The Bell Curve Wars." However, reactions to the publication were intense, ranging from a *Forbes* writer who claimed that *The Bell Curve* was being "seriously compared" with Darwin's *Origin of Species* (Brimelow 1994) to black intellectuals who called it "hate literature with footnotes" (Jones 1995) and "utterly racist" (Patterson 1995).

SEE ALSO *Education, Discrimination in Higher; Education, Racial Disparities; IQ and Testing.*

BIBLIOGRAPHY

PRIMARY WORKS

Herrnstein, Richard J. 1965. "In Defense of Bird Brains." *Atlantic Monthly* 216 (3): 101–104.

———. 1971. "I.Q." *Atlantic Monthly* 228 (3): 43–64.

———, and Charles Murray. 1994. *The Bell Curve: Intelligence and Class Structure in American Life*. New York: Free Press.

SECONDARY WORKS

Brimelow, Peter. 1994. "For Whom the Bell Tolls." *Forbes* (October 24): 153.

Fraser, Steven, ed. 1995. *The Bell Curve Wars: Race, Intelligence, and the Future of America*. New York: Basic Books.

Jones, Jacqueline. 1995. "Back to the Future with *The Bell Curve*: Jim Crow, Slavery, and 'G'." In *The Bell Curve Wars: Race, Intelligence, and the Future of America*, edited by Steven Fraser. New York: Basic Books.

Patterson, Orlando. 1995. "For Whom the Bell Curves." In *The Bell Curve Wars: Race, Intelligence, and the Future of America*, edited by Steven Fraser. New York: Basic Books.

William H. Tucker

HETEROSEXISM AND HOMOPHOBIA

Heterosexism and homophobia are two related forms of oppression that can exist alongside or interact with race and racism. Heterosexism can be defined as a system of power that privileges heterosexual ("straight") people on the basis of their sexual or affectional orientation, while homophobia can be defined as prejudice, discrimination, or violence against lesbian, gay, bisexual, transgender, queer, questioning, or intersex (LGBTQQI) people on the basis of their sexual or affectional difference from heterosexual people. Like racism, sexism, classism, caste prejudice, xenophobia, ageism, and other oppressions, heterosexism and homophobia share a common root: namely, the exercise of social domination based on a negative evaluation of social difference.

Heterosexism and homophobia uphold racism in three key ways: (1) by exacerbating the negativity directed at people who are already subject to racism (for example, gay black people); (2) by strengthening the existing social tendency to create hierarchies based on difference (for example, tacitly ranking black heterosexuals above black LGBTQQI people, or privileging white gay men above black gay men); and (3) by providing additional avenues of discrimination or violence for already vulnerable populations and thus confounding the source of discrimination or violence (such as the routine imprisonment or frequent assault of homeless black transsexuals).

Both heterosexism and homophobia can pertain to prejudice, discrimination, or violence against people on the basis of their gender presentation and its conformity to social norms in addition to prejudice, discrimination, or violence against LGBTQQI people and related systems of power. Thus, heterosexism and homophobia encompass virtually all forms of oppression that relate to physical sex, sexuality, sexual behavior, sexual orientation, sexual preference, affectional preference, sexual identity, gender identity, gender role, and gender expression, particularly when any of these fall outside what society deems normal or traditional. As such, heterosexism and homophobia often intersect with sexism in addition to race and racism.

Heterosexism and homophobia denote a broad general spectrum of experiences that involve negative, unfair, or discriminatory treatment on the basis of sexual orientation or gender expression. Other terminologies that have been used to encompass this spectrum include homonegativism, homoprejudice, gay-bashing, gay-baiting, and hate crimes. Although hate crimes have been the subject of much public discussion and policy development in the United States and globally, researchers agree that there are many forms of negative behavior directed toward LGBTQQI people that fall outside the definition of hate crimes due to their subtler, more informal, or less overtly violent nature. Both survey data and anecdotal reports suggest that the majority of LGBTQQI people have been the target of negative behavior directed at them as the result of their sexual orientation or gender expression. In addition, both research-based and personal accounts indicate that experiences of heterosexism and homophobia have often been compounded by forms of discrimination related to race, gender, class, nationality, culture, religion, ability status, age, or other vectors of social difference.

Intersectionality refers to the fact that various identities and oppressions overlap and interact. For instance, the experience of being white and gay may differ from the experience of being black and gay; the experience of being a lesbian of East Indian descent from a Hindu community may differ from the experience of being a lesbian of East Indian descent from a Muslim community; the experience of being a transgender person living in poverty may differ from the experience of being a wealthy transgender person. While there are commonalities to the LGBTQQI experience, there are also significant differences based on unique aspects of individuals' identity and social location. Even within groups of people claiming the same identity and sharing the same social location (black Christian middle-class lesbians, for instance), there are differences in experience and perspective based on personality and personal history.

EXAMPLES OF HETEROSEXISM AND HOMOPHOBIA

Heterosexism and homophobia, like all forms of oppression, may be expressed at the individual, collective, or institutional levels of society. Furthermore, heterosexism and homophobia, like other forms of oppression, may be reflected in attitudes and feelings, behaviors and practices, cognitions (including beliefs and stereotypes), policies and laws, and even material or symbolic culture. For example, an individual may hold a homophobic feeling, "I don't like gay people," possess a heterosexist belief, "Same-sex couples shouldn't marry," or enact a homophobic act, such as physically assaulting a man who dresses like a woman or a woman who dresses like a man. Groups of people, such as members of a church or a clique in school, may promote homophobic attitudes, as "Homosexuality is evil" or "Trannies (transsexuals) are rejects"; practice heterosexist discrimination, for example, barring homosexual individuals from positions of visibility or leadership in the church, such as the ministry; or engage in homophobic violence, such as vandalizing the locker of a student known to be a lesbian.

Social institutions, such as schools, jails, hospitals, or public welfare agencies, may develop heterosexist or homophobic policies that prevent LGBTQQI people from enjoying the same rights or privileges as heterosexual or gender conforming people. For example, schools may place on detention or expel same-sex student couples who hold hands or kiss, but not different-sex student couples who do the same thing. Furthermore, schools may tacitly discourage or explicitly disallow students of the same sex from attending a prom together, while similar disincentives or prohibitions are not placed upon students of different sexes. Jails may prevent condom distribution because of a desire to not condone or even not acknowledge same-sex sexual activity. Hospitals may deny visitation or consultation rights to the same-sex partner or children of a patient. In other cases, patients are rejected from care on the basis of their presumed sexual orientation or non-traditional gender expression, a particularly common problem for transgender people. In some cases, stereotypes linking LGBTQQI people to HIV/AIDS interfere with access to medical care.

Public welfare agencies may fail to recognize same-sex unions or parental relationships, thus denying access to certain benefits or programs that would be available if the clients were heterosexual. For example, non-biological mothers whose same-sex unions dissolve may lose custody of their children or even visitation rights despite strong bonds between them and their children and years of childrearing. LGBTQQI individuals who live in poverty may be faced with additional challenges. For instance, transgender individuals often have a hard time finding placement in gender-segregated facilities for the unhoused; queer people who are fired from their jobs on the basis of sexual orientation or who experience other forms of discrimination often cannot afford the legal expenses of a civil suit.

Heterosexism and homophobia exist in law as well. For instance, laws that bar same-sex partners from marriage or civil union disallow lesbian and gay couples from a number of rights and privileges that different-sex couples can take for granted, such as tax benefits, insurance benefits, property rights, inheritance rights, adoption rights, visitation rights, and immigration rights. These laws also disadvantage different-sex partners who choose not to marry, although such couples are not subject to

Candlelight Vigil for Matthew Shepard, 1998. *University of Wyoming student Matthew Shepard was beaten to death because of his homosexuality. His assailants were not charged with a hate crime as the state's hate crime law did not include sexual orientation or gender expression.* EVAN AGOSTINI/GETTY IMAGES.

the extra stigma and unique vulnerabilities attached to homosexuality in homophobic and heterosexist societies.

Heterosexism and homophobia abound at the level of material and symbolic culture, most evident in the mass media and everyday social practices. For example, heterosexual couples are common on television, in movies, and in advertisements, whereas homosexual couples are rare. The experiences of heterosexual couples are normalized and presented in great diversity, whereas the experiences of homosexual couples tend to be presented as pathological or comedic departures from the norm. For example, heterosexual couples from a variety of racial, ethnic, and cultural groups, socioeconomic classes (rich, poor, middle class), and religious communities (Christian, Jewish, Islamic) are frequently observed, unlike their lesbian or gay counterparts. (Notably scarce for both groups, however, are interracial, intercultural, or cross-religious unions and families.) Furthermore, individuals whose relational style or preference does not conform to the couple model—for example, people with multiple partners, people in open relationships, polyamorous or polygamous people, or people who are celibate by choice—are rarely represented, or, when they are, are treated as spectacle rather than normalized. The cumulative effect of these depictions is to perpetually reinscribe the notion that heterosexuality and traditional gender expression are normal and good, while homosexuality and non-traditional gender expression are abnormal and bad—producing what Adrienne Rich has termed "compulsory heterosexuality" (1986).

Even language encodes heterosexism and homophobia. In English, there are more words (most of them pejorative) to describe gay men than straight men and lesbian women than straight women. Conversely, there are few words that suggest the possibility of genders other than (or in between) male and female, excluding and minimizing the lived experiences of transgender and intersex people. It has been argued that the dearth of terminology and the lack of articulation of categories to reflect people's lived experience of their own gender and sexuality is partially responsible for contemporary phenomena like the down-low, in which men who appear straight and maintain relationships with women engage in secret homosexual sex while rejecting the label *gay.* While other forms of homophobia and heterosexism certainly contribute to this phenomenon, the absence of an appropriately diversified discourse about gender and sexual expression is likely an important factor.

Finally, social practices like gender-reassignment surgery (in the case of intersex children), gender reassignment therapy (in the case of transgender or intersex individuals who are diagnosed with gender identity disorder), and reorientation therapy (also known as reparative therapy, conversion therapy, or RT—designed to change homosexuality into heterosexuality or asexuality) further invalidate and render invisible the reality that not all people fit into the sexual, gender, and relational categories on which mainstream society has historically relied.

HETEROSEXISM AND HOMOPHOBIA IN HISTORICAL AND GLOBAL PERSPECTIVE

Perspectives on homosexuality, homosociality, gender role, and gender expression have varied across time and culture. Cultures vary with regard to how they define and label sex and gender, and not all cultures devalue same-sex sexual expression. Additionally, virtually all cultures have witnessed historical changes in how they define and label sex and gender as well as the value or stigma they place on same-sex sexual expression. While biological sex, gender expression, gender role, sexual or affectional orientation, and gender or sexual identity are all technically independent of one another (that is, capable of existing in a virtually infinite number of combinations), most societies package these variables in predictable ways and attach value to social scripts that contribute to heterosexism and homophobia.

For example, in the West, male bodies have typically been associated with masculine gender expression, certain "male" social roles, sexual attraction to or interaction with women, and straight identity. In numerous societies, however, particularly historically, latitude has existed for male bodies to be associated with feminine gender expression or female social roles, and/or sexual interaction with males and females. As Walter Williams has shown, a number of societies, from Native American to Southeast Asian, Pacific Islander, Middle Eastern, and African have defined valued gender statuses of this nature, often linked to special statuses within the larger society (1986). In many cases, these statuses have been associated with unique spiritual abilities or responsibilities. While seemingly less common, similar roles for female-bodied or intersex persons have also existed. Many societies have defined what are known as third-sex or third-gender statuses, some naming as many as six unique and identifiable sexes or genders based on different combinations of body (male, female, or intersex), gender role (male, female, or transgender), sexual orientation or behavior (homosexual, heterosexual, or bisexual), and other factors (spiritual, ritual, or preferential).

Societies have varied on (and scholars continue to debate) whether sex, gender, and sexual orientation are natural and fixed (the essentialist position) or arbitrary and historically constituted (the social constructionist position). Many societies have maintained religious doctrines or cosmologies (creation stories) explaining how gender, sex, and sexuality came into being and what are the acceptable variations. At the same time, a great deal of evidence suggests that homosexual behavior and variations in gender expression have always existed across all known societies. How societies have interpreted and explained homosexuality and gender variation, as well as the value societies have placed on these practices, has varied over time and across subpopulations within societies. Each of these perspectives has different implications for how heterosexism and homophobia manifest in society, as well as how each is combated.

ANTI-HETEROSEXIST AND ANTI-HOMOPHOBIC ACTIVISM

In the early 2000s, the rights of LGBTQQI people are the subject of debate and activism. Rights for homosexual and gender variant people are being linked with the larger human rights discourse. Activism focuses on gaining recognition, visibility, and rights, as well as parity in the representational realm, whether political, economic, or symbolic. Since the 1960s, marches for lesbian, gay, bisexual, and transgender rights, also known as pride marches, have become increasingly common around the globe, although LGBTQQI organizing continues to be risky in many countries. In 1996, South Africa achieved international renown by becoming the first nation in the world to incorporate LGBT rights into its national constitution.

In 2007, same-sex marriage was legal in the Netherlands, Belgium, Spain, Canada, and South Africa. Additional countries that recognize civil unions include Andorra, Argentina, Australia (Tasmania only), Brazil, Croatia, Czech Republic, Denmark, Finland, France, Germany, Hungary, Iceland, Israel, Luxembourg, New Zealand, Norway, Portugal, Slovenia, Sweden, and the United Kingdom. In the United States, same-sex marriages or civil unions are recognized to some degree in the states of California, Connecticut, Hawaii, Maine, Massachusetts, New Jersey, and Vermont, as well as the District of Columbia, although this acceptance is highly contested at the national level. At the same time that advances in LGBTQQI rights are taking place, however, anti-gay backlash continues to occur, threatening safety, well-being, and justice for LGBTQQI people around the world. Because LGBTQQI people are whole persons and not just embodiments of sexual orientation or gender expression, anti-heterosexist and anti-homophobic activism targets the elimination of *all* forms of prejudice, discrimination, and violence in society.

SEE ALSO *Feminism and Race; Gay Men; Lesbians.*

BIBLIOGRAPHY

Beam, Joseph, ed. 1986. *In the Life: A Black Gay Anthology.* Boston: Alyson.

Bell, Alan P., and Martin S. Weinberg. 1978. *Homosexualities: A Study of Diversity Among Men and Women.* New York: Simon and Schuster.

Curray, Paisley, Richard M. Juang, and Shannon Price Minter, ed. 2006. *Transgender Rights.* Minneapolis: University of Minnesota Press.

D'Emilio, John, and Estelle B. Freedman. 1988. *Intimate Matters: A History of Sexuality in America.* New York: Harper & Row.

Duneier, Mitchell. 1999. *Sidewalk.* New York: Farrar Straus Giroux.

Feinberg, Leslie. 1997. *Transgender Warriors: Making History from Joan of Arc to Dennis Rodman.* Boston: Beacon.

Foucault, Michel. 1978. *The History of Sexuality,* trans. Robert Hurley. New York: Pantheon.

Graupner, Helmut, and Phillips Tahmindjis, eds. 2005. *Sexuality and Human Rights: A Global Overview.* Binghamton, NY: Harrington Park Press.

Greene, Beverly, ed. 1997. *Ethnic and Cultural Diversity Among Lesbians and Gay Men.* Thousand Oaks, CA: Sage.

Harvey, Andrew, ed. 1997. *The Essential Gay Mystics.* San Fransciso: HarperSanFrancisco.

Hemphill, Essex, ed. 1991. *Brother to Brother: New Writings by Black Gay Men.* Boston: Alyson.

Herek, Gregory M., and Kevin T. Berrill, eds. 1992. *Hate Crimes: Confronting Violence Against Lesbians and Gay Men.* Newbury Park, CA: Sage.

Leong, Russell, ed. 1996. *Asian American Sexualities: Dimensions of the Gay and Lesbian Experience.* New York: Routledge.

Lorde, Audre. 1984. *Sister Outsider: Essays and Speeches.* Trumansburg, NY: Crossing Press.

Mason-John, Valerie, ed. 1995. *Talking Black: Lesbians of African and Asian Descent Speak Out.* London: Cassell.

Murray, Stephen O. 1995. *Latin American Male Homosexualities.* Albuquerque: University of New Mexico Press.

———. 2002. *Pacific Homosexualities.* Lincoln, NE: Writer's Club Press.

———, and Will Roscoe, eds. 1997. *Islamic Homosexualities: Culture, History, and Literature.* New York: New York University Press.

Patton, Cindy, and Benigno Sanchez-Eppler, eds. 2000. *Queer Diasporas.* Durham, NC: Duke University Press.

Peterson, K. Jean. 1996. *Health Care for Lesbians and Gay Men: Confronting Homophobia and Heterosexism.* Binghamton, NY: Haworth Press.

Pharr, Suzanne. 1988. *Homophobia: A Weapon of Sexism.* Inverness, CA: Chardon.

Phillips, Layli. 2006. "Deconstructing 'Down Low' Discourse: The Politics of Sexuality, Gender, Race, AIDS, and Anxiety." *Journal of African American Studies* 9 (2): 3–15.

Potgieter, Cheryl, ed. 2006. "Homosexuality." *Agenda* 67. Available from www.agenda.org.za. Special issue of the South African feminist journal on African homosexualities.

Preves, Sharon E. 2003. *Intersex and Identity: The Contested Self.* New Brunswick, NJ: Rutgers University Press.

Ratti, Rakesh, ed. 1993. *A Lotus of Another Color: An Unfolding of the South Asian Gay and Lesbian Experience.* Boston: Alyson.

Rich, Adrienne. 1986. "Compulsory Heterosexuality and Lesbian Existence." In *Blood, Bread, and Poetry, 1979–1985.* New York: Norton.

Roscoe, Will. 1998. *Changing Ones: Third and Fourth Genders in Native North America.* New York: St. Martin's Press.

Roscoe, Will, and Stephen O. Murray, eds. 1998. *Boy-Wives and Female Husbands: Studies in African Homosexualities.* New York: St. Martin's Press.

Rothblum, Esther D., and Lynne A. Bond, eds. 1996. *Preventing Heterosexism and Homophobia.* Newbury Park, CA: Sage.

Savin-Williams, Ritch C., and Kenneth M. Cohen, eds. 1996. *The Lives of Lesbians, Gays, and Bisexuals: Children to Adults.* Fort Worth, TX: Harcourt Brace.

Seidman, Steven. 2003. *Beyond the Closet.* New York: Routledge.

Smith, Barbara. 1998. *The Truth that Never Hurts: Writings on Race, Gender, and Freedom.* New Brunswick, NJ: Rutgers University Press.

Stryker, Susan, and Stephen Whittle, eds. 2006. *The Transgender Studies Reader.* New York: Routledge.

Warner, Michael, ed. 1993. *Fear of a Queer Planet: Queer Politics and Social Theory.* Minneapolis: University of Minnesota Press.

Williams, Walter. 1986. *The Spirit and the Flesh: Sexual Diversity in American Indian Culture.* Boston: Beacon.

Layli Phillips

HIGHER EDUCATION, DISCRIMINATION IN

SEE *Education, Discrimination in Higher.*

HIP-HOP CULTURE

Hip-hop culture has always had a complex relationship with race. From its inception, the relationship between hip-hop and race has been fragmented, decentralized, and, in many ways, fluid. Hip-hop emerged in the Bronx, New York, in the early 1970s. The economic environment that catalyzed its development reflected the negative effects of a postindustrial society and a rapidly changing economy. Inner-city communities were devastated by the emergent service economy and the shift from domestic manufacturing to overseas outsourcing.

At the same time, the social and racial environments in which hip-hop developed were multifaceted and have yet to be systematically studied. From hip-hop's inception, the youth involved in its genesis were from a diverse array of African, Latino, and European origins. Hip-hop itself would not exist in its current style without the various and diverse contributions of pioneers and artists from the Caribbean and Latin America, as well as their African American neighbors and counterparts in the Bronx.

Most observers identify four foundational elements of hip-hop culture. These components are DJ-ing/turntablism, B-boying/breaking, MC-ing/rapping, and visual/graffiti art. Each component stands on its own, however, with its own artisans, audiences, and commercial products. The intersection of these components in the West and South Bronx generated the cultural revolution of hip-hop. Although rap music and hip hop are often used interchangeably, rap is only one of (at least) four elements of hip hop. A brief explanation of these elements underscores their original emergence and sets the stage for the corresponding racial categorizations.

DJ-ing is the deliberate and technical manipulation of the turntable, ultimately transforming it from a simple musical platform into a full-blown musical instrument with its own arsenal of sounds, such as scratches, temporally manipulated tones, sonic cuts, and samples (short bits of other people's music). B-Boying refers to the kinesthetic or body responses to the DJ's isolation of "break" beats on vinyl records. B-boys would break during the isolation and looping of break beats at the original hip-hop jams (parties). The break is that part of a song where the track is stripped down to its most fundamentally percussive elements. The connection between the highly percussive or beat-oriented segments in hip-hop music and the power of the drum in African and African-American cultures should not be overlooked or underestimated. Hip-hop music captures and reflects the power of the drum in its dance and music.

The MC is the verbal arbiter of hip-hop culture. Originally cast as a tangential hype-man for the earliest well-known DJs in hip-hop, the MC has now graduated to the foreground of the culture. The poets, MCs, and rappers of hip-hop have become the main purveyor of rap music's dominance on the pop culture landscape. Graffiti art is the element of the culture that most clearly and singularly predates the genesis of hip-hop. Indeed, graffiti can be traced back to ancient times. However, its development in conjunction with the other foundational elements of hip-hop is striking. Graffiti provided a viable artistic platform for poverty-stricken inner city youth, whose artistic outlets were diminished in most public institutions. In addition, in the 1970s there was a drastic reduction of musical and arts programs in public schools, and of funds that supported recreational centers and other public platforms for creative production. Many scholars have referred to hip-hop's graffiti art as one of the most potent signals of young people's reclamation of public spaces, which have been utterly privatized in this postmodern era. One generation's rampant vandalism is indeed another generation's revolutionary movement.

At the risk of promoting racial essentialism in hip-hop culture, the following is a brief outline of several of the seminal figures in the origins, development, and growth of hip-hop underscores the postmodern quality of the racial dynamics within the culture. To begin with, the consensus founder of hip-hop culture is known as DJ Kool Herc (Clive Campbell). Born in Kingston, Jamaica, not very far from Bob Marley's neighborhood of origin, Herc moved with his family to the West Bronx in the late 1960s. Before long he borrowed elements of Jamaican "dub" and "yard" cultures and infused these public performance techniques with African-American soul music, the verbal styles of radio disc jockeys, and the aforementioned developing elements of hip-hop (especially graffiti art).

Herc's sensibilities for these forms, and his understanding of their potential to entertain inner city youth in postindustrial New York, bloomed suddenly in the summer of 1973, when he took over for a DJ at his sister's birthday party, held in the rec room of their housing project. From this point forward, the hip-hop "jam" became the fastest-growing and most engaging form of youth entertainment. In interviews and in public appearances, Kool Herc readily concedes the importance of his relationships with African-American and Latino youth, as well as his Jamaican heritage and love of African-American soul music. In particular, James Brown's soulful stylings and live music performances inspired Kool Herc's desire to

Breakdancer Performing in a New York Subway, 2003. *Breakdancing first became popular through local performances in parks and clubs in New York City during the early to mid-1970s. It found a mainstream audience through movies such as* Flashdance *and* Beatstreet. © JERRY ARCIERI/CORBIS.

isolate the break beats of records in order to extend the most danceable aspects of the original hip-hop jams.

At least two other DJs share the honor as founders of hip-hop: Afrika Bambaataa, of West Indian heritage, and Grandmaster Flash who is of Jamaican heritage. Aside from being one of the originally eclectic hip-hop DJs (e.g., using music from Japan and Germany, and borrowing and sampling from electronica and disco), Afika Bambaataa was also a leading figure in one of the largest and most notorious street gangs, the Black Spades. During the early stages of hip-hop culture, Bam was the leader of the movement within the Black Spades to transition away from the violent activity usually associated with gangs. The result was the birth of the largest and longest-lasting community arts organization in hip-hop culture: the Zulu Nation. DJ Grandmaster Flash learned the basic technique of scratching from Grand Wizard Theodore, and in the mid-1970s he developed it in a way that transformed the turntable into a bona fide instrument.

Although youth from all backgrounds have been influential in "breaking" (sometimes referred to as "break dancing"), the earliest pioneers are of Latin American origins. One of the first dominant breaking crews was the Rock Steady Crew. One of this group's leaders and most endearing personalities is Crazy Legs, who starred in a number of Hollywood films, including *Flashdance* (1983) and *Beatstreet* (1984). Though he witnessed the decline in mainstream popularity of breaking, he continues to be an ambassador for hip-hop dance forms all over the world.

One of the first MCs, Busy Bee starred in the groundbreaking docudrama *Wild Style* (1982). Of African-American origin, MCs and rappers such as Busy Bee, Coke La Rock, Grandmaster Caz, and Melle Mel extended the African-American oral tradition (including field hollers, ring shouts, spirituals, the blues, sermons, toasts, and playing the dozens) into the twenty-first century with their rap lyrics. The best rappers and MCs have generally been of African-American origin—Rakim, Jay-Z, Nas, and Tupac Shakur are usually included in this group, though this is not to exclude their West Indian counterpart,

Notorious B.I.G., whose Jamaican American heritage informed his milky and melodic lyrical delivery.

One of the most noted pioneers of graffiti art in hip-hop culture was a young Greek-American named Demetrius. His "graf tag," Taki 183, is credited as one of the first monikers to go "all-city" (i.e., to be recognized in all five boroughs of New York City) via its ubiquitous presence on subway trains and various neighborhoods. Many graffiti pioneers were of Latin American descent, such as the extraordinary Lady Pink, who braved the same dangers and pitfalls of graffiti writing as her male counterparts. Clearly, "graf art" is another element of hip-hop in which African-American ethnicity is not an essential prerequisite to artistic or commercial success.

It is admittedly a racially essentialist conclusion to assert that any of the aforementioned elements of hip-hop are dominated by any particular ethnic group. Yet each element, through its pioneers and most significant contributors, often suggests a particular ethnicity's penchant for artistic expression. So it may be appropriate to conclude that young people of European descent have (at least in America and Europe) been more prominent in graffiti artistry than in MC-ing or rapping. Likewise, Latin American acrobats have been more prominent in breaking and B-boying than in MC-ing or rapping. DJs tend to run the ethnic gamut, though various DJs of Asian ethnicity dominated international competitions in the early twenty-first century. These racial assignments and categorizations ultimately deconstruct the spirit of hip-hop culture, which tends to invite people of all hues to participate in and experience what is the most pervasive popular form of entertainment across the globe in the early twenty-first century.

SEE ALSO *Black Popular Culture; Rap Music.*

BIBLIOGRAPHY

Chang, Jeff. 2005. *Can't Stop, Won't Stop: A History of the Hip-Hop Generation.* New York: St Martin's Press.

Forman, Murray, and Mark Anthony Neal, eds. 2004. *That's the Joint! The Hip-Hop Studies Reader.* New York: Routledge.

George, Nelson. 1998. *Hip Hop America.* New York: Viking Penguin.

James Peterson

HIV AND AIDS

During 2005, around 4.1 million adults and children became infected with the human immunodeficiency virus (HIV), the virus that causes acquired immunodeficiency syndrome (AIDS). By the end of the year, an estimated 38.6 million people worldwide were living with HIV, according to the World Health Organization (WHO) and the Joint United Nations Programme on HIV/AIDS (UNAIDS 2006) report. Since the beginning of the epidemic in the 1980s, 32 million people have died from AIDS, but it is increasingly clear that this global health crisis has not impacted populations equally. Rather, patterns of social and economic inequality are evident in the hardest-hit AIDS epicenters around the world.

Of those living with HIV globally, 95 percent live in developing countries. In contrast to western and central Europe and North America where the number of people living with HIV is estimated to be 720,000 and 1.2 million, respectively, in Asia, 930,000 people were newly infected in 2005, bringing the total number of people living with HIV in the region to 8.3 million, with more than two-thirds of them living in India.

However, sub-Saharan Africa is by far the worst-hit region, with 24.5 million people estimated to be HIV infected. This region is home to just over 10 percent of the world's population, but almost two-thirds of all people living with HIV reside there. Across sub-Saharan Africa, HIV prevalence rates (proportion of people living with HIV) vary significantly between and within sub-regions and countries. While several southern African countries have HIV prevalence rates above 17 percent (with Botswana and Swaziland having the highest prevalence rates of 24% and 33%, respectively), prevalence rates in West African countries are much lower (with adult HIV prevalence rates lower that 2% in most countries). More serious epidemics are in Central and East Africa where HIV prevalence rates range from 4 to13 percent.

In the Caribbean region—which is the second most affected region—prevalence rates in the Bahamas (3.3%) and Haiti (3.8%) are the highest outside of the African continent. An estimated 330,000 people were living with the virus in 2005. In the same year, Latin America reported around 104,000 new HIV infection cases, and an estimated total of 1.6 million people living with HIV, about one-third are residing in Brazil.

In the United States, of the estimated 1.2 million people reported to be living with HIV in 2005, historically oppressed African American and Latino populations accounted for more than 73% of new HIV infections, although they represented only 12 and 11 percent, respectively, of the U.S. population (Centers for Disease Control 2003). Thus, in both resource-poor and resource-rich countries, HIV/AIDS has increasingly been concentrated in the poorest, most marginalized sectors of society (Parker 2002).

Three general factors have influenced the overlapping crises and the distinct dynamics of the epidemic: (1)

poverty and economic underdevelopment; (2) mobility and patterns of community instability, including migration and social disruption due to war and political or community marginalization; and (3) gender inequalities (Parker, Easton, and Klein 2000). These structural factors are at work across all countries and also help elucidate how HIV and AIDS disproportionately impact indigenous people of color, particularly people of African descent, for whom larger health and social welfare inequities are tied to the enduring legacy of racism. Accordingly, this discussion situates the disease within a sociocultural context and delineates the ways in which racism underlies the alarming rates of HIV-infection among African descent populations that have historically been the targets of inequity and racism on a global scale.

HISTORICAL RACISM, SOCIAL AND HEALTH INEQUITIES, AND HIV/AIDS

Globally, racism plays a role in vulnerability to health disparities, including HIV/AIDS. Long before AIDS, many of the issues that place people at risk for HIV/AIDS occurred along the contours of racial oppression for marginalized indigenous populations, specifically among people of African descent. In discussing global health disparities, Raymond Cox contends that "systematic and widespread discrimination over centuries has manifested itself in poor living conditions and poor health of indigenous peoples and people of African descent all over the world" (Cox 2004, p. 548). The experience of sub-Sahara Africa sets the stage for examining historical conquest, violence, and oppression as a backdrop to socio-political conditions which have enabled the rapid spread of HIV/AIDS across the African Diaspora.

European colonialism and imperialism, and the artificial boundaries these systems imposed on Africa, exacerbated sociopolitical upheaval. The disintegration of traditional socioeconomic structures led to conflicts, poverty, and family and community disruption; forced migration; and involuntary displacements. South Africa, a country whose racist apartheid system deprived blacks of education and access to health care, is home to the second largest number of AIDS cases. Apartheid pervaded South African culture and supported the treatment of nonwhite South Africans as second-class citizens. During the 1960s and1970s, the government implemented a policy of "resettlement" that forced nonwhites to move to government-specified areas, or "homelands," where blacks rarely had plumbing or electricity, and where access to transport, hospitals, and health-care facilities was sharply curtailed. Highly developed white hospitals were off limits to blacks, whose few hospitals were seriously understaffed and underfunded. Further, within the tragic pattern of forced removal of blacks to "resettlement zones" and the destruction of indigenous family life, black South African miners and other laborers worked long periods away from home and family. This became an underlying factor in increases in sex worker services and a major factor contributing to the HIV/AIDS epidemic (Sachs 2000, Robins 2005). Within this entrenched migrant-labor dynamic, it is estimated that AIDS may have been spreading at the explosive rate of more than 500 new cases per day. In 1982 the first recorded death from HIV occurred in the country, and by the mid-1990s the death toll had reached 10,000. In the United States, meanwhile, HIV/AIDS was ballooning into a health crisis, most notably for historically oppressed ethnic minority populations, African Americans and Hispanics. The U.S. epidemic ostensibly began as an epidemic of gay white males; however, the changing face of AIDS became evident in the mid-1990s as the percentages of AIDS cases among whites declined but grew disproportionately among people of color, especially African Americans. In 1985 blacks accounted for 25 percent of diagnosed AIDS cases but this figure rose to 50 percent by 2005 according to the Centers for Disease Control (CDC 2006). In 2003 the rate of AIDS diagnoses for African Americans was almost ten times the rate for whites and almost three times the rate for Hispanics. African-American men had AIDS rates eight times that of white men, while the rate of AIDS diagnoses for African American women was 25 times the rate for white women. In 2002 AIDS was the number one cause of death for African-American women between twenty-five and thirty-four years of age, and AIDS ranks in the top three causes of death for African Americans aged twenty-five to thirty-four (CDC 2006).

The AIDS epidemic among African Americans has been shaped by poverty, chemical dependency, lack of accessible health care, mistrust of medical and other institutions, isolation, institutionalized racism, and internalized oppression (Gilbert 2003). It unfolded parallel to a rise in intravenous drug use and crack cocaine use, a situation only worsened by biased law enforcement practices and the increased arrests associated with the 1980s "war on drugs," forcing a disproportionate number of black men to enter the penal system. Nearly half of all prisoners in state and federal jurisdictions and almost 40 percent of juveniles in legal custody are African Americans; and in 2003, the AIDS prevalence in state and federal prisons (0.51%) was more than 3 times higher than in the general U.S. population (0.15%) (Maruschak 2005).

Similar to people of African descent around the world, black Americans already suffered from serious health and standard of living disparities predating AIDS. The death rate for African Americans is higher than non-Hispanic Whites for heart diseases, stroke, cancer, chronic lower respiratory diseases, influenza and pneumonia, diabetes, and homicide. African Americans make up 40 percent of the homeless population; and infant mortality rates among U.S. blacks outpace those of some developing countries. Depression among African American women is almost 50 percent higher than that of white women. Not surprising, the U.S. Institute of Medicine released a report in 2002 that documented increasing evidence that, even after such differences as income, insurance status, and medical need are accounted for, race and ethnicity remained significant predictors of the quality of health care received by African Americans (Smedley, Stith, and Nelson 2003). The report confirmed racial and ethnic bias in the U.S. health care system, and that people of African descent suffer poorer health, use fewer health services, and are less satisfied with health-services encounters than almost any other ethnic group. Thus, issues such as providers' attitudes, communication with persons of color, and lack of cultural competence are factors in not only maintaining these disparities, but also in exacerbating them. Such patterns of health and HIV infection disparities are found in other countries where people of African descent are disproportionately poor and disenfranchised. In Brazil, which has the largest population of African descent outside the African continent, black and brown children are twice as likely as white children to die before the age of one (Cox 2004). Although the country has always boasted of its lack of racial problems, recent developments have highlighted racial disparities and pushed Brazilians to come to terms with how race affects virtually all aspects in their lives, from education to employment to justice. Around 47 percent of Brazil's 185 million people are black, and half of them live in poverty. Blacks in Brazil are twice as likely as whites to be poor and to receive less schooling, and they are more likely to die at a younger age than whites. These statistics underscore how HIV infection rates parallel color lines in Brazil. Brazilian blacks are nearly twice as likely as whites not to know how HIV is transmitted and, thus, to not know how to protect themselves from the virus (Hay 2005). Further, between 2000 and 2004, new cases of AIDS among people who declared themselves black or brown rose from 33.4 percent to 37.2 percent for men and from 35.6 percent to 42.4 percent for women (Hay 2005).

Even in countries such as the United Kingdom, Canada, Australia, New Zealand, and Columbia, where advanced risk-sharing systems of health care should protect its residents equally, people of color are not in fact protected as well as others. In Canada, for example, disparities among the indigenous population and among people of African descent exist, and cultural incompetence among healthcare workers has been acknowledged as a cause for these disparities. Poverty rates among persons of color in Canada are unacceptably high, reaching as high as 50 percent for some groups, such as recent black immigrants (Jackson 2001). As a result, blacks are highly overrepresented among those suffering from HIV/AIDS. In the 2001 census, black people accounted for 2.2 percent of Canada's population but represented 15.1 percent of AIDS cases with known ethnicity. At the same time, the proportion of cases among white Canadians declined from 87.5 percent in 1993 to 64.1 percent in the first half of 2002 (CDC 2003). In sum, across continents and within countries, the patterns of HIV infection rates underscore the reality of health vulnerabilities grounded in inequitable access and treatment.

RACE, CULTURAL IDENTITY, AND GLOBAL RESPONSES TO HIV/AIDS

Sociopolitical constructions frame society's responses to any epidemic, and people with HIV/AIDS have frequently been blamed for their condition, rather than being viewed in the contexts of marginalization and inequity. For example, the initial categories of "high risk" groups (i.e., gay men, Haitians, Africans, sex workers) obscured the sociopolitical constructions of HIV. Early responses to AIDS were crippled by a lack of knowledge about the sociocultural context of the lives of historically oppressed people, including an understanding of how structural impediments rooted in institutionalized racism often place people in "high risk situations" (Zwi and Cabral 1992) and limit the options people can choose as a means of survival. Among these impediments are poverty, sociopolitical inequity, underdevelopment of education, disparities in health and healthcare, and marginalized and inadequate living conditions. Life choices to avoid HIV infection typically depend on the extent to which individuals have access to, and personal agency to obtain, crucial societal resources such as food, shelter, safety, money, education, and appropriate mental and physical health care.

Further, negative stereotyping and devaluing one's group can lead to a weakening of self-regard and group pride, and can express itself in depression, despair, and self-abuse. Substance abuse, for instance, has been linked to deteriorating communities and hopelessness. In addition, in-group horizontal oppression often translates into the imposition of stigma, sexism, heterosexism, and oppression against less-empowered members, such as women and children, homosexuals, and other HIV infected persons. These internal group dynamics can, in turn, create added vulnerability to HIV infection. Further, the extent to which people of African descent are affected by a distrust of whites and the notion that Eurocentric health information is untrustworthy constitutes another hindrance. This distrust can foster conspiracy theories (i.e., AIDS is a manmade virus that is being

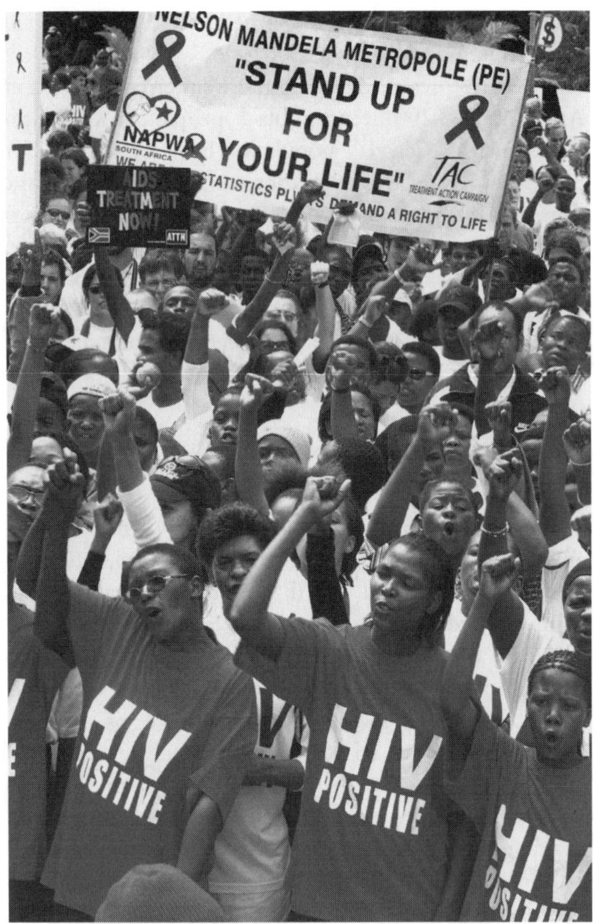

AIDS Activists Protest in Cape Town, South Africa, 2003. *HIV and AIDS is highly prevalent in Africa. Here AIDS activists gather in Cape Town to protest South African president Mbeki's failure to address the issue in his annual state of the nation address.* AP IMAGES.

employed against blacks) as a way to make meaning of the disease and tragedy when accurate information is missing. Lack of information and educational disparities also remain a major barrier. For example, in Botswana where the HIV prevalence rate is 24.1 percent, only one in ten survey participant knew three ways of preventing sexual transmission of HIV (UNAIDS 2006).

HIV/AIDS researchers and policymakers have only recently acknowledged the ways in which early responses failed to adequately address the needs of people of African descent. Nowhere has the slow response to address HIV transmission and treatment been more controversial than in South Africa where President Mbeki persistently questioned, rather than taking action against, the startling HIV infection rates and projections. Steven Robins (2004) notes that while there is a need to avoid the construction of AIDS as a "black disease," the government's slow response along with popularly held AIDS myths, stigma, and shame created a sense of denial among the general population as well as policymakers and politicians. Former South African president Nelson Mandela's 2005 announcement that his son died of AIDS sent a strong message about breaking down barriers surrounding the disease's public stigma and putting pressure on the government to take prevention and treatment efforts seriously. At the 2006 International AIDS Conference in Toronto, the South African government faced severe criticism about its policies encouraging traditional remedies such as beetroot and garlic over antiretroviral drugs. While there has been some treatment progress, less than 20 percent of the almost one million South Africans in need of antiretroviral treatment were receiving it in 2005 (UNAIDS 2006).

Advances in tackling HIV/AIDS around the world can occur through culturally congruent programs that address structural and cultural forces and the daily realities of people who contend with racial oppression. For example, despite poverty, war, and social disruption, Uganda's political leadership declared AIDS a national priority as early as 1986 and responded swiftly with educational programs backed by the participation of traditional religious and community leaders and prevention strategies that were integrated with media, popular culture, the arts, and school systems (Irwin, Millen, and Fallows 2003). As a result, while HIV infection rates rose sharply in late 1990s in many other African countries, Uganda saw a steep decline in HIV prevalence during the mid and late 1990s.

Brazil is noted for its universal free access to antiretroviral therapies that has nearly halved AIDS-related deaths. However, in 2005 leaders of Brazil's AIDS Program acknowledged that racism is an additional factor in HIV vulnerability, pointing to new statistics that AIDS among people of African descent was on the rise. The ministry launched the "AIDS is RACISM" campaign to encourage more blacks to seek information on HIV/AIDS (Hay 2005). Similarly, in the United States, despite treatment advances in antiretroviral medications that can allow people to live with HIV as a chronic illness, blacks have not realized the same benefits. Black Americans account for more AIDS-related deaths than any other racial/ethnic group and blacks with HIV/AIDS face greater barriers to treatment, including lack of transportation and health insurance. In his noteworthy 1989 essay "AIDS in Blackface," Harlon Dalton questioned how much whites would commit to sociopolitical action toward eradicating AIDS, a disease of the most politically weak and negatively socially constructed target population. Indeed, concern is mounting that as the disease has shifted away from whites to blacks, the general public has become less concerned and alarmed by the epidemic (Jaffe 2004).

Despite the fact that AIDS is a preventable and treatable disease, racism continues to play a strong force in structural impediments to effective prevention and intervention among African decent people worldwide. On a global scale, recent progress has been made through UNAIDS toward building a renewed international response to the HIV/AIDS epidemic; however, the path of progress remains unclear. Yet, it is clear that the health of people of African descent is inextricably tied to the broader struggles of equity and social justice in health, education, and social welfare. Therefore, organizations such as the Global AIDS Alliance, an organization dedicated to mobilizing the political will and financial resources needed to slow, and ultimately stop, the global AIDS crisis and reduce its impact on poor people and poor countries are of vital importance as a unified voice in continuing to focus attention on responsible and equitable treatment and global AIDS policies.

SEE ALSO *Brazilian Racial Formations; Caribbean Racial Formations; Cuban Racial Formations; Diseases, Racial; Haitian Racial Formations; Medical Racism; Social Problems; South African Racial Formations; Transnationalism; United Kingdom Racial Formations.*

BIBLIOGRAPHY

Centers for Disease Control and Prevention. 2003. "Aboriginals, Blacks Hit Hardest by AIDS." Bethesda, MD: CDC National Center for HIV, STD and TB Prevention.

———. 2006. *HIV/AIDS Surveillance Report, 2006*. Bethesda, MD: CDC. Available from http://www.cdc.gov/hiv/topics/surveillance/resources/reports/index.htm.

Cox, Raymond L. 2004. "Global Health Disparities: Crisis in the Diaspora." *Journal of the National Medical Association* 96 (4): 546–549.

Dalton, Harlon L. 1989. "AIDS in Blackface." *Daedalus* 118 (3): 205–227.

Gilbert, Dorie J. 2003. "Sociocultural Construction of AIDS among African American Women." In *African American Women and HIV/AIDS: Critical Responses*, edited by Dorie J. Gilbert and Ednita M. Wright. Westport: CT: Praeger Publishers.

Hay, Andrew. 2005. "Brazil Bucks AIDS Trend, but Blacks Are Hard-Hit." Reuters newsMedia. Available from: http://www.aegis.com/news/re/2005/RE051153.html.

Irwin, Alexander, Joyce Millen, and Dorothy Fallows. 2003. *Global AIDS: Myths and Facts*. Cambridge, MA: South End Press.

Jackson, Andrew. 2001. "Poverty and Racism." Canadian Council on Social Development. *Perception* 24 (4). Available from http://www.ccsd.ca/perception/244/racism.htm.

Jaffe, Harold. 2004. "Whatever Happened to the U.S. AIDS Epidemic?" *Science* 305 (5688): 1243–1244.

Joint United Nations Programme on HIV/AIDS (UNAIDS). *2006 Report on the Global AIDS Epidemic.*. Available from http://data.unaids.org/pub/GlobalReport/2006_GR_CH02-en.pdf.

Maruschak, Laura M. 2005. "HIV in Prisons, 2003." Washington, DC: U.S. Department of Justice, Bureau of Justice Statistics.

Parker, Richard. 2002. "The Global HIV/AIDS Pandemic, Structural Inequalities, and the Politics of International Health." *American Journal of Public Health* 92 (3): 343–346.

———, Delia Easton, and Charles H. Klein. 2000. "Structural Barriers and Facilitators in HIV Prevention: A Review of International Research." *AIDS* 14 (Suppl. 1): 22–32.

Robins, Steven. 2004. "Long Live Zackie, Long Live": AIDS Activism, Science, and Citizenship after Apartheid." *Journal of Southern African Studies* 30 (3) 651–672.

Sachs, Johnny. 2000. "South Africa as the Epicenter of HIV/AIDS: Vital Political Legacies and Current Debates." *Current Issues in Comparative Education* 3 (1). Available from http://www.tc.columbia.edu/CICE/Archives/3.1/31sachs.pdf.

Smedley, Brian D., Adrienne Y. Stith, and Alan R. Nelson, eds. 2003 2002. *Unequal Treatment: Confronting Racial and Ethnic Disparities in Healthcare.* Washington, DC: National Academic Press.

Zwi, Anthony, and A. J. R. Cabral. 1992. "Identifying 'High Risk Situations' for Preventing AIDS." *British Medical Journal* 303 (6816): 1527–1529.

Dorie J. Gilbert

HOAXING

A racial hoax is an instance when someone falsely places blame for a real or fabricated crime on another person because of that person's race. The crime may be real or staged, and the falsely accused person may be real or imaginary. Although a person of any race can perpetrate a racial hoax against a person of any other race, the most common racial hoaxes have historically involved whites falsely accusing blacks of criminal activity.

Racial hoaxes play on stereotypes about racial Others. Their believability depends upon the general public already possessing strong negative stereotypes about racialized groups, which form the basic premises of racial hoaxes. Throughout the whole of colonial and American history, whites have routinely developed, popularized, and generally believed negative stereotypes about people of color, especially African Americans. Negative stereotypes specific to African Americans, who are the usual targets of white-initiated racial hoaxes, include myths describing black people as hypersexual, randomly violent, lacking self-control, and emotionally and intellectually inferior to whites. As these myths spread through media, anecdotal stories, and popular culture, negative beliefs about people of color become rooted in whites' minds.

People who attempt racial hoaxes choose their racial targets and craft their stories to fit these stereotypes. A famous example occurred in 1994, when Susan Smith, a young white mother in South Carolina, claimed "a surly black man wearing a dark knit cap" had carjacked her and driven off with her two young children in the back seat. For several days, Smith issued public pleas for the safe return of her children, and the police publicized a composite image of a black man and asked residents to come forward with information. Large numbers of black men were suddenly under public suspicion of kidnapping. For nine days, Smith carried on her story before confessing to police that she had murdered her own children. She led police to where she had strapped her children in her car and rolled the car into a lake.

Smith's hoax exemplifies the relationship between racial hoaxes and stereotypes. Smith's story depended upon the belief that black men are dangerous and frequently commit acts of random violence. The massive official response, and the fact that most whites initially believed Smith's story, indicates the pervasiveness of the stereotype of black men as dangerous criminals. In this way, racial hoaxes clearly demonstrate the continuing reality of pervasive white racism in contemporary society.

The extreme number and popularity of negative stereotypes against people of color, especially black men, and the paucity of negative stereotypes about whites play a major role in the large disparity between incidents of white-initiated racial hoaxes and those initiated by people of color. Negative stereotypes against people of color make hoaxes believable. In the absence of stereotypes, hoaxes are often nonsensical and obvious lies *prima facie*. In addition, the widespread acceptance of negative stereotypes has produced an atmosphere in which whites are quick to believe racial hoaxes claiming black criminality but are more skeptical about claims of white criminality.

A second reason for the greater frequency of white-on-black hoaxes is the disproportionate amount of institutional power whites have over people of color in the United States. The story of Charles Stuart illustrates this point. In October of 1989, Charles Stuart, a white Bostonian, with the help of his brother and a friend, murdered his pregnant wife and then shot himself in the stomach. As part of the cover-up, Stuart telephoned police and claimed a black man in a jogging suit had committed the crime. At the mayor's direction, police detectives rushed to Stuart's aid. Police officers randomly stopped, harassed, and interrogated dozens of innocent young black men throughout the mostly black neighborhood where Stuart claimed the crime had occurred. During this process the police detained several innocent black men, and they nearly arrested one black man who Stuart had identified in a lineup. After two months of searches and investigations and a tip from Charles' brother, police finally decided to question Stuart about the events. Sensing their suspicion, Stuart took his own life rather than face murder charges.

White-on-black racial hoaxes are frequently effective because they receive massive institutional support from whites who control major institutions, such as police departments and judiciaries. Because anti-black stereotypes make claims about the fundamental nature and character of all black people, the white public and white-run institutions react to hoaxes by effectively considering all black people as suspicious and criminal. Hoaxes in which people of color falsely blame whites do not have this effect because negative stereotypes about the general character of white people are uncommon, and because people of color do not have the institutional power to effectively criminalize all whites. Instead, hoaxes initiated by people of color are often met with initial suspicion and, when taken seriously, result only in limited searches for guilty individuals rather than general searches through entire white neighborhoods.

The importance of unequal institutional power is even more apparent when one considers the history of racial hoaxes in the United States. During the slavery and Jim Crow periods (1619–1965), whites had complete control over every government institution, including the police and the courts. Extensive and overt white racism allowed whites to completely disregard the testimony of blacks and the objective evidence of cases. Mere accusations from whites were sufficient to convict people of color in a court of law. Often, black people never even reached a courtroom, while white mobs lynched unknown numbers of black men (official estimates are over 6,000), usually as scapegoats after whites accused them of petty theft or sexual promiscuity with white women, as occurred in the Rosewood, Florida, massacre of 1923. In this case, a white mob burned down the black community of Rosewood after a white woman falsely claimed that a black man had raped her.

Some racial hoaxes, however, have been perpetrated by people of color against whites. Most often these hoaxes involve people of color claiming to be victims of racial hate crimes. White-originated hoaxes are usually not classified as such until perpetrators confess their fabrications. Hoaxes against whites, however, are more frequently deemed hoaxes by white officials without confessions from the people of color who made the original claim.

Perhaps the most famous hoax of this type is the 1987 case of Tawana Brawley. Brawley, a fifteen-year-old black girl, was found in New York State covered in feces and racial slurs written in charcoal. She claimed that six white police officers had abducted and raped her before leaving her in the condition in which she was discovered. Several black community leaders, including the Reverend Al Sharpton, supported Brawley and brought national attention to the incident. Eventually, investigators claimed Brawley's accusation to be a racial hoax. Ten years after the event, Sharpton and other Brawley supporters were found liable for defaming the accused officers. Nevertheless, Brawley consistently claimed that the officers did in fact rape her and perpetrate a hate crime against her.

Racial hoaxes continue to be common. Kathryn Russell-Brown, the director of the Center for the Study of Race and Race Relations at the University of Florida, has found 68 examples of racial hoaxes that occurred in the United States between 1987 and 1996. Seventy percent of these involved whites falsely accusing people of color. Among these cases, several trends are worth noting. First, white-initiated racial hoaxes are more frequent and usually involve whites blaming black men for extremely violent actions such as rape and murder. Accusations from people of color usually falsely claim that whites have perpetrated hate crimes against them. Second, white law-enforcement officers were the most frequent initiators of racial hoaxes. This is especially disturbing when one considers the trust and power the public places in these officers. Finally, white-initiated hoaxes are usually classified as hoaxes only after offenders confess their dishonesty. Conversely, white officials often classify black claims as hoaxes in the absence of confessions. This trend and the ubiquity of stereotypes against people of color suggest that far more blacks have been victims of white-initiated racial hoaxes than history records.

SEE ALSO *Criminal Justice System; Criminality, Race and Social Factors.*

BIBLIOGRAPHY

Feagin, Joe R. 2000. *Racist America: Roots, Current Realities, and Future Reparations.* New York: Routledge.

———, Vera Hernán Vera, and Pinar Batur. 2001. *White Racism: The Basics,* 2nd ed. New York: Routledge.

Fine, Gary A., and Patricia A. Turner. 2001. *Whispers on the Color Line: Rumor and Race in America.* Berkeley: University of California Press.

Russell-Brown, Kathryn. 1998. *The Color of Crime: Racial Hoaxes, White Fear, Black Protectionism, Police Harassment, and Other Macroaggressions.* New York: New York University Press.

Glenn E. Bracey II
Joe R. Feagin

HOLOCAUST

Winston Churchill described the mass murder of European Jewry by Nazi Germany and its allies as "a crime without a name." The perpetrators, the National Socialist (Nazi) regime in Germany called it *Die Endlösung der Judenfrage* (the Final Solution of the Jewish Question). The number of Jewish victims is generally regarded to be between 5.8 and 6 million. Later, this extermination policy became known as the Holocaust, or "Shoah" in Hebrew. In a more generic and legalistic formula, the Holocaust was an example of genocide, a word invented by Raphael Lemkin in 1943. The word *holocaust* is derived from the Greek *holokaustos,* meaning a "burnt offering," as used in a religious sacrifice.

Since the end of World War II and the development of more critical studies of this event, other racial, religious, asocial and political groups have been identified and included as victims of the Holocaust. These include the Roma and Sinti (Gypsies), victims of the T-4 program (killings carried out because of genetic disorders), Jehovah's Witnesses, political prisoners, Poles, and homosexuals. The use of the word "Shoah" tends to limit the issue to Jews only, as is the case with the commemorative day on the Jewish calendar, the 27th day of the month of Nisan. In 2006, the United Nations adopted January 27 (the date on which the Auschwitz death camp was liberated in 1945 by troops of the Soviet Army) as an International Day of Commemoration in Memory of the Victims of the Holocaust.

RACISM IN NAZI GERMANY

Racism played a key role in defining the victims of Nazi persecution, and it became lethal when it was mixed with German nationalism, folk concepts of blood and soil that helped define insiders and outsiders, issues of degeneracy, fear of chaos and outside enemies, a world war, and the application of modern scientific and medical technologies to mass killing. In the case of the extermination of the Jews, race was also indistinguishable from Jewish religious practice. In 1931 the National Socialist Party established the Race and Resettlement Office (Rasse-und Siedlungshauptamt, or RuSHA), which became a Schutz-staffel (SS) Main Office in 1935. Ultimately, this office was concerned with population transfer policies and the extermination of the Jews and other undesirable groups.

However, while race was the defining issue in the Holocaust, other factors were also present, including economic motivations that involved German medical doctors, lawyers, and businesses getting rid of their Jewish competitors in order to improve wage conditions; the seizure or sale of property during a process called "Aryanization," in which the Jewish owners received only a small percentage of the property value; the seizure and sale in other countries of "degenerate art" from museum collections, and, later, the massive pilfering of private Jewish art collections. Aryanization and the subsequent ethnic cleansing of Jews in occupied countries made it easy to justify property transfers from Jews to members of the local nation, such as Poles, Slovaks, Croatians, and Hungarians. The seizure of property was all done with legal decrees. Hence, a long paper trail was left by the German bureaucracy, which later provided the basis for material claims against the postwar German government. In parts of Eastern Europe, especially those states created after 1918, local individuals saw the Germans and Jews as controlling industry. This was especially true in those sections of Poland that were formerly part of the German Empire. The historian Raul Hilberg has also pointed out that once the Holocaust commenced, there was no authorized budget for it. It was, therefore, the sale of Jewish assets that paid for the killing.

In the eyes of both perpetrators and bystanders, however (with variations from country to country), there were collateral factors that had developed during the long presence of the Jews within European Christendom. Among these were biblical allegations of responsibility for the crucifixion of Christ (particularly Acts 5:30, "The God of our fathers raised up Jesus whom you murdered by hanging on a tree.") and the multigenerational responsibility for this crime (Matthew 27:25, "His blood be on us and on our children."). Another factor was the fear of vertical social and political mobility by a formerly tolerated minority, the Jews, who had a generally supportive attitude on issues of democratization. In Claude Lanzmann's film *SHOAH* (1985), a Polish peasant woman remarks that Jewish women were seen as rivals for their "beauty," owing to the fact that they did not work and hence were sought after by Polish men. Whether this testimony is true remains conjectural.

All of these factors pointed to the Jew as "other" or "stranger," despite long residencies in the countries where the Holocaust would play itself out. Nevertheless, it is important to point out that Jews were often killed not by German killing squads but by local populations. The most notorious cases, perhaps, were in Kaunas (Kovno), Lithuania, and the Polish town of Jedwabne. In the latter massacre, which took place on July 10, 1941, approximately 1,500 Jews were killed by Poles. However, despite a 2001 apology for the massacre by President Aleksander Kwasniewski, both the facts and interpretation of this event remain contentious because of the nationalist view that the Poles were also victims of Nazism.

RACE AND RELIGION IN THE NAZI PERSECUTION OF THE JEWS

Race and cognate terms in Greek and Latin have been used for 2,000 years to describe the existence of social or ethnic groups of various kinds. However, in the late nineteenth century, the word *race* was applied to European Jews in a novel manner, combining a mixture of the new pseudoscience of eugenics, romantic ideas from the arts, and religious ideas to construct the idea of "the Jewish race." While Nazi theorists had constructed the idea of the "Aryan" along racial lines as having white skin, blond hair, blue eyes, and a right to rule because of natural selection, the Jews were constructed in an opposite light. Jews were often described as having Middle Eastern origins, no matter how long they had lived in Germany. According to Nazi propaganda, as indicated in the notorious 1940 film *Der ewige Jude* (*The Eternal Jew*), Jews were considered a mixed race "with negro admixture." In addition, racists considered the Jewish Diaspora to be a potential threat because Jews were situated in many places and hence difficult to defeat at once. Jews were also described as both inbred (unlike the "Aryans") and having a cunning power because of their intelligence. It was also held that the specific occupations that they held in society (bankers, intellectuals, etc.) put them in a position to dominate the modern world of the twentieth century. However, Jews were also said to be "feminized" because of their lack of a country and an army. They needed protection from others, and they were therefore vulnerable when policies of toleration broke down.

As Nazi racism developed, the issue of what constituted race became more complex. Religion entered the discourse not for Jews, but rather for Jews who had converted to Christianity but were still considered Jews by Nazi law. For example, the 1935 Nuremberg Laws imposed a state-defined racial definition on Jews based on grand parentage, irrespective of current religion. This was a negation of the Christian concept of religious conversion: After the Nuremberg Laws, Christian mission to the Jews was prohibited. In the long run, despite race theory being based on "blood," the racial attack on the Jews also necessitated attacks on synagogues and Jewish books, as well as on the Jews themselves.

Adolf Hitler attacked the Jews in his writings from 1920 onwards. However, the Nazi Party (officially, the National Socialist German Workers' Party) did not attempt to define Jews with specificity until 1935. Hitler's landmark book, *Mein Kampf* (1925), became the source of the essential ideology of Nazi Germany. In the book, a series of struggles of opposites were laid out: light against darkness, health against sickness, the visible against invisible, form against formlessness in the arts and thought, culture against decadence, and Aryan against Jew. Deviations from the worldview found in Hitler's thought were viewed as forms of sickness, which could be changed through surgery. For the Nazi state, that surgery took the form of genocide.

Under German National Socialism, the führer was viewed as a charismatic and authoritarian leader who emerged from the chaotic conditions in Germany at the end of World War I. While his rise was also linked to

Germanic nationalism and folklore, Hitler positioned himself as a new Siegfried prepared to avenge a betrayed nation and restore equilibrium. What followed in the Nazi program was a form of salvation that was both romantic and artistic: It was interested in a memory of the past, especially as it concerned race and spirit of a people. Using myths of the German past, Hitler and his cohorts constructed the new myth that no German hero could be defeated except by a "stab in the back," a phrase popularized by General Eric Ludendorff.

It was through this logic that the explanation of the German defeat of 1918 was revealed through two critical events. The first was the Russian Revolution of November 1917, described by its enemies as "Jewish Bolshevism." The second was the questioning within the nation-state of who was a true German and who was a stranger. The latter proved to be the Jews, who had a long history in Europe as being the "other," and who were often linked erroneously to the outbreak of chaotic situations. This included Christian myths of deicide in the Bible, accusations about the defiling of culture, and ultimately race mixing through conversion to Christianity. Thus, anti-Semitism, which minimally might be simply a dislike of Jews because of religious or cultural reasons, became infested with racism based on biological concepts.

Nazi rhetoric also had within it a strong relationship to Christian rhetoric. In November 1934 at Nuremberg, Deputy Führer Rudolph Hess stated: "The party is Hitler, but Hitler is also Germany, just as Germany is Hitler." This extravagant claim was derived from the language of the Gospel of St. John, which reads, "I am in the Father and the Father is in me." (John 14:10) The general propaganda of the era suggested that Hitler had been chosen to put the German universe back in order and that Nazism was a Christian movement.

AESTHETICS, PUBLIC HEALTH, AND LAWS OF EXCLUSION

Art and public health programs were also a part of Nazi race theory and biology, known as *Rassenkunde* (Race Science). The concept was sufficiently simple. It meant that good breeding creates a sense of race in a people. Race was a myth linked to art, bodily aesthetics, and racial hygiene, and it was an ideal to be accomplished. Any intrusion by aliens, such as Jews, threatened this process. Such eugenic ideas were not new, nor were they specifically German. Hitler's attacks on the Jews as a race, however, necessitated an attack both on Jewish art and creativity and on the physical characteristics of the Jews. Hitler believed that the idea of creative work had to be anti-Semitic. Thus, the Jewish presence in Germany, and later Europe, was seen as evil not only because of the threat of interbreeding, but also because of the infiltration of "inferior" Jewish art and music. The German word *entarte* (degenerate) was applied to modern art, swing music, people who had nontraditional life styles, and individuals with mental disorders and physical handicaps, as well as to Jews, Afro-Germans, and the Sinti and Roma (Gypsies). Many applications of "degeneracy" were made to the works of non-Jews, but ultimately all Jewish influences on culture were to be eliminated.

Once Hitler came into power on January 30, 1933, the Jews were the main focus of exclusionary laws based upon state-authored racism. Those laws were similar to the "Jim Crow" laws that established the segregation of races in the United States, although Jews in Germany were Caucasian, spoke German, and often had German family names. Some had in fact been Christians for generations, and were therefore not Jews according to the religious precepts of the Jewish community. More than 2,000 anti-Jewish laws were passed between 1933 and 1945 creating a wall of separation between newly defined "Jews" and "Aryans." The initial laws were more general in nature, including the Law for Restitution of the German Civil Service (April 1933), the Law to Prevent the Overcrowding of German Schools (April 1933), the Law for the Protection of Hereditary Health of the German People (July 1933), and the Editorial Law (October 1933). Later laws of exclusion grew more and more specific.

For the Nazis, the Jews were the group that caused fear and anomie. The solution, at first, was separation and a push for them to emigrate. Only later did the issue become one of extermination. The German laws that removed Jews from professions and left them without a livelihood were an invitation for them to leave the country. A decree of February 10, 1935, authorized the Secret State Police (or Gestapo) to forbid all Jewish meetings that propagandized for the continuing residence of Jews in Germany. On February 8, 1936, the Gestapo applied a ban on the Association of Jews Faithful to the Torah, because such an organization "cannot promote the emigration of Jews and is likely to impede the supervision of Jews." Other laws made it more and more difficult for Jews to live in Germany. Thus, through the "First Supplemental Decree" of the Nuremberg Laws, which was passed on November 14, 1935, the civil rights of Jews were cancelled, their voting rights were abolished, and those Jewish civil servants who were still working were retired (this process of removal began in April 1933). On December 21, 1935, the "Second Supplemental Decree" led to the dismissal of all professors, teachers, physicians, lawyers, and notaries who were state employees.

Other laws created racial and social separation between Aryans and Jews. This included a prohibition

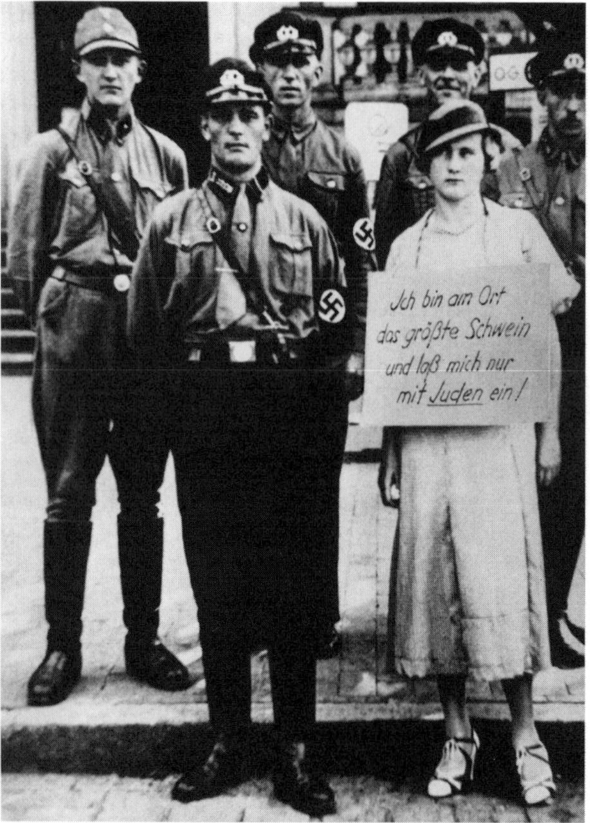

Jewish Sympathizer, 1935. *Jews and those who sympathized with their plight were publicly humiliated. This woman was forced by Nazi soldiers to wear a sign that reads: "I am the greatest swine form, and only get involved with Jews."* © HULTON-DEUTSCH COLLECTION/CORBIS.

on marriages between Jews and citizens of "German or kindred blood." In addition, sexual relations outside of marriage between Jews and nationals of "German or kindred blood" were forbidden, and Jews were not permitted to employ female citizens of "German or kindred blood" as domestic servants. A decree of August 17, 1938, required Jews to have a red "J" stamped in their passports, while Jewish men had to take the middle name "Israel" and women the middle name "Sara." These were clear identifiers of "Jewish race."

If any law is useful for understanding the political construction of "race" in Nazi Germany, it is the law of August 31, 1936, when the Reich Finance Ministry announced that religious affiliation had to be indicated on tax forms. Soon thereafter, on October 4, 1936, another decree indicated that the "conversion of Jews to Christianity has no relevance with respect to the question of race. The possibility to hide one's origin by changing one's religious affiliation will entirely vanish as soon as the offices for racial research begin their work."

FURTHER DEFINING THE VICTIMS

A major problem with the "Jewish Question," in Germany, as it was termed, was that there were no clear statistics about the number of Jews living among the German population of approximately 66 million people. The general belief was that the Jewish population in Germany was 530,000, or about eight-tenths of one percent of the total population. Statistics released in April 1935 indicated there were 750,000 half-Jews (*Mischlinge,* or "half-breeds") and 475,000 full Jews, totaling more than a million Jews. Other sources placed the total number of Jews and half-Jews at no more than 600,000. Certainly many German Jews were so assimilated they could not be differentiated from Germans by any objective criteria.

Thus, the dilemma of determining the number of Jews and half-Jews (who were also half-German) produced the necessity of a more precise law in order to enforce prior and future decrees. This discussion led, in September 1935, to the Law for the Protection of German Blood and German Honor (the first Nuremberg Law), and to the subsequent decrees of November 14, 1935, which attempted to perfect the definition of a Jew. However, these laws led to many anomalies over the question of half-Jews, or *Mischlinge.*

According to the Nuremberg Laws, a Jew was a person descended from three or four Jewish grandparents, regardless of their current religious affiliation. A "Mischling, First-Degree" was a person with two Jewish grandparents who fell into one of the following categories: he or she belonged to the Jewish community religiously; was married to a Jew; or was the offspring of legal or nonlegal sexual intercourse with a Jew. A "Mischling, Second-Degree" was a person with one Jewish grandparent. Thus, theoretically, an Aryan was someone with no Jewish grandparents. However, the law revealed some of the artificiality of the construction of race in the definition of a first-degree Mischling, which included membership in the religious community as a determinant of race. In Poland, which was occupied by Germany during World War II, a change in the law permitted children born to a Mischling family before May 31, 1941, to be regarded as Aryans, while those born after May 31, 1941, were considered Jews.

THE PUSH TO EMIGRATE

These decrees and laws took away German citizenship and made Jews technically "stateless," suggesting that the race policy of Germany between 1933 and the beginning of World War II was designed to promote the emigration of Jews rather than their extermination. The July 1938 Evian Conference was convened by thirty-two countries in an effort to solve the growing refugee problem, but little was decided and the conference had only a minor impact. The hypocrisy of the Western nations in criticizing the German policies on Jews but being unwilling to accept an extensive number of the refugees only encouraged and emboldened Hitler. However, the issue of accepting refugees was never popular among the populations of democratic countries and leaders often reflected that they were following democratic opinion on this question. Nonetheless, before the end of 1938, while hundreds of separation laws were being decreed, the violence against Jews was often lethal, but hardly genocidal.

Kristallnacht, or the "Night of Broken Glass" (November 9–10, 1938), was the first German nationwide outburst against the Jews. It was allegedly caused by the murder of a German official in Paris by a Jew upset with his parents' deportation to a "no-man's land" on the Polish border. On Kristallnacht, mobs throughout Germany, Austria, and the Sudetenland attacked Jews and Jewish property, including places of worship. Ninety-six Jews were killed and hundreds were injured, and hundreds of synagogues were subjected to arson and destroyed, as were 7,500 businesses. Cemeteries and schools were also vandalized. In the immediate aftermath, between 26,000 and 30,000 Jews, mostly men, were arrested and sent to concentration camps. Most were eventually released on the assumption that they would leave Germany. The difficulty, however, was finding a country of refuge. A heavy fine was levied on the Jewish community for their responsibility for the event. Most significantly, Kristallnacht marked the transfer of Jewish policies to the Schutzstaffel, or SS, headed by Reichsführer Heinrich Himmler.

Emigration did pick up after Kristallnacht. However, a major problem in successful emigration was the world economic depression, which limited entry visas into other countries. In addition, even the world's democracies had varying levels of anti-Semitism, which affected their immigration policies.

Some of the prohibitive laws that were passed before and after Kristallnacht limiting Jewish rights were dazzling in their specificity and emphasis on things usually considered trivial. For example, an April 1933 decree forbad the use of Yiddish in the State of Baden's cattle markets. A law passed on December 1, 1933, proclaimed: "The Association of Retail Traders in Frankfurt forbids Jewish shops from using Christian symbols during Christmas season sales." On June 21, 1934, the Hessian Education Ministry excluded the Old Testament from the Protestant religious educational curriculum, replacing it with additional passages from the New Testament. On September 28, 1935, the Mayor of Königsdorf, a village in Bavaria, decreed that cows purchased directly or indirectly from Jews could not be inseminated by the common village bull. However, it was not until September 3, 1941, that a decree mandated that Jews remaining in Germany had to wear the Yellow Star identification on their outer clothing. It is of note that this requirement was imposed on Jews in the occupied territories even earlier, after the beginning of World War II and occupation policies of 1939.

The T-4 Euthanasia Program that led to the killing of Germans who were physically and mentally impaired began officially on September 1, 1939. It included gassing operations, and an estimated 100,000 patients were killed. Others were killed through starvation or injections of phenol directly into the heart. The numbers killed by each method are imprecise, and more natural causes of death were often written into death certificates. Doctors who served in the T-4 program also aided in the selection process for arriving inmates at German death camps in occupied Poland after 1941.

RACIAL PROPAGANDA

Alongside the various decrees separating the Jews from "Aryans" was a constant barrage of racial epithets that came from the Ministry of Propaganda and the notorious anti-Semitic newspaper *Der Stürmer*, edited by Julius Streicher. *Der Stürmer* began publication in 1923, ten years before the Nazis achieved power. It was a perfect example of a "rag" newspaper, with stories that were sensationalist and anti-Semitic (and pornographic, in their own way). The stories were drawn often from standard anti-Semitic mythologies of the past, and from the *Protocols of the Learned Elders of Zion*, a notorious forgery from the turn of the twentieth century that purported to reveal a Jewish plot of world domination. There were exaggerated stories about alleged "ritual murders" of Christian children and about the alleged predatory nature of Jewish men seeking out pure Aryan women for sexual relations (a myth that Hitler obsessed about). Jewish men were almost always depicted in what would be considered a "racial" type of imagery—long hooked noses, rounded bodies, large ears, thick glasses, and long devilish fingernails—and these images were linked to images of capitalist as well as communist domination. The offensiveness of *Der Stürmer* was so intense that Streicher was sentenced to be hanged at the 1945 International Tribunal at Nuremberg, although he had never personally ordered or carried out a murder.

By the autumn of 1938, after five and a half years of National Socialist rule, the living conditions of the German Jews had worsened dramatically as the result of the discriminatory measures planned and executed by the state. Many were unable to believe that things could get worse. Others, however, were convinced that the openly declared threat of a "solution to the Jewish question" would be carried out.

Concurrent with the persecution of the Jews was the reclassification of the Gypsy population from "asocial" to a "race." After 1936, the Nuremberg Laws were applied to them, even though they were not mentioned in the decree. In 1937, German law classified Gypsies as "asocials," but in May 1938 they were reclassified as a racial group by the Central Office for Fighting the Gypsy Menace. The racial classification created some contradictions in strict Nazi racial policy, as the Roma were from India, thereby placing them in the structure of Indo-European peoples, and hence Aryans. Nevertheless, the Gypsies, already the subject of social ostracism because of their perceived lifestyle, became the subject of eugenic studies using the same pseudoscientific methods of bodily measurements as those used on the Jews. This included measurement of nose and skull size and descriptions of hair and eye color.

An SS decree of December 16, 1942 (referred to in other German documents, though the original has not been found), ordered the deportation of Gypsies to concentration camps. At Auschwitz, the Nazi medical researcher and eugenicist Dr. Joseph Mengele took particular interest in Gypsies. The artist and former Auschwitz prisoner Dina Gottlieb has testified about a series of paintings and drawings of Gypsy women she did on Mengele's order, emphasizing the structure of the ear. At least half a million Gypsies perished in concentration camps and killing centers, including Babi Yar near Kiev, Auschwitz, and a killing site called Lety in the Bohemian Protectorate.

Dutch Jews Leave for a Concentration Camp, 1942 or 1943. *A Jewish family in Amsterdam, Netherlands, has just been arrested and must leave their house to go to a concentration camp in Poland.* © BETTMANN/CORBIS.

FROM EMIGRATION TO GENOCIDE

The steps toward genocide, toward a "racial purification program" of mass killing, started with the German attack on Poland on September 1, 1939. While no written order apparently exists for what became the "final solution of the Jewish question," the general consensus of historians is that a written order should not be expected in a modern bureaucratic state such as Nazi Germany. However, the general idea of the removal of the German Jews had been in the air for a long time and is found frequently in Hitler's speeches. For example, in Hitler's speech given on January 30, 1939, he indicated that war would bring some sort of extermination program. He stated, "Today I will be once more a prophet: If the international Jewish financiers in and outside Europe should succeed in plunging the nations once more into a world war, then the result will not be the Bolshevizing of the earth and thus the victory of Jewry, but the annihilation of the Jewish race in Europe." The speech may be said to have paved the way to a further radicalization of anti-Jewish policies, although it was not until 1940 that extermination appeared to be a realistic goal.

In 1940 the highly propagandistic and racist film, *Der ewige Jude* was shown in German movie theaters. Produced by Minister of Propaganda Joseph Goebbels and filmed by Fritz Hippler in the Lodz ghetto, the film conjures up images of Jews as both a public health menace and a group racially inferior to the Aryans (they are ultimately compared with an infestation of rats). The film ends with Hitler's speech of January 30, 1939. Hitler repeated the threat of the destruction of the Jews in later speeches, including those given on January 30, 1941; February 24, September 30, and November 8, 1942; and February 24, 1943. Parallel to Hitler's pronouncements at this time were additional directives within the Nazi Party by Joseph Goebbels, Reichmarshall Hermann Goering, and Heinrich Himmler, the commander of the SS. Reinhard Heydrich, the head of the SS Main Office and the second-ranking officer in the SS, approached Hermann Goering in July 1941 and asked him to authorize his department to begin plans for a "total solution" of the "Jewish question." A return letter from Goering to Heydrich, dated July 31, 1941, seems to establish bureaucratic approval for the extermination of the Jews on a racial basis. In this document, Goering wrote: "I hereby commission you to carry out all necessary preparations . . .

for a total solution of the Jewish question in the German sphere of influence in Europe."

Early Executions. Heydrich had convened a conference on September 21, 1939, to discuss racial policy in Poland. A decision was made to evacuate up to 1.5 million Jews into the Lublin district, into what would be called, for the time being, a "reservation." The first Nazi ghettos were established for Jews in October 1939. The Star of David, in white and yellow colors, was introduced as an insignia for Polish Jews on November 23, 1939. Executions of Jewish male leaders in towns and cities followed. On December 10, 1942, the London-based Polish government in exile made the following request: "The Polish Government asks that the United Nations shall take effective measures to help the Jews not only of Poland but of the whole of Europe, three to four millions of whom are in peril of ruthless extermination."

The most well-known study of shooting units is Christopher Browning's 1992 book *Ordinary Men,* in which he examines *Ordnungspolizei* (Order Police) Reserve Police Unit 101, based in Hamburg. This unit killed over 38,000 Jews by shooting, beginning in July 1942 in the village of Jozefow, and it was later involved in the deportation of 45,000 others to Treblinka. Later, when the ghettos were better organized, they became the vehicle for a slower but consistent method of deportation to the death camps. Beginning in the summer of 1942, for example, more than 300,000 Jews were deported from the Warsaw Ghetto to Treblinka, a process that prompted the Warsaw Ghetto Uprising that began on April 19, 1943.

The beginning of the war against the Soviet Union on June 22, 1941, clearly mixed the territorial ambitions of the Reich with a policy of racial annihilation. Four mobile killing squads, the *Einsatzgruppen,* followed the regular army onto the territory of the USSR and began the liquidation of the Jewish population, and of anyone linked to the Soviet political class. Mass murder was carried out mainly by shooting the victims in pits, though there was some experimentation with killing people in gas vans. While the local population killed Jews in some of the Eastern countries under occupation, the SS preferred "organized killing" rather than spontaneous pogroms. Slovakia solved its Jewish problem in an interesting way: It paid the Germans 500 Reichmarks for the removal of each Jew.

The mechanism for killing the Jews had also been put in process early in 1941. Auschwitz, a Polish army camp, was taken over on June 14, 1940, and turned into a concentration camp. In October 1941, the SS leader Heinrich Himmler authorized the construction of the Auschwitz II-Birkenau camp for Soviet prisoners of war. After the first test gassings of prisoners at Auschwitz I in September 1941, the first selections and gassings took place in May 1942 at Birkenau, which had been converted from a place of incarceration for Soviet prisoners to the principal destination for the mass murder of the Jews. Eventually, the six major death camps were established on the territory of the former Polish state: Auschwitz, Majdanek, Belzec, Chelmno, Sobibor, and Treblinka.

While the death camps were being built on the territory of the prewar Polish Republic, which was now divided into occupation zones, on October 23, 1941, the Security Police forbade the emigration of Jews from Nazi-controlled territories for the duration of the war. This ended all emigration solutions, including the one most talked about in inner Nazi circles, that of sending the Jews to the island of Madagascar.

Wannsee and the Final Solution. The Wannsee Conference, convened at a lakeside resort south of Berlin on January 20, 1942, is best interpreted as a bureaucratic evaluation of extermination policy to date. Debates took place on strategies such as the immediate need for the Final Solution versus the labor needs of the Reich. The minutes from this conference taken, by Obersturmbannführer Adolph Eichmann, indicate the advanced plans to murder all of European Jewry and suggest the entire German bureaucracy was becoming involved in the process. They also suggest that the participants discussed creating a mood for compliance in mass murder among the diverse branches of the SS and the bureaucracy.

The Wannsee Conference also raised the question of race through a discussion of the fate of the Mischlinge, or the half-Jews. The discussion at Wannsee, as revealed in the minutes of the meeting, indicated the imprecision in the Nuremberg Laws of 1935, especially when related to the labor needs of the Third Reich. For example, it was decided at the conference that persons of mixed blood of the second degree were to be treated "essentially as Germans," probably because of the labor shortage in the country. There were some bizarre exceptions, however. For example, this policy did not apply to any person who, from a racial viewpoint, had an "especially undesirable appearance that marks him outwardly as a Jew," nor did it apply to anyone who had a "particularly bad police and political record that shows that he feels and behaves like a Jew."

The discussion on first-degree Mischlinge (those with two Jewish grandparents) indicated that many exemptions had already been made and that cases should be reexamined based on "personal merit." This pattern of reinterpretation indicates that racial definitions, so critical in 1935, were now being rethought. However, in order to prevent any additional mixed offspring, first-degree

Mischlinge were to be sterilized. Other very precise situations of marriages between Jews and Aryans, with or without children, were discussed, and remedies advanced for the deportation of Jews to what was called "the old-age ghetto" of Theresienstadt.

Reinhard Heydrich became the effective leader of early plans to implement the Final Solution. He and his subordinate, Adolf Eichmann, controlled the bureaucratic apparatus to implement this policy In addition, Heydrich also controlled the operations of the Einsatzgruppen and the work of SS-Obergruppenführer Odilo Globocnik in the Lublin district of the General-Government (the central part of occupied Poland). According to what is regarded as the "functionalist" model of the Holocaust, Heydrich created a coherent and systematic plan for the extermination of European Jews by merging a series of diffuse internal systems. After Heydrich's assassination in April 1942 near Prague, this phase of the destruction process adopted the name "Operation Reinhard." The death camps at Belzec, Sobibor, and Treblinka were associated with this destruction process. By the end of 1942, approximately 4 million Jews had been killed in the various extermination processes.

As German control of Europe expanded into military occupations, the extermination of Jews intensified. The killing process was more ruthless in the East, featuring mass shootings by Einsatzgruppen on Soviet territory; the use of gas vans; and two forms of gas chambers, using carbon monoxide and Zyklon B gas (prussic acid), at the Auschwitz and Majdanek extermination camps.

Execution in Poland, c. 1942. *Victims of the Holocaust were often buried in mass graves. It was not uncommon for victims to be marched to the edge of a pit filled with bodies before being shot in the back of the head by Nazi soldiers.* © CORBIS.

Poland, the Ghettos, and Forced Labor. The implementation of the Holocaust in Poland included a rapid identification and isolation of the Jews. On November 23, 1939, all Jews over the age of ten years were required to wear the Star of David as an identification mark. The Nazi occupation authorities would eventually establish 400 ghettos in occupied Eastern Europe. The two largest were in Warsaw and Lodz, Poland. The Warsaw Ghetto was created on November 23, 1939. From both a racial and a supposed public health point of view, the ghettos were designed to separate the Jews from the rest of the local populations.

However, a debate existed among the Nazi elite about the purpose of the ghettos. On one hand, because of a shortage of labor, the ghettos could provide, theoretically, a reserve of slave labor. On the other hand, the poor and dismal living conditions, combined with poor diet and the absence of health care created conditions for what would appear to be a natural decline of the Jewish community through an increased death rate. A third interpretation was that the ghettos were way stations to the death camps. Ghettos were subject to frequent raids by the SS, who often removed the very people who might be part of a useful slave labor force. German capitalist enterprises also benefited from the slave labor potential. Virtually every German company used some form of slave labor. Perhaps the most well-known case is that of I.G. Farben, which ran Auschwitz Camp III-Buna with slave labor supplied by the SS. Eventually, all of the ghettos were liquidated, with the remaining populations sent to death camps or other slave labor facilities, or else sent on death marches into Germany itself.

The ghettos began to be emptied in 1942 during "Operation Reinhard." As the war progressed and defeat became probable for the Germans after the loss at Stalingrad on February 2, 1943, the attempt to exterminate the remainder of European Jews under German control intensified. This is best documented in the deportation of Hungarian Jews, who had previously been protected by the Hungarian regent, Admiral Miklos Horthy. However, the Germans occupied Hungary in mid-March 1943, and the deportation of Hungarian Jews to Auschwitz began in May. Within a short time, 440,000 Jews were deported from Hungary.

THE AFTERMATH

By the time the Holocaust ended in the East, Jewish losses were severe: 2.8 million from Poland were killed; 1.5 million on the territory of the Soviet Union; 277,000 from Czechoslovakia; 560,000 from Hungary; and 270,000 from Romania, plus other losses in Greece (60,000) and Yugoslavia (65,000). However, the war between Germany and the Soviet Union has to be assessed as being a war not only between competing ideologies but also as a conflict that involved racial ideas.

In Western Europe, Jews were identified for deportation to the East and annihilation. The imposition of "Race Laws" or registration laws helped in defining Jews, especially by the wearing of a yellow star, and this was a prelude to isolation and deportation. In the Netherlands, the Jewish population was 159,000 at the outset of war. Registration was mandated there by the German occupation authorities in January 1941. Eventually, 107,000 were deported and 102,000 died. Up to 30,000 Dutch Jews were hidden, two-thirds of whom survived. Belgium's Jewish population was 66,000 at outset of the war, of whom 28,500 were deported, beginning in September 1942. France's Jewish population was approximately 225,000, and 77,000 of them were deported. Of Norway's approximately 1,500 Jews, 770 escaped to Sweden, while 761 were deported by ship to Stettin and on to Auschwitz. Jews were also deported from the British Channel Islands, which were occupied by the Germans.

Under Mussolini, Italy was generally reluctant to give up its Jews, despite imposition of the race law in 1938. However, after the initial fall of fascism, Mussolini established the Northern Italian Republic of Salo on September 23, 1943, with German support. This led to the beginning of the deportation of 8,000 Italian Jews (about 20% of Italy's Jewish population) in October 1943, and 95 percent of those who were deported died. About 40,000 Italian Jews survived the war without deportation.

The last phase of the Holocaust was defined by death marches and the liberation of the Western concentration camps in April and May 1945. As territory under German control contracted, the SS began to march inmates from the camps in the East to concentration camps in Germany. During these marches, stragglers who fell by the wayside were beaten and killed. The sadism of the guards during the death marches has been recalled with particular detail by many survivors, raising the question of whether they were obeying the orders of the SS guards, or whether this was a reflection of their own racism toward the prisoners. The survivors of the death marches and transports wound up in concentration camps at Bergen-Belsen, Dachau, Flossenburg, Buchenwald, Mauthausen, and other places inside pre-1938 German borders.

The Holocaust ended with the end of World War II on May 7, 1945. The Nobel Peace Prize Laureate Elie Wiesel has suggested that without Hitler, there would have been no Holocaust. However, the period before the Holocaust witnessed an intense development of race theory, anti-Semitism and racial hygiene in the realm of public health policies that demonized the "others" who lived in Germany. The whole issue of how non-Europeans, as the Jews and Roma/Sinti were defined, fit into the nation-state idea of the 1930s, when race became a political factor, suggests the explosive aspects of policies based on tolerance of "others" and "strangers."

The postwar International Military Tribunals (IMT) at Nuremberg, and the later zonal trials, clearly established the nature of the Nazi criminal offenses, not only in conspiracy and aggressive war, but also in war crimes and crimes against humanity that were racist and genocidal in nature. For those anti-Semitic states, individuals, and organizations that deny the event happened, the trials, the huge amount of documents from the event, and Germany's own admission of guilt are the most effective rebuttals. In addition, there is extensive documentation of the testimony of victims, particularly through such video projects as the Fortunoff Archive at Yale University, the University of Southern California's Shoah Foundation Institute for Visual History and Education, and the work done within research divisions of Holocaust museums, such as the United States Holocaust Memorial Museum in Washington, D.C. and Yad Vashem, the Holocaust Martyrs' and Heroes' Remembrance Authority in Jerusalem.

Since 1945 the study of the Holocaust has become a template for understanding acts of genocide that came before and after the Nazi era. The intensity of racism, especially as authored by a modern state, and the technological aspects of the German killing machine, as well as the extended time frame and the attempts to kill Jewish victims outside German borders (but in occupation zones) provide a certain uniqueness to the plan of the perpetrators. However, this assessment is not to suggest that the Holocaust is so different that it excludes comparisons with other genocides. On the contrary, the study of the genocide of the Herero, the Armenian genocide, and the genocides in Cambodia under the Khmer Rouge, in Bosnia-Herzegovina, in Rwanda, and in Darfur have been more identifiable and better understood because of the legacy and historiography of the Holocaust.

SEE ALSO *Anti-Semitism; Ethnic Cleansing; Genocide; Roma.*

BIBLIOGRAPHY

Aly, Götz, and Suzanne Heim. 1991. *Architects of Annihilation: Auschwitz and the Logic of Destruction*. Princeton, NJ: Princeton University Press.

Bauer, Yehuda. 2001. *A History of the Holocaust*, rev. ed. Danbury, CT: Franklin Watts.

Berenbaum, Michael, and Abraham J. Peck. 1998. *The Holocaust and History*. Bloomington: Indiana University Press.

Browning, Christopher R. 1992. *Ordinary Men: Reserve Police Battalion 101 and the Final Solution in Poland*. New York: Harper Perennial.

———. 2004. *The Origins of the Final Solution*. Lincoln: University of Nebraska Press.

Bytwerk, Randall L. 2001. *Julius Streicher: Nazi Editor of the Notorious Anti-Semitic Newspaper Der Sturmer*. New York: Cooper Square Press.

Cecil, Robert. 1972. *The Myth of the Master Race: Alfred Rosenberg and Nazi Ideology*. New York: Dodd, Mead.

Deichmann, Ute. 1996. *Biologists under Hitler*. Cambridge, MA: Harvard University Press.

Fischer, Klaus P. 1998. *The History of an Obsession: German Judeophobia and the Holocaust*. New York: Continuum.

Friedlander, Henry. 1995. *The Origins of Nazi Genocide: From Euthanasia to the Final Solution*. Chapel Hill: University of North Carolina Press.

Gilman, Sander L. 1991. *The Jew's Body*. New York: Routledge.

———. 1998. *Creating Beauty to Cure the Soul: Race and Psychology in the Shaping of Aesthetic Surgery*. Durham, NC: Duke University Press.

———. 2001. *Making the Body Beautiful: A Cultural History of Aesthetic Surgery*. Princeton, NJ: Princeton University Press.

Gobineau, Arthur Comte de. 1970. *Selected Political Writings*. Edited by Michael D. Biddiss. New York: Harper & Row.

Goldensohn, Leon. 2004. *The Nuremberg Interviews*. New York: Knopf.

Goodrick-Clarke, Nicholas. 1998. *Hitler's Priestess: Savitri Devi, the Hindu-Aryan Myth, and Neo-Nazism*. New York: New York University Press.

Issac, Benjamin. 2004. *The Invention of Racism in Classical Antiquity*. Princeton, NJ: Princeton University Press.

Levi, Neil, and Michael Rothberg, eds. 2003. *The Holocaust: Theoretical Readings*. New Brunswick, NJ: Rutgers University Press.

Lifton, Robert Jay. 1986. *The Nazi Doctors: Medical Killing and the Psychology of Genocide*. New York: Basic Books.

Michaud, Eric. 2004. *The Cult of Art in Nazi Germany*. Stanford, CA: Stanford University Press.

Muller-Hill, Benno. 1988. *Murderous Science: Elimination by Scientific Selection of Jews, Gypsies, and Others, Germany 1933–1945*. New York: Oxford University Press.

Proctor, Robert N. 1988. *Racial Hygiene: Medicine under the Nazis*. Cambridge, MA: Harvard University Press.

Rosenberg, Alfred. 1970. *Race and Race History, and Other Essays*. Edited by Robert Pois. New York, Harper & Row.

Schreckenberg, Heinz. 1996. *The Jews in Christian Art: An Illustrated History*. New York: Continuum.

Weinreich, Max. 1946. *Hitler's Professors: The Part of Scholarship in Germany's Crimes against the Jewish People*. New York: Yiddish Scientific Institute-YIVO.

Weitz, Eric. 2003. *A Century of Genocide: Utopias of Race and Nation*. Princeton, NJ: Princeton University Press.

Stephen C. Feinstein

HOMOPHOBIA

SEE *Heterosexism and Homophobia.*

HOTTENTOT VENUS

"Hottentot Venus" was the moniker given to a series of women exhibited in sexually suggestive, ethnic curiosity shows in England and France in the early nineteenth century. The woman who is most linked with the icon, Saartjie Baartman, was the first to take the role. Baartman, who was also called Sarah or Sara, was a native of South Africa. It is generally believed that she was born around 1788, and she may have been twenty years of age or older in 1810 when she arrived in London, England, to perform in the "Hottentot Venus" show. She died in Paris, France, in 1816. Even after Baartman's death, the "Hottentot Venus" show continued, featuring unnamed women, including one performing at the ball of a duchess in Paris in 1829 and another performing at Hyde Park in London in 1838.

Baartman was born during the period of Dutch colonization in South Africa. Her indigenous name is uncertain, but the name Saartjie is Dutch for "little Sara." Baartman was raised in a rural indigenous community of Khoisan, the descendants of the Khoi Khoi people (who were already rumored to have been wiped out) and the San. The Khoi Khoi were derogatorily referred to as "Hottentots," while the San were called "Bushmen." Both Khoi Khoi and San were labeled "missing links" between humans and apes in racist scientific arguments because of their hunter-gatherer lifestyles and unusual speech patterns, which the Dutch dismissed as guttural animal sounds. Such views dehumanized the Khoi Khoi and San, who were targeted for extermination and removal. Baartman was already a married woman when she experienced one of these extermination raids on her community. She lost her husband and family in the raid, and eventually she migrated to the urban center of Cape Town for survival, taking work as a servant to a Boer farmer named Peter Cezar.

Cezar's brother, Hendrik Cezar, noticed Baartman during a visit to the house and later conceived of the "Hottentot Venus" show. The show, which would take place in London at the famous Piccadilly Circus, would exploit European interests in African natives, especially the

"Hottentots," who had already become mythical in the European imagination. It would also exploit English interests in South Africa, since Great Britain had battled with the Dutch over control of the African colony. Aside from these racial and political elements, the "Hottentot Venus" show would also capitalize on prurient interests in so-called primitive sexuality, described in the tall-tale accounts of explorers who fabricated stories of "Hottentot" women's oversized buttocks and mysterious genitalia excess—rumored to be an extra flap of skin covering the vaginal area and known as the "Hottentot apron."

Hendrik Cezar formed a partnership with a British ship surgeon, Alexander Dunlop, both entertaining the idea of Baartman's exhibition in Europe. It is believed that both men convinced Baartman to enter into a contract on the "Hottentot Venus" show, in which she would share in the profits of her exhibition. They left the Cape for London in 1810 and arrived in September of that year. Dunlop eventually dropped out of the business transaction when a local merchant purchased a giraffe skin from the two men but refused to invest in Baartman. Nonetheless, Cezar advertised the show and billed Baartman as a "most correct specimen of her race." The "Hottentot Venus" exhibition, which took place at 225 Egyptian Hall in Piccadilly Circus, was instantly popular and inspired bawdy ballads and political cartoons, thus demonstrating how the icon of the Hottentot Venus became a fixture in the culture. This image created a fetish out of her backside, and it possibly served as the basis for a fashion development: the mid- to late-nineteenth-century bustle, which gave the illusion of a large bottom.

The show also provoked outrage, as various witnesses complained about what they perceived as an occurrence of slavery. These witnesses described Baartman as appearing in a cage nearly nude and being threatened with violence by her exhibitor. These complaints soon led to the intervention of the African Institution, an abolitionist organization that brought Hendrik Cezar to trial for practicing slavery and public indecency. Baartman testified on her own behalf, but she did not corroborate stories of being held against her will and only complained about not having enough clothes to wear. The courts eventually dismissed the case but mandated that Cezar discontinue the show's indecency. As a result, the show disappeared from London but may have surfaced in the English countryside. There is evidence that Baartman passed through Manchester, where a baptism certificate indicates her conversion to Christianity and her adoption of the name Sarah Baartman in December 1811.

In 1814, Cezar and Baartman arrived in Paris, where Cezar abandoned her to an animal trainer named Reaux. Baartman continued in the "Hottentot Venus" show, which caused the same sensation in Paris as it had in London. It is

Illustration and Description of Saartjie Baartman, 1811. *Hottentot Venus was the moniker given to a series of women exhibited in sexually suggestive, ethnic curiosity shows in England and France in the early nineteenth century. South African native Saartjie Baartman was the first to portray her.* **GEORGE ARENTS COLLECTION, THE NEW YORK PUBLIC LIBRARY, ASTOR, LENOX AND TILDEN FOUNDATIONS.**

possible that her audiences also included the Parisian elite, since she was featured at salons and private parties. Baartman later attracted the attention of three revered natural scientists George Cuvier (who served as Napoleon's surgeon general), Henri de Blainville, and Geoffroy Saint-Hilaire. In March 1815, these three men subjected Baartman to scientific observations in the Jardin du Roi (King's Garden) of the Muséum d'Histoire Naturelle. Baartman was already an alcoholic at the time, and the scientists enticed her with alcohol and sweets to pose nude. She refused, however, to reveal what they had hoped to witness: a view of her "Hottentot apron." Engaging scientific theories of "missing links," Cuvier posited that Baartman was really a San, and he began referring to her as "my Bushwoman." However, de Blainville remained convinced that she was a "Hottentot."

Less than a year after this scientific inquest, Baartman died from complications of alcoholism. Upon her death, Cuvier acquired her cadaver, using it to write his 1817 scientific thesis unveiling the mystery of her "apron." In this thesis, Cuvier compared her genitalia with those of apes and crafted racist scientific theories, which circulated for more than a century, on African women's oversexed and subhuman status. He also molded a plaster cast of Baartman's body and preserved her genitalia (considered "enormous" in comparison to white women) and her brain (considered "small" in comparison to white men) in jars of formaldehyde fluid, which remained on display at the Musée de l'Homme in Paris as late as the 1980s. Baartman's skeletal remains were also housed at this museum, alongside other skeletons displayed for scientific study.

In 1995, under Nelson Mandela's post-apartheid government, South Africa agitated for the return of Baartman's remains and began a nearly decade-long feud with the French government over this troubling history. Seven years later, in March 2002, the French Senate finally agreed to return Baartman's remains—including her preserved organs—for burial in her homeland. On August 9, 2002, National Women's Day in South Africa, thousands attended Baartman's centuries-delayed funeral in Cape Town. She was buried along the River Gamtoos.

SEE ALSO *Cultural Racism; Scientific Racism, History of.*

BIBLIOGRAPHY

Abraham, Yvette. 1998. "Images of Sara Baartman: Sexuality, Race, and Gender in Early Nineteenth-Century Britain." In *Nation, Empire, Colony: Historicizing Gender and Race*, edited by Ruth Roach Pierson, Nupur Chaudhuri, and Beth McAuley, 220–236. Bloomington: Indian University Press.

Altick, Richard. 1978. *The Shows of London*. Cambridge, MA: Belknap Press.

Fausto-Sterling, Anne. 1995. "Gender, Race, and Nation: The Comparative Anatomy of 'Hottentot' Women in Europe, 1814–1817." In *Deviant Bodies*, edited by Jennifer Terry and Jacqueline Urla, 19–48. Bloomington: Indiana University Press.

Gilman, Sander. 1985. "Black Bodies, White Bodies: Toward an Iconography of Female Sexuality in Late Nineteenth-Century Art, Medicine, and Literature." *Critical Inquiry* 12 (1) 204–242.

Gould, Stephen Jay. 1982. "The Hottentot Venus." *Natural History* 91 (1): 20–27.

Hobson, Janell. 2005. *Venus in the Dark: Blackness and Beauty in Popular Culture*. New York: Routledge.

Lindfors, Bernth. 1982. "'The Hottentot Venus' and Other African Attractions in Nineteenth-Century England." *Australasian Drama Studies* 1 (2): 82–104.

———. 1985. "Courting the Hottentot Venus." *Africa (Rome)* 40: 133–148.

Sharpley-Whiting, T. Denean. 1999. *Black Venus: Sexualized Savages, Primal Fears, and Primitive Narratives in French*. Durham, NC: Duke University Press.

Strother, Z. S. 1999. "Display of the Body Hottentot." In *Africans on Stage: Studies in Ethnological Show Business*, edited by Bernth Lindfors, 1–61. Bloomington: Indiana University Press.

Janell Hobson

HOUSTON, CHARLES HAMILTON
1895–1950

Charles Hamilton Houston was born on September 3, 1895, in Washington, D.C. He would go on to become one of the greatest lawyers in American history. Houston developed a systematic approach to the use of the courts to advance individual rights, and he trained a generation of lawyers to battle an entrenched system of racial oppression and segregation. Houston's colleague William H. Hastie defined Houston as "a genius," "the architect of the NAACP legal program," and "the Moses" of the civil rights movement. Houston believed that lawyers were "social engineers" who had a responsibility to work for the common good. He was instrumental in revamping Howard Law School as a training ground for generations of black lawyers, and he thus created a nationwide network of lawyers who could help fulfill his mission.

These efforts created a foundation that lawyers would use to topple the system of "separate but equal" and the assumptions of many about racial inferiority. Houston's strategic approach involved the preparation of hundreds of legal challenges to discrimination, which eventually led to the Supreme Court's 1954 decision in *Brown v. Board of Education* that "separate but equal" facilities are unconstitutional. Through his life's work, Houston exemplified an excellence of character and ability that transcended racial categories and spoke to the promise of equal opportunity and education.

Houston was born into a society in which segregation was both de facto and de jure in much of the country. Blacks and whites lived, worked, and were educated separately, either by custom or by law. Houston's father was a lawyer who, for a time, worked as a clerk in the federal Record and Pension Office to supplement his income from the practice of law. His mother was an accomplished hairdresser whose clients included the wives of senators and diplomats. Houston's parents had high expectations of their only son, and when he received a scholarship to attend the University of Pittsburgh they encouraged him to attend a more prestigious school. He therefore attended Amherst College in Massachusetts. While schools like Amherst and Harvard occasionally accepted blacks as students, they were not fully integrated into school organizations, and clubs and fraternities often barred their entry. As a result, Houston led a singular but not lonely existence at Amherst. He made some friends and acquaintances, but he was never fully accepted into the fabric of college life. Nonetheless, Houston distinguished himself as a student and was elected to Phi Beta Kappa. In 1915, he graduated *magna cum laude* and was one of the college's six valedictorians.

After graduation, Houston taught English at Howard University, the prestigious black college in Washington, D.C. His career was interrupted by World War I, in which he served as a second lieutenant in the field artillery. During his service, Houston experienced overt racism, and he observed that in the face of discrimination, intelligence, talent, skill, and character provided little, if any, protection. Systemic racial prejudice allowed whites to belittle, threaten, humiliate, and abuse their fellow soldiers of color with impunity. Houston began to recognize the impact that legal skill and strategy could have in combating the inequities of racism and segregation. He remarked, "I would never get caught again without knowing something about my rights; that if luck was with me . . . I would study law, and use my time fighting for men who could not strike back" (McNeil 1983, p. 42).

In 1919, Houston enrolled in Harvard Law School, where he again experienced the stings of de facto segregation. Nonetheless, he demonstrated a keen legal mind and distinguished himself as a law student, receiving praise from his professors. Based on his academic achievements, he became the first black student elected to the editorial board of the *Harvard Law Review*. He graduated from Harvard Law School in 1922, earned a doctorate in juridical science from the same institution in 1923, and then studied civil law at the University of Madrid. Houston's pursuit of an advanced legal education was driven, in large part, by his belief that a complete understanding of the Constitution and the legal structures of the nation was essential in the fight for justice and civil rights for African Americans.

Houston joined his father's legal practice, and from 1924 to 1929 he worked in the Washington, D.C. firm of Houston & Houston. At that time, he developed a reputation for a willingness to represent the underrepresented, despite their inability to pay. In 1924, Houston began teaching at Howard Law School, and in 1929 he became the vice-dean of the school. He helped to transform Howard from an evening program to a fully accredited law school that would become a training ground for some of the country's greatest lawyers. He worked at Howard until 1935, when he joined the National Association for the Advancement of Colored People (NAACP) as its first full-time salaried attorney and special counsel, and he became the "architect" of its legal civil rights program. After resigning from the NAACP in 1940, Houston returned to private practice, where he worked tirelessly against infringements on the right to work; unfair labor practices; and segregation in housing, land ownership, and transportation. He remarked to friends that his grandmother's stories of slavery inspired him to protect African Americans against discrimination and prejudice. He also applied this fundamental belief in equality to international struggles for human rights and freedom when he protested economic imperialism in Latin America and colonization in Africa.

Houston's work was grounded in a belief in equality in education, in lawyers as agents of social change, and in human rights. He firmly believed that discrimination in education had to be eradicated for racial equality to be possible. Houston's strategy involved attacking racial inequities in teacher's salaries, transportation, and graduate and professional education. He tied the inadequacy of advanced educational opportunities for blacks to efforts to impede the development of black leadership and economic development in the black community. His brilliance and success rested on his careful preparation of legal briefs and the use of the Constitution to advance equality and equal rights, and to force reforms where they could have no chance through politics. He advanced the idea of using law as an instrument to achieve equality.

The development of socially conscious and prepared lawyers was integral to Houston's strategy of attaining racial equity in education. He believed lawyers had to use their understanding of the Constitution in "bettering conditions of the underprivileged citizens." According to Houston, the lawyer was a "mouthpiece of the weak and a sentinel guarding against wrong" (McNeil 1983). He emphasized the role of black lawyers in these efforts in particular, and he worked to strengthen the National Bar Association, which represented the interests of black lawyers at a time when nonwhites were excluded from the American Bar Association.

Houston is perhaps best known as an advisor to the first black Supreme Court justice, Thurgood Marshall. He mentored and taught legions of lawyers and was always available for consultation in their work. Erin W. Griswold, a former dean of Harvard Law School, noted that "It is doubtful that there has been a single important case involving civil rights during the past fifteen years in which Charles Houston has not either participated directly or by consultation and advice" (Hine 1995, p. 39). Most important, however, according to Houston, was the need to "work for the social good." Houston stressed the role of law in advancing civil rights, stating that human beings are "each equally entitled to life, liberty, and the pursuit of happiness," and that good governments are bound to protect these rights "without prejudice or bias" (Hine 1995, p. 39).

SEE ALSO *Brown v. Board of Education; Civil Rights Movement; Marshall, Thurgood; NAACP; NAACP: Legal Actions, 1935-1955; Plessy v. Ferguson.*

BIBLIOGRAPHY

Greenberg, Jack. 1995. *Crusaders in the Courts: Legal Battles of the Civil Rights Movement*. New York: Basic Books.

Hine, Darlene Clark. 1995. "Black Lawyers and the Twentieth-Century Struggle for Constitutional Change." In *African Americans and the Living Constitution*, edited by John Hope Franklin and Genna Rae McNeil, 33–55. Washington, DC: Smithsonian Institution Press.

McNeil, Genna Rae. 1983. *Groundwork, Charles Hamilton Houston and the Struggle for Civil Rights*. Philadelphia: University of Pennsylvania Press.

Ogletree, Charles J. Jr. 2004. *All Deliberate Speed, Reflections on the First Half Century of* Brown v. Board of Education. New York: W. W. Norton.

Deseriee A. Kennedy

HUERTA, DOLORES

1930–

Dolores Huerta, a cofounder of the United Farm Workers of America, was born Dolores Clara Fernandez on April 10, 1930, in Dawson, New Mexico, to Juan Fernandez and Alicia Chavez. Her parents divorced when she was three years old, and she relocated with her mother and two brothers to Stockton, California. In her youth, Huerta was greatly influenced by her mother's independence as a businesswoman and activism as a community member. After graduating from Stockton High School in 1947, she attended college and received a certificate in teaching.

In 1955 she joined the Community Service Organization (CSO) and was trained in community organizing by Fred Ross. Through her work with the CSO, where Huerta met César Chávez, she was exposed to the unique needs of farmworkers. In 1962, she and Chávez resigned from the CSO and established the National Farm Workers Association (NFWA), which later became the United Farm Workers (UFW), the largest organization of its kind in the nation.

As a cofounder of the UFW, Dolores Huerta has dedicated her life to organizing farmworkers and lobbying for the rights of farmworkers and their families—a job many considered impossible, given the seasonal nature of much of farm work and the migratory patterns of workers. Huerta's work has included negotiating union contracts, directing national boycotts, organizing field strikes, speaking out against the use of toxic pesticides, and campaigning for political candidates. Her efforts have been essential to the establishment of a credit union and medical and pension plans for farmworkers. Huerta and her family have made many sacrifices while struggling for farmworkers' rights, and they have often struggled financially. Indeed, at times they have not even had enough money for bare necessities.

As one of the few women holding a leadership position within a union during the 1960s and 1970s, Huerta was both criticized and admired for her assertiveness and independence. She suffered accusations of putting her position within the union above her role as a mother to her eleven children, and she was resented by both men and women for her "manlike" role within the union. At the same time, Huerta has been considered a role model for Chicanas, Latinas, and other women, especially those seeking to carve out a space for themselves within contemporary social movements. Huerta's position within the union has been essential to breaking down gender stereotypes within the farmworker movement.

Through her work, Dolores Huerta has encouraged the maintenance of a strong sense of self, personal pride, service to others, and self-reflection. Throughout her life, she has maintained her commitment to social justice and community activism both in theory and in practice. It is her belief that "the power for change is predicated on the power of individuals to make moral choices for justice over personal welfare" (Griswold del Castillo and Garcia 1995, p.69). Her lifelong dedication to the farmworker movement has led her to travel throughout the United States promoting an awareness of the issues faced by farmworkers, immigrants, women, and youth.

SEE ALSO *Chávez, César Estrada; Farmworkers; United Farm Workers Union.*

BIBLIOGRAPHY

Dolores Huerta Foundation. "Dolores Huerta Biography." Available from http://www.doloreshuerta.org.

Griswold del Castillo, Richard, and Richard A. Garcia. 1995. *César Chávez: A Triumph of Spirit*. Norman: University of Oklahoma Press.

Brianne A. Davila

HUMAN AND PRIMATE EVOLUTION

The diversification and cultural development of humans occurred only in the last few million years, but the species has a much longer evolutionary background. Humans are primates, related to apes, monkeys, and lemurs, and many of the unique characteristics of the species are a result of the social and ecological interactions of our ancient primate ancestors. Human evolution built upon general primate adaptations by elaborating several major innovations, such as upright walking, tool use, culture, and, ultimately, language.

Since the late twentieth century, there has been an explosion of genetic information about humans and other primates. The Human Genome Project and subsequent projects exploring the genomes of related primates have made it possible to examine the genetic changes that underlie human and primate anatomy and behavior. This has led to a reevaluation of many old hypotheses concerning primate and human evolution, as well as the formulation of new ones, most notably, the recognition that humans and chimpanzees are sister taxa. Anthropologists can now employ a combination of genetic information and evidence of fossil form (morphology) to test hypotheses about human evolution.

HUMANS AMONG THE PRIMATES

Molecular comparisons of living primates suggest that the last time they all shared a common ancestor was sometime during the Late Cretaceous period, around 80 million years ago (Ma). The first primates would have been animals similar in form and adaptation to living tree shrews, which are small arboreal insectivores. The earliest fossil evidence of primates is from the Paleocene epoch, between 65 and 55 Ma.

The initial diversification of the primates may have been a case of coevolution with flowering plant species, for whom modern primates, bats, and plant-eating birds are important pollinators and seed dispersers. Today, nearly all primates retain a generalized, broad diet made up of a balance of fruits, leaves, plant gums, and insects or meat, with some primate lineages specializing to some extent on one or another of these sources. Early primates left humans an anatomical legacy: arboreal adaptations such as grasping hands, fingernails, and binocular vision. They also left a legacy of sociality, as most living primates form long-term social bonds that include mutual grooming.

The prosimian primates include living and fossil lemurs, lorises, and tarsiers. Lemurs live today only on Madagascar; East African bushbabies and South Asian lorises are their close relatives. Tarsiers now live on Southeast Asian islands. In the Eocene and Oligocene (c. 50–30 Ma), lemur-like adapid primates and tarsier-like omomyid primates were broadly distributed through the forests of North America, Europe, Africa, and Asia. The Eocene was the warmest period of the last 65 million years, and subtropical forest habitat suitable for primates covered areas as far north as Wyoming and France.

Monkeys, apes, and humans are grouped together as anthropoid primates. Living anthropoids share a number of features attributable to their common ancestry. These primates tend to invest more resources and time into their offspring, with longer developmental times and more extensive brain growth. These features allow more sophisticated social behaviors, with stable social groups that effectively share information. Nearly all anthropoids give birth to one offspring at a time, and females have a single-chambered uterus to enable longer gestations and larger fetal size.

Early anthropoids appeared during the Late Eocene (c. 40 Ma). Anthropoids like *Aegyptopithecus* from Fayum, Egypt, had skeletons like living monkeys in most respects, but with relatively smaller brains. Genetic comparisons of living humans and monkeys show that genes expressed in brain development have evolved rapidly during the last 30 million years, reflecting the recent evolution of cognitive functions in anthropoids (see Dorus et al. 2004).

MIOCENE APES

Humans and apes are hominoids, and they diverged from the cercopithecoids (Old World monkeys) around 30 Ma. The first hominoids were similar to earlier anthropoids. They were arboreal quadrupeds, unlike living apes, which have long arms for suspending their bodies beneath branches. The teeth of early apes were like those of earlier primates. *Proconsul* was an important fossil hominoid lineage in Africa from 24 to 15 Ma, with several species covering a range of size from monkeys like macaques up to chimpanzee-sized or larger. The diversity of these apes covered many of the size and diet niches now occupied by cercopithecoids. At the same time, a gorilla-sized African ape called *Morotopithecus* appears to have had a suspensory locomotor pattern. Genetic evidence suggests that the most diverse lineages of living apes, the gibbons and siamangs, diverged from the ancestors of the great apes sometime around 18 Ma.

A dispersal of hominoids into Eurasia during the Middle Miocene may have included the ancestors of living great apes. Several apes, including *Ankarapithecus* and *Pierolapithecus*, were relatively small apes, with arms suited to suspending their weight beneath branches like living gibbons. These apes divided into an Asian lineage, ancestral to living orangutans, and a European-African lineage, ancestral to humans, chimpanzees and gorillas. The number of genetic differences between living species can be used to estimate the length of time since they last shared a common ancestor, called their divergence time. For the Asian and European/African ape lineages, this divergence occurred around 13 Ma. An orangutan-like ape called *Sivapithecus* existed in South Asia by 12 Ma.

Toward the end of the Miocene, ape diversity declined. South Asian and European apes ultimately became extinct, coincident with climate changes that increased seasonal temperature and rainfall variations and reduced the area of forests. These climatic shifts favored the rise of the cercopithecoid (Old World) monkeys, whose geographic range increased during the Upper Miocene and Pliocene to include Europe and East Asia by the Early Pliocene (c. 5 Ma).

Both humans and the living great apes are survivors of these extinctions. Despite being limited to small geographic ranges in the tropical forests of Africa and Indonesia, great apes have substantial adaptive and genetic diversity. For example, the genetic differences between Sumatran and Bornean orangutans exceed those between many other primate species. Likewise, chimpanzees and gorillas retain behaviorally and genetically distinct subspecies across their African ranges. These primates depend on different foods, strategies for finding food, and styles of communication in different parts of Africa.

THE FIRST HOMINIDS

Unlike the other African apes, early hominids are exceptionally well preserved in the fossil record almost immediately after their origin. Three hominid species have been found dating to the Late Miocene: *Sahelanthropus tchadensis* (7 Ma) in Chad, *Orrorin tugenensis* (6 Ma) in Kenya, and *Ardipithecus kadabba* (5.5 Ma) in Ethiopia. Each is represented by a fragmentary sample that presents some evidence of bipedal locomotion or upright posture (e.g., the proximal femur of *Orrorin,* the cranial base of *Sahelanthropus,* and the foot of *Ardipithecus*). The dental remains of these genera are very similar and, except for their smaller canines, within the range of other Late Miocene apes (see Haile-Selassie et al. 2004; Wolpoff et al. 2006).

A rich record of early hominids exists from sites in eastern, southern and central-western Africa. These remains date from as far back as nearly 4 Ma. The famous "Lucy" skeleton, found in 1974 in Hadar, Ethiopia, represents the species *Australopithecus afarensis,* and an even more complete skeleton was found in Dikika, Ethiopia in 2001. Hundreds of other fossil fragments from Ethiopia, Kenya, and Tanzania also belong to this species, which lived between 3.8 and 2.9 Ma. An additional large sample of hominids found in South Africa and dating to between 3.0 and 2.5 Ma represents *Australopithecus africanus.* This was the first of the early hominid species to be discovered. It was first identified by the South African anatomist Raymond Dart in 1924. From the name *Australopithecus,* these early hominids are often called "australopithecines."

These samples confirm the importance of bipedal locomotion to the early hominid lineage. The shape of the pelvis, knees, and feet had evolved to a human-like form that precluded efficient quadrupedal locomotion. Footprint trails from 3.5 Ma found in Laetoli, Tanzania, also demonstrate their human-like bipedality. Several pieces of evidence suggest that these australopithecines retained an adaptation to climbing. In particular, this may explain their short legs, small body sizes, powerful arm bones, and curved hand bones. Their small size stands out as a contrast to recent humans, as they averaged only around 1.2 meters in height and 35 to 50 kilograms in mass.

Aside from bipedality, the other major anatomical pattern of early hominids involved dentition. Australopithecines had large molar and premolar teeth compared to living and fossil apes and humans. These teeth were low-crowned and had thick enamel, apparently adapted to a diet of grinding hard foods such as seeds. Isotopic evidence suggests that their diet was varied, with the main difference from other primates being a high consumption of plants with a C_4 photosynthetic cycle—including grasses and some sedges (see Sponheimer et al. 2005). As primates cannot digest grass, it has been suggested that this may represent the consumption of grass seeds, termites, and other grass-consuming animals (see Peters and Vogel 2005). Contrasting with their large molar teeth, early hominids had small canine teeth, which may hint at a reduction in male competition or a shift from threatening displays with the canine teeth to other kinds of displays, such as vocalizations or weaponry.

A later group of australopithecines greatly emphasized the adaptation to large grinding teeth. These "robust" australopithecines had molar and premolar teeth with as much as four times the area of present-day humans, together with immense jawbones and jaw muscles. Their diet presumably included a higher percentage of hard, brittle foods, which may have been increasingly important during the drier climates of the Late Pliocene. These were the last of the australopithecines to become extinct, a little less than 1.5 Ma.

FROM *AUSTRALOPITHECUS* TO *HOMO*

Alongside the robust australopithecines lived the earliest members of our own genus, *Homo.* Early *Homo* can be distinguished from contemporary australopithecines by its smaller molar teeth (although still larger than living people) and larger brain size. The transition to large brains and smaller teeth was accompanied by an increased dietary reliance on meat. Because of its high caloric and protein content, meat requires fewer digestive resources and can fuel more substantial brain growth. Primates with high-energy diets tend to have smaller guts, which also allows a higher proportion of metabolic resources to be allocated to brain tissue (see Milton 2003; Aiello and Wheeler 1995).

The archaeological record provides further evidence for a dietary shift, with the earliest-known stone tools occurring in Ethiopia about 2.6 Ma. Many primates are able to manipulate objects as tools, and wild chimpanzees have traditions involving the use of stones to crack nuts and shaping simple wooden spears or probing sticks. It seems probable that early hominids also shared these abilities, but they left no archaeological trace. The earliest flaked stone tools were used to cut flesh off animal bones and break into bones for marrow.

These early toolmaking hominids existed in regions with more extensive and seasonally arid grasslands, and they are found together with the robust australopithecines. Both fossil and archaeological evidence of *Homo* remain rare before 2 Ma, but after this time numerous fossils of a small-bodied, large-brained hominid species called *Homo habilis* have been found. *Homo habilis* is the first species to show evidence in the wrist and hand of toolmaking adaptations, and the traces of brain anatomy preserved on its endocast suggest a more advanced planning ability than in earlier hominids (see Holloway 1996).

A second species of early *Homo*, called *Homo erectus* had larger bodies and taller stature—an average of 1.6 to 1.8 meters compared to earlier hominids at 1.0 to 1.4 meters. With its longer legs and larger brain size, *Homo erectus* was adapted to the use of larger home ranges and more patchily distributed, high-energy food resources. The differences in size between males and females in this species, sexual dimorphism, were in the range of recent humans, possibly reflecting more human-like social interactions than in earlier hominids, including greater cooperation and food sharing.

The use of more open territory and larger home ranges may have enabled *Homo erectus* to colonize Eurasia. A series of fossils and archaeological remains from Dmanisi, Republic of Georgia, dates to about 1.8 Ma. Hominids also reached Java around this time, and indeed the first fossil specimens of *Homo erectus* to be found were discovered on Java by the Dutch colonial physician and scientist Eugene Dubois in 1891.

PLEISTOCENE HUMAN EVOLUTION

The populations of *Homo erectus* in Africa and East Asia developed some regional differentiation relatively early in their existence. The form of the cranium, the thickness and shape of the brow ridge, the size of neck muscle attachments, and other details overlap between regions but differ substantially on average. Also, the Dmanisi *Homo erectus* skeletons appear to have been smaller than those in Africa. Some researchers view these features as evidence that *Homo* was divided into different species in different parts of the world. Others consider these morphological differences to be analogous to features distinguishing human populations today (see Asfaw et al. 2002).

Homo erectus had reached China by 1.2 Ma, but hominids entered Europe later, after 1 Ma, and possibly as late as 800,000 years ago. Shortly after this time, fossils in Africa show a loss of some of the diagnostic cranial traits of *Homo erectus*, and, with a few exceptions, early European skulls never had them. The African and early European remains are often referred to as "archaic" members of our own species, *Homo sapiens*, or else by another species name, *Homo heidelbergensis*. It is not clear whether the anatomical evolution was accompanied by biological speciation, or whether it represents an increase in brain size and consequent changes in cranial morphology within a single evolving species. In either case, early European hominids also had morphological features distinguishing them from other regions, including a projecting face and nose and large sinuses. One of the most important sites of the last million years is Sima de los Huesos, Ataperca, Spain, at which the partial skeletal remains of more than 25 individuals, from around 300,000 years ago, have been found.

The emergence of regional morphological variants was one trend during the Pleistocene, and it was joined by other trends in common across different regions. The most important was a gradual increase in brain size. The earliest *Homo erectus* specimens had endocranial volumes averaging around 750 milliliters; these increased to an average of 1,400 milliliters by 50,000 years ago. This increase is evident everywhere ancient humans lived, including Africa, Asia, and Europe. It is logical to assume that brain size increased because of new cognitive abilities. Brains are energetically expensive, and the metabolic cost of an increase in brain tissue must be redeemed by more food acquisition or reproduction.

The archaeological record provides additional evidence about cognitive evolution. Stone tools gradually became more sophisticated over the Pleistocene. First, the development of bifacially flaked handaxes and cleavers in Acheulean industry shows that hominids could learn and replicate standardized, symmetrical forms by 1.5 Ma. Later, tools became more standardized, raw materials were obtained across longer distances, and techniques were shared across wider areas. These changes may reflect either more widespread contacts between cultural traditions or more efficient transfer of information. Finally, by 300,000 years ago, humans had mastered prepared-core toolmaking techniques, which required information transfer, not only about finished tool form but also about procedure. After this time, the technological properties of different human cultures began to diversify yet further, with industries changing more rapidly and occupying smaller areas. The fragmentation and acceleration of change in material culture would continue over the last 50,000 years as the complexity of culture and behavior increased further.

It is likely that the behavioral complexity after 300,000 years ago required some capacity for spoken language. Because people learn and coordinate their activities by talking to each other, language is a fundamental basis for human culture and behavior. But there is very little anatomical evidence relating to the evolution of language, for the necessary structures (e.g., tongue, larynx, brain) do not fossilize. Still, a few hints exist. At least one *Homo habilis* skull includes a marked enlargement of Broca's area in the frontal cortex, a brain structure important to planning complex activities and carrying out speech in living humans (see Holloway 1996). The hyoid bone, a small bone in the throat that supports the larynx, rarely fossilizes, but two hyoids from Sima de los Huesos and one from Kebara, Israel, have been found. These hyoids are essentially human-like in shape, in contrast to a preserved hyoid from *Australopithecus afarensis*, which is ape-like. Finally, at least one gene related to language, *FoxP2*, shows evidence of strong selection within the past 200,000 years (see Enard et al. 2002). Together, these hints suggest a long evolution of language from early, simple communication to the fully human language of today.

THE NEANDERTHALS

The most well-known group of ancient humans is the Neanderthals (or Neandertals), inhabitants of Europe and parts of West Asia between 200,000 and 30,000 years ago. The Neanderthals were specialists in hunting large game, with sites dominated by the bones of bison, horse, and red deer. Isotopic evidence suggests that their diet included a very high proportion of meat (see Bocherens et al. 2005). Early humans, including Neanderthals, had short lives compared to recent humans, including recent hunter-gatherers. They also had a very high rate of traumatic injuries. These factors may be attributable to their reliance on close-contact hunting of large animals using thrusting spears. With powerful long bones and muscular necks, the Neanderthals were highly adapted to this strenuous lifestyle.

The high mortality and risks of early human lifestyles had demographic consequences. Archaic humans maintained low population densities and low total numbers for thousands of generations. In contrast, recent humans have exploded exponentially in numbers. This rapid growth has been possible with a relatively small per-generation rate of increase, emphasizing that the reproductive potential of early humans must have been balanced by higher mortality. The risks of ancient lives may also be illustrated by the occurrence of cannibalism, both by Neanderthals and other archaic peoples.

Genetic evidence taken directly from Neanderthal skeletal remains has been recovered. Some of the diversity of ancient Neanderthals is evidenced by their mitochondrial DNA (mtDNA), which share a common ancestor with the mtDNA of living humans between 300,000 and 700,000 years ago (see Serre et al. 2004). No sequences like the Neanderthal mtDNA have been found in any living people, however, suggesting that at least this genetic element did not form part of the ancestry of present-day humans. The relationships concerning the rest of the genome are somewhat more complicated. The initial phase of the Neanderthal Genome Project found possible evidence for Neanderthal-human interbreeding, with Neanderthals differing only slightly more from humans than a random pair of humans do from each other. Other genetic evidence from recent people also suggests that genes from archaic humans may have entered recent human populations by interbreeding.

Neanderthals and other early humans were absorbed or displaced by the emergence of modern humans. This event may reflect the simple technology of earlier peoples and the more effective collection strategies of moderns, and it therefore may have been a primarily cultural transition with anatomical and behavioral consequences. Alternatively, there may have been a cognitive revolution between the earlier archaic and later modern humans. In any event, the later historical elaboration of human cultures and diversity would not have been possible without the evolutionary history of Pleistocene and earlier hominids. The anatomical and behavioral adaptations of our ancestors were the building blocks of the current human world.

SEE ALSO *Genetic Distance; Genetic Variation Among Populations; Human Biological Variation; Human Genetics; "Out of Africa" Hypothesis.*

BIBLIOGRAPHY

Aiello, Leslie C., and Peter Wheeler. 1995. "The Expensive-Tissue Hypothesis: The Brain and the Digestive System in Human and Primate Evolution." *Current Anthropology* 36 (2): 199–221.

Alemseged, Z., et al. 2006. "A Juvenile Early Hominin Skeleton from Dikika, Ethiopia." *Nature* 443: 296–301.

Antón S. C., W. R. Leonard, and M. L. Robertson. 2002. "An Ecomorphological Model of the Initial Hominid Dispersal from Africa." *Journal of Human Evolution* 43: 773–785.

Asfaw, B., et al. 2002. "Remains of *Homo erectus* from Bouri, Middle Awash, Ethiopia." *Nature* 416: 317–320.

Berger, T. D., and E. Trinkaus. 1995. "Patterns of Trauma among the Neandertals." *Journal of Archaeological Science* 22: 841–852.

Bocherens, H., et al. 2005. "Isotopic Evidence for Diet and Subsistence Pattern of the Saint-Césaire I Neanderthal: Review and Use of a Multi-Source Mixing Model." *Journal of Human Evolution* 49 (1): 71–87.

Coale, Ansley J. 1974. "The History of the Human Population." *Scientific American* 231: 40–52.

Dorus, S., et al. 2004. "Accelerated Evolution of Nervous System Genes in the Origin of *Homo sapiens*." *Cell* 119 (7): 1027–1040.

Enard, W., et al. 2002. "Molecular Evolution of *FOXP2*, a Gene Involved in Speech and Language." *Nature* 418: 869–872.

Glazko, Galina V., and Masatoshi Nei. 2003. "Estimation of Divergence Times for Major Lineages of Primate Species." *Molecular Biology and Evolution* 20: 424–434.

Green, R. E., et al. 2006. "Analysis of One Million Base Pairs of Neanderthal DNA." *Nature* 444: 330–336.

Haile-Selassie, Yohannes, Gen Suwa, and Tim D. White. 2004. "Late Miocene Teeth from Middle Awash, Ethiopia, and Early Hominid Dental Evolution." *Science* 303 (5663): 1503–1505.

Hawks, John, and Gregory Cochran. 2006. "Dynamics of Adaptive Introgression from Archaic to Modern Humans." *PaleoAnthropology* 2006: 101–115.

Hawks, John, and Milford. H. Wolpoff. 2001. "The Accretion Model of Neandertal Evolution." *Evolution* 55 (7): 1474–1485.

Holloway, Ralph. 1996. "Evolution of the Human Brain." In *Handbook of Human Symbolic Evolution*, edited by A. Lock and C. R. Peters, 74–116. Oxford, U.K.: Clarendon Press.

Kay, R. F., C. Ross, and B. A. Williams. 1997. "Anthropoid Origins." *Science* 275: 797–804.

Lee, Sang-Hee, and Milford H. Wolpoff. 2003. "The Pattern of Evolution in Pleistocene Human Brain Size." *Paleobiology* 29: 186–196.

McBrearty, S., and A. S. Brooks. 2000. "The Revolution that Wasn't: A New Interpretation of the Origin of Modern Human Behavior." *Journal of Human Evolution* 39 (5): 453–563.

McHenry, Henry M., and Katherine Coffing. 2000. "*Australopithecus to Homo*: Transformations in Body and Mind." *Annual Review of Anthropology* 29: 125–146.

Milton, Katherine. 2003. "The Critical Role Played by Animal Source Foods in Human (*Homo*) Evolution." *Journal of Nutrition* 133: 3886S–3892S.

Peters, Charles R., and John C. Vogel. 2005. "Africa's Wild C4 Plant Foods and Possible Early Hominid Diets." *Journal of Human Evolution* 48 (3): 219–236.

Serre, D., et al. 2004. "No Evidence of Neandertal mtDNA Contribution to Early Modern Humans." *PLoS Biology* 2: 0313–0317.

Sponheimer, M., D. de Ruiter, J. Lee-Thorp, and A. Späth. 2005. "Sr/Ca and Early Hominin Diets Revisited: New Data from Modern and Fossil Tooth Enamel." *Journal of Human Evolution* 48: 147–156.

Stern, Jack T., Jr., and Randall L. Susman. 1983. "The Locomotor Anatomy of *Australopithecus afarensis*." *American Journal of Physical Anthropology* 60: 279–318.

Tavaré, Simon, et al. 2002. "Using the Fossil Record to Estimate the Age of the Last Common Ancestor of Extant Primates." *Nature* 416: 726–729.

Warren, Kristin. S., et al. 2001. "Speciation and Intrasubspecific Variation of Bornean Orangutans, *Pongo pygmaeus pygmaeus*." *Molecular Biology and Evolution* 18: 472–480.

Wildman, D. E., et al. 2003. "Implications of Natural Selection in Shaping 99.4% Nonsynonymous DNA Identity between Humans and Chimpanzees: Enlarging Genus *Homo*." *Proceedings of the National Academy of Sciences USA* 100 (12): 7181–7188.

Wolpoff, Milford H., et al. 2006. "An Ape or *the* Ape: Is the Toumaï Cranium TM 266 a Hominid?" *PaleoAnthropology* 2006: 36–50.

Won, Y. J., and J. Hey. 2004. "Divergence Population Genetics of Chimpanzees." *Molecular Biology and Evolution* 22 (2): 297–307.

Wynn, Thomas. 2002. "Archaeology and Cognitive Evolution." *Behavioral and Brain Sciences* 25: 389–438.

John Hawks

HUMAN BIOLOGICAL VARIATION

To some people, "race" is a four-letter word associated with negative connotations, while for others it refers to actual biologically inherited traits. Skin color is the most readily visible signifier of race, and as such is the characteristic upon which most racial classifications are based. Historically, the ancient Egyptians were the first to classify humans on the basis of skin color. In 1350 BCE Egyptians classified humans into four races: "red" for Egyptians, "yellow" for people living to the east of Egypt, "white" for people living north of Africa, and "black" for Africans from the south of Egypt. The ancient Greeks, on the other hand, referred to all Africans as "Ethiopians." A major tenet of the biological concept of race is that the traits that identify a given race are unchangeable and have been fixed since the beginning of humankind. Since the early twentieth century, however, an evolutionary approach led by anthropologists and human biologists has emerged that calls into question the validity of the biological concept of race.

RACE IN THE TWENTIETH CENTURY

In the early 1900s, head shape was considered an innate "racial" trait that was inherited, with little environmental influence at work. This concept changed with the pioneering studies of Franz Boas (1858–1942). Boas demonstrated that the cephalic index (the ratio of head width to head length) of children born to immigrants to the United States changed because they grew up in a different environment than that of their parents. These and subsequent genetic studies have demonstrated that the biological features that distinguish racial groups are subject to environmental influence and are of recent origin. Furthermore, data and models from DNA studies suggest that common race definitions pertaining to humans have little taxonomic validity, because there is no correlation

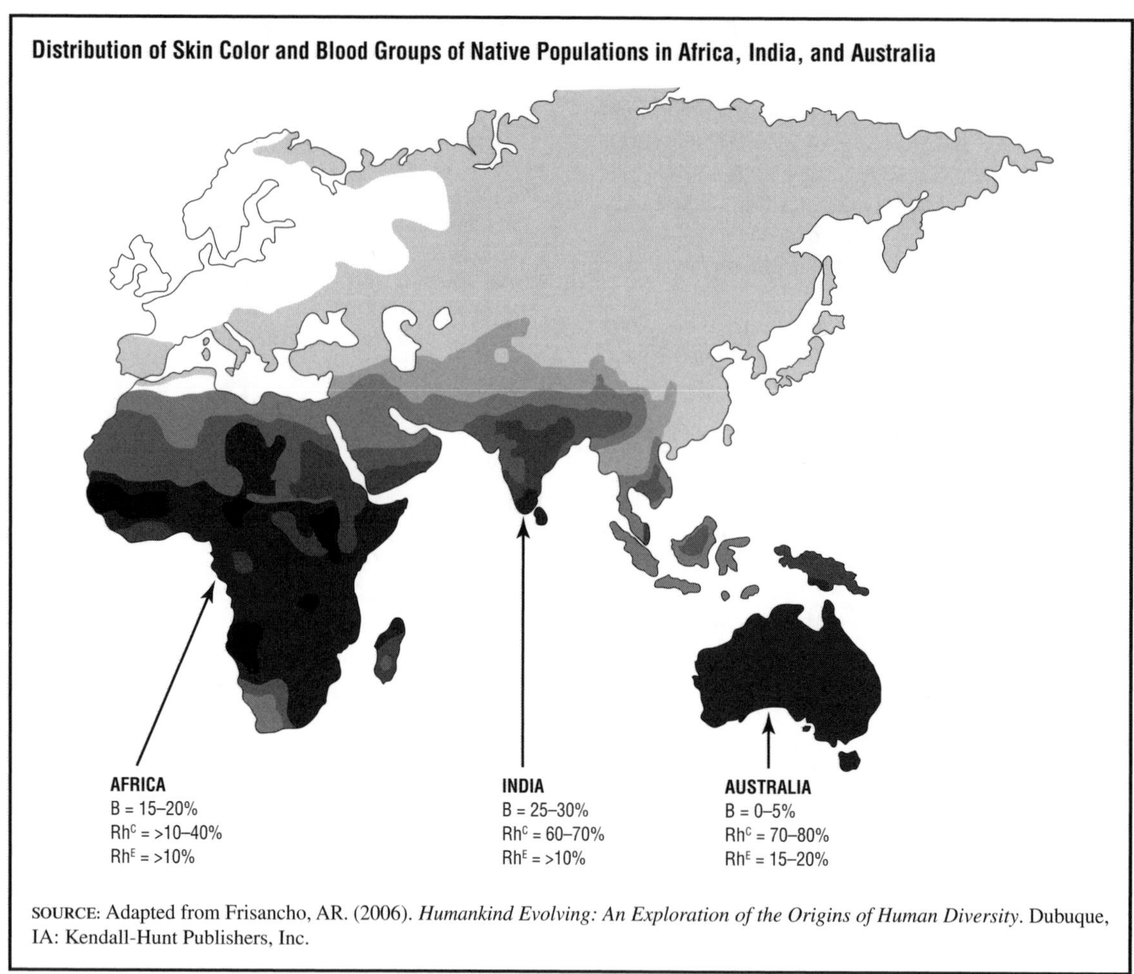

Figure 1. *Distribution of Skin Color, B Blood Group, and Rh Blood Group Rh^C and Rh^E in native populations of Africa, India, and Australia. Although Australian, African, and Indian populations have similar skin color, they have very different blood types.*

between genetic markers such as blood type and markers for race such as skin color. For example, as shown in Figure 1, the Australian aborigines, East and West African populations, and native populations from India have a similar dark skin color. Based on this trait, they could all be assigned to an "African race." However, with reference to frequencies of the B blood group and Rh blood genes C and E, the Australian aborigines are very different from the East African, West African, and Indian populations. In other words, there is no concordance between blood type and skin color. Likewise, the ABO blood type frequencies for natives of Taiwan and Greece are very similar (0 = 45.2 %, A = 32.6 %, B =18.0 %, AB = 3.4 %), but on the basis of geography and physical appearance these two populations clearly belong to different categories.

Likewise, the indigenous populations of sub-Saharan Africa, southern Europe, the Middle East, and India have similar frequencies of the sickle-cell trait (20 to 34 percent), yet they differ in skin color. The similarity of these populations in the frequency of sickle-cell trait is related to their common adaptation to malaria, not to a common racial origin. Similarly, lactose tolerance occurs both in European and African populations, not because they have the same racial origin, but because both were evolutionarily adapted to dairy products. In other words, the concept of "race" is both too broad and too narrow a definition of ancestry to be biologically useful. The reason that definitions of race lose their discriminating power for identifying races is due to the fact that humans share a common origin and have been constantly migrating throughout their evolutionary history. For example, the large-scale migrations between Africa and Europe, as well as the colonial expansion of European populations into Asia and the New World, have resulted in the mating of individuals from different continents and the concomitant mixture of genetic traits.

For these reasons, using the biological concept of race to describe biological diversity has largely been abandoned. Nevertheless, because the risks of some diseases have a genetic basis in some populations that may have originated in a geographic region that differs from their current area, there is still great interest in understanding how genetic diversity has been structured in the human species.

CRITERIA FOR RACIAL CLASSIFICATION

In the taxonomic literature, "race" is any distinguishable type within a species. Among researchers, however, "race" as a biological concept has had a variety of meanings. Some use frequency of genetic traits between and within groups as the point of reference, while others use geographical area.

Trait Frequency. Genetic studies demonstrate that about 85.4 percent of all the variation in the human species can be attributed to variation within populations and that there is only a 6.3 percent difference between "races," with less than half of this value accounted for by known racial groupings (see Lewontin 1972; Barbujani, Magani, Minch, et al. 1997). In other words, there is much more genetic variation within local groups than there is among local groups or among races themselves. This genetic unity means, for instance, that any local group contains, on average, 85 percent of the genetic variation that exists in the entire human species. As a result, there is about 15 percent genetic variation between any two individuals. Therefore, a randomly selected white European, although ostensibly far removed from black Americans in phenotype, can easily be genetically closer to an African black than to another European white. As summarized by Jeffrey Long and Rick Kittles in a 2003 article, the patterns of genetic variation within and between groups are too intricate to be reduced to a single summary measure. In other words, identification of trait frequencies and statistical partitions of genetic variation do not provide accurate information to justify claims for the existence of "races."

Geographical Race. Because some phenotypes, such as skin color, facial features, and hair form, differ between native inhabitants of different regions of the world, biological anthropologists and geneticists introduced the idea of geographical races (see Dobzhansky 1970, Brues 1977, Garn 1961, Mayr 2002). In this classificatory approach, each geographic region (e.g., South America, Australia, sub-Saharan Africa, East Asia, Polynesia) is associated with a race. According to these authors, "geographical races" refer to an aggregate of phenotypically similar populations of a species inhabiting a geographic subdivision. An underlying assumption of this approach is that in each geographical area there are clusters of genetic traits that, taken together, differentiate them from those of other geographic areas. Current evidence indicates that variability in the genotypic and phenotypic expression of genetic traits is affected by natural selection, migration, and genetic drift. As a result of these processes, genetic diversity follows a pattern characterized by gradients of allele frequencies that extend over the entire world. (Alleles are alternative versions of a particular gene.) In other words, when identified, the clustering of genetic traits in a given area reflects the demographic and evolutionary history of the population rather than a racial category. Therefore, there is no reason to assume that "races" represent any units of relevance for understanding human genetic history.

In summary, and as stated by the 1996 American Association of Physical Anthropologists' "Statement on Biological Aspects of Race": (1) all human populations derive from a common ancestral group, (2) there is great genetic diversity within all human populations, and (3) the geographic pattern of variation is complex and presents no major discontinuity. In other words, race is a consequence of social history and any variation is therefore transitory. For these reasons, among biological anthropologists at least, the biological concept of race for describing biological diversity has largely been abandoned.

IQ AND RACE: MISUSE OF SCIENTIFIC INFORMATION

An illustration of the dangers of misusing information on the intelligence quotient (IQ) and heritability is found in studies of IQ and race. The IQ test was developed by the French psychologist Alfred Binet in the 1910s to identify children's reading readiness. The IQ test was intended to measure "mental age" in various categories. Binet warned that the IQ test could not properly be used to measure intelligence "because intellectual qualities are not superposable, and therefore cannot be measured as linear surfaces are measured" (Binet and Simon 1916, p. 206). Intelligence was therefore not considered by Binet to be a fixed quantity, but rather one that could be increased through teaching. Yet in the United States, tests of IQ have been used to measure general intelligence.

As shown in Figure 2, the normal range for IQ for about 67 percent of the population falls between 85 to 115, while only 5 percent of the population attain IQ values greater than 140 and below 70. The use of IQ as a measure of an individual's innate intelligence is not valid for two reasons. First, there are many kinds of intelligence. There are some people with outstanding memories, some with mathematical skills, some with musical talents, some good at seeing analogies, some good at synthesizing information, and some with manual and mechanical expertise. These different kinds of intelligence cannot be subsumed into an IQ score.

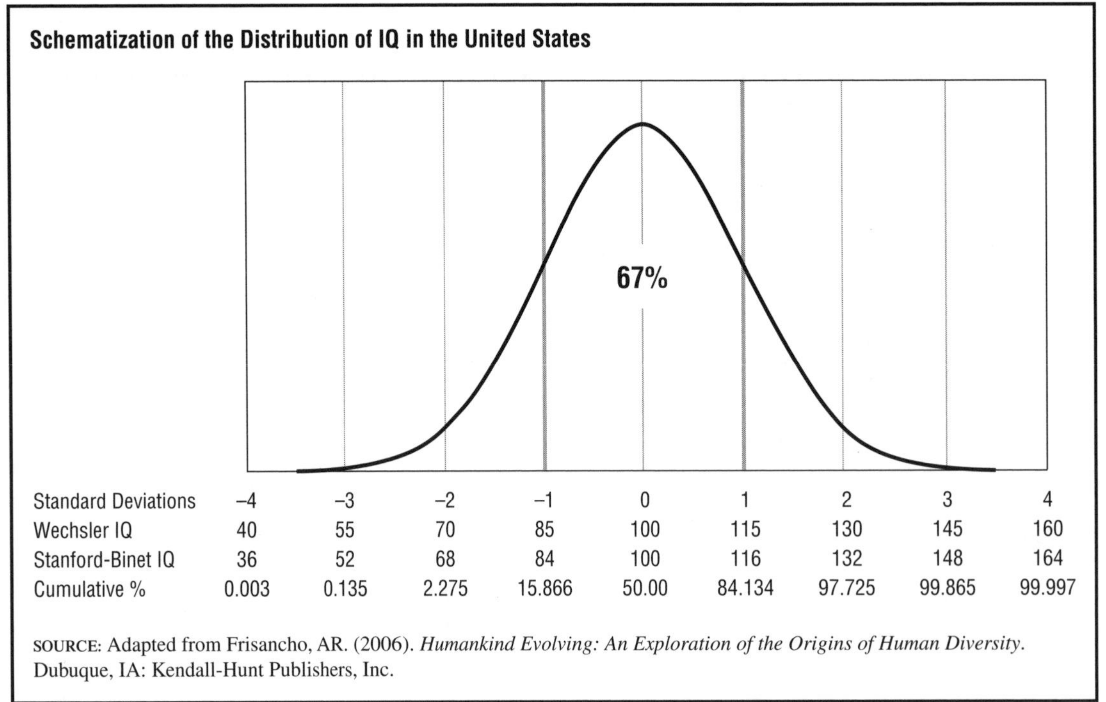

SOURCE: Adapted from Frisancho, AR. (2006). *Humankind Evolving: An Exploration of the Origins of Human Diversity.* Dubuque, IA: Kendall-Hunt Publishers, Inc.

Figure 2.

Second, there is no evidence that IQ is genetically determined. It is true that about 60 percent of the variability in IQ is inherited within family lines, but the fact that it is inherited does not mean that it is genetically determined. Discrete traits such as blood type that do not change through the life cycle are genetically determined and, therefore, have a high heritability, but continuous traits such as height, weight, or IQ are highly subject to environmental influence. Heritability is computed as the fraction of phenotypic variability due to genetic differences divided by total variability. It is expressed as $h^2 = G / P = G / (G + E)$, where G is variability in genotype, E is variability in environment, and P is variability in phenotype. Depending upon whether the environmental variance (E) is large or small, the phenotypic variance (P) can be either large or small, and the heritability (h^2) can be either large or small. Measures of heritability, especially of continuous traits such as intelligence, indicate the joint influence of genetic and environmental factors. Twin and family studies have shown that shared environmental factors have an important effect on educational attainment (see Silventoinen et al. 2004). Shared environmental factors such as education have a greater impact on intelligence during childhood than in adulthood. In other words, heritability of intelligence (unlike genetic determination) can be very different in different populations, depending upon the environmental condition in which each population develops. Therefore, a low IQ score reflects the effects of poor education during childhood and negative environmental conditions.

Despite these pitfalls, some researchers have attempted to show that difference in IQ reflects difference in genetic capabilities. For example, Richard Herrnstein and Charles Murray, in their book *The Bell Curve* (1994), argue that differences in IQ between white and black Americans reflect differences in the genetic capability of intelligence in each race. They point out that the distribution of IQ scores in black Americans is shifted to the left, so that there are higher frequencies of low IQ scores and lower frequencies of high IQ scores when compared to white Americans. However, this difference is more a reflection of the different educational experiences of black and white Americans. For example, a study by Dickens and Flynn (2006) shows that "in nine standardization samples for four major tests of cognitive ability blacks gained four to seven IQ points on non-Hispanic whites between 1972 and 2002. Gains have been fairly uniform across the entire range of black cognitive ability." Similarly, in the Barclay School of Baltimore, black children who previously scored at the 20th percentile were later attaining scores at the 85th percentile. These findings together indicate that the lower IQ scores associated with black samples is more a function of educational experiences than of genetic determinants.

It is evident that cultural environment is an important contributor to any measures of IQ. This inference can be illustrated by several examples. First, consider two hypothetical groups of eight-year-old children: one from a middle class U.S. school and one from a poor rural area in Guatemala. These children are asked the following question: "Suppose you have five eggs and you drop two, how many eggs do you have?"

The U.S. children will likely answer that they have three eggs left, but the rural children may answer that they have five eggs. Based on this result, one might conclude that the Guatemalan rural children do not know how to add or subtract. However, the rural children have been raised in an environment associated with food shortages, and they will likely believe that just because an egg has been dropped does not mean it cannot be eaten. Hence, for the Guatemalan rural children, there are still five eggs. The "correct" answer, therefore, depends on the children's past experience. In another example, suppose that Australian aborigine trackers and Peruvian Andean weavers are asked to identify a series of drawings that will make a complete square as fast as possible. It is likely that the speed of the Peruvian Andean weavers at this task will be faster than that of Australian aborigine trackers. This difference is related to the fact that Australian aborigine trackers have had little or no contact with the concepts of two-dimensional geometry, whereas the Peruvian Andean weavers are in an occupation that involves experience with two-dimensional geometric designs. Thus, differences in responses may reflect an individual's or population's past experience.

IQ should be defined as a measure of an individual's sum of cultural experience, rather than a measure of genetic difference. This does not mean that a person's genetic makeup is not a significant factor in individual intelligence in particular areas. Without the proper environment, however, this trait may not be expressed.

THE USE OF GEOGRAPHIC AREA AND RACE IN BIOMEDICAL RESEARCH

It is evident that the biological concept of race is poorly defined and cannot be used as a surrogate for multiple environmental and genetic factors in disease causation. Recent genetic studies of DNA polymorphisms have suggested that human genetic diversity is organized in continental or geographical areas (see Serre and Pääbo 2004; Feldman, Lewontin, and King 2004). This conclusion suggests that geographic area, rather than race per se, has a valid role in biomedical research because many medically important genes vary in frequency between populations from different regions. If, for example, there are major differences in allele frequencies between geographic areas, individuals from different origins may be expected to respond differently to medical treatments. In this case, the identification of the origin of people in a geographic area does have some justification as a proxy for differences in environmental and other factors of relevance for public health.

However, the ability to place an individual within a geographic region and range of variation does not mean that this variation is best represented by the concept of race. For example, sickle-cell disease is a characteristic of ancient ancestry in a geographic region where malaria was endemic (e.g., Africa, the Mediterranean, and southern India), rather than a characteristic of a particular racial group. Therefore, a diagnostic approach toward sickle-cell disease must take into account the individual's geographical ancestry. Similarly, populations who throughout their evolutionary history have developed an adaptive response to economize salt loss under the condition of tropic heat stress are more susceptible to developing high blood pressure than other populations when living in temperate climates. In other words, in biomedical research, it is not race that is relevant, but rather how the forces of evolution in a geographic area have shaped the individual's genes. Thus, because an individual's genes are grounded in his or her genealogy, identifying all contributions to a patient's ancestry is useful in diagnosing and treating diseases with genetic influences.

SEE ALSO *Australian Aborigine Peoples; Clines; Clines and Continuous Variation; Human and Primate Evolution.*

BIBLIOGRAPHY

Allison, Anthony C. 1954. "Protection Afforded by Sickle-Cell Trait against Subtertian Malarial Infection." *British Medical Journal* 1: 290–294.

———. 1956. "Sickle Cells and Evolution." *Scientific American* 195: 87–94.

American Association of Physical Anthropologists. 1996. "AAPA Statement on Biological Aspects of Race." *American Journal of Physical Anthropology* 101: 569–570. Available from http://www.physanth.org/positions/race.html.

Barbujani, Guido, Arianna Magani, Eric Minch, and L. Luca Cavalli-Sforza. 1997. "An Apportionment of Human DNA Diversity." *Proceeding of The National Academy of Sciences USA* 94: 4516–4519.

Binet, Alfred, and Théodore Simon. 1916. *The Development of Intelligence in Children (the Binet-Simon Scale).* Translated by Elizabeth S. Kite. Baltimore, MD: Williams & Wilkins.

Boas, Franz. 1912. *Changes in the Bodily Form of Descendants of Immigrants.* New York: Columbia University Press.

Boomsma, Dorret, Andreas Busjahn, and Lenna Peltonen. 2002. "Classical Twin Studies and Beyond." *Nature Reviews Genetics* 3 (11): 872–882.

Brace, C. Loring. 2005. *Race Is a Four-Letter Word: The Genesis of the Concept.* New York: Oxford University Press.

Brown, Ryan A., and George J. Armelagos. 2001. "Apportionment of Racial Diversity: A Review." *Evolutionary Anthropology* 10 (1): 34–40.

Brues, Alice M. 1977. *People and Races.* New York: Macmillan.

Dickens, W. T., and J. R. Flynn. 2006. "Black Americans Reduce the Racial IQ Gap: Evidence from Standardization Samples." *Psychological Science* 17 (10): 913–920.

Dobzhansky, Theodosius. 1970. *Genetics of the Evolutionary Process.* New York: Columbia University Press.

Feldman, Marcus W., and Richard C. Lewontin. 1975. "The Heritability Hang-Up." *Science* 190: 1163–1168.

———, and Mary-Claire King. 2003. "Race: A Genetic Melting Pot." *Nature* 424 (6947): 374–375.

Frisancho, A. Roberto. 2006. *Humankind Evolving: An Exploration on the Origins of Human Diversity.* Dubuke, IA: Kendall-Hunt.

———, et al. 1999. "Role of Genetic and Environmental Factors in the Increased Blood Pressures of Bolivian Blacks." *American Journal of Human Biology* 11 (4): 489–498.

Garn, Stanley M. 1961. *Human Races.* Springfield, IL: Charles C. Thomas.

Haldane, John B. S. 1949. "The Rate of Mutation of Human Genes." *Proceedings of the Eighth International Congress of Genetics*: 267–273.

Herrnstein, Richard, and Charles Murray. 1994. *The Bell Curve: Intelligence and Class Structure in American Life.* New York: Free Press.

Lewontin, Richard C. 1972. "The Apportionment of Human Diversity." *Evolutionary Biology* 6: 381–398.

———. 1976. "Genetic Aspects of Intelligence." *Annual Review of Genetics* 9: 387–405.

———. 2002. "Directions in Evolutionary Biology." *Annual Review of Genetics* 36: 1–18.

Lieberman, Leonard, and Fatimah Linda C. Jackson. 1995. "Race and Three Models of Human Origin." *American Anthropologist* 97 (2): 231–242.

Livingstone, Frank B. 1963. "On the Non-Existence of Human Races." *Current Anthropology* 3 (3): 279–281.

Long, Jeffrey C., and Rick A. Kittles. 2003. "Human Genetic Diversity and the Nonexistence of Biological Races." *Human Biology* 75 (4): 449–471.

Mayr, Ernst. 2002. "The Biology of Race and the Concept of Equality." *Daedalus* 131 (1): 89.

Serre, David, and Svante Pääbo. 2004. "Evidence for Gradients of Human Genetic Diversity Within and Among Continents." *Genome Research* 14: 1679–1685.

Silventoinen, Karri, et al. 2004. "Heritability of Body Height and Educational Attainment in an International Context: Comparison of Adult Twins in Minnesota and Finland." *American Journal of Human Biology* 16 (5): 544–555.

Wilson, James F., et al. 2001. "Population Genetic Structure of Variable Drug Response." *Nature Genetics* 29 (3): 265–269.

A. Roberto Frisancho

HUMAN GENETICS

Whether or not race is a useful construct in biology, medicine, and society has been debated for more than a century. Despite this attention, even the most elementary questions about race persist. What is a race? How many human races are there? What determines membership in a race? Is race a useful proxy for health or behavior?

Scientific interest in the relationship between race and human biological variation has intensified recently with advances in genomics. There is hope that an increased knowledge of the human DNA sequence and the discovery of DNA sequence variations within and among individuals will provide definitive answers to the long-standing questions about the biological aspects, and indeed the biological validity, of the idea of race. Genomic data have revealed the patterns of human genetic diversity in exquisite detail. However, it is still a challenge to understand how these patterns relate to the biological processes that generated them, and to discover the implications of these patterns for broader issues related to health and disease. While the purpose here is to focus on contemporary issues of race in genetics and disease research, it must also be remembered that race is not simply a biological topic; it is part of human social and political fabric as well.

IMPORTANT TERMS AND KEY CONCEPTS IN GENETICS

A basic familiarity with terms and concepts in genetics is essential to understanding human genetic variation. To begin, all hereditary information is encoded in DNA (deoxyribonucleic acid). Each DNA molecule is composed of two strands of basic building blocks called *nucleotides.* There are four different kinds of nucleotides, denoted by the letters A, C, G, and T. The letter designations for nucleotides are used as a shorthand for the chemical bases that give the four kinds of nucleotides their distinctive properties. The two strands of a DNA molecule are wound together lengthwise forming a *double helix* shape. At each position along the double helix, the nucleotide from one strand is paired with a nucleotide from the other, according to a basic rule: A with T and C with G. In essence, each DNA molecule exists as a long string of nucleotide pairs. The information in genes is encoded in the sequence of A, T, C, and G nucleotides (see Figure 1).

The DNA double helix is super-coiled and bundled with proteins into structures called *chromosomes.* Every person has twenty-three pairs of chromosomes, with one member of each pair inherited from their mother and the other member inherited from their father. One of the twenty-three chromosome pairs is special because it determines the person's chromosomal sex. The two members of this pair are different in males (they are denoted X and Y); while females carry two X chromosomes. The other twenty-two pairs of chromosomes are called *autosomes.* The autosomes are alike in males and females. Chromosomes are contained inside the nuclei of cells. Interestingly, humans and other life forms carry a small DNA molecule outside of the cell nucleus. This DNA molecule occurs in many copies in a

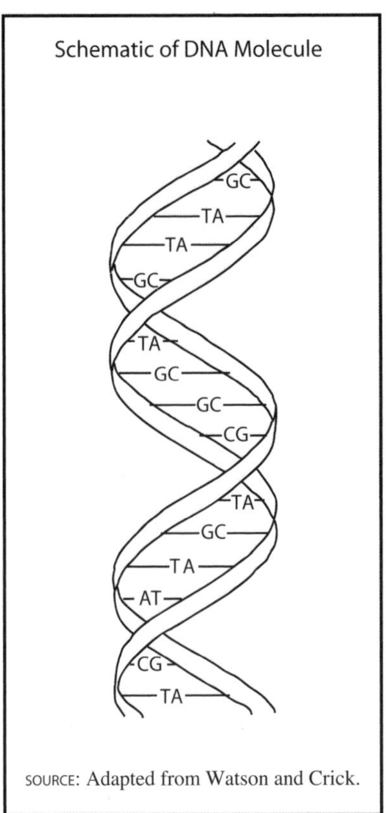

Figure 1. *Schematic of the DNA molecule illustrating the double helix form and base pairing rule T:A and G:C.*

cell component called the *mitochondrion*. Mitochondrial DNA (mtDNA) is easy to work with in the laboratory and has been studied extensively.

In the early twenty-first century, geneticists speak of the *genome*, which is a complete copy of the DNA for a species. The term *locus* refers to a specific physical location on a genome. Loci (plural of locus) vary in length: They can be small and hold only a single nucleotide, or they can be large and hold stretches of thousands or millions of nucleotides. *Alleles* are alternative nucleotide sequences that occupy the same locus. New alleles are created by the chemical process of mutation. The differences between alleles are usually minor; at some places one base is substituted for another, or a small number of nucleotides is inserted or deleted from the DNA sequence.

A *gene* is a nucleotide sequence that encodes the information for a specific product such as a protein. Every gene resides at a locus and there are often allelic forms of genes. Surprisingly, the genome contains far more DNA than is required to encode all of the information in human genes. In fact, only about 2 percent of the genome encodes genes, and about half of the genome consists of repeated nucleotide sequences with no known function.

HUMAN DIVERSITY AT THE DNA LEVEL

Genetic diversity is measured from DNA sequence differences between alleles. There are many methods for estimating genetic diversity. However, all of the methods reveal three major features that typify a unique pattern of human genetic diversity. The first feature is that the amount of diversity at the DNA level is only a fraction of what would be expected for a species that consists of billions of members. The second feature is that the genetic diversity in people living outside of sub-Saharan Africa is mostly a subset of the genetic diversity in populations within sub-Saharan Africa. The third feature is that, at most genetic loci, a variant allele that is common in one human population is common in the entire species. These three features have been reproduced by many independent studies and in many regions of the genome.

The three basic properties of human genetic variation are seen in patterns of *nucleotide diversity*, which is defined as the probability that a nucleotide at a random position in the genome will differ between two randomly chosen copies of the genome (Nei 1987). The first property, that humans have low diversity, is apparent when comparing humans and chimpanzees. Humans and chimps are each others' closest relatives and, in comparison to other animals, are remarkably similar genetically and behaviorally. In a study of mtDNA, nucleotide diversity in chimpanzees was 4.32 percent, which was more than seven times the value observed in humans, which is 0.609 percent. It would normally be expected that the human population, with more than six billion members, would harbor more diversity than the chimpanzee population, with only 100,000 to 200,000 members. Figure 2, modified from Gagneux et al. (1999), provides a further illustration of this finding. Each terminal branch on the trees represents a group of closely related mtDNA sequences, and the branch lengths represent the numbers of nucleotide changes among these sequence groups. Notice that the chimpanzee tree is bushier than the human tree.

The second and third basic properties of human genetic variation are illustrated by a study of DNA sequences from widely dispersed populations in Africa, Asia, and Europe (Yu, Chen, Ota, et al. 2002) that estimated nucleotide diversity at different levels of population structure; for example, the nucleotide diversity between two copies of the genome that were sampled from the same population (within group) or from different populations (between groups).

As shown in Figure 3, nucleotide diversity is lower if both copies of the genome are drawn from Europe or from Asia, than if both copies of the genome are drawn from Africa. That is, Africa has more within-group nucleotide diversity than Europe or Asia. However, what is even more interesting is that if one copy of the genome is drawn from Asia and the other

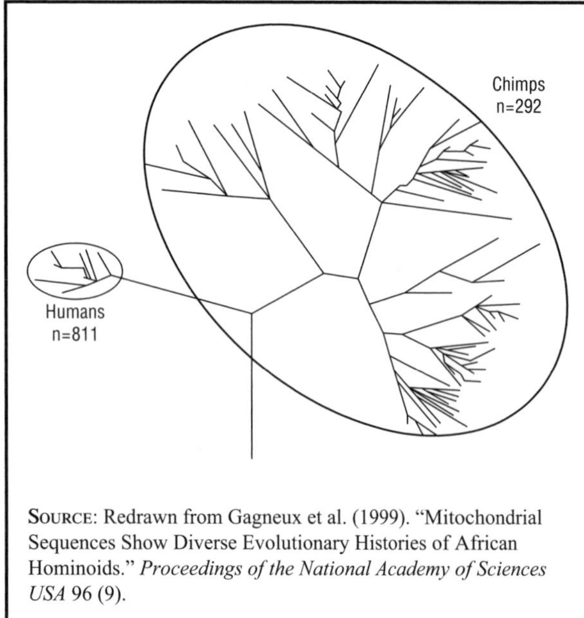

SOURCE: Redrawn from Gagneux et al. (1999). "Mitochondrial Sequences Show Diverse Evolutionary Histories of African Hominoids." *Proceedings of the National Academy of Sciences USA* 96 (9).

***Figure 2.** Lineage of mtDNA linking human and chimpanzee forms back to their common ancestor. Notice the "bushiness" on the Chimpanzee side of the family tree.*

copy is drawn from Europe, the nucleotide diversity is nearly the same as when both copies are drawn from Europe or both copies are drawn from Asia. On the other hand, if one copy of the genome is drawn from Africa and the other from Asia, the nucleotide diversity is higher than if both pairs were drawn from Asia. The result is the same for African-European pairs in comparison to European-European pairs. By contrast, if both copies of the genome are drawn from Africa, nucleotide diversity is higher than either the African-Asian or African-European pairs. This unexpected result comes from the fact that diversity in non-Africans is mostly a subset of the diversity in Africans. In other words, there is widespread diversity in Africans that is not found in non-Africans, but most of the widespread diversity in non-Africans is found in Africans.

Repeated DNA sequences further support the three primary features of genetic variation. In a study that included 4,199 alleles from 377 loci in 52 different populations from around the world, about half of the alleles (46.7%) were widely represented in populations across major geographic regions, and only 7.4 percent were exclusive to populations in a single region (Rosenberg et al. 2002). These region-specific alleles tended to be rare, even within their region of occurrence. This finding is consistent with a theory in population genetics that holds that common alleles are usually old and expected to be shared across populations either by descent from a common ancestor or because they have spread by migrations, whereas new alleles are rare and localized to the geographic region in which they arose because they have not had time to spread.

The low nucleotide diversity and nested subset pattern of genetic diversity is consistent with a model that postulates a succession of ancient founder events that occurred as the human species expanded its range and occupied new continents. In this view, the origin of the species was in Africa about 200,000 years ago, and the species expanded out of Africa beginning only 100,000 years ago (Rogers and Jorde 1995; Harpending and Rogers 2000; Rogers 2001). While the present data agree with the recent African-origin scenario, it must be recognized that there are active debates on the timing of human origin and the global expansion of the species (Wolpoff et al. 2001).

A final word of caution is that the patterns described above represent averages over many different loci. The variation at any single locus can deviate from the overall average. One reason for different patterns of variation across loci is that the order and timing of evolutionary change is a complex stochastic process. While each locus is potentially an outcome of the same process, no two outcomes are alike (Harpending and Rogers 2000). Another reason for different patterns at different loci is that natural selection can create deviations from the otherwise common patterns of genetic variation (Ruiz-Pesini et al. 2004). For instance, alleles that bestow a resistance to malaria are primarily found in regions with a history of malaria and reflect localized adaptations. Because natural selection can present a bias, DNA sequences that do not encode functional products are the most useful for understanding patterns of population history and relationships.

GENETIC VARIATION AND RACE

The word *race* should be used carefully because different meanings have been affixed to it in scientific, social, and historical contexts. Population geneticists typically define *race* as a group of individuals in a species showing closer genetic relationships within the group than to members of other such groups (Hartl and Clark 1997, p. 121). However, race defined in this way is not a very useful description for the overall pattern of DNA variation in humans. Figure 4 illustrates some of its shortcomings.

Panel 4A represents three hypothetical groups. Within each of the three groups, the members are, on average, more similar to each other than they are to the members of the other two groups. If one focuses on a pair of the groups, say A and B, a member of A is less similar compared with a member of B than with another member of A. The same is true the other way around: A member of B is less similar compared with a member of A than with another member of B. The relationship is symmetrical: A is a race when compared with B and B is a race when compared with A. The same pattern is evident when members of A are compared with members of C and when members of B are compared with members of

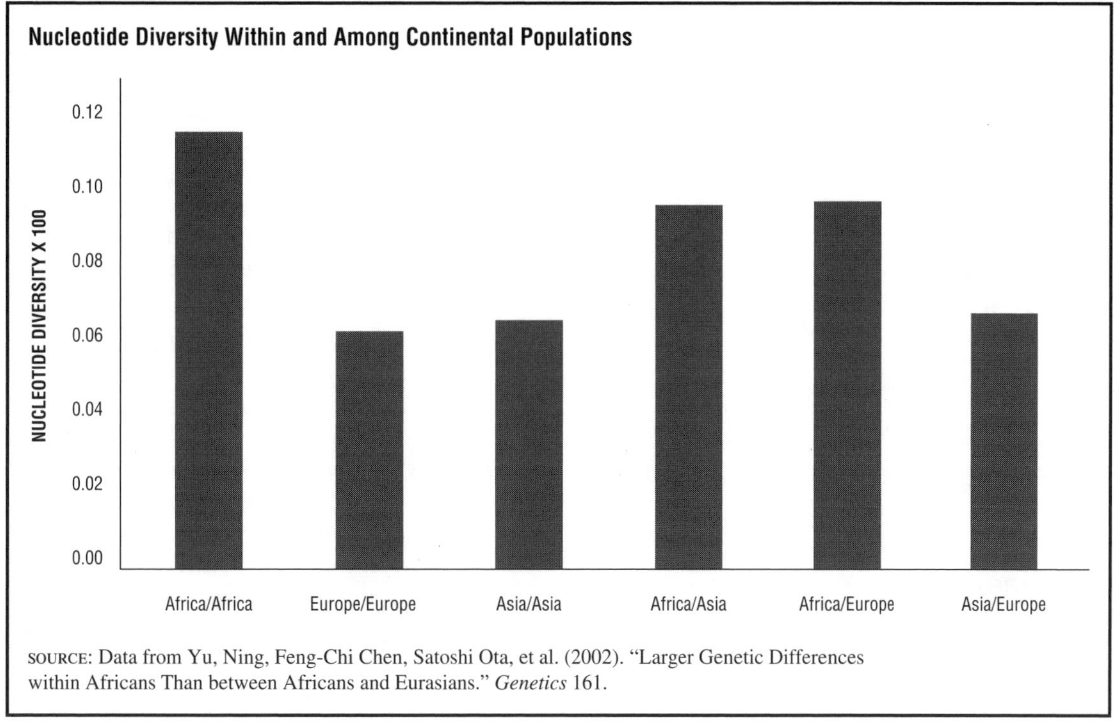

Figure 3.

C. Panel 4B shows that the actual pattern of variation in human DNA sequences lacks symmetry between populations. For example, the genetic variation found in Europeans and Asians is a subset of the variation found in Africa.

Genes from African populations are, on average, less similar to each other than they are to genes from European and Asian populations. Thus, Africans cannot be considered a race by the population genetics definition. Conversely, Europeans can be considered a race relative to Africans because the similarity between a pair of genomes drawn from Europe is greater than the similarity between a pair from Europe and Africa. The same sort of asymmetry holds in comparing genomes from Asia with genomes from Africa. However, one would be hard-pressed to argue that Europeans and Asians are races with respect to each other, because European-European pairs, Asian-Asian pairs, and European-Asian pairs are all similar to nearly the same degree. Thus, whether or not a particular group is a race, or how many races a group belongs to, is relative to whom that group is being compared.

PREDICTING POPULATION MEMBERSHIP FROM GENETIC VARIANTS

Several studies have successfully used sets of highly variable DNA markers from nonfunctional regions of the genome to reveal clusters of genetically similar individuals. Notably, the resulting genetic clusters tend to contain people sampled from the same region of the world (Pritchard et al. 2000; Rosenberg et al. 2002; Bamshad et al. 2003). It is now estimated that only a modest number of highly variable loci are required to correctly assign an individual to a continental cluster (Bamshad et al. 2003; Rosenberg et al. 2003). While only nonfunctional markers have been used for finding genetic clusters, one study has shown that the frequencies for alleles of drug metabolizing enzymes differ among clusters (Wilson et al. 2001).

To many scientists and nonscientists, these results seem to affirm the validity of race. After all, the correct assignment of individuals to populations has been traditionally viewed as a gold standard in validating races (Mayr 1969). Nevertheless, the ability to assign individuals to groups is unlikely to resolve the major issues surrounding race. The ability to classify individuals is ambiguous with respect to the pattern of variation among groups. Both of the patterns of variation illustrated in Panel 4A permit classification of individuals, but the asymmetrical pattern of actual human variation (Panel 4B) challenges conventional intuition about what race means.

PREDICTING GENETIC VARIANTS FROM POPULATION MEMBERSHIP

Though it is often possible to use genetic information to assign an individual to the geographical region from

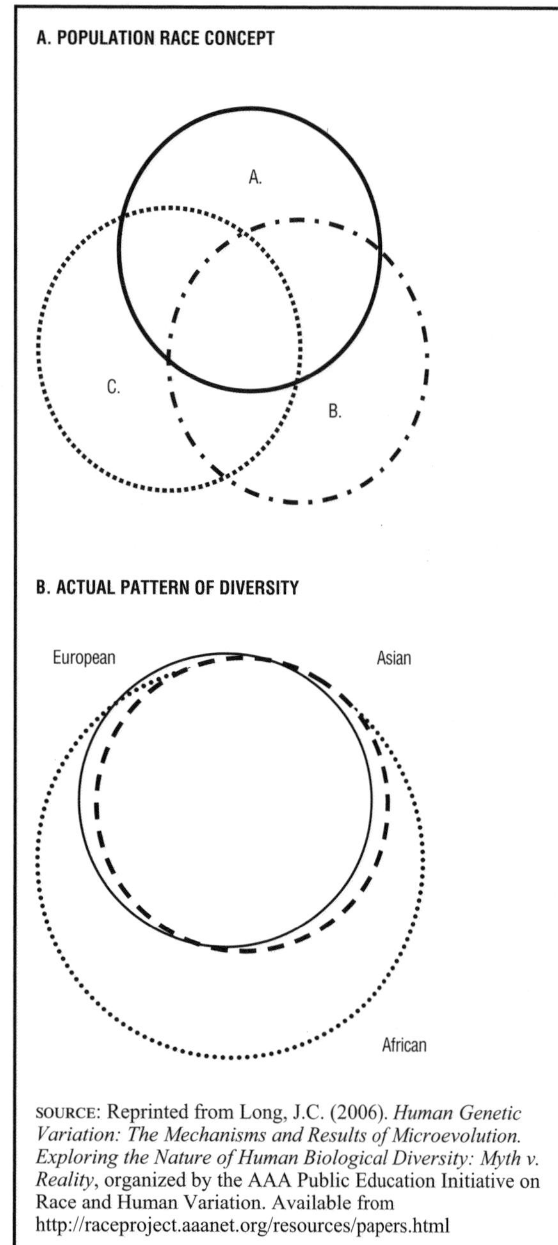

SOURCE: Reprinted from Long, J.C. (2006). *Human Genetic Variation: The Mechanisms and Results of Microevolution. Exploring the Nature of Human Biological Diversity: Myth v. Reality*, organized by the AAA Public Education Initiative on Race and Human Variation. Available from http://raceproject.aaanet.org/resources/papers.html

Figure 4. *Idealized race concept (A) and actual pattern of genetic diversity (B).*

which he or she came, the inference is not as strong in the reverse direction. An individual's ancestry conveys only a small amount of information about the specific genetic markers that they carry. This is true even when the occurrence of a particular marker is restricted to a localized geographic region. A prime example is the ALDH2-2 allele at the acetaldehydrogenase 2 locus (ALDH2). This allele encodes a dominant-acting deficiency that prevents formation of the active ALDH2 enzyme. A consequence of ALDH2 inactivity is the accumulation of the noxious metabolic intermediate acetaldehyde (Inoue et al. 1984). Elevated blood acetaldehyde is associated with alcohol sensitivity and symptoms such as increased blood flow, dizziness, accelerated heart rate, sweating, and nausea (Wolff 1972; Agarwal and Goedde 1990; Agarwal et al. 1991). These symptoms in combination define the "flushing response." The ALDH2-2 allele affects human health in an interesting way. Individuals who carry the ALDH2-2 are protected from heavy drinking and ultimately alcoholism by the unpleasantness of flushing.

Figure 5 presents data on the frequencies of four major allele complexes at the ALDH2 locus (Peterson et al. 1999; Mulligan et al. 2003). The ALDH2-2 allele is carried on H4. Notice that H4 is found only in Asian populations, where it is relatively common. Because ALDH2-2 is found only in Asians, it is a perfect indicator of Asian ancestry. Nonetheless, the converse cannot be claimed, because most Asians do not carry the ALDH2-2 allele. As a result, while the ALDH2-2 allele is a good indicator that an individual will not drink alcohol or become alcoholic, most Asians do not carry ALDH2-2, and some Asians do drink alcohol and become alcoholic.

Population membership, therefore, may not be a precise indicator of genetic susceptibility to, or treatment of, diseases. While many marker alleles can be used to accurately infer ancestry, ancestry will allow only a weak inference about whether an individual carries a particular disease-risk allele.

PREDICTING HEALTH FROM RACE

Health researchers are actively debating the value of race and ethnicity in the diagnosis and treatment of chronic diseases such as diabetes, high blood pressure, and cancers (Burchard et al. 2003; Cooper et al. 2003). It is well known that chronic diseases are unevenly distributed in the general population. Depending on the disease, some groups are more or less prone than others. However, chronic conditions are difficult to analyze because they are caused by a combination of many factors, including both genes and environment. This complexity makes it likely that people presenting the same diagnosis vary widely with respect to the underlying causes that led to their problem. The chief argument for using race in medicine is that it can serve as a proxy for the total mix of genes and environments experienced by the patient. As such, it will better enable doctors to tailor diagnoses and treatments to the patient. However, there are several arguments against using race in the practice of medicine. First, racial groups are often too poorly defined to serve as useful proxies for genetic populations or specific environments. Second, the known genetic differences among populations are too small for population membership to be a strong indicator of the genes carried by individuals. Third, analyses suggest that although disease-predisposing

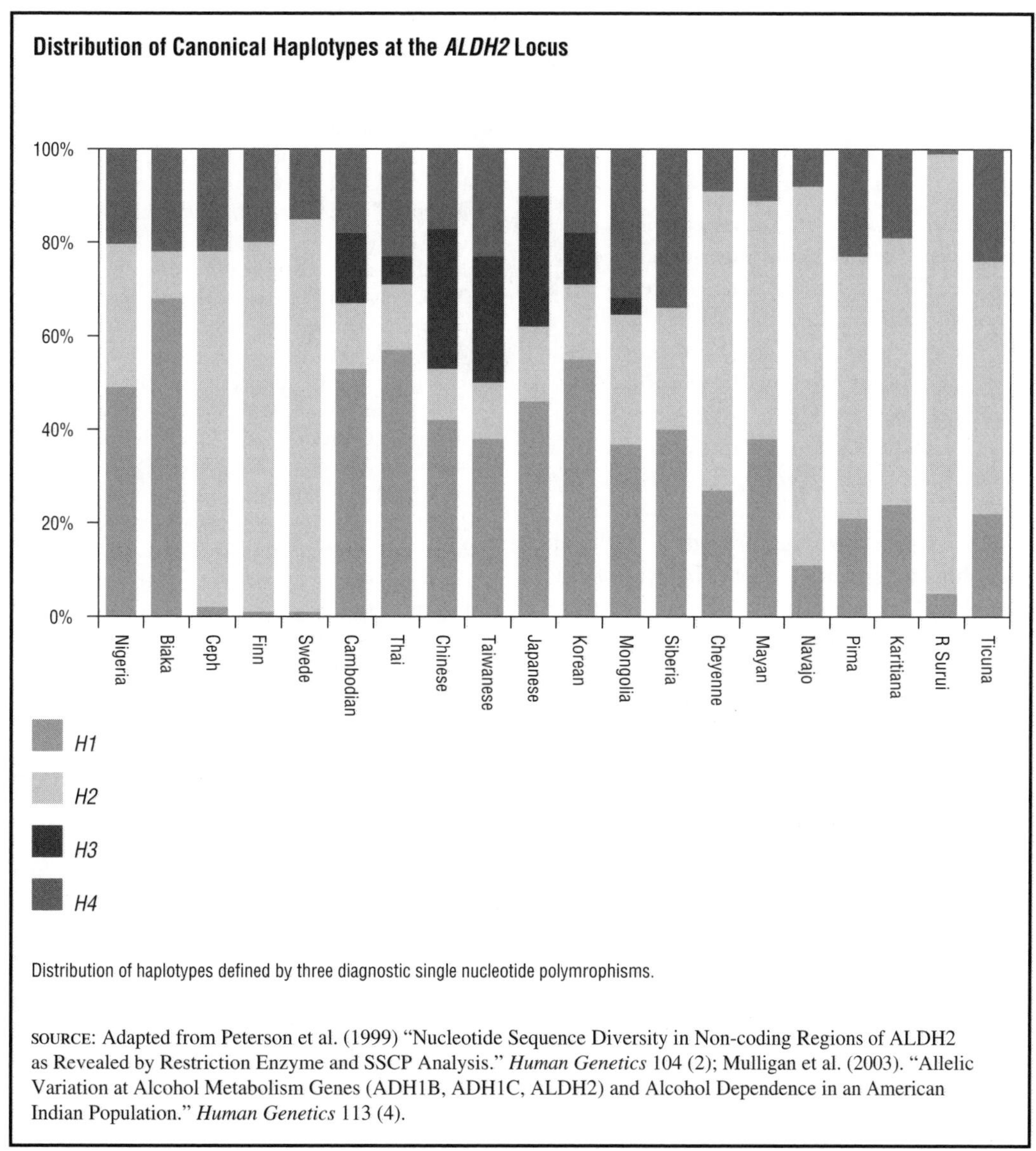

Distribution of haplotypes defined by three diagnostic single nucleotide polymrophisms.

SOURCE: Adapted from Peterson et al. (1999) "Nucleotide Sequence Diversity in Non-coding Regions of ALDH2 as Revealed by Restriction Enzyme and SSCP Analysis." *Human Genetics* 104 (2); Mulligan et al. (2003). "Allelic Variation at Alcohol Metabolism Genes (ADH1B, ADH1C, ALDH2) and Alcohol Dependence in an American Indian Population." *Human Genetics* 113 (4).

Figure 5.

alleles can vary in frequencies across population, the disease-predisposing alleles appear to have similar effects in people in different groups (Ioannidis et al. 2004). Fourth, a race-specific approach to medicine easily lends itself to misuses such as justifying unequal opportunity for health care. Despite these caveats, the U.S. Food and Drug Administration has recently approved the marketing of BiDil, a congestive heart failure medication, for a specific racial group: African Americans.

SUMMARY AND CONCLUSIONS

The genetic diversity in our species has three defining features. First, the level of diversity in humans is consistent with a much smaller population than is living in the early twenty-first century. Second, the geographic pattern of genetic diversity forms nested subsets. Third, at most genetic loci, an allele that is common in one human population is common throughout the species. The architecture of human genetic variation is ultimately explained by the evolutionary history of our species and best understood in that context.

These findings complicate genetic scholars' notions of human race by contradicting the intuitive expectation that a race classification is symmetrical (i.e., if A is a race with respect to B, then B is a race with respect to A). For example, non-African people are more homogeneous than the species as a whole, but there is nearly as much genetic diversity in African people as there is in the species as a whole. Despite the inadequacy of race concepts for describing patterns of genetic variation, genetic differences among human populations do exist, and one of the most striking ways that populations differ is in the overall level of variation. African populations harbor the greatest diversity. On average, non-African populations harbor less diversity.

A major question is: Do disease susceptibility alleles have the same distribution as the more-or-less neutral variations in the DNA sequence? The answer to this question is not yet known. Some speculation has led to the common disease–common variant hypothesis (Reich and Lander 2001), which holds that the alleles that contribute to common diseases will have population distributions much like neutral variants because they are only disadvantageous in the post-reproductive phase of life, and are therefore undetected by natural selection. To the extent that this is true, the susceptibility alleles for common diseases should be widely shared. In general, the findings from one population should be relevant to others. However, two important caveats must be raised. The first is that because Africans harbor more allelic variation than do non-Africans, studying non-Africans will not identify important genetic variants related to the health of people of African descent. The second is that effects of major genes may be modified by the rare variants that are specific to local populations or geographic regions.

Race is clearly a poor descriptor of the patterns of genetic variation. However, breaking the tradition of using it will be difficult. A major barrier to breaking this tradition is that lay people and scientists alike use what is known as the *implicit* definition of race. In this view, races represent a pattern of variation that is difficult to pinpoint but clear to most people. This position is imprecise and irrefutable because it is based on an article of faith: that races display a pattern of variation that is already clear to most people. It is easy for users of the implicit definition to talk past each other, and for them to unwittingly fall back on prejudices or use typological thinking that is inconsistent with biological processes. The utility and internal consistency of race concepts can only be validated or rejected to the extent that they are explicitly stated. It must also be remembered that race is as much a social phenomenon as it is a biological one. The ancestry of individuals and groups is hopelessly confounded with environment and social standing. Therefore, it is unlikely that one line of evidence, such as genetics or genomics, will clarify all of the important health issues surrounding race.

SEE ALSO *Clusters; Eugenics, History of; Forensic Anthropology and Race; Gene Pool; Genes and Genealogies; Genetic Distance; Genetic Marker; Genetic Variation Among Populations; Genetics, History of; Genetics and Athletic Performance; Human and Primate Evolution.*

BIBLIOGRAPHY

Agarwal, Dhram Pal, and H. Werner Goedde. 1990. "Pharmacogenetics of Alcohol Dehydrogenase (ADH)." *Pharmacology and Therapeutics* 45 (1): 69–83.

Agarwal, Dhram Pal, S. Harada, and H. Werner Goedde. 1991. "Racial Differences in Biological Sensitivity to Ethanol: The Role of Alcohol Dehydrogenase and Aldehyde Dehydrogenase Isozymes." *Alcoholism: Clinical and Experimental Research* 5 (1): 12–16.

Bamshad, Michael J., Stephen Wooding, W. Scott Watkins, et al. 2003. "Human Population Genetic Structure and Inference of Group Membership." *American Journal of Human Genetics* 72 (3): 578–589.

Burchard, Estaban G., Elad Ziv, Natasha Coyle, et al. 2003. "The Importance of Race and Ethnic Background in Biomedical Research and Clinical Practice." *New England Journal of Medicine* 348: 1170–1175.

Chen, W.J., E. W. Loh, Y. P. Hsu, et al. 1996. "Alcohol-Metabolising Genes and Alcoholism among Taiwanese Han Men: Independent Effect of ADH2, ADH3 and ALDH2." *British Journal of Psychiatry* 168 (6): 762–767.

Chimpanzee Sequencing and Analysis Consortium. 2005. "Initial Sequence of the Chimpanzee Genome and Comparison with the Human Genome." *Nature* 437: 69–87.

Cooper, Richard S., Jay S. Kaufman, and Ryk Ward. 2003. "Race and Genomics." *New England Journal of Medicine* 348 (12): 1166–1170.

de Waal, Frans B. M de. 2005. "A Century of Getting to Know the Chimpanzee." *Nature* 437: 56–59.

Gagneux, Pascal, Christopher Wills, Ulrike Gerloff, et al. 1999. "Mitochondrial Sequences Show Diverse Evolutionary Histories of African Hominoids." *Proceedings of the National Academy of Sciences USA* 96 (9): 5077–5082.

Hamblin, Martha T., Emma E. Thompson, and Anna Di Rienzo. 2002. "Complex Signatures of Natural Selection at the Duffy Blood Group Locus." *American Journal of Human Genetics* 70: 369–383.

Harada, Shoji, Dhram Pal Agarwal, H. Werner Goedde, et al. 1982. "Possible Protective Role against Alcoholism for Aldehyde Dehydrogenase Isozyme Deficiency in Japan." *Lancet* 2: 827.

Harpending, Henry C., Stephen T. Sherry, Alan R. Rogers, and Mark Stoneking. 1993. "The Genetic Structure of Ancient Human Populations." *Current Anthropology* 34: 483–496.

Harpending, Henry C., Mark A. Batzer, Michael Gurven, et al. 1998. "Genetic Traces of Ancient Demography." *Proceedings of the National Academy of Sciences USA* 95 (4): 1961–1967.

Harpending, Henry C., and Alan Rogers. 2000. "Genetic Perspectives on Human Origins and Differentiation." *Annual Review of Genomics and Human Genetics* 1: 361–385.

Hartl Daniel L., and Andrew G. Clark 1997. *Principles of Population Genetics,* 3rd ed. Sunderland, MA: Sinauer and Associates.

Inoue K, M. Fukunaga, T. Kiriyama, and S. Komura. 1984. "Accumulation of Acetaldehyde in Alcohol-Sensitive Japanese: Relation to Ethanol and Acetaldehyde Oxidizing Capacity." *Alcoholism: Clinical and Experimental Research* 8 (3): 319–322.

Ioannidis, John P., Evangelia E. Ntzani, and Thomas A. Trikalinos. 2004. "'Racial' Differences in Genetic Effects for Complex Diseases." *Nature Genetics* 36 (12): 1312–1318.

Jorde, Lynn B., Michael J. Bamshad, and W. Scott Watkins, et al. 1995. "Origins and Affinities of Modern Humans: A Comparison of Mitochondrial and Nuclear Genetic Data." *American Journal of Human Genetics* 57 (3): 523–538.

Jorde, Lynn B., Alan R. Rogers, Michael J. Bamshad, et al. 1997. "Microsatellite Diversity and the Demographic History of Modern Humans." *Proceedings of the National Academy of Sciences USA* 94: 3100–3103.

Long, Jeffrey C. 2006. Human Genetic Variation: The Mechanisms and Results of Microevolution. Exploring the Nature of Human Biological Diversity: Myth v. Reality, organized by the AAA Public Education Initiative on Race and Human Variation. http://raceproject.aaanet.org/resources/papers.html.

Marth, Gabor, Greg Schuler, Raymond Yeh, et al. 2003. "Sequence Variations in the Public Human Genome Data Reflect a Bottlenecked Population History." *Proceedings of the National Academy of Sciences USA* 100 (1): 376–381.

Mayr, Ernst. 1969. *Principles of Systematic Zoology*. New York: McGraw-Hill.

Mulligan, Connie J., Robert W. Robin, Michael V. Osier, et al. 2003. "Allelic Variation at Alcohol Metabolism Genes (ADH1B, ADH1C, ALDH2) and Alcohol Dependence in an American Indian Population." *Human Genetics* 113 (4): 325–336.

Nachman, Michael W., W. M. Brown, Mark Stoneking, and Charles F. Aquadro. 1996. "Nonneutral Mitochondrial DNA Variation in Humans and Chimpanzees." *Genetics* 142 (3): 953–963.

Nei, Masatishi. 1987. *Molecular Evolutionary Genetics*. New York: Columbia University Press.

Ning, Yu, Yung-Xin Fu, and Wen-Hsiung Li. 2002. "DNA Polymorphism in a Worldwide Sample of Human X Chromosomes." *Molecular Biology and Evolution* 19: 2131–2141.

Ning, Yu, Feng-Chi Chen, Satoshi Ota, et al. 2002. "Larger Genetic Differences within Africans than between Africans and Eurasians." *Genetics* 161: 269–274.

Peterson, Raymond J., David Goldman, and J. C. Long. 1999. "Nucleotide Sequence Diversity in Non-coding Regions of ALDH2 as Revealed by Restriction Enzyme and SSCP Analysis." *Human Genetics* 104 (2):177–187.

Pluzhnikov, Anna, Anna Di Rienzo, and Richard R. Hudson. 2002. "Inferences about Human Demography Based on Multilocus Analyses of Noncoding Sequences." *Genetics* 161 (3): 1209–1218.

Posada, David, and Keith A. Crandall. 2001. "Intraspecific Gene Genealogies: Trees Grafting into Networks." *Trends in Ecology and Evolution* 16 (1): 37–45.

Pritchard, Jonathan K., Matthew Stephens, and Peter Donnelly. 2000. "Inference of Population Structure Using Multilocus Genotype Data." *Genetics* 155 (2): 945–959.

Race, Ethnicity, and Genetics Working Group. 2005. "The Use of Racial, Ethnic, and Ancestral Categories in Human Genetics Research." *American Journal of Human Genetics* 77 (4): 519–532.

Reich, David E., and Eric S. Lander. 2001. "On the Allelic Spectrum of Human Disease." *Trends in Genetics* 17: 502–510.

Reich, David E., Stephen F. Schaffner, Mark J. Daly, et al. 2002. "Human Genome Sequence Variation and the Influence of Gene History, Mutation, and Recombination." *Nature Genetics* 32 (1): 135–142.

Rogers, Alan R., and Henry C. Harpending. 1992. "Population Growth Makes Waves in the Distribution of Pairwise Genetic Differences." *Molecular Biology and Evolution* 9 (3): 552–569.

Rogers, Alan R. and Lynn B. Jorde. 1995. "Genetic Evidence on Modern Human Origins." *Human Biology* 67 (1): 1–36.

Rogers, Alan R. 2001. "Order Emerging from Chaos in Human Evolutionary Genetics." *Proceedings of the National Academy of Sciences USA* 98 (3): 779–780.

Rosenberg, Noah A., Jonathan K. Pritchard, James L. Weber, et al. 2002. "Genetic Structure of Human Populations." *Science* 298 (5602): 2381–2385.

Rosenberg, Noah A., Lei M. Li, Ryk Ward, and Jonathan K. Pritchard. 2003. "Informativeness of Genetic Markers for Inference of Ancestry." *American Journal of Human Genetics* 73 (6): 1402–1422.

Sabeti, Pardis C., David E. Reich, John M. Higgins, et al. 2002. "Detecting Recent Positive Selection in the Human Genome from Haplotype Structure." *Nature* 419 (6909): 832–837.

Suwaki Hiroshi, and H. Ohara. 1985. "Alcohol-Induced Facial Flushing and Drinking Behavior in Japanese Men." *Journal of Studies on Alcohol* 46 (3): 196–198.

Thomasson, Holly R., Howard J. Edenberg, David W. Crabb, et al. 1991. "Alcohol and Aldehyde Dehydrogenase Genotypes and Alcoholism in Chinese Men." *American Journal of Human Genetics* 48: 667–681.

Tishkoff, Sarah A., Erin Dietzsch, W. Speed, et al. 1996. "Global Patterns of Linkage Disequilibrium at the CD4 Locus and Modern Human Origins." *Science* 271 (5254): 1380–1387.

Vigilant, Linda, Renee Pennington, Henry C. Harpending, et al. 1989. "Mitochondrial DNA Sequences in Single Hairs from a Southern African Population." *Proceedings of the National Academy of Sciences USA* 86 (23): 9350–9354.

Watkins, W. Scott, Christopher E. Ricker, Michael J. Bamshad, et al. 2001. "Patterns of Ancestral Human Diversity: An Analysis of Alu-insertion and Restriction-Site Polymorphisms." *American Journal of Human Genetics* 68 (3): 738–752.

Whiten, Andrew. 2005. "The Second Inheritance System of Chimpanzees and Humans." *Nature* 437: 2–55.

Wilson, James F., Michael E. Weale, Alice C. Smith, et al. 2001. "Population Genetic Structure of Variable Drug Response." *Nature Genetics* 29 (3): 265–269.

Wolff, Peter H. 1972. "Ethnic Differences in Alcohol Sensitivity." *Science* 175: 449–450.

Wolpoff, Milford H., John Hawks, David W. Frayer, and Keith Hunley. 2001. "Modern Human Ancestry at the Peripheries: A Test of the Replacement Theory." *Science* 291 (5502): 293–297.

Wooding, Stephen, Un-Kyung Kim, Michael J. Bamshad, et al. 2004. "Natural Selection and Molecular Evolution in PTC, a Bitter-Taste Receptor Gene." *American Journal of Human Genetics* 74 (4): 637–646.

Zhivotovsky, Lev A. 2001. "Estimating Divergence Time with the Use of Microsatellite Genetic Distances: Impacts of Population Growth and Gene Flow." *Molecular Biology and Evolution* 18: 700–709.

———, Noah A. Rosenberg, and Marcus W. Feldman. 2003. "Features of Evolution and Expansion of Modern Humans, Inferred from Genome-Wide Microsatellite Markers." *American Journal of Human Genetics* 72 (5): 1171–1186.

Jeffrey C. Long
Nicole Scott
Cecil M. Lewis Jr.

HUMAN TRAFFICKING

According to the United Nations (2002):

> Trafficking in human beings is the recruitment, transportation, transfer, harboring, or receipts of persons, by means of threat or the use of force or other forms of coercion, of abduction, of fraud, of deception, of the abuse of power or of a position of vulnerability or of the giving or receiving of payments or benefits to achieve the consent of a person having control over another, for the purpose of exploitation.

In short, human trafficking is the recruitment and transportation of persons through coercion, deception, or some other form of illicit influence.

The main reasons behind human trafficking are labor and sexual exploitation. Labor and sexual exploitation, however, are intertwined and in many cases proceed simultaneously. Each year, millions of women, children, and men, especially from developing nations, are trafficked within and across national boundaries to serve as bonded labor, domestic workers, farmworkers, and sex workers. Kathryn Farr (2005) reports that about 27 million people around the world live under some form of slavery. Most are women trafficked for prostitution. For example, about 35,000 women from Columbia, 25,000 women from Bangladesh, and 500,000 women from the former Soviet states have been trafficked and sold into prostitution in different countries. The trafficking of Nepali girls and women in Indian brothels has been considered the most intensive sexual slave trade anywhere in the world (Hynes and Raymond 2002). Trafficked women have become the new slaves of the global economy.

The trafficking of children has also become a major social problem. Children are trafficked around the world mainly for labor and sexual exploitation. They work in homes, farms, factories, carpet factories, sweatshops, restaurants, construction sites, and the sex and tourist industries. Conditions can include debt bondage. The International Labor Organization estimates that there are about 250 million working children ages five through fourteen. About 120 million children are working full-time in hazardous and exploitative types of work (Palley 2002). Trafficking has become one of the fastest growing crimes and generates up to $7 billion annually (Widgen 1994).

THE HISTORICAL CONTEXT

The exploitation of women is often rooted in imperialism and colonialism. Political, economic, and sexual exploitation of the weak and powerless, who are often people of the previously colonized and developing nations, continue today on a worldwide scale. During imperial and colonial expansion, whether in North America, the Caribbean, Europe, Africa, or Australia, colonizers extracted huge profits by exploiting and commodifying women. Women's sexuality and labor became a means to appropriate economic, political, and social gain for colonizers. By purchasing, hiring, and selling women, the colonizers made these women transferable commodities to be used and reused, sold and resold.

Kamala Kempadoo (2004) reports that during the colonial invasion of the Caribbean, "slave women were frequently hired out by white and free colored families as nannies, nurses, cooks, washerwomen, hucksters, seamstresses, yet the general expectation of individuals who hired female labor under whatever pretense was that sexual benefits were included" (p. 53). Kempadoo further reports that "concubines served as both mistresses and housekeepers and were sometimes hired out by their owners to sexually service other men in order to obtain cash" (p. 53). To rationalize such practices, these women were blamed for being sexually available and promiscuous. Referring to the sexual exploitation of black women during slavery in the United States, bell hooks (1981) states: "The use of the word prostitution to describe mass sexual exploitation of enslaved black women by white men not only deflected attention away from the prevalence of forced sexual assault, it lent further credibility to the myth that black females were inherently wanton and therefore responsible for rape" (p. 34).

Under slavery, African women in the United States were subject to bondage labor, captive slavery and prostitution, and breeding labor; they lived a barbaric slave life. The colonial white owners controlled their labor and bodies. Forced sex, rape, and brutal torturing and floggings of women's naked bodies were a common practice by white male slave owners. By coerced mating and oppressive massive breeding, slave women's bodies became machines to produce and reproduce slave labor. State agencies fostered racial and gendered violence through various discriminatory laws. Dorothy Roberts (1997) reports that "the law reinforced the sexual exploitation of slave women in two ways; it deemed any child who resulted from the rape to be a slave and it failed to recognize the rape of a slave woman as a crime" (p. 29).

Social, economic, and sexual exploitation and oppression of slave women in the United States is rooted in a white supremacist colonial patriarchal culture and ideology. As hooks (1981) points out, "Colonial white men expressed their fear and hatred of womanhood by institutionalizing sexist oppression" (p. 31). Slave women were forced to adapt to mainstream oppressive gender roles and relations defined and introduced by the colonial patriarch. Slave women were thus oppressed and exploited by a double-edged sword—their race and their gender.

Similarly, various anthropological studies illustrate the ways in which women became concubines, prostitutes, and entertainers after the colonial invasion in Australia. Eleanor Leacock and Mona Etienne (1980) report that the "history of relations between colonizers and aboriginal Australians meant that women's sexual freedom became transformed into its opposition: prostitution" (p. 11). The colonizers and those in authority had turned women's bodies and sexuality into a site for deriving sexual pleasure and economic profit.

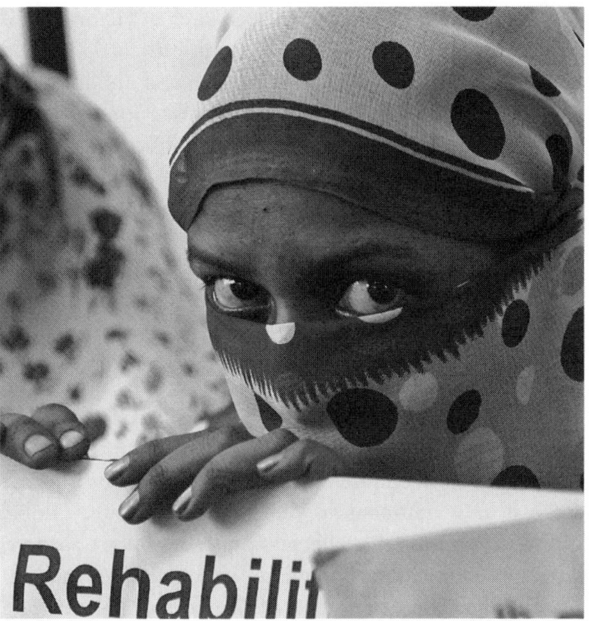

Sex Worker Protests Sexual Exploitation Reform Plans. *In 2004 the Indian government announced plans to curb human trafficking and require that victims of sexual exploitation receive rehabilitation. Dozens of sex workers staged a protest in New Delhi, worried that such legislation would threaten their livelihood.* © DESMOND BOYLAN/REUTERS/CORBIS.

GENDER AND STATE AGENCIES

Cases from different parts of the world also show ways in which war, political violence, and expansion of military bases have exacerbated various forms of gender-based violence—particularly sexual exploitation. Any kind of war, whether political, civil, or ethnic, and expansion of army bases and processes of militarization have fostered the sex trade and forced prostitution, with young girls and women as primary targets. Being a displaced refugee makes girls, women, and children even more vulnerable for sexual exploitation. War and conflict in Vietnam, the Persian Gulf, eastern Europe, and Africa have witnessed such sexual exploitation and political violence.

Trafficking, sexual exploitation, and gendered violence are also rooted in the low status and positions of girls and women. In addition, those who are already marginalized in society because of their low socioeconomic status, demographic characteristics, and culture and political location are more susceptible to being trafficked and sexually exploited. In caste-based societies such as India and Nepal, the poor, indigenous, low-caste ethnic minorities and uneducated girls and women are more likely to become victims of sexual labor exploitation. For example, in Nepal, under the "Deukis system," wealthy families buy young girls to offer to temple idols. These girls are forbidden to marry, and without alternative livelihoods, they are forced into prostitution. Similar to the Deukis system, under the "Devadasi system" in India, young girls are offered as gifts to various deities. Unable to earn their livelihood by the donations and gifts from their patrons and other visitors, the girls are compelled to sell their sex. Girls and women of the Badi community, the lowest caste in Nepal, traditionally earned their livelihood by singing and dancing. Because of economic factors, they were later pushed into prostitution.

Such cases suggest how state agencies and cultural practices through various religious and other institutions control women's labor and sexuality. Additionally, the cases indicate how some traditional practices have increased women's vulnerability to sexual labor exploitation.

INDUSTRIALIZATION, FACTORY WORK, AND TRAFFICKING

The processes of industrialization and modernization have also facilitated trafficking. The industrializing nations of Asia and Latin America have created conditions that brought a massive number of rural women and children into low-paying, labor-intensive manufacturing jobs in the cities. In Southeast Asia and South Asia, persistent poverty and debt have compelled many parents to sell their daughters and children. Many of these parents, however, do not know that their children are then tricked and lured into the sex trade. Customers' preference for virgins and the fear of AIDS have also accelerated the number of children and young girls forced into sex trafficking. UNICEF reports that there are at least a million child prostitutes in Asia alone, with the highest numbers present in India, followed by Thailand, Taiwan, and the Philippines (Banerjee 2002).

Industrial manufacturing jobs and a factory-based work culture provide favorable conditions for labor and sexual exploitation. Even those women and children who join manufacturing work voluntarily face long working hours and deteriorating working conditions, and they are subjected to sexual harassment, rape, and different forms of sexual violence and exploitation by owners and overseers.

GLOBALIZATION AND THE POLITICAL ECONOMY

The processes of globalization, global restructuring, and global capital accumulation have intensified sex trafficking and the exploitation of sexual labor. The trafficking of women and children, particularly girls, for the sex trade is now rampant in the global economy. Global capital expansion, neoliberal policies, open borders, structural adjustment programs, internal and international migration, transnational networks, globalization of communications and different modes of communications that facilitate international arranged marriage, mail-order brides, and the marketing of women and children in sex tourism have fueled the trafficking and sex trade industry. As Kamala Kempadoo and Jo Doezema (1998) put it, "Sexual labor today forms a primary source for profit and wealth, and it is a constituent part of national economies and transnational industries within the global capitalist economy" (p. 8).

Structural adjustment programs (SAPs) that have been imposed by the World Bank and the International Monetary Fund in the developing nations have become key features of global restructuring. Under SAPs, poor countries are pressured to privatize their state-owned enterprises, liberalize domestic markets, remove trade barriers, encourage foreign investment, and prioritize export-oriented manufacturing. A huge cut in state-owned health care and education; open borders; free flow of labor, capital, and commodities; and a highly competitive international market economy have exacerbated various social, economic, and global problems. After the privatization of public sectors, prices doubled for public goods and services in areas such as education, transportation, health care, telecommunications, drinking water, and electricity. Under trade liberalization, protection is removed from local industries. This negatively affects cottage, handicraft, and small and labor-intensive manufacturing industries, all of which depend on a large unskilled and semiskilled labor force.

Although the main goal of SAPs is that goods and services should be produced where they can be made most efficiently at the lowest cost, with nations increasing their prosperity by mutually opening their trade and markets, it has not worked out that way. By eroding national markets and industries, global restructuring has displaced many people, particularly women and children, from their work and livelihoods. These women and children, who are the most vulnerable of the labor force, then become primary targets for sex trafficking and the sex trade. For example, millions of women and children in Bangladesh have lost their work in the textile industry when work was moved to China, where production costs were lower. This pushed many women and children into the sex industry.

By allowing free competition, open markets, free enterprise, and deregulated labor markets, economic restructuring has on the one hand led to poverty, unemployment, risk, and social, economic, and political inequality, and on the other hand to the insecurity of low-paying jobs in the informal economic sectors. This duality has affected poor women and children the most, as they are now the preferred labor of informal economic sectors and constitute the largest labor force in the service sector. This has simultaneously accelerated the feminization of migration and of the labor force, as well as trafficking and the sex trade. In the service sector particularly, the demand for female labor has been greatest in domestic work, tourism, and the sex industry.

Interregional and international labor migration provides a route and a context for sex trafficking. As poor women and children from deprived regions seek employment in cities or foreign nations, they become more vulnerable to sex trafficking. Trafficking of girls and women, particularly in South Asia, occurs en route from rural to urban areas within the country and en route from one country to another. Shobha Hamal-Gurung (2003) notes the linkage between factory work, migration, and sex trafficking; and reports that sex trafficking of girls and women in Indian brothels occurred mainly in two ways: during the migration process—en route to destined employment cities and from the carpet factories where these girls and women worked.

By providing loans with high interest rates, SAPs push poor countries into becoming debt-ridden. Since women have become the ideal labor force of the global economy, many industrializing, debt-ridden nations then encourage their female citizens to migrate and become transnational workers in order to stabilize and boost their economies with the remittances they send back home. Transnational female labor migrants are more likely to be trafficked or subjected to economic and sexual exploitation in foreign lands, particularly if they are brought into the country illegally or if they become illegal aliens later.

The process of globalization and global restructuring has created a market for the sex industry in which millions of innocent women and children are turned into economic and sexual commodities, thereby becoming the new slaves of globalization. According to Goodwin (2003), quoting a UN spokesman, "Slavery is one of the most undesirable consequences of globalization" (p. 499).

Although a matter of choice for some, sex work is not a matter of choice for the majority of women and children who migrate to urban areas in search of wage work and a better life. It is not a matter of choice for the majority of women and children who are deceived by false jobs in urban or global cities and who are then smuggled during the internal and international migration process. Victims of trafficking and the sex trade are brought into the industry in various ways. They are often lured away from their country by recruiters who promise them high-paying jobs in a foreign country. They are either brought illegally or upon their arrival their passports and other legal documents are seized by the recruiter or pimp. The willingness to migrate in search of livelihood, legally or illegally, results in favorable conditions for traffickers and an impetus to trafficking. Consequently, these women and children become extremely vulnerable to various forms of exploitation. Because of their legal status, language and cultural barriers, and fear of the police and government authorities, these women and children are trapped—forced and coerced to become sex workers. Fear of deportation also makes them vulnerable to abuse. Even if they manage to escape, they may encounter trouble with the law and authorities, and they may end up in jail, where they may face another cycle of sexual violence.

The tourist industry in Southeast Asia is intertwined with the sex trade that brings billions of dollars annually. The Thai government, for example, promotes sexual tourism through advertising stating that "the only fruit sweeter than durian [a local fruit] is Thai women," according to Richard Poulin (2003, p. 38), citing David Hechler. No doubt the sex industry now flourishes with the interplay of the domestic and international political economic system. Cynthia Enloe (1989) states that the sex industry "requires Third World Women to be economically desperate to enter prostitution" and makes them dependent "on an alliance between local governments in search of foreign currency and local and foreign businessmen willing to invest in sexualized travel" (pp. 36–37).

The rampant, ever growing global sex industry is also analyzed within the demand and supply model in which the receiving countries with large sex industries create a demand for female bodies. On the demand side also are significant numbers of men with social, economic, and political power. The industry exists because those in power—the state, government, the political and economic systems, industrial capitalists, and patriarchy—hegemonize it and reap the profits. The majority of poor women and ethnic minorities from the industrializing nations or nations facing political and economic crises constitute the supply side, while businessmen and patriarchs, particularly from the rich nations, constitute the demand side. Women as a commodity serve the demand of those who can purchase them. Globalization has no doubt provided multiple sites and multiple agencies to operate and foster the transnational sex trade. H. Patricia Hynes and Janice G. Raymond (2002) report:

> In what becomes a predacious cycle, the growth of the transnational sex industry—with its unique profit potential from the reuse and resale of women, compared to the one-time sale of drugs and weapons—entices governments facing economic crisis to promote women for export within the global sex trade industry in order to attract a flow of remittance back to the sending country; or to directly and indirectly promote local sex industries to bring money into the country. (p. 205)

CONCLUSION

Historical factors, larger structural forces, the processes of global capital accumulation, sociocultural and political-economic factors, and the politics of race, class, gender, nationality, and citizenship are important when analyzing the nature, pattern, process, and victims of contemporary human trafficking.

Although in general the majority of slaves in the global economy are children and women, these children and women can also be described as members of a particular race, ethnicity, and class, and as nationals of particular Third World countries. Until the collapse of the former Soviet states, the majority of trafficked girls and women were from Asian, Latin American, and Caribbean nations, whose black, brown, and gold skin tone made them exotic and desirable to others in the global sex trade. The increasing numbers of *Natashas* (female sex workers from the former Soviet states) and other white women into the sex trafficking and sex trade, however, illustrates the historical overrepresentation of women in such practices.

Although patriarchal entrepreneurs extract profit from the labor of women and children, they often rationalize their interest and behavior by arguing that they are helping to alleviate poverty. The majority of enslaved sex workers who provide bondage labor are subjugated, exploited, and commodified not only because they are women but also because they are poor and typically members of racial-ethnic minority groups in their countries. As Hynes and Raymond (2002) put it, "The fact that it took blond and blue-eyed victims to draw governmental and public attention to trafficking in the United States gives the appearance, at least, of racism" (p. 200).

The inclusion of white women into the sex trade, nonetheless, helps us to see the racialized gendered aspect of human trafficking and the sex industry.

The processes of colonialism, industrialization, and globalization have eroded women's positions and status. Whether in the poorest developing nations of Asia, Africa, and Latin America, or in the cities of the richest and most developed nations, young girls' and women's labor and sexuality as a commodity has been colonized, subjugated, and globalized across continents, nations, and regions. What is common between the colonial expansion, industrialization, and globalization is that in all of these phases, women's labor and sexuality are highly commodified and exploited. This continuation of global colonialism and imperialism reflect a series of unequal power relations and hierarchical power structures in which poor girls and women in general, and poor girls and women of color in particular, are located at the bottom of global power structures.

SEE ALSO *Body Politics; Gender Ideology; Illegal Alien; Poverty; Rape; Sex Work; Sexuality; Violence against Women and Girls.*

BIBLIOGRAPHY

Banerjee, Upala Devi. 2002. "Globalization, Crisis in Livelihoods, Migration and Trafficking of Women and Girls: The Crisis in India, Nepal and Bangladesh 2002." Paper presented at the 111th International Congress of Women, Work and Health in Sweden.

Enloe, Cynthia. 1989. *In Banana Beaches and Bases: Making Feminist Sense of International Politics.* Berkeley: University of California Press.

Farr, Kathryn. 2005. Sex *Trafficking: The Global Market in Women and Children.* New York: Worth Publishers.

Goodwin, Jan. 2003. "The Ultimate Growth Industry: Trafficking in Girls and Women." In *Reconstructing Gender: A Multicultural Anthology,* 3rd ed., ed. Estelle Disch, 498–502. New York: McGraw-Hill.

Gurung, Shobha Hamal. 2003. "Women in Factory-Based and Home-Based Carpet Production in Nepal: Beyond the Formal and Informal Economy." Ph.D. diss., Northeastern University, Boston.

hooks, bell. 1981. *Ain't I a Woman: Black Women and Feminism?* Boston: South End Press.

Hughes, Donna M. 2000. "The 'Natasha' Trade: The Transnational Shadow Market of Trafficking in Women." *Journal of International Affairs* 53 (2): 625–651.

Hynes, H. Patricia, and Janice G. Raymond. 2002. "Put in Harm's Way: The Neglected Health Consequences of Sex Trafficking in the United States." In *Policing the National Body: Race, Gender, and Criminalization,* ed. Jael Silliman and Anannya Bhattacharejee, 197–229. Boston: South End Press.

Kempadoo, Kamala. 2004. *Sexing The Caribbean: Gender, Race and Sexual Labor.* New York: Routledge.

———, and Jo Doezema, eds. 1998. *Global Sex Workers: Rights, Resistance, and Redefinition.* New York: Routledge.

Leacock, Eleanor, and Mona Etienne. 1980. "Introduction." In *Women and Colonization,* ed. Eleanor Leacock and Mona Etienne, 1–24. New York: Praeger.

Palley, Thomas. 2002. "Child Labor Problem and the Need for International Labor Standards." *Journal of Economic Issues* 36 (3): 601–615.

Poulin, Richard. 2003. "Globalization and the Sex Trade: Trafficking and the Commodification of Women and Children." *Canadian Woman Studies* 22 (3–4): 28–43.

Roberts, Dorothy. 1997. *Killing the Black Body: Race, Reproduction, and Meaning of Liberty.* New York: Vintage.

United Nations. 2002. "United Nations Response to Trafficking in Women and Girls." Division for the Advancement of Women Department of Economic and Social Affairs. http://www.un.org/womenwatch.

U.S. Department of State. 2003. "Trafficking in Persons Report." http://www.state.gov.

Widgen, Jones. 1994. "Multinational Corporations to Combat Trafficking in Migrants and the Role of the International Organizations: International Responses to Trafficking in Migrants and Safeguarding of Migrants Rights." IOM Seminar on Trafficking in Migrants and Safeguarding Migrants Rights. Geneva, October 26–28, 1994.

Shobha Hamal Gurung

HYPERTENSION AND CORONARY HEART DISEASE

Persistent high blood pressure, or hypertension, became recognized as a diagnosable medical condition in the 1930s, with rudimentary treatments emerging in the late 1940s. A decade or more before this, colonial physicians in Africa had already developed an interest in the apparent paucity of hypertension among indigenous black populations, which they attributed, in part, to the absence of modern stresses and cultural dissonances. This explanation persisted for decades, especially in apartheid-era South Africa, where it conformed to the ideology of black homelands as salubrious respites from a more complex urban life for which native people were thought to be inherently unsuited (Donnison 1929; Packard 1989).

Hypertension is an important precursor of coronary heart disease (CHD), which involves a narrowing of the coronary arteries that supply oxygenated blood to the heart muscle. The blood-carrying capacity of the coronary arteries becomes restricted by fat and cholesterol deposits on the artery walls until the affected person experiences a chest pain called *angina,* or until a sufficient obstruction of the coronary artery occurs to precipitate a heart attack. Often, a heart attack results from a sudden closure of the artery due to a blood clot forming at a point where the artery is already narrowed.

HYPERTENSION AND AFRICAN AMERICANS

Observations of heightened levels of hypertension and average blood pressure in African Americans arose in the early 1900s, with primitive population-based survey results dating to at least as early as 1932. These findings were in direct contrast to the apparent absence of hypertension in rural African populations, and also with a relatively low risk for CHD among African Americans. By the 1960s there was extensive evidence from community-based surveys, such as the Evans County (Georgia) Study, to indicate that black Americans experienced nearly twice the clinically defined hypertension than that experienced by white Americans. At the same time, however, these epidemiologic surveys confirmed that CHD risk was lower for blacks than for whites in the United States. Rather than precipitating heart disease, untreated hypertension in African Americans was more likely to manifest in cerebrovascular disease and stroke mortality.

The observation of differential risk for hypertension and CHD between racial groups led many physical anthropologists and medical researchers in the first half of the twentieth century to focus on identifying inherent anatomic and physiological differences between groups that might explain this disparity. A large number of research reports resulted, with putative racial variation identified in nearly every component of the cardiovascular apparatus. For example, one study involved postmortem examinations of the hearts of seventeen whites, fifteen Africans, and two African Americans in the early 1950s. This study concluded that the Africans had an extra large branch of the left coronary artery, to which protection from coronary heart disease was attributed (Phillips and Burch 1960).

There was a similar preoccupation with the comparative sizes and weights of organs, such as the observation that blacks had smaller or lighter kidneys than whites. Similarly, it was widely held that blacks had a natural resistance to a number of common diseases, including hookworm, gall stones, tuberculosis, syphilis, pneumonia, and whooping cough, and thus it was thought that they might also possess a lower risk for coronary heart disease as an intrinsic racial trait (Lewis 1942; Phillips and Burch 1960).

A consequence of the persistent observation of racial/ethnic disparity in hypertension and CHD risk has been the ongoing use of language that casts blacks and whites as fundamentally distinct in terms of innate biology or physiology. For example, scientific articles often carry titles such as "Hypertension in Blacks: Is it a Different Disease?" (Megs 1985).

This predominant ideology of essential biologic difference has precipitated numerous unsubstantiated assertions in the peer-reviewed medical literature. For example, hypertension is often described as intrinsically more virulent among blacks. But assertions that blacks "tend to experience greater cardiovascular and renal damage at any level of [blood] pressure" (Kaplan 1994, p. 450) have no clear empirical basis.

Likewise, despite voluminous research on environmental and behavioral factors that contribute to hypertension and CHD risk, the long-standing paradigm of viewing racial/ethnic groups as representing human subspecies has led many discussions of the cardiovascular disease disparity in the biomedical literature to be couched reflexively in terms of hypothesized genetic factors. For example, in an exhaustive review of more than 400 articles on racial differences in cardiovascular disease in 1960, John H. Phillips and George E. Burch sought to caution against a completely essentialist interpretation by concluding, judiciously, that "it appears that many racial differences reflect not only genetic and racial factors but [also] variations in the medical care available and extended to the Negro, and the Negro's cooperation and participation in this medical care" (p. 274). In the subsequent four decades, however, the general emphasis on intrinsic as opposed to social factors remained largely intact. For example, writing in the *British Medical Journal* in 1997, Sarah Wild and Paul McKeigue concluded that "excess mortality from cerebrovascular and hypertensive diseases in migrants from both West Africa and the Caribbean suggests that genetic factors underlie the susceptibility to hypertension in people of black African descent" (p. 705).

THE SLAVERY HYPERTENSION HYPOTHESIS

An abiding faith in innate biologic predisposition as the explanation for observed racial patterning in disease has led to a surfeit of ad hoc hypotheses, such as relating blood pressure disregulation directly to skin pigmentation, or to excess testosterone levels in black men. The most widely disseminated of these "just so" stories is the slavery hypertension hypothesis, an evolutionary theory that relates excess hypertension risk in New World blacks to selection during the "Middle Passage" for phenotypes that were sodium retentive. The theory was posited at least as early as 1983, and it was adopted in the late 1980s by the hypertension researcher Clarence Grim, who has since championed the idea energetically. Grim speculated that sodium loss from sweating, diarrheal stools, and vomit during the transatlantic voyage led to high levels of mortality from dehydration, and therefore to selection pressure against genes coding for greater sodium excretion. Though the slavery hypertension hypothesis lacks any empirical support and has been widely criticized from the historical as well as the biomedical arenas, it continues to capture the popular and scientific imagination as a tidy explanation for elevated levels of hypertension in African Americans, and it is routinely cited in medical textbooks, scientific journal articles, and the popular press. For example, in a feature article about the young Harvard economist Roland Fryer Jr., published in the *New York Times Magazine* in March 2005, the hypothesis is depicted as a new and exciting idea from the rising academic superstar. (Grim, Henry, and Myers 1995; Kaufman and Hall 2003).

The unexpectedly low prevalence of coronary heart disease observed in African Americans in the first half of the century led to similar speculation regarding some categorical racial protection, either cultural or genetic. But these theories of innate resistance to atherosclerotic progression quickly evaporated as the racial disparity flipped in the 1960s and 1970s. Indeed, by the 1980s and 1990s it was black Americans who had a higher CHD risk than whites (driven largely by a wider disparity for women). This reversal in the racial disparity was largely explained by changes in risk-factor distributions in the two populations, such as more diabetes, more atherogenic lipid profiles, less physically active occupations, and greater levels of obesity among blacks. Nonetheless, the scientific discourse soon shifted to speculation about an innate characteristic that predisposed blacks to develop CHD, rather than to avoid it.

HEART DISEASE, RACIAL DIFFERENCES, AND MEDICAL CARE

By the last quarter of the twentieth century, the CHD death rate was falling for all groups, although more slowly for blacks, which further exacerbated the disparity. At younger ages (less than sixty-five years), the relative black excess became particularly pronounced. The mortality risk at these young ages is low in absolute terms, but the racial disparity is as much as two-fold. This produces a relatively small difference in the number of attributable cases of CHD death, but a larger number of excess years of life lost, due to the young ages of the cases.

Another important cause of cardiovascular mortality is congestive heart failure, which may result from CHD, hypertension, or any of several other cardiovascular pathologies. There are roughly five million Americans with congestive heart failure, and another half a million are diagnosed with the condition every year, making it the one major category of cardiovascular disease that has continued to increase in the United States over the last several decades. Like hypertension and CHD, a racial predisposition to heart failure incidence or mortality has been proposed numerous times in the medical literature, especially to account for a more extreme excess of black risk at younger ages.

Heart failure is unique in being the target of a race-specific pharmacotherapy. The new drug, marketed under the commercial name BiDil, is simply a combination of two previously existing generic vasodilators, isosorbide dinitrate and hydralazine. In June 2005, based on the successful results of a clinical trial called A-HeFT, which enrolled only self-defined African-American heart failure patients, this drug combination was approved by the U.S. Food and Drug Administration (FDA) for sale in the United States as the first "ethnic drug" (Taylor et al. 2004).

To justify a trial restricted to one racial group, the A-HeFT investigators proposed that African Americans have lower average rennin-angiotensin system activity, which leads to reduced tissue availability of nitric oxide, a molecule that facilitates the vasodilation necessary for healthy blood pressure regulation. The A-HeFT investigators then asserted that retrospective analyses of data from previous heart-failure trials strongly suggested that black patients had an especially pronounced response to the BiDil combination. However, in the only study that was cited to support this assertion, a statistical test for racial heterogeneity found no significant difference in response between blacks and whites (Carson et al. 1999). It has therefore been suggested that the decision to test and market the drug only for blacks appears to be motivated by concerns that are commercial, rather than scientific, in nature (Kahn 2004).

The whole notion of creating ethnic-specific drugs for cardiovascular conditions remains controversial. Racial groups are not discrete genetic categories, and they overlap considerably with respect to the relevant etiologic and physiologic factors that influence pharmacological effects. Therefore, all available data suggest that any drug determined to work on most blacks will also work on most members of any other group, and vice versa. This phenomenon was demonstrated quantitatively by a recent meta-analytic review by Ashwini Sehgal (2004). Despite numerous claims that antihypertensive therapies have differential efficacy across racial groups, Sehgal showed that the distributions of blood pressure reductions for various common classes of antihypertensive medications overlapped by 83 to 93 percent. This suggests that basing clinical decisions on race may disadvantage the majority of patients of any group, who would respond equivalently to a drug that is presumed to have an effect specific to some other group.

TREATMENT FOR CARDIAC DISEASE

In contrast to the very ambiguous basis for race-specific therapies, the evidence for differential treatment of cardiovascular conditions is now extensive, including differential access to screening and to diagnostic and therapeutic interventions. These differences persist even when controlling for insurance status and socioeconomic level. For example, in an experimental design in which physicians were shown videotapes of actors reading identical scripts of a case presentation of chest pain, the odds that a black woman actor would be referred for right-heart catheterization were only 40 percent of the odds for a white man, even though the vignettes contained identical medical and social histories and identical symptoms (Schulman et al. 1999).

A large number of factors may contribute to differences in access to care and to differential treatment within the medical system, including patient knowledge, patient trust in the physician (and in the healthcare system as a whole), patient-physician communication, patient noncompliance, physician stereotyping, and overt discrimination. For example, when a physician gains less information from a patient of a different race because of cultural or educational barriers in the communication process, the natural response is to stereotype the patient (i.e., to treat the patient based on assumptions about the average member of the group, instead of according to the patient's individual values). This stereotyping, even if entirely well-intentioned and factually unbiased, will tend to exacerbate disparities between groups by adding more random error to the transfer of information necessary for appropriate treatment. If the stereotype is factually incorrect, then the disparity may be exacerbated even further (Balsa and McGuire 2003). There is also extensive evidence to suggest that physicians have many irrational stereotypes about racial-minority patients. For example, in experimental studies, medical students rated black women as having a lower quality of life than white men (Rathore et al. 2000), while psychiatrists asked to make diagnoses from standardized patient vignettes rated black men as being more hostile and dangerous than males from other groups (Loring and Powell 1988).

Cardiovascular disorders have complex etiologies involving diet, physical activity, and genetic factors, as well as a person's psychosocial and physical environment. Moreover, they are ascertained and treated differentially with respect to social position and cultural identity. As such, these conditions are very sensitive to social contexts, and they tend to show wide disparities when the relevant factors vary across population groups. These disparities have long fueled hypotheses of innate group predispositions, but rapid shifts in patterns over space and time belie such facile speculation. For example, the West African diaspora, stretching from the population groups of origin through the Caribbean, Brazil, the United Kingdom, and the United States, represents a group of genetically related peoples who were dispersed widely over dramatically different social environments. Yet despite a common geographic origin, these groups now evidence some of the widest variations in cardiovascular risk factors and disease prevalences in the world (Cooper et al. 1997). Nonetheless, the emergence of race-based therapeutics as the latest approach to cardiovascular disease disparities demonstrates that many of the most important lessons of the last several decades of epidemiologic research have not yet been fully assimilated.

SEE ALSO *Diseases, Racial.*

BIBLIOGRAPHY

Balsa, Ana Inés, and Thomas G. McGuire. 2003. "Prejudice, Clinical Uncertainty and Stereotyping as Sources of Health Disparities." *Journal of Health Economics* 22 (1): 89–116.

Carson, Peter, Susan Ziesche, Gary Johnson, and Jay N. Cohn. 1999. "Racial Differences in Response to Therapy for Heart Failure: Analysis of the Vasodilator-Heart Failure Trials." *Journal of Cardiac Failure* 5 (3): 178–187.

Cooper, Richard S., et al. 1997. "The Prevalence of Hypertension in Seven Populations of West African Origin." *American Journal of Public Health* 87 (2): 160–168.

Crook, Errol D., et al. 2003. "From 1960s Evans County Georgia to Present-Day Jackson, Mississippi: An Exploration of the Evolution of Cardiovascular Disease in African Americans." *American Journal of the Medical Sciences* 325 (6): 307–314.

Donnison, C. P. 1929. "Blood Pressure in the African Native." *Lancet* 1: 6–11.

Grim, Clarence E., James P. Henry, and Hector Myers. 1995. "High Blood Pressure in Blacks: Salt, Slavery, Survival, Stress, and Racism." In *Hypertension: Pathophysiology, Diagnosis, and Management*, 2nd ed., edited by John H. Laragh and Barry M. Brenner, 171–207. New York: Raven Press.

Kahn, Jonathon. 2004. "How a Drug Becomes "Ethnic": Law, Commerce, and the Production of Racial Categories in Medicine." *Yale Journal of Health Policy Law and Ethics* 4 (1): 1–46.

Kaplan, Norman M. 1994. "Ethnic Aspects of Hypertension." *Lancet* 344 (8920): 450–452.

Kaufman, Jay S., and Susan A. Hall. 2003. "The Slavery Hypertension Hypothesis: Dissemination and Appeal of a Modern Race Theory." *Epidemiology* 14 (1): 111–118.

Lewis, Julian H. 1942. *The Biology of the Negro*. Chicago: University of Chicago Press.

Loring, Marti, and Brian Powell. 1988. "Gender, Race, and DSM-III: A Study of the Objectivity of Psychiatric Diagnostic Behavior." *Journal of Health and Social Behavior* 29 (1): 1–22.

Meggs, Leonard G. 1985. "Hypertension in Blacks. Is It a Different Disease?" *New York State Journal of Medicine* 85(4):160–161.

Packard, Randall M. 1989. "The 'Healthy Reserve' and the 'Dressed Native': Discourses of Black Health and the Language of Legitimation in South Africa." *American Ethnologist* 16 (4): 686–703.

Phillips, John. H., Jr., and George E. Burch. 1960. "A Review of Cardiovascular Diseases in the White and Negro Races." *Medicine* (Baltimore) 39: 241–288.

Rathore, Shailendra Singh, et al. 2000. "The Effects of Patient Sex and Race on Medical Students' Ratings of Quality of Life." *American Journal of Medicine* 108 (7): 561–566.

Schulman, Kevin A., et al. 1999. "The Effect of Race and Sex on Physicians' Recommendations for Cardiac Catheterization." *New England Journal of Medicine* 340 (8): 618–626.

Sehgal, Ashwini R. 2004. "Overlap between Whites and Blacks in Response to Antihypertensive Drugs." *Hypertension* 43 (3): 566–572.

Taylor, Anne L., et al. 2004. "Combination of Isosorbide Dinitrate and Hydralazine in Blacks with Heart Failure." *New England Journal of Medicine* 351 (20): 2049–2057.

Wild, Sarah, and Paul McKeigue. 1997. "Cross Sectional Analysis of Mortality by Country of Birth in England and Wales, 1970–92." *British Medical Journal* 314 (7082): 705–710.

Jay S. Kaufman

I

ILLEGAL ALIEN

On March 3, 1875, the United States established, for the first time, federal prohibitions on the entry of immigrants deemed undesirable. The legislation, known as the Page Law, excluded criminals and prostitutes from entry into the country, as well as Chinese contract laborers known perjoratively as "coolies." The act, driven by racial and economic fears and followed by a series of broader Chinese exclusion laws beginning in 1882, is often referred to as the genesis of the "illegal alien" category in the United States.

In the contemporary debate about undocumented migration to the United States, the term *illegal aliens* is widely perceived to be synonymous with Latino immigrants, and particularly with Mexican immigrants. Yet much is misunderstood about the legislative and social origins of the term. This history, in which the federal government created the category of "illegal aliens" by forbidding entry to a racially targeted class of undesirable immigrants, has engendered the conflation of noncitizenship, nonwhiteness, and criminality into a malleable racial euphemism readily available for private and public enforcement strategies.

DEFINING "ILLEGAL ALIEN"

In U.S. law, there is not a clear definition of an "illegal alien," despite the term's widespread use in popular and policy discourse. Although the conjoined phrase is not found in the *Oxford English Dictionary*, the word *illegal* is defined as "not legal or lawful; contrary to, or forbidden by law." *Alien*, in turn, is defined as "belonging to another person, place, or family"; "foreign, not of one's own"; or "of a foreign nation and allegiance." In broader immigration discourse, terms such as *illegals*, *undocumented workers*, or *unauthorized immigrants* are commonly used interchangeably, although they do not necessarily represent the same category. Rather, these terms are often a measure of political sensitivity and ideological position in the U.S. immigration debate. Undocumented workers, for example, are a subset of "illegal aliens" representing those who have entered the workforce. In addition, despite the extraterrestrial implications of the term *alien*, within U.S. immigration law an alien is "any person not a citizen or national of the United States," according to the Department of Homeland Security. This is a broad bureaucratic category that includes legal permanent residents, temporary visitors, and unauthorized migrants. An "illegal" alien can be a person who has entered the country without authorization or whose legal status has lapsed—either because the person violated the terms of his or her visa or committed a deportable offense. Consequently, lawful permanent residents, or green-card holders, can become illegal aliens, while some illegal aliens can be paroled into the country and thus be considered lawful persons.

PRECURSORS TO "ILLEGAL" MIGRANTS

Before 1875, federal and state restrictions on the mobility of persons also produced "illegality." In the antebellum period, for example, the mobility of both free blacks and slaves was regulated by state and federal laws. While not dubbed "illegal aliens," persons such as foreign black seamen were nonetheless the target of restricted entry into various states. The overall regulation of slavery notwithstanding, the movement of convicted criminals, the poor, indentured servants, and persons deemed a threat to public health were also variously controlled, restricted, and penalized prior to 1875. In fact, the Page Law, by restricting the "coolie trade," convicts, and prostitutes, only codified the central elements of pre-1875 restrictions. In this sense, illegal aliens "have always existed in the United States" (Neuman 1993, p. 1901). They are a constituent element of the nation.

ENFORCEMENT

The creation of the U.S. Border Patrol in 1924 operationalized border enforcement and the apprehension of illegal aliens. Prior to this, only a token force of mounted officers was commissioned to assist immigration officers in the capture of persons so categorized. The creation of an enforcement apparatus coincided with the Johnson-Reed Act of 1924, which created numerical limits on immigration from throughout the world. Deeply impacted by racism, and by a preference for northern European migrants, the numerical limits of the 1924 law expanded significantly the numbers of present and future "illegal aliens" (Ngai 2004, p. 4).

After 1924, deportation became the central strategy for confronting illegal aliens. The deportation process, which once abided by a statute of limitations (the illegal immigrant had to be caught within a range of zero to five years after entry), was streamlined over the twentieth century by removing the statute of limitations on a migrant's undocumented status, by denying due process for noncitizens, and by the use of "voluntary departures." In the latter example, a migrant would sign a prepared statement and then "voluntarily" depart, avoiding any lengthy adjudication process. Further, as Joseph Nevins points out in *Operation Gatekeeper* (2002), the immigration statute of March 4, 1929, explicitly criminalized "illegal" entry as a misdemeanor and "illegal" reentry as a felony punishable by fine or imprisonment (p. 54). It is during this time period that Mexicans immigrants became the quintessential "illegal aliens." They were subject to large-scale government repatriation and deportation campaigns in the 1930s and 1950s, with the latter campaign being termed "Operation Wetback" by the Immigration and Naturalization Service (INS).

MEXICANS, BRACEROS, AND "ILLEGALS"

The focus on Mexican undocumented migrants coincided with a twenty-two-year guest-worker program called the Bracero Program, which contracted an average of 200,000 male Mexican laborers per year between 1942 and 1964. The Bracero Program is said to have greatly increased the presence of undocumented migrants through job recruitment and competition, the stimulation of social and family networks, and the growth of Mexican communities in the United States that developed during the decades-long flow of sanctioned migration. The contradiction of large-scale recruitment simultaneous with large-scale deportation is illustrated by Operation Wetback in 1954. In her book, *Inside the State: The Bracero Program, Immigration, and the I.N.S.* (1992), Kitty Calavita describes the INS process of "paroling illegal aliens to employers as braceros and legaliz[ing] others with a symbolic step across the border" (p. 109). This process exemplifies not only the preference for illegal labor by employers, but also early strategies of legalization as a way to reconstruct and make the "illegal alien" legal. The end of the Bracero Program in 1964, followed by the equalization of numerical migration quotas for all nations in 1965, also stimulated, nearly overnight, the massive presence of Mexican illegal aliens, for the sanctioned flow of well over 200,000 Mexican persons annually exceeded the legal quota for the entire western hemisphere and would later be limited further to 20,000 per year (De Genova 2004, pp. 172–173).

CRIMINALIZATION AND POPULAR SENTIMENT

Since the middle of the twentieth century, illegal immigration has been followed by a pattern of popular outrage and tolerance closely tied to U.S. economic performance. These attitudes have generated a range of policies, including employer sanctions, militarization of the U.S.-Mexico border, denial of public services, reductions in due process, and an amnesty for longtime undocumented residents. These various strategies to halt, control, or regulate the flow of migration, which myopically focus on domestic enforcement instead of international cooperation and global economic development, have largely failed to permanently change the flow and presence of undocumented immigrants. Instead, these policies have heightened the costs of unauthorized migration—stimulating growth in human smuggling, labor exploitation, and vigilante movements against persons perceived to be "illegals," as well as increasing the migrant death toll along the U.S.-Mexico border. Whereas anti-immigrant activists blame uncaring human smugglers (known as *coyotes*) or the immigrants themselves, immigrant advocates fault U.S. enforcement practices that make unauthorized entry extremely dangerous, leading to more than 3,600 migrant deaths between 1994 and 2005 (Marosi 2005).

Popular responses to undocumented migration place heavy emphasis on migrants' "illegality" and suggest an

Sign Warns Drivers to Watch for Illegal Aliens. *In some areas, illegal border crossings are so prevalent that road signs have been posted to warn motorists.* © CHASE SWIFT/CORBIS.

inherent and self-evident unlawfulness that criminalizes the person rather than the action the person is purported to have committed. The criminalization of immigrants and persons perceived to be immigrants manufactures a sweeping form of illegality that fails to consider the economic, political, social, or historical factors explaining a person's "illegal" presence. Nevins calls this process *illegalization,* which he defines as "the process by which immigrants entering the United States without state sanction have become constructed and perceived as lawbreakers and alleged threats to the sociocultural and political fabric of the country" (Nevins 2002, p. 166). Legally, however, most undocumented migrants, while unsparingly referred to as "illegals," have technically not been charged or tried for the misdemeanor of first-time illegal entry. Roughly half of each year's cohort of new undocumented immigrants entered by legal means but have allowed their legal entry status to lapse, which is not a violation of the criminal code. Nevertheless, a presumably legal category becomes a cultural one, which envelopes all immigrants regardless of status, especially those most commonly marked as "illegal" in the early twenty-first century—Latinas and Latinos. Popular discourse, especially when racialized explicitly or implicitly, is a central component to the construction and management of "illegal aliens."

ILLEGAL ALIENS IN THE TWENTY-FIRST CENTURY

The nonpartisan Pew Hispanic Center estimates that there are 11.5 to 12 million illegal aliens in the United States (based on the March 2005 Current Population Survey), representing 30 percent of the nation's foreign-born residents. Undocumented migrants from neighboring Mexico make up more than half, or 56 percent, of the undocumented population, whereas Asia accounts for 13 percent. Europe and Canada, meanwhile, account for 6 percent. Two-thirds of undocumented persons reside in just six states (California, Texas, Florida, New York, Illinois, and New Jersey), according to the Urban Institute, while newer immigrant destinations, such as Arizona, Georgia, and North Carolina, have acquired concentrations of illegal aliens amounting to more than 40 percent of these states' foreign-born populations.

The presence of illegal aliens stimulates a wide-ranging debate about national resources such as jobs, housing, education, and the environment. It also raises cultural fears about bilingual education, racial composition, and crime. Policy issues about noncitizen I.D. cards, driver's licenses, guest-worker programs, and large-scale "legalization" have been known to polarize communities addressing undocumented migration. Both sides make arguments about what to each is clearly evident: Anti-immigrant activists oppose any policy that "rewards" illegal behavior, while immigrant advocates decry the stark inequality that undocumented immigrants and their families endure.

The issue of potential terrorists entering the United States with the flow of undocumented migration was introduced in the 1990s and reinvoked after September 11, 2001. Economic concerns, meanwhile, such as wage depreciation and job competition with undocumented workers, persist in animating activists and politicians on all sides of the issue. Among "illegal aliens" in the early twenty-first century, more than two-thirds are workers (including 94 percent of male undocumented migrants), representing nearly 5 percent of the total U.S. workforce. Whereas many industries or local economies cannot survive without this source of labor, undocumented workers' concentration in low-wage industries—such as agriculture, construction, janitorial services, domestic care, hotels and restaurants, and other service industries—perpetuates high poverty rates despite above-average workforce participation. In fact, many immigrant advocates argue that the purpose of most policy initiatives has never been to halt undocumented labor but simply to reduce the rights and protections of undocumented workers, thus making them invisible, exploitable, and a permanent underclass in the nation's economy.

Throughout U.S. history, illegal aliens have been subject to labor recruitment, deportation, and settlement into the margins of U.S. society. An undocumented status has, in turn, complicated family and community structures, expanding the impact of anti-immigrant sentiment and legislation onto "legal" migrants and U.S. citizens. For example, 3.1 million U.S.-born children have parents who are illegal aliens, and children under the age of eighteen make up almost 16 percent of undocumented migrants. The welfare of the citizenry is thus tied to the welfare of noncitizens. Family structures, transformed by immigrant status, suggest that undocumented migration is a permanent and complex feature of U.S. society, yet it is one that has been made invisible by the moniker "illegal alien."

SEE ALSO *Border Crossings and Human Rights; Border Patrol; Immigration to the United States.*

BIBLIOGRAPHY

Bender, Steven. 2003. *Greasers and Gringos: Latinos, Law, and the American Imagination.* New York: New York University Press.

Calavita, Kitty. 1992. *Inside the State: The Bracero Program, Immigration, and the I.N.S.* New York: Routledge.

De Genova, Nicholas. 2004. "The Legal Production of Mexican/Migrant 'Illegality.'" *Latino Studies* 2 (2): 160-185.

Lee, Erika. 2003. *At America's Gates: Chinese Immigration during the Exclusion Era, 1882–1943.* Chapel Hill: University of North Carolina Press.

Marosi, Richard. 2005. "Border Crossing Deaths Set a 12-Month Record." *Los Angeles Times,* October 1.

Neuman, Gerald. 1993. "The Lost Century of American Immigration Law (1776–1875)." *Columbia Law Review* 93 (8): 1833–1901.

Nevins, Joseph. 2002. *Operation Gatekeeper: The Rise of the "Illegal Alien" and the Making of the U.S.-Mexico Boundary.* New York: Routledge.

Ngai, Mae. 2004. *Impossible Subjects: Illegal Aliens and the Making of Modern America.* Princeton, NJ: Princeton University Press.

Passel, Jeffrey, Randolph Capps, and Michael Fix. 2004. "Undocumented Immigrants: Facts and Figures." Washington, DC: Urban Institute. Available from http://www.urban.org.

Schuck, Peter H. 1998. *Citizens, Strangers, and In-Betweens: Essays on Immigration and Citizenship.* Boulder, CO: Westview Press.

David Manuel Hernández

IMMIGRANT DOMESTIC WORKERS

Domestic work entails the duties of cleaning, caring, and nurturing in a private household. Domestic work is either "paid" or "unpaid" labor, and it has historically been done by women. When done by mothers and other kin, it is considered skilled work, but when done by others it is often disregarded as unskilled labor, and therefore minimally rewarded with low wages. The labor of domestic work is not inherently racist. However, it has been a vehicle for institutional racism in both the past and the present.

Paid domestic work continues to be relegated to poor women of color and migrant women around the world, and it is usually shunned by those with other labor market options. This is because it is considered a low-status occupation with low wages and poor labor-market conditions. Because it is difficult to enforce labor standards in domestic work, the work often entails excessive job responsibilities that include cooking, cleaning, and caring for the dependents of a household. In the United States, African-American women have historically performed paid domestic service in the South—a labor-market concentration that is a legacy of slavery. In the early twentieth century, African Americans began to enter domestic service in the North, and they were joined by poor immigrant women from Ireland, Italy, Japan, and Mexico. In the early twenty-first century, migrant women of color from Mexico, Central America, the Caribbean, and the Philippines make up a disproportionate number of domestic workers in the United States.

The United States is not the only country that depends on migrant women workers to fill the need for paid domestic work in private households. With globalization, domestic workers are increasingly migrating from poorer to richer countries. Polish and Albanian women, for instance, are moving west to respond to the demand for domestic work in private households in countries from Greece to Germany. Likewise, Filipinos, Sri Lankans, and Indonesians are filling the need for domestic workers in richer countries of Asia and the Middle East, while Filipinos, Caribbeans (e.g., Dominicans in Spain and West Indians in Britain), and Latinos (e.g., Mexicans and Central Americans in the United States and Peruvians in Italy) are filling the demand for domestic workers in the rich countries of North America and western Europe.

Native citizens tend to shun domestic work because of its low pay. Migrant domestic workers uniformly earn below minimum wage—generally reaching no more than $3.00 an hour for live-in work in Los Angeles, for example (Hondagneu-Sotelo 2001). Average salaries of domestic workers differ across the diaspora: Migrant domestic

Hong Kong Domestic Workers Protest Pay Cut. *In 2005 China announced a U.S. $50 pay reduction for foreign domestic workers. In response, maids from the Philippines, Indonesia, Thailand, and Nepal staged a protest march in downtown Hong Kong.* AP IMAGES.

workers earn, on average, $100 per month in Jordan, $500 per month in Israel, $1,200 per month in Italy, and $750 per month in Taiwan. In the United States they can earn up to $2,000 per month for full-time live-in employment, though they are also known to earn much less—sometimes not reaching $1,000 per month for the same work. Wage differences between domestic workers in a single country reflect the absence of a labor standard in domestic work and the dependence of domestic workers on the consciousness of employers. However, there are some good employers and bad employers. Good employers ensure domestic workers receive a day off regularly, a daily rest period, and their own private space in the household. In contrast, bad employers have been known to force domestic workers to sleep in the kitchen (Anderson 2000).

Across the globe, from Israel to Greece to Canada, ethnic and racial differences between domestic workers and their employers are not diffused by the intimacy of their interactions in the private space of a home. Instead, these differences tend to be magnified by the unequal relationship imposed by employers. The imposition of racial difference first takes place in hiring. Racist stereotypes shape the hiring practices of employers, a practice that aggravates the subordinated status of domestic workers while highlighting the racial difference between domestics and employers. In stereotyping an ethnic and racial group, certain characteristics are generalized and conflated, thereby ridding members of the group of their individuality. For example, in Canada, the two largest group of domestic workers—Caribbean and Filipinos—are racialized differently. Filipinos are often enforced with positive stereotypes. Many consider them to be excellent housekeepers who are docile and willing to tolerate the poorest of working conditions without any complaints. In contrast, Jamaicans are imbued with negative stereotypes. They are considered aggressive and less likely to be willing to do the extra work requested by employers. However, both positive and negative stereotypes enforce the marginal status of a group and their distinction as an "Other."

Xenophobia also mars the integration of foreign domestic workers in the host society (Parreñas 2001). Restrictive immigration laws impose partial citizenship on foreign domestic workers, so that they are not granted the rights of full membership in the society that depends on their labor. Domestic workers are usually relegated to a temporary visa, which is the case in Asian and European countries. Their legal status is usually conditional to their employment by one particular employer, and they often do not have the right to choose their employer regardless of their treatment—whether good or bad—by employers. This places domestic workers in a position of bonded servitude. This is the case in Hong Kong, but also in Canada and the United States. Under Canada's Live-In Caregiver's Programme, for example, domestic workers must reside for two years with their sponsoring employer to qualify for landed status. In the United States, under foreign labor certification programs, domestic workers must remain employed with their sponsoring employer regardless of work conditions until they receive their green card, a process that has been known to take ten years. In some countries, the exclusion of domestic workers extends to marriage and pregnancy. For instance, foreign domestic workers cannot marry Singaporean nationals, and they face immediate deportation from Singapore and Malaysia if they test positive for pregnancy.

In the workplace, racial inequalities also adversely shape employer-employee relations. Social divisions are manifested spatially and physically. For instance, some employers insist that domestic workers must wear uniforms and wash their clothes separately. Employers also impose "spatial deference" on their domestic workers, meaning the "unequal rights of the domestic and the employer to the space around the other's body and the controlling of the domestic's use of house space" (Rollins 1985, p. 171). Employers also control the spatial movements of domestic workers by deciding on the domestic's integration or segregation from the family. More often than not, they prefer segregation, as they tend to hire those who will demand very little resources in terms of time, money, space, or interaction. Thus, the access of domestic workers to household space is usually far more contained than for the rest of the family. In both Los Angeles and Rome, Filipina domestic workers have found themselves subject to food rationing, prevented from sitting on the couch, provided with a separate set of utensils, and told when to get food from the refrigerator and when to retreat to their bedrooms.

Finally, the inequality of an international and racial "division of reproductive labor" (Glenn 1992; Parreñas 2000) defines employer-employee relations, as women with greater privilege in the global economy pass down the burdens of housework to less-privileged women. Usually those with less privilege are working-class immigrant women of color. Since the 1970s, there has been an increase in the number of two-income families and women in the paid labor force in richer countries throughout the world. Yet states have not adequately responded to the different needs of these families, particularly their need for child-care assistance, but has instead continued to relegate child care as a private responsibility of the family. Likewise, men have not taken up the slack left by women's participation in the labor force and still do less housework than women (Hochschild 1989). To be free of the burden of housework so one is able to pursue the personally fulfilling challenges of paid work, women with greater resources rely on the low-wage labor of poor immigrant women of color. This inequality suggests that domestic work is not a "bond of sisterhood," but instead a "bond of oppression," allowing for the mobility of one group of women at the cost of the immobility of another (Romero 1992).

SEE ALSO *Caribbean Immigration; Immigration, Race, and Women; Immigration to the United States; Undocumented Workers.*

BIBLIOGRAPHY

Anderson, Bridget. 2000. *Doing the Dirty Work: The Global Politics of Domestic Labour.* London: Zed Books.

Bakan, Abigail, and Daiva Stasiulis. 1995. "Making the Match: Domestic Placement Agencies and the Racialization of Women's Household Work." *Signs* 20 (2): 303–335.

Glenn, Evelyn Nakano. 1992. "From Servitude to Service Work: Historical Continuities in the Racial Division of Paid Reproductive Labor." *Signs* 18 (1): 1–43.

Hochschild, Arlie. 1989. *The Second Shift.* New York: Avon.

Hondagneu-Sotelo, Pierrette. 2001. *Domestica: Immigrant Workers Cleaning and Caring in the Shadows of Affluence.* Berkeley: University of California Press.

Parreñas, Rhacel. 2001. "Transgressing the Nation-State: The Partial Citizenship and 'Imagined (Global) Community' of Migrant Filipina Domestic Workers." *Signs: Journal of Women in Culture and Society* 26 (4): 1129–1154.

———. 2000. "Migrant Filipina Domestic Workers and the International Division of Reproductive Labor." *Gender & Society* 14 (4): 560–580.

Rollins, Judith. 1985. *Between Women: Domestics and their Employers.* Philadelphia, PA: Temple University Press.

Romero, Mary. 1992. *Maid in the USA.* New York: Routledge.

Rhacel Salazar Parreñas

IMMIGRATION, RACE, AND WOMEN

Latin American women who migrate to the United States come with a set of social beliefs and practices with regard to race relations and racism that selectively shape their lives in the new land. Racial ideologies and practices in each Latin American country have been shaped by distinctive colonization histories and regional socioeconomics, politics, and cultures. A woman from Santiago de Cuba, for example, experiences these dynamics in a very different way than a woman from Santiago de Chile, or from Santiago, Nuevo León, in Mexico. But beyond these local and unique differences, the Spanish invasion and colonization, as well as its historical sequel, unite all the people of Latin America through a common denominator that has shaped their lives for centuries: white supremacy.

In any Latin American country, being *blanca,* or a white-skinned woman, has been socially established as superior to other standard racial identities that shape women's lives. In Mexico and other countries, these identities may include, but are not limited to: (1) *negra,* or "black," (2) *indígena,* or the derogatory expression "india," (3) *morena,* or "dark skinned," and (4) *mulata,* whose linguistic origin comes from *mula,* or "mule," and which indicates a racial mixture of *raza negra* with white. As a consequence of *el mestizaje*—a term of Spanish origin that identifies racial and cultural mixture following the Spanish colonization of the Americas—multiple skin tones, facial features, body shapes and sizes, hair textures, and eye shapes and color have selectively emerged along with their corresponding identity categories. Beyond these endless phenotype possibilities, the closer the combined effect gets to the superior European standard, the more privilege a woman is granted in a given society. Likewise, the more distant from the "ideal" a woman is, the greater the social disadvantage and inequality she will experience.

In the United States, Latin American immigrant women unpack their racialized baggage within a mainstream society that celebrates women with white skin, blond hair, tall and slender bodies, and blue eyes. As women from different Latin American cultures and societies coincide with people from different ethnic cultures and backgrounds living in the United States, the endless racial and cultural interactions that emerge follow distinct social avenues in a number of ways.

RACISM IN THE NEW LAND

Migration to and settlement in the United States does not automatically guarantee gender equality to Latin American women. Ironically, women who use migration as a coping mechanism to escape the violence they experienced in their countries of origin (e.g., domestic and sexual violence) may painfully encounter the very same form of inequality they were trying to escape. Some women encounter sexual violence as they partake in the dangerous journey to the United States. These women are raped in transit, while crossing the border, or after settlement in the new society.

After establishing a permanent life on the margins of society, racism becomes part of a large structure of inequality and everyday life for immigrants, uncovering new forms of danger. Racism is part of the new socioeconomic and sociopolitical scenarios that make immigrant women's routine at work a treacherous puzzle, and sexual violence may become part of their survival journeys. Women who were raped before migrating and who live and work on the margins of society in the United States become vulnerable to sexual violence and rape on their way to sweatshops and other deplorable spaces where they face exploitative and miserable labor conditions. A lack of transportation, linguistic limitations, a dangerous inner-city life, and uncertain citizenship status, among other factors, can exacerbate women's vulnerability.

More and more Latina women have been facing these challenges in the United States. Since the early 1980s, the numbers of Latina migrants coming from Mexico and Central America and settling in permanently in the United States has increased, and as Enrico Marcelli and Wayne Cornelius point out, by the early 1990s Mexican migrant women outnumbered Mexican migrant men. Groundbreaking research done by Pierrette Hondagneu-Sotelo in 1994 found that the migration and settlement of women in the United States can redefine gender relations in a way that may alter power dynamics in their households. These women actively nurture kinship networks and well-established migrant communities (further mediating the migration of women); they attain relatively stable paid employment; and they utilize various forms of financial assistance. Marcelli and Cornelius note that settlement patterns of women seem to be more permanent than that of men, who seem to move back and forth more frequently. Further, motherhood and the education of children raised in the United States may mediate this process.

THE GENDERED PRIVILEGES AND IMAGES OF LATINA WOMEN

In both Latin America and the United States, social images of women are racialized. For more than 500 years, racist beliefs, practices, and experiences of womanhood have made white and fair-skinned women the idealized expression of femininity vis-à-vis indigenous women, *negras, mulatas,* and *mestizas.* Before and after migrating, racist images of women have been internalized and reproduced by Latina women. For instance, it is common for people in Mexican and Mexican immigrant communities to celebrate the lighter skin or other attributes of relatives or people close to them, thereby implying some kind of racial superiority. For example, a mother may use the expression "my daughter is *blanca, blanca, blanca,*" or "my daughter has *ojos azules, azules, azules*" sharing her joy and pride with others as she describes the white skin or the blue eyes of a child born with these characteristics.

Racial privilege is reproduced within everyday life interactions and shaped by larger social and cultural contexts in Mexican and other Latino immigrant communities. Popular culture reinforces white supremacy, which is further emphasized when immigrant women are exposed to major Spanish-speaking television networks such as *Telemundo* and *Univisión*. Both of these broadcasting companies reproduce the same Western ideals of beauty in their racist, sexist, classist, and homophobic soap operas, or *telenovelas*. In *telenovelas* and other TV shows and movies, white skin goes hand and hand with socioeconomic class. The concept of "*una buena familia*" (literally, "a good family") represents the heterosexual nuclear family with an intact moral reputation from the middle, upper-middle, or elite socioeconomic strata. *Las buenas familias* in Mexico are usually light-skinned families, never poor or working-class families, and many of the Latino families portrayed in these TV shows follow the same pattern.

In Mexican society and other Latin American countries, a dark-skinned woman is very frequently the inspiration of love and passion in the lyrics of romantic songs, but rarely do such songs express these feelings for a white woman. In other popular culture expressions, race relations take different dimensions. The quintessential "sexy" Latina image—characterized by brown skin, exotic features, and a well-shaped (and at times voluptuous) body—may create both cultural pride and discomfort in women. This iconic archetype has produced racist stereotypes for the benefit of Hollywood filmmakers and U.S. and Latin American producers of images for mass consumption, leading to women's endless efforts to achieve unattainable standards of beauty. Even though a Latina immigrant may feel validated for her dark skin color, she now has to work on her body so she will look like actresses such as Salma Hayek and Jennifer López, or the statuesque models that are sexually harassed by Don Francisco in his popular *Sábado Gigante*, a Saturday evening television variety show that *Univisión* has aired for at least twenty years.

THE EXPERIENCE OF DAUGHTERS OF LATIN AMERICAN IMMIGRANTS

Becoming a woman in the United States—*ser mujer*—is not only about gender but also about culture, race, ethnicity, and class. Second-generation Latinas come of age being exposed to racialized stereotypical images of Latinas. In addition, they are also exposed to their immigrant mothers' expectations rooted in their Latin American countries of origin. These experiences are shaped by the women's cultural roots, their immigration experiences, and the ways young women are raised in the United States, particularly in relation to gender, sexuality, and romantic relationships. Some immigrant mothers may not want their daughters to experience premarital sex, but others are not concerned about their daughters' virginity, given the different values in the United States regarding the virginal status of a woman. In the end, immigrant mothers do their best to protect their daughters from the gender inequalities they experienced before and after migrating.

THE ROMANTIC AND SEXUAL LIVES OF IMMIGRANT WOMEN

Racially, "dating up" and "marrying up" are acceptable in these immigrant communities, but "dating down" and "marrying down" are frequently objected to. While being exposed to the racist ideologies they learned before migrating, immigrant women who date outside their group are subjected to their families' and friends' racial surveillance of their romantic choices. A frequent racist pattern views dating African-American men negatively and light-skinned Latino men or white men positively. This preference is related, in part, to the structure of opportunity: Dark-skinned individuals have historically encountered discrimination in education and employment vis-à-vis whites.

Accordingly, going back home with the "wrong" or the "right" man is either punished or celebrated. The act of visiting relatives back home in Latin America may reproduce both racially discriminatory and white supremacist practices, for these relatives may react to a woman's choice in a partner in racially stigmatizing ways. Ultimately, coming to the United States may help a heterosexual woman to "marry up" racially, providing an avenue for social mobility that many Latin Americans celebrate as a way to "improve one's race," as witnessed in the expression "*para mejorar la raza*." Finally, but not less importantly, in homophobic and sexist Latin American societies, same sex romantic relationships are always questioned regardless of racial differences. However, racism may exacerbate the above dynamics for immigrant women involved in interracial lesbian relationships. Similar patterns may interact with other factors including her family and friends' feelings of acceptance or discomfort toward same sex relationships.

Given the above complexities that reproduce racist dynamics, is racial-ethnic community integration and development possible for all Latin American immigrant women living in the United States? Entrepreneurs and politicians have worked hard to satisfy their own agendas through the construction of a pan-Latino or "Hispanic" identity that embraces all Latin American immigrants. Many women may not escape, however, from the forces that divided them before migrating from Latin America. Even though social networking and a sense of solidarity among Latina immigrants have been identified in migration research with Mexican women (Hondagneu-Sotelo 1994; González-López 2005), racism, classism, and homophobia, among other factors, selectively survive the migration test. And while a common language and similar colonization histories unite these women, intragroup diversity divides them based on socioeconomic class and occupation, racial background, modes of migration and incorporation, country of origin, sexual orientation, education, marital status, and political agendas and concerns in their countries of origin. The frequently romanticized concept of a "Latino culture" is therefore a theoretical fiction that has little to do with the social realities of Latina immigrant women and their families. The wider concept of "Latino cultures" is more appropriate, for it recognizes diversity in both Latin American societies and U.S. Latino communities.

BIBLIOGRAPHY

Anzaldúa, Gloria. 1987. *Borderlands/La Frontera*. San Francisco: Aunt Lute Books.

Argüelles, Lourdes, and Anne M. Rivero. 1993. "Gender/Sexual Orientation Violence and Transnational Migration: Conversations with Some Latinas We Think We Know." *Urban Anthropology* Vol. 22 (3–4): 259–275.

Baca Zinn, Maxine. 1982. "Mexican-American Women in the Social Sciences." *Signs: Journal of Women and Culture and Society* 8 (2): 259–272.

Castañeda, Antonia I. 1993. "Sexual Violence in the Politics and Policies of Conquest: Amerindian Women and the Spanish Conquest of Alta California." In *Building with Our Hands: New Directions in Chicana Studies*, edited by Adela De la Torre and Beatriz M. Pesquera, 15–33. Berkeley: University of California Press.

Comas-Díaz, Lillian, and Beverly Greene, eds. 1994. *Women of Color: Integrating Ethnic and Gender Identities in Psychotherapy*. New York: Guilford Press.

Gaspar de Alba, Alicia, ed. 2003. *Velvet Barrios: Popular Culture and Chicana/o Sexualities*. New York: Palgrave Macmillan.

González-López, Gloria. 2003. "*De madres a hijas*: Gendered Lessons on Virginity Across Generations of Mexican Immigrant Women." In *Gender and U.S. Migration: Contemporary Trends*, edited by Pierrette Hondagneu-Sotelo, 217–240. Berkeley: University of California Press.

———. 2005. *Erotic Journeys: Mexican Immigrants and Their Sex Lives*. Berkeley: University of California Press.

Hondagneu-Sotelo, Pierrette. 1994. *Gendered Transitions: Mexican Experiences of Immigration*. Berkeley: University of California Press.

———, and Ernestine Avila. 1997. "'I'm Here, but I'm There': The Meanings of Latina Transnational Motherhood." *Gender and Society* 11 (5): 548–571.

Hurtado, Aída. 2003. *Voicing Chicana Feminisms: Young Women Speak Out on Sexuality and Identity*. New York: New York University Press.

Marcelli, Enrico A., and Wayne A. Cornelius. 2001. "The Changing Profile of Mexican Migrants to the United States: New Evidence from California and Mexico." *Latin American Research Review* 36 (3): 105–131.

Skerry, Peter, and Stephen J. Rockwell. "The Cost of a Tighter Border: People-Smuggling Networks." *Los Angeles Times*, Opinion Section, May 3, 1998.

Gloria González-López

IMMIGRATION REFORM AND CONTROL ACT OF 1986 (IRCA)

Large-scale immigration and foreign-born populations routinely spur political controversy, and sometimes harsh xenophobic reactions, in receiving countries. Although the United States has been celebrated as an open society offering a "golden door" to all people, the historical reality is that American policymakers began to impose draconian restrictions on immigration when newcomers of unfamiliar racial and ethnic origin sparked nativist backlashes in the late nineteenth and early twentieth centuries.

Starting with Chinese exclusion in the 1880s and followed by the establishment of a literacy test and national origins quotas in the early twentieth century, dominant conceptions of ethnic and racial undesirability dramatically shaped policy outcomes. After the liberalizing reforms of the civil rights era, the ethnic and racial composition of new arrivals changed markedly as Asian and Latin American inflows overshadowed traditional European sources in the 1970s and 1980s. Against this backdrop of "new" immigration, American policymakers focused their attention on a divisive issue most closely associated in the public mind with Mexicans: illegal immigration. The Immigration Reform and Control Act of 1986 (IRCA) was the culmination of an acrimonious struggle among lawmakers over the issue of "porous borders." The history of this struggle illuminates how a changing polity resolved contentious debates about race, vulnerable populations, labor, and security, and its outcome cast a long shadow on American immigration reform politics.

Illegal immigration inspired more public concern and media attention than any other migratory issue of the 1970s. Dramatic increases in apprehensions and deportations of undocumented aliens by the U.S. Immigration and Naturalization Service (INS) were seen as evidence that illegal immigration had reached a crisis level. While 1,608,356 undocumented aliens were deported from 1961 to 1970, the number of deportations rose to 11,833,328 from 1971 to 1980. At the same time, legal immigration soared to 4.5 million in the 1970s, with most immigrants originating from Asian, Latin American, and Caribbean countries. During the early 1970s, Representative Peter Rodino (D-N.J.) championed an employer sanctions law that would punish employers who knowingly hired undocumented aliens. Employer sanctions legislation had been a goal of the AFL-CIO and other labor organizations for years, and pro-labor Democrats like Rodino eagerly led the charge once the issue of illegal immigration assumed prominence on the national agenda. But the proposal placed new strains on old alliances. Major Mexican-American and Latino groups and leaders, joined by civil rights organizations, entered the fray to argue that such penalties would lead to job discrimination against Latinos, legal aliens, and anyone who looked or sounded foreign. Business lobbies also openly challenged the measure as a burdensome and unjustified regulatory demand on employers. In the Senate, bills addressing illegal immigration were held up by Senator James Eastland (D-Miss.), the chairman of the Senate Judiciary Committee and a friend of agricultural interests that relied on Mexican labor.

As Congress became deadlocked on the issue, President Gerald Ford established the cabinet-level Domestic Council Committee on Illegal Aliens to develop policy options for addressing porous borders and the presence of millions of undocumented aliens in the United States. The Domestic Council Committee ultimately proposed a broad reform package that included employer sanctions, tough penalties for smugglers, and amnesty for undocumented aliens residing in the country. The administration of President Jimmy Carter advanced reform legislation in 1977 that reflected a similarly comprehensive package of employer sanctions, amnesty for undocumented aliens, and tougher border controls. Yet the proposal met its demise in Congress, where conflicts between organized labor, employer groups, and Mexican-American, Latino, and civil rights organizations once again derailed reform proposals. Reluctant to take no action, Congress established the Select Commission on Immigration and Refugee Policy (SCIRP) in 1978. The committee membership included a cross-section of lawmakers, administration officials, and prominent civilians charged with investigating immigration and the national interest and recommending policy solutions to problems like illegal immigration. SCIRP's final report endorsed a reform package of stronger border enforcement, legalization of undocumented aliens already living in the United States, and employer sanctions with tough worksite enforcement to weaken the magnet of jobs for migrants not authorized to enter the country. One of the controversial findings of SCIRP was that employer sanctions would not work in the absence of a secure system for verifying employee eligibility, raising the possibility of national identification cards (which would be linked to a national data bank) for all employees eligible to work in the United States. The legalization program recommended by SCIRP was billed as a "one-time only" measure.

Representative Romano Mazzoli (D-Ky.) and Senator Alan Simpson (R-Wyo.) took the lead from 1982 through 1986, championing immigration reform legislation that mirrored SCIRP's recommendations. Their initial efforts encountered fierce resistance on all sides, as opposition to key provisions of the comprehensive legislation remained as formidable in the 1980s as it had in the previous decade. Agricultural lobbies complained that access to unskilled Mexican labor was crucial for economic success, and defenders of reform such as Governor Pete Wilson (R-Calif.) proposed legislation that would establish a large farmworker program. Powerful business groups continued to argue that employer sanctions placed undue regulatory burdens on small and large firms alike, and they found support among members of Congress and the administration of President Ronald Reagan. Latino and civil rights organizations, joined by key leaders of the Congressional Hispanic Caucus, criticized employer sanctions for their potential to increase ethnic and racial discrimination against Latino job-seekers—or anyone else who might look or sound alien to an employer. Vilma S. Martinez, president of the Mexican-American Legal Defense and Education Fund (MALDEF) warned that "well-meaning employers, fearful of government sanctions, will shy away from persons who appear 'foreign.' Racist or biased employers will simply use the 'fear' of sanctions as an excuse to avoid hiring qualified minorities" (Fallows 1983). The American Civil Liberties Union (ACLU) and its allies challenged a national identification card linked with a national database on the grounds that it would endanger privacy by exposing confidential financial, medical, or other information. At the same time, the AFL-CIO and other labor organizations steadfastly defended tough employer sanctions backed by tight workplace enforcement. Finally, public opinion polls suggested that most Americans opposed a legalization or amnesty program for undocumented aliens already in the country, prompting several key lawmakers to echo these concerns.

Given these enormous political obstacles, Representative Mazzoli and Senator Simpson were not optimistic about the chances of enacting comprehensive immigration reform in 1985. But then, as Simpson quipped, "a finger on the corpse began to twitch." At the eleventh hour, a handful of congressional entrepreneurs hammered out a compromise package that included employer sanctions, enhanced Border Patrol resources, a seasonal agricultural worker program, a provision aimed at providing new job antidiscrimination rights for aliens, and a legalization program for immigrants who entered the United States prior to January 1, 1982, and lacked a serious criminal record. This controversial bargain was ultimately passed by Congress as the Immigration Reform and Control Act (IRCA) of 1986, surviving a number of tight votes on key provisions of the compromise. The final version of employer sanctions, the initiative at the vanguard of immigration reform efforts begun more than a decade earlier, was a mere shadow of the blueprints spelled out by SCIRP. The employer sanctions provisions of the IRCA lacked any reliable employee verification system, exempted small businesses from regulation, and included an "affirmative defense" clause that released employers of any obligation to verify the authenticity of documents presented to them. Thus, the major policy innovation that was originally meant to curb future illegal immigration lacked teeth.

Although President Reagan signed the IRCA bill into law, his administration was lukewarm about several of its provisions. For instance, Reagan officials openly refused to equip the Justice Department with sufficient resources to counteract potential job discrimination related to new employer sanctions. The administration, which had been instrumental in scrapping proposals for national identification cards tied to employee eligibility, also demonstrated little interest in tough worksite enforcement of the sanctions. To be sure, some Reagan officials shared the view that illegal immigration was a potent threat to national sovereignty. One of the most influential of these law-and-order conservatives, Attorney General William French Smith, argued that the country had "lost control of its borders," and that tougher border enforcement, employer sanctions, and national identification cards were necessary to restore "faith in our laws." But at a time when the Reagan White House pledged "regulatory relief," little effort was made to enforce employer sanctions vigorously. Moreover, the absence of a secure verification system of employee eligibility (which was crucial to the efficacy of employer sanctions, according to SCIRP) made it easy for undocumented aliens to secure jobs via fraudulent documents.

While IRCA's enforcement mechanisms were quite limited in discouraging unauthorized entries, it was more effective in extending new opportunities for legal status to undocumented aliens residing in the country before 1982, as well as to new seasonal agricultural workers. Consequently, the law marked a significant break with federal policies of the past in which Mexican undocumented aliens were targeted for mass deportations. One of the most infamous of these dragnet efforts was the so-called Operation Wetback of 1954, in which President Dwight Eisenhower authorized mass raids in Mexican-American neighborhoods across the southwestern United States, with local police and INS Border Patrol agents rounding up tens of thousands of "Mexican-looking" people for deportation. The IRCA legalization program reflected very different official conclusions about how to respond to the presence of millions of undocumented immigrants living in the shadows of American life. Tellingly, when Reagan administration officials attempted to exclude certain undocumented alien groups from the IRCA's amnesty program, a variety of immigration and civil rights defenders won judicial vindication of a more generous set of legalization program regulations. If national officials once responded to worrisome illegal immigration by launching dragnet raids and mass deportation campaigns, the IRCA ultimately conferred legal status to roughly three million undocumented aliens. Illegal immigration, however, though dampened briefly after the IRCA was enacted, soon returned to peak levels of the pre-reform era, requiring a new generation of leaders to confront the divisive politics of immigration reform.

BIBLIOGRAPHY

Cose, Ellis. 1992. *A Nation of Strangers: Prejudice, Politics, and the Populating of America.* New York: William Morrow.

Fallows, James. "Immigration: How It's Affecting Us." *Atlantic Monthly* November 1983.

Joppke, Christian. 1998. "Why Liberal States Accept Unwanted Immigration." *World Politics* 50 (2): 266–293.

Laham, Nicholas. 2000. *Ronald Reagan and the Politics of Immigration Reform.* Westport, CT: Praeger.

Lee, Kenneth. 1998. *Huddled Masses, Muddled Laws: Why Contemporary Immigration Policy Fails to Reflect Public Opinion.* Westport, CT: Greenwood Press.

Tichenor, Daniel J. 2002. *Dividing Lines: The Politics of Immigration Control in America.* Princeton, NJ: Princeton University Press.

Daniel J. Tichenor
Byoungha Lee

IMMIGRATION TO THE UNITED STATES

A disproportionately large part of the history of immigration to the United States, and much of the history of legal deliberations over U.S. immigration policy, has been shaped by a preoccupation with whether or not the migrants in question were understood to be racially "white." In other words, the determination of U.S. immigration and citizenship law—and thus the very definition of who has been recognized as eligible to become a genuine "American" and a legitimate member of the U.S. national polity—can only be adequately understood in relation to a sociopolitical order of white supremacy.

EARLY IMMIGRATION LAWS

In what was the first legislative determination of access to U.S. citizenship, and, in effect, the first official definition of U.S. nationality, the first Congress of the United States mandated in the Naturalization Act of 1790 that a person who was to become a naturalized citizen must be "white." What is perhaps most remarkable, however, is that this whites-only policy for migrant access to U.S. citizenship remained in effect until 1952. Although the law never specified what precisely was to be understood by the term "white," it established an enduring explicit racial barrier to all migrants' prospective access to U.S. citizenship, requiring individual migrants (and more often than not, entire migrant groups, defined by national origin) to either have their whiteness confirmed and accepted by authorities or have any possibility of

U.S. citizenship denied. Between 1878 and 1952, there were fifty-two legal cases, including two that were considered by the U.S. Supreme Court, in which various migrants contested their presumed ineligibility for citizenship by petitioning to be recognized as "white." When pressed to define whiteness in this manner, the courts variously resorted to virtually any definition that ensured that people of non-European origins would be excluded. Sometimes the rationalizations were based on the purportedly objective truths established by "scientific" or anthropological experts, and in other instances, when such expertise proved inconvenient for the purposes of racial exclusion, the courts upheld definitions of whiteness that were justified according to "common knowledge" and the accepted opinions of "the common (white) man." Exceedingly seldom were the instances when a petitioner was actually recognized to be white, and thereby eligible for U.S. citizenship.

Among the first actual U.S. immigration laws ever enacted was the Chinese Exclusion Act of 1882, which, following decades of large-scale Chinese labor migration, prohibited any further Chinese migration. Not only was the access of migrants to citizenship explicitly barred on the basis of "race," but this law began an era of unprecedented immigration regulation that would increasingly seek to exclude whole groups from entry into the country solely on the explicit basis of race or racialized "nationality." Chinese exclusion was followed by prohibitions against Japanese and Korean labor migration by a diplomatic "Gentlemen's Agreement" in 1907. Finally, the Immigration Act of 1917 established an "All-Asia Barred Zone," proscribing migrations from an area bordered by Afghanistan on the west and the Pacific on the east. The extension of the exclusions that were already in effect for China, Japan, and Korea to all of eastern and southern Asia was primarily intended to prohibit migration from British colonial India. Filipinos, however, having been designated as U.S. "nationals" due to their colonized status following the Spanish-American War of 1898, were a notable exception to the all-Asian exclusion. The Quota Act of 1921 and the Johnson-Reed Immigration Act of 1924, which imposed severe restrictions on migration from eastern and southern European countries on the basis of a national-origins quota system, reaffirmed the All-Asia Barred Zone. Thus, the formulation of "Asiatic" and "Asian" as overtly racialized categories became institutionalized by law and ensconced in U.S. immigration policy.

These expansive and rigid restrictions against Asian immigration were coupled with the absolute omission of Latin American migrations from any specific national-origins or hemispheric stipulations or regulations. This left the robust and enthusiastic importation of Mexican migration unhindered by any all-encompassing exclusions or other numerical quotas. But it remained sufficiently flexible to label such migrants "illegal" and subject to mass deportations as a routine technique of labor subordination and discipline. Beginning in the second half of the nineteenth century, in the decades following the U.S. war against Mexico, migration became an indispensable source of labor for burgeoning new industries such as mining, railroads, ranching, and, increasingly, mechanized agriculture, especially in the former Mexican regions that came to be known as the "American Southwest."

IMMIGRATION IN THE TWENTIETH CENTURY

Through the beginning of the twentieth century, this transnational movement back and forth between the United States and Mexico remained largely unhindered, and the border between the two countries went virtually unregulated. There was a widespread acknowledgement that Mexicans were encouraged to move freely across the border, and, in effect, come to work without any official authorization or immigration documents. Indeed, throughout the twentieth century, Mexicans remained the predominant Latino group in the United States, and for the first half of the century they accounted for the vast majority of Western Hemisphere migration as a whole. Although a dramatically restrictive system of national-origins quotas had been formulated in the 1920s for European migrations, this system of statutory numerical controls pertained exclusively to immigrations from the Eastern Hemisphere. Alongside this severe framework of immigration restrictions and prohibitions, and despite the vociferous opposition of many nativists who readily denounced Mexicans and other Latinos as racial inferiors to the "American" white race, the prospects for "legal" migration from Latin America remained numerically unhindered. Given the crucial role of Mexicans as a disposable migrant labor force within the United States, their numbers were left effectively unlimited.

This is not to say that there were no legal grounds by which U.S. immigration officials could selectively deny entry to prospective Latin American migrants, or to later deport them after the fact. Despite the absence of any statutory quotas to restrict their numbers, unofficial policies at the local level of U.S. consulates charged with issuing immigration visas in Mexico, for instance, were nonetheless imposed to periodically limit the number of prospective "legal" migrants. At the statutory level, there were other bases for the restriction of Latino migrants during this era, but these depended upon a selective enforcement of qualitative provisions in immigration law. The qualitative features of immigration law involve rules and regulations governing who may be allowed to migrate, with what characteristics, how they may do so, and how they conduct themselves once they have entered the country.

Thus, during the first half of the twentieth century, "legal" immigration could be (and frequently was) denied to many Latino migrant workers from relatively impoverished backgrounds due to a person's perceived "illiteracy" or presumed "liability to become a public charge" (often associated with having no pre-arranged employment). Attempted migration could also be refused for such infractions as a failure, upon entry, to pay a required $8 immigrant head tax and the $10 fee for a visa. Likewise, Latino workers could be subsequently deported if they could not verify that they held valid work visas, or if they could otherwise be found to have evaded inspection upon entry. In the case of a worker who later became unemployed, a migrant could be determined to have become a "public charge," which allowed immigration authorities to retroactively judge that the person had originally been culpable of a prior condition of "liability." In addition, a migrant charged with violating U.S. laws, or having engaged in acts that could be construed as "anarchist" or "seditionist," could also be summarily deported.

By the 1920s, all of these violations of the qualitative features of the law established deportation as a crucial mechanism of labor discipline and control, not only coordinated with the vicissitudes of the market's demand for migrant workers but also for the purposes of counteracting unionization and political organizing among Latinos. The abundant availability of such a mass migrant labor force encouraged the expectation among employers that it also be exceptionally flexible and tractable, and that its mobility could be effectively managed and subordinated to employers' needs. Indeed, it is revealing that the U.S. Border Patrol, from 1924 (when it was first created) until 1940, operated under the auspices of the Department of Labor.

The possibility of deportation arose as a consequence of successive changes in U.S. immigration law, and of the remarkably malleable, but increasingly restrictive, policies that summarily defined various migrations as "legal" or "illegal," thus creating an image of U.S. national sovereignty defined by the territorial integrity of its physical borders. It is important to emphasize, however, that the possibility for "illegal" migrants to be deported was almost always coupled with, and overwhelmingly overshadowed by, the more or less insatiable demand for their legally vulnerable labor, and thus for an effectively permanent importation of ever-greater numbers of undocumented migrant workers. The pervasive racialization of their specific national identity allowed for a commonplace disregard of the juridical distinction between undocumented Mexican migrants and U.S.-born birthright-citizen Mexicans (Chicanos or "Mexican Americans"). This was most dramatically demonstrated by the mass deportations and coercive "repatriations" of Mexicans who were

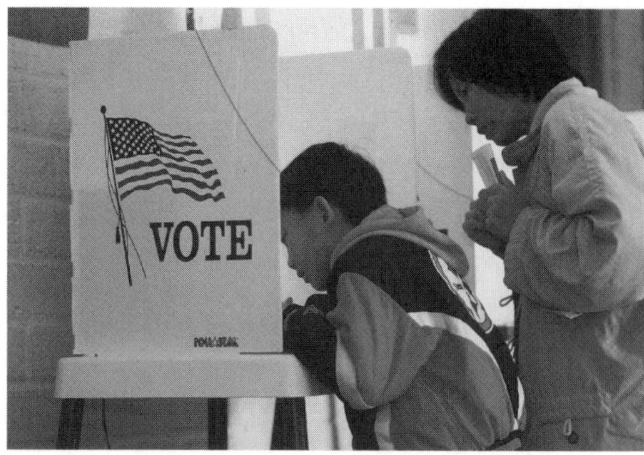

Immigrant Voter. *A Chinese boy helps his mother complete her ballot at a polling center in Chinatown near Los Angeles, California in 2004. Since the late 1960s and early 1970s, Latinos and Asians have provided the vast majority of new migrants to the United States.* ROBYN BECK/AFP/GETTY IMAGES.

U.S. citizens, usually alongside their migrant parents, during the Great Depression of the 1930s.

Over the course of the twentieth century, U.S. immigration policy toward Latin America came to be distinguished chiefly by increasing regulation and restriction. There was a dramatic overall shift from a policy of numerically unlimited possibilities for "legal" migration from anywhere in the Western Hemisphere (excluding colonies) to one of strict annual quotas for every country of origin, which began with specific immigration legislation in 1976. Latin American experiences of migration to the United States, and consequent U.S. Latino community formation, have been profoundly shaped by this history of calculated interventions in immigration law. Until the Hart-Celler Immigration Act of 1965, there were no numerical quotas whatsoever restricting the "legal" entry of migrants from any of the countries of the Western Hemisphere (excluding colonies). With the hemispheric quota enacted in 1965 and put into effect in 1968, and then, after 1976, with the individual country quotas, an alarmingly disproportionate number of Mexicans (and, increasingly, other Latin American migrants as well) found themselves with no other recourse than to become undocumented, and they were thus relegated to an indefinite condition as "illegal aliens."

Despite its unprecedented restriction of Latin American and Caribbean migrations, the Hart-Celler Immigration Act of 1965 is typically celebrated as a liberal reform. This is because it finally eliminated the national-origins quota system that had severely restricted European and Asian migrations. The actual exclusions against Asian migrations had been sporadically dismantled during the 1940s and 1950s because they came to be seen as an embarrassment that impeded diplomatic relations with China and Japan. Subsequently, Asian migrations remained subject to the very strict national-origins system that otherwise remained in place, thus ensuring that permitting migration from Asian countries did not in any significant way alter the fact that only miniscule numbers of Asian migrants would be allowed entry to the United States. This changed dramatically after the 1965 amendments to U.S. immigration law took effect. Notably, because of the absolute interruption in Asian migration during the Exclusion Era, new provisions for family reunification were very often irrelevant—at least initially—for people seeking to migrate from Asia. Therefore, the law's explicit preferences for professional or otherwise highly skilled migrants were commonly the only avenue available. In this way, the law effectively predetermined a middle-class social composition for the new Asian migrations. Over time, however, family reunification provisions created opportunities for somewhat greater class diversity in subsequent waves of Asian migration. Meanwhile, new restrictions limiting migration from Mexico and other Latin American countries ensured that the already massive Latino labor migrations would not only be overwhelmingly working-class in character, but also rigidly locked into a degraded social condition due to the legal vulnerability of these migrant's undocumented immigration status.

Since the late 1960s and early 1970s, Latinos and Asians have provided the vast majority of new migrants to the United States. These recent migrations are simply incomprehensible, however, without a critical appreciation of the instrumental role of the law in hierarchically evaluating, ranking, mobilizing, and regulating them. The operations of U.S. laws of citizenship and immigration reveal decisive features that determined how the variously racialized identities of Latinos and Asians have been profoundly shaped in historically specific relation to the U.S. policy. Furthermore, the racialized experiences of these non-European migrations reveal crucial aspects of how the wider U.S. sociopolitical order of white supremacy has continually been maintained and reproduced, not only in relation to its own internal racial dynamics but also in ever-changing relation to the rest of the globe.

SEE ALSO *Border Crossings and Human Rights; Border Patrol; Citizenship and Race; Illegal Alien; Immigrant Domestic Workers; Immigration, Race, and Women; Immigration Reform and Control Act of 1986 (IRCA).*

BIBLIOGRAPHY

Ancheta, Angelo N. 1998. *Race, Rights, and the Asian American Experience.* New Brunswick, NJ: Rutgers University Press.

Chang, Robert S. 1999. *Disoriented: Asian Americans, Law, and the Nation-State.* New York: New York University Press.

De Genova, Nicholas. 2004. "The Legal Production of Mexican/ Migrant 'Illegality'." *Latino Studies* 2 (2): 160–185.

———. 2005. *Working the Boundaries: Race, Space, and "Illegality" in Mexican Chicago.* Durham, NC: Duke University Press.

———, ed. 2006. *Racial Transformations: Latinos and Asians Remaking the United States.* Durham, NC: Duke University Press.

Haney-López, Ian. 1996. *White by Law: The Legal Construction of Race.* New York: New York University Press.

Hing, Bill Ong. 1993. *Making and Remaking Asian America through Immigration Policy, 1850–1990.* Stanford, CA: Stanford University Press.

Kim, Hyung-Chan. 1994. *A Legal History of Asian Americans, 1790–1990.* Westport, CT: Greenwood Press.

Lee, Erika. 2003. *At America's Gates: Chinese Immigration During the Exclusion Era, 1882–1943.* Chapel Hill: University of North Carolina Press.

Ngai, Mae M. 2004. *Impossible Subjects: Illegal Aliens and the Making of Modern America.* Princeton, NJ: Princeton University Press.

Salyer, Lucy E. 1995. *Laws Harsh as Tigers: Chinese Immigrants and the Shaping of Modern Immigration Law.* Chapel Hill: University of North Carolina Press.

Nicholas De Genova

IMPLICIT RACISM

Situated within the discussion of racism in the United States and elsewhere, particularly in relation to the study of social psychology, the term *implicit racism* is often erroneously used in oppositional comparison to *explicit racism*. Explicit racism is overt and often intentional, for it is practiced by individuals and institutions that openly embrace racial discrimination and hold prejudicial attitudes toward racially defined groups, which they assume to be scientifically identified through genetics. Implicit racism, however, is not the opposite of explicit racism but a different, yet no less harmful, form of racism. Implicit racism, broadly defined, refers to an individual's utilization of unconscious biases when making judgments about people from different racial and ethnic groups.

According to a number of observers, implicit racism is an automatic negative reaction to someone of a different race or ethnicity than one's own. Underlying and unconscious racist attitudes are brought forth when a person is faced with race-related triggers, including preconceived phenotypic differences or assumed cultural or environmental associations. Since this type of racism lies beyond the awareness of the person displaying the attitudes or actions, it is quite possible for someone to report that they hold few, if any, overt racist ideologies and yet display implicit racism in their everyday interactions with people of different racial groups. In particular, this can occur among whites when they are confronted by others not perceived as white. As discussed by the sociologist Joe Feagin, examples of everyday racism can include such things as being treated differently when exchanging money at cash registers, being seated at bad tables in restaurants, or being assigned undesirable rooms when checking into hotels. Each of these scenarios is a possible result of the implementation of implicit racism.

Project Implicit is a large and somewhat controversial psychological study that was designed as a demonstration project at Yale University in 1998 and later taken over by researchers from Harvard University, University of Virginia, and University of Washington. The study utilizes Internet testing as a primary research tool for subject recruitment and data gathering. The goal of the Implicit Association Test is to explore the "unconscious roots of thinking and feeling" in the contexts of particular words and pictures associated with gender, sexuality, age, weight, race, and other areas. In reference to implicit racism, it explores reactions to factors such as skin tone, ethnic groups, and race. The goal of these tests is to gauge participants' implicit preference for one group in comparison to another through responses to representative stimuli.

An average of 15,000 tests per week have been completed in the seven years Project Implicit has been gathering data via the Internet, for a total of 4.5 million tests administered and over 200 investigations published. Researchers have uncovered four main results from this large data set: People are unaware of their implicit biases, biases are pervasive, implicit biases predict behavior, and people differ in their levels of implicit bias. Specific to implicit racism, people harbor negative associations in reference to particular racial groups while reporting that they hold no such biases, resulting in statistically significant racial preferences such as 75 to 80 percent of white and Asian Americans showing an implicit racial preference for whites over African Americans. Individuals with higher levels of implicit racial prejudice engage in acts of discrimination including lower levels of friendliness, lack of racial inclusion, and lower evaluations of performance in the workplace.

Implicit racism has taken hold in our everyday lives, where decisions about individuals and groups continue to be based on racial identifications dictated by perceived clues pertaining to racial group membership. These split-second decisions are based upon non-definitive sensorial associations including, but not limited to, skin color, speech patterns, hair texture, and clothing style. In this day and age of many professing color-blind ideologies, there is strong evidence to show that a large portion of the population, albeit subconsciously, continues to discriminate according to race. Lines are drawn between individuals based on difference, in particular those not perceived as fitting into a category of white. As a result, limitations are placed on minorities in a myriad of societal arenas resulting in everyday racism, relatively low possibilities for interracial friendship formation, and inadequate access to and mobility within housing, education, and jobs.

SEE ALSO *Cultural Racism; Racial Hierarchy.*

BIBLIOGRAPHY

Dovidio, John. F., and Samuel L. Gaertner. 1996. "Affirmative Action, Unintentional Racial Biases, and Intergroup Relations." *Journal of Social Issues* 52 (4): 51–75.

Feagin, Joe R. 2000. *Racist America: Roots, Current Realities, and Future Reparations.* New York: Routledge.

Feagin, Joe R., and Melvin P. Sikes. 1995. *Living with Racism: The Black Middle-Class Experience.* Boston: Beacon Press.

Kawakami, Kerry, and John F. Dovidio. 2001. "The Reliability of Implicit Stereotyping." *Personality and Social Psychology Bulletin* 27 (2): 212–225.

Killen, Melanie, Jennie Lee-Kim, Heidi McGlothlin, and Charles Stangor. 2003. *How Children and Adolescents Evaluate Gender and Racial Exclusion.* Boston: Blackwell.

Project Implicit. https://implicit.harvard.edu/implicit/.

Sears, David O., Jim Sidanius, and Lawrence Bobo, eds. 2000. *Racialized Politics: The Debate about Racism in America.* Chicago: University of Chicago Press.

Ingrid E. Castro

INDIAN BOARDING SCHOOLS

In the fifty years following the American Civil War, federal Indian policymakers eagerly embraced boarding schools to assimilate Native people according to white, middle-class sensibilities. Convinced that race was not a limiting factor in the transformation of Indian culture, reformers embraced ideas that Thomas Jefferson and Albert Gallatin had articulated early in the nineteenth century, and they sought to remold Indian cultures by imposing new American models of behavior. Their optimism was short-lived, however, and the boarding schools had foundered by the turn of the twentieth century, when policymakers, politicians, and the public accepted an increasingly racialized and negative view of Indians and their cultures. The Indian school system was compromised and then largely destroyed when appeals to racialized thinking convinced policymakers that education for Native people was a waste of time, money, and effort.

RESHAPING AMERICAN INDIAN CULTURE

The U.S. government relied on a variety of programs to remold Native cultures between 1870 and 1920, but boarding schools quickly became a key element in the era's coercive assimilation policies. Schools could be built everywhere, they were less expensive than military action, and they were consistent with the nation's self-professed duty to lift up the oppressed and instruct the unenlightened. As Commissioner of Indian Affairs Thomas Jefferson Morgan put it in his 1889 annual report, schools would do for Indians "what they are so successfully doing for all the other races in this country—assimilate them" (*Annual Report of the Commissioner of Indian Affairs*, 1889, p. 23). Another bureaucrat reminded his audience in 1901 that education and civilization were practically synonymous. Annie Beecher Scoville's address to the Board of Indian Commissioners in the same year summed up the case for boarding schools as neatly as anyone ever had: "If there is an idol that the American people have," she insisted, "it is the school.... It is a remedy for barbarism, we think, and so we give the dose.... The school is the slow match.... It will blow up the old life, and of its shattered pieces [we] will make good citizens" (*Annual Report of the Commissioner of Indian Affairs*, 1901, pp. 809–810).

The belief in the power of education to reshape Indian culture rested implicitly on the assumption that race was not a barrier to transformation. As with other federal Indian policy initiatives designed to promote the acquisition of private property and to confer citizenship, many officials and reformers initially agreed that race posed no significant limitations for the educability of Indians. Morgan, for example, insisted there were "no insuperable obstacles" to the successful education and eventual absorption of Indian children (*Annual Report of the Commissioner of Indian Affairs*, 1892, p. 55). One participant at the 1895 annual meeting of the National Education Association observed that Indian children were "just as capable as any white pupil I have ever had," and when Richard Henry Pratt was queried as to whether the "intellectual faculties of the Indian are essentially different from those of the white race," the famous founder and superintendent of the Carlisle Indian School replied that he did not think they were (Pratt 1895, p. 764).

This kind of optimism led to a flurry of building, which created an impressive array of schools in the three decades following the Civil War. Between 1877 and 1900 the number of boarding schools increased from 48 to 153 (this figure includes 24 off-reservation boarding schools that opened between 1879 and 1898), and the number of day schools rose from 102 to 154. The total number of federally supported Indian schools doubled, from 150 to 307, and by 1900 more than 21,000 Indian children attended federal Indian schools of one kind or another, including 17,708 boarding students. The Indian education budget showed similar trends when it rose from a paltry $20,000 in 1877 to nearly $4,000,000 by 1907 (Ellis 1996, p. 22), and when measured against the Indian Bureau's other programs, the schools regularly claimed a larger share of the budget than any other item save annuities and payments required by treaties.

THE IMPORTANCE OF THE BOARDING SCHOOLS

Although the U.S. government opened day schools and boarding schools on every reservation, boarding schools quickly became the centerpiece of the Indian assimilation system. Day schools were inexpensive to build and operate, but many educators thought them fundamentally flawed because teachers saw their students for only a portion of the day. Because boarding-school students lived on residential campuses that were isolated from their communities, they were exposed—at least in theory—to influences from which it would be difficult to escape. Committed to giving students a thorough exposure to middle-class white values in the boarding schools, many reformers agreed with Richard Henry Pratt, who famously commented that "in Indian civilization I am a Baptist because I believe in immersing the Indians in our civilization and when we get them under holding them there until they are thoroughly soaked" (Pratt 2004, p. 335).

Whether at one of the large off-reservation campuses like Carlisle or Chemawa, or at a more modestly sized reservation boarding school, students encountered a curriculum designed to teach them gender-specific vocational skills and to expose them to a level of academic training that would prepare them for lives as independent, self-sufficient citizens. In the early decades of the school system, this meant that Indian children were expected to matriculate according to standards that reflected both the substantive and philosophical ideals that drove public school education all over the country. Thus, boarding-school students received instruction in mathematics, literature, geography, and art, in addition to working in the school's physical plant or in one of its numerous support systems. White audiences at civic and cultural events were regaled with demonstrations by Indian students (the Carlisle band led the way across the Brooklyn Bridge when it opened, for example), commissioners of Indian Affairs extolled the virtues of an educated and assimilated rising generation of Indian youth, and bureaucrats looked forward to the day when the boarding schools would solve the Indian question once and for all.

A CHANGE IN VIEWPOINT

But this optimism faded after the turn of the twentieth century, when policymakers came to believe with increasing certitude that Indians were racially backward, culturally deficient, and intellectually feeble. For example, Herbert Welsh wrote that as a race the Indian was "distinctly feebler, more juvenile than ours" (Welsh 1902, p. 178). Early-twentieth-century education expert Charles Dyke, meanwhile, struck an even more pessimistic note when he observed that the crucial issue facing Indian education was how to train the "child races" (Dyke 1909, pp. 928–932).

Seized by the racial determinism of the day, policymakers, reformers, and social scientists eagerly applied new standards of racial thinking to Indians and, not surprisingly, found them wanting in every important category of thought and behavior.

The fallout was immediate. Convinced that race had trapped Indians and made them unable to understand or use education except in its most remedial forms, educators eliminated much of the academic curriculum in favor of vocational training. The point was no longer to educate and assimilate, for racial realities apparently made any significant improvement impossible. Thus, the school supervisor for the Creek Nation commented in 1902 that "we should not try to make the Indian too much of a white man" (*Annual Report of the Commissioner of Indian Affairs*, 1902, p. 424), while federal Superintendent of Indian Education Estelle Reel observed in 1905 that it was a mistake to "attempt to make the Indian over and transform him into a white man, with the idea that this is necessary to bring him into harmony with the established order." Educators needed to recognize the Indian's "natural impulses," she continued, and "not attempt anything more than is consistent with those impulses" (Reel 1905, p. 931). For his part, Commissioner of Indian Affairs Cato Sells thought that racial limits had made it utterly impossible for Indians to do more than learn simple job skills, and so he ordered what he called "nonessentials" removed from the boarding school curriculum in 1918. As a result, geography, arithmetic, history, and physiology disappeared from the Indian boarding schools (*Annual Report of the Commissioner of Indian Affairs*, 1918, pp. 20, 26).

As Frederick Hoxie has observed in the most important work on this subject, racism and racialized policies not only emerged as the single most important factors during the early twentieth century for redefining the meaning of Indian assimilation, they also doomed the boarding schools and contributed to a legacy of racist thinking whose echoes may still be heard. Tsianina Lomawaima agrees with Hoxie. She notes that "federal boarding schools did not train Indian youth to assimilate into the American melting pot. Instead, they trained Indians to "adopt the work discipline of the Protestant ethic and accept their proper place in society as a marginal class" (Lomawaima 1993, pp. 236–237). As a result of this philosophy, the boarding school system began to be systematically dismantled by the 1910s, and many Indian communities were forced to contend with the prospect of sending their children to local white schools that often resented them and barely tolerated their presence.

SEE ALSO *Cultural Racism; Native American Popular Culture and Race.*

BIBLIOGRAPHY

Adams, David Wallace. 1996. *Education for Extinction: American Indians and the Boarding School Experience, 1875–1928.* Lawrence: University Press of Kansas.

Dyke, Charles Bartlett. 1909. "Essential Features in the Education of the Child Races." *Journal of the Proceedings and Addresses of the Annual Meeting of the National Educational Association*: 928–932.

Ellis, Clyde. 1996. *To Change Them Forever: Indian Education at the Rainy Mountain Boarding School, 1893–1920.* Norman: University of Oklahoma Press.

Hoxie, Frederick. 2001 (1984). *A Final Promise: The Campaign to Assimilate the Indians.* Lincoln: University of Nebraska Press.

Lomawaima, K. Tsianina. 1993. "Domesticity in the Federal Indian Schools: The Power of Authority Over Mind and Body." *American Ethnologist* 20 (2): 227–240.

———. 1994. *They Called It Prairie Light: The Story of Chilocco Indian School.* Lincoln: University of Nebraska Press.

Pratt, Richard Henry. 1895. "Industrial Training as Applied to Indian Schools." *Journal of the Proceedings and Addresses of the Annual Meeting of the National Educational Association*: 759–764.

———. 2004. *Battlefield and Classroom: Four Decades with the American Indian, 1867–1904.* Edited by Robert M. Utley; foreword by David Wallace Adams. Norman: University of Oklahoma Press.

Reel, Estelle. 1905. Untitled Comments and Remarks. *Journal of the Proceedings and Addresses of the Annual Meeting of the National Educational Association*: 931–933.

Trennert, Robert. 1988. *The Phoenix Indian School: Forced Assimilation in Arizona, 1891–1935.* Norman: University of Oklahoma Press.

U.S. Bureau of Indian Affairs. 1824–1949. *Annual Report of the Commissioner of Indian Affairs.* Washington, DC: U.S. Government Printing Office.

Welsh, Hebert. 1902. "Comments on Thomas Morgan's 'Indian Education'." *Journal of Social Science* 40 (December): 178.

Clyde Ellis

INDIAN RIGHTS ASSOCIATION

From the time of first European encounters with the Native peoples of the "New World" to the present time, much has been said and much time and money have been expended in an effort to "civilize the savage." But in fact, and depending on where one stands, one could also spend a great deal of time and energy in arriving at a just conclusion as to exactly who was the savage: the European bent on acquisition of land and riches at any cost, or the indigenous peoples of the Americas reacting in a mostly defensive posture to protect the lands that they had inherited from their ancestors. In the process of "civilization," the native population was reduced from tens of millions at the time of European contact to a low point of 248,000 in 1890, while the Anglo population increased from 107 with the founding of the Jamestown Colony in 1607 to an 1890 total U.S. population of 62,622,250.

CIVILIZING THE AMERICAN INDIAN

While most members of the dominant (Anglo) society were interested in exterminating the Native Americans, there were other groups who believed that Indian Peoples had souls worthy of converting to Christianity and that in this effort the "savages" could be civilized if they would lay aside their languages, traditions, tribal structures, and adopt a "civilized" yeoman-farmer type mentality. One such group was the Indian Rights Association (IRA).

Herbert Walsh and Henry Spackman Pancoast formed the IRA in Philadelphia in 1882. The Association was dedicated to providing equal protection of the law to Indian Peoples as well as education, citizenship, and ownership of land in a fee-simple title status (personal ownership). While these goals may sound altruistic and high-minded, it should be noted that most Indian Peoples believed that the Creator had given them title to the land, and they had little or no interest in attending Anglo schools or becoming U.S. citizens. In short, the IRA was concerned with turning Indians into a picture of the white person, a vision not shared by those to be converted. The IRA was also interested in civil-service reform and reorganization of the Bureau of Indian Affairs (BIA) to include employment of Indian people. In a move that set apart the IRA as a progressive organization, the Association placed the blame on avaricious whites and a corrupt and paternalistic government for the continuing existence of what had become known as the "Indian problem."

Groups such as the IRA were among a number of groups who considered themselves to be "Friends of the Indian," and although most were well intentioned and some of their activities proved to be beneficial, many of the policies they helped enact were tremendously destructive to Indian people. The IRA and other Friends of the Indian groups saw themselves as advocating equal status for Indians, and to that end they organized branch associations in cities across the United States, sent representatives on fact-finding missions into Indian Country, and published pamphlets and reports to the Congress, while maintaining a high public visibility through speeches and in the press. For the most part, members of the IRA and Friends of the Indian groups never left their comfortable urban homes in the East to venture into Indian Country to see the Indian experience first hand.

IMPLEMENTING GOVERNMENTAL CHANGE

To ensure passage of reform legislation, the IRA kept a full-time lobbyist in Washington. So effective was the association that most of its program was enacted before 1900. Among the IRA's projects were the formation of a comprehensive compulsory government Indian boarding school system; the passage of the General Allotment Act of 1887 (Dawes Act), which included land allotments and citizenship; and the extension of civil-service rules to the Indian Office. Of these three main initiatives, only the extension of civil-service rules and the reorganization of the BIA worked to the benefit of American Indian people.

The BIA had its beginnings in 1824. Because the U.S. government's view of Indians was one of savages, the BIA was placed under the War Department until 1949, at which time it was transferred to the Department of the Interior. Under the War Department the BIA became a powerful non-Indian organization that led tribes down a path toward poverty and extinction. The BIA was powerful, and in many instances the BIA superintendent's word was law. But following passage of the Indian Reorganization Act of 1934 and with the backing of the IRA, Congress extended Indian preference in employment to the BIA and the Indian Health Service (IHS). The intent of Congress in establishing Indian preference was to give tribes greater control over their own self-government. As a result, the BIA and IHS were required by law to give preference to persons of American Indian or Alaska Native descent. Over the ensuing years, Native people began to take control of the agency. At the time of passage of Indian preference, less than 15 percent of the BIA and IHS were of Indian descent or ancestry. In 2007, 95 percent of approximately 14,000 employees are recognized as Native people.

BOARDING SCHOOL SYSTEM

The IRA also endorsed a key component to the civilization of "the savage": the removal of Indian children from the Indian family and tribal environment and their education on a Western model. In 1877 the Congress appropriated $20,000 for the expressed purpose of the reeducation of Indian children, to "kill the Indian, and save the child." In 1879 Army Captain Richard H. Pratt founded the Carlisle Indian School at Carlisle Barracks, Pennsylvania, as a demonstration project to convince the government and the general public that Indians could be educated. Carlisle became the model for off-reservation boarding schools. The number of students enrolled in day schools on reservations and off-reservation boarding schools increased rapidly. From an enrollment of 3,598 in 1877, more than 20,000 Indian students were enrolled in 148 boarding schools and 225 day schools by the close of the nineteenth century.

Indian parents were demoralized and terrorized by the threat of their children being kidnapped by Indian agents (who for the most part were corrupt officials hired as the result of nepotism or favoritism) and soldiers and being taken to remote boarding schools, some as distant as 800 miles from their homes. Attendance was made mandatory, however. In 1891 Congress authorized the Commissioner of Indian Affairs "to make and enforce by proper means" rules and regulations to ensure that Indian children attended the schools. Native people resisted by sequestering their children in mountain hideaways or by taking them deep into reservations, where agents often pursued them on horseback and lassoed them like animals, bound them hand and foot, threw them into wagons and hauled them like freight to train terminals where they were then shipped off to distant schools (Rinaldi 1999).

In the Southwestern United States pressure to enroll children in boarding schools began in earnest in 1887, when the first government school was established at Keams Canyon. According to Indian agent E. H. Plummer, the Keams Canyon School was in dismal condition. The school was crowded and the buildings were poorly maintained. Plummer himself feared that disease would spread and children would die (Holliday 1998). As a result, many Hopi parents refused to send their children to a school so far away to learn the white man's ways. As an example to resistant families, the government arrested nineteen Hopi Indian men and sentenced them to confinement on Alcatraz Island because they had hidden their children and would not allow them to be taken to the boarding school. The prisoners were released in September 1895.

When Indian children arrived at the boarding schools, both boys and girls had their hair cut short and were given new "American" names. For most Indian people the cutting off of the hair represented a condition of mourning, and was associated with death. For Indian children in boarding schools this represented a life and death battle to retain their religion, language, and cultural identity. Many Indian children were required to select an Anglo name from lists that they could not possibly read or understand. Other children were simply assigned new names. Traditional clothing was taken away and miniature copies of military uniforms with high collars, stiff shirts, and leather boots were given to the boys and long cotton dresses and hard leather shoes were given to the girls (Lomawaima 1995).

The goals of the boarding schools were numerous. First and foremost was the belief that Indian children should be removed from parental and tribal influences. A summer "outing" program was added to the boarding school program, placing Indian children on farms and ranches near the boarding school. This prevented the child's return to the reservation during the summer months. The federal government paid the host family $50 per year per student for upkeep, and any money generated by the labor of the student was claimed by the boarding school. As a result of the distant schools and the outing program, Indian children typically were separated from their family for periods ranging from four to eight years.

Treatment at the boarding school varied, but most children endured harsh discipline, particularly if they were caught speaking their native language, performing a traditional ceremony, or practicing their native religion. Corporal punishment, solitary confinement, and withholding of rations were common punishments used to control Native students who insisted on retaining and practicing traditional ways.

For most Indian children the conversion to a copy of "the white man" proved to be more illusionary than real. Indian boys and girls were taught skills in the boarding schools that had little or no relationship to tribal or reservation life. Indian children who attempted to return to their families could no longer speak their native languages. Skills necessary for survival in a tribal or reservation setting had been crushed. The children were poorly trained for the non-Indian world as well. Some Indian boys found work on farms and ranches. To the disappointment of boarding school administrators, most returned to the reservations and attempted to reestablish themselves within the tribal culture. A small number of Native girls found work at the Bureau of Indian Affairs, but most met only with discrimination and unemployment.

ALLOTMENT ACT

The next step in the IRA's plan to civilize and Americanize Indian Peoples into the general U.S. population came with the passage of the Dawes General Allotment Act of 1887. The act is more generally known as "the allotment act" or "Allotment in Severalty." The intent of the Act was to abolish reservations and to allot land to individual Indian people as private property. It was the single most devastating development during this period, because it worked to undermine tribal self-sufficiency and tribal sovereignty. As more and more settlers moved west under the national ideology of Manifest Destiny, new lands were needed. Pressure mounted to abolish Indian reservations. Allotment, a thinly disguised way to break up tribal land holdings, was the answer. The chief provisions of the Allotment Act provided that each Indian family head would receive a grant of 160 acres of reservation land, in fee-simple title. Each single Indian person over eighteen years and each orphan under eighteen years of age received eighty acres, and each other single person under eighteen usually received forty acres of former reservation land, although the amounts varied from reservation to reservation. The key to the Allotment Act was that all land remaining after the allotment to Native Peoples would revert to the federal government and the government would in turn offer this "surplus" land for sale.

Proponents of the Allotment Act claimed that they had the endorsement of IRA chapters across the country. Allotment would break up communal holdings, they said, and instill the American ethos of individual ambition in the Indian. The overarching goal of the "Friends of the Indian," those who supported allotment, was to substitute white civilization for Indian culture. Individual landholding would break up extended families and further undermine traditional leadership patterns.

Congress passed the Allotment Act into law even though there was little or no support of the concept of allotment by Indian people. In 1888 Congress ratified five agreements with different Indian Nations providing for the allotment and sale of what the federal government now described as surplus reservation lands. In 1889 eight such laws were passed. In the first nine months of 1891 an additional 8,000,000 acres of former reservation lands passed into non-Indian hands. Oil speculators and timber companies bought up individual allotments. Minor Indian children who possessed allotment lands were declared wards of non-Indians so that oil could be extracted from their allotments or fertile farmlands could be exploited. Through these methods, the total of Indian land holdings was cut from 138,000,000 acres in 1887 to 48,000,000 acres in 1934. Many Indian people did become landless and Native people living on the remaining allotted reservation lands increasingly experienced extreme poverty, despondency, and despair.

It soon became evident that allotted land would be the target of Congressional theft as well, as evidenced in the 1903 legal case *Lone Wolf v. Hitchcock.* Following increased white migration and conflict, the Kiowa, Comanche, and Apache tribes signed the Treaty of Medicine Lodge in 1867, which created a sizable reservation for them in Indian Territory. Article 12 of that treaty states that no further land cessions would occur "unless executed and signed by at least three-fourths of all the adult male Indians" within the reservation. Although the U.S. government lacked the signatures of a three-fourths majority of Indians, the Secretary of the Interior directed the sale of more than two million acres of land ceded to the federal government. Lone Wolf and other Kiowa-Comanche landholders sued. In *Lone Wolf v. Hitchcock,* the Supreme Court affirmed the rulings of the lower courts and ruled that the land sale was legal, stating: "the power exists to abrogate the provisions of an Indian treaty. . . ." Congress has exercised this plenary authority over the tribal relations of the Indians from the beginning, and the power has always been deemed a political one, not subject to control by the judiciary.

The primary goal of the IRA as defined by its constitution is "to secure to the Indians of the United States the political and civil rights already guaranteed to them by treaty and statute of the United States, and such as their civilization and circumstances may justify." The founders of the IRA, Pancoast and Welsh, believed in the immediate acculturation of Native Peoples into American society. Pancoast and Welsh were instrumental in the passage of the Indian Reorganization Act (1834), the termination of tribal land holdings, the crushing of Indian culture, and "civilization" as the solution to the nation's Indian problem. Other early Indian advocacy groups, such as the Lake Mohonk Conferences of the Friends of the Indian and the American Indian Defense Association, supported the IRA.

The IRA was founded by individuals who were of the philanthropic sort who believed that American Indians' best hope for survival lay in a program of assimilation. They did not see the survival of Indians as a separate race of people as a viable option. The destruction of the Indian would require a dedicated effort of education, conversion to Christianity, adoption of Anglo-Saxon legal institutions, institution of private land ownership, and the abandonment of Indian culture and tradition. The organization's initial stated objective included racist goals, to "bring about the complete civilization of the Indians and their admission to citizenship." The IRA was not alone in this racist approach to the nation's Indian problem. The IRA was among several reform organizations that considered themselves to be friends of the Indian, but in reality had little understanding of the physical, cultural, or spiritual needs of Native Americans. Welsh and other IRA leaders lobbied heavily for allotment of Indian lands in severalty, believing that private property and the reduction of communal land holdings would replace tribal membership and place the Indian on the road to extinction as a separate race.

SEE ALSO *Native American Rights Fund (NARF).*

BIBLIOGRAPHY

Baxter, Jonathan. 1887. *Indian Rights Association.* Cambridge, MA: Harvard University Press.

Clinton, Robert N., Carole E. Goldberg, and Rebecca Tsosie. 2007. *American Indian Law: Native Nations and the Federal System,* 5th ed. Newark, NJ: Lexis/Nexis.

Getches, David H., Charles F. Wilkinson, and Robert A. Williams Jr. 1998. *Cases and Materials on Federal Indian Law,* 4th ed. St. Paul, MN: West Group.

Holliday, Wendy. 1998. "Hopi History: The Story of the Alcatraz Prisoners." Available at http://www.nps.gov/archive/Alcatraz/tours/hopi/hopi-h1.htm.

Lomawaima, K. Tsianina. 1995. *They Called It Prairie Light: The Story of Chilocco Indian School.* Lincoln: University of Nebraska Press.

Prucha, Francis Paul. 1981. *Indian Policy in the United States: Historical Essays.* Lincoln: University of Nebraska Press.

———. 1995. *The Great Father: The United States Government and the American Indians.* Lincoln: University of Nebraska Press.

Rinaldi, Ann. 1999. *My Heart Is on the Ground: The Diary of Little Rose, a Sioux Girl.* New York: Scholastic Press.

Rose, Cynthia, and Duane Champagne, eds. 2001. *The Native North American Almanac: A Reference Work on Native North Americans in the United States and Canada,* 2nd ed. Farmington Hills, MI: UXL.

Wilkins, David E. 1997. *American Indian Sovereignty and the U.S. Supreme Court.* Austin: University of Texas Press.

———. 2002. *American Indian Politics and the American Political System.* New York: Rowman & Littlefield.

Troy R. Johnson

INDIAN SLAVERY

Scholars have long held that the transatlantic slave trade initiated by the Portuguese in the mid-fifteenth century and carried to new heights by the Spanish, Dutch, and English prompted the rise of modern-day racism. From the sixteenth to the nineteenth century, European slave traders and slave owners increasingly propagated beliefs in African inferiority to justify and facilitate the enslavement of African men, women, and children on an unprecedented scale. Africans, however, were not the only peoples coerced into colonial enslavement. American Indians throughout North America were also enslaved in the seventeenth and eighteenth centuries. While never a majority in European colonies north of Mexico, American Indians nonetheless constituted a significant proportion of the slave population—in some cases up to 25 percent.

The seventeenth century marked the simultaneous rise of both Indian and African enslavement in the colonies that would become the United States. Indian slaves were often easier to acquire than Africans, particularly in the first decades of settlement, when mainland colonists were cash poor. Most African slaves were shipped to sugar plantations, where a booming cash crop combined with steep slave mortality rates resulted in a high demand, and high prices, for African slaves. Planters in Virginia and South Carolina, for example, could not attract slave ships coming directly from Africa until late seventeenth century when tobacco and rice cultivation made better trading prospects possible. In South Carolina African slave importation remained a small enterprise well into the 1720s, and Carolinians were forced to trade with Caribbean-based slavers, taking what slaves they could find.

Indian slaves were a highly desirable alternative to Africans. They could be easier to procure, and they were far cheaper. The long Middle Passage (the journey of the slave ships across the Atlantic) was costly: Many Africans died en route, and the shipping expenditures were high. Indian slaves, on the other hand, were often transported short distances on foot or in small boats to the nearest port of sale. Thus, less financial investment and infrastructure were needed. Moreover, both Europeans and Indians took Indian captives in the numerous wars that European colonialism spawned. As in Africa, some native communities were willing to sell their war captives to European slavers and the latter were eager to buy them.

INDIGENOUS AND EUROPEAN CONCEPTS OF SLAVERY

Indian slaves, like those from Africa, often began their enslavement as war captives. Indian societies throughout North America took war captives prior to contact with Europeans. Among the nations of the League of Iroquois, for example, "mourning wars" were waged by clans who had recently suffered the loss of loved ones to violence or disease. These wars could lead to long cycles of revenge warfare in which clans retaliated against other tribes for the killing or capture of their kin. Among the Iroquois this was known as "requickening;" among the Cherokees it was "crying blood." Motivated by grief, revenge, and a need to restore a cosmological balance, clan matriarchs sent out male warriors to make war on their enemies. Captives were brought back to the matriarchs, who then decided whether the traumatic loss of their family member would be better compensated for by adopting the captives into the community or by relegating them to torture and death or enslavement.

Women and children were usually adopted, and these captives quite literally replaced lost kin, assuming their names and identities. Men were more often killed, though the killing of a woman was a particularly assertive, powerful act.

Not all captives were killed or adopted, however: Some were kept as slaves. Unlike European chattel slavery, indigenous slavery was not labor based. While Indian slaves worked for their Indian masters, they were not enslaved to produce goods for a market economy. Some scholars object to the use of the term "slavery" to describe indigenous captives, preferring the term "adoption complex." However, this concept does not adequately describe the status of those who remained outside of the clan system. In Indian communities, slaves were enemies who were purposefully not incorporated into a clan, which was the source of all identity in Indian societies. Indigenous slaves lived out their days not simply as outsiders but as nonhumans. In many Indian languages, the same word was used to describe slaves and domestic animals. While indigenous slaves were not

Native American Abduction. *Native Americans constituted a significant portion of the slave population in the Americas because they were both cheaper and easier to acquire than African slaves.* PICTURE COLLECTION, THE BRANCH LIBRARIES, THE NEW YORK PUBLIC LIBRARY, ASTOR, LENOX AND TILDEN FOUNDATIONS.

chattel property in the European sense, they were slaves, as well as a decidedly political form of capital.

Europeans also understood the concept of enslaving enemies. They believed that if a war was waged for just reasons, the war captives whose lives were spared might reasonably be sentenced to servitude or enslavement. They also echoed Indian beliefs that slaves lived outside of human society, thus sharing the idea that slaves were subhuman. Nevertheless, slave status was less immutable in Indian societies' slaves than in European ones. In Indian communities slaves might gain their humanity and rights as citizens through adoption or intermarriage, and their children rarely inherited their status as slaves. In contrast, by the late seventeenth century, European colonies had enacted slave laws to prohibit just this kind of social mobility.

INDIAN SLAVE TRADES AND TRADERS

Seeking alternative sources of slave labor, European colonists in New France, Virginia, New England, South Carolina, New Mexico, and Texas established slave trades with Indian communities in these regions. Slave trades represented a middle ground where indigenous traditions of captive-taking and European desires for economic slaves met. Indians diverted their traditional war captives to this trade. In most cases, this meant that a larger number of women and children, who previously would have been adopted or kept as slaves, were now sold off as slaves.

In New France French officials and visitors found themselves the recipients of war captives, who were given to them by Iroquois, Illinois, and Ottawas to symbolize political alliance. Though Louis XIV had outlawed Indian slavery in 1689, French officials increasingly accepted these political gifts to promote peace with their Indian allies. The French also gave Indian slaves to Indian allies themselves in exchange for English captives taken during Queen Anne's War (1702–1713). These political exchanges, in turn, bred a small trade in Indian slaves purchased to work for French families.

French traders on the western borderlands of Louisiana established a brisk trade with Comanches and Wichitas for Indian women and children. In these frontier communities, single Frenchmen abounded, and a need for domestic help coupled with sexual motives prompted the establishment of a widespread slave trade. While much of Louisiana's labor force was African, Indian women were purchased in significant numbers for sexual companionship. By the early nineteenth century, one-quarter of all Europeans living in northwest Louisiana had an Indian ancestor.

The Comanches and Wichitas, who supplied French traders and soldiers with their Indian slaves, targeted their mutual enemies: the Apaches. The Spanish in Texas also focused on the eastern bands of Apaches, sending out punitive slave expeditions to take Apache women and children to stop or punish Apache horse raids. While the Spanish occasionally returned some of these captives, others were given to soldiers or citizens, while some were exported to Mexico City or the Caribbean. Unlike the French, the Spanish did not develop a system of intermarriage with Indian slaves. Rather, Spaniards tended to marry or have children only with Indian women who had become part of Spanish society.

Both the European demand for Indian slaves and the Indian desire for European trade goods prompted many of the Indian communities involved in the slave trade to intensify their war activities. Despite popular misconceptions to the contrary, war was not generally the main occupation of Indian communities prior to European colonization. The advent of Indian slave trades ushered in an unprecedented level of warfare, as Indian communities rose to meet European demand, often suspending their traditional customs in the process.

In many ways, Indian slave wars were driven by the "gun-slave cycle" that emerged in Africa as a result of the transatlantic slave trade. In North America, as in Africa, a desire or need for European goods (particularly guns, cloth, metals, and alcohol) led many Indian communities to war more frequently on their enemies and to take more captives than previously. Slaving communities acquired guns, waged more successful wars, took more captives, and in turn acquired more guns. These Indian slavers expanded their wars, traveling greater distances to acquire slaves. The Westo Indians are a quintessential example. The victims of Iroquoian mourning wars, the surviving Westoes had moved southwards into Virginia by 1661. Having selected Virginia because they hoped to trade with colonists there for guns and other goods, the Westoes discovered that Virginians would pay handsomely for Indian slaves. Hence, the Westoes turned into slavers, traveling down as far as Spanish Florida for slaves. When English colonists began to establish South Carolina in 1670, they quickly established a trade with the Westoes for Indian slaves. The slave trade proved politically and economically empowering for some Indian communities who capitalized on the trade, who first enslaved their traditional enemies then expanded their raids further afield. But this was also a dangerous business. When South Carolina traders began to see the Westoes as competitors in the slave trade, they sponsored the Savannahs in a campaign to enslave and kill the Westoes. By the eighteenth century, Indians who were not slavers in the Southeast were likely to fall victim to slave raids.

Colonists not only purchased war captives from Indian communities, they also enslaved Indians whom they captured in their own wars. In Virginia, colonists engaged in punitive slave expeditions after the wars of 1622 and 1644 with the Powhatan Indians. Similarly, in New England, colonists enslaved not only Indian warriors but also Indian women, children, and noncombatants following the Pequot War (1636–1637) and King Philip's War (1675–1676). King Philip's War represented a distinct turning point in New English attitudes toward Indians generally and Indian enslavement specifically. The war was a conflict between English and Indian neighbors who had lived in peace for over fifty years. Catalyzed by English expansion into Wampanoag territory, the war resulted in the enslavement of many New England Indians, including Indians allied with the English. In the wake of the war, southern New England Indians became subjects of the New English colonies. That being the case, it was harder to justify their enslavement, and New Englanders began to import Indian slaves taken from their western frontiers during King William's War (1689–1697) with the French, plus others from the Carolinas.

South Carolinians exhibited the largest, if most short-lived, Indian slave trade: From 1670 to 1715 they enslaved between 30,000 and 51,000 Indians. South Carolinians invested heavily in the Indian slave trade, and it quickly became the central facet of their economy. They exported many of their slaves to Virginia, New England, and the Caribbean, but a significant number were also kept in the colony. While economically crucial to the colony, the slave trade also served a keen geopolitical purpose. Traders and the colonial government directed their Indian trading partners to enslave Indians who were allied with the Spanish in Florida and the French in Louisiana. Indians vastly outnumbered Europeans in the colonial Southeast and European imperial wars were largely fought by Indian soldiers. Enslavement served both to weaken the Spanish and French and to enrich the English. Most active in this slave trade were the Creek Indians, who in turn used the slave trade to advance their own political ambitions and economic goals. Most notably, Creeks' slave raids (two of which were led by English officials) resulted in the near destruction of the Spanish Indian missions in Florida by 1706.

While the Indian slave trade and Indian slave wars could be mutually beneficial to European and Indian communities, they could also prove deadly if mishandled. South Carolina was nearly destroyed in 1715 when Indian nations throughout the region—Yamasees, Creeks, Cherokees, Chickasaws, Catawbas, and others—killed 90 percent of the traders and 400 settlers. Indian towns had become increasingly indebted to their traders over the course of the early eighteenth century. As the colony's population, wealth, and territory expanded, southeastern Indians watched their own power decrease. When, under the pretext of debt settlement, some traders began to enslave the kin of their Indian trading partners, southeastern Indians responded with war, effectively ending the Indian slave trade in the region. Though South Carolina's economic trade in Indian slaves ended, both Indians and Europeans continued to wage war against their enemies, and to turn some of their captives into slaves.

RACE AND INDIAN SLAVERY

While Carolinian traders had acted illegally when they enslaved free Indians with whom they traded in the 1710s, the colonial courts of New England began to involve themselves in the "judicial enslavement" of Indians for crimes and debts following King Philip's War. In the wake of that war, it proved more difficult to formally enslave Indians who were now considered English subjects. However, through punitive indentures—whose terms were either ill-defined or indefinitely extended (through the courts or illegally)—Indians charged with crimes or indebtedness became defacto slaves. In 1774 more than a third of all Rhode Island Indians lived as slaves with white families.

The codification of slave laws across North America from the 1660s through the 1720s effectively erased the Indian identity of large numbers of Indians who were living as slaves or servants. Though Indians were mentioned in colonial slave laws, the rise of a black majority (combined with binary ideas of race as black and white) doomed Indians who were enslaved to become effectively "black" in the eyes of most colonists. Nonetheless, Indian slaves maintained their own cultural identities. Their impact on slave cultures and slave religions has yet to be fully appreciated.

SEE ALSO *Racial Slave Labor in the Americas; Slavery, Racial; Slavery and Race.*

BIBLIOGRAPHY

Barr, Juliana. 2005. "From Captives to Slaves: Commodifying Indian Women in the Borderlands." *Journal of American History* 92 (1): 19–46.

Bossy, Denise. Forthcoming. "Indian Slavery in Colonial South Carolina: Indian and English Contexts, 1670–1730." In *Indian Slavery in Colonial America*, ed. Alan Gallay. Lincoln: University of Nebraska Press.

Braund, Kathryn E. Holland. 1991. "The Creek Indians, Blacks, and Slavery." *Journal of Southern History* 57 (4): 601–636.

Brooks, James F. 2002. *Captives and Cousins: Slavery, Kinship, and Community in the Southwest Borderlands.* Chapel Hill: University of North Carolina Press.

Forbes, Jack. 1993. *Africans and Native Americans: The Language of Race and the Evolution of Red-Black Peoples.* Urbana: University of Illinois Press.

Gallay, Alan. 2002. *The Indian Slave Trade: The Rise of the English Empire in the American South, 1670–1717.* New Haven, CT: Yale University Press.

Magnaghi, Russell M. 1998. *Indian Slavery, Labor, Evangelization, and Captivity in the Americas: An Annotated Bibliography.* Lanham, MD: Scarecrow Press.

Newell, Margaret. 2003. "The Changing Nature of Indian Slavery in New England, 1670–1720." In *Reinterpreting New England Indians and the Colonial Experience,* edited by Colin G. Calloway and Neal Salisbury, 106–136. Boston: Colonial Society of Massachusetts.

Perdue, Theda. 1979. *Slavery and the Evolution of Cherokee Society, 1540–1866.* Knoxville: University of Tennessee Press.

Ramsey, William. 2001. "'All and Singular the Slaves': A Demographic Profile of Indian Slavery in South Carolina." In *Money, Trade and Power: The Evolution of South Carolina's Plantation Society*, edited by Jack P. Greene, et al., 166–168. Columbia: University of South Carolina Press.

Rushforth, Brett. 2003. "'A Little Flesh We Offer You': The Origins of Indian Slavery in New France." *William and Mary Quarterly* 60 (4): 777–808.

Standwood, Owen. 2006. "Captives and Slaves: Indian Labor, Cultural Conversion, and the Plantation Revolution in Virginia." *Virginia Magazine of History and Biography* 114 (4): 434–463.

Usner, Daniel H., Jr. 1992. *Indians, Settlers & Slaves in a Frontier Exchange Economy: The Lower Mississippi Valley before 1783.* Chapel Hill: University of North Carolina Press.

Denise Ileana Bossy

INDIGENISMO IN MEXICO

The concept of race in Mexico is deeply rooted in the xenophobic tendencies of the Spanish colonization. It has been recorded that Hernán Cortés (c.1485–1547), the famous Spanish conquistador responsible for the downfall of the Aztec empire, once stated: "We Spaniards suffer from a disease of the heart which only gold can cure." Cortés therefore brought an exploitative political philosophy to the New World and its indigenous peoples. Since then Mexico has struggled to come to grips with its history and to define its nationalistic identity and place in the world. The historical periods of Mexico's development and public policies can be broken down into the following: colonization, independence, revolution, modernization, and neoliberalization. Each is marked by its own particular set of institutionalized and informal racist policies.

ROOTS OF *INDIGENISMO*: COLONIZATION, CONVERSION, AND CORRUPTION

Policies regarding race began with allegations of ideological superiority by the Spanish at the time of contact. Cortez's actions are deeply criticized to this day by the indigenous peoples of the Americas, and "Columbus Day" has been reformulated by Native peoples as "Indigenous Peoples' Day."

The imperialistic approach of the Spanish toward the New World was conditioned in large part by the earlier Christian Reconquest of Spain, during which Spanish soldiers battled the Moorish population from 711 to 1492 for control of the Iberian Peninsula. Viewing the Reconquest as a "holy war," a religious-military complex took shape in Spain. Freedom from Islamic rule was equated with Christian identity, and the religious conversion of Muslims and Jews was a critical ideological driving force behind the Reconquest. Using xenophobia (fear of the Other) as grounds to conquer new lands for god and country, the Spanish carried these ideas to their "New World" colonizations, beginning with Christopher Columbus's arrival in 1492.

The arrival of the Spanish in Mexico in 1519 marked the end of indigenous control over the region and the collapse of the Aztec empire. Those indigenous peoples not killed by the sword were subjected to a wealth of foreign illnesses from smallpox to influenza, which reduced the population of native peoples from an estimated 27.1 million to as few as 1.2 million shortly after Spanish arrival (Carmack 1996, p. 128). In 1552, the Dominican priest Bartolomé de las Casas (1474–1566) related the devastation that followed the arrival of the *encomenderos,* Spanish arrivals who earned land grants that included economic and political control over indigenous populations. Upon returning to Spain, Las Casas wrote about Spanish brutality under the *encomenderos* and about his doubts that the indigenous populations would ever truly be Christianized or fully integrated into Hispanic society.

Indigenismo is "public policy and institutions that address the educational, economic, health, and social needs of the Indian population, with the underlying goal of assimilating Indians into the mainstream culture" (Carmack 1996, p. 478). On the surface such policies appear beneficial to the well-being of the colonial empire, yet they also served to further marginalize the indigenous peoples into resettled communities known as *congregaciones* (or *reducciones*). These resettlements were close to towns where labor pools (*obrajes*) could come from the native communities to aid public work projects that developed the internal infrastructure of the towns (*municipios*), yet they did little for the rural countryside. Where indigenous labor was not accessible, such as along the coast, African slaves were imported. In the ideal, *indigenismo* would bring the indigenous people onto an equal footing with their European colonizers. It would, in essence, "civilize" them. Colonization, however, had quite the opposite effect. Chief among the bad consequences of this process was the imposition of a caste system based on a series of status rankings. This became known as the doctrine of *limpieza de sangre* (purity of blood).

Limpieza de sangre policies brought day-to-day reality to the caste situation in Mesoamerica. It was originally dictated in Spain to allow only those of "demonstratable Christian stock" to be allowed to attain noble status or to hold public office. The extension of the *limpieza de sangre* led to racial castes based on skin color, heritage, and Indian ancestry. The most prominent among these rankings (from highest to lowest) were the following:

- *Peninsulares*: Those born in Spain of Spanish descent (immigrants and dignitaries).
- *Criollos*: Those of Spanish descent born in the New World.
- *Mestizos*: Offspring of a Spanish man and an Indian woman.
- *Mulattos* (*Sambos*) and Free Blacks: Offspring of a Spanish man and an African woman.
- *Indios* (Indians): Indians of pure descent.
- African Slaves: Those brought from Africa to work on coastal plantations or in the mines (Carmack 1996, pp. 172–174).

The caste status of Indians and African slaves varied from one region to another. Frequently, an Indian death from excessive labor was of no concern to *encomenderos*, yet the loss of a slave meant a loss of paid property. This justified, at times, the higher status of slaves over Indians.

As can be seen from the categories above, even though both *criollos* and *peninsulares* had the same skin color, they were separate castes. A constant struggle between *peninsulares* and their lesser *criollo* elites led to the eventual uprising of *criollos* against the *peninsulares*, contributing to Mexican independence from Spain in 1810. The Indians were a prominent part of the uprising because of their resistance to colonial taxation of *obrajes* and their objection to dominant views of the indigenous populations as "passive, dependent, docile, stupid, incapable of higher civilization, lacking in emotions and sensitivity, impervious to pain and suffering, [and] unable to improve their miserable conditions of living" (Stavenhagen 1998, p. 16).

The prevailing attitude at this time was that the indigenous people needed to be "cared for" by missionaries. During this time, religious confraternities (*cofradías*) were formed by the missionaries, allowing indigenous peoples some degree of religious self-control over the practice of Christian ceremonies. This led to religious syncretism, or a blending of traditional native beliefs with those of Christianity. In the minds of rural friars, the Indians' inherent inferiorities kept them low on the caste scale and out of clergy positions. The derogatory nature of the word *indio* was created through the caste system and resulted in increasing levels of legal discrimination. The missionaries viewed the caste system as a way of interacting with the Indians in similar fashion as they had interacted with the uneducated peasantry of Europe.

This marginalization of the native peoples was met with resistance. In western Mexico, according to Beatriz Rojas (1993), missionaries did not make inroads into the isolated indigenous mountain communities until the 1550s. Thereafter, they met with varying levels of resistance. For example, from 1617 to 1618, the Tepehuán Indians revolted against the Spanish and the Cora were forcibly resettled into villages. In 1712 the Tzeltal revolted against the Spanish in Chiapas.

Mexican independence from Spain did little for the rights of indigenous peoples. *Criollo* elites simply replaced the *peninsulares* in positions of power. *Mestizos,* those of mixed Indian and Spanish ancestry, however, gained prominence as the dominant working class on the ranches (*haciendas*) of the *criollos* and as local authorities in the cities. In essence, they filled gaps in the social structure that the elites were unable or unwilling to fill. The indigenous peoples continued to be marginalized, and *indigenismo* returned in the guise of what was viewed as "the native problem" (*el problema indígena*).

EMERGENCE OF THE MIDDLE CLASS *MESTIZO*

The Mexican Revolution of 1910–1917 marked the rise of the *mestizo*. Although nationalistic sentiments were important for the independence movement, a new *mestizo* caste consciousness was also apparent in the years leading up to and during the Mexican Revolution. The denial of infrastructural development in the rural areas had led much of Mexico's population to continue to live in poverty and servitude to *hacienda* owners. In general, the period between independence from Spain and the Mexican Revolution encouraged the advancement of the *mestizo* as the dominant caste and racial classification.

Mexico's growing *mestizo* population was not without its problems. Although *mestizos* were more Indian in their ancestry than their political opponents, they nonetheless found it necessary ideologically to reject the significance of their Indian past to become a dominant political power in Mexico. This meant the denial of their indigenous heritage in an attempt to be more like their elite neighbors, the *criollos*. Being Christianized, rejecting the use of one's indigenous language in favor of Spanish, and changes in one's style of dress and place of residence were all critical to becoming *mestizo*.

When he became President, Benito Juarez (1806–1872), who was half Zapotec Indian and is considered the "founder of modern Mexico," instituted a series of seemingly liberal social policies that led to the breaking up of the large landholdings of the Church and others, but with the goal of privatizing the lands rather than restoring them to rural communities. This was known as the *Ley Lerdo* of 1856. Juarez viewed the destruction of collective lands as vital to the emergence of Mexico into a new age of progressivism that would require destruction of two communities—the Church and the indigenous peoples. As a result of his agenda, only the wealthy could afford to purchase the lands taken away by the state.

The *Ley Lerdo* had devastating effects on the indigenous lands, and indigenous-controlled communities, already outlawed for fear of their ability to influence local municipal governments, were subject to outside electoral control (i.e., *mestizo*). Indigenous collective lands were either absorbed into the nonindigenous-controlled municipalities to pay off state debts or they were auctioned off. This law affected indigenous communities from the Yucatan to Oaxaca and the Sierra Madre region in the northwest.

Arriving on the heels of Benito Juarez was Porfirio Díaz (1830–1915), who was driven by the need for foreign capital to modernize Mexico. A railroad infrastructure was built, and European arts, music, and literature were promoted. Intellectualism was equated with Europeanism and the wealthy middle and upper classes gained prominence, ushering in a new period of Mexican development in which the population doubled and the infrastructure expanded.

By 1910, 85 percent of mining companies were North American. Many of these companies favored hiring their own nationals instead of Mexicans. The situation became so bad that "only 2 percent of the population held title to land and 3 percent of the properties covered 58 percent of Mexico" (Foster 2004, p. 154). Seventy percent of the Mexican citizenry, however, continued to be farmers. Hunger was prevalent due to poor pay or displaced peasantries. By 1910, only 10 percent of Indian communities held collective land (Foster 2004, p. 155).

A subsequent economic decline during the early 1900s resulted in foreign debt and infrastructural collapse. It was during this time that the rural areas began to rebel against the policies effected by the Porfiriato regime, leading to the rebellion of Pancho Villa's forces in the north and Emiliano Zapata's forces of the south. The success of the rebellion was achieved in 1917, though at the loss of as many as 2 million lives.

BUILDING A MODERN MEXICO: LAND REFORM

The Mexican Revolution and the expansion of the *mestizo* race did little for the indigenous populations of Mexico. A nationalistic image of Mexico was created, which aimed to shroud the pluralistic nature of the country in a romantic image of the past, known as *Mexico profundo* (Bonfil Batalla 1996). In the world of the *Mexico profundo*, the de-Indianized peoples were reclassified as part of the rural peasantry. Stripped of their sense of identity, a romantic notion of the past was created and perpetuated by the *mestizo*. In this image, the indigenous peoples no longer existed except as part of the past Mexico—a modern Mexico required a unified nation-state, and indigenous identity represented a threat to that unity.

The Mexican Constitution of 1917 institutionalized the destruction of collectively owned lands (*ejidos*), even though one of the major goals put forth in the constitution was the restoration of communal lands that had been lost to wealthy owners and foreign companies. This ruling was known as the Agrarian Reform Law (*La Reforma Agraria*), or Constitutional Article 27, and its intended purpose was to restore power to the rural proletariat through land redistribution and certification.

With the passage of the Agrarian Reform Law and the rise of President Lázaro Cárdenas (1895–1970) in 1934, foreign control was to be reduced, if not eliminated all together. Lands were to be restored to rural village communities in collective fashion. In principle, the Agrarian Reform Law had great potential not only for the *mestizo*, but for indigenous peoples as well. The government failed to fully implement the ruling in all affected areas, however. In general, lands in indigenous areas that were determined to have worth to the now federalized resource associations were never restored. Chief among these government-controlled, nationalized industries was *Petroleos Mexicanos* (PEMEX), which came to control much of the oil rich lands of southern Mexico.

NEOLIBERALISM: CHALLENGES TO A PLURALISTIC SOCIETY

Neoliberalism is a term that was often used by indigenous peoples in the 1990s to refer to the renewed policies of governmental reforms, economic justice, and political ideology that benefited the elites and commercial centers at the expense of indigenous peoples and the poor. According to George Collier and Elizabeth Quaratiello, neoliberalism "looks to the marketplace to solve all of society's problems and meet all its needs. Neoliberalism has changed society, both for the better by contributing to dramatic growth of civil institutions independent of the government, and for the worse by leading the government to militarization and repression to hold onto power" (1999, p. 157). It is the belief of the native peoples of Mexico that neoliberalism is directly responsible for the continued violation of indigenous rights, economic justice, and sovereignty observed in the early twenty-first century.

In 1975 the first National Congress of Indian Peoples was held, organized in part by the Mexican anthropologist Guillermo Bonfil Batalla. The goals of the congress were the same as those to be later mentioned by the Zapatistas in their 1994 uprising in southern Mexico. These issues included:

- Much of the land was considered infertile or lacking in amount to prove useful.
- The lack of public health care facilities and services.
- The lack of basic human services, such as running water or electricity, despite tax payments.
- The prevalence of malnutrition and poverty brought about by the lack of arable land.
- The poor availability and quality of education, and educational institutions that did not benefit indigenous communities.
- Low salaries and unfair labor conditions.
- Exploitation of peasant and native industries by wealthy middlemen (Collier and Quaratiello 1999, p. 63–64).

In the twenty years after the First Indigenous Congress, it was apparent that the government was doing little, if anything, to address these basic human needs in Chiapas. In the 1970s, a number of indigenous organizations were begun in response to government inaction, among them the Emiliano Zapata Peasant Organization (OCEZ), the Independent Confederation of Agricultural Workers and Indians (CIOAC), and Popular Politics (PP). These organizations aided indigenous peoples with land reform and with organizing workers. The CIOAC enabled farmworkers to "sue ranchers under federal labor laws for back wages and improved working conditions," while PP was a Maoist-Marxist student organization that engaged university students to work with impoverished communities in eastern Chiapas (Collier and Quaratiello 1999, p. 71).

Indigenous organization largely failed amid a booming development phase of the Mexican economy in the 1970s, dominated by oil. Oil exports reached new heights until the market's decline in 1981, displacing thousands of indigenous farmworkers from their land and resulting in a two-class system of extreme wealth for the few and impoverishment for the majority.

While the population was booming in the highland region, there was increasingly little arable land available in the low-lying areas. This especially impacted the Tzotzil Indians of the region. Much land had been turned over to cattle ranching, was lost in the construction of hydroelectric dams to supply power to the cities, or was to be used for oil drilling by PEMEX. Industry, it was argued, could not lose these lands because of the wealth they provided.

By 1982, oil exports became 80 percent of the Mexican export economy, to the detriment of agriculture and other internal industries. The export market crashed in 1982, however, and left many with nowhere to go. The living situation had become untenable in the highland region. Pesticides and herbicides used to increase production on small plots of land had not only damaged much of the soil, but the debts incurred by farmers through loans to acquire these chemicals resulted in further land losses by the many who could not afford to repay their debts.

The succeeding events of the 1980s were no better for the Zincanteco peasantry and Tzotzil Maya. Basic government services were limited and budgets were slashed. Moreover, the indigenous Maya peoples were monolingual Tzotzil speakers and illiterate. These factors resulted in deep divisions between the indigenous and the literate Spanish-speaking peoples (*ladinos*) of the region. Not only did educational barriers prevent the *ladinoization* of the indigenous Maya, but political affiliation became a factor. Loyalty to the Institutional Revolutionary Party (PRI), which had held power since the revolution, determined whether or not one had access to certain governmental programs and services. Indigenous and *ladino* communities alike became divided. Native communities that had remained loyal to the PRI since the reforms of President Cardenas became angry with the cuts in agricultural subsidies that aided the poor. Only those regions where elections were being held or contested received government support, and affiliation with competing political parties, especially the growing Democratic Revolutionary Party (PRD) grew.

The 1988 Mexican national election resulted in the continued dominance of the PRI. Carlos Salinas de Gortari (b. 1948) became president amid allegations of corruption and ballot-box stuffing. Salinas continued to support free-trade policies, which led to inflated prices for foods such as the tortilla, a staple of the Mexican diet, yet eliminated farm subsidies. Assistance was supposed to be received regardless of one's political affiliation, but this was not the case. Forty-eight percent of the population lived below the official poverty level, and the distribution of funds to indigenous communities in Chiapas and elsewhere did not occur as planned. PRI officials continued to use literacy and legalism to take advantage of indigenous peoples. Salinas's worst mistake, perhaps, was the amendment of Article 27 of the Mexican Constitution in 1992 in order to again allow privatization of *ejido* lands. Fifty-four percent of Mexican lands were held as *ejidos,* including indigenous territories (Stephen 2002). In order for *ejidos* to remain as collectives, *ejidatarios* had to enroll through a complicated certification process. In addition, women could not vote under these rules, nor did the necessary electoral structure exist. Frustrated with the political impasse, the Zapatista National Liberation Army (EZLN) took matters into their own hands. In 1994 an army composed mostly of Zapotec and Tzotzil Indians revolted, timing their revolt to coincide with the implementation of the U.S.-led North American Free Trade Agreement (NAFTA). In the revolt, the Zapatistas took over government offices throughout Chiapas. An Internet posting called international attention to the event and detailed the 34-point agenda of the Zapatistas. Chief among these demands were the return of privatized lands to native communities, hospitals and medicine for indigenous communities, housing and basic services (e.g., water, plumbing, electricity), an end to illiteracy, fair prices for their farm products, and an end to hunger and malnutrition. Very few of these demands differed from those listed twenty years previously by the 1974 Indigenous World Congress, or those called for in the International Labor Organization's (ILO) Conventions 107 and 169, which had been ratified into the Mexican constitution in 1990. These ILO resolutions were specifically designed to protect indigenous collective rights on religious, political, labor, and land freedom issues. They were viewed by many merely as symbolic gestures, however, in order to show that Mexico was making progress in its commitment to a "plural-ethnic" state.

When the Zapatistas finally voluntarily withdrew from the government centers, an international conference was held between the Zapatistas and the government's Commission of Agreement and Peacemaking (COCOPA) officials to reach a consensus over demands. This agreement, known as the San Andreas Accords, was later signed by President Ernesto Zedillo, who later refused to implement any of the resolutions. However, the idea that indigenous people could organize themselves began to spread to other indigenous peoples.

The end of the rebellion and subsequent meetings resulted in several self-proclaimed autonomous communities by the Zapatistas, which continued to face armed vigilance from the Mexican military in 2005. The autonomous Zapatista communities reflect a socialistic model of social welfare by engaging the Indians themselves to construct and promote schools and bring basic services into their communities as well as to form artisan cooperatives to bring in funds to the autonomous communities.

THE NEW WAVE OF *ZAPATISMO*: GLOBALIZATION AND THE FUTURE

In the early twenty-first century, the term *Zapatismo* stands for the new indigenous rights movement. Reorganized as the *Fuerza Zapatista de Liberación Nacional* (FZLN) to emphasize nonviolence, *Zapatismo* is a pan-Indian consciousness that includes the indigenous peoples of Mexico and nonnative sympathizers around the world. The Mexican military's acts of social injustice have come to be closely watched by such organizations as Human Rights Watch and Amnesty International.

Mexico continues to deny the implementation of any plural-ethnic model of Mexican society, though outwardly promoting it, and the Mexican authorities continue to vigilantly police the indigenous areas of Mexico for fear of uprisings. The military and state police closely watch native gatherings and migrations, and human rights abuses against the indigenous peoples of Mexico continue, including the illegal detention of Huichol religious pilgrims on their way back from collecting peyote for use in community religious festivities (Valadez 1998) and military vigilance (searches and questioning) toward individuals coming into and out of the Huichol Indian communities. In addition, the Jaliscan State Police have appeared at biannual community meetings where natives were searched, questioned, and religious artifacts seized (Biglow 2001, p. 158–159). These events occurred despite protection for native religious practices expressly

Tzotzil Indians Trek Home, 2001. *Autonomous Zapatistas communities in Chiapas continue to face armed vigilance from the Mexican military. In this photo, hundreds of Tzotzil Indians and aid workers return home from a refugee camp in Chollep after violence between the two forces died down.* AP IMAGES.

being covered in the ratification of the ILO conventions into the Mexican constitution in 1990.

The idea of indigenous communities as "closed corporate communities" (Wolf 1957) is no longer a viable model to describe the changing peasantry. Indigenous identities blend interchangeably with regional identities, resulting in a sort of *polybian*, a person who can exist in two or more worlds (Kearney 1996, p. 141). These polybians are part of regional identities that are difficult to separate from other native or nonnative populations. Whereas ethnic identity and affiliation were previously based on appearance (dress and/or phenotype) and language, these can no longer be the sole criteria for ethnic classification. Self-identification has become the chief factor for this determination. This change was reflected in the 2000 Mexican national census, where 30 percent of the population now identify themselves as indigenous and descended from sixty-two different recognized ethnic groups (Foster 2004, p. 257).

Ongoing confrontations with missionaries further complicate the situation of indigenous rights. Despite the fact that many indigenous communities have passed local resolutions forbidding missionaries from residing in native areas, missionary activity continues due to support from both domestic and foreign missionary organizations. While some measures employed by missionaries are clearly clandestine and dishonest, other less blatant practices also seem to violate native conceptions of sovereignty, including the repeated aerial dropping of radios that receive evangelical shortwave stations, onto native lands where missionaries are forbidden (National Public Radio 2001b).

Injustices against native peoples have continued in the twenty-first century. The 2000 election of Vicente Fox as the first non-PRI party president in seventy-one years has done little to benefit the indigenous communities. The National Action Party (NAP) promised new economic growth in the indigenous areas, and President Fox maintained that NAFTA would both stabilize Mexico's economy and bring it firmly into status as a First World nation. This has not occurred, however, as maize imports continue to come from the United States, undercutting Mexican prices for the grain. Rural and indigenous farmers, particularly Zapotec farmers of Oaxaca, have been forced to turn to bio-engineered crops (transgenics) to increase production (Enciso 2001, National Public Radio 2001a). This was done despite a long-standing indigenous connection with corn production as the chief crop in their diet and the religious connection of corn fertility to human life (Sandstrom 1991; Biglow 2002).

The increase of services to some indigenous areas, such as the Huichol Indians of western Mexico, has brought about a rapid *Mestizoization* of the population. Traditional village politics are turning from an egalitarian socialistic model, with status based on age-prestige social rankings, to a class-based stratification whereby personal wealth and political affiliation largely determine one's place in society (Biglow 2001). This has been compounded by the downfall of cheap labor factories (*maquiladoras*) along the U.S.-Mexico border in 2002, in favor of cheaper labor in Asia.

Not only has lack of employment become a problem for Mexicans in general, but by 2002, nearly one in three Mexicans had been to work in the United States, either legally or illegally (Foster 2004, p. 251). Few realize, however, that the majority of the illegal immigrants are indigenous Mexicans who have become landless in Mexico and are forced to seek out agricultural jobs in the United States. It is therefore important to note the presence of indigenous peoples living in diaspora in the United States and Canada.

Mexican racial politics continue to play a large role as the nation struggles with the ideas of unity and nationalism in the early twenty-first century. A number of recurrent themes have come about, including: (1) the denial of an indigenous past and ethnic diversity, (2) the failure to recognize indigenous sovereignty and constitutional protections for their diverse peoples, and (3) a continued attention to the demands of industry over the will of its the people. While there are no easy solutions to these policies, Héctor Díaz-Polanco (1997), a prominent Mexican anthropologist, argues that at least some degree of indigenous self-determination or autonomy appear crucial if Mexico is to survive as a unified nation-state. Adding to this argument, the Mexican national Consultation of 1999 showed overwhelming support by the populace for Zapatista demands. The World Trade Center bombings in September 2001 and subsequent attention to border security and illegal immigration appear to have halted these initiatives but they will continue to dominate the political scene in the coming years.

SEE ALSO *Mexicans; Zapatista Rebellion.*

BIBLIOGRAPHY

Biglow, Brad M. 2001. "Ethno-Nationalist Politics and Cultural Preservation: Education and Bordered Identities among the Wixaritari of Tateikita, Jalisco, Mexico." Ph.D. diss., University of Florida, Gainesville, Florida.

———. "Maintaining the Sacred: Corn Varieties and Biogenetic Engineering among the Huichol." Paper Presented at the Society for Applied Anthropology Meetings, Atlanta, Georgia.

Bonfil Batalla, Guillermo. 1996. *Mexico Profundo: Reclaiming a Civilization.* Austin: University of Texas Press.

Cancian, Frank, and Peter Brown. 2002. "Who Is Rebelling in Chiapas?" In *Contemporary Cultures and Societies of Latin America*, 3rd ed., edited by Dwight B. Heath. Prospect Heights, IL: Waveland Press. Originally Published in *Cultural Survival Quarterly* 18 (1): 22–25.

Carmack, Robert M., et al. 1996. *The Legacy of Mesoamerica: History and Culture of a Native American Civilization.* Upper Saddle River, NJ: Prentice Hall.

"Chiapas: The View from Within." 2004. Translated by Zac Martin. *Cultural Survival Voices* 3 (1): 1, 8.

Collier, George, and Elizabeth Quaratiello. 1999. *Basta! Land and the Zapatista Rebellion in Chiapas,* rev. ed. Chicago: Food First Books.

De las Casas, Bartolomé. 1992 (1552). *A Short Account of the Destruction of the Indies.* Translated by Nigel Griffin. New York: Penguin Books.

Díaz Polanco, Héctor. 1997. *Indigenous Peoples in Latin America: The Quest for Self-Determination.* Boulder, CO: Westview Press.

Ejército Zapatista de Liberación Nacional (EZLN). 1993. "Declaración de la Selva Lacandona." Available from http://www.ezln.org.

Enciso, Angélica L. 2001. "Detectan contaminación por maíz transgénico en milpas oaxaquieñas." *La Jornada,* October 15, p. 26. Available from http://www.jornada.unam.mx/2001/10/15/026n1pol.html.

Foster, Lynn V. 2004. *A Brief History of Mexico,* rev. ed. New York: Facts on File.

Franz, Allen R. 1996. "Huichol Ethnohistory." In *People of the Peyote*, edited by Stacy B. Schaefer and Peter T. Furst. Albuquerque: University of New Mexico Press.

Kearney, Michael. 1996. *Reconceptualizing the Peasantry.* Boulder, CO: Westview Press.

Maybury-Lewis, David. 2002. *Indigenous Peoples, Ethnic Groups, and the State*, 2nd ed. Boston: Allyn and Bacon.

Nash, June C. 2001. *Mayan Visions: The Quest for Autonomy in an Age of Globalization.* New York: Routledge.

National Public Radio (NPR). 2001a. "Biotech Genes Found in Wild Maize in Mexico." *All Things Considered*, November 28.

———. 2001b. "Christian Group Drops Radios Chiquitos in Mexico." *All Things Considered*, November 19. Available from http://www.npr.org.

Rojas, Beatriz. 1993. "Los huicholes en la Historia." Mexico: Colegio de Michoacán, Instituto Nacional Indigenista.

Sandstrom, Alan R. 1991. *Corn Is Our Blood: Culture and Ethnic Identity in a Contemporary Aztec Village.* Norman: University of Oklahoma Press.

Stavenhagen, Rodolfo. 1998 (1992). "Challenging the Nation-State in Latin America." In *Crossing Currents: Continuity and Change in Latin America*, edited by Michael B. Whiteford and Scott Whiteford. Upper Saddle River, NJ: Prentice Hall.

Originally Published in *Journal of International Affairs* 45 (2): 421–440.

Stephen, Lynn. 2002. "Accommodation and Resistance: Ejiditario, Ejiditaria, and Official Views of Ejido Reform." In *Contemporary Cultures and Societies of Latin America,* 3rd ed., edited by Dwight B. Heath. Prospect Heights, IL: Waveland Press. Originally Published in *Urban Anthropology* 23: 233–265.

Valadez, Susana. 1998. "Huichol Religious Pilgrims Jailed for Possession of Peyote." *Native Americas* V.XV, No. 1 (March 31): 12.

Wolf, Eric R. 2002 (1956). "Aspects of Group Relations in a Complex Society: Mexico." In *Contemporary Cultures and Societies of Latin America,* 3rd ed., edited by Dwight D. Heath. Prospect Heights, IL: Waveland Press. Originally Published in *American Anthropologist* 58: 1065–1078.

———. "Closed Corporate Communities in Mesoamerica and Central Java." *Southwest Journal of Anthropology* 13 (1): 1–18.

Brad M. Biglow

INDIGENOUS

Indigenous peoples are the original inhabitants of a territory that has been colonized by a settler society, such as the United States, Australia, Canada, and New Zealand. As such, they are often minorities in their own homeland. The terms used to identify indigenous peoples vary depending on the colonial history and region, as well as historical period. For example, in Australia the term *Aboriginal* is common, whereas in Canada the terms include *Aboriginal* and *First Nations*, and *Indian peoples*. In New Zealand, the Maori tribes constitute the indigenous people. In Latin America, they are the *Indigenas*; in Japan, the Ainu people are the indigenous minority; and in Sweden, Norway, and Iceland, they are the Sami. In the United States, indigenous peoples include American Indians (made up of hundreds of tribal nations), Alaska Natives (including Inuits, Aleutians, and American Indians), Native Hawaiians, American Samoans, and Chamorros from Guam and the Northern Marianas Islands. In addition, there are Taino-identified people in Puerto Rico.

In the 1986 report of United Nations (UN) Special Rapporteur José Martínez Cobo titled *Study of the Problem of Discrimination against Indigenous Populations*, indigenous peoples are defined as "those which, having a historical continuity with pre-invasion and pre-colonial societies that have developed on their territories, consider themselves distinct from other sectors of the societies now prevailing in those territories, or parts of them." Cobo goes on to assert that "they form at present non-dominant sectors of society and are determined to preserve, develop and transmit to future generations their ancestral territories, and their ethnic traditional medicines and health practices, including the right to protection of vital medicinal plants, animals and minerals."

A key issue for indigenous peoples worldwide is the question of the right to self-determination under international law. Because the basic criteria defining colonies under international law includes foreign domination and geographical separation from the colonizer, indigenous peoples remain at a disadvantage in terms of the application of decolonization protocols to indigenous nations, an issue heatedly debated within the world community. UN General Assembly Resolution 1514 declares: "all peoples have the right to self-determination; by virtue of that right, they freely determine their political status and freely pursue their economic, social, and cultural development." However, there is no consensus that indigenous peoples have the right to full self-determination, an option that would allow for the development of nation-states independent from their former colonizers. In addition, it is not clear if such rights should be limited to internal self-determination within the existing nation-states in which indigenous peoples live. A key element in this debate is the use of the term *peoples* (plural), which signifies legal rights under international law, over and above the singular *people*, which is grammatically and legally different.

Indigenous peoples worldwide have worked for decades to ensure that their preexisting human rights are recognized and upheld by global nation-states, especially because the domestic laws in most settler states have not protected their ability to assert their self-determination. Key issues of struggle include the right of ownership and control of lands and resources, self-governance, and decision-making authority vis-à-vis the dominant population. As a result of indigenous global activism since the 1970s, a Declaration on the Rights of Indigenous Peoples is currently being considered in the UN Human Rights Council, and a vote by the UN General Assembly is possible at some time in the future. In its draft form, the declaration is currently being promoted as part of customary international law, and indigenous leaders are endeavoring to have states adopt this document in order to make it enforceable and legally binding. There is broad resistance to adopting the declaration, however, especially by the United States.

Histories of racism have varied across different global contexts, but histories of genocide are pervasive, as settler states have typically expanded their territory by waging wars against indigenous peoples. European nations, and later the United States and other nation-states, used the "Doctrine of Discovery," which rationalized the conquest of indigenous lands, to perpetuate the legal fiction of land possession, and these nations continue to impose this principle as a mechanism of control in their negotiations with indigenous peoples' legal status and land rights. One of the most common forms of racism against indigenous peoples in modern times is the pernicious falsehood that they are entirely extinct or diluted due to racial mixing. These populations are subject to a standard of authenticity based on a colonial logic of culture and purity. In the United States, the myth of the "Vanishing Indian" endures and has led to stringent criteria required of tribes seeking federal recognition. This recognition enables the exercise of internal self-determination by domestic dependent indigenous nations subject to the U.S. trust doctrine, which is supposed to be a unique legal relationship with the U.S. federal government that entails protection.

SEE ALSO *Fourth World; Genocide; Genocide and Ethnocide; Genocide in Rwanda; Genocide in the Sudan; Racial Hierarchy; Violence against Indigenous People, Latin America.*

BIBLIOGRAPHY

Barker, Joanne, ed. 2005. *Sovereignty Matters: Locations of Contestation and Possibility in Indigenous Struggles for Self-Determination.* Lincoln: University of Nebraska Press.

Calloway, Colin G. 1999. *First Peoples: A Documentary Survey of American Indian History.* Boston and New York: Bedford/St. Martin's Press.

Durie, Mason 1998. *Te Mana, Te Kawanatanga: The Politics of Maori Self-Determination.* Auckland: Oxford University Press.

Moreton-Robinson, Aileen, ed. 2007. *Sovereign Subjects: Indigenous Sovereignty Matters.* St. Leonard's NSW, Australia: Allen and Unwin Press.

Russell, Dan. 2002. *A People's Dream: Aboriginal Self-Government in Canada.* Toronto: University of Toronto Press.

Wilkins, David E., and K. Tsianina Lomawaima. 2001. *Uneven Ground: American Indian Sovereignty and Federal Indian Law.* Norman: University of Oklahoma Press.

J. Kehaulani Kauanui

INFANT MORTALITY AND BIRTH WEIGHT

Infant mortality refers to the death rate of babies less than one year old; it is expressed as the number who die per every thousand live births. The chances of dying are high among infants because they have not developed immunities to most infectious, parasitic, and communicable diseases, which are often associated with poor sanitary conditions and malnourishment. The infant mortality rate can thus be used as a gauge of the health of populations within and across countries.

IMR WORLDWIDE

The infant mortality rate (IMR) tends to decline as countries become more economically developed. For example, the IMR in the United States was about 100 per thousand live births in 1900, but in the early twenty-first century it is below 10 per thousand. Many countries have even lower rates than the United States, such as Japan (3.0), Finland (3.1), and Norway (3.4). In industrialized countries, differences in IMRs tend to be the result of disparities in the health status of women before and during pregnancy, as well as a reflection of the quality and accessibility of primary care for pregnant women and their infants. The IMRs for Peru (43), India (60), Laos (87), Ethiopia (116), Afghanistan (150), and Burundi (157) are very high, although most of these countries have witnessed a substantial decline in infant mortality since the 1960s (United Nations 2004). For example, the IMR in India was 146 in 1960 but reached a low of 60 in 2003. Nonetheless, many developing countries will continue to struggle in their efforts to eliminate adverse birth outcomes if they do not improve access to adequate health care facilities, improve the standards of living for all of their citizens, and put forth a more conscious effort at improving the health of women and children overall.

On a more positive note, the IMR has declined significantly around the world: It was 198 in 1960, 83 in 2001, and 54 in 2003. In the early 2000s, the most common causes of infant mortality worldwide are pneumonia and dehydration from diarrhea. The rate of children dying from dehydration is decreasing, however, due to the success of international efforts in providing mothers with information about Oral Rehydration Solution.

IMRS IN THE UNITED STATES

In the United States, the IMR has also steadily declined. It was 26.0 in 1960, but has dropped significantly, falling to 6.9 in 2000 (Iyasu and Tomashek 2000). A variety of factors have been proposed to explain the declining IMR across several different historical time periods in the United States. For example, in the early 1900s improved environmental and living conditions were responsible for initial declines in infant mortality, while the next few decades saw declines as a result of programs established to care for pregnant women and their infants (Meckel 1990). According to some scholars, infant mortality declined in the 1990s because of decreases in sudden infant death syndrome (SIDS) (Willinger 1998).

Although the United States has greatly reduced its IMR since the 1960s, it ranked only twenty-sixth among industrialized countries in infant mortality in 1999 (United Nations 2002). This ranking is in large part the result of disparities that continue to exist among various racial/ethnic groups in the United States, particularly between African Americans and whites. In 2000, infant mortality occurred at a rate of 14.0 per thousand live births among African Americans, compared to 5.7 for non-Hispanic whites (Iyasu and Tomashek 2000). By 2002 the IMR for African Americans had declined slightly to 13.9, but this was still more than double the rate of 5.8 for non-Hispanic whites. Infants of Native American (8.6) and Puerto Rican (8.2) mothers also have relatively high IMRs, while other ethnic groups in the United States, such as Mexicans (5.4), Japanese (4.9), Cubans (3.7), and Chinese (3.0), have relatively low IMRs (Mathews, Menacker, MacDorman 2002). Even though the infant mortality rate has declined throughout the twentieth century for all women, the comparative inconsistency between African Americans and whites remains unchanged.

LOW BIRTH WEIGHT AND RACE

Low birth weight is an important determinant of racial/ethnic differences in infant mortality in the United States. Low-birth-weight (LBW) babies are newborns weighing less than 2,500 grams (5 pounds 8 ounces) and very-low-birth-weight (VLBW) include newborns weighing less than 1,500 grams (3 pounds 4 ounces). The IMR for low-birth-weight infants is more than twenty times that of infants born at a normal weight (MacDorman and Atkinson 1999), putting them at a much greater risk for mortality.

In 2001 the percentage of LBW babies born to African-American mothers was 13.0. Although this figure represents a decline from a high of 13.6 in 1991, it is still considerably higher than the rate for Asian/Pacific Islander (7.5), American Indian (7.3), white (6.7), and Hispanic (6.5) births (Martin et al. 2003). In 2001 the rate of VLBW newborns remained at 1.4 percent of live births to U.S. women, but the rate of VLBW among African-American babies was more than two-and-a-half times higher than that among non-Hispanic whites (Martin et al. 2003). The black-white gap in infant mortality in the United States can be explained when adverse birth outcomes such as low birth weight are taken into account (Hummer et al. 1999).

According to the U.S. Centers for Disease Control and Prevention (CDC), other major contributors to infant mortality include congenital abnormalities, SIDS, and respiratory distress syndrome. In fact, SIDS rates are 2.4 times higher for African American babies and 2.6 times higher for Native American and Alaska Native babies than for non-Hispanic white babies.

RISK FACTORS FOR LBW

Some relevant lifestyle factors influencing the likelihood of having a LBW infant are maternal smoking, drug and alcohol abuse, poor nutrition, and insufficient prenatal care. For example, in 2001 there was a higher percentage of LBW infants born to smokers (11.9 percent) than to nonsmokers (7.3 percent), a pattern that has been observed among both African American and white infants. Other factors associated with increased risk of LBW include maternal poverty, low levels of educational attainment, and family medical history (Conley and Bennett 2001).

Social scientists have developed a number of theories to help explain the high infant mortality rate among African Americans.

The Weathering Hypothesis. Arline Geronimus argues that there is a more rapid decline in the reproductive health of African-American women than in other women in the United States. According to Geronimus, this partially explains why older African-American women (those in their mid-twenties) have higher neonatal mortality rates (IMR for babies younger than 28 days) and a higher risk for having a LBW baby than their younger counterparts. In her research, Geronimus has found the opposite pattern for non-Hispanic white women, who have the lowest neonatal mortality rates and LBWs among women in their mid-twenties. According to this view, "weathering" occurs among African-American women as a result of a lifetime of exposure to economic disadvantage, untreated health conditions, accumulated obligations to significant others, negative health behaviors, limited job choices, and racial/ethnic discrimination.

Additional empirical support for the weathering hypothesis is mixed, however. Elizabeth Wildsmith (2002) has found some evidence for the hypothesis among U.S.-born Mexican–American women in terms of maternal health. Narayan Sastry and Jon Hussey (2003), using data from birth records of mothers who resided in Chicago, report that an increase in age is associated with a decrease in birth weight among African Americans, but with an increase in birth weight among Hispanics of Mexican origin. Michael Klitsch (2003), on the other hand, reports few racial/ethnic differences in the general pattern of decreasing infant death rates with increasing maternal age in a study of African-American, white, and Mexican-American women.

Cumulative Disadvantage. The weathering hypothesis is consistent with the "cumulative disadvantage" perspective that is often proposed to explain disparities in physical health between elderly minorities and their white peers (Crystal and Shea 1990). Those who embrace the cumulative disadvantage perspective argue that individuals who start out with fewer resources will have poorer health outcomes across the life course. Within the weathering framework, age is a resource that decreases in value over time more rapidly for African Americans than for non-Hispanic whites. Age brings with it certain forms of capital such as high energy and a sense of optimism. These resources are higher among the young compared to the old. The difference between these two perspectives, however, is that the weathering hypothesis is multiplicative (it includes the interaction between age and race/ethnicity) while the cumulative disadvantage view is additive (it includes only the linear effect of age and race/ethnicity). These perspectives emphasize the complex etiology of racial/ethnic differences in infant mortality rates.

The Intersectionality Hypothesis. A second view of disadvantage, referred to as the "intersectionality hypothesis," also advocates a nonlinear relationship between race/ethnicity and health across groups (Mullings and Wali 2001; Weber and Parra-Medina 2003). This view suggests that a unique set of circumstances are created at the intersection of race, class, and gender that do not always support expectations. For example, African-American women who have graduated college have a higher infant mortality rate than white women who have not completed high school (Pamuk et al. 1998). Intersectionality theory provides a useful lens through which such health disparities may be more clearly viewed. In particular, attention is paid to the resources that are available to individuals as a result of the amount of power afforded to their group. It can be argued that African-American professional women must often navigate within the boundaries of organizations that are structured by both racial and gender divisions. In this case, it seems that middle-class status is experienced in a less profound and beneficial way for these women than for any other group. As a result, these women are not afforded the opportunity to organize resources that should be available to them given their social-class standing (Jackson and Williams 2005).

These perspectives are not contradictory. They simply draw attention to the accumulation of risk factors that produce disparities in IMRs. Many social scientists acknowledge the role that more general structures, such as residential segregation and neighborhood quality, play in producing racial disparities in health (Williams and Collins 2001). Residential segregation is directly associated with access to and quality of health care, as well as environmental hazards. In fact, because of segregation, middle-class African Americans live in poorer areas than do whites of similar economic status, and poor whites live in much better neighborhoods than do poor African Americans (Massey and Denton 1993). Predominantly African-American neighborhoods also have fewer quality health facilities (Williams and Jackson 2005), and their residents are more likely to be victims of environmental racism (Sexton et al. 1993). A related body of research highlights the role played by neighborhood disadvantage. Neighborhoods perceived as unsafe discourage residents from engaging in healthful behaviors such as walking (Ross and Mirowsky 2001). African-American babies born in more segregated cities have higher rates of infant mortality than those born in less segregated cities (Hogue and Hargraves 1993). A host of environmental and neighborhood-level factors are also associated with the risk of delivering a low-birth-weight baby (Sastry and Hussey 2003). Thus, residential segregation and other environmental factors play an important role in access to quality healthcare, the promotion of healthful behaviors during pregnancy, and resulting infant mortality rates.

The steady decline in infant mortality worldwide is an encouraging pattern for the future. It will be important, however, for scientists to continue to investigate a variety of factors (social, economic, environmental, biological) that contribute to infant deaths. On the other hand, some of the complex patterns found in racial/ethnic differences in infant mortality rates suggest that a concerted effort must also be made to carefully distinguish between these causes. For example, infant mortality rates among African Americans compared to non-Hispanic whites are primarily due to the higher incidence of LBW and preterm births. Similarly, Puerto Rican infants have higher IMRs because of higher LBW rates. On the other hand, the differential in the rate of SIDs helps explain the higher death rate among American Indian infants. Health officials must continue to document the causes of infant death, monitor the success of public health campaigns, and keep track of the increasing use of medical technologies, which can also help explain fluctuations in the infant mortality rate (Reuwer, Sijmans, and Rietman 1987; Zhang, Yancey, and Henderson 2002).

SEE ALSO *Life Expectancy.*

BIBLIOGRAPHY

Conley, Dalton, and Neil Bennett. 2001. "Birth Weight and Income: Interactions across Generations." *Journal of Health and Social Behavior* 42: 450–465.

Crystal, Stephan, and Dennis Shea. 1990. "Cumulative Advantage, Cumulative Disadvantage, and Inequality among Elderly People." *The Gerontologist* 30 (4): 437–443.

Geronimus, Arline, and John Bound 1990. "Black/White Differences in Women's Reproductive-Related Health Status: Evidence from Vital Statistics." *Demography* 27 (3): 457–466.

———. 1992. "The Weathering Hypothesis and the Health of African American Women and Infants: Evidence and Speculation." *Ethnicity and Disease* 2 (3): 207–221.

———. 1996. "Black/White Differences in the Relationship Between Maternal Age to Birthweight." *Social Science and Medicine* 42 (4): 589–597.

Hogue, Carol J., and Martha A. Hargraves. 1993. "Class, Race, and Infant Mortality in the United States." *American Journal of Public Health* 83 (1): 9–12.

Hummer, Robert A., et al. 1999. "Race/Ethnicity, Nativity, and Infant Mortality in the United States." *Social Forces* 77: 1083–1118.

Iyasu, Solomon, and Kay M. Tomashek. 2000. "Infant Mortality and Low Birth Weight among Black and White Infants: United States, 1980–2000." *Morbidity and Mortality Weekly Report* 51: 589–592.

Jackson, Pamela Braboy, and David R. Williams. 2005. "The Intersection of Race, Gender, and SES: Health Paradoxes." In

Gender, Race, Class, & Health: Intersectional Approaches, edited by Amy Schulz and Leith Mullings, 131–162. San Francisco, CA: Jossey-Bass.

Klitsch, Michael. 2003. "Youngest Mothers' Infants Have Greatly Elevated Risk of Dying by Age One." *Perspectives on Sexual and Reproductive Health* 35 (1): 52–53.

MacDorman, Marian F., and Jonnae O. Atkinson. 1999. "Infant Mortality Statistics from the 1997 Period, Linked Birth/ Infant Death Data Set." *National Vital Statistics Reports* 47 (23). Hyattsville, MD: National Center for Health Statistics.

Martin, Joyce A., et al. 2002. "Births: Final Data for 2001." *National Vital Statistics Report* 51 (2). Hyattsville, MD: National Center for Health Statistics.

Massey, Douglas, and Nancy Denton. 1993. *American Apartheid: Segregation and the Making of the Underclass.* Cambridge, MA: Harvard University Press.

Mathews, T. J., Fay Menacker, and Marian F. MacDorman. "Infant Mortality Statistics from the 2002 Period, Linked Birth/Infant Death Data Set." Available at http:www.cdc.gov.

Meckel, Richard A. 1990. *Save the Babies: American Public Health Reform and the Prevention of Infant Mortality, 1850–1929.* Baltimore, MD: Johns Hopkins University Press.

Mullings, Leith, and Alaka Wali. 2001. *Stress and Resilience: The Social Context of Reproduction in Central Harlem.* New York: Springer.

Pamuk, Elsie, Dianne Makuc, Katherine Heck, et al. 1998. *Socioeconomic Status and Health Chartbook.* Hyattsville, MD: National Center for Health Statistics.

Reuwer, P. J., E. A. Sijmans, and G. W. Rietman. 1987. "Intrauterine Growth Retardation: Prediction of Perinatal Distress by Doppler Ultrasound." *Lancet* August 22 (2): 415–418.

Ross, Catherine, and John Mirowsky. 2001. "Neighborhood Disadvantage, Disorder, and Health." *Journal of Health and Social Behavior* 42 (3): 258–276.

Sastry, Narayan, and Jon Hussey. 2003. "An Investigation of Racial and Ethnic Disparities in Birth Weight in Chicago Neighborhoods." *Demography* 40 (4): 701–725.

Sexton, Ken, Henry Gong, John C. Bailar, et al. 1993. "Air Pollution Health Risks: Do Class and Race Matter?" *Toxicology and Industrial Health* 9 (5): 843–878.

United Nations. *World Population Prospects: The 2004 Revision.* Vol. I, *Comprehensive Tables.* New York: United Nations Population Division.

Weber, Lynn, and D. Parra-Medina. 2003. "Intersectionality and Women's Health: Charting a Path to Eliminating Health Disparities." In *Advances in Gender Research.* Vol. 7, *Gendered Perspectives on Health and Medicine.* San Francisco: Elsevier.

Wildsmith, Elizabeth. 2002. "Testing the Weathering Hypothesis among Mexican-Origin Women." *Ethnicity and Disease* 12 (4): 470–479.

Williams, David, and Chiquita Collins. 2001. "Racial Residential Segregation: A Fundamental Cause of Racial Disparities in Health." *Public Health Reports* 116: 404–416.

Williams, David, and Pamela Braboy Jackson. 2005. "Social Sources of Racial Disparities in Health." *Health Affairs* 24 (2): 325–334.

Willinger, Marian, H. Hoffman, K. Wu, et al. 1998. "Factors Associated with the Transition to Non-Prone Sleep Positions of Infants in the United States." *Journal of the American Medical Association* 280 (4): 329–39.

Zhang, Jun, Michael K. Yancey, and Cassandra E. Henderson. 2002. "U.S. National Trends in Labor Induction, 1989–1998." *Journal of Reproductive Medicine* 47 (2): 120–124.

Pamela Braboy Jackson
Yasmiyn Irizarry

INFECTIOUS DISEASE, SUSCEPTIBILITY, AND RACE

Disparities in health status, whether measured by infant mortality, life expectancy, or rates of disease, have always existed between different groups. They have been especially stark during epidemics. HIV (human immunodeficiency virus), for instance, exhibits marked disparities between developing and developed countries and between different populations within developing countries. How can these disparities be explained?

Some observers have argued that disparities in disease and mortality reflect disparities in socioeconomic conditions, with impoverished populations being most vulnerable to a wide range of diseases. Others have argued that the disparities reflect biological differences between groups that have different genetic susceptibilities to infectious disease. Genetic explanations have been especially popular in the many cases in which health disparities have existed among racial and ethnic groups.

Two diseases, smallpox and tuberculosis, demonstrate this well. During epidemics of smallpox in the sixteenth and seventeenth centuries, and during epidemics of tuberculosis in the nineteenth and twentieth centuries, doctors and other observers debated the extent to which substantial disparities in mortality could be attributed to assumed biological differences between racial groups. These cases each suggest that biological differences between "races" might be less important determinants of disease than variations in social and economic conditions.

"VIRGIN SOIL" EPIDEMICS

Since ancient times, physicians have been aware that disease is distributed unevenly. Different people living in different places suffer from different diseases, or from different rates of the same diseases. In one of the most influential texts of ancient Greece, *On Airs, Waters, and Places*, the author traced disease to the source and quality of drinking water, the direction and intensity of the prevailing winds, and the topography of the land. Yet the susceptibility to disease went deeper than these environmental conditions. Because people who lived in a specific place became adapted to the local environment, environmental differences became embodied as biological differences (but not necessarily heritable differences) between different groups. Athenians who moved to Alexandria would have found themselves in a climate to which they were not adapted. They would therefore have been more vulnerable to the local diseases of Alexandria. In this way, ancient authors traced variations in rates of disease, in part, to biological differences between people.

Patterns in the distribution of disease among different peoples and places became more obvious and more relevant during the European voyages of exploration and colonization in the sixteenth and seventeenth centuries. As Europeans initiated sustained contact with foreign populations in Africa, Asia, and the Americas, they encountered new diseases and spread their own diseases throughout the world. Smallpox, measles, malaria, and many others spread from Europe and Africa to the Americas. Syphilis spread from America to Europe and then throughout the world. This exchange of diseases had devastating consequences, particularly for the indigenous inhabitants of the Americas. The population of Hispaniola, the first group subjected to Spanish Conquest, foretold the fate of other areas: The Arawak population fell from roughly 400,000 in 1496 to 125 in 1570. As the historian Alfred Crosby has shown, every encounter brought disease and decimation—to Mexico and Peru in the sixteenth century, to New France and New England in the seventeenth century, and throughout North America and the Pacific Islands in the eighteenth and nineteenth centuries. American and Pacific populations typically declined by 90 percent in the first century after contact, falling victim to smallpox, measles, influenza, and countless other epidemics.

The new encounters between people and disease inspired substantial speculation about the distribution of disease and the causes of susceptibility. Colonists produced a diverse range of explanations for the prevalence of disease among American Indians, including religion, diet, environmental conditions, and hygiene. Early colonists, at least in New England, did not see the mortality disparity in racial terms nor did they assume that there were intrinsic differences between European and Indian bodies. Instead, as Philip Vincent, who led English forces in the Pequot War, put it in 1637, "we have the same matter, the same mould. Only art and grace have given us that perfection which they yet want, but may perhaps be as capable thereof as we" (Jones 2003, p. 38). However, the disparities in health status became more and more striking over time. Colonists described epidemics that devastated American Indians but had no effect on the Europeans who lived among them. European populations grew steadily even as Native populations declined. As Joyce Chaplin has argued, these observations led more and more colonists in the seventeenth and eighteenth centuries to suspect that there were intrinsic differences between Europeans, Native Americans, and Africans. Within their starkly Eurocentric worldview, Europeans saw themselves as both more civilized and more resistant to disease.

Historians and medical researchers have debated for centuries why American Indians had such high mortality from epidemics. Many have favored explanations based in evolutionary theory and natural selection. According to the popular "virgin soil" theory of epidemics, European and Asian populations suffered a high burden of infectious disease throughout their history. As a result, they developed a genetic resistance to smallpox, measles, and many other infections. Because these diseases did not exist in the Americas before Christopher Columbus, the indigenous population never developed similar resistance. Alfred Crosby and Jared Diamond have argued that this differential susceptibility explains the outcome of the encounter: American Indians were doomed because they lacked genetic resistance to a wide range of Eurasian pathogens.

However, the theory of virgin soil epidemics has had many critics. Despite intensive study, medical researchers have not found any substantial evidence that different races have different genetic susceptibilities to smallpox, measles, or other acute viral infections. At the same time, Linda Newson, Stephen Kunitz, and other historians have shown that environmental conditions and social factors played a decisive role in shaping the outcome of encounters between Europeans and Native Americans. Many American populations barely eked out a subsistence living before the European arrival, with life expectancies as low as twenty to twenty-five years. When European colonizers disrupted patterns of subsistence and exposed Indians to warfare, slavery, and dislocation, the populations suffered terribly. The severity of the mortality varied between different groups, often depending on the intensity and intrusiveness of European contact. This suggests that American Indian populations were not born vulnerable to European pathogens. Instead, they may have been made vulnerable by the chaos of colonization and conquest.

TUBERCULOSIS, RACE, AND EXTINCTION

During the nineteenth century, tuberculosis replaced smallpox as the dominant cause of mortality in Europe and the United States. Smallpox declined for a variety of reasons, including the spread of vaccination and the emergence of a less virulent strain of smallpox. The rise of tuberculosis is more complex, with urbanization, overcrowding, working conditions in factories, and malnutrition all contributing. By the late nineteenth century, tuberculosis caused roughly 20 percent of all deaths in Europe and the United States. The impact was even more dire on some populations. Randall Packard has shown how Africans working in South African mines in the first half of the twentieth century suffered terribly from tuberculosis, even after it had receded among the white population of South Africa. Medical researchers at the time wondered whether the Africans were a "virgin soil" for tuberculosis. Packard argued instead that the epidemic arose from the poverty, malnutrition, and physical stress experienced by the black laborers.

In North America the most afflicted populations were American Indians who had been confined on reservations. Tuberculosis caused more than half of all deaths on the Sioux reservations in the Dakotas. Observers continued to emphasize environmental conditions, tracing tuberculosis to overcrowded housing, poor hygiene, and inadequate food. Racial theories, however, became more common. By the mid-nineteenth century, many scientists believed either that the races had been created separately or that they had diverged thoroughly from their common creation. In either case, there was no reason to think that the different races were equivalent. As a result, many scholars in the United States and Europe believed that whites were superior to both American Indians and blacks. This belief led to a widely held conclusion: Indians and blacks, unable to compete with whites, would inevitably go extinct. The burden of tuberculosis among the Native population was seen as proof of their eventual fate.

These theories of racial susceptibility to tuberculosis had many subtleties. White Protestants were not always seen as the most superior race. Just as American Indians were believed to be susceptible because they had only recently encountered tuberculosis, Jews were seen as particularly resistant because they had long lived in urban ghettos where tuberculosis had thrived. However, as the historian Alan Kraut has shown, Jewish doctors did not welcome this theory. Instead, they argued that there was no particular connection between Jews and tuberculosis. The disease simply assailed everyone who lived in suitable conditions.

During the twentieth century, tuberculosis receded from the United States and Europe but remained endemic in many other countries. By 2000, one-third of the world's population (two billion people) were infected. More than two million people died each year. It became clear over the twentieth century that socioeconomic factors have an enormous impact on tuberculosis. In many populations, everyone would become infected, but only those weakened by physical stress or malnutrition would die. This was seen clearly during wartime conditions, when famines, fatigue, and dislocation greatly increased tuberculosis mortality. Such observations led the microbiologist and author René Dubos to christen tuberculosis a "social disease." Any population, when weakened by poverty and malnutrition, can become devastatingly susceptible to tuberculosis.

Despite clear evidence of the importance of socioeconomic factors, researchers continued to seek and find evidence of genetic factors that influence susceptibility to tuberculosis. In the 1990s William Stead, Richard Bellamy, Adrian V.S. Hill, and other researchers identified a series of genetic variants that increased both the risk of infection with the bacteria that causes tuberculosis and the risk of active disease once infected. In 2006, Philip Liu and his collaborators showed a link between melanin concentration in skin (i.e., darkness of skin) and susceptibility to tuberculosis. It is possible that variations in the frequency of susceptibility genes between different populations contribute to the observed variations in the frequency of tuberculosis in different racial and ethnic groups. The discovery of new susceptibility genes became more common as the Human Genome Project and the International HapMap Project facilitated high-volume genomic analysis. The new genetic data, taken with the existing evidence of the importance of socioeconomic conditions, forced researchers to continue to debate the contribution of genetic and environmental factors to disease susceptibility and health disparities.

RACE, GENETICS, AND SUSCEPTIBILITY

Discussions of race and susceptibility to disease have not been limited to virgin soil epidemics and tuberculosis. Instead, racial disparities in disease incidence and mortality rates have been described for most diseases. Diabetes has been most prevalent among the Pima Indians, a problem attributed to the mismatch between scarce ancestral food supplies and the overabundance of modern life. Sickle-cell disease is largely a problem for people of African ancestry, a legacy of evolution in malarial environments. Tay-Sachs disease occurs almost exclusively among Ashkenazi Jews, a product, it has been speculated, of their long exposure to tuberculosis. Countless other "racial" diseases and susceptibilities have been described. This research benefited from increasingly fine-grained analyses of human genetics. Although it has become clear that humans are remarkably homogeneous genetically (much more so than fruit flies or dogs), there is enough variation between humans for genetic subpopulations to be identified. As Noah Rosenberg's analysis has shown, these genetically defined populations correlate well with conventional racial categories. These various lines of research are seen by some to support the conclusion that race is both biologically real and medically significant.

However, as happened with both virgin soil epidemics and theories of tuberculosis susceptibility, questions emerged about the significance of genetic differences between racial and ethnic groups. Even if a disease is distributed along racial lines, genetic differences between races might not be the cause. Race in the United States is correlated with education, living conditions, and socioeconomic status, each of which influences disease outcomes. The limitations of racial theories, and the discomfort with them, can be clearly seen in the case of HIV. From the earliest years of the epidemic, HIV/AIDS has exhibited striking disparities in morbidity and mortality. Few scientists or historians, however, have argued that the disparities between South Africans and Europeans, or between urban minorities and suburban whites, existed because the afflicted populations were genetically susceptible to HIV. Instead, the social contingency of HIV on a local and global scale has long been recognized.

Ironically, as more and more genetic data emerge to explain observed racial disparities in health status, the overall argument about the importance of genetics becomes harder and harder to sustain. For instance, disparities between American Indians and the general population of the United States have been described for acute infections, such as smallpox and measles; chronic infections, especially tuberculosis and trachoma; and for the endemic ailments of modern society, including heart disease, diabetes, alcoholism, and depression. A different, but equally diverse, set of disparities exists for African Americans. The persistence of disparities across changing disease environments is actually a powerful argument against the belief that disparities reflect the genetic susceptibilities of different racial groups. Instead, the disparities could arise from disparities of wealth and power that exist between different racial and ethnic groups.

Disparities in disease incidence and mortality rates among different racial and ethnic groups have existed for millennia. However, the causes of these disparities remain unclear. Many researchers have argued that biological differences between racial groups, especially variations in disease susceptibility genes, are the cause of the differential susceptibility. Others have rejected these claims and argued instead that environmental conditions and socioeconomic factors have a greater influence on patterns of disease. Until the questions are resolved, researchers, clinicians, and policymakers need to recognize the complexity of race and the many other factors that interact to produce patterns of disease and mortality.

SEE ALSO *Diabetes; Diseases, Racial; Genetic Variation among Populations; Health Disparities between Indians and Non-Indians; Heritability; HIV and AIDS; Human Genetics; Sickle Cell Anemia; Tay-Sachs and "Jewish" Diseases.*

BIBLIOGRAPHY

Bellamy, Richard, et al. 1998. "Variations in the *NRAMP1* Gene and Susceptibility to Tuberculosis in West Africans." *New England Journal of Medicine* 338: 640–644.

Chaplin, Joyce E. 2001. *Subject Matter: Technology, the Body, and Science on the Anglo-American Frontier, 1500–1676.* Cambridge, MA: Harvard University Press.

Crosby, Alfred W. 1972. *The Columbian Exchange: Biological and Cultural Consequences of 1492.* Westport, CT: Greenwood.

Diamond, Jared. 1997. *Guns, Germs, and Steel: The Fates of Human Societies.* New York: W.W. Norton.

Dubos, René, and Jean Dubos. 1987 (1952). *The White Plague: Tuberculosis, Man, and Society.* New Brunswick, NJ: Rutgers University Press.

Jones, David S. 2003. "Virgin Soils Revisited." *William and Mary Quarterly* 60: 703–742.

———. *Rationalizing Epidemics: Meanings and Uses of American Indian Mortality since 1600.* Cambridge, MA: Harvard University Press.

Kraut, Alan M. 1994. *Silent Travelers: Germs, Genes, and the "Immigrant Menace."* Baltimore, MD: Johns Hopkins University Press.

Kunitz, Stephen J. 1994. *Disease and Social Diversity: The European Impact on the Health of Non-Europeans.* New York: Oxford University Press.

Liu, Philip T., et al. 2006. "Toll-Like Receptor Triggering of a Vitamin D-Mediated Human Antimicrobial Response." *Science* 311: 1770–1773.

Newson, Linda A. 1985. "Indian Population Patterns in Colonial Spanish America." *Latin American Research Review* 20 (3): 41–74.

Packard, Randall M. 1989. *White Plague, Black Labor: Tuberculosis and the Political Economy of Health and Disease in South Africa.* Berkeley: University of California Press.

Rosenberg, Noah A., Jonathan K. Pritchard, James L. Weber, et al. "Genetic Structure of Human Populations." *Science* 298 (5602): 2381–2385.

Stead, William W., John W. Senner, William T. Reddick, and John P. Lofgren. 1990. "Racial Differences in Susceptibility to Infection by *Mycobacterium tuberculosis.*" *New England Journal of Medicine* 322: 422–427.

David S. Jones

INSTITUTIONAL RACISM

Institutional racism is the process by which racial oppression is imposed on subordinate racial groups by dominant racial groups through institutional channels. While individuals carry out single acts of discrimination, societal institutions are the primary settings where patterns of racial discrimination are established and perpetuated toward subordinate peoples. Central to the operation of institutional racism is a racial hierarchy of power, and, despite differences in historical development and racial-ethnic group composition among the world's countries, institutionalized racism tends to be prevalent in countries that have both dominant and subordinate racial groups.

BEYOND RACISM AS FEELINGS

Stokely Carmichael (later, Kwame Ture) and Charles V. Hamilton introduced the concept of institutional racism in their pioneering *Black Power* (1967), thus moving the scholarly understanding of racism beyond the traditional—yet still widespread—focus on individual bigots. While many race scholars now accept the systemic operations of racism, many people still view racism as a feeling of ill will directed toward any racial out-group. Thus, a common notion is that a person either is, or is not, a racist. Understanding that racism occurs at the institutional level adds a layer of complexity to the simple idea that racism is a feeling each individual can choose to either possess or deny.

All societies include institutional inequalities, but, as Louis L. Knowles and Kenneth Prewitt (1969) explain, "no society need use race as a criterion to determine who will be rewarded and who punished. Any nation that permits race to affect the distribution of benefits from social policies is racist" (p. 6). Knowles and Prewitt provide an illustrative example of institutional racism in U.S. history, claiming that the 1964 murder of civil rights workers by Ku Klux Klan members and white police officers in Mississippi was an act of individual racism, while the killers' acquittal, involving various state agencies in Mississippi, was an example of well-institutionalized racism. Even this delineation, however, is contested; other scholars would argue that the actions of the police officers should also be considered institutional racism because they acted within the police structure and with the support of the all-white police culture.

HISTORY AND POWER

Institutional racism does not arise spontaneously, but rather develops as institutions themselves are created and/or modified over the years. For example, in the United States, all major institutions, including education, government, and the economic and legal systems, were formed and underwent substantial entrenchment and evolution during the extreme racial oppression and inequality from the 1600s to the 1960s, eras of slavery and legalized segregation. According to Joe R. Feagin, in *Systemic Racism* (2006), each institution has embedded, maintained, and enhanced the unjust impoverishment of people of color and the unjust enrichment and privilege for whites. Indeed, the U.S. economic system was originally created to center around the exploitation and oppression of African Americans via enslavement and, to a lesser extent, the exclusion and discrimination of North American indigenous peoples. Thus, racial oppression is truly part of the bedrock of the United States, forming part of the country's foundation.

Most European countries differ markedly from the United States in that their racial oppressions and inequalities have historically been less rooted in national origins, less openly contested on the domestic front, and thus less visible to the world. Nevertheless, Europe too has a long history of racist ideology and practice, including the colonization of indigenous peoples across the globe and the support for slavery in many of these overseas colonies.

Central to institutional racism is the power differential whereby patterns of discriminatory practices reward those of the dominant group (typically whites and lighter-skinned peoples) and harm subordinate groups. White elites in many white-dominant countries, such as the Netherlands, Germany, the United Kingdom, France, and the United States, have firm control of the political, corporate, media, and academic arenas, and they are able to generate and reproduce racism through these powerful channels, consciously or unconsciously (Dijk 1993). This occurs not just through the establishment of discriminatory institutional practices but also through the creation of a white supremacist ideology, which gives people rationalizations for outcomes of even extreme levels of racial inequality.

THE ROLE OF INTENT

According to Joe R. Feagin and Clairece Booher Feagin (2003), institutional racism takes two major forms: *direct* and *indirect* institutionalized discrimination. The former type involves overt actions prescribed by dominant-group organizations that have a discriminatory impact on subordinate racial groups, such as legalized exclusion from certain types of well-paying jobs. The latter consists of less overt racialized acts that harm members of subordinate groups without the perpetrators necessarily having malicious intent. For example, when local tax bases are used as the basis for public school funding, communities of color—whose residents tend to be poorer—are more likely to wind up with the less-funded, often inadequate, schools. Students of color disproportionately receive meager educations, which in turn hinder their ability to compete in the higher education and employment arenas. By contrast, white students receive better than average educations and, therefore, receive unearned benefits from institutional racism practices. Thus, institutional racism in one area (e.g., education) can have substantial effects in another (e.g., employment) and interact with forms of direct and indirect institutional racism there, which results in a cumulative dynamic.

Importantly, indirect institutional racism is hardly reducible to class inequalities working themselves out in racial ways. Contemporary social science research strongly indicates that, even when controlling for all other possible factors (such as class status, education, experience, skills, and location), discrimination against people of color tends to occur at significant rates. These numerous studies include the areas of housing (e.g., Yinger 1995), employment (e.g.,

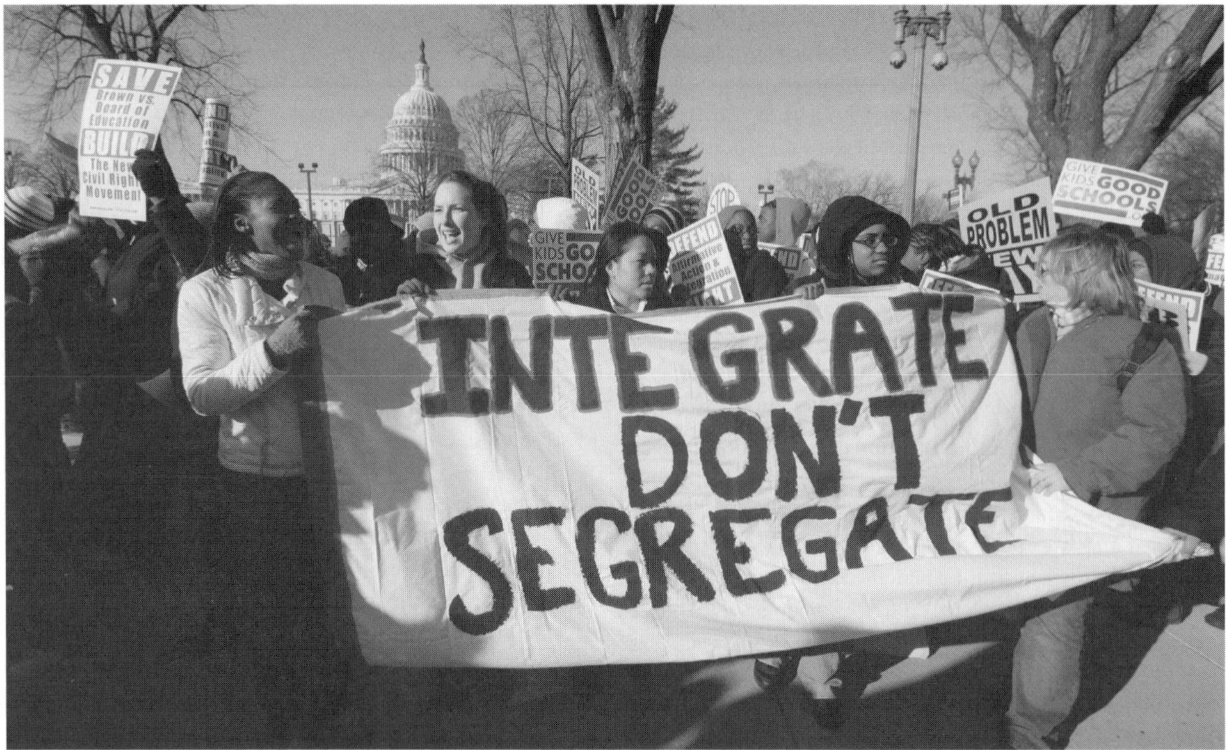

Supreme Court Protest, 2006. *In December 2006 the Supreme Court heard arguments in two suits challenging school admission policies. The court's ruling would decide how race can be used when assigning students to K-12 schools in an effort to achieve diversity.* AP IMAGES.

Bertrand and Mullainathan 2004; Pager 2003), education (e.g., Oakes 2005), and criminal justice. Notably, a 2005 study conducted by Devah Pager and Lincoln Quillian lends support to the assertion that individuals need not be aware of the racism in their actions for discrimination to be the effect: Employers who had favored white job applicants with criminal records over black applicants with clean records claimed to have no awareness of their recent discriminatory hiring decisions, when interviewed later.

If using the racism-as-feelings perspective, it can seem counterintuitive that the agents of racism can sometimes be oblivious of the discriminatory implications of their actions. Nonetheless, institutional racism can operate with or without the awareness of dominant group members, or their representatives, and does not require malicious intent. However, while institutions need not operate in an explicitly racist manner for the effects of their actions to be discriminatory, the persistence of institutional racism does rely on the active operation of negative attitudes toward people of color in the society (Carmichael and Hamilton 1967).

CUMULATIVE IMPACT

In the United States, overt racism, for the most part, is no longer inscribed in law. Nevertheless, this does not mean that racism is not still institutionalized. According to extensive research done by Harvard University's Civil Rights Project (2003), there is a striking "pipeline" leading from schools to prison. This funneling of students of color into prisons occurs through the systematic tracking of "high-risk" children of color and includes such practices as high-stakes testing, disproportionate special education placements, resource inequities, and stringent disciplinary procedures. This treatment of students of color (most significantly black and Latino boys) combines with law enforcement trends that treat these same juveniles with increasing harshness for both major and minor offenses (see also Oakes 2005).

Here again the cumulative impact of racial discrimination comes into focus. Because of institutional racism in the education system combined with discrimination by law enforcement, a young male of color is likely to enter the criminal justice system and then experience institutional racism there. An abundance of social science research shows that people of color (especially black men) are racially profiled and harassed by police, are likelier to be arrested and charged with crimes, receive harsher sentences, and have more difficulty achieving parole than their white counterparts. Additionally, beyond the prison, in the employment sector, a black man with a criminal record will have extreme difficulty finding a job, compared to his white counterpart (Pager 2003).

In education, institutional racism can also be seen operating through standard classroom materials, where textbooks omit or skew the truth about racial histories and seriously neglect any discussions of racism and anti-racism (Loewen 1995; Dijk 1993). Virtually all mainstream textbooks are controlled by elites, who most often have an interest in upholding the racial status quo and offering a "whitewashed" perspective on difficult matters such as slavery and colonization, a perspective that will play down the unfair advantages whites have gained through centuries of racial oppression.

All of these institutionalized racist practices are supported by a white supremacist ideology, including insidious stereotypes that rationalize these serious oppressions of people of color. Although media cannot be blamed for creating harmful, racist images of people of color, they certainly project them to the mainstream for consumption and, thus, fuel white conceptions of the goodness of whiteness and the criminality of people of color (Russell 1998). Also often overlooked is the extent to which American (and, to a lesser extent, European) media forms are broadcast to a global market. The world's populations consume the white supremacist ideology and images and receive ready-made rationalizations for racial inequality that leaves the darkest-skinned peoples at the bottom of a global racial hierarchy through the worldwide operation of institutional racism.

SEE ALSO *Color-Blind Racism; Critical Race Theory; Everyday Racism; Orientalism; Racial Formations; Scientific Racism, History of.*

BIBLIOGRAPHY

Bertrand, Marianne, and Sendhil Mullainathan. 2004. "Are Emily and Greg More Employable than Lakisha and Jamal? A Field Experiment on Labor Market Discrimination." *American Economic Review* 94 (4): 991–1,013.

Carmichael, Stokely, and Charles V. Hamilton. 1967. *Black Power: The Politics of Liberation in America.* New York: Random House.

Dijk, Teun A. van. 1993. *Elite Discourse and Racism.* Newbury Park, CA: Sage Publications.

Feagin, Joe R. 2006. *Systemic Racism: A Theory of Oppression.* New York: Routledge.

———, and Clairece Booher Feagin. 2003. *Racial and Ethnic Relations,* 7th ed. Upper Saddle River, NJ: Prentice Hall.

Harvard University. Civil Rights Project. 2003. "School to Prison Pipeline: Charting Intervention Strategies of Prevention and Support for Minority Children." Available from http://www.civilrightsproject.harvard.edu/convenings/schooltoprison/synopsis.php.

Knowles, Louis L., and Kenneth Prewitt, eds. 1969. *Institutional Racism in America.* Englewood Cliffs, NJ: Prentice-Hall.

Loewen, James W. 1995. *Lies My Teacher Told Me: Everything Your American History Textbook Got Wrong.* New York: New Press.

Oakes, Jeannie. 2005. *Keeping Track: How Schools Structure Inequality,* 2nd ed. New Haven, CT: Yale University Press.

Pager, Devah. 2003. "The Mark of a Criminal Record." *American Journal of Sociology* 108 (5): 937–975.

———, and Lincoln Quillian. 2005. "Walking the Talk: What Employers Say versus What They Do." *American Sociological Review* 70 (3): 355–380.

Russell, Katheryn K. 1998. *The Color of Crime: Racial Hoaxes, White Fear, Black Protectionism, Police Harassment, and Other Microaggressions.* New York: New York University Press.

Yinger, John. 1995. *Closed Doors, Opportunities Lost: The Continuing Costs of Housing Discrimination.* New York: Russell Sage Foundation.

Kristen M. Lavelle
Joe R. Feagin

INTELLIGENCE PROJECT

The Intelligence Project is a department of the nonprofit Southern Poverty Law Center (SPLC), a major civil rights organization based in Montgomery, Alabama, that specializes in monitoring, investigating, and curbing the American radical right. Started in 1981 under the name of Klanwatch, the Intelligence Project changed its name in the 1990s to reflect the expansion of its bailiwick to a large variety of other extreme-right individuals, groups, and movements.

The roots of the Intelligence Project stretch back to 1979. That year, Curtis Robinson, a black man, shot a Ku Klux Klansman (KKK) in self-defense in Decatur, Alabama, during an attack on peaceful civil rights marchers by more than 100 club-wielding members of the Invisible Empire Klan. When Robinson was convicted by an all-white jury of assault with intent to murder, the SPLC appealed the conviction and brought its first civil suit against the Klan. During trial proceedings, evidence was uncovered that convinced the FBI to reopen the case, ultimately resulting in the conviction of nine Klansmen on criminal charges. They also discovered the extent to which the KKK had rebounded after its decline in the 1960s. This led to the decision to create Klanwatch in 1981.

In the early years, Klanwatch operated essentially as the investigative arm of the SPLC's legal department, which was pioneering new legal avenues of attack against hate groups. In 1981, nineteen-year-old Michael Donald was on his way to the store when two members of the United Klans of America abducted him, beat him, cut his throat and hung his body from a tree on a residential street in Mobile, Alabama. The two Klansmen who killed Donald were arrested and convicted, but Klanwatch investigators also found evidence to support a civil suit alleging conspiracy, eventually winning a historic $7 million verdict against the United Klans and several individual Klansmen. The most violent Klan group of the civil rights era was forced to turn its headquarters building over to Beulah Mae Donald and to disband.

Klanwatch investigations supported a number of other path-breaking suits against hate groups. In the 1980s, an SPLC suit forced the White Patriot Party, then the South's most militant Klan group, to disband after investigators found it was using U.S. army personnel to train Klan recruits, and that it had acquired stolen military weapons. Another suit resulted in Tom Metzger and John Metzger and their neo-Nazi White Aryan Resistance (WAR) being found partly responsible for the 1988 murder of an Ethiopian student by racist skinheads in Portland, Oregon. In the 1990s, Klanwatch investigators built a case against the neo-Nazi Church of the Creator after one of its "reverends" murdered a black Gulf War veteran. Other suits resulted in judgments against the Christian Knights of the Ku Klux Klan and its leaders for conspiring to burn black churches, and, in 2000, against the neo-Nazi Aryan Nations and its leaders because of an attack on two hapless passersby by heavily armed Aryan Nations security guards.

EXPANDING ITS BAILIWICK

While the original purpose of Klanwatch was to gather information about the Klan, it expanded over the years to monitor hate crimes and an array of other kinds of extremists—including neo-Nazis, racist skinheads, Christian Identity adherents, academic racists, violent anti-abortionists, anti-immigrant vigilantes, black supremacists, neo-Confederates, and, notably, the militias that appeared in the mid-1990s. Well before the 1995 bombing of the Alfred P. Murrah Federal Building in Oklahoma City left 168 men, women, and children dead, Klanwatch investigators documented the rise of the antigovernment militia movement and its links to white supremacist groups and their leaders. In the aftermath of the bombing, officials of Klanwatch and the SPLC were called upon by law enforcement, media outlets and many others to provide expertise on the American radical right. SPLC cofounder Morris Dees testified before the Senate Judiciary Committee on terrorism just eight days after the attack, and Klanwatch staffers would go on to testify on numerous occasions to Congress, the United Nations, and a number of local and state legislative bodies. Their expertise is supported by a Klanwatch's remarkable database, dubbed "Beholder," the nation's most comprehensive on the radical right.

The Intelligence Project is known for the quality of its factual investigative work and the information it provides to reporters, scholars, and law enforcement agencies. Its prestige has risen to the point where *U.S. News & World Report*, for instance, said in 1999 that its "state-of-the-art tracking system" had "bested the nation's mighty law enforcement agencies" in connecting a man who shot up a Jewish community center in Los Angeles with the notorious Aryan Nations group.

THE STRATEGIES

The Intelligence Project pursues three basic strategies in carrying out its mission of curbing right-wing extremism: (1) Providing information to the public on the radical right and its activities; (2) educating law enforcement officials and supporting their efforts to counter criminal extremist activity; and (3) carrying out the investigative work necessary to pursue civil suits against hate and other extremist groups.

The Project's primary public education vehicle is its magazine, the *Intelligence Report*. The *Report* began as a Klanwatch newsletter of a few pages in 1981, but it evolved over time into a glossy, full-color quarterly magazine that has become the nation's pre-eminent periodical on the radical right. The *Report* is offered free to those whose work relates to right-wing extremism, including more than 60,000 law enforcement officials. In addition, journalists frequently use the groundbreaking stories as fodder to produce their own news articles and broadcast reports.

The magazine has covered a wide array of topics, from annual analyses of the radical right to major profiles of individual extremists and groups. It has examined such phenomena as the use of the Internet by hate groups; the development of White Power music and its importance, the rise and fall of the militias of the 1990s, the proliferation of hate activity on school campuses, and the development of radical new ideologies such as racist variants of Neopaganism and "pan-Aryanism." It has frequently used information dug up in investigations to damage or even destroy hate groups. On one occasion, a neo-Nazi group was completely wrecked when its leader's partly Jewish heritage was revealed. On another, a key leader left the white supremacist movement after the *Report* revealed he was secretly running a pornography Web site and a magazine that carried interracial and bisexual sex ads.

The *Intelligence Report* also carries listings once per year of all hate groups and antigovernment "Patriot" groups active in the previous year, including a map showing their locations and types. These listings typically result in hundreds of local newspaper and broadcast stories that raise local awareness about the groups. A few examples of some of the more important stories carried by the *Intelligence Report* help to give a sense of other ways the magazine works to damage hate groups.

In late 1998 the *Report* published a special edition detailing the white supremacist roots and ideology of the

Council of Conservative Citizens, a group that then had thirty-four members in the Mississippi state legislature and claimed to be merely a conservative organization. The story detailed the racism of the group and its leaders and pointed out its close relationship with Trent Lott of Mississippi, then the U.S. Senate majority leader. As a result, the head of the Republican National Committee asked Republicans to avoid the group. In 2004, the *Report* followed up with a story about politicians who ignored that advice, embarrassing a large number of legislators and effectively curtailing the group's ability to attract any kind of political legitimacy.

In 1999 a special issue of the *Report* explored the socioeconomic roots of racist youth in a group of stories that detailed how "an underclass of white youths, in many cases buffeted by the winds of huge social changes and dislocations," was "altering the face of American hatred." In 2000 an entire issue of the magazine was devoted to the burgeoning neo-Confederate movement, made up of racist groups that seek to justify slavery, Jim Crow segregation, and a number of other hateful doctrines. Subsequent investigative articles detailed the development of the movement and led to the severe disruption of the 32,000-member southern heritage group Sons of Confederate Veterans, which had been largely taken over by extremists.

A series of major reports in various issues have detailed the white supremacist and paramilitary strains that characterize large swaths of the organized anti-immigration movement. A particularly important piece explored the role of a Michigan ophthalmologist with bigoted ideas about Hispanics in constructing and building up most of the nation's anti-immigration organizations.

A 2001 article reported on a detailed Intelligence Project analysis of hate crime statistics, concluding that, nationally, hate crimes are undercounted by a factor of five. Other reports on hate crimes detailed how homosexuals are the group most targeted by violent hate criminals and, separately, explored a wave of fatal violence directed at transsexuals. Another, related report explored a rash of Georgia hate crimes that were part of a backlash against illegal aliens.

Beginning in 2002, a series of articles included extremely detailed and closely held information about the National Alliance, at that time the nation's leading neo-Nazi group. The first, published shortly after the Alliance founder's death, detailed a secret speech he had given recently that savaged members of other hate groups as "freaks and weaklings." The report severely damaged the group's reputation, and started a series of internal splits and other battles that have left the Alliance a mere shadow of its former self. By 2005, the Alliance had been reduced to less than a seventh of its size just three years earlier. In 2005, the *Report* ran a major cover story on the development of the religious right's crusade against homosexuals, a war that began some three decades earlier but heated up with a 2003 Supreme Court decision striking down state sodomy statutes. The story detailed the false "science" and bully-boy tactics employed by many Christian Right leaders to defame gays and lesbians.

OUTREACH

The Intelligence Project increasingly has used other methods to fight extremism as well. In the fall of 2003, Project investigators exposed a major attempt by anti-immigration zealots to take over the Sierra Club, a major environmental group with some 750,000 members. A letter was sent to the president of the Club warning him and others that the Sierra Club was "the subject of a hostile takeover attempt" and providing detailed factual material about that attempt. At the conclusion of a lengthy campaign, Sierra Club voters decisively rejected the takeover attempt.

Another form of outreach is the education and training programs that the Intelligence Project offers law enforcement. In 1992, the program's director was asked to help the Federal Law Enforcement Training Center (FLETC) develop a training program to improve the reporting, investigation, and prosecution of hate crimes. The next year, Project staffers wrote and began teaching courses that are a permanent part of FLETC's hate/bias crime training. In the early twenty-first century, Project staffers offer seminars and other training on hate groups, terrorism and related matters to law enforcement agencies around the country. In 2001 the Project began offering an online hate crimes training program for law enforcement officers that is co-sponsored by California State University at San Bernadino.

Probably the single best measure of the efficacy of the Intelligence Project is the virulent hatred directed against its staffers by members of the radical right. The SPLC has seen repeated rallies and demonstrations near its headquarters by neo-Nazis, Klansmen, and a variety of other white supremacists. In 1983 the SPLC's offices were burned by enraged Klansmen, forcing a move to a new building but raising the profile of the organization. In addition, over the decades, more than twenty people have been sent to prison in connection with plots against the SPLC.

SEE ALSO *Hate Crimes; Ku Klux Klan; National Alliance; Neo-Nazis; Southern Poverty Law Center; White Citizens' Council and the Council of Conservative Citizens.*

BIBLIOGRAPHY

Dees, Morris. 1991. *A Season for Justice: The Life and Times of Civil Rights Lawyer Morris Dees.* New York: Scribner.

Dees, Morris, with Steve Feiffer. 1993. *Hate on Trial: The Case against America's Most Dangerous Neo-Nazi.* New York: Villard.

Dees, Morris, and Ellen Bowden. 1995. "Courtroom Victories: Taking Hate Groups to Court." *Trial* 31 (2): 20–29.

Dees, Morris, with James Corcoran. 1997. *Gathering Storm: America's Militia Threat.* New York: Harper Perennial.

Gannon, Julie. 1997. "'We Can't Afford Not to Fight': Morris Dees Takes Bigotry to Court." *Trial* 33 (1): 18–24.

Intelligence Project. Available from http://www.splcenter.org/.

Intelligence Report. Montgomery, AL: Southern Poverty Law Center. Available from http://www.intelligencereport.org.

Stanton, Bill. 1991. *Klanwatch: Bringing the Ku Klux Klan to Justice*. New York: Grove Press.

Mark Potok
Heidi L. Beirich

INTERNALIZED RACIALISM

Racism is among the most written about forms of oppression that occur at the individual, institutional, and cultural levels. While levels of racism are studied by social scientists across disciplines, psychologists typically focus on the origins, manifestations, and impact of racism at the individual level. Racism is predicated on the belief that certain human groups, called races, are inferior, while other human groups are superior. Internalized racialism is of particular interest to mental health professionals because it involves beliefs about race that are usually uncritically accepted and subsequently become internalized.

Internalized racialism can broadly be defined as the process by which ethnic minorities internalize white stereotypes about ethnic minorities. In the scientific literature the term has been used primarily with blacks or African Americans, but in theory, if not practice, it can be applied to any racial or ethnic minority. The term has been used primarily with blacks or African Americans because they seem to be the most racialized of all ethnic groups in the United States.

Racist Memorabilia. *These items present some of the ethnic stereotypes of African Americans. As people of African descent begin to internalize these stereotypes, internalized racism develops.* AP IMAGES.

RACIALISM

Unlike *racism* the term *racialism* is harder to define because it is used in different ways by different people. In the psychological literature, racialism has been defined as a way of cognitively organizing perceptions of racial categories so that members of a race are believed to share immutable characteristics that they do not share with members of another race. The immutable traits believed to be shared by all members of a racial group usually include, but are not limited to, physical characteristics such as skin color, hair texture, width of nose, size of lips, shape of chin, the shape and size of the buttocks, and, for men, the size of their genitalia. Behavioral traits often associated with a particular race include law abidingness, sexual activity and reproduction, and athleticism. Cognitive processes are alleged to include intelligence and personality traits regarding temperament.

Racialism is related to the philosophical idea of essentialism, whereby things that look alike are believed to share similar properties. In the white separatist literature, racialism is usually described as involving a strong interest in racial matters, based on the premise that there are innate and immutable traits that define the nature of every racial group. This interest in racial matters can sometimes translate into advocating for or enacting racial policy, such as racial segregation. Consequently, people who are proponents of racialism, or racialists, do not see themselves as racists because they do not appear to advocate or promote the idea that racial groups are superior or inferior.

Social scientists and other social commentators often doubt the truthfulness of this claim, and they dispute the notion that one can believe in immutable racial traits without assigning value, and ultimately a hierarchy, to those traits. Proponents of racialism do not see themselves as promoting racism because they do not support behaviors that harm certain racial groups. Instead, they promote the idea that there should be laws recognizing that there are racial differences. In theory, racialism is usually a precursor to or a necessary condition for racism. It has been argued that racialism is not inherently problematic. Instead, in this view, it is only problematic when the beliefs lead to discriminatory and harmful behavior. In reality, there are instances when claims of racialism are synonymous with racism and other instances when racialism is truly distinct from racism. Because of white racial oppression, the expression of racialism by ethnic minorities may be more about promoting racial pride than promoting racial separatism.

STEREOTYPES

The term *stereotype* refers to negative or positive beliefs about the characteristics of a group of people. Like racialism, it has been argued that stereotypes are not necessarily problematic unless they influence the behavior of a member of one racial group toward a member of another racial group. Racialism is largely responsible for racial stereotypes. It has been found that the stereotypes applied to blacks are generally more negative than the stereotypes applied to other racial or ethnic groups. The negative stereotypes of blacks include the beliefs that blacks are more prone to violence and criminal behavior, and that they are lazy, low in intelligence, and sexually promiscuous. The so-called positive stereotypes of blacks include the beliefs that they are athletic, naturally good dancers, and that black men have large genitalia. The notion of positive stereotypes is somewhat controversial, in that members of groups to whom positive stereotypes have been attributed often believe that there are hidden harmful effects of positive stereotypes (e.g., the pressure on Asian-American students to excel academically because of the model minority stereotype). Racial stereotypes play an important role in influencing prejudiced behavior in the form of discrimination and racism.

INTERNALIZED RACISM

Internalized racism is the degree to which members of ethnic and racial minority groups agree with negative racist stereotypes attributed to their racial or ethnic minority groups, and consequently act on these beliefs. Examples of internalized racism may include: (1) Believing that members of one's racial or ethnic minority group are stupid, lazy, and inferior; (2) aggressive or violent behavior against members of one's racial or ethnic minority group because of the low regard or hatred one holds toward the group; (3) having low self-esteem associated with one's racial or ethnic group membership; (4) placing a higher value on members of one's racial or ethnic minority group who physically or phenotypically appear more white in their features (e.g., lighter skin, straight hair) while denigrating those who have darker skin or appear less white in their features; and (5) holding in higher regard members of one's racial or ethnic minority group who adopt the values or behaviors of the white majority because of the belief that the values and behaviors of one's racial or ethnic minority group are inferior. Internalized racism is generally believed to be negatively related to mental health and physical health. For example, psychologists examining black identity have found that low regard for being black is related to negative mental health outcomes. Internalized racism can take the form of Asians having plastic surgery to "fix" their eyelids to look more like the white majority, or of blacks bleaching their skin to be lighter. It can also involve dating individuals outside of one's racial or ethnic minority group because of the low regard one has toward members of one's own racial group.

INTERNALIZED RACIALISM

Internalized racialism is the degree to which members of ethnic and racial minority groups believe that racial groups have innate and immutable characteristics, and consequently act on these beliefs. This racialist thinking usually involves identifying with any negative or positive stereotype attributed to one's racial group. Internalized racialism differs from internalized racism in one important way. Unlike internalized racism, internalized racialism includes agreeing with so-called positive stereotypes attributed to one's racial group. The notion of positive stereotypes, as mentioned earlier, can be controversial. An African American who believes that blacks are naturally faster runners than whites and other racial and ethnic groups is experiencing a form of internalized racialism because being a naturally fast runner is a positive stereotype. Similarly, an African American who believes that blacks, on average, are genetically less intelligent or more prone to acts of violence and criminality is also experiencing a type of internalized racialism. Whether it involves agreeing with negative stereotypes (internalized racism), or a combination of negative and positive stereotypes (internalized racialism), individuals who have internalized these stereotypes believe that all individuals are a part of a definable racial group characterized by immutable traits.

RELATIONSHIP TO BLACK RACIAL IDENTITY

A disproportionate amount of academic discussions about internalized racism and internalized racialism focus on black people, specifically on African Americans. This is perhaps because of the legacy of slavery in the United States. The legacy of slavery, segregation, and discrimination has negatively affected the identity and self-conception of many African Americans. Consequently, many psychologists have focused on facilitating a positive black racial identity for African Americans. The process of constructing a positive black racial identity has been found to be related to racialist beliefs about black athleticism, black mental capabilities, and black sexuality.

SEE ALSO *Cultural Racism; Mental Health and Racism; Stereotype Threat and Racial Stigma.*

BIBLIOGRAPHY

Cokley, Kevin. 2002. "Testing Cross's Revised Racial Identity Model: An Examination of the Relationship between Racial Identity and Internalized Racialism." *Journal of Counseling Psychology* 49: 476–483

Devine, Patricia G. 1989. "Stereotypes and Prejudice: Their Automatic and Controlled Components." *Journal of Personality and Social Psychology* 56: 5–18.

Jones, James M. 1997. *Prejudice and Racism,* 2nd ed. New York: McGraw-Hill.

Taylor, Jerome, and Carolyn Grundy. 1996. "Measuring Black Internalization of White Stereotypes about African Americans: The Nadanolitization Scale." In *Handbook of Tests and Measurements of Black Populations,* Vol. 2, edited by Reginald. L. Jones, 217–221. Hampton, VA: Cobb and Henry.

Kevin O. Cokley

INTERRACIAL MARRIAGE

SEE *Black-White Intermarriage.*

IQ AND TESTING

This composite entry will cover:

OVERVIEW
Peter H. Knapp

ORIGIN AND DEVELOPMENT
Leon J. Kamin

CULTURE, EDUCATION, AND IQ SCORES
Mark Nathan Cohen

CRITIQUES
Wendy M. Williams
Susan M. Barnett
Jeffrey M. Valla

OVERVIEW

The place of racial groups in society has historically been determined by a variety of structures of segregation, inequality, and domination. However, as George Frederickson notes in *Racism: A Short History* (2002), conceptions of "scientific racism" that rest on ideas of innate differences in intelligence are distinctively modern. The conception of intelligence as a fixed, unitary, biological capacity was a product of the nineteenth century. Its application to the relationships between Europeans and people of color is the product of a particular historical and intellectual conjuncture.

SCIENTIFIC RACISM AND MEASURES OF INTELLIGENCE

Prior to the nineteenth century, invidious ranking of races, individuals, or groups on scales of beauty, ability, virtue, and level of civilization, did not focus on intelligence. The rise of science led to the increase of scientific rationales for race differences during the nineteenth century, based largely on the pseudoscientific disciplines of anthropometry and the use of brain size as an index of intelligence. In the early twentieth century, particularly after World War I, the increased importance of education led to the growth of intelligence tests and other timed paper and pencil tests, such as IQ tests widely interpreted as measures of "intelligence" to assign persons in education or jobs.

In the late nineteenth century, the British biologist Francis Galton (1822–1911) conceived of intelligence as being closely related to sensory discrimination (e.g., sight, hearing, touch, and weight). James McKean Cattell imported Francis Galton's idea to the United States, and he devised tests of sensory discrimination, reaction time, and memory. The scores on these tests, however, proved unrelated to each other and to complex intellectual performance. The French psychologist Alfred Binet (1857–1911), meanwhile, conceived of intellectual development as the cumulative mastery of increasingly difficult tasks of judgment, and he conceived of intelligence as the ratio of mental age (number of tasks mastered) to chronological age. In the United States, researchers used Binet's conceptions to develop standardized measures of IQ. However, early tests derived from Binet had to be administered one-on-one in a nontimed setting, and they were scored by examiner judgment.

In the early twentieth century, demands by the military for rapid testing of large numbers of people led to the development of the test format that has become familiar: paper and pencil questions that can be objectively scored, such as the Army Alpha test and the Wechsler test. Similar measures of academic achievement were developed, such as the SAT (called the Scholastic Achievement Test prior to 1941, then the Scholastic Aptitude Test, then the Scholastic Assessment Test, and then referred to by its initials) and the AFQT (Armed Forces Qualifications Test), and these were widely interpreted as measures of ability. However, they were based upon the presumption that those taking the test had been exposed to equivalent environments. In countries where students were exposed to the same curriculum, potential could be measured as mastery of the material in that curriculum, but where different students were exposed to different curricula, measures of ability came to focus on scores on such timed tests.

CONCEPTIONS OF RACIAL DIFFERENCE PRIOR TO THE NINETEENTH CENTURY

The relationship between Europeans and people of color has been based on many different conceptions of difference. Religious conceptions of difference dominated the relations of Europeans with Muslims and with a ghettoized Jewish population through most of the late medieval and early modern period. Ethnic and linguistic groups within Europe, such as the Celtic, Saxon, and Norman populations of Britain, were sometimes conceived of as "races." However, it was only after European colonialism superimposed European elites upon large populations of color that racism emerged in recognizable modern forms. In North America, the relations of Europeans with each other, with Native Americans, with imported African slaves, and with Asians formed a complex system. The compact between northern mercantile elites and southern plantation holders, based on the recognition of slavery, influenced the race relations between Europeans and peoples of color such as Chinese and Native Americans. All the other group relations were polarized around the color line generated by slavery. With the rise of abolitionist sentiment in the nineteenth century, there was a rise in theories of scientific racism, which was used to legitimize those structures.

RELIGIOUS AND BIOLOGICAL CONCEPTIONS OF RACE DIFFERENCE IN THE NINETEENTH CENTURY

In *The Mismeasure of Man* (1996), the paleontologist and evolutionary biologist Stephen J. Gould examines three kinds of purportedly scientific demonstration of innate superiority from the nineteenth century, all based on physical measures. Theories of polygenism, defended by creationist biologists such as Louis Agassiz (1807–1873), argued for the separate biological origin of distinct races of humankind. Theories of the atavism of criminals, defended by Cesare Lombroso (1835–1909), argued that different moral and social characteristics are associated with distinct body types. The craniology of theorists such as Paul Broca (1824–1990) argued that Europeans have larger brains, and that they therefore have a natural superiority to non-Europeans. Broca made similar arguments about men in comparison to women, and about the upper classes in comparison to the lower classes. In each case, it became evident that the bodies of evidence, which appeared incontrovertible at the time, resulted from a tissue of arbitrary methodological choices and special pleadings, all based on assumptions about group superiority.

The assumption that physical traits, such as brain size, skull shape, or ratio of arm length to height, had some relationship to development and to some unitary concept of intelligence was never demonstrated and is now recognized as mistaken. For example, brain size is mainly a function of body size, and the data allegedly establishing differences between groups were often a product of implicit assumptions stemming from group prejudice.

Within early nineteenth-century biology, attempts to secure the independence of biology from religion were often mixed with powerful ideological and emotional commitments to racism. For example, Gould showed that the published versions of Agassiz's letters were edited by his wife in order to obscure the transparent racism that was one of the main sources of his polygenism. The hundreds of skull-volume measurements made by Samuel George Morton were regarded by Agassiz as decisive evidence that Europeans had larger skulls, and therefore larger brains, and that they were consequently more advanced than Africans, Asians, or Native Americans. Gould shows that the Morton findings resulted from biased choices and decisions.

The idea that physical, inherited differences between persons and groups allow them to be ranked as superior or inferior was an essential component of the social Darwinist though that came to dominate political and social thought in the late nineteenth century, particularly in Britain and the United States. The superiority of men over women, of whites over people of color, of Europeans over non-Europeans, and of the upper classes over the poor were unquestioned assumptions of much of that thought. This superiority was often conceived in terms of morals, aesthetics, or emotional and physical energy, rather than in terms of intelligence. For example, the explicit distaste that Agassiz felt for nonwhites was expressed primarily in terms of qualities such as beauty, courage, and honesty, and was only secondarily attached to interpretations of alleged quantitative mean differences between "races," such as cranial capacity.

In the same way, the arguments used by Lombroso and his school to ascribe criminality to physical indicators of atavism, or to a more "primitive" type, illustrated an essential tendency of social Darwinist thought. Lombroso selected examples that attempted to prove that people with physical traits that he characterized as "atavistic stigmata," such as a flattened nose, prominent teeth, or joined eyebrows, were more likely to engage in criminal behavior. When he selected cases for illustration, there were always an indefinitely large number of characteristics that could be distinguished, and his choice of measures was often driven by the visceral reactions and conceptions that Gould has called "the apishness of undesirables" (Gould 1996, p. 142).

I. Q. Test
KEEP 'EM FLYING!
PHOTO COPYRIGHT BY F. M. KIRKPATRICK
Reception Center, Fort Benjamin Harrison, Indiana
2B417-N

Soldiers Take an IQ Test. *IQ tests were administered to Army draftees during World Wars I and II. The earliest administrators of the test claimed that racial differences in average IQ scores was evidence of genetic superiority and inferiority.* © LAKE COUNTY MUSEUM/CORBIS.

The choice of measures were in fact driven by preordained conclusions, illustrated by the arguments of Broca, who unintentionally selected the aspects and interpretations of the data in order to reach the conclusion that males, Europeans, the upper class, and whites were superior. The notion that brain size is proportional to some unitary quality of intelligence was a deceptively simple idea. In practice, the interpretation of skull size depended upon an indefinitely large number of decisions about measurement. The conclusions were driven by assumptions about such factors as the deterioration of different cadavers or differences in body size resulting from gender and nutrition. Gould notes that an analysis of Broca's arguments reveals a circle proceeding from the preordained conclusion (his certainty that men, whites, Europeans, and the upper class are more intelligent and must have larger brains) to assumptions about choices that would guarantee that conclusion. The presumption that there is some unitary biological capacity that could be called intelligence, and that it could be measured by some external trait such as brain size, drove a series of choices, assumptions, interpretations, and methodological decisions that generated bodies of data purporting to demonstrate the original presumption.

TWENTIETH CENTURY CONFLICTS CONCERNING INTELLIGENCE TESTS

During the nineteenth century, attempts to prove the superiority of privileged groups by physical measurements formed a component of the broad stream of social Darwinism. The idea that social progress results from competition between groups and individuals of different abilities, leading to survival of the fittest, took different forms. Conceptions of individual competition, directed against the status pretensions of the upper class, coexisted with conceptions of group competition, and these conceptions were connected to nativist and racist movements that were reacting to the waves of immigration to the United States and to the migration of African Americans from the American South to northern cities.

During the twentieth century, life chances came increasingly to depend upon educational credentials, and the development of paper-and-pencil measures of alleged ability, which were used to allocate people both within education and in businesses and the military, forced debates about race, class, gender, and ethnicity to focus upon the interpretation of those scores. Nicholas Lemann, in *The Big Test* (1999), analyzed the fact that in the absence of a common school curriculum in different communities, it was not possible to test a mastery of that curriculum in any depth. This led to an increased use of tests such as the ASQT and the SAT consisting of timed multiple choice answers to questions dealing with many bits of largely academic information.

In the 1970s the Harvard psychologist Richard Herrnstein argued that social class was and should be largely a function of intelligence, and in the 1990s Herrnstein and Charles Murray's controversial book *The Bell Curve* extended that argument to the view that poverty, low income, welfare dependency, unemployment, divorce, illegitimate pregnancy, crime, and a lack of "middle-class values" were all in large part produced by a lack of intelligence, and that race differences in such conditions were largely explained by race differences in IQ. This analysis was widely criticized. For example, Peter Knapp and his colleagues in *The Assault on Equality* found that virtually all of the alleged effects of IQ disappear if it is measured contemporaneously with social class.

Gould has noted that assumptions of unitary intelligence, which is greater among privileged groups, have invariably served as justifications of social inequality, and that Charles Darwin had recognized the central issue in his comment, "If the misery of our poor be caused not by the laws of nature, but by our institutions, great is our sin" (Gould 1996, p. 424). The assumptions and presumptions of the natural superiority of privileged groups are relatively pervasive, and like the spores of a fungus or like crab grass, they proliferate under favorable conditions. Specifically, the favorable conditions for the proliferation of theories concerning inherited group differences of ability have been political conflicts over group privilege and opportunity. There have been three main periods of recrudescence and increased popularity of such arguments during the twentieth century: the first was in response to the waves of immigration and migration at the beginning of the century; the second was in response to the civil rights movement in the middle of the century; and the third was in response to movements to cut back social policies at the end of the twentieth century.

BIBLIOGRAPHY

Frederickson, George M. 2002. *Racism: A Short History.* Princeton, NJ: Princeton University Press.

Gould, Stephen J. 1996. *The Mismeasure of Man*, 2nd ed. New York: W.W. Norton.

Herrnstein, Richard J., and Charles Murray. 1994. *The Bell Curve: Intelligence and Class Structure in American Life.* New York: The Free Press.

Knapp, Peter H., Jane C. Kronick, R. William Marks, and Miriam G. Vosburgh. 1996. *The Assault on Equality.* Westport, CT: Praeger.

Lemann, Nicholas. 1999. *The Big Test: The Secret History of the American Meritocracy.* New York: Farrar, Straus & Giroux.

Peter H. Knapp

ORIGIN AND DEVELOPMENT

The first intelligence test was devised by French psychologist Alfred Binet (1857–1911) in Paris in 1905. The test, designed for schoolchildren, assessed both the child's fund of acquired knowledge and academic skills. The child's performance was compared to the typical performance of children of various ages. If children did as well as other children of the same age, they were labeled "normal." If children did as well as older children, they were "bright." If the child could only do as well as younger children, Binet concluded that their intelligence was not developing properly and they should receive remedial education. Binet prescribed courses of "mental orthopedics" for those who did poorly on his test. The test was thus to be used as a diagnostic instrument, indicating a possible need for corrective treatment. Binet did not regard the test as measuring some fixed, unchangeable capacity, however, and he railed against the "brutal pessimism" of those who might think otherwise.

Within a decade of Binet's original work, adaptations of his test, including some designed for use with adults, were in use in the United States. The pioneers of the American mental testing movement (Henry Goddard [1866–1957], Lewis Terman [1877–1956], and Robert Yerkes [1876–1956]) all asserted that intelligence tests did measure a fixed, unchangeable capacity, largely determined by an individual's heredity. Familial resemblance in IQ scores was claimed to be evidence of the role of heredity. In addition, racial differences in average IQ were erroneously seized upon as evidence of genetic superiority and inferiority.

In 1912 Henry Goddard administered supplemented Binet tests to European immigrants arriving at Ellis Island in New York harbor. He reported that 83 percent of Jews, 80 percent of Hungarians, 79 percent of Italians, and 87 percent of Russians were "feeble-minded." Lewis Terman, who introduced the Stanford-Binet test to the United States, wrote that IQs in the 70–80 range, indicating borderline mental deficiency, were "very common among Spanish-Indian and Mexican families of the Southwest and also among negroes. Their dullness seems to be racial.... The writer predicts that... there will be discovered enormously significant racial differences which cannot be wiped out" (1916, pp. 91–92).

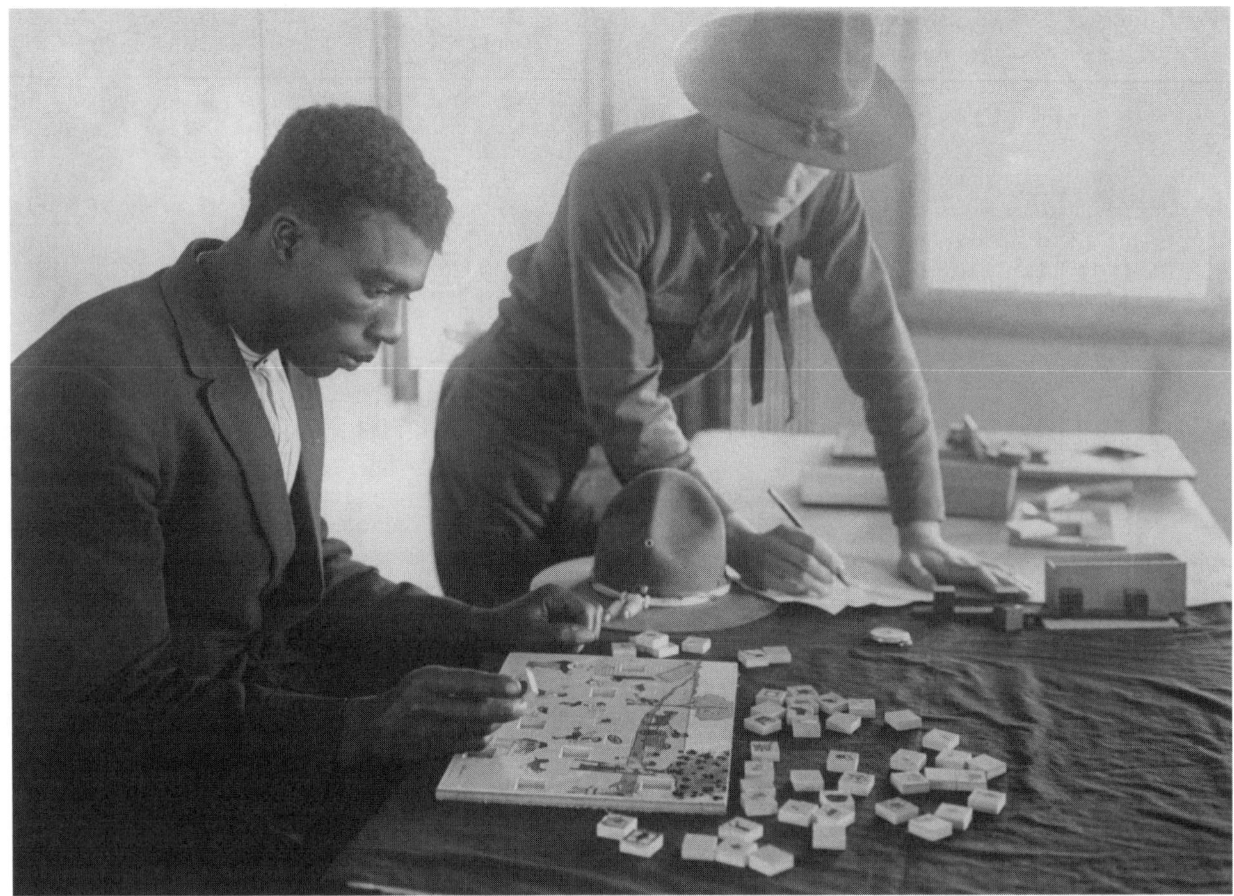

African American Army Recruit Takes IQ Test, 1918. *After World War I, the National Academy of Sciences published an analysis of IQ tests administered to army recruits. This was the first large-scale report to find that blacks scored lower on IQ tests than whites.* © BETTMANN/CORBIS.

A claim was soon made that Terman's prediction of racial differences had been verified. Robert Yerkes had been head of a massive program to administer specially developed IQ tests to draftees into the United States Army during World War I. Many of the draftees were foreign-born and either unfamiliar with the English language or illiterate in English. Yerkes and a committee of psychologists devised two "group tests" of intelligence. "Alpha" was a written test that could be administered to large groups. "Beta" was a "nonverbal" test designed for men either unfamiliar with English or illiterate. Instructions for Beta were given in pantomime to groups of soldiers.

After the war, in 1921, the National Academy of Sciences published an analysis, edited by Yerkes, of the data collected during the army's testing program. This was the first large-scale demonstration that American blacks scored lower on IQ tests than whites. Given the stereotypes that prevailed at the time, however, that finding occasioned little surprise. The data with immediate political impact were the IQ scores of foreign-born draftees. The Yerkes report indicated that the immigrants with the highest scores came from England, Scandinavia, and Germany. The lowest scorers were immigrants from Russia, Italy, and Poland, whose average IQs were not perceptibly higher than that of native-born blacks. The Army findings were supported in a 1923 textbook by Rudolf Pintner, who indicated that the median IQ found in six studies of Italian children in America was only 84—as low as the average of American blacks.

In 1923 Carl Brigham published a re-analysis of the Army data, concluding that the tests had demonstrated "a genuine intellectual superiority of the Nordic group" over "Alpine and Mediterranean blood." Yerkes, in a preface to Brigham's book, stressed the relevance of the Army data to "the practical problems of immigration." At the time, a flood of "New Immigration" from the "Alpine and Mediterranean" countries of southern and eastern Europe was replacing the earlier stream of immigrants from English-speaking and "Nordic" countries. Popular support for a new and restrictive immigration law was widespread. The Army data were cited repeatedly in Congressional debates that ended in the passage of a racist immigration law in 1924. The new law imposed "national origin quotas" on future immigration. The design and effect of the quotas was to reduce sharply the proportion of "Alpine and Mediterranean" immigrants.

Forty-five years later, racial differences in average IQ again came to the fore in a political context, but this time the genetically inferior groups were no longer Alpines and Mediterraneans—they were blacks. Arthur Jensen, in an influential and widely publicized review article published in 1969, maintained that efforts at compensatory education were doomed to failure. He argued that children who did poorly in school did so because of their low IQs. Further, IQ was in large measure hereditary, and not very malleable. The gap between blacks and whites in educational achievement, like the gap in average IQs, was said to be largely due to genetic causes. That view was repeated by J. Philippe Rushton and Arthur Jensen (2005), who argued that the underrepresentation of blacks in "socially valued outcomes" was genetically determined, and that policies such as affirmative action should be reconsidered in this light.

To claim that IQ scores are largely hereditary is to denigrate the importance of educational and other environmental influences. Taken to an extreme, Rushton and Jensen have straight-facedly reported that the average IQ of sub-Saharan Africans is 70—meaning that about half of the people in this part of Africa are mentally retarded. The desperate environmental conditions and inferior education to which most Africans have been exposed are ignored as causes of any differential in performance.

The political usage of purported low scores for Africans is clearly illustrated by Richard Lynn and Tatu Vanhanen, who wrote:

> Hitherto theories of economic development have been based on the presumption that the present gaps between rich and poor countries are only temporary and that they are due to various environmental conditions.... Because of the evidence we have assembled for a causal relationship between national IQ's and economic disparities, it has to be accepted that there will inevitably be a continuation of economic inequalities between nations. Intelligence differences between nations will be impossible to eradicate because they have a genetic basis (2002, p. 195).

Lynn and Vanhanen choose to interpret the correlation between IQ scores and ethnic and racial differences as a genetic effect, ignoring the obvious environmental and cultural differences between ethnic and racial groups.

SEE ALSO *Jensen, Arthur.*

BIBLIOGRAPHY

Brigham, Carl C. 1923. *A Study of American Intelligence.* Princeton, NJ: Princeton University Press.

Jensen, Arthur R. 1969. "How Much Can We Boost IQ and Scholastic Achievement?" *Harvard Educational Review* 39: 1–123.

Lynn, Richard, and Tatu Vanhanen. 2002. *IQ and the Wealth of Nations.* Westport, CT: Praeger.

Rushton, J. Philippe, and Arthur R. Jensen. 2005. "Thirty Years of Research on Race Differences in Cognitive Ability." *Psychology, Public Policy, and Law* 11 (2): 235–294.

Terman, Lewis M. 1916. *The Measurement of Intelligence.* Boston: Houghton-Mifflin.

Leon J. Kamin

CULTURE, EDUCATION, AND IQ SCORES

Differences in human behavior are overwhelmingly cultural not biological as anthropologists have understood since at least 1910. Known biological controls of subtle, sophisticated behavior (within the normal range) are trivial. Behavior patterns rarely match the visible biological variations or putative race categories.

Most anthropologists agree that "races" do not exist. People do not come in sharply bounded groups. Skin color, nose shape, lip form, hair color and form, length of limbs, and sickle cell anemia have distributions that do not match that of skin color, or of one another. Color is a graded variable, as are many of the others. The vast majority of the world's people, even those who are not blended, are neither black nor white, but a gradual continuum of shades that cannot be partitioned into sharply defined groups. Most important, genes are so thoroughly mixed among people, and so few correlate with color, that there is very little genetic unity beyond color itself to groups such as black Americans.

Culture is a much more complicated and powerful force than people realize. Culture is not merely composed of superficial things people do (art, music), it is a complex "grammar" that defines and controls every aspect of people's lives, including their actions, thoughts, identities, and self images. It defines appropriate behavior, values, morals, goals, and perceptions of cause and effect. It controls where people focus and what they selectively see and hear out of a stream of information otherwise too complex to comprehend. It controls methods of categorizing, analogies, and logic. It controls how and what people learn, and how they express what they have learned (e.g., medium, style, convention, meaning, and symbolism). It limits the available repertoire of thought and action, making behavior comprehensible and predictable within the group, while also enforcing group identity, and thus defining and separating "us" from of "them." One's culture can promote a sense of superiority over others, inculcating patterns, perceptions, and ethnocentrism, a kind of patriotism, through some form of both formal and informal learning of shared cultural perceptions, whether they are accurate or not.

Cultures, like languages, are arbitrary designs. Any viable culture fulfills basic human needs but they do it in different styles. Any child can learn any culture in which it is raised; but learning a new culture becomes more difficult with age. Adults are prisoners of their culture because each culture limits people's ability to understand others. Most people are not aware that there are other cultures, nor do they perceive what exists outside the blinders imposed by their own. Because fair-minded people rarely comprehend the power of cultural differences, they are easy prey for racist assumptions.

Intelligence quotient (IQ) tests, once designed to help individuals, have evolved to often act as cultural mechanisms to define an elite and to denigrate others. They purport to demonstrate the inherent abilities of certain individuals, in the process defending class, ethnic, and gender discrimination, segregation, and exclusion. For example, IQ tests can imply, erroneously, that blacks are inferior and that women lack essential abilities. If differences in IQ are assumed to be genetic and unchangeable, then privilege carries no guilt and no obligation to invest in closing the gap. It is thus a kind of "affirmative action" for the already advantaged.

IQ is defined as one's position along a distribution of scores earned by taking various tests. The average (i.e., white middle-class) score is arbitrarily defined as 100. Scores range from below 50 (unintelligent) to 150 or more (intelligent). Black Americans score a mean of about 90. The test data can be used as one wishes, particularly if one can choose the form of the test, and manipulate and interpret the results. Some interpreters of some tests have estimated the mean IQ of sub-Saharan Africans at 70 (implying largely dysfunctional individuals and societies, and, incidentally, a figure once applied to Ashkenazi Jews). This is an extreme manipulation of the interpretation of poor test choices.

COMMON ASSUMPTIONS ABOUT IQ

The common discriminatory use of the tests demands a chain of assumptions. If any assumption is wrong, the chain breaks, regardless of the validity of the other assumptions. In fact, it shall be seen that all the links break. Nine such assumptions will be discussed here.

The first of these assumptions is that genes significantly affect or control differences in intelligence among individuals and groups. There is in fact no known causal connection, and only one minor correlation between any gene (for an insulin-like growth factor) and intelligence within the normal range. Correlation does not prove cause because it may be indirect. For example, a gene may be shared by members of an ethnic group (e.g., Ashkenazi Jews), and members of this group may also, coincidentally, share a cultural commitment to education. Likewise, a particular gene may contribute to health, and only indirectly to higher IQ.

Estimates of genetic determination of IQ range from 40 to 80 percent. However, the power of genes is always context-specific and cannot be generalized, particularly not from individuals studied for group differences. Environmental and genetic factors are reciprocal variables. That is, the larger the environmental differences, the smaller the genetic factor appears. High concordance between identical twins reared separately partly reflects the fact that they are rarely reared in very different circumstances. If differences in their environments were greater, genetic concordance would be much less. If one twin were damaged, starved, malnourished, or raised amid deprivation (severe environmental differences), concordance would certainly be reduced, perhaps almost to zero. So marked differences in intelligence need not imply genetic differences at all. Environmental differences could account for all measurable differences in IQ between individuals or groups.

Moreover, IQs are increasing everywhere much faster than genes evolve (the widely recognized Flynn effect). The enormous increase in the IQs of Ashkenazi Jews through the late twentieth century is particularly striking. Such rapid changes are either cultural or a result of changes in the tests themselves.

A second assumption is that IQ tests actually measure innate, not learned, mental abilities that are important to the group. Even in Western society, success is obviously based on a large number of qualities that may have little to do with the "intelligence" measured on the tests.

A third assumption holds that intelligence is either one thing (a compendium of test scores referred to as "g") or a small number of things (multiple intelligences), and that it has been successfully defined by Euro-American scholars and is rankable on linear scales. However, most cultures informally evaluate individuals for performance (not potential) in a wide range of skills, without assuming that the skills correlate with one another or that one person is best over all. The fact that the core of "g," or general intelligence as measured on written tests, is vocabulary, which is obviously largely learned rather than genetic, further undermines the idea that intelligence is significant controlled by genes.

The fourth assumption is that intelligence combines the same attributes in all cultures. But culture-bound IQ tests do not measure facility in other languages, leadership potential, or social or organizational skills, although all are important in most other cultures.

It is also assumed that individuals who are tested have equal exposure to, and equal focus on, the content of the culture that constructs the tests and to the language in which the tests are given. Recent tests have eliminated some egregiously biased items (e.g., tennis courts), but poor inner-city children may have limited exposure to some obvious items. They may have never seen cows, fields, trees, free-standing houses, the horizon, many simple child's toys, and other items suburban children take for granted. Many questions on IQ tests also involve culture-biased visual stimuli, conventions, perceptions, and thought patterns. Cultural divides are far deeper than they first appear, but Americans, who wear cultural blinders, do not see them. IQ tests used across cultural boundaries are meaningless, but they still generate numbers.

The sixth assumption is that necessary skills can be measured by literate tests, even though human abilities (if genetic) obviously evolved in a nonliterate world.

Assumption number seven is that quick answers on simple questions, solved by isolated individuals, indicate "intelligence." Even in American culture, most significant problems are neither simple nor solved in isolation. Many cultures consider rapid, simple answers a sign of simple minds, and cooperative problem solving is often preferred.

The eighth assumption is that the biological conditions of all test takers are the same. But illness or malnutrition in the present, in childhood, or in utero are known to affect performance and are clearly related to class or "race."

The ninth assumption is that people taking a particular test are all equally motivated. Differences in motivation are obviously related to people's perception of the testing culture, their expectations of success, and their interpretation of the environment and process of testing. Oppressed classes may actually resist success on the tests (and pressure others to resist) as a mark of cultural solidarity and resistance to the culture that discriminates against them. Poor scores are common to minorities resisting involuntary inclusion in any society, regardless of their genes.

Most of the world's people take IQ tests across cultural boundaries and under inappropriate conditions. Black Americans are a culturally defined group, not a biological one, and their IQ scores must result from their common environment. Women, too, are culturally defined, despite a core of biological differences with men, and some of the same principles apply.

SEE ALSO *Scientific Racism, History of.*

BIBLIOGRAPHY

Alland, Alexander, Jr. 2002. *Race in Mind: Race, IQ, and Other Racisms*. New York: Palgrave.

Cohen, Mark Nathan. 1998. "Culture Not Race Explains Human Diversity." *Chronicle of Higher Education,* April 17, pp. B3–5.

———. 1998. *Culture of Intolerance: Chauvinism, Class, and Racism in the United States*. New Haven, CT: Yale University Press.

Devlin, Bernie, Stephen E. Feinberg, Daniel P. Resnick, and Kathryn Roeder, eds. 1997. *Intelligence, Genes, and Success: Scientists Respond to The Bell Curve*. New York: Springer-Verlag.

Fish, Jefferson, ed. 2002. *Race and Intelligence: Separating Science from Myth*. Mahwah, NJ: Lawrence Erlbaum.

Herrnstein, Richard J., and Charles Murray. 1994. *The Bell Curve: Intelligence and Class Structure in American Life*. New York: The Free Press.

Jensen, Arthur. 1969. "How Much Can We Boost IQ and Scholastic Achievement?" *Harvard Educational Review* 39: 1–123.

Rushton, J. Philippe. 1995. *Race, Evolution, and Behavior, a Life History Perspective*. New Brunswick, NJ: Transaction Publishers.

Sarich, Vincent, and Frank Miele. 2004. *Race, the Reality of Human Differences*. Cambridge, MA: Westview Press.

Mark Nathan Cohen

CRITIQUES

A variety of critiques have been offered by eminent scholars regarding the use of IQ tests to draw conclusions about racial/ethnic (particularly black-white) group differences. Before detailing these critiques, however, it is necessary to consider the nature of the argument about IQ and race to which these rebuttals respond. Briefly, the main argument is that racial differences in IQ equate to innate racial differences in intelligence. Proponents of this position include Arthur Jensen, J. Philippe Rushton, Richard Herrnstein, Charles Murray, and Richard Lynn. Their position can be summarized as follows: (1) The black-white IQ gap is generally about 15 points on a standard IQ test (one standard deviation), (2) the IQ tests used are equally fair and valid measures of actual intellectual ability in both blacks and whites, (3) differences in IQ are largely genetic in origin, and (4) the 15-point gap cannot be explained by environmental factors, such as whites' greater access to high-quality schooling, nutrition, health care, and overall economic advantage.

This notion of a genetic or inherent inferiority of blacks is then extended to explain the less optimal living conditions of blacks, within individual countries as well as across countries, with black communities and entire African nations being seen as economically lacking due to the

Louis Agassiz, 1861. *Creationist biologists such as Louis Agassiz argued for the separate biological origin of distinct races of humankind.* THE LIBRARY OF CONGRESS.

inherent intellectual deficiencies of their citizens. Another way to think of this argument is within the "nature-nurture" paradigm in science. The proponents of innate differences argue that the observed differences are due to genes or nature, whereas the opponents of this view argue that observed differences are a result of environmental deprivation, poverty, and racism. What follows is a selection of rebuttals to the "innate differences in intelligence" viewpoint, (this is not an exhaustive list, nor does it address the fundamental question of whether IQ tests measure true "intelligence," whatever that may be).

CULTURAL BIAS

Anyone who has taken an IQ test (or related tests, such as the SAT or the GRE) recognizes that the types of questions on the test may be more familiar to some people than to others. Questions from the Wechsler Intelligence Scale for Children, 3rd ed. (WISC-III) referring to, for example, "advantages of getting news from a newspaper rather than from a television news program" (Wechsler, p. 138), "why it is important for cars to have license plates" (Wechsler, p. 137), "why you should turn off lights when no one is using them" (Wechsler, p. 134), "what is an umbrella?" (Wechsler, p 108), and "in what way are a telephone and a radio alike?" (Wechsler, p. 78), would not be equally difficult, even when translated, for individuals from more and less developed countries, or even for people coming from upper-middle-class, working-class, or impoverished families. To be culturally fair, people must be tested using questions that tap knowledge to which the people have been equally exposed—and which is equally valued in the cultures of these people. Unless test equivalence is assured, comparisons across people and groups of people with differing backgrounds can be meaningless.

In response to the above argument, it has been suggested that assessments of IQ that are not as overtly culturally and linguistically bound as the WISC-III, should be used. An example of a potentially more culturally fair test is called the Raven Progressive Matrices, which relies on complex geometric shapes and pictures to assess IQ. However, the cultural neutrality of these tests may be illusory. In a review of potential environmental causes for the worldwide systematic increase in IQs for all developed nations, Wendy Williams noted in 1998 that the contemporary visual world offers many children mazes and games on the backs of cereal boxes and on placemats at fast food restaurants, in addition to their omnipresence on the computer. For children not exposed to such stimuli, the Raven tests may be a much less familiar—and thus more difficult—experience. In fact, a 1998 review of the literature by Nicholas Mackintosh noted that there is "no reason to suppose that the ability to solve arbitrary abstract problems, such as those found in Raven's tests, is any less a learnt skill than the ability to do mental arithmetic or answer questions about the meanings of words" (Mackintosh 1998, p. 171). Mackintosh cites a study (Sharma 1971) that showed that children's scores on Raven's Matrices varied as a function of how long they had been resident in Britain: Those still resident in India and those from the same district in India living in Britain for less than two years scored in the low 80s, while those originally from the same district who had been resident in Britain for more than six years scored more than 100 (Mackintosh 1998, pp. 171–172). Thus, the Ravens, like language-based IQ tests, may suffer from cultural bias.

An interesting parallel to the African-American situation is the historical experience of Caucasian immigrants to the United States. Richard Lynn's data from 1978 show that every ethnic group, when tested upon entrance to the United States, scored relatively poorly—approximately one standard deviation below the mean. This is true for immigrants from India, Yugoslavia, Greece, Spain, eastern Europe, southern Europe, Portugal, Iran, and Iraq. Subsequent generations of their offspring, however, show an increase in test scores, to the point where they equal or exceed the national average of the host country. In short, these immigrants came in with mean IQs of 85, while their children and their children's children have mean IQs of 103 (for people from India, for example). Clearly, this increase in scores is due to the effects of environmental factors (including cultural change and test familiarity) and not genetic factors.

On a broader note, the very concept of intelligence varies from place to place. For people from a culture that values scoring high on IQ tests, taking such a test is a different matter than it is for people who do not value high test scores. Robert Sternberg and colleagues summed up a discussion of the cross-cultural validity of IQ tests: "Scores from tests used in cultures and sub-cultures other than those for which the tests were specifically created are suspect, and probably of doubtful validity in many if not most cases" (Sternberg, Grigorenko, and Bundy 2001, p. 29).

NATURE AND NURTURE

Studies used to support claims of genetic causation of IQ differences often confound nature and nurture. This is a problem in adoption studies, both cross-race and within-race. Some studies of black and Asian infants reared by white families show intelligence consistent with the child's race rather than the race of the adoptive family, arguably providing support for innate racial differences. But there are problems with designing a perfect experiment using real adopted children. First, it is difficult to ensure that adoptive homes are truly randomly assigned and that the children are representative. For example, are adoption rights enforced at the same time (e.g., at birth or at identical ages) for adoptee-adoptee comparisons? Are the impacts of societal racism on the respective children's upbringing avoided? In such studies, race and environment are often confounded, rendering conclusions unclear.

Similar problems apply to within-race studies of identical twins adopted apart. The observed high correlation of identical twins has been used to argue for genetic causation, but this viewpoint ignores environmental interaction. Much attention has been paid to the extraordinary similarities of identical twins, even those who were separated at birth and meet up as adults, only to learn that they both collect balls of string and jiggle the toilet handle three times (Bouchard, et al. 1990). While these stories are fascinating and clearly reveal that genes are very important, it is essential to remember the dramatic similarity of the environments identical twins are generally raised in, even when they are adopted by separate families. Economic characteristics of these families are often very similar. They live in comparable communities, for example, and share a common culture—even more so than one might expect, because many adoptions are arranged by religious organizations and social workers who seek similar values and attributes across adoptive families. Heredity surely controls part of how intelligent any one person will be, but extrapolation from these studies to explain racial differences in intelligence is problematic.

APPLYING HERITABILITY MEASURES

The "innate differences in intelligence" argument depends on notions of heritability (percentage of variance explained by genes) of IQ and genetic causality. There is no such thing as a universal "heritability of intelligence," only the heritability of intelligence in such and such a population at a particular time. For example, the environmental component of variance is likely to be much greater in a sample where some children attend school and some do not, than it is within a sample where schooling is universal (such as the United States). Heritability must therefore be regarded as "sample specific," varying with population and cohort. Heritability is lower among poor people than wealthy people, for example. Imagine two children, both with innate or genetic gifts for music, growing up in homes with very different economic circumstances. One child is given music lessons and access to musical instruments virtually from the time she can walk; the other child has none of these advantages. The former will thus have the opportunity to develop and display more of her genetically rooted talents, yielding higher heritability.

More generally, the variance of a trait within a group does not predict the variance between that group and another, because the differences in genes and environments within a group do not say anything about the differences in genes and environments between groups. Each measure of heritability applies only to the population from which it came, at a particular time and place.

IQ TEST SCORES AND ENVIRONMENTAL FACTORS

Contrary to the "innate differences" argument, scores on IQ tests have been demonstrated to be affected by environmental factors, such as education, and by environmental changes over time. For example, exposure to schooling increases IQ, so that the more schooling an individual receives, and the higher the quality of this schooling, the higher the person's IQ score will be, on average (Ceci 1991). Schooling has been shown to increase IQ in studies of children tested before versus after school vacations (Jencks et al. 1972), of children leaving school early (Harnquist 1968) and starting school late (Schmidt 1967), of children with birthdays separated by a single day but whose number of years in school differs by a whole year due to school admissions cutoffs (Cahan and Cohen 1989), and so on. Schooling and IQ have also been shown to increase individual income, which further contributes to the cycle of wealth resulting in higher IQs (Ceci and Williams 1997). How does schooling exert these positive effects on IQ? Basic familiarity with the types of questions on IQ tests is one key mechanism. Another is that schools specifically train students in the types of abilities that help a person answer IQ test questions correctly. Wealthy countries and wealthy communities obviously have more money to spend on schooling, and these communities tend more often to be white.

IQ test scores also change over time. IQs have been increasing at a steady rate for the last century (Flynn 1987; 1999; 2000). Because test manufacturers change the norms over time and keep resetting the average score to 100, it took some time before anyone noticed that the number of questions the average person was answering correctly was steadily increasing. The Raven Matrices, show the most dramatic increase across generations. For example, there was a gain of 20 IQ points in thirty years for Dutch men. The significance of this worldwide rise in IQ scores (known as the Flynn Effect) to the "innate differences in intelligence" argument is that it provides clear evidence for the strong impact of environment on IQ test scores. Given the economic conditions that African Americans have experienced, dramatic differences in IQ could thus be possible with economic enrichment. As one example, in 1998 Min-Hsiung Huang and Robert Hauser analyzed scores on a vocabulary subtest of the general social survey, in which the exact same vocabulary words have been used over and over, and found that black adults showed the largest gains in scores over time. This finding argues for the dramatic effects of improving environments, access to better schooling, and other changes that have accompanied blacks' increased economic success. In sum, the Flynn Effect shows that an IQ score is not genetic destiny. Even within a given genotype, there is considerable room for IQs to increase substantially.

As a blue-ribbon panel of experts on intelligence concluded, "Heritability does not imply immutability" (Neisser et al. 1996, p. 86). Even highly heritable traits, such as height, can nevertheless change dramatically due to the environment. For example, the children of Japanese immigrants to the United States have usually been taller than their parents, due to better nutrition. Environment is an omnipresent contributing factor in every situation. For instance, it has been argued that racial IQ differences are due to differences between races in average brain size, and there is indeed a positive correlation between brain size and intelligence. But again, it is not clear whether any such differences are genetic or environmental in origin. It is simply not known if purported racial differences in brain size or IQ would be eradicated by equalization of environments.

RACES ARE NOT VALID BIOLOGICAL UNITS

Finally, the notion that there are "pure gene pools" for blacks versus whites ignores the biological reality that humans are a blended species, and that they are becoming even more so. Attempts to explain IQ differences using blood markers for African versus European ancestry have been unconvincing, revealing only a negligible relationship between IQ and European genes, which is itself potentially attributable to differential treatment of lighter-skinned versus darker-skinned blacks—an environmental effect itself (Nisbett 2005). Some proponents of the "genetic differences in intelligence" argument rely on evidence linking observed "racial characteristics" with underlying genetic differences, suggesting that, if races differ on other aspects such as skin and hair color, it is likely that they would differ on the genes for intelligence. However, genetic differences on one dimension imply nothing about differences on others, particularly when some traits under consideration are caused by individual genes and others are polygenic (i.e., caused by multiple genes—a classic example being intelligence, a broadly polygenic trait). In sum, the picture of how IQ test scores are used to make comparisons between races is often unfocused or muddled, and it suffers from inaccurate and incomplete reasoning on multiple dimensions.

SEE ALSO *Heritability.*

BIBLIOGRAPHY

Bouchard, Thomas J., Jr., et al. 1990. "Sources of Human Psychological Differences: The Minnesota Study of Twins Reared Apart." *Science* 250 (4978): 223–228.

Cahan, Sorel, and Nora Cohen. 1989. "Age versus Schooling Effects on Intelligence Development." *Child-Development* 60 (5): 1239–1249.

Ceci, Stephen J. 1991. "How Much Does Schooling Influence General Intelligence and Its Cognitive Components? A Reassessment of the Evidence." *Developmental Psychology* 27 (5): 703–722.

———, and Wendy M. Williams. 1997. "Schooling, Intelligence, and Income." *American Psychologist* 52 (10): 1051–1058.

Flynn, James R. 1987. "Massive IQ Gains in 14 Nations: What IQ Tests Really Measure." *Psychological Bulletin* 101: 171–191.

———. 1999. "Searching for Justice: The Discovery of IQ Gains Over Time." *American Psychologist* 54: 5–20.

———. 2000. "IQ Gains, WISC Subtests and Fluid G: G Theory and the Relevance of Spearman's Hypothesis to Race." In *The Nature of Intelligence* (Novartis Foundation Symposium 233), edited by Gregory R. Bock, Jamie A. Goode, and Kate Webb, 202–227. Chichester, U.K.: Wiley.

Grieco, Elizabeth M., and Rachel C. Cassidy. 2001. "Overview of Race and Hispanic Origin." In *Census 2000 Briefs*. Washington, DC: U.S. Census Bureau.

Harnquist, Kjell. 1968. "Relative Changes in Intelligence from 13 to 18." *Scandinavian Journal of Psychology* 9 (1): 50–64.

Herrnstein, Richard J., and Charles Murray. 1994. *The Bell Curve: Intelligence and Class Structure in American Life*. New York: Free Press.

Huang, Min-Hsiung, and Robert M. Hauser. 1998. "Trends in Black-White Test-Score Differentials: The WORDSUM Vocabulary Test." In *The Rising Curve: Long Term Gains in IQ and Related Measures*, edited by Ulric Neisser, 303–332. Washington, DC: American Psychological Association.

Jencks, Christopher, et al. 1972. *Inequality: A Reassessment of the Effects of Family and Schooling in America*. New York: Basic Books.

Lynn, Richard 1978. "Ethnic and Racial Differences in Intelligence: International Comparisons." In *Human Variation: The Biopsychology of Age, Race, and Sex*, edited by R. Travis Osborne, Clyde E. Noble, and Nathaniel Weyl. New York: Academic Press.

———, and Tatu Vanhanen. 2002. *IQ and the Wealth of Nations*. Westport, CT: Praeger.

Mackintosh, Nicholas J. 1998. *IQ and Human Intelligence*. Oxford: Oxford University Press.

Neisser, Ulric, et al. 1996. "Intelligence: Knowns and Unknowns." *American Psychologist* 51 (2): 77–101. Available from http://www.michna.com/intelligence.htm.

Nisbett, Richard E. 2005. "Heredity, Environment, and Race Differences in IQ: A Commentary on Rushton and Jensen." 2005. *Psychology, Public Policy, and Law* 11 (2): 302–310.

Plomin, Robert, John C. DeFries, and Gerald E. McClearn. 1980. *Behavioral Genetics: A Primer*. San Francisco, CA: W. H. Freeman.

Renner, Michael J., and Mark R. Rosenzweig. 1987. *Enriched and Impoverished Environments: Effects on Brain and Behavior*. New York: Springer-Verlag.

Rushton, J. Philippe, and Arthur R. Jensen. 2005. "Thirty Years of Research on Race Differences in Cognitive Ability." *Psychology, Public Policy, and Law* 11: 235–294.

Sharma, R. 1971. "The Measured Intelligence of Children from the Indian Subcontinent," Ph.D. diss., University of London (cited in Mackintosh 1998).

Schmidt, W. H. O. 1967. "Socio-Economic Status, Schooling, Intelligence, and Scholastic Progress in a Community in Which Education Is Not Yet Compulsory." *Paedogogica Europa* 2: 275–286.

Sternberg, Robert J., Elena L. Grigorenko, and Donald A. Bundy. 2001. "The Predictive Value of IQ." *Merrill-Palmer Quarterly* 47 (1): 1–41.

Williams, Wendy M. 1998. "Are We Raising Smarter Children Today? School- and Home-Related Influences on IQ." In *The Rising Curve: Long-term Changes in IQ and Related Measures*, edited by Ulric. Neisser. Washington, DC: American Psychological Association Books.

Wechsler, David. 1991. *Manual for the Wechsler Intelligence Scale for Children*, 3rd ed. San Antonio, TX: The Psychological Corporation.

Wendy M. Williams
Susan M. Barnett
Jeffrey M. Valla

IRISH AMERICANS AND WHITENESS

Throughout most of the eighteenth century, Ireland was governed under a series of codes known collectively as the Penal Laws, which regulated every aspect of Irish life and subjected Irish Catholics to a form of oppression that in another context would be labeled "racial." Judicial authorities in Ireland declared, "The law does not suppose any such person to exist as an Irish Roman Catholic?" A dictum whose similarity to the Dred Scott Decision, the 1857 U.S. Supreme Court ruling that denied blacks the rights of citizenship, is impossible to overlook. Indeed, the landlord system made the material conditions of the Irish peasant comparable to those of an American slave. The 1800 Union with Britain ruined Irish agriculture, creating a surplus population of farmers. Unable to find places in domestic industry, Irish agriculture workers were compelled to emigrate.

From 1815 to the end of the Great Irish Famine (1845–1850), between 800,000 and one million Irish went to America, where developing industry created a shortage of wage laborers. These displaced Irish peasants became the unskilled labor force in the free states. When they first began arriving in large numbers, they were, in the words of "Mr. Dooley" (the columnist Finley Peter Dunne), given a shovel and told to start digging up the place as if they owned it. They worked on the rail beds and canals for low wages under dangerous conditions. In the South they were occasionally employed where it did not make sense to risk the life of a slave.

As they arrived in American cities, they were crowded into districts that became centers of crime, vice, and disease, and they commonly found themselves thrown together with free Negroes. Irish and African Americans fought each other and the police, socialized (and occasionally intermarried), and developed a common culture of the lowly. Both groups also suffered the scorn of those better situated. Along with Jim Crow and Jim Dandy, the drunken, belligerent, and foolish Pat and Bridget were stock characters on the early American stage.

The Irish enjoyed one marked advantage over refugees from southern slavery, however: No one was chasing them with dogs. In spite of initial barriers, including

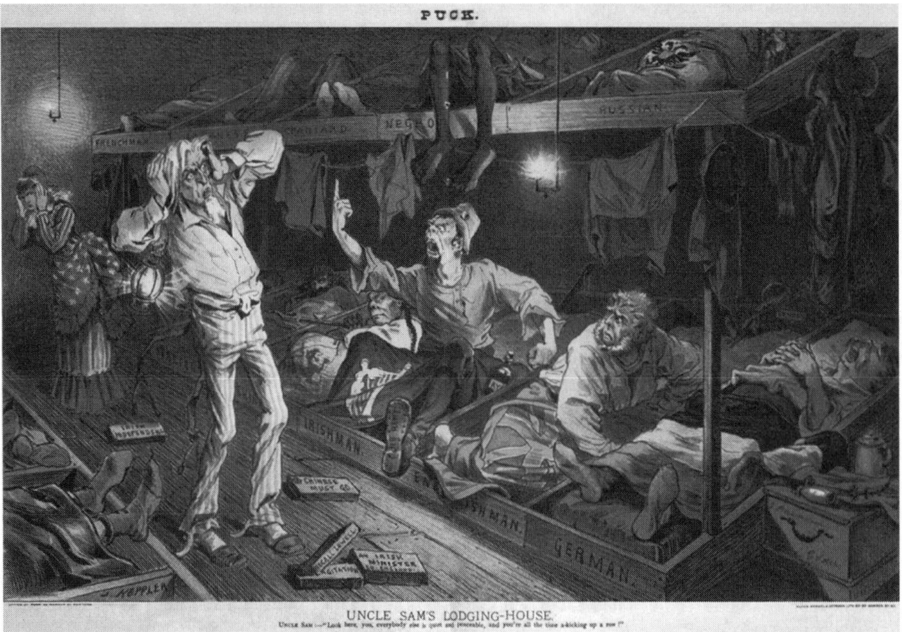

Uncle Sam's Lodging-House. *Irish immigrants to the United States met with considerable discrimination. In this political cartoon from 1882, the Irishman is presented as the troublemaker while immigrants from other nations are peaceful.* THE LIBRARY OF CONGRESS.

nativist hostility, they were able to make the transition from an oppressed race in Ireland to members of an oppressing race in America, that is, they became "white." To the Irish, to become white in America did not mean that they all became rich, or even "middle-class." Nor did it mean that they all became the social equals of the Saltonstalls and van Rensselaers; even the marriage of Grace Kelly to the Prince of Monaco and the election of John F. Kennedy as president did not eliminate all barriers to Irish entry into certain exclusive circles.

To Irish laborers, to become white meant that they could sell themselves piecemeal instead of being sold for life, and later that they could compete for jobs in all spheres instead of being confined to certain work. To Irish entrepreneurs, it meant that they could function outside of a segregated market. For all the Irish, it meant that they were citizens of a democratic republic, with the right to elect and be elected, to be tried by a jury of their peers, to live wherever they could afford, and to spend whatever money they managed to acquire without racially imposed restrictions. To enter the white race was a strategy to secure an advantage in a competitive society.

To the extent that color consciousness existed among newly arrived immigrants from Ireland, it was one of several ways they had of identifying themselves. To become white they had to subordinate county, religious, and national animosities (not to mention any natural sympathies they may have felt for their fellow creatures) to a new solidarity based on color—a bond that, it must be remembered, was contradicted by their experience in Ireland. America was well set up to teach new arrivals the overriding value of white skin. The spread of wage labor made white laborers anxious about losing the precarious independence they had gained from the American Revolution. In response, they sought refuge in whiteness. The dominant ideology became more explicitly racial than it had been during the Revolutionary era. The result was a new definition of citizenship, with the United States becoming a "white republic." Black skin was the badge of the slave, and in a perfect inversion of cause and effect, the degradation of the African Americans was seen as a function of their color rather than of their servile condition. The color-caste system meant that no black person could be free, even in the limited sense most whites were. It affected relations between employers and laborers, even in those areas where slavery did not exist.

In the decades following the War of 1812, as wage labor grew in the north, southern slavery became the foundation of world commerce and industry. The slaveholders strengthened their hold over the Republic, with the support of northern white laborers seeking to protect themselves from competition. As a consequence, the color line grew firmer in all parts of the country.

The Democratic Party was the chief instrument of the governing coalition, the party most strongly identified with white supremacy, and the Irish were a key element in it. By 1844 they were the most solid voting bloc in the country, and it was widely believed that Irish votes provided James Polk's margin of victory in that year. The Irish voted Democratic because the party championed their assimilation as whites, and because, more than any other institution, it taught them the meaning of whiteness. The party rejected nativism, not because of a vision of a nonracial society, but because their vision was for a society polarized between white and black. Even as the bulk of the northern population began to turn toward Free-Soilism and, later, the Republican Party, the Irish remained loyal to the Democratic slaveholder-led coalition. They were less attracted than any other group to the promise of land in the West, primarily because they simply could not afford it. Free-Soil did not imply free soil. Taking into account the costs of land purchase, clearing and fencing, implements, seed, and livestock, as well as travel costs and the cash needed to survive until the first crop was brought in and sold, a minimum of $1,000 was required to equip a family farm in the West; a sum so far beyond the reach of the savings possible on a laborer's wage that the available land for settlement might as well have been located on the moon.

"It is a curious fact," wrote John Finch, an English Owenite who traveled the United States in 1843, "that the democratic party, and particularly the poorer class of Irish immigrants in America, are greater enemies to the negro population, and greater advocates for the continuance of negro slavery, than any portion of the population in the free States" (quoted in Ignatiev 1995, p. 97), attributed the animosity between Irish and African Americans to labor competition between the two groups.

Citing "labor competition" without further specification raises more questions than it answers, however. Ideally, workers contracting for the sale of their labor power compete as individuals, not as groups. The competition gives rise to animosity among these individuals; but normally it also gives rise to its opposite, unity. It is not free competition that leads to enduring animosity, but its absence. Race becomes a social fact at the moment that group identification begins to impose barriers to free competition among atomized and otherwise interchangeable individuals. Competition among Irish and African-American laborers failed to form a mutual appreciation of the need for unity because the competition among these two groups did not take place under normal circumstances, but was distorted by the color line. Slavery in the United States was part of a bipolar system of color caste, in which even the lowliest of "whites" enjoyed a status superior in crucial respects to that of the most exalted "blacks." As members of the privileged group, white laborers organized to defend their caste status as a way of improving their condition as workers.

The initial turnover from black to Irish labor does not imply racial discrimination; many of the newly arrived Irish, hungry and desperate, were willing to work for less than free persons of color, and it was no more than good sense to hire them. The race question came up after the Irish had replaced African Americans in the jobs. Now it was the black workers who were hungry and desperate, and thus willing to work for the lowest wage. Why, then, were they not hired to undercut the wage of the Irish, as sound business principles would dictate? It is here that the organization of labor along race lines made itself felt. Only after the immigrants had established their place in America were they able to exert enough pressure on employers to maintain the factories as "white" preserves. In the labor market, "free" African Americans were prohibited by various means from competing with whites, in effect curtailing their right to choose among masters (a right that was pointed to by contemporary labor activists as the essential distinction between the free worker and the slave). Free black laborers were confined to certain occupations, which became identified with them. To be acknowledged as white, it was not enough for the Irish to have a competitive advantage over African Americans in the labor market; in order for them to avoid the taint of blackness it was necessary that no Negro be allowed to work in occupations where Irish were to be found.

Employment practices in the new industries had different consequences for African Americans, Irish, and native whites. Black workers were pushed down below the waged proletariat, into the ranks of the destitute self-employed. They worked as ragpickers, bootblacks, chimney sweeps, sawyers, fish and oyster mongers, washerwomen, and hucksters of various kinds. Native-born whites became skilled laborers and foremen. Irish immigrants were transformed into the waged labor force of industry. Access to the most dynamic area of the economy became a principal element defining "white" in the north.

There were several means by which the Irish secured their position as "whites." The Democratic Party was one. Another was the riot, in which mobs swept through the streets destroying property and attacking individuals. The year 1834 alone saw sixteen riots, and the following year there were thirty-seven. No less a witness than Abraham Lincoln warned in 1837 that "accounts of outrages committed by mobs form the every-day news of the times." The riots were often the work of "fire companies" organized along national or religious lines; it is significant that only black people were prohibited from forming such companies. In antebellum America a citizen (or potential citizen) was distinguished by three main privileges: He could sell himself piecemeal; he could vote; and he could riot. Among the causes of riots, antiblack sentiments were prominent. In one case, a committee investigating a riot identified the widespread belief that some employers were hiring black laborers over white, and it proposed to leave the solution "to the consideration and action of individuals." Sometimes the targets were abolitionists, who were hated not so much for their opposition to slavery as for their insistence on equal rights for Negroes.

Related to the riot was the police. At first, the police forces of large cities were drawn from the native-born population, and Irish immigrants were excluded. The Irish, with reason, regarded the police as nativist mobs with badges, and hostilities between them were common. As the Irish gained political influence, however, they were admitted to the ranks of the police, and were thus empowered to defend themselves from nativist mobs (while carrying out their own agenda against blacks, who, of course, were still excluded). The Irish cop is more than a quaint symbol; his appearance marked a turning point in the Irish struggle to become "white" in America. A pithy summary of the change in the racial status of Irish-Americans is found in the following ditty, which circulated in Philadelphia following the 1844 Kensington riots between nativists and Irish (which saw the burning of a Catholic Church, General Cadwalader's troops firing into a crowd, and a mob firing back from a cannon dragged from a ship docked nearby):

Oh in Philadelphia folks say how
Dat Darkies kick up all de rows,
But de riot up in Skensin'ton,
Beats all de darkies twelve to one.

An' I guess it wasn't de niggas dis time
I guess it wasn't de niggas dis time,
I guess it wasn't de niggas dis time,

Mr. Mayor,
I guess it wasn't de niggas dis time.

Oh, de "Natives" dey went up to meet,
At de corner ob Second and Massa' Street,
De Irish cotch dar Starry Flag,
An' tare him clean up to a rag.

An' I guess it wasn't, etc.

De Natives got some shooting sticks,
An' fired at dar frames and bricks,
De Pats shot back an' de hot lead flew,
Lord! what's creation comin' to?

Oh, guess it wasn't, etc.

Cat-wallader he walk in now,
An' wid his brave men stop de row,
Den wicked rowdies went in town,
An burn de St. Augustine's down,

Oh, whar was de police dat time,
Oh, whar was, etc.

Oh, den de big fish 'gin to fear,
Dey thought the burnin' was too near,
Dey call'd a meetin' to make peace,
An' make all white folks turn police.

If dey'd been a little sooner dat time
If dey'd been a little sooner dat time,
If dey'd been a little sooner dat time,

Mr. Mayor,
Dey might a stopt all dis crime.

SEE ALSO *Dred Scott v. Sandford; White Racial Identity.*

BIBLIOGRAPHY

Allen, Theodore W. 1994. *The Invention of the White Race.* Vol. 1, *Racial Oppression and Social Control.* New York: Verso.

Ignatiev, Noel. 1995. *How the Irish Became White.* New York: Routledge.

Miller, Kerby. 1985. *Emigrants and Exiles: Ireland and the Irish Exodus to North America.* New York: Oxford University Press.

Roediger, David R. 1999. *The Wages of Whiteness: Race and the Making of the American Working Class,* rev. ed. New York: Verso.

Saxton, Alexander. 1990. *The Rise and Fall of the White Republic: Class Politics and Mass Culture in Nineteenth-Century America.* New York: Verso.

Noel Ignatiev

J

JAPANESE AMERICAN REDRESS MOVEMENT

Japanese immigrants began arriving in the United States in the 1880s. This first generation of Japanese immigrants, called the Issei, found assimilation into the American mainstream difficult at best. Cultural differences, xenophobia, and a quota system for immigrants served to stigmatize and subordinate the Issei. Life was little better for the first generation of ethnic Japanese born in the United States (the Nisei). Some Nisei were sent by their parents to Japan to be educated in the old ways. When these educated Nisei returned to the United States, they were known as the Kibei, and they achieved a degree of cultural status within the ethnic Japanese community. Although the Nisei were American citizens, they faced many of the same barriers to assimilation as their Issei parents. In the eyes of many white Americans, the ethnic Japanese represented an "otherness" that could neither be trusted nor respected. Out of this prejudice grew many forms of discrimination. The Issei, for example, were denied the right of naturalization and the right to purchase land. In 1924, further immigration from Japan was banned under the National Origins Act. This poisonous atmosphere set the sociopolitical stage for the extraordinary level of hostility visited upon Japanese Americans in the aftermath of the 1941 attack on Pearl Harbor.

PEARL HARBOR AND INTERNMENT

On December 7, 1941, Japan attacked the American naval base at Pearl Harbor, Hawaii. After declaring war on Japan, President Franklin Delano Roosevelt issued an executive order that effectively denied the basic right of due process to thousands of Japanese Americans. Issued on February 19, 1942, Executive Order 9066 directed the secretary of war to identify military areas from which "any or all persons" deemed to be a threat to national security, "by sabotage or espionage," should be excluded. There was no requirement in the executive order that criminal charges be filed against the accused or that the accused receive a trial prior to his or her exclusion (evacuation and internment) from the designated areas. The right to be formally charged and the right to defend oneself from such charges were supposedly fundamental rights in this democracy. However, pursuant to the executive order, government officials and military personnel rounded up Japanese Americans on the West Coast and in western Arizona. Without indictment, trial, or conviction, they were forced to quickly sell or store their property, for they were taken away with little—and in many cases no—prior notice. They were taken first to assembly centers, and later to one of ten internment camps located in the western United States. More than 120,000 persons of Japanese ancestry, including over 77,000 American citizens, were confined to the internment camps under the authority of Executive Order 9066.

Life in the internment camps was harsh by any measure. The internees lived a highly regimented lifestyle in crowded, dilapidated quarters behind barbed-wire fences and watchtowers with armed guards. These conditions greatly affected the psychological state of the internees. A sense of being a POW or a convicted criminal pervaded the camps. Adding to this sense of incarceration was the attitude of the guards. To generate a little excitement in their monotonous job, the guards would often terrorize the internees by shooting at them. Hence, not only were Japanese Americans uprooted from their homes, deprived of their property, denied due process, and stripped of their freedom, they were also psychologically terrorized—all at the hands of their own government.

POSTWAR INVESTIGATION

The sociopolitical forces that allowed Executive Order 9066 to be used as a means to deprive Japanese Americans of their fundamental constitutional rights and freedoms were later detailed in a congressional investigation prepared by the Commission on Wartime Relocation and Internment of Civilians (CWRIC). Established in 1980 to review Executive Order 9066 and its impact on "American citizens and permanent resident aliens," the commission conducted a comprehensive series of hearings, which included testimony from over 750 witnesses. The commission concluded that Executive Order 9066 and its execution were not justified by military necessity or national security, despite claims to the contrary by officials in the Roosevelt administration. Rather, they were fueled by racial prejudice, war hysteria, and a failure of political leadership.

This conclusion is supported by the dramatically different treatment ethnic Japanese received in Hawaii after the attack on Pearl Harbor. Although residents of Japanese ancestry represented more than 35 percent of the Hawaiian population at the time, only 1 percent of them were detained in the aftermath of the attack. Given the fact that Hawaii was regarded as a strategically important area, the logical assumption would be that ethnic Japanese posed a great danger to national security in Hawaii. But government officials in Hawaii exercised better judgment than their mainland counterparts, due in large part to three factors: a history of greater racial tolerance, a larger percentage of ethnic Japanese in the population, and a restrained military commander who believed in a presumption of loyalty unless there was evidence to the contrary.

REDRESS

Despite the inherent injustice of interning innocent people, especially U.S. citizens, it seemed unlikely at first that Japanese Americans would receive any redress in the postwar years. Increasing numbers of the Nisei and their children (the Sansei, or grandchildren of the Issei) became members of the American middle class. The Issei became eligible for citizenship in 1952, and the ban on Japanese immigration was lifted (although a quota was instituted in its place). In 1959 Hawaii became a state, and Asian American legislators soon arrived in Washington. By the 1960s, Japanese Americans had become the "model minority." These developments made redress appear unnecessary and unwise.

Yet a sense of injustice remained for many Japanese Americans, especially the Sansei who participated in the civil rights movement of the 1960s. Conflicting attitudes about redress were largely drawn along generational lines. While the Nisei who experienced internment first-hand preferred to move beyond that traumatic experience, their Sansei children wanted to confront the past as a foundation for moving forward. These socially active children of the civil rights era wanted to restore ethnic pride to Japanese Americans. They also wanted to uncover the truth about the internment. As the myriad internal dialogues unfolded, one fact became clear: each group of Japanese Americans viewed internment as the central event in Japanese American history. It has often been said that internment is the event from which all other events in the lives of Japanese Americans are dated and compared.

This sense of shared history brought survivors of the internment forward to testify before the CWRIC. In addition, two sets of lawsuits were filed. The first was a *coram nobis* (Latin for "error before us") litigation brought in 1983 by three former internees: Gordon Hirabayashi, Minoru Yasui, and Fred Korematsu. These plaintiffs sought to overturn their convictions, which were upheld by the Supreme Court in 1943 and 1944, for violating the wartime curfew and exclusion orders. The *coram nobis* lawsuits were successful in overturning these criminal convictions. "The courts issuing the writs declared an injustice and sought to redress it by correcting the historical as well as the legal record on which the Supreme Court had relied in its prior decisions" (Brooks 2004, p. 114).

The second set of lawsuits sought redress for all internees, not just those criminally convicted of violating the wartime exclusion laws. The most important of these cases is *Hohri v. United States* (1986), in which the plaintiffs sought monetary relief for violations of their constitutional rights and for losses to their homes and businesses. Like similar lawsuits that have sought monetary relief for past governmental injustice, this case was dismissed on grounds that it was barred by the statute of limitations and by the government's sovereign immunity. The case was finally dismissed in 1988, the same year in which President Ronald Reagan signed the Civil Liberties Act into law.

The Civil Liberties Act of 1988 marked the successful culmination of the Japanese American redress movement. Among other things, the act contained: (1) a joint congressional resolution acknowledging and apologizing for the internment of Japanese Americans; (2) a presidential pardon for Japanese Americans who, like

Hirabayashi, Yasui, and Korematsu, refused to comply with exclusion orders; (3) the establishment of a foundation to sponsor educational activities; and (4) payment of $20,000 to each surviving internee.

In 1988, when the reparations bill was singed into law, Japanese Americans were less than 1 percent of the population, politically passive as a group, and divided over whether to pursue a legislative or litigeous path to redress. In addition, the redress movement reached its zenith in the 1980s, when the federal budget deficit was nearing an all-time high. By all accounts, the Japanese American redress movement should have failed, not unlike the African American redress movement for slavery and Jim Crow, or, at best, it should have gained only marginal success, similar to the Native American redress movement.

So why was the redress movement so successful? There were a number of factors that allowed Japanese Americans to break through the political barriers that had stymied other groups. First, the redress bill became essentially a "free vote" for members of Congress. This was made possible because veterans groups did not actively oppose the bill, primarily due to the remarkable war record of Japanese American veterans (Nisei soldiers), who fought valiantly for a country that held their relatives and friends captive. Second, Japanese American leaders were able to frame the legislative issue as a deprivation of equal opportunity rather than as a claim for preferential treatment. Third, Barney Frank (D-Mass.) made redress his top priority when he became subcommittee chair in 1987. And finally, four powerful Japanese American Republicans and Democrats in the House and Senate vigorously supported the bill, personalizing discussions with narratives of their own war experiences.

SEE ALSO *Civil Rights Acts; Immigration to the United States; Model Minorities; Reparations for Racial Atrocities.*

BIBLIOGRAPHY

Brooks, Roy L. 2004. *Atonement and Forgiveness: A New Model for Black Reparations.* Berkeley: University of California Press.

———, ed. 1999. *When Sorry Isn't Enough: The Controversy over Apologies and Reparations for Human Injustice.* New York: New York University Press.

Commission on Wartime Relocation and Internment of Civilians. 1982. *Personal Justice Denied.* Washington, DC: U.S. Government Printing Office.

Hatamiya, Leslie T. 1993. *Righting a Wrong: Japanese Americans and the Passage of the Civil Liberties Act of 1988.* Stanford, CA: Stanford University Press.

Hohri, William Minoru. 1988. *Repairing America: An Account of the Movement for Japanese-American Redress.* Pullman: Washington State University Press.

Irons, Peter. 1983. *Justice at War: The Story of the Japanese Internment Cases.* New York: Oxford University Press.

Yamamoto, Eric K., Carol L. Izumi, Jerry Kang, and Frank H. Wu. 2001. *Race, Rights and Reparation: Law and the Japanese American Internment.* Gaithersburg, MD: Aspen Law & Business.

Roy L. Brooks

JENSEN, ARTHUR
1923–

Arthur R. Jensen was born on August 24, 1923, in San Diego, California. He joined the faculty of the University of California, Berkeley, in 1958 and became the center of a major controversy in 1969 when his article "How Much Can We Boost IQ and Academic Achievement?" was published in the *Harvard Educational Review.*

Jensen argued that Americans socially classified as black and white had, on average, different genetic potentials for intelligence, which he identified with IQ. He concluded that if black and white Americans enjoyed environments of equal quality, blacks would reduce their 15-point IQ deficit (compared to whites) to only about 10 points. In his later works he introduced the concept of "g," sometimes called the "general intelligence factor," which measures the tendency of some people to do better (or worse) than others on a whole range of mental tasks. This tendency becomes more marked as the cognitive complexity of the task increases and Jensen notes that blacks tend to fall farther below whites when the "g-loading," or cognitive complexity, of an IQ test increases.

At Berkeley, the immediate reaction to Jensen's views was several weeks of violent demonstrations, and protests continued to flare periodically throughout the 1970s. He defended himself against charges of racism with four arguments:

1. Setting race aside, "black" and "white" are socially significant groups in America. Blacks are identified for purposes of affirmative action (different standards of entry to universities) and public debate. For example, the principal of a school may be criticized if the children of black professionals do worse than most white students.

2. There can be average genetic differences between socially constructed groups. For example, if people with higher intelligence become professionals and less intelligent people become unskilled workers, and if like tends to marry like, then a genetic difference for intelligence will emerge among social classes. This theme was later developed by Charles Murray and Richard Herrnstein in *The Bell Curve* (1994).

3. The truth can never be racist, and whether two groups differ for genetic potential is a scientific question to be settled by evidence. Knowing the truth is important. If black and white children, on average, do have different genetic potentials for academic achievement, it may be unjust to criticize a school principal when an achievement gap exists.
4. An average difference between groups does not justify discrimination against individuals because of their group membership. Jensen stresses that, even if his hypothesis is correct, under conditions of environmental equality the upper 25 percent of blacks would overlap with the upper 50 percent of whites for intelligence. Indeed, the brightest individual in America might be black.

The emotion that has surrounded Jensen's hypothesis has largely overshadowed the evidence both for and against it. For example, after World War II, the children of black American soldiers and German women matched the IQs of children fathered by white soldiers and German women, irrespective of the g-loading of IQ tests. This fact is by no means decisive of the debate, but it illustrates that the debate can be carried on in terms of evidence rather than epithet. Jensen's assessment of the evidence from postwar Germany appears in *The g Factor* (1998).

Emotion has also obscured the fact that had the IQ debate not occurred, certain advances in psychology might also not have occurred. For example, Jensen (1972) noted that identical twins have IQs far more alike than randomly selected individuals, which seems to show that genes are dominant and environment weak in determining intelligence. He calculated that the impotence of environment was such that the magnitude of the black-white IQ gap was too large to be purely environmental.

William Dickens and James Flynn responded to Jensen's theories to this point with a model suggesting that people who are alike genetically tend to have environments that are atypically similar. Two individuals born with the physical traits of being fast and tall are both likely to be selected for basketball teams and get professional coaching. Similarly two individuals born with more mental ability than average are likely to have the benefits of greater teacher attention, honors classes, and attending good universities. In other words, even when identical twins are separated at birth, they will have more than genes in common: they will have life histories that show the same powerful environmental factors at work. They both will have enjoyed professional coaching, or both will have enjoyed highly superior educational experiences. The model's mathematics demonstrated that large group differences in either basketball skills or IQ-test performance could be primarily environmental in origin. If correct, this would illuminate areas as diverse as special education and how to remain mentally acute in old age. The Jensen debate shows that racism and the scientific examination of group differences are two different things, and also that banning scientific debate always inhibits the pursuit of truth.

SEE ALSO *Heritability; IQ and Testing.*

BIBLIOGRAPHY

Dickens, William T., and James R. Flynn. 2001. "Great Leap Forward." *New Scientist* 170 (2287): 44–47.

Flynn, James R. 1980. *Race, IQ, and Jensen.* London: Routledge.

———. 1999. "Searching for Justice: The Discovery of IQ Gains over Time." *American Psychologist* 54 (1): 5–20.

Herrnstein, Richard J., and Charles Murray. 1994. *The Bell Curve: Intelligence and Class Structure in American Life.* New York: The Free Press.

Jensen, Arthur R. 1972. *Genetics and Education.* London: Methuen.

———. 1998. *The g Factor: The Science of Mental Ability.* Westport, CT: Praeger.

James R. Flynn

JEWISH DEFENSE LEAGUE

The Jewish Defense League (JDL) and its offshoots in the United States advocate a militant Jewish nationalism characterized by racism and violence against the perceived enemies of the Jewish people. Established by Rabbi Meir Kahane in 1968 in Brooklyn, New York, JDL's initial goal was to protect the local Jewish community from anti-Semitism through intimidation and violence.

Kahane taught his followers that all non-Jews, especially African Americans and Arabs, are potential threats to the American Jewish community. His preachings highlighted the perception of Jews as a defenseless and weak community, and he often denounced both the mainstream Jewish community and law enforcement agencies as unwilling or unable to protect Jewish neighborhoods. He concluded that only Jews could protect themselves.

In his writings and public appearances, Kahane echoed the rhetoric of the Black Power movement. He emphasized Jewish Power through the strength of arms and threats of violence to defend against anti-Semitism. In *The Story of the Jewish Defense League* (1975), he declared, "Vandals attack a synagogue? Let that synagogue attack the vandals. Should a gang bloody a Jew, let a Jewish group go looking for the gang. This is the way of pride, not evil pride, but the pride of nation, of kinship—the pride of the mountain (p.143)."

Kahane's vision was turned into reality in May 1969, when the JDL established training camps and schools in which young Jews learned militant Jewish nationalism, hand-to-hand combat, and how to use firearms. Premeditated violence and vigilante justice followed. In September 1970, armed JDL activists were arrested in an attempted hijacking of an Arab airline.

As the JDL gained national recognition and support, its violent activities escalated. Protests and terror attacks were staged, including bombings, kidnappings, and attempted hijackings. Soviet and Arab representatives were the most common targets, as JDL wanted to respond to the oppression of Jews in the Soviet Union and to participate in the Israeli-Arab conflict. However, anyone that the JDL believed was or could be a threat to Jews was threatened, including mainstream Jewish organizations, which denounced the JDL and its tactics.

In 1971 Kahane immigrated to Israel to establish the anti-Arab Kach Party. He continued to travel to the United States and direct JDL activities until he officially resigned from his position as the group's leader on April 17, 1974. Although Kahane continued to inspire his American followers and traveled to the United States to participate in JDL activities, the organization was left to less charismatic leaders such as Victor Vancier and Irv Rubin, under whose guidance JDL support was reduced.

At the end of the 1980s, JDL's significance declined. It had received some support from moderate American Jews for pressuring the U.S.S.R. to allow Jews to emigrate. When President Gorbachev finally permitted record numbers of Jews to leave in the late-1980s, Kahane's focus shifted almost entirely to Israel. In addition, many JDL activists were arrested, including Vancier in 1986. However, the movement was dealt a crippling blow on November 5, 1990, when Kahane was assassinated in Manhattan by El Sayyid Nosair, an Egyptian Islamic fundamentalist connected to Al Qaeda.

Thus, the already weak JDL lost its founder. In addition, a split occurred within the Kach Party in Israel. Binyamin Kahane, Meir Kahane's son, broke with Kach Party leader Baruch Marzel and founded Kahane Chai (Kahane Lives), based in the Israeli settlements in the West Bank and Gaza Strip. Kahane Chai also established operations in Brooklyn, encroaching on JDL's financial and political territory.

After Kahane's death, the JDL was overshadowed by the shocking actions of its ideological brethren in Israel, particularly the Hebron Massacre of dozens of Muslims while they were praying, perpetrated by Kahanist Baruch Goldstein on February 25, 1994, and the assassination of Prime Minister Yitzhak Rabin by Yigal Amir on November 5, 1995, in protest of the Oslo Peace Accords. The JDL leadership refused to condemn these crimes.

The JDL's continued use of violence eventually led to its failure. On December 11, 2001, Rubin, its longest serving national chairman, and Earl Krugel, the group's former West Coast coordinator, were arrested days before they were to carry out several terrorist attacks on Arab targets in retaliation for Islamic terrorism. While in jail, Rubin committed suicide in November 2002. Three years later, in November 2005, Krugel was murdered in jail. Following Rubin's death, his widow Shelley Rubin feuded with JDL leaders Bill Maniaci and Matthew Finberg, which led to the JDL splitting into two rival camps.

In 2005, JDL rallies and protests rarely attracted more than a dozen supporters. Activities remain on a small scale and include rallies against Arab and Islamic interests and protests of white supremacists, antiwar protestors, and anti-Israel events. Maniaci has intimated that the JDL would like to shed its image as a violent extremist group. However, indoctrination and combat training camps are occasionally reported, and the JDL continues to threaten Arabs, Muslims, and others it deems dangerous to the American Jewish community and Israel.

SEE ALSO *Anti-Semitism.*

BIBLIOGRAPHY

Anti-Defamation League. 1995. "Extremism in the Name of Religion: The Violent Record of the Kahane Movement and Its Offshoots." *ADL Research Report.* New York: ADL.

Kahane, Meir. 1971. *Never Again! A Program for Survival.* Los Angeles, CA: Nash.

———. 1975. *The Story of the Jewish Defense League.* Radnor, PA: Chilton Book Company.

Alexander M. Feldman

JOHNSON, MORDECAI WYATT

1890–1976

Mordecai Wyatt Johnson was born on January 12, 1890, in Paris, Tennessee. His father, the Reverend Wyatt Johnson, was a former slave and mill worker, and his mother, Carolyn Freeman Johnson, was a housewife. In 1926 he became the first African-American president of Howard University in Washington, D.C., an institution with an enrollment of 2,268 students and 160 teachers. When he retired in 1960, the enrollment was in excess of 6,000. In 2006, benefiting from the momentum of Johnson's guidance of thirty-four years, Howard

University had 11,000 students and more than 1,000 teachers. It offered degrees in ninety-three different fields, including law, medicine, business, nursing, education, and communication. This is a range of instruction unmatched by any other of the hundred predominantly black higher education institutions in the nation.

Mordecai's own eminence rested upon an unusually rich education. He earned a B.A. from Atlanta Baptist College (now Morehouse College) in 1911, another B.A. from the University of Chicago in 1913, a divinity degree from the same institution in 1920, and an M.A. in divinity from Harvard University in 1922. He gained distinction as a master orator while at Harvard, and over the years he become known as one of the nation's top preachers as well as the president of its premier black educational institution.

In his 1926 presidential inaugural speech, Johnson shared his vision of the social-uplift role Howard University should play as "the first mature university organization to come to pass among Negroes in the modern civilized world." In addition to a balanced undergraduate program, Johnson saw the schools of medicine, law, education and religion as having arisen "to meet definite needs of the Negro people." In subsequent years under his leadership, the medical school would turn out half of the nation's black physicians, nearly all of its lawyers, a disproportionate number of specialists in education, and trained ministers dedicated to "releasing their energies for constructive service to the common good."

Johnson also was responsible for hiring such prominent scholars as the Rhodes Scholar and philosopher Alain Locke, the sociologist E. Franklin Frazier, the political scientist and future Nobel Laureate Ralph Bunche, the medical school dean Numa P. G. Adams, the pioneer blood-bank researcher Charles Drew, the economist Abram Harris, the historians John Hope Franklin and Rayford W. Logan, the theologians Benjamin E. Mays and Wallace Thurman, the school of education giants Charles E. Thompson and Allison Davis, and the law school dean Charles Hamilton Houston. The achievements of these scholars solidified Howard's reputation as the "capstone" of black education. Thompson founded the *Journal of Negro Education,* Drew received international recognition for his work, and Mays's leadership placed the Howard University School of Religion in the vanguard of black religious education, an achievement that led to his presidency of Morehouse College.

In addition to supporting the work of individual scholars, Johnson saw that Howard's law school could be a national systemic catalyst in breaking the chains of "legal" racial discrimination and advancing African-American civil rights. Thus, Charles Houston, with Johnson's support, vastly improved the law school and stressed that African-American lawyers should look upon themselves as "social engineers." Through mock trials, lawyers such as Thurgood Marshall and James Nabrit III developed and rehearsed the legal arguments crucial to the school integration cases of the 1950s, and the historic *Brown v. Board of Education* decision of 1954. Marshall went on to become the first African-American U.S. Supreme Court Justice. Laying the foundation for the successful attack on official racism, the law school became the nation's tutor in the field of civil rights. Nabrit was to succeed Johnson as president of the university.

Some were critical of what they termed Johnson's "autocratic manner" on campus and his "messianic" complex when dealing with Howard's adversaries off campus. Like most college presidents of his era, Johnson saw himself as the captain of a ship, with the faculty being his crew. His unrivalled authority was also a result of his success in 1926 in persuading the U.S. Congress to make Howard's federal appropriation an annual part of the federal funding cycle, a situation that enabled him to contain conflicts and rivalries among some of black America's most brilliant individuals. At the same time, Johnson's belief in academic freedom shielded his faculty from the efforts of some legislators to curb this freedom, especially during the "Red Decade" of the 1930s, at time when many intellectuals were accused of being admirers of Stalin and Communism.

Some of Johnson's outspoken political views also drew negative attention, but he was able to survive these attacks and become a world-recognized advocate for social justice, not only for African Americans but for the peoples of the underdeveloped countries of the world. For years he was the national leader and advocate for black education, and his sermons and public lectures were special events. He embodied in full measure Howard University's motto of "Truth and Service," and the university's central administration building bears his name.

BIBLIOGRAPHY

Bridglall, Beatrice L., and Edmund W. Gordon. 2004. "The Nurturance of African American Scientific Talent." *Journal of African American History* 89 (4): 331.

Carson, Clayborne, Susan Carson, Kieran Taylor, and Adrienne Clay, eds. 2000. *Papers of Martin Luther King, Jr.* Vol. IV, *Symbol of the Movement, January 1957–December 1958.* Berkeley: University of California Press.

McKinney, Richard I. 1997. *Mordecai, The Man and His Message: The Story of Mordecai Wyatt Johnson*. Washington, DC: Howard University Press.

———. 2000. "Mordecai Johnson: An Early Pillar of African-American Higher Education." *Journal of Blacks in Higher Education* 27: 99–104.

Meier, August, and Elliott Rudwick. 1976. "Attorneys Black and White: A Case Study of Race Relations within the NAACP." *Journal of American History* 62 (4): 913–946.

Muse, Clifford L., Jr. 1991. "Howard University and the Federal Government during the Presidential Administrations of Herbert Hoover and Franklin D. Roosevelt, 1928–1945." *Journal of Negro History* 76 (1/4): 1–20.

Urquhart, Brian. 1994. "The Higher Education of Ralph Bunche." *Journal of Blacks in Higher Education* 4: 78–84.

George Tamblyn

K

KENNEWICK MAN

The relevance of the Kennewick Man discovery to the issue of race is a consequence of semantic confusion over the meaning of the term *Caucasoid* between the scientist who initially inspected the find and the public media that reported it.

THE DISCOVERY

In July 1996, two young men discovered a human skull on the banks of the Columbia River in Kennewick, Washington, on land owned by the U.S. Army Corps of Engineers. The county coroner enlisted the assistance of a local forensic anthropologist, who worked for the next month to recover the rest of the skeleton from the mud of the reservoir. Ultimately, he recovered a nearly complete skeleton in excellent condition.

Upon initial inspection, the skull and limbs appeared to more closely resemble those of a European than a local Native American; they were Caucasoid-like. The skull was long, high, and narrow, the mid-face projecting, and the chin prominent. The limbs were long, with proportionately longer lower arm and leg bones than are usually reported for Native American skeletal remains. These features, along with excellent preservation and association with late-nineteenth-century artifacts, led the anthropologist initially to suggest the remains might be from an early Euro-American settler. This inference came into question a few days later when, while cleaning the skeleton, he found a stone spearpoint embedded in the pelvis.

To resolve the apparent contradiction between the embedded artifact and the skeletal morphology, the coroner submitted a small bone for radiocarbon dating. The carbon-14 dating found the skeleton to be between 9,300 and 9,500 years old. This made the skeleton one of the oldest and best-preserved examples of human remains ever found in North America. Some in the media, as well as some public figures, quickly jumped to the conclusion that "Caucasoid-like" features meant that the first Americans had been Caucasians. To anthropologists who study the earliest Americans, however, it simply joined other discoveries, such as the Spirit Cave Mummy from Nevada, in suggesting that the first people in the Western Hemisphere had differed phenotypically from the historic indigenous inhabitants and that the peopling of the Americas may have been a more complex process than the immigration of a single, small group of ancestral eastern Siberians. Multiple episodes of migration from Asia may well have occurred toward the end of the last Ice Age, when that region was populated by disparate, morphologically distinct populations, most of whom would not fit the modern image of "Asians."

POLITICAL FIRESTORM

The discovery set off a political firestorm and led to an important legal decision. Five Native American tribes—the Umatilla, Yakama, Wanapum, Nez Percé, and Colville—quickly claimed the remains, citing the Native American Graves Protection and Repatriation Act of 1990 (NAGPRA). That act, intended to protect the remains of Native American skeletons from wanton desecration, and to facilitate the return of museum specimens to their probable descendants, requires a federal agency to turn over any inadvertently discovered Native American remains to an affiliated tribe or, without affiliation, to the tribe that the U.S. Court of Federal Claims had determined owned the land in historic times. The various tribes asserted that because their religion dictated they had originated in the territory they occupied in the nineteenth century, which included the place where Kennewick Man had been found, he was certainly their ancestor and should be returned immediately for reburial. The Corps of Engineers concurred and published its intent to turn the remains over to the Umatilla tribe. The corps had concluded that the Umatilla tribe had occupied the region around the discovery site at the time of European contact, meeting one of the criteria established for repatriation under NAGPRA.

Scientific interest among scholars was high. Numerous biological anthropologists and archaeologists sought the opportunity to study these unique remains. Initially, they sent study requests to the Corps of Engineers and to the concerned native governments, but, after being ignored, eight of them (Robson Bonnichsen, C. Loring Brace, George W. Gill, C. Vance Haynes Jr., Richard L. Jantz, Douglas W. Owsley, Dennis J. Stanford, and D. Gentry Steele) ultimately filed suit in the Federal District Court in Portland, Oregon, to halt the scheduled repatriation. The case, known as *Bonnichsen et al. v. United States*, lasted eight years. Two other claimants, a Norse revivalist religion known as the Asatru Folk Assembly, and Joseph Siofele, a Polynesian who hailed Kennewick Man as an ancestor of his people, also filed suits, but the first dropped out and the second case was dismissed.

Both the Asatru and Siofele appeared to take the opportunity provided by Kennewick Man's distinctive physical characteristics—the Asatru his supposed "Caucasoid-like" appearance and Siofele the statistical similarity of the Kennewick skull to that of some Polynesian peoples—to legitimize their rights to live in the Western Hemisphere. By having a legally acknowledged predecessor of their race in the New World, they seemed to believe, their later "re-immigration" might give them claims at least equal to those of Native Americans.

THE LEGAL CASE

Federal Magistrate John Jelderks heard arguments for and against dismissal of the case in 1997, and ordered the government to vacate its initial decision and properly follow the procedures of NAGPRA—that is, methodically attempt to determine affiliation. Working with non-plaintiff anthropologists, many of them approved by the native governments, the federal government conducted its own studies of the skeleton, local archaeology, folklore, and language. Ultimately, the decision, for affiliation to the claimant tribes, came down to folklore. The case then went back to court.

Legal arguments hinged on the interpretation of the NAGPRA legislation. Plaintiffs asserted, among other things, that Kennewick Man was not Native American under the statute; and if he were Native American, he could not be considered affiliated with any of the claimant tribes. Identity as Native American was the threshold issue. According to the statute, they noted, the term refers to "a tribe, people, or culture that *is* indigenous to the United States" (emphasis added). The law refers to the present, not all time. Living more than four hundred generations ago, Kennewick Man could not be a member of a present-day group, nor connected to them in any clear ancestor–descendant relationship. For its part, the government asserted the law meant that any person who predated Christopher Columbus's arrival is Native American. Tribes and Native American rights groups, who entered the case as amicus curiae, asserted verb tense did not matter; one never loses one's indigenousness.

Ultimately, the court found in favor of the plaintiffs, ordering the government to enter into negotiations with them over the timing and content of studies. The government and tribes appealed the case to the Ninth Circuit Court of Appeals, which unanimously upheld the initial ruling.

Studies by the plaintiffs' study team took place in June 2005 and again in February 2006, with more investigations planned. Kennewick Man is said to have been a well-muscled middle-aged man around 5 feet 9 inches tall who had survived head, chest, shoulder, and pelvic injuries before his death and possible burial. As with most of his North American contemporaries, his physical characteristics make him distinct from all modern "races."

Kennewick Man was a case of confused identity. The legal interpretation of Kennewick Man's identity hinged strictly on the reading of legal language. Kennewick Man was not "Native American" under the law because no cultural or biological link between him and any modern tribe could reasonably be made. The decision had nothing to do with an assignment of his "race." To the anthropologists who studied him, his distinctive phenotypic characteristics raised the intriguing question about greater diversity among America's earliest inhabitants, who arrived long before present-day "races" had evolved. Nonetheless, in the popular culture, the mistaken idea of Kennewick Man as evidence that Caucasians were the first Americans has taken a firm hold. Like the Asatru, many white Americans seemingly seek a moral right to live in America at a time when they feel embattled as illegitimate usurpers.

SEE ALSO *Folk Classification.*

BIBLIOGRAPHY

Chatters, James C. 2001. *Ancient Encounters: Kennewick Man and the First Americans.* New York: Simon and Schuster.

Cunningham, Richard B. 2005. *Archaeology, Relics, and the Law,* 2nd ed. Durham, NC: Carolina Academic Press.

"Kennewick Man Virtual Interpretive Center." Tricity Herald. Available from http://www.kennewick-man.com.

Thomas, David Hurst. 2000. *Skull Wars: Kennewick Man, Archaeology, and the Battle for Native American Identity.* New York: Basic.

James C. Chatters

KING, MARTIN LUTHER, JR.
1929–1968

Of political leaders, statesmen, and great figures with national and international influence during the nineteenth and twentieth centuries, the Reverend Martin Luther King Jr. is in a class by himself. Before the twentieth century faded into history and time, King, because of his commitment to humanitarian principles and values, had elevated himself into a universal political icon admired and beloved by millions. Before his death, he was a living legend. The international community, in awarding him the Nobel Peace Prize in 1963, recognized the global significance of his work and life. Twenty years later, in 1983, the U.S. government honored him for this same commitment with a national holiday. Beyond these international and national awards, many states, counties, and cities have named streets, highways, parks, buildings, bridges, centers, fellowships, prizes, and endowed academic chairs in his honor. Cultural institutions and individuals have created plays, songs, poems, pageants, bronze busts, and statues as tributes to him. There have been theater movies, television movies and programs, radio programs and presentations, public school presentations, and countless readings of his speeches, as well as grand orations and speeches about him and his influence. Since his death, every U.S. president has issued presidential proclamations on his birthday to honor him on behalf of the nation. Words of honor and praise have been continuous. In point of fact, they have never stopped.

Beyond the words and visual images, there have been the printed thoughts. Doctoral dissertations, senior and master's theses, books, book chapters, scholarly journal articles, newspaper and magazine articles, and children's works are in constant flow to the public and to the political elites of the nation and the international community. No year passes without some new discussion, debate, and revelation about Reverend King. But this steady stream of accounts is not necessarily singing his praises. Critics and criticism abound in this ever-growing voluminous literature. Yet most of it is positive and commemorative. His legendary status in life has not only grown with his death but has in retrospect also pushed his critics to the margins and sidelines. His own papers, letters, and writings are now headed for their own special archives for future generations of scholars and laypersons to study. He is becoming a man for the ages.

BIRTH AND FAMILY

Martin Luther King Jr.'s parents, Michael King and Alberta Williams, were married on Thanksgiving Day 1926 in Atlanta, Georgia, at Ebenezer Baptist Church, where his wife's father, the Reverend A. D. Williams, was the pastor. The newly married couple moved in with the wife's parents. It was in this household that Michael Luther King Jr. was born on January 15, 1929. He was the second child in the family, preceded by his sister, Christine, and later followed by a brother, Alfred Daniel (A. D.) in 1930. Shortly thereafter, tragedy struck when Reverend Williams died of a heart attack in March 1931. The son-in-law, King's father, who was already associate pastor, with the help of his outspoken mother-in-law became pastor of Ebenezer after about seven months. In a short time span, Reverend King rescued the bankrupt church, reformed its internal structure, put it on a sound financial footing, and launched an outreach program for the sick and shut-ins. His ministry proved so successful that at the end of his first year, he was the highest paid minister in Atlanta. By the end of his second year, he asked his church to send him on a summer tour of the Holy Land, Europe, and Africa. They did, and part of the tour carried him into Germany and the village where Martin Luther had defied the Catholic Church in 1517. Upon his return home, the Reverend Mike King changed his name and that of his son to Martin Luther King, senior and junior.

As his father moved up in the social, religious, and political circles in Atlanta, "M. L." or "Little Mike," began elementary school first at Yonge Street, then David T. Howard School, and by the seventh and eighth grades he attended the Atlanta University Laboratory High School. However, it closed at the end of King's eighth-grade year, and he returned to public education at Booker T. Washington High School, where he skipped the ninth and twelfth grades. Morehouse College, the all-male college that his father had graduated from in 1930, found its student enrollment declining as a result of World War II and instituted an early-admission program—taking bright young tenth and eleventh graders as freshmen. King was admitted to his father's college after the eleventh grade and, with a major in sociology, graduated in 1948. During his junior year at Morehouse College, King gave his trial sermon at Ebenezer and was shortly thereafter ordained and made an associate minister in his father's church. Prior to graduating in 1948, King applied to and was accepted at Crozier Theological Seminary in Chester, Pennsylvania. After three years of study of the dominant theologians of his time, such as Walter Rauschenbusch, Paul Tillich, Reinhold Niebuhr, and Mohandas Gandhi, King decided to attend graduate school and attain a Ph.D. in the philosophy of religion. During his last year at Crozier, he applied to Yale University, Boston University, and Edinburgh University in Scotland. Yale turned him down, and Edinburgh became less interesting. Thus, in September 1951 he began his doctoral studies at Boston.

Besides his study of more theologians, political philosophers, political activists, and the giving of guest sermons at churches where his father had connections, King kept an active social life, meeting once a week with his discussion group known as the Dialectical Society. During that first year, he met Coretta Scott, from Alabama, who was in Boston to attend the New England Conservatory of Music for training as a classical singer. The relationship grew to the point that he had her visit Atlanta and meet his mother and father. Things did not go well. When "Daddy King" and his wife visited their son in Boston to urge him to end the relationship, they discovered that King planned to marry Coretta. They were married on June 18, 1953, at the home of Coretta's parents near Selma, Alabama. King's brother served as best man and the affair went smoothly with the lone exception of Daddy King trying at the last minute to talk them out of it. He failed, and the couple spent their honeymoon at a local funeral parlor. Later they drove to Atlanta and moved in with King's parents.

King, with his wife, returned to Boston to finish up his coursework and find an agreeable dissertation topic as well as search for a job. His father wanted him to return to Atlanta and persuaded the president of Morehouse, Dr. Benjamin E. Mays, to offer him a teaching job at his alma mater, Morehouse College. The elder King wanted his son as a successor at Ebenezer. Before leaving school, King explored job possibilities at the First Baptist Church of Chattanooga, Tennessee, and Dexter Avenue Baptist Church in Montgomery, Alabama. In driving down to Montgomery, the previous pastor, Reverend Vernon Johns, hitched a ride with King to Montgomery from Atlanta. Once in the city, he dropped off Reverend Johns at the home of Reverend Ralph David Abernathy, who pastored the First Baptist Church. Johns was supposed to preach there while King was giving his trial sermon at Dexter. Instead of simply dropping off Johns, King stayed for dinner and struck up a friendship with the Abernathys that would last until his death.

Although one of King's best college friends was also up for the Dexter Avenue Church job, King accepted the church pastoral offer on April 14, 1954, agreeing to start that fall in September. On the fifth of that month King delivered his initial sermon. During that year he finished his dissertation and was awarded the Ph.D. in June 1955. Next came the birth of his first daughter, Yolanda Denise, on November 17, 1955. This was followed by the historic arrest of Rosa Parks on December 1, 1955, for refusing to give up her seat on a bus to a white rider. The results of this arrest would change the history of the South forever.

THE MONTGOMERY BUS BOYCOTT

After Parks was arrested, three major overlapping organizations, the NAACP, the Women's Political Council, and the Montgomery Improvement Association, mobilized to launch a bus boycott to protest the blatant racism and segregation inflicted upon black passengers.

For several years the NAACP had been looking for an appropriate case arising from an arrest of an African American for violating the city bus segregation ordinance. Several had come up during the early years after King's arrival at Dexter, but E. D. Nixon, the leading civil rights activist in the city, rejected them as inadequate test cases. However, it was a different story with the universally respected Rosa Parks, and when approached she agreed to permit herself to become the test case the NAACP wanted. Concerning tactics, the Women's Political Council, headed by Mrs. Jo Ann Robinson, an English professor at Alabama State University, wanted to plan a simple one-day bus boycott in the aftermath of Parks's arrest to protest the unfairness of the city's segregation bus law. In order to activate the protest, Robinson worked all night at her office at the university, mimeographing a leaflet to be circulated through the churches and other council contacts. In addition to her conceiving the boycott, Robinson was a member of King's church. After speaking to Robinson, Nixon called King and asked for his support as well as requesting that the city's fifty top African American leaders meet in the basement of his church to organize and plan an extended boycott. Those attending the meeting agreed to the legal challenge and the bus boycott and condensed the leaflet prepared by Robinson, which called for a mass meeting to spread the details about it. On that Sunday both King and Abernathy announced to their congregations that the boycott was on. The leading white newspaper, the *Montgomery Advertiser*, got copies of both leaflets from white women who had received them from their maids and printed a story to warn the white community about what was coming, but the article also informed other African Americans who had not heard about the forthcoming boycott. The boycott meant that some 20,000 of the 40,000 African Americans in the city would not use public transportation, making it necessary for the leaders of the action to establish private transportation arrangements for participants.

Once the white police chief heard about the Monday morning boycott, he declared that it would be effective only if "Negro goon squads" forcibly kept people off the buses. Hence, he ordered policemen to arm themselves and ride behind the buses to keep the "goon squads" from being effective. But this heavy show of police force scared away the few African Americans who wanted to

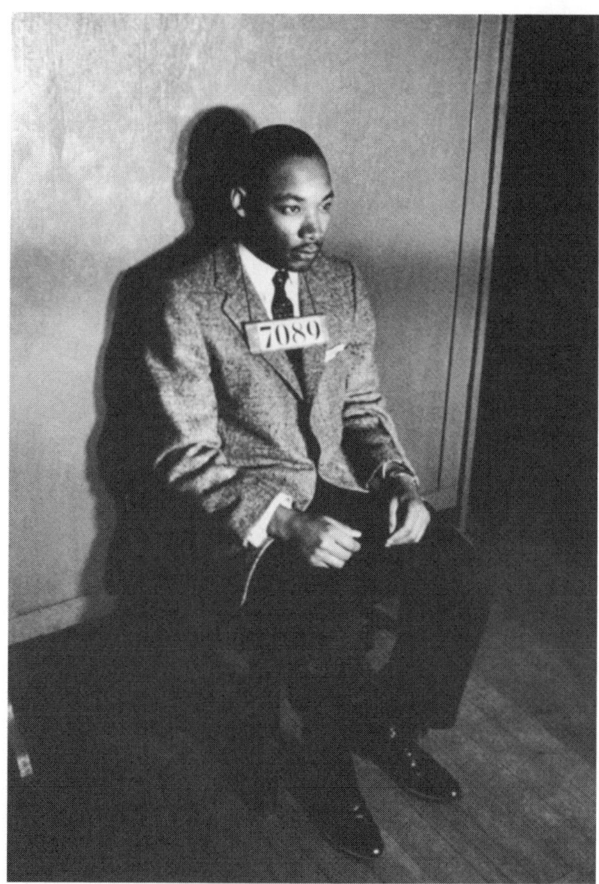

Martin Luther King Jr., 1956. *Martin Luther King Jr. sits for his mug shot after his arrest for directing the Montgomery, Alabama, bus boycott.* DON CRAVENS/TIME LIFE PICTURES/ GETTY IMAGES.

ride the buses but saw only trouble from such armed policemen. Parks was convicted in court; her lawyer, Fred Gray, filed an appeal; and Nixon posted her bond.

Just as they left the courtroom, a massive crowd of African Americans met them in the hallway and urged further action. Such an unexpected show of support led Nixon, Abernathy, and others to immediately assemble and call for a new mass meeting that evening. At that meeting, King was elected president of the organization and a name was voted on for the boycott organization. It was named the Montgomery Improvement Association. But before they decided on whether to make the one-day boycott a longer one, they decided to wait and see the actual turnout at the mass meeting that evening.

The first indication that the moment of decision had arrived was when King and his college friend, who was giving him a ride to the Holt Street Baptist Church, could not get within ten blocks of the church. Eventually, King had to exit the car and walk for nearly fifteen minutes to reach the church and push his way inside. He was called to the pulpit and gave a stirring address. Afterward, it was clear that the long boycott was on and only the details needed to be worked out. However, the extension of the boycott forced it to move from a taxi-based system providing transportation to the participants to a volunteer carpool arrangement. Such changes brought a host of problems and white pressures to cripple the MIA leadership and its system of helpful transportation. Scores of internal and external problems led Parks's attorney, Fred Gray, to file a suit in federal court on February 1, 1956, against the entire system of bus segregation in the city. This was two days after King's house was bombed with his wife and child in it.

On June 4, 1956, a panel of three federal judges voted 2 to 1 to declare bus segregation in Montgomery unconstitutional. Next came the Supreme Court decision on November 13, 1956, that upheld and affirmed the lower court decision. But the city had the right to ask the Court for reconsideration, which it did. On December 17 the Court rejected the city appeal, and the final court order to the city arrived on December 20. The successful boycott had lasted 382 days and in the process had made King a national figure.

THE CREATION OF SCLC

Out of the Montgomery protest came not only the ascendancy of King but also the creation of a new civil rights organization for African Americans in the South. During the wait for the final court order to the city, the MIA hosted a weeklong conference called Institute on Nonviolence and Social Change. A few notable outsiders and several ministers around the South who were leading bus boycotts in other cities or planning to set them in motion met on December 3–9. The meeting permitted the sharing of ideas and strategies and the creation of lifelong friendships.

Shortly after Christmas, King traveled to Baltimore to make a speech and met master march organizer Bayard Rustin and several of his friends. Rustin and a New York lawyer, Stanley Levison, told King that the now successful boycott showed that a regionwide movement against segregation was now possible. After discussing this with King, who was interested in a regional organization, Rustin and Levison drafted a memo of ideas and proposed a title: Southern Leadership Conference on Transportation. King moved to sell the idea and issued a call for the conference. On January 10 and 11, 1957, the Southern Negro Leaders Conference on Transportation and Nonviolent Integration held its initial meeting at Ebenezer Church in Atlanta and reacted to an agenda developed by Rustin. King and Abernathy left on January 10 after hearing that Abernathy's house in Montgomery had been bombed. They returned the next day when the conference approved a "Statement to the South and Nation" and made King the organization's temporary chairman.

On February 14 a second meeting of the conference was held in New Orleans, and King informed the group that President Dwight Eisenhower and his attorney general had failed to respond to their request for federal help and intervention. He told the conference that they should hold a prayer pilgrimage in Washington, D.C., at the Lincoln Memorial to put pressure on the Eisenhower administration to act. Before adjourning, the participants changed the organization's name to the Southern Leadership Conference.

Following the second conference meeting, King and his wife went to the independence celebration of the new African nation Ghana, where he met Vice President Richard Nixon and discussed a possible formal meeting with him. Back in the United States, he met with A. Philip Randolph, nationally known president of the Brotherhood of Sleeping Car Porters, and Roy Wilkins, executive director of the NAACP, and began making plans for a prayer pilgrimage in Washington. After a second meeting, May 17 was chosen because it was the third anniversary of the *Brown v. Board of Education* Supreme Court decision. Later, a third meeting of the conference was held on August 8 and 9 in Montgomery, and at that meeting the organization was renamed the Southern Christian Leadership Conference (SCLC). The SCLC would coordinate civil rights protests around the South, and when needed, King would arrive to help local leaders and local movements. The creation of this new organization angered the secretary of the NAACP, Roy Wilkins, for he knew it would attract monies that would otherwise have come to his organization. King was made the first president of this organization.

THE ALBANY MOVEMENT: 1961–1962

The successful Montgomery bus boycott created its own dynamism both inside the African American community and in white communities across the South. The civil rights gains in the black community of Montgomery, Alabama, were perceived by some in the white community as a loss. Nevertheless, there had been success in only one southern city, and numerous other southern cities were unaffected. Segregation in these cities stood firm. Such locales became targets for civil rights activists as well as rallying points for opponents of change. Albany, Georgia, was just such a place.

The Montgomery bus boycott not only illuminated these hamlets of white supremacy but also energized other groups in various African American communities. One of the first energized groups undertook the successful student soda fountain sit-ins in Greensboro, North Carolina, in February 1960. Their success led to another new African American student civil rights organization at Shaw University in Raleigh, North Carolina, known as the Student Nonviolent Coordination Committee (SNCC). This group was looking to mobilize in other locales, hoping to remove the shackles of the past. They got help from a new presidential administration. Democrat John F. Kennedy was elected in November 1960, and upon taking office he appointed his brother Robert Kennedy as his attorney general. Before they took office the Freedom Rides were under way.

The Supreme Court decision pertaining to Montgomery was supposed to lead the attorney general to forcing the Interstate Commerce Commission to set up new rules and regulations to integrate bus facilities across the South. Many southern locales ignored rules banning segregation, as they had ignored the Supreme Court decision in *Morgan v. Virginia* in 1946 that had banned racial discrimination in bus transportation. Local leaders and SNCC volunteers decided to test local compliance with the ICC ruling in the Albany bus terminal. Thus began a local protest movement that eventuated in a call to King for help because local white political resistance and intransigence and a creative and inventive sheriff had outmaneuvered the youthful and inexperienced leaders. Although King went to jail with the local leaders, many in the community, black and white, opposed inviting King from the outset and continued to do so even after he arrived. Shrewd white leaders who had stalled a settlement proffered one if he would leave. King exited the jail, and no settlement came. After more delays, Attorney General Kennedy, whose policy of "quiet persuasion" led to nonintervention, left the beleaguered protesters at the mercies of the local authorities. Eventually, they prevailed. The Albany Movement got little more than verbal promises and no implementation. From this event, King and his staff learned that it would be better if he selected his own sites to conduct battles rather than trying to rescue one that had already faltered and was in deep trouble. In addition, they learned that it was essential to have the federal government intervene rather than standing on the sidelines acting as a neutral observer. Thus, the stage was set for a new site and new struggle.

THE BIRMINGHAM PROTEST: 1963

The Birmingham protest began on April 3, 1963, just before the Easter shopping season. There, as elsewhere, marches and demonstrations led to the jailing of King, and from his cell he wrote the now famous "Letter from the Birmingham Jail." This letter garnered much national publicity for his efforts and attracted significant support from white churches and ministries, north and south. But the greatest generator of national and international publicity for the Birmingham protest was the police commissioner, Eugene "Bull" Conner. To protect segregation and white supremacy in the city, he unleashed dogs, fire hoses, billy clubs, cattle prods, police on horseback, police brutality, police beatings of women and children, and endless racial epithets and slurs.

This use of brute force shocked the nation, its political elites, and the international community. Internationally, colonialism was being displaced by the rise of new nations in African and Asia. The United States and the Soviet Union were competing for the loyalty and alignment of these new nations and their allegiance in the cold war. King's aide, Wyatt T. Walker, who chose Birmingham for the next confrontation, did so precisely because of the presence of Connor and his reputation for vigorously defending segregation at all costs. In his plans, Walker had dubbed the city "C," for "confrontation." Connor's response to the marches and demonstrations was even more violent than anticipated. It turned out to be a major media attention getter and created a national crisis for the federal government. Conner's reaction moved the Birmingham protests from a local struggle for civil rights and human dignity into a national effort to attain new civil rights legislation. While King struggled in Birmingham, efforts by labor leader A. Philip Randolph to create and set into motion a march on Washington were coming to fruition.

THE MARCH ON WASHINGTON: 1963

Eventually, Randolph persuaded all the major civil rights leaders to back the march on Washington plan, and on July 17, 1963, President Kennedy endorsed the march during a press conference. On August 28, 1963, in front of the Lincoln Memorial, King delivered his "I Have a Dream" speech and after the festivities were over, all the major leaders went to the White House for a meeting with the president to talk about how best to ensure the passage of his civil rights bill. Suggestions were made, and some were accepted by the president in the seventy-two-minute meeting. King had been in Washington before with his prayer pilgrimage in 1957, but this was even greater and much more was at stake. Unlike the 1957 march, this time King was not only a national figure but an international one.

Despite such lofty moments, there were numerous protests and endless acts of violence and resistance to attend to while the new civil rights bill worked its way through Congress. Throughout the South, local bastions of segregation still fiercely defended that institution. Albany still had not relinquished its stiff prosecutions of the protesters, hoping that their diehard resistance would reverse the favorable course of events for the protesters. The worst example of this violence came on September 15 when a bomb at the Sixteenth Street Baptist Church in Birmingham killed four young girls attending Sunday

"I Have a Dream" Speech, 1963. *Martin Luther King delivers his landmark "I Have a Dream" speech in Washington, D.C., during the March on Washington for Jobs and Freedom.* © BETTMANN/CORBIS.

school, and a resultant riot killed another black youth. By October 15, King was called into Selma, Alabama, to help local activists against Sheriff Jim Clark. By the next month, President Kennedy was assassinated. To King and other civil rights leaders, the pressure placed on the White House by Birmingham and the March on Washington eventuated into nothing. Little did he know what Vice President Lyndon Johnson would do when he assumed the presidency. With Johnson in the White House, national civil rights legislation would advance further and faster than ever before.

THE SELMA-TO-MONTGOMERY MARCH

In the aftermath of Johnson's ascendancy to the presidency and his subsequent speech to support Kennedy's civil rights bill, King and the SCLC selected St. Augustine, Florida, as a new site to attack segregation. On May 18, 1964, King made his first visit and prepared to lead demonstrations and marches against the city, which had decided to hold out against any kind of concessions. Despite King's intermittent visits, violence not only broke out but also escalated, with no resolution in sight.

Elsewhere, the SNCC and several other civil rights groups in Mississippi had instituted the Freedom Summer in 1963 to register as many African Americans as possible to vote. This effort resulted in the creation of the Mississippi Freedom Democratic Party (MFDP) and in a major seating challenge to the regular Democratic Party in Mississippi at the Democratic National Convention in Atlantic City, New Jersey. King was asked to intervene and help the challenge. He agreed, but before the challenge took place, the 1964 civil rights bill became law on July 2. There was a White House ceremony for the signing of this historic bill. Yet in other parts of the nation, race riots broke out and continued during what was called the long hot summer. At the Democratic National Convention, the MFDP challenge was heard by the Credential Committee, which was empowered to decide which delegation to seat, the MFDP or the regular party. King, despite a broken foot, stayed for the entire convention and was persuaded to talk with MFDP leaders to accept a compromise of two honorary seats. The compromise had been brokered by Senator Hubert Humphrey, whom President Johnson had sent to work out a settlement. Party member and cofounder Fannie Lou Hamer made an electrifying speech to the convention indicating that the party could not accept such a compromise given the terrible struggle in Mississippi simply to register her people to vote. This compromise of two seats was, as she saw it, only "token rights." In the midst of her speech, the national television coverage was abruptly cut off. Later, she would lead a demonstration on the convention floor and engage in singing several freedom songs.

For many in the civil rights struggle, this repulse of the MFDP was a clear-cut window on the weakness and shortcomings of liberalism in America. Some of the participants in this challenge, particularly the youthful SNCC activists, afterward struck out on another path, which led them to embrace the "Black Power" slogan and drop the "nonviolent" part of their name. King, in contrast, went on to win the 1964 Nobel Peace Prize and numerous other awards. Yet another fight lay ahead in Selma.

On December 31, 1964, the SCLC staff moved into Selma as its next protest site, and King followed on January 2, 1965, announcing to the people at Brown Chapel Church that the marches and demonstrations were about to commence. January 18 would become "Freedom Day." White officials in Selma decided to take a page out of Police Chief Laurie Pritchard's playbook in Albany, where quiet police action had stalled the movement. But Dallas County head Sheriff Jim Clark thought that Bull Conner had failed in Birmingham simply because he had not used enough force and violence to stop the marches and demonstrations. After more than a few arrests and jailings, King announced that he would lead a march from Selma to Montgomery to arouse public opinion and get more help and support. On March 7, in defiance of the courts, and against the wishes of the president and numerous civil rights leaders and activists, King began what is now called in the history books "Bloody Sunday," because the marchers were met on the Edmund Pettus Bridge just outside town on the highway to Montgomery. Although it had been prearranged with King that the marchers would go to the middle of the bridge, then kneel and pray, the sheriff and Alabama state troopers waded into the crowd with tear gas, billy clubs, and horses and proceeded to beat the nonviolent marchers for nearly two blocks back to Brown Chapel Church. This violent spectacle, viewed on television by millions of Americans, created a furor throughout the nation and in the international community. Sympathizers around the nation soon mobilized thousands of marchers who took buses to Alabama and completed the march from Selma to Montgomery on March 25, 1965, when 25,000 peaceable, orderly marchers gathered at the state capitol to hear a speech by King. President Johnson called a special session of Congress and submitted a Voting Rights Bill. On August 6 the Voting Rights Act became law.

THE CHICAGO MOVEMENT: 1965–1966

On June 28, 1965, when local protests in Chicago over the school system and its insensitive superintendent Benjamin Willis failed to budge Mayor Richard Daley, local leader Al Raby asked King to come to the city and assist with marches and demonstrations to deal with the city's nonresponsive mayor. King agreed and arrived first on July 6, then came back for neighborhood rallies on July 24 and 25. With this action, many saw the civil rights movement moving north. Although King also considered other cities such as Cleveland, New York, and Philadelphia problems, he focused on Chicago. But because of numerous commitments elsewhere and his increasing attention to the Vietnam War, the Chicago effort of the SCLC did not get under way until January 5, 1966, with King calling his program the Chicago Freedom Movement.

Elsewhere, James Meredith started to lead a march against fear through Mississippi but was shot on the second day of the march, June 6. The SCLC, SNCC, and the Congress of Racial Equality (CORE) completed the march, where the slogan Black Power was introduced on June 17. During the next weeks, the NAACP and President Johnson denounced the slogan, but King refused to sign a statement condemning it. CORE, led by James Farmer, embraced the slogan. Many saw the slogan as being strongly opposed to an interracial society, and King was heavily criticized for not attacking and condemning "Black Power," which became quite popular and was clearly opposed to the idea of nonviolence.

From July 12 to 15, riots broke out on the west side of Chicago, and King led mass marches from July 30 until August 25. Some of these marches engendered great violence and angry responses and outrage. They also met with serious resistance from Mayor Daley and some of his African American aldermen. Things went less well than in some southern cities, but on August 26 a "Summit Agreement" ended the demonstrations in the city and King eventually moved back south. Once again many criticized him for achieving only a set of paper concessions and little else. King himself noted that after living in his apartment in the Chicago ghetto, the problems he encountered were greater than what he had prepared for and more than his southern experiences had taught him to expect. The northern movement was over hardly before it had started.

THE POOR PEOPLE'S CAMPAIGN: 1968

After the withdrawal from Chicago in the fall of 1966, King in January and February 1967 wrote his fourth book, *Where Do We Go from Here?* and on February 25 delivered his first speech attacking U.S. policy in Vietnam. In July, President Johnson increased the number of troops in Vietnam, while the ghettoes in Newark, New Jersey, and Detroit, Michigan, witnessed large-scale riots. In Detroit federal troops had to be called in to restore order. Responding to these urban rebellions, Johnson created a presidential commission, the National Advisory Commission on Civil Disorders, to explore the causes and consequences and make recommendations to prevent them.

From September 12 to 17 King and his SCLC staffers held the first of their retreats to begin planning their Poor People's Campaign. A second retreat occurred in Frogmore, South Carolina, from November 27 to December 2. Although SCLC staffers James Bevel and Jesse Jackson spoke out against the campaign, a third retreat occurred in Atlanta on January 15–16, 1968. Before the end of the month, Bayard Rustin came out in opposition to the campaign. This new high-profile proposed action by King for the organization was running into significant opposition inside SCLC and among his trusted advisors.

At about the same time in Memphis, Tennessee, sanitation workers went on strike for recognition as a union and better wages. This occurred on February 12, 1968, and when they marched on February 23, the city police broke up the march. Within a month, on March 12, Senator Eugene McCarthy made a strong showing in the New Hampshire Democratic presidential primary, and four days later Robert Kennedy announced his candidacy for the Democratic nomination. Two days after Kennedy announced, King went to Memphis to meet with the striking sanitation workers and promised to lead marches in support of them. On March 28, King's first march turned into a riot, police had to disperse the crowd, and the governor of Tennessee sent in the National Guard. Two days later, the SCLC executive staff urged King to return to mapping out his Poor People's Campaign. One day later King, along with the rest of the nation, heard President Johnson announce that he would not run for reelection. King returned to Memphis on April 3 to lead a second march to prove to critics, skeptics, and cautious observers that nonviolence was still realistic and that he could keep his mass movement obedient and committed to this principal value.

However on April 4 King was assassinated at the Lorraine Hotel, where he had stayed during his first visit. His death forced the city to enter into an agreement with the union and approve it. His death also triggered the passage of the stalled 1966 civil rights bill, which now became the 1968 bill and contained a fair housing provision. Four days after King's assassination, Congressman John Conyers (D-MI) introduced the first bill to make King's birthday a national holiday. Shortly after Conyers's legislative initiative, numerous other bills were introduced to honor and commemorate the slain leader, with stamps, bronze busts, portraits, buildings, and national medals.

Ralph Abernathy succeeded King and led the Poor People's Campaign to Washington, DC, on June 19, but he proved ineffectual in managing the media spectacle surrounding the camp known as "Resurrection City." District police closed the city on June 24, and the campaign ended as a failure on July 16, 1968.

NATIONAL HOLIDAY: 1983

King's leadership, along with that of other civil rights groups and activists, led to the passage of three major civil rights bills and the evolution of African Americans to full citizenship. Not only was this unprecedented, but it restored America's democracy to a new level in world affairs. Thus, Conyers's efforts to honor this distinguished citizen led him to try to mobilize grassroots support to pressure Congress and the president to pass his national holiday bill. Previous efforts to make holidays for Booker T. Washington, Black Mammies, National Freedom Day (Emancipation Day), and George Washington Carver all ended in failure or were reduced to special observations.

Conyers enlisted Stevie Wonder, who wrote a popular song. Conyers also held rallies in Washington in front of the Capitol and inserted numerous items in the *Congressional Record* as well as reintroduced his bill every year from 1968 until 1983, but failed to get passage and support from Democratic presidents Johnson and Jimmy Carter.

However, in 1982, a congressman from Indiana died, and it fell to Gary's mayor, Richard Hatcher, to handpick and support State Senator Katie Hall to be a candidate to assume the office. In a special election, Hall won the right to serve the remainder of the congressman's term and win her own term. Upon coming to the House of Representatives, she learned that the chairmanship of the Subcommittee on Population and Census had not been filled because no one wanted such a low-prestige committee post. Yet she discovered that this subcommittee was in charge of considering bills for national holidays. She accepted the chair's position and introduced her own King holiday bill, which eventually came to her own subcommittee for consideration. She held a public hearing on the bill, voted the bill out of her subcommittee, and sent it back to the full committee. She lobbied the full committee, and they voted it out and sent it to the floor of the House of Representatives. After Hall lobbied all 434 members of the House, her bill passed.

Next, Hall lobbied all 100 members of the U.S. Senate, and Senate majority leader Robert Dole (R-KS) introduced the House bill in the Senate and put it on the Senate calendar. President Ronald Reagan not only declared that he would veto such a bill but asked Senator Jesse Helms (R-NC) to stop the bill with a filibuster. Once Helms started his stalling tactics, Dole asked the White House to call Helms off. When it did not, Dole and his majority whip, Howard Baker (R-TN), successfully invoked cloture to stop the Helms filibuster. Thus, the bill passed, and when it reached the White House, Reagan held a Rose Garden ceremony to sign it into law.

Legacy of Nonviolence Called Upon During Iraq War. *A man holds a portrait of Martin Luther King Jr. during a 2007 demonstration calling for President George W. Bush to bring U.S. troops home from Iraq.* GABRIEL BOUYS/AFP/GETTY IMAGES.

In 1983, King's birthday became a national holiday, and a Federal Holiday Commission was created to implement it. As of 2007, but not at first, all the states recognize this holiday. As a consequence, the King legacy still lives.

SEE ALSO *Civil Rights Acts; Civil Rights Movement; Hamer, Fannie Lou; NAACP; Rustin, Bayard.*

BIBLIOGRAPHY

PRIMARY SOURCES

King, Martin Luther, Jr. 1958. *Stride Toward Freedom The Montgomery Story.* New York: Harper & Row.

———. 1959. *The Measure of a Man.* Philadelphia: Christian Education Press.

———. 1964. *Strength to Love.* New York: Pocket Books.

———. 1967. *Where Do We Go From Here? Chaos or Community.* New York: Harper & Row.

SECONDARY SOURCES

Branch, Taylor. 1988. *Parting the Waters: America in the King Years, 1954–1963.* New York: Simon & Schuster.

———. 1998. *Pillar of Fire: America in the King Years, 1963–1965.* New York: Simon & Schuster.

———. 2006. *At Canaan's Edge: America in the King Years, 1965–1968.* New York: Simon & Schuster.

Carson, Clayborne, ed. 1992. *The Papers of Martin Luther King, Jr.* Vol 1. Berkeley: University of California Press.

———, ed. 1998. *The Autobiography of Martin Luther King, Jr.* New York: Intellectual Properties Management in association with Warner Books.

Carson, Clayborne, and Peter Holloran, eds. 1998. *A Knock at Midnight: Inspiration from the Great Sermons of Reverend Martin Luther King, Jr.* New York: Intellectual Properties Management in association with Warner Books.

Carson, Clayborne, and Kris Shephard, eds. 2001. *A Call to Conscience: The Landmark Speeches of Dr. Martin Luther King, Jr.* New York: Intellectual Properties Management in association with Warner Books.

Walton, Hanes, Jr. 1968. "The Political Leadership of Martin Luther King, Jr." *Quarterly Review of Higher Education Among Negroes* 36: 163–171.

———. 1971. *The Political Philosophy of Martin Luther King, Jr.* Westport, CT: Greenwood Press.

Hanes Walton Jr.

KLANWATCH

SEE *Intelligence Project.*

KU KLUX KLAN

The Ku Klux Klan is America's oldest domestic terrorist organization, and despite several cycles of growth and decline, it still exists and still commits violent acts in the early twenty-first century. With eight major groups and around forty minor ones, comprising roughly 110 chapters or "Klaverns," Klan groups are the most common type of hate group in the United States. An estimated 4,000 to 5,000 Klan members, with greater numbers of associates, sympathizers, and hangers-on, perpetuate its history.

Despite its age, the Klan has demonstrated amazing resiliency. This has allowed it to appeal to poor and working-class whites, addressing their economic and social frustrations, regardless of what those frustrations may be at any given point in history. Klan ideology and conspiracy theories provide members with scapegoats to blame for their failures and misfortunes, an enemy to absorb their attention, and activities on which to focus their energies. It also provides self-respect, pride, and empowerment.

The Klan's enemies are often minority groups in direct economic competition with the lower- and working-class whites who form the Klan's core constituency. Other perceived enemies are groups that threaten white control of society in some other way. At various times, Klan enemies have included African Americans, Jews, immigrants, Catholics, anti-prohibitionists, drug dealers, homosexuals, and others.

Klansmen (and Klanswomen) also have a strong sense of victimization. Many Klan members are motivated to commit acts of intimidation, murder, torture, and terrorism—and to rationalize these acts as "self defense" because of a twisted perception that they are under attack and have to protect their "way of life." In the minds of most Klan members, the Klan never attacks innocent victims—it simply responds with vigor and righteousness to encroachments on the God-given rights of whites.

THE KLAN IN THE TWENTY-FIRST CENTURY

In the early 2000s, the Ku Klux Klan is no longer a single entity. Instead, fragmentation and decentralization are the rule. Many of the approximately 110 Klan groups or chapters remain at least nominally independent, although some are attached to national organizations—Klan groups that claim a national or multiregional reach.

Various Imperial Wizards, who set the tone for their subordinate chapters, lead these national organizations. The larger Klans sometimes have an intermediate level of organization, called the "Realm," usually based within a state or a regional collection of states. Both independent local Klaverns and nationwide Klans tend to revolve around a central leader with a strong, charismatic personality, and the fortunes of the organizations typically rise and fall with those of their leaders.

Early twenty-first century Klans generally adopt one of two public stances. Some take a cue from David Duke. Duke was the Imperial Wizard of the Knights of the Ku Klux Klan during the late 1970s. He changed his title to "national director," stopped "burning crosses" and instead held "cross lightings," and encouraged his followers to run for political office at the local level. Like Duke, some Klansmen use euphemisms instead of racial epithets and proclaim pride in their "heritage" rather than hatred of other groups. Others, however, consider themselves "old school" and take pride in the Klan's heritage as a terrorist organization. They take a confrontational approach to law enforcement and make no effort to disguise or tone down their beliefs.

KLAN IDEOLOGY

Today's splintered Klan encompasses a wide range of beliefs. For the sake of clarity, the ideology is categorized into religious, political, racial, and anti-Semitic beliefs, but Klan members do not necessarily make the same categorical distinctions.

Klan ideology, at its core, is centered on the idea that white Americans are threatened by nonwhite minorities and that most of these threats are arranged or encouraged by a sinister Jewish conspiracy. The Klan promotes itself as a way for white Americans to right these perceived wrongs, protect themselves, and to strike back at their enemies. At the heart of Klan beliefs is the notion that violence is justified in order to protect white America.

POLITICAL BELIEFS

One basic assumption behind the Klan's political ideology is that nonwhites and immigrants threaten whites. Klan members therefore seek to remove these threats, either by themselves or through government action. Another assumption is that, because Klan members believe that the government sides with minorities and immigrants instead of with whites, the government itself has become an enemy. Specific political issues that concern Klan members include immigration, free trade agreements, "racial purity," affirmative action programs, foreign aid, gun control laws, gay rights, and what they perceive as an unconstitutional separation of church and state. Because of its emphasis on an America "by, for and of" whites, the Klan is also extremely opposed to immigration and often calls for military forces to be deployed along U.S. borders.

"Taking back" America is an important theme in Klan ideology. The Texas Knights of the Ku Klux Klan's Web site makes this clear: "Enemies from within are destroying the United States of America. An unholy coalition of anti-White, anti-Christian liberals, socialists, feminists, homosexuals, and militant minorities have managed to seize control of our government and mass media... We shall liberate our nation from these savage criminals and restore law and order to America."

KKK March, 2004. *Members of the Ku Klux Klan marched through the streets of Sharpsburg, Maryland in 2004. To prevent violence between the KKK members and spectators, police with riot gear were also present.* AP IMAGES.

RELIGIOUS BELIEFS

Traditionally, the Ku Klux Klan has held extremely conservative Protestant Christian beliefs. Since the early 1970s, many Klaverns have converted to strongly fundamentalist Protestant beliefs, Christian Identity beliefs, or an amalgam of the two.

Christian Identity. Christian Identity, which has become popular among many Klan groups, is a relatively obscure sect known primarily for its racism and anti-Semitism. Its core belief is that whites are actually descendants of the Biblical lost tribes of Israel, and are therefore God's "Chosen People." Most Identity adherents believe that Jews, in contrast, are descended from Satan and that other nonwhite peoples are "mud people" on the same spiritual level as animals.

One of the main teachings of Identity Christianity is that all other Christians are "false" Christians, followers of corrupt "Churchianity" and duped by a Jewish conspiracy. This is clearly explained on the White Camelia Knights Internet site: "I understand that most people have been educated to believe that the jewish [sic] people are God's chosen people. Christians have even gone as far as to call themselves judeo-christians [sic], they become extremely hostile at the Klan whenever this subject is mentioned. But, we are followers of Christ and even if our beliefs are unpopular, they are still correct. I am constantly told that Christ was a jew [sic]. That Moses and Abraham were jews [sic], but, this belief is incorrect" (Lee 2005, White Camilia Kights Internet site).

In effect, this belief system teaches that, because they are animals, blacks are subhuman, do not have souls, and therefore do not deserve equality before the law, much less American citizenship. Jews, as the descendants and representatives of Satan, are considered the root of all evil in the world.

Fundamentalism. While many Klan members have converted to Christian Identity, others have merely adopted some of its tenets or practice one of several extreme variations of Christian fundamentalism. There are three primary facets of extreme fundamentalism that are important in understanding Klan ideology.

First, fundamentalists, in general, are millennialists and believe that the world is fast approaching its end. They believe that a final, major event of apocalyptic proportions will "purify" the Earth and leave only true believers behind in a perfect world. Klan members intermesh these beliefs with their racism and anti-Semitism; thus, the final battles may be against racial minorities or Jews.

Second, extreme fundamentalism is an essentially dualist belief system that offers black-and-white answers to all questions. Anyone who does not share the fundamentalist view is wrong; compromises would be capitulations to evil.

Finally, and most importantly, fundamentalists are conspiracists. Their interpretations of history and society hold that there are secretive, manipulative, all-powerful entities operating behind the scenes.

Anti-Semitism. The Klan sees Jews as the source of virtually all evil in American society—as secretive, hidden manipulators operating behind the scenes to control government, education, banking, and the mass media. Most Klansmen refer to this supposed secret Jewish cabal as ZOG, or Zionist Occupied Government. Many Klansmen believe that Jews are behind the federal government's efforts to combat organizations such as the Klan. According to the White Camelia Knights' leader, Charles Lee, "the jews [sic] tried to entrap Jesus in a conspiracy against the government, just as they do to Christian Klansmen today" (Lee 2005, White Camelia Knights Internet site).

The ultimate goal of this alleged Jewish conspiracy, the Klan believes, is to first control and then destroy the white "race," primarily by encouraging miscegenation. Jews also serve another function by reconciling a glaring inconsistency in Klan ideology. Klan members believe that blacks are unintelligent, lazy, and inferior. But if whites are so superior to blacks, how can blacks be such a monumental threat? The Klan answer is that Jews control the blacks. Jews manipulate African Americans, encouraging them to commit crimes against whites, and they also manipulate the government to give blacks preference over whites. Therefore, if the "Jewish problem" could be solved, all of America's other minority "problems" would become easier to deal with. Klan leaders also insist that Jews are attempting to outlaw Christianity, and they often point to the Supreme Court's ban on mandatory prayer in public schools as proof.

RACE

Race has always been the central issue in Klan ideology. Klan activists believe that all nonwhite races are a threat to whites; most of the organization's history has revolved around its attempts to exert or retain white control over minorities. In the early twenty-first century, many Klan leaders offer a perverse variation on this theme: Not only have whites lost control of their country, but the future of the white race itself is now threatened. Only the Klan can save it.

African Americans. The typical Klan activist believes that African Americans are the cause of most crime in America. They also believe that blacks are intellectually inferior and have no moral sense, that they rely on welfare to survive, that they are drug users, and that black men are pathological rapists of white women.

Klan literature also blames the failure of whites to succeed or advance in their careers on "reverse discrimination." According to the National Knights of the Ku Klux Klan, for example, "anti-White discrimination is official government policy through 'affirmative action' schemes such as minority scholarships, minority business grants, contract 'set-asides,' and the hiring and force fed promotion of less qualified employees" (Ku Klux Klan Internet site). This is a key part of the Klan sense of victimization, especially its belief that white males are the "real" victims.

C. Edward Foster wrote in the November/December 1997 issue of *The Pennsylvania Klansman* that "the Pennsylvania Ku Klux Klan recognizes the simple fact that all African niggers are all savage, bloodthirsty Satanic beasts... In the last thirty years these cannibalistic apes have fiendishly murdered over 50,000 White Christians. A nigger cannot be a Christian. Voodoo is the only appropriate religion for these depraved, demonic, vile, ape-like creatures of jungle darkness" (p. 2). This sort of rhetoric attempts to dehumanize African Americans, to make them easier and more acceptable targets for violence and intimidation.

Hispanics. The fear of a foreign "invasion" is a source of great anxiety among Klansmen. This fear demonstrates the Klan tendency to hate those who might compete with lower-class whites in the job market, as well as the tendency to seek scapegoats to blame for economic and educational failures. Klan websites and newsletters are replete with calls for the military to "seal the border." Hispanics, of whatever background, are simultaneously and paradoxically seen as direct economic competition (stealing the jobs of white men) and as lazy welfare recipients.

KLAN CRIMINAL ACTIVITY

The hallmark activity of the Ku Klux Klan is the perpetration of violence. From the early days of the original Klan when "night riders" terrorized former slaves, through the firebombing and murders during the civil rights era, to the present day, the Klan has been America's most notorious and well-known domestic terrorist movement. The Klan is known for terrorism, murder, and assault.

Klan violence largely stems from a combination of Klan ideology combined with the lack of political power on the part of Klan members. Typical Klan members are poor, with low education levels and little or no access to political leaders. Thus, Klan groups rarely experience success using normal political and social means of achieving their goals. This makes violence a more attractive option for some Klan members.

Rather than being ashamed of the Klan's sordid past, many modern Klan members are quite proud of this history. As Grand Dragon C. Edward Foster once said of the Klan, "I'll tell you this, the Klan's here because we've been here for 131 years. The legacy is that, uh, we've had a lot of hangings, a lot of bombings, a lot of shootings. That don't bother me at all. If somebody wants to go out here and kill a nigger or something, I don't know... They're [African Americans] not our equal, they have got no right to breathe free air in America. This is not the Boy Scouts, this is the Ku Klux Klan... You know who we are and you know what our history is" (Brummel 1998).

THE FUTURE OF THE KLAN

Despite its age and fragmentation, the Ku Klux Klan's presence in the United States is still strong. Though smaller than in the Klan's heyday in the 1920s, or its resurgence in the 1950s and 1960s, the Klan continues to be the most common type of hate group in America.

The Klan is likely to become even more decentralized. Large, hierarchical Klan structures are more vulnerable to collapse than are smaller Klan groups. The future may also see more "hybrid" Klan groups, such as the Aryan Knights of the Ku Klux Klan, that combine Klan traditions and goals with those of newer neo-Nazi groups. The level of Klan criminal activity is likely to remain high. In addition to their rallies and publicity-gaining stunts, Klan groups routinely engage in more sordid forms of activity, from harassment and intimidation to hate crimes and acts of terrorism.

SEE ALSO *Anti-Semitism; Christian Identity; Duke, David; Hate Crimes; Intelligence Project; Second Klan; White Racial Identity.*

BIBLIOGRAPHY

Brummel, Bill. 1998. *The Ku Klux Klan: A Secret History.* Written and produced by Bill Brummel for A&E Home Video.

Chalmers, David. 1987. *Hooded Americanism: The History of the Ku Klux Klan*, 3rd ed. Chapel Hill, NC: Duke University Press.

Lee, C. 2005. "Christian Identity." White Camilia Kights Internet site. Available from http://www.wckkkk.com/identity.html.

Ku Klux Klan Internet site. Available from http://nationalknights.org.

Sims, Patsy. 1996. *The Klan*, 2nd ed. Lexington: University Press of Kentucky.

Telease, Allen W. 1971. *White Terror: The Ku Klux Klan Conspiracy and Southern Reconstruction.* New York: Harper & Row.

Wade, Wyn Craig. 1987. *The Fiery Cross: The Ku Klux Klan in America.* New York: Simon and Schuster.

Weller, Worth H., and Brad Thompson. 1998. *Under the Hood: Unmasking the Modern Ku Klux Klan.* North Manchester, IN: DeWitt Books.

J. Keith Akins

KU KLUX KLAN OF THE 1920s

SEE *Second Klan.*

L

LA MALINCHE

Easily the most elusive, eminent figure in the history of the Americas, Doña Marina, "La Malinche," defies basic biographical description. Indeed, very little is known about her, and nothing really of the date and place of her birth, the cause or place of her death, or even her very name. Some call her Malintzin Tenepal, based on deductive speculation pertaining to the birth sign *Malinalli* (twisted grass) found in the *tonalámatl* (the Aztec book of horoscopes) and the root word *tene* (sharp; cutting), which reflects a facility for language evident in Marina's later life (she could speak Nahuatl, Chontal Maya, the tongues of Potonchan, and eventually Spanish). This gift for speech secured her role as the translator on the Spanish expedition to, and conquest of, Tenochtitlan.

THE HISTORY OF LA MALINCHE

Doña Marina came to the attention of the Spaniards in March 1519, following the battle of Cintla, when the defeated Tabascans gave her and nineteen other women to the Spaniards as a token of friendship and alliance. The Spanish friar Bartólome de Olmedo baptized her "Marina" and later instructed her in the Catholic faith. As a Catholic convert and loyal campaigner, Marina held a pre-eminent role among the female *conquistadoras* of the European forces and their native allies. Both the Spaniards and Indians considered her important and indispensable to the colonial project. The Spaniards, for example, were overjoyed to learn that she had survived the debacle of *La Noche Triste* the evening of June 30, 1520, when they fled from Tenochtitlan losing hundreds of lives and large quantities of treasure. A native account of the conquest, *El Lienzo de Tlaxcala,* depicts Marina as larger in scale than all others, and as the recipient of greater amounts of gold tribute than that given Cortés. Her name, too, marked those closely associated with her. Juan Pérez de Arteaga, her guard, became "Juan Pérez Malinche" and Cortés himself was known as "el Malinche" among the natives. By the end of the conquest, in 1521, Marina's service and elevated status brought her considerable wealth and recognition.

Marina had settled in Coyoacán, just outside Mexico City, when she joined Cortés on his 1524 expedition to Las Hibueras (Honduras) in wasteful pursuit of the renegade Cristóbal de Olid. On route, she wed Captain Juan Jaramillo in Tiltepec on the *encomienda* (estate) of the conquistador Alonso de Ojeda; as a dowry she received the encomiendas of Olutla and Xaltipan in the Coatzacoalcos region, allowing her the tribute and labor of the people of these towns. On the return trip, in 1526, Marina gave birth to a girl, her second child by a Spaniard. The first was Martín Cortés (Cortés's son)—known as "el grande," for his Spanish half-brother was given the same name.

Two years later, in 1528, Cortes departed for Spain with his mestizo son, but not with the boy's mother. Nothing more is known about Marina and some authors speculate that she died that year, possibly of smallpox. Mention of her in the historical records surfaces on May 16, 1542, when Maria Jaramillo (Marina's daughter) sued her father (who tried to disinherit her) for the valued encomienda of Xilotepec. Maria was granted half the encomienda, in part due to her mother's distinguished achievements.

MALINCHE'S CULTURAL AND DISCURSIVE SIGNIFICANCE

In his book, *The Discovery and Conquest of Mexico,* an eyewitness account of the conquest, conquistador Bernal Díaz del Castillo, presents the first historical account of Marina. Mimicking the immensely popular chivalric literature of the time, as well as aspects of Joseph's biblical story of redemption and forgiveness, his tale transforms Marina into a heroine. Borrowing stylistic traits from Spanish medieval narrative, Díaz del Castillo presents Marina as an heir of Aztec aristocracy and refers to her by using the honorific prefix *doña.* As a child, he says, Marina was robbed of her birthright when her mother gave her away to be raised as a Mayan slave. Despite this betrayal, Marina forgave all and exalted her newfound Christian faith and Hispanic culture. She is thus presented as the good and virtuous "Angel of the Expedition."

By the nineteenth century, Mexican patriots had revised this image. Mexico's independence from Spain in 1821 forged a national identity largely antipathetic to Spain and those associated with its legacy; Marina was subsequently cast as a traitor and whore. Not surprisingly, Mexico's first historical novel, *Xicotencatl* (1826), faults her for the Spanish defeat of indigenous Mexico and as the root of all that had gone wrong in the new republican nation. Two decades later, as his country fought to keep its land and sovereignty during the Mexican American War of 1846–1848, the dynamic orator Ignacio Ramirez incited nationalist sentiment by evoking the image of La Malinche as Cortés's mistress and identifying her complicity with foreigners as the cause of the fall of ancient Mexico. It was not until the last quarter of the twentieth century that Mexican feminists such as Rosario Castellanos and Elena Garro challenged the patriarchal discourse concerning La Malinche.

By 1973, Chicana feminists were challenging patriarchal authority through the appropriation and revision of Malinche's image. The mere mention of her in a poem by Adaljiza Sosa Riddell, who laments "*Pinche, como duele ser Malinche*" ("Damn, how it hurts to be Malinche"), initiated a collective process by Chicanas of remembering Malinche piece by interpretive piece in narrative and literary form in order to contest a politics of sexism and historical erasure. To Norma Alarcón, Malinche is a "paradigmatic figure in Chicana feminism," for Chicana feminist discourse began with her and continues to be preoccupied with her signification. In 1974, frustrated by the dearth of information on Malinche, Adelaida R. Del Castillo offered a social scientific discourse of Malinche's life and role in the conquest as if historical authenticity were possible. For the poet and author Cherrie Moraga, Malinche bequeathed Chicanas a sexual legacy, which in its most radical form (lesbianism) represents the ultimate control of female sexual identity. To this day, Chicana discourse on the Malinche paradigm contests sexism, cultural nationalism, heteronormative sexuality, and patriarchal hegemony.

SEE ALSO *Chicana Feminism; El Mestizaje.*

BIBLIOGRAPHY

Alarcón, Norma. 1989. "Traddutora, Traditora: A Paradigmatic Figure of Chicana Feminism." *Cultural Critique* 13: 57–87.

Anzaldúa, Gloria. 1987. *Borderlands/La Frontera: The New Mestiza.* San Francisco: Aunt Lute Books.

Del Castillo, Adelaida R. 1977. "Malintzin Tenepal: A Preliminary Look into a New Perspective." In *Essays on La Mujer,* edited by Rosaura Sánchez and Rosa Martinez Cruz. Los Angeles: Chicano Studies Center Publications, University of California.

Díaz del Castillo, Bernal. 1996. *The Discovery and Conquest of Mexico.* Edited by Genaro García. Translated by A.P. Maudslay. New York: Da Capo Press.

Messinger Cypess, Sandra. 1991. *La Malinche in Mexican Literature: From History to Myth.* Austin: University of Texas Press.

Adelaida R. Del Castillo

LA RAZA

The term *La Raza* literally translates as "The Race," but it is more colloquially understood to mean "The People." It celebrates the multiracial and ethnic heritage of Latinos in the United States. The lineage of La Raza is the Spanish Conquest of the indigenous Indians of Mexico and the resulting mestizaje, or the mixed racial and ethnic identities, of indigenous, Europeans, and Africans unique to the Americas. The Raza Studies Department at San Francisco State University states on their Internet site: "In practical usage, the term *Raza* refers to mestizos or mixed peoples; we have the blood of the conquered and conqueror, indigenous (i.e., Aztec, Mayan, Olmec, Yaqui, Zapotec and numerous other Native Americans), European, African, and Asian."

The term became popularized during the Chicano movement of the late 1960s and early 1970s, but its roots lie in the philosophy of Jose Vasconcellos's "La Raza Cósmica." Vasconcellos was a Mexican educator, philosopher and writer, and he served as both the Mexican secretary of education and the president of the National University of Mexico. In his 1925 work *La Raza Cósmica,* Vasconcellos predicted the birth of a new race of people of multiple races and ethnic heritages—a "cosmic race"—that would take precedence over white Spanish or European hegemonic racial categories.

La Raza Cosmica, however, was an ideal that was far from real. At the time, people of mixed racial and ethnic heritage in the Americas were the objects of miscegenation laws, segregation, indentured servitude, and poverty. Arguably, Vasconcellos made some impact with this term. Mexico and other South American and Caribbean countries used this concept and term to rename October 12 from Columbus Day, a celebration of the discovery of the so-called New World, to *El Dia de la Raza*, a celebration of the anniversary of the birth of a new race. In many of these countries, October 12 is a national holiday celebrating the confluence of civilizations (European and indigenous) in the Americas. In 1928, México made *El Dia de la Raza* a national holiday.

LA RAZA UNIDA

By the mid-1960s, particularly among Chicanos, children born in the United States of Mexican parents began rediscovering Vasconcelos and incorporating "La Raza" into organizational names. In Texas, Chicano youth formed the Mexican American Youth Organization (MAYO) in 1967, and the used the slogan "La Raza Unida" to sponsor conferences and organize and rally their supporters. By 1970, MAYO had formed a new political party that spread to nineteen states and the District of Columbia under the name La Raza Unida (LRU). This party lasted as an independent political party for a decade.

Other groups followed suit. The Southwest Council of La Raza was formed and headquartered in Phoenix, Arizona, in 1968. It eventually became National Council of La Raza (NCLR), the premier civil rights advocacy organization for Chicanos and other Latinos. In the early twenty-first century, NCLR is headquartered in Washington, D.C., with a multimillion dollar budget and hundreds of staff members. In Seattle, Washington, in the late 1960s, a Chicano community development group named its building El Centro de la Raza. In Los Angeles, California, a Chicano student group began a journal titled *La Raza* at about the same time. Católicos por la Raza was the name chosen by a group of religious practitioners protesting the building of a new cathedral far removed from the barrios in East Los Angeles in the late 1970s. Law students on many campuses across the country organized themselves under the name La Raza Law Students Association. Upon graduation and admission to the various state bar associations, these lawyers formed La Raza Lawyers. There is also a Committee on Raza Rights. At the Boalt Hall School of Law at the University of California, Berkeley, *La Raza Law Journal* has been published since 1981. At San Francisco State, a group of students pressed the university to form La Raza Studies, an academic course of study, in the late 1960s. In 1999 the department's title was shortened to Raza Studies because of the redundancy of the article *La* in Spanish with "The" in English. In 2005, radio stations in Los Angeles and San Francisco began to advertise themselves as "Raza Radio."

LA RAZA: THE PAN-ETHNIC UMBRELLA

From the 1960s to the 1980s, grassroots leaders of the Chicano movement—such as César Chávez (California), Reies López Tijerina (New Mexico), Rodolfo "Corky" Gonzales (Colorado) and José Ángel Gutiérrez (Texas)—frequently incorporated the term *La Raza* into their political rhetoric. La Raza became synonymous with persons of Mexican ancestry in the United States. From 1970 to the present time, Mexicans are the largest group among those labeled "Hispanic" by the U.S. government.

The U.S. government persists in pressing Spanish-speaking people or those of Latino heritage to identify themselves by "race" on the U.S. Census form, and then to also identify themselves ethnically as "Hispanic." Hispanics are divided into racial groups and nationalities by the U.S. government, and thus essentially fractured from both within and without. Over the past four decades, La Raza has become an inclusive term that provides group shelter to those who reject the government-imposed term *Hispanic*, those that prefer *Latino* as a self-identifier, and many of the immigrants from Central America and the Caribbean who have arrived in the United States since the mid-1970s.

Ethnic labels for the diverse nationalities that have come to the United States blend into La Raza, an umbrella term of pan-ethnic identity and solidarity that promotes cohesion. Yet because of the racialized nature of U.S. politics, immigrants arriving in this society often learn to choose ethnic labels such as Latino and Hispanic, terms that lack meaning in their former countries of origin and that did not exist in the United States four decades ago. Such ethnic labels are U.S. products, and many people so labeled are rejecting them.

BIBLIOGRAPHY

Acuna, Rodolfo F. 2004. *Occupied America*, 5th ed. New York: Longman.

Gutiérrez, José Angel. 1998. *The Making of a Chicano Militant: Lessons from Cristal.* Madison: University of Wisconsin Press.

Navarro, Armando. 2000. *La Raza Unida: A Chicano Challenge to the U.S. Two-Party Dictatorship*. Philadelphia: Temple University.

Raza Studies Department, San Francisco State University. "Why the Term *Raza*." Available from http://www.sfsu.edu/raza/.

Vasconcelos, Jose. 1966 (1925). *La Raza Cósmica: Missión de La Raza Iberoamericana, Argentina, y Brasil.* Mexico: Espasa-Calpe.

———. 1997 (1925). *The Cosmic Race*, bilingual ed, translated by Didier T. Jean. Baltimore, MD: Johns Hopkins University Press.

José Angel Gutiérrez

LABOR, CHEAP

Racial oppression and cheap labor have historically gone hand in hand. From colonialism to Jim Crow, and from slavery in the Americas to apartheid in South Africa, social systems of discrimination against people of color have typically accompanied economic discrimination in the form of substandard wages and benefits. Cheap labor, however, means more than low pay. To maximize profits, employers have historically subjected workers of color to unsafe and inhumane working conditions. They have also cheapened these workers' labor by cutting costs on factory maintenance, farming equipment, and a variety of other workplace improvements. While race is not the only factor determining which workers are treated as labor, workers of color disproportionately earn less for their labor than their white counterparts, just as immigrants have earned less than native-born workers and women have earned less than men.

A RACE TO THE BOTTOM

In any society, employers drive the cost of labor downward by maximizing their control over the workforce. This is done in a variety of ways. First of all, employers must find the most vulnerable workers, those least able to pressure employers to spend more money on compensation or workplace improvement. Workers of color, for a variety of reasons, have often been among the most vulnerable. At the height of apartheid rule in South Africa, for example, black workers' average wage was one-fourteenth what their white counterparts earned. Although black South Africans were roughly 80 percent of the country's population, their share of the national income was less than 20 percent. Because apartheid law subjected blacks to severe punishment (from fines to whippings to indefinite imprisonment) for engaging in protest, their ability to fight for fair wages was severely hampered. In this case, the support of the apartheid government and a racist legal and political framework granted employers a great deal of power over black workers.

Displaced workers, from immigrants to slave laborers, have historically been among the most vulnerable and exploitable workers. Transplanted to new cities, countries, or continents, often lacking relevant language skills, knowing little of their new local legal systems and power structures, and lacking basic community support, displaced workers are easily isolated and exploited by their employers. Displaced workers are also often dependent upon employers for a variety of reasons. Employers may aid them in going through the immigration process or help them find housing, for example. While race and displaced status often intersect (as in the case of African slaves in the Americas or North African immigrants in western Europe), displaced status functions on its own to facilitate cheap labor for employers. For example, Polish immigrants in Vance, Alabama, were earning roughly $1,100 per month for working as much as 65 hours per week at an automobile factory (Dixon 2003). This was less than a third of what many of their native-born, unionized counterparts in the United States earned. Though these were white workers, their displaced status left them little leverage to demand better compensation and gave employers a great deal of control.

Another way that employers have driven wages downward is through "de-skilling," which literally means eliminating a particular skill required to perform a job so that workers become easier to replace. Deskilling is often accomplished through the introduction of new workplace technology. For example, the U.S. Postal Service (whose workforce has historically been dominated by workers of color) introduced sorting machines in the late 1950s that reduced postal sorting jobs to machine monitoring jobs. In the automotive industry, many skilled assembly jobs have similarly been reduced to "minding the machines," and the same holds true in agriculture. Workers of color have disproportionately been stuck in these unskilled positions, making them easily replaceable and leaving them with little leverage to demand improved working or living conditions. In 1970 an estimated 78 percent of black women workers and 74 percent of black men workers labored in unskilled jobs, compared to only 39 and 40 percent for their white counterparts.

In addition to removing skill from labor, new technologies often lead to job loss, which increases competition between workers for the few jobs that remain. This competition drives down the cost of labor, for workers who complain about poor compensation and working conditions are simply replaced. New technologies often also serve to fragment a workforce, isolating workers from each other. In modern auto plants, for example, robots now perform many of the functions formerly done by workers. As a result, workers have fewer opportunities to develop solidarity and collective strategies for achieving better pay and working conditions.

SLAVE LABOR

Slave labor in the Americas is perhaps the best and most dramatic illustration of how cheap labor relates to racial oppression under capitalism. First, and most obviously, slave laborers were displaced and transplanted into circumstances of maximum vulnerability. Beyond the linguistic and cultural barriers they faced, African slaves were brought into a social and legal system that isolated them from local communities, fragmented their own already fragmentary communities, denied them any basic legal rights, and engendered a culture of oppression and contempt for black skin. In such circumstances, while rebellion was possible, the obstacles to collective action in support of any form of compensation of improved working conditions were, to say the least, formidable. Beyond this social system of oppression, slave owners developed a tight system of workplace control. Dividing workers into "house" and "field" slave categories, demanding that they perform exhausting and humiliating labor, surveilling their workers closely, and maintaining a violent discipline system, slave owners did everything in their power to control their workers' activity and consciousness. Plantation owners profited handsomely from this interlocking system of racial and workplace oppression, which can be seen as a prototype for the use of workers of color as cheap labor under capitalism.

CONTEMPORARY WAGE DISCRIMINATION

Indeed, incidences of modern-day slavery illustrate how employers still use variations on the plantation model of slavery to drive labor costs down. Like former African slaves, in the early twenty-first century the cheapest laborers are usually displaced people, such as immigrants from developing regions, who often immigrate in response to economic pressure. While colonial and capitalist forces drove the Atlantic slave trade, contemporary migration is driven by neoliberalism and globalization. In North America, for example, the North American Free Trade Agreement (NAFTA) has led to massive migration and the cheapening of labor standards from Mexico to Canada. By eliminating trade restrictions, NAFTA has allowed U.S. agriculture companies to flood Mexican markets with cheap, mass-produced corn, pushing local Mexican farmers out of the market. These farmers then often migrate to the United States in search of new work. Once there, they face legal obstacles to citizenship, anti-immigrant nativism and anti-Mexican racism, and exploitative employers eager to provide them with back-breaking farm work for substandard wages and few, if any, benefits. Meanwhile, U.S. employers lobby the government for more restrictive immigration policies that force immigrant laborers further towards the social margin and render them increasingly vulnerable.

Whereas workers of color have been pressed into lower-paying, low-skilled jobs, women workers have found themselves facing parallel pressures. Historically and across cultures, women have typically been consigned to service (as opposed to productive) labor, including domestic work, nursing, cleaning and maintenance, and child care. This labor has been culturally devalued as "women's work," and it has consequently received lower pay than productive labor in the manufacturing and distribution sectors. This cultural attitude has been reflected in labor costs, as traditionally female occupations such as nursing and teaching have been consistently lower paid than traditionally male work in areas such as trucking and auto manufacturing. With the onset of industrial capitalism, more and more women entered traditionally male sectors of the economy, but they still received lower pay and found themselves excluded from supervisory positions as well as male-led unions. Indeed, some women workers, excluded from these unions, were forced to form women-only unions in shops where men had already won collective bargaining rights. As recently as 2003, women in the United States earned only 75 percent of the full-time salary of their male counterparts. Where gender and race intersect, wage discrimination is strongest. In 2002, black women earned just 68 cents for every dollar earned by a male worker, while Latina women earned just 56 cents for every male dollar.

Ultimately, the common determining factors for cheap labor (e.g., displacement, social vulnerability, low-skilled jobs, competition among workers) hold true across borders and are found in any Western, industrial, capitalist economy. The justifications for these exploitative labor practices are similarly universal—cheap laborers are consistently blamed for their circumstances, either due to innate, biological deficiencies or poor individual choices. These justifications skirt the plain truth, which is that cheap labor is actively pursued by the capitalist class, which uses racial, gender, and class prejudices to divide workers and render them vulnerable to employer coercion.

SEE ALSO *Workfare and Welfare.*

BIBLIOGRAPHY

Bacon, David. 2006. *Communities without Borders: Images and Voices from the World of Migration.* Ithaca, NY: ILR Press.

Dixon, Jennifer. 2003. "Firestorm over Foreign Workers." *Detroit Free Press* July 24.

Eisenstein, Zillah. 1979. *Capitalist Patriarchy and the Case for Socialist Feminism.* New York: Monthly Review Press.

Elkins, Stanley. 1959. *Slavery: A Problem in American Institutional and Intellectual Life.* Chicago: University of Chicago Press.

Marable, Manning. 1983. *How Capitalism Underdeveloped Black America: Problems in Race, Political Economy, and Society.* Boston: South End Press.

Moody, Kim. 1997. *Workers in a Lean World: Unions in the International Economy.* New York: Verso.

Wilhelm, Sidney. 1993. *Who Needs the Negro?* Hampton, VA: U.B. & U.S. Books.

Zinn, Howard. 1980. *A People's History of the United States.* New York: Harper & Row.

William Johnson

LABOR MARKET

Inequality in the labor market is an especially critical component of racial and ethnic relations in the United States. Virtually all aspects of peoples' lives are affected fundamentally by what they do for a living, how much they earn, and how much wealth they are able to accumulate. These factors have serious implications for the schools children attend and how long they stay in school, for their health and the kind of health care they receive, and for where and how long they live. The term *labor market* refers to the exchange of labor for a wage or salary, or to the matching of individuals to jobs. According to orthodox economic theory, the laws of supply and demand govern labor market processes in a capitalist economy. The race, ethnicity, or gender of a worker should not be of any consequence in determining whether he or she is hired or how much he or she is paid, yet, historically, women and members of subordinate racial and ethnic groups in the United States have not fared as well as their dominant-group counterparts in the labor market. Group differences, in fact, call into question the fairness of labor processes and the labor market.

One critique of orthodox economic theory is labor market segmentation theory, which states that the labor market is segmented into "primary" (core) and "secondary" (periphery) jobs (see Doeringer and Piore 1971). Secondary jobs pay lower wages, offer fewer possibilities for advancement and lower levels of job security, and require fewer years of education. In the primary sector of the economy, workers earn more, are better educated, are much more likely to have careers, are more likely to exercise discretion on the job, and are more likely to be unionized. Racial and ethnic minority-group members tend to fill secondary labor-market jobs disproportionately, and native-born white males predominate in primary jobs. Typical primary-sector jobs include most white-collar jobs, including teachers, engineers, managers, lawyers, and doctors. Examples of secondary-sector jobs include busboys, sales clerks, domestics, typists, and janitors. Meanwhile, the informal labor market has grown since the 1970s. This market involves the exchange of work and wages (between workers and employers) outside of the legal and regulatory context that regulates the formal economy, and it employs immigrant workers in disproportionate numbers.

INCOME AND EDUCATIONAL INEQUALITY

In the 2000 U.S. Census, 36.2 million people, or almost 13 percent of the population, reported they were black (12.2% of the population reported black as their only race). Latinos (or Hispanics), largely of Mexican descent, accounted for 12.5 percent of the population (35.2 million people). Latinos have since surpassed blacks in number. In 2004, the Latino population totaled almost 40.5 million and the black population was nearly 37.7 million, according to the U.S. Census Bureau. Both populations lag behind the white population in education, which accounts in some measure for the economic inequality between both groups and whites. In 2000 just over 80 percent of the total population were high school graduates, compared to 72.3 percent of blacks and 52.4 percent of Latinos. While 24.4 percent of the population had earned a bachelor's degree or higher, according to 2000 Census data, only 14.3 percent of blacks and 10.4 percent of Latinos had achieved this level of education (see McKinnon and Bennett 2005, Ramirez 2004). In some respects, the picture is more dismal than these figures suggest, since another important difference between minority and majority groups is the quality of the education they receive. White students are more likely than black and Latino students to attend better-funded and resource-rich schools, and they are more likely to attend more prestigious institutions of higher education. The networks they form in these institutions can be critical when they enter the labor market.

The labor force participation rates of blacks and Latinos are comparable to those of the total population, but the nature of their participation is not. In 2000, for example, 63.9 percent of the total population and 60.2 percent the black population participated in the labor force, but compared to the white population, blacks (and Latinos) were much more likely to work in low-wage, low-prestige jobs, earn appreciably less on average, and accumulate much less wealth. While 33.6 percent of the total population was employed in management, professional, and related jobs in 2000, the corresponding figure for blacks was 25.2 percent, and it was even lower for Latinos.

Both black and Latino workers are much more likely than white workers to be employed in the service sector. In both categories, whites are more likely to hold the highest-paying and most prestigious jobs. For example, white managers are more likely than their black and Latino counterparts to hold high-level management positions, and they are more likely to be promoted. Blacks and Latinos are disproportionately concentrated in, and are more likely to languish in, mid- and low-level positions. These and educational differences account for a portion of the wage differential (see McKinnon and Bennett 2005, Ramirez 2004, Oliver and Shapiro 1995).

In 1999 the median family income of Latinos ($34,397) was higher than that of blacks ($33,255), but both were well below the $50,046 median family income of the total population. However, the total population median family income for married couples ($57,345) was only $7,000 higher than the black median family income for married couples ($50,690). Income and education gaps between black and white Americans have narrowed significantly since the 1950s, but since 1990 the unemployment rate of blacks has been at least twice the rate of whites, with Latinos in the middle, and Asians closer to, but still higher than, whites. Furthermore, the return on education for whites and Asians is greater than it is for blacks and Latinos. Even when controlling for education, whites' average earnings are higher than those of blacks and Latinos (see McKinnon and Bennett 2005, Ramirez 2004, Reeves and Bennett 2004). In large cities, for example, one study found that for each year of education, whites chances of being employed in a position of authority increased by 9 percent, but for blacks they increased only 1 percent (see Mooney et al. 2002). An additional measure of inequality that is of growing concern to many is the racial wealth or assets differential.

WEALTH DISPARITIES

Black households have barely one-tenth the net worth of white households. The black middle class has expanded substantially since the 1950s, but it is fragile, principally because its status rests principally on income rather than on assets or wealth. In their book *Black Wealth, White Wealth: A New Perspective on Racial Inequality* (1995), Melvin Oliver and Thomas Shapiro argue that the racial wealth gap is the "fundamental axis of racial inequality" in the United States. In this landmark study they found a wealth gap of $60,980 in 1988. By 2002, however, the gap had increased to $82,663. Furthermore, they contend, residential segregation, "the lynchpin of race relations" in the United States, prevents blacks from producing the housing wealth generated by white homeowners and providing their children with the kind of education that they will need to produce more wealth as adults. As a consequence, blacks cannot weather economic storms as well as whites, and they are more likely to fall into poverty in the event of an unexpected decline in income.

The 2000 poverty rate in the United States was 12.4 percent, but for blacks it was 24.9 percent and for Latinos it was 22.6 percent. The rate for the American Indian and Alaska Native population was even higher, at 25.7 percent. Every major American Indian group had a poverty rate above the national average, but the Apaches, Navajos, and Sioux had poverty rates of more than 34 percent. The poverty rate for the Sioux was 39 percent. Not unexpectedly, the American Indian and Alaska Native population lagged behind the total population in virtually every area discussed thus far. Only 71 percent of this population completed high school or higher, compared to 80 percent of the total population. On reservations, where roughly one-third of American Indians reside, the figures are more disquieting. On the Fort Apache reservation in Arizona, for example, 49 percent of the residents did not complete high school.

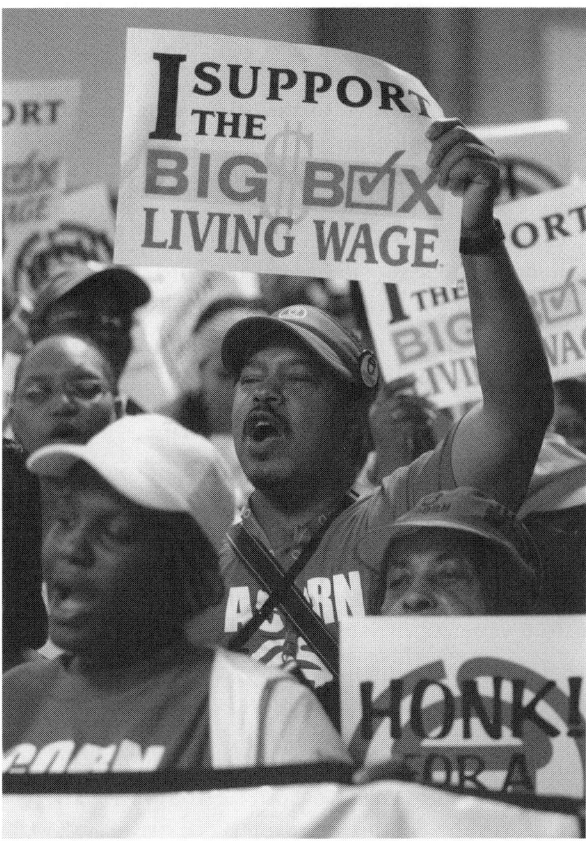

Wage-increase Supporters Demonstrate in Chicago, 2006. *In 2006 Chicago mayor Richard Daley vetoed the "big-box" living wage city ordinance that would require mega-retailers to pay higher wages. A group of supporters gathered outside City Hall as the city council decided whether or not to override the veto.* AP IMAGES.

In the labor force, Native Americans are underrepresented in the management, professional, and related ranks and overrepresented in service sector jobs. These educational and occupational differences are reflected in lower median earnings for American Indians relative to the total population (see McKinnon and Bennett 2005, Ramirez 2004, Ogunwole 2006).

A HISTORY OF RACIAL DISCRIMINATION AND EXCLUSION

Why are society's goods and services not shared equally by society's racial and ethnic groups? Some of the earliest explanations were biological and drew on Charles Darwin's work. At the turn of the twentieth century, social Darwinists argued that the fittest (intellectually and morally) were at the top of the social and economic hierarchy, and that the less fit were at the bottom. Slavery, for example, did not explain why blacks were at the bottom. Instead, they argued, slavery was simply evidence of African Americans' inferiority. Eventually, biological deficiency theories gave way to cultural deficiency theories, and these theories remain popular in the early twenty-first century. Advocates of the "culture of poverty" theory blamed the poor for their poverty, arguing that they were poor because of their inability to embrace the proper values to pull themselves out of poverty. These theorists posited that it was the inability to defer gratification, the propensity to engage in criminal activity, fatalism, and other cultural values that resulted in poverty.

Conservatives employ versions of this theory to oppose government programs designed to assist the poor and racial and ethnic minority groups. Predictably, critics of this and other individual-focused theories shift the focus from the individual and place it instead on structural factors and institutional forms of racial and ethnic discrimination. The institutional racism explanation relies heavily on the cumulative effects of historical discrimination and exclusion. (For an explanation and critique of the culture of poverty theory, see Leacock 1971.)

After the abolition of slavery, the United States, on the brink of becoming the most industrialized and wealthiest nation in the world, could have integrated black workers into the industrial mainstream. Instead, the South and North collaborated to "reconstruct black servitude" in the South (See chapter 7 in Steinberg 2001, pp. 173–200).

Freed slaves in the South labored as farm workers, sharecroppers, and tenant farmers and were subjected to a system of apartheid known as Jim Crow well into the twentieth century. In 1896 the Supreme Court of the United States established, in *Plessy v. Ferguson*, the doctrine of "separate but equal," which gave legal sanction to this system segregation. The ruling stood until the landmark *Brown v. Board of Education* in 1954, but by then the damage had been done, and the effects are still evident in the twenty-first century.

Denied the same opportunities as whites in education, politics, and the economy, blacks were unable to provide their progeny with the same opportunities as whites for a better life. De jure segregation may have ended with *Brown v. Board of Education*, but de facto segregation persists. Blacks, however, were not alone in being denied the fruits of industrialization. "Like European overseas colonialism, America had used African, Asian, Mexican, and, to a lesser degree, Indian workers for the cheapest labor, concentrating people of color in the most unskilled jobs, the least advanced sectors of the economy, and the most industrially backward regions of the nation" (Blauner 1972, p. 62).

In the Southwest, the United States seized from roughly half of Mexico's territory. Initially, it was the border that crossed Mexicans in the new Southwest, but subsequently it would be millions of Mexicans who would cross the border to perform the most menial and least desirable work in the mines, fields, and factories of the United States. Their contribution to the economic development of the Southwest was enormous, but they received very little of the wealth. They were denied, as were their African-American counterparts in the Southeast, full participation in the social, political, and economic life of the country, with similar effect. Indians fared no better. Uprooted from lands they and their ancestors had occupied for centuries, nearly wiped out by war and disease, their cultures decimated, and relegated to life on reservations as wards of the state, they remain in the early 2000s the poorest of the poor. Despite difficulties of their own, as Robert Blauner explains in *Racial Oppression in America*, European immigrants fared much better:

> In an historical sense, people of color provided much of the hard labor (and technical skills) that built up the agricultural base and the mineral-transport-communication infrastructure necessary for industrialization and modernization, whereas the European worked primarily within the industrialized, modern sectors. The initial position of European ethnics, while low, was therefore strategic for movement up the economic and social pyramid. The placement of nonwhite groups, however, imposed barrier upon barrier on such mobility, freezing them for long periods of time in the least favorable segments of the economy. (Blauner 1972, p. 62)

The consequences of this history of exclusion and discrimination are reflected in the twenty-first century labor market.

INSTITUTIONAL RACISM

Stiff resistance to the implementation of the Supreme Court's decision in *Brown v. Board of Education* underscored how entrenched racial and ethnic bigotry and inequality were in the United States. The ruling nonetheless helped to spur a movement that eventually resulted in civil rights legislation, legal rulings, and executive orders that generally improved the lives of blacks and other minority groups and created new opportunities in the labor market. Within a few decades, blacks, Latinos, and other minority groups were represented in all occupations. The number of blacks, Latinos, and other groups graduating from high school and college increased markedly in a relatively short period of time, and the dual-wage system and other "legal" means to deny minorities a fair wage became illegal. But blacks and Latinos continue to lag behind whites in education and the economy.

Proponents of structural theories insist that the racial and ethnic inequality that exists in the United States in the first decade of the twenty-first century in income, wealth, education, and jobs are best explained by the effects of a long history of discrimination and institutional racism, and by the persistence of overt and direct forms of discrimination. College admissions criteria that do not take into account conditions of poverty, for example, discriminate against blacks and Latinos, even if there is no intent to discriminate. This is an example of institutional racism. Refusing to hire an individual because she is Asian is an example of individual racism. Both of these forms of racism continue to be practiced in the labor market, and both reinforce economic and other forms of racial and ethnic inequality.

Employers continue to discriminate illegally against minorities in all phases of the employment process, including recruitment, the interview, the job offer, salary, and promotion. White males continue to hold the highest, most powerful positions in firms. Exclusion from exclusively or predominantly white male social clubs hamstring minority and women professionals, because important business is conducted and important connections are made over drinks and during a round of golf. Attempts to reduce the effects of unintentional racial discrimination have met with some success. Affirmative action, for example, has markedly improved the lives of many minorities and women. By the end of the twentieth century, however, affirmative action was disappearing in many parts of the country.

Two other theories are worth noting. Marxist economic theory postulates that the capitalist class benefits from and acts to create or deepen divisions among workers along racial and ethnic lines. By discriminating against blacks, for example, employers create and maintain a reserve army of cheap labor. In the process, labor solidarity is undermined, employers can appropriate more surplus from black workers, and white worker militancy can be dampened by replacing or threatening to replace white workers with black workers. Edna Bonacich, a professor of sociology at the University of California, Riverside, has proposed a related but alternative explanation, the split labor-market theory, to explain ethnic antagonism. In a 2001 essay, Bonacich argues that employers are interested in hiring the cheapest labor, regardless of race or ethnicity. Because the labor market is split along racial lines, higher-priced white labor is threatened by cheaper black or immigrant labor and therefore acts to restrict black and immigrant labor participation in the labor market.

GLOBALIZATION

Complicating (and worsening) the picture for minority workers in the United States is the globalization of the labor market. Because of globalization and trade and immigration policies that facilitate outsourcing, segments of the workforce in the United States compete, usually unsuccessfully, with low-wage workers in the developing world. Low- and middle-wage black and Latino workers in the United States have been hit especially hard by these policies. Globalization has increased the demand for well-educated and highly skilled workers in the United States, good manufacturing jobs have left the country, and increased immigration has swelled the ranks of workers performing the least desirable manual and service jobs that cannot be outsourced. Many of the jobs that have not left the country have left the inner city for the suburbs, and the upper middle class, which is predominantly white, has gone with them. As a result, tax revenue needed to support the city's services and infrastructure has been diminished. Left behind in the cities are poor people with deteriorating schools and high rates of unemployment. Between 1967 and 1987, for example, 65 percent of manufacturing jobs in Philadelphia disappeared (Kasarda 1995). The cost of transportation, discriminatory real estate practices, and the high cost of owning a home in the suburbs have made it all but impossible for many of the cities' poor to follow the jobs. Thus, globalization has sealed the fate of many of the cities' poor, who are disproportionately members of racial and ethnic minority groups.

The effects of historic discrimination are lasting, and they are aggravated by contemporary racial and ethnic discrimination in the labor market. The exclusion of racial and ethnic minority-group members from participation in the economic mainstream, especially during the late nineteenth century and the first half of the twentieth century, when the economy was expanding at a rapid pace and the demand for labor was unprecedented, resulted in disadvantages for these groups in virtually every area of social life, including education, housing, and health care. Despite legislation, executive orders, and court decisions protecting the rights of individuals in the labor market, discrimination persists. Along with the effects of prior discrimination and globalization, this makes it difficult for minority-group members to improve their labor market position.

SEE ALSO *Braceros, Repatriation, and Seasonal Workers; Day Laborers, Latino; Labor Market, Informal; Occupational Segregation.*

BIBLIOGRAPHY

Blauner, Robert. 1972. *Racial Oppression in America*. New York: Harper & Row.

Bonacich, Edna. 2001. "A Theory of Ethnic Antagonism: A Split Labor Market." In *Social Stratification: Class, Race, and Gender*, 2nd ed., edited by David B. Grusky. Boulder, CO: Westview Press.

Doeringer, Peter B., and Michael J. Piore. 1971. *Internal Labor Markets and Manpower Analysis.* Lexington, MA: Heath.

Kasarda, John. 1995. "Industrial Restructuring and the Changing Location of Jobs." In *State of the Union: America in the 1990s.* Vol. 1, edited by Reynolds Farley. New York: Russell Sage Foundation.

Leacock, Eleanor Burke. 1971. *The "Culture of Poverty": A Critique.* New York: Simon & Schuster.

McKinnon, Jesse D., and Claudette E. Bennett. 2005. "We the People: Blacks in the United States." Washington, DC: U.S. Census Bureau. Available from http://www.census.gov/prod/2005pubs/censr-25.pdf.

Mooney, Linda A., David Knox, and Caroline Schacht. 2006. *Understanding Social Problems,* 5th ed. Belmont, CA: Wadsworth/Thomson Learning.

Ogunwole, Stella U. 2006. "We the People: American Indians and Alaska Natives in the United States." Washington, DC: U.S. Census Bureau. Available from http://www.census.gov/prod/2006pubs/censr-28.pdf.

Oliver, Melvin L., and Thomas M. Shapiro. 1995. *Black Wealth/White Wealth: A New Perspective on Racial Inequality.* New York: Routledge.

Ramirez, Roberto R. 2004. "We the People: Hispanics in the United States." Washington, DC: U.S. Census Bureau. Available from http://www.census.gov/prod/2004pubs/censr-18.pdf.

Reeves, Terrance J., and Claudette E. Bennett. 2004. "We the People: Asians in the United States." Washington, DC: U.S. Census Bureau. Available from http://www.census.gov/prod/2004pubs/censr-17.pdf.

Shapiro, Thomas, and Melvin Oliver. 2005. "Closing the Racial Wealth Gap." Institute on Assets and Social Policy: Monthly Perspective. Available from http://iasp.brandeis.edu/pdfs/columns/sept05.pdf.

Steinberg, Stephen. 2001. *The Ethnic Myth: Race, Ethnicity, and Class in America,* 3rd ed. Boston: Beacon Press.

U.S. Census Bureau 2004. *The Black Population in the United States.* Available from http://www.census.gov/population.

———. 2004. Population by Sex, Age, Hispanic Origin, and Race: 2004. Available from http://www.census.gov/population.

Héctor L. Delgado

LABOR MARKET, INFORMAL

In the contemporary global capitalist economy, labor represents a commodity that is bought and sold. The labor market can be divided into two distinct spheres: the formal labor and the informal. State agencies monitor the formal labor market by tracking all income-generating activities that require routine censuses, regulation, and taxation. However, when the formal market fails and unemployment rises the informal sector can become the best available option for people, who either lack credentials (e.g., education, legal status) or have other types of barriers to entering the formal labor market (e.g., discrimination, age, care-work responsibilities). In *Affluent Players in the Informal Economy* (1997), Pierrette Hondagneu-Sotelo found that the informal economy is "synonymous with survival strategies used by the poor, the underprivileged, and those outside of the class system" (p. 134). Hence, the growth of the informal labor market becomes a survival mechanism for disenfranchised and vulnerable groups, such as people of color, undocumented immigrants and women.

Also known as the shadow economy, sub-economy or underground economy, the informal sector involves the production of legal goods and services in an unregulated system. It usually involves indiscretions such as tax evasion and unlicensed businesses, given that most transactions involve cash exchange to escape detection or records. Manuel Castells and Alejandro Portes posit that the informal labor market constitutes "the process of production and income-generating activity outside of regulatory institutions and the formal market system" (1989, p. 12). The informal economy is distinct, however, from the illegal economy, which includes activities such as prostitution, gambling, and drug-dealing. People labor in the informal labor market for a variety of reasons. Informal workers often do not have the legal means of obtaining secure employment or earning a living wage in the formal sector because they do not have legal documents or a valid social security card to secure employment. Nevertheless, the formal and informal labor markets function interdependently and are co-dependent. At times, an increased share of informality derives from subcontracts from the formal market, resulting in a greater need for informal workers increased profit.

The informal labor market is both an overt and covert activity where cash becomes the standard of exchange. This is commonly referred to as being "off the books" and "under the table." Some people who labor in the informal sector work within the private sphere of their own homes. This allows them to conceal offering services (e.g., babysitting) or the production and selling of goods, while at the same time minimizing detection. In the public sphere businesses are visible to the public eye and income generation takes place in open locations, such as the streets. In other instances people participate in the informal sector barter in exchange for goods and services. For example, an auto mechanic may barter labor expended on a vehicle in exchange for landscaping work on his or her yard. Ivan Light and Steven J. Gold characterize the informal labor market as "an industry that lacks a permanent mailing address, a telephone, regular business hours, tax identities, and inventory" (2000, p. 40). Day labor, housecleaning, gardening and landscaping, street vending (food and merchandise), and child care are all forms of work within the informal labor market. The changing face of the informal sector derives from the state's imposed constraints and opportunities enforced by the formal labor market. The formal economy rarely generates sufficient employment, which funnels surplus laborers into the informal labor market; this, in part, explains the persistence and expansion of the informal sector. There are three critical themes within the broad area of the informal labor market: self-employment, participants, and the social ramifications.

SELF-EMPLOYMENT

In the informal labor market, numerous individuals are self-employed in a range of activities. Informal enterprise often allows laborers and vendors to achieve a sense of agency, autonomy, and self-sufficiency by giving them the full control of their business operations. Some self-employed persons sell prepared fruits, clothes, crafts, pillows, or jewelry at conventional street locations by setting up stands on sidewalks or empty parking lots, or by transporting and peddling goods. Other vendors establish unlicensed businesses at local flea markets or swap meets that charge a daily fee for the use of an assigned space. Still others convert their living room spaces into pseudo-convenience stores where chips, sodas, and candies are sold. Taken together, self-employment in the informal sector takes various shapes and involves multiple forms of income-generation activities.

For some participants in the informal sector, self-employment is the principal source of income for people who are unauthorized to work in the United States. For others, informal income-generating activities are a viable way of supplementing wages from unstable jobs (e.g., temporary and part-time employment) in the formal sector. In this way, some people participate in both labor markets. In some instances, workers have regular employment in the formal sector and sell sodas and seafood cocktails at the local park to help them make a living. The formal economy often does not generate economic opportunities for all workers, and surplus labor gets funneled into the informal labor market, which contributes to the persistence and expansion of the informal sector. The informal sector is central to the economic subsistence of undocumented migrants, whose particular circumstances hinge upon a sort of anonymity, especially with regard to immigration and law enforcement officials, and to government agencies generally. Abel Valenzuela explains that some undocumented laborers undertake self-employment to regular wage work as a due to "labor force disadvantages such as physical disability, ethno-racial discrimination, unrecognized educational credentials, and exclusion from referral networks" (2001, p.349). In the same vein, Elaine L. Edgcomb and Maria Medrano Armington argue that "working in one's own business allows one to be more invisible. There is no need to be constantly showing documents to agencies or other prospective employers, and be at risk of being discovered to have fraudulent ones" (2003, p. 27). Therefore, the informal market empowers people to become economically sufficient without adhering to formal employment conventions.

PARTICIPANTS IN THE INFORMAL LABOR MARKET

While the formal labor market benefits those who control and own the means of production, the informal labor market attracts marginalized people of color, women, and undocumented immigrants who must innovate to achieve subsistence. In many instances the formal sector excludes undocumented laborers by forcing them to negotiate with employers for job provisions and pay without a contract. Immigrants often lack legal documentation required by employers. In other situations, corporations and businesses subcontract their labor to intermediaries, who later employ unauthorized workers for low wages. This arrangement is pivotal in the accumulation of huge profits for it allows people to do business in cash and to avoid taxes and record-keeping. Edna Bonacich and Richard Appelbaum in *Behind the Label* (2000) show how apparel industry elites contract small Korean garment factory (sweatshop) owners, who hire numerous undocumented Latinas, especially Mexicans, "under the table," thus avoiding both paying federal and state taxes and providing health and unemployment benefits that are more readily available to workers from the formal sector. This type of informal employment is actually connected to the formal sector but it can reduce labor costs and achieve higher profit margins, while also providing a cheap and expandable labor force. This organization of labor shows the interdependence between the informal and formal labor markets, which becomes central to the profit making machinery of certain industries.

Informal work often takes place in remote areas that are predominantly unregulated and in the private sector (e.g., homes), where detection is unlikely and the opportunity to benefit from an exploitable workforce increases. The sociologist Ivan Light argues that discriminatory practices in the labor market can force recently arrived immigrants to accept undesirable jobs with little lucrative payoff. Some of these jobs are also occupied by U.S. natives who have little human capital (e.g., education, job skills). Thus, the informal sector pits people of color, women, and undocumented immigrants against each other in fierce competition for low-status jobs.

It is important to keep in mind that the informal market provides economic opportunities for people from different backgrounds. For example, in his book *Day Laborers in Southern California* (1999), Abel Valenzuela notes that the overwhelming majority of day laborers in Los Angeles are undocumented male Latinos, with Mexicans being the single largest group of informal workers. Most of these unauthorized laborers experience overwhelming discrimination on the job. They wait on street corners or hiring sites hoping that employers will pick them up for work in construction, roofing, or landscaping. Undocumented Latinas and Chicanas participate in the informal labor markets as well. Pierrette Hondagneu-Sotello (2001) observes that Mexican undocumented immigrant women often become employed in the domestic sector of the informal economy, performing live-in and live-out housekeeping or nanny duties. Most domestic work is obtained through informal and personal networks consisting of family, friends, or acquaintances. Some women who participate in the informal sector prefer the flexible schedule that gives them ample time to perform household chores and spend time with their families. Both Valenzuela and Hondagneu-Sotelo demonstrate how undocumented Latinos become part of an exploitable and racialized enclave in both the public and private sphere.

Similarly, African-Americans are another racialized and exploited group within the informal sector. Mitch Duneier, in his book *Sidewalk* (1999), highlights how a group of low-income, often homeless black men participate in the informal labor market by selling used books and magazines on the sidewalks of Greenwich Village, New York City. For these men, the informal labor market has become a survival strategy and coping mechanism. Likewise, Yvonne V. Jones (1988) depicts how inner-city African-American men engage in two forms of street peddling involving the sale of clothes, food items, and household products. Jones found that peddlers relied on mobile peddling, in which their vehicles became a means of transporting products to communities of color, and sedentary peddling, in which they stay in one location and rely on pedestrian traffic. Most business transactions involving sedentary activities take place in different busy sectors of the community. In this case, informality is a viable and necessary option that benefits the vendor and the larger community. Finally, Paul Stoller and Jasmin Tahmaseb McConatha (2001) focus on undocumented West African traders who participated in the informal sector by selling counterfeit goods. Taken together, the informal labor market becomes instrumental in helping disenfranchised men and women achieve economic betterment in a system that traditionally keeps them in the fringes of society.

SOCIAL RAMIFICATIONS IN THE INFORMAL MARKET

For participants in the informal labor market, achieving economic success is too often accompanied by substantial risk factors for undocumented immigrants, women, and people of color. Thus, achieving economic success in the informal sector comes with consequences. In particular, informal sector work does not provide health or disability benefits, and continued employment is dependent on remaining injury-free. The informal labor market makes undocumented men and women run the risk of injury due to their participation in poorly paid, unskilled, physical and hazardous jobs where occupational regulations are often disregarded and workers receive inadequate training. In such settings, certain workers perform work that fails to conform to health and safety standards. The lack of social protections corresponds to the risks of injury, disability and untimely death. When an undocumented worker becomes injured on the job, the incident is often not reported because the worker's family depends on the day-to-day earnings. Other informal sector workers who get injured on the job may refuse services in order to conceal their undocumented status; these persons do not want to be stigmatized as "illegal aliens," and they fear deportation. Finally, informal sector workers may not have enough income to pay for services and medication, and they may instead turn to unconventional means of healing.

Some informal sector workers run the risk of not getting paid at all because most transactions are established through verbal agreements. In certain situations, the worker may complete a shift or assignment, but the employer will not pay the worker because there is no paper trail or timesheet that proves work was performed. The worker has little recourse in such a situation. Harassment and humiliation is also commonplace occurrence for street vendors as a result of clashes with local merchants and law enforcement personnel. Public displays of humiliation, as well as the destruction or confiscation of processed goods and materials are means by which law enforcement attempt to expel vendors from certain public spaces. People participating in the informal sector encounter constant threats from the Immigration and Naturalization Service (INS) officials and police repression because they are seen as a law-breaking and uncivilized group. The constant dehumanization of undocumented workers influences law enforcement personnel to react with repulsion and conflict.

With the continued expansion of a global economy, the displacement of people from peripheral nations, and the oppression of American ethnic and racial communities, most developed-capitalist nations will continue to simultaneously experience both increased migration and informal economic activities. In fact, formal and informal labor markets can not survive without an exploitable workforce of immigrants and people of color. It is likely, however, that anti-immigrant and nativist groups will continue to publicly express opposition to immigrants and people of color who participate in the informal sector by scapegoating these marginalized groups.

Thus, U.S. society will maintain and reproduce a racialized labor force and rhetoric that legitimizes hate and inequality.

SEE ALSO *Capitalism; Day Laborers, Latino; Immigrant Domestic Workers.*

BIBLIOGRAPHY

Bonacich, Edna, and Richard P. Appelbaum. 2000. *Behind the Label: Inequality in the Los Angeles Apparel Industry.* Berkeley, CA: University of California Press.

Castells, Manuel, and Alejandro Portes. 1989. "The World Underneath: The Origins, Dynamics, and the Effects of the Informal Economy." In *The Informal Economy Studies in Advanced and Less Developed Countries*, edited by Alejandro Portes, Manuel Castells, and Lauren A. Benton, 11–37. Baltimore, MD: Johns Hopkins University Press.

Duneier, Mitchell. 1999. *Sidewalk.* New York, NY: Farrar Strauss and Giroux.

Edgcomb, Elaine L., and Maria Medrano Armington. 2003. "The Informal Economy: Latino Enterprises at the Margins." FIELD (Microenterprise Fund for Innovation, Effectiveness, Learning, and Dissemination), The Aspen Institute. Available from http://fieldus.org.

Hondagneu-Sotelo, Pierrette. 1997. "Affluent Players in the Informal Economy: Employers of Paid Domestic Workers." *International Journal of Sociology and Public Policy* 17(3): 131–159.

———. 2001. *Doméstica: Immigrant Workers Cleaning and Caring in the Shadows of Affluence.* Berkeley, CA: University of California Press.

Jones, Yvonne V. 1988. "Street Peddlers as Entrepreneurs: Economic Adaptation to an Urban Area." *Urban Anthropology* 17(2-3): 143–170.

Light, Ivan. 1972. *Ethnic Enterprise in America: Business Welfare among Chinese, Japanese, and Blacks.* Berkeley, CA: University of California Press.

———, and Steven J. Gold. 2000. *Ethnic Economies.* San Diego, CA: Academic Press.

Valenzuela, Abel. 1999. *Day Laborers in Southern California: Preliminary Findings from the Day Labor Survey.* Center for the Study of Urban Poverty, Institute for Social Science Research, University of California, Los Angeles. Available from http://www.sscnet.ucla.edu/issr/csup.

———. 2001. "Day Laboureres as Entrepreneurs?" *Journal of Ethnic Migration Studies* 27 (2): 335–352.

Xuan Santos

LANGUAGE

The relationship between language and power, or more specifically, domination and racism, dates back to the colonial period when the colonial language became an aspect of cultural production that established dominance as well as cultural and linguistic superiority of one language group over the other (Pennycook 1998). In the case of the expansion of the British Empire, English was used to paint the world from the perspective of superior over inferior, culture over nature, and civilized over savage. It produced the constructions of "self and other" as superior and subhuman.

Many of these constructs continue in the early twenty-first century, specifically in the centrality English assumes in language policies that produce and reproduce ideologies and structures of inequality, a characteristic Skutnabb-Kangas and Phillipson (1990) call "linguicism." Closely associated with the biological form of racism—that is, the basing of superiority on racial traits—linguicism reproduces "unequal division of power and resources (both material and non-material) between groups which are defined on the basis of language" (p. 110). These structures of power grow out of the nature of language itself as a group identifier and the ideological discourses that produce and are produced by exclusionary legislation, news media, and pedagogical beliefs.

Language, for example, is a social phenomenon that shapes one's humanity and one's group membership. Like racism, it is not neutral. Rather, it is "dialectically related to society, and not an independent, isolated linguistic system" (Fairclough, quoted in Hruska 2000, p. 1). Rather, it is heavily weighted with the socioemotional experiences of the individual and the group, the history of intergroup relations, and the embodiment of power dynamics. Language is emblematic of identification, and as Fishman (1985) points out, is part and parcel of the "authentic doing and knowing of a particular kind of people" (p. 9) that generates a profound distinction between "us" and "them" in intergroup relations. This distinction is experienced at two levels of language contact: (1) the point at which the social, psychological, and linguistic features of language use affect the individual, the context, and the language itself and, (2) the point at which a particular language is culturally and politically legitimized, learned, and/or expanded (Appel and Muysken 1987).

Vulnerability to racist ideologies and structures—that is, the potential for evaluation of difference in terms of better or worse and the subsequent unequal access and distribution of resources based on that evaluation—is possible at either of these levels of language contact. Social and institutional conventions exert pressure on the individual or the group to shift to the dominant language and give up their identification with a non-dominant language and its beliefs, values, and worldview, often without the same benefit accorded to members of the dominant group. The compulsion to shift to the national language is conveyed in multiple ways: (1) in the dearth of institutional information available in the minority language to facilitate the acquisition of health care, social services, and justice; (2) the exclusion of the minority language as a viable tool for intellectual work; and (3) the promulgation of the primacy of English by the media. The highly publicized directive to immigrants made by California's governor Arnold Schwarzenegger to "turn off the Spanish television set" so they could learn English is an example of the chauvinism surrounding the value of English (Salinas 2007).

Intentional and unintentional—as most would classify Schwarzenegger's comments—language forms that racialize groups has a differential impact on inequality than language ideologies. For example, it is a common assumption that the use of racially charged language is intended to disparage the "other." It is inflammatory, marginalizing, and basically racist; however, individuals who use presumably harmless linguistic forms from a minoritized language such as "Hasta la vista, baby" (Spanish for "see you later," typically used for "good riddance"), "nappy-headed hos" (whores with naps in the hair), or "chinito" (Spanish for "little Chinese," a term used by Spanish speakers to refer to all Asians) in a state of innocence, also disparage the minority language and its speakers, at the same time they elevate the dominant language speaker and culture (Hill 2001). The use of language to racialize an individual or a group is implicated in the promotion of racist ideologies and structures of inequality and voices the hierarchical nature of the society (Asante 1998). However, offensive language does not have the direct impact on language rights and equal opportunity as does cultural and political ideologies and structures.

Language-based structures of inequality privilege the dominant language to the detriment of the minority language and its speakers. The imposition of monolingualism, seen as "a reflection of linguicism" by Skutnabb-Kangas (1988, p. 13) also comes at considerable cost to the sociohistorical legacy of the minority language speaker. In addition, these policies have an added disadvantage of diminishing the viability of the monolingual speakers to perform on the world stage where bilingualism is a social reality. The imposition of the dominant language—in the case of the United States, English—destabilizes, deculturates, and domesticates non-European groups (Wiley 2000). Shrouded in ideological rationality, the pressure to shift to the dominant language and abandon the native tongue is touted as the most logical thing to do given the circumstances. Reasons given for shifting to the dominant language such as the lack of resources, the economic necessity to learn the dominant language, or the importance for social mobility are typically taken as commonsensible without question. The common refrain "Speak English, you are in America!" is one of these seemingly rational imperatives that is loaded with ideological connotations about which language is valued and more tragically, which language is to be forsaken. These practices produce and reproduce exclusive and arbitrary systems of awards and access that establish, reaffirm, and promote structural inequality based on language. They also lay the burden of learning a second language, negotiating mainstream bureaucracies, and scaling the opportunity ladder squarely on the disempowered and dispossessed minority language speaker.

Such complex processes of linguistic privilege and favoritism shape and are shaped by legislation and the news media. Both ideological fields reflect the dominant perspective of the hegemonic language. Both base their formulations on uninformed, incomplete, and "linguicistic" assumptions of what is "good" and "bad" language and what is "right" for the country (Goldstein 2001). The media circulates national views on language at the same time that it racializes language in what Hill (2001) calls "language panics"—"intense public attention to 'language problems.'" (p. 249) It is the sheer intensity of these episodes, the low level of the discourse, and the maligning of the minority language speaker that classifies these media eruptions as racist. Gutiérrez and colleagues (2002) concur that these panics and "backlash politics" have little to do with language and more to do with race, specifically with the threat that the minority language and its speakers pose for national identity. In the discourse surrounding the proposed use of Ebonics by the Oakland School District in California and the consequent series of propositions in California between the 1980s and the 1990s (Hill 2001, p. 245), language became the proxy for race, facilitating a recategorizing of its speakers as deviant and semilingual (having an incomplete working knowledge of either the native or the second language) and their language as underdeveloped. The more recent media outburst in 2007, caused by former U.S. House Speaker Newt Gingrich's comments that "English is the language of progress" and bilingual education is teaching "the language of living in a ghetto" (Sanchez 2007), illustrates that the connection between language and national identity at the expense of the minority language and its speakers continues to have a major sway in the ideological discourses in the United States.

Nowhere is the connection between language and racism more potent than in the schooling process where income, class, ethnicity, and gender are interlinked with language into a synergistic process of inequality. The schooling process typically excludes the minority language and culture from the curriculum content, medium of instruction, and interpersonal communication cultivating long-lasting ideas of self as unfit and the world as unfair. This process creates a disequilibrium in which the individual is confronted with his or her language as unsuitable for personal expression or intellectual work, an experience best described by Adrian Rich as looking into a mirror and not seeing oneself. Thus, language is often used as a proxy for race to sort students into ability and interest groups, freeing the school to speak of deficiencies and rankings according to academic and social needs without repercussions. This is particularly true in states that have passed antinative language legislation such as California's Proposition 227, euphemistically called "Language for the Children." These types of legislation shape the educational content and curriculum to privilege the dominant language and deny access to the children's complete linguistic resources (Gutiérrez et al, 2002). As a result, minority language speakers are subjected to an education that is undemocratic, theoretically weak, and out of sync with the social and multilingual realities of an increasingly globalized and multilingual world.

SEE ALSO *American Colonization Society and the Founding of Liberia; Cultural Deficiency; Education, Racial Disparities; Slavery, Racial; Slavery and Race.*

BIBLIOGRAPHY

Appel, René, and Pieter Muysken. 1987. *Language Contact and Bilingualism.* Baltimore, MD: Edward Arnold.

Asante, Molefi Kete. 1998. *Identifying Racist Language: Linguistic Acts and Signs.* Thousand Oaks, CA: Sage Publications. Available from http://www.asante.net/newsmagazine/identifyingracistslanguage.html.

Fishman, Joshua, Michael H. Gertner, Esther G. Lowy, and William G. Milán. 1985. *The Rise and Fall of the Ethnic Revival: Perspectives on Language and Ethnicity.* New York: Mouton de Gruyter.

Goldstein, Lynn M. 2001. "Three Newspapers and a Linguist: A Folk Linguistic Journey into the Land of English as the Official Language." In *Language Ideologies: Critical Perspectives on the Official English Movement,* Vol. 2: *History, Theory, and Policy,* edited by Roseann D. González, 221–244. Urbana, IL: National Council of Teachers of English.

Gutiérrez, Kris. D., Jolynn Asato, Maria Santos, and Neil Gotanda. 2002. "Backlash Pedagogy: Language and Culture and the Politics of Reform." *The Review of Education, Pedagogy, and Cultural Studies* 24: 335–351.

Hill, Jane H. 1993. "Hasta La Vista, Baby: Anglo Spanish in the American Southwest." *Critique of Anthropology* 13: 145–176.

———. 2001. "Racializing Function of Language Panics." In *Language Ideologies: History, Theory, and Policy.* Vol. 2, edited by R. Dueñas González and I. Melis, 245–267. Mahwah, NJ: Laurence Erlbaum.

Hruska, Barbara. 2000. "Ideologies, Programs, and Practices: Implications for Second Language Learners." Paper presented at the Puerto Rican Studies Association Conference (Amherst, MA), October 28.

Pennycook, Alastair. 1998. *English and the Discourse of Colonialism.* New York: Routledge.

Salinas, Maria Elena. 2007. "Governor Is Wrong about Spanish Media." *Fresno Bee,* June 26. Available from http://www.fresnobee.com/columnists/salinas/story/69541.html.

Sanchez, Rick. 2007. Paula Zahn Now program: "Former House Speaker Newt Gingrich under Fire; Is Media Portrayal of Iraq Accurate?" April 2. Available from http://transcripts.cnn.com/TRANSCRIPTS/0704/02/pzn.01.html.

Skutnabb-Kangas, Tove. 1988. "Multilingualism and the Education of Minority Children." In *Minority Education: From Shame to Struggle,* edited by Tove Skutnabb-Kangas and Jim Cummins, 9–45. Clevedon, U.K., Multiligual Matters.

———, and Robert Phillipson. 1990. "Linguicism: A Tool for Analysing Linguistic Inequality and Promoting Linguistic Human Rights." *International Journal of Group Tensions* 20, no. 2.

Wiley, Terrence. 2000. "Continuity and Change in the Function of Language Ideologies in the United States." In *Ideology, Politics, and Language Policies: Focus on English,* edited by Thomas Ricento, 67–85. Amsterdam, Netherlands: John Benjamins.

Olga A. Vásquez

LANGUAGE, INCENDIARY

On April 4, 2007, signing off his CBS morning radio program, popular "shock jock" Don Imus apparently had no idea that he had just incited a firestorm of controversy. A cross between radio/TV shock jock Howard Stern and a bright, hard-driving investigative reporter, Imus often stated that he took special pride in offending everyone. But one typically derogatory remark made on that April day ultimately resulted in his downfall. In an on-air conversation with producer Bernard McGuirk, Imus described the Rutgers University women's basketball team, which consisted mostly of African American women, as "nappy-headed hos."

THE CONTROVERSY

Like other radio talk-show hosts such as Michael Savage and Rush Limbaugh, Imus had made a name for himself by being outrageous and making cruel, crude jokes. Audiences apparently loved him, driving his ratings up, which attracted generous sponsors. They could tune in weekdays for a blistering diatribe against politicians, celebrities, athletes, religious groups, and ethnic minorities—no one was safe. Frequent targets were New York Roman Catholic Cardinal John O'Connor ("a vulgar Irishman") and football players ("knuckle-dragging morons"). A *Washington Post* reporter and frequent guest was called a "beanie-wearing Jew boy," and Gwen Ifill, correspondent with the Public Broadcasting Company was the "cleaning lady." He and his sidekick had shticks playing off one another. (Impersonating poet Maya Angelou, an eloquent and dignified African-American writer, poet, and playwright, producer and sidekick McGuirk spoke in a lazy southern drawl, saying they should "kiss my big black ass.")

But "Imus in the Morning" was a major draw for guests as well as listeners. Guests were alternately flattered and ridiculed, but they were willing to put up with this trash talk because Imus gave them an opportunity to talk about political and global issues important to them. Journalists, authors, and politicians earned a kind of cachet for visiting the show, and every appearance boosted their celebrity status and helped put their books on best-seller lists.

No one might have noticed the remark about the Rutgers team if it had not been for a media-watch group called Media Matters for America. The group posted a recording of the remark on its Web site and on YouTube and notified civil rights and women's groups via e-mail. After the story was e-mailed to the National Association of Black Journalists, the association demanded an apology, then demanded that Imus be fired. The National Association for the Advancement of Colored People (NAACP) denounced him. National Organization for Women (NOW) encouraged its members to e-mail CBS, MSNBC, and individual radio stations with the message, "Dump Don."

At first, the network only suspended the media giant—essentially a slap on the wrist for bad-boy behavior—and Imus dutifully apologized. But when the public outcry continued, NBC executives met with their African American employees via satellite conference to hear their concerns. Al Roker, weatherman on the *Today* television show, was particularly outspoken: "That could have been my daughter Imus was joking about" (Kosova 2007, p. 24). The last straw for network executives was the withdrawal of support for the show from advertisers. Eight days after Imus made the racial/sexist remarks, he was fired.

THE DEBATE

Weeks were spent debating the issues in the media. Imus was criticized for using racially and sexually demeaning language—for criticizing decent, hard-working young scholar-athletes who had done nothing wrong. Some claimed a white male had no right to use those racial terms. Others countered that those words were standard fare for hip-hop rappers and black comedians, and they decried the double standard. Noted black journalist Bill Maxwell wrote that, with their acceptance of a gangsta rap music that insults black people, African Americans "have only ourselves to blame for the mainstreaming of 'nappy-headed hos.'" (Maxwell 2007, p. 3P). There was debate over whether the comments were primarily racial or gender slurs. Many defended Imus by calling up the tenets of freedom of speech, stirring up fears of media censorship.

Up to that point, criticism of the black cultural phenomenon, hip-hop, had been largely ignored. The Reverend Al Sharpton was one early critic, but most considered such trash talk in black music to be simply part of the act. TV talk-show host Oprah Winfrey dedicated two hours to the issue. Black women professionals began to speak out against rappers' derogatory behavior toward women, and a few rap executives and rappers seemed ready to change. Months after the incident, it seemed as though the Imus affair would blow over with time. Imus and his supporters insisted he will be brought back to radio. Imus was still popular and had brought in millions of advertising dollars to the networks. As Rutgers coach C. Vivian Stringer said pointedly, the affair was not about the color black or the color white—it was about the color green.

Hate talk over the airways and racial slurs by celebrities are nothing new. In the 1930s, Father Charles Coughlin, the so-called father of talk radio, routinely made anti-Semitic remarks in his American broadcasts—this in a climate of growing Nazism in Europe—often inciting violence against Jews. With the 1960s civil rights movement, the era of "political correctness" toned down bigoted comments, at least in public. The Fairness Doctrine of the U.S. Federal Communications Commission mandated that stations give airtime to opposing political views, effectively cutting off much divisive talk. But when that law was abolished in 1987, trash talk began to take off.

Broadcasters reacted in different ways to public complaints as talk-show hosts grew bolder. Howard Stern's career took off in the mid-1980s, although he was once fired from NBC radio for a "Bestiality Dial-A-Date" sketch. In the early 1990s in New York, a black-owned radio station was told to stop letting callers and guests make anti-Semitic and other racist remarks. For years, noted talk-show personality Bob Grant regularly targeted liberals, civil rights workers, and African Americans. He called then-president Bill Clinton a "sleazebag," Martin Luther King Jr., a "scumbag," a NOW president an "ugly dyke," and black mayor David Dinkins a "washroom attendant." In 1996, Grant went too far: He was fired for his tasteless sarcasm regarding the air-crash death of black U.S. Secretary of Commerce Ron Brown. But in the press Grant was considered a "consummate showman," "a man of wit and erudition." He had a million listeners every week and, at that time, generated around $7 million annually for his radio station. Within weeks of Grant's firing, he was hired at another New York radio station where he was treated as a superstar.

Celebrities caught making racial comments on- or off-air became a regular news item with their public apologies. White actor Ted Danson, known for the TV show *Cheers*, made racial jokes in blackface at a 1993 banquet and had to apologize, even though his then girlfriend, black comedian Whoopi Goldberg, claimed she had written the skit. In 2007, Michael Richards, from the TV show Seinfeld, shouted the word "nigger" and other epithets to a surly audience during a comedy routine. That same year, actor/director Mel Gibson, known for his academy-award winning movie *Braveheart* and the critically acclaimed *The Passion of the Christ*, railed against the "f—-ing Jews" when pulled over for drunk driving.

THE CONSEQUENCES

In the immediate wake of the Imus affair, a few other "shock jocks" were suspended or fired for racist or sexist jokes, including JV and Elvis in New York for their slurs against Asian Americans, and Gregg Hughes and Anthony Cumia for "jokes" about raping black Secretary of State Condoleezza Rice. Disc jockey Luis Jiménez of Univision Radio sparked controversy for reportedly making homophobic comments on his radio talk show. But "shock jocks" are, as the term indicates, supposed to be shocking and outrageous. In his own defense, Imus claims that controversy—tasteless humor and all—was what he was hired to promote, and he hired a lawyer to sue the networks for breach of contract.

In the twenty-first century, North American societies tend to be multicultural and diverse, and once-taboo subjects can be discussed frankly. Despite freedom of speech, most people believe that there is a line between talk that is acceptable and talk that is not. Society tends to accept profanity when it is used for socially redeeming purposes. Social critics such as the late black comic Dick Gregory used language that was intended to make people uncomfortable and make them think. Lenny Bruce, a white comic and satirist repeatedly arrested in the 1950s and 1960s for using profanity in his performances, wanted to repeat the "N word" over and over until it had no meaning. The difference between acceptable and unacceptable use of language is defined by some as a matter of hostility—whether given with a smile or not, the difference is between social critique and cruelty.

The issue is complex. Fear of censorship and loss of free speech are real concerns of U.S. citizens. But in an increasingly uncivil society where name-calling, racism, homophobia, and misogyny are the norm, there are increasing calls for government intervention, such as a return of the Fairness Doctrine—a real fear of radio executives supervising talk shows.

In the case of restraining the trash talk and bigotry of talk-show hosts, it appears that corporate profits make the difference. Tasteless humor, it seems, is lucrative. The media caved in to criticism of Imus, but his firing came only after advertisers such as General Motors and American Express pulled their ads from the show. *Adweek* magazine claimed that advertisers never intended to kill Imus's show and they are amenable to sponsoring him again. With an annual sum of $11 million taken by Imus's radio station owners, $33 million for MSNBC on which the show was simulcast, and $15–$20 million for CBS Radio, the name Imus meant high profits. Perhaps Don Imus will be able to put this episode behind him and follow the path of the once-fired Bob Grant, the talk host who made a quick comeback and still regularly appears on New York radio. Ranked as one of the greatest talk-show hosts of all time, Grant proved to be a major influence on the careers of many current high-profile shock jocks.

BIBLIOGRAPHY

Asim, Jabari. 2007. *The N Word: Who Can Say It, Who Shouldn't, and Why*. Boston: Houghton Mifflin.

Fish, Stanley. 1994. *There's No Such Thing as Free Speech, and It's a Good Thing, Too*. New York: Oxford University Press.

Gates, Henry Louis, Jr. 1994. *Speaking of Race, Speaking of Sex: Hate Speech, Civil Rights, and Civil Liberties*. New York: New York University Press.

Kennedy, Randall. 2002. *Nigger: The Strange Career of a Troublesome Word*. New York: Pantheon.

Kosova, Weston. 2007. "The Power That Was." *Newsweek* April 23: 24ff.

Kurtz, Howard. 1996. *Hot Air: All Talk, All the Time*. New York: Times Books.

Maxwell, Bill. 2007. "Black Critics of Imus are Hypocrites." *St. Petersburg Times*: 3P.

Shelley Arlen

LATIN AMERICAN RACIAL TRANSFORMATIONS

The term *ethnogenesis* refers to the emergence of a people within recorded or oral history. Throughout the Americas, people have surged into history as independent nationalities or ethnicities, sometimes as allies in wars between colonial powers or, later, wars of independence. In the late twentieth century, waves of previously unrecognized people—in cultural alliance with others—appeared in Latin America in protest movements and in performances that celebrated a new, alternative modernity, as historical peoples in new contemporary places. People have also been placed in various categories historically, whether or not they wanted to be in such categories or deserved to be there. In the twentieth and twenty-first centuries, cultural systems have emerged to confront nationalist ideologies of "racial hybridity" that signify the oneness of the *mestizo* body of the nation, and to reject or transform stereotypic categories such as the Spanish *indio* (Indian) and *negro* (black). In such rejections, aggregates of people with multicultural or intercultural orientations often come to the forefront of ethnic resurgence. During such resurgence, emphasis is placed on culture as interethnic, and on ethnicity as intercultural.

In his edited book *History, Power, and Identity: Ethnogenesis in the Americas, 1492–1992* (1996), Jonathan D. Hill writes: "ethnogenesis can be understood as a creative adaptation to a general history of violent changes—including demographic collapse, forced relocations, enslavement, ethnic soldiering, ethnocide, and genocide—imposed during the historical expansion of colonial and national states in the Americas" (p. 1).

In a 2000 article in the journal *Current Anthropology*, the archaeologist Alf Hornborg argues that ethnogenesis was prevalent throughout prehistoric America, but as destruction and devastation occurred during the European conquest and the subsequent extended colonial period, ethnogenetic processes became increasingly important in response to the catastrophic disruptions that occurred in the varied lifeways of the vanquished. *Transculturation* is part of the process of ethnogenesis. It refers to the appropriation of cultural features by people in one system from those in another for specific purposes. Such purposes include trade, alliance against enemies, and religious conversion.

NAPO RUNA: MODERNITY, ETHNOGENESIS, AND TRANSCULTURATION

In the Quichua language, a variant of Incaic Quechua, *runa* means "people," or "fully human beings." Napo is a province in Ecuador named for the Napo River, which has its headwaters in the Andes mountains and runs down through Ecuador and part of Peru into the Amazon River. While Quechua is an Andean language, the Napo Runa are Amazonian people in an Andean nation. The origins of their language, spoken by perhaps 100,000 Amazonian people in Colombia, Ecuador, and Peru, remains obscure, but "conservative" features in it negate migration theories from the Ecuadorian Andes to Amazonia. In his book *The Napo Runa of Amazonian Ecuador* (2004), Michael Uzendoski offers a dramatic illustration of historical cultural emergence (in the sixteenth century, and again in the eighteenth century) that manifests a twenty-first century cultural resurgence oriented to the establishment of self-determination in a known territory (the Napo river region of Ecuador) and general recognition in the Ecuadorian nation-state.

The drama of transculturation is documented in the sixteenth-century revolt of shamans (called *pendes*) led by the indigenous leader Jumandy. In his chapter "The Return of Jumandy," Uzendoski writes about the indigenous uprising of 2001, during which Quichua concepts of transformation of space-time and power generated a collective sense of ancient resistance to conquest and colonialism, thereby strengthening an affirmation of oneness by a people in intercultural interaction with other Andean and Amazonian people. During the 2001 indigenous uprising, Napo Runa people blocked the airport and bridge in Tena, in northern Ecuador. Even after one person was shot and killed, waves of indigenous people came to replace one another, and in the face of death proclaimed a victory modeled on the historical revolt led by Jumandy.

The sixteenth-century uprisings in the Quijos territory of what is now Napo Runa cultural territory was nearly coterminous with another great uprising, that of the Shuar people to the south. Both rebellions spread to the Andes, where they were viciously crushed by the Spanish, but the former is commemorated in the early twenty-first century in north Andean Ecuador in a major festival of the Otavalan people, who still celebrate the "revolt of the shamans" in their annual ritual of the Pendoneros.

On the southern fringe of Quito, the capital of Ecuador, there are indigenous people who have thus far not participated in the sporadic indigenous uprisings that well up in the countryside and flow into the capital. These people celebrate cultural diversity and interculturality in two extended annual festivals, the Day of the Dead, celebrated throughout Latin America, and the local festival that is dedicated to Saint Bartolomé. Although as yet unpublished, important research by the anthropologist Julie Williams demonstrates that the people of Lumbisí, who speak Spanish and work as lower- and middle-class people in Quito, regard themselves as multicultural and indigenous, separate from all processes of *mestizaje*. In their celebrations they build ties to other indigenous communities as they celebrate "the future's past," itself a metaphor for the emerging identity referent of the Ecuadorian people.

To understand the early underpinnings of ethnogenesis and transculturation more fully, it helps to look at the Caribbean region, the area that took the first brunt of the conquest and suffered the brutal changes of the colonial era. This is the region where the miracle of interculturality, often known as *créolité*, uniting indigenous people with African and African-descended people, first emerged in the Americas.

COLONIAL ARAWAK AND CARIB PEOPLE

Probably nothing captured the interest of Europeans in the Americas like the image of the "savage cannibal." This image of man-eating people, long existent in European thought, became codified into a Spanish religious and secular canon in a royal proclamation, signed by Queen Isabella in 1502, that created what Michael

Palencia-Roth calls "The Cannibal Law of 1503." This extraordinary law established the people who became known as the "Carib" as veritable cannibals. These people were also called *indios* (Indians), and because of their alleged cannibalism they became legal victims of "Just Wars." Anyone named as "Carib" could be legally enslaved and sold at a profit—no proof was needed of anthropophagy. To "be Carib" was to be fair game for legal servitude or annihilation. In many cases, indigenous people with long hair were taken to be Carib and treated as subhuman eaters of other humans.

The idea of Caribs apparently came to Columbus from people he encountered in his first voyage. They called themselves Taíno (meaning talented people, crafts people) and spoke an Arawak language of the greater Antilles. On his second voyage in 1493 Columbus, at the suggestion of his Arawak peons and slaves, took a more southerly route across the Atlantic and the flotilla made landfall in islands in the lesser Antilles. There, in an island household, human bones were found. At this point the living legend of the savage cannibals, dangerous to "peaceful" Arawaks and Europeans, was born, and it has been maintained right up into the present century.

Arawaks, or those said to be Arawaks, were recruited by European powers such as the Spanish, who regarded them as malleable to European needs, but those who resisted the Spanish were called Caribs. These latter people, whatever language they may have spoken, were recruited by the enemies of the Spanish, such as the Dutch and the English, in a system known as "ethnic soldiering." In the early twenty-first century, learned scholars still debate relationships, historical and contemporary, among the Caribs and the Arawaks. The languages still exist in the mainland of South America, and a mixture of Carib and Arawak is spoken on the Caribbean Island of Dominica. But the actual ethnic affiliations and cultural characteristics of this great dichotomy in history, as well as the present lifeways of these peoples' descendents, remain very controversial.

BLACKNESS, *ZAMBAJE*, AND COMPLICATIONS WITH INDIGENOUS CULTURES

The characterization of Caribs and Arawaks—as fierce and friendly, respectively—became complicated in the Americas almost from the outset due to the presence of African-descended peoples in the same region, and due to the phenomenon of *cimarronaje*, self-liberation by African-descended and indigenous-descended people who mixed, merged, and defended their traditional and new territories on the fringes of the growing capitalist enterprise. Two people who became known (and feared) in early colonial times are the Garífuna and the Miskitu. Each is the representative of a segment of the population of Central America in the early twenty-first century, and each has been studied from a variety of scholarly perspectives. The Garífuna are usually regarded as African American, and the Miskitu as indigenous American, but both share a deep history of *cimarronaje*, ethnogenesis, transculturation, and emergent cultural orientations. Many of these features speak against the facile, racialized Western contrast of African and Indian.

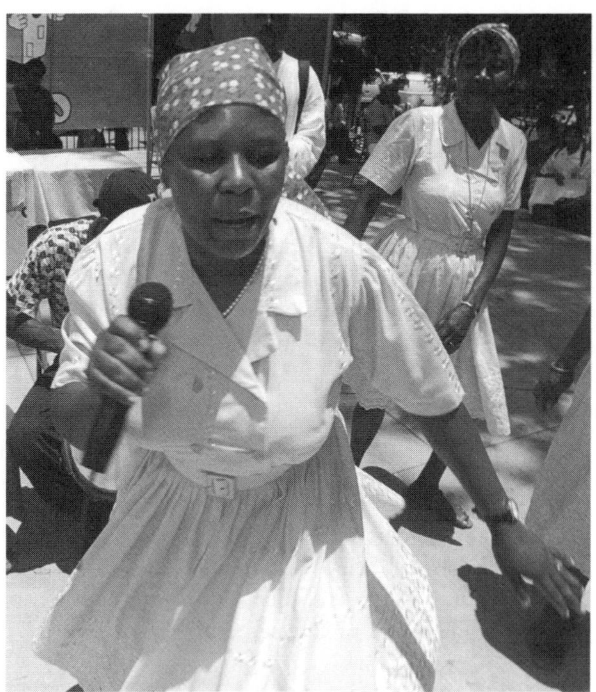

Garífuna Celebration, 1999. *The Garífuna are blacks who came to Honduras, Nicaragua, Belize, and Guatemala to escape slavery in the Caribbean.* AP IMAGES.

The Garífuna of Honduras, Nicaragua, Belize, and Guatemala have large local populations with specific cultural organizations in Los Angeles and Chicago. They were first known in the seventeenth century as the "Black Carib" because they came into historical view on St. Vincent Island in the Lesser Antilles through interbreeding between native people (known as "Island Carib") and black Maroons (and perhaps enslaved Africans). The name *Garífuna* (plural *Garinagu*), which these Central American people call themselves, derives from "Kalinago," the name Christopher Columbus learned as the plural of the "Carib" of Eastern Venezuela and the Guianas. All Carib speakers, and other native peoples who resisted Columbus's profitable advances, were called "Cannibals" (from whence came the name "Caribbean").

The Miskitu people of Honduras and Nicaragua became famous during the U.S. sponsored Contra war against the Sandinista government of Nicaragua. They got their name through their colonial alliance with the British, from whom they obtained muskets that they used against the Spanish. The name for the weapons they used (muskets) was applied to the weapon bearers in the form "mosquitoes" (like "musketeers"), which then became "Miskitu." Missing the major point of *zambaje*—the mixture of African-descended and indigenous-descended peoples without European "admixture"—many anthropologists and historians have debated whether the Garífuna and Miskitu, among many other similar people, should be studied "as Africans" or "as Indians." Once such a debate is engendered, the tendency is to see what is "retained" from African heritage and what is "retained" from indigenous heritage. When this happens, a colonial mentality prevails, and people living their ways of life are stifled in expressing their existence, presence, and emergent cultural systems to a global audience. To use the Spanish vernacular, they become *negreado*—darkened, blackened, diminished, and silenced by a spurious hegemonic, racialized, diffusionist debate.

ALTERNATIVE MODERNITIES AND EMERGENT CULTURES

Two concepts that relate specifically to ethnogenesis are *alternative modernity* and *emergent culture*. A third idea, which has become prevalent throughout Latin American nation-states, is that of *interculturality*, which contributes to the process of transculturation. Emergent culture confronts racial categories of the conquest and colonial era of Latin America, drawing upon previous moments of ethnogenesis for strength and self-assertion. This idea of emergent culture refers to how people present themselves in various settings, ranging from everyday greetings to stylized ritual performances for varied audiences. In the 1980s, for example, indigenous people in many nations organized themselves into nationalities to reflect their individual cultures grounded in specific localities, as well as their common identity through specific histories of oppression. By 2001, more than twenty different nationalities had emerged in Ecuador, and they have coalesced into regional organizations located in the coastal, Andean, and Amazonian regions of that country. With such emergence, regional commonalities are stressed that may clash with other commonalities in different regions. Nonetheless, with all this diversity, coastal, Andean, and Amazonian people have arisen as one group to confront national leaders in Ecuador, even contributing to the ousting of several national presidents.

Alternative modernity is the idea that one can live in the contemporary world but adhere to cultural values and social practices at odds with the dictums of dominant modernity, where racial stratification, profit seeking, and forced conformity define an ideal way of life. Indigenous nationalities reflect the notion of alternatives in modern life, as do celebrations of Kwanzaa by North American African Americans near the time of the winter solstice. Indigenous nationality is an alternative to standardized, Western nationalist life, and Kwanzaa is an alternative to Christmas and Hanukah.

In Bolivia, Peru, and Ecuador, many Andean indigenous peoples present themselves as Inca (or Inka), not as remnants of a conquered people, but as people transformed in the twentieth and twenty-first century as self-determined peoples in control of their own lives. In Andean Ecuador, for example, indigenous festivals of Corpus Christi, once a blending of Catholic and local indigenous (not Incaic) traditions, have been reconfigured into a celebration of Inti Raymi, the Festival of the Sun. This festival has come to be promoted in Ecuador, the United States, Canada, and European nations as "authentic" Ecuadorian indigenous performance, and it is being adopted outside of Ecuador as essential Ecuadorian culture by people identifying as nonindigenous.

In the Amazonian region of Ecuador, however, indigenous Quichua-speakers generally reject any Incaic heritage, lumping the conquering Inca with the conquering Spanish and identifying "Andean" with a clear hierarchy, in contradistinction to individualistic and egalitarian Amazonian values. However, Andean and Amazonian people, together with various peoples of the coast, have allied repeatedly since the indigenous uprising of 1990 to proclaim themselves as united, intercultural, indigenous people opposed to the national ideology of "blending" and "hybridity." These peoples are opposed to a national, hierarchical socioeconomic system that places them together with Afro-Ecuadorians at the bottom of the social ladder of power, privilege, and life chances. In such movements, the twin phenomena of interculturality and transculturation stand in strong relief.

INTERCULTURALITY AND TRANSCULTURATION

As a vibrant ideological and educational motif in many Latin American nations, interculturality lies just beneath the surface of public publications, radio broadcasts, and television presentations of the oneness of the people of a nation-state and on the vestiges of indigenous and African-descended cultures. Emerging in the 1980s and early 1990s, interculturality represents an indefatigable social movement called *interculturalidad*, which is conjoined with its seemingly paradoxical complement of reinforced cultural and ethnic boundaries. Interculturality is very different from an ethos of hybridity or social or cultural pluralism. It is multicultural, but it is also intercultural.

Interculturality stresses a movement from one cultural system to another—the phenomenon of transculturation—with the explicit purpose of understanding other ways of thought and action. Social and cultural pluralism, by contrast, stress the institutional separation forced by the *blanco* (white) elite in Latin American nations on its varied and diverse peoples. The ideologies of hybridity and pluralism are national, regional, and static, while a formal consciousness of interculturality and transculturation is local, regional, diasporic, global, and dynamic.

The transformations of ethnicity and cultural systems in the twenty-first century in the Americas have roots in the European conquest and colonization of the New World. Now, as then, people throw off their stereotypical otherness to affirm and reaffirm their own dynamic lifeways. In their assertions one finds revolt and rebellion as well as celebration and festivity. The significance of ethnogenesis and interculturality must be sought in the symbolic and pragmatic systems of people themselves, and not in the oppressive categories that continue to reflect conquest and colonial mentality.

SEE ALSO *Blackness in Latin America; El Mestizaje; Racial Formations.*

BIBLIOGRAPHY

Bilby, Kenneth. 2006. *True-Born Maroons.* Gainesville: The University Press of Florida.

Hill, Jonathan D, and Fernando Santos-Granero, eds. 2002. *Comparative Arawakan Histories: Rethinking Language Family and Culture Area in Amazonia.* Urbana: University of Illinois Press.

Hornborg, Alf. 2005. "Ethnogenesis, Regional Integration, and Ecology in Prehistoric Amazonia: Toward a System Perspective." *Current Anthropology* 46 (4): 589–620.

Hulme, Peter, and Neil Whitehead, eds. 1992. *Wild Majesty: Encounters with Caribs from Columbus to the Present Day.* New York: Oxford University Press.

Palencia-Roth, Michael, 1993. "The Cannibal Law of 1503." In *Early Images of the Americas: Transfer and Invention,* edited by Jerry M. Williams and Robert E. Lewis. Tucson: University of Arizona Press.

Redstall, Mathew, ed. 2005. *Beyond Black and Red: African-Native Relations in Colonial Latin America.* Albuquerque: University of New Mexico Press.

Silverblatt, Irene. 2004. *Modern Inquisitions: Peru and the Colonial Origins of the Civilized World.* Durham, NC: Duke University Press.

Uzendoski, Michael. 2004. *The Napo Runa of Amazonian Ecuador.* Urbana: University of Illinois Press.

Whitten, Norman E., Jr., Dorothea Scott Whitten, and Alfonso Chango. 1997. "Return of the Yumbo: The Caminata from Amazonia to Quito." *American Ethnologist* 24 (2): 355–391.

Whitten, Norman E., Jr., and Rachel Corr. 2001. "Contesting the Images of Oppression:" *North American Congress of Latin America (NACLA)* 34 (6). Special Issue: *The Social Origins of Race: Race and Racism in the Americas,* Part I, pp. 24–28, 45–46.

Whitten, Norman E., Jr., ed. 2003. *Millennial Ecuador: Critical Essays on Cultural Transformations and Social Dynamics.* Iowa City: University of Iowa Press.

Norman E. Whitten Jr.

LATINA GENDER, REPRODUCTION, AND RACE

Race, fertility, and immigration have formed a fearsome trinity for much of United States history. During each wave of immigration, "natives" have feared that the new immigrants would have deleterious impacts on American culture and society. Predominant among these fears was that of immigrant fertility levels, which a wary public often perceived as dangerously high, and thus as a threat to the education, welfare, and medical care systems. Immigrant fertility has also been viewed as a harbinger of demographic shifts that would lead to the diminishing power of the dominant racial/ethnic group, however it was conceived at the historical moment. During the most recent wave of immigration, commonly referred to as post-1965 immigration, Latina reproduction and fertility, especially of Mexican immigrant women, has become ground zero in a war not just of words but also of public policies and laws. Indeed, anti-immigrant sentiment during the last decades of the twentieth century focused specifically on the biological and social reproductive capacities of Mexican immigrant and Mexican-origin (U.S.-born) women. This trend continued into the first decade of the twenty-first century.

LATINA FERTILITY AND THE "BROWNING OF AMERICA"

The post-1965 period witnessed a continuous fertility decline among U.S. women, which has contributed to a demographic shift in which white, non-Hispanic Americans have declined as a proportion of the overall population. The concept that emerged in popular discourse in response to this demographic shift was "the browning of America." Latina reproduction and fertility has been center stage in the often vitriolic public debate over the meaning of this demographic change. National magazines, for example, have consistently represented the fertility levels of Latinas, especially Mexicans and Mexican Americans, as "dangerous," "pathological," "abnormal," and even a threat to national security. These representations of Latina fertility have been evident in two interrelated themes prevalent in the public discourse on immigration: (1) high fertility and population growth, and (2) invasion and reconquest (Chavez 2001).

HIGH FERTILITY AND POPULATION GROWTH

The demographic changes to the nation's racial and ethnic composition began slowly after 1965, and they did not therefore become a central component of public discourse in the 1970s. Latina reproduction and fertility, however, were becoming an object of social-science inquiry and public concern. In the 1970s, the contribution of Latino immigrants and their children to population growth was particularly problematic for some environmental and population groups, such as Zero Population Growth, Inc. Academic researchers noted that "the fertility of Mexican Americans is substantially higher than other groups," with the average size of Mexican American families (4.4 persons) about one person larger than that of all Americans (3.5 persons per family) in 1970 (Alvirez and Bean 1976, pp. 280–281).

National magazines also warned readers of the threat of Latina reproduction. *U.S. News* & *World Report*'s July 4, 1977, cover carried the headline: "Time Bomb in Mexico: Why There'll be No End to the Invasion of 'Illegals.'" The accompanying article clarified that the "time bomb" was Mexico's population and its expected growth rate. The article stressed that the fertility of Mexicans, combined with Mexico's inability to produce jobs for its population, would lead to greater pressure for immigration to the United States in the future. Although the story drew the reader's attention to the external threat posed by the reproductive capacity of Mexican women, the internal threat posed by their U.S.-born children's high fertility levels were also implicated in the rapidly growing U.S. Latino population.

In the 1980s, stories about the growth of the U.S. Latino population were often paired with stories about the decline in immigrants from Europe and the declining proportion of whites in the U.S. population. For example, *Newsweek*'s January 17, 1983, issue reported that the number of Latinos in the United States grew by 61 percent between 1970 and 1980. This growth was attributed to immigration and higher fertility rates, and to the fact that since the mid-1960s there were 46.4 percent fewer immigrants from Europe. The fertility rates of immigrant Latinas and U.S.-born Latinas were characterized as "high" and responsible for demographic changes occurring in the nation's racial composition. For example, John Tanton—an ophthalmologist from Michigan who had been president of Zero Population Growth, a cofounder of the Federation for American Immigration Reform in 1979, and an ardent promoter of population control, restricting immigration, and making English the official language of the United States—wrote a now infamous memorandum in 1988 about Latina fertility and "the Latin onslaught." He asked, "Will Latin American immigrants bring with them the tradition of the *mordida* (bribe), the lack of involvement in public affairs, etc.? Will the present majority peaceably hand over its political power to a group that is simply more fertile? … On the demographic point: Perhaps this is the first instance in which those with their pants up are going to get caught by those with their pants down!" (Conniff 1993, p. 24).

By the 1990s, "race" and "multiculturalism" had become dominant themes in U.S. public discourse about the changing composition of the nation's population. For example, in its April 9, 1990, issue, *Time* magazine focused on the implications of the United States becoming a multiracial and multicultural society, with no single social group demographically dominant. As *Time* put it: "The 'browning of America' will alter everything in society, from politics and education to industry, values and culture. … The deeper significance of America becoming a majority nonwhite society is what it means to the national psyche, to individuals' sense of themselves and the nation—their idea of what it is to be American." (Henry 1990, p. 31).

Public concern over Latina reproduction has led to changes in public policy. Proposition 187, the "Save Our State" initiative on the 1994 California ballot, sought to control undocumented immigration by eliminating education, certain social services, and medical care for pregnant undocumented women and their children. Bette Hammond, one of the organizers of Proposition 187, explained the reason for the initiative: "They come here, they have their babies, and after that they become citizens and all those children use social services" (quoted in Kadetsky 1994, p. 418). Proposition 187 was passed overwhelmingly by the California voters, but most of its key components were later deemed unconstitutional by the courts. At about the same time, California's governor, Pete Wilson, made denying undocumented immigrant women prenatal care a top priority of his administration. The 1996 federal welfare reform law also denied many medical and social services to immigrants, including women.

In 2004, Samuel P. Huntington, a professor at Harvard University, repeated what had become a three-decades-long national narrative about the threat posed by Latina fertility. Writing in *Foreign Policy,* Huntington noted: "In this new era, the single most immediate and most serious challenge to America's traditional identity comes from the immense and continuing immigration from Latin America, especially from Mexico, and the fertility rates of those immigrants compared to black and white American natives" (Huntington 2004, p. 32).

INVASION AND RECONQUEST

The threat posed by Latina biological and social reproduction is central to the second theme in the public discourse: the Mexican "invasion," or "reconquest," of the southwestern United States. Key to this theme is evoking the ideology of the Quebec separatist movement, whereby French-speaking Canadians sought separation from English-speaking Canada. The Quebec separatist movement has provided the lens through which Mexican-origin population growth has been viewed (and its threat elaborated) over decades of public discourse. It is important to note that although the reconquest theme is repeated over and over, no empirical evidence for such a movement is provided.

The reconquest theme surfaced in the *U.S. News & World Report*'s December 13, 1976, issue, which featured the headline "Crisis across the Borders: Meaning to U.S." The cover's image is a map of North America with two arrows, both beginning in the United States, one pointing to Mexico and one pointing to Canada. The problem in Canada was Quebec, where many French-speaking residents were pushing for greater sovereignty and even separation from the English-speaking provinces. The problem in Mexico was the economic crisis and the pressure for increased migration to the United States.

The "Mexican invasion" theme has often been intertwined with Latina biological and social reproduction and the overuse by this population of social services. Both *U.S. News & World Report* (March 7, 1983) and *Newsweek* (June 25, 1984) published covers that serve as examples. *U.S. News & World Report*'s cover announced: "Invasion from Mexico: It Just Keeps Growing." The image on the cover was a photograph of a line of men and women being carried by men across a canal of water. At the head of the line was a woman being carried to the United States on the shoulders of a man. *Newsweek* had a similar cover, a photographic image of a man carrying a woman across a shallow body of water. The woman is wearing a headscarf and a long shawl. The man carries the woman's handbag, which suggests she is traveling somewhere, moving with a purpose and intending to stay for an extended amount of time. She holds a walking cane. The caption states: "Closing the Door? The Angry Debate over Illegal Immigration."

Featuring women so prominently on the covers of these two national magazines and warning of an "invasion" sends a clear message about fertility and reproduction. Rather than an invading army, or even the stereotypical male migrant worker, the images suggest a more insidious invasion, one that includes the capacity of the invaders to reproduce themselves. The women being carried into U.S. territory carry with them the seeds of future generations. The images signal not simply a concern over undocumented workers, but also a concern with immigrants who stay and reproduce families and, by extension, communities in the United States. These images, and their accompanying articles, allude to issues of population growth and the use of prenatal care, children's health services, education, and other social services related to reproduction.

Reproduction, immigration, and "reconquest" come together in *U.S. News & World Report*'s cover of August 19, 1985. Its headline announces: "The Disappearing Border: Will the Mexican Migration Create a New Nation?" The accompanying article provides a fully embellished rendition of the "reconquest" theme:

> Now sounds the march of new conquistadors in the American Southwest.... By might of numbers and strength of culture, Hispanics are changing the politics, economy and language in the U.S. states that border Mexico. Their movement is, despite its quiet and largely peaceful nature, both an invasion and a revolt. At the vanguard are those born here, whose roots are generations deep, who long endured Anglo dominance and rule and who are ascending within the U.S. system to take power they consider their birthright. Behind them comes an unstoppable mass—their kin from below the border who also claim ancestral homelands in the Southwest, which was the northern half of Mexico until the U.S. took it away in the mid-1800s. (Lang and Thornton, p. 30)

In 2000, Samuel P. Huntington repeated the alarm of a Mexican reconquest when he wrote the following: "The invasion of over 1 million Mexican civilians is a comparable threat [as 1 million Mexican soldiers] to American societal security, and Americans should react against it with comparable vigor. Mexican immigration looms as a unique and disturbing challenge to our cultural integrity, our national identity, and potentially to our future as a country" (Huntington 2000, p. 22).

The persistent focus in popular discourse on immigration is on Latina fertility and reproduction (both biological and social). U.S.-born Latinas and Latin American immigrants, according to this discourse, have extreme, even dangerous, levels of fertility in comparison to an "imagined" native population.

LATINA FERTILITY RECONSIDERED

The racialization of fertility and reproduction reinforces a characterization of white Americans as *the* legitimate Americans who are being supplanted demographically by less-legitimate Latinas. The characterization of Latina reproduction and fertility as a threat to U.S. society, culture, and demographic stability is one that has been repeated often and developed along various dimensions over many decades. These characterizations are propelled by powerful stereotypes that can make it difficult to perceive contrary evidence. Indeed, empirical data on Latina reproductive behavior may not be able to refute the deeply-held beliefs upon which these cataclysmic stories of threat, doom, and destruction are based.

However, it must be noted that Latinas are not static when it comes to fertility. Like other women in the United States, Mexico, and the world in general, Latinas have sometimes experienced rather dramatic declines in fertility. In Mexico, for example, fertility rates declined from 7 to 8 children per woman in the pre-1970 period to 4.4 children per woman in 1980, to 3.8 children in 1986, to 3.4 in 1990, and to 2.4 in 2000 (Hirsch 1998, pp. 540-541; Zuniga et al. 2000). In addition, declines in fertility are undoubtedly greater for younger Mexican women than these averages indicate.

In the United States, the fertility of Mexican-origin women has also declined dramatically. David Alvirez and Frank Bean associate this trend with urbanization and social mobility. The average size of Mexican-American families in 1970 was about one person larger than the 3.5 persons per family for all Americans at the time. By the late 1990s, all Mexican-origin women in the United States between 18 and 44 years of age had 1.81 children, well below the zero population level. Non-Hispanic white women between the same ages had 1.27 children at this time (Bean et al. 2000; Chavez 2004). When examining the fertility of the children of immigrants, second-generation, Mexican-American women had 1.4 children per woman in the late 1990s, much closer to the fertility of non-Hispanic white women (Bean, Swicegood, and Berg 2000). Moreover, research has shown that age, education, marital status and increasing facility with English are better than ethnicity (i.e., being Latina or non-Hispanic white) as predictors of whether women will have more or less children (Chavez 2004).

Despite such information, Latino reproduction is often viewed in the popular imagination as a threat, mainly because it is conflated with the decline in the reproduction of the white population. The specter of fewer white Americans and more Latinos in the United States is represented in ways that play to the fears of the general population. It is as if races are buckets, and that as one fills up the other drains out. The social and cultural construction of "races" posits firm boundaries between categories. But such boundaries are increasingly porous, intermixing, and disappearing. Perhaps the real threat of Latino reproduction is that it exposes the limitations and contradictions of racial categories that evolved during previous economic, social, and demographic contexts, but which no longer fit the realities of the early twenty-first century.

SEE ALSO *Caribbean Immigration; Day Laborers, Latino, Illegal Alien; Immigrant Domestic Workers; Immigration, Race, and Women; Immigration Reform and Control Act of 1986 (IRCA); Immigration to the United States; Mexicans; Motherhood; Nativism.*

BIBLIOGRAPHY

Alvirez, David, and Frank D. Bean. 1976. "The Mexican American Family." In *Ethnic Families in America*, edited by Charles H. Mindel and Robert N. Haberstein, 271–291. New York: Elsevier.

Bean, Frank D., C. Gray Swicegood, and Ruth Berg. 2000. "Mexican-Origin Fertility: New Patterns and Interpretations." *Social Science Quarterly* 81: 404–420.

Chavez, Leo R. 1997. "Immigration Reform and Nativism: The Nationalist Response to the Transnationalist Challenge." In *Immigrants Out!: The New Nativism and the Anti-Immigrant Impulse in the United States*, edited by Juan F. Perea, 61–77. New York: New York University Press.

———. 2001. *Covering Immigration: Popular Images and the Politics of the Nation*. Berkeley: University of California Press.

———. 2004. "A Glass Half Empty: Latina Reproduction and Public Discourse." *Human Organization* 63 (2): 173–188.

Chock, Phyllis Pease. 1996. "No New Women: Gender, 'Alien,' and 'Citizen' in the Congressional Debate on Immigration." *Political and Legal Anthropology Review* 19: 1–9.

Conniff, Ruth. 1993. "The War on Aliens: The Right Calls the Shots." *The Progressive* 57: 22–29.

Fix, Michael E., and Jeffrey S. Passel. 1999. *Trends in Noncitizens' and Citizens' Use of Public Benefits Following Welfare Reform: 1994-97*. Washington, DC: Urban Institute.

Gerstle, Gary. 2004. "The Immigrant as Threat to American Security: A Historical Perspective." In *The Maze of Fear: Security and Migration After 9/11*, edited by J. Tirman. New York: New Press.

Gould, Stephen J. 1981. *The Mismeasure of Man*. New York: Norton.

Gutiérrez, Elena Rebeca. 1999. "The Racial Politics of Reproduction: The Social Construction of Mexican-origin Women's Fertility." Ph.D. diss., University of Michigan, Ann Arbor.

Henry, William A., III. 1990. "Beyond the Melting Pot." *Time* 135 (15).

Hirsch, Jennifer S. 1998. "Migration, Modernity, and Mexican Marriage: A Comparative Study of Gender, Sexuality, and Reproductive Health in a Transnational Community." Ph.D. diss., Johns Hopkins University.

Hondagneu-Sotelo, Pierrette. 1995. "Women and Children First: New Directions in Anti-Immigrant Politics." *Socialist Review* 25 (1): 169–190.

Huntington, Samuel P. 2000. "The Special Case of Mexican Immigration: Why Mexico is a Problem." *American Enterprise* 11 (December): 20-22. Available from http://www.taemag.com.

———. 2004. "The Hispanic Challenge." *Foreign Policy* (March/April): 30–45.

Kadetsky, Elizabeth, 1994. "'Save Our State' Initiative: Bashing Illegals in California." *The Nation* 17 (October): 416–418.

Lang, John S., and Jeannye Thornton. 1985. "The Disappearing Border: Will the Mexican Migration Create a New Nation?" *U.S. News & World Report*. August 19: 30.

Lesher, Dave, and Patrick McDonnell. 1996. "Wilson Calls Halt to Much Aid for Illegal Immigrants." *Los Angeles Times*, August 28.

Marks, Jonathan. 2002. *What it Means to be 98% Chimpanzee: Apes, People, and Their Genes.* Berkeley: University of California Press.

Roberts, Dorothy E. 1997. "Who May Give Birth to Citizens? Reproduction, Eugenics, and Immigration." In *Immigrants Out! The New Nativism and the Anti-Immigrant Impulse in the United States*, edited by Juan F. Perea, 205–219. New York: New York University Press.

Wilson, Tamar D. 2000. "Anti-immigrant Sentiment and the Problem of Reproduction/Maintenance in Mexican Immigration to the United States." *Critique of Anthropology* 20 (2): 191–213.

Zuniga, Elena, Beatriz Zubieta, and Cristina Araya. 2000. *Cuadernos de salud reproductiva: Republica Mexicana.* Mexico City: Consejo Nacional de la Poblacion.

Leo Chavez

LATINO SOCIAL MOVEMENTS

Latinos in the United States have been involved with numerous social movements over the past 150 years. Despite legislation that granted them full legal, political, and social rights, Latinos (mostly Mexicans during this particular time period) became "second-class" citizens after the U.S.-Mexico War ended in 1848. They faced widespread discrimination in housing, education, and employment, which severely limited their opportunities for social mobility. These harsh conditions (which came close to those that African Americans encountered in the South after the Civil War) sparked the establishment of various labor, immigrant rights, feminist, and political organizations in the late nineteenth and early twentieth centuries.

LULAC, MENDEZ, AND THE STRUGGLE FOR CIVIL RIGHTS

The League of United Latin American Citizens (LULAC) was founded in Corpus Christi, Texas, in 1929 (Kaplowitz 2005). LULAC might be best understood as the Chicano/Latino version of the National Association for the Advancement of Colored People (NAACP), an interracial organization that African-American scholar, writer, and activist W.E.B. Du Bois helped form in 1905 (Jonas 2004). The NAACP challenged segregation through legal means, largely eschewing civil disobedience and nonviolent direct action. It also did not critique nor call for the abolition of capitalism, nor did it openly question U.S. foreign policy before and after World War II, though some black scholars and activists claimed these policies were racist and imperialist (Von Eschen 1997). The NAACP also included many middle-class individuals who favored segregation's demise but rejected calls for more radical social change.

These positions generally mirrored LULAC's political orientation. LULAC actively resisted segregation through the courts, playing a key role in the landmark 1946 *Mendez v. Westminster School District* decision that ruled that California's segregated public school system was unconstitutional. NAACP lead counsel Thurgood Marshall later cited *Mendez* as a precedent when and he and his fellow colleagues argued the *Brown v. Board of Education* case before the United States Supreme Court in 1954 (Johnson 2005; Robbie 2002). The *Mendez* case thus helped reshape the entire nation.

SECOND-CLASS CITIZENS

Mexicans were called "greasers," "*cholos*," "bloodthirsty savages," and other demeaning epithets for decades after the U.S.-Mexico War. Vigilante groups regularly hunted down Mexicans and lynched them without any legal proceedings. The legal system was largely based on "gringo justice," and the implicit assumption was that Mexican Americans constituted a separate, inferior "race" that did not deserve equal treatment under the law. The United States used this same ideology during the U.S.-Mexico War, claiming it was their "Manifest Destiny" to take territory controlled by "uncivilized people" (Horsman 1981).

LULAC believed that Mexicans-Americans were neither inferior nor uncivilized. They flatly stated that they were American citizens and should receive equal, fair, and just treatment. To achieve that goal, LULAC's leaders pushed for incremental social change through legal reforms, but it distanced itself from more militant positions. LULAC implicitly assumed that Mexican Americans would become assimilated and accepted over time by becoming more Americanized. English, therefore, became LULAC's official language. LULAC also called for stricter immigration controls and, unlike the Spanish-Speaking People's Congress, a much more radical Mexican-American organization that maintained close ties with the Communist Party in the late 1930s, it did not play an active role in organizing the labor unions that included mostly Mexican-American workers. LULAC also did not challenge political repression (e.g., McCarthyism), and it supported an anti-immigrant program called Operation Wetback in the mid-1950s. The organization also largely excluded women from leadership positions, even though some, such as Alice Dickerson Montemayor, fought for greater inclusion (Orozco 1997).

Most Chicano scholars and activists in the 1960s criticized LULAC for taking these fairly conservative positions, asserting that the organization was too tepid and

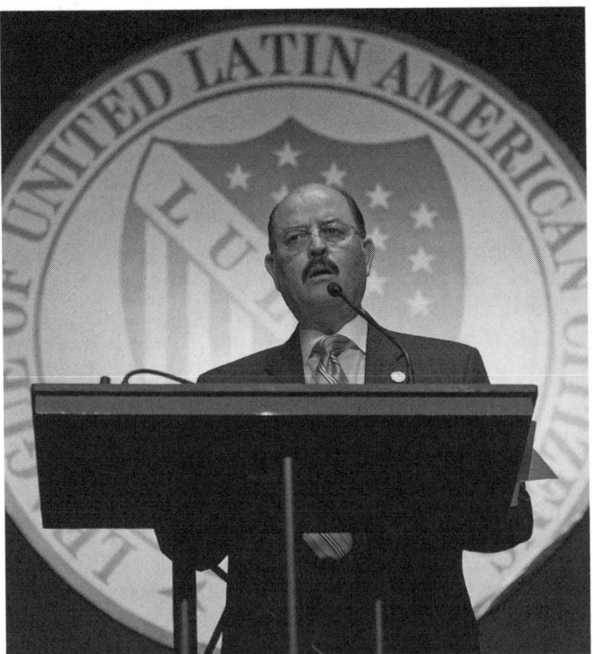

LULAC President Hector M. Flores, 2006. *The League of United Latin American Citizens (LULAC), founded in 1929, was one of the first organizations established to address Latino issues.* AP IMAGES.

mainstream. Some even called LULAC members "*vendidos*," or "sell-outs." This assessment was probably too harsh, however, because LULAC helped dismantle school segregation and racially based jury discrimination, though it did very little to transform the harsh lives of working-class Mexican Americans who faced sweatshop conditions in factories and fields all over the United States.

MEXICAN AMERICANS AND UNIONS

Between the 1930s and 1950s, two organizations—the Spanish-Speaking People's Congress (also known as *El Congreso*) and the *Asociacion Nacional Mexico-Americana* (National Association of Mexican-Americans [ANMA])—focused on organizing and supporting union campaigns that primarily involved Mexican Americans. Luisa Moreno and Josefina Fierro de Bright were El Congreso's two most notable activists. Moreno, a native-born Guatemalan, focused her efforts on organizing agricultural workers in California and Texas, while Fierro de Bright concentrated on fighting racial discrimination in Los Angeles (Ruiz 2004). Moreno helped organize, for instance, the Sleepy Lagoon Defense Committee (SLDC) to fight for the release of eleven Mexican Americans and one Euro American who had been falsely prosecuted for the murder of José Diaz in August 1942. The SLDC was a multiracial coalition that received financial support mostly from labor unions affiliated with the Congress of Industrial Organizations (CIO), a progressive labor federation that emerged in the 1930s (Barajas 2006).

CIO-affiliated unions spearheaded numerous campaigns involving Mexican Americans in the Midwest and Southwest in the middle and late 1930s. The United Cannery, Agricultural, Packing, and Allied Workers of America (UCAPAWA), for example, targeted workers in pecan-shelling plants in San Antonio, Texas. Emma Tenayuca, a young Mexican-American woman, led this campaign, organizing a strike that included 10,000 workers in 1938. Tenayuca and her Euro-American husband, Homer Brooks (who both were Communist Party members), wrote a crucial pamphlet during that two-week strike called "The Mexican Question in the Southwest." They claimed that Mexican Americans were not an "oppressed national minority" within the United States, and that they should, therefore, form alliances with working-class people of all racial backgrounds to create a "united front against fascism" (Vargas 2005).

These various elements indicate that the historical period that preceded the Chicano movement was ideologically and politically diverse. Moderate groups such as LULAC and the American GI Forum, which was created in the late 1940s to protest the interment of the World War II veteran Felix Longoria in a segregated cemetery in Texas, resisted racial discrimination, but they generally overlooked issues such as economic and class exploitation (Carroll 2003). The International Union of Mine, Mill, and Smelter Workers opposed this trend, however. "Mine-Mill" (as many called it) was one of eleven Left-leaning unions that the CIO purged in the late 1940s (the federation became increasingly conservative as the cold war between the United States and the Soviet Union, erstwhile allies during World War II, heated up). Despite being ousted from the CIO, Mine-Mill remained active, organizing a miners' strike in Bayard, New Mexico, that was immortalized in the classic blacklisted 1954 film *Salt of the Earth*. The National Association of Mexican Americans (ANMA) supported the strike and the making of the film, but McCarthyism and the ensuing "Red Scare" dramatically weakened Mine-Mill and ANMA (Lorence 1999). Political repression effectively drove *Salt of the Earth* underground over the next two decades and virtually wiped out the Mexican-American Left, leaving more politically mainstream organizations such as LULAC and the American GI Forum intact.

THE CHICANO MOVEMENT

LULAC and the American GI Forum were the most influential Mexican-American civil rights organizations in the late 1950s and early 1960s, but their prominence soon faded. The Mexican American Political Association (MAPA), Viva Kennedy clubs, the Political Association of Spanish-Speaking Organizations (PASSO), the National Farm Worker Association (NFWA), and *Alianza Federal de las Mercedes* were all established between 1959 and 1963. George Mariscal, the director of the Chicano/Latino/Arts and Humanities Program at the University of California, San Diego, contends that these groups marked the emergence of a new "more militant ethnicity-based politics throughout the Southwest" (Marsical 2005, p. 7). The United Farm Workers (UFW) probably symbolized this trend more than any other organization.

Back-breaking conditions, very low pay, no bathrooms or drinking water, and an overall lack of respect and dignity for workers, among other factors, sparked the union's formation in 1965 (Ferriss and Sandoval 1997). Filipino and Mexican farm workers, harvesting table grapes, launched the UFW's first strike—the infamous *huelga* and eventual boycott that lasted five years and resulted in contracts that guaranteed better wages and working conditions. Larry Itilong, Phillip Vera Cruz, Dolores Huerta, Jessie de la Cruz, Gilbert Padilla, Eliseo Medina, Marshall Ganz, and César Chávez were some of the union's key leaders (Scharlin and Villanueva 1997). Chávez was a former farm worker himself, and he was an organizer with the Community Service Organization (CSO) for ten years. He left the CSO in 1962 and helped establish the NFWA, the UFW's predecessor.

Much has been written about César Chávez and the UFW. Chávez was not a fiery or charismatic speaker, but he was a deeply spiritual person who moved people through his humble demeanor and savvy organizing skills. He understood quite well how culture and memory could facilitate social movements. Chávez therefore suggested that the UFW be established on September 16, Mexican Independence Day (Ferriss and Sandoval 1997). That strategic decision tied together, in a rather subtle manner, Mexico's struggle for independence from colonial rule and the farm workers' struggle for independence from exploitative working conditions. Chávez also personally helped create the UFW's trademark red-and-black eagle flag. He purposefully chose the eagle because it closely resembled the indigenous pyramids outside Mexico City, while the colors were chosen because most Mexican-based unions used them while they were on strike. Red and black also symbolize revolution and anarchy, respectively.

Despite these connotations, the UFW was not a radical organization. The union struggled for better wages and working conditions through strikes, boycotts, marches, fasts, and improvisational ("guerrilla") theater, particularly through *El Teatro Campesino* (the Farm Workers' Theater). The UFW consistently displayed banners depicting the Virgen de Guadalupe during their demonstrations, including the 250-mile pilgrimage from Delano to Sacramento held in 1966. The El Teatro Campesino leader, Luis Valdez, famously stated that the images showed the public that the union's members were "followers of the Virgin Mary, not Karl Marx" (Ferriss and Sandoval 1997). The UFW also formed close alliances with liberal Democrats such as Robert F. Kennedy.

The UFW was thus militant, but it was also a fairly reformist, organization. The Crusade for Justice, Alianza Federal de las Mercedes, La Raza Unida Party, Movimiento Estudantíl Chicano de Aztlán (MEChA), and the Brown Berets, in contrast, were seen as more radical than the UFW. They gained that reputation because they rejected the label "Mexican American" as being too closely associated with "conservative" groups such as LULAC and the American GI Forum. "Chicano" was the collective identity that these new organizations preferred. Most older and middle-aged Mexican Americans shunned the label "Chicano," however, because they associated it with backwardness, inferiority, and indignity. But younger Chicanas and Chicanos transformed those meanings into something that connoted cultural pride, militancy, and political engagement (Munoz 1989). In the same way that lesbian, gay, bisexual, and transgender activists took the epithet "queer" and turned into a positive, politicized, and self-affirming identity, Chicanas and Chicanos transformed "Chicano."

These new groups were also seen as more radical because they claimed that Chicanos were a people or nation that had a shared history, culture, and language. They asserted that Chicanos had been historically oppressed for decades, if not centuries, and that they had bravely resisted and struggled for their liberation. The Crusade for Justice leader Rodolfo ("Corky") Gonzales excavated that "genealogy of resistance" in his epic, masculine-oriented poem *Yo Soy Joaquín* (I Am Joaquín). *Joaquín* and *El Plan Espiritual de Aztlán* (The Spiritual Plan of Aztlán) implicitly claimed that Chicanos were "brown-eyed children of the sun" who would obtain their freedom once they "reclaimed Aztlán" (Mariscal 2005). Aztlán was the mythical homeland of the Aztecs who migrated from the U.S. Southwest to Mexico City in 1325. The United States, of course, captured the Southwest from Mexico in the 1840s during the U.S.-Mexico War.

In 1967, taking the story of Aztlán literally, a group of Chicanos (or *Hispanos*, as they are sometimes called) associated with Reies López Tijerina's New Mexico–based Alianza Federal de las Mercedes (or La Alianza for short) walked into a courthouse in Tierra Amarilla, New Mexico, with guns to claim lands granted under the Treaty of Guadalupe Hidalgo. For the Denver-based

Crusade for Justice, "reclaiming Aztlán" meant controlling local school boards, community-based organizations, police review panels, city councils, businesses, and so on. For still others, "reclaiming Aztlán" became associated with resisting police brutality, tracking students into non-college prep courses, high drop-out (or "push-out") rates, and Eurocentric history. Ten thousand Chicano high school students from East Los Angeles were focused mostly on the latter three issues when they walked out of their classes in March 1968, chanting "blow-out" and "Chicano power" (Bernal 1997; Haney-López 2003).

Those demonstrations took place alongside growing dissatisfaction with the Vietnam War. Chicanos, like African-Americans and working-class whites, were disproportionately drafted at high rates into the armed services and suffered high casualty rates (Oropeza 2005). To protest these conditions, and partially to express solidarity with the Vietnamese people and their struggle for national liberation, activists organized the Chicano Anti-War Moratorium in East Los Angeles on August 29, 1970. This peaceful march included 25,000 people. It ended tragically, however, when the Los Angeles Police Department shot and killed three people, including the Chicano journalist Ruben Salazar, who worked as a reporter for the *Los Angeles Times* and had criticized the Vietnam War (García 1994).

Salazar's death, combined with the Black Power, anti-war, and student movements in the United States and the national liberation, anti-imperialist struggles outside the United States, radicalized the Chicano movement. Some activists started questioning cultural nationalism, the *movimiento*'s prevailing ideology, for focusing too heavily on race while virtually ignoring class. Those who held this viewpoint turned towards Marxism and suggested that there was no fundamental difference between Mexican Americans and Mexicans. They therefore rejected the "Chicano" label and maintained that Mexican Americans and Mexicans were all "Mexicans" who faced a common foe—capitalism (Pulido 2005).

This was the ideological perspective behind Centro de Acción Social Autónomo (The Center of Autonomous Social Action, or CASA). CASA's key slogans were *"el pueblo unido, jamas será vencido"* (the people united, will never be divided) and *"sin fronteras"* (without borders). CASA activists focused on labor-organizing campaigns that mostly included undocumented workers in Southern California, and they opposed anti-immigrant legislation. CASA was also heavily involved with cases involving police brutality and the forced sterilization of Mexican women (E. Chávez 2002; M. Chávez 2000). Bert Corona, a former labor organizer with the CIO in the 1930s, a socialist, and a member of the SLDC, was one of CASA's founding members (García 1994).

CASA and the August Twenty-Ninth Movement (ATM—a small, Maoist-inspired organization that claimed Mexican-Americans were "Chicanos" and that they constituted a "nation" struggling against capitalism and colonialism) represented the Chicano Left. These organizations gained many committed followers, but they clashed ideologically and never really expanded their activities very far outside the greater Los Angeles area. Both groups eventually disbanded—CASA in 1978 and ATM in 1982.

Most scholars maintain that the *movimiento* ended around 1975, the same year that the Vietnam War ended. They also primarily focus on the so-called four horsemen—César Chávez, Reies López Tijerina, Corky Gonzalez, and José Angel Gutiérrez—and the organizations that they led—UFW, Alianza Federal, Crusade for Justice, and La Raza Unida Party, respectively. These scholars also largely view the Chicano movement through a binary ideological lens; that is, as being either liberal or nationalist. These assumptions have been challenged, however.

The Chicano movement lasted until the late 1970s and early 1980s, and it included both socialist organizations (CASA and ATM) and religious ones (Católicos por la Raza, Priests Associated for Religious, Educational, and Social Rights [PADRES], and Las Hermanas). Research done since the early 1990s (e.g., E. Chávez 2002; Mariscal 2005; Medina 2004; R. Martínez 2005) demonstrates that the Chicano movement was actually a "movement of movements" (to borrow language from the contemporary global justice movement) that included many different actors, ideologies, organizations, and regional or spatial locations. These studies should be praised for making these contributions, but with one exception, they overlook gender and sexuality.

WOMEN AND THE *MOVIMIENTO*

Much has been said about the sexism and heterosexism that were embedded within the movements that made up the larger Chicano movement. Drawing upon pioneering Chicana scholars, writers, and activists such as Gloria Anzaldúa, Cherrie Moraga, Anna Nieto-Gómez, Chela Sandoval, Emma Perez, Carla Trujillo, and many other U.S. "Third World women," Maylei Blackwell persuasively contends in *Geographies of Difference* (2000) the movement's dominant ideology, cultural nationalism, privileged heterosexual masculine subjects, and heroes. When Chicanas were represented, they were portrayed either as traditional mothers, holding together overly romanticized notions of *la familia* (the family), or as brave *soldaderas* (soldiers) fighting during the Mexican Revolution in the 1910s. These images existed alongside ones depicting Chicanas as helpless Aztec goddesses being carried by strong Aztec gods. These patriarchal representations were extremely problematic because they circumscribed Chicana agency, but even more troubling were the numerous texts that never even mentioned Chicanas. Blackwell calls this process the "mechanics of erasure."

Mexicanas, Mexican-American women, and Chicanas have been, until quite recently, literally erased from most Chicano movement–oriented texts. Despite being virtually forced into cooking, typing, and even making love, numerous studies have showed that Chicanas were deeply involved with the UFW, Brown Berets, the East Los Angeles high school blow-outs, CASA, La Raza Unida, MEChA, and the Crusade for Justice (Bernal 1997; M. Chávez 2000; Espinoza 2001). This participation was often divided: Either Chicanas submerged gender-based concerns and worked alongside Chicanos in order to "reclaim Aztlán," or they claimed that racism and sexism should be challenged simultaneously. The women who fell into the first category were called "loyalists," while those who fell into the latter group were called "*vendidas,*" or "sell-outs" (Ruiz 1998). These Chicana activists often faced tremendous harassment from some of their male counterparts.

The Chicana student leader Anna Nieto-Gómez, for example, was the "democratically elected" MEChA president in 1969-1970, but some male activists opposed her, holding clandestine meetings and hanging women activists in effigy. Dionne Espinoza's research documents the mass resignation of every single Chicana member of the East Los Angeles chapter of the Brown Berets because of its sexist practices. Marisela Chávez similarly found that most men within CASA retained public leadership roles, while women did behind-the-scenes tasks such as fundraising and writing newspaper articles. During the April 1969 *El Plan de Santa Barbara* conference, Yolanda García helped type the actual plan (a blueprint for creating Chicano Studies programs and incorporating Chicanas/os into institutions of higher education), but the text never mentioned her name.

These incidents, and many more just like them, demonstrate that various organizations or movements within the larger *movimiento* marginalized women. Despite these activities, Chicana activists did not back down. On the contrary, some established new organizations that challenged race, class, and gender inequality. Anna Nieto-Gómez and her female colleagues at California State University, Long Beach, for instance, formed a Chicana feminist group called *Hijas de Cuahutémoc* (and created a newspaper with the same name) in 1971. *Hijas* (the newspaper) became *Encuentro Femenil* two years later. Other Chicana organizations founded in the late 1960s and early 1970s include the Chicana Welfare Rights Organization, *La Adelitas de Aztlán,* and *Comisión Femenil Mexicana Nacional* (Blackwell 2000). Chicanas were also critical in community papers such as *El Grito del Norte* and *Regeneración* and feminist journals like *La Comadre*, *Hembra*, *Imagenes de la Chicana*, and *La Cosecha* (Blackwell 2000).

These organizations and publications laid the foundation for extensive writings published by Chicanas (straight and queer) in the late 1970s and early 1980s, the most notable one being Cherrie Moraga and Gloria Anzaldúa's classic co-edited anthology, *This Bridge Called My Back: Writings By Radical Women of Color* (1981). The publication of *This Bridge,* combined with the establishment of *Mujeres Activas en Letras y Cambio Social* (MALCS, Women Active in Research and Social Change) in 1983 and community-based groups such as the Mothers of East Los Angeles (who successfully blocked the construction of a prison and a toxic incinerator plant) in 1984, provides evidence against the widely accepted assumption that the Chicano movement declined in 1975. Seen from a masculine viewpoint, this analysis may seem valid, but seen from various feminist and queer standpoints the movement did not end in the mid-1970s.

On the contrary, while many scholars bemoan the movement's demise in the mid-1970s, feminist and queer writers and activists emphasize that it "took off" at that time. Horacio Roque Ramírez's research on the San Francisco-based Gay Latino Alliance (GALA) illustrates this point quite clearly. GALA was established in 1975, the very year the movement was supposedly falling apart. Luis Aponte-Páres and Jorge Merced, in "Páginas Omitídas: The Gay and Lesbian Presence" (1998), and Horacio Roque Ramírez, in "That's My Place!" (2003), note that groups such as Third World Gay Liberation, *El Comité de Orgullo Homosexual Latino-Americano, Comunidad de Orgullo Gay,* and Greater Liberated Chicanos also emerged before and around the same time period as GALA. In the 1980s, *Latinas Lesbianas Unidas, Ellas,* and the National Latina and Latino Lesbian and Gay Organization (LLEGO) were created (Chávez-Leyva 2000).

MARGINALIZED MOVEMENTS

Chicana feminist and queer movements and writings have occasionally sparked a negative backlash. Some scholars apparently long for the "good old days" when gender and sexuality were not substantively addressed and the movement was militant and male-centered. Maylei Blackwell criticizes this approach because while militancy is still sorely needed, women and queers can no longer be excluded.

Nor, one might add, can "other" Latinos be marginalized any longer. For many years, and in the early twenty-first century, most Chicana/o studies scholarship and activism has largely ignored Latino-based social movements such as the Young Lords Party. There are several studies on the Young Lords, which was patterned after the Black Panther Party and existed in Chicago, New York City, and Philadelphia in the late 1960s and early 1970s (Melendez 2003; Morales 1998; Torres and Velásquez 1998). The Young Lords challenged racism through programs that "served the people" (e.g., conducting tuberculosis testing, establishing a free breakfast and clothing program), and rhetorically called for gender equality, but sexism and ideological conflicts plagued the organization. The Young Lords also embraced the Puerto Rican independence movement, and the group was later infiltrated by COINTELPRO, the FBI's notorious counterintelligence program. Puerto Rican activists also formed the Puerto Rican Student Union, the Puerto Rican National Left Movement, and the U.S. branch of the Puerto Rican Socialist Party (*Partido Socialista Puertorriqueño,* or PSP), in the 1970s. The latter organization formed close ties with CASA, but it did not address sexuality and gender, leading some PSP members to form their own organizations within the party or leave it altogether.

Some writers have also examined the Central American solidarity movement of the 1980s. This movement emerged from the United States' support for authoritarian, right-wing governments in Guatemala, El Salvador, Nicaragua, and Honduras in the late 1970s and early 1980s (Davidson 1988; Golden and McConnell 1986; Nepstad 2004; Smith 1996). Based on cold-war, anticommunist logic, the United States provided these countries with extensive military aid, despite the fact that it was used to brutally massacre, torture, and disappear hundreds of thousands of people during this time period.

Many Central Americans fled to the United States and Canada, where they sought refuge inside progressive Protestant and Catholic churches. A number of activists (mostly white, but also some Chicana/o activists such as Father Luis Olivares) were involved with this movement, which operated like a modern-day underground railroad (Davidson 1988; Golden and McConnell 1986). Whereas various groups such as *El Rescate,* the Committee in Solidarity with the Salvadoran People (CISPES), and the Central American Resource Center (CARECEN) emerged in the 1980s, not much has been written about Central Americans who participated in the solidarity movement. Central Americans have been rather extensively examined, however, in novels such as Demetria Martínez's *Mother Tongue* (1994) and films including Gregory Nava's *El Norte* (1983), *Mi Familia* (1995), and Cheech Marin's *Born in East L.A.* (1987).

LATINO MOVEMENTS IN THE 1990S AND BEYOND

In the 1990s, Latina/o social movements emerged around numerous issues; the most notable ones seemingly being immigration, globalization, and gender violence. In 1994, three events took place simultaneously—the North American Free Trade Agreement (NAFTA) went into effect, Operation Gatekeeper was introduced, and the Zapatista National Liberation Army came out into the open. These issues were all interrelated. NAFTA deepened the economic crisis in Mexico that started in the early 1980s, sparking significant migration throughout the decade and into the 1990s. Operation Gatekeeper was designed to curtail that migratory wave through an increase in border patrol agents and high-technology equipment. The Zapatistas challenged NAFTA because they understood how U.S. policies were driving *campesinos* off their lands and pushing them north as migrants looking for work.

The debate over NAFTA intersected with the "femicide" in Cuidad Juarez, Mexico, in the 1990s. Over a ten-year period, about 500 women, many of whom worked in *maquiladora* factories making products for U.S.-based corporations, were brutally murdered. These cases have not yet been solved, and a vibrant transnational social movement involving Chicanas, Latinas, and Mexican women has been established. The Zapatistas have also attracted tremendous attention from Chicanas/os and Latinas/os, and especially white social-justice activists.

The broader movement that the Zapatistas are loosely affiliated with has gained great momentum since 2001, when activists from all over the world met in Porto Algere, Brazil, for the first World Social Forum. The Forum's motto is "Another World Is Possible." With war raging across Iraq and the Middle East and billions living in poverty and misery, one can only hope that this slogan will become a reality, and that, in the Zapatistas' words, a "world where many worlds fit" will finally be established.

SEE ALSO *Anzaldúa, Gloria; Chávez, César Estrada; Corona, Bert; La Raza; Labor Market, Informal; Zapatista Rebellion.*

BIBLIOGRAPHY

Aponte-Páres, Luis, and Jorge Merced. 1998. "Páginas Omitídas: The Gay and Lesbian Presence." In *The Puerto Rican Movement,* edited by Andrés Torres and José Velásquez, 296–315. Philadelphia: Temple University Press.

Barajas, Frank. 2006. "The Defense Committees of Sleepy Lagoon: A Convergent Struggle against Fascism, 1942–1944." *Aztlan* 31(1): 33–62.

Blackwell, Maylei. 2000. *Geographies of Difference: Mapping Multiple Feminist Insurgencies and Transnational Public*

Cultures in the Americas. Ph.D. Diss., University of California, Santa Cruz.

Carroll, Patrick. 2003. *Felix Longoria's Wake: Bereavement, Racism, and the Rise of Mexican American Activism*. Austin: University of Texas Press.

Chávez, Ernesto. 2002. *"Mi Raza Primero!" (My People First!): Nationalism, Identity, and Insurgency in the Chicano Movement in Los Angeles, 1966–1978*." Berkeley: University of California Press.

Chávez, Marisela. 2000. "'We Lived and Breathed and Worked the Movement': The Contradictions and Rewards of Chicana/Mexican Activism in el Centro de Acción Social Autónomo-Hermandad General de Trabajadores (CASA-HGT), Los Angeles, 1975–1978." In *Las Obreras: Chicana Politics of Work and Family*, edited by Vicki Ruiz, 83–106. Los Angeles: Chicano Studies Research Center, UCLA.

Chávez Leyva, Yolanda. 2000. "Breaking the Silence: Putting Latina Lesbian History at the Center." In *Unequal Sisters: A Multicultural Reader in U.S. Women's History*, 3rd ed., edited by Vicki Ruiz and Ellen Carol DuBois, 403–408. New York: Routledge.

Davidson, Miriam. 1988. *Convictions of the Heart: Jim Corbett and the Sanctuary Movement*. Tucson: University of Arizona Press.

Delgado, Bernal Dolores. 1997. *Chicana High School Resistance and Grassroots Leadership: Providing an Alternative History on the East Los Angeles Blow-Outs*. Ph.D. diss., UCLA.

Espinoza, Dionne. 2001. "'Revolutionary Sisters': Women's Solidarity and Collective Identification among Chicana Brown Berets in East Los Angeles, 1967–1970." *Aztlán* 26 (1): 17–58.

Ferriss, Susan. 1996. "Junctures in the Road: Chicano Studies since 'El Plan de Santa Barbara.'" In *Chicanas/Chicanos at the Crossroads*, edited by David Maciel and Isidro Ortiz, 181–204. Tucson: University of Arizona Press.

———, and Richardo Sandoval. 1997. *The Fight in the Fields: César Chávez and the Farmworkers Movement*. New York: Harcourt Brace and Company.

———, and Ignacio García. 1997. *Chicanismo: The Forging of a Militant Ethos among Mexican Americans*. Tucson: University of Arizona Press.

García, Mario T. 1989. *Mexican Americans: Leadership, Ideology, and Identity, 1930–1960*. New Haven, CT: Yale University Press.

———. 1994. *Memories of Chicano History: The Life and Narrative of Bert Corona*. Berkeley: University of California Press.

Golden, Renny, and Michael McConnell. 1986. *Sanctuary: The New Underground Railroad*. Maryknoll, NY: Orbis Books.

Haney-López, Ian. 2003. *Racism on Trial: The Chicano Fight for Justice*. Cambridge, MA: Harvard University Press.

Horsman, Reginald. 1981. *Race and Manifest Destiny: The Origins of American Racial Anglo-Saxonism*. Cambridge, MA: Harvard University Press.

Johnson, Kevin. 2005. "*Hernández* v. *Texas*: Legacies on Justice and Injustice." *UCLA Chicano-Latino Law Review* 25: 153.

Jonas, Gilbert. 2004. *Freedom's Sword: The NAACP and the Struggle against Racism in America, 1909–1969*. New York: Routledge.

Kaplowitz, Craig. 2005. *LULAC, Mexican Americans, and National Policy*. College Station: University of Texas A & M Press.

Lorence, James J. 1999. *The Suppression of Salt of the Earth: How Hollywood, Big Labor, and Politicians Blacklisted a Movie in Cold War America*. Albuquerque: University of New Mexico Press.

Mariscal, George. 2005. *Brown-Eyed Children of the Sun: Lessons from the Chicano Movement, 1965–1975*. Albuquerque: University of New Mexico Press.

Martínez, Demetria. 1994. *Mother Tongue*. Tempe, AZ: Bilingual Press.

Martínez, Richard Edward. 2005. *PADRES: The National Chicano Priest Movement*. Austin: University of Texas Press.

Medina, Lara. 2004. *Las Hermanas: Chicana/Latina Religious-Political Activism in the U.S. Catholic Church*. Philadelphia: Temple University Press.

Melendez, Miguel. 2003. *We Took the Streets: Fighting for Latino Rights with the Young Lords*. New York: St. Martin's Press.

Moraga, Cherrie, and Gloria Anzaldúa, eds. 1981. *This Bridge Called My Back: Writings by Radical Women of Color*. Watertown, MA: Peresphone Press.

Morales, Iris. 1998. "PALANTE, SIEMPRE PALANTE! The Young Lords." In *The Puerto Rican Movement: Voices from the Diaspora*, edited by Andrés Torres and José Velásquez, 210–227. Philadelphia: Temple University Press.

Muñoz, Carlos. 1989. *Youth, Identity, Power: The Chicano Movement*. London: Verso.

Nepstad, Susan Erickson. 2004. *Convictions of the Soul: Religion, Culture, and Agency in the Central American Solidarity Movement*. New York: Oxford University Press.

Oropez, Lorena. 2005. *Raza Si, Guerra No! Chicano Protest and Patriotism during the Vietnam War Era*. Berkeley: University of California Press.

Orozco, Cynthia. 1997. "Alice Dickerson Montemayor: Feminism and Mexican American Politics in the 1930s." In *Writing the Range: Race, Class, and Culture in the Women's West*, edited by Elizabeth Jameson and Susan Armitage, 435–456. Norman: University of Oklahoma Press.

Pulido, Laura. 2005. *Black, Brown, Yellow, and Left: Radical Activism in Los Angeles*. Berkeley: University of California Press.

Ramírez, Horacio Roque. 2003. "'That's My Place!': Negotiating Racial, Sexual, and Gender Politics in San Francisco's Gay Latino Alliance, 1975–1983." *Journal of the History of Sexuality* 12 (2): 224–258.

Robbie, Sarah. 2002. *Mendez* v. *Westminster: For All the Children/Para Todos Los Niños*. VCR. Written and Produced by Sarah Robbie. Huntington Beach, CA: KOCE-TV.

Ruíz, Vicki. 1998. *From Out of the Shadows: Mexican Women in Twentieth Century America*. New York: Oxford.

———. 2004. "Una Mujer Sin Fronteras: Luisa Moreno and Latina Labor Activism," *Pacific Historical Review* 73: 1–20.

Salazar, Ruben. 1995. *Border Correspondent: Selected Writings, 1955–1970*. Edited by Mario T. García. Berkeley: University of California Press.

Scharlin, Craig, and Lilia Villanueva. 1992. *Philip Vera Cruz: A Personal History of Filipino Immigrants and the Farmworkers' Movement*. Los Angeles: UCLA Labor Center, Institute of Industrial Relations, and UCLA Asian American Studies Center.

Smith, Christian. 1996. *Resisting Reagan: The U.S. Central American Peace Movement.* University of Chicago Press: Chicago.

Soto, Gary. 2000. *Jessie de la Cruz: A Profile of a United Farm Worker.* New York: Persea Books.

Torres, Andrés, and José Velásquez, eds. 1998. *The Puerto Rican Movement: Voices from the Diaspora.* Philadelphia: Temple University Press.

Vargas, Zaragosa. 2005. *Labor Rights Are Civil Rights: Mexican American Workers in Twentieth-Century America.* Princeton, NJ: Princeton University Press.

Von Eschen, Penny. 1997. *Race against Empire: Black Americans and Anticolonialism, 1937–1957.* Ithaca, NY: Cornell University Press.

Ralph Armbruster-Sandoval

LATINOS

The rapid growth of the Latino population was one of the key features of the American landscape in the last part of the twentieth century. All population projections show that the Hispanic population will continue to grow rapidly. Latinos do not fit easily into the racial framework as it is socially constructed in most of the United States, especially outside the Southwest and California. Most of the country has a bipolar racial structure—black and white. Secondarily, the bipolar structure is white and nonwhite (the latter including Asian, Native American, and African American, in that order from highest to lowest status). The construction of race differs between the United States and Latin America in terms of fluidity, degrees and social recognition of race mixture, and the mitigation of racial discrimination by social class. Many Latinos are mestizos—the result of the mixture of European colonizers and the indigenous population. Phenotypically, their appearance ranges from light "white" skin with European hair types and facial features to very dark skin with indigenous characteristics. Many Latinos have African ancestors and a few have immediate Asian ancestors. Many Latinos can phenotypically be distinguished from Anglos (white non-Latinos) on the basis of their physical appearance, as well as other identity markers.

THE RACIALIZATION OF LATINOS

Michael Omi and Howard Winant define racial formation as "the process by which social, economic and political forces determine the content and importance of racial categories, and by which they are in turn shaped by racial meanings" (1994, pp. 61–62). "The meaning of race is defined and contested throughout society.… In the process, racial categories are themselves formed, transformed, destroyed and re-formed." Importantly, race is a social and historical construct. The term *racialization* describes "the extension of racial meaning to a previously racially unclassified relationship, social practice or group" (1994, pp. 64–65). This process describes the racial situation of Latino immigrants in new receiving areas. Even though they exhibit a range of appearances, birthplaces, and legal statuses, through the process of racialization they are lumped together as "Mexicans"—a subordinate, nonwhite group who, because of their frequently presumed illegal status, have been denied claims to the rights and privileges that Anglos take for granted. The label *Mexican* appropriately applies to Mexican citizens, and the fact that many Latinos have had this label applied to them even if they were U.S. citizens or the U.S.-born children of U.S.-born parents confirms their racialization. The meanings attached to their distinguishing characteristics have been key in determining where they lived, what work they could do, their privileges as citizens, and the educational opportunities available to their children.

DISCRIMINATION

Latino civil rights have faced severe restrictions since the mid-nineteenth century. Observers of that period found that the Mexican-origin residents of Texas were subject to prejudice and contempt. This ignominious beginning of restricted Latino civil rights in the United States was the foundation for other gross civil rights violations in the twentieth century, such as blocked access to the ballot box, de jure segregation into inferior schools, residential segregation, and widespread employment discrimination.

Such violations of civil rights are not only part of Latino history. There are several instances of late-twentieth- and early-twenty-first-century social science research that provide very strong evidence of present-day discrimination against Latinos in many areas. For example, researchers have found that among defendants, sentences of Hispanics resemble those of blacks and tend to be harsher than the sentences of whites (Demuth and Steffensmeier 2004; HRW 1997). A number of matched-pair "audits" where Anglos and Latinos with substantively identical credentials apply for jobs, housing, or mortgage loans convincingly show a high degree of discrimination against Latinos (Bendick et al. 1992; Cross et al. 1990).

Latinos are far from attaining equal access to higher education. Since the early 1970s, the Latino proportion of the U.S. college-aged population—those between eighteen and twenty-four years old—has more than doubled. However, the proportion of Latinos among all B.A. degree recipients has increased at a much lower rate. Jorge Chapa and Belinda De La Rosa found, for example, that in 2002, 43 percent of all Latino adults had less than a high school education, compared with 16 percent of all adults. Similarly, 8 percent of Latino adults had a bachelor's degree and 3 percent had an advanced degree, compared to 18 percent of the total population with a bachelor's and 9 percent with advanced degrees (Chapa and De La Rosa 2004). Similarly, the percentage of Latino high school graduates ever enrolled in college has decreased since the mid-1970s. In 1975 the proportion of Latino high school graduates attending college was within 2 percent of that for the total U.S. population. Since that time, the Latino proportion has decreased so that among high school graduates, 15 percent fewer Latinos went to college. At each successive step or level, the higher education pipeline is increasingly leaky, and it is losing and leaving out larger numbers and proportions of the rapidly growing Latino population. In spite of increased opportunities that may have resulted from earlier lawsuits to increase Latino access to public education, like the Edgewood and League of United Latin American Citizens (LULAC) suits, the low levels of Hispanic parental educational attainment, high poverty levels, and a number of other demographic characteristics all work to create severe educational barriers. The low levels of attainment and high school completion are not merely artifacts of high levels of immigration. U.S.-born Latinos have much lower educational levels than non-Latinos. This is true even when different generations among the U.S.-born are distinguished and analyzed separately. While de jure segregation of Latinos may have been eliminated, de facto segregation in public education has continued to grow. In many states, Latinos are the most segregated group.

HISPANIC/LATINO IDENTIFIERS

The U.S. Census concept of Hispanic ethnicity and the various identifiers by which the conceptualization was made concrete have changed many times since the first crude effort of the 1930 Census to conceptualize and identify Hispanics who were not immigrants or the children of immigrants. These changes reflect the substantial shifts in the composition of this population that occurred over the course of the twentieth century. They also reflect the increase in Latino population size and in the Census Bureau's and the nation's awareness of this group. During the early part of the twentieth century, almost all of the population now identified as Hispanic were people of Mexican origin who were largely concentrated in a few southwestern states. In contrast, the 2000 Census reports data on more than twenty categories of national origin groups of Hispanics who are to be found in increasingly large numbers in all fifty states.

Conflating Immigrants, Race and National Origin. The U.S. Census has counted by race since its inception and has kept track of immigrants since 1850, and their children from 1880 to 1970, by the use of nativity and parentage questions. Censuses from 1910 through 1970, excluding 1950, determined the language spoken by respondents at home as a child, also known as their mother tongue. The mother tongue questions were typically reported only for immigrants or the children of immigrants. Thus the enduring Census concerns with race and immigration excluded many U.S.-born Hispanics from enumeration. The first significant population of Hispanics in the United States was found among the residents of Texas when it became a state in 1845. The lands annexed in 1848 as a result of the Mexican War added substantially to the total Hispanic population. This population grew again when many Mexicans came to the United States as refugees from the Mexican Revolution (1910).

The current Census concept of race (black or white) has not worked well. Motivated by generally xenophobic concerns, the 1930 Census attempted to enumerate Hispanics by using the concept of a Mexican race. There were many serious problems with this approach. Many Hispanics were U.S. citizens and the U.S.-born children of U.S.-born parents. The *Mexican* identifier appropriately applies to citizens of Mexico. Additionally, many Hispanics did not want to be identified as members of a socially subordinate group commonly referred to as Mexicans, regardless of their nativity or how many generations their ancestors had resided in the United States. The preferred and polite term used as an alternative at the time was Latin.

For example, the name of the organization known as LULAC, the League of Latin American Citizens (founded in Texas in 1929), is an example of this preference. The name also emphasizes the U.S. citizenship of many Hispanics. One of the clear indications of the inadequacy of the Mexican race approach is that many people were identified as being of Mexican birth or parentage, but not of Mexican race. This highlights another problem, that this identifier depended on the judgment of the enumerator, which apparently was neither consistent nor reliable. Finally, and perhaps most important, being racially designated as Mexican excluded the possibility of being classified as white. At the time, many rights and privileges, including the right to become a U.S. citizen, were explicitly available to whites only. Because of these problems and in response to protest and litigation, the Census Bureau dropped the use of the Mexican race identifier after 1930. This experience also set the precedent for the current practice of separating race and Hispanic ethnicity into two items on the census questionnaire.

Standardizing Subjective Self-Identification as Spanish/ Hispanic Origin. The 1970 Census long-form questionnaire, administered to five percent of the population, asked, "Is this person of Spanish/Hispanic origin?" The possible responses were "Mexican," "Puerto Rican," "Cuban," "Central or South American," "Other Spanish," and, "No, none of these." Extensive analysis of several Hispanic identifiers used in 1970 showed that this identity question produced the most consistent responses and distinguished between Mexicans, Puerto Ricans, Cubans, and other major Latino populations as well as included Latino respondents who were neither foreign born nor of foreign parentage. The demographic advantages of this question coincide with political and legal considerations. In 1976, Congress passed Public Law 94–311, known as the Roybal Resolution, requiring the use of a self-identified Hispanic question on federal censuses and surveys. The use of such a question was further promulgated in the Office of Management and Budget (OMB) Directive 15, first released in 1977. However, it is worth noting that Directive 15 permits the use of a combined race and Spanish origin question. The data collected from a combined question are significantly different from data collected using separate race and Hispanic questions. Self-identification has now become the accepted standard for determining Hispanic origins. Slightly modified and improved versions of the question were part of the standard Census questionnaire in 1980, 1990, and 2000. One modification in these subsequent censuses was to make the "Mexican" origin response category more inclusive by changing it to "Mexican, Mexican American, Chicano."

WILL LATINOS BECOME WHITE?

Some of the most interesting recent books on the history of European immigrants in the United States are the works that elucidate the process by which European immigrants became white. Many European immigrants were initially seen as outcasts who were not fit to be part of mainstream American society. They achieved white identity as they advanced economically and educationally.

One of the key concerns in the policy debates concerning Latinos focuses on the future incorporation or lack of incorporation of the children of immigrants. Both institutional barriers and perceptions of discrimination may explain the apparent low levels of educational and economic mobility of second- and third-generation Latinos. This lack of mobility and more pronounced indigenous features may prevent many Latinos from ever being accepted as white. In a "country of immigrants," as the United States has so often been called, achieving the status of white has been the hallmark of the full incorporation into the mainstream of U.S. society. At this point in time, it seems likely that only some Latinos will be accepted as white. The question is, will American society be open to the complete incorporation of a people who are not white?

SEE ALSO *Central Americans; Mexicans; Puerto Ricans; Sweatshops.*

BIBLIOGRAPHY

Bendick, Marc, Jr., Charles W. Jackson, Victor A. Reinoso, and Laura E. Hodges. 1992. "Discrimination against Latino Job Applicants: A Controlled Experiment." Washington, DC: Fair Employment Council of Greater Washington.

Chapa, Jorge, and Belinda De La Rosa. 2004. "Latino Population Growth, Socioeconomic and Demographic Characteristics, and Implications for Educational Attainment." *Education and Urban Society* 36 (2): 130–149.

Cross, Harry E., Genevieve M. Kenney, Jane Mell, and Wendy Zimmerman. 1990. *Employer Hiring Practices: Differential Treatment of Hispanic and Anglo Job Seekers.* Washington, DC: The Urban Institute Press.

del Pinal, Jorge. 1996. "Treatment and Counting of Latinos in the Census." In *The Latino Encyclopedia,* edited by Richard Chabran and Rafael Chabran. New York: Marshall Cavendish.

Demuth, Stephen, and Darrell Steffensmeier. 2004. "Ethnicity Effects on Sentence Outcomes in Large Urban Courts: Comparisons Among White, Black, and Hispanic Defendants." *Social Science Quarterly* 85 (4): 994–1011.

Feagin, Joe R. 2000. *Racist America: Roots, Current Realities, and Future Reparations.* New York: Routledge.

———. 2006. *Systemic Racism.* New York: Routledge.

Foley, Neil. 1997. *The White Scourge: Mexicans, Blacks, and Poor Whites in Texas Cotton Culture.* Berkeley: University of California Press.

Hernandez, Jose, Leo Estrada, and David Alivirez. 1973. "Census Data and the Problem of Conceptually Defining the Mexican American Population." *Social Science Quarterly* 53 (4): 671–687.

HRW (Human Rights Watch). 1997. "Cruel and Unusual: Human Rights Violations in the United States; Disproportionate Sentences for New York Drug Offenders." HRW 9 (2 (B)). http://www.hrw.org/reports/1997/usny/.

Ignatiev, Noel. 1995. *How the Irish Became White.* New York: Routledge.

Lopez, Ian F. Haney. 1996. *White by Law: The Legal Construction of Race.* New York: New York University Press.

Millard, Ann V., and Jorge Chapa, et al. 2004. *Apple Pie and Enchiladas: Latino Newcomers in the Rural Midwest.* Austin: University of Texas Press.

Nieto-Phillips, John M. 2004. *The Language of Blood: The Making of Spanish-American Identity in New Mexico, 1880s–1930s.* Albuquerque: University of New Mexico Press.

Omi, Michael, and Howard Winant. 1994. *Racial Formation in the United States,* 2nd ed. New York: Routledge.

Roediger, David. R. 2005. *Working Toward Whiteness: How America's Immigrants Became White: The Strange Journey from Ellis Island to the Suburbs.* New York: Basic Books.

Teller, Charles H., Jose Hernandez, Leo Estrada, and David Alivirez, eds. 1977. *Cuantos Somos: A Demographic Study of the Mexican-American Population*. Austin: Center for Mexican American Studies, University of Texas.

Jorge Chapa
Ann V. Millard

LEAGUE OF REVOLUTIONARY BLACK WORKERS

Few organizations have challenged racism as creatively and systematically as the League of Revolutionary Black Workers and its affiliate organizations, the various Revolutionary Union Movements (RUMs) of the late 1960s and early 1970s. Based in Detroit, Michigan, the league fused the local fight against racism with broader social struggles in the areas of workers' rights, economic justice, public education, and municipal political power. The league grew from African-American workers' struggles in Detroit's teeming automotive manufacturing plants. Because of this, in all the league's work the struggle for racial justice was connected to the struggle against what the league saw as worker exploitation.

Though the league is less well remembered than another group of the period, the Black Panthers, it challenged what it saw as the racist practices of some of the world's most powerful corporations. In the United States and abroad, activists looked to the league's work in Detroit as a model for strategies and tactics in the fight against racism and injustice.

A CITY IN FLAMES

To understand the league, one must understand the city from which it emerged—Detroit in the late 1960s. Many American cities experienced serious racial unrest and rioting in the 1960s, but none matched the scale and ferocity of the Detroit race riots of 1967, known at the time to many of the city's African-American residents as the Great Rebellion.

For five days in July 1967, large swaths of Detroit burned to the ground in an explosion of racial violence. Stoked by anger over what black residents saw as persistent police harassment and racial injustice, the Great Rebellion could only be subdued by a major mobilization of the National Guard. By the time the smoke had cleared, forty-one people had died, 1,300 buildings had been leveled, and $500 million in damage had been done. Late-1960s Detroit was a powder keg of racial tension that seemed ready to blow at any moment.

Unrest among the city's 600,000 African-American residents—roughly 40 percent of the city's population—was mirrored by unrest in the Detroit area's many automotive plants. Detroit, long known as the "Motor City," relied heavily on the Ford, Chrysler, and General Motors (GM) automobile companies as the chief suppliers of jobs for the city's residents. There were some 250,000 black workers at these "Big Three" automakers, and they were almost always relegated to the lowest-paying, most dangerous jobs. At Chrysler's Dodge Main plant, for example, 95 percent of all foremen were white, 90 percent of all skilled trades workers (higher-paying, higher-skilled jobs) were white, and 100 percent of superintendents were white.

Autoworkers, and disproportionately African-American autoworkers, were regularly injured or maimed on the job at Big Three plants. Nor were workplace deaths uncommon; —a 1973 study of the U.S. automotive industry found a rate of sixty-five workplace deaths per day. Temperatures in the plants rose to well over 100 degrees in the summer and fell close to freezing in the winter. Heart attacks were the most common cause of workplace death.

Anger and frustration mounted among African-American workers, who continually saw white workers promoted ahead of them into more desirable jobs. In one famous 1970 incident, James Johnson, a black worker at Chrysler's Eldon Avenue Gear and Axle plant, one of the most dangerous manufacturing plants in the United States, shot and killed two of his foremen and one other coworker. He was acquitted, largely due to a legal defense that placed responsibility for his actions in the persistent racism and abominable working conditions he had encountered. Though such extreme cases were rare, violent tensions were in the air at Detroit's auto plants.

THE REVOLUTIONARY UNION MOVEMENTS

When frustrated black workers turned to their union, the United Auto Workers (UAW), for support or protection, they usually found their frustrations exacerbated. Though the UAW had a reputation as a strong advocate for workers' rights and racial equality, the union in many ways reflected the same problems workers saw in their workplaces and in their city.

The UAW, which sprang up in Detroit in the 1930s as a militant expression of workers' demands for justice, had by the 1960s become a calcified, bureaucratic institution. In most cases, the union's function was more to keep the auto plants running smoothly than to advocate for their workers' interests. Workers' grievances would gather dust for months and years, and workers who rocked the boat were targeted by a tandem of union and management, who operated more like business partners than adversaries.

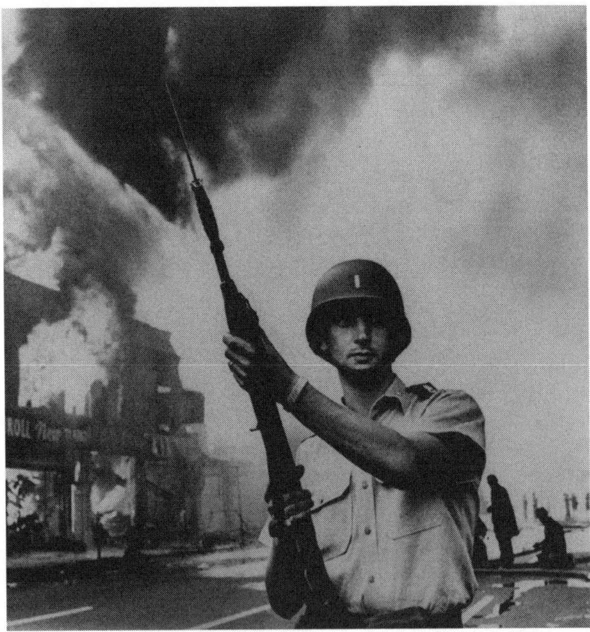

National Guardsman at the Detroit Riots, 1967. *Unrest among the city's 600,000 African-American residents—roughly 40 percent of the city's population—was mirrored by unrest in the Detroit area's many automotive plants.* AP IMAGES.

Although by the 1960s about one-third of the UAW's one million members were African American, workers of color were almost completely excluded from leadership or even staff roles in the union. Black workers, fed up with both management and the union, sought other avenues to demand justice on the job. From this dissent and the broader social unrest in Detroit grew the Revolutionary Union Movements (RUMs), the League of Revolutionary African American Workers' predecessor organizations.

The Dodge Revolutionary Union Movement (DRUM), the first of the RUMs, was born at the Dodge Main plant in May 1968. DRUM exploded onto the scene during a one-day, 4,000-worker strike at the Dodge plant on May 2, protesting management's speed-up of the assembly lines. By speeding up the lines, Chrysler not only produced more cars per hour, but it also produced a greater risk of injury and a more stressful work environment.

The strike brought operations at Dodge Main to a halt. This was a wildcat strike, one not called or sanctioned by the union's leadership, but it clearly had substantial support within the plant. Management responded quickly: Several workers were fired and disciplined, and punishment for the strike was meted out disproportionately to African-American workers, even though white workers had also been involved. This inequity fueled support for DRUM, whose supporters now saw that they had enough power to stop production at a Chrysler facility.

In the days and weeks that followed, DRUM began distributing a weekly newsletter called *DRUM.* This newsletter publicized instances of workplace racism and rallied African-American workers to DRUM's cause—namely, Black Power in the auto plants. The newsletter also attacked the UAW for its failure to represent black workers, and DRUM proposed that black autoworkers should struggle for power independently of the UAW.

BEYOND DODGE MAIN

Writings in the newsletter also focused on racism outside the plant gates. Particular attention was paid to incidences of police brutality, a hot-button issue for blacks in Detroit. As the newsletter became more and more visible, support for DRUM grew. Emboldened, DRUM next targeted two bars frequented by Dodge Main workers. These bars, both close to the plant, served African-Americans customers but would not hire them. DRUM called for a boycott of the bars and received overwhelming support. The bars quickly acquiesced to DRUM's demands, and DRUM leaders decided they would try to carry the momentum to Chrysler, presenting the company with a list of fifteen demands. These included fifty black foremen and ten black general foremen at Dodge Main, black medical and security personnel at the plant, equal pay for South African workers, and an African-American head of Chrysler's board of directors. If their demands were not met, DRUM threatened a series of demonstrations and another work stoppage at Dodge Main.

When Chrysler failed to respond, DRUM took a series of actions that illustrated their uniquely systematic and militant approach. On July 7, 1968, DRUM and more than 300 of its supporters rallied in the parking lot across the street from Dodge Main. The demonstrators marched to the hall of UAW Local 3 (which represented Dodge Main workers), where the union's executive board was meeting. Hoping to pacify the workers, union officials agreed to hear their grievances and demands. Unimpressed with the officials' responses, the workers announced they would defy the union and strike at Dodge Main.

The morning of July 8 found DRUM activists picketing outside Dodge Main. In addition to the 3,000 black workers who gathered to picket outside the plant gates that morning, many white workers also participated in a show of solidarity. Dodge Main's assembly lines slowed to a snail's pace. Within a few hours, police arrived in riot gear, prepared for a confrontation, but when they ordered the demonstrators to disperse, most of the strikers left the line, with some 250 quickly departing for a demonstration at Chrysler headquarters. When police arrived to break up this second demonstration, DRUM's car pool took the demonstrators home.

The strike lasted three days and cost Chrysler 1,900 cars. DRUM's approach—causing maximum disruption without taking unnecessary risks or submitting to law enforcement—differed radically from many protest groups who sought confrontations with police for either symbolic purposes or media attention.

THE LEAGUE IS BORN

Though it looked like a spontaneous uprising of angry workers, DRUM's rapid emergence was the product of a great deal of planning and organizing by a core group of leaders, some of whom would later be leaders of the League of Revolutionary Black Workers. These included Dodge Main workers General Baker and Chuck Wooten, as well as black radicals who did not work at Dodge Main. This core group's first collective work was on the Detroit-based newspaper *Inner City Voice* (*ICV*). First appearing just months after the Great Rebellion in October 1967, *ICV* was in many ways a testing ground for the RUM's approach to workplace organizing. *ICV* covered local community struggles against racism and injustice, but it always placed these struggles in the context of a broader, revolutionary perspective. The skills this core group developed working on *ICV* served them well as DRUM continued to grow.

In September 1968, DRUM ran a candidate for UAW Local 3 executive board. DRUM's candidate, Ron March, won the initial vote, but lost a runoff election fraught with irregularities and police harassment of DRUM supporters. As word of DRUM's successes spread, black workers at other plants followed their lead. FRUM (at Ford's River Rouge complex), JARUM (at Chrysler's Jefferson Avenue plant), CADRUM (at Cadillac's Fleetwood plant), and a number of other RUMs sprang up around the city. ELRUM, at Chrysler's Eldon Avenue plant, emerged in the winter of 1968 and soon had more members than DRUM.

The RUM movement spread beyond the auto industry. UPRUM represented United Parcel Service (UPS) workers, and NEWRUM was founded by workers at the *Detroit News*.

It became clear that a body would be needed to coordinate all this work, and the League of Revolutionary Black Workers was formed in June 1969. Aside from Baker and Wooten, the league's core leadership included former *ICV* editor John Watson, the lawyer Kenneth Cockrel, two former leaders of the Detroit Black Panther Party, and another of *ICV's* original founders.

Though the league emphasized workplace organizing, it also coordinated other areas of activity. In the fall of 1968, Watson had maneuvered himself into the editorship of the *South End*, the student newspaper at Detroit's Wayne State University. Watson and the league used the *South End*, with its daily circulation of 18,000, to promote their work and political perspective. The league's media activities were not limited to the printed word, however. In 1969 the league began work on a documentary film about its activities. *Finally Got the News* was completed in 1970 and distributed (on a very small scale) throughout the United States and parts of Europe.

As it grew, the league became a presence in Detroit politics. Watson and other league members took the lead in a battle with the Detroit Board of Education over community control of public schools. In addition, the Black Student United Front was formed to serve as a youth wing of the league, and branches were established in twenty-two high schools.

POLITICAL DIRECTION

Beyond coordination, the league's leadership provided political vision and coherence. Baker, Watson, and the league's other leaders had been devoted Marxists since well before the league's inception, and Marxist revolutionary thought permeated their work. This was most evident in their emphasis on the workplace as the point where black workers could leverage the most social and economic power. In 1969 the word *revolutionary* was not just grand sloganeering—the league's ultimate goal was to overthrow capitalism and replace it with a more just economic system.

The 1960s had seen a rush of political movements aimed at overthrowing colonial governments throughout the developing world, and league members were inspired by these international developments. Anticolonial uprisings in Vietnam, Algeria, and elsewhere galvanized league members, who saw African-Americans' struggles in the United States as an anticolonial struggle.

Central to the league's ideology was their assertion that company, union, and government formed an interconnected system of oppression, each supporting the other in efforts to maintain dominance over minorities and working people. To combat this system, the league worked in coalition with community groups, Arab-American groups, and groups of white activists. Though the league remained an African-American organization, they encouraged other groups to organize themselves and work with the league in coalition.

There were, however, political differences among the league's leaders. Some, like Baker and Wooten, believed that the league should focus the vast majority of its resources on workplace organizing, expanding and consolidating their network of RUMs. These leaders thought that the emphases on media work and education were spreading the league's resources too thin and diluting their political message. Others, like Watson and Cockrel, believed that media work had the potential to grow the pool of African-American supporters. Only focusing on workers, they pointed out, excluded the many African Americans not in workplaces with league members, as well as those not in workplaces at all.

As the league expanded, these divisions grew deeper and internal tensions increased. Activists from groups such as the Black Panthers and the Student Nonviolent Coordinating Committee (SNCC) joined up with the league, bringing their own agendas and ideologies and increasing these divisions. Pressures also increased from employers, as workers involved in RUMs were disciplined and fired. In June 1971, the league's leadership split over these political differences, though by that time its activity had already begun to diminish. This was likely due in equal parts to internal political divisions, external pressures (from employers and law enforcement), and a lack of adequate financial resources.

Though it was short-lived, the league's impact can be measured by the response it generated. Organizations as powerful as the Chrysler Corporation and the UAW went to great lengths to destroy the league, targeting its members for harassment and unjust disciplinary action. Though often compared to the Black Panthers, whose flair for dramatics gave them more visual appeal, the league's message was ultimately different. Dressed not in leather and berets, the league's leaders were blue-jeaned working-class revolutionaries; they sought to create a movement of working African Americans, fighting to transform a society they saw as fundamentally racist, exploitative, and unjust.

BIBLIOGRAPHY

Elbaum, Max. 2002. *Revolution in the Air: Sixties Radicals Turn to Lenin, Mao, and Che.* New York: Verso.

Georgakas, Dan, and Marvin Surkin. 1998. *Detroit: I Do Mind Dying,* 2nd ed. Cambridge, MA: South End Press.

Kelley, Robin D. G. 1999. "Building Bridges: The Challenge of Organized Labor in Communities of Color." *New Labor Forum* 5: 42–58.

Moody, Kim. 1988. *An Injury to All: The Decline of American Unionism.* New York: Verso.

Serrin, William. 1973. *The Company and the Union: The "Civilized Relationship" of the General Motors Corporation and the United Automobile Workers.* New York: Knopf.

Sugrue, Thomas J. 1996. *The Origins of the Urban Crisis: Race and Inequality in Postwar Detroit.* Princeton, NJ: Princeton University Press.

Thompson, Heather. 2001. *Whose Detroit? Politics, Labor, and Race in a Modern American City.* Ithaca, NY: Cornell University Press.

William Johnson

LESBIANS

The word *lesbian* is derived from the poet Sappho of Lesbos, who lived in the sixth century BCE and is renowned for her lyric poetry praising romantic love between women. Lesbians are women who have same-sex desires or engage in same-sex relationships. The term *lesbian* has also, at times, been extended to include political lesbianism, in which women choose primary relationships with women and place primary importance on these relationships. This construction of the political lesbian was popularized by Adrienne Rich in her essay *Compulsory Heterosexuality and Lesbian Existence* (1980), in which she discussed society's role in making heterosexuality the norm.

A diverse array of lesbian communities have been active in constructing a safe haven for lesbians, creating both social spaces and political spaces. Lesbian bars have existed since the early 1800s in France and the late 1800s in the United States. Political groups have been a more recent phenomenon with the establishment of the organization Daughters of Bilitis in 1955 and still further after the Stonewall riots of 1969. Some of these are virtual communities via the Internet, which can reach lesbians in rural communities. In addition, lesbian studies has been a growing field in academia, adding to the work done on lesbianism within women's studies and queer studies.

LESBIANS OF COLOR

In "Multiple Jeopardy, Multiple Consciousness" (1988), Deborah King describes the "triple jeopardy" of racism, sexism, and homophobia faced by lesbians of color. This triple jeopardy can lead to a separation of lesbians of color from both their racial/ethnic communities and from the lesbian community. Every culture has norms about appropriate sexual behavior for women, and many cultures also have a history of oppression based on how the dominant society views the sexuality of women and men. In many communities of color, lesbians are close to their families of origin, and they live close to their families, so that the threat of estrangement is a serious one. Immigrant families that do not speak English at home may not have a word for "sexual orientation," or they may know only negative terms for lesbianism. Thus, lesbians of color may be closeted to their families of origin, and they might not use the term *lesbian* in identifying themselves. Finally, communities of color may view lesbianism as a Western or American concept, when in fact there is a rich tradition of same-sex relationships among women across the world (see, for example, both Gloria Wekker's [2006] research on same-sex relationships in Latin America and the work of Will Roscoe and Stephen Murray [2001] on same-sex relationships in Africa).

AFRICAN-AMERICAN LESBIANS

African-American lesbians have a long history within popular culture, and they have ensured their own visibility at various times throughout history. Many African-American blues singers of the early 1900s, including Gertrude "Ma" Rainey and Bessie Smith, were not only known to engage in same-sex relationships, but they also sang about it in their music. Lesbianism was also a recurring theme during the Harlem Renaissance, as seen in Nella Larson's novella *Passing* (1929).

In the 1970s, the discussion of lesbianism within the African-American community became more visible, due in part to both the Black Power movement and the women's movement. Audre Lorde's biomythography, *Zami: A New Spelling of My Name* (1983), examined the intersections of sexism, racism, and antilesbian attitudes. The authors Alice Walker and Toni Morrison have also included descriptions of intense relationships between African-American women in their works, including overt lesbian relationships.

African-American women often have more flexible gender roles, and a large percentage of African-American women work outside the home. Because of this, African-American women are often depicted as independent and "masculine," similar to the stereotypes of lesbians. Over the years, the African-American family has developed as a protective barrier and survival tool, so it can be hard for African-American lesbians to "come out" and risk alienation from their families. This may mean that families are less likely to disown or reject a lesbian daughter, though they may not want to talk about her sexual orientation or acknowledge her lover.

NATIVE AMERICAN LESBIANS

Native American cultures have a long history of fluid gender roles. In these cultures, people could change their gender, become transgendered, have multiple gender identities, or marry someone with the same gender. European-American anthropologists first used the term *berdache* to describe a Native American with a fluid gender, but today the term *two-spirit* is often used. The anthropologist Sabine Lang, in *Men as Women, Women as Men* (1998), describes how in the past the status of two-spirits varied from tribe to tribe, noting that sometimes they had special powers or served as healers or leaders. For example, if only women were healers in a tribe, then a man would become a "woman-man" in order to be a healer. Two-spirit social roles were still part of Native American culture in the 1940s, and they are still honored in some tribes. Carrie House, a lesbian of Navajo/Oneida descent, writes:

> Our oral traditions acknowledge that the he-shes and she-hes (those who hold in balance the male and female, female and male aspects of themselves and the universe) were among the greatest contributors to the well-being and advancement of their communities. They were (and we are) the greatest probers into the ways of the future, and they quickly assimilated the lessons of changing times and people. (1997, p. 225)

Despite the positive history of fluid gender roles, lesbianism is not accepted on many current Indian reservations due to the historical influence of colonizing Europeans. As a result, Native American lesbians may feel torn to leave their community for a new lesbian community that may be racist or refuse to address their specific needs. Paula Gunn Allen is a Native American poet and one of the first scholars to discuss the tradition of lesbianism within Native American culture. She argued that Native American lesbians existed and were an integral part of tribal life, though silenced to serve the patriarchal interests of the European colonization, and thus are systematically forgotten in most contemporary history.

LATINA LESBIANS

Latina and Chicana women are also a very diverse group, encompassing Mexican American, Puerto Rican, Cuban, Caribbean, and Central and South America women. Latino communities often have defined gender roles for women and men, with strong expectations of heterosexuality. Many Latino communities are also Catholic, and unmarried women are expected to remain virgins. Yet the psychologist Beverly Greene has described the close relationships that develop among Latinas in this gender-segregated society.

There is a thriving literature about Chicana lesbians. Gloria Anzaldúa identifies herself as a "Chicana dyke-feminist, tejana patlache poet, writer, and cultural theorist" (Anzaldúa 2006, Internet site). Cherrie Moraga identifies as a lesbian and Chicana; as a Chicana she hid her sexuality and it was not until she confronted her lesbianism that she became aware of the need to be vocal to open the doors of understanding about herself and others.

ASIAN-AMERICAN LESBIANS

Asian Americans include Japanese, Chinese, Filipino, Korean, and Pacific Island Americans. In many Asian languages there is no word that means "lesbian," and open discussions about sex are frowned upon. The family is highly valued and gender roles are based on tradition and stereotypes. Thus, because their culture requires that a daughter become a wife and mother, Asian-American lesbians may be blamed for tarnishing their family's honor. However, outward appearance may be more important than private acts, so women may be allowed to have same-sex relationships as long as they are married to men and do not discuss sex. Asian-American families

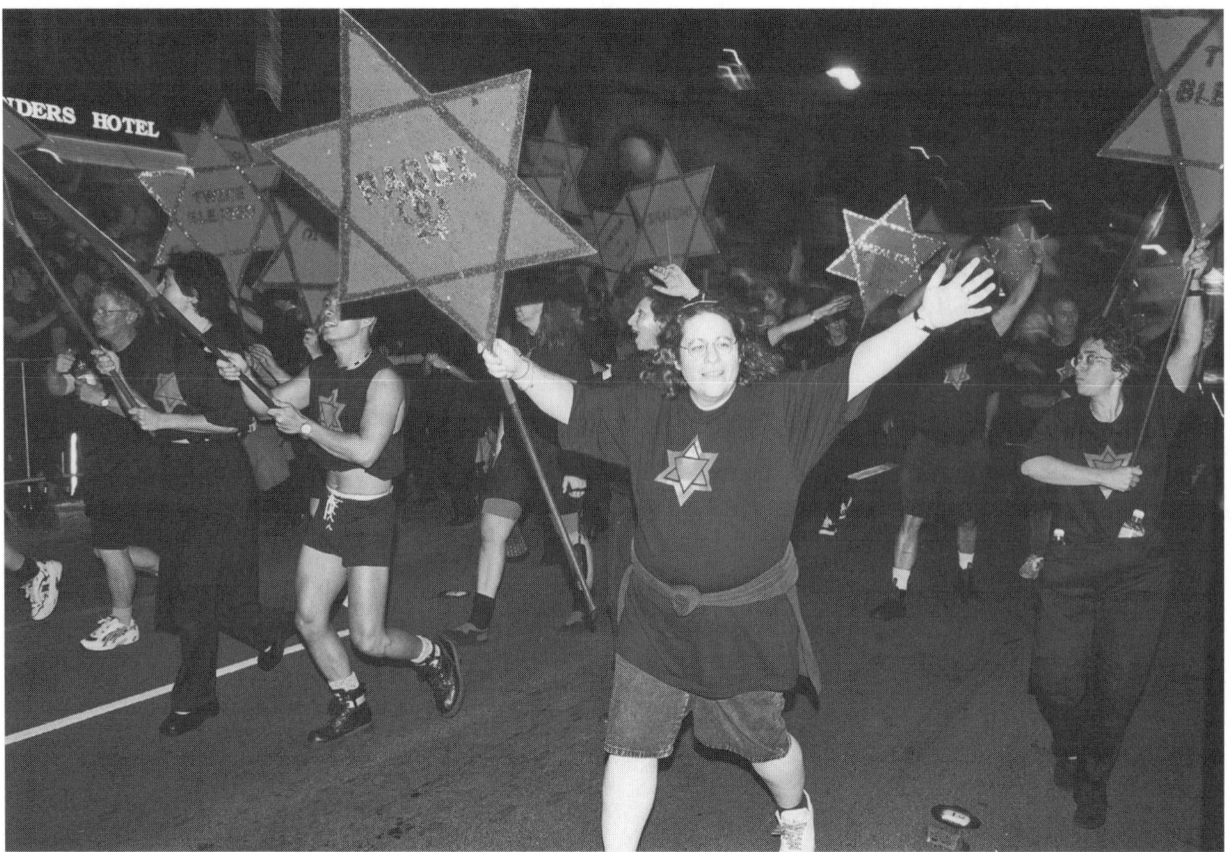

Gay and Lesbian Carnival. *Every culture has norms about appropriate sexual behavior for women. Here gay members of the Australian Jewish community join in a celebration of gay pride.* © JOHN VAN HASSELT/CORBIS SYGMA.

who are not Christian may have fewer religious taboos against lesbianism.

There has been very little focus from scholars and writers on U.S. lesbians from India and other South Asian countries. India is a vast country with many languages, religions, and cultures, so it can be hard for U.S. lesbians from India to find each other and communicate. Cultures in which men and women are separated (e.g., Moslem cultures) give women the opportunity for close, intimate contact even if this contact is not sexual or not considered lesbian.

Asian-American lesbians are becoming more outspoken, and they are publishing articles, making films, and establishing activist groups to ensure their continued existence. Yau Ching, for example, produced the film *Ho Yuk* (*Let's Love Hong Kong*) in 2002. Films about Indian and Indian-American lesbians include the critically acclaimed film *Fire* (1996) by the heterosexual Indian-Canadian director Deepa Mehta, and Indian-Canadian filmmaker Nisha Ganatra's "Chutney Popcorn" (1999), which is set in the United States.

WHITE LESBIANS

Studies in the early part of the twentieth century on "deviant" same-sex desires were conducted by medical researchers and focused almost entirely on lesbians of European descent. This focus on white lesbians was due in part to the construction of normative female sexuality as white, heterosexual, and passive. In the early to mid-1900s, these socially normative white women were assumed to have little or no sexual desire, so that any suggestion of female same-sex desire was viewed as a psychological illness and a desire to be male. Beginning with the removal of "homosexuality" as a mental illness from the American Psychological Association's *Diagnostic and Statistical Manual of Mental Disorders* in 1973, research became more affirmative for lesbians. A large body of research since then has focused on the coming-out process, lesbian relationships, lesbian mothers, lesbians in the workplace, and lesbian health and mental health.

Nevertheless, the vast majority of research on lesbians continues to focus on white women, so it is important to remember that white lesbians are not necessarily the norm.

For example, white lesbians tend to be more removed from their family of origin and from religion than lesbians of color. Research done by Jessica Morris and Esther Rothblum in 1999 found white lesbians to be less cohesive on dimensions of lesbianism (e.g., the interrelationship of self-identity, sexual behavior, degree of "outness") than African-American, Latina and Native American lesbians. Finally, lesbians of color often find that lesbian communities are racist or ignore the needs of lesbians of color, leading them to form their own communities.

SEE ALSO *Gay Men; Heterosexism and Homophobia; Lorde, Audre; Sexuality.*

BIBLIOGRAPHY

"Gloria Anzaldúa 1942–2004." 2006. Regents of the University of Minnesota. Available from http://voices.cla.umn.edu/vg.

Greene, Beverly. 1994. "Lesbian Women of Color: Triple Jeopardy." In *Women of Color: Integrating Ethnic and Gender Identities in Psychotherapy*, edited by Lillian Comas-Diaz and Beverly Greene. New York: Guilford Press.

House, Carrie. 1997. "Navajo Woman Warrior: An Ancient Tradition in a Modern World." In *Two-Spirit People: Native American Gender, Identity, Sexuality, and Spirituality*, edited by Sue-Ellen Jacobs, Wesley Thomas, and Sabine Lang. Urbana: University of Illinois Press.

King, Deborah. 1988. "Multiple Jeopardy, Multiple Consciousness: The Context of a Black Feminist Ideology." *Signs* 14 (1): 42–72.

Lang, Sabine. 1998. *Men as Women, Women as Men: Changing Gender in Native American Cultures.* Austin: University of Texas Press.

Lorde, Audre. 1983. *Zami: A New Spelling of My Name.* Trumansburg, NY: Crossing Press.

Morris, Jessica, and Esther Rothblum. 1999. "Who Fills Out a 'Lesbian' Questionnaire? The Interrelationship of Sexual Orientation, Years Out, Disclosure of Sexual Orientation, Sexual Experience with Women, and Participation in the Lesbian Community." *Psychology of Women Quarterly* 33: 537–557.

Rich, Adrienne. 1980. *Compulsory Heterosexuality and Lesbian Existence.* London: Onlywomen Press.

Roscoe, Will, and Stephen Murray. 2001. *Boy-wives and Female Husbands: Studies in African Homosexualities.* New York: St. Martin's Press.

Wekker, Gloria. 2006. *The Politics of Passion: Women's Sexual Culture in Afro-Surinamese Diaspora.* New York: Columbia University Press.

Zimmerman, Bonnie, ed. 2000. *Lesbian Histories and Cultures: An Encyclopedia.* New York: Garland.

Joselyn Leimbach
Lisa Chavez
Esther Rothblum

LIBERIA

SEE *American Colonization Society and the Founding of Liberia.*

LIFE EXPECTANCY

Race is widely understood as a sociocultural phenomenon, not a biological one. This view is based on evidence that conventional racial categories fail to capture global patterns of human genetic variation. Yet severing the link between race and human biological variation may create an unintended blind spot: Race is biological in the sense that racial differences in life experiences are linked to biological outcomes, including death and disease. Historically, these health inequalities were interpreted as evidence of innate biological differences between racially defined groups. But researchers increasingly seek to understand them as the biological consequences of social inequalities among racialized groups.

Racial inequalities in health are often summarized by reference to life expectancy, a standard indicator of population health. This entry first defines life expectancy and then presents evidence for current and historical racial inequalities in life expectancy in the United States. It then reviews explanations for the persistent gap in life expectancy and identifies key needs for research to improve our understanding of racial inequalities in health.

RACIAL INEQUALITIES IN LIFE EXPECTANCY

Life expectancy is calculated on the basis of age-specific death rates for a population at a given point in time. It estimates the average number of years people who have reached a particular age would continue to live, if current death rates at each age remained constant over time. Because death rates do not remain constant, life expectancy does not measure the longevity of actual birth cohorts. Rather, it summarizes the overall mortality profile of a population at a particular point in time.

Life expectancy can be calculated for any age, but the most common summary of a population's health status is life expectancy at birth. However, this measure is heavily influenced by rates of infant and child mortality, especially if these rates are high. When researchers wish to exclude the impact of early mortality on population health, they typically calculate life expectancy at ages five or fifteen.

Black and White Americans. In the United States, research on racial inequalities in life expectancy focuses largely on inequalities between black and white Americans.

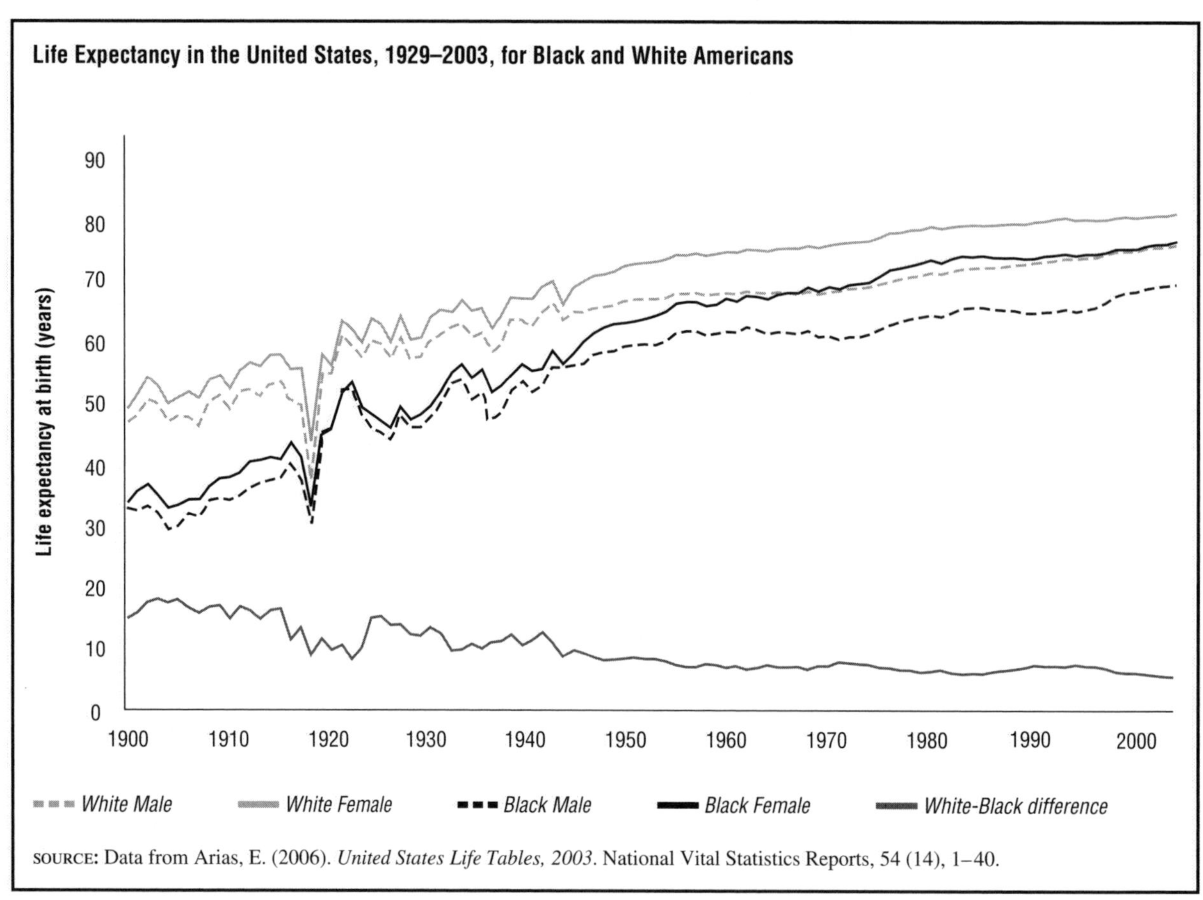

SOURCE: Data from Arias, E. (2006). *United States Life Tables, 2003.* National Vital Statistics Reports, 54 (14), 1–40.

Figure 1.

Figure 1 shows how these inequalities persisted over the twentieth century. At the beginning of the century, the black-white gap in life expectancy at birth was 14.6 years. This gap reached a peak in 1903 (17.8 years) and declined through World War II. (It narrowed considerably but temporarily during the "colorblind" 1918 flu pandemic.) By 1955, the black-white gap in life expectancy had fallen to less than seven years.

However, during the second half of the century, racial inequalities in life expectancy scarcely changed, despite substantial gains in life expectancy for the population as a whole (Figure 1). Indeed, in 1995 the black-white gap in life expectancy was the same as it was in 1956 (6.9 years). Only in the last few years has this gap narrowed again, reaching a historic low of 5.3 years in 2003.

The apparent stability of this inequality masks the diverging fortunes of black men and women, as Figure 1 shows. From 1950 to 2003, the gap in life expectancy between black and white women fell from 9.3 to 4.4 years, such that black women's life expectancy at birth now exceeds that of white men. During the same period, the gap between black and white men climbed to a peak of 8.5 in 1982, before falling again to 6.3 years in 2003. This gap between black and white men is still greater than it was in 1955.

The historical depth of inequalities between black and white Americans explains the usual focus on black-white comparisons of health and life expectancy. But these comparisons are limited in at least three ways. First, crude black-white comparisons neglect the diversity of health and mortality profiles within racial categories. Second, they ignore the changing racial demography of the United States in the wake of increasing immigration from Asia and Latin America since the 1960s. Third, they imply that race per se is the most important determinant of health disparities, rather than identifying the specific causal influences on racial inequalities of health.

"Eight Americas." One group of researchers addressed these concerns by dividing the U.S. population into eight distinct groups based on race and the socioeconomic attributes of counties where people lived (Murray et al. 2006). The resulting "Eight Americas," shown in Table 1, capture the striking range of inequalities in life expectancy in the United States.

Life Expectancy and Socioeconomic Inequalities across "Eight Americas"

America	Description	Population (millions)	Average income per capita	Percent completing high school	Male life expectancy at birth	Female life expectancy at birth
1	Asian	10.4	$21,566	80	82.8	87.7
2	Northland low-income rural white	3.6	$17,758	83	76.2	81.8
3	Middle America	214.0	$24,640	84	75.2	80.2
4	Low-income whites in Appalachia and the Mississippi Valley	16.6	$16,390	72	71.8	77.8
5	Western Native American	1.0	$10,029	69	69.4	75.9
6	Black Middle America	23.4	$15,412	75	69.6	75.9
7	Southern low-income rural black	5.8	$10,463	61	67.7	74.6
8	High-risk urban black	7.5	$14,800	72	66.7	74.9

SOURCE: Reprinted from Murray et al. (2006). "Eight Americas: Investigating mortality disparities across races, counties, and race-counties in the United States." PLoS Medicine 3: e260.

Table 1.

Relative to global inequalities in life expectancy, racial disparities within the United States are massive. The gap between Americans with the longest and shortest life expectancies—Asian-American women and black men in high-risk urban settings—is an astonishing 21 years, more than the difference between Japan and Bangladesh, for example. Within sexes, the gap between the longest and shortest life expectancies is 13.1 years for women and 16.1 years for men. These gaps are 2.6 to 3 times greater than the inequalities between black and white women in the United States as a whole. They also rival the nearly 14-year gap in life expectancy between high-income OECD (Organisation for Economic Co-Operation and Development) countries and low-income developing countries (United Nations Development Programme 2005). Indeed, the life expectancy of high-risk urban black men in the United States is more typical of life expectancy in developing countries than it is of high-income countries like the United States (Figure 2).

Table 1 also highlights diversity within conventional racial categories. Murray and colleagues identify three black and three white Americas. Across the white Americas, the gap in life expectancy is 4.0 years for women and 4.4 years for men. Across the black Americas, the gaps are smaller but still substantial—1.3 years for women and 2.9 years for men. These gaps cannot be attributed simply to socioeconomic inequalities. Despite low per capita income, rural whites in the northern plains and Dakotas have a significant mortality advantage over high-income whites in America. Likewise, despite greater poverty, rural black men in the South have a slight edge in longevity over black men in high-risk urban environments.

Murray and colleagues emphasize that inequalities in life expectancy across the eight Americas are not the result of differential mortality among children or the elderly. Although racial inequalities in infant mortality persist, the largest mortality differences are among young (ages 15–44) and middle-aged (ages 45–64) adults. These differences are the result primarily of noncommunicable causes such as cardiovascular disease, diabetes mellitus, cancer, and liver cirrhosis. Injuries and HIV/AIDS also contribute significantly to excessive mortality among young adults. In separate analyses, Wong and colleagues (2002) estimate that eliminating hypertension, or chronic high blood pressure, would have the largest impact on reducing racial differences in life expectancy, followed by HIV,

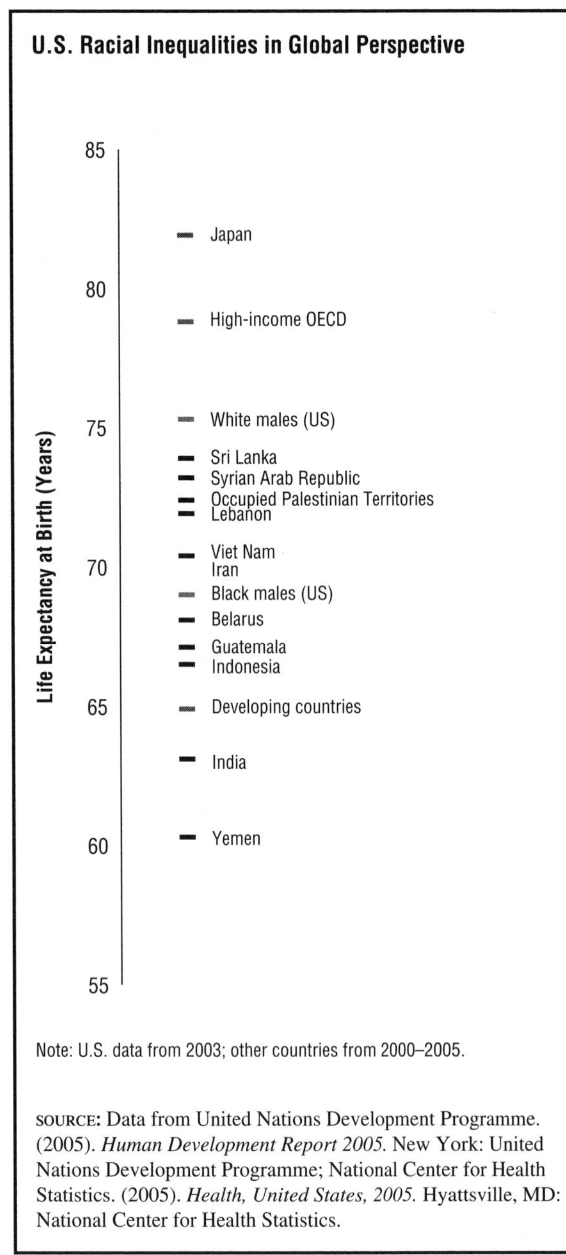

U.S. Racial Inequalities in Global Perspective

Note: U.S. data from 2003; other countries from 2000–2005.

SOURCE: Data from United Nations Development Programme. (2005). *Human Development Report 2005.* New York: United Nations Development Programme; National Center for Health Statistics. (2005). *Health, United States, 2005.* Hyattsville, MD: National Center for Health Statistics.

Figure 2.

homicide, diabetes, colon cancer, pneumonia, and ischemic heart disease.

EXPLANATIONS FOR RACIAL INEQUALITIES IN LIFE EXPECTANCY

There remains debate about why these inequalities exist. Many critics note that the debate often ends prematurely with the assumption that race is biology and that racial differences in health are largely determined by genetic differences. However, in the last twenty years, clinicians and health researchers have become increasingly aware of the problems with race as a biological construct, and there is growing emphasis on the social and cultural factors that shape racial inequalities in health.

In a recent review, Dressler, Oths, and Gravlee (2005) identify five models for explaining racial inequalities in health:

1. A racial-genetic model
2. A socioeconomic model
3. A health-behavior model
4. A psychosocial stress model
5. A structural-constructivist model.

Although the review focuses largely on infant mortality and high blood pressure, the five models apply to explanations for racial health inequalities in general.

The *racial-genetic* model holds that racial inequalities in health are primarily genetic in origin. This view has a long history in American medicine (Krieger 1987). Indeed, many key figures in the history of scientific racism were physicians and medical scientists who asserted the natural biological inferiority of blacks as the basis of their greater susceptibility to disease and premature death. For example, during the first years of Reconstruction, as many as one-quarter to one-third of former slaves may have died in parts of the southern United States. Many white physicians interpreted this trend as evidence of African Americans' innate biological inferiority, not of fundamental social inequality.

The basic assumptions of this period remain surprisingly common today. Whereas social scientists generally take it for granted that race does not correspond to meaningful genetic differences, many physicians and biomedical researchers still assume that there are innate racial differences in the susceptibility to disease. Some prominent researchers explicitly defend race as a useful framework for identifying the genetic basis of common diseases (Risch et al. 2002). Yet there remains little reason to think that genes are to blame for racial inequalities in life expectancy (Goodman 2000).

Most research on the nongenetic basis of racial inequalities in health has focused on the role of *socioeconomic status* (SES), usually defined as some combination of education, occupation, and income. The rationale is that race and SES are confounded, such that controlling for differences in SES should either eliminate racial disparities in health or reveal the true causal effect of race. As a rule, accounting for SES reduces but does not eliminate racial inequalities in health. This pattern also holds for life expectancy, as the Eight Americas study suggests (Table 1).

Some researchers have interpreted the residual relationship between race and health, after controlling for SES, as support for the racial-genetic model. But this interpretation is untenable because race cannot be reduced to class; racial inequality affects health through mechanisms other than socioeconomic deprivation. Thus, controlling for SES, even when it is measured well, does not eliminate differences between racially defined groups in noneconomic factors that influence population health (Kaufman, Cooper, and McGee 1997).

The *health behavior* model is in part a response to the limitations of the socioeconomic model. One possible reason that SES does not account for racial inequalities in health is that it does not capture the unequal distribution of health-related behaviors across racially defined groups. The health behaviors most often discussed include dietary intake and physical activity (resulting in excessive weight and obesity), alcohol consumption, and smoking. These factors clearly impact health and longevity. However, there is little evidence that they account for the relationship between race and health (Dressler, Oths, and Gravlee 2005).

The incomplete success of socioeconomic and health-behavior models has stimulated research on the contribution of *psychosocial stress* to racial inequalities in health. Research in this tradition begins from the premise that institutional and interpersonal racism create stressful life circumstances that adversely impact the health of racially oppressed people. The literature in this area is enormous and growing. Dressler and colleagues (2005) distinguish three streams of research on psychosocial stress, including (1) studies that measure general markers of stress exposure such as depression and anxiety, (2) studies that assess the perceived experience of discrimination, and (3) studies that adapt general models of the stress process to the unique stressors and coping resources in African-American communities.

Each approach has produced novel insights, confirming the importance of psychosocial stress in the origin of racial inequalities in health. Yet much research in this tradition remains vulnerable to the limitations of stress research in general. First, many stressors, including exposure to racism, are difficult to measure apart from individuals' efforts to cope with those stressors. Second, research on psychosocial stress traditionally focuses on individual experience, with too little consideration of how stressors and coping resources are socially distributed and culturally constructed.

The *structural-constructivist* model addresses these limitations. This approach seeks to explain racial inequalities in health at the intersection of social structure and cultural meaning. For example, Dressler (2005) shows that racial inequalities in mental and physical health are associated with one's ability to obtain culturally valued resources, which is partly constrained by structural inequalities. Gravlee, Dressler, and Bernard (2005) show that the association between skin color and blood pressure in Puerto Rico is shaped both by the meaning people attribute to skin color and by access to socioeconomic resources. These examples illustrate the promise of research that examines how social structural forces condition exposure to culturally defined stressors and coping resources.

RESEARCH NEEDS

Racial inequalities in life expectancy pose three critical challenges for the social and biomedical sciences. First, given the persistence of racial-genetic determinism, it remains necessary to clarify the fallacy of race as a framework for understanding human biodiversity. Second, there is a need for research on how hidden assumptions about race shape biomedical research and clinical practice and how clinical practice and biomedical research, in turn, perpetuate prior beliefs about race. Third, researchers need to integrate multiple levels of analysis—sociocultural, environmental, behavioral, physiological, molecular—to understand how the sociocultural phenomena of race and racism become embodied in biological outcomes over the life course.

SEE ALSO *Demographics and Race; Diseases, Racial; Hypertension and Coronary Heart Disease; Infant Mortality and Birth Weight; Infectious Disease, Susceptibility, and Race; Social Class and Mortality.*

BIBLIOGRAPHY

Arias, Elizabeth. 2006. United States Life Tables, 2003. *National Vital Statistics Reports* Vol. 54, No. 14. Available from http://0-www.cdc.gov.mill1.sjlibrary.org/nchs/data/statab/lewk3_2003.pdf.

Dressler, William W. 2005. "What's *Cultural* about Bio*cultural* Research?" *Ethos* 33 (1): 20–45.

———, Kathryn S. Oths, and Clarence C. Gravlee. 2005. "Race and Ethnicity in Public Health Research: Models to Explain Health Disparities." *Annual Review of Anthropology* 34 (1): 231–252.

Goodman, Alan H. 2000. "Why Genes Don't Count (for Racial Differences in Health)." *American Journal of Public Health* 90 (11): 1699–1702.

Gravlee, Clarence C., William W. Dressler, and H. Russell Bernard. 2005. "Skin Color, Social Classification, and Blood Pressure in Southeastern Puerto Rico." *American Journal of Public Health* 95 (12): 2191–2197.

Kaufman, Jay S., Richard S. Cooper, and Daniel L. McGee. 1997. "Socioeconomic Status and Health in Blacks and Whites: The Problem of Residual Confounding and the Resiliency of Race." *Epidemiology* 8 (6): 621–628.

Krieger, Nancy. 1987. "Shades of Difference: Theoretical Underpinnings of the Medical Controversy on Black/White Differences in the United States, 1830–1870." *International Journal of Health Services* 17 (2): 259–278.

Murray, Christopher J. L., C. Sandeep, Catherine Michaud Kulkarni, et al. 2006. "Eight Americas: Investigating

Mortality Disparities Across Races, Counties, and Race-Counties in the United States." *PLoS Medicine* 3 (9): e260.

National Center for Health Statistics. 2005. Health, United States, 2005. Hyattsville, MD: National Center for Health Statistics. Available from http://www.cdc.gov/nchs/hus.htm.

Risch, Neil, Esteban Burchard, Elad Ziv, and Hua Tang. 2002. "Categorization of Humans in Biomedical Research: Genes, Race and Disease." *Genome Biology* 3: comment2007.1–comment2007.12.

United Nations Development Programme. 2005. *Human Development Report 2005*. New York: United Nations Development Programme.

Wong, M. D., M. F. Shapiro, W. J. Boscardin, and S. L. Ettner. 2002. "Contribution of Major Diseases to Disparities in Mortality." *New England Journal of Medicine* 347 (20): 1585-1592.

Clarence C. Gravlee

LORDE, AUDRE

1934–1992

The author and activist Audre Lorde was born in Harlem on February 18, 1934, the youngest child of West Indian immigrants. Lorde viewed art and social protest as inseparable, although *The First Cities* (1968), her first volume of poems, is not as overtly political as the fourteen books that followed. Among her best-known works are *The Black Unicorn* (1978), a poetry collection with a strong African emphasis; *The Cancer Journals* (1980), a feminist perspective on Lorde's struggles with breast cancer; *Zami: A New Spelling of My Name* (1982), an experimental memoir; and *Sister Outsider: Essays and Speeches* (1984), which includes "Uses of the Erotic: The Erotic as Power," "The Master's Tools Will Never Dismantle the Master's House," "Age, Race, Class, and Sex: Women Redefining Difference," "The Uses of Anger: Women Responding to Racism," and several other examples of Lorde's persuasive rhetoric.

In *Zami,* Lorde details how her parents tried to protect their three daughters from American racism by warning them not to trust white people, but without giving them any reasons. Because Lorde's mother and aunts were light-skinned, prohibitions based on color confused the children, as did the odd excuses their mother made to explain the behavior of white adults who avoided sitting near the Lorde family in crowded buses. On a trip to Washington, D.C., to celebrate her grade school graduation, Audre was enraged when the family was refused service in a segregated restaurant across the street from the Supreme Court. She felt betrayed by the nation, but also by her father's failure to prepare her for the shock of rejection.

Lorde worked at several blue-collar and pink-collar jobs to support her undergraduate studies at Hunter College. A book lover who believed in the power of language to change social systems, she earned a master's degree in library science from Columbia University while she was employed by the Bureau of Child Welfare. In 1968, a pivotal experience as a creative writing teacher at Mississippi's historically black Tougaloo College convinced her to focus on a career as a poet and teacher. Lorde said that this first trip to the Deep South, working with African-American students for the first time, made her feel that a library career was "not enough" (Hall 2000, p. 95). At Lehman College and John Jay College of Criminal Justice in New York, she developed courses on racism. During the 1970s and the 1980s, she lectured in Australia, Africa, and other places. In the United States she helped to found Kitchen Table Women of Color Press, and in Berlin she encouraged the Afro-German women in her writing workshops to publish an anthology.

As a "black lesbian feminist mother poet warrior," Lorde said she was always an outsider, even in the major movements for equal rights. She argued that sexism and racism were both rooted in white male authority; she exposed race prejudice within the predominantly white and middle-class women's movement; and she criticized African Americans who denied sisterhood to black lesbians. Lorde concluded that these various forms of injustice kept women from achieving the erotic power of female creativity and a true depth of feeling. According to the biographer Alexis De Veaux, Lorde gradually came to see "the necessity for linking analyses of racial, class, and sexual oppressions" (De Veaux 2004, p. 170), and as her "multiple identities" evolved, eroticism became essential to her "self-actualization" (p. xi). Two years before her death on November 17, 1992, Lorde was honored by more than 2,000 people from twenty-three countries at a conference titled *I Am Your Sister: Forging Global Connections across Difference.*

SEE ALSO *Black Feminism in the United States; Feminism and Race; Heterosexism and Homophobia; Lesbians.*

BIBLIOGRAPHY

PRIMARY WORKS

1978. *The Black Unicorn*. New York: W.W. Norton.

1980. *The Cancer Journals*. San Francisco: Aunt Lute Books.

1982. *Zami: A New Spelling of My Name*. Watertown, MA: Persephone Press.

1984. *Sister Outside: Essays and Speeches*. Trumansburg, NY: Crossing Press.

SECONDARY WORKS

De Veaux, Alexis. 2004. *Warrior Poet: A Biography of Audre Lorde*. New York: W.W. Norton.

Hall, Joan Wylie, ed. 2004. *Conversations with Audre Lorde*. Jackson: University Press of Mississippi.

Joan Wylie Hall

M

MACHISMO

The concept of "machismo" is a culturally defined attribute associated with U.S. Mexican and other Latino men. It has come to have a number of negative connotations, such as a chauvinistic and tyrannical male character, an exaggerated masculine posture, extramarital sexual activity, involvement in physical abuse and violence, displays of physical courage or daring, heavy drinking, and the imposition of restrictions on women's freedom of movement. However, there is a contrasting view holding that machismo embodies the desirable combination of fearlessness, self-sufficiency, and courage. In this view, a macho is a *hombre noble* (noble man) who sacrifices to economically support and protect his family at all costs. This article explains the etiology and veracity of these two views of machismo and suggests how it may be used analytically.

MACHISMO'S ETIOLOGY

In the social sciences, the words *macho* and *machismo* have become shorthand for labeling male characteristics in Mexican and other Latino cultures. Machismo is thought to be more dominant among U.S. Hispanic groups than non-Hispanic populations. However, these gender role characteristics are more likely to be attributed to men from more traditional cultures. The cornerstone of machismo is the traditional Mexican family, stereotyped as having a patriarchal structure characterized by the unquestioned and absolute supremacy of the husband and the self-sacrifice of the wife. Within this family structure, major decisions and privileges flow from the male patriarch to all others, from whom he demands unquestionable allegiance, respect, and obedience.

Mexican women and other Latinas are seen as submissive women who are not only forced into this type of situation but also accept this position. *Marianismo* defines the Hispanic female ideal. Like the Virgin Mary, the ideal woman in Hispanic culture is regarded as morally and spiritually superior to men. She is seen as centering her life around her husband and children; she is unfailingly submissive and obedient; she avoids self-indulgence and sensuality; she is expected to be chaste before marriage and accept her husband's *macho* behavior when married; and she is expected to endure whatever suffering men may impose on her. The family is perceived as the institution in which these clearly delineated gender roles are perpetuated and reproduced from one generation to the next. In contrast, the woman who does not adopt these characteristics is labeled "*la mujer mala*" or "the bad woman."

Traditionally, social scientists tend to reinforce these images by imposing an assimilationist paradigm on this population. This paradigm promotes the perspective that Mexican Americans immigrated to the United States from rural agricultural regions of Mexico with strong traditional cultures and values. These images are based on early anthropologists such as Robert Redfield, whose description of Mexican rural society in the mid-twentieth century was transferred to Mexicans living in the United States. This paradigm was reinforced by early settlement patterns, which found Mexicans living in rural areas of the Southwest. Even though most Mexican Americans were living in cities by the 1960s, the existing literature on this population was heavily weighted by studies of rural and traditional life.

The cornerstone of the assimilation model is that a minority group's disadvantaged status decreases as it

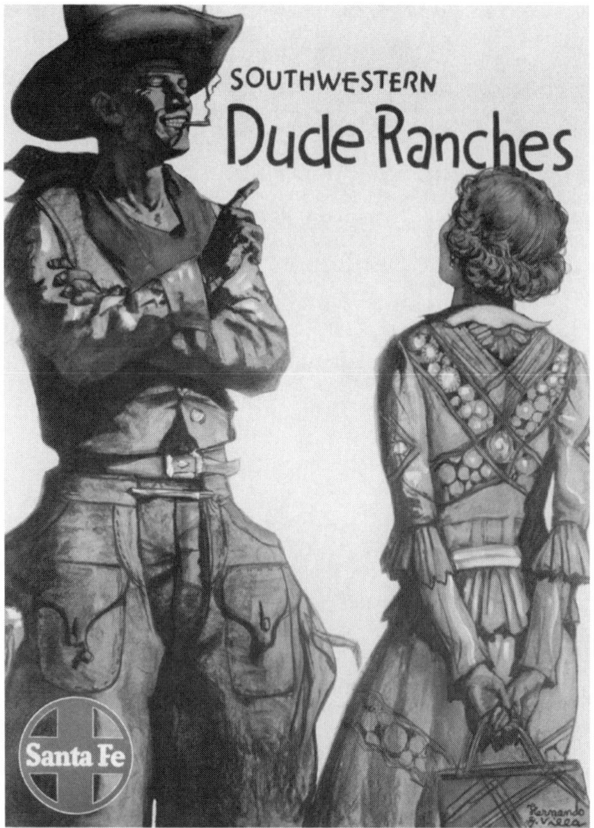

Southwestern Dude Ranches (Hernando G. Villa, 1938). *This poster portrays the exaggerated masculinity of Mexican and Latin American men.* SWIM INK 2, LLC/CORBIS.

adopts the values of the majority society. In the case of Mexican Americans, the model assumes that what impedes the advancement of this population is that they stubbornly adhere to a deficient traditional culture that is incompatible with modern urban societies such as the United States. One of the most pejorative cultural characteristic ascribed to this population is that of machismo, which is assumed to permeate all aspects of family life. The family places a great emphasis upon children learning submission and strong obedience to the dictates of the father and other authority figures, and the family is seen as orbiting the strong domination of the male in the family. This idea, however, conceptualized as "machismo," was accepted without any empirical verification, resulting in a distorted view of the family and gender roles.

Although some social scientists have challenged the portrayal of Mexican American (and other Latino) machismo (Baca-Zinn 1982), research has found that gender roles within the family are more egalitarian than previously presented. For instance, the women's role is more independent and assertive than previously described, and decisions are shared by both the husband and wife (Cromwell and Cromwell 1978; Vega 1990). These findings support a view of Latino husbands and fathers as caring individuals who have an active role in their children's upbringing. Contrary to the stereotypes and the popular view of machismo, the bond between fathers and children is one that is inherent in the culture, independent of the child's relationship to the mother. In this more sympathetic view, a macho is the protector of the family and defender of family honor.

A result of current empirical evidence, a less pernicious and nuanced view of machismo has emerged in some social-science literature. More recent research suggests that—just as in the broader area of family sociology—marital power, division of labor, and kinship orientation are found to be influenced not only by culture but also by structural factors such as class position, employment status, and residential patterns.

THE CONSEQUENCES OF MACHISMO

Despite this contemporary research, the association of machismo with Mexican Americans and other Latinos has endured as a major stereotype of these populations. These exaggerated and prejudicial views are reinforced by societal institutions (e.g., religion, education) and, in particular, by the mass media. In the first half of the twentieth century, films and literature largely portrayed Mexican males as sleazy bandits, sleepy peons, Latin lovers, fun-loving buffoons, or some variation of these characterizations. These images have been modernized for twenty-first century audiences and have evolved into urban versions of these earlier portrayals. The new imagery of Mexican Americans is dominated by the gang member, drug user, dealer, and illegal immigrant, and they tend to be men that are violent, sexual predators, criminals, or cowards. Mass media researchers have proven that long-term exposure to misrepresented stereotypes can have what is called a cumulative effect, leading persons to believe that the dominant image is the norm.

These negative machismo stereotypes result in prejudice and discriminatory behavior towards Mexican American and other Latino men. Regardless of whether these characterizations are true or false, the stereotype leads to what Robert Merton identified in 1957 as a *self-fulfilling prophecy*. For example, if Mexican American men are widely believed to be sexist, people will behave toward them, have certain expectations of them, or interpret their behavior in such a manner that fulfills their stereotype. Even if these beliefs are false, they become real in their consequences.

Further, the prescribed male roles associated with machismo among Mexican Americans and other Latino men have various negative consequences. One of these is that these characteristics become internalized by Latino males themselves. The relationship between these stereotypes, self-image, and subsequent behavior needs further exploration. However, it is clear that Mexican-American youth are highly influenced by their exposure to the mass media. In particular, the urban life culture promoted in the hip-hop and rap music subculture has had a pervasive influence on young urban Latino males. Many of this musical genre's lyrics promote an oppositional culture centered on a lifestyle expressed through distinct clothing styles, tattoos, language, and body jewelry. Of more concern is that some artists involved in this genre condone violence and crime by promoting a "gangsta" way of life. Some of the most vociferous critics of this musical genre argue that it also promotes a hypermasculinity, sexism, and an objectification of women.

When this message is delivered to Mexican-American (and other Latino) males living in economically disadvantaged urban Mexican-American communities, it reinforces an already established predisposition to machismo. As Elijah Anderson (1999) points out, in many economically depressed areas of inner cities, the rules of civil law have been replaced with what is identified as a "code of the streets." Here, youth and adult subcultures are involved in street violence, drug use, crime, and confrontational behaviors toward authority. Specifically, this subculture revolves around a street socialization process that emphasizes the development of collective and individual coping strategies that use violence as a means of resolving conflicts, especially among males. The repercussions for Latinos may be more severe than among blacks or whites. In this regard, machismo is highly embedded in situated activities and an environment that is based on a male-dominated patriarchal hierarchy.

MACHISMO AS ANALYTICAL CONCEPT

Mexican-American culture, reinforced by social context, magnifies the differences between gender roles to a greater degree than the culture of many other groups. The magnification of gender reflects a family-ethnic community complex tied to structural features of the family, and to more general conditions of social solidarity that stem from Mexican Americans' subordinate status. There is a complex intersection of patriarchy (male domination/female subordination) and machismo with class and ethnicity. As Denise Segura (1999) notes, patriarchy refers to the development and institutionalization of male dominance over women in society. Machismo is how a patriarchal ideology is operationalized by males of Mexican descent or other Latinos. When using machismo as an analytical construct, class and ethnicity need to be theorized together because they emerge at the points at which stratification articulates structure. Christopher McCall (1999) has shown that class privileges are maintained by a pervasive social control made possible by ethnic labeling. Within ethnic communities, however, the structure of opportunity often operates through the mediations imposed by a patriarchy, which, in turn, may derive legitimacy from class and ethnicity. This is important to consider when using machismo as an analytical tool.

An illustration of how this approach can be used is taken from a recent study of intimate-partner violence. In this 2005 study, Avelardo Valdez and Raquel Flores attempted to understand the situational processes that contribute to the escalation of an argument to a physical and violent confrontation between Mexican-American gang-affiliated adolescent females and their dating partners. They found that "disrespect" was one of the precursors to the unfolding of a violent incident. This precursor implies that one of the partners has demonstrated a lack of good will, esteem, or deference to the other partner through behavior, symbolic gesture, or language. What is important here is that one party has perceived the other as engaging in behavior that is disrespectful. Differences in what is perceived as disrespect is influenced by gender and culture. For instance, a male will escalate the violence if the incident results in a "loss of face," as dictated by the "code of the street." Similarly, the inability to dominate one's female partner is a challenge to a socially structured male hierarchy, particularly within a male gang subculture with clearly defined gender barriers. The violent response of a man in this position will be interpreted as somewhat instrumental and rational. On the other hand, a female will more likely escalate the violence if she perceives a threat to an emotional relationship or connection. For women, this is often based on witnessed behavior (i.e., seeing the man flirting with another woman) or validated behavior. For men, jealousy is often based merely on suspicion. This type of violence on the part of women is often interpreted as emotional or expressive, while the men's violence is seen as more rational or instrumental. This is just an example of how the concept of machismo can be used as a construct in conducting research on Latino populations.

Machismo is a socially constructed concept that needs to be used judiciously when applied to Mexican-American and other Latino males. The degree of machismo associated with these men will vary depending on a constellation of variables, such as income, generation and education. Nonetheless, it would be a fair statement, considering culture and class variables, to say that machismo may be more salient among Latinos than other groups. This is certainly the case among young men living in disadvantaged communities, where it is a socially valued ideal that emphasizes aggression and control, venerates dominance, and has wide currency on the streets. However, this street machismo may be different than that represented in the home that is associated with prosocial characteristics. As a cultural model for male behavior, machismo provides important standards and motivations for the attainment of social goals. In the application of this construct, however, researchers must recognize the importance of considering structural factors, including economic marginality, in explaining these phenomena.

BIBLIOGRAPHY

Abad, V., J. Ramos, and E. A. Boyce. 1974. "A Model for Delivery of Mental Health Services to Spanish-Speaking Minorities." *American Journal of Orthopsychiatry* 44 (4): 584–595.

Aday, Lu Ann, Grace Y. Chiu, and Ronald Andersen. 1980. "Methodological Issues in Health Care Surveys of the Spanish Heritage Population." *American Journal of Public Health* 70 (4): 367–374.

Alvirez, David, Frank D. Bean, and Dorie Williams. 1981. "The Mexican American Family." In *Ethnic Families in America*, 2nd ed., edited by Charles H. Mindel and Robert W. Habenstein, 269–292. New York: Elsevier North Holland.

Anderson, Elijah. 1999. *Code of the Street: Decency, Violence, and the Moral Life of the Inner City*. New York: W. W. Norton.

Baca-Zinn, Maxine. 1982. "Chicano Men and Masculinity." *Journal of Ethnic Studies* 10 (2): 29–44.

Christensen, Elia Hidalgo. 1979. "The Puerto Rican Woman: A Profile." In *The Puerto Rican Woman*, edited by Edna Acosta-Belen, 51–63. New York: Praeger.

Comas-Diaz, Lillian. 1982. "Mental Health Needs of Puerto Rican Women in the United States." In *Latina Women in Transition*, edited by Ruth. Zambrana, 1–10. Monograph Series. New York: Hispanic Research Center, Fordham University.

Cromwell, Vicky L., and Ronald E. Cromwell. 1978. "Perceived Dominance in Decision Making and Conflict Resolution among Anglo, Black, and Chicano Couples." *Journal of Marriage and the Family* 40 (4): 749–759.

Grebler, Leo, Joan W. Moore, and Ralph C. Guzman. 1970. *The Mexican American People*. New York: Free Press.

Hawkes, Glenn R., and Minna Taylor. 1975. "Power Structure in Mexican and Mexican American Farm Labor Families." *Journal of Marriage and the Family* 37 (4): 807–811.

McCall, Christopher. 1990. *Class, Ethnicity, and Social Inequality*. Montreal: McGill-Queens University Press.

Medina, Carmen. 1987. "Latino Culture and Sex Education." *SIECUS Report* 15 (3): 1–4.

Merton, Robert K. 1957. *Social Theory and Social Structure*, rev. ed. Glencoe, IL: Free Press.

Mirandé, Alfred. 1997. *Hombres y Machos: Masculinity and Latino Culture*. Boulder, CO: Westview Press.

Redfield, Robert. 1958. *Tepoztlan, A Mexican Village: A Study of Folk Life*. Chicago: University of Chicago Press.

Segura, Denise. A. 1994. "Working at Motherhood: Chicana and Mexican Immigrant Mothers and Employment." In *Mothering: Ideology, Experience, and Agency*, edited by Evelyn N. Glen, Grace Chang, and Linda R. Forcey, 211–233. New York: Routledge.

Stevens, Evelyn. 1973. "Machismo and Marianismo." *Transaction Society* 10 (6): 57–63.

Valdez, Avelardo, and Raquel Flores. 2005. "A Situational Analysis of Dating Violence Among Mexican American Females Associated with Street Gangs." *Sociological Focus* 38 (2): 95–114.

Vega, William A. 1990. "Hispanic Families in the 1980s: A Decade of Research." *Journal of Marriage and the Family* 52 (4): 1015–1024.

Wurzman, Ilyana, Bruce J. Rounsaville, and Herbert D. Kleber. 1983. "Cultural Values of Puerto Rican Opiate Addicts: An Exploratory Study." *American Journal of Drug and Alcohol Abuse* 9 (2): 141–153.

Ybarra, Lea. 1982. "When Wives Work: The Impact on the Chicano Family." *Journal of Marriage and the Family* 44 (1): 169–178.

Avelardo Valdez

MAGIC FLUTE, THE

The sublime music of Wolfgang Amadeus Mozart's *Die Zauberflöte* (*The Magic Flute*) is frequently contrasted with the banal philosophy, purloined symbolism, obvious misogyny, and crude racism of its libretto, attributed to German librettist Emanuel Schikaneder (1751–1812). The series of contradictions between noble music and offensive text is of signal importance, not only as it relates to Mozart but as it relates to other operatic composers, notably Richard Wagner (1813–1883). Some of the most exalted music in opera is tied to the least attractive characters and most offensive situations. Indeed, the most interesting music of *Die Zauberflöte* is associated with words in the libretto that are not only embarrassing to modern ears, but that were completely unacceptable to the best minds of the Enlightenment.

Does this mean that Mozart was, in the words of his contemporary William Blake (1757–1827), "of the devil's party?" The least generous interpretation is that he was, in fact, aware of and intentionally endorsed racist and sexist ideas in the libretto. This refocuses attention on the problem raised by Aristotle and Plato of whether music can communicate philosophical intent. The problem is furthermore related to the question raised in Gotthold Ephraim Lessing's *Laokoon* (1766): "How it is possible to derive aesthetic pleasure from works of art that embody painful, horrifying, or disgusting subjects?"

While the opera was first performed in September 1791, its origins have been traced to a story by August Liebeskind, *Lulu, oder Die Zauberflöte* (Lulu, or the magic flute), which was published in a collection of fairy tales by Christoph Martin Wieland in 1789. The text is usually attributed to Emanuel Schikaneder, although shortly after its appearance Karl Ludwig Giesecke claimed authorship, and some historians safely assign coauthorship. Regardless, the libretto is no masterwork of artistic integrity, but rather an incoherent semiplagiarized text. It provides no definitive evidence, however, as to Mozart's attitudes on gender, race, and class.

The text of *Die Zauberflöte* celebrates human brotherhood in lyrics similar to those of Friedrich Schiller's *Ode to Joy,* which Ludwig van Beethoven used in his Ninth Symphony, another expression of Enlightenment values. The opera's text, like the writings of Thomas Jefferson, reveals the moral paradoxes and intellectual inconsistencies of Enlightenment attitudes on race. The "Age of Reason," was also an age of romantic nationalism, religious enthusiasm, and maudlin sentimentality. Mozart composed in an age dominated by the madness of crowds and the febrile passions of gender, race, and class. His music is the epitome of crystalline regularity, but in the *Magic Flute* it is set in a plot that is disruptive and irrational. The philanthropy and interpretive Freemasonry, with its preachments of liberty, fraternity, and equality, are blandly superficial. They fall miserably short of the more inclusive philanthropy of William Blake, whose *Songs of Innocence* (1789) and *Songs of Experience* (1794) are critiques of Enlightenment hypocrisy.

Mozart made no pretensions to being a philosopher, nor did he leave behind a corpus of writings on the social, political, religious controversies of his time. Indeed, in both the stage and screen versions of Peter Schaffer's *Amadeus*, he is portrayed as a case of arrested development, as an infantile prodigy struggling for independence from a dominant father, and this portrait has not helped his reputation.

In contrast to *Die Zauberflöte,* Mozart's great Italian operas, including *La nozze di Figaro* (*The Marriage of Figaro*), for which Pierre de Beaumarchais provided the ideology and Lorenzo Da Ponte wrote the libretto, demonstrate enlightened, even revolutionary attitudes towards gender and class. Susanna, the heroine of *Figaro,* is not the passive victim of Count Almaviva, but a shrewd calculator, who exposes the clumsiness of his passions, and repeatedly makes a fool of him. *Don Giovanni* is an undisguised commentary on the meanness of the aristocracy, for the Don is not portrayed as a man of refinement, but as a pig whose insatiability at the dining table recapitulates the theme of his sexual gluttony. *Die Zauberflöte* contains no such obvious elements of political satire or social protest.

The serpentine structure of *Die Zauberflöte* recoils on itself through numerous illogical twists and turns, justifying the long-held view that it was wantonly assembled from a hodgepodge of incoherent ideas. In the opening scene, Prince Tamino, shrieking for help, is chased on stage by a serpent and he faints without putting up a fight. This unlikely *Heldentenor* is rescued by three spear-bearing women who cut the snake to pieces with their *Walküre* spears. On awakening from his swoon Tamino encounters Papagano, a comic figure attired in bird feathers, whom he mistakenly believes to be his savior. Papageno willingly allows him to persist in the delusion until the women reappear to set matters right. The *Walküres,* it turns out, are servants of the Queen of the Night, who enters in a thundercloud to charge Tamino with the task of rescuing her daughter Pamina from Sarastro, whom she describes as an evil priest. Eventually, the plot changes direction when it turns out that the Queen is merely a misguided and spiteful woman who foolishly attempts to upset the natural order by her unwillingness to submit to masculine authority.

The overt sexism of the opera is accompanied by acute racism located in the character of Monostatos, Sarastro's cowardly and lascivious black servant. Monostatos contemplates raping Pamina in the second act, but he is interrupted by the thunderings of the wrathful Queen. Later, however, Monostatos woos the Queen and teams up with her to oppose Sarastro. In the meantime, Tamino decides to join Sarastro's priesthood and submits to a rite that, by all accounts, resembles a Masonic initiation. By the end of the opera, Tamino is betrothed to Pamina, the Queen's plottings have been foiled, and Papageno has happily discovered his feminine counterpart, Papagena, a bird-woman with whom he will sensibly settle down and raise a family.

The opera's racism is most excruciating in the aria Monostatos sings in the second act, as he creeps toward the sleeping Pamina with loathsome intent. Monostatos is repugnant, not only because of the cowardice and fawning subservience that mark his character, but because he intends to violate the helpless innocence of Pamina:

> Everyone feels the joy of love; bill and coo, flirt, and squeeze and kiss. But I'm supposed to do without love because a black man is ugly! Is there no heart set aside for me? Am I not flesh and blood? It would be hell to live forever without a woman! And as I live and breathe, I want someone to rub noses with, and feel some tenderness. I'll get myself a white girl. Whiteness is beautiful; I must kiss her! Hide yourself, oh Moon! If you find this sight too vexing, then shut your eyes!

The music of this aria, composed in Mozart's celebrated mock-Turkish style, certainly deserved better than these sentiments. But it is unclear whether the opera, with its misogynistic slurs and racial derision, should be considered a guide to Mozart's thoughts on any subject. While the lyrics of *Die Zauberflöte* range from the banal to the opprobrious, some of them reveal an inadvertent comic wisdom. Papageno is a wise fool, and he seems to be the only character endowed with common sense. His famous aria, *Ein Mädchen oder Weibchen,* seems artless, unless one pays attention to the complicated glockenspiel accompaniment. Papageno's music in contrast to his clownish, cowardly, and hedonistic manner, is the essence of classicism, if by classicism is meant strophic integrity and Pythagorean symmetry.

The racism and sexism that undermine the egalitarianism of *The Magic Flute* display both the strengths and limitations of Enlightenment philanthropy. The clichés about all men being created equal, mouthed by Sarastro and his council of priests, is crippled by embarrassing racial and sexual stereotypes. While its idealism is inspiring and its arcane symbolism superficially linked to an ostensibly enlightened Freemasonry, *Die Zauberflöte,* with its inconsistent character development and ideological defects, hardly represents the best that was thought and said about human brotherhood in the world of the eighteenth-century Enlightenment.

BIBLIOGRAPHY

Biancolli, Louis Leopold. 1954. *The Mozart Handbook: A Guide to the Man and His Music.* New York: World Publishing Co.

Chailley, Jacques. 1971. *The Magic Flute, Masonic Opera: An Interpretation of the Libretto and the Music.* New York: A. A. Knopf.

Keefe, Simon P. 2003. *The Cambridge Companion to Music.* New York: Cambridge University Press.

Wilson J. Moses

MALCOLM X
1925–1965

Malcolm X was a minister, orator, American Black Muslim, and a prominent leader of the Nation of Islam until his break with the organization. He was born Malcolm Little in Omaha, Nebraska, on May 19, 1925, and he was also later known by his Islamic name, El-Hajj Malik El-Shabazz. Along with other African Americans in Omaha, he and his family lived in segregated North Omaha. His mother, Louise, was a homemaker who looked after the family's eight children, of whom Malcolm was the fourth. She was a Grenadian by birth, the daughter of a white man. Her son Malcolm acquired the nickname "Red" because of a reddish tinge to his hair in his early years. In his youth, Malcolm regarded his light complexion as a status symbol, but he later said that he came to hate the white blood he inherited from his maternal grandfather. Malcolm's father, Earl, was a fiery Baptist lay preacher, a proponent of the ideas of Marcus Garvey, and a founder of the Omaha chapter of Garvey's Universal Negro Improvement Association.

EARLY LIFE

Malcolm's early life was one of turmoil. Because of his outspokenness on matters of civil rights, Earl Little attracted the hatred of the local chapter of the Ku Klux Klan, which harassed the family and on two occasions forced them to move to escape threats. Thus, before Malcolm was four years old, his family relocated first to Milwaukee, Wisconsin, and then to Lansing, Michigan. In 1929, however, the family's Lansing home was burned. Earl Little and the black community believed that the fire was the work of a white supremacist group called the Black Legion. In 1931 Earl Little was run over by a streetcar, and after his mutilated body was found, the family was convinced that he died at the hands of the Black Legion, but the police ruled the death a suicide. Although Earl Little had two life insurance policies, the company that had issued the larger of the two refused to pay the family because of the finding of suicide. Later, in 1938, unable to cope with her grief over her husband's death, Louise Little had a nervous breakdown and was institutionalized for twenty-six years. The eight children were split up and placed in various orphanages and foster homes.

Malcolm was a bright student and, in fact, was at the top of his class in junior high school. In the eighth grade, however, one of his favorite teachers told him that his dream of becoming a lawyer was "no realistic goal for a nigger" (Malcolm X 1965, p. 36). At that point he lost interest in formal education and dropped out of school. He moved to Boston to live with his half-sister (one of Earl's children by a previous marriage) and he worked there in an assortment of odd jobs. His "street" education began in the early 1940s, when he moved to Harlem, New York, and embarked on the life of a petty criminal. Using the nickname "Detroit Red," he was involved in running drugs, gambling, racketeering, burglary, and prostitution. He also became addicted to cocaine. From 1943 to 1946 he lived intermittently in Harlem and Boston, often accompanied by his close friend Malcolm Jarvis. He escaped the military draft by telling the examining officer that he could not wait to organize black soldiers so that he could "kill some crackers."

Malcolm X returned to Boston in January 1946. On the twelfth of that month he was arrested for burglary, and he was quickly convicted of grand larceny and breaking and entering. He was sentenced to ten to twelve years in prison and he began serving his sentence on February 27, 1946. In prison Malcolm acquired the nickname "Satan" because of the inveterate hatred he expressed for God, religion, and the Bible. He used those years, though, to further his education by reading extensively from the prison library and pursuing a course of self-enlightenment. He became so absorbed in his studies that, he later claimed, he lost awareness that he was in prison and felt spiritually free. When he entered prison, he was barely literate, but he developed his ability to read and write by

Malcolm X at a Harlem Rally, 1963. *Malcolm X became one of the most important icons of twentieth-century African American life after his 1965 assassination, but stirred tremendous public debate about racial injustice in the United States in the years just before his death.* AP PHOTO.

copying the pages of a dictionary, one at a time, until he had copied the dictionary in its entirety. He requested and received a transfer to a prison with a larger library, and he said that after lights out at 10:00 p.m., he continued to read by sitting on the floor near the door of his cell, where light filtered in from a bulb in the corridor. When the prison guards conducted their hourly rounds, he would climb back into bed and feign sleep until they passed, then read for another hour, often continuing this ruse until 4:00 AM. His reading program was broad, including the works of Socrates, Gandhi, Herodotus, W.E.B. Du Bois, and numerous other philosophers and scientists. He used their works to test his own emerging religious beliefs.

THE NATION OF ISLAM

While he was in prison, Malcolm X received letters and visits from his brother Reginald, who was a recent convert to Islam and a member of the Nation of Islam, an organization that promulgated the teachings of its founder, Elijah Muhammad (1897–1975). Often referred to as the Black Muslims, the Nation of Islam believed that white society achieved social, economic, and political success while acting to deny such success to African Americans. The Nation of Islam rejected integration, but perhaps its most controversial belief was that blacks should form a separate state of their own, free of white domination and white religious, economic, political, and cultural institutions.

While in prison, Malcolm extensively studied the teachings of Elijah Muhammad and maintained contact with him. Committed to the organization's goals, he began to gain a measure of fame among his fellow prisoners for his growing convictions. Prison authorities regarded him as a potential troublemaker, however, and refused to grant him an early release, as would have been customary after five years. Finally, after serving nearly seven years of his sentence, he was paroled in 1952. At that time he took the name Malcolm X, believing that "Little" was a slave name. The "X" represented not only the brand that was often burned into the upper arms of slaves, but also the unknown tribal name he would have had but was lost to him. Numerous members of the Nation of Islam followed his example and took X as their surname.

Malcolm X was highly intelligent and a forceful orator. After meeting with Elijah Muhammad, he gained appointment as a minister in the Nation of Islam at its Boston mosque, and in 1954 Elijah Muhammad gave him the task of establishing mosques in Harlem, Philadelphia, Detroit, and other cities. He also served as the Nation of Islam's national spokesman. Throughout the 1950s and early 1960s he used the radio, newspaper columns, and the new medium of television to spread the message of the Nation of Islam. He typically relied on fiery rhetoric, such as his frequent assertion that whites were "devils" who had been created in a misbegotten breeding program established by a black scientist. The media could always count on him for a provocative quotation, such as his famous statement, when asked about the assassination of President John F. Kennedy in 1963, that it was a matter of "chickens coming home to roost." In 1959 he took part in a television documentary with the journalist Mike Wallace titled "The Hate that Hate Produced." He was also sharply and publicly critical of the 1963 March on Washington led by Martin Luther King Jr. Whereas King advocated nonviolence in his approach to race relations, Malcolm X believed that "turning the other cheek" led nowhere and that violence was sometimes necessary. Blacks would attain their freedom, he said, "by any means necessary."

By the early 1960s, Malcolm X was eclipsing Elijah Muhammad as the most prominent member of the Nation of Islam. In 1952 the organization had only 500 members, but by 1963 it claimed some 30,000 members, and many historians credit this exponential growth to Malcolm X and his powers of persuasion. His growing prominence drew the attention of the Federal Bureau of Investigation (FBI), which labeled him a communist and infiltrated the organization. One of Malcolm X's bodyguards was in fact an FBI agent, and the FBI conducted wiretaps and other forms of surveillance. In time, the bureau's file on him would run to 2,200 pages. Meanwhile, in 1958, he married Betty X, born Betty Sanders, and the two had six daughters, all with the surname Shabazz. Malcolm himself later adopted Shabazz as part of his Islamic name, and it became a popular surname among American Black Muslims. According to Malcolm X, it was the name of a black African tribe from which African Americans descended.

BREAK WITH THE NATION OF ISLAM

Malcolm X, despite being the Nation of Islam's brightest rising star, broke with the organization in the early 1960s. He had begun to hear rumors that Elijah Muhammad was committing adultery with young organization secretaries and that some of these liaisons had produced children. Islam strictly forbids adultery, and Malcolm X, deeply committed to the teachings of Islam, had remained celibate himself until his marriage. At first, Malcolm X did not want to believe the rumors, but when they were confirmed by Muhammad's son and several of the women involved (and later by Muhammad himself, who asked him to keep the matter quiet), his disillusionment with the Nation of Islam and its message of religious (as opposed to economic) nationalism was complete.

Malcolm thus believed that the Nation of Islam was fraudulent, for its chief prophet had betrayed Islam's teachings. On March 8, 1964, he publicly announced his departure from the Nation of Islam, and just a few days later he founded his own organization, Muslim Mosque, Inc. Later that year he founded the Organization of Afro-American Unity, which was built around four major goals: (1) the restoration of connections with Africa; (2) reorientation, or learning about Africa through reading and education; (3) education, to liberate the minds of children; and (4) economic security.

A number of Malcolm X's followers urged him to become an orthodox Sunni Muslim. He acquiesced, but to complete his conversion he decided to make a pilgrimage to the city of Mecca in Saudi Arabia, Islam's holiest site. Every able-bodied Muslim who can afford to do so is required to make such a major pilgrimage to Mecca, a journey known as the *hajj,* at least once during his or her life. He departed for Mecca in April 1964, but when he arrived in Saudi Arabia the authorities detained him because they did not believe he was an authentic Muslim and because he was traveling with an American passport. After some twenty hours in detention, he was released with the help of a friend. Later, Prince Faisal of Saudi Arabia met with him at his hotel and declared him a state guest. In this way he was allowed to make his pilgrimage to Mecca. His journey, however, was not *hajj* but *umrah,* referring to a "minor" rather than a "major" pilgrimage.

Malcolm X performed all the rituals associated with the *umrah*. These included making seven circuits around the Kaaba, a large cubical monument contained within Mecca's mosque that Muslims believe was built by the prophet Abraham. He drank water from the well of Zamzam, located near the Kaaba and believed to be the well provided to Hagar, Abraham's wife, when she was in desperate need of water for her infant son Ishmael. He completed the ritual running between the hills of Safah and Marwah seven times, an act that commemorates Hagar's frantic search for water until she found it in the well of Zamzam. In short, Malcolm X carried out all of the rituals that any Muslim would be expected to carry out on a minor pilgrimage to Mecca.

Malcolm X's trip to Saudi Arabia had a transforming effect on him. For two decades or more, he had been angry and bitter, filled with hatred directed at whites for centuries of injustice and exploitation of blacks. He had called himself the "angriest black man in America." After his trip to Mecca, though, he softened his rhetoric considerably and adopted a new attitude to race relations, one that he admitted his followers would find surprising. For example, while he was in Mecca he wrote a letter to his followers in Harlem in which he stated:

> Never have I witnessed such sincere hospitality and overwhelming spirit of true brotherhood as is practiced by people of all colors and races here in this ancient Holy Land, the home of Abraham, Muhammad and all the other Prophets of the Holy Scriptures. For the past week, I have been utterly speechless and spellbound by the graciousness I see displayed all around me by people of all colors.... There were tens of thousands of pilgrims, from all over the world. They were of all colors, from blue-eyed blondes to black-skinned Africans. But we were all participating in the same ritual, displaying a spirit of unity and brotherhood that my experiences in America had led me to believe never could exist between the white and non-white. (Malcolm X 1965, p. 340)

When he returned to the United States, Malcolm X was again a media magnet. Reporters and the public were interested in whether his trip to Saudi Arabia had changed him in any way. At a press conference on his arrival, he made the following statement, which indeed did come as a surprise to many:

> In the past, yes, I have made sweeping indictments of *all* white people. I never will be guilty of that again—as I know now that some white people are truly sincere, that some truly are capable of being brotherly toward a black man. The true Islam has shown me that a blanket indictment of all white people is as wrong as when whites make blanket indictments against blacks. Yes, I have been convinced that some American whites do want to help cure the rampant racism which is on the path to destroying this country! (Malcolm X 1965, p. 362)

In the year before his death, Malcolm X became an international ambassador. Chief among his activities was an eighteen-week trip to Africa, during which he addressed African heads of state at the first meeting of the Organization of African Unity. He also spoke in Paris and in Birmingham, England, on issues having to do with race relations; in Birmingham, he paid a visit to a pub that held to a "non-coloured" policy.

ASSASSINATION

Malcolm X's break with the Nation of Islam was marked by animosity. One member of the group confessed to Malcolm that he had been given orders by Nation of Islam leaders to kill him. In March 1964, *Life* magazine published a picture of Malcolm X holding a rifle and peeking out from curtains in his home, resolved to defend himself and his family against the death threats he had received. The Nation of Islam used the courts to reclaim his home in Harlem, which the group claimed was its property. He received an eviction order, but the night before a court hearing to postpone the eviction, the house was burned to the ground. No one was ever charged with the crime.

On February 21, 1965, Malcolm X was assassinated. He had just begun giving a speech at the Audubon Ballroom in New York City when a disturbance erupted. He and his bodyguards tried to restore order, but at that point a man rushed forward and shot him in the chest with a shotgun. Two other men, armed with handguns, pumped bullets into his body; in all, he was shot sixteen times. He was taken to Columbia Presbyterian Hospital, where he was pronounced dead. Eventually, three men were charged with the crime: Malcolm 3X Butler, Thomas 15X Johnson, and twenty-two-year-old Talmadge Hayer. All three were convicted, although Hayer was the only one to

Malcolm X. *Malcolm X was legendary during his lifetime. In death, he ascended to mythic status.* © BETTMANN/CORBIS.

confess to the crime. Hayer stated in affidavits that Butler and Johnson had taken no part in the crime and were not even present, but he named two other men who, he said, had participated in the crime. To this day, questions remain about who was behind the murder.

LEGACY

For many Americans, particularly white Americans, Malcolm X was and remains a frightening figure. He was outspoken and incendiary, and he held that violence was acceptable when other means of achieving respect and racial equality failed. He fell under the watchful eye of the J. Edgar Hoover's FBI—though in that respect, so did Martin Luther King Jr. and a host of other black activists. He used the language of religion and the cadences of the Christian Bible to announce to Americans that a day of judgment for three centuries of exploitation was at hand. His words often seemed prophetic during the turbulence and racial unrest of the 1960s.

Time, however, has softened the image of Malcolm X, at least to some extent. His 1965 *Autobiography of Malcolm X* was written with the help of Alex Haley, himself the author of *Roots,* which entered American homes, both black and white, as a television miniseries about the history of slavery. The *Autobiography* is commonly read in schools. A popular 1992 movie, *Malcolm X,* directed by Spike Lee, won its star, Denzel Washington, an Academy Award nomination for best actor. In 1999, this once feared black militant earned a mainstream honor when his picture was placed on a U.S. postage stamp.

The chief legacy of Malcolm X is that he sharpened and clarified the racial debate in America during the 1950s and 1960s. Like Martin Luther King Jr., he has become an icon of the debate, but whereas King, from Malcolm X's point of view, advocated turning the other cheek, Malcolm X believed that turning the other cheek only meant getting the other cheek slapped. Thus, he was a caustic critic of exploitation, poverty, racism, oppression, and violence against blacks. His militancy, feared at the time, is admired by many in the early twenty-first century. He spoke to the collective consciousness of the African diaspora, giving it a sense of economic, political, and social independence from dominant white America.

BIBLIOGRAPHY

Asante, Molefi K. 1993. *Malcolm X as Cultural Hero: And Other Afrocentric Essays.* Trenton, NJ: Africa World Press.

Breitman, George. 1967. *The Last Year of Malcolm X: The Evolution of a Revolutionary.* New York: Pathfinder.

———, Herman Porter, and Baxter Smith. 1976. *The Assassination of Malcolm X.* New York: Pathfinder.

DeCaro, Louis A., Jr. 1996. *On The Side of My People: A Religious Life of Malcolm X.* New York: New York University Press.

Dyson, Michael Eric. 1995. *Making Malcolm: The Myth and Meaning of Malcolm X.* New York: Oxford University Press.

Gallen, David, ed. 1992. *Malcolm A to Z: The Man and His Ideas.* New York: Carroll and Graf.

Jenkins, Robert L., ed. 2002. *The Malcolm X Encyclopedia.* Westport, CT: Greenwood Press.

Malcolm X. 1965. *The Autobiography of Malcolm X.* New York: Grove Press.

———. 1970. *By Any Means Necessary: Speeches, Interviews, and a Letter, by Malcolm X.* Edited by George Breitman. New York: Pathfinder.

———. 1971. *The End of White World Supremacy: Four Speeches.* Edited by Benjamin Goodman. New York: Merlin House.

———. 1989. *Malcolm X: The Last Speeches.* Edited by Bruce Perry. New York: Pathfinder.

———. 1992. *Malcolm X: February 1965, The Final Speeches.* Edited by Steve Clark. New York: Pathfinder.

Marable, Manning. 1992. "By Any Means Necessary: The Life and Legacy of Malcolm X." Speech delivered at Metro State College, Denver, CO, February 21. Available from http://www.black-collegian.com/african/lifelegacy200.shtml.

Perry, Bruce. 1991. *Malcolm: The Life of a Man Who Changed Black America.* New York: Station Hill.

Wood, Joe, ed. 1992. *Malcolm X: In Our Own Image.* New York: St. Martin's Press.

Michael J. O'Neal

MANDELA, NELSON
1918–

Rolihlahla Mandela was born on July 18, 1918, in the village of Mvezo, a Thembu tribal area that was part of the Xhosa nation in the Eastern Cape Province of South Africa. At the age of seven he was given the name "Nelson" by an African teacher who insisted on English nomenclature, thereby establishing a moniker that was to surpass in world renown the English naval officer after whom he was named. Nelson Rolihlahla Mandela was to become the leader of the African National Congress (ANC), the world's most famous political prisoner (1962–1990), and the overseer (along with F. W. de Klerk) of the political and constitutional negotiations that ended apartheid in South Africa.

The acknowledged "father" of the "new" South Africa, Mandela became president of the country (1994–1999) following its first democratic elections in 1994, when the ANC won 62 percent of the vote. For their role in helping to dismantle South Africa's racial formations, Mandela and de Klerk won the 1993 Nobel Peace Prize. Mandela's achievements in encouraging both a peaceful transition to nonracialism and an acceptance of black majority rule will prove his lasting legacy.

Mandela had a relatively privileged upbringing as a minor member of a royal household. His father died when

Mandela was nine years old, and he was brought up under the guardianship of Chief Dalindyebo, Regent of the Thembu people. The Grand Palace in Mqhekezweni was next to a Methodist Mission School, where the young boy excelled under what was, for the time, the very best of education available to Africans. While at school, Mandela converted to Methodism, and he was encouraged to challenge the boundaries that colonialism and apartheid imposed on South Africans. He encountered a number of people who seemed to exemplify this challenge to the status quo, being taught, for example, by the first female African graduate, Gertrude Ntlabathi.

Around 1937, Mandela went on to attend the University of Fort Hare (originally known as the South African Native College), which was established in 1916 as the first university for black South Africans. But his experience there only served to impress upon him some of the paradoxes of apartheid. The widening of educational and socioeconomic opportunities to a small African elite made him aware of how further development for blacks was restricted by race laws, while simultaneously heightening his awareness of the gulf between him and the rest of the African population. This awareness radicalized Mandela, ultimately forcing his expulsion from Fort Hare for organizing student protests.

After leaving Fort Hare, Mandela moved to Johannesburg—partly to escape a traditional tribal arranged marriage—and he found work as a guard at a mine (he was suited to this work because he was also an amateur boxer). He then drifted into law, not on the basis of formal qualifications but as a result of assisting miners to negotiate their way through apartheid's iniquities. Mandela eventually entered a law firm as a clerk, during which time he obtained a law degree by correspondence. He then went on to study law further at the University of Witwatersrand.

While practicing law, Mandela became involved with the African National Congress (ANC), which had been established in 1912, and he helped to reinvigorate the organization. There was a sense among many younger radicals that the ANC needed to expand recruitment and broaden the base of its coalition to include Communists and community opposition groups, who were themselves mobilizing against the progressive creep of apartheid's restrictions to Indian and Colored peoples. In addition, many of these radicals thought the group was misguided in putting its faith in white trusteeship, whereby blacks relied on the paternalism of liberal whites to assist them. Under such a system, blacks unwittingly endorsed subservience to white leadership. In 1943, the newly formed ANC Youth League was at the vanguard of these challenges, with Oliver Tambo as secretary, Walter Sisulu as treasurer, and Mandela as a member of its National Executive. The broadening nonracial coalition within the ANC was reinforced in the 1950s by the imposition of even more repressive legislation following the victory of the Afrikaans National Party in the 1948 election. This legislation deepened the level of suffering and intensified the effects of racial discrimination in the country, and it led to the famous Freedom Charter of 1955, a declaration of human and civil rights established by political opposition and community groups in South Africa, deliberately couched in terms redolent of the American Declaration of Independence, outlining the case for freedom and political liberty for South Africans irrespective of race. Despite opposition from radicals who wished to continue with an exclusive form of African nationalism, which would lead eventually to the formation of the rival Pan African Congress, Mandela helped maintain the ANC's historic commitment to nonracialism.

Periods of detention and arrest followed for Mandela, including a long period spent out on bail, along with 194 other defendants, for the charge of high treason. While he was eventually found not guilty, Mandela was temporarily detained under emergency powers imposed in response to growing political unrest, and he decided to go on the run in 1960 after the ANC was banned. In November 1961 the ANC decided to establish an armed wing, *Umkhonto we Siswe* (Spear of the Nation), or MK for short, with Mandela as its leader. Mandela would later admit that he never fired a gun in anger, so making him the leader of an armed struggle seems, in retrospect,

Mandela and de Klerk Accept Nobel Peace Prize, 1993. *For their efforts toward bringing an end to South African apartheid, Nelson Mandela and South African president F. W. de Klerk were jointly awarded the Nobel Peace Prize.* AP IMAGES.

an odd choice. Indeed, the relative ineffectiveness of MK's sabotage campaign between 1961 and 1962 lies in part in Mandela's reluctance to commit the organization to terror. Nevertheless, the threat of such actions ensured that massive energy was expended in an attempt to arrest him, and Mandela was eventually captured in August 1962. He later ridiculed the speculation that the CIA tipped off the South African police, admitting to having become lax about his own security.

In July 1963 most of the prominent ANC leaders were captured near Rivonia, and the suburb of Johannesburg lent its name to their treason trial, in which Mandela was also a defendant. Those still at large fled overseas (Tambo escaped to London to lead the ANC in exile) or went so deep underground that the ANC essentially had no presence inside the country until at least after the 1976 Soweto uprising. Mandela went to Robben Island, to be freed on February 11, 1990, nine days after the ANC was reinstated as a political entity. He refused early release in 1985, insisting that his freedom had to be part of a comprehensive freeing of the country from racism, one part of which had to be the legalization of the ANC.

Mandela's commitment to the twin pillars of nonracialism and nonviolence did much to slow the descent into conflict that occurred between 1990 and 1994. There was a political vacuum during this period, and the number of deaths due to political violence was greater than during the worst apartheid years. Mandela's role in keeping the violence from escalating even further won him respect around the world. He came to be revered as a peacemaker, and he involved himself in many peace processes and issues of conscience throughout the ensuing years. Life-long personal commitments affected other parts of the new South African government's policies as well, for Mandela resisted economic policies that were anticapitalist or anti-Western, ensuring that tight monetary and fiscal policies would prevent the massive redistribution of wealth that seemed to cripple the economies of other postcolonial societies in Africa. The legitimacy of the man among many white South Africans—founded ironically on the stoicism and dignity with which he bore twenty-eight years of imprisonment imposed in their name—did much to ensure the acceptance of black control of the political system. Likewise, his position as the unrivalled leader of the campaign against apartheid did much to help Africans reconcile themselves to lowered expectations of economic redistribution from the new ANC government. As the figurehead for a moral cause against apartheid, Mandela served as a beacon that shone light around the world and into the hearts of most South Africans. His charisma and steadfastness guided the country during its most difficult period of transition.

SEE ALSO *Anti-Apartheid Movement; Apartheid; South African Racial Formations.*

BIBLIOGRAPHY

PRIMARY WORKS

Mandela, Nelson. 1994. *Long Walk to Freedom*. Boston: Little, Brown.

SECONDARY WORKS

African National Congress. "Nelson Rolihlahla Mandela." Available from http://www.anc.org.za/people/mandela.html.

Brewer, John D. 1986. *After Soweto: An Unfinished Journey*. Oxford, U.K.: Clarendon Press.

Meer, Fatima. 1988. *Higher than Hope: The Biography of Nelson Mandela*. Durban, South Africa: Madiba Publishers.

Nelson Mandela Foundation. http://www.nelsonmandela.org/.

Sampson, Anthony. 1999. *Mandela: The Authorised Biography*. London: Harper Collins.

John D. Brewer

MARINA, DOÑA

SEE *La Malinche.*

MARSHALL, THURGOOD
1908–1993

Thurgood Marshall was born in Baltimore, Maryland, on July 2, 1908. Later known as "Mr. Civil Rights," Marshall devoted his life to advancing individual rights for African Americans, the poor, and the disadvantaged. He served as legal counsel for the National Association for the Advancement of Colored People (NAACP), on the U.S. Court of Appeals for the Second Circuit, and as solicitor general; and he became the first African American Supreme Court justice. A talented advocate and jurist, Marshall argued for decisions striking down "white primaries," which prevented southern blacks from voting in primary elections; "restrictive covenants," or agreements not to sell land to blacks; and segregation in schools, transportation, parks, and other public accommodations. Former Supreme Court justice William Brennan Jr. described Marshall as "probably the most important legal advocate in America and the central figure in this nation's struggle to eliminate institutional racism" (Davis 1994, p. 14). Marshall believed that lawyers can be social reformers and that equal protection was a right guaranteed to all regardless of race. His mission, according to Marshall, was to make "the law a reality for those to whom it is now largely meaningless" (Ball 1998, p. 382).

Marshall was born into a society that practiced racial segregation of people by law or custom in employment, housing, schools, parks, and stores, especially in states of the ex-Confederacy. Segregation meant inferior treatment, limited educational and job opportunities, and legal and social harassment on the basis of race. The lines were strict and rigidly drawn in the South, and Marshall was influenced by the arbitrariness and violence of racism that resulted in restricted opportunities, violations of equal rights, threats, violence, and death.

Marshall attended historically black Lincoln University in Chester, Pennsylvania, graduating with honors. He then matriculated at the historically black Howard University School of Law, where he met his lifelong mentor and friend, Charles Hamilton Houston. Houston believed that black lawyers were to be "social engineers" who had a responsibility to advocate to advance the interests of the group. Houston's influence bolstered Marshall's conviction that the U.S. Constitution could be a powerful tool against discrimination and to advance and protect the rights of African Americans.

After graduating magna cum laude in 1933, Marshall opened a private practice in Baltimore, Maryland. During this time he began his successful civil rights practice. In 1935, he filed suit against the University of Maryland Law School for its failure to admit Donald Murray based on his race. With Houston's counsel, Marshall won the first case to require the admission of a black student to an all-white school. Marshall argued that Murray's exclusion from the Maryland law school violated the "separate-but-equal" doctrine because Maryland did not offer an "equal" law school for its black citizens. *University of Maryland v. Murray* (1935) became one in a series of cases that relied on constitutional principles to topple the "separate-but-equal" system. In response to the *Murray* decision, a fellow civil rights lawyer said of Marshall. "He brought us the Constitution as a document like Moses brought the people the Ten Commandments" (Davis 1994, p. 18).

Marshall was appointed as the NAACP assistant special counsel in New York City in 1936. He later became director counsel of the NAACP, serving in that position for twenty-one years. While at the NAACP, Marshall implemented the legal strategy for the Legal Defense and Educational Fund, which involved attacking segregation in housing and education and racial discrimination in the judicial process and voting. Marshall also traveled throughout the United States talking to people about the unjust system of white supremacy that denied opportunity and justice to African Americans. During his employment at the NAACP, Marshall argued thirty-two cases before the Supreme Court and won twenty-nine of them. Through his work as a tireless advocate for equality, he became known as "Mr. Civil Rights." Marshall successfully argued against excluding blacks from primary elections and convinced the Court that the enforcement of "restrictive covenants," or private agreements not to sell land to blacks, violated the Constitution. In a series of cases beginning with *Brown v. Board of Education* (1954), Marshall's work led to findings that segregation in public education, transportation, parks, and swimming pools is unconstitutional.

The 1954 decision in *Brown v. Board of Education* is perhaps the single most important case in which Marshall participated. Marshall and his team eloquently argued the unconstitutionality of "separate but equal," relying heavily on scientific and sociological research that challenged the concept of race and racial distinctions. Grounded in research by noted historians and psychologist Dr. Kenneth Clark, Marshall argued that separate was inherently unequal and, therefore, offended the Constitution's guarantee of equality. Clark's work demonstrated that segregation by race resulted in psychological and emotional harms to blacks, who were stamped with a "badge of inferiority." Marshall argued that segregation violated the Fourteenth Amendment of the Constitution. The Court agreed with Marshall and his cocounsel and unanimously ruled that "in the field of public education the doctrine of 'separate but equal' has no place. Separate educational facilities are inherently unequal."

His influence on the country and Supreme Court jurisprudence gained significant praise and attention. In 1961 President John F. Kennedy appointed him to the U.S. Court of Appeals for the Second Circuit. Faced with a broader spectrum of cases than he argued as a civil rights advocate, Marshall wrote ninety-eight opinions as an appellate court judge and, in many, continued to express concern for the poor and underprivileged in America. In 1965, President Lyndon B. Johnson appointed Marshall as the solicitor general of the United States. Marshall won fourteen of the nineteen cases he argued for the government, many of which involved civil rights and privacy.

Marshall was nominated to the U.S. Supreme Court in 1967, becoming the Court's first black justice. He served on the Court for twenty-four years until he retired in 1991 at the age of eighty-two. During his time on the bench, Marshall was a tireless supporter of the rights of the poor, opposing governmental action that unfairly or disproportionately affected the poor. In addition, he embraced First Amendment right of free speech and consistently opposed capital punishment as excessive. Marshall worked to protect the privacy and civil liberties of Americans and believed firmly in race and gender equity, as well as the need to remedy the ongoing effects of discrimination.

A champion for civil rights, Marshall was one of the country's greatest advocates for racial justice and was responsible for a transformation of the American system of racial segregation. He believed firmly in the potential of the Constitution to protect the rights of the underserved, and after retirement from the Court he noted: "Americans can do better. … America has no choice but to do better to assure justice for all Americans, Afro and white, rich and poor, educated and illiterate … Our futures are bound together" (Davis 1994, p. 369). Marshall died on January 24, 1993. His death was mourned and his life was celebrated by thousands. At his funeral Vernon Jordan, former head of the National Urban League, remarked, "He was a teacher who taught us to believe in the shield of justice and the sword of truth, a role model whose career made us dream large dreams and work to secure them, an agent of change who transformed the way an entire generation thought of itself, of its place in our society, and of the law itself" (Davis 1994, p. 388).

SEE ALSO *Bates, Daisy; Brown v. Board of Education; Houston, Charles Hamilton; NAACP.*

BIBLIOGRAPHY

Ball, Howard. 1998. *A Defiant Life: Thurgood Marshall and the Persistence of Racism in America*. New York: Crown.

Davis, Michael, D., and Hunter R. Clark. 1994. *Thurgood Marshall, Warrior at the Bar, Rebel on the Bench*. Secaucus, NJ: Carol Publishing Group.

Tushnet, Mark V. 1994. *Making Civil Rights Law: Thurgood Marshall and the Supreme Court, 1936–1961*. New York: Oxford University Press.

Williams, Juan. 1998. *Thurgood Marshall: American Revolutionary*. New York: Times Books.

Deseriee A. Kennedy

MAYAN GENOCIDE IN GUATEMALA

Genocide is the physical destruction of an ethnic group and the most extreme expression of racism. During the 1970s and 1980s, the Mayan people of Guatemala experienced a brutal genocide, perpetrated mainly by the Guatemalan state under a racist and terrorist policy designed to protect and strengthen the political and economic power of an embattled social elite.

This episode of genocide was part of the "Silent Holocaust" in Guatemala, which grew out of thirty-six years of internal armed conflict between different guerrilla organizations and the Guatemalan Army. The Commission for Historical Clarification, set up in 1996 to investigate "human rights violations and acts of violence linked to the period of armed conflict," has pointed out that this military confrontation had a high human cost for Guatemalan society as a whole. Nevertheless, 83 percent of the victims were Mayan civilians, predominantly older adults, children, and women.

The Guatemalan state forces were responsible for 91 percent of the total human rights violations and genocidal acts, while guerrilla organizations accounted for around 3 percent. A trilogy of genocidal campaigns—named "Scorched Earth," "Model Villages," and "CPR Persecution"—were introduced by the Guatemalan Army between 1981 and 1983. These campaigns clearly demonstrated the racism and cruelty inherent in the application of counterinsurgency forces.

In December 1996, a peace accord was signed by the government of Guatemala and the *Unidad Revolucionaria Nacional Guatemalteca* (Guatemalan National Revolutionary Unity, or URNG), and a fragile peace process began, which at least stopped the prolongation of the conflict. The two sides committed to resolving the causes that triggered the conflict and initiating the painful process of reconstructing and understanding the recent historical events.

BACKGROUND

Guatemala is a small Central American country characterized by its extraordinary geography and great ethnic and linguistic diversity, reflected in its indigenous populations of Mayan, Xinca, and Garífuna people. This cultural mosaic comprises more than half of the population of Guatemala, estimated at 12 million inhabitants. The Ladino population (mixed Amerindian-Spanish heritage) constitutes the other half. The multicultural composition of Guatemalan society is the fruit of a millennial civilizing process, which had its beginnings with the splendor of the Mayan civilization that flowered about 1500 BCE. The European invasion of America, beginning in the sixteenth century, began the first genocide in this region, destroying Mayan peoples and cultures and putting their societies under a colonial system.

Yet after three centuries of Spanish colonization, the indigenous peoples miraculously survived the genocide and ethnocide perpetrated by both the conservative and liberal states of the nation, which had excluded them from the national project and reduced them to laborers on the great plantations.

The triumph of the 1944 "October Revolution" in Guatemala began a democratic, national modernization process that implemented deep social reforms, such as the promulgation of a new constitution, labor legislation, and agrarian reform. However, agrarian reform adversely affected North American economic interests and invited retaliation, especially from the United Fruit Company.

The North American intervention in Guatemala in June 1954 marked the beginning of the first U.S. Central

Intelligence Agency (CIA) operations in Latin America, which were in line with the general anticommunist policy adopted during the cold war. The Commission for Historical Clarification points out that following the counterrevolutionary triumph of General Carlos Castillo Armas on July 8, 1954, Guatemala began a period of historical regression that provoked the causes of the genocidal violence of the late twentieth century.

The first guerrilla attacks in Guatemala began during the 1960s in the East, on the South Coast, and in Guatemala City, all nonindigenous regions. The first guerrilla organizations, such as the *Movimiento Revolucionario 13 de Noviembre* (November 13th Revolutionary Movement, or MR-13), *Frente 12 de Octubre* (October 20th Front), and later the *Fuerzas Armadas Rebeldes* (Rebel Armed Forces, or FAR), implemented a *guerrilla focus* strategy, inspired by the Cuban revolution of 1959.

In 1965, the Guatemalan army initiated a ferocious counterinsurgency campaign that prevailed against the guerrillas. The new *Doctrina de Seguridad Nacional* (National Security Doctrine, or DSN) implemented a new and more modern counterinsurgency method that resulted in more than 8,000 victims, mostly civilians.

WAR IN MAYAN LANDS

The Commission for Historical Clarification has concluded that the beginning of the violence in Guatemala was the result of racist and exclusionary national policies, which made it impossible for the state to achieve a social consensus in Guatemalan society.

During the 1970s, a number of guerrilla groups emerged in the Mayan region, including the *Organización del Pueblo en Armas* (Organization of the People in Arms, or ORPA), which appeared in 1971. The following year, the *Ejército Guerrillero de los Pobres* (Guerrilla Army of the Poor, or EGP) arose in the Guatemalan Highlands. The FAR was decimated in the 1960s, but resumed its military actions in 1979. After suffering ferocious political persecution and kidnappings, the *Partido Guatemalteco del Trabajo* (Guatemalan Labor Party, or PGT) decided to participate in the armed warfare in 1979.

The military-political strategy adopted by the new guerrilla groups sought to incorporate the indigenous masses into what was becoming a war of national liberation. They considered that the previous guerrilla experience had largely failed, partly because they had been forced to limit their operations to discrete geographic areas in eastern Guatemala, a region populated mostly by Ladinos.

A major earthquake struck Guatemala in 1976. This natural disaster caused a social cataclysm that demonstrated the corruption of the state, as well as its limited capacity to respond to a disaster and organize a response. In the following years, numerous social organizations arose in Guatemala, mainly cooperatives and unions that mobilized protests of various kinds against the violence and repression and that fought for better labor conditions, wages, and benefits.

THE MAYAN EARTH GENOCIDE

In response to this emergent social movement, the state unfolded a counterinsurgency plan that intensified repression and violence. Beginning in 1980, state forces increased the practices of "kidnappings" and "disappearances" against union leaders, university students and faculty, and political candidates. Violence against the Mayan people took the form of "selective murders" of community leaders. The Commission for Historical Clarification has provided evidence that at least 100 Mayan community leaders were assassinated in Chajul, Cotzal, and Nebaj between February of 1976 and November of 1977.

As this repression increased, the first massacres of Mayan communities began. In 1980, in Panzós, a Q'eqchí community in the department of Baja Verapaz, 150 *kaibiles*, or military elites, assassinated more than 300 farmers in the town square. This action was in response to Q'eqchí peasants making claims to lands that had been alienated by military officials and plantations owners.

The *Comité de Unidad Campesina* (Campesino Unity Committee, or CUC) founded in the mid 1980s by Mayan farmer leaders and poor Ladinos, soon initiated a series of strikes, both as a strategy to gain better labor conditions and as a protest against the violence. By January 1981, CUC leaders had peacefully occupied the Spanish Embassy, enabling them to make their protests heard outside the country. This mobilization ended when state forces burned the embassy killing more than thirty people. That same year, CUC members organized a meeting in Tecpán, in the department of Chimaltenango, and wrote the Declaration of Iximche, which denounced the oppression, exclusion, racism, and cultural intolerance in Guatemala. At about this time, the Catholic Diocese of the El Quiche department was closed due to acts of repression against its members.

In 1980 the four guerrilla organizations, encouraged by the triumph of the 1979 Sandinista revolution in Nicaragua and the apparently weak position of the Guatemalan Army, spread its military operations over a vast geographic area. This move has since been viewed as a serious military mistake, for the army was well prepared to confront the guerrilla organizations and had already planned its genocidal military campaigns in response. Previous to the military counteroffensive (between July and August 1981), the Guatemalan Army managed to capture all the "secure houses" of the ORPA and the EGP in Guatemala City. Although military aid from the

United States had been suspended indefinitely due to increased human rights violations, the Guatemalan Army still managed to receive military aid approved years before.

FIRST MILITARY CAMPAIGN: SCORCHED EARTH

In the middle of 1981, the government of President Lucas Garcia began a military counter-offensive plan designated "Ash 81." This operation was in fact a well-planned genocide against the Mayan peoples, who were accused of being "communists" and supporting the rebel groups, thereby justifying the campaign called "Scorched Earth."

The main objective of this genocidal campaign was to "drain the water to the fish"—that is, to isolate the guerrillas from the civil population, and thus from their base of support. The anthropologist Robert Carmack, in *Harvest of Violence: The Maya Indians and the Guatemalan Crisis* (1988) points out that the military intelligence was used to draw a map demarcating the different communities with different colors. Each color designated the military actions to be made, depending on the political proximity of each community to the guerrillas. The "Green" communities were considered "free" of the "internal enemy." Those communities where some persons or leaders were believed to be supporting the guerrillas were designated as "Pink" or "Yellow." In these areas the army applied a selective repression, including "kidnappings," "disappearances," and "killings" of social leaders and "suspects." "Red" communities were selected for total destruction because there was intelligence information that they were fully supporting the guerrillas.

The racism and code colors significantly helped the Guatemalan Army, mostly directed by Ladinos, in the conception and planning of this genocide. The "Scorched Earth" military campaign that followed began with the taking of the city of Chimaltenango and other strategic places in order to surround the "internal enemy."

The guerrillas were not able to stop the bloody military counteroffensive of the Guatemalan Army, despite the fact that they had about 6,000 combatants and a base of support exceeding 250,000 people. Forty-five massacres were committed by the Guatemalan Army from March 1981 to March 1982, with 1,678 victims. The average number of victims per massacre was 37.29 people.

The "Scorched Earth" military campaign was directed by the High Guatemalan Commander using "kaibiles," or elite forces, and Mayans that were forcibly recruited. Once military control had been gained over the populations that had not been destroyed, the Guatemalan Army organized the *Patrullas de Autodefensa Civil* (Civil Self-Defense Patrols, or PACs) in order to "take care of" the population and defend the community from the threat of communism.

The army intelligence apparatus and a mechanism of social control were increased, using military commissioners, the police, customs guards, and secret agents, who conducted a "witch hunt" against those who protested the violence. The G-2 (military intelligence) used paid informants, or "orejas," to gain intelligence about the guerrilla groups.

SECOND MILITARY CAMPAIGN: MODEL VILLAGES

In 1982 the government of Lucas Garcia was overthrown in a coup d'état that made General Efraín Ríos Montt the new president. Ríos Montt then inaugurated a new military plan, "Victory 82," with well-directed and improved military actions. This genocide campaign promised to "eliminate," "annihilate," and "exterminate" the "internal enemy" very quickly and "gain the hearts of the population."

From March 1982 to March 1983, thirty-two selective massacres were carried out, killing 1,424 people. The massacre in Plan de Sánchez in Rabinal, Alta Verapaz, claimed the lives of children, women, and the elderly. The Inter-American Commission on Human Rights in its Report 31/99, Case 11.763 Plan de Sánchez, Guatemala, describes this massacre as follows:

> ... early on the morning of July 18, 1982, two grenades fell to the east and west of Plan de Sánchez. A group of approximately 60 men dressed in military uniforms and armed with assault rifles, and four "judiciales" allegedly arrived in Plan de Sánchez between 2:00 and 3:00 p.m. Those four judiciales were identified by witnesses, and the two officials in charge were identified as Lieutenants Solares and Díaz. The petitioners report that soldiers monitored points of entry into the community, while others went house to house rounding up the population. Girls and young women were held in one location, while older women, men and children were gathered in another. Approximately 20 girls between 12 and 20 years of age were taken to one house where they were raped and then killed. The rest of the population was forced into another house and the adjoining patio. The petitioners allege that, at about 5:00 p.m., soldiers threw two hand grenades into that house, and then sprayed it and the patio with sustained gunfire. Small children were hit or kicked to death. Shots were reportedly heard in another location, where four bodies were later found. The petitioners describe the soldiers as having subsequently set fire to the house where the majority of the victims had been killed before leaving the community some hours later. (Inter-American Commission on Human Rights 2007 Internet site)

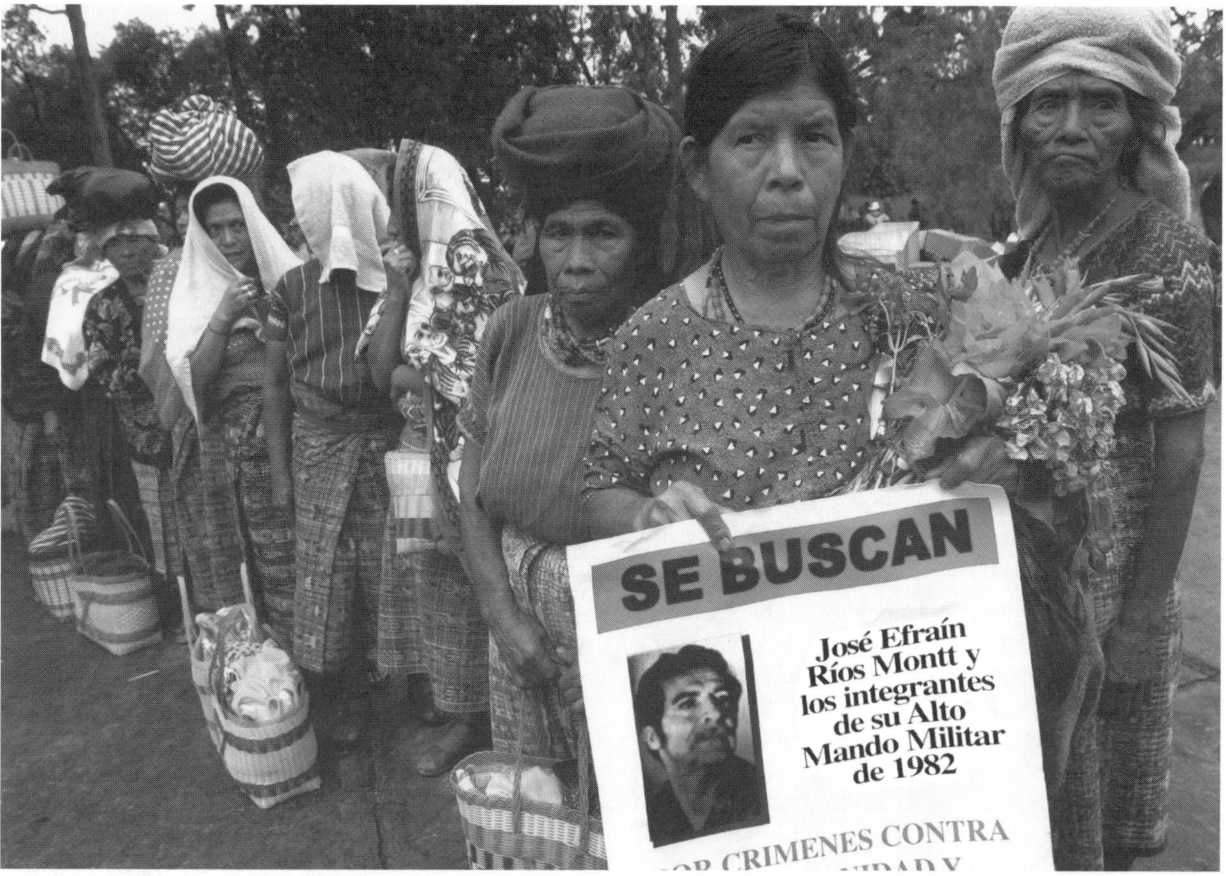

Mayan Protest March. *A Mayan woman holds an anti-Efraín Ríos Montt sign during a protest march in 2003. During the dictatorship of Efraín Ríos Montt, 200,000 people were assassinated or "disappeared."* AP IMAGES.

The extreme cruelty of these military actions against a noncombatant population, as well as various atrocities, such as the extraction of the viscera of victims who were still alive or the opening of the wombs of pregnant women, demonstrate the genocide and racism of this period. Thousands of Maya fled from Guatemala seeking refuge in Mexico, while others fled from the army into the mountains to join the *Comunidades y Pueblos en Resistencia* (Communities of Populations in Resistance, or CPRs).

Ríos Montt's military campaign was more selective than its predecessor, and the number of victims per massacre was increased. Victoria Sanford, in her book *Buried Secrets* (2003), has pointed out that the percentage of victims per massacre was increased from 37.29 during Lucas Garcia's regime to fifty. Ríos Montt introduced new military projects for civilians, the "Model Villages." These were very similar to the "Strategic Hamlets" program implemented by the U.S. Army during the Vietnam War. Thousands of Mayans were forced to live in the model villages, which were under permanent military control by the Guatemalan Army.

The government of Ríos Montt also implemented the "Fusiles y Frijoles" (guns and beans), and "Techo, Trabajo y Tortillas" (roof work, and tortillas) policies as part of the counter-insurgency project. Through these policies, the Guatemalan Army offered protection and assistance to Mayan civilians in exchange of their incorporation to the PACs. In addition, the Special Privilege Tribunal was created to punish the political opponents in summary judgments. As a result of these policies, the guerrilla organizations, realizing their weakened condition, saw the urgent necessity to reorganize. In February of 1982, the four guerrilla organizations reunited to form *Unidad Revolucionaria Nacional Guatemalteca* (Guatemalan National Revolutionary Unity, or URNG).

THIRD MILITARY CAMPAIGN: PERSECUTION OF THE CPRs

The genocidal atrocities committed during the Ríos Montt regime ended in August 1983, when Montt was deposed by another coup d'état. The new president, General Oscar Mejía Víctores, promised a transition to democracy and the end of armed conflict. Nevertheless, his government implemented another military plan, denominated "Firmness 83," whose main objective was the removal of the last "resistance focus" of the guerrillas and the destruction of the CPRs, who still miraculously survived in the mountains and jungle. The Guatemalan Army succeeded by isolating the civilian population from the guerrillas and by "annihilating," "exterminating," and "destroying" several Mayan communities. The "Scorched Earth," "Model Villages" and "Persecution of the CPRs" genocide campaigns helped the army dominate the military confrontation with the guerrillas.

Reduced in number, without their support base, and crowded into a reduced geographic area, the guerrillas also suffered a "surgical attack" from the Guatemalan Army. Though they still maintained a considerable number of members, there was no real possibility that they could challenge the army.

The control of the population through the Civil Self-Defense Patrols (PACs), the Model Villages program, military commissioners, and military intelligence was also crucial in this process. The Commission for Historical Clarification points out that at least a million Mayan people were forced to belong to PACs by 1983. In 1984, under the military plan known as "Re-Encounter 84," a new Constitutional Assembly was created that initiated the work of elaborating a new constitution.

In 1985, the plan "National Stability 1985" was implemented, allowing a new presidential election to be held. The victor was Vinicio Cerezo, the Christian Democratic Party candidate. The Guatemalan leftist organizations did not participate in this election, however, and the URNG actively boycotted it. In an effort to end military hostilities, Cerezo initiated a dialogue with the guerrillas in Madrid in October 1987. The Esquipulas I and II meetings, held under the mediation of the Mexican government, gave an impulse to the peace process. During the dialogue process, numerous nongovernmental organizations arose and began to demand land, respect for human rights, a search for "disappeared," the return of refugees, and indigenous peoples' rights. They formed the *Coordinadora Nacional de las Viudas de Guatemala* (National Coordination of Guatemalan Widows, or CONAVIGUA), the *Grupo de Ayuda Mutua* (Mutual Support Group, or GAM), the Vicente Menchú and Myrna Mack foundations, and the *Academia de Lenguas Mayas* (Mayan Languages Academy, or ALM), among other groups.

Peace accords between the government of Guatemala and the URNG were finally signed in December of 1996 after years of negotiation. Since then, advances in the peace agenda have been minimal, despite efforts by the United Nations Verification Mission in Guatemala (MINUGUA) and the *Secretaría de la Paz* (Secretariat for Peace, or SEPAZ), creating conditions for new social conflicts, particularly in the matters of land, human rights, and labor.

AFTERMATH

The Commission for Historical Clarification has provided evidence that the human cost of this tragedy includes the 626 Mayan communities destroyed by fire, 200,000 people assassinated or "disappeared," 1.5 million people displaced, 150,000 refugees who fled to Mexico, and several hundred people exiled into other countries.

There is evidence that 91 percent of the violations to the human rights and genocidal acts were committed by the state forces and that 83 percent of the victims were Mayan people. This evidence comes from first-hand accounts, such as that of Rigoberta Menchú, a survivor of the massacres and a Nobel Prize winner in 1992; from the human rights report *Guatemala: Nunca Más* (*Guatemala: Never More,* 1998); from the Interdiocesan Project for the Recuperation of Historical Memory (1998); and from the Commission for Historical Clarification, with the support of the United Nations.

The Guatemalan state participated in genocide, a crime against humanity forbidden by the UN Convention for the Prevention of the Crime of Genocide. The massacres perpetrated against noncombatant populations demonstrates the barbarity and racism of the state during this period. The state also participated in ethnocide, the destruction of Mayan culture in the form of ceremonial centers, language, dress, systems of authority, and exercise of spirituality.

Lamentably, public knowledge of this truth has provoked more victims. For example, Monsignor Juan Gerardi, a Catholic archbishop and the main force behind the report *Guatemala: Never More*, was assassinated two days after the publication of the report. In addition, as of 2007, none of those responsible for these acts has yet faced justice, despite the judgments that have been made against them.

SEE ALSO *Genocide; Zapatista Rebellion.*

BIBLIOGRAPHY

Carmack, Robert M., ed.1988. *Harvest of Violence: The Maya Indians and the Guatemalan Crisis.* Norman: University of Oklahoma Press.

Centro de Investigaciones para el Desarrollo. 1988. *Guatemala, polos de desarrollo: El caso de la desestructuración de las comunidades indígenas.* México City: Editorial Praxis.

Commission for Historical Clarification. 1999. *Guatemala: Memory of Silence*, Vols. 1–2. Guatemala City: Commission for Historical Clarification.

Le Bot, Yvon. 1995. *La guerra en tierras maya.* México City: Fondo de Cultura Económica.

Manz, Beatriz. 2003. *Paradise in Ashes: A Guatemalan Journey of Courage, Terror, and Hope.* Berkeley: University of California Press.

Oficina de Derechos Humanos del Arzobispado de Guatemala. 1998. *Guatemala: Nunca Más*, 4 Vols. Guatemala City: ODHAG.

Ordóñez, José Emilio. 1996. *Rostros de las prácticas etnocidas en Guatemala*. Mexico City: Universidad Nacional Autónoma de México.

"Report Number 31/99, Case 11.763, Plan de Sánchez Massacre." Inter-American Commission on Human Rights. Available from http://www.cidh.org/annualrep.

Sanford, Victoria. 2003. *Buried Secrets: Truth and Human Rights in Guatemala*. New York: Palgrave Macmillan.

Schirmer, Jennifer. 1998. *The Guatemalan Military Project: A Violence Called Democracy*. Philadelphia: University of Pennsylvania Press.

Carlos Salvador Ordóñez

MAYS, BENJAMIN E.

1894–1984

One of the most influential religious black intellectuals of the twentieth century was Benjamin Elijah Mays. Born in South Carolina, Mays grew up in the system of Jim Crow that mistreated African Americans by denying them equal public services and restricting them to inferior segregated schools that were barely funded by state governments and municipalities—in short, denying them justice under the law. Mays was born two years before the U.S. Supreme Court in 1896 rendered its doctrine of separate but equal in *Plessy v. Ferguson*, legalizing the practice of racial segregation. Under these conditions it is not surprising that racial issues became a central concern in his life. His autobiography, *Born to Rebel* (1971), opens with the story of a crowd of white men with rifles surrounding and cursing his father. The episode was not uncommon for blacks in the South. Mays declared, "Since my earliest memory was of murderous mobs, I lived in constant fear that someday I might be lynched" (p. 49).

Mays was raised in abject poverty by ex-slave parents who eked out a living as tenant farmers. Despite poverty, racial injustice, and economic inequality, Mays was determined to succeed in life. He credited his parents for his strong work ethic. As a child he had a craving for education. However, he had to overcome separate and unequal educational opportunities and the opposition of a father who wanted him to work on the farm. Despite these obstacles, at the age of twenty-one Mays graduated as valedictorian of his high school class in 1916.

Mays spent one year at Virginia Union College before he transferred to Bates College in Lewiston, Maine. He excelled in academics at Bates, ranking fifth in his graduating class in 1920. While at Bates, Mays became an ordained minister and decided to pursue graduate work at the University of Chicago's School of Religion. However, after a short time there, he accepted a position at Morehouse College in Atlanta to teach mathematics and psychology. He spent six years at Morehouse before going back to the University of Chicago and earning his master's degree in 1925. After receiving his graduate degree, he took a position teaching English at South Carolina State College from 1925 to 1926. He served as executive secretary of the National Urban League in Tampa, Florida, from 1926 to 1928 and as student secretary for the National Men's Christian Association.

One of Mays's greatest accomplishments occurred when he, along with Joseph W. Nicholson, was commissioned by the Institute of Social and Religious Research to carry out a national study of black churches. After two years of research and writing, Mays and Nicholson completed their study, entitled *The Negro's Church*, which was published in 1933. It was the most comprehensive work on black churches in the United States, examining more than 600 black churches in twelve urban cities and close to 100 churches in rural areas of the South.

Mays eventually went back to Chicago and earned his Ph.D. However, before he received the degree in 1935 from the University of Chicago's School of Religion, Mordacai Johnson, president of Howard University, offered him the deanship of the School of Religion at the university. Mays spent six years at Howard's School of Religion and was able to increase graduate enrollment and strengthen the faculty. Under his leadership, the school received accreditation by the American Association of Theological Schools, becoming the second historically black college to receive such accreditation. He also increased the number of volumes in the library.

In 1940 Mays became president of Morehouse College and went on to transform the institution into one of the nation's premier historically black colleges. He increased the number of black faculty and faculty with doctorates. He also increased the number of buildings from eight to twenty-five. Additionally, Mays was responsible for the growth of the number of graduates who went on to medical schools, law schools, and Ph.D. programs, and under his leadership the college attracted major donors, thereby increasing the college's endowment.

Besides becoming one of the leading educators in the nation, Mays also was a crusader for civil rights. As a graduate student at the University of Chicago, he challenged housing and other forms of racial discrimination on campus. Represented by Thurgood Marshall and other attorneys of the NAACP's Legal Defense Fund, Mays took the Southern Railway Company before the Interstate Commerce Commission after he was refused service in one of the company's dinning cars in October 1944. He contended that his actions were not motivated by personal concern but "for the sake of justice." Working along with a "roving editor" for *Reader's Digest*, Mays helped reveal patterns of discrimination in hotels, restaurants, and other places of public accommodation in Chicago. Moreover, President Harry Truman appointed him to the National Committee of the Mid-Century White House Conference on Children and Youth. President John F. Kennedy considered Mays for a seat on the Commission on Civil Rights, but southern segregationists red-baited the Morehouse president and he was never appointed. It was Mays's outspokenness against segregation that galvanized southern opposition to his appointment to the commission. He was the chair of the national conference on religion and race in 1963, and also became vice president of the Federated Council of Churches, the first African American to hold that position.

One of Mays's greatest talents was to inspire generations of young people to work for social justice. Martin Luther King Jr. was one of several Morehouse students who asserted that Mays became a role model for him. After Mays retired as president of Morehouse in 1967, he became a close adviser to President Jimmy Carter. Throughout his career, he published seven books and numerous scholarly articles. In 1982 the National Association for the Advancement of Colored People (NAACP) awarded him the coveted Spingarn Medal, its highest award recognizing outstanding service in the fight against racism. Mays died in 1984.

BIBLIOGRAPHY

Carter, Lawrence E. 1998. *Walking Integrity: Benjamin Elijah Mays, Mentor to Martin Luther King, Jr.* Macon, GA: Mercer University Press.

Colson, Freddie. 2002. *Benjamin E. Mays Speaks: Representative Speeches of a Great American Orator.* Macon, GA: University Press of America.

Mays, Benjamin E. 1971. *Born to Rebel: An Autobiography.* New York: Scribner's.

Clarence Taylor

MEDICAL EXPERIMENTATION

Throughout history, humans have routinely used other human beings for scientific research and medical experimentation. Vivisection was practiced for centuries by ancient civilizations to augment their knowledge of anatomy. Physicians in the Middle Ages honed their craft not only on cadavers and animals, but also on condemned criminals. By the eighteenth century, Europe and the United States had ushered in the scientific revolution, with prisoners, heretics, and slaves providing a steady stream of bodies to help researchers better understand their fields of science.

During the last 200 years, human experimentation has added its own chapter to a long and nefarious history. Deadly medical procedures, eugenics programs, chemical and radiation exposure, mind-altering drugs, and dubious vaccine trials have been part and parcel of what many historians believe were the seeds that ultimately took root in the experimental race and genetics programs of Nazi Germany. As technology and medicine advanced at breakneck speed, at no time in history had there been such a willingness to exploit human life for the benefit of scientific progress.

It did not take long after the first slaves reached the shores of the New World before physicians started using them as a ready source of material. Beginning in the 1800s, radical surgeries and vaccinations were performed to test medical treatments and to verify the safety of new vaccines. Dr. J. Marion Sims (1813–1883), considered a pioneer in gynecological surgery, performed numerous operations on slaves to perfect his techniques. Robert Jennings (1824–1893), credited with the development of a typhoid vaccine, did so only after experimenting with dozens of slaves. And Dr. Crawford Long (1815–1878), one of the first physicians to use ether as a general anesthetic, used slaves in many of his early experiments, the rationale being that blacks were thought to be biologically inferior both physically and mentally.

TUSKEGEE SYPHILIS STUDY

Although the end of slavery greatly diminished the practice of medical experimentation on African Americans, it did not eliminate it. In 1932 the Tuskegee Institute, in conjunction with the U.S. Public Health Service, initiated "The Tuskegee Study of Untreated Syphilis in the Negro Male." Six hundred African-American men, most in various stages of syphilis, were recruited for the purpose of recording the natural history and progression of the disease. Records describe the painful and often debilitating effects of spinal taps followed by treatment with mercury for what was called "bad blood," a local term used to describe severe ailments. In exchange for their participation, the men received small cash payments, free medical exams, and burial insurance. What they were not told was that even though the study had officially ended six months after it began, it would continue for another forty years with no one receiving treatment, even after penicillin became the drug of choice for treating syphilis in 1947. Dr. Raymond Vonderlehr, one of the Tuskegee researchers who became director of the Division of Venereal Disease, argued that should the cases be followed over a period of five to ten years, many interesting facts could be learned regarding the course and complications of untreated syphilis.

Once the decision was made to continue, the men who had previously been diagnosed with syphilis were recruited with official letters that enticed them back for further treatment. The deception was brilliant. A living laboratory was assembled in which men with a progressive yet treatable disease could be observed through their terrible stages until the final autopsies were done. Brought to Macon County, the unsuspecting victims would gather for their annual examination and treatment with aspirin and tonic. The incentive for young doctors was a chance to learn diagnostics in a clinical setting and to participate in a-once-in-a-lifetime experience.

As the years went by, the men's health worsened. An increase in eye disorders, headaches, and other discomforts grew into unbearable pain due to invasion by microbes into vital organs and bone marrow that was gradually eaten away. In the worse cases, in which patients survived long enough to reach the tertiary stage, syphilis infected the brain and spinal cord, causing excruciating pain that was described as electricity surging through their bodies. For these victims there was often paralysis, seizures, mental deterioration, toxic psychosis, convulsions, and dementia. The final months brought horrible personality disorders that reduced patients to helpless vegetables with little or no brain function.

During the forty-year study, subjects were allowed to grow progressively sicker until they died. Had it not been for a 1972 *New York Times* front-page story, the study would have continued even longer. The fact that penicillin was purposely withheld in order to encourage the disease to spread is one of the most shameful examples of racial medicine in U.S. history. Though a formal apology was issued, the Tuskegee study would forever be linked to subsequent human experiments throughout the twentieth century.

NAZI GERMANY

The atmosphere of racism and racial hygiene gained momentum and reached an epidemic in 1930s Germany, where the eugenics torch was passed from moderates seeking birth control to zealots wanting nothing less than to eliminate the unfit from the human population. Adolf Hitler, a student of the American eugenics movement, assumed that many in the West shared his philosophy that only healthy individuals reproduce, when editors of the prestigious *New England Journal of Medicine* wrote in a 1934 article that "Germany is perhaps the most progressive nation in restricting fecundity among the unfit."

In the beginning, it was simply a matter of sterilization; the disabled, the mentally ill, and those with genetic disorders were targeted. But soon euthanasia was added to eliminate anyone who placed an undue burden on society. The final step was human experimentation, in which individuals or races thought inferior were used in medical research for the benefit of superior races. The horror of experiments in places such as Auschwitz was so shocking that it would eventually hatt the eugenics movement.

The medical blocks were areas within concentration camps where prisoners were kept and special medical procedures done. In one of the blocks, victims were submerged in vats of water and ice until they froze into subconsciousness before awakening to screams of pain as their limbs thawed out and felt as if they were being torn off. In an adjacent block, other victims had blistering hot water injected into their stomachs and intestines. In another, subjects whose intentionally administered wounds were infected with gangrene cultures had their blood vessels tied off and shards of glass, mustard gas, and sawdust placed into open wounds to see how quickly the lethal gangrene would set in. Still other blocks were used for mass sterilizations, where caustic agents were injected into the uterus to see how much they would obstruct the oviducts.

Two of the blocks were especially frightening. Block 41 in Birkenau was notorious for vivisections, in which prisoners were used for surgeries, often without anesthesia, and limbs were cut open to expose muscles and apply medications. In block 28 of Buchenwald, victims had toxic chemicals rubbed into their bodies to cause severe abscess, infection, and painful burns, or were forced to ingest toxic powders to study stomach and liver damage. Virtually every medical block was manned by SS doctors who viewed their subjects as less than human and justified their experiments in the name of improving the lives of German citizens. The atrocities committed were a culmination of a eugenics movement that crossed the line from birth control to mass murder. Because the Nazis had destroyed many of the documents, laboratories, and evidence before Allied forces liberated camps such as Auschwitz, the world would never know the full extent of Germany's medical experiments.

POST–WORLD WAR II EXPERIMENTATION

Not long after the horrors of World War II, American physicians began a decades-long foray into human medical experimentation. In a 1963 study, for instance, physicians at the Jewish Chronic Disease Hospital of Brooklyn injected live cancer cells into twenty-two unwitting African-American patients. A few years later, African-American women were receiving abortions with experimental devices that caused such severe bleeding that they required hysterectomies. By the 1970s, developing nations throughout the world, financed by the U.S. Agency for International

Development, were using a host of experimental drugs and medical procedures on their own populations.

Mass sterilization, an outgrowth of the earlier eugenics movement, was also common throughout the 1960s and 1970s. In Puerto Rico, as much as 35 percent of the female population was sterilized during the 1960s, ostensibly as a way to moderate growth and maintain economic development. Similar programs were started at the same time in most Third World countries. In the United States, family planning and abortion clinics greatly expanded in black and Hispanic communities, with some women being refused abortions or welfare benefits if they did not consent to sterilization. As recently as the 1990s, public health officials encouraged a disproportionate number of African-American women to have themselves and their teenage daughters sterilized as a means of controlling population growth among select minorities. In a 1970s program exposed by Senator James Abourezk, more than 25,000 Native American women were sterilized, many without their knowledge or permission. In all these cases, race played a key role in determining who would be sterilized.

Human experimentation, often justified in the name of science, began as a blight on humankind and was allowed to grow like a cancer because of racism, nationalism, and paranoia. From early medical research to modern human experiments, history is replete with examples of inhumanity that took root simply because few stood up until it was too late. Many who witnessed these events later feared that unless those in positions of power became vigilant protectors against such abuses, it could very well happen again.

SEE ALSO *Forced Sterilization; Forced Sterilization of Native Americans.*

BIBLIOGRAPHY

Annas, George J., and Michael A. Grodin. 1992. *The Nazi Doctors and the Nuremberg Code: Human Rights in Human Experimentation.* New York: Oxford University Press.

Goliszek, Andrew. 2003. *In the Name of Science: A History of Secret Programs, Medical Research, and Human Experimentation.* New York: St. Martin's Press.

Jones, James H. 1993. *Bad Blood: The Tuskegee Syphilis Experiments*, rev. ed. New York: Free Press.

Katz, Jay. 1972. *Experimentation with Human Beings: The Authority of the Investigator, Subject, Professions, and State in the Human Experimentation Process.* New York: Russell Sage Foundation.

Kühl, Stefan. 1994. *The Nazi Connection: Eugenics, American Racism, and German National Socialism.* New York: Oxford University Press.

Larson, Edward J. 1995. *Sex, Race, and Science: Eugenics in the Deep South.* Baltimore, MD: Johns Hopkins University Press.

Lifton, Robert Jay. 1986. *The Nazi Doctors: Medical Killing and the Psychology of Genocide.* New York: Basic Books.

Andrew Goliszek

MEDICAL RACISM

Racist ideologies are the foundation for the belief that human biological/genetic diversity among racially defined groups is the reason for social and cultural differences between these groups. Racism emerges when racist ideologies are used to claim that biological differences are a legitimate reason for differential treatment of human populations. Racism is based on the belief that *Homo sapiens* are composed of distinct biological groups (races) with biologically based cultural characteristics and that races can be ranked.

Medical racism is prejudice and discrimination in medicine and the medical/healthcare system based upon perceived race. Racism in medicine can occur in at least four ways. First, on a conceptual level, it can occur as members of a society learn about races and racism as well as the validity of white privilege. Healthcare providers are a product of their social environment. They learn negative attitudes and beliefs about human biological diversity from society that may be brought to the work/health setting. They may be unaware of this racism, and it can be subtle or overt. Second, collective racial discrimination, based on shared cultural beliefs, can result in differential medical treatment and health care. Third, experiences with racism in society and the medical setting can result in stress that negatively impacts health. Lastly, institutional racism in the medical/healthcare system can affect the quality and quantity of health care for minorities.

RACE AND HEALTH

Genes linked to skin color have not been shown to be determinants of disease. Genes "are almost always a minor, unstable, and insufficient cause" of disease (Goodman 2000, p. 1700). Rather skin color (race) is a centrally determining characteristic of obligations and social identity and a determinant of access to desirable resources.

Medical studies include race in the demographic triad of age, sex, and race, where race is considered a biological trait and a predictor of health in the same way as age and sex. It is assumed that any association with the race category is the result of genes, although there is no evidence that genetic markers for race or geographic region of origin are linked to those that determine health. Rather than race being used as a risk factor, it should be viewed as a risk marker. Race is a risk marker for exposure to health risks such as occupational health hazards, environmental toxins, and poor quality of medical care.

From a biological perspective, races do not exist in nature. Human biological diversity does not conform to groups described as races. For example, physical criteria for assignment to racial groups such as skin color, facial features, and hair texture are inconsistent and discordant. That is, a person with blond hair may or may not have blue eyes. Also, there are no qualitative differences between groups. Rather, one finds a clinal distribution, or overlapping gradients, for traits in nature without boundaries between populations. In any population, individual variability overwhelms group differences. It may seem easy to identify characteristics perceived to represent races, but the differences dissolve when one scans the genome for deoxyribonucleic acid (DNA) hallmarks of race. Data from the Human Genome Project indicate that the percentage of genes contributing to physical differences between populations account for only 0.1 percent of the human genome (Angier 2000). Since there is greater variation within populations than between them, group differences are very small.

Race is a social rather than a biological construct. Characteristics chosen to identify races are subjective and can vary over time and among countries. For instance, race can change between birth and death. In addition, individuals may change their racial classification over time. For example, using NHANES I data, it was reported that 42 percent specified different ancestries at different interviews (Hahn, Truman, and Barker 1996).

The contemporary idea of race is not based in nature or biology but is the product of U.S. colonization and slavery. With increased desire for profits from agriculture, settlers wanted more slaves. And with ideas of freedom and equality written into the Declaration of Independence, a justification and legalization of the institution of slavery and simultaneously a way to legitimize racism, especially institutional racism, was needed. To increase and maintain a large, cheap labor force, the rights of blacks and other people of color were eliminated. A legacy of this chapter in U.S. history is continued beliefs about minorities as diseased populations with lowered mental abilities.

While race is not real from a biological perspective, racism still exists and is harmful. In epidemiological surveillance, medicine, and public health, race as a variable suggests a genetic basis for the differences in prevalence, severity, or outcome of health conditions. This leads readers to assume that specific races have a certain predisposition, risk, or susceptibility to the illness or behavior under study. Since such assumptions are not substantiated, this type of comparison may represent a subtle form of racism because "racial differences in mortality are in all likelihood not due to fundamental biological differences, but are in large part due to racism and discrimination" (Herman 1996, p. 13).

RACISM AND MEDICAL/HEALTHCARE PROVIDERS

Since at least the colonial period, health providers conformed to a model of health that viewed race as a function of biological homogeneity and black-white differences in health as mainly biologically determined. This model is based on the belief that race is a valid biological category and that genes that determine race are linked to those that determine health. Although no scientific evidence supports these assumptions, in the medical community and in public health, a genetic etiology for disease is equated with racial-genetic susceptibility to that disease.

Physicians' perceptions of patients are influenced by gender, socioeconomic status, and race/ethnicity. These perceptions affect physicians' behavior in medical encounters. For example, Wilson et al. (2004) reported that perceptions of unfair treatment in health care varied among medical students and physicians. They found that first-year medical students were more likely to perceive unfair treatment in health care compared to fourth-year medical students, who were more likely to perceive unfairness relative to physicians. The process of acculturation into the medical profession may account for perceptions of unfair treatment. In other words, during the educational process, medical students become less likely to view health disparities as the result of unequal treatment by their peers and the health-care system. Medical students and physicians are less likely to accept the possibility that their peers harbor prejudice and practice discrimination in health care, although physicians are aware that inequalities in treatment exist.

Barbee (1993) argued that racism is unacknowledged in nursing education to avoid conflict and to emphasize empathy, where all patients are treated the same. Also, a nursing population similar to the faculty is perceived as efficient, and nurses are geared toward an individual paradigm that does not focus on societal structures that impact health. She argues that these factors result in racism being ignored in nursing education.

Examination of third-year medical students' perceptions of social and cultural issues in medicine showed a lack of awareness. Canadian medical students either failed to recognize or denied the importance of race, class, gender, culture, and sexual orientation in their medical encounters with patients and colleagues. Those who acknowledged social differences denied social inequality and their own privilege in society (Beagan 2003).

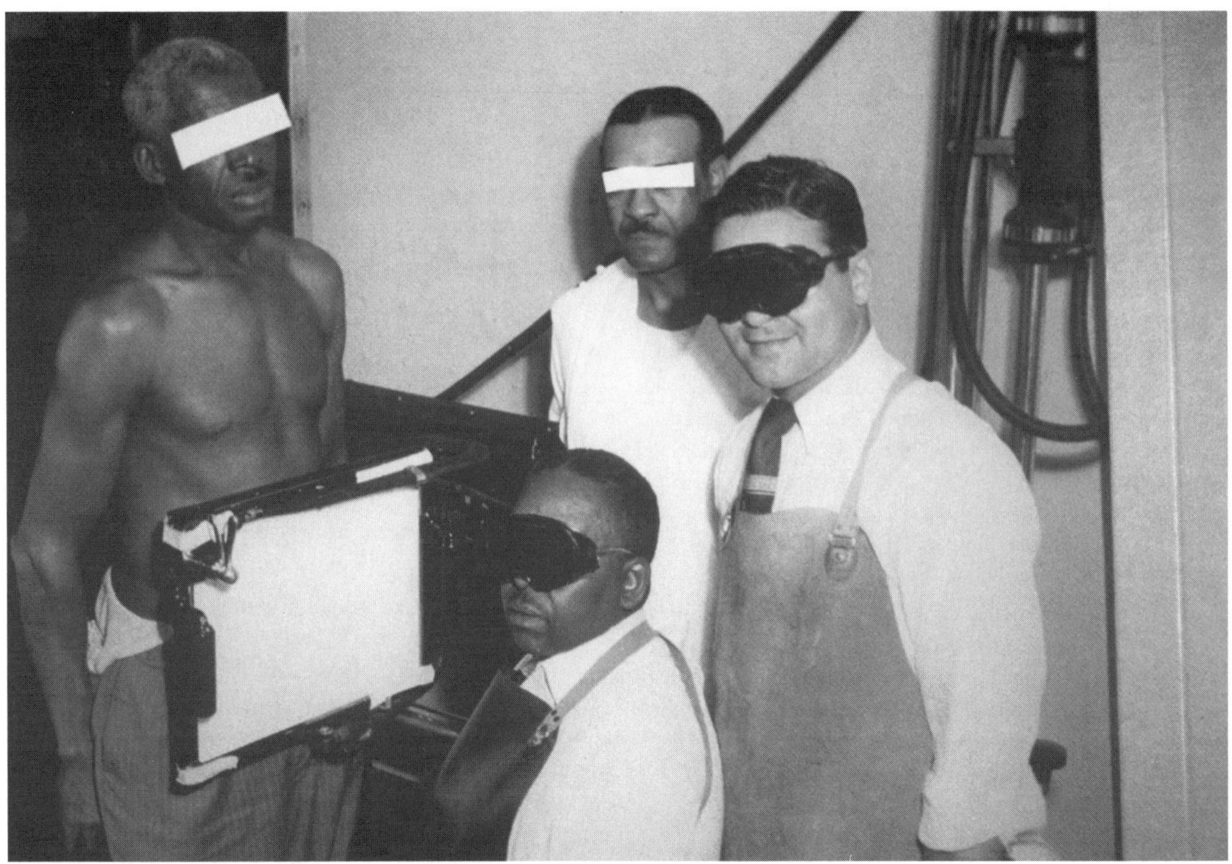

Tuskegee Syphilis Study, 1947. *The Tuskegee Syphilis Study took place over a 40-year period and was meant to discover how syphilis affected blacks as opposed to whites. The test subjects were never told what disease they were suffering from or its seriousness. Nor were they given treatment for the disease.* © CORBIS SYGMA.

In another study, medical students viewed ethnic groups as discrete and "well defined" groups, and they had difficulty with issues of cultural diversity in medical practice. White medical students did not consider themselves advantaged, were less likely to believe that doctors harbor prejudices, and had problems believing that racism exists in the United States (Dogra and Karnik 2003). Training as a physician, nurse, or other health-care provider does not prepare one to interact with people of other races/ethnicities. Physicians, nurses, and other health-care workers are part of society and subject to the same biases and prejudices that are found in society.

RACISM IN MEDICINE

The previous discussion described the conceptual underpinnings of medical racism. In this section racism in medicine is examined from a structural and institutional perspective. In order for racism to operate in medicine and the medical care system, institutions must collaborate in a systematic way. Carmichael and Hamilton (1967) stated that institutional racism occurs when one or more of the institutions of a society function to impose more burdens on and give less benefit to members of one racial or ethnic group than another on an ongoing basis. Bowser and Hunt (1996) stated that racism is an expression of "institutionalized patterns of white power and social control that were rooted in the very structures of society" (p. xiii). The medical care system is an institution and like other institutions reflects the racial culture of the wider society.

Experimentation. Historically, since blacks were viewed as a separate species that were biologically, mentally, and morally inferior, they were considered appropriate subjects for experimentation. Although the Tuskegee Syphilis Experiment illuminated the enormity of problems in the recruitment of disenfranchised people in medical research, this type of racism has a long history. For example, James Marion Sims, the father of gynecology and president of the American Medical Association (1875–1876), experimented on slave women between 1845 and 1849 in an attempt to find a cure for vaginal fistula. Experimentation on these women was considered acceptable because of their "inhuman" status.

Experiments on disenfranchised people continue into contemporary times. For instance, Jones (1993) and Brandt (1978) examined the Tuskegee Syphilis Experiment (1932–1972) and its sponsorship by the United States Public Health Service (USPHS). From the beginning it was assumed that blacks in Macon County, Alabama, constituted a "natural" syphilitic population. The USPHS believed the study might show that treatment for syphilis was unnecessary for blacks and that existing knowledge concerning treatment for latent syphilis did not apply to them. To the USPHS, syphilis was a different disease in blacks as opposed to whites (Jones 1993). Even in the early 2000s one finds evidence of this logic in medical journals; for example, in 2001 the *American Journal of Surgery* included an article titled "Is Breast Cancer in Young Latinas a Different Disease?"

By the mid-1970s the Department of Health, Education and Welfare (HEW) report suggested that failure to provide penicillin (by 1947 the treatment of choice for syphilis) was the major ethical problem with the study, but Brandt (1978) suggested that lying to the men about treatment was the major problem. The fact that a comparative sample of whites was not included in the research design shows the racial orientation of the USPHS. Nothing scientifically useful resulted from this experiment.

Racial underpinnings of this experiment are shown by the fact that the study was widely reported for almost forty years without evoking widespread protest within the medical community and at the USPHS (Brandt 1978). Examples of these publications include: *Environmental Factors in the Tuskegee Study of Untreated Syphilis* (Public Health Reports 1954); *Untreated Syphilis in the Male Negro; Background and Current Status of Patients in the Tuskegee Study* (*Journal of Chronic Disease* 1955); and *The Tuskegee Study of Untreated Syphilis: The 30th Year of Observation* (Archives of Internal Medicine 1964).

Access to Health Care. A number of epidemiologic studies reported differences in access to health care and differential treatment based on race. Giachello (1996) examined the sociodemographic disadvantages of Latinos in the United States, especially women. Latina access to health care is restricted by lack of health insurance, white male orientation of health services, institutionalized sexism and racism, and the inability of the medical system to recognize and adapt to the needs of the poor and those of diverse cultures and languages.

Numerous studies report differences in recommendations for specific medical treatments by race and sex of patient. After adjustment for clinical status and health insurance, whites were more likely than blacks to receive coronary angiography, bypass surgery, angioplasty, chemodialysis, kidney transplants, and intensive care for pneumonia. Blacks and women were less likely than whites and males to receive cardiac catheterization or coronary-artery bypass graft surgery when they were admitted to the hospital for myocardial infarction or chest pain. Although blacks and whites had similar hospitalization rates for circulatory disease or chest pain, whites were one-third more likely to undergo coronary angiography and were twice as likely to receive bypass surgery or angioplasty. This disparity persisted after controlling for income and severity of disease (Wenneker and Epstein 1989).

In a study of physicians, Schulman et al. (1999) found that women and blacks were less likely to be referred for cardiac catheterization than men and whites, respectively. The authors suggested that the race and sex of a patient independently influenced the decision-making process for physicians' management of chest pain. In other words, after adjustment for symptoms, the physicians' estimates of the probability of coronary disease and perceptions of the personalities of the patient, along with clinical characteristics, race, and sex, still affected the physicians' decisions about whether to refer patients with chest pain for cardiac catheterization. This suggests a bias on the part of the physician that may represent overt prejudice or subtle racism.

Individual racism can operate as aversive or subtle racism when individuals of the dominant group unknowingly or without intent express prejudice and discrimination against subordinate groups. Prejudice, negative stereotypes, ethnocentrism, and discrimination can be incorporated into individual racism, the negative attitudes and behaviors expressed by members of the dominant group toward the minority group. With this type of racism individuals believe that biological traits are determinants of morality, intellectual qualities, social behavior, and health. Ultimately, it is assumed that biological differences are a legitimate basis for differential treatment.

BIOLOGICAL CONSEQUENCES OF RACISM

Stress. The state of stress alerts physiological mechanisms to meet the challenge imposed by stressors (stimuli that produce stress). One of the first responses to stress is an increase in sympathetic activity. Sympathetic fibers innervate blood vessels and stimulate the secretion of epinephrine, which increases blood sugar, blood pressure, and heart rate. Denial of racism, experiences with racism, and acceptance of racist ideology may serve as stressors that adversely impact mental and physical health.

Numerous studies show a positive association between racial discrimination and mental distress. Racism can lead to self-hatred and impact how individuals view themselves relative to the dominant group. For instance, experiences with discrimination, as measured by being Mexican American, have been associated with depression.

Racial discrimination is related to decreased measures of personal life satisfaction and more psychological distress. Using data from the National Survey of Black Americans, Jackson et al. (1996) found that unfair treatment because of race was inversely related to subjective measures of well-being. Perceived racism (whites want to keep blacks down) was associated with increased psychological stress and lower levels of subjective well-being. Perceived racism and discrimination resulted in poorer mental health but over time better physical health. They posit that life satisfaction and psychological distress are transitory and situational, whereas physical health problems are chronic with intervening and mediating factors that modify the relationship between racism and health. For instance, those who perceive whites as "holding blacks down" may be more vigilant about their own physical health. Alternatively, recognizing racism and discrimination may be a protective mechanism for combating stress related to racism (Jackson et al. 1996).

Studies indicate that racial discrimination is associated with increased cardiovascular responses (CVR). Exposure to and attributions of racial discrimination can increase CVR and maintain a heightened CVR among African Americans. Racist stimuli have been associated with significantly elevated CVR among African Americans. In another study, African Americans who viewed racist scenarios had increased electromyography (EMG) and heart rates (Sutherland and Harrell 1986; Jones et al. 1996).

Numerous studies show a relationship between racism and blood pressure. For instance, denial of racism may lead to higher blood pressures. Black women who did not report discrimination and who were passive when treated unfairly may have higher blood pressures, but those who reported discrimination may have lower pressures (Krieger and Sidney 1996). In another study, African Americans who viewed scenes of racial harassment by white police officers had elevated systolic and diastolic pressures (Morris-Prather et al. 1996). James and colleagues (1984) found higher diastolic pressures among successful black men who worked hard to overcome obstacles, their race (John Henryism), compared to those who saw their race as helpful. These studies indicate that experiences with racism can impair the cardiovascular system.

Aversive racism, a subtle form of racial discrimination, commonly experienced by blacks, was examined in a laboratory stress test. Black men who perceived aversive racism had higher systolic and diastolic blood pressures compared to those who did not acknowledge racism and those who considered it a blatant form of racism. Since blacks show more vascular responses to laboratory stressors, these situations, aversive racism, may be important in black-white disparities in CVR. It is also important because blatant forms of racism are giving way to more subtle forms in U.S. society.

Dressler (1993) suggested a social structural model to explain health inequalities. This model incorporates the concept of incongruence. For example, in a study of African Americans, variation in skin color was used as a proxy for socioeconomic status, where it was hypothesized that darker skin color is equated with lower social class regardless of education or lifestyle. He found that African Americans with darker skin color had higher blood pressures than lighter-skinned blacks. He theorized that this was the result of incongruence, where darker-skinned blacks with a high-status lifestyle have more negative interactions because they are not treated in a way commensurate with their social status (Dressler 1991).

Amputation. A variety of studies indicate an association between race/ethnicity and lower extremity amputation. For instance, the NHANES Epidemiologic Follow-up Study (1971–1992) found that while blacks were 15.2 percent of the cohort, they were 27.8 percent of the subjects with amputations (Resnick et al. 1999). In a national study of veterans, being black and Hispanic were independent risk factors for lower extremity amputation after controlling for atherosclerosis in veteran patients with peripheral artery disease (Collins et al. 2002).

Organ Transplants. Racism is found in patterns of organ donation. Blacks wait for a first kidney transplant twice as long as whites. In a review of patients who received long-term dialysis in the United States, nonwhite dialysis recipients were two-thirds less likely as white patients to receive a kidney transplant. Also, whites were disproportionately on waiting lists for transplants. Many observers believe that there is a two-tiered health-care system.

HEALTH CONSEQUENCES OF MEDICAL RACISM

Health disparities between minorities and the majority population in the United States are well documented. Such health gaps are demonstrated in, for instance, higher mortality rates among blacks than whites in the United States. In 1900 the life expectancy at birth for whites in the United States was 47.6 years compared to nonwhites (mainly blacks), who had a life expectancy at birth of only 33 years. Life expectancy at birth for black men in 1992 was 65.5 years compared to 73.2 years for white males. For black and white women the figures were 73.9 years and 79.7 years respectively.

Health disparities between whites and other minorities continue to exist. Death rates for heart disease are more than four times higher for African Americans than whites. Hispanics are almost twice as likely to die from diabetes as non-Hispanic whites. While Asians and Pacific Islanders are among the healthiest populations in the United States, there is great diversity within these groups. For example, women of Vietnamese origin suffer from cervical cancer at nearly five times the rate for white women (National Center for Health Statistics 1999).

Medical racism is based on stereotypical folk beliefs about minority groups that have been socially transmitted from one generation to the next. Those who use genetics to explain health disparities between groups ignore alternate explanations. Race/ethnicity should be used to understand individuals' lived experience. It is a risk marker for life experiences and opportunities as well as access to valued resources. Medical racism is the antithesis of the medical motto: First, Do No Harm.

SEE ALSO *Aversive Racism; Clines and Continuous Variation; Diseases, Racial; Hypertension and Coronary Heart Disease; Institutional Racism; Life Expectancy; Medical Experimentation; Mental Health and Racism; Skin Color.*

BIBLIOGRAPHY

Angier, Natalie. 2000. "Do Races Differ? Not Really, DNA Shows." *New York Times* August 22. Available from http://nytimes.com.

Barbee, E. 1993. "Racism in U.S. Nursing." *Medical Anthropology Quarterly* 7 (4): 346–362.

Beagan, B. L. 2003. "Teaching Social and Cultural Awareness to Medical Students: It's All Very Nice to Talk About It in Theory, But Ultimately It Makes No Difference." *Academic Medicine* 78 (6): 605–614.

Bowser, B. P., and R. G. Hunt, eds. 1996. *Impacts of Racism on White Americans,* 2nd ed. Thousand Oaks, CA: Sage.

Brandt, A. M. 1978. "Racism and Research: The Case of the Tuskegee Syphilis Study." *Hastings Center* 8 (6): 21–29.

Carmichael, S., and C. V. Hamilton. 1967. *Black Power: The Politics of Liberation in America.* New York: Random House.

Collins, T. C., M. Johnson, W. Henderson, et al. 2002. "Lower Extremity Nontraumatic Amputation among Veterans with Peripheral Arterial Disease: Is Race an Independent Factor?" *Medical Care* 40 (1) Suppl: 106–16.

Dogra, N., and N. Karnik. 2003. "First-Year Medical Students' Attitudes Toward Diversity and Its Teaching: An Investigation at One U.S. Medical School." *Academic Medicine* 78 (11): 1191–1200.

Dressler, W. W. 1991. "Social Class, Skin Color, and Arterial Blood Pressure in Two Societies." *Ethnicity and Disease* 1: 60–77.

———. 1993. "Health in the African American Community: Accounting for Health Inequalities." *Medical Anthropology Quarterly* 7 (4): 325–345.

Giachello, A. L. 1996. "Latino Women." In *Race, Gender, and Health,* ed. M. Bayne-Smith, 121–171. Thousand Oaks, CA: Sage.

Goodman, A. 2000. "Why Genes Don't Count (for Racial Differences in Health)." *American Journal of Public Health* 90 (11): 1699–1701.

Hahn R. A., B. I. Truman, and N. D. Barker. 1996. "Identifying Ancestry: The Reliability of Ancestral Identification in the United States by Self, Proxy, Interviewer, and Funeral Director." *Epidemiology* 7 (1): 75–80.

Herman, A. A. 1996. "Toward a Conceptualization of Race in Epidemiologic Research." *Ethnicity and Disease* 6 (1–2): 7–20.

Jackson, J. S., T. N. Brown, D. R. Williams, et al. 1996. "Racism and Physical and Mental Health Status of African Americans: A Thirteen-Year National Panel Study." *Ethnicity and Disease* 6: 132–147.

James, S. A., A. Z. LaCroix, D. G. Kleinbaum, and D. S. Strogatz. 1996. "John Henryism and Blood Pressure Differences Among Black Men. II. The Role of Occupational Stressors." *Journal of Behavioral Medicine* 7: 259–275.

Jones, D. R., J. P. Harrell, C. E. Morris-Prather, et al. 1996. "Affective and Physiological Responses to Racism: The Roles of Afrocentrism and Mode of Presentation." *Ethnicity and Disease* 6: 109–122.

Jones, J. H. 1993. *Bad Blood: The Tuskegee Syphilis Experiment.* New York: Free Press.

Krieger, N., and S. Sidney. 1996. "Racial Discrimination and Blood Pressure: The CARDIA Study of Young Black and White Adults." *American Journal of Public Health* 86 (10): 1370–1378.

Morris-Prather, C., J. P. Harrell, R. Collins, et al. 1996. "Gender Differences in Mood and Cardiovascular Responses to Socially Stressful Stimuli." *Ethnicity and Disease* 6: 123–131.

National Center for Health Statistics. 1999. *Healthy People 2000 Review, 1998–1999.* Hyattsville, MD: Public Health Service.

Resnick, H. E., P. Valsania, and C. L. Phillips. 1999. "Diabetes Mellitus and Nontraumatic Lower Extremity Amputation in Black and White Americans: The National Health and Nutrition Examination Survey Epidemiologic Follow-Up Study, 1971–1992." *Archives of Internal Medicine* 159 (20): 2470–2475.

Schulman, K. A., J. A. Berlin, W. Harless, et al. 1999. "The Effect of Race and Sex on Physicians' Recommendations for Cardiac Catherization." *New England Journal of Medicine* 340: 618–626.

Sutherland, M. E., and J. P. Harrell. 1986. "Individual Differences in Physiological Responses to Fearful, Racially Noxious and Neutral Imagery." *Imagination, Cognition and Personality* 6 (2): 133–150.

Wenneker, M. B., and A. M. Epstein. 1989. "Racial Inequalities in the Use of Procedures for Patients with Ischemic Heart Disease in Massachusetts." *Journal of the American Medical Association* 261: 253-257.

Wilson, E., K. J. Grumbach, J. Huebner, et al. 2004. "Medical Student, Physician, and Public Perceptions of Health Care Disparities." *Family Medicine* 36 (10): 715–721.

Janis Faye Hutchinson

MENTAL HEALTH AND RACISM

President Bill Clinton's 1997 Initiative on Race identified racism as one of the most toxic forces in society, with detrimental consequences on racial and ethnic minorities in education, employment, income, housing, and access to health care. Within the field of mental health, the deleterious effects of racism for people of color have been well documented. A survey of studies examining racism and mental health concluded that racism is a major cause of unhappiness, lower life satisfaction, poor self-esteem, and feelings of powerlessness (Williams, Neighbors, and Jackson 2003). African Americans and Latino/Hispanic Americans report higher levels of global stress, experience greater physiological distress, and have more trauma-related symptoms than do white Americans. Racism has also been found to be associated with depressive symptoms and stress for Asian Pacific Americans as well. Racism not only predisposes an individual to socio-emotional disorders, but it can also result in a depletion of cognitive and emotional resources. The inevitable conclusion is that racism is a social risk factor for mental illness among people of color.

UTILIZATION PATTERNS

Unfortunately, racism not only causes emotional distress for people of color, but it may infect the delivery of mental-health services as well. Significant racial and ethnic disparities in health care for racial and ethnic minorities, when compared to their white counterparts, are remarkably consistent in studies (Smedley and Smedley 2005). In brief, racial minorities (1) receive an inferior quality of health care across many diseases, including mental disorders, (2) receive less desirable services, (3) are more likely to receive an inaccurate diagnosis, and (4) suffer higher mortality. In a major report, *Mental Health: Culture, Race, and Ethnicity* (2001), the U.S. surgeon general concluded that major disparities in the delivery and utilization patterns of mental-health services for people of color were due to bias and cultural insensitivity.

In one study cited in this report, only 16 percent of African Americans with a diagnosable mood disorder saw a mental health professional, and less than one-third saw a health provider of any kind. When sociodemographic factors such as income and insurance coverage were controlled for, the percentage of African Americans receiving any mental-health treatment was half that of whites. Less than 25 percent of Asian Americans who experienced symptoms of a mood or anxiety disorder, and 32 percent of Native American/Alaska Natives with a diagnosable mental disorder received treatment from a mental-health professional. Among Latino/Hispanic Americans, only 11 percent with a mood disorder and 10 percent with an anxiety disorder utilized mental-health services.

However, although minimal numbers of racial and ethnic minorities seek mental health treatment from private providers and treatment centers, they are often overrepresented in public mental health treatment facilities, such as hospital emergency rooms. Perhaps this is due to ease of accessibility or because the person waited to treat a problem due to mistrust of mental health providers until it was unavoidable. Because African Americans are significantly more likely to have inpatient psychiatric care than are whites, and because African Americans and Native Americans are more likely to receive emergency care, these groups are greatly overrepresented in inpatient settings. Ironically, among the small numbers of African Americans, Asian Americans, Latino/Hispanic Americans, and Native Americans who do seek mental-health services, the majority are more likely to prematurely terminate treatment than are whites. This high drop-out rate can be directly attributed to the person of color's experience of mental-health care, which is often invalidating and antagonistic to their life experiences and cultural values.

Societal, community, and organizational biases often make mental-health services unavailable and inaccessible to people of color. For example, in rural communities inhabited by many Native Americans and Alaska Natives, there is a dearth of mental-health services. In addition, psychologists and psychiatrists in private practice tend to be inaccessible to those in lower socioeconomic classes, due to high hourly rates and a tendency not to accept government-funded programs such as Medicare. Further, people of color are significantly less likely to have adequate insurance than whites.

Not only is treatment less available to many people of color, but research supports the idea that mental-health services for people of color are often inferior to the treatment received by whites. For example, many African Americans and Latino/Hispanic Americans feel that providers have judged them unfairly or treated them with disrespect because of their race or ethnic background. African Americans were found to be less likely to receive appropriate care than whites for depression and anxiety and African Americans and Latino/Hispanic Americans experiencing a mood or anxiety disorder are less likely to receive good guideline-adherent treatment.

The prescription of psychotropic medication is also distributed unevenly among whites and people of color.

In a trial study of Medicare recipients, African Americans were less likely than whites to be prescribed an antidepressant medication, and African Americans were significantly more likely to be prescribed antipsychotic drugs, even when indications for this treatment did not exist. Misdiagnosis of people of color is a pervasive issue in mental-health-care settings. Oftentimes, the mental-health provider will mistakenly see differences in cultural determined behaviors as pathology. Clinicians have been shown to be predisposed to diagnosing African Americans as schizophrenic, whereas widely held stereotypes of Asian Americans as the "model minority" may prompt clinicians to overlook their mental-health problems.

BARRIERS TO EFFECTIVE MENTAL HEALTH SERVICES

Various factors act as barriers to mental-health treatment for people of color. The culture-bound and class-bound values of therapy may work against minority clients from seeking such treatment. For example, researchers have shown that the under-utilization of mental-health resources by Asian Americans can be attributed to a mismatch between Asian cultural values and the values inherent in Western mental-health services. In particular, Asian Americans were significantly less likely than whites to discuss their mental-health problems with a mental-health specialist because of the shame and stigma associated with disclosing family and personal issues. African Americans have described such a stigma and the "cold," "detached," and objective manner of professionals as affecting their willingness to seek help. Indeed, therapists who are unaware of how cultural values influence the helping process are likely to misinterpret and misdiagnose racial and ethnic minorities in a pathological manner.

Cultural mistrust is also a major barrier to mental-health treatment. Mistrust of white clinicians by people of color derives from historical persecution and continuing experiences of racism. The field of psychology has a history of exploiting people of color and utilizing racist and culturally ignorant practices. The alienation and lack of trust felt by people of color toward mental-health services is well documented and is considered to be compounded by cultural misunderstanding (Sue 2003). Clients of color are likely to approach the helping professional with a healthy suspiciousness about whether the clinician's biases, preconceived notions, and lack of cultural understanding will prevent them from obtaining the help needed. Unfortunately, they often conclude that they will not receive the help they need and fail to return for sessions.

The heavy reliance on the use of Standard English and "talking" may also serve as barriers to mental-health services for people of color. It is estimated that access to mental-health care is limited for approximately half of the Asian-American population due to lack of English proficiency, as well as to the shortage of providers who have the necessary language skills. Among Native Americans and Alaska Natives, cultural differences in the expression of distress often compromises the ability of both clinicians and assessment tools to capture the key signs and symptoms of mental illness. For example, the words "depressed" and "anxious" do not exist in some American Indian and Alaska Native languages. Further, many cultural groups rely heavily on nonverbal rather than verbal communication to transmit information about themselves and their problems. A culturally unaware provider may miss or misinterpret important nonverbal messages being imparted by the client.

The limited availability of mental-health professionals who can be ethnically matched with clients is problematic, especially as it often relates to language barriers. For example, there are very few African American, Latino/Hispanic American, Native American/Alaska Native, and Asian American mental-health professionals, so making an ethnic match between therapist and client is difficult at best. Studies have shown that both an ethnic match between therapist and client and services that respond to the cultural needs of the client can prevent early termination of treatment and lead to better outcomes for racial and ethnic minorities.

In conclusion, there is overwhelming evidence supporting the notion that racism is a risk factor for mental illness among racial and ethnic minorities. Unfortunately, research also suggests that mental-health systems are often inappropriate, antagonistic, inferior, and inaccessible to populations of color and may only serve to marginalize them. Only if society and the mental-health professions begin to address these disparities in a serious way will we be able to improve the mental health of populations of color and provide culturally relevant services. In general, it is important for mental-health professionals to acknowledge the insidious effects of racism in their profession and themselves. No helping professional is free from racial or ethnic bias, and only if racism is honestly acknowledged and confronted will the profession begin to minimize the psychological harm of racism, enhance physical and psychological well-being, and increase access to health care for all minorities.

SEE ALSO *Health Care Gap; Medical Racism; Model Minorities.*

BIBLIOGRAPHY

President's Initiative on Race. 1998. *One America in the Twenty-First Century: The President's Initiative on Race.* Washington, DC: U.S. Government Printing Office. Available from http://www.ncjrs.org.

Smedley, Audrey, and Brian D. Smedley. 2005. "Race as Biology Is Fiction, Racism as a Social Problem Is Real." *American Psychologist* 60 (1): 16–26.

Sue, Derald W. 2003. *Overcoming Our Racism: The Journey to Liberation*. San Francisco, CA: Jossey-Bass Publications.

U.S. Department of Health and Human Services. 2001. *Mental Health: Culture, Race and Ethnicity—A Supplement to Mental Health: A Report of the Surgeon General.* Washington, DC: U.S. Government Printing Office. Available from http://www.surgeongeneral.gov.

Williams, David R., Harold W. Neighbors, and James S. Jackson. 2003. "Racial/Ethnic Discrimination and Health: Findings from Community Studies." *American Journal of Public Health,* 93(2): 200–208.

Christina M. Capodilupo
Derald Wing Sue

MEXICANS

Beginning with the conquests of the sixteenth century and the subjugation of the indigenous population, race and racism have been a major stratifying dynamic in Mexico. Throughout this history, the Native peoples of the land have been made to feel inferior because of their physical appearance and cultural traditions. After hundreds of years of adjustments and struggle, this colonial legacy persists in Mexico. The Zapatista resistance, which began in the 1990s, is living testimony to the continuing significance of this problem.

This tradition of race and racism has also affected the Mexican American, not only as a result of the legacy of the earlier experiences in Mexico, but also as a consequence of the annexation of northern Mexico by the United States after the Mexican-American War of 1846–1848. In the early twentieth century, immigration to the United States from Mexico reinforced these animosities and racial conflicts. Moreover, Mexicans who appeared "Indian" in appearance were treated much the same as Americans had traditionally treated Native peoples, so that segregation, discrimination, and a denigration of race and culture were the order of the day. These older practices were added to in the late twentieth century, when increasing waves of immigration fanned other racist practices. Mexicans became "illegal aliens" and, ironically, outsiders in the land of their ancestors.

Race and racism are critical and related social constructions. In the United States, racism is a social construction of the dominant Euro-American elite who have exerted power to subordinate other groups who are physically or culturally distinct, particularly Native Americans, African Americans, and Hispanics, in an effort to justify inequality in wealth, power, and prestige.

THE MEXICAN CASE

The social construction of racism in Mexico has informed the way racism toward Mexican Americans has been expressed in the United States. Both countries inherited miscegenation laws from the colonial era. In Mexico, a *mestizo* (mixed-race) population developed and ranged from Indian to Spanish (and later African) in physical attributes and appearance. Strict racial barriers and laws were in place throughout the colonial period, with the darker-hued groups held in lower esteem The hierarchical ordering of races was intensified by the arrival of Africans, who further complicated the racial mixing then underway. The skin color and phenotypic traits of the white ruling elites set the standard to which all others had to measure up, and this generated a new strategy among the mestizo population, who attempted to "pass" if they had lighter skin or were European in appearance. In both Mexico and the United States, many adopted this strategy in order to increase their chance of upward mobility.

In Mexico, being a mestizo helped blur class and cultural differences, as many could claim that the country was mostly mestizo. The notion of *La Raza Cósmica* (the Cosmic People) made the mestizo heritage a popular one and took hold after the 1910 Mexican Revolution. The ruling elites favored building a mestizo ideology around nineteenth-century notions that racial problems had been resolved because intermarriage was transforming the population into a hybrid people. Problems persisted, however, and were exacerbated by indigenous people migrating to cities both at home and abroad. With the rise of the Zapatistas in 1994, the term *dignidad* (dignity) came to the fore as a principle to generate pride in an indigenous struggle for rights and recognition.

Nevertheless, the outcome of some of these developments is that acculturation and integration into the mainstream of Mexico by Indians have been mediated by racial appearance, and the customs of a region and people have helped to guide and direct acceptance based on race. Cultural transformations have thus been an aid in escaping one's racial heritage. For example, many Indians pass themselves off as mestizos and not of pure Indian heritage. (Because females are usually the transmitters of indigenous culture, this path is more often taken by males.) Thus, a large portion of the Mexicans are not only dark in appearance but actually have Indian ancestry. The additional pressures of urban migration, communal land privatization, and population growth among the indigenous have only compounded Mexico's "Indian problem" in modern times.

The indigenous population began to be taken more seriously by elites after the Mexican Revolution of 1910, if for no other reasons than the Indians were key participants and many revolutionary goals were grounded in their experiences. In the aftermath of this conflict, the Mexican government and people initiated programs of language and cultural integration, and great strides were made in integrating the Indians and darker mestizos. A more pluralistic model of diversity began to emerge in Mexico as much-neglected problems were addressed. However, the unspoken government policy has been to rate all citizens equal but treat Indians differently.

Racial discrimination always takes its psychological toll. Most Indians who assimilated and learned to dislike (or hate) their phenotype were left with psychological trauma. They repressed and despised their own indigenous (and Mexican) heritage in order to conform to the ways of the larger society. The result is a commonly traversed path of marginality, conflict, and ambiguity for many people who must reconcile two cultural (and, in reality, racial) worlds.

It is no surprise, then, that in Mexican society there is a social myth of the superiority of white skin. This myth is promulgated by the media and often reinforced by physical threats to the well-being of darker skinned individuals. Internal and external migration have acted as both a safety valve and as an integration strategy for the Indian problem, but these movements have also brought deep and old racist sentiments to the surface. Nevertheless, indigenous migration to urban places had become commonplace by the end of the twentieth century. There have also been attempts to "deport" indigenous people to the interior, where much of the general public believes they belong. Even border town leaders often take a position against Indians, and they encourage the U.S. police to "clean up" the area around the border crossings on the pretense of protecting the Americans. Such actions can subject Indians to human rights violations, however.

The proximity of this region to the United States (sometimes referred to as "Mexiamerica") helps generate feelings of shame among the population there. Most Americans cannot claim an Indian heritage, but the view Americans have of Mexico is of both an Indian past and present: The people look and act like Indians. Many Mexican border residents, who are largely mestizo, feel that this association does them a disservice, and they feel disgraced "by association" as a result.

THE SITUATION IN THE UNITED STATES

In the United States, race and racism take on another dimension. Margarita Melville defined racism as "pejorative social discrimination based on phenotypic (observable biological) characteristics" (1994, p. 92). In the aftermath of the Mexican-American War, conditions and practices of racism permeated Anglo-Mexican relationships, and racial attitudes and practices from the colonial era played a role in this new context. But as Mexican immigration increased to become a critical factor, there was a regeneration of Mexican culture in the United States. Yet large-scale immigration in the late twentieth century also served to reawaken the Anglo racism of the past, creating an intense anti-immigrant sentiment.

Attitudes based on prejudices shape discriminatory behavior. To situate Mexicans in the lowest positions, the dominant U.S. group prejudged their behavior negatively and set up social barriers to their inclusion in good neighborhoods, schools, and jobs. Thus, their social aspirations were dampened and their paths to success were curtailed. In a very short time, the subordinate status of Mexicans became socially constructed as being a consequence of their own inadequacy. Up until the 1960s, Mexican workers in the United States were seen to be careless, lackadaisical, and poorly disciplined. Since then, there has been some relaxing of these stereotypes. There is still, in the early 2000s, a ready association between Mexicans and functionary service labor.

Throughout the twentieth century, the strain of gaining social acceptance made Mexicans in the United States always want to catch up and rid themselves of such stereotypes. Passing as Spanish, especially among light-skinned Mexicans, was one strategy Mexicans used to "elevate" themselves. This strategy was based on racial ideologies that held that darkness signified inferiority. Anglo feelings of superiority to people of color were so deep-rooted that only lighter-hued Mexicans might avoid negative treatment, and even "swarthy" Spaniards were looked down upon (see Almaquer 1994). Yet American leaders often fought against such attitudes and practices. The civil rights movement and the 1964 Civil Rights Act exemplify this type of striving for equality. However, successes were slow and hard won, as overt racism gave way to covert versions, such as disparities in school district budgets and the elimination of job training programs. In short, the structure of society in the late twentieth-century was imbued with racist feeling and actions. As in the earlier colonial confrontation, the struggle over resources and social power is an important motivating factor in modern racist behavior, and racist ideology has been used to prevent the acquisition of land and wealth among minority groups. Impoverished in this manner, Mexicans and others have been blamed for their own poverty and socioeconomic failures. As recently as the early 1960s, the police departments in various southwestern cities held negative views of Mexicans just for being darker and speaking a foreign language. Such reasoning translated into policies that were extremely detrimental in most heavily populated Mexican regions of the Southwest. Later, when other parts of the United States such as the East and Southeast, experienced an influx of Maya, Mixtec, and Zapotec Mexicans, the police

Justice and Dignity for All Immigrants Rally, 2006. *A Mexican woman waves the U.S. and Mexican flags at a rally protesting proposed immigration legislation that many Latino groups consider discriminatory.* AP IMAGES.

departments in these areas displayed similar attitudes (see Escobar 1998).

There were occasional successes, though, especially in the celebrated cases involving segregated schools, including the successful desegregation of the Lemon Grove (California) School District in the 1930s and the 1946 *Mendez v. Westminster* case, in which separate schools for Mexican students were held to be unconstitutional under the Fourteenth Amendment. Most other societal sectors were interwoven with racial standards that were implicitly or even explicitly aimed at the exclusion of ethnic minorities. In some regions and cities, racism continued in social realms outside the school as late as the 1950s. Swimming pools, recreation centers, movie theaters, shopping districts, and restaurants were considered off limits to Mexicans. In certain heavily racist towns, even something as mundane as a haircut was touched by racism. In the 1930s, a barber in Texas stated: "No, we don't wait on Mexicans here. They are dirty and have lice, and we would lose our white trade. The Mexicans also have venereal diseases, most of them, but of course some whites do, too. The Mexicans go to their own barbershop. The Negroes barber each other" (Taylor 1934, p. 250). While some individuals internalized this type of treatment to nurture feelings of self-hate, there were others who resisted in different ways.

RESISTANCE

Chicano resistance against racism erupted in the nineteenth century. It took such forms as social banditry (e.g., armed combat against police and vigilante authorities) and has continued to recent times, as in the Los Angeles riots of 1992 in the aftermath of the Rodney King verdict. In the early twenty-first century, marches and protests associated with immigrant rights have been packed with racial overtones. The national hysteria in the United States regarding the overwhelming presence of undocumented Mexicans and the problems with the border regions are also loaded with racist motifs.

One major example of this propensity for resistance against racism is the so-called Zoot Suit Riots of the early 1940s in Los Angeles. This was a clear, united stand against racist persecution. Chicanos grouped together for defensive purposes, as both the police and civilians subjected the community to angry attacks, and the rioting continued for several days. Mexican Americans were held responsible for the entire affair, but public attention eventually zeroed in on the barriers and obstacles affecting Mexican Americans, especially the ones that were based on racism, and some programs were introduced to counter them.

Mexican-American veterans also took a stand against racist institutions. As first-class citizens in the front lines of both world wars, they could not accept second-class citizenship when they returned home. Steadfast in their resolve, they organized as the American GI Forum and fought to eliminate racist practices. Institutional discrimination was reinforced, however, by the proliferation of derogatory images of Chicanos, and by labels such as "greaser," "Mecskin," "wetback," and "beaner." Negative stereotyping was also a common practice among social-science writers and other academicians, who needed to rationalize the experiences of the ethnically defined underclass. Mexicans were described as being unable to delay gratification, fatalistic, too collective in nature, lazy, dumb, immoral, and culturally deficient. These and other disparaging stereotypes were still popular in the 1950s and 1960s. While many social scientists subsequently rid their work of such imagery, the legacy lives on elsewhere. One need only look to Hollywood movies and television programs to document the occurrence of stereotyping. In films, Mexican female and male characters (as well as Indians) are often depicted as mostly a bad sort, and they are generally associated with gangs, terrorism, illegal immigration, and drug trafficking.

Over time, Chicanos have adjusted to this treatment and fashioned a self-protective shell. Many have become "reverse racists," even toward other racial minorities. As an adaptive mechanism, this racist attitude has helped Mexican Americans survive the onslaught and reclaim some sense of self-dignity. Even after immigration to the United States, however, intragroup racism persists among Mexicans, with the darker-skinned people treated more shabbily. Generational distance from Mexico has also affected intragroup relations. To some degree, Mexicans in the United States have mistreated and verbally abused Mexican immigrants on the basis of cultural attributes, calling them *mojados* (wetbacks), *chuntaros*, and T. J.s (meaning "from Tijuana"). Occasionally, Chicano leaders have tried to stop this name-calling.

In the United States, hiring practices have often been racially based. In addition, socioeconomic variation among Mexicans has contributed to intraethnic relations and conflicts. Mexican immigrants compare their socioeconomic status to the status they had in Mexico, whereas Mexican Americans born in the United States compare their status with that of Anglos. Darker-skinned Mexicans have sometimes sought a status change through intermarriage. Thus, up to the early 2000s, the Mexican-American community has faced tremendous problems stemming from racial discrimination. In employment and social standing there have been major barriers for advancement.

Thus, many race-based problems still persist in the United States. In the past, racial discrimination was blatantly practiced. The breaking down of the most extreme barriers has come faster in urban areas, due to the successes of the civil rights movement and the increase in minority populations in these areas. As racial and cultural myths are challenged and eliminated, Chicanos have made advances in mainstream America, but individuals and groups still struggle to gain some level of parity.

IMMIGRATION AND RACISM

Discrimination toward indigenous people in Mexico proper has often been carried north into the United States as well. Mexican immigrants to the United States are both nonindigenous and indigenous, forcing these two groups to live and work side by side. As in many societies, people who are darker skinned are also more susceptible to harassment. There seems to be a paradoxical mentality that exists in Mexico and in the United States among nonindigenous Mexicans. Mestizos like to identify with the glorious past of the indigenous people, such as their Aztec cousins of five hundred years ago. On the other hand, they see the living indigenous Mexicans as being inferior to themselves.

Some people are confused and saddened that they are treated badly by the people who are supposed to be their countrymen. One of the effects of this discrimination is that people from indigenous regions have become ashamed of who they are. To be Indian is a stigma in some quarters of American society, although with the resurgence of Indian rights this attitude is changing somewhat.

One strategy used to deal with this ambiguous situation is to become bilingual and bicultural, a strategy that has worked for many Indians in Mexico. Recent cultural and ethnic reclamation efforts, as part of a general pan-Indian movement, have assisted in making Indians more autonomous. Indigenous dictionaries, novels, and poems have been written, and indigenous organizations have sprung up, heralding a renaissance in Native culture. Ethnic identity is being reaffirmed as Indians strive to achieve what was once ascribed to them.

Indian Mexico has changed for the better and recent political and social disturbances reflect this ascendancy. Jan Rus, the director of the Native Language Publishing Project, maintains that discontent among the indigenous population goes back decades, to when the Mexican government failed to deliver on the promises made after the 1910 Revolution and capitulated to landowners. Nevertheless, the initial Zapatista thrust in January 1994 caught many citizens and observers by surprise. Remarkably, with each political episode, more defenders and supporters have materialized. This is one instance where "identity affirmation" has bolstered a self-esteem with definite political overtones.

LEGACIES OF RACISM

The legacies of the racial hierarchy that was introduced to Mexico by the Spaniards include discrimination and racism toward indigenous people. In its neo-caste form, this hierarchy still functions to create barriers to integration and acceptance. Worse yet, postcolonial and neoliberal regimes have reformed rather than eliminated such practices. To speak of racism in Mexico is to be "unpatriotic," and racism and discrimination are seen as existing only in the minds of indigenous people. Yet the historical record and the recent Zapatista movement suggest a different picture.

In spite of the Indians' presence in Mexican life, to many they are to be glorified as a dead culture that represents the seeds of the modern Mexican state. Those who have used indigenous ideologies to create a Mexican identity have manipulated the Indian identity to empower themselves under a *mestizocracia*. Indigenous people are thus in a double bind: they are losing their culture in the process of acculturation and assimilation, and yet they are not accepted in the mestizo society.

There is constant friction between Mexican social scientists who wish to accentuate Spanish culture and those who want to emphasize indigenous culture. This push to take on a new identity has persisted in the twentieth century, as the Mexican government has tried to incorporate indigenous people into mainstream life through the educational system. Given the complexity and intractability that exists in Mexico, a more inclusive strategy needs to be formulated to expedite race relations studies in Mexico, one that takes into account all the disparate facets of the realities of old and new forces.

The Spaniards who conquered Mexico neither accommodated nor appreciated Indian culture. Later, Anglos were similarly disdainful of Mexican culture. Almost without exception, the subordinate culture was forced to assimilate to the culture of the aggressor. In both Mexico and the United States, this shift required a glorification of the dominant culture and a vilification of other cultures. Despite this pressure to assimilate, many Native people took the creative bilingual-bicultural approach of amalgamating their culture with that of the dominant group. Thus, they innovated a new cultural style, a blend of elements generating a new cultural orientation and identity. Although feelings of inferiority and acts of socioracial "passing" are still prevalent, it appears that a more confident and accepting attitude is emerging to underscore recent improvements in self-image. Notwithstanding these advances, and to reiterate, racism has generated a pronounced impact on almost every single facet of Chicano life.

Mexicans are not one homogeneous group, however, nor will there be any overnight changes in the way indigenous people are perceived and treated in Mexican society (or in the way Mexican Americans are treated in the United States). Acknowledging the issue of racism will initiate a much-needed dialogue to assist in unraveling the many issues marking the inequality within Mexican society. Debates over issues of discrimination and power relations within the Mexican community are still lacking because of a number of interrelated factors, such as who determines the research that gets undertaken and who has the social status, power, and access to institutions of higher learning. In the United States, the mounting hysteria over immigration and the rights of immigrants has taken a very negative turn, eroding some of the gains of past decades. Racism fades slowly, and it recurs when seemingly intractable problems arise as a reminder of how deeply rooted it can be.

SEE ALSO *Citizenship and "the Border"; Colonialism, Internal; Immigration, Race, and Women; Nativism; Treaty of Guadalupe Hidalgo; Zapatista Rebellion.*

BIBLIOGRAPHY

Almaquer, Tomáas. 1994. *Racial Fault Lines: The Historical Origins of White Supremacy in California.* Berkeley: University of California Press.

Alvarez, Roberto. 1988. "National Politics and Local Responses: The Nation's First Successful Desegregation Court Case." In *School and Society: Learning Content Through Culture*, edited by Henry T. Trueba and Concha Delgado-Gaitan, 37–52. New York: Praeger.

Escobar, Edward J. 1999. *Race, Police, and the Making of a Political Identity: Mexican Americans and the Los Angeles Police Department, 1900–1945.* Berkeley: University of California Press.

Gonzales, Gilbert. 1990. *Chicano Education in the Era of Segregation.* Philadelphia: The Balch Institute Press.

Harris, Marvin. 1964. *Patterns of Race in the Americas.* New York: Walker and Sons.

Knight, Alan. 1990. "Racism, Revolution, and Indigenismo: Mexico, 1910–1940." In *The Idea of Race in Latin America, 1870–1940*, edited by Richard Graham. Austin: University of Texas Press.

McWilliams, Carey. 1949. *North from Mexico: The Spanish-Speaking People of the United States.* Philadelphia: J.B. Lippincott.

Melville, Margarita. 1994. M. "'Hispanic' Ethnicity, Race, and Class." In *Handbook of Hispanic Cultures in the United States: Anthropology*, edited by T. Weaver. Houston, TX: Arte Publico Press.

———. 1993. "Chicano Indianism: A Historical Account of Racial Repression in the United States." *American Ethnologist* 20 (3): 583–603.

Menchaca, Martha. 2001. *Recovering History, Constructing Race: The Indian, Black, and White Roots of Mexican Americans.* Austin: University of Texas Press.

Mörner, Magus. 1967. *Race Mixture in the History of Latin America.* Boston: Little, Brown.

Nagengast, Carole, and Michael Kearney. 1990. "Mixtec Identity: Social Identity, Political Consciousness, and Political Activism." *Latin American Research Review* 25 (2): 61–91.

Nagengast, Carole, Rodolfo Stavenhagen, and Michael Kearney. 1992. *Human Rights and Indigenous Workers: The Mixtecs in Mexico and the United States.* San Diego: UCSD Center for U.S.-Mexican Studies.

Santa Ana, Otto. 2002. *Brown Tide Rising: Metaphors of Latinos in Contemporary American Public Discourse.* Austin: University of Texas Press.

Stonequist, Everett. 1937. *The Marginal Man: A Study in Personality and Culture Conflict.* New York: Scribner.

Taylor, Paul S. 1934. *An American Mexican Frontier.* Chapel Hill: University of North Carolina Press.

Vasconcelos, Jose. 1997. *The Cosmic Race,* bilingual ed. Translated by Didier T. Jaen. Baltimore: Johns Hopkins University Press.

Wagley, Charles. 1965. "On the Concept of Social Race in the Americas." In *Contemporary Cultures and Societies of Latin America,* edited by Dwight B. Heath and Richard N. Adams. New York: Random House.

Wievioska, Michel. 1995. *The Arena of Racism.* Thousand Oaks, CA: Sage.

James Diego Vigil
Felipe H. Lopez

MILITARY

SEE *Black Civil War Soldiers; Soldiers of Color.*

MISSIONARIES AMONG AMERICAN INDIANS

The loss of Native homelands through the movement of tribes by means of warfare, treaty, and political policy, coupled with the strategy to "civilize" Native peoples through religious conversion, represents the common experience shared by First Peoples in what is now North America. Political and religious attempts to dismantle the cultural and spiritual existence and the familial structures of Native tribes varied from place to place, whereas the timeline and severity of these efforts were connected to the unfolding of European contact experienced by each tribe. The enactment and enforcement of European and subsequent U.S. federal policy are clearly marked both in time and experience. Religious conversion efforts, however, varied significantly among tribes and bands.

The identification and labeling of Native people as "less than human," "heathen," "neophytes," "soulless," "wild," "uncivilized," or "pagan" by those charged with the efforts to religiously convert and educate them solidified the racialized construct of Indian people. Family structures that deviated from biblical charges, such as polygamy, gay relationships, and matriarchal systems, were marked for genocidal, or at the very least, ethnocidal policies that have impacted Native life ever since.

CHRISTIANITY AND INDIGENOUS PEOPLES

To fully understand the complexities of the contemporary American Indian situation, one must consider how Christianity was used by Europeans to further their goals of conquest and capitalism. The so-called Doctrine of Discovery, which had its origins in the Crusades and the papal bull *Romanus Pontifex* issued by Pope Nicholas V, was tantamount to a declaration of war on all non-Christians. This carte blanche understanding of the rights of conquest was furthered by papal documents issued to Spain and Portugal by Pope Alexander VI in 1493. Subsequent decrees from European monarchs, such as the English Charters, also utilized the language of conquest that originated in these papal documents. In other words, Christian nations believed that they had God's blessing to lay claim to all "discovered" lands and their non-Christian peoples. These documents and their supporting ideology laid the groundwork for the largest and most violent land grab in the Western Hemisphere.

The resulting dehumanization of Native peoples was grounded in the Europeans' archetype of "humanity," which they defined as white and Christian. Both of these components—being white and being Christian—are inherently intertwined and must be understood as such. This dehumanization process allowed Europeans to wage extreme violence and brutality against indigenous peoples on both the North and South American continents. The historical record includes numerous examples of Europeans hunting and killing Native people for sport, including playing sword games in which they tried to kill a Native child with one swipe, or using their dogs to hunt down Native peoples and subsequently feeding them to the dogs as a reward for catching their prey (Churchill 1997).

Jesuit communications recounting their first contacts with American Indians continually and systematically describe them as neophytes and savages, terms that were also in common use in communications among the church hierarchy and with non-Indian parishioners. A neophyte, according to the *Catholic Encyclopedia*, is one who lately entered a new and higher state or condition of life, such as those who have entered the Christian ecclesiastical life. It was also used to describe people who had recently converted from heathenism to the higher life of the Church. The Council of Nicaea (325 CE) decreed that, after baptism, each neophyte must undergo a period of "fuller probation," the duration of which was left to the discretion of individual bishops, before they could be declared Christians. This probationary status clearly inferred that the newly converted were not yet wholly human, meaning that they could not be trusted to act in the manner of white Christian Europeans.

CONVERSION AND CIVILIZING THE POPULATION

In the North American colonies, the English settlers' legal system followed English common law. It was also in direct conflict with many American Indians' traditional methods of maintaining social order. The settlers' understanding of God's will and vision of themselves as bringing salvation to the savages perpetuated their racist attitudes and actions toward American Indians. This is evidenced by the formation of "Praying Towns" inhabited by "Praying Indians" in the New England and New York colonies. A corporation formed by the English Parliament in 1646 allotted sums to establish these towns, which were formed on the outskirts of colonies and used as a political and physical barrier to encroaching non-English white settlers. Some Native groups in the area did not succumb to conversion and were hostile to these towns, and these groups were often used as scouts by non-Puritan settlers. Ironically the "Praying Towns" were decimated during King Philip's War (1675–1676), and the English settlers did not come to their aid. The inference is that they were in a racialized neophyte status and not worthy of being saved.

As the land changed from a conglomeration of settlers and colonies to the United States, government policies towards Native peoples remained rooted in the antiquated and racist pillars of the Doctrine of Discovery. When, for financial and political reasons, the United States' policy towards its Native inhabitants evolved, the views rooted in this doctrine also justified using religious conversion and education as means of "civilizing" or assimilating American Indians. Many politicians during the formation of the United States government saw American Indians as "sons of the forests" (in the words of George Washington) and part of nature (according to Thomas Jefferson). Again, the inference was that, as creatures of the land and nature, they were inherited by the Christians of the United States along with conquest of the land. As such, it was as much a duty to civilize (i.e., Christianize) the Indians as it was to civilize (i.e., conquer and cultivate) the wilderness. Further, if these efforts failed, the duty was to extinguish those who would not comply.

It is also important to note the historical shift in language that occurred before the Revolutionary War. Although the religious terminology of *heathen* and *neophyte* began to be replaced by the more secular term *savage*, the equation of Christianity with civilization remained. Indeed, as a result of continual contact with Euro-Americans settlers and the importance of the fur trade, some American Indian Nations succumbed to the forces of civilization, and missionaries taught them to become Christians and farmers. The early political leaders of the United States advocated either Christianizing (civilizing) or exterminating American Indians. So, in essence, Christianizing and civilizing were reduced to one ideology in federal Indian policy.

The Indian Trade and Intercourse Act, passed by the first U.S. Congress in 1790, was the first step in dealing with the "Indian problem" in the newly formed United States. This act allowed the government to license traders as agents of the United States to trade with American Indians. This is the birth of the ubiquitous "Indian Agent" and the imposition of the federal government in every aspect of American Indian affairs. Another important feature of this act was that land was no longer taken under the auspices of conquest. Instead, it was acquired through the "sale" of American Indian lands under the authority of the U.S. government and in the form of a treaty. During this first Congress, the government also put in place the bureaucracy that has surrounded American Indians since the formation of the United States. The "Indian problem" was subsumed under the office of the secretary of war, and the 1802 Congress reinforced this relationship between American Indians by giving the secretary of war control over all American Indian affairs.

THE ROLE OF THE SETTLERS

Non-Indian settlers believed that, by living among the Indians and serving as exemplars of the highest Christian values, they could inspire and teach them to become like the archetypical white yeoman farmer; that is, they could make the Native peoples both civilized and Christian. The Massachusetts legislature bought land and established Stockbridge as a township for converts (not unlike the "Praying Indians") and interested white Christian families. In response to the encroachment of increasing numbers of white settlers, many American Indians moved to this settlement, where the Mahikan language was used in church and as the shared language of the settlement. Many Indian warriors from Stockbridge fought with the Americans in the Revolutionary War. While the Native males were gone to war, however, the missionaries divided the church into Indian and English congregations, and the Christian Indians' were forcibly removed to Central New York.

By the time the Indian Trade and Intercourse Act became law, the Stockbridge Mission Indians could speak, read, and write English; they had developed a stable farming community modeled after the white yeoman farmer; and were serving as cultural brokers between other American Indians and white settlers. Shortly after the first Congress, the War Department held the Stockbridge Indians up as models and argued that the rest of the American Indians should also become "civilized." Even as model American Indians, however, the Stockbridge Indians could never fully escape being thought of as neophytes or savages. They were forcibly relocated seven times before obtaining a small piece of land from the Menominee in what is now Wisconsin. As late as 1982, the Stockbridge Indians (known as the Mohican Nation) had to sue a museum in Massachusetts to have their original Bible and communion set recognized as their patrimony and returned to them.

SOLIDIFYING THE SUBJUGATION

A version of the Christian-influenced Doctrine of Discovery was institutionalized in the 1823 Supreme Court ruling in the case of *Johnson v. McIntosh.* The Court decided unanimously that Indian peoples were subject to the ultimate authority of the first nation of Christendom and the government was allowed to claim possession of a given region of Indian lands (Wheaton 1855, p. 270). In his opinion, Chief Justice John Marshall specifically cited the English Charter issued to John Cabot, which authorized Cabot to take land regardless of the occupancy of "heathens" or non-Christian people. Marshall claimed that this authorization carried over to the United States government. The Supreme Court reiterated the premise of the Doctrine of Discovery in its 1831 ruling in *Cherokee Nation v. Georgia* that the Cherokee Nation was not wholly sovereign and the United States did not have to recognize Indian Nations as free from United States control (Newcomb 1993, p. 4).

These rulings infused the religious doctrine of Christianity directly into United States law regarding the Indian problem. Hence, it could be said that the U.S. government became the ultimate missionary. By implicitly incorporating the distinction between Christian people and Native peoples, these rulings became the premise on which all legislation towards American Indians was based, beginning with the Indian Removal Act of 1830 and extending all the way through the Native American Graves Protection and Repatriation Act of 1990.

Thus, the Doctrine of Discovery became incorporated into the law of the land, subsumed under the nationalistic ideology of Manifest Destiny, the belief that it was the Christian God's will to expand "white American's liberty" from the Atlantic to the Pacific, and used by politicians and expansionists to further the goals of conquest. Andrew Jackson, a politician who had long been involved militarily in Indian conquest, cleared the way for the southeastern land grab by putting forth and signing legislation known as the 1830 Indian Removal Act. Explicitly allowing the government to "negotiate" land-based treaties with the tribes and "encourage" them to relocate on land acquired through the Louisiana Purchase west of the Mississippi, the unscrupulous tactics used in obtaining treaties and subsequently removing Indians from their lands was far from voluntary. For instance, the Treaty of New Echota, which required Cherokee removal, was not signed by the leaders of the tribe, but it was enforced at gunpoint. Many southeastern Indians were strong stewards of their land and quite proficient in agriculture, making their land prime real estate. Even though many Native communities in this region had welcomed missionaries, established churches, and sometimes used enslaved Africans to farm their land, the intersection of Western capitalism and the ideology of Manifest Destiny continued to fuel the push for land. The Five Civilized Tribes (the Cherokee, Chickasaw, Choctaw, Creek, and Seminole Nations) were removed from their land and several thousand Native people died on the trek to the newly named "Indian Territory" because the government did not provide adequate transportation and provisions. The federal government had contracted these services out to the lowest bidder and did not follow up to see if the supplies and health care were adequate. This forced genocidal trip is known as the "Trail of Tears."

As romantic stories from explorers such as Lewis and Clark about the available fertile land on the other side of the Mississippi spread eastward, the ideology of Manifest Destiny became even more pronounced, fueled by visions of a transcontinental railroad and great wealth in the form of natural resources such as gold. Another factor that played into expansionism and Manifest Destiny was the addition of more than a million square miles of land in what is now the western United States. This land was acquired through war with Mexico and the Treaty of Guadalupe Hidalgo. The United States also "inherited" the indigenous peoples of this area. The Indians of the western United States had previous contact with the Spaniards and had already experienced the Doctrine of Discovery through Spanish rule. The Mission Indians of southern and central California were used as forced labor on their own land by the twenty-one Spanish missions established from 1769 to 1823. Part of their "education" was being indoctrinated into the Catholic faith. The Pueblo Indians of the Southwest had also encountered the Spanish settlers, and by the 1500s many of them had faced forced conversion to the Catholic religion.

ASSIMILATION

In 1849 the Bureau of Indian Affairs (BIA) transferred administrative responsibilities from the War Department to the Department of the Interior. The shift was based on

PUCK.
PUCK'S SOLUTION OF THE INDIAN QUESTION.
If the Regular Army can't Handle the Hostiles, let us send a Detachment of the Salvation Army to Frighten them into Submiss

Native Americans Afraid of the Salvation Army, 1890. *The efforts of missionaries to Christianize and "civilize" American Indians also served to destroy the traditional Native way of life.* THE LIBRARY OF CONGRESS.

fiscal reasoning, for it was getting more and more expensive to guard the settlers as more of them continued to pour westward. It was simply less expensive to assimilate American Indians than kill them. Carl Schurz, the commissioner of Indian Affairs after the Civil War, argued that the estimated cost of killing an Indian in warfare was approximately a million dollars and educating them was approximately twelve hundred dollars (Adams 1995, p. 20). Thus the emphasis on an assimilationist educational policy was based on fiscal reasoning rather than any recognition of humanity.

A war-weary United States changed its policy towards American Indians after the Civil War. The Peace Commission of 1867 was developed to study the "Indian Problem," resulting in the onset of President Ulysses S. Grant's Peace Policy in 1869. The policy marked a significant transition in religious conversion efforts, which now came to include more Protestant influences, including Quakers and Episcopalians. Furthermore, the policy continued to solidify "civilization" efforts through assimilationist Christian policy versus warfare. Orthodox "Friends" were appointed by President Grant to serve as Indian agents and superintendents. A group of highly religious men, their purpose was to promote civilization of Indians via Christianity conversion. The "Friends," upon the request of Grant, met to identify and provide recommendations for appointments to the Indian agent posts. Once in place, not unlike previous conversion efforts, agents were empowered to assess the seriousness with which Indians repented their past ways and converted fully to Christianity. The position of agent and superintendent was delicate and ripe with power and reward.

The Dawes Act of 1887 created a land allotment system that would divide tribal lands into parcels for individual Indians. The intent was to break up the communal land holdings of tribes and establish tribal adult males as the archetypical freeholding yeoman farmers often associated with the formation of the United States.

The dismantling of traditional economic systems through individualizing and taxing Indian lands was imperative in bringing forth Christian civilization. Politicians and missionaries alike argued that allotment was necessary in order to transform the tribal heathens into Christians and productive taxpaying members of Christendom. The "Indian Problem" would resolve itself as Native people became fully assimilated as landholding, taxpaying Christians.

INDIAN SCHOOLS

Again, the imposition of Christianity was to play a significant role in federal education policy. Missionaries played a considerable role in enacting the concept of "killing the Indian and saving the man." The government awarded tribal lands to churches with the understanding that they would support the government's goal of assimilation. Often, when the federal government did not want to follow through on their treaty obligations to educate, they would pay missionaries to set up schools or contract with established churches on the reservations to educate American Indians. The Tulalip Indian Mission School, located in the Puget Sound area in the American Northwest, became the first contracted school in 1857. Mission schools followed a curriculum that attempted to indoctrinate Native students into a Christian lifestyle.

Most of the educational opportunities offered to reservation Indians during this era were in federal or church-run boarding and day schools. Children were often forcibly removed from parents to attend the twenty-five off-reservation schools. Parents were often left with no choice but to send their children away, as the Indian agent used this as a bargaining chip for provisions. Parents were told that their children would be taken care of and would have food to eat on a regular basis. The goal of these institutions, whether federal or church-based, was to eradicate any cultural traits that white society deemed as savage or heathen. These schools were the first "English Only" educational institutions, and they integrated biblical principles into the curriculum. There was no separation of church and state in the educational process, a core theme that ran through the educational process was one of equating civilization with Christianization.

Thus, the shift away from physical genocidal policies allowed the federal government to use more subtle methods of cultural ethnocide. The idea was to focus on the younger generations and teach them that Indianness was bad and uncivilized, whereas whiteness was good and civilized. Further, one could not be civilized or "good" without being Christian. Most of these schools stressed vocational and agricultural training, limited contact with families, and boarded students out during school vacations with "good Christian families." These students were to practice the vocational or domestic skills they were "learning" in schools at these white homes, which were often affiliated with community churches.

In 1926, at the behest of the Secretary of the Interior Hubert Work, a government study of Indian conditions was undertaken. The Merriam Report (named for Lewis Merriam, who headed the study) came out in 1928. The report was exceptionally critically of this type of "education," and the system soon began to be dismantled. However, it is important to note that some federal boarding schools for American Indians still exist in the first decade of the twenty-first century. This failed ethnocidal federal policy may have been one of the most damaging undertaken in Indian Country, for it removed children from their families and cultures and taught them that Indianness was shameful.

TRIBAL GOVERNMENT, TERMINATION, AND RELOCATION

By the turn of the twentieth century, Christianity and Indian Policy in the United States were so entangled that they could not be separated, though not many policymakers were concerned about the enmeshment. One official did recognize how assimilationist policies were damaging American Indian cultures. John Collier became Indian commissioner in 1933, and he challenged the entanglement of missionaries in American Indian affairs. His concerns led to the Indian Reorganization Act, also known as the Wheeler-Howard Act of 1934. The act allowed tribes to establish tribal governments and govern themselves, at least to some extent. However, these newly established tribal governments were modeled after the U.S. legislative model, not on traditional Native social, political, and economic systems.

Collier's reforms and ideals about preserving traditional cultural patterns encountered a response movement among Protestant missionaries and certain politicians to advocate for the end of federal guardianship of American Indians and the eradication of the BIA. Their philosophy of "rapid assimilation" advocated that the BIA and trust relationships inhibited assimilation into white Christian society. Gustavus Lindquist, a leader of the Home Missions Council, was at the forefront of the termination and urban relocation policies of the mid-twentieth century.

The termination policy was first termed "liquidation" and was supported by politicians and Christian organizations alike. According to the Menominee Nation Web site the "termination" program was a federal policy of forcing tribes to assimilate by withdrawing federal supervision. This meant releasing the government from its obligation to protect the sovereign rights of American Indian tribes. This policy also served as a catalyst for urban relocation. The idea of urban relocation was to remove American Indians from their culture and force them into white society. Relocation agents often met the relocated individuals and families the first time in urban centers and provided them with nominal assistance to get started in their "new life." It was very common for the relocation officer to arrive with a local minister or pastor in tow to help the removed American Indians adjust to their new surroundings. Relocation was quite simply an extension of termination. The congressional termination of tribal status would resolve the "Indian Problem" and force American Indians to adapt once and for all to white society. It was common for politicians and religious advocates of this ethnocidal policy to use assimilated Indians as examples, and these individuals also misrepresented the implications of termination. These assimilated Indians were often referred to as "mixed-bloods" by religious leaders and politicians with the clear inference that their "white blood" and acceptance of Christianity made them "acceptable" Indians.

Like numerous other genocidal and ethnocidal federal policies, termination and relocation forced many American Indians into an underclass in urban centers and created another land grab in Indian Country. Many terminated tribes, such as the Menominee Nation in Wisconsin and the Klamath in Oregon, had rich timber resources and lumber mills. Termination allowed lumber companies and land developers to encroach on these lands that were formerly held in trust. Termination eroded more of the land base of numerous tribes that had the misfortune to experience this federal policy. However, many tribes fought back. The Menominee people established grass roots efforts such as the Determination of Rights and Unity of Menominee Shareholders (DRUMS), and Menominee social reformers worked to halt the sale of land within the reservation boundaries and restore the federal status it had formally held. The Menominee Restoration Act (Public Law 93-197) was signed into law by President Nixon on December 22, 1973. Tribal assets and land were returned to trust status; however, the development of Legend Lake (prime lake-front real estate largely owned by whites) and the establishment of Menominee County were not reversed.

THE LATE TWENTIETH CENTURY: THE STRUGGLE CONTINUED

Federal policies regarding American Indians during the late twentieth century had a less religious overtone than previously, but the ideals of the Doctrine of Discovery still existed. The federal government continued its nonrecognition of American Indians as completely separate sovereign entities. Without such a change, the perception of "domestic dependency" creates an environment in which American Indians must negotiate a highly politicized system created and reinforced by the Doctrine of Discovery at several levels. Federal, state, and local governments continually demand that tribal political entities not be treated as equals, and each level of government creates obstacles for sovereign tribal governments.

While many American Indian Nations exercise their political power through the United States court systems, they are continually forced to negotiate their cultural and spiritual beliefs. The constitutional framers appropriated Christian language when creating the separation of church and state. The language was crafted in such a way that only Christian theology defined sacredness. Indigenous sacredness, because it did not fall under the auspices of this theology, was completely disregarded. In the twenty-first century, concepts of sacredness in the United States continue to be framed in a Christian context, forcing American Indian people who adhere to traditional belief systems to have to define what is sacred against a Christian backdrop.

The unfairness of this is illustrated by the way that places sacred to Native peoples, such as Devil's Tower in Wyoming and the Black Hills of South Dakota and Wyoming, are a common tourist site for mainstream Americans. It is very uncommon to see people climbing or using the Vatican as a recreational activity, or having to explain the use of a rosary during a religious ritual, but American tourists see no problem in climbing Devil's Tower or using other sacred Native sites as recreation areas. Many American Indian Nations have had to fight to claim their ancestors' remains and sacred objects from museums, universities, and private collections, even after the Native American Graves Protection Act was passed in the late twentieth century. Some scientists fail to recognize the sacredness or "ownership" of tribal cultural patrimony.

The Doctrine of Discovery was forced upon Native peoples by missionaries, who used languages the Indians did not completely understand. As this absolute ideology was put into effect, it brought disease, exploitation, and violence. It has been more than five hundred years since Pope Nicholas issued his edict against non-Christian peoples, and American Indians are still resisting efforts to be subjugated to the Doctrine of Discovery.

BIBLIOGRAPHY

Adams, David Wallace. 1995. *Education for Extinction: American Indians and the Boarding School Experience, 1875–1928.* Lawrence: University Press of Kansas.

Berkhofer, Robert, Jr. 1971. "Protestants, Pagans, and Sequences among the American Indians, 1760–1860." In *The American Indian: Past and Present,* edited by Roger Nichols and George Adams, 120–131. Waltham, MA: Xerox College Publishing.

Brasser, Ted. 1974. *Riding on the Frontier's Crest: Mahican Indian Culture and Culture Change.* Ottawa: National Museums of Canada.

Churchill, Ward. 1998. *A Little Matter of Genocide: Holocaust and Denial in the Americas, 1492 to the Present.* San Francisco: City Lights Books.

Coleman, Michael C. 1985. *Presbyterian Missionary Attitudes toward American Indians, 1837–1893.* Jackson: University Press of Mississippi.

Daily, David W. 2004. *Battle for the BIA: G.E.E. Lindquist and the Missionary Crusade against John Collier.* Tucson: University of Arizona Press.

Newcomb, Steve. 1993. "The Evidence in Christian Nationalism in Federal Indian Law: The Doctrine of Discovery, Johnson and McIntosh, and Plenary Power." *The New York University Review of Law and Social Change* 20 (2).

Wheaton, Henry. 1855. *Elements of International Law,* 6th ed. Boston: Little Brown, and Co.

L. Marie Wallace
Amy Fischer Williams

Korean Market in Los Angeles. *This market was ransacked during riots in 1992, but in just five years it was rebuilt and has become a successful part of the community. The representation of Asian immigrants as models for others has bred resentment against Asian Americans.* AP IMAGES.

MODEL MINORITIES

The term *model minority* refers to a racialized or ethnic minority that has achieved success within the parameters of a dominant culture. Such groups are held up as a model of behavior for less successful or problem minorities. The representation of Chinese and Japanese Americans as model minorities was popularized in the mid-1960s through the publication of two essays: "Success Japanese American Style," which appeared in the *New York Times Sunday Magazine* in January 1966, and "The Success Story of One Minority in the U.S.," a story about Chinese Americans that was published in *U.S. News and World Report* in December 1966. Both articles contrasted a narrative of Asian-American self-sufficiency and assimilation with the militant demands placed on the American polity by African Americans demanding recognition of civil and economic rights.

Japanese and Chinese Americans might have been surprised to read of their histories described as models of successful assimilation. For Japanese Americans the price of assimilation had been very high. During World War II they were subject to mass incarceration and the theft of their property, and after the war they witnessed the dispersal of their communities. And while there was an emergent Chinese-American middle class in the mid 1960s, American Chinatowns had some of the most overcrowded and dilapidated housing in the country. Rates of tuberculosis and other diseases of poverty were epidemic in these communities. Nevertheless, in the early 1960s the political repression of these communities was nearly complete. The Japanese communities had been dismantled and dispersed, while the Chinese communities, which included a large number who had entered the United States in violation of the Chinese Exclusion Acts, had faced the threat of deportation if they did not conform to the anticommunist orthodoxy of the 1950s. The resulting political silence of these communities was precisely the quality that critics of black empowerment and affirmative action policies valued most highly. The myth of successful assimilation into the American way of life by eschewing political struggle became an enduring racial stereotype of the Asian-American community.

The Asian-American community grew, due to immigration, from just under one million in 1970 to just over 12 million in 2000. The Asian-American immigrant population in the early twenty-first century is characterized by a large percentage of middle-class professionals alongside a high percentage of poor and less skilled immigrants. The claim of Asian-American upward mobility is disputed however with the relatively large number of professional and managerial immigrants in the population accounting for the statistical claim that the Asian-American population as a whole has been successful. The myth of Asian-American academic success based on supposedly traditional Asian cultural values of obedience, hard work, self-sufficiency, and discipline has been held up as a model for other "problem" groups, notably African Americans, Latinos, and, more recently, the "slacker" children of working-class and middle-class whites.

The use of racial stereotypes of Asian Americans to control or discipline other groups is an old political ploy. In the 1870s the image of Chinese workers as nimble, quick-witted, docile, and disciplined was commonly counterpoised in newspapers and trade journals with stereotypes of the "problem" Irish, who were portrayed as drunkards and troublemakers.

Not surprisingly the representation of Asian immigrants as models for others has bred resentment against Asian Americans. In the nineteenth century the image of Chinese workers as docile fuelled claims by opponents of Chinese immigration that the Chinese were "coolies," servile and unfit for organization. In the late twentieth century the tale of Asian-American success through thrift and self-sufficiency gave rise to resentment on the part of African Americans and Latinos, about whom the reverse is often claimed. It also caused resentments among white middle-class families who see their children pitted "unfairly" against Asian-American students in academic settings.

Many Asian Americans, especially those who come from working-class and refugee families, do not meet the expectations that teachers and colleagues have formed, based on the stereotype of the high-achieving "model minority" student. These students and workers are often consigned to invisibility in academic and work settings. As a matter of public policy, Asian Americans are often excluded from educational programs designed to benefit underrepresented minorities, despite the fact that certain Asian ethnic groups, such as the Hmong and Khmer, are dramatically underrepresented in higher education. Some Asian Americans have themselves adopted a belief in the model minority stereotype, leading them to believe in a cultural or even genetic superiority, and hence an attitude of racial superiority.

SEE ALSO *Film and Asian Americans.*

BIBLIOGRAPHY

Bascara, Victor. 2006. *Model-Minority Imperialism*. Minneapolis: University of Minnesota Press.

Klineberg, Stephen. 1996. *Houston's Ethnic Communities, Third Edition: Updated and Expanded to Include the First-Ever Survey of the Asian Communities, Executive Summary*. Houston, TX: Rice University. Available from http://cohesion.rice.edu/centersandinst.

Lee, Robert G. 1999. *Orientals: Asian Americans in Popular Culture*. Philadelphia, PA: Temple University Press.

Pettersen, William. 1966. "Success Story: Japanese American Style." *New York Times Magazine*. January 9: 180.

Tuan, Mia. 1998. *Forever Foreigners or Honorary Whites?: The Asian Ethnic Experience Today*. New Brunswick, NJ: Rutgers University Press.

U.S. News & *World Report*. 1966. "The Success Story of One Minority Group in the U.S." December 26: 73–76.

Wu, Frank. 2002. *Yellow: Race in America beyond Black and White*. New York: Basic Books.

Robert G. Lee

MONTAGU, ASHLEY
1905–1999

One of the most successful and prolific scholars of anthropology of the twentieth century, Ashley Montagu is most noted for addressing important social issues in terms accessible both to scholars and to the lay public. Born in London in 1905 (as Israel Ehrenberg), he was educated at University College, London and at the London School of Economics. After leaving England and settling in the United States, Montagu taught anatomy at the Graduate School of Medicine, New York University, from 1931 to 1938. After earning his Ph.D. in anthropology from Columbia University in 1937, he taught at the Hahnemann College of Medicine in Philadelphia and then at Rutgers University from 1949 to 1955 (as well as, briefly, at New York University, Harvard, and Princeton). He was a scholar with a significant record of scientific work and a record of iconoclastic ideas about anthropological problems. He had a history of challenging anthropological shibboleths and some of their famous proponents. In one instance, he attacked a physical typology of criminals proposed by the enormously influential anthropologist E. A. Hooton.

After retiring from Rutgers in 1955, Montagu shifted his focus increasingly toward the study of social problems, becoming a very effective social critic. He became widely renowned as a public speaker, occasionally appearing on television. His success as a "popularizer" of anthropological ideas and his own iconoclastic ideas made him anathema to a discipline priding itself on its relative inaccessibility to the public. But despite his "outsider" status, he was ultimately awarded both the Distinguished Achievement Award of the American Anthropological Association and the Darwin Award of the American Association of Physical Anthropologists.

Montagu wrote about an enormous range of topics, including the nature of humanity; "race" and racism; evolution and genetics; sexuality, reproduction, childbirth, and breastfeeding; gender and women's rights; anatomy; aggression, violence, criminality and war; creationism; and even Joseph Merrick (the "Elephant Man"). Of a total of more than eighty books, his most important works include *Man's Most Dangerous Myth: The Fallacy of Race* (1942, with multiple revisions through 1977), *The Natural Superiority of Women* (1953; revised ed. 1970), *The Concept of Race* (1964), *The Elephant Man* (1971), *The Nature of Human Aggression* (1976), and *Science and Creationism* (1984).

Montagu was an early "feminist" and an early critic of the concept of "race." Much of his most important work focused on dispelling the myth of "race." His analysis embraced not only blacks but also Native Americans and Jews. He has been called the most important theorist of race and race relations of the twentieth century. Montagu was one of the first to argue forcefully that the human species could not, scientifically, be divided into "races" despite the assumption, very widespread in both scholarly and popular circles, that such races were not only well defined but blindingly obvious. A key argument was (at first in theory, later as a matter of fact) that the various traits thought to be packaged in stereotyped groups actually had independent and only partly overlapping distributions. A second key argument was that the boundaries of traits such as color were not abrupt but gradual, over geographic space, a pattern that had earlier been described as "clines." Neither concept was entirely original to Montagu, as he admitted, but he was responsible for their broadest and most broadly influential presentation.

His stance on race, racism, and inherent human equality figured in the 1954 *Brown v. Board of Education* decision by the U.S. Supreme Court, and he was the primary author of the *United Nations Statement on Race* (1949). His book *Man's Most Dangerous Myth: The Fallacy of Race*, first issued at the height of Nazi power and American racism, is arguably his most important work, standing as a landmark criticism of both race and racism that anticipated and helped frame much of the subsequent debate over racial issues by defining (and to a significant degree anticipating and answering) the questions involved: human biology and the erroneous perception of the existence of "races" and "racial" diversity; eugenics and genetic equality; the interaction of biological and social forces in defining human behavior; cultural definitions of race; and the role of race perceptions in social issues such as aggression, war, the measure of intelligence, and democracy itself. This book and a later edited volume, *The Concept of Race* (1964), still stand as significant rebuttal of contemporary racist assertions.

SEE ALSO *Clines and Continuous Variation; Genocide; Genocide and Ethnocide; Great Chain of Being; Racial Hierarchy.*

BIBLIOGRAPHY

PRIMARY WORKS

Montagu, Ashley. 1942. *Man's Most Dangerous Myth: The Fallacy of Race.* New York: Columbia University Press.

———. 1953. *The Natural Superiority of Women.* New York: Macmillan.

———. 1964. *The Concept of Race.* New York: The Free Press of Glencoe.

———, ed. 1975. *Race and IQ.* New York: Oxford University Press.

———. 1976. *The Nature of Human Aggression.* New York: Oxford University Press.

SECONDARY WORKS

Brace, C. Loring. 1997. "Foreword." In *Man's Most Dangerous Myth: The Fallacy of Race,* 6th ed., by Ashley Montagu, 13–23. Walnut Creek, CA: AltaMira Press.

Marks, Jonathan. 2000. "Ashley Montagu: 1905–1999" *Evolutionary Anthropology* 9 (3): 111–112.

———. 1979. *The Elephant Man: A Study in Human Dignity.* New York: Outerbridge and Dienstfrey.

———, ed. 1984. *Science and Creationism.* New York: Oxford University Press.

Mark Nathan Cohen

MORTON, SAMUEL GEORGE
1799–1851

Samuel George Morton, anatomist, physician, and "ethnologist," has been called the father of physical anthropology in America. Morton was born in Philadelphia, and his Irish immigrant father died when the boy was only six months old. His mother enrolled him in Friends' boarding schools for his education. The visits of many doctors during his mother's illness in 1817 brought Morton into contact with the medical profession. After her death, he entered the service of Philadelphia physician Dr. Joseph Parrish and earned his medical degree from the University of Pennsylvania in 1820 (Hrdlička 1943). At the same time, he was elected into the Philadelphia-based Academy of Natural Sciences.

After attaining his degree, Morton traveled to Ireland to visit his uncle, James Morton, with whose financial support he undertook further medical training at the University of Edinburgh (Stevens 1856). At Edinburgh, Morton encountered the phrenologist George Combe and became acquainted with the most current trends in craniological research. This included phrenology, in the midst of a wave of support across Europe, as well as the researches into racial differences by Johann Blumenbach.

When he returned to Philadelphia to establish his medical practice in 1824, Morton also pursued his interest in natural history. This interest was quite varied: Some of his earliest scientific work concerned the description of fossils from Cretaceous and other geological contexts, including his description of invertebrate fossils collected by Lewis and Clark (Morton 1834). He was elected to the American Philosophical Society in 1828, and became professor of anatomy at Pennsylvania College in 1839 (American Philosophical Society 2002). During his early career he also advanced within the ranks of the Academy of Natural Sciences, attaining the office of secretary in 1831. Ultimately, he acceded to the presidency of the academy in 1849; by this time he had become one of the most celebrated scientists in the United States.

Morton attained renown for his study of the craniological variation between human races. What made the work distinctive was Morton's large collection of skulls, which at the time of his death was the largest such collection anywhere in the world. Morton acquired skulls by correspondence with naturalists, scientific authorities, explorers, and many others. In some instances, he exchanged skulls to build his collection, some were gifts, and others came at considerable expense. After Morton's death in 1851, his collection was entrusted to the Academy of Natural Sciences and was augmented by further skulls solicited by Morton and others. The collection was later housed at the University of Pennsylvania Museum, where it continued to be a valuable resource for anthropological and medical research.

Morton's first major work of anthropological import was the book *Crania Americana* (1839), in which he investigated the craniological characters of present and ancient Americans in relation to the races of the Old World. This book is notable for Morton's conclusions that all the indigenous peoples of the Americas shared a common origin, that their features at once join them together and render them distinct from the races of the Old World and that these craniological differences were present in ancient specimens from the Mound Builders. Because of the antiquity of these cranial characters, Morton inferred that racial differences must have been inherent from creation, not induced by the environment or climate later in history. *Crania Americana* is notable for Morton's relatively neutral approach to measurement and comparison, as he did not interpret the features in phrenological terms, although he did include an essay on this subject by George Combe, who held that Native Americans but not blacks were naturally "savage" and impervious to training.

The interpretation of racial antiquity was the subject of his second major work, *Crania Aegyptaica* (1844). Morton had acquired a substantial sample of ancient Egyptian remains through the efforts of the American consul to Alexandria, George R. Gliddon. Gliddon himself argued for the antiquity of races based on pictorial representations on ancient Egyptian monuments. On the basis of the crania, Morton concluded that racial differences were in fact as pronounced 4,000 years or more ago as in the present day. This result conflicted with the belief in unitary origins of humanity, as described in Genesis, and Morton approached a polygenic interpretation of human races. Polygenism was developed further by Gliddon and Josiah Knott, who argued for the specific diversity of Europeans and Africans.

Like most of his contemporaries, Morton took for granted an implicit ranking of human races. Accepting Blumenbach's five-race categorization, Morton focused particularly on cranial capacity as the important factor differentiating them in terms of mental capacity. In his measurements, Caucasians (Europeans) sat at the highest rank, proceeding through Mongolians (Asians), Malay, Americans, and Ethiopians (Africans) at the lowest cranial capacity. He assumed a one-to-one relationship between cranial size and intelligence level. According to an 1849 study by Morton, his skull size measurements yielded these results: English skulls capacity, 96 cubic inches; Germans and Americans, 90 cubic inches; blacks, 83 cubic inches; the Chinese, 82 cubic inches; and Native Americans, 79 cubic inches (Gossett 1963, p. 74)

These results and his researches into the antiquity of racial differences gained political importance, as Morton—at the urging of Gliddon—advised Secretary of State John C. Calhoun on African racial qualities in support of the continuation of slavery (Stanton 1960) as a positive good.

In the late twentieth-century, Morton's empirical work came under scrutiny. After reanalysis of Morton's data tables, paleontologist Stephen Jay Gould suggested that Morton's summary statistics reflected "unconscious finagling," reinforcing interracial differences (Gould 1978, 1981). Gould noted a number of potential biases, in particular the inclusion of a higher proportion of small and female crania—as well as Australians—in Morton's "African" sample, the exclusion of small "Hindu" crania from Morton's "Caucasian" sample, and apparent discrepancies between measurements of the same crania taken using shot versus seed. However, a later consideration of these points by Michael (1988) found that Gould had mischaracterized Morton's tables and had disregarded errors that weighed *against* Morton's racial ranking. Michael interpreted Morton's work as having been "conducted with integrity" (1988, p. 353), although the work did contain errors and sample biases attributable to the haphazard collection strategy.

Morton's death in 1851 followed several years of illness from pleurisy, during which his work slowed. He was survived by his wife of twenty-four years, Rebecca Grellet Pearsall, and all eight of their children.

SEE ALSO *Cranial Index; Genesis and Polygenesis; Racial Hierarchy.*

BIBLIOGRAPHY

American Philosophical Society. 2002. "Background Notes." In Samuel George Morton papers. Philadelphia: American Philosophical Society. Available from http://www.amphilsoc.org/library/mole/m/mortonsg.htm.

Gossett, Thomas F. 1963. *Race: The History of an Idea in America.* Dallas, TX: Southern Methodist University Press.

Gould, Stephan Jay. 1978. "Morton's Ranking of Races by Cranial Capacity: Unconscious Manipulation of Data May Be a Scientific Norm." *Science* 200: 503–509.

———. 1981. *The Mismeasure of Man.* New York: Norton.

Hrdlička, Ales. 1943. "Contribution to the History of Physical Anthropology in the United States of America, with Special Reference to Philadelphia." *Proceedings of the American Philosophical Society* 87 (1): 61–64.

Michael, J. S. 1988. "A New Look at Morton's Craniological Research." *Current Anthropology* 29: 349–354.

Morton, Samuel G. 1834. *Synopsis of the Organic Remains of the Cretaceous Group of the United States*. Philadelphia: Key and Biddle.

———. 1839. *Crania Americana; or, a Comparative View of the Skulls of Various Aboriginal Nations of North and South America*. Philadelphia: J. Dobson.

———. 1844. *Crania Aegyptiaca; or, Observations on Egyptian Ethnography Derived from Anatomy, History, and the Monuments*. Philadelphia: J. Pennington.

Stanton, William. 1960. *The Leopard's Spots: Scientific Attitudes Toward Race in America 1815–59*. Chicago: University of Chicago Press.

Stevens, A. 1856. "Samuel George Morton and Ethnology." *The National Magazine* 9: 336–343.

John Hawks

MOTHERHOOD

It is tempting, especially in terms of feminist discourse, to define "motherhood" as a unifying, universal vocation that women can look to and through for a common ground on which to stand and understand each other. After all, as Naomi Lowinksy has stated, "Women are the carriers of the species, the entry way to life. Although a woman may choose not to have children or be unable to do so, every woman is born of woman. Every woman alive is connected to all the women before her through the roots of her particular family and culture" (2000, p. 230). This oft-assumed connection, however, can be lost or severed because of each woman's particular family and cultural roots and the interlocking structures of class and race that work together to create different definitions, ideas, stereotypes, and experiences of motherhood.

Every day, Americans are confronted by normative constructions of "ideal motherhood." The socioeconomic culture in the United States benefits and adheres to majority rule: White is right. Because the privileged American position is wealthy, white, and male, those in that position (or those who benefit from someone in that position) define the ideal American mother. Susan J. Douglas and Meredith W. Michaels, in their 2004 book, *The Mommy Myth: The Idealization of Motherhood and How It Has Undermined Women*, examine the constraints placed on even the most privileged (which they acknowledge) of American mothers, the middle- to upper-class white woman of the early twenty-first century. Through the media, and as a result of the progress that women, especially white women, have made in America via the women's movement (or because of the backlash against this movement), women are being coerced into believing "the new momism": that is, "that motherhood is eternally fulfilling and rewarding, that it is *always* the best and most important thing that you do, that there is only a narrowly prescribed way to do it right, and that if you don't love each and every second of it there's something really wrong with you" (Douglas and Michaels, p. 4). That white women especially are bombarded with such an idealization of motherhood in the first place is indicative of their recognition as normative mothers. As such, they are supposed to embody American expectations of motherhood and women: Have a career, but do not neglect your children, while looking good, consuming, and protecting your children from a seemingly endless number of internal and external threats. This stress is aggravated not only by the so-called mommy wars, which pit working (white) mothers against stay-at-home (white) mothers, but also by the pitting of white, ideal, supposedly capable mothers against unfit mothers—that is, women of color.

Whereas middle- to upper-class white women are ushered into fertility clinics when they have difficulty conceiving, women of color are still often scorned for having children, viewed by society as indiscriminate breeders. Patricia Hill Collins, in her 1994 essay, "Shifting the Center: Race, Class, and Feminist Theorizing about Motherhood," analyzes how race affects women's expectations and experiences of motherhood. Collins recognizes that "racial domination and economic exploitation profoundly shape the mothering context not only for racial ethnic women in the United States but for all women" (p. 56). Often, even feminist analysis of motherhood is done through a middle-class, white perspective: That is, women's experiences with motherhood are defined via a family with a male head of household—a nuclear family in which the father brings home the bacon, the mother/wife cooks it, and then Father and children eat it together while Mom hovers over them expectantly, anticipating needs for drink refills and napkins.

Experience for women of color mothers (and many white mothers) may be vastly different, as men may play an altogether different role in their lives, "since work and family have rarely functioned as dichotomous spheres for women of color" (Collins 1994, p. 58). To hold not only their own families, but entire communities together, mothers of color often work not just in the home, but outside it, in economically fragile positions, in contrast to ideals of stay-at-home motherhood.

AFRICAN-AMERICAN MOTHERS

Collins examines how survival itself is a prominent theme in the lives of mothers of color. Whereas "physical survival is assumed for children who are white and middle class ... racial ethnic children's lives have long been held in low regard. African-American children face a mortality rate twice that for white infants ... [and] one-half who survive infancy live in poverty" (p. 61). These grim statistics, however, are counteracted by the power and respect that can accompany motherhood for African-American women. "In a racist culture that deems black children inferior, unworthy, and unlovable, maternal love of black children is an act of resistance; in loving her children the mother instills in them a loved sense of self and high self-esteem, enabling them to defy and subvert racist discourses that naturalize racial inferiority and commodify blacks as other and object" (O'Reilly 2000, p. 151). The logic may follow, then, that if "motherhood is the pinnacle of womanhood," African-American women will strive to reach that pinnacle (O'Reilly, p. 150). In the process, African-American mothers may be sensationalized, served up by the media as "the hideous counter-examples good mothers were meant to revile … and were disproportionately featured as failed mothers in news stories about 'crack babies,' single, teen mothers, and welfare mothers" (Douglas and Michaels 2004, p. 20). What the news does not feature is the strength African-American women may draw from their communities, their children, and each other. "Many African-American women receive respect and recognition within their local communities for innovative and practical approaches to mothering not only their own biological children, but also the children in their extended family networks and in the community overall" (Collins 1994, p. 67). In spite of, or in response to, cultural standards of motherhood, African Americans can empower themselves through ways of mothering that do not fit the ideal.

NATIVE AMERICAN MOTHERS

The struggle for power can be a common one for women of color, as they "are concerned with the power and powerlessness within an array of social institutions that frame their lives" (Collins 1994, p. 64). Native American women (like African-American women and other women of color) traditionally relied on extended family formations to help raise children and maintain their power. However, as Mary Crow Dog describes in her 1990 autobiography, *Lakota Woman*, the white government of the United States worked to dissolve such family arrangements in order to promote nuclear family formation, which depleted women's autonomy. Government controls over and influence on Native American life have had serious impacts on how women have been able to mother. One way in which this can clearly be seen is through implementation of forced sterilizations of Native American women. Crow Dog's account reveals that her mother was sterilized without her permission after the birth of Crow Dog's youngest sister, "which was common at the time, and up to just a few years ago, so that it is hardly worth mentioning. In the opinion of some people, the fewer Indians there are, the better" (p. 9). Her sister was also sterilized after the birth of her first and only son, who died within a few hours of his birth. For Crow Dog, the attempted extermination of her people made her own motherhood more triumphant.

Sterilization was not the only form of powerlessness Native American women faced. For years, children were taken from their families and put into white (often religious) boarding schools, where attempts were made to strip them of their culture. Not only does the separation of child from mother create feelings of powerlessness for the mother, but, as Collins points out, "In contrast to middle-class white children, whose experiences affirm their mothers' middle-class values, culture, and authority, children [of women of color] typically receive an education that derogates their mothers' perspective" (p. 66). However, as Collins further explains, "A culture that sees the connectedness between the earth and human survival, and that sees motherhood symbolic of the earth itself holds motherhood as an institution in high regard" (p. 72). It is this view of motherhood, and firm connections to their culture, that can empower Native American women in their motherhood.

LATINA AND ASIAN-AMERICAN MOTHERS

Ideals of motherhood for Latina and Asian-American women are convoluted by American's mixed feelings about immigration. White Americans may view Latinas and Asian-American women as outsiders even when they are native citizens. On the other hand, Latina's mothering abilities are valued not only in their own communities, but by families who employ Latinas as nannies. When immigration is discouraged or actively fought against, as is often the case for Latin Americans, the message sent to these women is often "we don't want you; we certainly don't want your children." This sentiment can be seen not only through media, but also through various welfare reforms. As Lisa C. Ikemoto asserts in her 1999 essay, "Lessons from the *Titanic*: Start with the People in Steerage, Women and Children First": "Since employers use gender, race, ethnicity, and immigration status to structure the labor sectors, and since welfare reform is part of a larger economic restructuring that has a disproportionately negative impact on women. … [I]mmigrant Latinas and Asian women are among those who are taking the heaviest blows" (p. 159). While the media may focus on welfare abuse, immigrant women must negotiate ways in which to obtain work and help support their families. For Latina women, this may include a redefinition of conventional motherhood. Though traditionally motherhood has been emphasized in relation to the home, and therefore separate from employment and embodied in cultural figures such as the Virgin de Guadelupe, the economy may demand that mothers work for pay (Hondagneu-Soptela, Avila 1997, p. 551). Transnational mothers who must leave their children in their home country to work, often as domestics, for better pay in America, may define themselves as better mothers than the mothers they work for who can afford to pay for in-home care for their children while they pursue their own careers. Latinas' experiences and definitions of motherhood may vary widely depending upon their own economic condition and their necessity to alter their ideas of "good-motherhood" to include their own position.

Tied to the struggle of work and defining good motherhood is the struggle to form a bridge between two (or more) cultures, to teach the children they may be separated from or working alongside that leaving one land for another does not mean abandoning one's culture, even while the dominant American culture seeks to assimilate the children. Joonuk Huh, in her 2000 account, "Constantly Negotiating: Between My Mother and My Daughter," explains how when she is with her Korean mother, "I wish my mother would let me be my own person instead of insisting that I be a Korean woman.... [W]hen I resume my mother role ... I am confronted by my daughter's question. ... She is not happy with me for reminding her that she is Asian-American, not American" (p. 268). M. Elaine Mar reveals a similar struggle with her Chinese mother in her 1999 memoir, *Paper Daughter*. Working with her mother in her aunt's home and in their family restaurant, Mar struggles with her mother's seemingly contradictory pressures to both assimilate and remain a loyal Chinese daughter. "Many Asian-American mothers stress conformity and fitting in as a way to challenge the system" (Collins 1994, p. 71). This claim to American identity through performance, regardless of ethnicity, is one more way that women of color negotiate their roles as mothers.

The differences and similarities between motherhood for women of color and white women cannot be broken into sections, or easily summarized, and certainly not all can be included in an explanation as brief as this. For all mothers living in a system that privileges some and devalues the lives and experiences of others, motherhood cannot be viewed as a simple vocation. It must be examined through the many ways in which it is influenced by race, class, sexuality, ability, and other institutions that affect women's lives. Through multiracial feminism, it can be further understood how race affects everyone, in every social location. Motherhood, like other women's experiences, must be analyzed and understood with race as a crucial aspect of that understanding. Analyzing motherhood through only one lens provides a distorted and incomplete view. Only by incorporating race as one of these lenses can one hope to form a cohesive understanding of motherhood for the diverse women who define it how they may.

SEE ALSO *Adolescent Female Sexuality; Families; Sexuality.*

BIBLIOGRAPHY

Collins, Patricia Hill. 1994. "Shifting the Center: Race, Class, and Feminist Theorizing about Motherhood." In *Representations of Motherhood*, edited by Donna Bassin, Margaret Honey, and Meryle Mahrer Kaplan, 56–74. New Haven, CT: Yale University Press.

Crow Dog, Mary, and Richard Erdoes. 1990. *Lakota Woman*. New York: Harper Perennial.

Douglas, Susan J., and Meredith W. Michaels. 2004. *The Mommy Myth: The Idealization of Motherhood and How It Has Undermined Women*. New York: Free Press.

Hondagneu-Sotelo, Pierette, and Ernestine Avila. 1997. "I'm Here, but I'm There: The Meanings of Latina Transnational Motherhood." *Gender & Society* 11 (5): 548–571.

Huh, Joonuk. 2000. "Constantly Negotiating: Between My Mother and My Daughter." In *Mothers and Daughters: Connection, Empowerment, and Transformation*, edited by Andrea O'Reilly and Sharon Abbey, 267–275. Lanham, MD: Rowman and Littlefield.

Ikemoto, Lisa C. 1999. "Lessons from the *Titanic*: Start with the People in Steerage, Women and Children First." In *Mother Troubles: Rethinking Contemporary Maternal Dilemmas*, edited by Julia E. Hanigsberg and Sara Ruddick, 157–177. Boston: Beacon Press.

Lowinsky, Naomi. 2000. "Mother of Mothers, Daughter of Daughters: Reflections on the Motherline." In *Mothers and Daughters: Connection, Empowerment, and Transformation*, edited by Andrea O'Reilly and Sharon Abbey, 227–235. Lanham, MD: Rowman and Littlefield.

Mar, M. Elaine. 1999. *Paper Daughter: A Memoir*. New York: HarperCollins.

O'Reilly, Andrea. 2000. "'I Come from a Long Line of Uppity Irate Black Women': African-American Feminist Thought on Motherhood, the Motherline, and the Mother–Daughter Relationship." In *Mothers and Daughters: Connection, Empowerment, and Transformation*, edited by Andrea O'Reilly and Sharon Abbey, 143–159. Lanham, MD: Rowman and Littlefield.

Zinn, Maxine Baca, and Bonnie Thornton Dill. 1996. "Theorizing Difference from Multiracial Feminism." *Feminist Studies* 22 (2): 321–332.

Mary Alice Long

MOTHERHOOD, DEFICIENCY IN

Deficiency in mothering is an ideological construction that refers to the ways in which mothering among women of color in the United States has been racialized as inferior. This ideological construction is both supported and negated in the scholarly and popular literature on family, gender, race, and class. Historically framed through discussions of minority group family structure, patterns of intergenerational poverty, and the problems of deviant subcultures, these discussions have more recently taken shape around assertions of problems related to teen pregnancy and the ongoing presence of an urban underclass. Minority women, including African-American women and other women of color, are frequently presented in these discussions as bad mothers, women whose patterns of mothering deviate in significant ways from those of good mothers in ideal families. Alternative viewpoints, presented by feminist scholars beginning in the 1970s, suggest that these ideological constructions posit an idealized image of mothering that reifies the subordinate status of women, the public/private split, and the state-sanctioned family structure (Collins 2000, Neubeck and Cazenave 2001, Moynihan 1965, Wilson 1987).

THE IDEAL FAMILY AND THE GOOD MOTHER

The deficiency in mothering framework is developed against the backdrop of the ideal family and interpretations of the good mother. The ideal family form, which serves as the norm against which minority family behavior is compared, has been framed by scholars and policymakers alike as a family in which the mother is a heterosexual, white female who is wife to a family wage-earning white-male father and who is responsible for the care of her biological children (Coontz 1992, Collins 2000). The good mother in this ideal is not just a caregiver, but a primary caregiver who remains within the feminine private sphere while leaving the world of work safely framed as public and masculine. Not only is the good mother responsible for the physical care of her children, she is also responsible for their emotional and moral development. She is a natural mother standing ready to guide future generations toward public and private success as individuals, workers, and citizens. In order to accomplish this, the ideal mother must not undertake work in a public arena that would remove her from her children and her role as the guardian of civilization. It is against this normative ideal that racialized images of the bad mother are constructed.

THE BAD MOTHER

The ideal family and good mother images, based in the public/private split, with women in the home and men in the world of work, have never been viable options for women of color. Yet the experiences of these women have been measured by this standard, have been used as a warning against those who question the standard, and are blamed for the deterioration of social norms, social relations, and social structures in a social system they did not institute. By examining the assumptions of the discourses within which the idealized concept of motherhood is created, it is possible to see how the "bad" mother/"deficient" mother idea has played out over time.

The first assumption of the discourse on deficiency is that real men work and real women care for families. Against this ideal the experience of the enslaved African-American woman or the migrant Latina worker is immediately found to be deficient. For example, the African-American woman's experience has been shaped by the necessities of a capitalist system that initially required her to perform forced labor, and then segregated labor, before subsequently requiring her to either work in the lower segments of the economic sector or face an often hostile welfare system. Against the idealized criteria of the public/private split these women are immediately found to be deficient both as workers and as mothers. While her presence as a laborer supports the dominant social order, her presence at the work site as a laborer also breaks down the masculinized elements of the public sphere and undermines the ability of African-American men to claim the wage earner status of "real men." Women of color are nevertheless employed in various sectors of the work world. As chief executive officers of companies, as instructors in schools, on meatpacking lines, or in sweatshops, these women find themselves struggling against stereotypes of the masculinized public sphere. In essence the African-American, Latina, or Asian woman who works outside the home is not a real woman, and her presence in the workplace means that African-American, Latino, or Asian men cannot behave as real men (Collins 2000, Kimmel 2006).

Second, women of color are often labeled deficient because of their status as absent mothers. Immediately deficient as a woman, her presence in the paid workforce and absence from the home labels her family as abandoned and her children as neglected. While propping up the racial status quo by caring for the children of white owners or employers in place of the biological mother (e.g., women of color acting as mammies and nannies), the minority woman's absence from her own home also means an absence from her children and an abandonment of her duty as mother. The image that emerges from these analyses is one of a self-interested, authoritative abandonment of the traditional family and the authority of men and masculinity.

By the mid-1960s the image of the matriarch had been racialized. Patricia Hill Collins (2000) notes that before the 1960s connections between higher rates of African-American female-headed households and persistent poverty had been interpreted as an outcome of poverty, not its cause. Between the early 1960s and the mid-1970s, however, the perception of scholars and policymakers had changed. For example, Daniel Patrick Moynihan (1965) and Lawrence Mead (1986, 1992), writing about the experiences of women of color during this period, assert that the African-American matriarchal family no longer ascribed to core American values, including self-discipline, motivation, and perseverance. Since that point, matriarchy has been associated with bad mothering and the causal relationship reversed so that in the new analysis matriarchy causes deviant values and poverty. According to this viewpoint, the new norms of these families support single motherhood, out-of-wedlock births, criminal behavior, and the irresponsibility of men. Dependency scholars assert that because individuals socialized in these families will have low social mobility aspirations, teen pregnancy and intergenerational poverty will persist (Wilson and Neckerman 1986, Jarrett 1994).

Negative stereotypes of women of color and their families posit moral or psychological failure as the cause of numerous social problems. Analysts using this perspective suggest that matriarchal households are part of the underclass and that these households are the key contributors to the growth of this class, a class composed of the long-term poor and those who deviate from societal norms and values (Moynihan 1965, Wilson 1987, McLoyd et al. 2000, Neubeck and Cazenave 2001). From this viewpoint, matriarchs who call on the state for support are not recharacterized as good mothers trying to establish adequate care for their children, but are labeled as irresponsible. The failure to recharacterize these women as good mothers not only is due to a welfare racism interpretation of the matriarch, but is also associated with ideological constructions of the deserving poor. Because welfare is perceived as charity rather than an entitlement, and because the criteria for distribution is based on who is deserving, women of color who receive assistance find themselves labeled as needy and deficient rather than good and caring. Defining welfare as charity immediately places mothers who seek assistance outside the deserving category. As Nancy Fraser and Linda Gordon (1994) note, programs that many of these women have relied on, including Aid to Families with Dependent Children (AFDC), emphasize the criteria of "deserving," which by definition suggests that women who collect AFDC are getting something for nothing. For women of color there are few criteria outside of being self-sufficient or meeting the stereotype of a good (state-) dependent woman (i.e., white and widowed) that provides appropriate grounds for receipt of support or characterization as a good mother. Because under these ideological constructions being a self-sufficient worker is not possible for a person who is defined as a primary parent (i.e., mother), and because a recategorization as white is not feasible, it is impossible by definition for these women to ever meet the good mother criteria.

In the 1980s a new deficiency argument emerged that focused on the African-American, unmarried, teenage mother who is welfare dependent (Fraser and Gordon 1994, Neubeck and Cazenave 2001). Frequently discussed as a new syndrome, these young women are described as baby-making machines who obtain welfare dollars by having more children. Reports by various agencies and national campaigns point to teen pregnancy to explain poverty, welfare dependency, abuse, neglect, incarceration rates, low levels of educational attainment, and future out-of-wedlock births (Wilson and Neckerman 1986, National Campaign to Prevent Teen Pregnancy 2002). The teen mother is "caught in the 'welfare trap' and rendered dronelike and passive" (Fraser and Gordon 1994, p. 327). The new cultural image synthesizes previous stereotypes and establishes a characterization of deficient motherhood as a permanent passivity based in biology, psychology, socialization, and/or poverty (Fraser and Gordon 1994, Mead 1986, Wilson 1987). The beginning of the 1990s found such terms as *welfare queen*, *welfare chiselers*, and *children having children* within the public discourse, further racializing the practice of mothering among women of color in the United States.

PROPOSALS FOR SOLVING DEFICIENCY

Within the deficiency discourse is included a set of solutions meant to reify the existing social structure and maintain the racial status quo. Education programs aimed at "deficient" mothers are historically associated with Americanization programs initially designed during the Progressive Era of the late nineteenth and early twentieth centuries to educate and support immigrant women (Hartmann 1967 [1948]). These programs provided English skills, child-care instruction, and housekeeping classes that were intended to improve the immigrant woman's skills so that she could appropriately fit into American society and could socialize her children to be productive workers and good citizens.

Contemporary approaches to deficient mothers have been based in the constructed problems of matriarchy, teen pregnancy, and welfare dependency. Beginning in the 1960s, presented solutions have been based on strengthening the legitimate authority of the traditional family, reasserting the value systems of the dominant culture, increasing job opportunities for men who are racial minorities, and reforming the welfare system.

Since the 1960s suggestions for strengthening the African-American family have included encouraging the reduction of black male unemployment and reestablishing patriarchy in African-American families. In the 1960s and 1970s many scholars and policymakers thought that by engaging the structural issues of opportunity and employment for ethnic and racial minority men, and by reasserting a male-dominant authority structure for the family, dependency problems and motherhood deficiency issues could be alleviated. By the 1980s these changes had not occurred, and new ideological constructions suggesting deficiency in the form of teen pregnancy and the underclass took their place. Subsequent responses to these deficiency problems suggest eliminating women's independent income acquired through programs such as AFDC, and relying on retraining programs that eliminate state dependency and instill dominant values and norms associated with ideal family forms.

Since 1996, programs designed to meet the requirements of that year's Personal Responsibility and Work Opportunity Reconciliation Act have been put in place to provide incentives to mothers to get off welfare and become self-sufficient. The Temporary Assistance for Needy Families program is implemented at the state level with various regulations that are tied to receiving temporary assistance. In many instances mothers who were previously on AFDC and are still in need of state assistance are either required to receive a short period of training (i.e., twenty-four months) linked to employment or they must find immediate employment or volunteering opportunities. Women who do not participate will not receive assistance (Collins 2000, Jennings and Santiago 2004, Seccombe 2007). In addition to this self-sufficiency solution, women of color have also been encouraged to rely more directly on the fathers of their children for support. Both the self-sufficiency model and the reliance on fathers model emphasize the ideological constructions of motherhood deficiency and dependence, and they posit solutions that racialize and genderize both the problem and the solution.

THE FEMINIST RESPONSE

Feminist responses to motherhood deficiency arguments turn the tables on both structural and cultural understandings used by dependency scholars and policymakers alike. They assert that proposed solutions that accept the deficiency interpretation fail to adequately interpret structural problems associated with ghettoization, industrial flight, mechanization, school segregation, and other macro factors that affect female and male economic vulnerability. In addition, dependency interpretations that reinsert a patriarchal structure as a solution fail to recognize the subordinate place of minority men in the racial power structure and the implications of this fact for the lives of racial minorities. When a privileged white form of legitimacy within the family is the proposed solution, alternative family forms are undermined and dismissed. Establishing a system in which there is an adequate income may be more important to the well-being of the family than reshaping the family around patriarchal patterns of power. The welfare reform practices of the early twenty-first century have also racialized poverty and its solutions. By ignoring the fact that the majority of people on welfare are white, and by instituting programs that fail to establish long-term self-sufficiency for poor families, proposed solutions continue to label women of color as deficient and dependent, and problematize them and their families (Glenn, Chang, and Forcey 1994; Collins 2000; Jennings and Santiago 2004).

SEE ALSO *Adolescent Female Sexuality; Families; Sexuality.*

BIBLIOGRAPHY

Collins, Patricia Hill. 2000. *Black Feminist Thought: Knowledge, Consciousness, and the Politics of Empowerment*, rev. ed. New York: Routledge.

Coontz, Stephanie. 1992. *The Way We Never Were: American Families and the Nostalgia Trap*. New York: Basic.

Fraser, Nancy, and Linda Gordon. 1994. "A Genealogy of *Dependency*: Tracing a Keyword of the U.S. Welfare State." *Signs* 19 (2): 309–336.

Glenn, Evelyn Nakano, Grace Chang, and Linda Rennie Forcey. 1994. *Mothering: Ideology, Experience, and Agency*. New York: Routledge.

Hartmann, Edward George. 1967 (1948). *The Movement to Americanize the Immigrant*. New York: AMS Press.

Jarrett, Robin. 1994. "Living Poor: Family Life among Single Parent, African American Women." *Social Problems* 41: 30–49.

Jennings, James, and Jorge Santiago. 2004. "Welfare Reform and 'Welfare to Work' as Non-Sequitur: A Case Study of the Experiences of Latina Women in Massachusetts." *Journal of Poverty* 8 (1): 23–42.

Kimmel, Michael. 2006. *Manhood in America: A Cultural History*, 2nd ed. New York: Oxford University Press.

McLoyd, Vonnie C., Ana Mari Cauce, David Takeuchi, and Leon Wilson. 2000. "Marital Processes and Parental Socialization in Families of Color: A Decade Review of Research." *Journal of Marriage and the Family* 62 (4): 1,070–1,093.

Mead, Lawrence M. 1986. *Beyond Entitlement: The Social Obligations of Citizenship*. New York: Free Press.

———. 1992. *The New Politics of Poverty: The Nonworking Poor in America*. New York: Basic.

Moynihan, Daniel Patrick. 1965. *The Negro Family: The Case for National Action*. Washington, DC: U.S. Government Printing Office.

National Campaign to Prevent Teen Pregnancy. 2002. *Not Just Another Single Issue: Teen Pregnancy Prevention's Link to Other Critical Social Issues*. Washington, DC: Author.

Neubeck, Kenneth J., and Noel A. Cazenave. 2001. *Welfare Racism: Playing the Race Card against America's Poor*. New York: Routledge.

Seccombe, Karen. 2007. *Families in Poverty*. New York: Allyn and Bacon.

Wilson, William Julius. 1987. *The Truly Disadvantaged: The Inner City, the Underclass, and Public Policy*. Chicago: University of Chicago Press.

———, and Kathryn M. Neckerman. 1986. "Poverty and Family Structure: The Widening Gap between Evidence and Public Policy Issues." In *Fighting Poverty: What Works and What Doesn't*, edited by Sheldon H. Danziger and Daniel H. Weinberg, 232–259. Cambridge, MA: Harvard University Press.

Colleen Greer

MOVIES AND THE POLITICS OF RACE

SEE *Filmography* in the Appendix at the end of Volume 3.

MULTICULTURALISM

The 1997 publication of Nathan Glazer's *We Are All Multiculturalists Now* signaled the ubiquity and apparent inescapability of multiculturalism in general, and multicultural education in particular, within the United States. Yet this characterization is also applicable to various other Anglophone nations, such as Canada, Britain, and Australia, each of which is a multicultural society, characterized by both racial and sociocultural diversity and by multicultural discourse. Despite its ubiquity, or perhaps because of it, multiculturalism has developed multiple meanings, depending on who employs the term and the context in which it is employed. Multiculturalism has been adopted internationally and is variously employed as a description of contemporary societies and communities characterized by racial, ethnic, and cultural diversity; as an official national and institutional policy that recognizes diversity; as a unifying national concept; as a principal marker of national identity and guideline for citizenship; as a collective description of various forms of identity politics; and as a political stance on how to address social and cultural diversity in society and in communities. Apart from this multiplicity of usages, a continuum of political positions (e.g., conservative, liberal, left-essentialist, radical left) is reflected in various expressions of the term. Thus, multiculturalism has multiple, and competing, meanings.

The consideration of issues of race and racism is an integral aspect of multiculturalism. In fact, one of the principal ways in which one can distinguish between different forms of multiculturalism is by the degree to which they address race and racism specifically, and more generally how they address the larger context of social and cultural discrimination based on difference and equity. Because racial classification has mutated repeatedly (e.g., from being based on religion, then phenotype, then culture, and, most recently, on population genetics), the attendant problem of racism has proven to be something of a moving target while remaining doggedly enduring. Some forms of multiculturalism have downplayed or euphemized race and racism as "culture" and "cultural difference," while others have taken them up as a crucial aspect of multiculturalism.

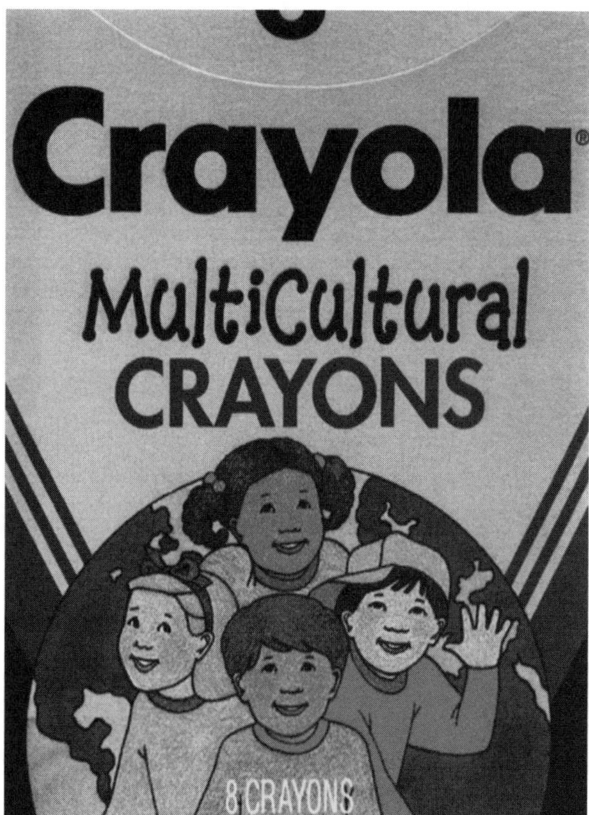

Multicultural Crayons. *To help children embrace the many cultures that surround them, Crayola developed crayons in eight different skin hues which provide a more realistic palette for coloring the world.* AP IMAGES.

THE ORIGIN AND EMERGENCE OF MULTICULTURALISM

The term *multiculturalism* was coined by a Royal Commission in Canada in 1965, and Canada was the first country to establish multiculturalism as national policy (through the Multicultural Policy of 1971 and the Multicultural Act of 1988). As other countries have developed multiculturalism as a discourse and educational approach (e.g., the United States), and in some cases as policy as well (e.g., Australia), they have understandably concentrated on their national narratives of origin, and their accounts almost never mention the Canadian origins of the term. In every country in which multiculturalism has emerged, it has done so in response to the need to address or manage increasing diversity, which is often linked to changes in immigration policy and the coming to voice of minority groups. In the Australian context, immigration led to the doubling of the population between World War II and 2002. At the same time, countries like Lebanon (in the 1970s), Hong Kong (in the early 1990s), and China and South Africa (since the 1990s) have rivaled the United Kingdom as the principal source of immigrants in Australia (see Hill and Allan 2004). Similarly, in Canada, increased migration from continental Europe (and the flexing of these minority groups' political clout) disrupted the "two solitudes" (French and English settler peoples) conception of Canada. This change led to Prime Minister Pierre Trudeau creating the "Policy of Multiculturalism within Bilingual Framework" in 1971.

While the emergence of multiculturalism has served to strengthen democracy by espousing a cultural (and presumably, racial) level playing field and celebrating diversity, multiculturalism has had a very awkward relationship with indigenous peoples in the Australian,

American, and Canadian contexts. For indigenous peoples, struggles by relatively late-coming European occupiers or colonizers to move beyond the "two solitudes" in Canada, or to open up immigration beyond predominantly British migrants in Australia, stand outside their own struggles to be recognized as the original peoples of the land—and to have historical treaties honored and atrocities against them addressed.

THE POLITICAL CONTINUUM OF MULTICULTURALISM

The form of multiculturalism that is most well known all over the world—and on which multiculturalism policy is usually based, and which most people have encountered and think of when they conceptualize multiculturalism in the singular—is liberal, celebratory multiculturalism. This form of multiculturalism breaks with assimilationist, monocultural conceptions of nation and posits a multicultural conception that identifies and celebrates both broad cultural categories and the cultural diversity that results from their juxtaposition with each other. Canada, for example, often employs the metaphor of the mosaic to describe itself. A mosaic of cultures cemented together by nationalism conjures an image of a multicolored beauty and a vibrancy of difference and variety, as well as the unity of the Canadian nation. Such an image stands in sharp contrast to the blandness of monoculturalism. There is resistance to liberal multiculturalism, however, from both the left and the right. Right-wing critics are suspicious of liberal multiculturalism, considering it a threat to the unity of the nation and established, supposedly unifying, traditions. Critics on the left assert that liberal multiculturalism, especially liberal multicultural education, concentrates altogether too much on celebrating rather than interrogating sociocultural difference. They point to the emphasis on a sharing of music, national dress, and foods, claiming this creates a "steel band, sari, and dim-sum" multiculturalism. Leftists hold that multiculturalism pays little attention to the pivotal issue of power differentials between the racial and ethnic groups within a nation, and that it does not address the resulting problems of sociocultural inequalities and discrimination in general, and white racism more specifically.

Responses to liberal multiculturalism have not been limited to critiques. Rather, in the United States in particular, they have also fostered the development of various types of multiculturalism, which are reflective of a continuum of political positions. A few leftist American cultural critics and educators have undertaken the useful work of identifying what might be conceptualized as discrete forms of multiculturalism, or as points on a political multicultural continuum. For example, Peter McLaren, a professor of education at the University of California, Los Angeles, identifies these points as conservative, liberal, left-liberal, and critical multiculturalism. The leftist category of "critical multiculturalism" has been expanded by other figures such as Henry Giroux, Shirley Steinberg, and Joe Kincheloe to include resistance, insurgent, and revolutionary multiculturalism. These leftist forms have some variations in emphasis, but they share the general approach of addressing power and working for social justice, equity, and a radical democracy. They consider overtly addressing sociocultural difference and discrimination based on difference, and particularly the central problem of white racism, as integral to their efforts.

ANTIRACISM AND OTHER ALTERNATIVES TO MULTICULTURALISM

While critical figures in the United States have chosen to put forward alternative interpretations and discourses of multiculturalism to compete with the dominant liberal, celebratory multiculturalism, their counterparts in Britain and Canada have chosen to eschew multiculturalism as inherently flawed, opting to develop British and Canadian versions of antiracism instead. Antiracist theory, policy, and discourse cut straight to what is seen as the heart of the matter, namely the need to address two central issues: (1) the power differential between whites and people of color, and (2) racism at various levels (e.g., individual, institutional, and social). Critiqued for not addressing other forms of sociocultural difference, antiracists have developed versions such as "integrative antiracism," which does address sociocultural difference in general but keeps race and racism as pivotal issues of concern.

Indigenous peoples have been wary of and had an awkward relationship with multiculturalism in countries such as Australia, Canada, and the United States. The struggles of indigenous peoples to be recognized as original people of the land (literally "First Nations" in Canada) means they have positioned themselves outside multiculturalism, so that Native education in the United States, Aboriginal education in Australia, and indigenous education in Canada are separate discourses from multicultural education (see Archibald 1995). In contrast with its former colonies, multiculturalism in the United Kingdom does not have to deal with the added wrinkle of the place of indigenous peoples in relation to dominant, settler populations (though the Irish in Northern Ireland might well beg to differ).

The Quebecois in Canada also position themselves outside of multiculturalism. They have struggled to maintain their identity and culture as a people, and they see multiculturalism as a policy that diminishes their status and stake in both Canada and North America. This is seen as reducing them from being one part of two solitudes to being merely one culture among many in the Canadian mosaic, and as threatening the viability of a small French-language culture in a North American continent dominated by the English language. There were several attempts to constitutionally recognize Quebec and the Quebecois as a "distinct society," (e.g., in failed Meech Lake Accord of the late 1980s and Charlottetown Accord of the early 1990s), and Canada's Parliament voted in 2006 to recognize Quebec as "a nation within the nation of Canada." Furthermore, the policy of "interculturalism" (which espouses French language and francophone culture as dominant and integrates newcomers into both) has been implemented in the province of Quebec.

THE STATUS QUO OF MULTICULTURALISM

Despite the challenges to it, multiculturalism has remained the dominant discourse and policy of choice in Anglophone countries, and its presence and presumed permanence is not taken for granted. There are new challenges facing multiculturalism, however, particularly from globalization, late capitalism, and the waning of the very notion of the nation-state. The increased movement of people, goods, and information around the world (and the attendant establishment of new discourses such as transnationalism and cosmopolitanism) threatens to render multiculturalism obsolete. Furthermore, the 9/11 bombings in the United States and the 7/7 bombings in Britain have led to a rise in Islamophobia and questions about cultural diversity in both countries (especially about official multiculturalism in Britain). The argument can be made—and indeed ought to be made—that what is needed is a strengthening rather than a questioning of multiculturalism. Meanwhile, even though Glazer's declaration still holds true in the twenty-first century, multiculturalists are left to wonder not whether we are all multiculturalists, but how much longer we will be multiculturalists.

SEE ALSO *Australian Aborigine Peoples; Brazilian Racial Formations; Canadian Racial Formations; Immigration to the United States; Indigenous; Language; Nativism; Social Welfare States; United Kingdom Racial Formations.*

BIBLIOGRAPHY

Archibald, Jo-Ann. 1995. "To Keep the Fire Going: The Challenge for First Nations Education in the Year 2000." In *Social Change and Education in Canada*, 3rd ed., edited by Ratna Ghosh and Douglas Ray. Toronto: Harcourt Brace.

Braham, Peter, Ali Ratansi, and Richard Skellington, eds. 1992. *Racism and Antiracism: Inequalities, Opportunities and Policies.* London: Sage.

Dei, George. 1996. *Anti-Racism Education: Theory and Practice.* Halifax, NS: Fernwood Press.

Gagnon, Allaine. 2002. "Problems and Limits of Multiculturalism: A View From Quebec." In *Multiculturalism in Contemporary Societies: Perspectives on Difference and Transdifference*, edited by Helmbrecht Breinig, Jürgen Gebhardt, and Klaus Lösch. Erlangen, Germany: University of Erlangen-Nurnberg Press.

Glazer, Nathan. 1997. *We Are All Multiculturalists Now.* Cambridge, MA: Harvard University Press.

Government of Canada. 1988. *Canadian Multiculturalism Act.* Statues of Canada, c.31.

Hill, Bob, and Rod Allan. 2004. "Multicultural Education in Australia: Historical Development and Current Status." In *Handbook of Research on Multicultural Education*, 2nd ed., edited by James Banks and Cherry A. McGee Banks. San Francisco: Jossey-Bass.

McLaren, Peter. 1994. "White Terror and Oppositional Agency: Towards a Critical Multiculturalism." In *Multiculturalism: A Critical Reader*, edited by David Theo Goldberg. Oxford, U.K.: Blackwell.

Quebec Ministry of Community, Culture, and Immigration. 1990. "Let's Build Quebec Together: A Policy Statement on Immigration and Integration." Montreal, Quebec: Minitere des Communautes Culturelles et de l'Immigration du Quebec.

Handel Kashope Wright

MULTIRACIAL IDENTITIES

Racial boundaries in the United States have historically been constructed in such a manner that racial groups and identities have been viewed as rigid and mutually exclusive categories of experience. These boundaries have been constructed and reinforced through *rule of hypodescent*—a social code that forces the offspring of interracial unions to identify with only one of their backgrounds—coupled with pervasive state laws prohibiting interracial marriage. Together, these mechanisms have helped to obfuscate, if not completely obscure, the complex history of racial blending in the United States. However, since the removal of the last antimiscegenation laws in 1967 (through the U.S. Supreme Court decision in *Loving v. Virginia*), growing numbers of individuals, especially the offspring of interracial marriages, have asserted multiracial identities that reflect their various backgrounds. The growth of a multiracial consciousness is reflected in a movement initiated in the late 1970s to change standards in racial-data collection at the federal, state, and municipal levels to allow for the expression of these multiracial identities.

THE RULE OF HYPODESCENT

The rule of hypodescent has historically suppressed the expression of a multiracial identity by relegating the racial group membership of the offspring of unions between European Americans and Americans of color exclusively to their background of color (e.g., Native American, Asian American, Pacific Islander American, Latino American, African American). This rule has been such an accepted part of U.S. racial "common sense" that its oppressive origins have often been obscured. European Americans began enforcing the rule of hypodescent in the late 1600s in order to draw social distinctions between themselves and subordinated groups of color. The rule was implemented primarily to regulate interracial sexual relations and, more specifically, interracial marriages in an attempt to preserve so-called white racial purity. However, hypodescent has also helped maintain white racial privilege by supporting other legal and informal barriers to racial equality in most aspects of social life, reaching extreme proportions at the turn of the twentieth century with the institutionalization of Jim Crow segregation. These barriers have existed in various forms in public facilities and other areas of the public sphere, such as the educational, occupational and political structure, as well as in the private sphere (e.g., neighborhoods, associational preferences, and interpersonal relationships).

The rule of hypodescent has been applied most stringently (depending upon the background of color) to the first-generation offspring of European Americans and Americans of color. Meanwhile, successive generations of individuals with European ancestry and a background of color have typically not been designated exclusively, or even partially, as members of that group of color if the background is less than one-fourth of their lineage. For these multigenerational individuals, self-identification with the background of color has been more a matter of choice. However, this flexibility has not been extended to individuals of African American and European American descent. Both the first-generation offspring of interracial relationships between African Americans and European Americans and later-generation descendants have experienced the most restrictive variant of the rule of hypodescent: the one-drop rule.

The one-drop rule designates everyone with any amount of African American ancestry ("one-drop of blood") as black. It precludes any choice in self-identification and ensures that all future offspring of African-American ancestry are socially designated as black. Though variations of the rule of hypodescent have been applied elsewhere to individuals with varying degrees of African ancestry (such as in South Africa), the one-drop rule is unique to the United States. It emerged between the late seventeenth and early eighteenth centuries and had the benefit of exempting white landowners (particularly slaveholders) from the legal obligation of passing on inheritance and other benefits of paternity to their multiracial offspring. By the 1920s, the one-drop rule had become the common-sense definition of blackness, and it had been internalized among the vast majority of African-descent Americans.

U.S. attitudes toward the offspring of unions between African Americans and other groups of color (e.g., Native Americans) have varied. More often than not, these individuals have been subject to the one-drop rule. However, there has been greater ambivalence regarding the classification of offspring whose ancestry reflects the combination of groups of color other than African Americans. This is partially due to the fact that these other groups of color have occupied a more ambiguous position in the U.S. racial hierarchy. For example, individuals of Mexican or Asian-Indian ancestry have been alternately classified as either white or nonwhite, according to federal court decisions, state legislation, and policies of government bureaucracies (such as the Census Bureau). Membership in these groups—except perhaps in the case of Native Americans—has also been less clearly defined in U.S. law. Consequently, the racial subordination of Americans of color by European Americans, while oppressive, has not been the same as that of African Americans. Some members of these groups have sought a more intermediate position in the racial hierarchy by avoiding contact with what they perceived as more subordinate groups of color. Still others have forged multiethnic communities of color. For example, Karen Leonard has traced the formation of Punjabi Mexican American communities in California's agricultural valleys, while Rudy Guevarra has researched the Mexipino (Mexican and Filipino) community in San Diego.

In the 1960s and 1970s, notions of racial purity that had supported the ideology of white supremacy were increasingly repudiated in the United States. Many European Americans, nevertheless, continued to maintain identities and privileges based on white racial exclusivity that originated in the rule of hypodescent. Moreover, this rule has had some unintended consequences for groups of color, especially African Americans. By drawing boundaries that would exclude Americans of color from having contact as equals with European Americans, it has legitimated and forged group identities among the former that have become the basis for mass mobilization and collective action in the struggle against racial inequality. These dynamics have thus helped reinforce, even if unintentionally, the notion that European Americans (and whiteness) and Americans of color inhabit categories of experience that are mutually exclusive, if not hierarchical, and that they each have an objective and independent existence of their own.

RESISTANCE TO HYPODESCENT

Though many individuals of African-American and European-American descent have internalized the one-drop rule, identifying themselves solely as black, some have engaged in various tactics of resistance to this rule. One historical form of resistance is "passing," in which individuals of a more European-American phenotype and cultural orientation have made a covert break with the African-American community, either temporarily or permanently, in order to enjoy the privileges of the white community. Though commonly viewed as a form of opportunism, G. Reginald Daniel has argued that "passing may be seen as an underground tactic, a conspiracy of silence that seeks to beat oppression at its own game" (2002, p. 49). Those individuals who were unwilling or unable to pass distanced themselves from the black masses by forming elite groups known as "blue-vein societies." These societies flourished in the nineteenth and early twentieth centuries in cities such as Charleston, Philadelphia, Nashville, Louisville, New Orleans, Boston, New York, Atlanta, and particularly Washington, D.C. to mention only a few. Entrance into these exclusive societies depended upon one's physical and cultural approximation to European Americans. Though such elites vigorously opposed any forms of segregation that would restrict them to African-American social spaces, they understood themselves to be a privileged class of a stigmatized minority. Thus, many were sympathetic to the plight of less fortunate African Americans.

While blue-vein societies constituted an urban elite situated within the African-American community, other multiracial individuals formed communities apart from both blacks and whites, either on the fringes of villages and towns or in isolated rural enclaves. These communities are known as "triracial isolates" because the members of such communities often have varying degrees of European-American, Native American, and African-American ancestry. These groups have historically affirmed only two components of their ancestry, Native American and European American, and some have fought for federal recognition as "nontreaty Native Americans." Meanwhile, "Creoles of color" in Louisiana and the Gulf ports of Mobile, Alabama, and Pensacola, Florida, sought to maintain the racial privilege and intermediate status they enjoyed during the period of French and Spanish rule in the region. Some resisted the decline in their status after the U.S. annexation of Louisiana (1803) and the Floridas (1810, 1819) by denying any similarity or community with English-speaking African Americans, while others openly challenged the onslaught of segregationist policies in the post-Reconstruction period. Still others attempted to pass for white, while some left for Mexico or the Caribbean.

Generated by racist pressure that has rewarded whiteness and punished blackness, all of the above tactics of resistance devised by multiracial individuals have been less of a reaction to the forced denial of their European-American ancestry than to the denial of the privileges that have accrued to such ancestry. Though challenging and subverting the one-drop rule, these tactics were rarely aimed at challenging the hierarchy between whiteness and blackness. In particular, tactics such as passing and the formation of blue-vein societies shaped and perpetuated a pernicious *colorism* among African-descent Americans, resulting in the preferential treatment of individuals who have more closely approximated whites in terms of consciousness, behavior, and phenotype.

Though the centrality of regulating racial blackness in U.S. jurisprudence and the entire legal apparatus supporting racial segregation gave African-descent Americans a more immediate impetus for racial passing, ultimately, some degree of social stigma has been attached to all groups of color in the United States. This stigma would provide an incentive for multiracial individuals with other ancestries of color and European background to pass as white. However, the key distinction between the experience of African-descent Americans and other groups of color lies in the more flexible application of the rule of hypodescent to the latter ancestries of color. Typically, individuals with less than one-fourth of a non-African ancestry of color in their lineage may not have even been designated as partially of color, obviating the need for racial passing. Indeed, a number of multiracial individuals have successfully negotiated white identities, despite having known Mexican or other Latino ancestry or Native American ancestry. These have included some of the offspring of intermarriages between elite Mexican landowners and white settlers in California, as well as a few film actors and entertainers of partial Mexican or other Latino descent or Native American descent.

MULTIRACIALITY AND MARGINALITY

Due to the multidimensional nature of their identity, multiracial individuals operate on the margins of several racial groups. Prior to the 1970s, this marginality, or sense of being "betwixt and between," was seen as the source of lifelong personal conflict, necessarily resulting in psychological maladjustment and pathology. Admittedly, such theories emerged at a time when the United States was significantly more hostile to the affirmation of a multiracial identity. However, these theorists did not focus on the sociological forces that made psychological functioning difficult for multiracial individuals. Rather, multiracial individuals were characterized as psychologically dysfunctional because this image reinforced what Cynthia Nakashima calls an existing "multiracial mythology" that discouraged racial blending, thereby protecting so-called white racial purity and racial dominance (1992, p. 164). These traditional frameworks were largely based on misinterpretations of the sociologist Robert E. Park's "marginal man" thesis. Though Park envisioned the marginal man as a person who stood on the margin of two racial/cultural worlds, and thus not fully a member of either world, he nevertheless argued that such a position could provide an individual with a broader vision and wider range of sympathies due to the ability to identify with more than one racial or cultural group.

THE EMERGENCE OF MULTIRACIAL IDENTITY

Increasingly, growing numbers of individuals have begun to embrace a multiracial identity. These individuals consider themselves to be members of more than one racial group, and they have thus challenged traditional U.S. racial categories and boundaries. The expression of this new multiracial identity originated in changes that have taken place since the dismantling of Jim Crow segregation—particularly the removal of the last laws against intermarriage in the 1967 decision in *Loving v. Virginia*—and the implementation of civil rights legislation during the 1950s and 1960s. The comparatively more fluid intergroup relations led to more extensive interracial marriage and a substantial increase in the number of multiracial births. However, up until the 2000 census, statistical surveys did not make it possible to tabulate reliable figures on the population of offspring from these unions. Nevertheless, census data indicate that the number of children born of interracial parentage grew from less than a half million in 1970 to about two million in 1990.

THE MULTIRACIAL MOVEMENT

As the number of interracial marriages and of births of multiracial offspring have increased, parents of multiracial children and multiracial-identified individuals have formed support groups and organizations. Such groups have sought to promote healthy images of multiracial children, and they have pursued, among other agendas, the official recognition of a multiracial identity from local, state, and federal agencies. The oldest of such organizations currently in existence, I-Pride (Interracial/Intercultural Pride), founded in 1979 in Berkeley, California, successfully petitioned the local school district to implement an "interracial" category on school forms. Though it was the first such category in U.S. history, it was later restricted to internal district uses only, based on federal regulations that did not allow such a category.

By the 1990s, I-Pride had become part of a coalition of more than fifty other grassroots organizations that had come into existence since the late 1970s, and this coalition began pressuring the federal government to revise its racial-data collection standards, particularly with regard to the decennial censuses. This coalition included the Association of MultiEthnic Americans (AMEA), a national umbrella organization that represented fourteen support groups based in various metropolitan areas in the United States, and Hapa Issues Forum (HIF), a national organization consisting of individuals of partial Asian/Asian American or Pacific Islander descent. Other organizations included A Place for Us National, a nondenominational religious support network for interracial families, and Project RACE (Reclassify All Children Equally), an activist, informational and educational organization that had successfully advocated for the implementation of a multiracial category on various municipal and state government forms. In terms of the census, these and other organizations, along with individual activists, sought the implementation of a "combined format" that would include a separate multiracial category but would also allow individuals to check all applicable boxes corresponding to their racial backgrounds. (Though an "other" category had been provided on each census since 1910, write-in responses to this category had been reassigned to one of the traditional racial categories until the 1990 Census).

The movement to revise federal data-collection policy was not without controversy. Several traditional civil rights organizations initially objected to the proposed inclusion of a multiracial category to the race question on the census, expressing concern over how such a category might impact the tabulation of data for underrepresented groups of color for the purposes of enforcing civil rights legislation. Specifically, they argued that a stand-alone multiracial identifier would lead to a loss of numbers. Consequently, their opposition was informed in part by the perception that multiracial movement activists were merely seeking to add a stand-alone multiracial category to the race question. Various factors contributed to this erroneous interpretation, including media coverage and the somewhat ambiguous statements of movement leaders themselves.

Furthermore, activists in the movement ultimately split over the racial data collection format they sought to implement. Faced with likely opposition from both traditional civil rights organizations and various government agencies that require data on race and ethnicity, multiracial movement leadership met on June 7, 1997 in Oakland, California, and ultimately withdrew its support for the combined format. Instead, they settled on a revised model presented by Project RACE that recommended a "check more than one box" option without a separate multiracial category. However, the leadership of Project RACE—perhaps under pressure from its constituents—eventually retracted support for its own revised model and returned to its original goal of implementing a "combined format."

On July 9, 1997, the Office of Management and Budget (OMB), the branch of government responsible for implementing changes in federal statistical surveys, announced its recommendations for "check more than one box" format without a multiracial category or any mention of the word multiracial in the race question. (Officials in Washington, D.C., were unaware that multiracial movement leaders had arrived earlier at a similar proposal.) Following the OMB recommendations, organizations such as Hapa Issues Forum and the AMEA elicited support from traditional civil rights organizations, including the NAACP, the Japanese Americans Citizens League, and the Mexican American Legal Defense and Education Fund, for the check more than one format. Meanwhile, Project RACE, joined by APUN and other individual activists, continued to advocate for a multiracial category in the combined format.

Their objections were based in part on the fact that individuals who checked more than one box would be retrofitted into the single-racial categories comprising their ancestry for the purposes of civil rights enforcement rather than being counted as a distinct "multiple race" population. Consequently, these activists did not consider the OMB's recommendations to be a significant advance over methods of data collection and tabulation in previous censuses. Nevertheless, the OMB's final decision on October 31, 1997 supported the "check one or more" format. Following the OMB's final decision, the AMEA itself was incorporated in an oversight committee related to the census.

Since the OMB announcement in 1997, some multiracial organizations (such as the AMEA and Project RACE) have focused on securing compliance with recent changes in federal racial classification standards from school districts and state universities. Meanwhile, a number of organizations (such as Swirl, Inc., and the MAVIN Foundation) have been initiated by multiracial adults with the purpose of building and strengthening a pan-multiracial community among the growing population of individuals who claim more than one racial background. Swirl Inc. is a New York–based organization with chapters in several major metropolitan areas in the United States and Japan. The MAVIN Foundation is a Seattle-based nonprofit organization that has developed a host of projects, including a magazine, a resource book on multiracial children, and a bone marrow drive, aimed at raising awareness about the needs of multiracial offspring and at fostering a sense of community.

In the early twenty-first century, both the MAVIN Foundation and the AMEA are working together on a national resource center for research on multiracial families and offspring. Similarly, multiracial student organizations have proliferated on college and high school campuses through the United States. Furthermore, the growth of the Internet has facilitated the formation of an online multiracial-identified community, reflected in a variety of Web sites and Web logs (or blogs) that encompass a range of perspectives with regard to the politics of race. These include online journals that have been established since the mid- to late-1990s, such as *Interracial Voice* and the *Multiracial Activist,* as well as more recently formed sites, such as Mixed Media Watch.

THE MULTIRACIAL IDENTITY PARADIGM

A multiracial identity is not indicative of someone who simply acknowledges the presence of various ancestries in their background. Consequently, this identity differs from members of traditional U.S. racial groups, such as African Americans or Latino/Hispanic Americans, who may have (and acknowledge) multiple racial backgrounds but affirm monoracial (i.e., single-racial) identities. Multiracial individuals seek to replace these one-dimensional identities with more multidimensional configurations. In addition, a multiracial identity bears similarity to, yet is not synonymous with, a multiethnic identity. The latter is displayed by individuals who consider themselves to be members of several groups that are thought to be racially similar but culturally different (e.g., English American–Swedish American or Chinese American–Japanese American). Though both sets of identities may incorporate and reflect the sense of bridging culturally distinct communities, a multiracial identity incorporates the axis of racial difference that has been the more significant basis for social inequality in the United States.

Likewise, a multiracial identity is not the same as a multicultural identity. A multicultural identity is applicable to any individual who, irrespective of ancestry, displays a general openness and sensitivity to racial and cultural differences. Thus, they have an affinity with the values, beliefs, and customs of more than one racial or cultural context due to an exposure to multiple racial and cultural groups. By comparison, multiethnic individuals feel a sense of kinship with several groups directly in response to the multiple cultural backgrounds in their genealogy. Similarly, multiracial individuals feel a sense of kinship with several groups directly in response to the multiple racial backgrounds in their genealogy. Exposure to these backgrounds enhances this feeling of kinship, though simple awareness of them can bring about this sentiment.

The new multiracial identity, unlike previous forms of resistance to the rule of hypodescent, is not premised on the desire to gain privileges that would be precluded by identifying oneself as a person of color. Consequently, this identity is not synonymous with the divisive colorism perpetuated by tactics such as passing and the formation of blue-vein societies. Nor it is the equivalent of efforts to claim and maintain a less subordinate position in the racial hierarchy, as with the strategies of the triracial isolates and some Creoles of color. Rather, the new multiracial identity contests the mutually exclusive nature of U.S. racial boundaries, and it challenges the hierarchical valuation of racial (and cultural) differences. This identity recognizes the commonalities among various communities in the manner of integration while simultaneously appreciating their differences in the manner of pluralism. Moreover, this identity is premised upon the equal valuation of racial and cultural differences and similarities between various communities. Consequently, those communities are seen as relative, rather than absolute, extremes on a continuum of grays.

RECENT DATA AND RESEARCH ON MULTIRACIAL IDENTITY

Beginning in the 1980s, a new wave of research emerged that challenged and refuted earlier theories of marginality that stressed psychological dysfunction. The researchers doing this work have agreed that multiracial-identified individuals may experience various ambiguities, strains, and conflicts in a society that views racial identities as mutually exclusive categories of experience. Yet such potentially negative feelings associated with marginality can be counterbalanced by an increased sensitivity to commonalities and an appreciation of racial and cultural differences in interpersonal and intergroup situations. More recent studies have shown little difference between multiracial offspring and their monoracial counterparts on various measures of psychological adjustment and self-esteem. Furthermore, researchers have focused on how the articulation of a multiracial identity has become more commonplace among the offspring of interracial marriage (even among black-white offspring), although some individuals may select more traditional monoracial identities.

Figures from Census 2000 indicate that, nationwide, 2.4 percent of the population, or 7.3 million people, identified with more than one race in 2000. The largest combination was White and "Some Other Race," constituting 32 percent of the "Two or More Races" population, followed by White and American Indian/Alaskan Native (17%), White and Asian (12%), and White and Black (11%). These four combinations constituted more than 70 percent of the Two or More Races population. Given that the Census Bureau treats Latinas/os separately as an ethnic group with the option of selecting one or more racial categories, it is difficult to discern which multiple-race responses are representative of the products of Latino intermarriage. However, nearly one in three (31%) of those who identified with two or more races also identified as of Hispanic or Latino origin, perhaps reflecting the more extensive historical patterns of racial blending and the more widespread acknowledgment of this phenomenon in some Latino countries of origin. The largest percentage of the Two or More Races population (40%) was concentrated in the western United States, with Hawaii, Alaska, and California reporting the highest percentages of multiracial-identified individuals out of the fifty states. Considering the ever-increasing racial and ethnic diversity of the United States, as well as the increased opportunities for intergroup contact due

The Twelve Largest Two or More Race Combinations on the 2000 Census

Combination	Number	% of U.S. Pop.	% Two or More Races Pop.
Total	7,270,926	2.58	100.1[a]
White; Some other race	2,322,356	0.83	31.9
White; American Indian and Alaska Native	1,254,289	0.45	17.3
White; Asian	862,032	0.31	11.9
White; Black or African American	791,801	0.28	10.9
Black or African American; Some other race	206,941	0.16	6.4
Asian; Some other race	280,600	0.10	3.9
Black or African American; American Indian and Alaska Native	206,941	0.07	2.8
Asian; Native Hawaiian and Other Pacific Islander	138,556	0.05	1.9
White; Black; American Indian and Alaska Native	116,897	0.04	1.6
White; Native Hawaiian and Other Pacific Islander	111,993	0.04	1.5
American Indian and Alaska Native; Some other race	108,576	0.04	1.5
Black or African American; Asian	106,842	0.04	1.5
All other combinations[b]	507,340	0.18	7.0

[a]Note: The percentages do not sum to 100.0 due to rounding.

[b]"All other combinations" includes the remaining 45 combinations of individuals reporting more than one race. None of the remaining combinations totaled more than 100,000 people.

SOURCE: Adapted from U.S. Bureau of the Census. 2005. "We the People of More Than One Race in the United States." *Census 2000 Special Reports*, table 1 and figure 1.

Table 1.

to the greater integration of persons of color into the public and private sphere, the numbers of multiracial-identified individuals will certainly continue to grow in the United States.

BIBLIOGRAPHY

Association of MultiEthnic Americans. Available from http://www.ameasite.org.

Daniel, G. Reginald. 2002. *More than Black? Multiracial Identity and the New Racial Order.* Philadelphia, PA: Temple University Press.

Guevarra, Rudy P. 2005. "Burritos and Bagoong: Mexipinos and Multiethnic Identity in San Diego, California." In *Crossing Lines: Race and Mixed Race Across the Geohistorical Divide*, edited by Marc Coronado, Rudy P. Guevarra, Jr., Jeffrey Moniz, and Laura Furlan Szanto. Lanham, MD: Altamira Press.

Hapa Issues Forum. Available from http://www.hapaissuesforum.org.

Interracial Voice. Available from http://www.interracialvoice.com.

Leonard, Karen Isaken. 1992. *Making Ethnic Choices: California's Punjabi Mexican Americans.* Philadelphia, PA: Temple University Press.

MAVIN Foundation. Available from http://www.mavinfoundation.org.

Mixed Media Watch. Available from http://www.mixedmediawatch.com.

Multiracial Activist. Available from http://www.multiracial.com.

Nakashima, Cynthia L. 1992. "An Invisible Monster: The Creation and Denial of Mixed-Race People." In *Racially Mixed People in America*, edited by Maria P. P. Root. Newbury Park, CA: Sage.

Project RACE. Available from http://www.projectrace.com.

Root, Maria P. P., ed. 1992. *Racially Mixed People in America.* Newbury Park, CA: Sage.

———. 1996. *The Multiracial Experience: Racial Borders as the New Frontier.* Thousand Oaks, CA: Sage.

———, and Matt Kelley, eds. 2003. *Multiracial Child Resource Book: Living Complex Identities.* Seattle: MAVIN Foundation.

Spickard, Paul R. 1989. *Mixed Blood: Intermarriage and Ethnic Identity in Twentieth-Century America.* Madison: University of Wisconsin Press.

Swirl. Available from http://www.swirlinc.org.

U.S. Bureau of the Census. 2005. "We the People of More than One Race in the United States." *Census 2000 Special Reports*, series CENSR-22. Washington, DC: U.S. Government Printing Office. Available from http://www.census.gov.

Winters, Loretta I., and Herman L. DeBose, eds. 2003. *New Faces in a Changing America: Multiracial Identity in the 21st Century.* Thousand Oaks, CA: Sage.

G. Reginald Daniel
Josef Castañeda-Liles

MUSLIMS

While there is a persistent tendency to give the term "Muslim" a racial connotation, "Muslim" and "race" constitute in fact very different categories. Although now recognized as a sociocultural construction, the notion of "race" is based on assumptions of some sort of common ancestry, and even on a degree of physiognomic homogeneity. The denotation "Muslim," however, refers to an adherent of Islam, one of the world's main religions. In 2006, there were close to 1.5 billion Muslims spread over all inhabited continents of the world. One can be a Muslim by birth, but a person can also become a Muslim through conversion, regardless of ethnic background. Consequently, the historical interrelations between the categories of "Muslim" and "race" are extremely complex, and any conflation of the two must generally be considered erroneous. In discussing this problematic connection, it is also important to make a distinction between, on the one hand, Islam as a religious tradition and the attitudes of Muslims toward race, and, on the other hand, the treatment of Muslims at the hands of non-Muslims.

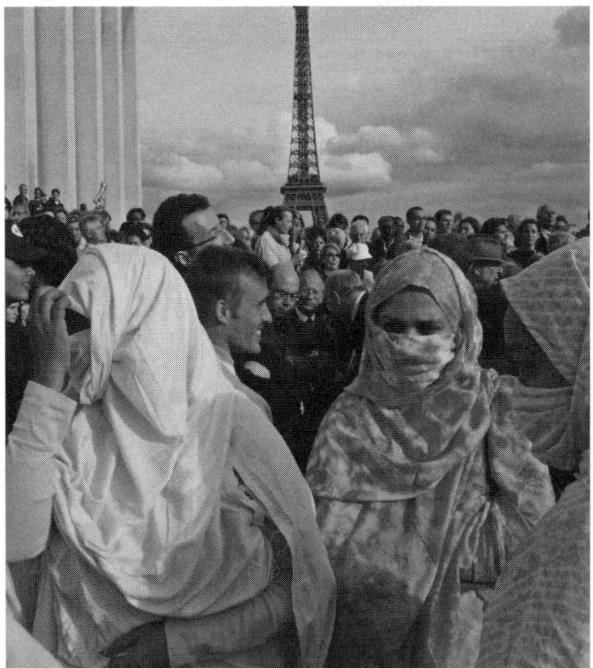

Muslim Community Demonstrates in France. *Muslim women take part in a protest in Paris, France, against the detention of French journalists held hostage in Iraq in 2004.* AP IMAGES.

ISLAM'S HISTORICAL ATTITUDES TOWARD RACE

As a monotheistic religion claiming universal validity, Islam makes an appeal to all of mankind. In this respect, the most frequently quoted injunctions from the Islamic sacred scripture, the Qur'an, are: "O mankind, We have created you male and female, and appointed you races and tribes, that you may know one another" (49:13), and "Among God's signs are the creation of the heavens and of the earth and of your languages and of your colors. In this indeed are signs for those who know" (30:22). The Prophet Muhammad's selection of a black slave, Bilal, as the first *muezzin* (the person who announces the times for the obligatory five daily prayers) is cited as an example of Islam's nondiscriminatory attitude toward race or ethnic affiliations.

Islam emerged in early seventh-century Arabia, and the culture-specific conditions of that time and place have had an influence on its outlook. In pre-Islamic times, the only factor holding the social fabric of Arab society together was tribal affiliation, and all tribes inhabiting the Arabian peninsula traced their lines of descent back to either one of two eponymous ancestors: the South Arabian Qahtan and the North Arabian Adnan. These two Arabian branches eventually converge again in their common forefather: Ismail (identical to the Biblical Ishmael). Traces of this historical setting in which the new faith initially took shape can also be found in the Koran. At various instances the scripture emphasizes the special position of the Arabs and the Arabic language: "And so We have revealed to thee an Arabic Koran that thou mayest warn the Mother of Cities [Mecca] and those who dwell about it, and that thou mayest warn of the Day of Gathering, wherein is no doubt—a party in Paradise, and a party in the blaze. If God had willed, He would have made them one nation" (42:7–8).

When, due to political pressures of his adversaries, the Prophet moved in 622 CE from his hometown Mecca to the oasis settlements now known as Medina, the tiny Muslim community came face-to-face with another ethnic group: Jewish tribes co-inhabiting the oasis alongside Arab tribes. As certain political and religious tensions began to develop, the relationship between Arab Muslims and Jews became more antagonistic, making Islam's aspects of "Arabness" more pronounced.

ISLAM'S SPREAD BEYOND THE ARABIAN PENINSULA

After the Arabian Peninsula had fallen under the sway of Islam, the Muslim armies, consisting of Arab tribesmen, swarmed out over the adjacent regions. Over the course of the second half of the seventh century CE, the areas of what are now Jordan, Syria, Palestine, Iraq, Iran, and North Africa were incorporated into the Muslim Empire. Conquest had priority over conversion, however, and this Islamic state remained very much an Arab entity. A major incentive for the Arab tribes to take part in these campaigns was namely the entitlement of all Muslims to share in the spoils of war. At the same time, this economic benefit acted as a restraint on the Arabs' attempts to convert the subjugated non-Arab peoples.

The gradual acceptance of Islam by non-Arabs—such as Aramaeans, Persians, Egyptians, and Berbers—actually caught the Arab conquerors unaware, and it was initially only possible because converts were being "adopted" as *mawali*, or "clients," into Arab tribes. Although this legally entitled them to a share in the spoils of war, for a considerable period of time the Arabs maintained a contemptuous attitude toward these non-Arab Muslims. The latter's growing discontent with this Arab attitude found a religious expression in their increased siding with a movement known as the *Shi'a 'Ali* or "Party of Ali." Shi'ism had started out as a purely Arab political faction supporting the claims of the Prophet Muhammad's cousin and son-in-law Ali's claims to succession. When the movement's epicenter moved from Arabia to Iraq, it began to draw increasing support from the non-Arab Muslims there, who were mostly of Persian origin.

The opposing party, known as the Sunnis, was led by the Caliph, and in 661 CE they shifted the capital of the Muslim Empire away from Medina in the Arabian Peninsula to Damascus, bringing them into closer contact with Aramaeans and Greeks. With the Caliph's seat first moving to Syria, and then to Baghdad in Iraq (in 750 CE), the Muslim Empire became more cosmopolitan. As intermarriage between Arab troops and non-Arab women became more common, Arab "racial purity" became diluted, and the ethnic diversity of the Muslim world increased. Moreover, with its continuous expansion, the empire faced a human resources crisis and had to rely on increasing numbers of non-Arabs to staff its bureaucracy and armies. In fact, Arabs soon constituted a minority, as large numbers of Persians, Syrians, southern Europeans, and later Turks from Central Asia began occupying influential positions in the realm.

In this context, a word should be said about the position of those who did not convert. As an Islamic legal system took shape, a special position was created for "Peoples of the Book," or Jews, Christians, and Zoroastrians. With the payment of a special tax, they could acquire the status of *Dhimmi*, which entitled them to continue their religious practices and allowed them also to serve the state in certain capacities. Christian Aramaeans, for example, played a prominent role in the transmission of classical Greek learning through their involvement in translation efforts undertaken by the Baghdad Caliphate. Their position compared favorably to the treatment of non-Christians in Christendom until relatively recent times. One discriminatory practice that remained in place was the prohibition of non-Muslim men marrying Muslim women without the formers' conversion to Islam, even though the reverse was permissible. The reason for this is that, under Islamic Law, children are considered to belong to their father's religion. Consequently, it is considered unacceptable that Muslim women contribute to the natural growth of non-Muslim communities.

Thus, Islam's historical roots in the Arabian Peninsula, aided by the spread of Arabic as the sacred language of Islam and as a *lingua franca* throughout many parts of the Middle East and North Africa, have contributed to the erroneous tendency to conflate the categories "Muslim" with "Arab," or at least with people of Middle Eastern origin. In regard to the latter, the fact that Persians and Turks are not Arabs, and that their languages are not even related to Arabic, is often ignored.

NOTIONS OF RACE AND ETHNICITY

As Islam continued its spread beyond the Middle East, the conflation of Islam—or the designation "Muslim"—with a particular race, as well as its own supposed non-discriminatory stance toward race from a doctrinal point of view, were increasingly at odds with reality.

In his 1971 study *Race and Color in Islam,* Bernard Lewis provides ample examples from actual Islamic history that run counter to the universalism of Islamic doctrine. As is often the case in other civilizations, Muslim attitudes toward skin color and the alleged inferiority of certain races is closely associated with slavery, an institution to which Africans in particular fell victim, even in the Muslim world. Racial distinction was also discussed by the geographer al-Jahiz (776–869), who used the Greek theory of the four humors to explain the characteristics of the various races in the world. The descriptions he formulated were not free from value judgments, which were often uncomplimentary.

In the early twenty-first century, the great majority of Muslims in the world are found outside of the Middle East. The largest Muslim nation in the world, Indonesia (with close to 200 million Muslims), is located in Southeast Asia, while the South Asian states of Pakistan, India, and Bangladesh together have more than 450 million Muslim citizens. Substantial numbers are also found in populous sub-Saharan African countries like Nigeria (65 million). In addition, after an intermezzo of nearly half a millennium, there are again increasing numbers of Muslims in Europe. Of more recent date is the entry of large numbers of Muslim immigrants into the Americas and Australia, and there is the growing phenomenon of Europeans and North American descendants of Europeans converting to Islam. This continued expansion of the Muslim presence throughout the world makes associations between religious and racial affiliations increasingly untenable.

As a world religion, Islam has therefore experienced an enormous internal cultural diversification. It has also been exposed to encounters with cultures holding on to different religious traditions, which has given rise to complicated ethno-religious issues, in which it is often difficult to disentangle the religious from wider cultural and ethnic aspects.

ISLAM IN RUSSIA AND CENTRAL ASIA

Before the arrival of the Proto-Russians, the areas of the Lower and Middle Volga were settled mainly by Bulgar and Turkish tribes, who were only Islamized at the beginning of the tenth century. The interactions between pagan Russians (and later Christianized Slavic Russians) and Turkic Muslims date back to these times. Following the Mongol invasions of the 1230s, a poly-ethnic and multicultural empire emerged, known as the "Golden Horde." This empire became increasingly Islamized from the early fourteenth century onward. In the 1480s the tide began to turn, and the Muslims of the Golden Horde, Caucasus, and Central Asia faced an increasingly expansive Russian state encroaching on their territories.

Under the relatively tolerant policy of Catherine the Great (1684–1727) toward the Muslims, the former Golden Horde and Caucasus experienced something of an Islamic renaissance. By the 1860s, however, when the tsar's eye began to fall on Kazakhstan and the Central Asian regions, tsarist politics became more consciously "Russian." In the late nineteenth century, this nationalist tendency carried over to the (Turkish-speaking) Uzbek, Turkmen, and (Persian-speaking) Tajik Muslims of Central Asia, who by then had been incorporated into the Russian realm. Overlaid with elements of Islamic Renewal (*Jadidism*) as well as traditionalism, a drive toward cultural, ethnic, and linguistic self-realization within the Russian state took hold of Russia's Muslims along the Black Sea, in the Northern Caucasus, and in Central Asia.

After the Russian Revolution of 1917, it was Josef Stalin who reorganized all inhabitants of the Soviet Union into "first-class" and "second-class" nationalities, based on commonalities in language, territory, economics, and culture—but not on religion. With respect to the Muslim citizens, this resulted in the "first class" union republics of Kazakhstan, Uzbekistan, Turkmenistan, Tajikistan, Kyrgyzstan, and Azerbaijan. The Tatars and Muslims of the Northern Caucasus were relegated to a patchwork of less-privileged "second-class" autonomous republics.

The blurring of the lines between the realm of the "religious" and other elements of ethnicity sporadically resulted in attempts at unification among the Muslims—at times driven by Pan-Turkic sentiments, at other times by Pan-Islamic sentiments. In particular, the latter turned into political dynamite following the events of the 1970s and 1980s in Iran and Afghanistan. Alongside attempts to affirm the specific ethnic identifications of these "nationalities," these unifying trends were suppressed by both tsarist Russia and the Soviet Union's "Russification" of its Muslim-inhabited territories, only to remerge again when Communism's fortune dwindled in the 1990s.

ISLAM IN CHINA

Islam has been present in China since the time of the Tang dynasty, and throughout history it was commonly regarded as a challenge, if not an outright threat, to the Chinese establishment. However, in discussing the racial dimensions of this tension, one runs into the same complications as elsewhere. Muslims differ from other minority groups in China in that they—although concentrated in certain geographical margins of the empire—are found in every province and every sizable urban agglomeration. This makes it difficult to reduce the differences between the Chinese Muslim minorities and the majority Han Chinese to an issue of race alone.

In fact, Chinese history evinces that both Chinese and Muslim identities are social-cultural constructs, since the root of the tensions between the two groups is the failure or refusal of the Chinese Muslims, both Han Chinese and others, to subscribe to the values of dominant Chinese culture, which is strongly informed by Confucian teachings that often run counter to Islamic dogmas. At the same time, this did not prevent certain Chinese Muslims from attaining prominent positions in Chinese society, such as the famous marine explorer Zheng He under the Ming dynasty. The glossing of all Chinese Muslims into one category can be traced to the Yuan dynasty, when the term *Hui* became the common denominator for referring to Muslims (and Jews and Christians as well).

More recently, the Chinese Muslim rebellions of the nineteenth century, such as the one resulting in the short-lived sultanate of Dali in the southwestern province of Yunnan, raised the awareness of the numerical significance of Muslims, particularly in certain frontier regions such as Yunnan and Xinjiang. This led, in the early twentieth century, to the recognition of the Muslims as one of the "five peoples of China" by the young republic under Sun Yat Sen. This conflation of Muslim identity with a discrete "nationality" was continued by the People's Republic after 1949. Then, however, the authorities began (not unlike Stalin's initiatives of the 1920s and 1930s) to differentiate between the *Hui* of China proper, the Uighurs of Xingjiang, and other Turkic minorities of China's Central Asian fringes, such as the Uzbeks, Kyrgyz, and Kazakhs. While these ethnic identifications may constitute an implicit and partial recognition of Muslim identity, any overriding tendencies toward "Pan Islamism" or—in the case of the Central Asian Muslims—"Pan-Turkism" have been strongly opposed by the central state. This is again an illustration of the ambivalence prevailing in the association of Muslim identity with any discrete form of ethnicity.

ISLAM IN SOUTHEAST ASIA

Since its independence, the political leadership of the largest Muslim nation in the world—the multiethnic Indonesia—has always steered clear of any unifying policies based on the Islam factor. This is in marked contrast with Malaysia, where "being Muslim" is considered an inherent part of "Malayness." Since the 1970s, the government has implemented a policy of "affirmative action" benefiting the Malay majority in the educational, social, and economic fields. Its aim is to emancipate the Malays from their backward positions in comparison with the often economically more affluent Chinese and Indian minorities. This policy was reinforced with an "Islamization" drive in Malaysian public life following the Malay-Chinese riots of 1969.

The position of the Malay Muslims of southern Thailand is another example of the politicization of an ethno-religious issue. Constituting a numerical majority in Thailand's border provinces with Malaysia, these Malays were severed from their counterparts south of the border as a result of a demarcation treaty signed between Thailand and the colonial authorities of British Malaya in 1909. As a result, close to three million ethnic Malay Muslims had to be incorporated into a predominantly Buddhist nation-state of ethnic Thai.

These Malay Muslims shared neither linguistic, religious, nor cultural commonalities with the majority population, but the policies of successive Thai governments emphasized loyalty and adherence to the monarchy (which is regarded as divine), Buddhism, and Thai language and culture. This policy has resulted in very antagonistic relations between the southern Muslim minority and the rest of the country. In political terms it led to frequently violent attempts by the Malay Muslims to secure secession and independence, or at least a degree of autonomy.

MUSLIMS IN THE WEST

Prior to the arrival of large numbers of Muslim immigrants, especially from countries in North Africa and South Asia in the 1960s and 1970s, Europe can be said to have at least a dual Muslim heritage. Until the fall of Granada in 1492, the Iberian Peninsula had been home to a thriving "Moorish" culture, in which Muslims, Jews, and Christians participated. In the eastern Mediterranean and in the Balkans, the Ottoman Empire had been making inroads into Christendom since its capture of Constantinople, the capital of the Byzantine Empire, in 1453 CE.

While Muslims disappeared from Spain and Portugal following the Christian *Reconquista*—either by extermination, going into exile, or through forced conversion—countries like Albania and the former Yugoslavia are still home to substantial Muslim minorities. Here again, state policies followed a strategy similar to those of the Soviet Union, regarding nationality and Muslim as analogue categories, while simultaneously downplaying the significance of religious beliefs and practices. The dissolution of the Federation of Yugoslavia in the 1990s has shown that such conflations can have disastrous results, for Serbian nationalists were pitted against Muslim Bosnians and Kosovars.

In connection with the migrant communities from Muslim countries found throughout western Europe, North America and Australia, it appears that religion has become an additional ingredient in a more complex mix of ethnic factors that set these communities apart from the majority population. These factors include physical appearance, language, and cultural and social mores, such as dietary requirements and dress codes.

Typically groups within these communities become affected by and actively take part in an Islamic resurgence (often with distinctly political overtones) that has swept the Muslim world since the late 1970s. The politicized manifestations of this new Muslim assertiveness are, to a considerable degree, a result of unresolved political conflicts in various parts of the Muslim world (e.g., Palestine, Afghanistan, Iraq), in which Western powers are often implicated or regarded as being involved.

When the politicization of this increasing Muslim assertiveness results in acts of violence, the authorities responsible for national security tend to include the tool of "racial profiling" in their repertoire of measures for defining potential threats. The most striking example in recent history of such a policy is the introduction of the Patriot Act and other Homeland Security measures in the United States following the 9/11 attacks on New York City and Washington D.C. However, as the above survey shows, such associations between religion and other elements of ethnicity are extremely diffuse and misleading.

BIBLIOGRAPHY

Carrère d'Encausse, Hélène. 1988. *Islam and the Russian Empire: Reform and Revolution in Central Asia*. Comparative Studies on Muslim Societies 8. Berkeley: University of California Press.

Israeli, Raphael. 2002. *Islam in China: Religion, Ethnicity, Culture and Politics*. Lamham, MD: Lexington Books.

Kappeler, Andreas, Gerhard Simon, George Brunner, and Edward Allworth, eds. 1994. *Muslim Communities Reemerge: Historical Perspectives on Nationality, Politics, and Opposition in the Former Soviet Union and Yugoslavia*. Translated by Caroline Sawyer. Durham, NC: Duke University Press.

Kersten, Carool. 2004. "The Predicament of Thailand's Southern Muslims." *American Journal of Islamic Social Sciences* 21 (4): 1–29.

Lewis, Bernard.1971. *Race and Color in Islam*. New York: Harper and Row.

Yemelianova, Galina M. 2002. *Russia and Islam: A Historical Survey*. London: Palgrave.

Carool Kersten

N

NAACP

The National Association for the Advancement of Colored People (NAACP) is the oldest and largest civil rights organization in the United States. Since its founding in the first decade of the twentieth century, it has been a leader in efforts to guarantee that all racial minorities receive equal protection under the law.

RACISM AT THE TURN OF THE TWENTIETH CENTURY

The NAACP was established when the direct racism of the Deep South had become a national problem, as reflected in race riots that occurred in New York City and New Orleans, Louisiana, in 1900; in Atlanta, Georgia, in 1906; in Springfield, Illinois, in 1908; and throughout mainstream America in 1910 when heavyweight boxing champion Jack Johnson, an African American, brutally defeated James Jefferies, the "great white hope" of the era. Between 1900 and 1910, at least 505 blacks were lynched, and for the first time since 1866, no person of color was to be found in the U.S. Congress. In 1896 the U.S. Supreme Court ruled, in the case of *Plessy v. Ferguson*, that racial segregation was not unconstitutional, a decision that accelerated a trend that had begun a generation earlier. A year before *Plessy*, at a time when the first wave of industrial millionaires was cresting, Booker T. Washington, the founder and principal of the Tuskegee Institute in Alabama, shot to international fame with his call for blacks to temporarily withdraw from political struggle and concentrate on cooperating with whites in economics, although the only asset blacks possessed was their physical labor.

Race relations were so poor that blacks held a conference at Atlanta University in 1893 on the theme of migration. Between 1895 and 1896, two shiploads of blacks sailed for Liberia, in what was meant to be the beginning of a mass migration of blacks back to Africa. Because of boll weevils in the cotton and the terror of Ku Klux Klansmen in white sheets, black southerners were also migrating north to Harlem and Philadelphia and Chicago. Thomas Dixon's play *The Clansman* (1905), based on his 1902 novel of the same name, was a multimedia tribute to the real Klan and became a hit in the North as well as in the South. Blacks had tried to rally in defense of their rights in several organizations prior to the NAACP. One was the National Afro-American League (1890–1893), which was organized by T. Thomas Fortune, the militant editor of the *New York Age*. This organization failed in its efforts to convert principle into practice, however, though it reformed from 1898 to 1908 as the Afro-American Council.

THE NIAGARA MOVEMENT

The other protest association was the Niagara Movement, which was founded to counter the dire effects of Washington's doctrine of status quo accommodation on racial issues.

Led by William E. B. Du Bois; William Monroe Trotter, the editor of the Boston *Guardian;* John Hope, a professor of classics and destined to become the first black president of Morehouse College in 1906; and Harry Clay Smith, the editor of the *Cleveland Gazette,* a group of twenty-nine likeminded African Americans held a conference in 1905 on the Canadian side of Niagara Falls (thus the name, the Niagara Movement). The fact that the conference was held in Canada is symbolic of the racial strife and discord in the United States at that time, for the group could not secure a hotel site in New York. Out of this conference emerged a call for an end to racial discrimination and an extension of full civil liberties to African Americans in the United States.

The Niagara Movement had many points in its platform, including the right to manhood suffrage, freedom of speech, the abolition of caste based upon race and color, and a belief in the dignity of labor. The organization also felt that the practice of universal brotherhood should be recognized. The group took the opportunity to issue a condemnation of Booker T. Washington's accommodationist philosophy, which he advocated in his Atlanta Compromise speech in 1895. The group held subsequent meetings in Harpers Ferry, West Virginia, the site of John Brown's 1859 raid designed to free enslaved blacks.

The Niagara Movement was a black organization that saw its role as using the legal system to fight for civil rights. By 1910 several of the nation's ablest black lawyers were affiliated with the organization and arguing civil rights cases. The organization was dying, however, hampered by a lack of funds. When the opportunity arose to join forces with another organization whose platform was nearly identical to its own, the Niagara Movement merged with the new group.

THE FOUNDING OF THE NAACP

Spearheaded by Mary White Ovington, the NAACP was organized in New York City in 1909, in the wake of a major riot in Springfield, Illinois, in 1908. It seemed ironic to many that this riot occurred in the hometown of President Abraham Lincoln, the great emancipator. During the riot many of the city's leading white citizens organized themselves into mobs, and over a two-day period they killed two blacks and five whites, wounded scores of African Americans, and ran thousands more out of town. Forty homes were destroyed.

The Springfield Riot became the subject of countless newspaper and magazine articles. One article, written by the socialist William English Walling of the *Independent*, was entitled "Race War in the North." Walling described in detail the atrocities launched against African American citizens, not only in Springfield but throughout the South. He raised the question of whether the spirit of abolitionism could be revived so that black citizens might one day be treated equally in the political and social arenas, or whether the voices of race-baiting southern segregationists, such as Senator Ben "Pitchfork" Tillman of South Carolina and Senator James K. Vardaman of Mississippi, would become the norm, even in the North. His final question was "Yet who realizes the seriousness of the situation, and what large and powerful body of citizens is ready to come to their aid?"

Ovington was one of the individuals who responded to Mr. Walling's challenge. Ovington had founded the Greenpoint Settlement in Brooklyn and had spent much of her time studying the housing and employment status of blacks in New York. She felt that the spirit of abolitionism had to be revived, and she wanted to pursue the struggle for civil and political rights with the same spirit that had motivated the abolitionists. With that as a mission, she sent a letter to Walling who agreed to meet with her in his New York apartment. Along with the social worker Henry Moskowitz and John Mitchell, the mayor of New York, they met in January 1909.

Ovington, Walling, Moskowitz, and Mitchell discussed the various issues and concerns they felt were pertinent to the mistreatment of black people. They wanted to move quickly in putting together a national forum, so they set the date of February 12, 1909, Abraham Lincoln's 100th birthday, on which to hold a conference on the "Negro question." They planned to use the opportunity to organize that body of citizens that Walling alluded to in his article. The meeting was not held on that date, however, but in May 1909. From the adjournment of this initial meeting to the date of the national meeting, this group appealed to others to participate. One person they called upon was Oswald Garrison Villard, the president of the New York Evening Post Company and a grandson of the abolitionist William Lloyd Garrison, the editor of the *Liberator*, a radical antislavery newspaper of the antebellum era. Through his own newspaper, the *New York Evening Post,* Villard publicized a call for a national meeting to consider the racism involved in repressing blacks. There were many prominent Americans who signed the call. Among them were Jane Addams, Ida Wells Barnett, William Dean Howells, the Reverend Francis J. Grimke, Rabbi Emil Hirsh, J. C. Phelps Stokes, Lincoln Steffens, Rabbi Stephen J. Wise, and the African Methodist Episcopal Bishop Alexander Walters, as well as the group from the original meeting. The signatures of all those who signed "The Call" was issued on February 12. The conference opened on May 30, 1909, and after a series of organizational meetings, the NAACP opened its doors with two offices in the Evening Post building in New York. The first national president of the NAACP was Moorfield Storey, a constitutional attorney and past president of the American Bar Association. DuBois became the director of publicity and research and the editor of the official magazine, *The Crisis: A Record of the Darker Races,* which ran to sixteen pages and was available for a dime. The first publication was issued in November 1910.

The NAACP was founded by an interracial group intent on working on behalf of all minorities, which led

NAACP Pilgrimage to Harpers Ferry, 1932. *After their first meeting, the NAACP held subsequent meetings at the site of John Brown's raid designed to free enslaved blacks, in Harpers Ferry, West Virginia.* THE LIBRARY OF CONGRESS.

to their use of the term "colored." Many of the original white members came from socialist and progressive organizations, while much of the African American membership was pulled from participants in the Niagara Movement. The organization would work on behalf of Native Americans, Hispanics, Asian Americans, African Americans, and Jews. Its purpose was to secure for all people the rights guaranteed under the Thirteenth, Fourteenth, and Fifteenth Amendments to the United States Constitution. Its principal objective was to ensure the political, educational, social, and economic equality of minority groups in the United States. Its efforts would be directed toward eliminating racial discrimination through established democratic processes. The early leadership and membership felt that civil rights could be secured through the enactment and enforcement of federal, state, and local laws, and by becoming a forum for informing the public about the negative effects of discrimination, segregation and racist public policies.

The newly formed organization was criticized by some in the African-American community, notably Booker T. Washington, who felt that the NAACP's tactic of openly condemning racist policies contrasted with his policy of quiet behind-the-scenes diplomacy. It was this strategy, however, that had been criticized by the Niagara Movement.

THE EARLY YEARS

As the first major civil rights organization, the NAACP took on the responsibility of righting the wrongs that burdened people of color through legal action. The primary means by which the NAACP operated was through the filing of lawsuits or supporting legal issues that would further its cause.

In the first few years of the organization, the NAACP was faced with the president of the United States, Woodrow Wilson, approving legislation (in 1913) that officially segregated the federal government. The organization launched a public protest against Wilson's segregation policies. This was followed by the release of D. W. Griffith's movie *The Birth of a Nation* (based on Dixon's *The Clansman*) in 1915. The NAACP organized a nationwide protest against the bigoted and racially inflammatory silent film, which promoted negative stereotypes and glorified the Ku Klux Klan. The film's release led to riots in major cities across the United States. Some cities, including Chicago, Pittsburgh, and St. Louis, refused to allow the film to be shown. President Wilson, with his daughters, viewed the film at a White House screening. He was alleged to have commented that "it's all so terribly true," though one of his aides denied that he ever made the statement. As the controversy over the film continued to grow, Wilson finally issued a statement indicating that he disapproved of the "unfortunate production." The organization also forced the hand of President Wilson on one of its major issues, lynching. Wilson issued a public statement against lynching in 1918.

As the NAACP began to gain national recognition, its membership grew from approximately 9,000 in 1917 to approximately 90,000 in 1919. There were more than

300 local branches, and it was well on its way to becoming the nation's premier civil rights organization. The battle against lynching then began in earnest.

The anti-lynching battle was fought in both the courts and legislature. The NAACP strongly supported the Dyer Bill, which would have punished those who participated in or failed to prosecute lynch mobs. The bill was introduced by Senator Leonidas C. Dyer of Missouri in 1918. The NAACP was the major lobbyist in support of the legislation and issued a report titled "Thirty Years of Lynching in the United States, 1889–1919." This report resulted in substantive public debate and is credited with causing a decline in incidences of lynching, but it did not end the atrocities. The legislation was never passed by Congress.

The NAACP also challenged the military's exclusion of African Americans from being commissioned as officers. This battle was won and, as a result, more than 600 black officers were commissioned and 700,000 registered for the draft. One of the newly commissioned officers was Charles Hamilton Houston, a 1915 Phi Beta Kappa graduate of Amherst College. Houston pointed to his experience in the military, facing the hatred and disrespect shown to black officers, as the catalyst for his decision to attend law school to fight such atrocities. He earned a law degree from Harvard Law School and in 1934 he became the first full-time attorney for the NAACP.

THE LEGAL ADVOCACY STRATEGY

The NAACP began its history of fighting legal battles in 1910 with the Pink Franklin case (*Franklin v. State of South Carolina*). Franklin, a black South Carolina sharecropper, had been put on trial for killing a white policeman. He had received an advance on his wages, but shortly afterward left his employer. A warrant was issued for his arrest under an invalid state law. Armed police went to his home at 3:00 a.m. to arrest him. When they did not state their purpose, a gun battle followed and one officer, H. E. Valentine, was killed. Franklin was convicted of murder and sentenced to death. The NAACP intervened and eventually had Franklin's sentenced commuted to life imprisonment. He was freed in 1919. The case prompted Joel Spingarn, a prominent NAACP official, and his brother Arthur to begin fighting such cases in earnest. This effort became the forerunner of the NAACP Legal Defense Fund.

Between 1915 and 1927, the NAACP appealed to the Supreme Court to rule that several laws passed by southern states concerning voting rights, education, and housing were unconstitutional. They won several major victories. In 1915, in the case of *Guinn v. United States*, the Supreme Court struck down the grandfather clause (a technique used to disenfranchise black voters) as a barrier to voting rights granted in the Fifteenth Amendment. The grandfather clause imposed a literacy and "understanding" test on individuals whose ancestors were not entitled to vote prior to 1866. This requirement virtually eliminated all African Americans who were freed from slavery in 1865 by the Thirteenth Amendment. In 1917, the Court ruled that municipal ordinances that mandated segregation were unconstitutional in *Buchanan v. Warley*. The case was argued before the court by Moorfield Storey, the NAACP's first president and a constitutional attorney. The ruling in the case led whites to develop the use of restrictive covenants to accomplish the same objective. In the covenants, white property owners agreed to sell or rent to whites only. In 1923, in the case of *Moore v. Dempsey* the Supreme Court ruled that the exclusion of African Americans from juries was inconsistent with the right to a fair trial.

The NAACP began to attack "white primaries" in 1927. The white primary was an electoral mechanism used by the Democratic Party in the South as a means of excluding African-American voters. For all intents and purposes, a candidate for office was chosen in the primary election, from which blacks were excluded by racial membership rules adopted by the party, a situation that made the November general election perfunctory. In a series of cases originating in Texas, the argument was put forward that the white primary deprived African Americans of their rights under the Fifteenth Amendment. The Court had always interpreted the amendment to mean that "state action" could not deprive voters of their rights. In the first case, the state of Texas had established the white primary through statute. In *Nixon v. Herndon* (1927) and *Nixon v. Condon* (1932), therefore, the Supreme Court found state action in the establishment of the white primary. The Texas Democratic Party then limited participation in the primary to whites on its own. Thus, in *Grovey v. Townsend* (1935) the Supreme Court did not find state action, ruling that the party was a private entity. Nine years later, the Court reversed itself in *Smith v. Allwright* (1944), stating that the party was inextricably linked to the state and that the primary was a violation of the Fifteenth Amendment. Thus, white primaries were finally outlawed.

The case of *Hocutt v. Wilson* (1933) was one of the first test cases involving segregation in higher education. Thomas Hocutt, a student at North Carolina College for Negroes, was denied admission to the University of North Carolina's School of Pharmacy. His attorneys, Conrad Pearson and Cecil McCoy, sought the assistance of the NAACP. William Hastie directed the litigation on behalf of the NAACP. Despite the praise given Hastie and his team, the case was undermined by the North Carolina College president's refusal to release Hocutt's transcript.

Victories in the majority of these cases set the stage for the more in-depth litigation strategy that the NAACP would use to fight injustice. In its early efforts the organization relied on lawyers who volunteered their services. Its first full-time attorney, Charles Hamilton Houston, began to use the courts in earnest. In 1935 Houston started a legal campaign to end school segregation. He was assisted by one of his former Howard University students, Thurgood Marshall.

Houston began the higher education litigation in 1938. The first case was *Missouri ex rel. Gaines v. Canada.* Lloyd Gaines was denied entry to the University of Missouri Law School, and the Supreme Court ruled that Missouri must offer Gaines an equal facility within the state or admit him to the university's law school. The state legislature attempted to build a makeshift law school, which caused Houston to renew litigation. Gaines disappeared, however, and the litigation ended. Shortly afterwards, in 1940, Houston resigned his position and Thurgood Marshall was made chief counsel of the new legal branch, the NAACP Legal Defense and Educational Fund (LDF). The LDF would become a separate entity in 1957.

Marshall focused on other areas of Jim Crow before returning to education cases. In 1946 he and his team won the *Morgan v. Virginia* case, in which the Supreme Court banned states from having segregated facilities on buses and trains that crossed state borders. They then argued against restrictive covenants in the *Shelley v. Kraemer* case. The Supreme Court struck down the use of restrictive covenants in 1948. With these successes, the Marshall team then began the series of education cases for which the NAACP is most noted. Marshall decided to attack the doctrine of "separate but equal" head on as being unconstitutional.

In 1950 the Supreme Court ruled in *Sweatt* v. *Painter* that racial segregation in professional schools (in this instance, the University of Texas law school) was inherently unequal and unconstitutional. Also in 1950, the Supreme Court ruled in *McLaurin v. Oklahoma State Regents* that if a student was admitted to a school, then the student was entitled to equal treatment and could not be segregated from other students, as McLaurin had been at the University of Oklahoma. This case and others before it paved the way for the NAACP landmark legal cases, which culminated in 1954 with *Brown v. Board of Education of Topeka.*

The organization spent years fighting racial segregation in schools in the thirteen southern states. The NAACP proved that children at "white only" schools were allotted more money and better resources than children at "black only" schools. Marshall pointed out that the South Carolina school system spent $179 per year for white students but only $43 for black children. They also used research from the psychologist Kenneth Clark's doll experiments to demonstrate the psychological impact of segregated schools on black children. Clark studied the effects of segregation on children by using black and white dolls. When shown the dolls, children liked the white dolls better and saw the black dolls as "bad." They also saw themselves as the white doll, but when asked which doll looked most like them, the children were upset because they had to pick the doll that they had rejected. The experiment thus demonstrated that the children had an internalized sense of inferiority. The Supreme Court accepted Marshall's argument and ruled that "separate but equal" was unconstitutional, effectively overturning the earlier decision in *Plessy v. Ferguson.* Under Marshall's leadership, the NAACP was very successful in many of its legal challenges to Jim Crow.

THE TURBULENCE OF THE LATE 1950S AND THE 1960S

In the late 1950s, the NAACP saw its membership dwindle to less than 500. This decline was attributed to accusations that labor unions and black groups had been infiltrated by communists. In its battle with the Soviet Union, the United States inspired loyalty and patriotism through anticommunist rhetoric. The effort to associate organizations with communist influence wreaked havoc. Following the successful year-long Montgomery Bus Boycott, the state of Alabama banned the NAACP from the state. Many states also prohibited state employees from participating in the organization, which impacted teachers in these states. Members of the organization, once discovered, were also subject to harassment and job loss.

The NAACP was also faced with new organizations emerging out of the struggle in the South. After his successful leadership in the Montgomery bus boycott in 1955, Reverend Martin Luther King Jr. became a powerful voice in the movement. In 1957 he founded the Southern Christian Leadership Conference (SCLC), which became the political arm of the black church. Unlike the legal and legislative approach favored by the NAACP, the SCLC used direct action techniques to accomplish its goals. Although the NAACP was opposed to extralegal popular actions, many of its members, such as Medger Evers, the Mississippi field secretary, participated in nonviolent demonstrations such as sit-ins and marches. The organization also collaborated with the SCLC and other civil rights organization such as the National Urban League on issues important to advancing the civil rights cause.

Following Houston's original plan, the NAACP Legal Redress Committee took the lead in the continued focus on education at the high school level. The state president in Arkansas, Mrs. Daisy Bates, organized a group of students to integrate Central High School in Little Rock in 1957. A lawsuit was filed in federal district court to force the immediate integration of schools in

Little Rock. Thurgood Marshall joined in the appeal. He lost the case in the Eighth U.S. Circuit and decided against pursuing further action. Bates, however, proceeded with plans to integrate. By the start of the school year, the group of students led by Bates had dwindled to nine. The "Little Rock Nine" gained national prominence when the National Guard was federalized by President Dwight Eisenhower and sent in to protect the students. In the 1958 case of *Cooper v. Aaron*, the Supreme Court ruled that the Arkansas governor, Orval Faubus, could not interfere with the desegregation of Central High School. In response, the Little Rock school board closed the schools.

Following the *Brown* decision, some states and cities took similar action as Little Rock and chose to close their schools rather than integrate. The school system in Prince Edward County, Virginia, closed for the longest period of time, from 1959 to 1964. The NAACP managed to get legislation through the Congress in the form of the 1957 Civil Rights Act. The civil rights movement then entered the direct action phase.

The new direct action tactics were tested in Greensboro, North Carolina, when four students from North Carolina Agricultural and Technical State University staged sit-ins at the Woolworth lunch counter. The city of Greensboro had had an active NAACP chapter in the 1930s, and in 1943 Ella Baker, a NAACP staffer, had established a youth group in the city. Two of the four students who participated in the sit-in had been members of the youth group. During the 1950s students were further inspired by their teachers and the pastor of the Shiloh Baptist Church to become more involved. The pastor had led a successful membership drive that doubled membership in the NAACP chapter. The Greensboro sit-in sparked similar action in more than sixty cities across the south.

THE STRUCTURE AND LEADERSHIP OF THE NAACP

The NAACP's basic organizational structure has not changed since its founding. Ultimate decisions are made by the annual national convention. Between conventions, decisions are made by the sixty-four-member board of directors. The executive director, staff, and the chairman of the board are instrumental in making day-to-day decisions, and the national headquarters maintains significant control over the actions of local branches.

The organization has had eight executive directors: William Walling, James Weldon Johnson, Walter White, Roy Wilkins, Benjamin Hooks, Benjamin Chavis, Kweisi Mfume, and Bruce Gordon. Since the appointments of the writer and diplomat James Weldon Johnson as executive secretary in 1920 and Louis T. Wright, a surgeon, as the first black board chair in 1934, neither position has been held by a white person. Walter White followed James Weldon Johnson as executive director in 1930. White was very fair-skinned and had used his color to infiltrate white groups, which allowed him to conduct significant research on lynching. He used his position in the NAACP to block the nomination of a segregationist judge, John J. Parker, from the Supreme Court.

Under White's leadership, the NAACP saw a significant growth in its membership, boasting approximately 500,000 members by 1946. In 1941 the Washington bureau was established as the legislative advocacy and lobbying arm of the organization. The bureau was directly responsible for strategic planning and coordinating the political action and legislation program. The Washington bureau also holds an annual Legislative Mobilization, which is a forum to provide information about the NAACP's legislative agenda. It also publishes an annual "Report Card" to publicize how members of Congress vote on significant civil rights legislation.

White was succeeded by Roy Wilkins, who became executive secretary in 1955. Wilkins led the organization through the turbulent times of pitting its moderate, integrationist goals against those of more direct action organizations such as the Southern Christian Leadership Conference (SCLC), Congress of Racial Equality (CORE) and Student Nonviolent Coordinating Committee (SNCC). It was under his leadership that the first significant legislative victory occurred, the Civil Rights Act of 1957. He worked with A. Philip Randolph, Martin Luther King Jr., and others in planning and executing the 1963 March on Washington. Wilkins also participated in the Selma-to-Montgomery March in 1965 and the March Against Fear in 1966. He led the organization through the legislative victories of the 1964 Civil Rights Act, the 1965 Voting Rights Act, and the 1968 Fair Housing Act.

Benjamin Hooks became executive director upon the retirement of Wilkins in 1977. He entered the office at a time when the civil rights movement had all but ended. Job discrimination still existed, however, as did de facto segregation, and urban poverty and crime were on the rise. The NAACP, as an organization, was experiencing internal problems, specifically tensions between the executive director and the board of directors. Although these tensions had existed almost from the beginning of the organization, they escalated to outright hostility during Hooks's tenure. This served to weaken the organization. The NAACP was also faced with several setbacks during the 1970s. In the 1978 *Regents of California v. Bakke* case, the Supreme Court placed limits on affirmative action programs. This case was followed by a further eroding of the rights that had been won during the 1950s and 1960s.

NAACP Leaders, 2006. *NAACP president Bruce Gordon (left) and chariman Julian Bond talk after a news conference at the start of the organization's 97th annual conference in Washington, D.C.* AP IMAGES

The NAACP had a large membership base and had always been more financially self-reliant than other civil rights organizations. However, it experienced a severe budget crisis in the 1980s. To help stabilize its finances, the organization moved its national headquarters from New York to Baltimore, Maryland. The move was made possible with the help of more than one million dollars from the state of Maryland and the City of Baltimore, and by a half-million dollar grant from the Kresge Foundation.

Benjamin F. Chavis succeeded Hooks as executive director in 1993. However, he was ousted a year later due to several controversies. Chavis, a nationalist, attempted to take the NAACP into a new direction. He offended many liberals and supporters of the organization by reaching out to Minister Louis Farrakhan, the head of the Nation of Islam. This period led to additional internal problems for the organization. Kweisi Mfume, a former Maryland congressman, followed Chavis as executive director in 1996.

Under Mfume, the NAACP focused on economic development and educational programs for young people. It also continued its role in legal advocacy for civil rights issues. To return the NAACP to strong financial health, Mfume cut the national staff by a third. In 1997 he launched the Economic Reciprocity Initiative (ERI), and in 2000 he negotiated the TV Diversity Agreements with various television networks. Also in 2000, the NAACP retired much of its debt, and the organization operated with a budget surplus for the first time in many years. The NAACP was also successful in massive voter registration drives that year, and it witnessed the largest black voter turnout rate in twenty years. Mfume led the organization in working through its political differences with major Latino civil rights organizations, such as the League of United Latin American Citizens and the National Council of La Raza.

In 2003 the United Nations designated the NAACP as a nongovernmental organization (NGO). The NGO designation meant that the organization could advise and consult with foreign governments and the UN Secretariat on issues involving human rights. Mfume developed an action agenda that included an emphasis on civil rights, political empowerment, educational excellence, economic development and health and youth outreach. The board, under the leadership of Julian Bond, began to streamline and strengthen the governing procedures of the organization. The board also began to revise and update its constitution and bylaws for the first time since its inception in 1909. And, with Mfume's leadership, the NAACP developed a five-year strategic plan.

Bruce Gordon, a retired Verizon executive, followed Mfume as executive director in 2004. His tenure was short lived, however. Citing differences with the board of directors, he resigned in March 2007, just nineteen months after taking the helm. Gordon was replaced by Dennis Courtland Hayes as interim president and CEO. Hayes previously served as the NAACP's general counsel in charge of the historic legal program.

THE NAACP IN THE TWENTY-FIRST CENTURY

The most significant change in the NAACP over the years has been the decline in the interracialism that was present at the founding of the organization and lasted well into the 1960s. Until that time, whites held leadership roles and were part of the staff. This change was largely a function of the 1960s Black Power ideology and its emphasis on racial solidarity and organization. Black Power advocates challenged the NAACP's purpose and tactics. With its traditional approach, the NAACP found itself attracting fewer members, as many African Americans became sympathetic to the more militant and separatist philosophies of the Black Power movement. However, the organization remained steadfast in its mission, and under the leadership of Mfume membership steadily increased.

The NAACP maintains its strategy of lobbying and litigation. In the post-civil rights era, the organization supported extension of the Voting Rights Act, the Civil Rights Act of 1991, and amendments to the Fair Housing Act. It has also lobbied against the confirmation of conservative judges to the federal bench. Although its strategy has remained virtually unchanged, the NAACP has adopted some new approaches through negotiating what is called "Fair Share" agreements. These agreements are made with both public- and private-sector organizations to promote the hiring of black workers and contracts with black businesses. The organization has also begun to focus on nontraditional civil rights issue such as alcohol and substance abuse, teenage pregnancies, black-on-black crime, and other issues impacting the underclass. It continues to engage in voter registration campaigns, but being nonpartisan inhibits the mobilization of black voters for particular candidates. As the NAACP approaches its centennial in 2009, it continues to be the nation's premier civil rights organization, with more than 500,000 members in 1,700 chapters and 450 college and youth chapters.

SEE ALSO *Affirmative Action; Marshall, Thurgood; NAACP: Legal Actions, 1935–1955; White, Walter Francis; Wilkins, Roy.*

BIBLIOGRAPHY

Charles Hamilton Houston Institute for Race & Justice. Available from http://www.charleshamiltonhouston.org.

Lawson, Steven F. 1991. *Running for Freedom: Civil Rights and Black Politics in America since 1941*. New York: McGraw-Hill.

Library of Congress. *"With an Even Hand": Brown v Board at Fifty*. Available from http://www.loc.gov/exhibits/brown/brown-segregation.html.

National Association for the Advancement of Colored People Internet home page. Available from http://www.naacp.org.

Ovington, Mary White. 1914. "How the NAACP Began." Available from http://www.naacp.org/about/history/howbegan.

Smith, Robert. 1996. *We Have No Leaders: African Americans in the Post-Civil Rights Era*. Albany: State University of New York Press.

Toonari Corporation. *Black American History: NAACP*. Available from http://www.africanaonline.com.

Williams, Juan. 1987. *Eyes on the Prize: America's Civil Rights Years, 1954–1965*. New York: Viking Penguin.

Mamie E. Locke

NAACP: LEGAL ACTIONS, 1935–1955

From the 1920s through the 1950s, the National Association for the Advancement of Colored People (NAACP) pushed the country toward racial equality through organized protests and highly strategic law suits that challenged the racist laws that promoted discrimination against blacks. The organization was founded in 1909, and from its inception it was devoted to the fight against legalized racial discrimination.

THE RIGHT LEADERSHIP

In 1930, Walter White became the NAACP's national executive secretary. Under White's leadership, which lasted until 1955, the NAACP began focusing its legal challenges on five areas: voting rights, housing discrimination, equality of due process, segregation in institutions of higher education in the South, and segregation in elementary and secondary education. Legalized racial discrimination (also known as Jim Crow laws) prohibited black and white people from using the same water fountains, attending the same public schools, and having access to the same public accommodations, including restaurants, public libraries, and buses.

In a departure from other legal strategies focusing on civil rights, the NAACP pursued these cases at all levels of judicial review, including state and federal courts and before state and federal administrative agencies. In 1935 Walter White recruited Charles Hamilton Houston to lead the NAACP's legal strategy. Houston had already displayed remarkable legal talent and vision by transforming, with minimal resources, Howard University Law School into the nation's foremost school for training black lawyers. One of Houston's brilliant moves at the NAACP was his recruitment to the NAACP of one of his former students, Thurgood Marshall. During this time, Marshall became one of the nation's leading legal civil rights advocates. Prior to joining the NAACP, Marshall practiced law in Baltimore, Maryland, where he had been born and raised. In 1965, after thirty years with the NAACP, Marshall was named the United States Solicitor General, the lawyer who decides what position the United States will take when the federal government appears before the U.S. Supreme Court. On October 2, 1967, President Lyndon Johnson appointed Marshall as an Associate Justice of United States Supreme Court, making him the first black American to sit on the Supreme Court.

In 1935 Marshall became chief counsel to the Baltimore branch of the NAACP, and shortly thereafter he joined Charles Hamilton Houston in the NAACP's New York office. For the next twenty years, the NAACP engaged in legal challenges that ultimately developed into a significant body of civil rights law. Many of the civil rights cases litigated by the NAACP during this period are studied in U.S. law schools in the early twenty-first century. As counsel for the NAACP, Marshall took thirty-two cases to the Supreme Court, and he was victorious in twenty-nine of them.

Since one of the NAACP's litigation goals from 1935 through 1955 included bringing an end to Jim Crow laws, the organization focused on issues deemed necessary to gain and maintain full U.S. citizenship. The most important of these issues was voting rights. Since the end of the Reconstruction era, Southern racism had eliminated black Americans as a political force by restricting or interfering with their right to vote through violence, poll taxes, and the election primaries limited to white voters. These forms of legalized discrimination ultimately eliminated most black American southerners from eligibility to vote during most of the Jim Crow era.

BROWN V. BOARD OF EDUCATION

Jim Crow laws restricted the educational opportunities of black Americans by requiring racially segregated elementary, secondary, and undergraduate education. The NAACP's challenge against unequal educational opportunities is most famously illustrated by the case known as *Brown v. Board of Education of Topeka Kansas.* This landmark decision of the U.S. Supreme Court struck down laws permitting government support of racial segregation in public schools.

Like a mantra for equal justice, *Brown v. Board of Education* is so widely recognized by Americans that the name of the case has become a symbol unto itself. On May 17, 1954, the U.S. Supreme Court, in a unanimous decision, declared that "in the field of public education the doctrine of separate but equal" has no place in America, thus affirming that separate educational facilities are inherently unequal. The Court squarely held that racial segregation in public schools violates the Fourteenth Amendment of the U.S. Constitution, which guarantees equal protection of the law, and the Fifth Amendment of the Constitution, which guarantees due process. This case overturned a nineteenth-century legal doctrine that disregarded the pernicious effects of discrimination against black Americans. Thus, the case marked a major turning point in the struggle for civil rights. Given the history of Jim Crow, how did the Supreme Court come to issue such a groundbreaking decision? Why would the nation's highest court depart from its prior decisions approving legal racial segregation? Of course, the right question is: How did the NAACP achieve its victory?

One of the hallmarks of the NAACP's success up until 1954 was the careful selection of test cases. The victory in *Brown v. Board of Education,* and in various cases that preceded it, illustrates how the law may be used to work toward social change and equal justice. This point, however, should not overwhelm the fact that after a half century, the promise of *Brown v. Board of Education* is still subject to legal controversy. In 1992, for example, in the case of *United States v. Fordice,* the U.S. Department of Justice persuaded the Supreme Court that two southern states, Alabama and Mississippi, had not yet complied with the Court's direction in *Brown* to dismantle all systems of legal segregation in higher education.

LEGAL STRATEGIES

Resistance to racial segregation and discrimination during the pre- and postwar eras of the twentieth century was undertaken by the use of a number of different strategies, including civil disobedience, nonviolent resistance, political marches, boycotts, rallies, and proposed legislation. Increasingly, access to the courts became a formal method of resistance to segregation and a dominant strategic means to achieve racial equality. The NAACP and the NAACP Legal Defense Fund (LDF) adopted the strategy of using legal cases to promote civil rights and seek equality, dignity, and self-respect for black Americans. The NAACP adopted strategies that promoted civil rights as a response to the role legal racism played in restricting the educational and political opportunities of black Americans, and the nation's understanding of what it means to discriminate on the basis of race would shift in response to the legal challenges raised by the NAACP. The nation's courts, and ultimately Congress, were persuaded to reorient the nation toward genuinely supporting the political participation and education for all Americans

The NAACP adopted a legal strategy based upon the use of the test case. This is a strategy involving the use of a case or controversy to establish a point of law as precedent to be relied upon in future cases. The early twentieth-century civil rights lawyers focused upon convincing the courts that no matter how concealed they were, discriminatory laws based on race could not blind the courts to the role of the state in legal racism. State laws imposing racial injustice therefore could, and should, be challenged on constitutional grounds.

Other forms of legal racism often involved private individuals, private acts, or private conduct. Consequently, it became an important objective among civil rights lawyers to develop legal strategies that could pinpoint state action when legal racism was at issue in public or nonpublic settings. The LDF and local NAACP activists searched for test cases that would get them before the U.S. Supreme Court. Since the test-case strategy was primarily designed to attack laws or government conduct, the goal would be to persuade the nation's highest court to view racial injustice through the lens of due process and the Fourteenth Amendment's equal protection clause. In this respect, successful arguments to the Court would ultimately lead the Court to the dismantling of discriminatory laws on the basis of their unconstitutionality.

Despite the overall success of the NAACP's legal strategy, NAACP lawyers from time to time suffered from false starts or dead ends, and some of the cases that became crucial precedents may not have seemed important to the litigators of the time. Yet legal victories achieved by the NAACP during the mid-twentieth century provided a framework to implement public policies that began to generate social change in American race relations, especially with regard to public education.

SMITH V. ALLWRIGHT

Because Jim Crow laws were predominately enacted by states and local governments in the South, the NAACP necessarily involved litigants in southern states. The 1944 case of *Smith v. Allwright* set the stage for *Brown v. Board of Education* ten years later. The case involved a black Texas voter, Lonnie E. Smith, who sued for the right to vote in a primary election conducted by the Democratic Party. Thurgood Marshall represented Smith. The law he challenged mandated that all voters in primary elections be white. At the time, the Republican Party was weak in most of the South, with its adherents being only a fraction of the eligible voters in any given locality. Thus, elections were essentially decided by the outcome of the Democratic primary.

Marshall argued that the state law at issue disenfranchised black voters by denying them the ability to vote in the only meaningful election in their jurisdictions. The U.S. Supreme Court agreed with this view of racial injustice, and found in Smith's favor. The Court held that the State of Texas, by its statute, had denied Smith the equal protection secured by the Fourteenth Amendment. This case overruled the Court's earlier doctrine in *Grovey v. Townsend* (1935), which ruled that political parties were not agents of the state but voluntary associations. Now, however, the Court seemed to signal that it was prepared to ensure that the right of citizens of the United States to vote could not be denied or abridged on the basis of race by any state or any association taking part in elections. Political parties operating as private organizations, freely electing officers from candidates of their own membership could not exclude African Americans from their primary elections. What was at issue was whether the opportunity to vote in a primary election for seats in the Congress of the United States used the apparatus of the state. In Texas, the answer was yes.

The State of Texas, by its own constitution and state laws, provided that every person qualified by residence in the district or county "shall be deemed a qualified elector." The Supreme Court reasoned that whereas a state was free to conduct elections and limit electorate participation, the Fourteenth Amendment forbade the states from abridging the right to vote on account of race. As such, the Democratic Party of Texas, although it was a voluntary organization freely able to select its own membership, could not legally limit participation in the party primary to whites.

The Court rejected the argument that the protections of the Constitution are applicable only to general elections. Primaries, the state argued, are political party affairs, handled by the party and not by governmental officials. The state's argument, however, did not square with the Court. Instead, the Court sided with the NAACP's lawyers, who argued that the right to vote in a primary for the nomination of candidates, like the right to vote in a general election, is a right secured by the U.S. Constitution, and that that right may not be abridged by any state on account of race. Accordingly, the Court did not allow the use of private organizations or political parties in the election system to camouflage the role of the state in the electoral process. Racial discrimination in this case was clearly traceable to the state, and the white-only primary was a clear instance of legal racism that the Court was prepared to strike down.

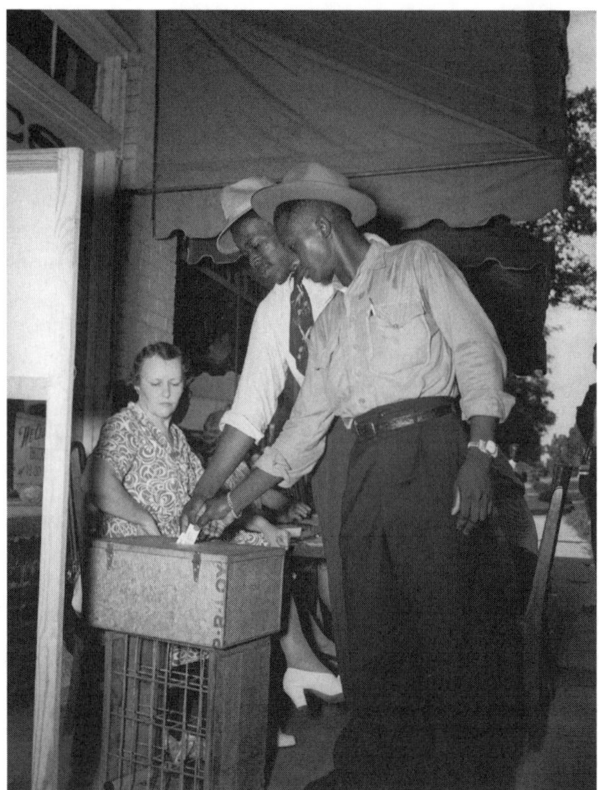

Democratic Primary Vote. *African Americans vote in the Mississippi Democratic primary in 1946. The Supreme Court's decision in* Smith v. Allwright *started a political revolution in the South.* © BETTMANN/CORBIS.

SHELLEY V. KRAEMER

In another case, NAACP lawyers raised the issue of whether the use of a private agreement or contract could insulate a state from the reach of the federal Constitution. In 1945 a black family by the name of Shelley purchased a house in St. Louis, Missouri, but a "restrictive covenant" had been placed on the property in 1911. Restrictive covenants were used to limit an owner's right to sell property to whomever he or she desired. Such covenants were used by white property owners to prevent future home sales to black

Americans. In *Shelley v. Kraemer,* the restrictive covenant at issue barred blacks and Asians from owning the property the Shelleys had purchased, and neighbors sued to restrain them from taking possession of the property. Thirty out of a total of thirty-nine owners in the area had signed an agreement containing a restrictive covenant, which held that "the said property is hereby restricted ... that hereafter no part of said property or any portion thereof shall be ... occupied by any person not of the Caucasian race."

At the time the agreement was signed, black Americans owned five of the parcels in the district, and black families had occupied one of those since 1882. The trial court found that some of the owners of homes within the restricted area of the premises in question had failed to sign the restrictive agreement in 1911. On August 11, 1945, pursuant to a contract of sale, the Shelleys obtained a deed to their new home. On October 9, 1945, the owners of other property subject to the terms of the restrictive covenant brought suit in Circuit Court of the City of St. Louis, requesting that the court divest the Shelleys of the title to the property. The trial court denied the requested relief on the ground that the restrictive agreement had never become final and complete because it had not been signed by all property owners in the district.

The Supreme Court of Missouri reversed this decision and directed the trial court to grant relief for the neighbors, holding that the agreement was legal and that enforcement of its provisions violated no rights guaranteed by the Constitution. Notably, at the time the court rendered its decision, the Shelleys were occupying the property.

The NAACP recognized that this case could allow the civil rights movement to build on legal precedent, while also attacking a discriminatory restriction on equal access to housing. Charles Hamilton Houston, the first African American to earn a Doctor of Juridical Science degree at Harvard, and Thurgood Marshall, argued the case before the U.S. Supreme Court. At issue two questions: (1) Are (race-based) restrictive covenants legal under the Fourteenth Amendment of the U.S. Constitution? and (2) Can they be enforced by a court of law?

Although this case focused on an economic opportunity, it followed closely upon the context of *Smith v. Allwright.* In both cases, the Supreme Court was faced with the task of drawing a line between presumptively permissible private discrimination based on race and unlawful state discrimination based on race. The Supreme Court held in this case that it is unconstitutional under the Fourteenth Amendment for the government to enforce such a restrictive covenant, because to do so requires judicial action by the state.

The only pertinent arguments that the Shelley's neighbors could raise was that judicial enforcement of private agreements did not amount to state action, and that the participation of the state is so attenuated that its participation could not constitute state action within the meaning of the Fourteenth Amendment. The Court determined, however, that there had indeed been state action in the case. The Court observed that the Shelleys were willing purchasers of the property, and that the owners were willing sellers. It was clear that but for the active intervention of the state courts, the Shelleys would have been free to occupy the property without restraint. The freedom from discrimination by the states in the enjoyment of property rights was among the basic objectives sought by the framers of the Fourteenth Amendment. For the Court, whatever else the framers sought to achieve, it was clear that the matter of primary concern was the establishment of equality in the enjoyment of basic civil and political rights, and the Court sought to preserve those rights from discriminatory action on the part of the states based on considerations of race or color.

SWEATT V. PAINTER

In *Sweatt v. Painter,* Herman Sweatt, a black American, was denied admission to the University of Texas Law School on the grounds that substantially equivalent facilities were offered by a law school open only to blacks (thus meeting the requirements of the 1896 decision in *Plessy v. Ferguson*). At the time the plaintiff first applied to the University of Texas, there was no law school in Texas that admitted blacks. The Texas trial court, instead of granting the plaintiff a *writ of mandamus* (a court order from a superior court to a lower or trial court to comply with a legal command in order to safeguard an individual's legal interest), postponed the trial for six months, allowing the state time to create a law school only for blacks. Ultimately, the U.S. Supreme Court reversed a trial court opinion that the newly established state law school for black Americans met the "separate but equal" judicial doctrine prevailing after *Plessy v. Ferguson.*

The University of Texas Law School had sixteen full-time and three part-time professors, 850 students, a library of 65,000 volumes, a law review, moot court facilities, scholarship funds, an Order of the Coif affiliation, distinguished alumni, and prestige. The separate law school for black Americans had five full-time professors, twenty-three students, a library of 16,500 volumes, a practice court, a legal aid association, and one alumnus admitted to the Texas Bar. At issue in this case was whether the legal education offered by the new school was substantially equal to that offered by the University of Texas Law School. W. J. Durham and Thurgood Marshall argued the case before the Court, recognizing that it could prove exceptionally useful as a test case, and perhaps help overturn the *Plessy* standard of separate but equal facilities.

Leading up to *Sweatt v. Painter,* the civil rights movement obtained a couple of additional helpful victories. In *Missouri ex rel. Gaines v. Canada* (1938), the U.S. Supreme Court invalidated state laws that refused black students access to all-white state graduate schools when no separate state graduate schools were available for African-Americans. In *Sipuel v. Oklahoma State Regents* (1948) the Court reaffirmed and extended *Missouri ex rel. Gaines v. Canada,* ruling that Oklahoma could not bar a black student from its all-white law school on the ground that she had not requested the state to provide a separate law school for black students. Perhaps forecasting the NAACP's focus on attacking legal racism in public education, Marshall had won a case in 1935 in the Maryland Court of Appeals against the state's law school, which gained admission for Donald Murray, a black graduate of Amherst College who had been denied admission to the law school based on the separate but equal doctrine. While significant, this ruling did not apply outside of Maryland. Marshall himself had been denied admittance to the University of Maryland Law School on the basis of race.

Following these precedents, the Supreme Court ruled in *Sweatt v. Painter* that, "with such a substantial and significant segment of society excluded, we cannot conclude that the education offered petitioner is substantially equal to that which he would receive if admitted to the University of Texas Law School." The court also considered whether excluding Sweatt from the University of Texas Law School was no different from excluding white students from the state's new law school. It concluded that it was unlikely that a member of a group so decisively in the majority and attending a school with rich traditions and prestige would seriously claim that the opportunities afforded him for legal education were unequal to those held open to Sweatt. Here, the Court concluded: "Equal protection of the laws is not achieved through indiscriminate imposition of inequalities."

Ruling that Sweatt could claim his full constitutional right, the Court held that a black American had a right to a legal education equivalent to that offered by the state to students of other races. Although the Court refused to expressly overrule *Plessy v. Ferguson,* and thus leaving the doctrine of separate but equal in place, the Court acknowledged that the equal protection clause of the Fourteenth Amendment required that Herman Sweatt be admitted to the University of Texas Law School.

Notwithstanding the success of Sweatt, the fact that the doctrine of *Plessy v. Ferguson* was not flatly rejected illustrates why *Brown* was necessary to complete the objectives of the civil rights lawyers. The constitutional evil of the separate but equal doctrine was that blacks were told to go to one set of schools, while whites could go to another set that, in practice, clearly provided a better education. This form of legal racism was pernicious because of its implicit stigmatization of black students. In *Brown,* the Court acknowledged that to separate black students from others of similar age and qualifications solely because of race generates a feeling of inferiority that affects the individual in a manner unlikely ever to be undone.

SEE ALSO *Brown v. Board of Education; Marshall, Thurgood.*

BIBLIOGRAPHY

Abernathy, Charles. 2006. *Civil Rights and Constitutional Litigation: Cases and Materials.* 4thd ed. American Casebook Series. St. Paul, MN: West Publishing Company.

Alderman, Ellen, and Caroline Kennedy. 1991. *In Our Defense: The Bill of Rights in Action.* New York: William Morrow.

Ball, Edward. 2001. *The Sweet Hell Inside: A Family History.* New York: William Morrow.

Bell, Derrick. 2004. *Silent Covenants: Brown* v. *Board of Education and the Unfulfilled Hopes for Racial Reform.* Oxford: Oxford University Press.

Blumberg, Rhoda. 1991. *Civil Rights: The 1960s Freedom Struggle.* Rev. ed. Boston: Twayne.

Branch, Taylor. 1988. *Parting the Waters: America in the King Years, 1954–63.* New York: Simon and Schuster.

Cottrol, Robert J., Raymond T. Diamond, and Leland B. Ware. 2003. *Brown* v. *Board of Education: Caste, Culture, and the Constitution.* Landmark Law Cases and American Society Series. Lawrence: University Press of Kansas.

Holt, Thomas. 1977. *Black over White: Negro Political Leadership in South Carolina during Reconstruction.* Urbana: University of Illinois Press.

Jonas, Gilbert. 2005. *Freedom's Sword: The NAACP and the Struggle against Racism in America, 1909–1969.* New York: Routledge.

Klarman, Michael J. 2004. *From Jim Crow to Civil Rights: The Supreme Court and the Struggle for Racial Equality.* Oxford: Oxford University Press.

Kluger, Richard. 1976. *Simple Justice: The History of Brown v. Board of Education and Black America's Struggle for Equality.* New York: Alfred A. Knopf.

Ogletree, Charles J. 2004. *All Deliberate Speed: Reflections on the First Half-Century of Brown* v. *Board of Education.* New York: W. W. Norton.

Ransom, Roger L., and Richard Sutch. 1977. *One Kind of Freedom: The Economic Consequences of Emancipation.* Cambridge, UK: Cambridge University Press.

Williams, Juan. 1998. *Thurgood Marshall: American Revolutionary.* New York: Times Books.

Rod Dixon

NAGPRA

SEE *Native American Graves Protection and Repatriation Act (NAGPRA).*

NATION OF ISLAM AND NEW BLACK PANTHER PARTY

The Nation of Islam (NOI) and the New Black Panther Party (NBPP) are the largest and most active black racist organizations in America. The NOI—modeled after other socioreligious groups such as Noble Drew Ali's Moorish Science Temple and Marcus Garvey's Universal Negro Improvement Association—is the oldest black nationalist organization in the United States. Since its founding in the 1930s, it has both instilled African Americans with a sense of empowerment and maintained a consistent record of racism and anti-Semitism.

Fard Muhammad, the founder of the NOI, taught his followers in Detroit that he was the personification of Allah. Fard's disciple, Elijah Muhammad, assumed leadership of the group when Fard disappeared in the mid-1930s. He continued to advance the NOI's radical religious beliefs promoting the doctrine that whites are "devils" created by a black scientist, and that blacks are superior and should have a separate nation within the United States.

The group significantly expanded in the 1950s and 1960s when Malcolm X, a captivating orator who joined the group while in prison, became its spokesman. His militant and charismatic style attracted many adherents, including the group's future leader, Louis Farrakhan. In 1964, however, Malcolm altered his views, denounced Elijah Muhammad, and left the organization (he was shot to death while addressing a rally in New York in 1965).

When Elijah Muhammad died ten years later, his son Warith Deen Mohammed began to steer the group toward a nonracist, more traditional form of Islam. Farrakhan, by then a popular leader, elected to perpetuate Elijah's separatist teachings by forming his own organization in 1978, and many members who preferred to keep the teachings of Elijah left with him.

More than any other NOI leader, Farrakhan marked himself as a notable figure on the extremist scene by making hateful statements targeting whites, Jews, and homosexuals. Under Farrakhan, the NOI has used its various institutions and programs to disseminate his message of hate. A major NOI publication, *The Secret Relationship of Blacks and Jews*, published in 1991, is one of the most significant anti-Semitic works produced in decades. It presents a multilayered attack against Jews, arguing essentially that slavery in the New World was initiated by Jewish ship owners and merchants. This alleged domination of blacks by Jews has continued into the present day, according to Farrakhan.

The NOI experienced a notable growth in media visibility and acceptance by the mainstream African-American community in the period leading up to the 1995 Million Man March in Washington, D.C. This popular reception of the NOI stressed the group's focus on black self-reliance and minimized the group's well-established record of racism. Although he has continued to make racially divisive comments—in the wake of Hurricane Katrina, Farrakhan alleged that levees were purposely destroyed in African-American sections of New Orleans—some observers suggest that Farrakhan's message has changed, and he has maintained a level of mainstream support.

Farrakhan has also reached out to the New Black Panther Party for Self-Defense (NBPP), which since the late 1990s has become the most blatantly racist and anti-Semitic black militant group in America. The NBPP takes its name from the original Black Panther Party, a radical black nationalist group active in the 1960s and 1970s. The roots of the New Black Panthers can be traced to Michael McGee, former Milwaukee alderman. In 1990, at a "State of the Inner City" press conference at city hall, McGee announced his intention to create the Black Panther Militia unless the problems of the inner-city improved. McGee then appeared on Dallas county commissioner John Wiley Price's nightly radio show "Talkback" in 1990. Aaron Michaels, who produced the radio show, was inspired to found the NBPP after McGee's appearance, registering the New Black Panther Party name in 1991. Although the group continues to use "for Self-Defense" on its Internet site and in other places, the group is often referred to as simply the New Black Panther Party.

Michaels organized a group of like-minded followers, borrowing the militant style and confrontational tactics of the original Panthers. The group apparently established a nationwide base during the next few years. In 1993 the Dallas chapter hosted the National Black Power Summit and Youth Rally, which drew about 200 people. In an effort to make common cause in favor of racial separatism, the white supremacist Tom Metzger was invited to speak.

Under Michaels' leadership, the NBPP embraced racist leaders, most notably Khallid Abdul Muhammad, a former member of the NOI who had previously served as an NOI minister in Los Angeles, Atlanta, and New York, and as Farrakhan's national spokesman. Muhammad's rise through the NOI hierarchy was abruptly halted in November 1993, after he delivered a notoriously anti-Semitic, anti-Catholic, homophobic, and racist speech at New Jersey's Kean College. In his remarks, Muhammad called for genocide against whites and referred to Jews as "bloodsuckers." Farrakhan responded to the controversy by removing Muhammad from the group's leadership, and Muhammad never regained a significant place in the NOI.

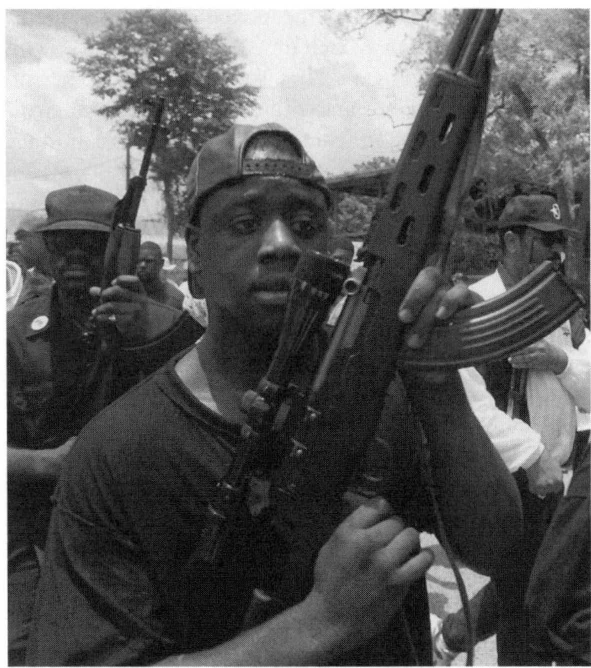

New Black Panther Party Demonstration, 1998. The New Black Panther Party (NBPP) is one of the largest black racist organizations in America. AP PHOTO/PAT SULLIVAN.

With his connection to NOI waning, Muhammad focused on raising the visibility of the NBPP and consolidating his leadership over it. Even without NOI backing, Muhammad remained a popular (if divisive) and publicity-generating speaker at colleges and universities and at public events across the country. By the summer of 1998, Muhammad became de facto leader of the NBPP, taking on high-profile, racially charged causes and seeking to recruit young men attracted to his racist message and militant tone. In June 1998, Muhammad led a group of fifty NBPP followers to Jasper, Texas—including a dozen carrying shotguns and rifles—to "protect" the streets in the wake of the racial murder of James Byrd Jr.

Muhammad then organized the "Million Youth March" in Harlem, New York, which provided a forum to showcase the emergent NBPP as an alternative to other groups interested in guiding black youth, specifically the NOI. The event would be remembered for reaffirming black separatism and antiwhite prejudice, as well as fomenting hostility toward local police.

In addition to organizing high-profile demonstrations, Muhammad's accomplishments with the NBPP include filling the organizational hierarchy with figures from the NOI and other Black Muslim groups. In February 2001, Muhammad died suddenly in Atlanta from the effects of a brain aneurysm. Control of the NBPP was left to Malik Zulu Shabazz, a Washington D.C.–based attorney and Muhammad's closest advisor.

Like Muhammad, Shabazz's long record of extremist speech can be traced to the NOI. In 1988 he founded Unity Nation, a Howard University group of NOI supporters. As the group's leader, Shabazz lashed out at whites and Jews in an ostensible effort to promote black pride and consciousness.

Shabazz, who could not match his mentor's oratorical intensity, compensated by quickly organizing protests across the country to capitalize on media attention. For example, Shabazz and the NBPP exploited the fear and anger that the September 11 terrorists attacks caused in the U.S. by spreading anti-Jewish conspiracy theories during a televised meeting at the National Press Club in Washington D.C.

By linking up with the NOI and feeding off of the nostalgia for the original Panthers, the NBPP has been able to attract some followers under the guise of championing the causes of black empowerment and civil rights. However, like the NOI, its record of racism and anti-Semitism has overshadowed many of its efforts to promote black pride and consciousness. Farrakhan's outreach to Shabazz and the NBPP in 2005 represents a significant development in the relationship between two groups that once competed with each other.

BIBLIOGRAPHY

Historical Research Department of the Nation of Islam. 1991. *The Secret Relationship between Blacks and Jews.* Nation of Islam.

Lincoln, Charles E. 1973. *The Black Muslims in America.* Boston, MA: Beacon Press.

Muhammad, Elijah. 1965. *Message to the Blackman in America.* Chicago, IL: Muhammad's Temple No. 2.

White Jr., Vibert L. 2001. *Inside the Nation of Islam.* Gainesville: University Press of Florida.

Oren Segal

NATIONAL ALLIANCE

For more than three decades, the National Alliance, headquartered at a rural hilltop compound outside Mill Point, West Virginia, has been one of the most important and best-organized hate groups in America. Founded and long led by William Pierce, a one-time university physics professor, the neo-Nazi group's influence peaked in the 1990s, when it perfected a remarkably successful business model and Pierce's ideological influence stretched across much of the Western Hemisphere. Over the years, it produced huge amounts of very effective propaganda, including Pierce's novel *The Turner Diaries,* which inspired numerous acts of terror, including the 1995 bombing of an Oklahoma City federal building that left

168 people dead. The group, which mentions in its platform statement the "temporary unpleasantness" that will follow its accession to power, is explicitly genocidal in intent. Pierce once described how he hoped to lock Jews, "race traitors," and other enemies of the "Aryan" race into cattle cars and send them to the bottom of abandoned coal mines. It has produced a large number of extremist assassins, bank robbers, and bombers. The Alliance has been a major player in the white-power music business, running an operation called Resistance Records that was, for a time, the leading label of its type. But the group, which was in many respects a cult of personality, has had severe difficulties surviving the 2002 death of its founder. Since then, the Alliance has been riven by internal divisions and repeatedly embarrassed by antiracist organizations. By 2005 its membership had fallen to fewer than two hundred, less than a seventh the number it had when Pierce died.

A native of Atlanta, William Luther Pierce became an assistant professor of physics at Oregon State University in 1962. He joined the rabidly anticommunist John Birch Society during his three years at OSU. In 1965 he left the university for the private sector, but he abandoned that work the following year to take up with the American Nazi Party, based in Arlington, Virginia. There, he edited the *National Socialist World*, a quarterly published by the party and meant to appeal to intellectuals, until 1967, when the group's leader, George Lincoln Rockwell, was assassinated by a disgruntled follower. Pierce then became a principal leader of Rockwell's renamed organization, the National Socialist White People's Party, before leaving in 1970 for the National Youth Alliance. That group had emerged from the rubble of the 1968 presidential campaign of the segregationist Alabama governor George Wallace, and it had been taken over by Willis Carto, a leading anti-Semitic activist. After a feud between Pierce and Carto, Pierce finally won control of the organization and, in 1974, shortened its name to the National Alliance.

The next year, Pierce serialized *The Turner Diaries* in *Attack!*, a publication he had started while he was with the National Socialist White People's Party. The manuscript, which would be published as a book in 1978 under the pseudonym of Andrew Macdonald, described a future race war in which Jews and others are slaughtered by the thousands, with its hero at one point promising to go "to the uttermost ends of the earth to hunt down the last of Satan's spawn" (meaning Jews). Along with others of Pierce's writings he edited *National Vanguard* (the renamed *Attack!*) and the members-only *National Alliance Bulletin* until his death, and also wrote another race-war novel, *Hunter*. *The Turner Diaries* became one of the most important pieces of extremist literature ever written in America.

In 1985 Pierce moved the group from the Washington, D.C., area to a 346-acre piece of land in Pocahontas County, West Virginia, where it would remain even after his death. Although he initially managed to win tax-exempt status for the property by describing it as owned by the "Cosmotheist" church (a pseudo-theology dreamed up by Pierce as a tax dodge) in 1986 officials stripped that exemption from all but 60 acres of the property, the part where "religious" activities supposedly prevailed. An earlier attempt by Pierce to win tax-exempt status as an "educational" institution ultimately failed when a federal appeals court upheld the initial IRS denial.

The National Alliance produced or harbored a large number of serious criminals. In 1983, for instance, the group's Pacific Northwest coordinator, Robert Mathews, broke away to form a terrorist group called The Order (clearly patterned on The Organization described in *The Turner Diaries*) that carried out a series of murders and armored car heists before Mathews was killed in a shootout with the FBI. Twelve years later, the Oklahoma City bomber Timothy McVeigh had photocopies of pages of *The Turner Diaries* when he was arrested, apparently to explain his motivation in the deadly attack. (McVeigh called an Alliance telephone line seven times the day before the bombing.) In all, Alliance members were connected to at least fourteen violent crimes between 1984 and 2005, including bank robberies, shootouts with police, and a plan to bomb the main approach to Walt Disney World in Florida.

The National Alliance's chief asset was always Pierce. In addition to his writings, Pierce appeared regularly on "American Dissident Voices," a shortwave radio show broadcast (and later simulcast on the Internet) by the group. He was explicitly Hitlerian in ideology, seeking to create a Nazi-like state in which the Alliance would rule the nation. He was also, in effect, a Leninist, in the sense that he never believed that the white masses (whom he regularly referred to as "lemmings") could lead themselves. Instead, the Alliance would lead them in a racially based authoritarian society that would be marked by Germanic music and "healthy" racial values.

As rabid as Pierce could sound—he once described Hitler as "the greatest man of our era," and elsewhere he wrote about the "relatively brief period of bloodletting" needed to return America to health—he was widely admired on the radical right for his ability to interpret world events in terms of neo-Nazi ideology. His disdain for Klansmen, racist skinheads, and neo-Nazis, with their penchant for parading in costume, won him plaudits from many leading racists. In the 1990s, Pierce built bridges to neofascist leaders in Europe, becoming an increasingly important figure there as well.

It was during that decade that the National Alliance became the most important hate group in America. In

1992, the Alliance had only three units, or chapters. By 1997, after years of careful recruiting, the group had grown to twenty-two units. Two years later, it boasted of chapters in eleven South American and European countries, and *The Turner Diaries* was translated and made available free in half a dozen languages. By 2002, the year of Pierce's death, the Alliance had 1,400 members in fifty-one U.S. units.

It was also profitable, thanks to the business model Pierce devised. For years the Alliance derived its income from members (who paid at least $10 per month in dues) and sales from its National Vanguard Books division. In 1999 Pierce added a key component, Resistance Records, a music label started by racists associated with another neo-Nazi group that had gone almost belly up. Pierce paid some $250,000 for the company, which he quickly built up through the addition of a warehouse on the West Virginia compound and a slick advertising campaign. By the year of Pierce's death, the National Alliance was grossing a total of almost $1 million from these sources, allowing Pierce to pay salaries to seventeen full-time national staff members—an accomplishment unmatched by any other contemporary hate group.

On July 23, 2002, at the age of sixty-eight, Pierce died unexpectedly of kidney failure and cancer, leaving control of the group in the hands of Cleveland unit leader Erich Gliebe, a man who used to box professionally as the "Aryan Barbarian." A hard-edged and humorless leader, Gliebe faced an uphill battle in holding the group together.

It did not help when the Southern Poverty Law Center's *Intelligence Report* obtained a tape of Pierce's last speech, given three months earlier at one of the semiannual secret "leadership conferences" held at the compound. Just weeks after Pierce's death, the *Report* published details of the speech, in which Pierce, parroted later by Gliebe, pilloried members of other hate groups as "freaks and weaklings" and "human defectives." That story, and others that followed it, had the effect of setting off a firestorm among non-Alliance hate-group members—in particular, the skinheads and others who had formed the customer base for Resistance Records. A boycott of Resistance quickly developed, and many radicals attacked the group.

The *Report* also published a series of other embarrassing facts in the following months, including the revelation that a Resistance calendar meant to highlight Aryan female beauty in fact featured a bevy of strippers from an all-nude men's club near Alliance headquarters. The magazine also reported details of wasted money and political infighting within the group. Gliebe's 2005 marriage to a former stripper and *Playboy* model hurt his prestige even further.

Between these kinds of revelations and massive resentment against Gliebe and his second-in-command, Shaun Walker, for their dictatorial management style, the National Alliance lost most of its key activists and unit leaders. Both Resistance Records and National Vanguard Books became unprofitable. In a desperate bid to keep the group alive, Walker replaced Gliebe as chairman in early 2005, while Gliebe was relegated to running Resistance. By the spring of that year, the group was down to under 200 members and had lost almost all its prestige. Meanwhile, two other neo-Nazi groups—White Revolution and National Vanguard, both started by men expelled from the Alliance by Gliebe—began to grow, largely on the basis of former National Alliance members who no longer trusted their once-proud alma mater.

SEE ALSO *Neo-Nazis.*

BIBLIOGRAPHY

Anti-Defamation League. 1996. *Danger: Extremism—The Major Vehicles and Voices on America's Far-Right Fringe.* New York: Anti-Defamation League.

Griffin, Robert S. 2001. *The Fame of a Dead Man's Deeds: An Up-Close Portrait of White Nationalist William Pierce.* Bloomington, IN: 1st Books Library, 2001.

Kaplan, Jeffrey. 2000. *Encyclopedia of White Power: A Sourcebook on the Radical Racist Right.* Lanham, MD: AltaMira Press.

Pierce, William. 1996. *The Turner Diaries.* 2nd ed. New York: Barricade Books.

Potok, Mark. "Money, Music and the Doctor." 1999. *Intelligence Report* 96: 33–36. Montgomery, AL: Southern Poverty Law Center.

———. 2000. "Darker Than Black." *Intelligence Report* 100: 6–15. Montgomery, AL: Southern Poverty Law Center.

———. 2000. "Paying the Price." *Intelligence Report* 97: 53–56. Montgomery, AL: Southern Poverty Law Center.

———. 2002. "Divided Alliance." *Intelligence Report* 108: 30–35. Montgomery, AL: Southern Poverty Law Center.

———. 2002. "Facing the Future." *Intelligence Report* 107: 30–38. Montgomery, AL: Southern Poverty Law Center.

———. 2003. "Against the Wall." *Intelligence Report* 111: 8–14. Montgomery, AL: Southern Poverty Law Center.

———. 2003. "In Sheep's Clothing." *Intelligence Report* 110: 20–24. Montgomery, AL: Southern Poverty Law Center.

———. 2004. "Raunchy Revolutionaries." *Intelligence Report* 115: 6–9. Montgomery, AL: Southern Poverty Law Center.

———. 2005. "Meltdown." *Intelligence Report* 118: 6–7. Montgomery, AL: Southern Poverty Law Center.

Mark Potok
Heidi L. Beirich

NATIONAL ASSOCIATION FOR THE ADVANCEMENT OF COLORED PEOPLE

SEE *NAACP; NAACP: Legal Actions, 1935-1955.*

NATIONAL STATES RIGHTS PARTY

From 1958 to the mid-1980s, the National States Rights Party (NSRP) was an influential force in the white supremacist movement in the United States. The party organized protests against the civil rights movement and other perceived enemies, published and distributed racist propaganda, and used intimidation tactics against religious and ethnic minorities. It also effectively networked factions of the Ku Klux Klan, neo-Nazi organizations, and other racist and anti-Semitic groups, intertwining these hardcore factions with traditional forms of racism and segregation common in the southern United States. The NSRP was the creation of two extremely active and avowed white supremacists, Edward R. Fields (b. 1932) and Jesse B. Stoner (1924–2005), who led the organization for more than two decades during the most intense period of the civil rights struggle in the United States.

FOUNDING

The NSRP was founded in 1958 in Jefferson, Indiana, as a political party primarily advocating anti-Catholic, anti-Semitic, antiblack, and white supremacist ideals. It moved its headquarters briefly to Atlanta, Georgia, and then to Birmingham, Alabama, in 1961. It remained in Birmingham until 1971, when it relocated to Marietta, Georgia. Its founders met in 1952 while attending Atlanta Law School, where Fields joined Stoner's Christian Anti-Jewish Party, which aimed to make being Jewish punishable by death. Stoner earned a law degree, but Fields dropped out and relocated to Davenport, Iowa, where he earned a degree in chiropractics while continuing to promote anti-Semitism. The degrees earned by Fields and Stoner were seen by their typically less-educated following as prestigious, helping them garner wide respect for the NSRP after the two reunited to form the group in 1958. Stoner served as chairman and general counsel for the group, and Fields was secretary and editor of the *Thunderbolt,* the NSRP newsletter.

NSRP MARKS CIVIL RIGHTS BATTLES

On June 29, 1958, soon after the founding of the NSRP, Stoner placed a dynamite bomb outside of Bethel Baptist Church in Birmingham, Alabama. Because the black church was empty, no casualties resulted from the blast. The FBI, investigating violence against black and Jewish places of worship in the 1960s, suspected that Stoner had participated in at least a dozen bombings of churches and synagogues throughout the southern states. He was only convicted once, however, in 1980, for conspiracy to commit murder in the bombing of Bethel Baptist. Law enforcement agents also suspected that Stoner, due to a distinct limp resulting from childhood polio, resigned himself in the early 1960s to inciting sympathizers to carry out similar attacks in his stead.

In addition to intimidation tactics, the NSRP published the *Thunderbolt,* in which Fields touted traditional anti-Semitic rhetoric, promoted the ideas of Hitler, and often called for violence. In one piece he opined that racial tension in America would be solved if all Jews were expelled to Madagascar and blacks to Africa. In another, Fields called for the execution of the justices on the U.S. Supreme Court.

The NSRP's rise to prominence in the white supremacist movement came during a time of passionate opposition to the civil rights movement by segregationists in the southern United States. The NSRP went beyond mere advocacy of segregation and voiced what are still staples of white supremacist ideology. Fields and Stoner's organization blatantly attacked Jews, whom they believed were behind a conspiracy to eliminate the white race by promoting integration. Decades later, neo-Nazi groups commonly voiced the same theory with regard to Hispanic and Latino immigration to the United States.

By the early 1960s, the NSRP outreach had grown to include some powerful individuals, including the Alabama governor George Wallace and the head of the Alabama State Patrol, Al Lingo. According to a 1993 missive from Fields to the author Dan T. Carter, Fields and his NSRP cohort James Warner met with Lingo, who informed them that if the NSRP were able to manage a "boisterous campaign" against the integration of schools, that the governor would be forced to close such schools.

The NSRP organized demonstrations in several southern states, often resulting in violence. In 1964, an NSRP rally in St. Augustine, Florida, resulted in injuries to forty people after sympathizers attacked civil rights demonstrators. The attack was incited by NSRP member Connie Lynch, who told hundreds of supporters, "I favor violence to preserve the white race ... some niggers are going to get killed in this process." ("Edward Fields," Anti-Defamation League Internet site).

In 1972, Stoner attempted to enter politics, running for the U.S. Senate in the Georgia Democratic primary on the platform of segregation. Stoner appeared in approximately 120 radio and television campaign advertisements, stating "the niggers want integration because the niggers want our white women," and urging Georgians to "vote white" (Forster and Epstein 1974, p. 301). Stoner lost the primary but received more than 40,000 votes, which Fields later elated in the *Thunderbolt* as "sensational."

DECLINE AND LEGACY OF THE NSRP

The group's impact on the white supremacist movement waned in 1983, when Stoner was imprisoned for conspiracy to commit murder and Fields was ousted by his own members for diverting NSRP funds. By 1987 the NSRP was defunct. In November 1986, Stoner, fresh from serving an abbreviated ten-year prison sentence for the 1958 bombing, founded the Crusade Against Corruption, which included a public awareness campaign regarding the disease AIDS. Stoner claimed, according to a 1986 article in the *Atlanta Constitution,* that only blacks were vulnerable to the disease and that whites were immune, unless they were homosexuals. Stoner ran in a primary for lieutenant governor of Georgia in 1990, and though he lost he garnered 31,000 votes. He suffered a stroke in 2001 and died in April 2005.

In the late 1980s, Fields, attempting to increase declining readership for the *Thunderbolt,* changed the newsletter's title to *The Truth At Last.* He still publishes the periodical despite a far lower circulation. In 1993 Fields attempted to resurrect a group similar to the NSRP called the America First Party, co-founded by A. J. Barker, the head of the North Carolina chapter of the ultraconservative Council of Conservative Citizens. Fields, in addition to writing racist tracts, continued his activism by occasionally delivering speeches at neo-Nazi gatherings and associating with Aryan Nations, the National Alliance, the Creativity Movement, and the former Ku Klux Klan leader David Duke.

In 2005, a small group of white supremacists in Philadelphia, Mississippi, led by Thomas Pou, formed a group with the same name, the National States' Rights Party. The group materialized during the Philadelphia murder trial of former Klansman Edgar Ray Killen, who was convicted of killing three civil rights activists in 1964. While there is not a direct connection between this neo-NSRP and the group founded by Stoner and Fields, the legacy of ideals promoted by the latter are maintained in extreme circles of the far right, including the Philadelphia-based NSRP.

SEE ALSO *Neo-Nazis.*

BIBLIOGRAPHY

Carter, Dan T. 1995. *The Politics of Rage: George Wallace, the Origins of the New Conservatism, and the Transformation of American Politics.* New York: Simon & Schuster.

Chalmers, David M. 1965. *Hooded Americanism: The First Century of the Ku Klux Klan, 1865–1965.* Garden City, NY: Doubleday.

"Edward Fields." Anti-Defamation League. Available from http://www.adl.org/learn.

Forster, Arnold, and Benjamin R. Epstein. 1974. *The New Anti-Semitism.* New York: McGraw-Hill.

Allen Kohlhepp

NATIONAL URBAN LEAGUE

SEE *Urban League.*

NATIVE AMERICAN GRAVES PROTECTION AND REPATRIATION ACT (NAGPRA)

In 1990, the U.S. Government began a historic repatriation process that would return to the native peoples of the United States the remains of some of their dead, as well as cultural property that was wrongfully taken in earlier times. This process is occurring under the Native American Graves Protection and Repatriation Act (NAGPRA), which was signed into law by President George H. W. Bush in 1990. NAGPRA is a human rights law enacted as part of Congress's Indian trust responsibilities. It protects Native American graves, prohibits the sale of native dead or their body parts, and establishes procedures and legal standards for returning this material, along with other cultural items, to Native American communities and owners.

THE BACKGROUND AND NEED FOR NAGPRA

Native Americans have experienced a long history of grave robbing by non-Indians. While the graves and dead bodies of white Americans have always been strictly protected by law, Indian graves were actively dug up and the contents removed by soldiers, pot hunters, curiosity seekers, scientists, and museum collection crews. As early as 1620, Pilgrims were opening Indian graves, "looking for underground stashes of food" (Mann 2005, p. 51). Since then, historians have documented the widespread collection of Native American human remains social norms making it acceptable to dig Indian graves but a crime to dig the graves of other races.

The roots of this double standard stem largely from the notions of race and racial theories among American scientists in the mid-1800s. Their interest in racial biology prompted great interest in collecting Indian skulls for cranial research. The craniologists assumed that "each race possessed a uniquely shaped skull," and they believed that "cranial measurements provided an index of brain size and hence intelligence" (Bieder 1990, pp. 5–6). To that end, Samuel G. Morton, the founder of physical anthropology in America, bought thousands of skulls. His pseudoscientific findings of nonwhite racial inferiority colored racial thinking for many years.

Consequently, "civilization for Indians was virtually impossible" and they "faced inevitable extinction" (Bieder 1990, p. 11). These predictions gave rise to the "Vanishing Red Man" theory, which was widely embraced and used to justify government Indian policies.

The appropriation of human remains was also spurred by America's newly founded museums, which competed to collect all aspects of the Native Americans' "procurable culture" (Cole 1985, p. xi.), including the bodies of their dead. Franz Boas, a leading museum collector, noted that "stealing bones from a grave was 'repugnant work' but 'someone has to do it.'" (Cole 1985, p. 119). To enhance the collection of the Army Medical Museum, founded in 1862, the U.S. Surgeon General ordered army personnel to collect Indian skulls beginning in 1867. More than 4,000 heads were obtained under that order. This government policy no doubt contributed to the rampant and clandestine taking of Native American remains by museums and private individuals.

Between 1875 and 1925 a staggering quantity of material, both secular and sacred, left native hands for American museums. By the time this scramble for native cultural property ended, more indigenous material lay in museums than in tribal communities. Virtually every Native American tribe and community in the United States had been victimized by grave looting. Hundreds of thousands of dead relatives, sacred objects, and objects of cultural patrimony lay stored or on display in museums, tourist attractions, art houses, private collections, and universities.

THE PASSAGE AND IMPLEMENTATION OF NAGPRA

NAGPRA established procedures and legal standards for museums and federal agencies to use in repatriating improperly acquired human remains, funerary objects, sacred objects, and objects of cultural patrimony to Native American claimants. These cultural items must be returned to lineal descendants or culturally affiliated Indian tribes or Native Hawaiian groups under prescribed evidentiary and procedural guidelines. In addition, NAGPRA prohibits trafficking in Native American body parts and the excavation of Indian graves found on federal or tribal land without tribal consent. If any remains are accidentally discovered on such lands, the affected tribes must be notified.

Repatriation under NAGPRA occurs on a case-by-case basis. The law will take years to fully implement due to the massive number of human remains, museums, and federal agencies involved. Meanwhile, agencies, museums, and the courts are promulgating, interpreting, clarifying, and applying the provisions of the law. By 2004 the remains of 30,261 Native Americans and 581,679 associated funerary objects had been repatriated to Native American claimants. In addition, 92,298 funerary objects unassociated with particular human remains, 1,222 sacred objects and about 800 objects of cultural patrimony had been repatriated. After a decade of implementation, there is a strong consensus that NAGPRA's repatriation process, which is based upon consultation among all interested parties, has been beneficial. There is also general agreement that the process has not harmed legitimate scientific interests, but has instead led to a better understanding of Native American cultural history and closer collaboration between Indian tribes and museums.

Almost 120,000 dead have not been repatriated, however, because their cultural affiliation is unknown, including 16,000 skeletal remains stored in the Smithsonian Institution. It is expected that NAGPRA regulations will be issued to recommend the appropriate disposition of these unknown American Indian dead. Some scientists wish to permanently retain these remains due to their potential value as scientific specimens. Native Americans disagree, however. They assert that these dead are entitled to a decent burial, pointing to mainstream social values found in the laws of every state that ensure a burial for all persons, including paupers, unclaimed strangers, or persons who die without next of kin.

Implementation of the social changes mandated by NAGPRA has not always come quickly or easily. Some scientists have sought to limit NAGPRA in order to protect their research interests. They have argued, in cases such as the "Kennewick Man" litigation, that NAGPRA is not an "Indian law statute," and that it must be narrowly construed and should not apply to early American remains. Historically, minority and ethnic groups have experienced different forms of discrimination. The historical mistreatment of Native American graves and dead relatives is one type of discrimination, and it has been repudiated by NAGPRA, which seeks to rectify centuries of disparate racial treatment.

BIBLIOGRAPHY

Bieder, Robert E. 1990. *A Brief Historical Survey of the Expropriation of American Indian Remains.* Boulder, CO: Native American Rights Fund.

Cole, Douglas. 1985. *Captured Heritage: The Scramble for Northwest Coast Artifacts.* Seattle: University of Washington Press.

Echo-Hawk, Roger C., and Walter R. Echo-Hawk. 1994. *Battlefields and Burial Grounds: The Indian Struggle to Protect Ancestral Graves in the United States.* Minneapolis, MN: Lerner Publications.

Gould, Stephen Jay. 1996. *The Mismeasure of Man,* rev. ed. New York: Norton.

Mann, Charles C. 2005. *1491: New Revelations of the Americas before Columbus.* New York: Alfred A. Knopf.

Trope, Jack F., and Walter R. Echo-Hawk. 1992. "The Native American Graves Protection and Repatriation Act: Background and Legislative History." *Arizona State Law Journal* 24 (1): 35–77.

Walter R. Echo-Hawk

NATIVE AMERICAN POPULAR CULTURE AND RACE

Native Americans have been historically represented in American popular culture as fitting into one of two categories, either the noble savage or bloodthirsty savage. Robert Berkhofer, in *The White Man's Indian* (1978), traces these categories as far back as Columbus's journals. Other scholars credit American author James Fenimore Cooper (1789–1851) with solidifying these categories in his *Leatherstocking Tales* (1823–1841). Both categories represent racist attitudes toward Native Americans because both construct a deficient model attributed to race. The bloodthirsty savage is violent and aggressive, animalistic in nature, and a constant threat to the dominant culture; therefore, violent action in retaliation is justified. The noble savage is friendly to Europeans and Americans and inherently wise but must ultimately vanish in the face of progress. The "Indian Princess" is the female version of the noble savage and was a popular icon in early American popular culture, becoming the subject of poems, plays, art, and later film. All of these represent models to which the dominant culture compared itself to validate its perceived superiority based on race.

EARLY AMERICAN LITERATURE

Captivity narratives are considered one of the first popular American literatures. These stories were written primarily in the sixteenth and seventeenth centuries by colonists who were taken captive by various Native American nations in the region. While the taking of captives had been practiced by both Native Americans and colonists alike, the phrase generally refers to the stories written by colonists "rescued" from Native American captivity and returned to their colonial villages. In the early stories, the Native Americans might be noble or savage, but in later versions bloodthirsty savages dominated as editors embellished the stories to add more drama. The underlying threat of miscegenation (the mixing of two different races) and the perceived threat of rape kept audiences on the edge of their seats. Taboos against miscegenation would continue well into early Hollywood film, as would the general theme of captivity, becoming a recognizable formula in the Hollywood western.

The western as a specific genre of literature and film followed logically from the frontier novels of Cooper, whose works are thought to have influenced everything from the extremely popular dime novels of the late 1800s to American films. Cooper's *Leatherstocking Tales* featured both bloodthirsty and noble savages, as demonstrated in his most famous novel, *The Last of the Mohicans* (1826). While many critics thought Cooper overly romanticized Native Americans, others claimed the bloodthirsty savages ultimately outnumbered the noble savages in his works. The bloodthirsty savage became a major figure in a continuing literary form, the dime novel.

Dime novels were fast paced, formulaic, serialized novels that featured heroic cowboys and savage Indians. Playing to the public's interest in westward expansion, the gold rush, and the Oregon Trail, these novels featured action-packed conflict between cowboys and Indians and glorified American heroes such as Buffalo Bill Cody (1846–1917). First published by Irwin P. Beadle & Company in 1860, these stories portrayed Native Americans largely as bloodthirsty and ignorant, speaking in grunts and broken English, thus validating the ideology of westward expansion and dismissing its devastating impact on Native Americans. The "Indians" in these stories were characterized as barely human, so their defeat by the hero was cause for celebration, not concern. This was also true of the later stage shows created by Buffalo Bill, the star of many dime novels.

Buffalo Bill Cody was an actual frontiersman and scout in the U.S. military. In 1883 Cody took advantage of his popularity with American audiences and created Buffalo Bill's Wild West, a traveling show that featured reenactments of western adventures, including conflicts between Native Americans and white Americans heading west. The show borrowed from the stage, vaudeville, and the circus in an effort to re-create the Old West for those who could only dream of such adventures. These included both American and European audiences, including European kings and queens who sometimes participated in the shows. The Wild West further cemented the theme of "cowboys and Indians" in the American imagination, and these live shows later became the subject matter of early American films.

NATIVE AMERICANS IN FILM

A Native American presence in film is as old as American film itself. Yet the filmic "Indian" is rarely a developed, complex character. Tribal specificity and cultural and historical accuracy seem not to have been a concern for the majority of filmmakers. When Thomas Edison premiered his kinetoscope at the Chicago Colombian World's Exposition in 1893, he showed *Hopi Snake Dance*, an "actuality" or ethnographic film displaying the "exotic cultures" of the newly defeated Native Americans. Despite the terms "actuality" and "ethnographic," these films were not historically or ethnographically accurate. They were one-sided interpretations of Native American culture that continued the Eurocentric tradition of presenting Native Americans as other and lesser. The premier of the film *Parade of Buffalo Bill's Wild West* (1894) launched the beginning of the most popular film genre: the western.

The western is the most common location to find Native Americans, or more accurately "Hollywood Indians." The Hollywood Indian belongs to a fictional group that lacks tribal specificity. For example, one of the most famous directors of westerns was John Ford. His films often featured the iconic actor John Wayne and portrayed Native Americans as generic tribes. They might be called Cheyenne or Comanche, but often the extras were played by Navajos in Navajo clothing speaking Navajo. Ford did not concern himself with historical accuracy and assumed that the audience would not either. These kinds of films contributed to a historically inaccurate mythology that persists despite later efforts to address it.

In the 1950s, the sympathetic western made its debut with *Broken Arrow* (1950) staring Jimmy Stewart. This film addressed the impact of westward expansion on Native Americans but still fell into the familiar traps of utilizing the noble savage as part of its formula. In particular, Stewart's wife is an Indian Princess who reinforces the stereotype of the vanishing American when she dies tragically but romantically, implying that the two races cannot coexist. Later films take the sympathetic western one step further, creating what are known as revisionist westerns. These westerns seek to revise the classic western often by inverting the classical elements. For example, in the revisionist western the Native Americans are the moral characters and the townspeople or settlers are amoral and westward expansion is viewed in light of its negative impact on Native Americans. The film *Little Big Man* (1970) is an example of this. The Cheyenne call themselves the "human beings," and protagonist Jack Crabb (Dustin Hoffman), when given the choice of whether to live as a "white man" or a Cheyenne, ultimately chooses the Cheyenne. They are clearly the superior people in the film. Or are they? Ultimately, they must, like all noble savages, vanish. In an eloquent speech to Jack Crabb the Cheyenne chief Old Lodge Skins (Chief Dan George) says, "There has always been a limited number of human beings but there is an endless supply of white men.… We won today, we won't win tomorrow," thus validating the audience's understanding that Indians—a defeated people—belong to the past.

In terms of historical accuracy, some later westerns tried to be more culturally sensitive. After a long dry spell in Hollywood the western resurfaced with Kevin Costner's Oscar Academy Award-winning *Dances with Wolves* (1990). As a film that billed itself as historically accurate, *Dances* did make some breakthroughs. The Sioux characters speak Sioux, and numerous Native American consultants were on the set. Still, the film heavily romanticizes the Sioux as noble and casts the Pawnee as bloodthirsty, failing to escape the formulas of the past. The film also continues to promote the notion of the vanishing race, ending with the eventual capture of the Sioux community by the cavalry.

NATIVE AMERICAN FILMMAKERS

Native American filmmakers have tried to address this history by making films about contemporary Native Americans, proving that Native Americans have not vanished and are not defeated. Sandra Osawa (Makah) has been involved in film and television since the 1960s, and her films *Lighting the Seventh Fire* (1995) and *On and Off the Res' with Charlie Hill* (1999) show Native American people dealing with contemporary issues. *On and Off the Res'* is especially interesting regarding the topic of film and media because it documents the career of stand-up comedian Charlie Hill, an Oneida who addresses Hollywood stereotypes in his comedy sketches. Victor Masayesva Jr. (Hopi) directly attacks both Hollywood stereotypes and the movie industry in his documentary *Imagining Indians* (1992), which looks at the history of Native American people's participation in Hollywood films and the way the industry has exploited Native American people and communities. The most prolific Native American feature filmmaker of the late 1990s and early 2000s is Cheyenne/Arapaho director and producer Chris Eyre. His films feature present-day urban and reservation Native Americans dealing with contemporary life.

Racist depictions of Native Americans in American popular culture are so entrenched that it is often difficult to escape them, but Native American filmmakers are making an effort, as are other independent filmmakers. Ideally, a more human depiction of Native Americans will become prevalent over time, replacing the simplified stereotypes of noble and bloodthirsty savage with images of complex human beings.

SEE ALSO *"Playing Indian"; White Settler Society.*

BIBLIOGRAPHY

Benshoff, Harry M., and Sean Griffin. 2004. *America on Film: Representing Race, Class, Gender, and Sexuality at the Movies.* Malden, MA: Blackwell.

Berkhofer, Robert F., Jr. 1978. *The White Man's Indian: Images of the American Indian from Columbus to the Present.* New York: Vintage.

Kilpatrick, Jacquelyn. 1999. *Celluloid Indians: Native Americans and Film.* Lincoln: University of Nebraska Press.

Rollins, Peter C., and John E. O'Connor, eds. 1998. *Hollywood's Indian: The Portrayal of the Native American in Film.* Lexington: University Press of Kentucky.

Singer, Beverly R. 2001. *Wiping the War Paint off the Lens: Native American Film and Video.* Minneapolis: University of Minnesota Press.

Angelica Lawson

NATIVE AMERICAN RIGHTS FUND (NARF)

Since its founding in 1970, the presence of the Native American Rights Fund (NARF) in Indian country in the United States has become very evident. But the continuing need in Indian country for creative legal assistance to enable Indian tribes, as sovereign governments, to regain control over their resources and their destiny is equally evident. Permeating native relations with the dominant society are 400 years of persistent racism, resulting in a complex modern agenda for NARF that includes, among other things: (1) Protecting human health and environmental integrity for Indian people on Indian lands; (2) safeguarding their children through the improvement of Indian education; (3) improving the structure of tribal communities so they can provide economic infrastructures and more responsive governments; (4) continuing the struggle to insure their rights to practice their religious beliefs and protect their cultures in the face of religious bigotry from the dominant culture; and (5) combating racism directly in such matters as voting practices, environmental degradation of Indian lands and resources, and bias in the judicial system.

Over the years, NARF has learned to listen hard and long to its clients, to present all the options open to them, and to help them make legal decisions based on the best information possible. During its history, NARF has represented more than 200 tribes in thirty-one states in such areas as tribal restoration and recognition, jurisdiction, land claims, water rights, hunting and fishing rights, the protection of Indian religious freedom, Indian child welfare, and voting rights. In addition, one of its greatest distinguishing attributes has been its ability to bring quality ethical legal representation to tribes.

INDIAN LAW

Modern Indian law and policy began to come to life in the late 1950s and early 1960s, when a consensus was reached among tribal leaders, young Indian professionals, and traditionalists. There was no formal declaration or stated agenda. Indeed, on one level there was nothing more than a few seemingly unconnected meetings, protests, and musings on the shores of Puget Sound, in the red-rock landscape of the Southwest, on the high plains of the Dakotas, in the backwoods of Wisconsin, and on the farms of Oklahoma.

These superficially unrelated stirrings were tightly and irrevocably bound together by an indelible reverence for the aboriginal past, an appreciation of the consequences of five centuries of contact with Europeans, and by desperation concerning the future of Indian societies as discrete units within the larger society.

An implicit oath of blood was made during the termination era of the 1950s, when the United States severed its government-to-government relationship, based on a legal trust relationship with American Indian tribes. Native Americans felt the federal policy of termination had to be slowed, halted, and then reversed. In a larger sense, the most persistent aspects of federal Indian policy since the mid-nineteenth-century—the assimilation of Indians, reduction of the Indian land and resource base, and the phasing out of tribal governments—had to be stopped and reversed. Even more generally, the tribes had to become more proactive in dealing with U.S. government policy.

The Indian initiatives would be premised on tribalism. In the 1832 Supreme Court case *Worcester v. Georgia,* Chief Justice John Marshall's opinion had carved out a special, separate constitutional status for Indian tribes. Within their boundaries, tribes had jurisdiction and the states could not intrude. They were recognized in their own right as sovereigns, a status that left the tribes with authority over their resources, economies, disputes, families, and values.

To outsiders, it might seem astonishing that reservation Indians know of concepts such as "sovereignty" and "jurisdiction." But they do, and they did in the 1950s and 1960s. The reason for this is simple: The tribal leaders bargained to reaffirm these things when treaties were made. Generation after generation, tribal elders passed down information about the talks at treaty time and about the fact that American law, at least in Marshall's time, had been faithful to those talks.

It was not through choice that modern Indian people have placed so much reliance on federal law. But there was no real alternative. Outside forces were bent on obtaining Indian land, water, fish, and tax revenues, and on assimilating the culture of Indian people, especially the children. Underlying this current was racism. There could be no internal development or harmony until the outside forces and racism were put at rest.

The program conceived of at the end of the termination era was successful in many ways. In this new century, however, the forces of termination and the challenges to tribal sovereignty have once again reared their heads, riding on the currents of racism. For every victory, a new challenge to tribal sovereignty arises from state and local governments, Congress, or the courts. The continuing lack of understanding, and in some cases blatant racism and lack of respect for the sovereign attributes of Indian nations, has made it necessary for the struggle to continue.

HISTORY OF THE NATIVE AMERICAN RIGHTS FUND

In the 1960s, the U.S. government began a widespread effort to address some of the social ills affecting the nation. As part of the "War on Poverty," the nation began to provide legal representation to the disadvantaged. Those running these programs came to realize that the legal problems of their Indian clients were, for the most part, governed and controlled by a little known area of law—"Indian Law"—which was driven by treaties, court decisions, and federal statutes, regulations, and administrative rulings. They also found that few attorneys outside of the legal services system were willing to represent Indians, and those who did generally worked on a contingency basis, only handling cases with anticipated monetary settlements. Thus, many issues would not get to court.

During this same period, the Ford Foundation, which had already assisted in the development of the NAACP Legal Defense Fund and the Mexican American Legal Defense Fund, began meeting with California Indian Legal Services (CILS) to discuss the possibility of creating a similar project dedicated to serving all of the nation's indigenous people. CILS had already established a reputation for taking on Indian legal cases. The Ford Foundation awarded CILS a planning grant in 1970 and start-up funding to launch the Native American Rights Fund in 1971.

As a pilot project of CILS in 1970, NARF attorneys traveled throughout the country to find out firsthand from the Indian communities what legal issues they were dealing with. They also began a search for a permanent location for the project, which was initially housed at CILS's main office in Berkeley, California. In 1971, NARF selected its new home and relocated to Boulder, Colorado.

An eleven-member all-Indian Steering Committee (now a thirteen-member Board of Directors) was selected by the CILS Board of Trustees to govern the fund's activities. Individuals were chosen (as they continue to be in the early twenty-first century) based on their involvement with and knowledge of Indian affairs and issues, as well as their tribal affiliation.

NARF continued to grow at a rapid pace over the next several years. In 1971, the project opened its first regional office in Washington, D.C. An office close to the

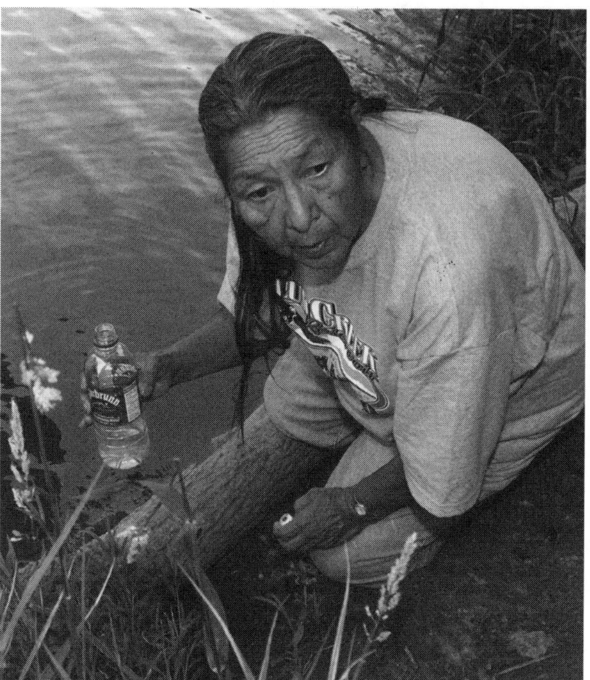

Kickapoo Nation Drinking Water. *The Native American Rights Fund (NARF) represented the Kickapoo Nation in their federal lawsuit to enforce promises made to the tribe to build the Plum Creek Reservoir Project. The tribe's drinking water is well below federal standards.* AP IMAGES.

center of the federal government would prove critical in future interaction with the White House, Congress, and federal administrative agencies. The Carnegie Corporation of New York awarded NARF start-up funding in 1972 for the creation of the National Indian Law Library, a national repository for Indian legal materials and resources. More than ten years later, in 1984, NARF established its second branch office, in Anchorage, Alaska, where it could take on the Alaska Native issues of tribal sovereignty and subsistence hunting and fishing rights.

NATIVE AMERICAN RIGHTS FUND'S MISSION

One of the initial responsibilities of NARF's first Steering Committee was to develop priorities that would guide the fund in its mission to preserve and enforce the legal rights of Native Americans. The committee developed five priorities that continue to lead NARF in the early 2000s: (1) The preservation of tribal existence; (2) the protection of tribal natural resources; (3) the promotion of Native American human rights; (4) the accountability of governments to Native Americans; and (5) the development of Indian law and educating the public about Indian rights, laws, and issues.

Preservation of Tribal Existence. NARF works to construct the foundations that are necessary to empower tribes so that they can continue to live according to their Native traditions, to enforce their treaty rights, to insure their independence on their homelands, and to protect their inherent sovereignty. Specifically, NARF's legal representation centers on sovereignty and jurisdiction issues, federal recognition and restoration of tribal status, and economic development. The focus of NARF's work relates to the preservation and enforcement of the status of tribes as sovereign governments. Jurisdictional conflicts often arise with states, the federal government, and others over tribal sovereignty.

Protection of Tribal Natural Resources. Throughout the process of European conquest and colonization of North America, Indian tribes experienced a steady diminishment of their land base down to a mere 2.3 percent of its original size. There are now approximately 55 million acres of Indian-controlled land in the continental United States and about 44 million acres of Native-owned land in Alaska. An adequate land base and control over natural resources are central components of economic self-sufficiency and self-determination, and as such are vital to the very existence of tribes.

Promotion of Native American Human Rights. Although basic human rights are considered a universal and inalienable entitlement, Native Americans face an ongoing threat of having their rights undermined by the United States government, states, and others who seek to limit these rights. NARF strives to enforce and strengthen laws designed to protect the rights of Native Americans against racism in order to allow them to practice their traditional religion, to use their own language, and to enjoy their culture. NARF also works with tribes to improve education and ensure the welfare of their children, which has often been threatened by long-standing racism. NARF is also active in efforts to negotiate declarations on the rights of indigenous peoples worldwide.

Accountability of Governments to Native Americans. Contained within the unique trust relationship between the United States and Indian nations is the inherent duty for all levels of government to recognize and responsibly enforce the many laws and regulations applicable to Indian peoples. Because such laws impact virtually every aspect of tribal life, NARF maintains its involvement in the legal matters pertaining to the accountability of governments to Native Americans.

Development of Indian Law and Educating the Public about Indian Rights, Laws, and Issues. Protecting Indian rights depends upon establishing favorable court precedents, distributing information and law materials, encouraging and fostering Indian legal education, and forming alliances with Indian law practitioners and other Indian organizations. NARF recognizes the importance of the development of Indian law and continues to manage and participate in a variety of projects specifically aimed at achieving this goal.

NARF strives to protect the legal and sovereign rights of tribes and Native people within the American legal system. This effort certainly could not exist without the contribution of the thousands of individuals who have offered their knowledge, courage, and vision to help guide NARF. Of equal importance, NARF's financial contributors have graciously provided the resources to make these efforts possible. NARF will thus continue to combat racism against Native Americans and pursue its mission of securing the sovereignty and right to self-determination to which all Native American peoples are entitled.

BIBLIOGRAPHY

Native American Rights Fund. Available from http://www.narf.org.

Mark C. Tilden

NATIVISM

In general, nativism is a form of ethnocentrism that considers previous residence in a country or region to constitute a claim to superiority in culture or a higher class of citizenship. In the United States, *nativism* has been defined as "the intense opposition to an internal minority on the grounds of its allegedly un-American characteristics" (Higham 1963). This fear and hatred of "aliens" in the United States has been typically directed against religious or ethnic minorities and political radicals. Despite having expelled and dispersed the previous residents and being surrounded by other ethnicities, races and religions, nativists have viewed themselves as somehow special—"Anglo Saxons" and other Protestant descendents of northern and western European settlers—the only people worthy of being called "American."

Nativists always seem to have felt that they were the only "real" Americans; in fact, they dismissed indigenous groups, like so many others, as inferiors. In their passionate crusades to protect the land from so-called "unassimilatables" unworthy of being citizens, religious and social constructions of race were the central concerns.

EARLY NATIVISM

The earliest form of nativism was anti-Catholic hostility rampant in England before the era of colonization and rooted in the imperial rivalries with Catholic Spain and France and the founding of what became the Church of England. Religious nativism gained new life in the American colonies and became the most enduring part of the nativist tradition in America until the mid-twentieth century. The Catholic population in the colonial era was minuscule—there were only 35,000 Catholics as late as the American Revolution. Almanacs, tracts, sermons, and periodicals of various kinds during this period vilified Catholicism. Public school primers instructed children to "abhor that arrant Whore of Rome and all her blasphemies." Fireside games such as "Break the Pope's Neck" were standard fare. The stubby tail of a baked turkey was dubbed "the Pope's nose."

Nativism declined in the Revolutionary era, but in the 1830s, as immigration from Ireland and Germany swelled the Catholic population, new anti-alien movements emerged, launching violent attacks on Catholic institutions and publishing numerous anti-Catholic tracts. Nativist fears shaped a new political party, the American-Republicans. These political nativists elected mayors of New York and Philadelphia and six members of Congress in 1844. They played a key role in the brutal street confrontations between Catholics and Protestants in Philadelphia on Independence Day 1844; hundreds were injured and fires ravaged the city.

This early nativist party did not endure; it was dead by 1847. But the forced migrations of Irish people to the western provinces of Ireland, and the resulting catastrophic potato famine, stimulated a vast migration to America in the next five years from which there emerged a new and more formidable nativist political movement.

Destitute newcomers fleeing Ireland and Germany in this period changed the social landscape. In the port cities, crime rates and "juvenile vagrancy" rose and were linked to increases in the foreign-born population. As almshouses and aid to "paupers" strained public budgets, "lunatic asylums" reported more immigrants in confinement, and immigrant-oriented bars and "gin houses" proliferated, nativists argued that these migrants were clearly a race of inferior peoples threatening the future of the nation. And they were Catholic; the number of their churches had increased from fewer than 100 to more than 1,800 by 1855. For anti-alien nativists, these events stimulated fear that priests under the control of a foreign prince—the pope—would manipulate members of an autocratic and centralized church opposed to individual judgment and intolerant of dissent. Nativists believed that Catholics would undermine the public school system by insisting on parochial education. And so democracy itself was at risk in America.

Out of the numerous nativist secret societies created at this time came the American Party. Because members were told to respond "I know nothing" when asked about the party (because "Jesuitical conspirators" allegedly menaced the movement, requiring it to remain secret), the new organization was called the Know-Nothings. With the Whig Party fractured by the abolitionist and free-soil issues, the Know-Nothings became the second largest political party in America by 1854. But this would not last. Like the Whigs and the Democrats, the Know-Nothing Party split apart over the issue of slavery after 1856 and disappeared in the crisis leading to the Civil War. But nativism would not disappear with it.

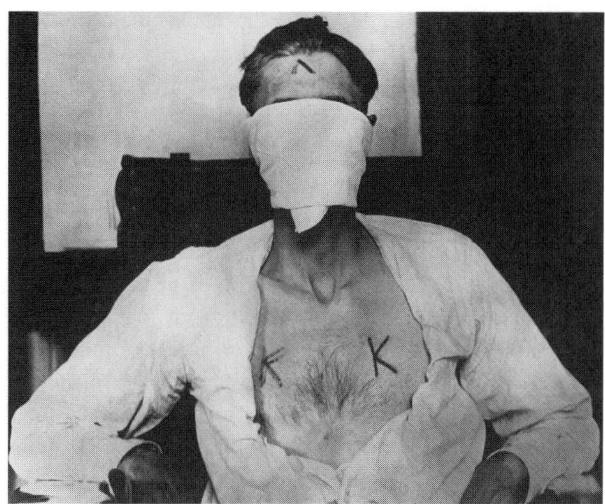

Anti-Catholic KKK Victim, 1924. *Anti-Catholic hostility was one of the earliest and most enduring forms of nativism.* © HULTON-DUETSCH COLLECTION/CORBIS.

THE "NEW IMMIGRATION"

In the last two decades of the nineteenth century, as the immense "new immigration" from southern and eastern Europe brought millions of Italian Catholics, Jews, Russians, and South Slavs, nativism gained strength, particularly during the depression years of the 1890s. Jewish immigrants, the non-Catholic target, were assailed as dirty, bearded foreign degenerates. New anti-alien groups proliferated, calling for immigration restriction and attacking Catholic political control in the big cities. The largest of these groups was the American Protective Association, with a membership reaching 500,000.

This new nativist effort emerged in a period when influential public figures, including such major reform leaders as Woodrow Wilson and Theodore Roosevelt, embraced racist theories. (Wilson contrasted the "men of the sturdy stocks of the north of Europe" with "the more sordid and hopeless elements which the countries of the south of Europe were disburdening ... men out of the ranks where there was neither skill nor energy nor quick intelligence.")

Like nativists in earlier decades, the focus was on the threat of Catholics (and now Jews) to Protestant America and on the social problems accompanying the newcomers. Again, ethnic differences were linked to racial inferiority.

While nativism declined in the Progressive Era during the first decade and a half of the twentieth century, World War I and the postwar Red Scare briefly revived it. German-Americans were attacked during the war. In 1919, the Palmer raids, organized by the attorney general and executed by future FBI chief J. Edgar Hoover, temporarily made the federal government the instrument of protecting America from communist aliens and other advocates of "un-American" ideas. Jewish radicals were seen as a particular threat, with Palmer describing the "Red" leadership as marked by a "small clique of autocrats from the lower East Side of New York."

THE KU KLUX KLAN

In the 1920s, a new organization with an old name, the Ku Klux Klan, recruited over two and a half million members to an anti-Catholic, anti-Semitic, anti-alien, antiblack movement. It offered a sense of community to many who felt left out or left behind during the economic boom of the "Roaring Twenties," with its skyscraper cities housing what Klan leaders called "the immigrant masses." Jews were again singled out by some nativist publications, with Henry Ford's *Dearborn Independent* characterizing them as "dark, squat figures, a strange Slovanic-Oriental admixture" influencing labor unions in service of their radical ideologies.

Weakened by scandals involving its leaders, the Klan did not survive the decade. But it did have a political impact, attacking the presidential candidacy of the Irish Catholic governor of New York, Al Smith, and strongly supporting passage of the Immigration Act of 1924, which restricted immigration and established national quotas directed against peoples from southern and eastern Europe.

THE 1930S AND BEYOND

In subsequent years, nativism faded from the American scene. In the 1930s, the New Deal championed diversity and shaped economic policies that made it hard to project anger about depression-bred privation on ethnic or religious outsiders. In the 1940s, GIs of all ethnic groups were fighting in World War II and assailing the traditional objects of nativist hostility as "un-American."

The 1950s brought a postwar prosperity that removed some of the economic anxieties that helped stimulate some earlier nativist outbreaks. Efforts to block access to those victimized by previous anti-alien movements became unacceptable in academia, commerce, and the professions. Indeed, the climate of repression pervading the early cold war era targeted not religious or ethnic groups but alleged political radicals. In fact, an Irish American Catholic senator, Joseph R. McCarthy Jr., became the chief communist hunter of the 1950s, and his targets were often members of the native-born elite.

In the last few decades, despite concerns on the southern border of the United States, old-style nativism has not returned in America. It is true that fears of a "flood" of undocumented Latino peoples—"feet people"—have stimulated efforts to curb "illegal aliens." Fragmentary extremist cells—the Aryan Nations, tiny neo-Klan chapters, skinhead gangs—have assailed these newcomers as un-American and a danger to the nation. Nativist rhetoric has been used by some politicians calling for border enforcement and expulsions. But on balance, the public debate over limiting immigration has not been conducted "in the spirit of the Know Nothings," as one congressman alleged in the 1980s. Instead, it has been economic and security arguments, not ethnic, religious, or racial issues, that have been used by those favoring new restrictions.

Scholarly analyses in the early years of the twenty-first century have focused on "the invention of the white race," the "wages of whiteness," and "how Irish Catholics and Jews became white folks" in explaining what has become of traditional nativism. While offering stimulating new perspectives on the nature and fate of nativism, these "whiteness studies" may lead some readers to underestimate the powerful tradition of anti-alien hostility that marked the history of America until the middle of the twentieth century. For nativists did fear and despise Catholic immigrants and other ethnic outsiders. They viewed them as inferiors, a population that could never be part of the American democratic community. And like its growth, development, and power across the years, the reasons for the decline of nativism are part of a complicated story.

SEE ALSO *Citizenship and "the Border"; Ethnocentrism; Irish Americans and Whiteness; Ku Klux Klan.*

BIBLIOGRAPHY

Bennett, David H. 1995. *The Party of Fear: From Nativist Movements to the New Right in American History*, 2nd ed. New York: Vintage Books.

Billington, Ray Allen. 1964. *The Protestant Crusade, 1800–1860: A Study of the Origins of American Nativism.* Chicago: Quadrangle Books.

Brodkin, Karen. 1998. *How Jews Became White Folks and What That Says About Race in America.* New Brunswick, NJ: Rutgers University Press.

Higham, John. 1963. *Strangers in the Land: Patterns of American Nativism, 1860–1925*, 2nd ed. New York: Atheneum.

Ignatiev, Noel. 1995. *How the Irish Became White.* New York: Routledge.

Perea, Juan F., ed. 1997. *Immigrants Out! The New Nativism and the Anti-Immigrant Impulse in the United States.* New York: New York University Press.

Roediger, David R. 1991. *The Wages of Whiteness: Race and the Making of the American Working Class.* New York: Verso.

David H. Bennett

NEO-NAZIS

Neo-Nazism is a loosely organized movement operating mainly in Europe and the Americas that promotes white supremacy, particularly hatred of Jews, and hearkens back to the Nazi regime led by Adolf Hitler in Germany from the 1930s through 1945. Among the hundreds of racial hate groups in the United States, neo-Nazis are among the largest, along with the Ku Klux Klan. To understand neo-Nazis today it is helpful to review their foundations in German Nazi politics of the early twentieth century.

The term *Nazi* is an acronym of the National Socialist German Workers Party (*Nationalsozialistische Deutsche Arbeiterpartei*). The original Nazi Party in Germany arose after World War I. Under the Treaty of Versailles that ended the war in 1918, Germany was required to pay reparations to the countries it had invaded. This international condemnation imposed a heavy economic burden on the people and the state, which fostered deep resentment. During the 1920s the Nazi, with Hitler among its top leaders, tapped into this resentment and inspired many Germans with ideas about patriotism and German supremacy, despite the earlier defeat. Hitler advocated rejecting the Treaty of Versailles and returning to German expansionism. The worldwide economic collapse and high unemployment of the Great Depression starting in 1929 made the Nazi Party's ideas attractive to more people, and they began to gain power both through elections and as a street strategy of recruiting veterans and the unemployed into paramilitary groups.

Hitler came to power through elections in 1932 that gave the Nazi Party a parliamentary majority. After he was appointed chancellor in 1933, he quickly moved to consolidate power. The Nazi regime, also known as the Third Reich, pursued a policy of invasion and expansion, beginning with annexing Poland in 1939. This was the precipitating event for the commencement of World War II. Hitler and the Nazis tapped the long-existing and underlying anti-Semitism of European societies to scapegoat Jews as a major cause of their economic and social instability.

Most infamously, the Nazis engineered genocide against the Jews, commonly called the Holocaust. The Holocaust was a carefully planned government program of extermination of Jews that lasted from 1941 through 1945. Long before the policy of organized mass murder was implemented, however, Jews were targeted by the Nazi regime with increasing harassment, violence, and restrictive laws. For example, after the coordinated attack on Jewish homes and businesses known as *Kristallnacht* (Night of Broken Glass) in 1939, Jews were required to pay fines for the damage caused, even though they were its victims. The Nazis revived the medieval policy of the ghetto, a term that refers to walled-off sections of towns in which Jews were segregated from the rest of the population, which facilitated rounding them up as the Nazi policies progressed toward genocide. Six million Jews from across Europe were killed. Initially, paramilitary groups committed mass murder in the towns where Jews lived. Later, men, women, and children were shipped by train to concentration camps, where some were forced to work under slave conditions until they died of disease or starvation, while those judged too weak to work were murdered en masse, eventually through a highly industrialized death machine. The so-called Final Solution was also applied to other social and racial groups the Nazis considered undesirable, including Roma (previously known as Gypsies), homosexuals, communists, and the disabled.

The foundation of Nazi ideology was belief in the racial superiority of the German or Aryan people. The crisis in German society provided a context for the development of an ideology of ethnic and racial superiority and a cultural movement that celebrated a romanticized image of the German *Volk* through the revival and creation of mythology, music, theology, and ritual. The Nazis drew on nineteenth-century theories of racial difference, superiority, and inferiority. Nazis viewed the German people as the "master race," invoking theories that ancient peoples from the Indus region and Iran had migrated to settle modern-day Germany. Descendants of this "Aryan race" were seen as biologically and culturally superior, and thus deserving of all society's goods. All other races, by definition in Nazi racial theories, were inferior and parasitic, which justified subjecting them to control and destruction.

Most analysts have characterized the Nazi state as fascist, meaning it was based on authoritarian principles with all power centralized in the state (although some scholars argue that the term *fascism* should be used more narrowly to apply to Benito Mussolini's movement in Italy that developed at the same time). This extreme form of state power facilitated the imposition of Nazi ideology and political programs, including its official policies of racism.

AFTER WORLD WAR II: THE NEO-NAZIS

The term *neo-Nazi* refers to groups since World War II that seek to revive the ideology and political movement of Nazism. In the last decade of the twentieth century and the first decade of the twenty-first century there has been a resurgence of neo-Nazi activity worldwide, but especially in Europe and North America. While neo-Nazis form a distinct subset of modern right-wing extremism, in their ideology and sometimes social groups they overlap with other groups, notably racist skinheads, white nationalist groups, Christian Identity (a white supremacist religious movement), and in the United States, the Ku Klux Klan. In their various guises, neo-Nazis espouse white supremacy, extreme nationalism, and an authoritarian fascist social structure. In the second half of the twentieth century, many European countries made Nazi political parties illegal. Nevertheless, groups that are not technically political parties continued to exist on a small scale. By the end of the twentieth century, such groups were growing. In some regions these movements developed close ties to extreme right-wing political parties that gained substantial representation in parliaments. Neo-Nazi groups also fomented street violence against targeted groups, especially immigrants.

Neo-Nazis in Europe. The neo-Nazi movement is found in every country in Europe. After World War II, Europe was divided between the West, allied with the United States, and the East, allied with the Soviet Union. Germany, the birthplace of the Nazi movement, was divided into West and East. The Federal Republic of Germany, or West Germany, outlawed Nazi political parties in its post-war constitution in 1949. In Eastern Europe, the Soviet and communist systems suppressed other forms of political organization, including nationalist and fascist movements. However, since the breakup of the Soviet Union and the reunification of Germany, a resurgence of neo-Nazi activity has appeared, especially in the countries of the former Eastern bloc, including the former East Germany, Poland, the Czech Republic, Hungary, and Bulgaria. Western European countries have also seen an increase in extreme right-wing activity beginning in the 1980s.

The ideology of European neo-Nazis continues to echo the original Nazi ideas, centered on nationalism, authoritarianism, and white supremacy. But as European societies have become more multicultural, xenophobia and anti-immigrant sentiment have become prominent themes. While the Jews of early twentieth-century Europe had been present for hundreds of years when they were targeted by Hitler, today's targets are more recent immigrants and refugees who, as part of globalization, have moved to Europe in search of economic opportunity or political asylum. Many of these immigrants are from African countries, the Middle East, and Turkey and are perceived by right-wing extremists as threatening the core of Western civilization. Right-wing movements have long been analyzed as a backlash by social groups who perceive that they are losing their place in society. The growth of Islam with immigration has led to cultural clashes that provide neo-Nazis and similarly minded activists with fodder for spreading hatred against anyone they decide is "other"—that is, non-European. Perceived competition for jobs also leads to anti-immigrant views, as in the United States. The creation of the European Union (EU) in 1992 added a layer of threat to traditional national identity in Europe. The EU human rights standards of tolerance for religious and cultural diversity create a context in which transnationalism is valued above nationalism. This sparks resentment against the state, the transnational entity of the EU, and people who symbolize the profound shifts in society of recent decades

European neo-Nazi activity ranges from highly institutionalized organizations that fall short of being actual political parties to more fluid, grassroots entities that engage in terrorist violence, commonly against foreigners. Ami Pedahzur and Leonard Weinberg (2001) suggest that while neo-Nazi political parties are banned in some European countries, the neo-Nazi movement in other guises supports political parties of the extreme right wing, creating a threat to European democracy. The activities of these neo-Nazi organizations include operating think tanks to influence policy indirectly, sponsoring Holocaust denial events, operating publishing houses, and producing music that appeals to young extremists. The neo-Nazi Internet presence has grown dramatically, and like the Internet itself, is an international phenomenon.

Neo-Nazis in the United States. Unlike Europe, neo-Nazi groups in the United States have never been criminalized. American neo-Nazis are part of a wider extreme right-wing, white supremacist movement that also includes the Ku Klux Klan. While they have little overall influence on U.S. politics, they have had a serious impact locally, where they have engaged in intimidation and committed violence against particular groups and recruited disaffected youth into their organizations.

The Intelligence Project, begun by the civil rights organization Southern Poverty Law Center, has monitored hate groups in the United States since 1979 and provides a respected clearinghouse of information about neo-Nazis and related groups operating in the United States. Its *2006 Year in Hate* report lists 844 active groups, of which 191 are neo-Nazi.

The National Alliance, the largest U.S. neo-Nazi organization, claims to represent a worldview based on beliefs about "nature" and the place of Aryan or white people within the "natural order." Their ideology is framed in language that attempts to sound scientific. For example, the National Alliance Web site promotes their "law of inequality" as the idea that evolution produced superior white people in northern Europe, where the necessity of "surviving a winter required planning and self-discipline, advanced more rapidly in the development of the higher mental faculties—including the

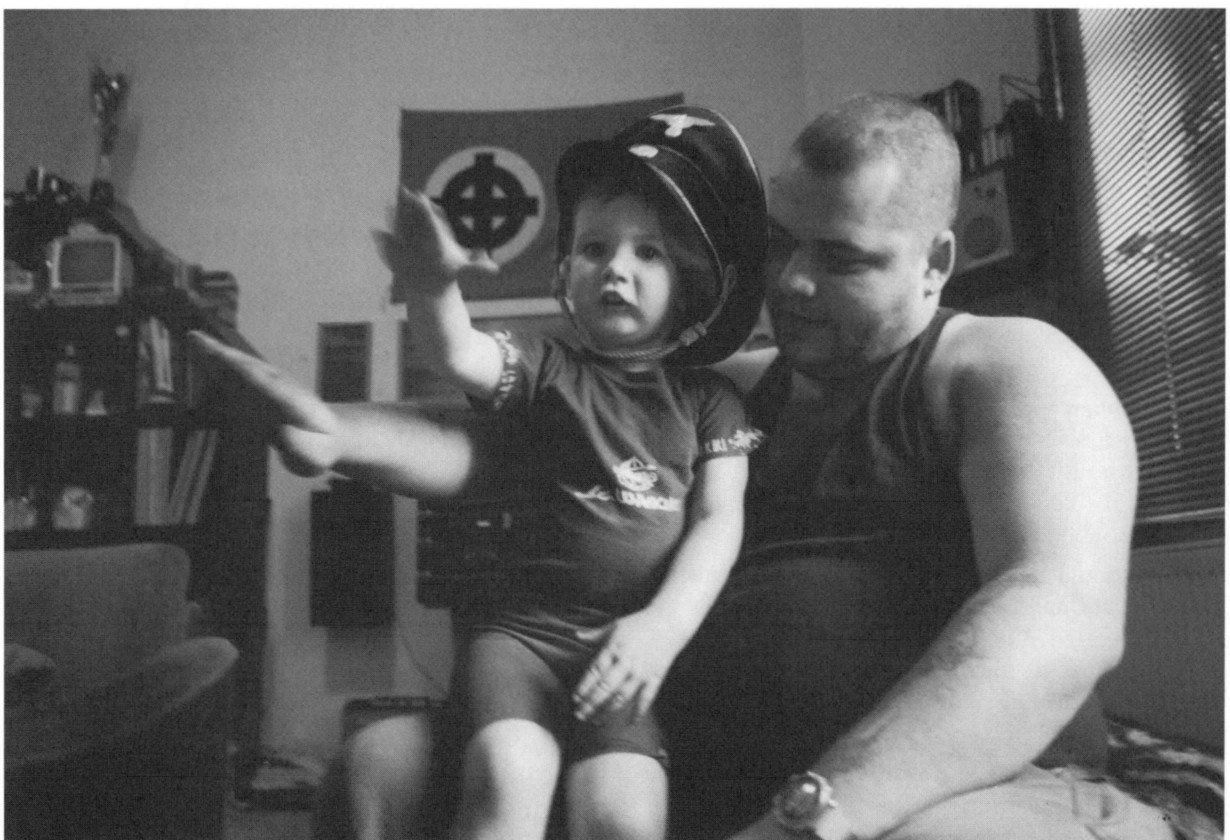

Neo-Nazi and Son Give Salute, 1994. *A German man and his young son give the Nazi salute. A resurgence of neo-Nazi activity has appeared since the break-up of the Soviet Union and the reunification of Germany.* © DAVID TURNLEY/CORBIS.

abilities to conceptualize, to solve problems, to plan for the future, and to postpone gratification." On its Web site the National Alliance claims to believe that this natural superiority of white or Aryan people imposes a "hierarchy of responsibilities" on members of the race to be as strong as they can be, to be "collective agents of progress," and to strive for higher levels of consciousness. Thus, much of their rhetoric sounds rather high-minded.

However, among the National Alliance's social and political goals are establishing "white living space" and "Aryan society." This means "rooting out of Semitic and other non-Aryan values and customs everywhere," which is elaborated to mean removing Jewish artists from museums, Jewish musicians from music, and any nonwhite face from films or other media. Ironically, the National Alliance has to defend its advocacy of a strong, centralized state, since there is a strong tradition on the U.S. right of complaining about the evils of "big government," as the following quote from the Web site illustrates:

> Many patriots look back fondly at the government as it was in its first phase, when it was less democratic and less intrusive in the lives of citizens. Perhaps the time will come when we can afford to have a minimal government once again, but that time lies in the remote future. The fact is that we need a strong, centralized government spanning several continents to coordinate many important tasks during the first few decades of a White world: the racial cleansing of the land, the rooting out of racially destructive institutions, and the reorganization of society on a new basis.

The discourse of the National Alliance uses language that appeals to pride, fear, and resentment. Its members invoke patriotism, which continues to be seen as a positive value in American culture, though it easily merges into nationalism, and from there to racism and xenophobia. For white Americans frustrated by their inability to get ahead, the National Alliance program offers explanations that sound reasonable (e.g., that multiculturalism contradicts nature) couched in pseudoscientific grounding (e.g., through evolution and natural selection). Some of its language resonates with New Age notions of pursuing "higher consciousness," although this is achieved through racial purity rather than the universal tolerance usually associated with that spiritual tradition. Aside from the actual content of National Alliance beliefs and programs, the tone of its discourse is dangerous because it is so soothing and inspiring.

By contrast, the second largest U.S. neo-Nazi group, the National Socialist Movement, adopts a more strident tone and directly invokes Nazism and Hitler. This group claims symbols of that era as its own: the swastika and the brown shirt uniform of the SA (*Sturmabteilung,* or storm troopers who operated in the 1930s in Germany to terrorize the population into submission to the Nazi program). The National Socialist Movement's Twenty-five Point Program, posted on its Web site, contains a hodgepodge of mandates that range from banning non-white immigration and ejecting nonwhites from the United States to demands for a living wage and land reform that includes affordable housing. These demands illustrate the combination of traditionally "right" and "left" ideas found in National Socialism.

As a social movement, the neo-Nazi movement is not static but undergoes change constantly; groups split and merge, and new groups form out of other social contexts. This is true worldwide, as the movement responds to changing societies and draws on the legacies of racism everywhere.

The growth of the Internet has facilitated the growth of neo-Nazi movements in the first decade of the twenty-first century. The Internet has given neo-Nazi organizations, like other social movements, a low-cost way to reach sympathizers and recruit adherents. Cyberspace has enabled European neo-Nazi groups to escape state controls by having their Web sites hosted by groups in the United States. American neo-Nazi groups have links to European neo-Nazi groups on their Web sites and vice versa. This may be the precursor to the growth of a more coordinated international movement, which would be a threat to democracy and racial equality worldwide.

SEE ALSO *Anti-Semitism; Christian Identity; English Skinheads; Holocaust; Transnationalism; White Racial Identity.*

BIBLIOGRAPHY

Lipset, Seymour Martin, and Earl Raab. 1970. *The Politics of Unreason: Right Wing Extremism in America, 1790–1970.* New York: Harper and Row.

Lukacs, John. 2002. "The Universality of National Socialism (The Mistaken Category of 'Fascism')." *Totalitarian Movements and Political Religions* 3 (1): 107–121.

National Alliance. Available from http://www.natall.com/.

Pedahzur, Ami, and Leonard Weinberg. 2001. "Modern European Democracy and Its Enemies: The Threat of the Extreme Right." *Totalitarian Movements and Political Religions* 2 (1): 52–72.

Nancy A. Matthews

NEW BLACK PANTHER PARTY

SEE *Nation of Islam and New Black Panther Party.*

NEW DEAL AND OLD RACISM

The Great Depression, which began in 1929 and lasted through the 1930s, was a time of great hardship for most Americans. Approximately one-fourth of the nation's entire labor force—or over 15 million people, both skilled and unskilled—lost their jobs, and malnutrition and hunger were rampant. The economy had collapsed, and the financial system was in disarray. Millions of Americans struggled to survive from day to day, and the administration of the Republican president Herbert Hoover offered the people little hope and no effective action to address this dire situation. When the Democrat Franklin Delano Roosevelt assumed the office of president in 1933, he immediately launched an ambitious set of programs known as the "New Deal." President Roosevelt's initiatives began to bring some economic relief and stability to the nation. Nevertheless, the New Deal was not able to solve the burning issues of justice and equality for poor people and people of color.

Americans who had little to begin with were among the hardest hit by the Great Depression. People who had already been living in poverty, a disproportionate number of whom were people of color, had fewer resources to call upon in this time of want. Across the nation, but particularly in regions of prolonged drought (known as the "Dust Bowl" in Texas and Oklahoma), poor farmers were forced from their land when they were unable to pay their rent or mortgage. White farmers from these regions left their homes by the thousands. Known as "Okies," they traveled westward looking for work and opportunity, and they met with widespread discrimination along the way.

If life was difficult for poor white farmers, people of color faced even greater hardships as they contended with the added burdens of racism and segregation. African Americans were often the "last hired and first fired"; unemployment in African-American communities was extremely high, and many families existed on the brink of starvation, especially in the urban South. In the Southwest, Mexican Americans faced deportation and hostile treatment because many whites blamed them for taking their jobs. Native Americans across the country simply tried to survive in what, for them, had been hard times for decades. Roughly 65 percent of people of color worked in sectors such as tenant farming, migrant farm work, and domestic work. These types of jobs were not covered by most New Deal programs, meaning that these workers were not even eligible for most forms of assistance.

However, when President Roosevelt took office in 1933, his new programs and "fireside chats" over the radio waves brought hope to many people. Americans from all walks of life waited for the end of hard times, expecting the New Deal to make it happen. New Deal programs attempted to focus on a few key areas, including welfare programs, business and industrial recovery, and systemic reform. The idea was to provide economic assistance to people in the short term and generate jobs to improve the economy over the long term. Reform in labor and business laws and practices were designed to help prevent a similar occurrence in the future.

The New Deal took place in two waves. Its first incarnation, in 1933 and 1934, included programs and legislation such as the Federal Emergency Relief Act, the National Industrial Recovery Act, the Agricultural Adjustment Act, and the National Labor Relations Board. The Second New Deal, begun in 1935, sought to move beyond the more immediate foci of the first and reestablish a stable, national economy. This effort included new structures like the Works Progress Administration and the National Youth Administration, as well as legislation like the Social Security Act, the Fair Labor Standards Act, and the Agricultural Adjustment Act of 1938. Unfortunately, these programs did not always live up to the ideals of national unity and opportunity from which they ostensibly emerged. Although the nation as a whole benefited in many ways from these initiatives, the gains were not equally distributed. In many ways the New Deal seemed to reinforce the same old system of privilege and preference from which middle- and upper-class whites gained and others lost.

AFRICAN AMERICANS AND THE NEW DEAL

By the early 1930s, close to half of all African-American workers were no longer employed, and the establishment of equal job opportunities had become a crucial issue for the black community. The National Recovery Administration (NRA), established in 1933, sought to establish fair rules and codes with regard to wages, prices, and competition in the labor market. In order to try to provide workers with a better standard of living and more purchasing power to stimulate economic growth, the NRA established relatively high standards for wages. In the South, where blacks were always paid much less than whites, many employers did not want to hire blacks under the new wage structure. Nevertheless, NRA rules would not allow wage differentials. It was an impossible dilemma for an administration not willing to challenge segregation. NRA leadership did not want to allow different pay structures for blacks and whites, but in general they did not have the political will or power to force white employers to hire blacks in positions with equal pay. White employers tried to find ways around the NRA policy by changing job descriptions so that jobs were not covered by these rules, and many employers simply refused to hire blacks.

Black newspapers and community organizations tried to work with government officials to publicize violations of NRA rules and gain justice for blacks facing discrimination. But they struggled vainly to find government officials who would take meaningful action against white business owners. Some African-American workers quietly accepted lower wages when faced with the choice between less money and no money. A few black organizations even advocated for different pay rates, arguing that the lower-paying jobs would provide some security in an atmosphere in which blacks were not getting hired at all. Blacks in the labor force worked in the agricultural and domestic sectors of the economy, and these types of jobs were not deemed eligible for assistance through the NRA. Thus, not only was the NRA ineffective in helping those African Americans it did include, it excluded a large proportion of them from the outset.

The Agricultural Adjustment Act (AAA) of 1933 addressed a different area of the economy. This act was an attempt to improve the situation of American farmers by cutting back on agricultural production in order to cause an increase in the price of agricultural commodities. In 1935, however, approximately 40 percent of the nation's farmers were sharecroppers and many of these people were forced to leave the land where they worked and lived when it went out of production. African-American tenant farmers, already living in poverty, debt, and oppression, received very little assistance from this program. Cotton plantations, in particular, decreased production and forced thousands of sharecroppers, black and white, from their homes. Black sharecroppers who managed to stay on their land often did not receive subsidy payments directed to them because white landowners kept the money for "debts" and rent.

Overall, other New Deal programs also accepted the status quo and allowed existing discriminatory practices to continue. The Federal Housing Authority acquiesced to the practice of segregating real estate markets in hopes of maintaining social stability through segregation. This policy contributed to the development of racial ghettos in urban areas. The Social Security Act excluded jobs in which large proportions of people of color were employed and had no specific prohibitions against discrimination, while the National Labor Relations Act established precedents allowing largely white unions to refuse admission to blacks. At bottom, the legislation establishing these programs was written with subtle exceptions and loopholes favored by a U.S. Congress containing one black representative and dominated by southern Democrats committed to the racial status quo.

SHIFTING ALLIANCES: AFRICAN AMERICANS TURN TO THE DEMOCRATS

Even though New Deal programs did not adequately address the needs of black people, many blacks began to switch their political loyalties from the Republicans to the Democrats. The Republican Party was the party of Lincoln and black emancipation, yet it had lost much of its appeal to black voters. When Roosevelt and the New Deal arrived, many blacks thought that economic improvement would be accompanied by an improvement in their sociopolitical status in the United States. Furthermore, the Roosevelt administration appointed several black leaders to relatively high positions in the New Deal administration, something never before seen in Washington. Among those given positions were Robert C. Weaver, who worked in the Interior Department and would later become America's first black member of the president's cabinet (under Lyndon Johnson); William H. Hastie, a pioneering black federal judge who also worked in the Department of the Interior; Eugene Kinckle Jones, advisor on Negro affairs for the Commerce Department from 1933 to 1937 and a former executive directory of the Urban League; Edgar Brown, an adviser on Negro Affairs in the Civilian Conservation Corps; Lawrence Oxley, head of the Negro Division of the Department of Labor; William J. Trent, a race relations officer in the Federal Works Agency; and Mary McLeod Bethune, who worked in the National Youth Administration. With Bethune as their leader in an informal group called the "Black Cabinet," these and many other black appointees gave voice to the concerns of African-Americans. There were more than a few sympathetic white leaders in the administration, including Eleanor Roosevelt, who was a personal friend of Bethune, and Secretary of the Interior Harold Ickes, a former head of the NAACP's Chicago chapter. Although the influence of these black and white New Deal officials was limited, the fact that such influence even existed was an important precedent. The mere establishment of African-American administrative units within government agencies represented the nation's first outreach toward the national black community since the Bureau of Freedmen, Refugees, and Abandoned Lands was set up in 1865.

Up until 1936, most black voters chose Republicans when they went to the polls, but the gradual move to the Democrats picked up steam, and Roosevelt received much of the black vote that year. Paradoxically, Roosevelt did nothing to improve the political rights of blacks, particularly with regard to voting rights in the South, nor did he promote anti-lynching legislation. The National Association for the Advancement of Colored People (NAACP) had been working for years on getting an anti-lynching bill through Congress, and in April 1937, after several well-publicized lynchings of African-Americans in the South, Representative Joseph A. Gavagan of New York succeeded in getting a version of the anti-lynching bill passed in the House of Representatives, despite opposition from southern Democrats. Getting it through the Senate was an entirely different matter, however. In the Senate, southern Democrats organized a filibuster that lasted six weeks and effectively stopped the bill.

During these dramatic events, Roosevelt was largely silent, despite the fact that he had the support of most African Americans. It is likely that his need for the political support of southern Democrats won out over any thoughts about taking a stand against racist violence in the South. The desire to maintain his office and keep the Democratic Party in the majority seemed to take precedence over ideals of equality and justice. At that point in history, blacks were prevented from exercising their political rights in many parts of the country, so concerns about whether or not they would continue to be loyal to the party were not paramount. White southern Democrats, however, controlled most of the votes and money in the South, and the political status quo remained unchanged.

LATINOS AND THE NEW DEAL

During the Great Depression, and throughout the New Deal, all members of politically marginalized communities in the United States faced a desperate struggle. Blacks and many Latinos living in cities like Detroit and Chicago were fired so that whites could take their positions. In the Southwest there were organized movements to force Mexican Americans out of jobs in order to provide openings for whites. Mexicans living in the United States, as well as Mexican-American citizens, provided a useful scapegoat for white fears and anxiety during the Great Depression. In the states of the Southwest, where segregation policies discriminating against people of Mexican descent were already in full force, public outcry in the white community painted a stereotyped picture of white jobs being taken by Mexican workers. In response, the Roosevelt administration carried out mass deportations, during which hundreds of thousands of people, perhaps as many as one million, were detained and sent to Mexico. Within that group were many Mexican-American citizens who had been born in the United States. Anyone appearing to be from Mexico was subject to arrest and deportation. Families and lives were disrupted, children were separated from their parents, and some who had never lived in Mexico found themselves ejected from their country of birth.

NATIVE AMERICANS AND THE NEW DEAL

As for Native Americans, they were among the poorest of the poor before the Depression hit. It could be argued that most Native American communities were already living in economic depression. Even so, the 1930s meant even fewer opportunities and resources in their communities. Nationally, there was considerable variety in the experience of Native Americans, depending upon their tribal affiliation and the region in which they lived. Yet Native people did have an advocate in the New Deal in the person of John Collier, the man appointed by Roosevelt as Indian Affairs Commissioner. The Indian Reorganization Act (IRA) of 1934, spearheaded by Collier, ostensibly advocated religious and cultural autonomy for Native peoples, yet the programs established by the act were implemented in a way that promoted assimilation and the loss of indigenous culture. Collier had hoped to help promote self-determination for Native American communities, but he was not able to persuade Congress to pass a strong bill that offered what he considered adequate support for Native Americans. The version of the IRA that did pass was not well funded or well structured in its approach.

Programs were pushed on Native American communities without the involvement or input of local leaders. The overall structure of what is often called the "Indian New Deal" was guided by the historical stereotype held by many whites that all Native American peoples were the same. Regional and tribal differences—in terms of needs, values, and organization—were not taken into account in the one-size-fits-all approach of the New Deal. Programs seeking to provide employment to Native Americans were limited and often did not provide them with real opportunities to move beyond low-wage jobs. Economic development programs promoted assimilation and devalued traditional ways. Native Americans living in urban areas faced the same struggles as blacks and Latinos, including losing their jobs before whites did and getting hired only when there were no whites applying. Native people living on reservations away from towns and cities received very few services, and outreach to them was not effectively implemented. For their part, many Native American communities and organizations found ways to adapt to the changing world without giving in to the pressure to assimilate. There was a resurgence of cultural pride and a recognition that the diverse Native groups shared a common struggle.

LOST OPPORTUNITIES AND THE MOVE TOWARD CHANGE

The Roosevelt administration and the programs of the New Deal are often seen as the beginning of a liberal movement in America favoring working families, and the interests of people of color are often assumed to have been included. The reality of the New Deal policies and their implementation is not so simple, however, and careful examination of the time period suggests that the New Deal did very little to address institutionalized social inequality based on race in the United States. With a focus on getting and keeping the economy moving again, the New Deal sought first to address the needs of those groups most instrumental in developing and maintaining the productive capacity of the nation. By and large this meant that it was concerned with the interests of big business, large landowning farmers, and the dominant trade unions. Poor people and people of color were grossly underrepresented in these interest groups; the New Deal attended to them only as parts of the larger system. Even so, Roosevelt and his administrative leadership did not completely ignore them, and for the first time in American history people of color gained some access to the power structure of the nation.

Moreover, during this process, organizations representing the needs of poor people and people of color did not stay silent or inactive. Perhaps heartened by the fact that at least some government officials were beginning to notice them and recognize inequality, the Urban League and the NAACP, along with a score of smaller interracial groups, supported the formation of the Joint Committee on National Recovery (JCNR), founded by John P. Davis and Robert C. Weaver. While the JCNR was unable to seriously influence Congress, it succeeded in making public the inequalities and inequities of the many recovery programs. So while the New Deal programs were altogether ineffective at addressing racial injustice, people concerned with social justice were able to sense a possible opening and began to push for more equality. At the end of the New Deal, World War II diverted the energy and attention of the whole nation, but as the war ended and the country returned its focus to domestic issues, the discussion of equality and justice began again, eventually evolving into the civil rights struggles that began in the 1950s—and that in many ways continue in the early twenty-first century.

SEE ALSO *Antiracist Social Movements; Bethune, Mary McLeod; Cultural Racism; Institutional Racism; Mexicans; Nativism; White Racial Identity.*

BIBLIOGRAPHY

Balderrama, Francisco, and Raymond Rodríguez. 1995. *Decade of Betrayal: Mexican Repatriation in the 1930s.* Albuquerque: University of New Mexico Press.

Holmes, Michael. 1972. "The Blue Eagle as 'Jim Crow Bird': The NRA and Georgia's Black Workers." *Journal of Negro History* 57 (3): 276–283.

Kennedy, David. 1999. "How FDR Lost the Struggle to Enact an Antilynching Bill." *Journal of Blacks in Higher Education* (25): 120–121.

Kersey, Harry A., Jr. 1989. *The Florida Seminoles and the New Deal, 1933–1942.* Boca Raton: Florida Atlantic University Press.

Sitkoff, Harvard. 1978. *A New Deal for Blacks: The Emergence of Civil Rights as National Issue.* New York: Oxford University Press.

Sullivan, Patricia. 1996. *Days of Hope: Race and Democracy in the New Deal Era.* Chapel Hill: University of North Carolina Press.

Taylor, Graham. 1980. *The New Deal and American Indian Tribalism: The Administration of the Indian Reorganization Act, 1934–1945.* Lincoln: University of Nebraska Press.

Valocchi, Steve. 1994. "The Racial Basis of Capitalism and the State, and the Impact of the New Deal on African Americans." *Social Problems* 41 (3): 347–362.

Zinn, Howard. 1980. *A People's History of the United States.* New York: Harper & Row.

Darin B. Stockdill

NIAGARA MOVEMENT

By 1905, when the Niagara Movement began, fewer than one black man in ten could vote and none held a national elective office. Public education, where it existed for black southerners, was separate and grossly unequal. Many blacks were lynched: More than 1,000 blacks were lynched during the final decade of the nineteenth century. For most whites, America's race problem was "solved" by de facto segregation in the North and legal racial segregation in the South.

Thus, blacks were totally subordinated within a white-dominated society. Booker T. Washington, the founder and president of Tuskegee Institute in Alabama, became the most prominent national black leader when he tacitly sanctioned this reality in his Atlanta Cotton States and International Exposition speech in 1895. Washington advised blacks against agitation for political and civic equality, instead counseling cooperation with whites for economic opportunities in the so-called New South, as it was proclaimed to be a decade earlier by Henry W. Grady, an influential Georgia newspaper editor.

Contrary to its widespread acceptance by whites, Washington's ascendancy to leadership status was challenged by younger urban and mostly northern-based, well-educated African Americans, including two Harvard alumni: W. E. B. Du Bois, a historian and sociologist, and William Monroe Trotter, a Harvard-trained militant black newspaper editor. Du Bois, Harvard's first black Ph.D. graduate, initially refrained from public attacks on Washington, who actually invited him to join the Tuskegee faculty. Sensing that he and Washington had conflicting ideas on racial matters, Du Bois declined the invitation but accepted a position at Atlanta University as head of its sociology department. Trotter became a Realtor in Boston, and in 1901 he began publishing *The Guardian,* in which he called for full citizenship rights for blacks. In a 1901 review of Washington's autobiography, *Up from Slavery,* Du Bois made a veiled attack on the deeper implications of Washington's accommodationist philosophy. Du Bois openly criticized Washington himself in *The Souls of Black Folk,* a 1903 publication that instantly became a widely read classic. In a chapter titled "Of Mr. Booker T. Washington and Others," Du Bois decried Washington's views, which he felt relegated practically all blacks to a politically impotent, servile existence.

Du Bois was fully aware of the anointing of Washington and his views by the white political and philanthropic elite. Among black Americans, Washington alone possessed delegated power, but for many he misused that power. In 1905, Du Bois called for an ideological leadership cadre composed of those in the African American community whom he referred to as "the Talented Tenth" with "sufficient ability and education to assume leadership among negroes" (Kellogg 1967, p. 23). Aware that Washington had the funds to control the black press, Du Bois said that conference was also to "to establish and support proper organs of new and public opinion."

Some twenty-seven black male professionals from fourteen states responded by meeting with Du Bois and Trotter on July 11, 1905, near Niagara Falls at the Erie Beach Hotel in Ontario, Canada, to plan for a national organization.

Among the attendees were Frederick McGhee, a practicing attorney; William Hart, a Howard University Law School professor; Charles E. Bentley, a physician; Harry Clay Smith, an editor; Freeman H. M. Murray, a print shop owner; and Jesse Max Barber, an educator and periodical publisher. After three days of intensive discussion and debate the Niagara conveners advocated the following goals, which were printed in Barber's periodical, *The Voice of the Negro*:

1. Freedom of speech and criticism
2. An unfettered and unsubsidized press
3. Manhood suffrage
4. The abolition of all caste distinctions based simply on race and color
5. The recognition of the principle of human brotherhood as a practical present creed
6. The recognition of the highest and best human training as the monopoly of no class or race

Founding Members of the Niagara Movement, 1905. *The Niagara Movement called for the right of black men to vote, an end to discrimination in public accommodations, equal justice before the law, equal educational opportunities, and the right to travel freely.* **PHOTOGRAPHS AND PRINTS DIVISION, SCHOMBURG CENTER FOR RESEARCH IN BLACK CULTURE, THE NEW YORK PUBLIC LIBRARY, ASTOR, LENOX AND TILDEN FOUNDATIONS.**

7. A belief in the dignity of labor
8. United effort to realize these ideals under wise and courageous leadership

At the second meeting of the Niagara Movement, held at Harper's Ferry, West Virginia, in 1906, Du Bois made it clear in his address that their goals were distinct from Washington's limited vocationalism:

> And when we call for education, we mean real education. We believe in work. We ourselves are workers, but work is not necessarily education. Education is the development of power and ideal. [sic] We want our children trained as intelligent human beings should be, and we will fight for all time against any proposal to educate black boys and girls simply as servants and underlings, or simply for the use of other people. They have a right to know, to think, to aspire.

Thus, the line was drawn between the accommodationists and the integrationists.

Indeed, allegedly during the 1905 meeting itself, one participant, the attorney Clifford Plummer, secretly kept Washington informed of its details. It was later alleged that other Washington allies persuaded white-owned newspapers to not cover the conference.

Du Bois, the guiding figure of the gathering, was named general secretary to coordinate the work among several committees. He proposed the creation of local branches in every state. Conspicuously absent that first year were women, but several were invited the next year. Few members lived south of the Potomac, and none had much daily contact with the black masses. Later, Du Bois admitted his own failings as a popular leader who could make small talk with those from humbler backgrounds. In addition to their social distance from the masses, the Niagara Movement adherents, by and large, were geographically separated from the southern rural masses who were bearing the brunt of direct and unremitting racial oppression.

Nevertheless, in 1906 Du Bois tried to broaden the movement's base and increase its support through a weekly publication, *The Moon Illustrated,* which ceased publication after only a year. Beginning in 1907, yet another periodical, *The Horizon: A Journal of the Color Line,* partially subsidized by Du Bois, was published monthly until 1910, when it was folded into the NAACP's *The Crisis,* which has appeared monthly ever since.

In 1906, the movement's adherents met in Harper's Ferry, made famous by John Brown's raid there in 1859. The delegates made a bare-footed pilgrimage to the site consecrated by the martyred Brown, and they called again for the right of black men to vote, an end to discrimination in public accommodations, equal justice before the law, equal educational opportunities, and the right to travel freely. Three years later, these became the goals of the Niagara Movement's successor organization, the National Association for the Advancement of Colored People (NAACP).

The 1907 Niagara Movement meeting was held at Faneuil Hall in Boston, and its report to the public called for "freedom from labor peonage, a fair and free ballot, the denial of representation to states who deny rights of citizens" and a demand for federal legislation "forbidding the exclusion of any person from interstate carriers on account of race or color." Less than fifty people showed up at the 1908 meeting, held at Oberlin College in Ohio. At this meeting, McGhee reported that the group had filed a suit against the Pullman Company for denying sleeping-car service to one of its members, and that local units of the group had met in a half dozen cities. It proudly reported that black voters in the South were being advised to vote against presidential candidate William Howard Taft because of his approval, as secretary of war, of the dishonorable discharge of 167 black soldiers for failing to identify one of their comrades as the person guilty of fatally wounding a white civilian in Brownsville, Texas, in 1906.

The Niagara Movement expanded into more than half the states, although its membership never exceeded 300 individuals. It had no white members until 1908, when Mary W. Ovington, a social worker, was invited to join. The 1908 Springfield Race Riot spurred white reformers into action. Some descendants of white abolitionists, such as Oswald Garrison Villard, the grandson of the great abolitionist editor William L. Garrison, called for concerted action for social justice by black and white leaders of all philosophical views. The target date to convene the meeting in New York City was February 12, 1909, the centennial of Lincoln's birthday. "The Call," as it was known, went out, urging "all believers in democracy to join in a national conference for discussion of present evils, the voicing of protests and the renewal of the struggle for civil and political liberty." This was the birth of the NAACP, which was backed by white and black luminaries and had a broader membership base than the Niagara Movement.

The initiative now passed from the black-controlled Niagara Movement to a white-dominated steering committee, which included Du Bois. Washington was invited, and initially expressed support, but he declined to attend. He promised to send a representative but never did, and he secretly opposed the new organization. This caused other black leaders to withhold support until after Washington's death in 1915. Trotter refused to follow Du Bois into a white-dominated organization, which he protested could not speak effectively for black people. He continued his protests in a newly formed Equal Rights League.

While the Niagara Movement formally disbanded, its stated goals became the NAACP's agenda for nearly a century. The movement lacked a secure financial base and broad appeal, but the NAACP quickly became the nation's premier civil rights organization, largely through the efforts of Du Bois, its first director of research and publicity. Du Bois also successfully launched *The Crisis*, which popularized the association to both black and white Americans.

SEE ALSO *Du Bois, W. E. B; Trotter, William Monroe; Washington, Booker T.*

BIBLIOGRAPHY

Du Bois, W.E.B. 1903. *The Souls of Black Folk*, Chicago: A. C. McClurg.

———. 1968. *The Autobiography of W. E. Burghardt DuBois: A Soliloquy on Viewing My Life from the Last Decade of Its First Century*, New York: International Publishers.

Franklin, John H., and Alfred A. Moss Jr. 2000. *From Slavery to Freedom: A History of African Americans*, 8th ed. New York: McGraw Hill.

Harlan, Louis. 1972. *Booker T. Washington, the Making of a Black Leader, 1856-1901*. New York: Oxford University Press.

Kellogg, Charles F. 1967. *NAACP: A History of the National Association for the Advancement of Colored People*. Baltimore, MD: Johns Hopkins University Press.

Lewis, David Levering, 1993. *W.E.B. DuBois: Biography of a Race*. New York: Henry Holt.

Medley, Keith W. 2003. *We as Freemen: Plessy v. Ferguson*. Gretna, LA: Pelican Publishing.

Raphael Cassimere Jr.

NONCONCORDANT VARIATION

Nonconcordant variation and *discordant variation* are the phrases that have historically been used to describe the commonly found noncorrelative and nonassociated nature of variation between pairs of genetically controlled traits. Said more positively, the phrases mean that traits tend to vary independently from each other.

A common example of a pair of nonconcordant traits is skin color and height. On both an individual and group level, skin color is independent of height (and height is reciprocally independent of skin color). As skin colors become lighter or darker, heights do not change in a predictable, dependent, or concordant way. Similarly, as heights increase or decrease, there is no predictable change in skin color. One trait is independent of the other.

Indeed, skin color appears to be independently distributed compared to all size traits and to virtually all phenotypic and genetic traits. The obvious exceptions are those few such as eye and hair color that are likely to share pigmentation genes with skin color. These exceptions can literally be seen with the eyes, and perhaps because they are so obvious, one might think that these are more common than they are. In fact, they are one of just a few known exceptions to the rule of trait independence.

The significance of this pattern of independent variation is that generally one cannot predict the distribution of one trait from that of another. Skin color does not reveal deeper (genetic) variation. More generally, from a biological perspective, racial traits such as skin color are just skin deep: they do not have deeper biological meaning.

HUMAN BIOLOGICAL VARIATION

The notion of discordant trait variation can be traced back to at least the 1950s. Evolutionary biologists observed that instead of varying together, geographic variation in one trait is usually discordant with geographic variation in other traits. One implication of this finding was a debate over the taxonomic classification "subspecies." In an influential 1953 article, "The Subspecies Concept and Its

Taxonomic Application," zoologists Edward O. Wilson and William L. Brown Jr. observed that because so few traits are concordant (vary together), a focus on different traits produces different subspecies. They also observed that most traits used to define subspecies are arbitrary.

In 1964, anthropologist Ashley Montagu edited a groundbreaking volume titled *The Concept of Race* in which zoologists Paul Ehrlich and Richard Holm used the terms *concordance* and *discordance* to describe the distribution of human traits relative to each other. They noted that if traits are largely concordant, then the study of the variation in one trait will reveal the pattern in the other. However, if the opposite is true, and traits are discordant or nonconcordant, then population variation must be studied one trait at a time.

Along with anthropologists C. Loring Brace and Frank Livingstone in the same volume, Ehrlich and Holm noted that rather than abrupt ruptures or boundaries in traits, the mean probabilities of traits vary continuously or gradually over geographic space. This type of geographic variation is now commonly referred to as clinal or continuous variation. They further noted that these traits tend to vary in different ways from each other. Thus, for example, human skin color tends to vary along a north to south gradient, with darker skin, on average, near the equator and lighter skin, on average, toward the poles. However, the distribution of other traits tends to follow different and less predictable patterns.

Trait independence is also a rule of variation on an individual (as well as a group) level. Thus, if one knows that someone is tall, one cannot predict if that person is dark or light, handsome or ugly. Tall, dark, and handsome is just as unlikely as tall, light, and handsome or tall, light, and ugly.

A useful diagrammatic illustration of trait independence was also published by Ehrlich and Holm (Figure 1). This diagram of discordant variation in four traits or characteristics has been frequently reproduced and redrawn in many textbooks. Each layer in the cube represents geographic variation in a trait. The top trait, for example, might be skin color. In this case, the individuals to the right have light skin, whereas the individuals to the left have darker skin. Similarly, the next layer down represents another trait, such as eye color, the next still another trait, such as the percent of type A blood, and the bottom layer represents a fourth and last trait.

Each core represents a specific individual or the average of a group of individuals in a region. (Remember: trait independence works at both an individual and a group level.) If the top layer represents skin color, then the two cores (individuals, groups) to the right appear to be the same for skin color. In the other levels, it becomes clear that skin color does not predict for the variation in the other traits. For example, the two individuals who have the same skin color differ with respect to all other traits. One might imagine millions of traits and any number of individual or group cores. Any one level/trait will predict very little about the other levels/traits.

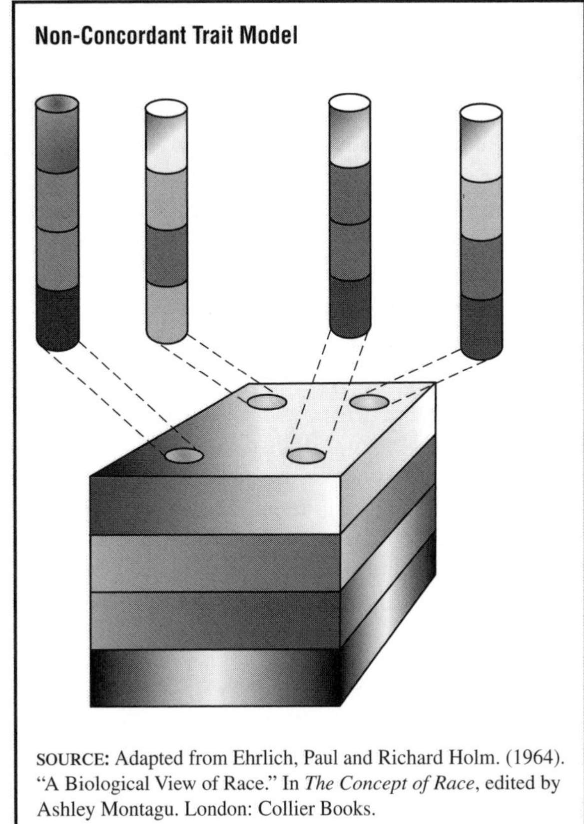

SOURCE: Adapted from Ehrlich, Paul and Richard Holm. (1964). "A Biological View of Race." In *The Concept of Race*, edited by Ashley Montagu. London: Collier Books.

Figure 1. *The layers represent traits and the cores represent individuals or groups from four different locations. Note that the first trait does not predict for the other traits.*

Although the general point of nonconcordant traits is modeled very well in Figure 1, in reality traits are rarely either completely independent or completely concordant. Another way to think about trait independence is in relationship to statistical concepts of correlation and association. If two traits are perfectly positively correlated, then as one increases, the other increases in a proportionate fashion. Similarly, if two traits are perfectly inversely correlated, then as one increase, the other decreases in a proportionate fashion. This is rare, but some traits are highly correlated, such as length of legs and height or hair color and eye color. On the other hand, most traits are nearly totally independent of each other; that is, as one trait changes, the change in the other trait is for all intents and purposes random and unpredictable. Trait independence is both a general taxonomic rule and a hallmark of human variation.

Why, then, would traits vary independently? The answer depends on the specific traits under consideration.

But, one can say that trait independence is probably related either to the forces of natural selection, if the trait is adaptive, or to random genetic factors.

In the case of skin color, variation appears driven by the relative adaptive advantages of dark skin pigmentation under conditions of maximal solar radiation and the advantages of lighter skin pigmentation under conditions of reduced solar exposure. The distribution of sickle cell anemia follows a pattern of variation that seems to be related to areas where malaria is greatest. The ability to digest lactose (milk sugar) in adulthood seems to be related to histories of dairying.

The majority of genetic and phenotypic traits appear to be adaptively neutral. Their distributions are also generally continuous across the globe. While the distribution of other traits seems more random and unpredictable, all of these traits are clinally distributed. Finally, the key point is that all of their clinal distributions are different. They are not concordant. They are independent.

NONCONCORDANCE AND RACE

The idea of biological races presupposes that traits are concordant; that is, the distribution in one trait tells us something or predicts for the distribution in another. In a sense, the idea of race is based on the notion that one can "read" a phenotype. For example, seeing someone who is overweight is often "read" in our society to mean someone who has an impulse-control problem. In this racist culture, seeing someone as dark skinned is "read" to conjure up a number of negative attribute associations. This is how the ideology of racism works.

As anthropologist Alan Goodman (1997) has noted, nonconcordance variation helps to make the case against meaningful biological races. For example, just as Wilson and Brown found that a subspecies could be redefined according to different traits, Jared Diamond (1994) created racial classifications based on the distribution of fingerprint patterns that were strikingly different from traditional models based on skin color.

Further, the overwhelming nature of nonconcordant variation tells us that what one sees does not predict for deeper characteristics. Genetic research suggests that traits such as skin color do not necessarily reflect shared evolutionary lineages. Nor are they useful for predicting behavior. Despite the social importance they may carry, racial traits are not useful markers for understanding human variation.

In describing the relationship between traits, nonconcordance captures part of the structure of human variation. That part is at complete odds with the idea of race.

SEE ALSO *Clines; Clines and Continuous Variation; Genes and Genealogies; Genetic Variation among Populations; Human and Primate Evolution; Human Genetics; Montagu, Ashley.*

BIBLIOGRAPHY

Brace, C. Loring. 1964. "A Nonracial Approach Towards the Understanding of Human Diversity." In *The Concept of Race*, ed. Ashley Montagu, 103–152. New York: Free Press of Glencoe.

Diamond, Jared. 1994. "Race Without Color." *Discover* 15 (11): 82–89.

Ehrlich, Paul, and Richard Holm 1964. "A Biological View of Race." In *The Concept of Race*, ed. Ashley Montagu, 153–179. New York: Free Press of Glencoe.

Goodman, Alan H. 1997. "Bred in the Bone." *The Sciences*. March–April: 20–25.

Livingstone, Frank B. 1964. "On the Nonexistence of Human Races." In *The Concept of Race*, ed. Ashley Montagu, 46–60. New York: Free Press of Glencoe.

Park, Michael Alan. 2002. *Biological Anthropology*, 3rd ed. Boston: McGraw-Hill.

Wilson, Edward O., and William L. Brown Jr. 1953. "The Subpecies Concept and Its Taxonomic Application." *Systematic Zoology* 2: 97–111.

Alan Goodman
Joseph Jones

NOTT, JOSIAH
1804–1873

Josiah Nott was a leading exponent of polygenism, the belief in the idea of multiple origins of the human species. He was a key figure in the American school of ethnology, which dominated the scientific understanding of race in the decades before Charles Darwin's *Origin of Species* appeared in 1859. In 1856 he helped to edit the first American translation of Arthur de Gobineau's *Essai sur l'inégalité des races humaines* (Essay on the inequality of the human race), a polemical work extolling Teutonic natural supremacy and warning against racial mixing.

In 1854, with George Gliddon, Nott published *Types of Mankind*, a tribute to their mentor, Samuel G. Morton, and a summation of their evidence that the races were separate and unequal species of *Homo sapiens*. He was determined to prove his belief in African natural inferiority, informally calling his research "niggerology" and "the nigger business." The underlying aim was to confound the abolitionists with evidence of the natural and permanent inferiority of blacks, and thus show that their liberation would be a disaster to both races. He asserted that "Caucasians" have been rulers throughout the ages, prepared and destined by nature.

Nott was born in Columbia, South Carolina, on March 31, 1804. He received his medical degree from the University of Pennsylvania, after which he traveled widely in Europe studying natural history and furthering his medical knowledge. He eventually settled in Mobile, Alabama, and built a flourishing practice treating the slaves of the wealthy. Nott sought to protect his clients, the slaveholders, both politically and scientifically by arguing that blacks and whites were of different species, and that nature itself had preordained their proper relationship to each other. The abolitionists, he claimed, were in error to think otherwise. For Nott, the impure mulatto population was proof of his theory: Being neither black nor white, mulattoes represented a dilution of fixed characteristics unhelpful to either race. This view was in line with several other prominent "ethnologists" of the era who believed that the human species had multiple origins, thus accounting for the diversity of humankind.

Nott had good company in pursuing the polygenist theory: Samuel G. Morton, Ephraim George Squire, James D. B. DeBow, and later Louis Agassiz also championed the fixity of species and the multiple origins of human races. They made this argument from the evidence derived from the study of "hybrids," crania, Egyptology, and philology. Ignoring the popular slaveholder's "Hamitic curse" argument for black enslavement, Nott argued that both natural history and slaveholder hegemony constituted evidence in support of his theory.

Nott tried to use scientific debates, lectures, and articles to advance his arguments. Among the scientific opponents of polygenism, the abolitionist churches were certainly united against the theory, as were Professor J. L. Cabell of the University of Virginia, and Rev. John Bachman of Charleston, the latter raising many questions about "exceptional human hybrids" and mixed-race fecundity. Nott dismissed Bachman's scientific objections as disguised religious positions from a "hypocritical parson," and he characterized Bachman as a failed scientist and a false minister.

The secular ideology of race was established in the years before Darwin's work eroded the dominance of polygenism. Nott immediately recognized Darwin's *Origins* as finally giving monogenesis an unshakable scientific basis, and in later life he gracefully admitted that Darwin's answer to the species question had settled the matter of origins, but not the issue of stratified racial diversity. Nott did not abandon his views on race, holding that inequality of status and competence had always characterized black-white race relations.

Having lost two sons in the Civil War, one from wounds received at Gettysburg, Nott could not endure a South transformed, he said, into "Negroland." He settled in New York City, drawn to a place "without morals, without scruples, without religion, & without niggers." There he rebuilt his practice, joined Squire's Anthropological Institute, and flourished until age and health forced his final return to Mobile. He died on March 31, 1873.

Nott's importance in developing and promoting the theory of polygenism left an enduring legacy of race as a scientific concept. Darwin believed natural selection would cause polygenism "to die a silent and unobserved death" (Darwin 1998 [1874], p. 188), but its supporters continued to justify using race as a secular explanation for human variety. Nott's work demonstrates how scientific theories often produce definitions of truth that are deeply embedded in the social relations of a given time and space. Nott and his fellow polygenists developed "race" as a construct, the use of which has continued as both a scientific ideology and a common-sense notion, largely due to the influence of Nott.

BIBLIOGRAPHY

Canguilhem, Georges. 1988. *Ideology and Rationality in the History of the Life Sciences.* Cambridge, MA: MIT Press.

Darwin, Charles. 1998 (1874). *The Descent of Man.* Amherst, NY: Prometheus Books.

Gould, Stephen Jay. 1996. *The Mismeasure of Man,* revised and expanded edition. New York: W.W. Norton.

Nott, Josiah. 1846. "Unity of the Human Race." *Southern Quarterly Review* 9 (17): 1–57.

———. 1850. "Ancient and Scripture Chronology." *Southern Quarterly Review* 2 (4): 385–426.

———. 1850. "Yellow Fever Contrasted with Bilious Fever: Reason for Believing It a Disease Sui Generis—Its Mode of Propagation—Remote Cause—Probably Insect or Animalcular Origin." *New Orleans Medical and Surgical Journal* 4: 563–601.

———. 1851. *An Essay on the Natural History of Mankind, Viewed in Connection with Negro Slavery Delivered before the Southern Rights Association, 14th December, 1850.* Mobile, AL: Dade, Thompson.

———. 1852. "Geographical Distributions of Animals and the Races of Man." *New Orleans Medical and Surgical Journal* 9.

———. 1853. "Aboriginal Races of America." *Southern Quarterly Review* 8 (3).

———, and George R. Gliddon, 1854. *Types of Mankind: Or, Ethnological Researches, Based upon the Ancient Monuments, Paintings, Sculptures, and Crania of Races, and upon Their Natural, Geographical, Philological and Biblical History.* Philadelphia: Lippincott Grambo & Co.

Stanton, William. 1960. *The Leopard's Spots: Scientific Attitudes toward Race in America, 1815–1859.* Chicago: University of Chicago Press.

B. Ricardo Brown

O

OCCUPATIONAL SEGREGATION

Occupational racial/ethnic and sex segregation—the separation of non-Hispanic white men and women and workers of color into different occupations—is more than a pattern of physical separation of the races and sexes at work. Rather, occupational segregation is a fundamental process in sustaining and perpetuating social inequality because occupations dominated by white men tend to offer more pay, fringe benefits, access to promotions, training, and authority than occupations dominated by white women and people of color. Occupational segregation also limits the bargaining power of minorities and white women, making it difficult for them to improve their labor-market positions. Segregation at work also limits female and minority workers' access to health insurance and retirement benefits. In no small way, then, occupational segregation reduces the quality of life for white women and racial/ethnic minority workers and plays an integral role in keeping a greater share of minorities compared to whites below the poverty line.

PREVALENCE BY RACE, ETHNICITY, AND SEX

Occupational racial/ethnic and sex segregation are common and persistent features of the U.S. labor market. In fact, it is rare to find Latinos, Asians, blacks, and other racial/ethnic minorities working in the same occupations. Within and across racial/ethnic groups, men and women are also segregated into different occupations. In their book *Women and Men at Work* (2002), Irene Padavic and Barbara Reskin documented the top occupations in the year 2000 for men and women belonging to selected racial/ethnic categories. The top occupation for black women was nurses' aide, orderly; for black men it was truck driver. For Hispanic women it was cashier and Hispanic men, truck driver. White women's top occupation was secretary, while white men's was salaried manager/administrator.

The occupations employing white men, white women, and male and female racial/ethnic minorities have different pay levels. Median pay levels in the occupations that employ mainly non-Hispanic whites (henceforth, whites) versus those that employ mainly minorities are significantly different, given their skill levels. According to the 2000 Census Bureau (see Fronczek and Johnson 2003), roughly 36 percent of employed whites and 45 percent of employed Asians work in managerial/professional occupations, where the 2000 median annual pay level was $42,844. Employed blacks, Hispanics of any race, and Native Hawaiian and other Pacific Islanders were concentrated mainly in sales and office occupations where the median annual pay level was just below $30,000.

Although the causes of racial/ethnic occupational segregation and occupational sex segregation are similar, occupational sex segregation is more prevalent in the United States. In other words, it is less common for women and men to work in the same occupation than it is for whites and minorities to hold the same occupation, mainly because racial/ethnic minorities make up a much smaller share of the labor force than women. The U.S. Department of Labor Bureau speculates that minorities will be 29 percent of the labor force by 2008, but women already comprise over 60 percent of the labor force. So, for example, integrating male minority workers into occupations dominated by white men is easier than integrating the tens of millions of female labor force participants into male-dominated occupations (see Padavic and Reskin 2002).

THEORETICAL EXPLANATIONS

Social scientists have put forth a number of theories to explain the persistent occupational segregation of white men, white women, and racial/ethnic minorities. This section reviews some of the major theoretical explanations of occupational segregation. The review begins with supply-side explanations of segregation, or explanations that focus on individuals' behaviors, then moves to demand-side explanations, or those that focus on the behaviors and actions of employers. The theories have related and overlapping components because the ideologies of race and gender are widespread in the U.S. labor market and beyond.

The first set of supply-side theoretical explanations view job seekers' personal choices and incentives as the root cause of occupational segregation. For example, gender-role socialization theory argues that women and men pursue different lines of work because of differences in their childhood socialization (i.e., girls are given dolls and raised to be nurturers; boys are given trucks and taught to be aggressive). Although there is little empirical support for the socialization explanation of occupational sex segregation, it remains a point of debate among researchers.

Human capital theory is another supply-side explanation of occupational sex segregation. According to this theory, women are more oriented toward family than men, so they seek lower levels of education, training, and work experience than men. Consequently, women and men are not as prepared for the same occupations. The education gap between employed women and men is closing, but they tend to major in different subjects and men have more job training and work experience, on average, than women. Many researchers view these differences as a function of demand-side factors rather than women's choice (see Padavic and Reskin 2002).

Supply-side theories look to somewhat different prelabor market forces to explain occupational racial/ethnic segregation. Supply-side theorists argue that discriminatory practices outside the labor market lead to racial residential segregation. As a result of residential segregation, whites and minorities have access to different schools. Because of the higher concentration of poverty among minorities, their neighborhood schools are not as well funded as the schools whites attend, so minorities enter the labor force with fewer job-related skills and lower quality education, on average, than whites. Consequently, minorities and whites are qualified for and hired into different occupations.

Even if their skills are similar, because of race-based stereotypes employers may perceive that whites have higher education levels, more job-related skills, and more work experience than racial/ethnic minorities. Phillip Moss and Charles Tilly's interviews with urban employers, reported in their 2001 book *Stories Employers Tell: Race, Skill, and Hiring in America*, revealed that employers tend to stereotype racial/ethnic minorities (especially black men) as lacking "soft skills," that is, nontechnical job skills such as friendliness, self-motivation, and responsibility. Almost half of the employers in their urban sample criticized black workers' soft skills and technical skills (i.e., math ability, reading, writing, computer knowledge), while a smaller share criticized Latinos' and Asians' skills. Despite the real and perceived differences in white and minority job-related skills and education quality, these differences are not enough to explain the segregation of whites and racial/ethnic minorities at work.

A second and related theoretical explanation blames employers' intentional racial and gender biases for occupational segregation. Some employers stereotype women as weak, emotional, and submissive, while they view men as aggressive, decisive, and strong. Thus, they see the sexes as suited to different types of work. Likewise, some scholars have asserted that employers' stereotypes of minority workers channel whites into "good," high-paying occupations and racial/ethnic minorities into poor, low-paying ones. Robert L. Kaufman explained in "Assessing Alternative Perspectives on Race and Sex Employment Segregation" (2002) that employers viewed jobs requiring high skill and authority as "inappropriate" for minority workers but considered jobs with poor working conditions, subservient tasks, low prestige, and low pay as "appropriate" for minorities. Of course, some race stereotypes operate in conjunction with stereotypes of women and men; for example, employers may stereotype black men as dishonest (see William Julius Wilson's 1996 book *When Work Disappears: The World of the New Urban Poor*) and black women as single mothers.

Occupational segregation is not always the result of intentional processes to harm minorities and white women. Nonconscious cognitive processes may also predispose employers to prefer hiring workers who share their race and sex. In the case of occupational race and sex segregation, this means that an Asian female employer may unintentionally favor an Asian female job applicant, perhaps by smiling more at her during the job interview or overlooking small problems on her job application. These nonconscious behaviors increase the likelihood that a job applicant who shares the employer's race and sex will receive a job offer. Since most employers in charge of hiring in U.S. workplaces are white men, these nonconscious preferences mainly benefit white men.

A third theoretical explanation views occupational racial/ethnic and sex segregation as the result of discriminatory employment practices and policies. In one case, policies or rules designed to treat all applicants, regardless of their race or sex, equally can have a different, negative impact on racial/ethnic minorities and white women during the employment process. This phenomenon, known as disparate impact, can lead to occupational segregation. One example of a practice with disparate negative impact on women and racial/ethnic minorities is word-of-mouth recruitment. Although this recruitment practice is not motivated by discriminatory intent and is designed to treat all job applicants the same, because white men dominate most high-paying occupations and people tend to have social ties to others that share their race/ethnicity and sex, this practice systematically excludes women and minority members from white-male-dominated occupations.

Employment policies and rules can differently affect white women and minorities—what scholars refer to as disparate treatment. Disparate treatment occurs when an employer treats a worker or job applicant differently because of his or her race/ethnicity. For example, disparate treatment happens when an employer requires a Latina job applicant to score 50 out of 100 on an employment test to be considered for a job but hires a white female applicant with a score of 25 out of 100. Another example occurs when an employer refuses to hire a mother based on the assumption that as a mother, she is not committed to the labor force. One consequence of policies and practices that have a negative disparate impact or yield disparate treatment of the races and sexes is occupational segregation.

A fourth theoretical explanation, called spatial mismatch, identifies the physical space that separates inner-city (mainly minority) workers from suburban jobs as a contributing factor to the segregation of minority and white workers at work. The theory does not apply to explaining occupational sex segregation because women and men are not segregated outside of the workforce; women and men live in the same neighborhoods and the same households and attend the same schools. Spatial mismatch theory argues that racial/ethnic minority men and women are overrepresented in central cities. Because of the movement of businesses to the suburbs in the 1970s and the closing of urban manufacturing plants, few businesses remain in urban settings, and those that do often pay low wages. Whites, on the other hand, live mainly in suburban areas where businesses with high-paying jobs are plenty. Because transportation to the suburbs from central cities is often unavailable (or expensive) in many U.S. cities, minorities have limited access to good job opportunities and thus have little choice but to take low-paying occupations while whites take high-paying ones in the suburbs.

POTENTIAL REMEDIES

U.S. workplaces are characterized by the segregation of white men, white women, and racial/ethnic minorities into different occupations. This segregation has negative consequences for minority men and women and white women because the occupations in which they are concentrated pay less, award fewer promotions, offer fewer benefits, and have less authority than occupations filled mainly by white men. A number of factors—many of them overlapping—contribute to occupational segregation. Undoubtedly, race and gender-based stereotypes about the "appropriateness" of jobs for one sex or the other or one race/ethnicity or the other play a role in maintaining occupational segregation. Given the prevalence of residential segregation by race/ethnicity in U.S. cities, the de facto segregation of the races at school, the informal ways employers go about finding potential workers, the continued flow of good jobs out of inner cities, and the difficulty of proving disparate impact and disparate treatment, occupational segregation based on race/ethnicity and sex are likely to be common in workplaces of the future.

Although stereotypical thinking on the part of employers and racial segregation in neighborhoods and schools cannot be entirely eliminated, occupational segregation is not inevitable. Formal workplace policies and rules whose goal is the equal treatment of white women, white men, and minorities at work are necessary for ending occupational segregation. Most notably, employers will have to change the way they recruit workers. The common practice of recruiting job applicants through referrals from current workers (i.e., word-of-mouth recruiting) hurts minorities and white women because most high-paying occupations are dominated by white men, and more often than not, people refer others who share their race and sex. Formalizing the employment process is one way to remove barriers that prevent racial and gender integration at work. For example, companies can establish a race/sex-blind application process by having job applicants submit their job applicants on a computer in the first stage of the application process. A race/sex-blind application process minimizes the extent to which employers' conscious hostility toward one race or sex or preference for workers of another race or sex matter in the employment process. Likewise, companies can establish equal employment offices to both monitor the employment process and help ensure the equal treatment of all applicants, regardless of their race or sex.

Changing the hiring process and establishing a system of oversight are only two small steps employers can take to integrate occupations. Cities can implement policies to integrate neighborhoods, design strategies to racially integrate public schools, and offer tax incentives for businesses with high-paying jobs to locate in neighborhoods predominated by racial/ethnic minorities. Communities can provide job training for workers interested in lines of work dominated by the opposite sex. Workplaces can subsidize childcare to help parents, especially women, remain in the labor force. As the nation's workforce continues to diversify along racial and ethnic lines and women continue to comprise a large share of the labor force, all workers will benefit from integrated workplaces.

SEE ALSO *Education, Racial Disparities; Labor Market; Racial Desegregation (U.S.); Sexism; Underemployment.*

BIBLIOGRAPHY

Fronczek, Peter, and Patricia Johnson. 2003. *Occupations: 2000.* U.S. Census Bureau, Washington, DC: U.S. Government Printing Office.

Kaufman, Robert L. 2002. "Assessing Alternative Perspectives on Race and Sex Employment Segregation." *American Sociological Review* 67 (4): 547–572.

Moss, Phillip, and Chris Tilly. 2001. *Stories Employers Tell: Race, Skill, and Hiring in America.* New York: Russell Sage Foundation.

Padavic, Irene, and Barbara F. Reskin. 2002. *Women and Men at Work,* 2nd ed. Thousand Oaks, CA: Pine Forge Press.

Tomaskovic-Devey, Donald. 1993. *Gender and Racial Inequality at Work: The Sources and Consequences of Job Segregation.* Ithaca, NY: ILR Press.

U.S. Department of Labor. 2007. "Working in the 21st Century." Available from http://www.bls.gov/opub/working/chart4.pdf.

Wilson, William Julius. 1996. *When Work Disappears: The World of the New Urban Poor.* New York: Knopf.

Julie A. Kmec

OLYMPIC GAMES OF 1904

The 1904 Olympic Games were held in St. Louis, Missouri, as an adjunct to a world's fair, the Louisiana Purchase International Exposition, usually called the Louisiana Purchase Exposition. The fair titularly celebrated the centennial of Thomas Jefferson's purchase of the Louisiana territory from the French, although that had occurred in 1803. The fair was originally scheduled for 1903, but plans could not be finished in time, so it was moved ahead to 1904. The Olympics themselves were less than memorable. With the 1900 Olympics, they have been termed "the farcical Olympics."

The 1904 Olympic Games were originally awarded by the International Olympic Committee (IOC) to Chicago. But James Sullivan, president of the Amateur Athletic Union (AAU), planned to hold competing sporting events during the world's fair. Chicago did not have the money that the fair organizers did, and people there realized that athletes would choose between the two, and likely compete in St. Louis. Eventually, Chicago capitulated and ceded its rights to the Olympics to St. Louis.

Sullivan was then put in charge of organizing the Olympic Program. He planned a huge program that lasted from early July until late-November of 1904. Sullivan considered everything that was contested during the world's fair as part of the Olympics. It is noted in the *Official Guide to the Louisiana Purchase Exposition,* "By a decision of the International Olympic Committee all sports and competitions during the World's Fair are designated as Olympic events, with the exception of competitions for the championships of local associations" (p. 138). It is more likely that this was a decision made by Sullivan, as he had little consultation with the IOC in 1904. He has left a quagmire for Olympic historians, who still debate which events should be considered Olympic in 1904.

Former Missouri governor David Francis ran the Louisiana Purchase Exposition. Francis and the director of exhibits, Frederick Skiff, planned the exhibits to demonstrate man and his works, emphasizing education, with the exhibits separated into twelve categories. The pertinent ones to the study of race were Section 10 on Anthropology and Section 12 on Physical Culture. The Olympic Games were considered a part of Section 12.

The exhibits at the 1904 fair were designed to demonstrate the progress of humanity from barbarism to the pinnacle of Anglo-Saxon civilization, and this was exemplified by a series of historical and anthropological exhibits contrasting various races and peoples. Emphasizing this, there were American Indian exhibits and exhibits of Philippine natives both of which contrasted modern civilization against the relative barbaric cultures of those two groups at that time.

The Louisiana Purchase Exposition opened on Saturday, April 30, and drew an estimated crowd of 200,000 on the first day. There were over 540 amusements and concessions, mostly located around the main thoroughfare, the Pike. The Pike featured "Cliff Dwellers, Zuni tribes, and Moku Indians who had never been shown before." Sections of the Pike demonstrated "Mysterious Asians with camel rides along its winding streets, and the Geisha Girls entertaining visitors to Fair Japan" (Mallon 1999, p. 10).

The 1904 Olympic Games took place primarily on the campus of Washington University, with the one-third mile track and its accompanying stadium having been specially built for the occasion. Alongside the track was a new building containing a gymnasium and locker rooms, which was then state-of-the-art for physical culture. The building and stadium still exist today.

The Olympic Games can be considered to have opened on July 1, with a series of gymnastic events. But on May 14, Sullivan staged the Missouri State High School Meet at the Olympic Stadium. He called it the

George Poage, 1904. *University of Wisconsin athelete George Poage won the bronze medal in the 200- and 400-meter hurdles at the 1904 Olympic Games.* THE LIBRARY OF CONGRESS.

Olympic Interscholastic Meet and a small opening ceremony preceded it.

The track and field athletic events were considered the showcase of the Olympic Games and were held from August 29 until September 3. It was one of the few Olympic sports in 1904 that had a true international flavor, as 117 athletes from ten nations competed.

It is often written that George Poage of the University of Wisconsin and the Milwaukee Athletic Club was the first person of African descent to win an Olympic medal, at the 1904 Games. This is incorrect. In 1900, a French team won a medal in rugby football, and one of the players was Constantin Henriquez de Zubiera, an Algerian doctor who played for the French team.

But Poage competed in the 200-meter hurdles, the 400-meter hurdles, and the 400-meter race at the 1904 Olympic Games. He won a bronze medal in both hurdles events and finished sixth in the 400. His 400-meter hurdle bronze came on August 31 and this is the "first medal" to which many writers have alluded. However, there are further documentary problems with the simple assertion that he was the first black Olympic medalist. On that same day, Joseph Stadler of the Cleveland Athletic Club, an African American, competed in the standing high jump, and won a silver medal.

Perhaps more ironic was the presence of the first black African competitors in the Olympic Games. In the marathon, two runners represented South Africa. They had been workers at the South African exhibit during the world's fair. They had been dispatch runners during the recent Boer War and were noted to be "the fleetest in the service." They have been listed in most record books as Lentauw and Yamasani, but Professor Floris van der Merwe (University of Stellenbosch) has found that they were Tsuana Tribesmen named Len Taw and Jan Mashiani. They both finished the marathon, Taw in ninth place and Mashiani in twelfth.

ANTHROPOLOGY DAYS

More important to any study of race and racism may be the so-called Anthropology Days that were held as a sideshow to the Olympic Games on August 12 and 13. These were a series of events open to minority, aboriginal, or native people from various lands who were present at the Physical Culture exhibits of the Louisiana Purchase Exposition. Among the tribes that competed were Pygmies, Patagonians, Filipinos, Native American Indian tribes, Japanese Ainus, and certain Asian tribes. The events included throwing bolos, mud fighting, and climbing a greased pole.

Sullivan later wrote of the rationale for the Anthropology Days by commenting that he had several conferences with William John McGee, chief of the department of anthropology for the Fair, related to the athletic abilities of many of the foreign tribes that were being exhibited at the Fair. McGee described startling rumors pertaining to the speed, stamina, and strength of many of the athletes at the exhibits and he and Sullivan decided to set up a two-day athletic meet for them.

McGee was well-qualified for his position. He was at the time the president of the American Anthropological Association. From 1893 to 1903 he had been ethnologist in charge of the government Bureau of American Ethnology, resigning only to assume duties as chief of the department of anthropology for the World's Fair.

Reflecting the mores of the time, Sullivan and McGee planned the Anthropology Days for August, "so that the many physical directors and gentlemen interested in scientific work could be present and benefit by the demonstrations" (Mallon 1999, p. 205). In fact, reading Sullivan's rationale for the Anthropology Days, it is apparent that this was intended to be a scientific study of the athletic abilities of the "savages." Interestingly, one of the spectators for the contests was the Apache chief Geronimo (1829–1909).

In addition to the so-called aboriginal events described above, several standard athletics events were contested: 100-yard run, shot put, 440-yard run, broad jump, high-hurdle race, one-mile run, and the weight throw event. In most cases, the events were separated into heats, or perhaps one could more accurately say, segregated. As an example, in the 100-yard run there

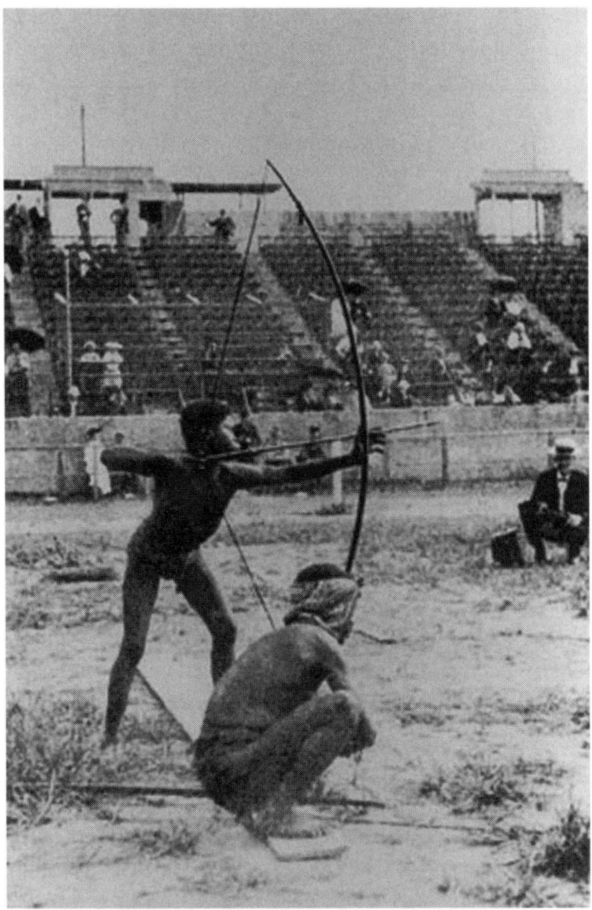

Anthropology Days, World's Fair, 1904. *A member of the Pygmy tribe competes in the archery contest. The so-called Anthropology Days were held as a sideshow to the 1904 Olympic Games.* © IOC/OLYMPIC MUSEUM COLLECTIONS.

were sections for Africans, Lanao Moros (Filipinos), Patagonians, Asians (Syrians from Beirut), Native Americans of the Cocopah tribe, and Native American Sioux. There were no finals, in which the winners of the heats would have competed against each other.

The results were the opposite of the rumored superb athletic abilities of the various tribes. In fact, the athletes performed very poorly. In most cases, this was attributed to the fact that the events were strange and unnatural to them, and not ones that they usually practiced. Sullivan noted of the running events, "With eight or ten men on the mark it was a pretty hard thing to explain to them to run when the pistol was fired. In running their heats, when coming to the finish tape, instead of breasting it or running through, many would stop and others run under it" (Mallon 1999, p. 209). Sullivan eventually concluded:

> It may have been a mistake in not having another day, when perhaps, the different interpreters could have explained to the savages more about what was expected of them, but nevertheless, the 'Anthropology Days' were most successful and interesting, and ones that scientific men will refer to for many years to come. It taught a great lesson. Lecturers and authors will in the future please omit all reference to the natural athletic ability of the savage, unless they can substantiate their alleged feats. (Mallon 1999, p. 209)

John Wesley Hanson's full report on the World's Fair contained a chapter on the Department of Anthropology entitled "The Study of Mankind." In it he noted, "The special object of the Department of Anthropology was to show each half of the world how the other half lives, and thereby to promote not only knowledge but also peace and good will among the nations; for it is the lesson of experience that personal contact is the best solvent of enmity and distrust between persons and peoples" (Hanson 1904, p. 265). The chapter had subsections on "Central African Pygmies," "Tehuelche Giants of Patagonia," "Northern Japanese Ainus," and several sections on Native American Indians. Interestingly, that report contains not one word on the Olympic Games.

The *Guide to the Louisiana Purchase Exposition* noted: "The Ethnological exhibit includes representatives of 23 Indian tribes, a family of nine Ainus, the Aborigines of Japan, seven Patagonian giants, and many other strange people, all housed in their peculiar dwellings, such as the wigwam, tepee, earth-lodge, toldo, or tent. Among the strangest people assembled are the Batwa pygmies from Central Africa. The various Filipino tribes constitute a complete anthropological display in themselves" (Lowenstein 1904, p. 92).

The 1904 Olympic Games are considered to have ended on November 23, at the finish of an Olympic football (soccer) tournament, won by a Canadian team from Galt, Ontario. But numerous non-Olympic sporting events were contested during the Louisiana Purchase Exposition, including a series of American football exhibition games held from September through November. The last sporting event contested during the 1904 World's Fair was such a football game, played appropriately enough by two schools devoted to training Native Americans, the Carlisle Indian School and the Haskell Indian School. Carlisle, which would later train the redoubtable Jim Thorpe, won the game, 38–4.

The founder of the modern Olympic Movement, Baron Pierre de Coubertin, was not present in St. Louis. He was only informed of the happenings there by the Hungarian International Olympic Committee member, Ferenc Kémény, who did attend and wrote de Coubertin, "I was not only present at a sporting contest but also at a fair where there were sports, where there was cheating, where monsters were exhibited for a joke." Later writing of the Anthropology Days, Coubertin presciently said, "As for that outrageous charade, it will of course lose its appeal when black men, red men, and yellow men learn to run, jump, and throw, and leave the white men behind them" (Coubertin 1931, p. 79).

Thus in many ways, the 1904 Olympic Games are important to the early study of race and racism at the Olympic Games. They saw the first American blacks win medals. They saw the first South African competitors who, pre-dating the days of apartheid, were also black men. But most importantly, they were the only Olympic Games at which aboriginal and native peoples were paraded about on exhibition and exposed to ridicule under the guise of a scientific study.

SEE ALSO *Olympic Games of 1936; Track and Field.*

BIBLIOGRAPHY

Barnett, C. Robert. 1996. "St. Louis 1904: The Games of the IIIrd Olympiad." In *Historical Dictionary of the Modern Olympic Movement,* edited by John E. Findling and Kimberly D. Pelle. Westport, CT: Greenwood Press.

Bennitt, Mark, ed. 1905. *History of the Louisiana Purchase Exposition.* St. Louis: Universal Exposition Publishing.

Coubertin, Pierre de. 1931. *Mémoires olympiques.* Lausanne, Switzerland: Bureau international de pédagogie sportive.

Findling, John E. 1990. "World's Fairs and the Olympic Games." *World's Fair* 10 (4): 13–15.

Hanson, John Wesley. 1905. *The Official History of the Fair St. Louis, 1904: The Sights and Scenes of the Louisiana Purchase Exposition. A Complete Description of the Magnificent Palaces, Marvelous Treasures and Scenic Beauties of the Crowning Wonder of the Age.* St. Louis, MO.

Lennartz, Karl, and Thomas Zawadzki. 2004. *Die Spiele der III. Olympiade 1904 in St. Louis.* Kassel, Germany: Agon Sportverlag.

Lowenstein, M. J., ed. 1904. *Official Guide to the Louisiana Purchase Exposition.* St. Louis, MO: Official Guide Co.

Lucas, Charles J. P. 1905. *The Olympic Games 1904.* St. Louis, MO: Woodward & Tiernan.

Mallon, Bill. 1999. *The 1904 Olympic Games: Results for All Competitors in All Events, with Commentary.* Jefferson, NC: McFarland.

Sullivan, James E. 1905. *Spalding's Official Athletic Almanac for 1905: Special Olympic Number, Containing the Official Report of the Olympic Games of 1904.* New York: American Sports Publishing.

Bill Mallon, M.D.

OLYMPIC GAMES OF 1936

Commonly referred to as the "Nazi Olympics" (Mandell 1971, Krüger and Murray 2003, Rippon 2006), the Olympic Games of 1936 in Berlin changed the Olympic movement in scope and political awareness. As an "Aryan" festival it demonstrated German superiority, yet the star of the Nazi Olympics was Jesse Owens, the African American sprinter who won four Olympic Gold medals. The Nazi Olympics highlighted race relations in sports on a world scale.

Organized since 1896, the Olympic Summer Games had become ever more important, developing into the focal point of amateur sports and its specialized press worldwide (Young and Wamsley 2005). Every four years the Olympic Games drew the attention of the sports world. With more than 4,000 athletes from forty-nine nations, participation in Berlin in 1936 was one-third larger than ever before. The games were attended by 3.77 million spectators, more than three times the previous record set at the Los Angeles Olympics of 1932. More spectators attended the opening ceremony of the 1936 Olympic Winter Games in Garmisch-Partenkirchen than had attended all events at the 1932 Winter Games in Lake Placid, New York, combined. More than 300 million people on all continents followed the Nazi Olympics over the radio, by far the largest radio audience of any event up to that date. Early television transmitted the Berlin Olympics into the center of town and brought even more people into contact with the games.

When the young French educator Pierre de Coubertin (1863–1937) revived the Olympic Games, he had the ancient Greek Olympic Games (776 BCE–393 CE) in mind and was looking for a sporting event that would bring the best youth together in something like a world exhibition of sports. Early Olympic Games were therefore often staged as sideshows of world exhibits. Coubertin, having a paternalistic attitude toward Africans, never questioned the superiority of the "white" race. The 1904 Olympic Games in St. Louis, Missouri, even contained Anthropological Days in which "natives" were to demonstrate their "sports" and prove white physical superiority.

The Olympic Games of 1936 had been granted to Germany in 1931, and everyone would have been happy with the grandiose staging of the games had the liberal German government persisted. In 1933, however, the National Socialist Party (NSDAP), the Nazis, with its long history of fundamental racism, came to power in Germany. The Nazis had previously questioned the legitimacy of such international events as the Olympics, as so noble a sporting event should be for "whites" only. After all, the ancient Greek Olympics had been one of the key features of the cradle of "Aryan" civilization. Now that the Nazis had the chance to organize the games themselves, they went about it in a far more sophisticated manner to impress world public opinion with their idea of "Aryan" supremacy (Krüger 2004).

RACE AND SPORTS AT THE OLYMPICS

Like many French, Coubertin followed the pre-Darwinist racial ideas of Jean-Baptiste Lamarck (1744–1829), who insisted on the inheritance of acquired characteristics. Physical training and sport were therefore supposed to have direct benefits not only for the generation practicing them but also for their children, who were supposed to become fitter by birth. To be French was, therefore, defined by culture. If people spoke French and soaked up French culture, they and their offspring were supposed to become culturally improved. By contrast, Germany was influenced by Gregor Mendel (1822–1884), whose theory had been developed using peas, but it became the dominant genetic theory for all living beings in the twentieth century. To be German was defined by blood. Just as with a racehorse, a person had to have a long lineage of German blood to be a "pure" German. The Nazis, aware of the German melting pot since the Middle Ages, called themselves "Aryan," thus claiming a long line of Germanic tradition that went back into Greek antiquity, the cradle of European civilization.

From the very beginning, the modern Olympic Games were a forum for international comparison of national strength, which was interpreted as a sign of national vitality and the dominance of a certain race. The International Olympic Committee (IOC) kept an official medal count to demonstrate the national ranking of nations. At the height of nationalism prior to World War I, Sweden used the Olympics of 1912 to demonstrate the superiority of its system, kicking off an international surge for national superiority at the 1916 Olympics, later canceled because of World War I. The use of sports to demonstrate national superiority was later used by Fascist Italy, Nazi Germany, and the communist Soviet Union. In the case of Germany, the demonstration of the superior system went hand in hand with the superior "Aryan" race, as German law started to exclude all non-Germans from the public sphere following the Nazi takeover.

RACE AND SPORTS IN GERMANY

Long before the Nazis came to power in Germany, Germans had been used to their government involving itself in areas that elsewhere were the province of the private sphere. This *Sonderweg*, the way in which Germany took a radically different course from other European countries, could be seen in the German interpretation of Social Darwinism: Whereas countries such as Great Britain and the United States saw it as survival of the fittest individual, in Germany it was interpreted as the survival of the fittest race. The selection and preparation of Olympic athletes had been paid for by German governments since 1914 (Krüger 1998) to demonstrate national—that is, racial—superiority in international sport.

The racial ideas of the party were not very consistent before Nazis came to power, as the Nazis had successfully attempted to soak up different kinds of racists in their political party. Nazi statements and publications before 1933 and private opinions even of prominent Nazi leaders after 1933 should therefore not be confused with official Nazi policy after the party gained control of the German government.

Privately, African Americans were considered "animals," and it was regarded as unfair that the American Olympic Committee would field them against human beings. Although Germany had a minute Afro-German minority, particularly in the Rhineland, the prime racial concerns in Germany were Jews and to a much smaller extent Sinti and Roma (Gypsies). Although less than 1 percent of the German population was Jewish according to the census of 1933, faith was not what racists targeted.

German Jews on the whole were well integrated into the mainstream sports movement, although a number of sports clubs in Germany prohibited Jewish membership. The German-Austrian Deutscher Turnerbund, the smallest of the three national gymnastics associations, was even outright anti-Semitic. Only about 20,000 Jews were members of Jewish sports clubs in Germany. There was no separate organization for Sinti and Roma. Because many of them traveled continually from town to town, they were difficult to count (Krüger 2001).

PROPAGANDA VALUE OF THE GAMES

During the race riots of early 1933, German clubs, including sports clubs, expelled their Jewish members of long standing. Although the German authorities closed social-democratic and communist sports clubs, Jewish sports clubs were maintained and tripled their membership in the following years, as they absorbed Jews that had been excluded elsewhere. Following the boycott of Jewish shops and the destruction of Jewish property, a worldwide boycott of Germany in cultural matters threatened to include the Olympic Games among its banned events.

At the same time, the newly appointed Nazi propaganda minister, Joseph Goebbels, realized the propaganda value of the games to advertise the "new" Aryan Germany and started to play by the rules of the IOC. The IOC insisted to German authorities that foreign teams could field athletes of any race and that Germany could not exclude any German athlete on the basis of race or creed. Although this was more than the IOC had asked from any previous organizer of the games, the German government accepted the terms in 1933 to avoid losing the games, although a transfer of the games would not have been feasible given the time necessary to stage them successfully.

To capitalize on the Olympic Games, the German government took a threefold approach: (1) the organizing committees for the Summer and for the Winter Games received full government support and financial backing; (2) sports organizations acquired full government support to select, train, and finance a full range of athletes for all Olympic sports beyond the scope of amateur rules customary at the time; and (3) extensive press and propaganda services were initiated worldwide to spread the word of the "new" Germany.

ANTHROPOMETRY TO SELECT GERMAN ATHLETES

Craniology, the exact measurement of the human skull, was first used by Henri de Boulainvilliers (1732), who alleged that there was a link between racial origin, skull shape, and intelligence. Similar connections were alleged in the first half of the twentieth century throughout the international scientific community. Not only did such tests link IQ to racial traits, but athletic ability was also said to be genetically defined. The United States was a particularly fruitful ground for such eugenic measurements, as men and women of a multitude of racial origins were readily available.

The first International Hygiene Exhibition in Dresden in 1911, which led to the establishment of the German Hygiene Museum, provided an avenue for bringing the German notion of "racial hygiene" (a term created by Alfred Ploetz in 1895) to the attention of the majority of the population. It also brought sports into direct contact with racial hygiene, as the various athletic systems competed with each other about which would be best methods to improve the fitness of the nation.

The scientific instruments used to measure the different forms and shapes of the body, formerly applied for craniology, were now used for "scientific racism"; in Dresden they were also introduced to the sports world. Anthropometry was used to measure the outcome of training at Harvard as much as in Berlin. German scientists soon realized, however, that anthropometry could not yet be the basis for talent identification and selection. Only after World War II did young scientists of the German Democratic Republic start to use anthropometric instruments for talent identification on a national scale. During the 1920s and 1930s selection competitions were staged to find athletic talents in any country. Anthropometric measurements were also used to explain the skill of certain nations and races, beginning on an international scale at the 1928 Olympics.

QUALIFYING AS AN AFRICAN AMERICAN

African American athletes had taken part in the Olympics since 1904, winning their first gold medal in 1908. To qualify for a spot on the team that was to participate in the 1936 Olympics, Americans had to take part in a final selection meet. To qualify for such a selection meet, the athletes had to do well in regional qualifying meets. Colleges in the American South were segregated in the 1930s. Although there were both white and black colleges, only white athletes could take part in qualifying meets in the South. If, however, the athletes or their college were sufficiently prosperous, they had the right to take part in qualifying meets in the North.

Jesse Owens on the Victor's Podium. *Owens's tremendous performance at the 1936 Olympics greatly contradicted the Nazi doctrine of Aryan supremacy.* AP IMAGES.

Track and field athletes such as Jesse Owens (born in Alabama) could not participate in many track meets during the college season. Whenever his Ohio State University team traveled south, Owens and other black athletes had to stay home because a northern team did not want to embarrass its southern counterparts. In Berlin in 1936, sixteen African American men and two women were part of the U.S. team, and they won fourteen of the fifty-six American medals.

QUALIFYING FOR THE GERMAN TEAM

On September 15, 1936, the Nuremberg Racial Laws were passed, defining what was "Aryan" ("German and racially similar"). Although German racial hygienists had hoped that their theory would get a stamp of approval in the laws, a Jew was defined culturally and racially to include persons of Jewish ancestry. Anybody who had three Jewish grandparents (no matter whether they or their children had later converted to Christianity) was by definition "Jewish"; a person having two Jewish grandparents, a "half-Jew," had to be closely inspected. A person of Jewish faith or married to a Jew was considered Jewish; a single person or one married to an Aryan was considered "non-Jewish." Members of the Nazi Party had to trace their Aryan linage back to the year 1800, thus showing that their ancestors four generations back had not been Jewish and had converted to Christianity at the earliest convenience.

Although the German government had guaranteed that athletes of Jewish descent could qualify for the German team, they could not. As the Jewish sports clubs were not part of the German Sports Federation, their members, Jewish athletes, could not take part in the German championships—the final selection meet. Gretel Bergmann, one of the best German high jumpers and a potential medal hopeful, was thus deprived of a place on the German team. But the decision was made to include the "half-Jews" (single, of Christian faith) Helene Mayer (foil fencing) and Rudi Ball (ice hockey) on the teams for the Summer and Winter Games as a move to placate international public opinion. Internationally, the token "half-Jews" were taken for Jews, which seemed to demonstrate that Germany played by the rules.

AN "ARYAN" SHOW?

The Olympic Games were a successful show, demonstrating the German ability to run a gigantic event. Germany won the official medal count, clearly ahead of the United States (89 to 56). Jesse Owens and the other African Americans dominated the speed events in the Olympic stadium and were the darlings of the German crowd. Several American sports organizations had threatened to boycott the Berlin Olympics because of race relations in Germany. For many African Americans athletes this was pure hypocrisy, as they were concerned more about segregation at home than about the exclusion of Jews in Germany at events they did not witness.

During the Olympics German authorities dressed up their public relations façade and took a pause in Jew baiting. For the German stormtroopers it was, however, foreseeable: "Once the Olympics are through—we beat up the Jew" (Krüger 1999).

SEE ALSO *Olympic Games of 1904; Track and Field.*

BIBLIOGRAPHY

Fröhlich, Elke, ed. 1987. *Die Tagebücher des Joseph Goebbels. Samtliche Fragmente* [The Joseph Goebbels diaries. Collected fragments]. Munich, Germany: Saur.

Krüger, Arnd. 1998. "A Horse Breeder's Perspective: Scientific Racism in Germany. 1870–1933." In *Identity and Intolerance. Nationalism, Racism, and Xenophobia in Germany and the United States,* edited by Norbert Finzsch and Dietmar Schirmer, 371–396. Cambridge, U.K.: Cambridge University Press.

———. 1999. "'Once the Olympics are through, we'll beat up the Jew.' German Jewish Sport 1898–1938 and the Anti-Semitic Discourse." *Journal of Sport History* 26 (2): 353–375.

———. 2001. "How 'Goldhagen' Was the German System of Physical Education, Turnen, and Sport?" In *Europäische Perspektiven zur Geschichte von Sport, Kultur und Politik* [European perspectives of the history of sport, culture, and politics], edited by Arnd Krüger, Angela Teja, and Else Trangbaek, 82–92. Berlin: Tischler.

———. 2004. "'What's the Difference between Propaganda for Tourism or for a Political Regime?' Was the 1936 Olympics the First Postmodern Spectacle?" In *Post-Olympism? Questioning Sport in the Twenty-first Century,* edited by John Bale and Mette Krogh Christensen, 33–50. Oxford: Berg.

———, and Murray, William, eds. 2003. *The Nazi Olympics: Sport, Politics and Appeasement in the 1930s.* Champaign: University of Illinois Press.

Mandell, Richard D. 1971. *The Nazi Olympics.* New York: Macmillan.

Rippon, Anton. 2006. *Hitler's Olympics: The Story of the 1936 Nazi Games.* Barnsley, South Yorkshire: Pen & Sword Military.

Young, Kevin, and Kevin B. Wamsley, eds. 2005. *Global Olympics: Historical and Sociological Studies of the Modern Games.* Amsterdam: Elsevier.

Arnd Krüger

OPERATION GATEKEEPER

Operation Gatekeeper is the name of the U.S. government's enforcement strategy along the California section of the U.S.-Mexico boundary. Launched by the Clinton administration on October 1, 1994, Gatekeeper is a "territorial denial," or "prevention through deterrence," strategy that attempts to thwart migrants and smugglers from entering the United States through the forward deployment of Border Patrol agents and the increased use of surveillance technologies and support infrastructure. (The previous strategy was to apprehend individuals after they crossed the border.) While initially limited to the sixty-six westernmost miles of the boundary (the Border Patrol's San Diego Sector), the operation eventually spread eastward to cover the entire California-Mexico border.

Operation Gatekeeper was devised as the centerpiece of a much larger national strategy, which has seen the implementation of similar operations across Arizona and Texas. This strategy has resulted in almost a tripling of the size of the Border Patrol (to approximately 11,000 agents in 2005), and a huge increase in surveillance equipment and enforcement infrastructure, including walls and fences.

The period during which Gatekeeper was first implemented was one of economic recession as well as anti-immigrant bravado by Republican politicians (and many of their Democratic counterparts) eager to curry favor with an increasingly anxious electorate receptive to scapegoating the poor, non-whites, and "illegals." Both state actors and anti-immigrant groups created a sense of crisis regarding the social, political, and economic consequences of a southern boundary "out of control," and of what many characterized as excessive levels of immigration. Thus, the early 1990s saw the outbreak of what would soon become a historically unparalleled level of official and public concern about the U.S. government's ability, or the lack thereof, to police the U.S.-Mexico border and prevent unauthorized, or "illegal," immigration from Mexico. The geographical epicenter of these concerns and efforts was California, whose southern boundary with Mexico, especially in the area of San Diego, was the gateway for the majority of unauthorized entries into the United States. It was in this context that California voters in November 1994, overwhelmingly approved Proposition 187, which sought to deny public education (from elementary to post-secondary levels), public social services, and public healthcare services (with the exception of emergencies) to unauthorized immigrants. It was in this context that the Clinton administration launched Gatekeeper—in large part to undercut any electoral advantages gained by the Republican championing of Proposition 187 and enhance the election prospects of Democrats (including his own re-election).

While such short-term factors were decisive in Gatekeeper's implementation, the operation and the larger national strategy are manifestations of much longer-term processes involving what is in many ways a hardening of the social and territorial boundaries between U.S. citizens and those from without—especially "Third World" and nonwhite peoples. Thus, it is not surprising that much of the anti-immigrant sentiment that led to Gatekeeper scapegoated immigrants, especially "illegals," for a whole host of social ills. And much of this sentiment was clearly racist in terms of its assumptions and notions of what the United States is and should be.

On a structural level, Gatekeeper and the larger border enforcement strategy it represents further institutionalize the social, political, and economic distance between a nationally defined "us" and "them." In doing so, this strategy strengthens the bases that allow the United States to treat noncitizen "others" (especially of the "illegal" variety) in ways that would be deemed unjust or unfair if applied to U.S. nationals. Given the material consequences involved in determining where one can live and work in a world of profound socioeconomic inequality, such differential treatment furthers the construction of an unjust global order—one in which socioeconomic differences often correspond to conventional notions of race, and one that many have characterized as apartheid-like.

In terms of Gatekeeper's direct effects, what is striking about the operation and the larger strategy are their marked failure to reduce unsanctioned immigration. One result of the enhanced boundary strategy has been to push border crossers away from urbanized areas and to curtail short-term and local unauthorized migrants. However, it does not appear to have significantly diminished the crossings by long-distance or long-term migrants. Research has consistently found that migrants have adapted to the new enforcement regime by relying increasingly on professional smugglers and utilizing new and more dangerous routes across the boundary. In addition, these individuals are staying in the United States longer than they might have previously. It has also led to increased human suffering: It is conservatively estimated that more than 3,000 unauthorized migrants died while trying to cross the international divide between 1995 and 2005. Given the vast and harsh terrain of the border region, the real number is undoubtedly higher. Further, despite much-touted efforts by U.S. authorities to address the resulting humanitarian crisis by warning would-be migrants of the dangers of crossing and increasing search-and-rescue missions, the growth of the death toll since 1995 has not slowed.

SEE ALSO *Border Crossings and Human Rights; Border Patrol; Citizenship and "the Border"; Immigration to the United States.*

BIBLIOGRAPHY

Andreas, Peter. 2000. *Border Games: Policing the U.S.-Mexico Divide.* Ithaca, NY: Cornell University Press.

Massey, Douglas S., Jorge Durand, and Nolan J. Malone. *Beyond Smoke and Mirrors: Mexican Immigration in an Era of Economic Integration.* New York: Russell Sage Foundation, 2002.

Nevins, Joseph. 2002. *Operation Gatekeeper: The Rise of the "Illegal Alien" and the Making of the U.S.-Mexico Boundary,* New York: Routledge.

Joseph Nevins

OPERATION WETBACK

The Immigration and Naturalization Service (INS) launched Operation Wetback in June and July 1954. It was a massive, coordinated effort involving the U.S. Border

Patrol and local law enforcement agencies to curtail illegal immigration along the U.S.-Mexico border. The term *wetback*, which came into widespread use in Texas during the late 1940s and early 1950s, was a derogatory term used to describe Mexicans who waded or swam across the Rio Grande River into Texas illegally. In Spanish they were referred to as *espaldas mojadas* ("wet backs").

The impetus for Operation Wetback stemmed from a tour along the southern border of California by U.S. attorney general Herbert Brownell in 1953. Initially Brownell was not supportive of increased security along the border. However, in April 1953 he was convinced by proponents of immigration reform and control to tour the Southwest border. During his trip to California, he witnessed firsthand the illegal crossing of Mexican workers into the United States. Shortly thereafter Brownell began a two-pronged campaign to bring the border under control. One prong involved the enactment of legislation imposing a penalty on any employer who "knowingly" hired undocumented workers. Brownell also sought increased funding for the understaffed Border Patrol and money with which to construct a 150-mile fence along the California-Mexico border. The other part of his plan was to conduct a massive roundup of illegal immigrants who had crossed the border from Mexico. This part of the plan came to be known as Operation Wetback.

At the urging of Brownell and President Dwight D. Eisenhower, Congress increased funding for the Border Patrol. The congressional response was also influenced by national media coverage of illegal immigration's growing threat to national security and the American economy. Proponents of immigration control argued that the number of Mexicans entering the United States illegally had increased by 6,000 percent between 1944 and 1954. When the economy took a downturn in the early 1950s, organized labor blamed the widespread use of illegal immigrant workers. Labor leaders argued that undocumented workers deprived American citizens of jobs, lowered wages, and disrupted unionization efforts by serving as strike breakers or "scab" labor. Undocumented immigrants were also accused of increasing crime in border communities, affecting the health of those communities by bringing with them communicable diseases, and of serving as a smokescreen for the infiltration of communists and subversives who crossed into the United States through its "unprotected" southern borders.

In 1952 Congress passed the McCarran-Walter Act, which in part allowed for the deportation of immigrants or naturalized citizens engaged in subversive activities. It also permitted the government to bar suspected subversives from entering the United States. President Harry Truman vetoed the bill, stating that "it would make a mockery of the Bill of Rights." Congress overrode the president's veto. The law, which disproportionately affected Mexican Americans engaged in civil rights struggles, effectively silenced activists and critics of immigration policies.

SUPPORT FOR IMMIGRATION REFORM

Ideologues were not the only ones who supported immigration reform. President Dwight D. Eisenhower felt a sense of urgency about illegal immigration when he assumed office. He was concerned that powerful grower interests who benefited from illegal immigration had bribed and intimidated federal office holders and enforcement agencies into not enforcing immigration laws. He considered this unethical, and decided he would move against government officials who engaged in this kind of conduct.

Mexican-American civil rights groups supported stricter enforcement of immigration laws as well. Organizations like the League of United Latin American Citizens (LULAC) and the American G.I. Forum believed that undocumented workers had a deleterious effect on Mexican-American farm workers' employment and earnings. They believed that illegal immigrants impeded assimilation and undermined efforts to achieve civil rights for Mexican Americans. They also held that illegals added to problems of health, crime, and unemployment—all of which reflected poorly on the Mexican-American community.

The popular media's increased coverage of illegal immigration brought national attention to the problem. Most of the coverage emphasized the lack of enforcement, attributing to illegals the blame for growing rates of crime, illiteracy, ill health, and unemployment in border communities. This media coverage further fueled fears that the uncontrolled influx of "alien hordes" from Mexico had caused the nation to lose control of its own borders.

Mexico, too, joined in the chorus for stricter enforcement. Long criticized by its own citizens for failing to protect Mexicans who had entered the United States illegally, the Mexican government had undertaken measures to dissuade its citizens from emigrating illegally. Critics of illegal emigration in Mexico believed that it represented the loss of valuable and much-needed labor. They chafed at the ill treatment accorded Mexicans, and believed that illegal immigration undermined the Bracero Program, which ostensibly provided contract guarantees to Mexican laborers in terms of wages, housing, and transportation. However, measures by Mexican officials to stem illegal emigration to the United States had proven ineffective. Therefore, Mexico was eager to work with the United States in stopping illegal immigration.

ENFORCEMENT

In the years preceding Operation Wetback the Border Patrol's ability to carry out its functions had steadily deteriorated. This was due to inadequate funding, the influence of powerful agribusiness interests in Congress who benefited greatly from a plentiful supply of cheap labor, and from internal problems stemming from poor organization and inadequate officers to patrol the vast border region. Renewed concerns about enforcement resulted in efforts to reorganize the Border Patrol. To lead this process, Eisenhower appointed a former West Point classmate, Joseph Swing, to serve as commissioner of Immigration. Swing immediately reorganized the Border Patrol along military lines. He brought a new look, greater professionalism, and new leadership to the organization. One of the agents who emerged as a new driving force in the Border Patrol was Harlon Carter, who initially laid out the plan for what became known as Operation Wetback.

It was Carter who proposed the creation of mobile task forces. These task forces would bring concentrated numbers of agents and equipment to designated areas to carry out sweeps to round up "illegal aliens" and transport them back to Mexico. Each operation was preceded by a massive publicity campaign designed to alert citizens and "aliens" alike of the impending roundup. The idea was that such a media blitz would cause illegals to flee across the border before the sweep began. Staging areas along the U.S.-Mexico border were established. To discourage immediate reentry by those captured in the sweeps, arrangements were made with the Mexican government to transport the deportees on trains to the interior parts of Mexico.

The first phase of Operation Wetback began in California in May 1954. As planned, a media campaign was launched announcing the intended sweep by the U.S. Border Patrol and local agencies. The media blitz, probably the most important factor in the success of the campaign, made it sound as if a veritable army of Border Patrol agents was being assembled to conduct the sweep. In truth, the task force consisted of about 800 agents. Nonetheless, the announcements created fear and uncertainty in Mexican communities throughout California. People still recalled the deportation drives in the early 1930s, when citizens and noncitizens alike were sent back to Mexico. Local observers reported that they witnessed large numbers of Mexicans leaving the United States.

On June 10, Border Patrol agents launched the opening phase of the operation. The raids targeted local businesses, parks, recreation centers, and any other places that were known to attract undocumented workers, according to information provided by local authorities. The sweeps served as a clear reminder to Mexicans and Mexican Americans of their precarious status in the United States. Mexicans apprehended in this initial sweep were placed on buses and driven to staging areas, where they awaited transportation on Mexican trains into the interior. On June 17, the Special Mobile Task Force shifted its operation to agricultural areas in California and Arizona because of the significant decline in apprehensions in the urban areas.

Mexican border cities, completely unprepared to handle the large influx of refugees, found themselves inundated by those fleeing the sweeps. They lacked the facilities to house, feed, and care for the number of people who poured into their communities. To make matters worse, there were delays in getting enough rail cars for the trains to transport people into Mexico's interior.

By the end of June the number of undocumented Mexicans picked up by the mobile task force had declined significantly. Border Patrol leadership decided to continue mop-up activities on a smaller scale in California, and to begin the second phase of the operation in Texas. That phase began in July 1954. Whereas in California growers and proponents of immigration control had widely supported the roundup of undocumented workers, the Border Patrol faced a far different situation in Texas.

In 1948 Mexico had blacklisted Texas growers from the use of braceros because of their blatant disregard of the contract agreement. Texas growers, who cared little for the requirements imposed on them by the Bracero Program, preferred to use illegal labor. They resisted all attempts at enforcement and federal interference. Many growers and the communities that depended on them viewed the Border Patrol as an "army of occupation" and made many of the agents feel unwelcome in the districts to which they were assigned. When news of Operation Wetback reached Texas, agricultural interests launched a full-scale attack on the plan. Herbert Brownell visited the Rio Grande region to gain their cooperation, and that of the Mexican-American community. He assured growers and local leaders that there would be plenty of affordable labor available to them. His words fell on deaf ears. The Border Patrol and the INS received little support from the growers for their campaign. They did, however, have the support of groups like LULAC and the American G.I. Forum.

Despite the widespread resentment and lack of cooperation, the Border Patrol began operations in the Rio Grande region. Again the operation was preceded by a publicity campaign that caused an unknown number of Mexicans to flee across the border. The actual sweeps began on July 15 and continued until the end of the month. The initial sweep netted the Border Patrol about 4,000 apprehensions. Thereafter apprehensions fell off to about 1,100 per day. Again, those apprehended were placed on buses and taken across the border into Mexico.

Others were placed on board two ships, the *S.S. Emancipación* and *S.S. Mercurio,* and transported to the port of Vera Cruz. The total number of Mexicans who left South Texas as a result of the drive and the attendant publicity was estimated at between 500,000 and 700,000 by the Border Patrol. The INS proclaimed the operation a great success, but not everyone applauded it. Critics, including Mexican-American civil rights activists, described Operation Wetback as heartless and xenophobic.

The campaign ended in mid-September 1954, both because the drive had pretty well exhausted the funding for the operation and mid-September marked the end of the growing season. Therefore the reduction in employment opportunities, the drive, and the attendant publicity campaign all served to discourage illegal entry at this time. According to the INS the entire campaign had resulted in the departure of more than 1.3 million undocumented Mexicans from the country through deportation, repatriation, or voluntary departures spurred by publicity of the impending roundup. There was, however, no way to prove the accuracy of these estimates.

Meanwhile, attempts at enacting legislation designed to curb illegal immigration by imposing fines and imprisonment on employers foundered in Congress. Instead Congress voted increased appropriations for the INS to control the influx of undocumented workers from Mexico as a way of mollifying those who wanted employer sanctions.

SEE ALSO *Border Patrol; Braceros, Repatriation, and Seasonal Workers.*

BIBLIOGRAPHY

Craig, Richard B. 1971. *The Bracero Program: Interest Groups and Foreign Policy.* Austin: University of Texas Press.

García, Juan R. 1980. *Operation Wetback: The Mass Deportation of Mexican Undocumented Workers in 1954.* Westport, CT: Greenwood Press.

Hadley, Eleanor. 1956. "A Critical Analysis of the Wetback Problem." *Law and Contemporary Problems* 21 (2): 334–357.

Hernández, Kelly Lytle. 2006. "The Crimes and Consequences of Illegal Immigration: A Cross-Border Examination of Operation Wetback, 1943 to 1954." *Western Historical Quarterly* 37 (4): 421–444.

Morgan, Patricia. 1954. *Shame of a Nation: A Documented Story of Police-State Terror Against Mexican-Americans in the U.S.A.* Los Angeles: Los Angeles Committee for the Protection of the Foreign Born.

"Operation Wetback." *The Handbook of Texas Online.* Available from http://www.tsha.utexas.edu/handbook/online/articles/OO/pqo1.html.

Juan R. García

ORGANISATION ARMÉE SECRÈTE (SECRET ARMY ORGANIZATION)

In January 1961, after more than six years of war, a popular referendum held by the government of France showed that extending the right of self-determination to the French colony of Algeria was favored by 75 percent of voters in both France and Algeria, but by only a small minority of *colons* (French colonists). The following month a group of *colons* created the *Organisation armée secrète* (OAS, or Secret Army Organization) determined to use all means necessary, including the most violent, to prevent the government of President Charles de Gaulle from granting Algeria independence.

The emergence of the OAS and its extremism represented the culmination of a roughly three-year process during which elements of the officer corps and *colons* turned increasingly against a government they believed was inept at protecting European rights and fighting the *Front de libération nationale* (FLN), the dominant revolutionary coalition in Algeria. In 1958, the military, led by Commanding General Raoul Salan, received a government reprimand for killing scores of civilians in the unauthorized February bombing of Sakiet, a western Tunisian town harboring FLN fighters. *Colon* riots in May of that year triggered the collapse of the Fourth Republic and the return of the World War II hero Charles de Gaulle to the presidency. Even though a great patriot, de Gaulle increasingly recognized the determination of the FLN to maintain the struggle for independence. Subjected to growing domestic and international pressure, he moved away from strategies of repression and toward proposals for reconciliation, including the integration of racially excluded Muslim Algerians into the colonial system, followed by self-determination. By the fall of 1959, angry *colons* had created the *Front national français,* whose leaders set up barricades in the heart of Algiers in January 1960 and fired at police while the army looked on. In the fall of 1960, many officers joined them in creating the *Front de l'Algérie française,* which almost succeeded in driving the governor general out of office before it was defeated and dissolved in January 1961.

The OAS took its place the next month. Key leaders were *colon* activists Jean-Jacques Susini and Pierre Lagaillarde who were joined on the military side by former commanding general Raoul Salan, General Marie-André Zeller, General Edmond Jouhaud, and the newly retired general Maurice Challe, who had been appointed by de Gaulle to replace the intransigent Salan in 1958. Challe agreed to coordinate a military putsch in Algiers that was launched on April 21, 1961. Using a Foreign Legion parachute regiment as its main instrument, the

OAS seized control of all key governmental, communications, and security facilities in Algiers and detained many officials, including the commanding general and governor general. Unfortunately, the movement had mobilized less effectively outside the capital city. After a stirring appeal by de Gaulle to the troops for loyalty, the putsch was defeated four days later. Challe surrendered, and hundreds of other insurgents were arrested or fled into hiding. Although the coup failed, the movement survived and spread underground. There were attempts to undermine government authority through bombings and targeted assassinations of officials, leftists, liberal intellectuals, and prominent Muslim leaders. As negotiations with Algerian emissaries proceeded at Evian, in eastern France, the organization switched to a campaign of terror against Muslims in general. Finally, after France agreed to independence, they reverted to a policy of massive destruction of Algerian infrastructure. On June 17, 1962, just two and a half weeks before Algeria received its independence, the OAS and the FLN signed a cease-fire.

BIBLIOGRAPHY

Horne, Alistair. 1977. *A Savage War of Peace: Algeria, 1954–1962*. London: Macmillan.

Ruedy, John. 2005. *Modern Algeria: The Origins and Development of a Nation,* 2nd ed. Bloomington: Indiana University Press.

John Ruedy

ORIENTALISM

Orientalism refers to a system of beliefs and practices through which Europeans and Americans have viewed and represented the Middle East and Asia, often in unfavorable and subordinate terms. According to Edward Said, the author of the influential and controversial book *Orientalism,* published in 1978, the discourse of Orientalism is predicated on an imagined divide between "the Occident" and "the Orient"—or "the West" versus "the Rest." He theorized that the Orient had been constructed and appropriated as a projection of Western desire in an effort to mask the power abuses of imperialism and colonialism. He defined Orientalism as follows:

> The corporate institution for dealing with the Orient—dealing with it by making statements about it, authorizing views of it, describing it, by teaching it, settling it, ruling over it: in short, Orientalism as a Western style for dominating, restructuring, and having authority over the Orient. (Said 1978, p. 2–3)

Early Orientalists constructed a monolithic notion of the Middle East and Asia as a single region characterized as timeless, sensuous, decadent, backwards, and feminized. These views of a despotic Orient were instrumental in rationalizing imperialism and colonialism, and they continue to influence contemporary political and cultural perspectives.

Said identified two basic forms of Orientalism—latent and manifest. Latent Orientalism refers to unquestioned beliefs characterizing the Orient as lazy, backwards, sensuous, passive, and inherently different. Manifest Orientalism refers to actions based on latent Orientalism, such as writing, teaching, cultural interchange, and policy enactment (Said 1978, p. 206.) Orientalism has been expressed in both positive and negative depictions, but, according to Said, unequal power relations are implicated either way. In different historical moments and contexts, Orientalism has taken a variety of forms, such as the racialization of *Orientals*, the exoticism and essentialism of Oriental people and cultural practices, eroticizing Oriental women while emasculating Oriental men, the gendering of civilizations, commodification and consumption, primitivism and demonization, and institutionalized racism. Orientalist cultural productions are inherently political because they originate in unequal power relations. In other words, the amassing of Western knowledge of the East is inextricable from Western power over the east.

HISTORY

Orientalism emerged from and evolved in relation to historical and political contexts, and it has transitioned between positive and negative perceptions depending on political circumstances. It is generally believed that the first *Orientalists* were nineteenth-century scholars who translated the writing of the Orient into European languages. Along with travel writers and artists, these scholars contributed greatly to the dissemination of Orientalist views to the public. However, Zachary Lockman, the director of the Center for Near Eastern Studies in New York, argues that Orientalism has a much longer history that can be extended back beyond the eleventh century. As a result of the Crusades, transcontinental trade, and increased travel, a concept of the West as a conglomerate, distinctive, and superior civilization developed. Orientalism was instituted as a field of scholarly inquiry in relation to the Ottoman Empire during the Renaissance.

With European exploration and the rise of European global hegemony beginning in the fifteenth century, Orientalism took a different turn. European empire was bolstered by notions of cultural evolution that characterized the Orient as degenerate and Europe as the beacon of civilization. The result of these interactions was that, by the eighteenth century, a large body of literature on the Orient had already been amassed. In the nineteenth century, Orientalism would be inextricably bound up with the mechanisms of empire.

Nineteenth-century Orientalists produced an astonishing array of texts and images, among them linguistic studies and translations, as well as histories and artistic images representing the Orient in ways that accorded with social and racial ideologies popular at the time. Alongside scholarly and artistic renderings of the East, the Orient was represented in home décor, fashion, popular literature, and music.

DEBATES

A number of scholars have debated the premises and limitations of Said's *Orientalism*. Initially, Orientalist scholars defended their turf against what they perceived to be accusations that they were complicit in the subordination and manipulation of the people they studied. Some scholars criticized Said's limited focus on French and English Orientalists, and they claimed his work was overly reliant on literary texts as a reflection of dominant cultural ideology. Said was accused of having participated in the same binary between Orient and Occident that he was critiquing, constructing the West as not only monolithic, but also as having the supreme power to misrepresent and dominate "the Rest." Other critics have objected to a perceived implication that there is no objective truth about the non-Western world, and they have found Said's views too cohesive to take into account the particularities of history and region. Some have also objected to his omission of non-Western writers, colonial resistances, and gender issues, arguing that without the inclusion of non-Western voices and accounts of resistances, all agency is relegated to the Western power structure that is being critiqued. As a result of these critiques, Said qualified and expanded his original views on more than one occasion, amending them to say that he did not believe that all representations are misrepresentations, and to encompass resistance and align himself with some anticolonial protests.

APPLICATIONS

Since the publication of *Orientalism*, Said's scholarship, which applied the theories of the French philosopher Michel Foucault (1926–1984) to representations of the Middle East, have been variously applied and expanded. Many scholars have applied his theory to views of Asia and Asians. Critiques of Orientalism have also taken on unique forms within the parameters of American multiculturalism, perhaps because of their resonance with American discourses of race. In *New York before Chinatown* (1999), John Kuo Wei Tchen limits his study to American Orientalism toward the Chinese between 1776 and 1882. He identifies three types and phases of American Orientalism—patrician, popular, and political—which correlate to American early contact and trade with China and the immigration of Chinese to America. According to Tchen, patrician Orientalism was characterized by an admiration for the products and institutions of China; popular Orientalism involved the commodification and popularization of *Chinese-ness* (such as the career of Chang and Eng, the Siamese twins); and political Orientalism was characterized by a view of the Chinese as a racially inferior social and national pollutant (the "Yellow Peril"). Increasingly negative views of the Chinese paralleled perceptions of them as an increased presence and were exacerbated by the application of racial stereotypes that had been honed on blacks. In *Orientals* (1999), Robert Lee explores the role of representations of the Chinese in American popular culture genres, such as music and yellowface performances, in engendering stereotypes.

Orientalism manifests in a variety of venues, so its critiques span disciplinary boundaries. For example, Mari Yoshihara examines a variety of ways in which white American women of the nineteenth century empowered themselves through Orientalism in the forms of household decoration, fashion, art, and cultural expertise, which allowed them to escape prescribed gender roles by appropriating the goods, labor, or knowledge of Orientals. Yayoi Everett and Frederick Lau analyze appropriations of Oriental sounds into Western art music, and Gina Marchetti examines Orientalism in film representations. Other studies cover a broad range of focuses (e.g., travel literature, popular culture, history, and the body) and employ a variety of methodologies; however, they share a common denominator in their implicit or explicit relationship to Said's construction of Orientalism as a foundational concept. In some cases, new limitations have appeared as the result of new theoretical applications. For example, in many cases, Said's theory has been applied exclusively to Asians and Asian Americans, and Sadik Jalal al 'Azm has suggested that *Orientalism* provided avenues of privilege for those who can construct a history of oppression based on its premises (Lockman 2004, p. 201).

Although Said has been criticized for an avoidance of the overtly political in favor of politicizing the cultural, his views have been applied directly to politics by some thinkers. John Dower, in *Embracing Defeat* (1999), looks at Orientalist representations as instrumental to demonizing the Japanese during World War II, and Cristina Klein, in *Cold War Orientalism* (2003), analyzes how cultural productions during the cold war era were instrumental in creating a narrative of cultural integration. In

Epic Encounters, Melani McAlister updates Orientalist views of the Arab world to illustrate how Orientalist representations have influenced views on U.S. relations with nations in the Persian Gulf region. Zachery Lockman, meanwhile, traces the history and politics of Orientalism in relation in that region in *Contending Visions of the Middle East* (2004).

While Lockman points out that Said was not the first scholar to critique Orientalist practices, critical theory on Orientalism has become inextricably linked to his work. That the critiques of Orientalism have proliferated and expanded is evidence of the continued practice of Orientalism in new forms. Said's work has served as a point of departure for a new generation of scholars, many of them non-Western and indigenous scholars speaking from a postcolonial perspective. These individuals have expanded the discourse by pointing out its limitations. Meanwhile, as the United States has expanded its military presence in the Middle East, discussions of Orientalism's political ramifications have been reinvigorated.

SEE ALSO *Institutional Racism; Racial Formations; Scientific Racism, History of.*

BIBLIOGRAPHY

Behdad, Ali. 1994. *Belated Travelers: Orientalism in the Age of Colonial Dissolution*. Durham, NC: Duke University Press.

Bernstein, Matthew, and Gaylyn Studlar. 1997. *Visions of the East: Orientalism in Film*. New Brunswick, NJ: Rutgers University Press.

Dower, John W. 1999. *Embracing Defeat: Japan in the Wake of World War II*. New York: W. W. Norton.

Everett, Yayoi, and Frederick Lau. 2004. *Locating East Asia in Western Art Music*. Middletown, CT: Wesleyan University Press.

Klein, Christina. 2003. *Cold War Orientalism: Asia in the Middlebrow Imagination, 1945–1961*. Berkley: University of California Press.

Lee, Robert G. 1999. *Orientals: Asian Americans in Popular Culture*. Philadelphia. PA: Temple University Press.

Macfie, Alexander Lyon, ed. 2000. *Orientalism: A Reader*. New York: New York University Press

Marchetti, Gina. 2004. *Romance and the "Yellow Peril": Race, Sex, and Discursive Strategies in Hollywood Fiction*. Berkeley: University of California Press.

McAlister, Melani. 2005. *Epic Encounters: Culture, Media, and U.S. Interests in the Middle East since 1945*, updated ed. Berkeley: University of California Press

Palumbo-Liu, David. 1999. *Asian/American: Historical Crossings of a Racial Frontier*. Stanford, CA.: Stanford University Press.

Lockman, Zachery. 2004. *Contending Visions of the Middle East: the History and Politics of Orientalism*. Cambridge, U.K.: Cambridge University Press.

Rodinson, Maxime. 1987. *Europe and the Mystique of Islam*. Translated by Roger Veinus. Seattle: University of Washington Press.

Said, Edward. 1978. *Orientalism*. New York: Pantheon.

———. 1985. "Orientalism Reconsidered." *Race & Class* 27 (1985): 1–5.

———. 1993. *Culture and Imperialism*. New York: Knopf.

Tchen, John Kuo Wei. 1999. *New York before Chinatown: Orientalism and the Shaping of American Culture, 1776–1882*. Baltimore, MD: Johns Hopkins University Press.

Yoshihara, Mari. 2003. *Embracing the East: White Women and American Orientalism*. New York: Oxford University Press.

Heather A. Diamond

"OUT OF AFRICA" HYPOTHESIS

The "Out of Africa" hypothesis is an evolutionary theory of modern human origin that posits that modern humans arose in the late Pleistocene, about 100,000–200,000 years ago, in Africa. There are different versions of "Out of Africa," but its major tenet is that modern humans originated as a discrete population or species that rapidly expanded and replaced archaic humans that were indigenous to other parts of the Old World: *Homo erectus* (or its descendents) in East and South Asia, and Neanderthals in Europe. In the most common version of Out of Africa, modern humans are considered a new species, with negligible gene-flow (mating) between the migrating African people and the indigenous archaic groups. Therefore, the Out of Africa hypothesis, as it is most generally understood, posits that the African population is the unique Pleistocene ancestor of all living humans. The other groups of archaic humans essentially died out and became evolutionary dead ends.

The Out of Africa hypothesis gained rapid acceptance in the late 1980s, with pioneering analyses of mitochondrial DNA (mtDNA), which revealed very low mean nucleotide variation between the mtDNA of individuals from diverse populations (Cann, Stoneking, and Wilson 1987). This suggested that the species was young, since one interpretation of low levels of variation is that there was a genetic bottleneck in the recent past, such as would occur at speciation, and little time since then for subsequent variation to accrue. Moreover, the fact that more variation occurred in African groups suggested Africa as the source. The Out of Africa, or mitochondrial "Eve Theory" as it is also known, has been promoted as underscoring the close relationship between all living humans, and the theory therefore gained ascendancy for sociopolitical reasons as well as scientific ones (Gould 1988).

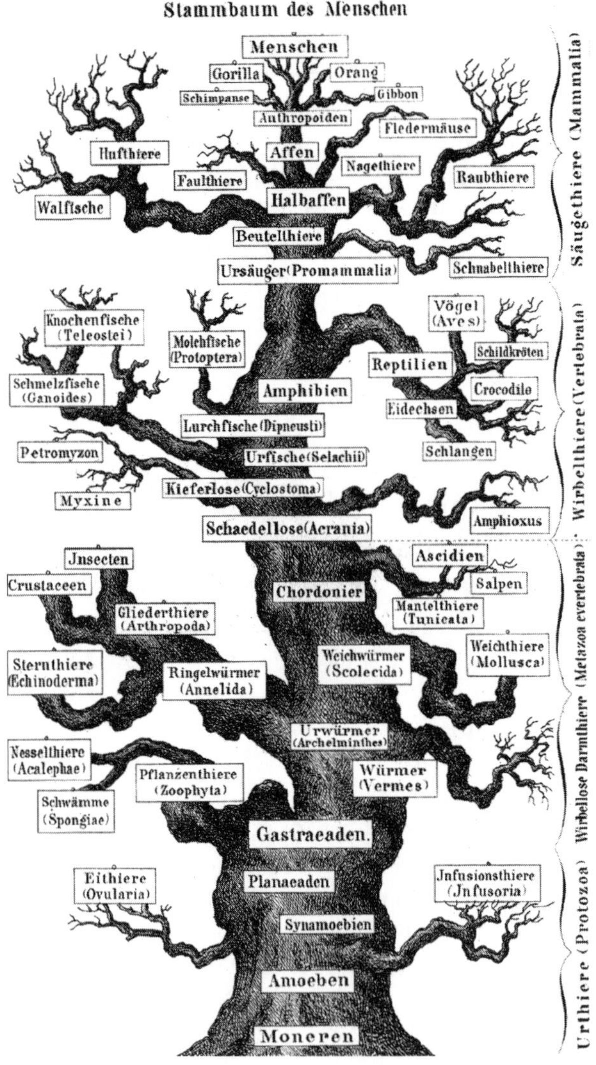

Figure 1. *Evolutionary tree depicting the place of humans in the tree of life. The small branches under Menschen depict the independent evolution of various species. While tree models are appropriate for understanding the relationships between species, they do not accurately depict the relationships between interbreeding populations. However, they continue to be commonly used to depict relationships between human populations.* FROM HAECKEL, E. 1884.

DEVELOPMENT OF THE HYPOTHESIS

The Out of Africa hypothesis is sometimes dubbed "Out of Africa 2" because it is not the first migration of *Homo* out of Africa. It is well accepted that the hominid lineage (the unique human lineage since divergence from the last common ancestor with chimpanzees) evolved in Africa, and for two-thirds of its 6-million-year history was an exclusively African clade. However, at the beginning of the Pleistocene 1.8 million years ago, soon after the emergence of the genus, *Homo,* hominids are found outside of Africa. These archaic *Homo* populations expanded from Africa to parts of Eurasia in the early Pleistocene, and subsequent populations were able to adapt to more temperate, colder, and even glacial environments in the Ice Ages. The question that the Out of Africa hypothesis addresses concerns the emergence of *modern* humans: Do modern human beings represent a new species that arose in Africa recently (in the last 200,000 years) and that replaced the earlier migrants?

Throughout the nineteenth and much of the twentieth centuries, the question of modern human origin was subsumed into the context of the "origin of races" (Howells 1942). Racial thinking dominated the science of human variation; the human species was thought to be composed of a number of discrete types of people ("races") who had separate origins (Stanton 1960), and after the rise of Darwinian thinking, separate evolutionary histories (Figure 1). These separate evolutionary histories were envisioned and depicted as nonreticulating (nonrecombining) branches of phylogenetic trees (Brace 1981). Workers differed on the number and constituents of different racial groups and when in the past they shared a common ancestor, but the "tree" model of human variation, implicit in the race concept, generally prevailed (Caspari 2003). Many workers believed in a few (three to five) primary races (such as Africans, Europeans, and Asians), and then multiple "secondary" and "tertiary" races, all of which could be represented as branches, or twigs, on an evolutionary tree (Coon, Garn, and Birdsell 1950).

Tree models are unrealistic representations of the relationships between human populations because they fail to represent gene-flow between human groups (Moore 1994). However, they are a part of the construction of "race" because they represent an easily conceived and visualized mechanism to explain human differences—a process of continual isolation, branching, and separation (Caspari 2003).

Evolutionary trees were also used to explain inequality. Some influential nineteenth-century evolutionary trees (Figure 2) depicted European racial groups with longer branches than other groups, implying that they are "more evolved." The perceived inferiority, and shorter branches, of other racial groups were considered the consequence of their unique evolutionary histories. Racial thinking and the concomitant branching models were so widely accepted that the alternative view—that of a "network" or "trellis" depicting the evolution of the human species as interconnected groups—was largely ignored, or misinterpreted (Figure 3).

Thus, the question of "the origin of races" focused on whether human races had a recent or an ancient common ancestor. Some models, reminiscent of the polygenism of the "American School" of the early

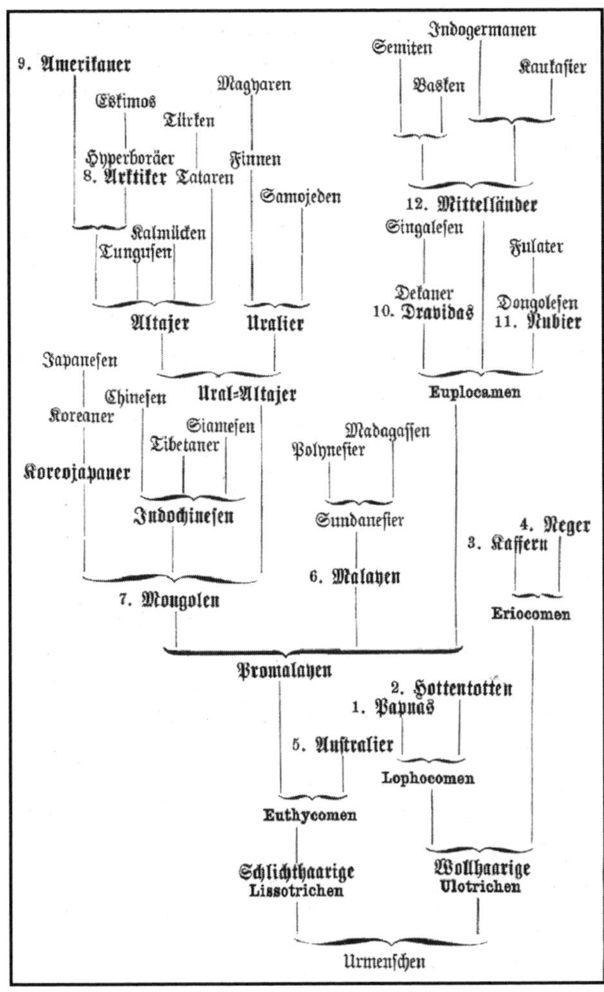

Figure 2. *Haeckel's racial phylogeny represents higher resolution than the tree in Figure 1, but its premise is the same. Races are treated as species, as independently evolving branches. As in many racial phylogenies, inequalities are "explained" evolutionarily; some races are considered more primitive and "less evolved" than others.* FROM HAECKEL, E. 1884.

nineteenth century, postulated a very ancient origin of races. This was epitomized by Carleton Coon's *The Origin of Races* (1963), in which the five major races Coon recognized were thought to have very long and separate evolutionary histories, sharing a common ancestor prior to the emergence of *Homo sapiens*. According to Coon, the five races crossed the threshold between *Homo erectus* and *Homo sapiens* at different times, and the length of time that races were in the "*sapiens*" state was related to their cultural "advancement." Coon wrote that Europeans and Asians crossed the threshold earlier and Africans and Australians considerably later.

This work, first published in 1963, had clear political implications, and was used as propaganda against school desegregation in the early 1960s (Jackson 2001). While Coon's overt linkage of polygenism to racial discrimination caused a backlash in the anthropological community, with many anthropologists and other scientists denouncing Coon (Dobzhansky 1963; Hulse 1963; Montagu 1964), the tree premise on which his model was based has been more ingrained. For most, tree versus network thinking as applied to human variation was not a focus of the debate. The tree was the dominant model and the question was whether the root of the tree was recent or ancient. By equating gene trees with population trees, tree metaphors are still inappropriately used to reflect relationships between human populations.

Modern thinking on Out of Africa began in the 1970s with the argument that because fossils phenotypically resembling recent humans are found in Africa earlier than anywhere else, "modern humans" originated there (Protsch 1975). Gunter Bräuer (1978, 1984) subsequently used new evidence to argue that Europeans must be of African descent. However, in arguing for African ancestry, neither Protsch nor Bräuer contended that early humans of modern form in Africa implied *unique* African origins. The Out of Africa hypothesis—the idea of an *African origin* for a recent modern human *species*—owes its genesis to interpretations of mtDNA, which suggested that the ancestors of recent humans first appeared in Africa and replaced other populations because they were a new species that did not interbreed (Cann, Stoneking, and Wilson 1987; Stoneking and Cann 1989). This model of replacement without mixture in the process of recent human origin was accepted by some paleoanthropologists (Stringer and Andrews 1988) and remains an influential model in the early 2000s.

THE GENETIC FOUNDATIONS

The Out of Africa hypothesis, the theory of a recent *unique* African origin for the modern human species, was supported by early interpretations of the variation of mtDNA (Cann, Stoneking, and Wilson 1987; Stoneking and Cann 1989). Advances in gene sequencing technology in the 1980s provided the techniques to sequence the mitochondrial genome, and Rebecca Cann initially compared mtDNA variants from representatives of several different populations. Mitochondria are organelles in the cytoplasm of cells, which play an important role in cell metabolism. Their DNA consists of a single chromosome, which is inherited maternally and does not recombine. It reproduces by mitosis, so all variation between mitochondria is a consequence of mutation. Assuming that mtDNA is selectively neutral and assuming constant population size, the amount of variation (number of nucleotide differences) between individuals and populations was interpreted to be a consequence of two factors: mutation rate and time since divergence of the mtDNA

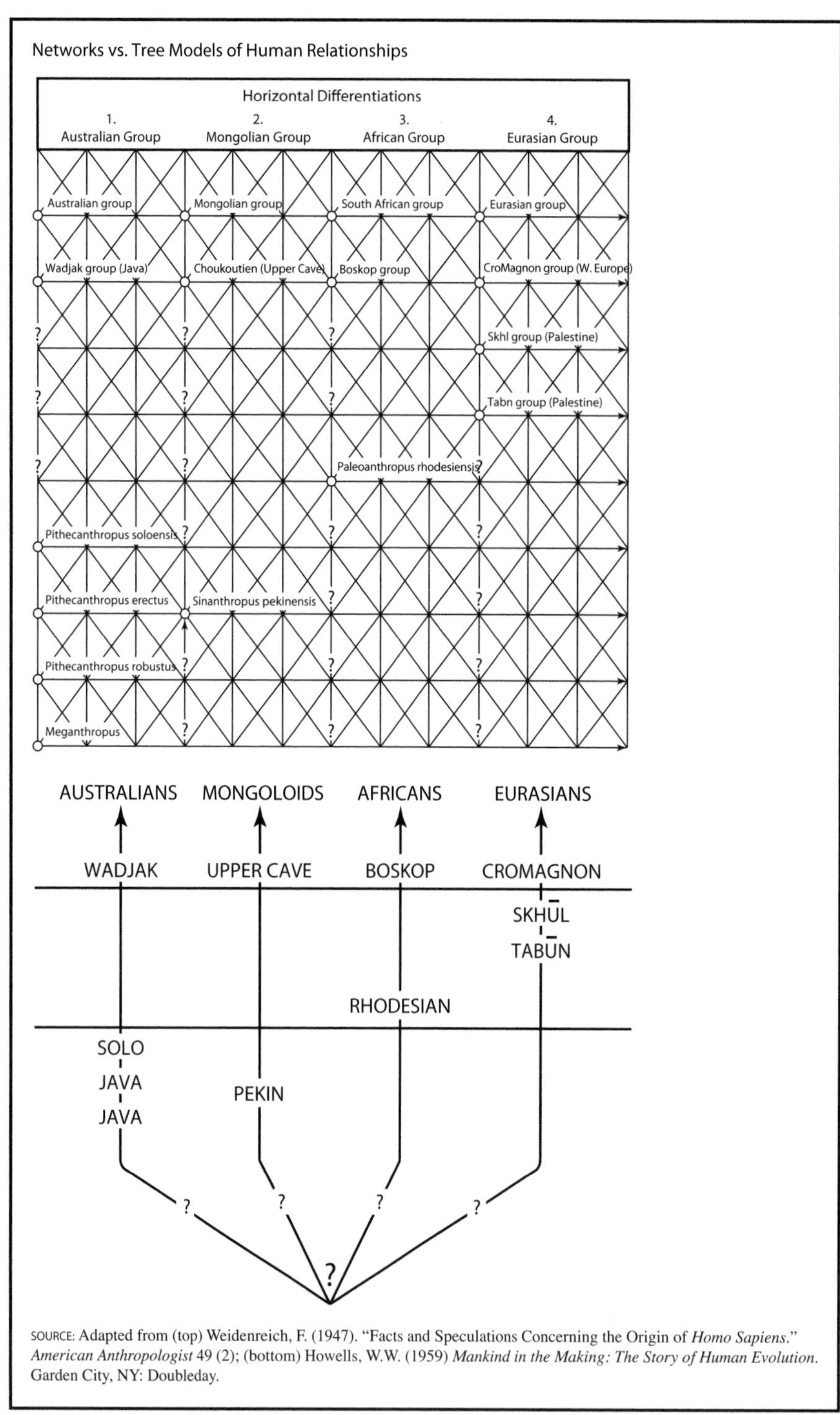

SOURCE: Adapted from (top) Weidenreich, F. (1947). "Facts and Speculations Concerning the Origin of *Homo Sapiens*." *American Anthropologist* 49 (2); (bottom) Howells, W.W. (1959) *Mankind in the Making: The Story of Human Evolution*. Garden City, NY: Doubleday.

Figure 3. *Network vs. Tree models of human relationships. Networks or other models depicting reticulation are more appropriate metaphors for human relationships (Moore, 1994), yet they were ignored or misunderstood in theories of human origin. In particular, multiregional evolution has consistently been interpreted as parallel evolution. Here, Weidenreich's trellis (top) in the original (1947) is shown, and its depiction in an influential secondary source (bottom), in this case from Howells (1959). In the original, the horizontal and diagonal lines depict potential avenues of gene-flow and are as important as the vertical lines. The trellis was converted into a "candelabra" that depicts parallel evolution, a model held by Carleton Coon (1963), one that is still falsely attributed to Weidenreich in the early 2000s. It has been argued that racial thinking (or its underlying essentialism) is partially responsible for such misunderstandings (Wolpoff and Caspari 1997).*

lineages. Therefore, given the same mutation rate, two mitochondria with fewer nucleotide differences would have a more recent common ancestor than two with a larger number of nucleotide differences.

Gene trees, like evolutionary trees in general, are hierarchical structures based on a particular gene or locus (these may be single nucleotides, haplotypes, genes, or the entire genome, which can be practical when the genome is short); variants of a gene that share more mutations are clustered together. The mtDNA gene trees derived from Cann's work were rooted in Africa, based on the observations that more variation was found in Africa and that all human populations had some African mitochondrial variants. The time of this root, based on the mutation rate derived for mtDNA (assuming neutrality), was estimated to be between 100,000–200,000 years ago. In the creation of the "Eve Theory" (as the Out of Africa hypothesis was frequently called), this gene tree was interpreted as a population tree and the root was thought to represent a population bottleneck, a massive reduction in population size where variation is greatly reduced. Such population bottlenecks often accompany speciations, and hence the mtDNA data were thought to reflect the time and place of the birth of the modern human species.

In the twenty years since this early research, genetic analyses have become far more sophisticated; in addition to mtDNA (which, because it does not recombine and is inherited as a single unit, can be considered only one gene), many nuclear genes now contribute to our understanding of human evolution, and the evolutionary models based on genetics have become more complicated. It is now widely understood that many factors, from population size and structure to natural selection, affect genetic variation and that different genes have different histories; in other words, gene trees are not population trees. Because of recombination, autosomal genes within the *same individual* will have very different evolutionary trees. Different genes reflect different aspects of our ancestry; moreover, if natural selection is acting on a gene, it may give no information about population history at all. The trees of some genes, particularly those on chromosomes that do not recombine, such as mtDNA and part of the Y chromosome, have shallow roots; other loci have roots that are millions of years old.

The Out of Africa theory is based on the loci whose evolutionary trees have shallow roots through the assumption that the recent root of the gene tree represents the recent root of the human species. However, it is now recognized that there are many potential explanations for the shallow roots of these gene trees: The relative effective population size of haploid loci is four times smaller than that of the autosomes, which alone causes the roots of their gene trees to be four times shallower; variations in past population sizes affect the structure and roots of gene trees; and perhaps most importantly, natural selection may have a larger effect on nonrecombining loci because of the effects of linkage. For example, selection favoring one locus on the mitochondrial genome affects the entire mitochondrial chromosome because it is inherited together. Given the importance of mitochondria in many functions of cell metabolism, such selection and selective sweeps are highly probable. Any selective sweep affecting mtDNA (or any other locus) will reduce variation and give gene trees an even shallower root. Therefore, Out of Africa (or a population bottleneck at speciation) is only one of many possible explanations for the genetic observations of loci with shallow rooted gene trees (Garrigan and Hammer 2006; Templeton 1998, 2002; Relethford 1998, 2001).

ALTERNATIVES: THE ROLE OF AFRICA

Much of the current genetic evidence is incompatible with the Out of Africa scenario because it does not reflect a bottleneck associated with recent speciation. While there are a number of nuclear loci that do fit the hypothesis (i.e., autosomal loci with roots four times as deep as the mtDNA and loci on the nonrecombining Y), the rate of discovery of loci with deep genealogical histories is rapidly increasing, and some of these have roots outside of Africa (Garrigan and Hammer 2006). The new evidence argues against a recent population bottleneck (speciation) because many genetic loci did not undergo reduction in variation at that time and there is no evidence of the postspeciation population expansions in Africa that would be expected under the Out of Africa model. Moreover, genealogical roots outside of Africa provide evidence of gene-flow between archaic humans in different regions, indicating that they were not separate species. Therefore, recent genetic research suggests that a simple, single origin model for the evolution of modern humans is incorrect, and that the genome of modern humans consists of contributions from multiple archaic populations. However, the many loci that have a recent common ancestor in Africa, as well as the early appearance of many modern skeletal features there, indicate the importance of Africa for the origin of modern humans.

The alternatives to the Out of Africa hypothesis are versions of "Multiregional Evolution," a model that hypothesizes evolutionary change within the human species with gene flow between "archaic" and "modern" humans rather than evolution due to recent speciation. The multiregional theory does not recognize Pleistocene Africans and archaic groups from Europe and Asia as different species. According to the multiregional model, gene-flow was an integral part of the evolution of modern peoples, dispersing adaptive genes throughout the species, and any one living human is likely to have had Pleistocene ancestors from different parts of the globe. Developed by Franz Weidenreich (1947) as "polycentric theory" in the 1940s, it differed from the prevailing evolutionary models in being network based rather than tree based; it was a reticulating model depicting the evolution of human populations as an intraspecific process, with gene-flow at its core.

Weaker versions of the Out of Africa hypothesis, such as the "Assimilation Theory" (Smith, Jankovic, and Karavanic 2005), where modern humans are a population, or deme, rather than a species are consistent with the multiregional gene-flow model because they do not involve speciation. Contemporary versions of multiregionalism reflect the importance of Africa in modern human origins. The contemporary multiregional model (Wolpoff, Wu, and Thorne 1984; Wolpoff 1989), in its center-and-edge contention, proposed that Africa was a significant source of new genetic variants during human evolution, because throughout human evolution the predominant direction of gene-flow was from the more densely occupied center (Africa) to the more sparsely occupied edges (Europe, East Asia, Australia). The hallmarks of the Out of Africa hypothesis are also addressed by multiregional evolution: Low genetic diversity among human populations is explained through gene-flow rather than recency of origin, and the greater genetic diversity in Africa is explained by larger population size, greater ecological diversity, and natural selection. The inequality of Pleistocene population sizes and the evolutionary consequences of the dominance of African population size have been widely discussed (Harpending, Batzer, and Gurven 1989; Harpending 1996; Relethford 2001; Hawks and Wolpoff 2003). Because of these factors, Africa has provided the strongest regional contribution to modern humans, which is observable genetically and morphologically, but genetic and morphological data also suggest that gene-flow occurred between African and non-African populations. Therefore, while current evidence suggests that the Out of Africa speciation model is incorrect, Africa played a predominant role in Pleistocene human evolution and the origin of modern humans.

RACIAL IMPLICATIONS

Race is intricately involved in human origin theories because these theories address the origin and nature of human biological variation. For many historical reasons, and perhaps some psychological ones, race impacts our understanding of human variation in a circular way: Folk (or social) understandings of variation (race) influence science, and conversely, science has been used to validate social meanings of race (Wolpoff and Caspari 1997).

The Out of Africa hypothesis is no exception. When it was first proposed, it was used to validate progressive political positions; it gained considerable publicity as underscoring the close relationships of living humans. As Steven J. Gould put it in 1988 (p. 21), "Human unity is no idle political slogan . . . all modern humans form an entity united by physical bonds of descent from a recent African root."

The idea that the mtDNA ancestor reflected the root of all human populations meant that we all share common ancestors from less than 200,000 years ago, underscoring the "brotherhood of man," and this view was thought to undermine the race concept. Conversely, the Out of Africa hypothesis has also been used to emphasize the importance of racial difference. Sarich and Miele (2004), for example, have argued that since the species is young, "race" must be biologically important: With little time for differences to accrue, there must have been isolation, strong selection, and different evolutionary histories. Thus, the same theory can be used to support conflicting political ideologies.

STATUS OF THE OUT OF AFRICA HYPOTHESIS

This entry has explored the relationship between the concept of race and evolutionary theories of the origin of modern humans, in particular the Out of Africa hypothesis. It is ironic that the Out of Africa theory, while recently promoted as proof of the "brotherhood of man," inadvertently undermines this important concept because the assumptions that underlie the model are dependent on an unrealistic "tree model" of human variation—a view that is a legacy of the race concept. Fossil and genetic data support the hypothesis that there was gene-flow both between modern and archaic populations, and between geographic groups of modern humans after their emergence.

However, while recent evidence no longer supports the Out of Africa hypothesis per se, Africa remains important in all theories of modern human origin. Africa was the center of Pleistocene human evolution: Modern human form appears there first, and Africa made the largest regional contribution to the gene pool of modern humans. Africa is central to both single origin and multiregional models of modern human origin. Therefore, while it seems increasingly likely that some gene-flow occurred between African and non-African populations both before and after the emergence of modern humans, and the "new species" version of the Out of Africa hypothesis appears to be incorrect, the importance of Africa as a central region for the evolution of recent humans is well supported.

SEE ALSO *Human and Primate Evolution; Human Genetics.*

BIBLIOGRAPHY

Brace, C. L. 1981. "Tales of the Phylogenetic Woods: The Evolution and Significance of Evolutionary Trees." *American Journal of Physical Anthropology* 56 (4): 411–429.

Bräuer, G. 1978. "The Morphological Differentiation of Anatomically Modern Man in Africa, with Special Regard to Recent Finds from East Africa." *Zeitschrift für Morphologie und Anthropologie* 69 (3): 266–292.

———. 1984. "The 'Afro-European Sapiens Hypothesis' and Hominid Evolution in East Asia During the Late Middle and Upper Pleistocene." In *The Early Evolution of Man, with Special Emphasis on Southeast Asia and Africa,* ed. P. Andrews and J. L. Franzen. *Courier Forschungsinstitut Senckenberg* 69: 145–165.

Cann, R. L., M. Stoneking, and A. C. Wilson. 1987. "Mitochondrial DNA and Human Evolution." *Nature* 325: 31–36.

Caspari, R. 2003. "From Types to Populations: A Century of Race, Physical Anthropology and the American Anthropological Association." *American Anthropologist* 105 (1): 63–74.

Coon, C. S. 1963. *The Origin of Races.* New York: Knopf.

———, S. M. Garn, and J. B. Birdsell. 1950. *Races: A Study of the Problems of Race Formation in Man.* Springfield, IL: C. C. Thomas.

Dobzhansky, T. 1963. "Possibility that *Homo Sapiens* Evolved Independently 5 Times Is Vanishingly Small." *Current Anthropology* 4: 360–367.

Garrigan, D., and M. Hammer. 2006. "Reconstructing Human Origins in the Genomic Era." *Nature Reviews Genetics* 7: 669–680.

Gould, S. J. 1988. "A Novel Notion of Neanderthal." *Natural History* 97: 16–21.

Haeckel, E. 1884. *The History of Creation, or the Development of the Earth and Its Inhabitants by the Action of Natural Causes. A Popular Exposition of the Doctrine of Evolution in General, and That of Darwin, Goethe, and Lamark In Particular.* 2 vols. Trans. E. Ray Lankester. New York: Appleton.

Harpending, H. C. 1996. "Genetic Evidence About the Origins of Modern Humans." In *Colloquia of the XIII International Congress of Prehistoric and Protohistoric Sciences.* Vol. 5, *The Lower and Middle Paleolithic. Colloquium X: The Origin of Modern Man,* ed. O. Bar-Yosef, L. L. Cavalli-Sforza, R. J. March, and M. Piperno, 127–132. Forlì, Italy: ABACO.

———, M. A. Batzer, M. Gurven, et al. 1998. "Genetic Traces of Ancient Demography." *Proceedings of the National Academy of Sciences USA* 95 (4): 1961–1967.

Hawks, J., and G. Cochran. 2006. "Dynamics of Adaptive Introgression from Archaic to Modern Humans." *PaleoAnthropology* 2006: 101–115.

———, and M. H. Wolpoff. 2003. "Sixty Years of Modern Human Origins in the American Anthropological Association." *American Anthropologist* 105 (1): 87–98.

Howells, W. W. 1942. "Fossil Man and the Origin of Races." *American Anthropologist* 44 (2): 182–193.

———. 1959. *Mankind in the Making: The Story of Human Evolution.* Garden City, NY: Doubleday.

Hulse, F. S. 1963. Review of *The Origin of Races,* by C. S. Coon. *American Anthropologist* 65: 685–687.

Jackson, J. P., Jr. 2001. "'In Ways Unacademical': The Reception of Carleton S. Coon's *The Origin of Races.*" *Journal of the History of Biology* 34: 247–285.

Montagu, A. ed. 1964. *The Concept of Race.* New York: The Free Press.

Moore, J. H. 1994. "Putting Anthropology Back Together Again: The Ethnogenetic Critique of Cladistic Theory." *American Anthropologist* 96 (4): 925–948.

Protsch, R. 1975. "The Absolute Dating of Upper Pleistocene Sub-Saharan Fossil Hominids and Their Place in Human Evolution." *Journal of Human Evolution* 4: 297–322.

Relethford, J. H. 1998. "Genetics of Modern Human Origins and Diversity." *Annual Review of Anthropology* 27: 1–23.

———. 2001. *Genetics and the Search for Modern Human Origins.* New York: Wiley-Liss.

Sarich, V., and F. Miele. 2004. *Race: The Reality of Human Differences.* Boulder, CO: Westview.

Smith, F. H., I. Jankovic, and I. Karavanic. 2005. "The Assimilation Model, Modern Human Origins in Europe, and the Extinction of Neandertals." *Quaternary International* 137: 7–19.

Stanton, W. 1960. *The Leopard's Spots: Scientific Attitudes Toward Race in America 1815–59.* Chicago: University of Chicago Press.

Stoneking, M., and R. L. Cann. 1989. "African Origins of Human Mitochondrial DNA." In *The Human Revolution: Behavioural and Biological Perspectives on the Origins of Modern Humans,* ed. P. Mellars and C. B. Stringer, 17–30. Edinburgh, Scotland: Edinburgh University Press.

Stringer, C. B., and P. Andrews. 1988. "Genetic and Fossil Evidence for the Origin of Modern Humans." *Science* 239: 1263–1268.

Templeton, A. R. 1998. "Human Races: A Genetic and Evolutionary Perspective." *American Anthropologist* 100 (3): 632–650.

———. 2002. "Out of Africa Again and Again." *Nature* 416: 45–51.

Weidenreich, F. 1947. "Facts and Speculations Concerning the Origin of *Homo sapiens.*" *American Anthropologist* 49 (2): 187–203.

Wolpoff, M. H. 1989. "Multiregional Evolution: The Fossil Alternative to Eden." In *The Human Revolution: Behavioural and Biological Perspectives on the Origins of Modern Humans,* ed. P. Mellars and C. B. Stringer, 62–108. Edinburgh, Scotland: Edinburgh University Press.

———, and R. Caspari. 1997. *Race and Human Evolution.* New York: Simon and Schuster.

———, Wu Xinzhi, and A. G. Thorne. 1984. "Modern *Homo sapiens* Origins: A General Theory of Hominid Evolution Involving the Fossil Evidence from East Asia." In *The Origins of Modern Humans: A World Survey of the Fossil Evidence,* ed. F. H. Smith and F. Spencer, 411–483. New York: Alan R. Liss.

Rachel Caspari

OVERSEAS CHINESE

SEE *Chinese Diaspora.*

P

PAN-AFRICANISM

Pan-Africanism is variously portrayed as a set of ideas and actions, a social and political resistance movement, an ideology, or a general philosophy challenging the effects of colonization and racial discrimination in Africa. Its goal is to foster development of an Africa-wide supranational identity and promote development of African nations in all sectors. Pan-Africanism also denotes cross-national and cross-group participation and identity. Thus, it is an attempt to link all peoples of African descent on the African continent or residing in the Americas and Caribbean, Europe, and elsewhere in the global African community, including black-skinned people in India, Australia, New Guinea, Melanesia, and the Andaman Islands. Pan-Africanism emerged in response to African experiences with Europeans in the colonial and postcolonial worlds. It is a vehicle for regenerating and unifying Africa, and for promoting a feeling of oneness among all peoples of the African world.

Pan-Africanism originated in the eighteenth century among early activists in the United States, the West Indies, and England who focused on the legacy of slavery and oppression. In the twentieth century it evolved into an intergovernmental movement focusing on postcolonial development. The term came to be used as an adjective attached to a variety of activities in which peoples of Africa and African descent participate in the black experience, including, but not limited to, labor, economic development, education, the arts, literature, sports, media, and religion. Common threads include matters of race, identity, equality, development, and community and unity. There is disagreement, however, on the scope, meaning, and goals of Pan-Africanism, particularly regarding leadership, political orientation, and national versus continent-wide interests.

HISTORICAL CONTEXT FOR PAN-AFRICANISM

Pan-Africanism originated in the New World, not in Africa. Among the early activists who campaigned against slavery and promoted the repatriation of slaves to Africa were Prince Hall, a black cleric in Boston in the late 1700s, and Paul Cuffe, a Bostonian shipbuilder who in 1815 founded a repatriation settlement in Sierra Leone (initially established by the British as a refuge for freed and runaway slaves in 1787). Frederick Douglass, David Walker, James Horton, James Weldon Johnson, and many others were also involved in this effort. Another slave refuge, Liberia, was established as a result of the efforts of the American Colonization Society. The 1884 Congress of Berlin, at which the European imperial powers partitioned Africa into colonial possessions, galvanized the Pan-African movement, and the African Emigration Association was established in the United States in 1886. In 1893, Pan-Africanists convened a conference on Africa in Chicago, at which they denounced the partition of Africa. In 1897 the African Association was formed under the leadership of Henry Sylvester Williams, a Trinidadian sometimes referred to as the grandfather of Pan-Africanism. He convened the first Pan-African Congress in London in 1900.

In the early twentieth century, two notable Pan-Africanists were Marcus Garvey and W. E. B. Du Bois. Garvey, a Jamaican, promoted black pride, repatriation to Africa, and African self-determination. His ideas on Pan-Africanism remained popular for decades, particularly in the Caribbean, where they melded with reggae and liberation ideology in the 1970s. Du Bois, sometimes credited as the father of Pan-Africanism, was a cofounder of the National Association for the Advancement of Colored People (NAACP) in the United States. His scholarly writings on the struggle against white domination, the social conditions of African Americans, and the connections between black Americans and Africans gave Pan-Africanism a truly global scope.

During the early twentieth century, the movement in the Americas was also linked to the Harlem Renaissance and to black writers and artists such as Claude McKay, Langston Hughes, and Paul Robeson. Pan-Africanism also contained a focus on negritude, or the idea of a shared African personality and identity, as portrayed by activists and intellectuals in the French Caribbean and African colonies such as Léopold Senghor and Aimé Césaire. Frantz Fanon and other writers criticized this strand of Pan-Africanism as being elitist and in consort with French colonial power.

A series of Pan-African Congresses were held in this period largely under the leadership of Du Bois in Paris (1919), London and Brussels (1921), London and Lisbon (1923), and New York City (1927). Participants were drawn largely from the Caribbean, American, and European diaspora rather than from Africa itself, and the conferences focused on gradual self-government and interracialism rather than on African independence.

After World War II, the primary focus of Pan-Africanism shifted to independence movements on the continent of Africa. In 1944 the Pan-African Federation united several African groups in the first organization promoting African independence and autonomous development. In 1945, the federation convened the Sixth Pan-African Congress in Manchester, England. Participants included future African leaders such as Kwame Nkrumah of the Gold Coast (Ghana), Jomo Kenyatta of Kenya, S. L. Akintola of Nigeria, Isaac Theophilus Akunna Wallace-Johnson of Sierra Leone, and Ralph Armattoe of Togo. At this Congress, Nkrumah founded the West African National Secretariat to promote a "United States of Africa." In 1957, Nkrumah led the Gold Coast to independence, with the nation renamed Ghana. He also promoted the cause of liberation of the whole continent. The First Conference of Independent African States, held in 1958 in Accra, Ghana, launched Pan-Africanism as an intergovernmental movement on the continent.

In subsequent years, as more colonies achieved independence, different configurations of new states and interpretations of Pan-Africanism emerged: the Union of African States (1960); the African States of the Casablanca Charter (1961); the African and Malagasy Union (1961); the Organization of Inter-African and Malagasy States (1962); and the African-Malagasy-Mauritius Common Organization (1964). However, the East African leaders Julius Nyerere of Tanganyika, Milton Obote of Uganda, and Jomo Kenyatta of Kenya were unsuccessful in creating a regional union of states. Indeed, Pan-African unity repeatedly came into conflict with goals for national independence of individual former colonies. While Nkrumah's dream of a united Africa was not realized at this time, the Organization of African Unity (OAU) was established in 1963, with headquarters in Addis Ababa, Ethiopia.

In the latter half of the twentieth century, most African colonies had attained independence and Pan-African activism waned. However, the civil rights movement in the United States brought social and political changes, and some observers would place leaders such as Malcolm X and Martin Luther King within the Pan-Africanist tradition. From the 1970s to the 1990s, many of the underlying goals of Pan-Africanism were kept alive in liberation struggles in places such as Jamaica and Zimbabwe, and in the black nationalist struggle against the apartheid regime in South Africa. In addition, transatlantic connections persisted, such as in the Rastafarian movement of Jamaica, which looked to Haile Selassie I of Ethiopia as its leader. The music of Bob Marley and other reggae artists came to symbolize the struggle of Jamaica and other colonies for autonomy. Pan-Africanist ideals found expression in many forms of music, literature, and other cultural forms that linked Africans and the diaspora and enriched the larger heritage.

Other dimensions of Pan-Africanism emerged too, such as the Afrocentric movement to represent history from an Afrocentric perspective rather than the conventional Eurocentric perspective, as well as the effort to advance Pan-African nationalism rather than Eurocentric Pan-Africanism (Nantambu 1998). The scholarly field of Pan-African studies, or African studies, emerged in North American and European universities in the 1960s.

In its historical forms, Pan-Africanism contributed significantly to solidarity and black consciousness on both sides of the Atlantic, as well as to decolonization and postcolonial national development in Africa. The tripartite heritages of indigenous African, Islamic, and Western cultures were articulated in the writings of Nkrumah as "consciencism," and in those of Ali Mazrui as Africa's "triple heritage." However, the movement was less than successful in achieving its goals, being criticized for its Eurocentric depictions of the problems of Africans. Pan-Africanist leaders were criticized for focusing on personal interests and micronationalism, and for failing to advance nation-building and continental unity as a foundation for development. Pan-Africanism failed to acknowledge ethnic and cultural differences in African and diasporic contexts, and it did little to alleviate African poverty and underdevelopment.

CONTEMPORARY FORMS OF PAN-AFRICANISM

In the late 1990s and early 2000s, as globalization accelerated and global attention turned to the new economic powers in Asia (and to the crises in southwestern Asia), renewed African marginalization became the concern of Pan-Africanists. Conflicts in Sudan, Rwanda, Zaire/Congo, and Sierra Leone prompted international efforts to restore peace and stability. These circumstances created the impetus for a revitalized Pan-Africanism. The original goals of solidarity and identity remained in place, but the development focus shifted to overcoming neocolonialism and recolonization, resurrecting the goals of continent-wide economic development and supranational identity, incorporating new forms of solidarity and ways to bring Africa into the global arena, and, once more, rescuing Africa from being regarded as chaotic, underdeveloped, and oppressed.

By 1995 the fifty-three-member OAU had dealt with many struggles, including border disputes, conflicts and aggression among member states, separatist movements, and independence struggles in the continent's last remaining colonial states. In 2002 the OAU was replaced by the African Union (AU), modeled on the European Union as an organization designed to promote even greater African economic, social, and political integration. As noted by Mazrui in 2001, Africans assumed globally prominent leadership positions toward the end of the twentieth century, including Amadou Mahtar M'Bow of Senegal, who served as director-general for UNESCO from 1974 to 1987; Boutros Boutros-Ghali, the first African to serve as Secretary General of the United Nations (from 1992–1996; Kofi Annan, the second African Secretary General of the UN (from 2007); Mohammed Bedjaoui, who served as president of the International Court of Justice at the Hague from 1994 to 1997; and Callisto Madavo of Zimbabwe and Ismail Serageldin of Egypt, who have both served as a vice president at the World Bank. Black and African Nobel Peace Prize winners in the twentieth century were Ralph Bunche (1950), Albert Lutuli (1960), Martin Luther King, Jr. (1964), Anwar al-Sadat (1978), Desmond Tutu (1984), Nelson Mandela (1993), and F. W. de Klerk (1993).

The South African leader Nelson Mandela became the most universally revered of African postcolonial leaders. Under his guidance as president, South Africa, the continent's economic powerhouse, assumed leadership in peacekeeping, diplomacy, and continent-wide development. In the early 2000s, President Thabo Mbeki continued South Africa's leadership in diplomatic and economic initiatives that sought to promote all aspects of African development within and across countries, to cultivate a Pan-African supranational identity, and to carve out an effective role for African states on the world stage. Specific initiatives included recognition of the historical legacy of oppression; moral renewal and restoration of African values; cultural, educational, political, and economic transformation; science and technology development; and development in media and telecommunications.

New Partnership for Africa's Development (NEPAD). *South African President Thabo Mbeki (right) and Amadou Toumani Toure, President of Mali, attend the 2004 NEPAD summit. The organization was designed to attract foreign investment in Africa.* AP IMAGES.

In 2002, Mbeki launched a related initiative. His Millennium African Recovery Plan (2001) was renamed as the New Africa Initiative (NAI) after consultations with Senegalese President Aboulaye Wade. Mbeki proposed the revised plan to a meeting of the G8 leading industrial nations in Italy in 2001. The plan was launched as the New Partnership for Africa's Development (NEPAD) and designed to attract foreign direct investment in Africa for development in energy, agriculture, communications, and human resources. Other regional organizations, such as the Southern African Development Community (SADC), would function collaboratively. NEPAD broadened into a wide variety of development initiatives and programs, many in new areas such as health care and HIV/AIDS programs. The long-term effectiveness of NEPAD in realizing Pan-African development goals remains to be seen, however.

Many other dimensions or uses of Pan-Africanism have emerged in expanded forms as a result of global interconnectedness. Early features of the movement have persisted, such as the tricontinental ideology linking Africa, the Americas, and the Caribbean; links between Pan-Africanism and Pan-Asianism; and a sense of solidarity, unity, and shared legacy and needs. However, globalization has also enhanced the interconnected activities of Africans and the African diaspora in the fields of television, radio, and print media; theology and religion; theater, art, music, and literature; sport; trades unions and worker organizations; and other civic, economic, and social organizations. In addition, increases in the number of African refugees and immigrants settling in the West have added new infusions to the diasporic mix abroad. Consequently, Pan-Africanism has retained much of its original spirit and goals, but it has also evolved into an extremely broad variety of forms and interpretations that are ever more global in scope.

The original goals and elements of Pan-Africanism have thus proved enduring. Contemporary Pan-Africanism, however, and within it the African Renaissance and NEPAD, have been challenged for still framing African development needs and goals in terms of external superpower influences and solutions; for failing to break patterns of conflict and underdevelopment on the continent; and for failing to reconcile internal development with wider continent-wide development. NEPAD has been challenged as a vehicle for promoting South African development interests disguised as continental development leadership (Africa Confidential 2005).

Twenty-first-century Pan-Africanism still faces its original challenges of overcoming racism, promoting African identity and postcolonial development, fostering unity of Africa and the diaspora worldwide, and resolving the ambiguities of identity and loyalty that resulted from African and European interactions. Additional challenges include the AIDS pandemic on the continent; increases in the numbers of displaced persons and refugees; chronic poverty and famine; a "brain drain" of skilled labor; and crime, violence, and corruption. Some also argue that the contemporary strengthening of black American cultural and capitalistic influences in Africa and the Caribbean at the expense of indigenous values could possibly undermine the traditionally radical spirit of Pan-Africanism (Ackah 1999). In addition, because membership in Pan-African institutions has largely comprised intellectuals, activists, and politicians, it never became a mass movement.. However, as noted by Abisi Sharakiya in 1992, the endurance and recognition of the Pan-African movement remains unchallenged, and it is likely to persist in some form in the future.

SEE ALSO *African Diaspora; African Economic Development; American Colonization Society and the Founding of Liberia, Black Consciousness; Capitalism; Racial Formations; Transnationalism; White Settler Society.*

BIBLIOGRAPHY

Ackah, William B. 1999. *Pan-Africanism: Exploring the Contradictions, Politics, Identity, and Development in Africa and the African Diaspora*. Aldershot, U.K.: Ashgate.

Adi, Hakim, and Marika Sherwood. 2003. *Pan-African History: Political Figures from Africa and the Diaspora since 1787*. New York: Routledge.

Africa Confidential. 2005. "Pan-Africanism Meets Market Economics." *Africa Confidential* 46 (1): 1.

Davidson, Basil. 1994. *Modern Africa: A Social and Political History*, 3rd ed. New York: Longman.

Du Bois, William E. B. 1965. *The World and Africa: An Inquiry into the Part Which Africa Has Played in World History*. New York: International Publishers.

Esedebe, P. Olisanwuche. 1994. *Pan-Africanism: The Idea and Movement, 1776–1991*, 2nd ed. Washington, DC: Howard University Press.

Makgoba, Malegapuru W., ed. 1999. *African Renaissance: The New Struggle*. Cape Town: Mafube/Tafelberg.

Mazrui, Ali A. 2001. "Pan-Africanism in the Era of Globalization." Binghamton, NY: SUNY Institute of Global Cultural Studies. Available from http://igcs.binghamton.edu.

———, and Toby K. Levine, eds. 1986. *The Africans: A Reader*. New York: Praeger.

Mbeki, Thabo H. 1998. *Africa: The Time Has Come. Selected Speeches*. Cape Town: Mafube/Tafelberg.

Nantambu, Kwme. 1998. "Pan-Africanism versus Pan-African Nationalism." *Journal of Black Studies* 28 (5): 561–175.

Nkrumah, Kwame. 1966. *Neo-Colonialism: the Last Stage of Imperialism*. New York: International Publishers.

Sharakiya, Abisi. M. 1992. "Pan-Africanism: A Critical Assessment." *TransAfrica Forum* 8 (4): 39–53.

Diane Brook Napier

PAY EQUITY

Pay equity is a social policy that seeks to compensate workers on the basis of the skill, required effort, responsibility, and working conditions of their jobs, rather than the gender, race, or ethnicity of the worker, or the gender and racial/ethnic composition of all workers in a particular job. Pay equity advocates point to evidence of persistent earnings inequality between men and women, and between whites and people of color, to justify the implementation of pay equity policies. Wage inequalities between men and women (called the "gender pay gap") and between whites and racial/ethnic minority groups (the "racial pay gap") are substantial and have persisted over time, despite some decline since the 1970s. Gender gaps within racial/ethnic groups are presented for three points in time in Table 1, with the figures representing women's earnings as a percentage of men's earnings.

Women's Earnings as a Percentage of Men's Earnings Within Their Racial/Ethnic Group, and Black and Hispanic Earnings as percentage of White Earnings, 1980–2003

	1980			1990			2003		
	White (Non-Hispanic)	**Black** (Non-Hispanic)	**Hispanic** (any race)	**White** (Non-Hispanic)	**Black** (Non-Hispanic)	**Hispanic** (any race)	**White** (Non-Hispanic)	**Black** (Non-Hispanic)	**Hispanic** (any race)
Overall Gender Gap	58	74	68	67	90	82	71	94	85
Occupation									
Professional or Manager	65	73	68	71	89	80	70	96	81
Non-Professional/ Non-Managerial	56	70	66	64	80	78	71	86	80
Industrial Sector									
Service Sector	71	92	70	76	105	83	71	107	76
Public Sector	64	70	66	70	79	70	70	86	77
	Black-White	**Hispanic-Black**	**Hispanic-White**	**Black-White**	**Hispanic-Black**	**Hispanic-White**	**Black-White**	**Hispanic-Black**	**Hispanic-White**
Female Race Gap	99	89	88	99	82	82	100	73	73
Male Race Gap	77	97	75	74	90	67	76	81	62

Note: Analysis includes only full-time, year-round workers, ages 25 and 55.

SOURCE: Data from the 1980, 1990, and 2003 Current Population Surveys (CPS), U.S. Census Bureau.

Table 1.

Among full-time, year-round workers, white women earned 58 percent of white men's earnings in 1980. This increased to 71 percent in 2003. The gender gap among blacks and Hispanics exhibit a similar trend. Black women earned 74 percent of black male earnings in 1980, but by 2003 this had increased to 94 percent. Hispanic women earned 68 percent of Hispanic men's earnings in 1980 and 85 percent in 2003. Thus, while the gap is closing, women still earn less than men within their racial group.

PAY EQUITY: POLICIES AND POLITICS

Given such unequal pay by gender, pay equity (also known as comparable worth) emerged in the 1980s as one legal remedy. The 1963 Equal Pay Act (EPA) made it illegal to pay different wages to men and women who perform the same job. However, men and women often work in different jobs that have different pay scales, even if they involve the same level of skill, effort, responsibility, and working conditions. Pay equity policies seek equal pay for work of equal value. To do this, employers must evaluate jobs along these objective criteria and pay objectively similar jobs the same wage. While developing and applying objective criteria for job evaluation are complex and arduous tasks, the pay equity political movement successfully convinced several states to pass laws requiring pay equity in the public sector. However, employers in the private sector are exempt from these laws, and U.S. courts have consistently refused to apply EPA legislation to private sector employers, accepting the argument that these gender and racial pay gaps are due to differing "market wages" for workers beyond the employer's control (and therefore responsibility). In addition, some economists argue that pay equity would reduce economic efficiency and women's employment opportunities. In general, neoclassical economists argue that any job evaluation process is subjective and prone to bias; they propose instead that any discriminatory gender pay gaps will be eroded by competitive market processes.

In comparison to other policies that aim to mitigate gender and racial pay gaps, such as the EPA or affirmative action, pay equity is fundamentally a more radical policy. The EPA seeks to eliminate gender and racial pay disparities within the same jobs, while affirmative action seeks to move women and racial minorities into more highly rewarded jobs and thereby reduce overall gender and racial pay gaps. In contrast, pay equity challenges the devaluation of certain kinds of work because it is associated with women or racial minorities. Pay equity advocates argue that white women and people of color who are in different jobs than white men should not be paid less if the job they perform is similar in its skill and educational requirements, its job tasks, and its responsibilities.

WHY IS THERE A PAY GAP?

Clearly, men earn more than women but overall pay gaps hide the various ways that such earnings inequality is created. One mechanism behind pay inequality is the segregation of men and women, and of racial/ethnic groups, into different jobs. Men and women continue to work in different occupations, as do whites and people of color. White men are most likely to be either managers or professionals, while African-American men tend to be in unskilled laborer occupations. Both white and African-American women are most likely to be in administrative support occupations, but black women are almost twice as likely to be in service occupations. (McKinnon 2003). Taking for example the hierarchy in the medical field, whereas only 31 percent of surgeons in 2003 were women, 93 percent of nurses were women. As well, whereas only 17 percent of surgeons were African-American, 31 percent were of medical technicians. When the kinds of jobs individuals hold are held constant, the pay gap decreases dramatically and when men and women are working in the same job the pay gap between is significantly smaller. Thus, much of this overall gap is accounted for by the segregation of men and women into different jobs. Men and women are not equally represented in all occupations, and the occupations where women are overrepresented tend to pay less than occupations where men predominate. Similarly, researchers have found that pay gaps vary across organizations. That is, some organizations pay more equal wages while others pay less equal wages to men and women. Researchers find that this occurs, in part, due to differing organizational policies on setting pay scales, such as having objective criteria for pay and promotions.

Another crucial explanation of women's lower earnings is that women disproportionately work part-time jobs and have lower labor-force participation rates. The overall gaps reported in Table 1 are only for full-time, year-round workers, and thus exclude many women workers. When part-time workers are included, in 2003, white women's earnings relative to white men's drops to 46 percent. For black women in 2003, their earnings relative to black men's drops to 70 percent, and for Hispanic women it drops to 56 percent. The major reason women work part-time so much more than men is because they bear the burden of family expectations. That is, women are expected to raise children and perform the majority of the housework, leading to what Arlie Hochschild has termed a "double shift" for working women, where they have to work one shift at a job and another shift doing housework. These demands lead some women to opt out of the labor force, while many others must work part-time. However, both of these options are most common among married women with employed husbands. These women can afford to reduce their employment to reallocate more time to unpaid caring work.

In earlier decades, part of the gender and racial pay gaps were due to the lower educational attainment of white women and people of color, compared with white men. However, these educational differences have lessened. That wage gaps persist despite this lessening implies that increased education for minority groups will not eliminate pay inequity. Moreover, when the pay gaps are broken down by education, they remain very similar to the overall gap; Irene Padavic and Barbara Reskin have shown that, at every level of education, men consistently outearn women with similar educational degrees.

PAY GAPS AND EMPLOYER DISCRIMINATION

Even when occupational segregation and differences in human capital are accounted for, men continue to earn more than women. This remaining gap may be explained by employer discrimination. A range of discriminatory mechanisms, both overt and unconscious, are used by employers to maintain earnings inequality. Sometimes employers assume that women are less productive (often because they assume women are distracted by family responsibilities), and they therefore do not hire or do not promote women into higher-paying jobs. Researchers have also documented the impact of preference for members of one's own social group on the hiring of women. Men are often responsible for hiring employees, and tend to be more comfortable around other men than they are around women. This leads them to prefer hiring men over equally qualified women. In addition, employers often hold stereotypical beliefs about what kinds of work men and women are supposed to do, leading them to hire women for some jobs and men for others. All of these processes lead to segregating men and women into different jobs. Employers also reward jobs that men and women are in differently. Through often unrecognized beliefs about the value of work women perform, employers reward the jobs women are segregated into less than the jobs into which men are segregated.

TRENDS TOWARD PAY EQUITY

The pay gap between men and women was smaller in 2003 than it was in 1980. But the pace at which this gap has declined has slowed since 1990. Social scientists have noted that much of these actual gains are a result of men's relative decline in earnings in the 1980s, when manufacturing jobs were moved overseas (Padavic and Reskin 2002). This helps explain why the decline from 1980 to 1990 was greater than the decline from 1990 to 2003.

In contrast to the slow erasure of the gender pay gap, the racial pay gap has actually grown, except for the gap between black and white women. Just as the trend in the pay gap between men and women has largely stemmed from men's declining earnings due to the loss of manufacturing jobs, so has the race gap been affected by the decline in manufacturing jobs. Scholars have noted that as manufacturing jobs are lost, less skilled workers have a harder time finding a job. Because people of color are stuck in occupations requiring less skill, their earnings decline when jobs for less-skilled workers decline.

THE FUTURE OF PAY EQUITY

Pay equity movements have attempted to eliminate the employer discrimination that leads to men and women in the same jobs being paid different wages, as well as the employer discrimination that leads to men and women in similarly valuable jobs being paid unequal wages. A crucial practical problem in pay equity policies is determining the value of skills. What skills, job tasks, and responsibilities should be considered comparable? Nevertheless, pay equity does address the inequalities produced through job segregation that policies addressing only unequal pay for the same work ignore. If pay were to equalize across the exact same occupations, it would not address the underlying causes of pay inequality: occupational segregation. While pay equity has often failed as a practical policy, it begins to address these underlying causes of pay inequality, whereas equal pay for the same work cannot address this structural inequality.

SEE ALSO *Affirmative Action.*

BIBLIOGRAPHY

England, Paula. 1992. *Comparable Worth: Theories and Evidence.* Hawthorne, NY: Aldine de Gruyter.

Hochschild, Arlie. 1997. *The Time Bind: When Work Becomes Home and Home Becomes Work.* New York: Henry Holt.

McKinnon, Jesse. 2003. "The Black Population in the United States: 2002." *Current Population Reports*, Series P-20-541. Washington, DC: U.S. Census Bureau.

Nelson, Robert, and William Bridges. 1999. *Legalizing Gender Inequality: Courts, Markets, and Unequal Pay for Women in America.* New York: Cambridge University Press.

Padavic, Irene, and Barbara Reskin. 2002. *Women and Men at Work*, 2nd ed. Thousand Oaks, CA: Pine Forge Press.

Reskin, Barbara. 2001. *The Realities of Affirmative Action in Employment.* Washington, D.C.: American Sociological Association.

Treiman, Donald, and Heidi Hartmann, eds. 1981. *Women, Work and Wages: Equal Pay for Jobs of Equal Value.* Washington, DC: National Academy Press.

Dustin Avent-Holt
Michelle J. Budig

PEONAGE CASES

The peonage cases were a rare but notable example of judicial protection of African-American rights during the highly racist era of the early twentieth century. In *Bailey v. Alabama* (1911), the United States Supreme Court invalidated an Alabama peonage law on the ground that it violated the Thirteenth Amendment's ban on involuntary servitude. The Alabama law criminalized a worker's breach of a labor contract in any case where he had received an advance payment from his employer (as was common practice in southern agricultural labor contracts at the time). Criminal punishment, usually including prison time, was a far more severe sanction than the standard civil remedy for reneging on a labor contract (which usually involved only financial compensation to the employer). This made it far more difficult for African-American farm workers to leave their employers in search of better opportunities elsewhere.

In the 1914 case of *United States v. Reynolds*, the Supreme Court struck down a second pillar of the peonage system: "criminal surety" laws. Such laws gave convicted criminals a choice between paying a fine, serving time in prison (usually on a chain gang), or working for a planter in exchange for sufficient funds to pay off the fine. Although these laws were less clearly unconstitutional than those at issue in *Bailey*, criminal surety statutes were part of a system in which poor African-Americans were routinely arrested for minor or nonexistent offenses for the purpose of using them as forced labor for the benefit of white planters.

The peonage cases arose from efforts by white southern planters to restrict the mobility of African-American agricultural labor after the abolition of slavery between 1863 and 1865. Planters initially attempted to force down African-American laborers' wages by organizing cartels under which they agreed to keep wages low and refrain from hiring away each other's workers. However, such private arrangements repeatedly broke down in the face of competitive pressures that gave planters an incentive to compete for workers by offering higher pay and superior working conditions. As a result, the planters turned to state governments for assistance, hoping that government action would suppress the competitive pressures that had stymied private efforts.

In the late nineteenth and early twentieth centuries, therefore, southern states enacted a variety of laws intended to restrict the mobility of African-American labor. Early peonage laws were even harsher than those invalidated in *Bailey* and *Reynolds,* forcing workers into involuntary servitude in order to pay off debts to their employers. The federal Peonage Act of 1867, upheld by the Supreme Court in the 1905 case of *Clyatt v. United States,* banned such laws. Southern state governments then had to rely on other measures to restrict black labor mobility, and the laws struck down in *Bailey* and *Reynolds* were among the results.

The history of the peonage cases shows that, in at least some situations, oppressed minorities can benefit from free labor markets. Although nearly all the planters who employed African-American agricultural laborers in the segregation-era South were white and most held racist views, competition between employers still led to improved pay and working conditions. Despite their commitment to racial hierarchy, white planters were usually unable to curtail the mobility of African-American labor without the aid of government intervention. In the aftermath of the peonage cases, hundreds of thousands of African Americans were able to improve their social and economic prospects by switching employers or moving to the North, where—despite widespread racism—opportunities for black workers were often better than in the South.

The Supreme Court's decisions in the peonage cases were not the only, or even the most important, factor enabling increased African-American mobility in the early twentieth century. Rising black education levels, lower transportation costs, and the availability of new job opportunities in the North also played key roles. Nonetheless, the Court's actions had an impact as well. Peonage complaints decreased after *Bailey*, and several southern states removed peonage laws from the books or stopped enforcing them.

The peonage cases were not a simple morality play in which a heroic court triumphed over racist public opinion. Although racism was endemic in the North as well as the South, peonage laws were a sufficiently blatant affront to the Constitution that most northern whites, and even some southerners, disapproved of them. Nonetheless, the Supreme Court probably went further in attacking peonage than most white elected officials were inclined to do. Although the peonage cases hardly revolutionized early twentieth-century race relations, they did measurably improve the lives of poor African Americans in the South.

SEE ALSO *Black Codes; Chain Gangs; United States Constitution.*

BIBLIOGRAPHY

Bernstein, David E., and Ilya Somin. 2004. "Judicial Power and Civil Rights Reconsidered." *Yale Law Journal* 114 (3): 591–657.

Bickel, Alexander M., and Benno C. Schmidt. 1984. *The Judiciary and Responsible Government, 1910–21*. New York: Macmillan.

Cohen, William. 1991. *At Freedom's Edge: Black Mobility and the Southern White Quest for Racial Control, 1861–1915*. Baton Rouge: Louisiana State University Press.

Daniel, Pete. 1990. *The Shadow of Slavery: Peonage in the South, 1901–1969*, rev. ed. Urbana: University of Illinois Press.

Klarman, Michael J. 2004. *From Jim Crow to Civil Rights: The Supreme Court and the Struggle for Racial Equality*. New York: Oxford University Press.

Ilya Somin

PHILLIPS, WENDELL
1811–1884

Wendell Phillips, antislavery leader and crusader for the rights of women, labor, and the oppressed everywhere, was born November 29, 1811, "the child," as he put it, "of six generations of Puritans" (Phillips 2001, p. 26). His father was the first mayor of Boston. His mother was Salley Walley, daughter of a Boston merchant. When Phillips was fourteen, he attended a meeting conducted by the famous revivalist Lyman Beecher. Shortly before his death, Phillips said, "From that day to this, whenever I have known a thing to be wrong, it has held no temptation. Whenever I have known it to be right, it has taken no courage to do it" (Korngold 1950, p. 111). He attended Boston Latin School, distinguishing himself as an athlete, and Harvard College, graduating with high honors in 1831. According to biographer Ralph Korngold (1950), he was "six feet tall, deep-chested, broad-shouldered and with a soldierly bearing." A college friend described him as "the most beautiful person I had ever seen … a young Apollo." All his life he conducted himself like an aristocrat, "always well-dressed—not a speck on his clothing" (pp. 119–120). He graduated from Harvard Law School in 1833 and was admitted to the bar the next year. He opened a law office, but his heart was not in it. Later he said that, left to follow his own course, he should have studied mechanics or history.

Phillips was fond of telling friends that his wife, the former Ann Terry Greene, whom he had met while he was in law school, had converted him to abolitionism. In 1835 he witnessed a mob determined to lynch William Lloyd Garrison leading him up the street with a rope around his neck. It was not that episode but another that won him to the cause of abolition. In November 1837 abolitionist editor Elijah Lovejoy was murdered in Alton, Illinois, while trying to defend his printing press from a mob. The following month, at a public meeting at Faneuil Hall called to discuss the case, Phillips, angered by the speech of the Massachusetts attorney general, who defended the mob and condemned Lovejoy as "presumptuous and imprudent," took the floor and delivered an address that linked the right of free speech and the antislavery cause. His address won over the audience, most of whom had started out hostile, and led to his being immediately recognized as one of the outstanding orators of the day. He would later come to be known as "the golden trumpet of abolition."

Phillips gave up his law practice, such as it was, because he found it impossible to take an oath to defend the Constitution, regarding it as "a covenant with death and agreement with hell," a description used by many abolitionists. For thirty years he labored in the ranks of the abolitionists. Whereas most northerners opposed slavery, they hated abolitionism more. Business interests depended on slave-grown cotton and sugar, and laborers feared the sudden appearance of a million former slaves in the labor market. As a result, abolitionists regularly found themselves the targets of violent mobs. Phillips carried a pistol to defend himself. His family responded to his course by seeking to have him declared insane. "We do not play politics," he declared. "Anti-slavery is no half-jest with us; it is a terrible earnest, with life or death, worse than life or death, on the issue" (Phillips 2001, p. 51).

In addition to speaking, Phillips wrote, traveled, and organized for the cause. He helped popularize the slogan "No union with slaveholders," part of a strategy aimed at bringing down slavery by removing northern support. Phillips frequently addressed northern audiences as "fellow subjects of Virginia," reminding them that it was their taxes that paid for the armed force that held down the slave. "All the slave asks of us," he declared, "is to stand out of his way, withdraw our pledge to keep the peace on the plantation, withdraw our pledge to return him" (Phillips 2001, pp. 14–15). At rallies he asked his audiences to pledge never to return the fugitive who set foot on northern soil, and he himself took part in efforts to defend fugitives by direct action, in defiance of federal law.

When South Carolina and other states announced their secession from the Union, Phillips and other abolitionists were outcasts, living under threat of attack from northern mobs who blamed them for the breakup of the nation. Yet as the Civil War continued and it became increasingly clear that no policy of conciliation could lure the seceded states back into the Union, public opinion turned. Over the winter of 1861–1862, five million people heard him speak or read his speeches calling for emancipation, the enlistment of black soldiers, and an active military strategy. When he visited Washington, the vice president welcomed him to the Senate chamber, the Speaker of the House invited him to dinner, and the president received him as a guest. He had gone from pariah to prophet.

When the Thirteenth Amendment passed in December 1865, some abolitionists, including Garrison, concluded that their work was done. Phillips disagreed, believing that their work was not over until full equality was guaranteed. He assumed formal leadership of the Anti-Slavery Society and continued his efforts on behalf of the freedpeople. While not forgetting the slave, he took up new issues. He ran for governor of Massachusetts in 1870 on the Labor Reform ticket, resisting the anti-Chinese campaign that had gained the support of many labor reformers. He joined the International Workingmen's Association and declared his support for the Paris Commune of 1871.

Summarizing his career, Phillips said he had "worked 40 years, served in 20 movements, and been kicked out of all of them" (Phillips 2001, p. 27). He died on February 2, 1884. His death was announced in newspapers across the country. His funeral was a state occasion, with offerings sent from workers, Irish, and other groups whose cause he had championed. Thousands waited in line for a last look at him. Two companies of black militia, marching to the roll of muffled drums, served as an honor guard (Korngold 1950, p. 397). A statue of him stands by the Boston Public Garden.

SEE ALSO *Abolition Movement.*

BIBLIOGRAPHY

PRIMARY WORKS

Phillips, Wendell. 1968 [1863]. *Speeches, Lectures, and Letters.* Boston: James Redpath Publishers. Reprint, New York: Negro Universities Press.

———. 1969 [1891]. *Speeches, Lectures, and Letters.* Second Series. Boston: Lee and Shepard. Reprint, New York: Arno Press.

———. 2001. *The Lesson of the Hour: Wendell Phillips on Abolition and Strategy.* Edited by Noel Ignatiev. Chicago: Charles H. Kerr.

SECONDARY WORKS

Korngold, Ralph. 1950. *Two Friends of Man: The Story of William Lloyd Garrison and Wendell Phillips.* Boston: Little Brown.

Martyn, W. Carlos. 1891. *Wendell Phillips: The Agitator.* New York: Funk and Wagnalls.

Stewart, James Brewer. 1986. *Wendell Phillips: Liberty's Hero.* Baton Rouge: Louisiana State University Press.

Noel Ignatiev

PLANTATIONS

The rise of the plantation complex was both a major economic force in commercial agricultural production and a major social and socializing institution. In the Americas, plantations were organized and managed through the maintenance and enforcement of strict social codes steeped in a racial doctrine of white supremacy and black inferiority. The implementation of chattel slavery as a form of absolute control over enslaved African people served to further codify and solidify social hierarchies, myths, and perceptions based on race. A critical examination of the plantation system reveals a pervasive dependence on the labor, services, and skills of enslaved Africans and their descendents. Starting with a definition and general description of plantations, followed by an overview of some of the major types of plantations, and concluding with a detailed analysis of a specific antebellum plantation, this article challenges myths and fixed perceptions about race as defined by the plantation experience.

Although the plantation as a form of agriculture has existed in a variety of places over a range of time periods, the term has become distinctly associated with European expansion. Nineteenth century plantations were typically large tracts of land owned and operated by a planter and his family. They were primarily developed and cultivated by groups of laborers under the autocratic control of the plantation owner, who generally concentrated on the production of a single "cash" crop that was exported and distributed globally. In the Americas, cash crops included sugar, cotton, tobacco, rice, and indigo.

At the start of the sixteenth century, an explosive and unprecedented demand for sugar in Europe resulted in the establishment of sugar plantations in South America and the Caribbean, most notably in Brazil. By the first two decades of the seventeenth century, sugar cultivation on European-owned plantations in places such as Antigua and Barbados had become the cash-crop production model of choice.

In North America, plantations dominated southern agriculture, and the premier cash crop was cotton. Throughout most of the eighteenth and nineteenth centuries, cotton plantations could be found across the South. In addition, during the seventeenth and early eighteenth centuries an increased demand for tobacco in European markets led to a rise in tobacco plantations in the Chesapeake colonies, particularly in the Piedmont and Tidewater regions of Virginia. Beginning in the seventeenth century, rice plantations were abundant in low-lying areas near a significant water source in South Carolina and parts of Georgia and East Florida.

The growth of the plantation system as an agricultural unit of production and commercial enterprise was fueled by a massive dispersion of people. From the late fifteenth century to the mid-nineteenth century, enslaved Africans became an increasingly significant factor in Europe's (especially Britain's) and America's growth and development. Slavery became the labor solution of choice for advancing economic and sociopolitical ambitions within the context of agricultural land units known as plantations.

Discussions of plantations are important in the early twenty-first century for a variety of reasons. Colonial and antebellum accounts of plantation life typically caricature persons of African descent solely as slaves, with no merit beyond the contributions of their physical labor. But to reduce the discussion of Africans on plantations to "slave life portraits" is to perpetuate a narrow vision of American history. In South Carolina, census records from as early as 1790 confirm that enslaved Africans and their descendents made up the majority of the population within plantation communities, and that they performed a wide range of jobs and tasks, enabling plantation-based agricultural centers to function relatively self-sufficiently. In addition, public history and National Heritage interpretations often provide merely one perspective of antebellum plantations—with a primary focus on life as experienced by plantation owners and their families and a generic profile of slave life. This leaves out important issues of race and power as experienced by the Africans on the plantations.

The sociologist Edgar T. Thompson, in selected papers published in *Plantation Societies, Race Relations, and the South* (1975), provides a rigorous analysis of some of the distinguishing aspects of the plantation as a unit of production. Thus, the plantation was: (1) a settlement institution actively involved in the process of occupying space, acquiring territory, and organizing people, land, and material structures; (2) an economic institution actively involved in the selection and production of a specific agricultural product mix for external market distribution and wealth generation; (3) a political institution with territorial autonomy and autocratic levels of control over its jurisdiction; and (4) a cultural institution with distinct norms and rules governing behavior and ways of interacting, with hierarchical assumptions about race being particularly pervasive.

TYPES OF PLANTATIONS

Plantation enterprises not only differed from other land-use enterprises in distinguishable ways, they also differed with respect to each other. The historical anthropologist Michel-Rolph Trouillot concludes that "the plantation, as such, never existed historically, not even in the Americas of slavery" (1998, p. 22). Instead, thousands of plantations existed, each offering challenges to the plantation ideal. One of the primary areas of distinction between different plantations involved labor requirements and socialcultural orientation—particularly the degree of autonomy and interdependence that existed between enslaved Africans (and their descendents) and plantation owners. What follows is a brief look at the labor requirements and social organization of four of the major plantation types (sugar, tobacco, cotton, and rice).

Sugar Production. Sugar plantations were typically large, privately owned enterprises in which enslaved African populations outnumbered whites in significant proportions. According to Ira Berlin and Philip Morgan, nearly two-thirds of all Africans arriving in the Americas ended up working on sugar plantations. In addition, women played a significant role in sugar production and accounted for more than 50 percent of the labor force on British-controlled sugar plantations throughout the Caribbean. In places where sugar was an important commodity, such as Barbados, Antigua, Martinique, St. Kitts, St. Croix, Guadeloupe, Jamaica, and Haiti, the African-descendent population continues to remains significant.

In the cash-crop production hierarchy, sugar plantations were generally regarded as being the most labor intensive and demanding. Sugar production contains both an agricultural and industrial component, commanding a range of skills and a complex division of labor. The production of granulated sugar, molasses, rum, and other sugar end products consists of a series of steps, including planting and harvesting; the grinding of harvested cane to extract cane juice; boiling the juice at extremely high temperatures to produce crystallized sugar; the curing of crystallized sugar; and distilling molasses and other sugar by-products into rum, a very popular and lucrative export item. The cane, once harvested, had to be processed immediately to avoid spoiling. During this aspect of the cycle, labor was required around the clock for up to a month or more. In addition to the very specific labor requirements involved in sugar production, Africans were required to perform an inexhaustible list of other labor and service activities in support of sugar plantation maintenance, including cooking, childcare, laundry, artisan services (e.g., masonry and carpentry), machine operation, and sexual services.

On a social level, because Africans made up an overwhelming majority of the population on sugar plantations, planters generally focused less attention on the assimilation and acculturation of slave populations and more attention on preserving their own identity. They instituted policies, rules, and laws aimed primarily at segregation, intimidation, and control. These segregation policies severely restricted the freedom of movement of the slave population. However, as a response, a greater focus on and commitment to African ways of being, independent of European norms, was fostered among the slaves. Africans formed and sustained their own communities outside the direct control of plantation owners, and a range of cultural practices—such as ways of obtaining, growing, cooking, and sharing food; spiritual practices, and patterns of speech—were encouraged.

A defining feature of the British and French plantation systems was their dependence on African labor and services. The work required to grow, harvest, process, and manage the production of sugar throughout the Americas reveals the importance of African labor and knowledge to European plantation owners and the success of their plantation ventures, but it also underscores the heavy toll exacted on the lives of Africans in the process.

Tobacco Cultivation. By the start of the eighteenth century, an increased demand for tobacco in European markets, particularly France, resulted in an expanded focus by planter families on tobacco in the Chesapeake colonies of Virginia and Maryland. The rise in tobacco production and its expansion inland from the Tidewater into the Piedmont region was coupled with an increase in the purchase of enslaved Africans by planters. This was followed by an increase in laws, legal practices, and other forms of control aimed at restricting and discouraging African autonomy (enslaved and free) and protecting and expanding white power and control. Such restrictive practices were applied on the basis of skin color alone, and all blacks, both free and enslaved, were collapsed into one category and treated the same, leading to an exodus of sizable numbers of free blacks from the Chesapeake region.

Tobacco was generally regarded as being less demanding and less labor intensive to produce than sugar, rice, or cotton. Tobacco plantations were generally small (with larger plantations being defined as having more than thirty slaves). Sugar plantations, by comparison, were typically described as having enslaved populations totaling into the hundreds at one plantation site.

Tobacco planters were also able to avoid major seasonal fluctuations in labor requirements because tobacco cultivation retained a consistent flow throughout the year. Tobacco leaves ripened seasonally and had to be picked at the right moment for optimal value. Work on tobacco plantations centered entirely on the planting and harvesting of tobacco leaves, which required constant attention throughout the year, but limited additional processing after harvesting was required. However, tobacco production did require a steady supply of good soil (soil that had never been planted or soil that had been left unplanted for several years). This dictated that enslaved Africans and their families adhere to a cycle that required them to move from location to location every two to three years in order to take advantage of fresh or unexhausted soils for planting.

African cultural autonomy from European norms in tobacco plantation environments was often harder to sustain because many enslaved Africans lived in close proximity to European planter families. As a result, opportunities to adapt to or share cultural practices such as language, foods, and religion with Europeans were greater. Although the degree of freedom gained from constant migration and resettlement, as dictated by the tobacco-plantation production cycle, was something many Africans valued, household and family stability was compromised with each required

Georgia Cotton Plantation, c. 1917. *Cotton was an important cash crop in the South and cotton plantations were a common feature in the region throughout most of the eighteenth and nineteenth centuries.* THE LIBRARY OF CONGRESS.

move. However, this arrangement enabled Africans to form extended communities, learn more about locations and opportunities outside their plantation setting, and obtain knowledge about a range of cultural practices. Thus, a larger mixture of old and new cultural ways and ideas was integrated into family and community practices by Africans in the Chesapeake region.

During the middle part of the eighteenth century, a decline in tobacco productivity coupled with a rise in small-grain production (such as wheat, rye, and oats) began to alter life and the nature of agricultural labor in the region. A demand for skilled laborers and artisans to support grain production resulted in the flow of enslaved African males to work outside the tobacco industry. The tobacco plantation economy in the Chesapeake region became increasingly dominated by women and their children, who were often considered ideal laborers by tobacco plantation owners.

Cotton. While tobacco production relied on fresh soils and encouraged short-range migration, the expansion of cotton and its status as the dominant crop in southern agriculture, was responsible for a massive migration of enslaved Africans from the coast to interior regions of America. Between 1790 and 1860, more than 800,000 blacks moved to cotton-producing states, whose boundaries extended from South Carolina to Texas and from Florida to Tennessee. Many of these Africans were from tobacco areas in the Chesapeake region or from rice areas in South Carolina and Florida.

On the cash-crop production hierarchy, cotton was considered more demanding to cultivate than tobacco, although it was far more regimented in terms of labor requirements. The growing market for cotton in the early 1800s led to a rise in the establishment of large cotton plantations (greater than twenty slaves) in regions of fertile soils and easy access to markets. Plantations that produced cotton (and little if anything else) ranged in land area from forty acres to one thousand acres.

Cotton plantations required two types of labor—an initial labor force dedicated to clearing uncultivated land and making it ready for cultivation (a rigorous and exhausting task), and an established workforce dedicated to planting and harvesting cotton according to its yearly cycle. After the initial clearing of the fields, which was dominated by the labor of young males, field labor on mature cotton plantations required no special strength or skills thought to advantage males over females. Women ranked among the most productive workers, especially during the harvesting period. The harvest period for cotton extended from as early as August into late February. During this time, production quotas were imposed on enslaved Africans and they were typically required to labor in tightly supervised units known as "work gangs" from sun-up to sundown. Because cotton production had limited requirements in terms of processing following the harvest period, workers were called upon to utilize a narrow range of skills in order to maintain plantation operations. Many Africans forced to labor on cotton plantations had lives more restricted and regimented than those on tobacco or rice plantations, and their ability to utilize their skill and knowledge in negotiating various liberties was severely diminished.

The gang system of labor, with its tight supervision requirements, created a relationship that pitted enslaved African workers against plantation owners. Africans fought to minimize exhausting labor demands, while owners sought to maximize production, often employing brutal methods of punishment and control in the process. These tensions escalated to a greater degree on cotton plantations in the southern agricultural region of the United States because of the number of people involved—including the high ratio of blacks to whites, the regimented production demands and high production quotas, and the diversity of African experiences with other labor systems.

Increasingly large populations of enslaved Africans in concentrated areas typically resulted in the institution of restricted laws, (black) codes of conduct, and prohibitions against social interaction between whites and blacks. White citizens in communities dominated by cotton plantations continually sought measures, passed laws, and participated in acts of violence aimed at limiting the autonomy of blacks. On cotton plantations, African autonomy was often compromised as plantation owners worked to limit worker focus and discourage outside activities. Owners of cotton plantations tended to be more driven to supply food and clothing rations to enslaved Africans, partly to maximize slave dependence and minimize outside distractions on their time.

Cotton dominated markets in the South between the Civil War and World War I. Because cotton plantations commanded such large land areas and employed such large numbers of people, a common culture and basis of connection formed among laborers. On mature cotton plantations, almost everyone engaged in the same tasks, participated in the same routines, and faced the same challenges and threats to freedom exacted by racist laws. In general, enslaved Africans created new traditions, honored old ones, and developed ways of being that emphasized ways of living and surviving.

Rice Production. In comparison to cotton, tobacco, and sugar production, rice was a small enterprise, but for more than 200 years (between 1690 and 1890) it was important for the U.S. Sea Island plantations along the coasts of South Carolina, Georgia, and Florida. Successful rice planter families and merchants created an elite social and political society, and they exercised a high degree of autonomy within and beyond plantation borders. After the Revolutionary War, many individuals in this society served as key figures in American nation-building. In 1843, the rice planter Robert F. W. Allston wrote the following regarding the significance of rice planting in South Carolina: "The cultivation of Rice in South Carolina has added materially to the wealth of the Province—the Colony—the State; and has enhanced, in no inconsiderable degree the value of the active commerce of both the kingdom of Great Britain, and the Federal Republic of the United States" (Allston 1843, pp. 5–6).

Water management is crucial in rice production because rice thrives on land that is saturated in water during all or part of its growth cycle. In much the same ways as cotton, the production of rice on U.S. Sea Island plantations required a tremendous amount of work, both in terms of the initial development of rice fields and the ongoing maintenance of the fields. The historian Mart Stewart concluded that a "massive application of human energy" went into the initial clearing of swamplands in order to transform them into commercial rice enterprises (1996, p. 147). In many instances, swampland contained cypress forests that had to be cleared, after which miles of ditches, dikes, and canals were constructed in order to provision the huge irrigation system on which tidal-swamp rice production depended. Once created, these artificial systems required constant maintenance to remain productive, and a steady influx of African labor made the creation of these rice ecosystems possible.

Africans dominated the geographic landscape in which the production of rice took place, and population figures affirm the significance of the African presence in commercial agriculture production in the U.S. Sea Islands. In South Carolina, African population growth paralleled the rise in rice production, with over two-thirds of the population being classified as black between 1740 and 1760. Additionally, between 1720 and 1765 the majority of Africans in South Carolina were imported directly from West Africa in European slaving ships. In *Slaves in the Family*, Edward Ball notes that Europeans, such as his ancestors, knew little about rice at first, and thus relied on the knowledge of enslaved Africans who worked for them:

> The cultivation of rice was, at least initially, something Elias and his peers knew nothing about. In parts of West Africa, however, rice was an old staple, grown along the Gambia River, for instance, and in Sierra Leone. It wasn't long before the planters recognized that some of the Africans they owned possessed a knowledge that could earn them profits. The strain of rice grown by Carolina slaves, refined through years of experiment, became known as Carolina Gold. (Ball 1998, p. 108)

The global movement of rice and African people links West African, European, and the U.S. Sea Island cultures in ways not typically discussed.

RICE PRODUCTION ON JEHOSSEE ISLAND

Imagine an island off the coast of South Carolina on which more than 95 percent of the people are Africans or descendants of Africans. Imagine as well a successful rice business being run on this very same island. The Jehossee Island Plantation off the Edisto and Dawho rivers, about twenty-five miles southeast of Charleston, South Carolina, in what was then St. John Colleton Parish, was such a place. The site of a thriving rice plantation in the 1800s, Jehossee was a community planned and managed around the cultivation and exportation of rice. Between the periods 1830 and 1887, it was owned by William Aiken, a one-time governor of South Carolina.

In the early twenty-first century, Jehossee was owned by the U.S. Fish and Wildlife Service (USFWS) and was part of the ACE Basin National Wildlife Refuge. The wetlands of Jehossee Island are considered of national and international importance, primarily because of alterations to the landscape that took place during the period of commercial rice production. Jehossee's undeveloped estuaries are home to a variety of flora and fauna.

Public discussion and knowledge of Jehossee generally revolve around the life, wealth, and social and political prominence of the Aiken family, primarily William Aiken Jr. (1806–1887), a respected planter and well-known political figure. However, Jehossee was mainly an African community. When Aiken inherited his share of the family's wealth, he began to focus his attention on agricultural pursuits, particularly rice. In 1830 he began his acquisition of Jehossee. According to U.S. Census records for St. Johns-Colleton County, by 1850 there were 897 enslaved Africans living on the island, and by 1860 there were still 699. These demographics suggest that Aiken actively purchased and retained the labor and services of large numbers of enslaved Africans.

Aiken's notoriety as a major producer and exporter of rice, coupled with his success in the political arena, placed Jehossee in public view. It was the destination of many visitors, who have supplied portraits of their experiences and glimpses into the daily life of Africans living on the island. Solon Robinson, a well-known writer and the agricultural editor for the *American Agriculturist* magazine, made a series of tours throughout rural America, most extensively between 1840 and 1860. After arriving at Jehossee in 1850, by way of a twelve-hour steamboat journey from Charleston (located thirty miles away), Robinson provided the following description of the island:

> This island contains about 3,300 acres, no part of which is over ten or fifteen feet above tide, and not more than 200 to 300 acres but what was subject to overflow until diked out by an amount of labor almost inconceivable to be performed by individual enterprise, when we take into account the many miles of navigable canals and smaller ditches. There [are] 1,500 acres of rice lands, divided into convenient compartments for flooding, by substantial banks, and all laid off in beds between ditches 3 feet deep, only 35 feet apart. Part of the land was tide-water marsh, and part of it timber swamp. Besides this, Gov. A. cultivates 500 acres in corn, oats, and potatoes. (Kellar 1936, pp. 364–365)

Robinson also explicitly highlights Jehossee's majority African community as being responsible for every aspect of rice production and plantation maintenance throughout the year, even during the months in which the threat of contracting malaria was especially high. According to Robinson enslaved Africans performed most of the jobs on the plantation from engineers to sailors:

> The average annual sales of the place do not vary materially from $25,000, and the average annual expenses not far from $10,000, of which sum $2,000 is paid the overseer, who is the only white man upon the place, besides the owner, who is always absent during the sickly months of the summer. All the engineers, millers, smiths, carpenters, and sailors are black. A vessel belonging to the island goes twice a week to Charleston, and carries a cargo of 100 casks. The last crop was 1,500 casks. (Kellar 1936, p. 367)

Solon Robinson, like many other visitors, described Jehossee Island plantation under the ownership of Governor William Aiken as having provided the best living and working conditions afforded enslaved persons during that time—primarily with respect to housing, medical care, daily labor demands, and quality of overseer management. He wrote that Governor Aiken's primary concern was making his people "comfortable and happy" (Kellar 1936, p. 368).

However, the severity of the toll exacted on the health of those forced to engage in tidal-swamp rice production, though seldom emphasized, cannot be ignored. For human populations, rice plantation ecosystems present a variety of environmental hazards and stresses, the primary problem being the threat of malaria. Countless numbers of people in rice plantation environs died from diseases resulting from living and working in conditions of high humidity and standing water—considered prime breeding grounds for mosquitoes. Most planters and their families lived away from their plantations, especially between the months of May and November, when malaria was especially prevalent. Many argued that Africans were protected against malaria because they possessed the gene that causes sickle-cell, which provides substantial protection from malaria. The gene is not restricted to Africans, however, and not all Africans carry this gene. In the Sea Islands, sizable portions of the population of enslaved Africans remained vulnerable to malaria and died as a result of living in malaria-infested areas.

The historian William Dusinberre's explicit analysis of the child mortality rate on rice plantations serves to further temper portrayals of Jehossee as a business enterprise in which the owner's interests in the comfort and happiness of the workforce superseded the goal of generating wealth and profit. According to Dusinberre, "A conservative modern estimate suggests that a least 55 percent of the children born on nineteenth century rice plantations died by age fifteen" (1995, p. 80). In addition to malaria, other conditions (such as sunstroke, dysentery, cholera), escalated by overwork and the requirements of

African Americans Hoeing Rice, Early 1900s. The plantation system relied heavily on the labor, services, and skills of enslaved Africans and their descendents. THE LIBRARY OF CONGRESS.

standing in ankle deep mud and water during periods when the fields were flooded, contributed to the high number of deaths amongst Africans on rice plantations.

According to research conducted by the historian Edda Fields, the sole reliance on tidal-swamp rice production by planters in South Carolina proved counter to the broad range of strategies for producing rice and other agricultural products practiced by coastal rice planters in many West African societies. The reluctance of many planter families in West Africa to focus exclusively on swamp-rice production because of unhealthy conditions was a sentiment that was recognized by Sea Island planters, but only with respect to their own health and safety.

An analysis of rice production on Jehossee plantation provides a specific example of plantation-owner dependence on majority African communities to sustain plantation-based economies and lifestyles. In spite of a social order based on race that dictated their place as chattel—thus subjecting them to adverse environmental conditions, health disparities, and unequal treatment—enslaved Africans were a dominant force in rice plantation environments in terms of cultural knowledge, population size, and the scope and range of labor and services performed.

In rice-plantation environments, African autonomy was another salient characteristic. Nowhere is the evidence for both the interdependence between whites and blacks and the autonomy of enslaved Africans more evident than in the kitchen and food-provisioning practices exhibited throughout southern plantations, particularly on Sea Island rice plantations. Here, enslaved Africans not only prepared food for plantation owners and their families, they also proactively secured and prepared food for their own survival above and beyond what was appropriated to them. They often maintained supplementary garden plots; consumed lesser grade foods or foods deemed less marketable by plantation owners; hunted local game; fished; and gathered wild plants for food and medicine. Solon Robinson observed that, in addition to rations, Africans on Jehossee Island grew and ate a great many vegetables; caught large numbers of fish, oysters, and crabs; and raised pigs and poultry (primarily to sell). Edmund Ruffin, another visitor to Jehossee Island in 1843, described the place where Africans resided as a "negro village," noting that each house had a garden ground attached. This type of culinary initiative stands in stark contrast to the notion that enslaved Africans waited to be fed and survived only on plantation-provided rations.

It can thus be seen that while Africans may have been assigned the status of "slave" on plantations in America, a closer look at plantation life and management reveals something far different. It shows instead how Europeans and Africans were economically and culturally connected within plantation environments around cash-crop production. In addition, it shows how crops such as rice served not only as a cash crops for European planters, but also as a means of securing cultural autonomy for Africans living in plantation environments. Highlighting the dependence of plantation owners on African skill, labor, and services for their economic autonomy is important because it destabilizes fixed notions about race in plantation spaces.

BIBLIOGRAPHY

Allston, Robert F. W. 1843. *Memoir of the Introduction and Planting of Rice in South Carolina: A Description of the Grass.* Charleston, SC: Miller and Browne.

Ball, Edward. 1998. *Slaves in the Family.* New York: Farrar, Straus and Giroux.

Berlin, Ira. 1998. *Many Thousands Gone: The First Two Centuries of Slavery in North America.* Cambridge, MA: Belknap Press of Harvard University Press.

———, and Philip D. Morgan, eds. 1993. *Cultivation and Culture: Labor and the Shaping of Slave Life in the Americas.* Charlottesville: University Press of Virginia.

Bieber, Judy, ed. 1997. *Plantation Societies in the Era of European Expansion,* Vol. 18. Brookfield, VT: Variorum.

Carney, Judith A. 2001. *Black Rice: The African Origins of Rice Cultivation in the Americas.* Cambridge, MA: Harvard University Press.

Dusinberre, William. 1995. *Them Dark Days: Slavery in the American Rice Swamps.* New York: Oxford University Press.

Fields, Edda L. 2001. "Rice Farmers in the Rio Nunez Region: A Social History of Agricultural Technology and Identity in

Coastal Guinea, ca. 2000 BCE to 1880 CE." Ph.D. diss., University of Pennsylvania, College Station.

Kellar, Herbert A., ed. 1936. *Solon Robinson, Pioneer and Agriculturist: Selected Writings*, Vol. II. Indianapolis: Indiana Historical Bureau. Reprint, New York: Da Capo Press, 1968.

Littlefield, Daniel C. 1981. *Rice and Slaves: Ethnicity and the Slave Trade in Colonial South Carolina.* Baton Rouge: Louisiana State University Press.

Mintz, Sidney W. 1985. *Sweetness and Power: The Place of Sugar in Modern History.* New York: Penguin Books.

Stewart, Mart A. 1996. *"What Nature Suffers to Groe": Life, Labor, and Landscape on the Georgia Coast, 1680–1920.* Athens: University of Georgia Press.

Thompson, Edgar T. 1975. *Plantation Societies, Race Relations, and the South: The Regimentation of Populations. Selected Papers of Edgar T. Thompson.* Durham, NC: Duke University Press.

Trouillot, Michel-Rolph. 1998. "Culture on the Edges: Creolization in the Plantation Context." *Plantation Society in the Americas* 5 (1): 8–28.

Antoinette T. Jackson

"PLAYING INDIAN"

"Playing Indian," the performance of American Indian identities by non-Indians, has likely been going on since the first contact between people of European descent and indigenous people of North America. It encompasses a wide variety of practices and behaviors, including Halloween costumes, elementary school Thanksgiving pageants, athletic team mascots, the Boston Tea Party, ethnography, and New Age spiritualism. When people play Indian, they put into motion their assumptions about what constitutes "Indianness." They enact racial tropes or stereotypes of Indianness. Although the most common usage of the term "playing Indian" is in reference to white performance of Indianness, even indigenous Americans can be said to play Indian by acting out non-Indian assumptions, stereotypes, and fantasies of Indianness.

Playing Indian reduces Indianness to a set of racial stereotypes at the expense of a dynamic political and cultural identity derived from the unique powers of tribal sovereignty. Despite this objectionable promotion of racial caricatures and stereotypes, playing Indian is arguably the most widespread form of racial mimicry in the world. People the world over immediately recognize a small set of powerful images—feathered headdresses, breach cloth, beaded moccasins, or bows and arrows—as standing for Indianness. Decontextualized from their origins in the Native communities of the North American plains, these symbols metonymically stand in for American Indians as a whole. These are also the key components of the most familiar form of playing Indian: dressing up. School and professional sports team mascots and all the "team spirit" rituals that accompany them—cheers, music, and live action performers—mobilize notions of Indianness to evoke strength and courage, qualities associated with the noble savage, or ruthlessness, a quality associated with the barbaric savage. In so doing, they reinforce the common racial stereotypes of Native savagery and continually reenact essentialized assumptions about Indians.

Playing Indian has been used as a strategy to gain and maintain Euro-American social and political power. Two of the most significant scholarly works on playing Indian—Philip J. Deloria's *Playing Indian* (1998) and Shari M. Huhndorf's *Going Native* (2001)— have found that playing Indian revolves around two sociopolitical tensions in American life: the need to prove the legitimacy of American nationhood and recurring anxieties over the meaning of modernity and its impact on American culture. Perhaps one of the most famous American historic examples of playing Indian is the Boston Tea Party of 1773. Protesting British colonial trade and taxation policies, American patriots dressed as Mohawk Indians stormed a ship in Boston Harbor and threw its cargo of tea overboard. In other instances, Revolutionary-era Americans protested British rule by taking on Indian personas through their own fabricated versions of Indian clothing, chants, and even names. Doing so dramatized white American colonists' claims that they—not the British—were the rightful governors of the land. During the early national era agrarian protesters played staking claims to rural land against landlords and state governments. For example, in the Whiskey Rebellion of the early 1790s rural farmers called on the same traditions of playing Indian used against the British to rally against the incipient federal government's newly exerted taxation, rent, and land distribution policies.

Decades later white fraternal organizations based around the performance of Indianness, such as Tammany Societies, flourished across New England. Members took "Indian" names, wore face paint and Indian clothes, performed rituals and held public parades and ceremonies to honor a purported Delaware Indian leader (named Tamenend) as a patron saint of America. After the War of 1812, Tammany Societies began to be replaced by organizations like the Improved Order of Red Men that sprouted up throughout the Eastern seaboard. These Indian-themed versions of Masonic organizations allowed the growing middle class to act out elaborate rituals of playing Indian. Red Men organizations claimed to harbor secret knowledge of supposed Native rituals and were structured around hierarchies of Indian-titled leadership. The influence of these Indian-themed fraternal organizations continued late into the antebellum years. The historian and proto-ethnographer Lewis Henry Morgan and the poet Henry Rowe Schoolcraft researched Native American customs and lore in an attempt to recreate and reenact this knowledge for each other in full "traditional" regalia at monthly campfire meetings in New York forests. Morgan's New Confederacy of the Iroquois allowed antebellum American cultural arbiters such as historians, writers, poets, and artists to play Indian as a way of forging a national-cultural identity. All of these forms of playing Indian provided white American men with esoteric connections to Native culture and the concept of aboriginality on which they could stake political claims to super-patriotism and position themselves as the legitimate and natural inheritors of Native American customs, traditions, and, most importantly, land.

Playing Indian resurfaced at the end of the nineteenth century and persisted into the twentieth. Americans were growing anxious about sociocultural changes brought about by modernity, including social alienation, urbanization, and the putative "closing" of the Western frontier. Thus "getting back to nature" by playing Indian functioned as a kind of remedy for the social decay of the urban center and the loss of clear notions of masculinity. Boy Scouts, Camp Fire Girls, and a host of Indian-themed summer camps provided opportunities for upper- and middle-class youth to purify themselves and build their moral character through enacting supposed Indianness. These years also saw significant growth in the field of American anthropology as ethnographers "went Native" through living in Native communities as participant-observers. This ethnographic form of playing Indian was popularized through ethnographic texts, exhibits, photography, and cinema seen in museums and at World's Fairs and through the works of Frank Hamilton Cushing, Edward Curtis, and Robert Flaherty. These recreational and ethnographic enactments of Indianness coincided with and were connected to the rise of the popular notion of Indians as a "vanishing race" doomed to extinction by modernity.

After World War II playing Indian became less about reenacting a disappearing racial identity and more about individual efforts to recover a sense of authenticity. This kind of playing Indian is exemplified by hobbyists, white Americans who participate alongside Native performers in powwows and who are highly devoted to detail-oriented performances of Indianness. Hobbyists spend a great deal of time and energy on creating their dance regalia to produce an authentic performance that aims to be indistinguishable from Native powwow dancers. This quest for personal distinction can be interpreted as a response to the conformist, consumer culture of postwar America. Indianness provided an authenticity and individuality lacking in the sameness of postwar, mass-culture America.

Adherents of the counterculture and New Age spiritualism movements of the 1960s through the present have followed in the footsteps of hobbyists and antimodernists of the early twentieth century. Although perhaps not with as much attention to detail, they have appropriated Native culture and tradition to critique the purported greed, pollution, and spiritual vapidity of modern America. Though often involving dress and paraphernalia, this kind of playing Indian has been more concerned with channeling a supposed Native ethos that was proverbially at one with nature and that placed communal welfare over individual wealth. Many indigenous communities do hold such values, but counterculturalists and New Agers disregard specific tribal histories and traditions and instead combine a hodge-podge of tribal customs. New Agers often make vague claims to Indian ancestry or suggest that all cultures ought to be open to anyone desiring to learn about and practice them. Many American Indians have strenuously rejected New Agers' Indian play as a form of cultural appropriation or ethnic fraud. For them, non-Indians' financial profiteering from playing Indian through spiritual and self-help literature and seminars is especially objectionable.

Playing Indian inflicts damage on Native peoples because it reduces Indianness to a set of racialized tropes and stereotypes. This affects the way Native people, especially children, see themselves. This act of racial formation also overrides the self-determining cultural and political identities of tribal communities, the foundations of tribal sovereignty. The strongest argument for and substantiation of American Indian self-determination and land rights is not based on a collective racial identity, fabricated by phenomena such as playing Indian, but the historical fact of inherent sovereignty and self-governance that Indian communities possessed long before colonization of the Americas.

BIBLIOGRAPHY

Berkhofer, Robert F., Jr. 1978. *The White Man's Indian: Images of the American Indian from Columbus to the Present.* New York: Knopf.

Deloria, Philip J. 1998. *Playing Indian.* New Haven, CT: Yale University Press.

Dilworth, Leah. 1996. *Imagining Indians in the Southwest: Persistent Visions of a Primitive Past.* Washington, DC: Smithsonian Institution Press.

Huhndorf, Shari M. 2001. *Going Native: Indians in the American Cultural Imagination.* Ithaca, NY: Cornell University Press.

King, Thomas. 2004. "Let Me Entertain You." In *The Truth About Stories: A Native Narrative,* 61–90. Minneapolis: University of Minnesota Press.

Mechling, Jay. 1980. "'Playing Indian' and the Search for Authenticity in Modern White America." In *Prospects,* Vol. 5, edited by Jack Salzman, 17–34. New York: Burt Franklin.

Powers, William K. 1988. "The Indian Hobbyist Movement in North America." In *Handbook on North American Indians,* Vol. 4: *History of Indian-White Relations,* edited by Wilcomb

Washburn, 557–561. Washington, DC: Smithsonian Institution Press.

Taylor, Alan. 1990. *Liberty, Men, and Great Proprietors: The Revolutionary Settlement on the Maine Frontier, 1760–1820.* Chapel Hill: University of North Carolina Press for the Institute of Early American History and Culture.

David Kamper

PLESSY V. FERGUSON

In the 1896 case of *Plessy v. Ferguson*, the United States Supreme Court upheld the constitutionality of a Louisiana law that required railroads to provide "equal but separate accommodations for the white and colored races." The case enshrined the constitutional validity of racial segregation laws under what came to be known as the "separate but equal doctrine," and it permitted the proliferation of mandatory segregation laws across the American South during the late nineteenth and early twentieth centuries. These laws formed a pervasive web of racial rules, known as Jim Crow laws, requiring the separation of the races in public accommodations, schools, hospitals, and even cemeteries. Although most Jim Crow laws called for equal facilities, public accommodations and services under the segregated system were glaringly unequal. In addition, laws requiring racial segregation were extended in many jurisdictions to include not only African Americans and "people of color," but also Native Americans and people of Chinese or Mexican descent.

The separate but equal doctrine operated to enforce a racial caste system that subordinated and disenfranchised nonwhites, denied them basic public services, isolated them in poor neighborhoods and schools, and limited their employment and educational opportunities. In the 1920s the *Plessy* case became the target of a litigation campaign by the National Association for the Advancement of Colored People (NAACP), which, after many years of litigation, succeeded in overturning the separate but equal doctrine in the landmark 1954 case of *Brown v. Board of Education.*

HISTORICAL BACKGROUND

Before the American Civil War, racial distinctions existed in the law of virtually every state and territory of the United States. These laws prohibited or limited the migration of slaves and free Negroes, excluded Negroes from public accommodations, prohibited intermarriage, and imposed various civil disabilities on nonwhites. The codes governing the behavior of slaves in the South were particularly onerous, for they prohibited slaves from such activities as learning to read and write, carrying a weapon, or testifying in court. In the immediate aftermath of the Civil War, Southern legislatures—still controlled by members of the former Confederacy—enacted Black Codes that resurrected much of the prewar slave-control legislation. Radical Republicans in Congress saw the actions of the former Confederate leaders as a threat to the Union and reacted by enacting federal civil rights statutes and extending federal protection to the civil and political rights of the former slaves.

During this postwar period, known as Reconstruction, three amendments were added to the federal Constitution to achieve these goals. The Thirteenth Amendment formally abolished slavery and involuntary servitude, except as punishment for a crime. The Fourteenth Amendment extended federal and state citizenship to all persons born or naturalized in the United States and prohibited the states from enacting any law abridging the privileges and immunities of citizenship. It further declared that the states may not "deprive any person of life, liberty, or property, without due process of law" or deny any person "the equal protection of the laws." The Fifteenth Amendment promised that the right to vote would not be denied or abridged because of "race, color, or previous condition of servitude."

While federal troops occupied the South, former slaves voted in large numbers across the states of the former Confederacy and began to enjoy some level of political clout. Blacks served on juries, were elected to political office, and opened schools. In some areas a black middle class began to emerge and some public accommodations were desegregated. In 1877, however, when federal troops were withdrawn from the South following the Hayes-Tilden Compromise, the social and political position of blacks in Southern society began a long decline. White "Redeemers" regained control of Southern legislatures; the Ku Klux Klan enlarged its campaign of terror; the number of lynchings increased; whites used poll taxes, literacy tests, violence and fraud to prevent blacks from voting; and new racial segregation laws began to be passed.

In 1890, when the Louisiana legislature enacted a bill requiring the separation of the races in railroad travel, a group of black and mixed-race citizens in New Orleans determined to test the legislation in court. Led by prominent "persons of color" in the Creole community, notably Louis A. Martinet, they formed a Citizens' Committee and hired Albion Tourgée, a well-known white lawyer, judge, carpetbagger, and activist for civil rights, to begin planning an appropriate test case.

The test case was initiated on June 7, 1892, when Homer Plessy, an octoroon (a person of one-eighth Negro ancestry), bought a first-class ticket for a trip from New Orleans to Covington, Louisiana, on the East Louisiana Railroad. As arranged in advance, Plessy was arrested when he refused to be seated in the car reserved for the colored race. In the state court, Plessy admitted that he had refused to take the assigned seat, but he asserted that he could not

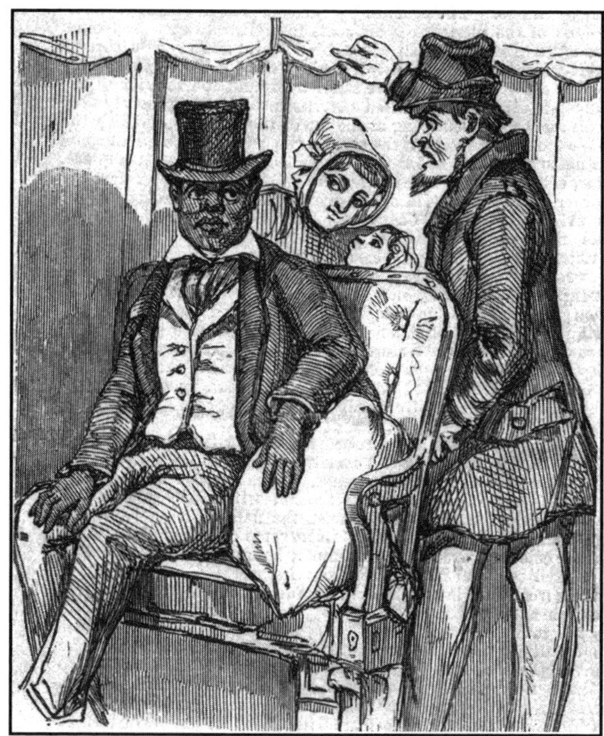

Expulsion from a Whites-Only Railway Car. *Homer Plessy was arrested after he refused to be seated in a train car reserved for African Americans.* PICTURE COLLECTION, THE BRANCH LIBRARIES, THE NEW YORK PUBLIC LIBRARY, ASTOR, LENOX AND TILDEN FOUNDATIONS.

be punished because the statute was unconstitutional. The Louisiana Supreme Court upheld the statute, and an appeal was taken to the U.S. Supreme Court.

THE MAJORITY DECISION

Before the Supreme Court, Plessy's lawyers argued that the Louisiana statute violated the Thirteenth Amendment to the Constitution because it was designed to degrade blacks and impose a badge of servitude on them. Further, they claimed that the statute violated the Fourteenth Amendment guarantee of due process, because any passenger wrongly identified as a colored passenger would be deprived of the status and reputation of being white, which were valuable property. They also argued that the statute violated the Fourteenth Amendment equal protection clause by restricting the personal right of citizens to freely enjoy all public privileges and by unjustly discriminating against one class of citizens.

In a seven-to-one ruling against Plessy, the Supreme Court rejected all of Plessy's arguments. Justice Henry Billings Brown, writing for the majority, found no violation of the Thirteenth Amendment because the statute "merely implies a legal distinction between the white and colored races" and has "no tendency to destroy the legal equality of the two races, or reestablish a state of involuntary servitude." Further, the statute presented no violation of the Fourteenth Amendment due process clause because any white man wrongly assigned to the colored coach could bring an action for damages against the railroad company. Most importantly, the statute did not violate the equal protection clause of the Fourteenth Amendment because it was a reasonable exercise of the state's police power to legislate for the public good, taking into account "the established usages, customs and traditions of the people."

In response to the argument that the separation of the races stamps the colored race with a badge of inferiority, Brown wrote, "If this be so, it is not by reason of anything found in the act, but solely because the colored race chooses to put that construction upon it." Finally, Brown rejected the idea that social prejudices may be overcome by legislation, saying, "If the two races are to meet upon terms of social equality, it must be the result of natural affinities, a mutual appreciation of each other's merits and a voluntary consent of individuals." Brown did not note that members of different races would face criminal penalties if their natural affinities inclined them to sit together on the train.

THE DISSENT

Justice John Marshall Harlan, a former slaveholder from Kentucky who became a Republican and a Union Army Colonel during the Civil War, wrote a lone dissenting opinion. For Harlan, the denial of equal civil rights to freed blacks in the South presented an affront to the federal power embodied in the Civil War Amendments, as well as a threat to the stability of the federal government. The states did not have the power, he asserted, to regulate the use of a public railroad by citizens on the basis of race. If a white man and black man chose to occupy the same public conveyance, he argued, it was their right to do so. The statute thus violated the personal liberty of members of both races.

Harlan rejected the majority's conclusion that the statute did not discriminate against either race because it applied equally to both, saying "Everyone knows that the statute in question had its origin in the purpose, not so much to exclude white persons from railroad cars occupied by blacks, as to exclude colored people from coaches occupied by or assigned to white persons." Harlan concluded that the law impermissibly stamps the colored race with a badge of inferiority. Although Harlan acknowledged the dominance of the white race in prestige, achievements, education, wealth, and power, he denied the authority of the legislature to draft laws that regulated the enjoyment of civil rights on the basis of race. "There is no caste here," he wrote, "Our Constitution is color-blind and neither knows nor tolerates classes among citizens." To permit the states to legislate based on race would ignore the fact that "the destinies of the two races, in this country, are indissolubly linked together," and it would allow the states "to plant the seeds of race hatred under the sanction of law." Harlan predicted what would happen if similar statutes were enacted across the nation:

> Slavery as an institution tolerated by law would, it is true, have disappeared from our country, but there would remain a power in the States, by sinister legislation, to interfere with the full enjoyment of the blessings of freedom; to regulate civil rights, common to all citizens, on the basis of race; and to place in a condition of legal inferiority a large body of American citizens, now constituting a part of the political community called the People of the United States.

Harlan's dissent accurately predicted the effect of judicial approval of mandatory segregation laws. Such laws proliferated in the wake of *Plessy* and played an important role in consigning people of color to a second-class version of American citizenship. Harlan's dissent also became important for its articulation of the concept of the color-blind Constitution. Legal color blindness, in the sense of the elimination of legal distinctions based on race, was a central goal of civil rights activists of the mid-twentieth century. Many believe that the ideal of color blindness still holds promise as a tool to be used in achieving racial equality.

On the other hand, the color-blind principle came to be used in the late twentieth century as a rallying cry for conservatives who sought to dismantle programs designed to remedy past discrimination, such as affirmative action programs or minority set-asides. Race-conscious measures designed to benefit historically disadvantaged racial groups are "color conscious" rather than "color blind." Thus, color blindness is presently viewed by many as a weapon in a battle against minority efforts to improve equality.

SEE ALSO *Color-Blind Racism.*

BIBLIOGRAPHY

Kluger, Richard. 1976. *Simple Justice: The History of Brown v. Board of Education and Black America's Struggle for Equality.* New York: Alfred A. Knopf.

Lofgren, Charles A. 1987. *The Plessy Case: A Legal-Historical Interpretation.* New York: Oxford University Press.

Stephenson, Gilbert Thomas. 1969 (1910). *Race Distinctions in American Law.* New York: Negro Universities Press.

Woodward, C. Vann. 1964. "The Case of the Louisiana Traveler." In *Quarrels That Have Shaped the Constitution,* edited by John A. Garraty. New York: Harper & Row.

Molly Townes O'Brien

PORNOGRAPHY

In the image-based society of the early twenty-first century, images of sexuality circulate widely in advertisements, movies, television, and music videos. Beyond these venues, pornography constitutes a prominent place where cultural notions of sexuality are most clearly articulated. Moreover, whether in mainstream movies and television or in pornography, images of sex never just portray sex, for they also construct representations that are based on collective ideologies of what constitutes both normal and deviant sexuality. James Snead, in his discussion of images of African Americans in white film, argues that "in all Hollywood film portrayals of blacks . . . the political is never far from the sexual" (Snead 1994, p. 8). Indeed, one of the ways in which whites demonize people of color is to define their sexuality as deviant, and thus in need of (white) policing and control.

From the image of the Asian woman as geisha to the black male as sexual savage, mainstream white representations have coded nonwhite sexuality as deviant, excessive, and a threat to the white social order. These images, while somewhat muted in mainstream Hollywood movies, are very much dominant in the pornography that is defined as "interracial" by the industry. While all pornography attempts to push the limits of what is acceptable sexual practice, representations of people of color operate within a regime of representation that defines them as "Other," and thus outside the realm of "normal" (white) humanity. There has been very little critique of these overtly racist images by academics studying pornography, suggesting that they have become so normalized that they now constitute common-sense assumptions regarding the sexuality of people of color.

DEFINITIONS OF PORNOGRAPHY

There is considerable academic debate concerning what constitutes pornography. Definitions are often political in nature, with pro-pornography writers such as Wendy McElroy defining pornography as "the explicit artistic depiction of men and/or women as sexual beings." (McElroy 1995, p. 43). However, antipornography scholars such as Catherine MacKinnon and Andrea Dworkin tend to take a more critical perspective, seeing pornography as material that sexualizes subordination through pictures and words. An example of such a definition that is widely accepted within antipornography feminist literature is that of Helen Longino, who defines pornography as any material that "represents or describes sexual behavior that is degrading or abusive to one or more of the participants in such as way as to endorse the degradation" (Longino 1980, p. 29). While Longino points out that in most cases it is women and children who are the ones degraded, men must also be included here, because they are the ones degraded in gay pornography.

While debating definitions may be an interesting academic practice, the reality is that there is a massive global pornography industry that generates estimated revenues of more than $57 billion dollars per year.

Those working in the pornography industry know what constitutes pornography, for as Gail Dines and Robert Jensen document in "The Content of Mass-Marketed Pornography" (1998), its products are highly formulaic and genre bound. A useful working definition for any discussion that attempts to map out specific genres of pornography is thus those products (in print or image form) produced, distributed, and sold with the aim of sexually arousing the viewer.

IMAGES OF RACE IN PORNOGRAPHY

The two largest moneymakers for the pornography industry are feature films and Gonzo movies. The former attempts to mirror mainstream movies. Thus, they include some story line and plot, and they employ a high degree of technological sophistication. Gonzo pornography, on the other hand, strings together a number of sex scenes devoid of a story line. These tend to look quickly made and amateurish and consist of body-punishing, often violent, sex acts where the women are penetrated (orally, anally and vaginally) by a number of men at the same time. The aim here is to facilitate masturbation in the male user as quickly and economically as possible. People of color dominate in Gonzo, which has none of the status or chic associated with the up-market features produced by companies such as Vivid Video. Indeed, in the emerging world of celebratory pornography, it is white women who are fronted by the industry, with regular appearances on syndicated television shows such as *The Howard Stern Show* and photo shoots in mainstream, best-selling men's magazines such as *FHM* and *Maxim*.

The Gonzo pornography has a sub-category called interracial. Although there are films with Asian and Latina women and men, much of the focus is on sex between black men and white women. Films in this subgenre typically trade in the long-standing racist myth that black men are more animalistic, sexually violent, and less evolved than white men. A central part of this myth is that black men use their sexual savagery mainly against white women, who are coded as "sluts." One recurring sentence on many interracial pornography sites is "once they go black, they never go back," thus suggesting that black men are sexually more enticing and exciting because of their lack of restraint.

This visual depiction of black men is actually part of a much larger regime of racial representation that—beginning with *The Birth of a Nation* (1915) and continuing with pornography—makes the black male's supposed sexual misconduct a metaphor for the inferior nature of the black race as a whole. *Hustler*, the most widely distributed hard-core pornography magazine in the world, regularly depicts caricatured black men as having oversized genitalia but undersized heads, thus signifying mental inferiority. They are frequently shown as pimps with gold chains, expensive cars, and a stable of black and white women. When not pimping women to make money, the black man is often shown cheating the government by cashing fraudulent welfare checks. The *Hustler* images clearly speak to the dominant racist ideology that black men are criminals and, if left unchecked, will financially drain law-abiding whites.

Representations of black women in pornography also draw on broader racist ideologies embedded in the dominant culture. Black women are repeatedly referred to as ebony whores, sluts from the ghetto, and bad black "sistas." They are defined as being less attractive than white women, and therefore desperate for sex with anything or anyone. One site, for example, focuses on the supposed inability of black women to dress in a way that attracts men.

In contrast to black women, Asian women in pornography are constructed as the feminine ideal. Referred to as sweet, cute, shy, and vulnerable, these images trade on the long-standing stereotype of Asian women as submissive and coy. A magazine called *Asian Beauties* tells the readers that these "exotic beauties" are "born and bred with the skills to please a man." Many Internet pornography sites make veiled reference to trafficking in women, but rather than depicting this as sexual slavery, the men are told that "she was imported for your delight." Totally commodified, these women cease to have any humanity but are instead goods to be traded internationally for white men.

Interestingly, Asian men rarely appear in straight pornography but are a major commodity in gay pornography. Also referred to as submissive, shy, and in many cases young, these men are offered up to a presumably white gay male audience. Black men in gay pornography, however, are represented in the same way that they are in straight pornography. Thus, black men are hypermasculinized in gay pornography, while Asian men are feminized. Commenting on the racialized hierarchy in gay pornography, Christopher Kendall notes that such imagery "justifies through sex the types of attitudes and inequalities that make racism and sexism powerful and interconnected realities" (Kendall 2004, p. 60).

Indeed, all pornography uses sex as a vehicle to transmit messages about the legitimacy of racism and sexism. Hiding behind the facade of fantasy and harmless fun, pornography delivers reactionary racist stereotypes that would be considered unacceptable were they in any other types of mass-produced media. However, the power of pornography is that these messages have a long history and still resonate, on a subtextual level, with the white supremacist ideologies that continue to inform policies that economically, politically, and socially discriminate against people of color.

SEE ALSO *Feminism and Race; Violence against Women and Girls.*

BIBLIOGRAPHY

Dines, Gail, and Robert Jensen. 1998. "The Content of Mass-Marketed Pornography." In *Pornography: The Production and Consumption of Inequality*, by Gail Dines, Robert Jensen, and Ann Russo, 65–100. New York: Routledge.

Dworkin, Andrea, and Catherine MacKinnon. 1988. *Pornography and Civil Rights: A New Day for Women's Equality*. Minneapolis, MN: Organizing against Pornography.

Kendall, Christopher. 2004. *Gay Male Pornography: An Issue of Sex Discrimination*. Vancouver: University of British Columbia Press.

Logino, Helen. 1980. "Pornography, Oppression, and Freedom: A Closer Look." In *Take Back the Night: Women on Pornography*, edited by Laura Lederer, 26–41. New York: Bantam Books.

McElroy, Wendy. 1995. *XXX: A Woman's Right to Pornography*. New York: St. Martin's Press.

Snead, James. 1994. *White Screens, Black Images: Hollywood from the Dark Side*. New York: Routledge.

Wiegman, Robyn. 1993. "Feminism, 'The Boyz,' and Other Matters Regarding the Male." In *Screening the Male: Exploring Masculinities in Hollywood Cinema*, edited by Steven Cohan and Ina Rae Hark, 173–193. New York: Routledge.

Gail Dines

PORRES, MARTIN DE, ST.

1579–1639

The patron saint of racial and social justice, Martin de Porres was born on December 9, 1579, in Lima, Peru. He was the illegitimate son of a Spanish nobleman and a young, freed black slave named Ana Velasquez. Because of Martin's dark skin, his father refused to acknowledge him as his own and left Martin and his mother alone. Without the support of his father, Martin and his mother lived in terrible poverty.

As a young boy, Martin became a servant in the Dominican priory and would beg money from the rich citizens of Lima in support of the poor and the sick. Eventually, the Dominican superiors accepted Martin as a brother of the order, ignoring the rule that disallowed a black person from taking vows and receiving the Dominican habit.

As a Dominican brother, Martin dedicated himself to working on behalf of the impoverished and oppressed. For the children living in the slums, he established an orphanage, a children's hospital, and a school where they could receive a complete education or learn a trade. He oversaw the Dominicans' infirmary and was known for his tender medical care of those who were ill or suffering. He provided food, clothing, and medicine for the most destitute of Lima's citizens, and he was especially concerned for those who were oppressed because they were black or of mixed-race ancestry. Drawing on his own experience of racial prejudice and discrimination, and on his commitment to the "poor, rejected Christ," his actions on behalf of African slaves and the poor who lived in the slums of Lima demonstrated his deep commitment to racial and social justice.

Martin's kindness toward the impoverished masses and his actions on behalf of justice sometimes led to difficulties between himself and his superiors in the Dominican order. He literally brought the struggles of the poor right into the center of the order's life—often by giving hospitality to the homeless and hungry at the priory itself, sharing his own living space, or even giving up his bed for a sick person who had no place else to turn. For Martin, this practice of solidarity with those who suffered because of economic or racial injustice was an extremely important value of the religious life. All of Martin's skills were placed at the service of those who were oppressed and marginalized, and he never ceased in promoting a world where poverty and prejudice were no more.

Martin died from a fever on November 3, 1639, at the age of sixty. His journey toward sainthood began when he was beatified by the Roman Catholic Church in 1873. He was officially named a saint on May 16, 1962, by Pope John XXIII. He was the first black American saint and is the patron saint of racial and social justice. Many Catholics in the Americas continue to draw inspiration from his life in their own work on behalf of racial reconciliation.

BIBLIOGRAPHY

Ellsberg, Robert. 1997. *All Saints: Daily Reflections on Saints, Prophets, and Witnesses for Our Time*. New York: Crossroads.

García-Rivera, Alejandro. 1995. *St. Martin de Porres: The "Little Stories" and the Semiotics of Culture*. Maryknoll, NY: Orbis Books.

John J. Zokovitch III

POVERTY

The term *poverty* has many different and complex meanings. Similar terms exist in various languages, but they often connote different and particular conditions of landlessness, destitution, deprivation, and inequality. In the Anglo-Saxon world, the usage of the term can be traced to the Middle Ages, though its emergence as a concept is more appropriately located in the writings of Thomas Malthus (1766–1834), specifically in an evolutionary theory that interpreted poverty and famine as natural outcomes of population growth.

INDUSTRIALIZATION AND POVERTY

In contemporary times, the concept of poverty as a social problem, and particularly as a problem to be addressed by the modern state, has its origins in the late nineteenth century. In England, the long process of "enclosures," which started in the thirteenth century and displaced and dispossessed English peasants through the privatization of agrarian and common lands, set the stage for the Industrial Revolution by freeing up labor and concentrating capital. But the system of industrial capitalism was to generate intense forms of poverty. England's rural poor made their way to cities such as London and Manchester, where they clustered in slums and worked under conditions akin to sweatshops. These conditions made poverty more visible than it had been previously, and social reformers and urban planners set about to create some of the first mappings and categorizations of poverty, sorting the poor into "deserving" and "undeserving" categories. There was charity for the former group and stiff penalties, in the form of poorhouses and vagrancy laws, for the latter. The French philosopher Michel Foucault (1926-1984) later theorized that such institutions of "discipline and punish" are the foundations of modern power.

In England, in France, and elsewhere in Europe, there was also concern that the urban poor would organize in rebellion and revolution, as they did in Paris in 1798, and again in 1848, and as had the rural poor in various peasant revolts. The Second Empire of France thus sought to break up urban enclaves of poverty, vesting Baron Georges-Eugène Haussmann with the powers of urban modernization, including the capacity to demolish the slums of Paris and displace the poor to scattered peripheries of the city. Such techniques of poverty management, both in England and France, were precursors to, and paradigms of, twentieth-century sociospatial control.

RACISM AND POVERTY IN THE UNITED STATES

American cities were also convulsed with the visible poverty of industrial capitalism. These cities had large immigrant populations, initially from Europe and then from other parts of the world. The concern with poverty was thus inevitably a concern about racial and ethnic differences. The social reform efforts of the late nineteenth century, such as the settlement houses, intended to assimilate the immigrant into an American way of life. However, these liberal tendencies did not apply to two social groups that were seen as the racial Other. On the West Coast, Chinese laborers were building the infrastructure that was to make the settlement of the American frontier possible. However, by the early twentieth century, the Chinese were seen as a threat. Racist cartoons depicted the "Chinaman" as an evil and alien figure. Legal mechanisms, such as the Chinese Exclusion Act of 1882, restricted the ability of Chinese workers to bring their families to America. Urban planning codes made it impossible for the Chinese to rent or own property in any part of the city other than Chinatown, which became a space of quarantine and control.

On the other side of America, large numbers of black families were making their way from the Deep South to the factories of the Northeast and Midwest. This Great Migration made visible the failure of post-Civil War Reconstruction. Despite the formal end of slavery, the American South was a racialized space marked by segregation, violence, and lynchings. But in the cities of the North, black Americans were to find other forms of state-tolerated, even state-sponsored, segregation. These included racially restrictive covenants that protected white neighborhoods in the name of property values; redlining policies that devalued property in black neighborhoods; and segregated public housing that, when integrated, saw massive white flight and a concentration of poor black families. This was in fact an "American apartheid" (Massey and Denton 1998).

In the American context, this racialized experience of poverty has been explained in various ways. In the 1920s, the Chicago School of urban sociology put forth a conceptual model of American cities as ecological zones of social and spatial mobility (Park, Burgess, and McKenzie 1925). This liberal interpretation envisioned the city as a spatial equilibrium where all social groups could be fully accommodated. The political scientist Edward Banfield was to later claim that the explanation for ghettoization and segregation of black Americans lay in the fact that black Americans had simply arrived late to the city, and were thus unable to access jobs and neighborhoods in the same way as European immigrants. Poverty, in other words, had nothing to do with structural racism, but was instead a historical idiosyncrasy. More important, Banfield argued that black Americans did not want to leave their racial enclaves: "there was nothing to stop them from doing so," he famously argued, concluding the chapter "Race: thinking may make it so" (Banfield 1974). Other scholarship, of course, such as the pathbreaking work of St. Clair Drake and Horace Cayton (1945), had already demonstrated why the argument "there was nothing to stop them from doing so" could not have been further from reality. Drake and Cayton delineated a "Black

Metropolis," a stubborn and persistent spatial concentration of racialized poverty in the heart of Chicago. But Banfield's work proved influential, reinforcing themes of a "culture of poverty." Liberal policymakers such as Daniel Patrick Moynihan (1965) argued that black poverty could be partly explained by a tangle of pathologies, including a distinctive matriarchal family structure. Culture-of-poverty arguments have even made their way into the work of the eminent African-American sociologist William Julius Wilson. In his famous research on the American underclass, Wilson noted that the economic restructuring of the 1970s sharply worsened the conditions of black Americans. Work disappeared from the ghetto and, in a "spatial mismatch," new jobs existed far away, often in the suburbs. He notes that with the civil rights movement, as restrictive covenants and redlining were struck down, black middle-class families did manage to leave the ghetto, but they left behind an underclass mired in a culture of poverty. These liberal frameworks of poverty have faced scathing criticism in the work of Loïc Wacquant. In an essay titled "Three Pernicious Premises in the Study of the American Ghetto" (1997), Wacquant insists that to state that poverty creates the ghetto is to reverse causation. Instead, the ghetto is a space created through the institutional mechanisms of ethnoracial closure and control, and such forms of institutionalized racism create poverty.

THE EFFECTS OF COLONIALISM

It is, of course, not enough to understand poverty, and its racial dimensions, solely in the Euro-American context. Poverty, in modern times, is inextricably located within structures of colonialism and imperialism. Such forms of colonialism include colonies of settlement that destroyed and wiped out indigenous populations, as in the settlement of the American frontier. They also include colonies of rule, where European powers established rule over colonized populations and lands, as the British did in India or the French did in North Africa. Using the world-systems perspective of theorists such as Immanuel Wallerstein (b. 1930), poverty can therefore be understood as a structural feature of the global extraction of resources. This unequal exchange is expressed as a core-periphery relationship, where colonizing (core) countries exploit colonized (periphery) countries. The core-periphery relationship is replicated at various scales—within the periphery, the primate city (one that is more than two times as large as others in a nation) exploits the countryside, and within cities the formal sector exploits the informal sector. Such a condition is often described as "dependency" or the "dependent city," a space where poverty is determined not only through internal mechanisms but also through the extractive and exploitative nature of global linkages (Cardoso and Faletto 1978).

While colonialism formally ended in much of the world in the mid-twentieth century, dependency theorists argue that the core-periphery structure persists through new institutions of international development, such as the World Bank and International Monetary Fund (IMF). While these institutions claim to enable economic growth, stabilize international financial markets, and alleviate poverty, their critics see them as instruments of "neocolonialism" (Escobar 1995). The World Bank stands accused of the widespread displacement and dispossession of vulnerable social groups in the name of development and modernization. The International Monetary Fund is seen to be responsible for severe austerity policies that have sharply restricted the ability of nation-states to maintain social safety nets or subsidize basic consumption. Various global poverty campaigns, such as Jubilee 2000 and Make Poverty History (2005), have called for an overhaul of these institutions and pushed for debt relief for formerly colonized countries.

Colonialism, or neocolonialism, is much more than the extraction of material resources, of course. It is also a racial ideology that claims a "mission of civilization" as a "white man's burden" (Fanon 1952). In the late nineteenth century, as London and Paris were being reformed and modernized, colonial cities such as Algiers and Calcutta were being managed and rationalized by colonial administrators. Colonial cities were often divided into "white town" and "black town," with natives cordoned and quarantined in the black town in a manner reminiscent of the slums and ghettos of Europe and America. This "dual city" also emerged under conditions of semicolonialism in cities such as Cairo and Mexico City, which were formally independent but remained within the sphere of control and authority of European powers. Here, native elites sought to enclose and contain the urban poor, and in some instances, as in Mexico City, they did so to enforce complex hierarchies of whiteness and color. Colonialism also returned "home" to shape ideologies of race. As analyzed in the seminal work of Edward Said (1977), Europe produced the "Orient" through military conquest and economic rule as well as through discourse—through the power to create an image and declare it to be reality. Such forms of "Orientalism" were applied to the colonized Other, but they were also applied to the urban poor in Euro-American cities. Jacob Riis, in his passionate documentation of urban poverty in New York in the 1890s, presented the poor as the "other half," and designated poor street children as "street Arabs." Wacquant, therefore, labels more recent instances of American ghetto poverty as the "new urban Orientalism." Indeed, American public debates about the "Latino metropolis" (i.e., about large numbers of Latino immigrants in U.S. cities), has taken a racist turn. Much like Banfield's earlier arguments, Samuel Huntington argued in 2004 that

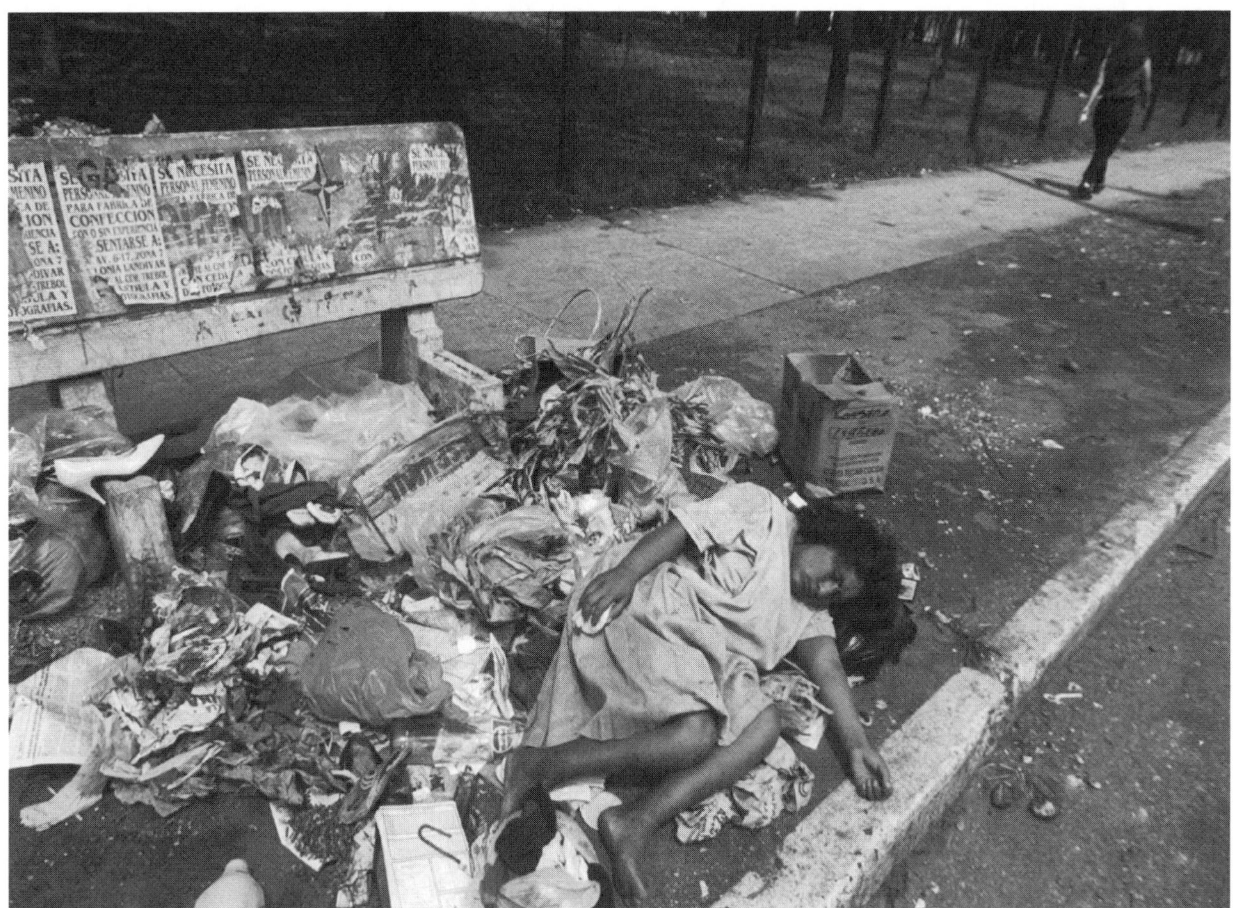

Poverty in Guatemala. *A homeless woman sleeps on the street in Guatemala. Approximately 80 percent of the population in the former Spanish colony lives in poverty.* AP IMAGES.

American culture is under threat from Latinos and their alleged enclave mentality. Similar racial tensions have erupted in France, where the failure of postcolonial integration and assimilation has become evident in the joblessness and frustration of North African immigrants.

THIRD WORLD POVERTY

While the Euro-American debates about poverty remain marked by racial anxieties, the "Third World" poverty debates have partly moved on. The late 1970s witnessed an important paradigm shift in the study of poverty in the Global South. Social scientists such as Janice Perlman undermined the "myth of marginality" (1976) and drew attention to the ways in which the urban poor create their own informal economies, urban settlements, and forms of social organization. In the important theoretical work of Manuel Castells (1983), these ideas were formalized as a theory of urban social movements. In the early twenty-first century, there is a vast body of research that indicates the tactics, quiet encroachments, and negotiations through which the urban poor carve out spaces of livelihood in the cities of the Global South (Roy 2003). Such work restores agency to the urban poor and presents an important challenge to "culture of poverty" arguments, while also remaining acutely aware of the structural exploitations and vulnerabilities of poverty. Third World poverty has also been presented in rather romanticized ways. In *The Mystery of Capital* (2000), for example, Hernando de Soto celebrates the poor as heroic entrepreneurs. Such ideas are gaining popularity because of their resonance with neoliberalism, which is the practice and ideology of privatization. Taking hold in the 1980s, neoliberalism has crucial implications for poverty and inequality. Neoliberal practices, such as the dismantling of the welfare state, often deepen poverty. Neoliberal ideology legitimizes such action by making a case against dependency on state welfare and by making a case for the work ethic and family ethic, tropes that are inevitably racialized. As an urban process, neoliberalism also involves an engagement with the inner city. In the 1950s and 1960s, the slums and ghettos of American cities were demolished to make way for state-led urban development. This was reminiscent of late nineteenth-century Haussmann-led modernization, but such forms of urban renewal also came to be known as "Negro removal." In the 1980s and 1990s, a second round of urban renewal unfolded. This was a more privatized process of gentrification that scripted the inner city as a new urban frontier of elite consumption and leisure. As covenants and redlining once protected prosperous neighborhoods, so walls and gates and paramilitary forces have come to protect the high-end enclaves of cities around the world. Neoliberal enclave urbanism is made possible through new and renewed forms of displacement and dispossession. These evictions can be understood as part of the long genealogy of colonialism and capitalism, and particularly of their mechanisms of primitive accumulation (Harvey 2005). Race, as a practice and ideology, is an integral part of such accumulation.

SEE ALSO *Brazilian Racial Formations; Capitalism; Children, Racial Disparities and Status of; Cuban Racial Formations; Education, Racial Disparities; Haitian Racial Formations; Health Care Gap; HIV and AIDS; Medical Racism; South African Racial Formations; United Kingdom Racial Formations; Violence against Women and Girls.*

BIBLIOGRAPHY

Banfield, Edward. 1974. *The Unheavenly City Revisited.* Boston: Little, Brown.

Caldeira, Teresa. 2000. *City of Walls: Crime, Citizenship and Segregation in Saõ Paulo.* Berkeley: University of California Press.

Cardoso, Fernando Henrique, and Enzo Faletto. 1979. *Dependency and Development in Latin America.* Berkeley: University of California Press.

Castells, Manuel. 1983. *The City and the Grassroots: A Cross-Cultural Theory of Urban Social Movements.* Berkeley: University of California Press.

Davis, Mike. 1990. *City of Quartz: Excavating the Future in Los Angeles.* London: Verso.

De Soto, Hernando. 2000. *The Mystery of Capital: Why Capitalism Triumphs in the West and Fails Everywhere Else.* New York: Basic Books.

Drake, St. Clair, and Horace Cayton. 1945. *Black Metropolis: A Study of Negro Life in a Northern City.* New York: Harcourt, Brace & World.

Escobar, Arturo. 1995. *Encountering Development: The Making and Unmaking of the Third World.* Princeton, NJ: Princeton University Press.

Fanon, Frantz. 1952. *Black Skin, White Masks.* New York: Grove Press.

Foucault, Michel. 1977. *Discipline and Punish: The Birth of the Prison.* Translated by Alan Sheridan. New York: Vintage Books.

Harvey, David. 2005. *The New Imperialism.* Oxford: Oxford University Press.

Huntington, Samuel. 2004. *Who Are We? The Challenges to America's National Identity.* New York: Simon & Schuster.

Malthus, Thomas. 1798. *An Essay on the Principle of Population.* London: J. Johnson.

Massey, Douglas, and Nancy Denton. 1993. *American Apartheid: Segregation and the Making of the Underclass.* Cambridge, MA: Harvard University Press.

Moynihan, Daniel Patrick. 1965. *The Negro Family: The Case for National Action.* Washington, DC: United States Department of Labor.

Park, Robert, Ernest W. Burgess, and Roderick D. McKenzie. 1925. *The City.* Chicago: University of Chicago Press.

Perlman, Janice, 1976. *The Myth of Marginality: Urban Poverty and Politics in Rio de Janeiro.* Berkeley: University of California Press.

Riis, Jacob. 1890. *How the Other Half Lives.* New York: Charles Scribner's Sons.

Roy, Ananya. 2003. *City Requiem, Calcutta: Gender and the Politics of Poverty.* Minneapolis: University of Minnesota Press.

Said, Edward. 1978. *Orientalism.* New York: Pantheon.

Smith, Neil. 1996. *The New Urban Frontier: Gentrification and the Revanchist City.* New York: Routledge.

Wacquant, Loïc. 1997. "Three Pernicious Premises in the Study of the American Ghetto." *International Journal of Urban and Regional Research* 21 (2): 341–353.

Wallerstein, Immanuel. 1974–1988. *The Modern World-System,* 3 vols. New York: Academic Press.

Wilson, William Julius. 1980. *The Declining Significance of Race: Blacks and Changing American Institutions.* Chicago: University of Chicago Press.

———. 1987. *The Truly Disadvantaged: The Inner City, the Underclass, and Public Policy.* Chicago: University of Chicago Press.

———. 1996. *When Work Disappears: The World of the New Urban Poor.* New York: Knopf.

Ananya Roy

POWELL, ADAM CLAYTON, JR.

1908–1972

Adam Clayton Powell Jr. was a flamboyant U.S. civil rights leader and clergyman from New York. He became the first African American to wield extensive structural power in the U.S. Congress. Representing New York City's community of Harlem in the U.S. House of Representatives from 1945 to 1971, Powell rose to be chairman of its powerful Education and Labor Committee (1961–1967), where he insured that key laws against racial discrimination and for economic and social justice were enacted.

The only child of Mattie Fletcher Schaefer Powell and the Reverend Adam Clayton Powell Sr., Adam Jr. was born on November 29, 1908, in New Haven, Connecticut, where his father was pastor at the Emmanuel Baptist Church and studied at the Yale Divinity School. It was in that same year that his father accepted the position of pastor at the famed Abyssinian Baptist Church (ABC) in New York City.

Founded in 1808 by blacks refusing to abide any longer the racial segregation in Manhattan's First Baptist Church, ABC was a venerable African-American institution. In its pulpit, Powell Sr. became one of the leading clergymen of his day. After earning a bachelor's degree from Colgate University (1930) in Hamilton, New York, and a master's degree from Columbia University (1932), Powell Jr. was hired by his father, first as the church's business manager and community center director, and then as assistant pastor. The Depression-era soup kitchen and community outreach programs he developed at the ABC facilities on West 138th St. helped expand the congregation into a megachurch, boasting 14,000 members in the mid-1930s. This experience served as a solid basis for the younger Powell's assaults on racial injustice after he succeeded his ailing father as pastor in 1937.

Powell Jr. led rent strikes to improve living conditions in Harlem and organized boycott campaigns designed to achieve better jobs for blacks. His work helped to improve public health care for blacks, particularly at the city's Harlem Hospital, and to break employment barriers on city transport and other public utilities, as well as in many department stores and at the 1939–1940 World's Fair held in New York City.

Powell never shirked the limelight. His ABC position and work focused further attention on him, which only grew as he matured. He represented a less restrained and more demanding "New Negro" community. He was a major supporter of the union leader A. Philip Randolph's successful effort in setting up the National Negro Congress in Chicago in 1936. The aim of the congress, which was attended by more than 800 delegates, was to get the government to address the needs of blacks during the Depression.

Powell saw the potential of blacks' concerted economic and political power. He believed that the large number of blacks drawn to Chicago in the Great Migration from the South to the North earlier in the century had illustrated that strength. It was in Chicago in 1928 that Oscar DePriest, whose family had moved north from Alabama in the 1878, became the first black in the twentieth century to be elected to the U.S. House of Representatives. Subsequently, Chicago's black voters elected Arthur W. Mitchell and William L. Dawson to that same seat.

Powell believed this process could be repeated in Harlem. He therefore entered electoral politics and was elected to the New York City Council in 1941. Using ABC as a base within the larger community of Harlem, Powell was elected to the U.S. House of Representatives in 1945. Almost immediately he clashed with the legislative establishment, which was dominated by whites from the South. Rejecting practices that restricted blacks from certain congressional facilities, he demanded the same access as other members of Congress. On the House floor, he challenged segregationist members and programs. He routinely attached antidiscrimination clauses (initially ridiculed as the "Powell Amendment") to federal spending measures, presaging federal antidiscrimination practices that became common in the 1960s. He also championed Third World independence and development in the years following World War II.

Powell rode the crest of the civil rights movement of the 1950s and 1960s. Through the rigid seniority rules of Congress, he became chairman of the House Committee on Education and Labor in 1961. He used this position to advance desegregation and antipoverty legislation, raise the federal minimum wage, and increase funding for public education. A key figure behind the landmark Civil Rights Act of 1964, he also championed aid for persons with disabilities.

Powell's open disregard for convention and his being one of only a half-dozen African-American congressmen in the mid-1960s made him conspicuous. His high living-style, notorious womanizing, and three marriages grated against traditional images of a suitably religious pastor. His political outspokenness made him an alluring target in the hotly contested civil rights era. Powell paid the consequences of his personal and political flamboyance in 1967. After charges of corruption, tax evasion, and misappropriation of funds, the House Democratic Caucus stripped him of his committee chairmanship, and in March 1967 the full House voted 307 to 116 to exclude him from membership. He challenged the action, appealing all the way to the U.S. Supreme Court, which in *Powell v. McCormack* (1969) ruled his exclusion unconstitutional. In the interim, Powell's Harlem constituency twice reelected him. But he had other legal problems, having become something of a fugitive from his own district because of an unpaid 1963 libel judgment against him.

Fading but still fiery in the late 1960s, Powell represented a militancy that bridged black generations since the 1920s in their struggle against racism and segregation. His 1967 sermon "Black Power: A Form of Godly Power," along with his six-sermon record album titled "Keep the Faith, Baby!" (1967), resonated for yet another generation insistent on more immediate racial and social justice. Emperor Haile Selassie in 1969 personally bestowed on Powell the Golden Cross of Ethiopia for his internationally recognized work. Yet Powell's long peccadilloes, particularly his congressional absenteeism, finally exhausted his Harlem constituency's patience, and in 1970 it replaced him with Charles B. Rangel. In decreasing health from a heart attack, chest tumor, and cancer, Powell withdrew to his Bahamian island retreat of Bimini. He died at sixty-three in Miami, Florida, on April 4, 1972.

BIBLIOGRAPHY

Hamilton, Charles V. 1991. *Adam Clayton Powell, Jr.: The Political Biography of an American Dilemma.* New York: Atheneum.

Haygood, Wil. 1993. *King of the Cats: The Life and Times of Adam Clayton Powell, Jr.* Boston: Houghton Mifflin.

Powell, Adam Clayton, Jr. 1945. *Marching Blacks: An Interpretive History of the Rise of the Black Common Man.* New York: Dial Press.

———. 1971. *Adam by Adam: The Autobiography of Adam Clayton Powell Jr.* New York: Dial Press.

Smith, Jessie Carney, ed. 1998. *Black Heroes of the Twentieth Century.* Detroit: Visible Ink Press.

Thomas J. Davis

PREJUDICE

SEE *Social Psychology of Racism.*

PROSTITUTION

SEE *Sex Work.*

PUERTO RICANS

In a republic established by colonizing European settlers and shaped by succeeding waves of immigrants, the Puerto Rican experience is exceptional. Other than the indigenous peoples of North America and the African Americans whose ancestors were brought to the United States as slaves, most U.S. residents are descended from immigrants of many nations, or else are among the current arrivals in a centuries-old progression. The people of Puerto Rico, however, have the distinction of being declared U.S. citizens by a single act of Congress in 1917 after the United States seized possession of Puerto Rico in 1898–1899 following four centuries of Spanish colonial rule.

The identity issues that have arisen from these circumstances are unique, leaving Puerto Ricans as a large ethnic minority among U.S. citizens but without a "hyphenated" identity. Even those born Stateside call themselves Puerto Ricans, not "Puerto Rican–Americans," and their identification with the island is quite strong. Many scholars, among them Ramon Grosfoguel and Angelo Falcón, have noted the extent to which multiple-generation Stateside Puerto Ricans retain a sense of belonging to the Puerto Rican imagined community even if they have never visited the island.

So many Puerto Ricans have migrated from the island in the last century that today the diaspora in the fifty U.S. states (estimated by the 2003 census at 3,855,608) matches the population of the island nation itself (3,808,610 people in the 2000 census), raising the prospect of a future in which the Puerto Rican majority is "Diasporican." The political and economic dependency between the United States and Puerto Rico, and U.S. governmental policies with intended and unintended consequences to Puerto Ricans, are critical to understanding the ethnoracial experience of Puerto Ricans Stateside as "people of color," regardless of skin color (Urciuoli 1996). How complicated these issues become in the racially charged and conflicted context of U.S. society is reflected in data showing that fewer Puerto Ricans (46%) in the U.S. diaspora identified themselves in the 2000 census as "white" compared to 80 percent of island residents.

"Puerto Ricans' racialization is evident through their imposed racial categorization," sociologist Vidal-Ortiz wrote in 2004 (p. 188). As the United States worked to Americanize Puerto Rico—for example. with a five-decade-long failed attempt to impose English language education in island schools—and as more island residents traveled Stateside, Puerto Ricans experienced the American racial dichotomy of black and white, as well as divisions based on proficiency in English and Spanish and economic conflicts based on social class under capitalism. The colonial history of the island still matters to the process of racial formation today.

HISTORY

Taínos, the inhabitants of Puerto Rico at the time of the first Spanish expeditions after 1500, left no written records and died out almost entirely as the result of the brutal Spanish conquest. Survivors were assimilated into the populations of the Spanish colonists: Creoles, Mestizos, African slaves, and Mulattoes who supplanted the Taínos, and from whom modern Puerto Ricans are descended. The Taínos called the island Borikén, meaning "land of the valiant warrior" (later transposed to Borinquén). Today Puerto Ricans self-refer as "Boricuas," one of many ways in which a link to the island's indigenous population is kept alive.

European writings from the time of the Spanish conquest described two different indigenous peoples of Puerto Rico, the Taínos—considered "gentle"—and the "warlike" Caribs. There is debate about the degree to which these distinctions were imagined by the Europeans. Modern scholars added confusion through the ambiguous categorization of Taínos as Arawak, based on a linguistic link to South America. The Taíno language is not Arawak but belongs to that family of languages and is sometimes called "Island Arawak." In recent decades the term Taíno has come into popular use as part of a revival in Caribbean indigenous self-identification. Some scholars argue that by focusing on the Amerindian past, Puerto Ricans may be obscuring or downplaying the connections to their African heritage and hence to blackness.

Puerto Rico, including the inhabited islands of Vieques and Culebra and the uninhabited islands of Culebrita, Palomino, and Mona, was colonized by Spain in the sixteenth century. Sovereignty was transferred from one colonial power to another in 1899 with the ratification that year of the Treaty of Paris, ending the Spanish-Cuban-American War. A militarily defeated Spain ceded the Philippines and Guam and dominion over Cuba and the Puerto Rican islands to the United States. Washington passed the Jones Act in 1917, granting U.S. citizenship to Puerto Ricans and all persons subsequently born on the island. Under the island's first elected governor, Luis Muñoz Marín, the Puerto Rican electorate in 1952 ratified Puerto Rico's status with the Constitution of the Commonwealth of Puerto Rico.

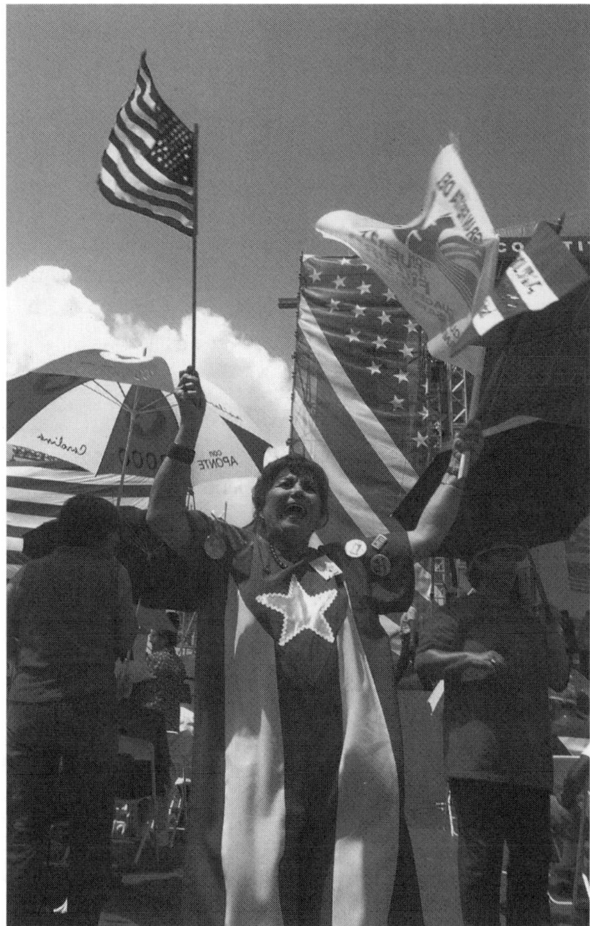

Puerto Rico Anniversary. *Puerto Ricans celebrate the 51st anniversary of the commonwealth's constitution in 2003. In 1952, voters ratified the Constitution of the Commonwealth of Puerto Rico, affirming the island's status as a self-governing territory under U.S. sovereignty.* AP IMAGES.

STATUS OF PUERTO RICO

Although they are U.S. citizens with the right to travel freely and reside in the fifty states, the island's residents are denied representation in the federal government. While island residents are ineligible to vote for president, they elect a governor. They pay no federal income tax, but they do pay Social Security and Medicare taxes. The island remains subject to the sovereignty of Congress under the Territorial Clause of the U.S. Constitution, leaving open the question of whether its status is properly described as an independent territory or a colony: Congress has all plenary power over Puerto Rico.

Puerto Rican citizenship in the United States is considered second class by many, politically as well as culturally. Some argue that second-class citizenship is evident as Puerto Ricans have long served in the U.S. military—islanders have been subject to conscription in the United States but cannot vote for the commander in chief. Citizens who live Stateside but then move to Puerto Rico cannot exercise the right to vote in federal elections on an absentee ballot in their last state of residence. That same citizen moving to Iran would be able to cast an absentee ballot at the U.S. embassy in Iran. Finally, because the terms of relationship between the island and Washington could change at any time on the authority of Congress, Puerto Rico's ability to govern its own affairs is seriously limited and, according to many, demonstrates policy that maintains the island and its residents as separate and unequal.

OPERATION BOOTSTRAP

Operation Bootstrap began in 1948 under the colonial government as an attempt to improve the fortunes of Puerto Rico, thereby improving the fortunes of the United States. In effect, the program industrialized Puerto Rico and changed the economy from an agricultural base to one reliant on manufacturing and tourism. Whereas sugar corporations dominated the island in the 1940s, today electronics and pharmaceutical companies are drawn there because of the favorable tax laws. Despite the wealth of those industries, the unemployment rate in Puerto Rico stands at about 10 percent.

While Operation Bootstrap encouraged the outmigration of men and the factory employment of the island's women, Puerto Rican elites and U.S. backers behind the transformation also actively sought to reduce the island's population growth. During this period, but having begun in the 1930s, increasing numbers of Puerto Rican women were sterilized. By the 1960s approximately 35 percent of Puerto Rican women had had "la operación," the highest rate of sterilization in the world. Puerto Rican women were also used as a test population for the development of the birth control pill.

The Great Migration of Puerto Ricans to the United States in the 1940s and 1950s was prompted by the changing labor picture and urbanization on the island brought about by Operation Bootstrap. Tens of thousands of migrants from Puerto Rico went Stateside just before United States industry shifted from manufacturing to office work, which required technical and professional skills that left these workers, without high levels of education, at a particular disadvantage.

THE NEW YORK CITY DIASPORA

Among U.S. Latinos, Puerto Ricans remain the most residentially segregated, which evidences housing discrimination. People living in segregation face low-performing schools, low-wage jobs, reduced physical and mental health—in short, the exhausting impacts of living in poverty. While Puerto Ricans can be found in increasing density in large and small cities around the country, including Chicago, Philadelphia, Newark, and Hartford, New York City has long been and remains a hub for those migrating from the island.

According to the 2000 census, New York City is still home to the highest concentration of Stateside Puerto Ricans. They were most active in building cultural, educational, and political institutions in New York from 1945 to 1970, when the majority of Stateside Puerto Ricans lived in the city. Even with steady decline since then, 23 percent of Diasporicans live in the city's five boroughs. The term Nuyorican became widely used when Miguel Algarín coedited an anthology of poetry in 1973 with Miguel Piñero titled *Nuyorican Poetry: An Anthology of Puerto Rican Words and Feelings*. When asked about his coinage, he explained that the term was used in the San Juan airport as an insult against him and Piñero because they spoke fluent English; they appropriated the word to remove its sting. He would go on to found the still-flourishing Nuyorican Poets Café in the Lower East Side (Loisaida) of Manhattan.

A rich cultural tradition of art—including literature, poetry and music, particularly salsa—was born in Nueva York. By 1964, Puerto Ricans were 9 percent of the city's population. Their art was sometimes born of the pain of exclusion, racism, and hostility faced Stateside. It can be difficult to document or measure discrimination, but looking at the history of education of Puerto Ricans Stateside provides concrete evidence of that manifestation of racism.

When Puerto Rican children began attending New York public schools in the 1900s, the environment placed no value on their ethnic heritage and held low expectations for their academic performance. As detailed by Rodríguez-Morazzani, the New York City Chamber of Commerce issued a report in 1935: *Study on Reactions of Puerto Rican Children in New York City to Psychological Tests*. Based on the results of an English-language exam administered to Puerto Rican children whose mother tongue was Spanish, they scored quite poorly. Concluding that Puerto Rican children were "retarded in school according to age," the report claimed that "the majority of Puerto Rican children here are so low in intelligence that they require education of a simplified, manual sort, preferably industrial, for they cannot adjust in a school system emphasizing the three R's" (Rodríguez-Morazzani 1997, p. 61). The committee also determined that Puerto Ricans would tend to become delinquents and criminals.

Having conceptualized the presence of Puerto Rican children as a problem, both reflecting and setting the tone for the school system's interaction with these students for decades to come, another study undertaken by the Board of Education was released in 1958. Whereas previous studies had no participation from the Puerto Rican community, "The Puerto Rican Study, 1953–1957" did include some Puerto Rican staff and consultants. The release of the study overlapped with the growing organization of Puerto Rican groups pushing for school reform, including the Puerto Rican Forum, Aspira, and United Bronx Parents, as well as the beginning of the "great school wars" of the late 1960s. Eventually a consent decree was won for bilingual education in city public schools, but the negative impact of early experience, combined with minimal funding and discrimination against Spanish-English education, would impact generations of Puerto Ricans.

FUTURE STATUS

Ongoing and fierce political debate over the status of Puerto Rico vis-à-vis the United States frames the development of Puerto Rican identity on the island and Stateside. Several options on a continuum of sovereignty are advanced: independence, free association, commonwealth, and statehood. Independence would mean full self-governance for Puerto Rico and international recognition as a sovereign state. Free association would involve a treaty between two nations assumed to be independently sovereign. Statehood means integration with the United States, including seats in the House and Senate as well as liability for federal taxes. Many argue that the status-quo option for the commonwealth in its current form would maintain colonial status for Puerto Rico, although the United States considers Puerto Rico an unincorporated territory, not a colony.

In 1998, a nonbinding referendum was held asking residents of Puerto Rico which option they wanted for the island. A fifth answer, "None of the above," received a slim majority of votes (50.3%), followed by statehood (46.5%). The referendum excluded an option that had won a plurality of votes in a 1993 plebiscite: enhanced commonwealth status (48%), which would shift power away from Congress to Puerto Rico.

Although the island's lack of sovereignty encourages the devaluation of its people and land, and although the people's lack of self-determination fosters an institutionalized racism, there has been no lack of resistance. In April 1999, a civilian U.S. Navy security guard living on Vieques, David Sanes Rodríguez, was killed, and four others were injured, when Marine jets on a training mission for the Kosovo war missed their target and fired two 500-pound bombs at the communications tower where he was working. The event brought together the three Puerto Rican political parties, religious organizations, politicians, and citizens—on the island and Stateside—in what to some represented an unprecedented unity call for the withdrawal of the navy from Vieques. Terms included a return of the two-thirds of the island the United States had purchased in 1941 as a weapons proving ground and a significant cleanup of damage done to the environment by military exercises. With repeated protests and civil disobedience, and after hundreds of people were arrested at a protest camp on Vieques, Viequenses eventually voted in a nonbinding referendum to remove the navy from their island. In May 2003, the navy withdrew, although Congress has yet to provide funds for a cleanup.

More recently, U.S. politicians have been prompted to support change by congressmen of Puerto Rican ancestry. In April 2007, two House members from New York introduced bills to demand that Congress act in deciding permanently on Puerto Rico's political future. One bill, the Puerto Rico Democracy Act of 2007, with ninety-six cosponsors, calls for a federally sanctioned self-determination process, but the bill is criticized as being pro-statehood. Another bill, the Puerto Rico Self-Determination Act, with thirty-four cosponsors, by contrast, would recognize the right of Puerto Ricans to call a constitutional convention through which they would exercise their right to self-determination. These recent bills will likely raise calls for a resolution to Puerto Rico's political status by 2009.

Despite concentrated poverty, Stateside Puerto Ricans are increasingly diverse economically, with a small, growing middle class. While still experiencing prejudice and discrimination, Puerto Ricans stand poised for a new era of self-determination. Cultural nationalism remains strong, for there is a consistent circular migration of people between the fifty states and the island (known as *vaíven*, or "coming and going"). The possible imminent resolution of the island's status is likely to redefine the future form of this coming and going and the relations between Puerto Ricans Stateside and those on the island.

SEE ALSO *Blackness in Latin America; Central Americans; Immigration to the United States; Latin American Racial Transformations; Latinos.*

BIBLIOGRAPHY

Acosta-Belén, Edna, and Carlos E. Santiago. 2006. *Puerto Ricans in the United States: A Contemporary Portrait.* Boulder, CO: Lynne Rienner.

Duany, Jorge. 2002. *The Puerto Rican Nation on the Move: Identities on the Island and in the United States.* Chapel Hill: University of North Carolina Press.

Falcón, Angelo. 2004. *Atlas of Stateside Puerto Ricans.* Washington, DC: Puerto Rico Federal Affairs Administration.

Grosfoguel, Ramón. 2003. *Colonial Subjects: Puerto Ricans in a Global Perspective.* Berkeley: University of California Press.

Louis de Malave, Florita Z. 1999. "Sterilization of Puerto Rican Women: A Selected, Partially Annotated Bibliography." Wisconsin Bibliographies in Women's Studies. http://www.library.wisc.edu/libraries/WomensStudies/bibliogs/puerwom.htm.

Rodríguez Domínguez, Victor M. 2005. "The Racialization of Mexican Americans and Puerto Ricans: 1890s–1930s." *Centro journal* 17 (1): 70–105.

Rodríguez-Morazzani, Roberto P. 1997. "Puerto Ricans and Educational Reform in the U.S.: A Preliminary Exploration." *Centro journal* 9 (1): 58–73.

Urciuoli, Bonnie. 1996. *Exposing Prejudice: Puerto Rican Experiences of Language, Race and Class.* Boulder, CO: Westview Press.

Vidal-Ortiz, Salvador. 2004. "On Being a White Person of Color: Using Autoethnography to Understand Puerto Ricans' Racialization." *Qualitative Sociology* 27 (2): 179–203.

Michelle Ronda

R

RACE RIOTS (U.S.), 1900–1910

The racial situation of the early twentieth century was presaged by the last black-dominated local government in the nation being swept away in the Wilmington, North Carolina white riot of 1898, and by the last nineteenth-century black member of the U.S. House of Representatives, George White of South Carolina, leaving Congress in 1901, a victim of vicious black exclusion politics. Three years into the new century, Booker T. Washington—the most powerful black man in America, who had urged blacks to eschew politics in return for social peace—would be attacked by W. E. B. Du Bois for aiding and abetting whites in their oppression of blacks. The turn of the century found blacks increasingly urbanized and competing with lower-income whites for jobs and living space. This process of change occurred as whites defined the Progressive era as one of Anglo-Saxon superiority and hegemony. Blacks attempting to escape the racism of the old order encountered it in the new, the results being nearly three decades of riots between the races.

RIOTS OF 1900

In 1900, the same year James Weldon Johnson wrote "Lift Ev'ry Voice and Sing" to celebrate thirty-five years of black emancipation, there were two major race riots—one in New York City's Tenderloin District, and the other in the city of New Orleans and in scattered locations in the Deep South—and at least 106 blacks were lynched. The New York City riot began with a series of misperceptions between one Arthur Harris, a black newcomer to New York, who thought a white undercover policeman, Robert Thorpe, was making improper advances toward his female friend on August 2. For his part, Thorpe thought the friend was soliciting. When Harris approached Thorpe, an argument ensued; Thorpe hit Harris with his billy club, and Harris knifed Thorpe, who died of his wounds several days later. Harris fled to Washington, D.C. Between this initial event and Thorpe's funeral on August 12, rumors circulated that the black community was heavily armed. On the day of Thorpe's funeral, rumors turned to rioting between whites and blacks in the low-income Hell's Kitchen neighborhood. For four days, some 10,000 young whites, the city police among them, attacked virtually every black they encountered, leaving scores of both races injured and one black man dead.

In the case of New Orleans, the riot began when one Robert Charles, a black man, shot a white police officer to death while fleeing from an earlier encounter with other officers. While a mob began burning black homes and attacking and killing blacks, other whites tracked down Charles, who had holed up in a house and refused commands to come out and surrender. When they began shooting into the residence, Charles returned the fire, killing seven of them. The house was set ablaze and Charles was shot to death as he fled the flames. In addition to burning a number of black properties, the rampaging white mob killed at least twenty-seven other blacks.

RACE RIOT IN ATLANTA, GEORGIA

The 1906 riot in Atlanta was caused by reasons very similar to other riots and violence against blacks all over the South. The city had seen a tremendous population growth in the last decades of the nineteenth century, especially of the black citizenry. This had led to an additional pressure on the city's public services, increased competition among the races for work, heightened social distinctions and stratifications, a widening of the gap between the elite and working-class blacks, and an increase in fears of miscegenation.

The presence of a black intelligentsia created a competition for control over the administration and organization of the city, while the presence of lower-class businesses like saloons, bars, and barbershops created a fear of moral and social pollution due to the myths the media perpetuated about the degeneracy of the black male and his unreliable, brutish character. The fear of black people's capability to organize businesses and create social capital, and their aspirations to political and social equality, further strengthened the resolve of the political parties to snuff out the idea of black enfranchisement. This is what the gubernatorial campaign set up as its main agenda during 1906. The white elite tried to control the black population in predictable ways: They imposed severe restrictions on public conduct and increased segregation through Jim Crow laws in public transportation and housing.

As a result, Democratic gubernatorial candidate M. Hoke Smith (with the aid of Populist politician Tom Watson), and the opposing candidate Clark Howell vied with each other in provoking white sentiment against black people by promising to control black "uppity-ness" and to disfranchise the black male. To achieve this, the political parties covertly sponsored a campaign against black men by making unsubstantiated charges of black males attacking white women. This was the easiest and surest way of provoking mob violence against blacks. By the last week of September 1906, several such allegations had repeatedly appeared in the local newspapers, and on Saturday, September 22, the newspaper published four such accounts, which immediately provoked a mob to gather in the city's Decatur Street and the violence to start. The mob raided black businesses, killed several barbers, stopped streetcars and beat and killed black men and women, attacked households and other known black dwellings. The city leaders could not calm the mob down, and eventually, around midnight, the state militia was called in. While the mob was off the main streets, violence continued in sporadic outbursts in the smaller back streets. Walter White, a future secretary of the National Association for the Advancement of Colored People (NAACP), was an eyewitness to the rioting. His father was a mailman who had finished the mail delivery route early that day upon hearing rumors of the riot. Later that night, White helped his father defend their home and family against the rioters. The intense hatred and brutality of the mob against poor and helpless black children and women made White aware of his racial position and the need to fight against that hatred.

The Progress of Civilization, ***c. 1897.*** *This political cartoon depicts an emancipated slave shaking John Brown's hand (left), while on the right a former slave is burned at the stake. As this illustration shows, the abolition of slavery did not alter the racist mindset of white Americans.* MANUSCRIPTS, ARCHIVES AND RARE BOOKS DIVISION, SCHOMBURG CENTER FOR RESEARCH IN BLACK CULTURE, THE NEW YORK PUBLIC LIBRARY, ASTOR, LENOX AND TILDEN FOUNDATIONS.

On Monday, September 24, some blacks armed themselves and organized a defensive group in Brownsville, a community south of Atlanta. The county police heard of the gathering and attacked the group; one police officer was killed in the shootout that ensued. Over 200 black men were then disarmed and arrested, while the white mobsters had gone unpunished. By Tuesday, the city's businessmen and clergy had called for a stop to the violence as the incidents were reported nationwide and would sully Atlanta's reputation as a prosperous city. The rioting stopped but its repercussions were felt deeply by Atlanta's black community, which had to limit its political activities. The failure of Washington's "accommodationist" strategies and the setback to black suffrage through the passage of statewide prohibition and restrictions on black franchise gave an added impetus to the growing discontent among the more radical black leadership that had never adhered to Washington's policies. The riot was one among the many incidents that served to violently negate the reforms promised for blacks by the Reconstruction. This was a setback that would not be overcome until the civil rights era five decades later.

RACE RIOT IN SPRINGFIELD, ILLINOIS

While a higher concentration of blacks in the population could be assigned as one reason for violence against blacks in other regions, in a city like Springfield, Illinois, the population of blacks had been steadily declining (from 7.2 percent in 1890 to 5.7 percent in 1910) (Senechal 1990, p. 60) as compared to the white population, which had risen. Black and white coalminers had coexisted mainly peacefully (Senechal 1990, pp. 58–59). Blacks generally occupied menial positions in Springfield and were not a threat to the economic prosperity of the whites. There were a few middle-class black families in the city who were mentioned in biographical accounts of city residents before 1880.

Before the 1908 riot the white majority had decried the behavior of black people living in the Badlands and Levee neighborhoods as the major reason for animosity toward them. Newspaper editorials lambasted their "drinking, gambling, drug use, criminal acts and general disorderliness" (Senechal 1990, p. 73). Several influential whites in the city felt after the fact that the riot was a sign of the decaying morality of the population as a whole.

The incident that sparked the riot was the jailing of two black men. One of them, Joe James, was allegedly involved in a sexual attack on the daughter of a well-liked white man, Clergy Ballard, on July 4, 1908. The fleeing James killed Ballard. The other was George Richardson, accused of molesting Mabel Hallam, a poor white woman, on August 13, 1908. Hallam later recanted her accusation. The attack on white purity, even among the lowest of the citizenry, was a strong incitement to an angry response. The mob wanted to carry out a more public justice by lynching the as yet untried black men. When the jailers refused to release the men to the angry mob (and transferred them secretly to a jail in Bloomington), the mob, led by an irate woman, Kate Howard, decided to direct its violence against the representatives and supporters of black people in the city. The hesitation of Sheriff Charles Werner to call in the militia (National Guard), even when asked directly by one of the citizens, caused an unnecessary delay in restoring peace and order, and the deaths of many black people, as well as the destruction of property worth thousands of dollars.

It seems that anti-black race riots were not uncommon in northern cities early in the twentieth century. White people were just as hostile toward blacks in the North as in the South at this time. In Springfield and elsewhere blacks were barred from many restaurants, hotels, parks, and other public facilities. Numerous race riots had occurred in the North as early as the first half of the 1800s. From 1900 to 1908, anti-black riots had broken out in cities like New York, and in smaller places like Evansville and Greensburg, Indiana, and Springfield, Ohio. But the riot in the Illinois capital brought attention to the issue as many of the nation's newspapers reported the riot. It was even more shocking as all this happened in the city where Abraham Lincoln practiced Law as a young man. It has been widely debated why this one black man's crime led to so much violence against blacks.

In 1908, Springfield did not seem to be such a volatile place. It had a stable, mixed economy based on coal, transportation, and manufacturing, as well as many businesses that catered to the large number of travelers. The reason for the riot was definitely not economic. Jobs were not scarce and blacks were kept out of respectable and more lucrative jobs systematically. Since whites almost had a monopoly on the well-paid, skilled jobs, the fear of losing jobs to a population that was rapidly declining in numbers was highly unlikely. The major threat was to the idea of white superiority.

Local politicians used the racism prevalent in the political sphere to garner support from the marginalized poor white people, setting the stage for the riot. Division across racial lines was one of the ways that politicians could gain power. The blacks were definitely pro-Republican in the South, while the Democratic Party candidates were anti-liberal.

The newspapers, politicians, and other influential actors in mainstream society raised the specter of miscegenation again by publishing highly falsified and inflammatory accounts of black men assaulting and defiling white women. It seems they had forgotten about the miscegenation already achieved through white slave owners and white men generally coercing black women into sexual relationships and raping them without any fear of reprisal. The large number of light-skinned, at times almost white "black" people did not register in the consciousness of most white people. Defiling white womanhood was sacrilegious, while defiling black women for two centuries had been of economic and sociopolitical advantage to white men. This also showed the clear-cut demarcation of ideas associated with whiteness and blackness: Whites were pure and superior, while blacks were inherently inferior, lewd, uncontrolled, sexually aggressive, and without a moral core.

In the riots in Atlanta, Springfield, and other cities, the immediate cause of the riot was the fear of defilement and the sexual and moral degeneration presumably caused by the presence of black people. The white newspapers kindled public outrage by inflaming already existing prejudice, hatred, and fear of black people. In each case police action proved reluctant and inadequate.

The mobs were mainly composed of the lower classes, the unruly, uncouth elements of white people from the cities. They were the main actors in the rioting, burning, looting of black businesses and homes, and the brutal killing of black people, but they had the moral support and silent acquiescence of the middle- and upper-class white citizens.

In each riot the number of reported black deaths was probably much lower than the actual number. For instance, the records showed only two black men dead (William Donnegan and Scott Burton, both lynched) and twelve injured, while further research revealed serious injuries (which may have resulted in deaths as the black people were afraid of reporting their injuries to the police or taking the injured to the hospital) to 83 victims of the riot in Springfield, Illinois (Senechal 1990, pp. 130–131). The cases of rioting were reported in the American as well as European press, which pushed the political authorities to intercede and prevent further violence from spreading. They had to keep up the pretense of being fair and concerned about the violence against black people.

In each riot, black people did arm themselves and group together to fight any more violence against them. But in each case they were disarmed and disbanded by the authorities that had failed to disarm the white mob. In some instances, they were forced to give up and were even attacked, arrested, and put on trial by the authorities. The incident that occurred in Brownsville, Texas, was inspired by very similar prejudices.

THE TEXAS BROWNSVILLE INCIDENT

When the black soldiers of the 25th Infantry moved into Fort Brown, Texas, they arrived in a place that had already had problems with the presence of armed troops in its midst. Several sections of the town resented the soldiers' presence and openly expressed their hostility. The soldiers were subjected to racial slurs and taunts, and received biased or surly hospitality from the white businesses. Customs inspector Fred Tate pistol-whipped Private James W. Newton for "jostling" Tate's wife and another white woman (Christian 1995, p. 72). Private Oscar W. Reed was pushed into the river for being seemingly drunk and loud (Christian 1995, p. 72). On August 12, 1906, rumors circulated that a black soldier had attacked a white woman, Mrs. Lon Evans, near the red-light district (Christian 1995, pp. 72–73), which provoked the post commander to impose an eight o'clock curfew on the men. However, the peace was disturbed permanently between the townspeople and the troops when shots, allegedly fired by some black soldiers, were heard around midnight and reports of attacks by black soldiers spread through town. Many witnesses surfaced, claiming that they had actually seen black soldiers, while others asserted that the shots were from military Springfield rifles. These reports were dubious and inspired at best. Mayor Frederick Combe brought forth some spent shells that proved the guilt of the black soldiers beyond doubt for many people, for whom this was only a confirmation of their racist beliefs and paranoia about armed black men (Christian 1995, p. 73). Even though Major Charles W. Penrose had checked the presence of all his men on the night of the shooting, and found all enlisted men accounted for and their weapons clean and undischarged, he still believed in the veracity of the mayor's "evidence."

Despite the questionable circumstantial evidence, it seems everyone believed in the guilt of the black soldiers. U.S. senators Charles Culberson and Joseph Weldon Bailey wrote to the secretary of war William Howard Taft for immediate removal of the black troops (Christian 1995, p. 74). The editors and writers at several newspapers, mainly the *Houston Post, Dallas Morning News*, and *Austin Statesman*, further stoked the public sentiment against the black troops by publishing inflammatory editorials and irresponsibly exaggerated accounts of assaults against white citizens by armed soldiers. They described the soldiers' provocations to be minimal and unjustified and actively called for the soldiers to be removed from Texas.

Major Augustus P. Blocksom, assistant inspector-general of the Southwestern Division, was in charge of the investigation and found twelve members of the garrison of companies B, C, and D guilty, and arrested them (Christian 1995, pp. 76, 78). Later, President Roosevelt ordered the dismissal of 167 men of the regiment without a trial in December 1907 (Christian 1995, p. 81). He did not offer a reprimand to the white men who had been guilty of assault or decry the racism of the townspeople, but commented that blacks were more proud and unaccepting of rude treatment than before. He gave more credence to the accounts of the raid given by the townspeople than to the protestations of the black soldiers of their innocence. He did not even credit the testimony of the white officers of the division who claimed that assertions of the men's involvement were not creditable. Major Blocksom recommended that all enlisted men in the battalion be discharged dishonorably unless they gave up the names of the guilty parties.

Twelve men of the garrison were arrested subsequently under the persuasion of Texas Ranger William Jesse McDonald (Christian 1995, p. 78). This openly defied the stance of General William S. McCaskey that there was no evidence of the direct involvement of any of the men. Further removal of the troops to Fort Reno, Oklahoma Territory, and the twelve incarcerated men to Fort Sam Houston did not resolve the situation. President Theodore Roosevelt asked General Ernest A. Garlington to discharge the 167 men of the companies A, B, and C if they did not give forth the guilty men's names (Christian 1995, p. 79). The investigations of General Garlington did not provide any conclusive results, and subsequently, on November 4, Roosevelt's dismissal order was signed and published. The fact that Roosevelt withheld his decision until after Election Day provoked charges from black newspapers and leaders that his act was politically motivated and unconstitutional. Du Bois urged black men to vote Democratic in the next election in 1908, while Washington remained silent and loyal to the white administration, resulting in increasing criticism of his conciliatory policies. The Military Affairs Committee convened on February 4, 1907, and nine of its members eventually suggested that the decision was justified, while four members found considerable flaws and gaps in the evidence (Christian 1995, p. 82). The campaign by Ohio senator Joseph B. Foraker to provide the 167 men due process through trial and possible acquittal did not succeed. Foraker and Senator Morgan Bulkeley (of Connecticut) submitted a minority report, which suggested that the eyewitnesses were unreliable and the shells produced as evidence had been brought from a firing range at Fort Niobrara (Christian 1995, p. 83). Roosevelt only conceded to allowing fifteen of the men to reenlist in the face of growing criticism of his decision. This event only highlighted the racism present in the social and political system, which denied black men justice. The men were subsequently given an honorable discharge by the Richard Nixon administration in 1972, which did not result in due reparations to more than one survivor from among the 167 men. Another casualty of this incident was Corporal Edward A. Knowles, who was charged with a shooting attempt on Captain Edgar A. Macklin of the 25th; despite lack of direct evidence, Knowles was sentenced to fifteen years of hard labor. He never received an honorable discharge posthumously. It was widely felt by black leaders, newspapers and their editors, black ministers, and even W. E. B. Du Bois (Christian 1995, p. 80) that the government was merely catering to racist public sentiment and evincing support for itself by acting highhandedly in disallowing due process to black soldiers.

All of these incidents reinforced the racism that prevailed in the country and clearly defined the different moderate and extremist ideologies of black leaders, politicians, and organizers. The failure of the political strategies of Washington and Du Bois led to the more radical movements of Marcus Garvey and A. Philip Randolph. While neither movement quite succeeded, both helped continue the struggle of black people toward attaining full citizenship and leading lives of dignity and equality.

BIBLIOGRAPHY

Christian, Garna L. 1995. *Black Soldiers in Jim Crow Texas, 1899–1917.* College Station: Texas A&M University Press.

Gaines, Kevin Kelly. 1996. "Living in Jim Crow: The Atlanta Riot and Unmasking 'Social Equality.'" *Uplifting the Race: Black Leadership, Politics, and Culture in the Twentieth Century.* Chapel Hill: University of North Carolina Press.

Meier, August. 1963. *Negro Thought in America, 1880–1915: Racial Ideologies in the Age of Booker T. Washington.* Ann Arbor: University of Michigan Press.

Rudwick, Elliott M. 1964. *Race Riot at East St. Louis: July 2, 1917.* Carbondale: Southern Illinois University Press.

Senechal, Roberta. 1990. *The Sociogenesis of a Race Riot: Springfield, Illinois, in 1908.* Urbana: University of Illinois Press.

Wintz, Cary D., ed. 1996. *African American Political Thought 1890–1930: Washington, Du Bois, Garvey, and Randolph.* Armonk, NY: M. E. Sharpe.

Abha Sood Patel

RACE RIOTS (U.S.), 1917–1923

Race riots have played a pivotal role in the social construction of race and racism throughout U.S. history. Since the early nineteenth century, race riots have shed light on race and class relations as well as the political dynamics in the nation. In general, riots—and the way a society responds to those riots—reveal which groups in the polity wield power at the expense of others. Race riots also fit within the histories of racism and colonialism in Western civilization. In *The Origins of Totalitarianism,* the philosopher Hannah Arendt observed that the brutality that culminated in the Holocaust was rooted in a long "subterranean stream of Western history." Arendt noted:

> When the European mob discovered what a "lovely virtue" a white skin could be in Africa, when the English conqueror in India became an administrator who no longer believed in the universal validity of law, but was convinced of his own innate capacity to rule and dominate ... the stage seemed to be set for all possible horrors. Lying under anybody's nose were many of the elements which gathered together could create a totalitarian government on the basis of racism. (Arendt 1958, p. 221)

Race riots expose underlying tensions in societies undergoing rapid technological and economic changes. The riots that transpired in the aftermath of World War I happened during a time characterized by segregation, white rule in the South, and the Great Migration of African Americans to the North. This was also an age marked by rapid social changes including industrialization, the transition to a war production economy, and technological advances in many fields. Technology was implicated in racial bloodshed as a new generation of vigilantes used telephones, electronic signboards, and telegraph messages to mobilize their forces. Night riders used motor vehicles instead of horses to inflict widespread carnage.

This era also witnessed the invention of the modern motion picture and the emergence of the mass viewing audience. The most popular and technically sophisticated film of the age was D. W. Griffith's *The Birth of a Nation* (1915). *Birth* was a complex film. It attacked African-American political aspirations during the Reconstruction era as inherently corrupt even as it celebrated the Ku Klux Klan's paramilitary decimation of black politics after emancipation. One famous scene depicted hooded Klansmen routing federal soldiers in battle, an acceptable scenario to the general public because the troops were black. *The Birth of a Nation* celebrated white national unity on the fiftieth anniversary of the end of the Civil War. According to the civil rights historian Philip Dray, the first modern motion picture in U.S. history "carried Americans back to what now appeared as a simpler, heroic time when a divided America had reunited, and rediscovered its purpose, by suppressing the unruly minority populace in its midst" (Dray 2002, p. 191). *The Birth of a Nation* was based in part on Woodrow Wilson's *A History of the American People* (1902), published when Wilson was a Princeton University historian. In 1915, while serving as president of the United States, Wilson heartily endorsed *Birth* and marveled that the film "is like writing history with lightning." *The Birth of a Nation* sparked the rebirth of the new Ku Klux Klan, which soon boasted chapters in every state of the union. Some of these chapters were implicated in race riots. Equally important, the film was part of a larger mass media culture that routinely depicted antiblack violence as a necessary and even admirable dimension of U.S. culture.

The race riots that occurred from 1917 to 1923 may be understood as a continuation of the tradition of publicly sanctioned assaults against the progress of African Americans as a group. This national wave of riots was in part a response to the fact that black people were waging increasingly effective struggles against white supremacy. In 1909 a group of liberal whites and African Americans founded the National Association for the Advancement of Colored People (NAACP). The NAACP scored a major victory in 1915 with the Supreme Court's *Guinn v. United States* decision. This decision outlawed the "grandfather clauses" in certain state constitutions that had allowed white men to vote without passing a literacy test as long as their grandparents had voted prior to 1867. It also gave registrars the discretion they needed to exclude black southerners whose grandparents had not been legally able to vote prior to the end of the Civil War, 1866, or 1867, depending on the state. The *Guinn* decision encouraged African Americans across the South to undertake new initiatives to becoming registered voters.

Meanwhile, large numbers of black southerners were moving to the North in order to take factory jobs in the burgeoning war economy. By the time thousands of black World War I veterans returned from France demanding their civil rights, the NAACP was becoming a mass-membership protest organization with hundreds of new branches forming in the South and Midwest. African Americans in Florida organized the first statewide civil rights movement of the century, and black voters began to flex their political muscles in Chicago, East St. Louis, New York, and other cities. Many white citizens, however, interpreted black advancement as threatening their own interests. The leadership of the Democratic Party in Miami, Florida, responded to African-American voter registration with the following broadside published in the *Miami Herald*:

> WHITE VOTERS, REMEMBER!
>
> WHITE SUPREMACY
>
> IS BEING ASSAULTED IN OUR MIDST, AND THE MOST
>
> SACRED
>
> INSTITUTIONS OF THE SOUTH
>
> ARE BEING UNDERMINED BY THE ENEMY FROM WITHIN (Ortiz 2005, p. 206)

A VIOLENT ERA

African Americans endured a renewed wave of riots, massacres, and acts of racial terrorism between 1917 and 1923. All too often, rising black aspirations were met with violence. The peak period of recorded violence occurred during the tumultuous months between April and October 1919, a season James Weldon Johnson called the "Red Summer." Race riots broke out in Washington, D.C.; Charleston, South Carolina; and Longview, Texas, among other places. Lynching was also prevalent during these years. Eleven African-American men were burned alive at the stake in 1919. In the same year lynch mobs murdered sixty-nine black people, including ten World War I veterans whose military service was viewed by some whites as a threat to the racial status quo. Antiblack race riots were often waged over the course of several days, and garnered international attention. The riots cost hundreds of lives and incalculable property damage. The riots also undermined the political and economic status of African Americans in numerous communities across the nation.

The intensity of these riots may be explained in part by examining the social context of violence in this period. White rioters enjoyed an almost universal immunity from prosecution, whereas their black counterparts were often incarcerated for defending their homes and neighborhoods. White citizens who shot or beat a black person to death in broad daylight had little to fear from law enforcement authorities, who in any case often participated in vigilante activities themselves.

Race riots were not inspired by blind racist hatred. White citizens who rioted were motivated by political and economic, as well as social, factors. For example, the 1920 Election Day massacre of African Americans who attempted to vote in Orange County, Florida, was

Tulsa Riot, 1921. *African American detainees, rounded up by the National Guard, are marched to the Convention Hall in Tulsa during the race riot in 1921. The guardsmen failed to disarm white citizens as they looted and destroyed black property.* AP IMAGES/ TULSA HISTORICAL SOCIETY.

designed to enforce black disfranchisement. The East St. Louis Race Riot of 1917 was aimed in part at keeping African Americans from moving up the occupational ladder. The Tulsa, Oklahoma, Race Riot of 1921 destroyed a thriving black business district, and white rioters explicitly targeted properties owned by African Americans. Remembering the years she spent building up a successful hairdressing practice in Tulsa, Mabel Little recalled decades later, "At the time of the riot, we had ten different business places for rent. Today, I *pay* rent" (Hirsch 2002, p. 8). Riots in small towns and rural areas drove African Americans off the land and often allowed white residents to take control of black property for drastically reduced rates or for nothing at all. The massacre and forced removal of the African-American community in Rosewood, Florida, in 1923 wiped out generations of black land ownership.

It is important to place these riots in historical context. In terms of lives lost per capita, these riots were far bloodier than the 1960s race riots but not as deadly as the antiblack riots of the nineteenth century. In each of the major race riots between 1917 and 1923—with the partial exception of the Houston Race Riot of 1917—the instigators and perpetrators of violence as well as property destruction were white citizens. This does not mean that white people in the United States were somehow biologically or culturally predisposed to violence. Instead, white rioters were acting on behalf of perceived pressures, interests, and ideologies. It is necessary to examine the roots of white violence in order to understand the genesis of the race riots. The savagery of the riots, the losses African-American communities suffered, and the effects on race relations between whites and blacks continue to echo down into the twenty-first century.

GLOBAL CONTEXT

W. E. B. Du Bois, A. Philip Randolph, and other African-American leaders believed that the social forces unleashed by World War I would help blacks challenge the system of white supremacy in the United States. In addition, a number of industrial labor union organizing committees undertook major interracial unionizing campaigns in Chicago, Birmingham, and other urban areas. The most powerful unions had traditionally operated with color bars that excluded African Americans, Chinese, and others. Black workers, however, responded with guarded optimism to organizers' efforts to build interracial locals. James Weldon Johnson sensed a revived spirit of hope among African Americans as he traveled throughout the country during the war:

> I was impressed with the fact that everywhere there was a rise in the level of the Negro's morale. The exodus of Negroes to the North . . . was in

> full motion; the tremors of the war in Europe were shaking America with increasing intensity; circumstances were combining to put a higher premium on Negro muscle, Negro hands, and Negro brains than ever before; all these forces had a quickening effect that was running through the entire mass of the race. (Johnson 1933, p. 315)

It was not long, however, before the forces of reaction regained the upper hand. Anticolonial and revolutionary movements were defeated, many by military force. In the United States, fear of working-class and black militancy led to a right-wing political backlash known as the "Red Scare." J. Edgar Hoover, the attorney general Alexander Mitchell Palmer, and others used their authority to arrest, detain, and ultimately expel thousands of "alien" political activists. As "law and order" types such as Hoover gained ascendancy, spaces for social and economic justice organizing diminished rapidly. State and federal authorities used powers gained through the Espionage Act of 1917 and the Sedition Act of 1918 to disrupt legitimate protest groups while ignoring the real crimes that exacerbated racial tensions. For example, in the two years leading up to the Chicago Race Riot of 1919, scores of African-American homes were bombed, and yet state authorities conducted no meaningful investigations nor were any of the perpetrators ever found. When similar bombing attacks rocked black homes in Miami, Florida, undercover federal agents appeared more interested in spying on African Americans than in catching the guilty parties. In contrast, the African-American soldiers who were involved in the Houston Race Riot of 1917 were vigorously prosecuted and nineteen were executed.

The Red Scare and the federal government's campaign to uncover "agitators" reinforced white supremacy and increased the likelihood of racial violence. As Department of Justice investigators bullied and interrogated African Americans in Chicago and East St. Louis about their true reasons for coming North, the larger public was encouraged to see black people as subversive outcasts in a virtuous "White Republic." The mainstream media fueled the fire of antiblack racism by publishing sensational headlines such as: "Negroes Flock in from South to Evade Draft" (*St. Louis Times*), "North Does Not Welcome Influx of South's Negroes" (*Chicago Herald*), "Negro Migration: Is It a Menace?" (*Philadelphia Record*), and "Negro Influx On, Plan to Dam It" (*Newark [N.J.] News*) (Gregory 2005, p. 47.)

Rising postwar unemployment and inflation added fuel to the competitive fire. The race riots that broke out in East St. Louis (1917) and Chicago (1919) occurred in the wake of failed strikes as well as stillborn attempts to create multiracial trade unions. As corporations and their organizations methodically destroyed the most important vehicle for collective working-class economic improvement—unions—a sense of anger and desperation swept through urban neighborhoods. As competition between workers intensified, racial tensions flared anew. The economic dimensions of the riots cannot be overestimated.

SEGREGATION AND THE RACE RIOTS

The race riots of 1917 to 1923 occurred during the era of legal segregation (or Jim Crow as it was commonly called). Segregation was designed to generate chronic interracial strife and distrust. In his monumental study of segregation, *An American Dilemma* (1944), Gunnar Myrdal pointed out that one of the major goals of segregation was to separate black and white working-class people so that southern elites would be able to quash social reforms. Thus, the once-promising moments of solidarity between whites and blacks in the post-Reconstruction years were replaced by the ascendancy of "Judge Lynch" in the latter half of the 1880s. The defeat of the Federal Elections Bill of 1890, which had been introduced by the Massachusetts senator Henry Cabot Lodge, quickened the federal government's general retreat from its role as a guarantor of Constitutional equality and civil rights. Between 1877 and the eve of the East St. Louis Race Riot of 1917, antiblack violence was viewed by the majority of white Americans as an inevitable albeit sometimes embarrassing fact of U.S. political life.

Why was the segregation era marked by so much violence and so many race riots? Segregation—like slavery—was a labor system designed to extract surplus labor power, property, tax revenue, wealth, and economic opportunities from African Americans and redistribute these resources to the dominant society. "Race prejudice," the sociologist Oliver C. Cox observed, "is a social attitude propagated among the public by an exploiting class for the purpose of stigmatizing some group as inferior so that the exploitation of either the group itself or its resources or both may be justified" (Cox 1948, p. 393).

Industrial and agricultural employers were the major beneficiaries of this racial wealth redistribution, and they treated black workers' efforts to organize or even assert themselves in their workplaces with repressive measures. Convict labor, debt peonage, and the chain gang may be seen in this context as institutionalized forms of economic—and often physical—violence.

Thus, when African Americans attempted to seize the opportunities offered by the improved economic climate of the early war years, it was not hard to predict that employers would react in a visceral manner. As African Americans began to leave the South in large numbers in 1916, state and local authorities in some areas ordered police forces to try to halt the exodus. African-American workers in Macon, Georgia, and Jacksonville, Florida, among other towns, were beaten and driven away from train stations. African-American sharecroppers in the Arkansas Delta began organizing an agricultural labor union as well as challenging large farm owners for a larger share of King Cotton's profits. Landowners responded by assaulting the union's meeting place, and ordering law enforcement officials to crush the sharecroppers. These activities led to the Elaine, Arkansas, Race Riot of 1919, which destroyed agricultural unionism in the Delta and drove cotton wages back down. When African Americans in Longview, Texas, began experimenting with cooperative purchasing and marketing of farm produce—thus bypassing creditors and merchants—whites in the area launched a major assault against the black community. While the Longview Race Riot of 1919 was allegedly sparked by a black man's presence in a white woman's bedroom, the NAACP and local African Americans understood that the violence had been sparked by the cooperative venture and growing black assertiveness. The racial dynamics exposed in the Arkansas Delta and Longview, Texas, would be repeated over and over again between 1917 and 1923 as the white elite responded—sometimes with violence—to black gains by acting to reassert the status quo.

SEX AND RACIAL VIOLENCE

One common excuse used to rationalize racial terrorism was black male sexual violence—rape or assault—against white women. A careful study of the historical record, however, shows that alleged sexual assault was given as the stated reason in only about 15 to 20 percent of all lynching incidents. In spite of the pioneering investigative work of Ida B. Wells-Barnett, the NAACP, and the Association of Southern Women for the Prevention of Lynching—all of whom demolished the myth of the black rapist—racial violence is still associated with sexual assault in the popular mind. In *At the Hands of Persons Unknown* (2002), Philip Dray noted that "Wells was one of the first people in America to perceive that the talk of chivalry and beastlike blacks ravishing white girls was largely fallacious, and that such ideas were being used to help maintain a permanent hysteria to legitimize lynching, as it reinforced the notion that the races must be kept separate at all costs" (p. 64). One white North Carolinian disavowed this racial hysteria in an editorial letter that appeared in the *Raleigh News and Observer* on February 5, 1922:

> We have a reputation of being bloodthirsty murderers down here in North Carolina, and it is our industrious lynchers who have secured that reputation for us.... All this snorting about the fierce pride of the Anglo-Saxon race is the most disgusting poppycock ever invented. If no [N]egro were ever lynched for anything but rape, it might have some shadow of excuse. But alleged rapists constitute only a small proportion of the victims of mobs in the south these days. Negroes are lynched for all manner of crimes, ranging down to simple misdemeanors.

The Jim Crow system did sanction one form of sexual license: white exploitation of black women. African-American domestic workers who toiled in white households were frequently subjected to sexual assaults. Cleaster Mitchell, who worked as a domestic in Arkansas, recalled in *Remembering Jim Crow* that "one time in the South, it's bad to say, white men was crazy about black women. They would come to your house. They would attack you. They took it for granted when they saw a black lady that they could just approach her, that it was not an insult to her for them to approach her" (Chafe, Gavins, and Korstad 2001, p. 214). In fact, while white supremacists often cloaked their attacks on black communities with the excuse of black-on-white sexual violence, they understood that white men and women often initiated interracial sexual unions. In 1921 the Houston, Texas, Ku Klux Klan issued a warning to white male citizens against interracial sex. The warning was reprinted in the February 4 edition of the *Afro-American*:

> Proclamation: Co-habitation of white men with Negro women is against the laws of this state, is against the interest of both races and is the direct cause of racial trouble. Such practices must stop. We want no more half-breeds.... This warning will not be repeated. Mene Mene Tekel Upharsen. Knights of the Ku Klux Klan.

POSTWAR RIOT PATTERNS

The Philadelphia Race Riot of 1918 illustrates many of the dominant patterns of the urban conflagrations of 1917 to 1923. The Philadelphia riot started after African Americans began purchasing homes in predominantly white residential communities. White homeowners protested black homeownership because they believed it would devalue their own investments. The political scientist Michael Jones-Correa argues that urban race riots occurred more often in areas with higher rates of preexisting white homeownership. According to Jones-Correa, "The higher the number of white homeowners, the greater the chances of an urban disturbance. This provides some confirmation to the notion that it was the resistance of white homeowners to the increasing movement of blacks into formerly all-white residential neighborhoods that helped contribute to the civil disturbances of the period" (Jones-Correa 1999, p. 13).

It was the newly purchased home of Adelia Bonds, a black probation officer, that became the flashpoint of the Philadelphia Race Riot. Bonds had violated an unwritten rule by purchasing a house in a predominantly white area. Bonds's neighbors began harassing her on a daily basis, threw objects at her home, and attacked nearby African-American churches in retaliation. On July 26, a group of white citizens gathered in front of Bonds's residence at 2936 Ellsworth and began throwing large stones at the house. Fearing for her safety, Bonds fled to the top story of the house and fired warning shots at the crowd. One of these rounds hit Joseph Kelly, a white person, and the riot began. The Philadelphia police were unable to quell the violence, and in any case, many sided openly with the white rioters. The Philadelphia Race Riot resulted in four deaths and approximately sixty wounded. Leaders of the Methodist ministers' Meeting of Philadelphia lodged a formal protest with the mayor's office, stating:

> We desire you to understand that we put the whole blame upon your incompetent police force. But for the sympathy of the police, their hobnobbing with the mob, what has now become the disgrace of Philadelphia would have been nothing more than a petty row, if that much.
>
> Your police have for a long time winked at disorder, at the beating up of Negroes, the stoning of their homes and the attacking of their churches. In this very neighborhood divine worship has time and again been disturbed by white hoodlums and there has been no redress. In nearly every part of the city, decent law-abiding Negroes have been set upon by irresponsible white hoodlums, their property damaged and destroyed, while your police seemed powerless to protect.
>
> We also call your attention to the fact that this riot was not started by Negroes; that the Negroes who were annoyed were of the orderly, law-abiding type; that your police arrested Negroes almost exclusively and let the white hoodlums roam the street to do more damage. … Further, your police disarmed only colored people and permitted whites to pursue them with guns. This is the cause of this condition and the whole blame is on your own police force. ("Race Riots in Philadelphia," *Afro-American* [Baltimore, MD], August 2, 1918).

Many of the social behaviors demonstrated in the Philadelphia Race Riot were repeated in the much larger Chicago riot the following year as well as in the other Red Summer race riots. In general, when these riots broke out local police and law enforcement officers openly fraternized with white citizens who were assaulting African Americans. In some instances—Philadelphia for example—the eventual presence of state troops appears to have quelled the violence. In the Tulsa Race Riot, however, state guardsmen contributed to an already disastrous situation by failing to disarm white citizens as they looted and destroyed black property. Some white troops openly referred to African Americans as "the enemy," as if the rioters were engaged in an Allied military invasion. In East St. Louis, William Tuttle reports that "State troops fraternized and joked with lawbreaking whites and many were seen helping in the murders and arson" (Tuttle 1970, p. 13).

African Americans attempted to defend their neighborhoods—sometimes using armed self-defense—during the Philadelphia Race Riot, and this was also a pattern played out in Chicago, Tulsa, and East St. Louis among other places that experienced riots. This was not a new phenomenon. African Americans had periodically engaged in armed self-defense in order to prevent lynching or other acts of racial violence. For example, some antebellum northern black communities created "vigilance committees" in order to protect escaped slaves from being recaptured and re-enslaved by their masters. In regard to the riots that occurred between 1917 and 1923, it is also important to remember that many black men of the period had received military training, and it is likely such expertise was used in the thick of the urban riots. Armed self-defense was a double-edged sword, however. African Americans might prevent an immediate act of violence from occurring only to incur the wrath of whites who simply regrouped and called for reinforcements. For example, the Tulsa Race Riot began after a group of armed African Americans gathered to help law enforcement officials prevent the lynching of a young man accused of bumping a white woman in an elevator. When white Tulsans realized that the black community was organizing to stop the lynching, they attempted to disarm a group of black veterans. Gunshots broke out and the riot commenced.

Active-duty military members as well as recently discharged white veterans played a major role in sparking and sustaining antiblack violence in the Charleston, South Carolina, and Washington, D.C., race riots of 1919. African Americans and their communities expected that their military service and patriotic support for the war effort would lead to first-class citizenship. White officers however, tried to convince black troops that they should continue to play a subordinate role to their white peers. Even the relatively liberal General C. C. Ballou ordered the African-American soldiers of the 92nd Infantry Division to respect segregation and to "refrain from going where their presence will be resented" ("Soldiers Must Not Ask for Legal Rights," *Afro-American*, April 12, 1918).

Ironically, the all-black 92nd Division went on to become one of the most highly decorated infantry units in U.S. history. Its record of facing and defeating numerous elite German combat units earned this division high honors. White officers and soldiers, however, were alarmed that African-American soldiers in the 92nd and other black units had received a hero's welcome in occupied France, and they sought to show after the war that

Rosewood Riot, 1923. *A cabin burns during the massacre in Rosewood, Florida, January 4, 1923. An unknown number of African Americans were killed and landowners were driven out of the community.* COURTESY OF STATE ARCHIVE OF FLORIDA.

black war service would not change race relations in the United States. One letter writer in Florida warned:

> The Negro returned soldier who is full of the "equal rights" treatment he got in Europe during the past months will do exceedingly well to remember that for every one of him there are about a thousand white returned soldiers who were completely fed up on the same equal rights stuff over there, and they are not going to stand for one moment any internal rot started by any yellow-faced coon who has the hellish idea that he is as good as a white man or a white woman (Ortiz 2005, p. 162).

THE ROSEWOOD MASSACRE IN FLORIDA

The final race riot of the period, the Rosewood Massacre, is shrouded in mystery. One explanation for the white riot that killed an undetermined number of African Americans is that it began after a black man sexually assaulted a married white woman on New Year's Day, 1923. However, Sarah Carrier, an African-American woman who worked as a maid for the white woman in question, testified that this woman was actually assaulted by her white lover. Because Carrier was subsequently murdered by white citizens who claimed they were looking for the alleged rapist, her side of the story was quickly suppressed. Another explanation for the riot's origin was given by a white eyewitness who later claimed that area whites were jealous of the relative prosperity of African Americans in Rosewood. Whatever the case, whites from the nearby sawmill community of Sumner and other places further away gathered in Rosewood in the first week of 1923 and completely annihilated the African-American community. Black landowners were permanently driven out of Rosewood, and many of their descendents were financially impoverished. In 1994 the State of Florida granted partial restitution to some of the Rosewood survivors and their descendents.

The race riots of 1917 to 1923 were not driven primarily by what later analysts would refer to as "racial hatred." White rioters were motivated by economic, political, and social considerations. There are several common assumptions about race relations that are unsustainable after a careful survey of these riots. The role of so-called poor whites in initiating racial violence has been exaggerated. In fact, many of the whites involved in the riots appear to have been homeowners (especially in Chicago and East St. Louis) or large landowners and employers (especially in the Arkansas Delta). These groups sought to defend their material interests against perceived African-American gains or accomplishments. Class conflict played a major role in the making of racial violence.

Local police forces as well as military units played crucial roles in these riots. In general, law enforcement officers sided with the rioters in the early stages of these conflicts, and this led to an escalation in the violence. The rioters, however, did not need police officers to lend credibility to their activities; they were acting in a long tradition of antiblack violence that was supported by the media and many political leaders of the day.

African Americans suffered enormous material, physical, and psychological damage as a consequence of the riots. Some historians have argued that the riots of 1917 to 1923 led to an eventual quickening of black protest activity. In the short term, however, the riots dispersed black communities, destroyed black businesses, and wiped out fragile economic gains that African Americans had made in the preceding half-century. U.S. society continued to wrestle with the troubling legacies of these race riots into the early twenty-first century.

BIBLIOGRAPHY

BOOKS

Arendt, Hannah. 1958. *The Origins of Totalitarianism*, 2nd ed. New York: Meridian Books.

Chafe, William H., Raymond Gavins, and Robert Korstad, eds. 2001. *Remembering Jim Crow: African Americans Tell About Life in the Segregated South*. New York: New Press.

Cox, Oliver C. 1948. *Caste, Class, and Race: A Study in Social Dynamics*. Garden City, NY: Doubleday.

Curriden, Mark, and Leroy Phillips Jr. 1999. *Contempt of Court: The Turn-of-the-Century Lynching that Launched 100 Years of Federalism*. New York: Faber and Faber.

D'Orso, Michael. 1996. *Like Judgment Day: The Ruin and Redemption of a Town Called Rosewood*. New York: Putnam.

Dray, Philip. 2002. *At the Hands of Persons Unknown: The Lynching of Black America*. New York: Random House.

Ellsworth, Scott. 1982. *Death in a Promised Land: The Tulsa Race Riot of 1921*. Baton Rouge: Louisiana State University Press.

Espada, Martin. 1990. *Rebellion Is the Circle of a Lover's Hands*. Willimantic, CT: Curbstone Press.

Franklin, John Hope, and John Whittington Franklin, eds. 1997. *My Life and an Era: The Autobiography of Buck Colbert Franklin*. Baton Rouge: Louisiana State University Press.

Gregory, James N. 2005. *The Southern Diaspora: How the Great Migrations of Black and White Southerners Transformed America*. Chapel Hill: University of North Carolina Press.

Grimshaw, Allen D., ed. 1969. *Racial Violence in the United States*. Chicago: Aldine Publishing.

Grossman, James R. 1989. *Land of Hope: Chicago, Black Southerners, and the Great Migration*. Chicago: University of Chicago Press.

Hirsch, James S. 2002. *Riot and Remembrance: The Tulsa Race War and Its Legacy*. Boston: Houghton Mifflin.

Johnson, James Weldon. 1933. *Along This Way: The Autobiography of James Weldon Johnson*. New York: Viking Press.

Litwack, Leon F. 1961. *North of Slavery: The Negro in the Free States, 1790–1860*. Chicago: University of Chicago Press.

———. 1998. *Trouble in Mind: Black Southerners in the Age of Jim Crow*. New York: Knopf.

Loewen, James W. 2005. *Sundown Towns: A Hidden Dimension of American Racism*. New York: New Press.

Meier, August, and Elliott M. Rudwick. 1976. *From Plantation to Ghetto*, 3rd ed. New York: Hill and Wang.

Myrdal, Gunnar. 1944. *An American Dilemma: The Negro Problem and Modern Democracy*. New York: Harper.

Oliver, Melvin L., and Thomas M. Shapiro. 1995. *Black Wealth/White Wealth: A New Perspective on Racial Inequality*. New York: Routledge.

Ortiz, Paul. 2005. *Emancipation Betrayed: The Hidden History of Black Organizing and White Violence in Florida from Reconstruction to the Bloody Election of 1920*. Berkeley: University of California Press.

Rudwick, Elliott M. 1964. *Race Riot at East St. Louis, July 2, 1917*. Carbondale: Southern Illinois University Press.

Slotkin, Richard. 1992. *Gunfighter Nation: The Myth of the Frontier in Twentieth-Century America*. New York: Atheneum.

Tuttle, William M., Jr. 1970. *Race Riot: Chicago in the Red Summer of 1919*. New York: Atheneum.

White, Walter. 2001 (1929). *Rope and Faggot: A Biography of Judge Lynch*. Notre Dame, IN: University of Notre Dame Press.

Woodruff, Nan Elizabeth. 2003. *American Congo: The African American Freedom Struggle in the Delta*. Cambridge, MA: Harvard University Press.

GOVERNMENT PUBLICATIONS AND RIOT STUDIES

Hoffman, Peter M., comp. 1920? *The Race Riots: Biennial Report, 1918–1919, and Official Record of Inquests on the Victims of the Race Riots of July and August, 1919, Whereby Fifteen White Men and Twenty-three Colored Men Lost Their Lives and Several Hundred Were Injured*. Chicago: Cook County Coroner.

Jones, Maxine D., Larry E. Rivers, David R. Colburn, et al. 1993. *A Documented History of the Incident Which Occurred at Rosewood, Florida, in January 1923*. Tallahassee: Florida Board of Regents.

Oklahoma Commission to Study the Tulsa Race Riot of 1921. 2001. *Tulsa Race Riot: A Report*. Oklahoma City: Author.

U.S. House. *Report of the Special Committee Authorized by Congress to Investigate the East St. Louis Riots*. 65th Congress, 2nd session, 1918. H. Doc. 1231.

ARTICLES

Jones-Correa, Michael. 1999. "American Riots: Structures, Institutions, and History." Working paper, Russell Sage Foundation, New York.

Reich, Steven A. 1996. "Soldiers of Democracy: Black Texans and the Fight for Citizenship, 1917–1921." *Journal of American History* 82 (4): 1478–1504.

Tuttle, William M., Jr. 1972. "Violence in a 'Heathen' Land: The Longview Race Riot of 1919." *Phylon* 33 (4): 324–333.

White, Walter. 1919. "The Causes of the Chicago Race Riot." *Crisis* 18: 25–29.

Paul Ortiz

RACIAL DEMOGRAPHICS IN THE WESTERN HEMISPHERE

Africans, Europeans, and Asians migrated to the Americas for a variety of reasons, and the volume, motives, and circumstances of this migration changed over time. In the Western Hemisphere, the majority of Africans were forced to work on sugar, coffee, tobacco, and rice plantations, as well as in mines, but there were a few free Africans who willingly made the journey. Europeans also migrated for different motives, including religious persecution, economic opportunities, or judicial condemnation.

The arrival of Europeans and Africans resulted in the near annihilation of the Amerindian population. The indigenous societies that originally inhabited the continent were displaced, massacred, or alienated from their land in order to accommodate the settlement of Europeans. Asians also came to the Americas, mainly in the nineteenth century. With the end of the transatlantic slave trade, plantation owners used Asian indentured laborers to replace slaves in Jamaica, Guyana, and elsewhere.

In many countries in Latin America and the Caribbean, after the decimation of the local populations prior to the nineteenth century, Africans and their descendents constituted the majority of the population. Their influence was vital for the formation of various societies, from Canada to the Mexican highlands, and from the Peruvian Pacific coast to the Brazilian Atlantic shore. Slavery and its stigma became associated with the descendents of Africans, becoming a key issue in race relations in the Americas. From the fluid race classifications that occurred in Latin America to the more bipolar race perception that occurred in the United States, people's skin color became associated with four centuries of slavery.

During the four centuries of the transatlantic slave trade, which occurred approximately from 1519 to 1867, it has been conservatively estimated that around 10 million Africans arrived in the Western Hemisphere. Most of the slaves disembarked in the Americas, with 40.6 percent being shipped to Brazil. The territories under British control absorbed 29 percent of all African slaves, while Spanish America imported 14.3 percent. Around 12 percent of the total African slaves that were imported went to the territories under French subjugation. A smaller number, somewhere around 2.7 percent, ended up in the Dutch Americas, and about 1 percent went to Danish America. The majority of these Africans disembarked in the Western Hemisphere during the nineteenth century (see Table 1).

Total of Africans Disembarked, 1519–1867

1519–1600	73,400
1601–1700	540,970
1701–1800	1,427,900
1801–1867	1,561,350
1519–1867	3,850,000

SOURCE: Reprinted from Eltis et al. (1999). *The Transatlantic Slave Trade: A Database on CD-ROM.* Cambridge, UK: Cambridge University Press.

Table 1.

NORTH AMERICA

Following the European overseas expansion and conquest of the Americas, there were several waves of forced and free migrations to the Western Hemisphere (see Table 2). Estimates on the indigenous population of North America suggest that around the year 1500 approximately 4.5 million people lived in what is referred to as the mainland region of the United States of America in the early twenty-first century. Until the end of the seventeenth century, most of the immigrants who went to British America were Europeans (approximately 152,000 Europeans, compared to 22,000 Africans). This pattern changed in the first half of the eighteenth century, when the volume of European and African immigrants was almost equal. However, for most of the period, Europeans constituted the majority of the incoming immigrants. Sometimes, however, such as the period from 1740 to 1759, the number of African slaves imported into British Americas was up to twice the number of European immigrants.

In the eighteenth century, British North America received 522,400 African slaves. However, this number decreased significantly during the following century. By the eve of the American Revolution, less than 20 percent of the slave population was African born. Instead, most of the slaves were born in the Americas. From 1801 to

Estimated Migration to British America, 1620–1779

Date	European	African	Total
1620-1639	22,000	0	22,000
1640-1659	34,000	1,000	35,000
1660-1679	60,000	5,000	65,000
1680-1699	36,000	16,000	52,000
1700-1719	33,000	38,000	71,000
1720-1739	70,000	78,000	148,000
1740-1759	35,000	69,000	104,000
1760-1779	68,000	40,000	108,000
Total	358,000	247,000	605,000

SOURCE: Adapted from Menard, Russell. (1991). "Migration, Ethnicity, and the Rise of an Atlantic Economy: The Re-Peopling of the British America, 1600–1790." In *A Century of European Migration*, 1830–1930, edited by Rudolph Vecoli and Suzanne Sinke. Chicago: University of Illinois Press.

Table 2.

1808, when the importation of new slaves was outlawed, 14,450 slaves (less than 1 percent of all the African slaves forcibly transported to the Americas during the nineteenth century) arrived in the United States. Unlike other slave societies in the Western Hemisphere, slave populations in the United States increased through natural reproduction rather than by the arrival of new slaves. The slave population of the United States increased from approximately one million in 1800 to more than four million by the 1860s (see Table 3).

In the territories of modern Canada, which were controlled by the British after 1759, most of the indentured laborers were whites from Ireland or Germany, despite the fact that African slavery was also a source of labor. Unlike other places in the Americas, African slave labor was utilized in urban centers and in domestic spheres. In New France, 1,132 African slaves arrived directly from Africa between 1628 and 1759. After that, traders did not import slaves directly from Africa, but did so either through the British colonies in North America or the French West Indies. However, most of the immigrants were still Europeans. By the mid-eighteenth century, 96 percent of the inhabitants of Montreal were classified as whites, while Amerindians and blacks represented 3 and 0.7 percent of the population, respectively. Until the end of the American Revolution, there were relatively few blacks in the northern colonies. Their number increased only after the arrival of white loyalists fleeing the new American Republic, who brought over 2,000 black slaves to British Canada. Besides their slaves, Loyalists also brought with them 3,500 free blacks. These new immigrants, both whites and blacks, settled mainly in Nova Scotia and New Brunswick, where local Amerindian populations had also been established. In addition, a wave of runaway American slaves migrated to Canada beginning in the 1790s. Most of them headed for Ontario, where a 1793 act guaranteed the freedom of any former slave entering the province. By the time of the American Civil War, it is estimated that about 30,000 blacks had found their way to Canada, establishing themselves near the American border, in places such as Chatham, Toronto, London, Windsor, St. Catherine, and Hamilton. The black population of Canada did not increase substantially again until the 1960s, when immigration restrictions, based on color and origin, were removed.

African American Population in the United States

Years	Number	Percent of total population
1790	757,208	19.3
1800	1,002,037	18.9
1810	1,377,808	19.0
1820	1,771,656	18.4
1830	2,328,642	18.1
1840	2,873,648	16.8
1850	3,638,808	15.7
1860	4,441,830	14.1
1870	4,880,009	12.7
1880	6,580,793	13.1
1890	7,488,788	11.9
1900	8,833,994	11.6
1910	9,827,763	10.7
1920	10,500,000	9.9
1930	11,900,000	9.7
1940	12,900,000	9.8
1950	15,000,000	10.0
1960	18,900,000	10.5
1970	22,600,000	11.1
1980	26,500,000	11.7
1990	30,000,000	12.1
2000	34,600,000	12.3

SOURCE: Adapted from *Time Almanac 2005*, Needham, 2004, p. 377.

Table 3.

In Mexico, a smaller white immigration and a larger Amerindian population contributed to the idea that it was a nation composed solely by Spaniards and Amerindians (and their descendents). The local population of the territory now known as Mexico was estimated to be at least 4.5 million by the time of the Spanish Conquest. African slaves arrived with the first Spaniards and were employed in the exploitation of the new territory. In the 1500s and 1600s, it was estimated that the number of blacks was double the number of whites in Mexico. By the 1650s the African slave population was estimated to be around 35,000. On the other hand, it is estimated that there were thirty Amerindians to every black and white combined. The result is that African descendents are almost invisible in the modern population of Mexico.

African and Amerindian labor were employed together in mixed farming enterprises, urban activities, and domestic tasks. Given its large local population, European settlers used local labor, which was cheaper than African slaves. This resulted in a decline in the number of African slaves over time, and by the end of the eighteenth century there were only 6,000 in Mexico.

CARIBBEAN

In the Caribbean and Latin America, a small number of white settlers controlled a large slave population, and modern societies still reflect this dichotomy. Unlike British North America, race classification was very fluid, which led to race distinctions that were very arbitrary and ambiguous. Cultural ascriptions, such as hairstyle and dressing, contributed just as much as physical appearance in classifying someone as being white or black. The legacy of slavery played a major role in defining people's classifications and shaped the way nations were created in the Caribbean.

The British and the French Caribbean each accounted for about one-fifth of the total slave trade to the Americas. This trade supplied plantation economies with cheap labor. In the eighteenth century, Jamaica and Saint Domingue were the largest plantation economies in the region and the principal destination for most African captives. In the nineteenth century, Cuba emerged as the main destination for African slaves.

Slavery is intrinsically associated with Jamaica, though the slave boom only took place after Jamaica fell into British control in the 1650s. Many Amerindians died in the first decades of contact with the Spaniards due to harsh conditions and diseases introduced by European settlers and later by African slaves. By 1611, a century after the Spanish arrived, 558 slaves were present in Jamaica, one for every Spanish settler. During the first two centuries of Spanish occupation, there were no major plantations established on the island and the number of African slaves never exceeded 1,000. Under British control, however, the transatlantic slave trade expanded. In 1661, six years after the British invasion and occupation of the island, the number of immigrants started to increase. It is estimated that there were 3,000 whites and 500 blacks on the island at that time. In 1673, however, the number of blacks exploded, and 55 percent of the total population of 17,272 was classified as black.

The 1673 census indicated the presence of approximately 7,768 whites and 9,504 blacks in Jamaica. In 1690, however, the black population was three times larger than the white (10,000 whites and 30,000 blacks). African slaves from the Gold Coast, the Bight of Benin, and modern-day Nigeria were exported to Jamaica to work on the sugar plantations. Jamaica became a major British port in the transatlantic slave trade, and it served as a commercial transshipment center for ships going to British North America.

Population of Cuba, 1774–1877

Years	Slaves	Free Blacks	Whites	Total
1774	44,333	30,847	96,440	171,620
1792	84,590	54,152	133,559	272,301
1817	199,145	114,058	239,830	553,033
1827	286,942	106,494	311,051	704,487
1841	436,495	152,838	418,291	1,007,624
1846	323,759	149,226	425,767	898,752
1862	370,553	232,493	793,484	1,396,530
1877	199,094	272,478	963,394	1,434,747

SOURCE: Adapted from Knight, Franklin. (1970). *Slave Society in Cuba during the Nineteenth Century*. Madison: University of Wisconsin Press.

Table 4.

In 1713 there were approximately 7,000 whites and 55,000 blacks. By the early 1730s blacks represented 90 percent of the total population, and by the end of the 1730s the white population increased to 10,000 people, while the number of black slaves jumped to 100,000.

The slave trade and the introduction of sugar plantations changed Jamaican society, imposing a strict hierarchical division in which race played a major role. A small number of white settlers regulated labor and controlled the slave population. Even when slavery was abolished in 1833, freeing 800,000 slaves, a strict racial hierarchy continued to inhibit the political and economic achievements of blacks, and power remained in the hands of the white elite. Between 1834 and 1845, more than 4,000 European indentured servants migrated to Jamaica, mostly from England, Ireland, Germany, and Scotland, in an effort to replace slave labor. Up to 10,000 African indentured servants were also recruited between 1841 and 1867. Between 1845 and 1930, more than 20,000 Indians and 6,000 Chinese migrated to Jamaica as indentured or contract workers seeking a better life.

Similarly, in Cuba, the local population was quickly decimated after the arrival of the Spaniards. The first shipment of slaves disembarked in Cuba in 1526, but it was not until more than two centuries later that a massive African migration took place. The slave imports expanded first with the British occupation of the island (1762–1763) and exploded after the Haitian Revolution (1791–1804). In the fifty years after the Haitian Revolution, an estimated one million slaves landed in Cuba (see Table 4).

African slaves who arrived in Cuba came from different parts of Africa; estimates indicate that no single part of Africa supplied more than 28 percent of arrivals to Cuba. In addition to Africans, an estimated 150,000 to 250,000

Population of Barbados, 1655–1715

Years	Whites	Black Slaves
1655	23,000	20,000
1673	21,309	33,184
1676	21,725	32,473
1680	-	38,782
1684	19,568	46,602
1696	-	42,000
1712	12,528	41,970
1715	16,888	

SOURCE: Reprinted from Dunn, Richard. (1972). *Sugar and Slaves: The Rise of the Planter Class in the English West Indies, 1624–1713.* New York: W. W. Norton.

Table 5.

Chinese indenture laborers were taken to Cuba between 1847 and 1887.

The situation was different in Barbados. Since the beginning of its occupation, white settlers established plantation economies on the island. Tobacco plantations came first, then cotton and sugar, which required large numbers of highly regimented enslaved workers. In 1655, 23,000 whites and 20,000 blacks lived on the island (see Table 5). In 1673 the number of whites decreased slightly to 21,309, while the number of blacks jumped to 33,184. The growth of the black population was associated with the economic shift to sugar plantations and the increased demand for African slaves. In 1684 approximately 19,568 whites controlled a black population estimated at 46,602.

First called La Isla Espanola, the island of Saint Domingue (modern-day Haiti and the Dominican Republic), was the wealthiest colony in the Caribbean. It was considered the "Pearl of the Antilles," by the French. By the end of the eighteenth century, the more than 450,000 black slaves on the island produced half of the world's sugar and coffee, plus indigo and cotton. Some 40,000 white settlers and 30,000 free people of color also lived on the island. The enslaved Africans came from diverse backgrounds. Before 1725, most of the Africans who landed at Saint Domingue came from the Bight of Benin, and were mostly Adja speakers. From 1725 to 1750, half of the slaves who disembarked in Saint Domingue came from Angola. From 1750 onward, different African regions supplied slaves to this Caribbean island. In 1791, slaves rose up to free themselves from bondage, and after thirteen years of war, Haiti became a free country.

CENTRAL AMERICA

Only a few settlements were established in Central America. The presence of only a small number of mines and the existence of only small-scale agricultural production prevented a large importation of African slaves. Initially, the Amerindian population fulfilled the labor requirement. However, the number of African slaves increased when the Amerindian population started to decline. In many parts of Central America, the number of slaves was so small that descendants of Africans were not visible by the 1800s, because many had integrated with the local population. They became virtually indistinguishable from the *mestizo* (descendants of Amerindians and Europeans). After emancipation, the expansion of infrastructure and the establishment of plantations attracted impoverished blacks from the Caribbean islands. They contributed to the construction of bridges, railroads, and channels, but employment was temporary and social integration was extremely difficult.

By the early nineteenth century, blacks and their descendents made up as much as 17 percent of the population of Costa Rica. More African descendents arrived by the end of the nineteenth century to work in the banana fields, but they remained marginalized and segregated from mainstream society. In 1992 the black population of Costa Rica was estimated at 2 percent.

In Honduras, the first slaves arrived in 1540, at the beginning of Spanish presence. In 1545, approximately 5,000 slaves were imported to carry out domestic tasks or labor on small farms. Yet the number of slaves never attained the proportion of the Caribbean island settlements. As was the case in Costa Rica, by the early twentieth century, plantations geared towards the external market attracted the immigration of workers, mainly free blacks from West Indies. Estimates of African descendents in Honduras varied from 1.8 to 5.8 percent of the total population.

Panama had the largest black community in Central America. Since the arrival of the Spaniards, Panama grew in importance because it offered the narrowest land route from the Atlantic to the Pacific. At first, Spaniards relied primarily on Amerindian labor as porters to transport goods from the Atlantic to the Pacific coast. However, in less than fifty years following the arrival of the Spanish, hard labor and diseases decimated the Amerindian population, which was estimated at being more than a half million by the late fifteenth century. In 1610, some 1,057 whites, 294 free persons of color, and 3,500 slaves lived in Panama City. By 1625, blacks numbered 12,000 in Panama City. By 1789, there were 22,504 blacks, representing 64 percent of the total population of 35,920 persons in the Province of Panama. In exchange for the support for Panama's secession from Colombia, the U.S. government received the right to build a channel unifying the Atlantic and the Pacific. By the early twentieth century, about 44,000 blacks had arrived in

Brazilian Population Demographics, 1819–1940

Years	White	Mulattos	Blacks	Asians	Total Population
1819			1,081,174		3,598,132
1872	3,787,289	4,188,737	1,954,452		9,930,478
1890	6,302,198	5,934,291	2,097,426		14,333,915
1940	26,171,778	8,744,365	6,035,869	242,320	41,236,315

SOURCE: Adapted from Reis, João José. (2000). "Presença Negra: conflitos e encontros." In *Brasil: 500 anos de povoamento*. Rio de Janeiro: IBGE.; Skidmore, Thomas. (1993). *Black into White: Race and Nationality in Brazilian Thought*. Durham, NC: Duke University Press.

Table 6.

Panama, mainly from Jamaica, Barbados, and Trinidad, to work on the Panama Canal.

SOUTH AMERICA

At the time of the arrival of the Portuguese, an estimated 2 to 5 million Amerindians lived in what has become Brazil. The growing Portuguese presence after 1530 changed the lives of the Amerindians who lived along the coast. From the early sixteenth century until the mid-nineteenth century, almost 4 million African slaves arrived in Brazil, the largest number of slaves in any colony in the Americas.

By the early seventeenth century, the establishment of sugar plantations had accelerated the importation of slaves, and by the eighteenth century, the expansion of the mining economy in Minas Gerais had had a similar effect. By the end of the eighteenth century, Africans and their descendents in Brazil represented the majority of the population in the four major regions of the colony: Minas Gerais (75%), Pernambuco (68%), Bahia (79%) and Rio de Janeiro (64%). Only in São Paulo did whites constitute a larger percentage of the population than blacks (whites were 56% of the population).

The transfer of the Portuguese Crown to Brazil in 1808 led to a high demand for cheap labor to attend the court that was installed in Rio de Janeiro. The expansion of coffee and sugar plantations also contributed to this demand. As a result, the demand for slaves continued until 1850, when the slave trade was finally abolished. Slavery lasted in Brazil until 1888.

For more than 300 years, the societies of the Western Hemisphere depended on the forced labor of imported Africans. No other social institution surpassed slavery in its demands on all aspects of social organization and intergroup relations. Force, both military and moral, was the ultimate factor in its survival. Once established, slavery required its primary victims, Africans, to do its bidding without question or recourse, and its European advocates and managers had to be more vigilant about its continuation than about their own liberties. The abolition of slavery as an institution did not, however, mean the immediate end of the values and attitudes that shaped it, or of the consequences that flowed from it.

BIBLIOGRAPHY

Altman, Ida, and James Horn, eds. 1991. *"To Make America": European Emigration in the Early Modern Period.* Berkeley: University of California Press.

Beckles, Hilary. 1990. "A 'Riotous and Unruly Lot': Irish Indentured Servants and Freemen in the English West Indies, 1644–1713." *William and Mary Quarterly* 47 (4): 503–522.

Dunn, Richard. 1972. *Sugar and Slaves: The Rise of the Planter Class in the English West Indies, 1624–1713.* New York: W. W. Norton.

Eltis, David, Stephen Beherendt, David Richardson, and Herbert Klein. 1999. *The Transatlantic Slave Trade: A Database on CD-ROM.* Cambridge, U.K.: Cambridge University Press.

Kiple, Kenneth. 1976. *Blacks in Colonial Cuba.* Gainesville: University Press of Florida.

Knight, Franklin. 1970. *Slave Society in Cuba during the Nineteenth Century.* Madison: University of Wisconsin Press.

Menard, Russell. 1991. "Migration, Ethnicity, and the Rise of an Atlantic Economy: The Re-Peopling of the British America, 1600–1790." In *A Century of European Migration, 1830–1930,* edited by Rudolph Vecoli and Suzanne Sinke. Chicago: University of Illinois Press.

Reis, João José. 2000. "Presença Negra: conflitos e encontros." In *Brasil: 500 anos de povoamento.* Rio de Janeiro: IBGE.

Skidmore, Thomas. 1993. *Black into White: Race and Nationality in Brazilian Thought.* Durham, NC: Duke University Press.

Telles, Edward. 1994. "Industrialization and Racial Inequalities in Employment: The Brazilian Example." *American Sociological Review* 59 (1): 46–63.

Vecoli, Rudolph, and Suzanne Sinke, eds. 1991. *A Century of European Migration, 1830–1930.* Chicago: University of Illinois Press.

Mariana P. Candido
Paul E. Lovejoy

RACIAL DESEGREGATION (U.S.)

The process of desegregation is connected to the evolution of segregation and the simultaneous resistance to segregation by African Americans. It is equally important to see that segregation in some places developed as a middle path between outright exclusion and integration. Thus, for example, in the 1830s Ohio excluded blacks from all public schools, then later allowed them to attend segregated schools, and then later integrated its schools.

The same evolution can be seen in the U.S. Army, which went from exclusion, to segregation, to integration.

FROM THE REVOLUTION TO THE CIVIL WAR

Starting with the growth of a free black population during the American Revolution, whites sought to separate themselves from blacks. With few public institutions and little legal regulation of personal behavior, most early segregation was based on private decision making. Thus, many churches welcomed blacks and offered to save their souls but required them to sit in separate pews, usually in the back of the church, off to one side, or in a gallery. Most schools were private or only quasi-public, and in northern cities they were usually segregated. At the beginning of the Revolution most of the northern militias were integrated, and blacks fought side by side with whites in the early battles. The former slave Peter Salem fought at Lexington and Concord and at Bunker Hill. Salem Poor, also a former slave, was one of the heroes of Bunker Hill. When George Washington took over the Revolutionary Army in early 1775, he was shocked to see scores of black soldiers in the New England regiments and initially ordered that they be discharged. When unable to accomplish this, he demanded that no new blacks be allowed to enlist.

This was the first formal attempt at racial segregation in the new nation. By the end of the year, however, Washington had changed his mind and welcomed black troops. Both Salem Poor and Peter Salem reenlisted and served throughout the war, as did thousands of other blacks. At the end of the war one of Washington's favorite units was the First Rhode Island, which was made up of mostly former slaves and free blacks from that state. After the war, however, Congress quickly forgot about the many contributions of the thousands of blacks who fought for American liberty. In the Militia Act of 1792 Congress prohibited blacks from serving in the state militias. This was the new nation's first statutory requirement of racial exclusion. Shortly after this Congress prohibited blacks from serving as postmasters.

From the early national period to the eve of the Civil War, segregation developed in a variety of ways. In the South churches continued to segregate pews, but most white-dominated churches did not exclude blacks. Some masters took their slaves to church but did not sit with them. Southern free blacks and slaves also created their own religious institutions, particularly in urban settings, but whites often came to watch these services, fearing that these gatherings would lead to slave revolts. Thus, by the time of the Civil War a pattern of segregation in churches was well entrenched. Every southern state prohibited slaves from being educated and most prohibited the education of free blacks as well. No southern state provided public education for blacks and in only a few places were they able to attend private schools. Thus, for example, in 1860, only about 2,800 school-aged blacks, out of a school-age population of about 95,000, were in any school in the South. More than half of these lived in the four slave states that did not join the Confederacy.

Other antebellum southern institutions were not segregated, in the sense that there were separate accommodations for blacks. Whites often traveled with slaves attending to them as personal servants, and thus segregation would have been impractical. Moreover, to the extent that exclusion and segregation developed to support white supremacy, such rules were unnecessary in a society where over 95 percent of all blacks were slaves, and thus already legally and socially subordinated. Free blacks were excluded from most public accommodations, although no laws required this. The antebellum South was a totally closed society, where race was a symbol of enslavement and free blacks lived on the edge of society, with no claims to citizenship or rights beyond the most basic legal protections. Laws requiring or even allowing segregation were unnecessary in such a world.

In the North, free blacks formed their own churches after facing discrimination and exclusion in white churches; although in many places blacks attended the same churches as whites. Before the 1830s most states initially provided no public education for blacks, and then later segregated their public schools by providing separate schools for blacks. Practices varied greatly between states and within states. In the 1830s most of the public schools in New York State's growing cities were segregated, but within a decade the public schools in Syracuse, Rochester, and Utica were integrated, whereas those in New York City, Albany, and Buffalo were segregated. By the 1840s most of the schools in Massachusetts were integrated, including the Boston Latin School and Boston English, both prestigious high schools; however, the city's 117 grammar schools were segregated with the exception of the Smith School, a white school open to blacks. Similarly, while the city had 161 primary schools (for children ages four through seven), blacks were allowed to attend only two, including the Belknap Street School, where Sarah Roberts was assigned. In 1849 Benjamin Roberts sued the school board to allow his daughter, Sarah, to attend the school nearest to her house.

In many ways *Roberts v. City of Boston* (1850) anticipated the Supreme Court case—but not the outcome—in *Brown v. Board of Education* (1954). Both cases were brought against northern schools. Like Linda Brown, who passed by a number of elementary schools for whites to get to her school for blacks only, Sarah Roberts had to pass five elementary schools every day to get to her designated school. Charles Sumner, who would later become a U.S. senator, argued that the segregated school was inherently inferior, even though it had the same books and some other facilities as the schools for white children. He also argued the segregation itself was psychologically damaging to black children.

Lawyers in the *Brown* case would make similar arguments. Unlike the U.S. Supreme Court in *Brown*, however, the Massachusetts Supreme Judicial Court rejected integrationist arguments. Chief Justice Lemuel Shaw framed the question of this case just as the Supreme Court would in 1954: "Conceding, therefore, in the fullest manner, that colored persons, the descendants of Africans, are entitled by law, in this commonwealth, to equal rights, constitutional and political, civil and social, the question then arises, whether the regulation in question, which provides separate schools for colored children, is a violation of any of these rights." He concluded that under the Massachusetts Constitution the school board was free to assign students in whatever manner it chose, and that segregation was neither against state law nor unconstitutional. This case established the judicially created doctrine of "separate but equal," with Shaw holding that as long as the schools for blacks has the same facilities as the schools for whites, the city could maintain separate schools. Black activists and white abolitionists in Boston did not cease their struggle for equality, and in 1855 the state legislature prohibited all public schools from segregating blacks.

By the time of the Civil War, segregation in schools across the North varied. In the 1830s Ohio had refused to provide public schools for blacks and also prohibited them from attending public schools for whites. However, blacks were also exempt from paying school taxes. This led to private schools in such places as Cincinnati, but in other parts of the state blacks attended the public schools by paying tuition that was roughly the same as the taxes their parents might otherwise have paid. By the 1850s the legislature had mandated that all communities provide a free public education for blacks, but it allowed districts to do so on either an integrated or a segregated basis.

In 1860 ten times as many black children attended school in the North (about 27,000) as in the South, even though the northern free black population was smaller. Northern black attendance rates were not as high as those for whites, but they were much greater than in the South. For example, in 1860 with a school-age population of more than 22,000, only forty-one black children were enrolled in schools in Virginia, while in Pennsylvania more than 7,000 black children (out of fewer than 20,000) were in school. Some blacks also attended northern colleges that were otherwise overwhelmingly white. In some places in the North, public accommodations (inns, restaurants, theaters, railroad cars, streetcars) were open to blacks on the same basis as whites, but more commonly, private owners segregated these facilities and the states did little to stop them. Almost everywhere in the North, blacks protested these conditions with some success. Some states, such as Massachusetts, banned segregation in railroad cars, and protests in New York City forced streetcar companies to allow patrons to sit anywhere. Most businesses in the North, however, were able to segregate without any interference from the courts or the legislature. On the eve of the Civil War it was possible to find substantial integration and substantial segregation in the same states and even in the same cities across the North.

FROM THE CIVIL WAR TO WORLD WAR II: THE NORTH

The Civil War brought vast changes to race relations. From the moment the war began, blacks volunteered for the army to fight the Confederacy. Initially the U.S. Army did not allow blacks to enlist, although the navy did. In late 1862 the Lincoln administration authorized the enlistment of blacks in segregated regiments, with mostly white officers. By the end of the war approximately 180,000 blacks had served in the army and another 20,000 or so in the navy. Initially black soldiers were paid at a lower rate than their white counterparts, but Congress rectified this by 1864. After the war the army did not revert to the exclusionist policy as it had done in the wake of the Revolution. Blacks, however, would remain in separate units and only a token few were allowed to rise above the rank of noncommissioned officer.

A few other racial barriers began to break down during the war. Congress, which had jurisdiction over the District of Columbia, granted charters to streetcar companies that were obligated to seat patrons without regard to race. During the war the state department began to issue passports for blacks, thus rejecting the logic of the *Dred Scott* decision—that blacks, even if free, could never be considered "citizens" of the United States. President Lincoln met with some black leaders at the White House and invited Frederick Douglass to have tea with him at his summer residence, The Soldiers' Home. This was a symbolically powerful moment, as the Kentucky-born president of the United States treated a leading African American as a social equal by sitting down with him to share food, drink, and conversation. After his reelection, Lincoln invited Douglass to his inauguration party. When a guard, not knowing who Douglass was, barred his entry, Lincoln personally escorted him into the room.

Immediately after the war a number of southern states, still dominated by legislatures elected during the war, passed laws requiring segregation in public facilities. In 1865 Florida became the first state to require segregation on railroad cars, with other states following close behind. Texas, for example, passed a law requiring a separate railroad car for blacks. However, during Reconstruction these laws were repealed, and some were replaced with laws requiring integration of public facilities. Southern public schools were open to children of all races, but most whites boycotted them. Louisiana passed laws prohibiting segregation on railroad cars and steamships. In 1870 Louisiana allowed interracial marriage, as did Arkansas in 1874. Other southern states dropped their ban on interracial marriage as well during this period. Meanwhile, in the Civil Rights Act of 1875 Congress required integration at the national level of most places of public accommodation. That year Congress also allowed black immigrants to become naturalized citizens. The law was drawn carefully, however, to exclude immigrants from Asia.

After 1877 this brief moment of racial fairness for former slaves began to fade. Southern states began to segregate transportation, schools, and other public facilities. In *The Civil Rights Cases* (1883) the Supreme Court struck down the Civil Rights Act of 1883, paving the way for rampant private discrimination in the South. In *Pace v. Alabama,* decided the same year, the Court also upheld an Alabama law making it a criminal offense for blacks and whites to marry each other.

Most northern states responded to these decisions by passing their own civil rights acts, banning restaurants, hotels, theaters, streetcars, and the like from discriminating on the basis of race. In 1883, for example, Michigan specifically allowed interracial marriage, and two years later the state passed a sweeping equal accommodations law that did at the state level what the Congress had tried to do nationally in the Civil Rights Act of 1875. Almost every other northern state passed a similar law in the next decade. Many northern states also prohibited school districts from maintaining separate schools for blacks. Courts in many northern states enforced these laws.

By 1900 segregation was not legal in most of the North. In theory schools, hotels, restaurants, theaters, streetcars, and railroad cars were open to blacks on the same basis as whites. By the eve of World War II, however, a decidedly different practice had emerged. Most northern blacks lived in cities and were increasingly ghettoized through real estate practices that were rarely regulated by statutes. Thus, segregation—in fact, de facto segregation—became the norm. In most places schools were not officially segregated, but neighborhood schools led to segregated schools in cities where blacks were concentrated into specific neighborhoods. In smaller towns and rural areas discrimination was often the practice if not the law. Paul Robeson, for example, was denied the right to be valedictorian at his high school in a small town in New Jersey simply because the principal did not want a black speaker at graduation. When he entered Rutgers University in 1915, he was the only black on campus and only the third in the history of the school. As the state university of New Jersey, Rutgers was not officially segregated, but it was effectively so.

Similarly, when future federal judge A. Leon Higginbotham entered Purdue University in Indiana, in 1944, only twelve black civilian students attended this large state university. Higginbotham was allowed to attend classes on an equal basis with whites but was not given dormitory space and was instead forced to live in an unheated attic. The university president told Higginbotham that the law did not mandate integration of the dormitories, only of the classrooms. On the other hand, blacks attended colleges on an equal basis with whites in many urban public universities throughout the North. Higginbotham left Purdue for the integrated, private Antioch College and then Yale Law School. At the time it would have been illegal for him to attend an integrated private college or law school anywhere in the South.

In 1947, the President's Committee on Civil Rights reported that "New York State, in particular, has an impressive variety of civil rights laws on its statute books" and that "few other states and cities have followed suit, especially in the fair employment practice field." However, many, perhaps most, privately owned businesses ignored such laws and rarely had to defend their actions in the courts. Blacks reported to the President's Committee that despite laws that prohibited discrimination, it was "difficult to find a meal or a hotel room in the downtown areas of most northern cities." Enforcement of such laws was lax and businesses "discouraged [blacks] from patronizing places by letting them wait indefinitely for service, charging them higher prices, giving poor service, and publicly embarrassing them in various ways." Although illegal, "whites only" signs could be found in some places in the North. Generally, though, such signs were unnecessary, as some businesses simply refused to accommodate or serve blacks.

By the end of World War II the practices of the North were mixed. In smaller cities and towns schools were integrated because neighborhoods were integrated or because there was only one school to attend. In southern Indiana, Illinois, and New Jersey some local districts maintained segregated schools for blacks even in small towns, despite state laws prohibiting such schools. Almost every northern state had civil rights laws prohibiting all sorts of discrimination, but hotels, restaurants, and landlords nevertheless often successfully ignored such laws. Beaches, pools, and parks were officially integrated, but local prejudice led to de facto segregation. However, blacks throughout the North could vote, run for office, and in many places find public-sector jobs.

Urban ghettoization led to de facto segregation but also to political power; by the end of World War II both Chicago and New York had black representatives in the U.S. Congress, and scores of blacks served on city councils and in state legislatures across the North. Blacks had access to public and private higher education. Most state universities were integrated, although a few northern states, such as Ohio and Pennsylvania, established public institutions that were not officially segregated but nevertheless had student bodies that were almost entirely black. Private-sector employment was mixed. Small employers easily evaded the fair employment practices acts in such states as Michigan and New York. But by the end of World War II in the industrial states of the Northeast and Midwest, blacks found relatively high paying jobs in steel mills, auto factories, and with similar large employers. Even in these industries, however, promotions were few and management positions almost always were closed to blacks.

On the West Coast a different kind of segregation emerged in the 1840s as Chinese laborers came to the nation during the California gold rush. They were segregated and often faced incredible violence. The phrase "a Chinaman's chance" emerged in the nation's lexicon to describe the likelihood of a Chinese gold miner surviving if he was lucky enough (or unlucky enough) to actually find gold. The Chinese faced segregation in schools, were not allowed to testify in cases involving whites, and were prohibited from marrying anyone outside their own race. During the Civil War, California repealed its laws prohibiting blacks from testifying against whites but did not do the same for Chinese. After the war, discrimination against Chinese was so blatant that in at least one case, *Yick Wo v. Hopkins* (1886) the Supreme Court rendered a decision in favor of Chinese laundry owners, who protested a law that required all laundries to be built of brick unless the sheriff gave the owner an exemption. All white owners got this exemption, but not Chinese. In 1882 anti-Chinese sentiment led to the first racially based immigration restriction in U.S. history, the Chinese Exclusion Act.

After 1886 Japanese began to come to the West Coast, where they also faced segregation. At the turn of the century, President Theodore Roosevelt complained that the mistreatment of Japanese immigrants and Japanese American citizens in California threatened international peace. This crisis led to the "Gentlemen's Agreement," by which Japan agreed to limit the number of immigrants coming to the United States. Until the 1950s Asian immigrants were prohibited even from becoming naturalized citizens. The West Coast states, especially California, continued to segregate Japanese, passing laws to prevent aliens "ineligible for citizenship"—which only applied to Asian immigrants—from owning real estate or obtaining certain licenses. After World War II the Supreme Court would strike down most of the laws, but before then Asians on the West Coast faced segregation. The final chapter of this grim history was the internment during World War II of more than 100,000 Japanese Americans, most of whom were citizens because they had been born in the United States. This was done by the federal government, but with the full support of officials in California, Oregon, and Washington.

During this period Hispanics in California, New Mexico, Arizona, and Texas faced some form of de jure segregation, especially in schools, and a significant amount of informal segregation. In *Wysinger v. Crookshank* (1890) the California Supreme Court prohibited the segregation of blacks in the state's public schools, although de facto segregation developed in the early twentieth century. In 1931 the legislature specifically allowed segregation of Asians and Hispanics in the state's schools. But between 1944 and 1948 state and federal courts in California banned all forms of segregation in the state and legalized interracial marriage. The key case was *Mendez v. Westminster* (1947), in which the Ninth Circuit Court of Appeals became the first federal court to strike down racially based segregation in the public schools. This case was not appealed, because shortly after the decision Governor Earl Warren signed the Anderson Bill, prohibiting all school segregation in the state. A year later, in *Perez v. Lippold* (1948), the California Supreme Court struck down the state's ban on interracial marriage, making it the first court in the nation to take such a position.

SOUTHERN SEGREGATION: FROM RECONSTRUCTION TO *BROWN*

The story in the South was entirely different. Starting with the end of Reconstruction in the 1870s, the southern states began to segregate every institution in southern society. In the 1870s and 1880s the U.S. Supreme Court struck down laws that blatantly prohibited blacks from voting or serving as jurors but gave its blessing to segregation. In *Hall v. DeCuir* (1878) the Court struck down a Louisiana law passed during Reconstruction that prohibited segregation on boats and trains in the state. The Court said this violated the powers of Congress to regulate interstate commerce. In *Louisville, New Orleans & Texas Railway Co. v. Mississippi* (1890), however, the Court upheld a Mississippi law that required segregation, even though presumably that law also placed a burden on interstate commerce. Both cases were argued on issues of interstate commerce and did not focus per se on the constitutional rights of blacks. This issue was brought directly before the Court in *Plessy v. Ferguson* (1896), in which the Supreme Court held that the Thirteenth and Fourteenth Amendments did not prevent Louisiana from segregating railroad cars and other public transportation in the state.

This decision opened the floodgates to massive segregation of everything in the South, where 90 percent of all blacks lived in 1900 and where 70 percent still lived in 1950. In 1898 a South Carolina newspaper mocked the growing penchant for southerners to segregate all facilities, noting:

> if there must be Jim Crow cars on the railroads, there should be Jim Crow cars on the street railways. Also on all passenger boats. . . . If there are to be Jim Crow cars, moreover, there should be Jim Crow waiting saloons at all stations, and Jim Crow eating houses. . . . There should be Jim Crow sections of the jury box, and a separate Jim Crow dock and witness stand in every court—and a Jim Crow Bible for the colored witnesses to kiss. It would be advisable also to have a Jim Crow section in county auditors' and treasurers' offices for the accommodation of colored taxpayers. The two races are dreadfully mixed in these offices for weeks.

However, as the historian C. Vann Woodward noted in his classic book *The Strange Career of Jim Crow* (1974 [1955]), within a few years, except for the "Jim Crow witness stand, all the improbable applications of the principle suggested by the editor in derision had been put into practice—down to and including the Jim Crow Bible" (p. 68).

By 1945 virtually every facet of life in the South was segregated. Southern blacks faced discrimination at every turn in their lives. If born in a hospital, southern blacks entered the world in a separate hospital; they would be buried in segregated cemeteries. As the President's Committee noted, in the South "it is generally illegal for Negroes to attend the same schools as whites; attend theaters patronized by whites; visit parks where whites relax; eat, sleep, or meet in hotels, restaurants, or public halls frequented by whites." Virtually all public and private educational institutions in the South, from nursery school to college, were segregated. The only exceptions were a few small private historically black colleges that occasionally had a white student or two. At the beginning of the century, Kentucky's Berea College was integrated. In 1904, to stop this breach of southern racial etiquette, Kentucky passed legislation banning private integration, and Berea sued, attempting to remain integrated in the face of laws mandating segregation. In *Berea College v. Kentucky* (1908) the U.S. Supreme Court upheld Kentucky's law mandating that private colleges be segregated, giving a green light to legally mandated segregation everywhere in the South, even where parties wanted to be integrated.

Most southern states ignored the education of their black citizens as much as they could. Louisiana, for example, created some twenty "trade schools" between 1934 and 1949 for whites but did not provide any trade schools for blacks. At the primary and secondary levels the disparity in public expenditures guaranteed that blacks would have inferior educational facilities. Almost without exception, white principals, supervisors, and teachers were paid more than blacks. Classes for blacks had more children than classes for whites, schools for blacks were open fewer days, and the facilities were vastly inferior. The situation in Clarendon County, South Carolina, illustrates the reality of segregated education. In 1949, the county spent $179 per pupil for white children and $43 per pupil for black children. The county had sixty-one school buildings for its 6,531 black students, which were worth $194,575. The 2,375 white students went to twelve different schools, worth $673,850.

Segregation profoundly affected criminal justice in the South. By the end of World War II a few southern cities had at least a few black police officers, but most southern blacks still lived in rural areas and small towns, where policing was segregated and often oppressive. Police brutality toward blacks was the norm, and only the most egregious cases ever reached the federal courts where some relief might be found. If arrested, blacks went to segregated jails and, when convicted, to segregated prisons. In Florida, for example, it was illegal for any sheriff or other law enforcement officer to handcuff or chain blacks and whites together, whereas in Georgia black and white prisoners were to be kept separate "as far as practicable." Segregated facilities meant that black prisoners would face worse conditions than their white counterparts. No matter how bad jail and prison conditions were for whites, they would always be worse for blacks. Furthermore, a convict leasing system gave county and state officials an incentive to prosecute vigorously all black lawbreakers because convicts were laborers who could be rented out to various southern farms and businesses. In court, blacks were invariably represented by white attorneys, if they had representation at all. They faced white judges and all-white juries. In the Deep South, prison often meant laboring on a chain gang or in a rural work camp.

Virtually all other facilities were equally segregated. Southern states segregated homes for the aged, orphanages, and homes or institutions for juvenile delinquents. Industrial schools were segregated where they existed. Louisiana had three industrial schools: one each for young white males, white females, and black males. Black female youthful offenders were not offered the option of learning a skill or trade in preparation for their rehabilitation. In most southern states, African Americans with a hearing problem, a mental illness, or tuberculosis went to special institutions for blacks only. Ironically, state schools for the blind were segregated in the South, even though, presumably, most of the students could not actually see each other. While all these institutions were in theory "separate but equal," in practice they were never equal. No matter how bad conditions might be for whites, they were invariably worse for blacks.

As the South became increasingly industrialized after World War II, segregation helped keep blacks economically marginalized. South Carolina provided $100 fines and up to thirty days' imprisonment at hard labor for textile manufacturers or their officials who failed to follow elaborate rules for racial separations. The law set out in great detail that no company engaged in textile or cotton manufacturing—the most important industry in the state—could allow members of

> different races to labor and work together within the same room, or to use the same doors of entrance and exit at the same time, or to use and occupy the same pay ticket windows or doors for paying off its operatives and laborers at the same time, or to use the same stairway and windows at the same time, or to use at any time the same lavatories, toilets, drinking water buckets, pails, cups, dippers or glasses.

Other states had similar rules. In Oklahoma, Tennessee, and Texas, mines were required to have both separate shower facilities and clothing lockers for workers when they emerged from the ground. These laws did more than just humiliate blacks and remind them of their inferior legal status: The laws also prevented them from advancing in their jobs, or even getting jobs. Separate facilities for blacks meant that factory owners would have to invest more money in their mills, mines, and factories. Where possible, it made greater economic sense simply to hire only whites, leaving blacks outside the growing industrial job market.

Everywhere in the South, public accommodations were segregated by law—separate, but almost never actually equal. The South required that there be separate drinking fountains, restrooms, motels, hotels, elevators, bars, restaurants, and lunch counters for blacks. Trains had separate cars for blacks, and buses reserved the last few rows for blacks, always keeping them, symbolically, at the back of the bus. Taxis served whites or blacks, not both. Waiting rooms at bus stations, train stations, and airports were separate as well. At theaters, blacks sat in separate sections at the back or in the balcony. Practice on these issues always varied. While many states mandated separate waiting rooms at train and bus stations, Florida found yet one more way to segregate, separate, and humiliate blacks, by requiring that railroads also provide separate ticket windows for black travelers.

Beyond public accommodations, schools, and the workplace, everything else was segregated. Louisiana required separate ticket windows and entrances at circuses and tent shows. The law required that these ticket offices be at least twenty-five feet apart. Southern states banned interracial meetings of fraternal orders, whereas cities and states followed Birmingham's segregation of "any room, hall, theatre, picture house, auditorium, yard, court, ball park, public park, or other indoor or outdoor place." Mobile, Alabama had a 10:00 p.m. curfew for blacks. Florida stored textbooks from black and white schools in different buildings, and New Orleans segregated its red light district. Texas specifically prohibited interracial boxing, most cities and towns segregated seating at baseball fields. Local ordinances or customs made it illegal or unlikely that blacks and whites would compete against each other in sporting events, but some states made certain this would not happen. Georgia specifically segregated billiard rooms and poolrooms. South Carolina and Oklahoma segregated public parks and playgrounds. In Louisiana, it was illegal for blacks and whites to reside in the same dwelling, and the existence of "separate entrances or partitions" would not be a defense to a charge under this law. Oklahoma provided for "segregation of the white and colored races as to the exercises of rights of fishing, boating, and bathing" as well as "to the exercise of recreational rights" at parks, playgrounds, and pools. The state required "telephone companies . . . to maintain separate booths for white and colored patrons."

Even the sacred was not protected from the need of southern whites to separate themselves from blacks: Tennessee required that houses of worship be segregated. Texas and North Carolina segregated their public libraries by statute, whereas other states did not, presumably because they did not imagine blacks using public libraries. Nevertheless, when blacks tried to use them, they were either refused access or forced into segregated facilities. Georgia never seemed to tire of finding things to segregate, and, thus, in its 1937–1938 legislative session, the state provided that the names of white and black taxpayers be made out separately on the tax digest. Beyond the statutes, there were customs and extralegal forms of segregation. Woodward was unable to find a statute requiring separate Bibles in courtrooms, but everywhere that was the practice. As Woodward noted, writing in 1955:

> It is well to admit, and even to emphasize, that laws are not an adequate index of the extent and prevalence of segregation and discriminatory practices in the South. The practices often anticipated and sometimes exceeded the law. It may be confidently assumed—and it could be verified by

> present observation—that there is more Jim Crowism practiced in the South than there are Jim Crow laws on the books.

Thus, banks in the South refused to give loans to blacks, even after World War II when housing loans for black veterans were guaranteed by the GI Bill. Southern blacks could usually shop at the same department stores as whites, but they had to take separate elevators (usually the freight elevators) to the different floors. They might buy the same clothing as whites but were usually not allowed to try on the clothing before purchasing it.

What the historian Woodward described for the turn-of-the-century and beyond, the economist Gunnar Myrdal observed in the 1940s. His classic study of American race relations, *An American Dilemma* (1944), detailed the existence of an elaborate system of segregation throughout the American South, as well as less pervasive and systematic, but equally pernicious, forms of discrimination in the North. Myrdal noted:

> Every Southern state and most Border states have structures of state laws and municipal regulations which prohibit Negroes from using the same schools, libraries, parks, playgrounds, railroad cars, railroad stations, sections of streetcars and buses, hotels, restaurants and other facilities as do the whites. In the South there are, in addition, a number of sanctions other than the law for enforcing institutional segregation as well as etiquette. Officials frequently take it upon themselves to force Negroes into certain action when they have no authority to do so. (p. 628)

Even before *Plessy v. Ferguson* (1896) the Supreme Court had upheld numerous southern regulations of race while striking down attempts by Congress and the southern states to create a more racially equal society. After *Plessy* the southern states segregated every private and public institution they could. Under President Woodrow Wilson—the first southerner elected president since the Civil War—almost all facilities in Washington, D.C., were segregated, and blacks were forced out of many civil service jobs. The army remained segregated, and blacks were limited to kitchen work and similar "service jobs" in the navy and totally excluded from the marines. When World War I began, the army forced into retirement its most senior black officer, Colonel Charles Young, because otherwise Young would have been in the position of commanding white soldiers and junior officers.

In 1909 black and white opponents of segregation formed the National Association for the Advancement of Colored People (NAACP), which would become the nation's largest civil rights organization. The NAACP organized chapters throughout the nation, although in the South member identities had to be kept secret in many places. The NAACP focused much of its energy on fighting segregation and racism through litigation, winning its first case in 1915 when the Court, in *Guinn v. United States*, struck down Oklahoma's grandfather clause that effectively disfranchised blacks in the state. In *Buchanan v. Warley* (1917) the NAACP won again when the Court struck down a Kentucky law that prohibited the sale of real estate to members of one race or the other, on the grounds that this would unduly restrict private property. In *Corrigan v. Buckley* (1926), however, the Court upheld the right of private parties to sign restrictive covenants, which prevented white landowners from selling their property to blacks. The Court maintained this public/private distinction in other ways, ruling, for example, that the state of Texas could not prohibit blacks from voting in primary elections, but if the political parties ran the primaries as private organizations, the parties themselves could exclude black voters. In *Missouri ex rel. Gaines v. Canada* (1938) the Court ordered the integration of the University of Missouri School of Law, but only because the state had not provided a similar school for blacks.

On the eve of World War II states were free to establish "separate but equal" facilities for blacks and whites, such as schools and colleges, and require "separate but equal" seating on public transportation and other areas of public life. Private enterprises were free to segregate without any laws. Most southern states also required that private enterprises segregate the races, or if that was not possible, be open to only one race. Similarly, the Court struck down laws that restricted the vote to whites but did not interfere with literacy tests, poll taxes, or the privatization of primary elections, which disfranchised most southern blacks and simultaneously kept them off juries. In 1940 most blacks—about 70 percent—lived in the South, where segregation was a way of life, discrimination an everyday fact, and economic opportunity severely limited. The North offered better jobs, housing, educational opportunity, and even some political power, but not full equality.

BROWN AND DESEGREGATION

The New Deal and World War II undermined the South's system of segregation in a number of ways. New Deal programs were often segregated, but they nevertheless provided some opportunities for blacks in the South. The Roosevelt Court also began to chip away at segregation, starting with the *Gaines* case in 1938. In *Mitchell v. United States*, decided in the spring of 1941, the Court held that state laws requiring segregation on interstate railroads violated the commerce clause and that only the Interstate Commerce Commission could authorize such segregation. In *Morgan v. Virginia* (1946) the Court applied the logic of this case to interstate bus transportation. Significantly, the opinion was written by a southern justice, Stanley Reed of Kentucky. Neither case was a "civil rights case" per se, since the Court used the commerce clause to overturn the state laws, but both cases clearly indicated that segregation was no longer constitutionally sacrosanct. While both cases were victories in the Court, buses and trains mostly remained segregated in the South.

In between these two cases, the United States fought World War II. During the war millions of northerners saw segregation for the first time, as they were stationed in military bases all over the South. Even northerners who were not sympathetic to civil rights were shocked by seeing blacks sent to the back of a bus or not even allowed on a bus. Segregation in the North was residential, de facto, and often not much in evidence. In the South it was bold, brutal, and evident everywhere one turned. Segregation in the army was also surprising to many men and women who simply never imagined that fellow soldiers would be separated on the basis of race. The ideology of the war was even more damaging to segregation. Nazism was the logical conclusion of racism. The war itself was a statement against racism. Moreover, for the first time in American history the United States was allied with nonwhites—the Chinese, Filipinos, and Koreans—in the war against Japan. Surely there was racism in the antiwar propaganda against the Japanese, but at the same time American propaganda extolled the virtues of the nation's nonwhite allies. After the war a significant number of GIs came home with Japanese wives, and after 1949, Korean wives. These returning veterans found that in about twenty states—almost all of them in the South—their marriages were void and it was illegal for them even to live with their nonwhite wives.

Returning black veterans were particularly incensed by the segregation that greeted them after risking their lives for American democracy. Using the GI Bill, they gained education and bought houses and stood up to the wall of segregation that awaited them. More blacks tried to vote, although with mixed results. Other blacks, such as Irene Morgan, who had been arrested for not moving to the back of a bus in Virginia, were more aggressive about asserting their rights.

The NAACP, which had rallied against segregation on the margins since the 1920s, fought for equality in housing, voting, and interstate transportation. In the 1930s the organization began to plan for an assault on segregated education, reasoning that without education blacks could never be equal in the workplace or any other part of society. The attack first began by testing the meaning of the "equal" provision of the "separate-but-equal doctrine" that had allowed segregation since the 1890s. Suits in Missouri and Texas forced the integration of graduate and professional schools by arguing that such separate schools could *never* be equal. In *Sweat v. Painter* (1950) the Supreme Court accepted this argument and forced the integration of the University of Texas Law School. This set the stage for the assault on segregation in public schools in *Brown v. Board of Education* (1954).

Other events also helped prepare for *Brown*. The most important may have been the decision of Branch Rickey to sign Jackie Robinson to play for the Brooklyn Dodgers, thereby breaking the color line in baseball. In 1947 Robinson became the first black to play in the major leagues since the 1890s. Other teams quickly followed suit, and soon black stars became common in both leagues and essential to the success of most teams. Teams that had not won the World Series in decades (or ever)—the Cleveland Indians, New York Giants, Brooklyn Dodgers, and Milwaukee Braves—won with black stars. By the mid-1950s black players were common, and as television invaded American homes, the whole nation became used to seeing integrated teams winning ball games. In an eleven-year period (from 1949 to 1959) nine of eleven most valuable players in the National League were black, as were most of the rookies of the year in that league.

While baseball made integration seem possible, the cold war and the Korean War made it necessary. As the United States competed with the Soviet Union for international prestige, segregation became increasingly embarrassing. Thus, in 1948 President Harry Truman ordered the integration of the military, ending nearly a century of separate units for blacks. Long an opponent of segregation in his home state of Missouri, Truman also saw that justice dovetailed with both good foreign policy and good politics. Segregation continued in all the services for a few more years, but by the end of the Korean War the military was no longer segregated, although the officer corps in all branches was overwhelmingly white. In 1948 the Democratic Party placed a strong civil rights plank in its platform, which led to a walkout by "Dixiecrats" led by Strom Thurmond of South Carolina. Thurmond contended for the presidency that year as a segregationist, but his poor showing, and his failure to derail Truman, could be seen as an indication that it was politically safe to challenge segregation. Thus, when the *Brown* case finally made it to the U.S. Supreme Court, the Eisenhower administration supported desegregation as a matter of foreign policy necessity, but with knowledge that it was politically acceptable to do so.

In 1952 the Supreme Court heard four cases consolidated as *Brown v. Board of Education*. The Court did not decide the case that year but ordered reargument for the following year. In the interim, California governor Earl Warren, who had signed the law banning segregation in that state, became chief justice. Warren fashioned a unanimous Court to support an end to segregation in the public schools but strategically held the decision until the end of the term in May 1954, when most public schools were no longer in session for the year. The key issue was whether segregation in public schools violated the equal protection clause of the Fourteenth Amendment. The Court found that it did. As Chief Justice Earl Warren put it in his opinion: "We come then to the question presented: Does segregation of children in public schools solely on the basis of race, even though the physical facilities and other 'tangible' factors may be equal, deprive the children of the minority group of equal educational opportunities?" In other words, could separate schools *ever* be equal. The Court held they could not be equal. Warren wrote:

> We conclude that in the field of public education the doctrine of "separate but equal" has no place. Separate educational facilities are inherently unequal. Therefore, we hold that the plaintiffs and others similarly situated for whom the actions have been brought are, by reason of the segregation complained of, deprived of the equal protection of the laws guaranteed by the Fourteenth Amendment.

This unanimous decision was narrowly limited to schools. It nevertheless signaled a revolution in American society. For the first time since Reconstruction a branch of government—the Supreme Court—had taken a firm stand against racial inequality and segregation. Southerners responded with grim opposition. In 1956 all but three southern members of the Senate and seventy-seven southern House members signed a "Southern Manifesto" denouncing the decision and integration. The nonsigning senators were three men with national ambitions: Lyndon Johnson of Texas and Estes Kefauver and Albert Gore Sr. of Tennessee. Across the South defiant school administrators warned that they would never submit to integration. A few counties in Virginia closed their schools rather than integrate. Schools developed "freedom of choice" programs to allow children to voluntarily choose which schools they would attend, knowing that whites would choose the former white schools and most blacks would be too intimidated to attend them. In 1957 President Eisenhower was forced to send federal troops to Little Rock, Arkansas, to enforce a federal court order requiring the integration of Central High School. Armed airborne troops, with bayonets in place, guarded nine children who entered the previously all-white high school. Federal troops and U.S. marshals would later be used to end segregation in state universities in Mississippi and Alabama.

While *Brown* was directed only at schools, the logic of the decision affected everything else in the South. Scores of federal court decisions struck down one form of segregation after another in the South. Meanwhile, a mass movement spread across the South, as blacks and white allies (often from the North) organized boycotts and demonstrations. In December 1955 Rosa Parks, a longtime member of the NAACP, was arrested when she refused to give up her seat to a white man on a public bus in Montgomery, Alabama. This sparked a 381-day boycott of the buses by blacks. The boycott thrust a young black preacher, the Reverend Martin Luther King Jr., into the national limelight. After the boycott, King organized the Southern Christian Leadership Conference (SCLC), which became the most important force for grassroots organizing.

Meanwhile, lawyers for the NAACP challenged bus segregation in the courts and in November 1956, in *Gayle v. Browder*, the U.S. Supreme Court upheld a lower court decision declaring the bus segregation unconstitutional. In late December the Court rejected final appeals from Alabama, and on December 20 the order to desegregate the buses arrived in Montgomery. A day later the boycott ended as blacks were able to sit wherever they wanted on the public buses. This was, in a formal sense, the reversal of *Plessy v. Ferguson*. It also meant that most state laws requiring or mandating segregation were unconstitutional. It would take another decade of demonstrations, court decisions, and interventions by the U.S. government to finally end all state-sponsored segregation in the South. The southern segregationists were, in the end, fighting a losing battle as long as the Supreme Court remained firm in its position that the states could not discriminate.

The Court's decisions, however, applied only to state laws requiring segregation. Private businesses were still free to discriminate. In February 1960 four students from the historically black North Carolina A&T University in Greensboro, North Carolina, sat down at a lunch counter in a Woolworth's to order coffee. When they were refused service, they in turn refused to leave. This was not the first "sit-in" to challenge segregation, but it gained national publicity. Within days hundreds of black students, joined by some whites, were demanding service at downtown stores and lunch counters. In the next two months there were more than fifty sit-ins in nine southern states. For national chains such as Woolworth's the sit-ins were an embarrassment and a threat to business outside the South, as its stores were picketed throughout the North. The sit-ins and demonstrations in Greensboro continued until July, when Woolworth's finally agreed to serve blacks. Because the southern states could no longer require segregation, sit-ins were successful where they focused on national stores and where the public mood led to lethal or near-lethal violence. In big cities of the

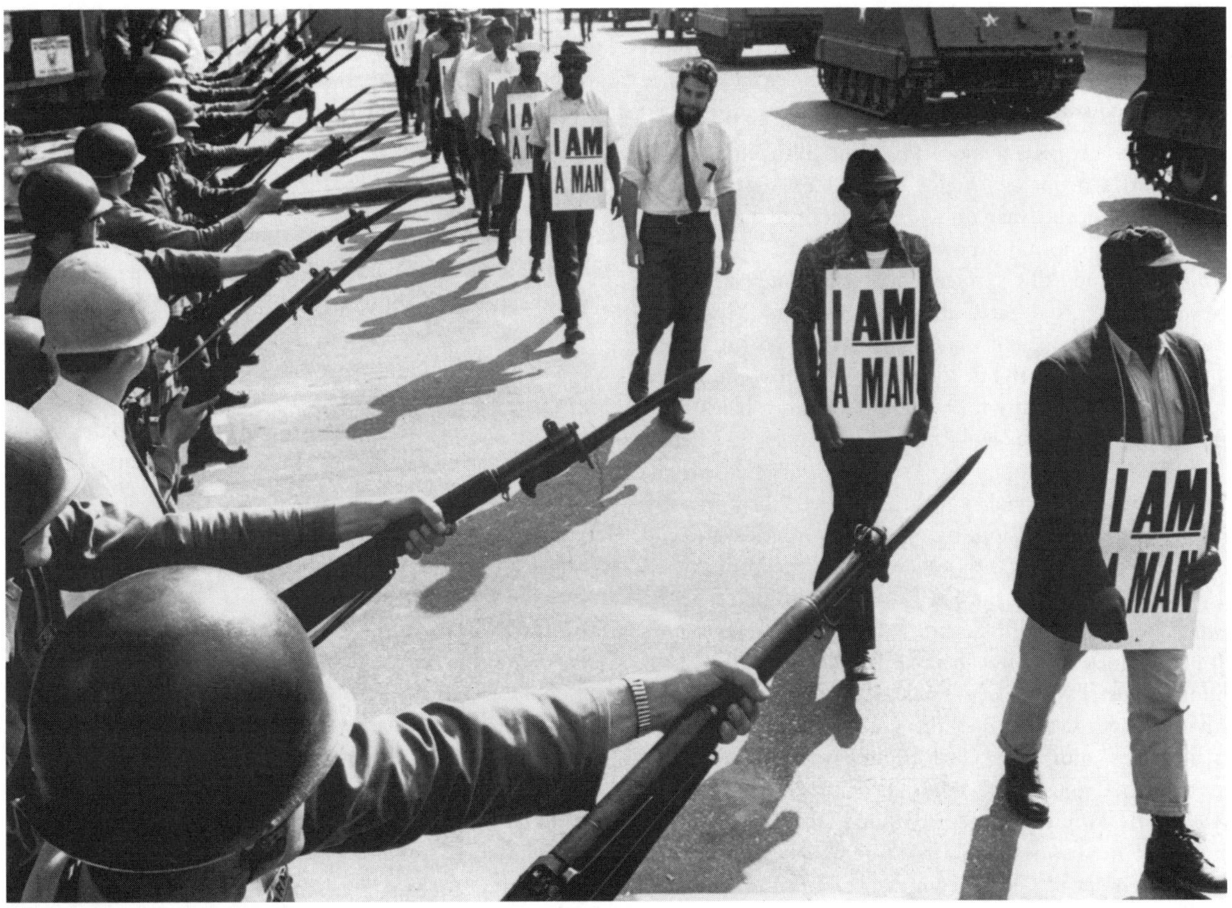

Civil Rights March, 1968. *Civil Rights activists stage a protest in Memphis, Tennessee. Civil Rights marches continued until the late 1960s, as blacks still struggled for equality and economic opportunity.* © BETTMANN/CORBIS.

upper and mid-South this tactic worked to force an end to segregation.

The Greensboro sit-in stimulated some cities—such as Atlanta and Nashville—to quietly desegregate public space. This led activists to organize "sit-ins" on the road in the spring of 1961. Hundreds of mostly students from the North and the upper South boarded interstate buses, with blacks and whites sitting next to each other. The Freedom Riders, as they were called, integrated lunch counters, rest rooms, and other facilities as their buses headed south. The buses passed peacefully through the upper South, but mobs began to attack the buses once they reached South Carolina. On May 14, 1961—Mother's Day—a mob in Anniston, Alabama, set a bus on fire and blocked the doors to prevent the Freedom Riders from escaping. The riders were able to leave the bus only when it exploded. But as they exited the bus they were brutally beaten, and only the presence of an armed undercover agent prevent a lynching. The federal government arranged for the National Guard to escort the buses to Jackson, Mississippi, where all the Freedom Riders were peacefully arrested. In November 1961 the Interstate Commerce Commission ordered the integration of all interstate buses and trains in the nation.

The firebombing of the bus in Alabama helped make that state the symbol of southern white resistance to change. In May 1963 Birmingham's Eugene "Bull" Connor ordered the use of fire hoses and police dogs to suppress peaceful marches sponsored by the SCLC. These attacks—showing young children being lifted off the ground by the high-pressure fire hoses—were broadcast on national news shows, to the shock of most northerners. In June, Governor George C. Wallace personally blocked the admission of two black students to the University of Alabama. That summer, civil rights leaders from around the nation organized their famous March on Washington to protest segregation. The highlight of the march turned out to be King's "I Have a Dream Speech," which in tone and substance was more sermon than speech, more conciliatory than angry. Seen by millions on television and repeated on news programs, the speech became a symbol of the civil rights movement and contrasted the movement's call for peaceful change and legal equality with the violence of police officials.

Before his assassination, President John F. Kennedy submitted a major civil rights bill to Congress, where it languished. In the wake of his assassination Lyndon Johnson used his enormous power and longtime Washington knowledge and skills to force Congress to vote on the law. While Congress debated the bill, events in Mississippi riveted the nation and underscored the need for federal protection for civil rights. In June 1964 three young men aged twenty to twenty-four, James Chaney, a black from Meridian, Mississippi, and Andrew Goodman and Michael Schwerner, both from New York, were arrested on the pretext of a traffic violation, briefly jailed, then released. They were in Mississippi trying to help blacks register to vote. After their release they were captured and murdered by local members of the Ku Klux Klan (some of whom were also in the sheriff's department). Their burned car was found immediately, but their bodies were not discovered until August. Events like this pushed Congress to act on the civil rights legislation. Once the Senate broke a filibuster of southern senators, the Civil Rights Act of 1964 easily passed both houses and was signed into law on July 2, 1964. The law prohibited segregation in restaurants, hotels, and all other forms of public accommodation. Litigation was necessary to secure compliance. In *Katzenbach v. McClung* (1964) the Court upheld the law, ruling that a barbecue restaurant (owned by Ollie McClung) many blocks from an interstate highway was still sufficiently involved in interstate commerce to fall under the law. Lester Maddox sold his Atlanta restaurant rather than integrate and used his status as a "victim" of the federal government to successfully run for governor of the state. Despite laws, equality remained elusive. Civil rights marches—and violence by the police and community—continued until the late 1960s, as blacks still struggled for equality and economic opportunity.

CONCLUSION

The movement for integration had mixed success. A half century after the *Brown* decision most blacks in the nation attended majority black schools and most whites attended school with very few blacks. Colleges and universities became fully integrated, but black enrollment was slight as huge numbers of blacks lacked the financial means to go beyond high school and blacks in inner-city and rural southern schools continued to receive substandard educations. On the fiftieth anniversary of *Brown* many scholars declared it a failure.

On the other hand, legal segregation is an artifact of history. Many blacks have successfully entered previously segregated schools and graduated from universities and colleges across the nation. A few blacks have reached the highest levels of the corporate world, such as Richard Parsons, the president of the media giant Time-Warner. Blacks have served in presidential cabinets and on the Supreme Court. When President George H. W. Bush nominated Clarence Thomas to the Supreme Court, his strongest advocate in the Senate was the old Dixiecrat candidate Strom Thurmond of South Carolina. Throughout the hearings southern senators praised the nominee, never once commenting on the fact that he had a white wife and that thirty years earlier it would have been a felony for them to live together in Virginia. The emergence of Barack Obama as a presidential candidate for the 2008 presidency illustrates the enormous change in race relations in the nation.

In the early years of the twenty-first century, residential patterns remain segregated, but at the day-to-day level the nation is integrated as blacks and whites work together, ride next to each other on buses and trains, and share meals at restaurants. Blacks still face discrimination in jobs, and there are persistent attempts in the Deep South to prevent blacks from voting and to prevent the creation of districts that will lead to black elected officials. Nevertheless, blacks have significant political power in the South, serving in Congress, as mayors, and in the case of Douglas Wilder, as the governor of Virginia. In the North, blacks have held all possible public offices, including terms as mayor in the three largest cities (New York, Los Angeles, and Chicago), even though none had a black voting majority. In Birmingham, Alabama, Ollie's Bar-B-Q has moved to a bigger space, where blacks and whites serve food to black and white patrons.

SEE ALSO *Brown v. Board of Education; NAACP; NAACP: Legal Actions, 1935-1955; Occupational Segregation; Plessy v. Ferguson.*

BIBLIOGRAPHY

Clotfelter, Charles T. 2006. *After* Brown: *The Rise and Retreat of School Desegration.* Princeton, NJ: Princeton University Press.

Dalfiume, Richard M. 1969. *Desegregation of the U.S. Armed Forces: Fighting on Two Fronts, 1939–1953.* Columbia: University of Missouri Press.

Finkelman, Paul. 2004. "The Radicalism of *Brown.*" *University of Pittsburgh Law Review* 66: 35–56.

———. 2005. "Civil Rights in Historical Context: In Defense of *Brown.*" *Harvard Law Review* 118: 973–1029.

Klarman, Michael. 2004. *From Jim Crow to Civil Rights: The Supreme Court and the Struggle for Racial Equality.* New York: Oxford University Press.

Murray, Pauli. 1997 (1951). *States' Laws on Race and Color.* Athens: University of Georgia Press.

Myrdal, Gunnar. 1944. *An American Dilemma: The Negro Problem and Modern Democracy.* New York: Harper and Row.

Raffel, Jeffrey A. 1998. *Historical Dictionary of School Segregation and Desegregation: The American Experience.* Westport, CT: Greenwood Press.

Smith, J. Clay. 1993. *Emancipation: The Making of the Black Lawyer.* Philadelphia: University of Pennsylvania Press.

Taylor, Nikki. 2005. *Frontiers of Freedom: Cincinnati's Black Community, 1802–1868.* Athens: Ohio University Press.

Woodward, C. Vann. 1974 (1955). *The Strange Career of Jim Crow.* New York: Oxford University Press.

Paul Finkelman

RACIAL DISEASES

SEE *Diseases, Racial.*

RACIAL FORMATIONS

Racial formations are social and historical processes by which racial categories are created, inhabited, transformed, and destroyed. They are also the product of state practices and policies. Michael Omi and Howard Winant outline a theory of racial formations in *Racial Formation in the United States: From the 1960s to the 1990s* (1994). They note that "racial formation is a process of historically situated projects in which human bodies and social structures are represented and organized" (pp. 55–56). Rejecting a nation-based theory of race, Omi and Winant argue that a global perspective on racial formation is essential to understanding all the elements of racial oppression. In their theory of racial formation in the post–civil rights United States, which Winant further elaborates in *The World Is a Ghetto* (2001), Omi and Winant further argue that "colonialism in the age of capitalism differed from previous imperial systems in that it came to encompass the entire world. … Racial groups are the outcome of relationships that are global and epochal in character" (p. 37). They identify inequality, political disenfranchisment, territorial and institutional segregation, and cultural domination as the central elements of racial oppression and thus, racial formations.

EARLY HISTORY OF RACIAL FORMATIONS

During the period of European colonialism, the territorial consolidation of the Americas, the Caribbean, Africa, parts of Asia, and the South Pacific and their control by a minority of European nations (Britain, France, Spain, Portugal, Holland) were the product of state practices such as extermination, enslavement, forced assimilation, segregation, and discrimination. These practices were part of the racial formation process. Europeans and their descendants established legal and political structures in the colonies and settler nations that racialized non-Europeans and subordinated them. State-sanctioned racism, including diverse practices such as legal statutes, municipal ordinances, private regulations, federal censuses, police practices, and mob violence, were used to establish and enforce white supremacy and racial hierarchies in multiethnic nations.

Carolus Linnaeus (1707–1778), a Swedish botanist, produced the first modern classification of human populations in 1735. Linnaeus, the founder of scientific taxonomy, divided the genus *Homo* into four racial types: Eurapaeus, Americanus, Asiaticus, and Africanus. During this period the dominant view was monogenesis—the view that all humans were the descendants of a common original ancestor. Johann Blumenbach (1752–1840), a German professor of medicine, became the most influential of the scientists who classified human populations. Between 1770 and 1781 Blumenbach proposed the division of humans into four and later five "varieties" that represented the worlds' major regions: Caucasian, Mongolian, Ethiopian, American, and Malay.

Blumenbach introduced "Caucasian" into the classification scheme to describe a variety of humankind—the Georgian—that had originated on the southern slopes of Mount Caucasus. He considered women from the Caucasus region in Russia to be the most beautiful of all Europeans, so he chose them to represent the European ideal type, and all other human groups were a departure and degeneration from this ideal. These racial typologies were ranked and were not considered equal in aesthetic beauty, intelligence, temperament, or morality. The racial typologies Blumenbach created reflected a belief in European supremacy, legitimated racialized slavery, and the subordination of groups of people based upon their physical and cultural differences. These racial classification schemes linked physical traits such as eye color, skin color, hair texture, nose shape, and mouth size to intellectual capacities, cultural traits, and moral temperaments. To formulate these classification schemes Blumenbach and other scientists relied primarily on the written observations and descriptions of "ordinary" men who earned their living as slave traders, slave owners, merchants, or others in dominant positions over peoples whom they considered "savages."

Blumenbach and his contemporaries studying the varieties of the human race laid the foundation for the idea that distinct races existed and that they were inherently unequal. Following the 1770s historians begin to see a general shift in thought from the universal, that is what nations and people shared in common, to an interest in the particular, on what made some races "special" and unique.

RACIAL FORMATIONS IN THE UNITED STATES

How did the belief get established in the United States that Anglo Saxons were racially superior to other groups, and thus that it was their "destiny" to racially and culturally dominate all other groups in what became the United States? American historian Reginald Horsman identifies the last decade of the eighteenth century and the first decade of the nineteenth century as a crucial moment in the development of racial Anglo-Saxon superiority. He argues that these two decades witnessed the growth of a European romantic movement that shifted the emphasis from "a continuity of institutions to the continuity of innate racial strengths" (1981, p. 25). Horsman notes:

> in the first decades of the nineteenth century, Englishmen and Americans increasingly compared Anglo-Saxon people to others and concluded that blood, not environment or accident, had led to their success. England and America had separated their institutions, but both countries were surging forward to positions of unprecedented power and prosperity. It was now argued that the explanation lay not in the institutions but in the innate characteristics of the race. (p. 63)

Europeans established and employed racial classification systems to establish their control over the people whom they conquered, enslaved, and colonized. By the eighteenth century, racial classification systems were firmly established and economic, political, and social resources were distributed along racial and ethnic lines. Race was firmly established as a "legal" identity, and the state regulated all aspects of an individual's life. In nations such as the United States and South Africa, one's racial classification determined where one could reside and attend school, whom one could marry, whether one could hold elected office, and what occupations were suitable. In other words, all aspects of one's economic, intimate, social, and political life were structured along racial lines.

People who were classified as "white" were granted citizenship rights, property rights, immigration rights, residence rights, the freedom to control their labor, religious freedom, and the ability to freely travel. In the United States, European Americans established laws and state policies that effectively denied citizenship rights to indigenous Americans, individuals of multiracial heritage, and individuals of visible or known African and/or Asian ancestry. For example, Native Americans were not citizens of the United States until 1924 and were classified by the U.S. government as "wards of the government and citizens," thus denying them political autonomy and subordinating them to European Americans. Between 1800 and 1858 the U.S. Congress passed a series of laws giving the president and commissioner of Indian affairs absolute powers. Indians were forbidden to sell, rent, or lease reservation lands or to sell minerals, timber, fish, cattle, or agricultural products without the prior consent of the government.

CHANGES IN U.S. RACE CLASSIFICATION SCHEMES

Racial classification schemes have been central to racial formations, and they produced political constituencies and racial inequalities reflecting unstable power relations. For example, in the United States racial categories have been added, removed, revised, and altered during the past 300 years in response to demographic changes, immigration, political mobilization, technologies, cultural shifts, and economic interests.

The U.S. government uses census figures to allocate some resources to members of racialized groups. In the past it distributed citizenship rights, land rights, immigration quotes and other political rights exclusively to Europeans and European-Americans while denying people of African, Indigenous/American Indian, and Asian ancestry the same rights. Consequently, there have always been political and economic stakes involved in the criteria for inclusion and exclusion in specific racial and ethnic minority categories. Racial classification schemes are one dimension of racial projects that reconstitute "racial" groups. Although they are socially produced, they continue to have real material, social, and economic consequences for members of racialized groups.

The United States is unique from all other nations in the Americas in its historical enforcement of what has become known as the "one-drop rule," in which a person of multiracial ancestry who had known or visible African ancestry is legally classified as "black" regardless of appearance, cultural training, and self-identification. The one-drop rule has been consistently upheld by state and federal courts. In states such as Louisiana, there were so many people of African ancestry socially classified and living as "white" that "race clerks" were hired to strictly enforce the one-drop rule.

In 1918, the U.S. Census Bureau estimated that at least three-fourths of all native blacks were racially mixed, and it predicted that pure blacks would disappear. Consequently, after 1920 the mulatto category was removed from the census and the U.S. government made no further attempt to systematically count the number of visible mulattos in the United States, partly because so many persons with some black ancestry appeared white. Social scientists have documented the inconsistencies in the logic employed by the census and the disparity between social-cultural and scientific definitions of race. By 1960 the practice of self-identification by race replaced the earlier practice in which the census taker assigned race. Beginning in 1960 the head of household indicated the race of all of its members. This change in policy did not introduce any noticeable changes in the number of blacks in the U.S. population.

In 1970 the Hispanic category was added to the census for the first time. And in 1980, for the first time, a question on ancestry was included in the census. In response to increased political mobilization by members of interracial or multiracial families, the United States added the category "multiracial" to the 2000 census. In the following year the United Kingdom also added a "mixed race" category to its 2001 census. These changes in the official census reflect political struggles over the boundaries between and within racial groups, and they produce new racial formations in the post-civil rights United States. In the late twentieth century, as state-sanctioned racial inequality such as Jim Crow segregation in the United States and apartheid in South Africa were dismantled, nations established a range of public policies designed to remedy past group-based discrimination. These policies have taken various forms, such as affirmative action in the United States and positive discrimination in the United Kingdom. Although nation-states have dismantled de jure (legal) racial segregation and formally criminalized discrimination against members of racial and ethnic minorities, racial status continues to over-determine an individual's life chances and access to resources in multiracial societies.

SEE ALSO *Brazilian Racial Formations; Canadian Racial Formations; Caribbean Racial Formations; Cuban Racial Formations; Haitian Racial Formations; South African Racial Formations; United Kingdom Racial Formations.*

BIBLIOGRAPHY

Horsman, Reginald. 1981. *Race and Manifest Destiny: The Origins of American Racial Anglo-Saxonism*. Cambridge, MA: Harvard University Press.

Lipsitz, George. 1998. *The Possessive Investment in Whiteness: How White People Profit from Identity Politics.* Philadelphia: Temple University Press.

Omi, Michael, and Howard Winant. 1994. *Racial Formation in the United States: From the 1960s to the 1990s*, 2nd ed. New York and London: Routledge.

Winant, Howard. 2001. *The World Is a Ghetto: Race and Democracy since World War II.* New York: Basic Books.

France Winddance Twine

RACIAL HIERARCHY

This composite entry will cover:

OVERVIEW

Racial hierarchy refers to the idea that races can be usefully categorized as being higher or lower on a given dimension. Historically, the dimensions of hierarchy have been intelligence and behavior, with behavior falling into the realm of "civilized" versus "uncivilized." Because race is seen as a fixed characteristic, linking race to a hierarchy of intelligence or behavior essentially fixes the capabilities of whole groups of people. There can be no "civilized" Africans if all Africans are categorized as "uncivilized" in a racial hierarchy. The utility of such hierarchies was in conquest and exploitation, since they made it both logical and necessary to control the "uncivilized" and "unintelligent" races.

Distinguishing one's own social group from others has been part of human life from its beginnings, and the earliest written records describe others in what are often unflattering terms. The Greek historian Herodotus (484–425 BCE), for example, describes the non-Greek peoples living around the Black Sea as "barbarians" and "primitive" because they lacked things that to Herodotus made civil life possible—stable communities with clear legal structures. However, Herodotus does not define a racial hierarchy. It is their lifestyle and not their biology that makes them barbarians, and they are, at least in theory, transformable into civilized people.

The classification of plants and animals into distinct biological groups began in the Enlightenment, and the first universal taxonomy was by Swedish naturalist Carolus Linneaus (1707–1778). In his groundbreaking work of taxonomy, *Systema Natura* (1758), Linneaus classified humans into four distinct races (American, European, Asiatic, and African), each defined not only by physical characteristics but also by emotional and behavioral ones. Similarly, Johann Blumenbach (1752–1840), a founder of the field of physical anthropology, divided humans into five races (Caucasian, Mongolian, Malayan, Ethiopian, and American) and is credited with coining the term Caucasian in his doctoral dissertation *On the Natural Varieties of Mankind* (1755). It is interesting that each of his races relates to peoples of recently colonized areas, and Blumenbach makes clear that the purpose of his division of humanity is to help classify the variety of humans that were being encountered by European colonists at the time.

A hierarchy of behavior is implicit in the work of Linneaus and Blumenbach, but neither scholar focused on behavior. Samuel Morton (1799–1851), a Philadelphia physician, was the first to explicitly link race with behavior and intelligence. Morton collected and measured the skulls of American Indians and in *Crania Americana* (1839) concluded that not only were American Indians a separate race but their behavioral differences from European Americas was rooted in the physical structures of their brains. Expanding his study, he examined skulls of ancient Egyptians, and in *Crania Aegyptiaca* (1844) concluded that race differences were ancient and unchanging.

Morton's work became important in establishing the alleged inherent inferiority of American Indians and Africans, and influenced a generation of scholars. His work had profound implications, for as Morton's acolytes Josiah Nott and George Glidden argue in a volume dedicated to Morton, "It is the primitive organization of races, their mental *instincts*, which determine their characteristics and destinies, and not blind hazard. All history, as well as anatomy and physiology, prove this" (*Types of Mankind* 1854, p. 460). Or, to reverse the stated causality, history proves that anatomical differences explain why some peoples are the victims of conquest, others the victors.

Fixity of these racial differences was essential, not only to maintain the exploitive relationships of colonialism and slavery but also to fight against the idea of evolution put forward by Charles Darwin in *The Origin of Species* (1859). If God created the world in a fixed and stable form, then racial hierarchy should be fixed as well. Thus, it is not surprising that one of the nineteenth century's strongest critics of evolution, Harvard naturalist Louis Agassiz (1807–1873), was also one of the century's most outspoken supporters of racial hierarchy. From 1863 to 1865 Agassiz measured thousands of Civil War soldiers and used the data he collected to argue that significant and stable differences existed between blacks and whites. He implied that these differences illustrated God's purposeful creation of racial hierarchy.

The concept of racial hierarchy also led some to suggest allegedly profound links between race and society. In his *Essay on the Inequality of the Human Races* (1853–1855), French novelist Arthur de Gobineau (1816–1882) argued that miscegeny (particularly between members of the allegedly superior "Aryan" race and other races) caused social unrest. Gobineau's ideas were widely discussed, and later became central in Nazi efforts to create a pure "Aryan" society. Eminent British scientist Francis Galton (1822–1911) promoted a social and political movement aimed at manipulating racial hierarchy by selectively breeding humans with desirable characteristics and preventing those with undesirable ones from having offspring. Eugenics, as this movement was called, was widely accepted in Europe and had strong supporters in the United States. The eugenics movement was a direct inspiration for the genocidal policies of the Nazis and continues to influence public thought through works such as Richard Herrnstein and Charles Murray's 1994 book, *The Bell Curve*.

The scholarly use of racial hierarchy declined precipitously following World War II, when Nazi genocide against races they viewed as inferior exposed the idea's dangerous potential. At the same time, advances in physical anthropology began to demonstrate that race itself was an analytical concept with very little utility. By the 1970s biologists were able to show that genetic races of humans did not exist. Still, the idea of racial hierarchy has not disappeared completely.

Canadian psychologist J. Philippe Rushton (b. 1943) argued in *Race, Evolution, and Behavior* (1995) that there are three distinct races of humans (Mongoloid, Caucasoid, and Negroid), each of which retains a reproductive strategy adapted to the unique environmental conditions under which it evolved. Rushton's ideas are erroneous, in terms of both the evolutionary theory he adopts and the data he employs to support them, yet Rushton has supporters and is widely published. The persistence of arguments based on racial hierarchy in the face of more than a half century of unambiguous refutation suggests that this outmoded concept has a powerful ideological attraction and is not likely to disappear from public debate.

SEE ALSO *Colonialism, Internal; Facial Angle; Genetic Distance; Genetic Variation Among Populations; Great Chain of Being; Human Genetics; Morton, Samuel George; Nott, Josiah; Racialization.*

BIBLIOGRAPHY

Brace, C. Loring. 2005. *"Race" Is a Four-Letter Word: The Genesis of the Concept*. New York: Oxford University Press.

Gould, Stephen J. 1996. *The Mismeasure of Man*, rev. ed. New York: Norton.

Lieberman, Leonard. 2001. "How 'Caucasoids' Got Such Big Crania and How They Shrank: From Morton to Rushton." *Current Anthropology* 42 (1): 69–95.

Montague, Ashley. 1997. *Man's Most Dangerous Myth: The Fallacy of Race*, 6th ed. Walnut Creek, CA: AltaMira Press.

Nott, J. C., and George R. Glidden. 1854. *Types of Mankind; or, Ethnological Researches Based Upon the Ancient Monuments, Paintings, Sculptures, and Crania of Races*. Philadelphia: Lippincott, Grambo.

Rushton, J. Philippe. 1995. *Race, Evolution, and Behavior*. New Brunswick, NJ: Transaction Publishers.

Peter N. Peregrine

RACES RANKED BY EARLY SCIENTISTS

Prior to the sixteenth century, human biological variation was not seen as characterized by separate and non-overlapping units, or what have come to be called "races." Instead, human variation was perceived as a gradual phenomenon with no discernible boundaries between adjacent populations. In his travels, Marco Polo (1254–1324) moved largely over land, one twenty-five-mile segment after another, and nowhere in the world did he find that the people of adjacent segments differed in appearance.

The Renaissance, starting in the fifteenth century, completely changed this outlook. Ocean-going ships and navigational capabilities enabled people to sail from one continent to another without seeing anything in between. The native inhabitants of the end points of such voyages seemed categorically distinct, providing the mind-set that led to the establishment of the idea that human variation was represented by a finite number of separate entities called "races," although that term did not enter common usage until the nineteenth century.

In the Enlightenment world of the eighteenth century—the "Age of Reason"—it was assumed that the pursuit of science would not only bring the greatest benefits to humankind but would also demonstrate the glory of the "Creator of the world." The figure credited with naming the categorical distinctions of the living entities of the world was the Swedish botanist Carolus Linnaeus (1707–1778) in his *Systema Naturae* (*The System of Nature*, 1735, especially the 10th edition of 1758). Linnaeus designated all living things by "Class, Order, Genus, and species." For common usage, he established his "binomial nomenclature," or two-name designation, using only *Genus* and *species* as the standard way of categorizing all living creatures. Thus, humans were called *Homo sapiens*. This single human species was then divided into four subspecies, in a kind of perpetuation of the old flat earth outlook where there were four sides of the world: north, south, east, and west. The four categories of *Homo sapiens* were *H. s. Europaeus*, *H. s. Afer*, *H. s. Asiaticus*, and *H. s. Americanus*, and each of these subspecies was described in terms of what Linnaeus regarded as its distinguishing behavioral characteristics, which were based on the four "humors" of the Greco-Roman physician, Galen of Pergamon (129–c. 216 CE). Europeans were said to be "sanguine," Africans "bilious," Asians "melancholic," and Americans "choleric."

The eighteenth-century systematists still honored the traditional Christian assumption of a single creation of all beings, as described in Genesis, a view that did not change fundamentally until the end of Enlightenment in the nineteenth century. Europeans were assigned the most favorable, and Africans the least favorable, of Galen's four humors, but this only hardened into a picture of permanent "racial" distinctions in the fourth decade of the nineteenth century.

Johann Friedrich Blumenbach. *Anatomist Johann Friedrich Blumenbach classified the races with five categories: Caucasian, Mongolian, Ethiopian, American, and Malay.* PRINT COLLECTION, MIRIAM AND IRA D. WALLACH DIVISION OF ART, PRINTS AND PHOTOGRAPHS, THE NEW YORK PUBLIC LIBRARY, ASTOR LENOX AND TILDEN FOUNDATIONS.

The most influential of the eighteenth century formulations was that of the Göttingen anatomist, Johann Friedrich Blumenbach (1752-1840) in the third edition (1795) of his doctoral dissertation, *De generis humani varietate native*, translated as *On the Native Varieties of the Human Species* by Thomas Bendyshe (1865). Blumenbach expanded on the four "varieties" of Linnaeus to recognize five, which he labeled Caucasian, Mongolian, Ethiopian, American, and Malay. The Caucasian variety he named after the Caucasus, the strip of land between the Caspian and the Black seas running from southeastern Russia to northwestern Iran. He regarded the Caucasian form of the skull the most beautiful in the human spectrum and believed that there was reason to accept it as representing the original human form, declaring "white . . . we may fairly assume to have been the primitive colour of mankind" (1865 [1795], p. 269). After all, Mount Ararat is located at the southwestern corner of the Caucasus, and in the traditional Christian view of things the ancestors of all living people got off Noah's Ark there.

Blumenbach declared that living people depart from that presumed original form by easy gradations on all sides. Because there are no hard and fast lines between the different human varieties, he acknowledged that the recognition of those varieties is more or less arbitrary. He was also clear that there was no innate inequality between the several varieties. He did note that the differences that had accrued since the time of common origin had occurred by a process of "degeneration," but in Latin that term simply means "departure from origin," without the pejorative connotation that the word *degenerate* has taken on in English.

Blumenbach's attempt to meld the scientific and the Biblical was a classic Enlightenment effort. Things changed in the next century. The most powerful and influential formulation was that of the Philadelphia physician and anatomist Samuel George Morton (1799–1851). In his *Crania Americana* (1839), he was the first to label Blumenbach's five varieties as "races," although he used the same identifying adjectives that were in Blumenbach's scheme. He preferred "race," rather than "variety," because it left open the possibility that the various groups might eventually be shown to be fully different species. He certainly specified the differences in innate capabilities and "worth" that characterized his various "races"—and "races" they have been ever since, although virtually no one remembers that it was Morton who pioneered this usage. After Morton's death, his views were taken up in the American South to justify the institution of slavery. When the South lost the Civil War, the views that had been associated with its "cause" were downgraded, and Morton was largely obliterated from memory.

Morton's views, however, had been adopted by the founder of French anthropology, Paul Broca (1824–1880), and they have remained at the core of French biological anthropology ever since. When the English-speaking peoples joined the French side in World War I, they adopted many French views, one being the validity of "race." It had been completely forgotten, however, that those views had been predominantly American in the first place. The American experience of the daily confrontation of people originally from radically different parts of the world initially led to the reification of the concept of "race."

BIBLIOGRAPHY

Blumenbach, Johann Friedrich. 1865 (1795). *On the Natural Varieties of Mankind.* Translated by Thomas Bendyshe. London: Longman, Green, Longman, Roberts and Groom.

Brace, C. Loring. 2005. *"Race" Is a Four-Letter Word: The Genesis of the Concept.* New York: Oxford University Press.

C. Loring Brace

DISPROVEN

The perception of humans as belonging to "racial" categories dates from the time of the Renaissance and the European colonization of the New World and those parts of the Old World remote from Europe itself. The aboriginal inhabitants in these areas were perceived, in hierarchical fashion, as being inferior in complexity and categorically different from the colonists, and they were referred to in somewhat derogatory descriptive terms. The European colonizers had technological capabilities that were largely lacking, or at least less developed, in the areas being colonized. The marine technology that created the ships that got them there in the first place was something they took understandable pride in, although it was this technology that got people from one part of the world to another without seeing anything of the inhabitants of the areas in between. This was one of the things that contributed to the perception of the people of the world in categorical "racial" terms. In addition to their marine technology, the literacy of the colonizers and the navigating skills they had learned led them to assume a categorical distinction in their capabilities and achievements as compared to the original inhabitants of the areas being colonized. Inevitably, they looked down on these peoples as being of a lesser order of intellectual worth.

Throughout history, all human groups have felt that they were the best of humankind, and those that looked different and lacked technological sophistication were considered inferior. More than a few psychologically oriented writers of the late twentieth and early twenty-first centuries have regarded the idea that different human groups had differences in average intellectual capacity as a valid expectation, just as they have gone along with the assumption that "races" are valid biological categories. These writers include J. Philippe Rushton, the author of *Race, Evolution and Behavior: A Life History Perspective* (1995), Arthur R. Jensen, who wrote *The g Factor: The Science of Mental Ability* (1998), and Richard Lynn and Tatu Vanhanen, the authors of *IQ and the Wealth of Nations* (2002).

During the colonial period, both Europeans and Americans assumed that there were no cities in sub-Saharan Africa, and that Africans did not pursue an agricultural way of life. In fact there were many urban centers in Africa, and agriculture was well-established and widespread. Furthermore, African religious sophistication has been widely documented (see Glazer 2001).

The assumption that "races" are valid biological categories has been essentially disproven by the fact that the variance of inherited dimensions of the subjectively assumed categories within "races" is many times greater than that of the variance of those same dimensions between such "racial" categories. Quantitative work on this subject clearly demonstrates that "race" is not a valid biological category (see, for example, Fish 2002, and Templeton 2002). When genetic diversity is tested, it can be shown that well over 80 percent of the known range of variation occurs between the individuals of any given population while only 6 percent occurs between the populations of different geographical regions.

There is another major reason to deny the folk assumption that various locally identified human groups should be expected to have different biologically inherent capabilities, and this is the appreciation of the nature of the selective forces that demanded a considered understanding and response on the part of the members of the human groups in question. This outlook is derived from an appreciation of what a full anthropological perspective can give, including an assessment of how human populations lived during the distant past, when their physical and mental characteristics were shaped by the forces of evolution that influenced human chances for survival. As it stands, most of the assessments of the survival problems faced by different human populations only consider the way they are living now, not what the lifeways of their ancestors were in the past.

Looking at the human populations of the world, one thing that needs to be emphasized is that virtually none of them are living the way their ancestors did in the Pleistocene era, which ended just over 10,000 years ago. Even the Australian aborigines, so often taken as typifying the lifeway of the "primitive," were living a late to post-Pleistocene way of life at the time of European invasion and settlement late in the eighteenth century. Starting nearly two million years ago, all ancestral hominid populations were living a hunting-and-gathering way of life, which was essentially the same type of existence in all the occupied portions of the Old World. This lifestyle involved selecting a prey animal, trotting after it for a number of days until it could go no more, and then moving in for the kill. This existence put the same pressures on people throughout the inhabited world. The same was true for the knowledge needed to collect edibles from the plant kingdom. Selective pressures did not differ from one part of the inhabited world to another in regard to what people had to figure out. Of course, selective forces maintaining pigment in the skin did differ from the tropics to the temperate parts of the world, but this had nothing to do with human problem-solving capabilities.

If there are differences in the capabilities of human populations, these tend to be very different from what so many ethnocentric commentators have assumed. Those whose survival has depended upon certain capabilities that have been relaxed in other human populations have retained what almost certainly had been common to all populations during the Pleistocene. For example, tests in the late twentieth century have shown that Australian aborigines have less near-sightedness and astigmatism than the European-derived people who were testing them. Peoples whose ancestors had most recently survived by hunting have tended to retain more fast-twitch muscle capabilities, which are more frequently found among those who are the best sprinters in the world (see Entine 2000).

If the lifeways of our Pleistocene ancestors required the same problem-solving capabilities throughout the world, it had to have taken just as much wit or intelligence to cope with the problems of making a farm work in the absence of any written instructions. The amount of rote learning needed to carry out such a project had to be every bit as daunting as outwitting prey animals was for the Pleistocene hunters, or as figuring out what was edible and what was not. There is thus no reason to expect that the innate intellectual capabilities of any of the populations of the world differ to any significant extent from those of any other population.

SEE ALSO *Forensic Anthropology and Race; Genetic Distance; Genetic Variation Among Populations; Great Chain of Being; Human Genetics.*

BIBLIOGRAPHY

Brace, C. Loring. 1995. *The Stages of Human Evolution,* 5th ed. Englewood Cliffs, NJ: Prentice-Hall.

———. 2005. *"Race" Is a Four-Letter Word: The Genesis of the Concept.* New York: Oxford University Press.

Connah, Graham. 2001. *African Civilizations: An Archaeological Perspective,* 2nd ed. Cambridge, U.K.: Cambridge University Press.

Ehret, Christopher. 1998. *The African Classical Age: Eastern and Southern Africa in World History, 1000 BC to AD 400.* Charlottesville: University Press of Virginia.

Entine, John. 2000. *Taboo: Why Black Athletes Dominate Sports and Why We Are Afraid to Talk About It.* New York: Pacific Affairs.

Fish, Jefferson M., ed. 2002. *Race and Intelligence: Separating Science from Myth.* Malwah, NJ: Lawrence Erlbaum.

Glazier, Stephen D., ed. 2001. *The Encyclopedia of African and African-American Religions.* New York: Routledge.

Jensen, Arthur R. 1998. *The g Factor: The Science of Mental Ability.* Westport, CT: Praeger.

Lynn, Richard, and Tatu Vanhanen. 2002. *IQ and the Wealth of Nations.* Westport, CT: Praeger.

Rushton, J. Philippe. 1995. *Race Evolution and Behavior: A Life History Perspective.* New Brunswick, NJ: Transaction Publishers.

Templeton, Alan R. 2002. "Genetic and Evolutionary Significance of Human Races." In *Race and Intelligence: Separating Science from Myth,* edited by J. M. Fish, 31–36. Malwah, NJ: Lawrence Erlbaum.

C. Loring Brace

RACIAL PURITY (U.S.), 1900–1910

The ideology of racial purity has been embraced by various cultures throughout history. Racial purity relates to the idea that human beings can be ranked on a hierarchical scale where one ethnoracial group, or "race," is ranked as more advanced than another group. For those that subscribe to this ideology, all cultures can be situated within this hierarchy, but there is only one culture and/or race that ranks supreme. Hence, it is not surprising to find that the importance of maintaining a racial hierarchy has been promoted historically by self-defined elite members of society in an attempt to uphold their status. In some cases the purity philosophy has been overt state policy, as in Hitler's Third Reich.

THE PROGRESSIVE MOVEMENT

In the United States, the period from 1900 to 1920 witnessed a large-scale racial purity crusade exceeding those of previous decades. The endeavor to protect white, Anglo-Saxon racial purity was applauded by President Theodore Roosevelt in a letter to Charles Davenport, head of the Eugenics Records Office, in 1913. In order to prevent "race suicide"—the envisioned tragic result of a decrease in reproduction by a superior race—"good citizens of the right type" should multiply themselves to cancel out rampant breeding by "citizens of the wrong type." This attitude went hand in hand with a movement that had begun in 1890: progressivism. Made up of primarily white, middle-class men and women, Progressives faced the new century fearing the further development of what they considered ever-increasing social disorder. In a time of incredible wealth, ease, and leisure for only a small minority of elite white Americans and of ever-increasing poverty and hardships for the lower classes, especially African Americans and eastern European immigrants, many members of the white middle class envisioned a coming world of peace, cleanliness, healthy bodies, and quiet minds. Progressives, through social transformations, desired to create a middle-class paradise patterned on their own idea of Utopia.

Although the urban white middle class lacked the monetary power of the upper elite and was small in number compared to the agrarian and working classes, Progressive Era social reformers did not shirk from decrying the economic control of big businesses, promoting temperance, striving to end prostitution and gambling, and trying to find ways to ameliorate poverty, mainly among the white "deserving poor."

Black proscription through discrimination and segregation was seen as the proper means of safeguarding the common good from a race deemed decidedly inferior. Preventing miscegenation and removing any potential for African Americans to gain political power were both viewed as strategies to maintain the social order and, therefore, ensure economic progress and white supremacy.

ROOTS OF RACIAL PURITY DOCTRINES

In order to understand why racial purity was embraced by Progressives in the 1890s and continued to grip the United States in the early years of the twentieth century, one must examine how race was constructed in the early decades of the nation's social history and how these constructions were reified by social and evolutionary theory in the latter half of the nineteenth century. Differences between humans in skin color, hair color and texture, language, and customs had been noted by various explorers and philosophers throughout history. European kingdoms, spurred by global exploration and the potential for the exploitation of untapped resources, found it convenient to expand the definition of "resources" to include people, especially people who varied in their appearance and culture from northern Europeans.

In the Western hemisphere, white settlers found themselves in possession of extremely large tracts of land far beyond their individual capacity to cultivate. A huge labor force was required to work in the rice, tobacco, and cotton plantations in the North American colonies. At first, the British attempted to fill this labor gap by enslaving Native Americans and using indentured English servants. They found quickly, however, that enslaved African workers were both more efficient and easier to control. Slaves could be owned for life, while a white indentured worker's labor tenure usually lasted a maximum of seven years. Moreover, it was believed that an African worker could be forced to do more than twice as much work as white workers, who would eventually become fellow citizens. Enslaved Africans were to work as slaves for the rest of their lives on terms set by others. All in all, African laborers were seen as cheaper and thus more profitable to use.

Karen Brodkin notes in her discussion on race making in *How Jews Became White Folks and What That Says about Race in America* (1998, p. 68) that Africans were chosen to be slaves not necessarily because they were black, but because they could not escape as easily. As a result, various cultures along the western coast of Africa were subjected to continual threats of enslavement and kidnappings by European slave traders, and slavery became one of the primary economic systems of the colonies and eventually, the United States.

Whiteness as a measure of purity and superiority in the United States fluctuated according to reactionary sentiments against various immigrant groups in the nineteenth century. For example, in the 1840s Irish immigrants—many of whom were impoverished, Catholic, and poorly educated—were met with ostracism and hatred when they arrived in American cities. Although the Irish, like enslaved and freed African Americans, filled a crucial niche in the American labor market by working primarily as manual laborers and domestic servants, their presence was considered a threat by established whites because of the sheer number of them arriving daily along the northeastern seaboard. Their devout Catholicism was seen as subversive, their deepest allegiance being to Rome rather than the United States with its pristine Protestantism. Stereotypes of the Irish as alcohol abusers, criminals, and beggars were widespread, and although the Irish for all intents and purposes appeared "white," they were not actually considered or treated as white. Instead, the Irish were socially equated with formerly enslaved African Americans. Embracing this sentiment rather than resisting it, many neighborhoods sprang up that were populated by a mix of Irish settlers and free African Americans. Hell's Kitchen in New York City was the most notorious of such group combinations. A common saying was that "An Irishman is a nigger turned inside out." Job discrimination against the Irish was quite common; "the NINA system" meant that "No Irish Need Apply."

On the other hand, the advantage that the Irish and other "off-white" groups had over African Americans, Native Americans, and other immigrants such as the Chinese was that since they looked white, they had the opportunity eventually to achieve the status of whiteness. As the cities became increasingly populated with scores of Irish immigrants by midcentury, the Irish slowly began to assume positions of power and, as a group, raise their social status on a broader scale. African Americans, Native Americans, and Chinese immigrants faced stronger obstacles to raising their social status because not only were they socially stigmatized, they could never actually *be* white in appearance. African Americans were still bound by the chains of slavery, and Native Americans were continually being pushed west to make way for westward expansion. Chinese immigrants, filling another niche of the labor market, had a much more difficult time being accepted in society than European immigrants and frequently faced violence and hostility as they landed on the shores of California beginning in the late 1840s.

SCIENCE AND RACE

During this time of economic and population growth and its concomitant societal changes, the white, privileged sector of society felt that their position at the top of the social ladder was being threatened by the influx of foreign immigrants. To maintain their sense of racial and intellectual supremacy, many members of the white elite attempted to justify subjugation of other non-whites by publicly portraying them as less intelligent and lazy. Rarely were blacks portrayed during this time as positive individuals to be feared lest this imagery become a reality. For many whites blacks' assertiveness often was seen as savagery, an additional indicator of their unsuitability for full freedom. For others, blacks were frequently portrayed as childlike, ignorant, and groveling. Caricatures, such as Uncle Tom and the ever-nurturing Mammy, suggested that not only were African Americans suited for slavery, but most of them embraced their roles in bondage. If African Americans required paternalistic treatment, then it could be argued that not only was slavery justifiable, but also morally right.

Another way white supremacy was reinforced was through the realm of science, specifically, scientific inquiry into the origin of races. Men such as Samuel George Morton amd Josiah Nott, among others, held blacks to be of a different species from whites. The great Swiss naturalist, Louis Agassiz, held that all humans, wherever located, lived under moral rules common to the universe, although he was convinced that blacks were of a different species from whites. He worried that the presence of large numbers of blacks would result in the collapse of the nation. For him and many other commentators, the physical attributes of blacks were clear indications of their being a different and much lower species. These men felt that one could prove once and for all that a natural racial hierarchy existed and should be upheld by society rather than challenged. In this racial ideology, those blessed by God (i.e., the white elite) were situated at the top of civilization and everyone else ranked somewhere below.

As a means of discovering the origin and character of racial and cultural differences, social theorists developed a classification system of what were dubbed essential natural human types. These essential natural types were based on physical as well as mental and behavioral characteristics, and they were also regarded as intrinsic and unchanging. Traits were passed from one generation to the next, and each race had essential characteristics distinguishing it from other races. Diverse traits such as skin color and intelligence were then measured and used as evidence that cultural and/or racial differences were representative of distinct types of humans (or even that some groups were non- or subhuman, as enslaved African Americans were often categorized).

The question of racial origins spurred many philosophers, biologists, zoologists, naturalists, and early anthropologists to grapple with how these racial differences had developed. Some leaned toward proving the assertion that all groups of people derive from a single, human line (monogenism), but some felt that physical differences observed between groups of people throughout the world were the result of several different human types, or species, that spontaneously generated at different times (polygenism). For monogenists, the human species was analogous to the trunk of a tree, where races made up the branches and twigs. Polygenists, in contrast, viewed races as separate species or subspecies of humanity created at separate places on the earth.

A consequence of this inquiry into the origins of race and the creation of human typologies was the establishment of racial hierarchies. Science, as opposed to speculation, carried more weight with lawmakers and the public because science was deemed to be based on nature and truth rather than intangible ideas. Although monogenists and polygenists differed in how they viewed racial origins, diversity, and the process of human inheritance, both perspectives regarded white Anglo-Saxons as the superior, ideal human type. To most scientists at the time, races were like individuals with different strengths and weaknesses, and to them, white Europeans had historically proven themselves to have higher willpower, strength, and intelligence. One only had to observe European and American economic and military global dominance to see the truth behind the science (Claeys 2000). Following this train of thought, unique physical characteristics differentiating groups around the world from northern Europeans implied permanent physical as well as mental inferiority that could not be remedied. According to Theodor Waitz in *Anthropologie der Naturvölker* (1859): "All wars of extermination, whenever the lower species are in the way of the white man, are then not only excusable, but fully justifiable, since physical existence only is destroyed, which, without any capacity for higher mental development, may be doomed to extinction in order to afford space to higher organisms" (p. 21).

SOCIAL DARWINISM

When Charles Darwin published *On the Origin of Species* in 1859, the notion of inherited characteristics was generally accepted. However, what Darwin suggested in opposition to the monogenists and polygenists of the day was the process of natural selection, wherein very simply, those members of a species that survive are those that are best able to adapt to an ever-changing environment. Additionally, contrary to polygenism, new species are created through the process of natural selection rather than spontaneous generation. For Darwin, natural selection was a means for improving species as well as creating new ones. Survival of a species relied upon genetic fitness, which was measured by a species' ability not only to reproduce but also to have one's offspring reproduce. Some scientists and social theorists were troubled by these assertions, because if the ability to reproduce in great numbers increased a species' chance of survival, then what they viewed as the fecundity of the urban poor could potentially drive the white elite into extinction.

Darwin did not discuss human evolution in *Origin*, but he addressed the issue in his 1871 work, *The Descent of Man and Selection in Relation to Sex*. In this book, Darwin attempted to address the fears of the elite who felt that his theories promoted the advancement of the poorer classes over the affluent. He posited in *Descent* that he felt that the "domestic race" was degenerating at a rapid rate because the poor members of society were allowed to reproduce unchecked while the more refined members of society married later in life. To Darwin, this was causing a retrograde effect on human progress, and the elite needed to address this problem (Claeys 2000). However, he also posited that while his theories rested on the premise that all "races" diverged from a single human evolutionary chain, some groups were more evolutionarily advanced and better able to survive than other groups. Contrary to his previous works, he did not focus on the similarities between groups of people throughout the world and the adaptive strategies inherent in different skin tones and other morphological characteristics. Darwin himself was a man of his day and supported the popular tenets that human intelligence could be measured and stratified according to race, and to Darwin, this meant that intelligence was also subject to natural selection. Hence, he conceived that civilized, intellectual, and moral societies could triumph over the lower and more degraded, savage races.

Social Darwinism, a paradigm based on cultural evolution that was embraced by social theorists in the late nineteenth and early twentieth centuries, has often been viewed as a bastardization of Darwin's theories. However, Darwin expressed some of these same racist ideas with his position on the superiority of civilized races and classes. Social Darwinism did not follow Darwin's theories as much as the foundation of Social Darwinism was already present as a social theory before he published his first book. Social Darwinism holds not only that humans do evolve but that different races and/or cultures also evolve at different rates and are subject to the processes of natural selection. Hence, one culture may be more evolutionarily advanced than another, and all races/cultures can be viewed as being in a constant state of evolution. However, a major tenet of Social Darwinism is that the lower, or more "primitive" and immoral cultures, are never as evolved as the more "civilized" and moral cultures.

Social Darwinists used a variety of ways to measure the level of evolutionary advancement in a society or culture. For example, skulls of white Europeans and African Americans (as well as other ethnoracial groups) were often measured in various ways to gauge cranial capacity, and therefore intelligence. In some cases, these skulls were filled with various materials, such as mustard seeds, which were then weighed to determine the cranial capacity and intelligence of each race. Various experiments placed one culture over another in the evolutionary hierarchy, but not surprisingly, all these experiments resulted in the conclusion that those of northern European descent had larger brains and were therefore more evolutionarily advanced than other ethnoracial groups.

THE POST–CIVIL WAR PERIOD

The development of evolutionary theory in the late nineteenth century occurred during a time of significant social change in the United States. The defeat of the Confederacy and the ending of slavery created a new dynamic between the races, especially between ex-masters and ex-slaves. The presence of large numbers of emancipated African Americans made many whites uneasy, for they no longer had personal control of their darker fellow citizens. Blacks were quickly discriminated against in employment by white workers and employers alike. Employers occasionally used blacks to keep down wages, thus angering white employees, who resisted any decrease in the value of their services. The Civil War promise of forty acres and a mule went unfulfilled, with neither being given to penniless ex-slaves. Black farmers were residentially segregated to marginal lands. Northern whites, however, were not much different in these sentiments because although many had supported abolition, they did not necessarily consider blacks equal to themselves in any measure. Whites on both sides of the former Mason-Dixon line began publishing books and articles disparaging the end of slavery and arguing that, with freedom, blacks had become socially intolerable and were reverting back to their "savage" roots, and, as a result, respectable society would have to be protected.

While these sentiments were being expressed throughout the nation, relations between poor whites and blacks began to worsen. Before the Civil War, poor whites were sometimes equated with African Americans in terms of intelligence and, at times, considered as being less evolved than their affluent brethren. Following the war, poor whites, with little power to change their economic circumstances as factory workers in the cities and tenant farmers and sharecroppers in the rural areas, had to compete economically with blacks. This competition increased racial hostility between working-class whites and blacks, especially since this competition arose at a time of major labor surplus. As freed blacks and poor whites flocked to the cities in search of work, there were not enough jobs for all who sought them, and many had to face returning to the rural hinterlands to compete for low wages as sharecroppers.

392. A TYPICAL MULATTO FARMER OF THE SOUTHERN UNITED STATES

Shrewd, virile, and thrifty

Photo from the book* The Negro in the New World, *1910. *Blacks and people of mixed race were often presented in a negative light in order to justify treating them as inferiors.* GENERAL RESEARCH & REFERENCE DIVISION, SCHOMBURG CENTER FOR RESEARCH IN BLACK CULTURE, THE NEW YORK PUBLIC LIBRARY, ASTOR, LENOX AND TILDEN FOUNDATIONS.

These setbacks only served to create even further hostility as poor whites then blamed blacks for their inability to secure employment. The white master class did not want the working classes to unite and challenge their control of politics and the economy; therefore, they frequently fostered bad relations between the poor along racial lines by stressing their common physical inheritance (Wilson 1976). Overt antiblack attitudes and conduct gave whiteness an added value, so much so that the white poor of the South eventually became the most rabid of racial purists.

The emergence of a widely dispersed white middle class served only to increase the urge for racial purity. One unanticipated result of the end of the Civil War was the rapid rise of the middle class. The middle class, primarily comprising local politicians, factory owners, merchants, bankers, and the owners and operators of mines and railroads, achieved a measure of economic power during the postwar years, and together with the white ruling elite, became increasingly wary of the prospects of black and white working-class cohesion. Hence, instead of ignoring the plight of the white working class as the master class had done for years, the white middle class helped poor whites push politically for black disenfranchisement and legal segregation.

Race would still be a status marker, now reinforced by class. What the white working and middle classes wanted was for segregation to extend from education to residency to public transportation. Ultimately, they desired separate facilities for whites and blacks in all public places. By the late 1880s, several states, such as Florida, Mississippi, and Texas, conceded to the concerns of poor whites and enacted laws requiring separate accommodations for blacks on railcars. Hence, the wheels were put in motion for an era of legalized segregation, disenfranchisement, and antimiscegenation regulations known as Jim Crow.

THE JIM CROW ERA

The Jim Crow era officially began two decades before the Progressive movement. The price of the North and South reunion was the withdrawal of federal supervision of southern race relations. This left blacks open to informal segregation through the violence of vigilante groups such as the newly organized Ku Klux Klan, beginning shortly after the Civil War ended. In the *Civil Rights Cases* (1883), the U.S. Supreme Court declared that the Fourteenth Amendment's equal protection provisions applied only to state action, not to individual acts, and the court was not meant to tell states how to handle race relations. This type of decision led directly to the infamous *Plessy v. Ferguson* (1896) doctrine of separate-but-equal. Blacks and whites alike understood that this decision was intended to *prevent* equality in transportation. White status purity was to be preserved, the immediate emergence of the "Negro car" being a visible symbol of the racial differences. Of course, this situation did not bar whites from being attended by their black servants or employees. From Reconstruction forward, not only to provide service for upper-status white travelers, but also to reassure them of their personal superiority, George Pullman, inventor of the "sleeping car" for long-distance train travel, took great pains to hire only those black porters who appeared to display unadulterated black genetic inheritance. Their bodies made clear the ranks of all.

Progressives, focused on transforming the nation from a defective society to a middle-class paradise, supported segregation policies and black proscription because many reformers felt that it would increase social stability. Many blacks resisted these policies, however, refusing to use segregated facilities and public transportation. However, African Americans as a group lacked the political leverage to overturn these racist policies. As the turn of the twentieth century neared, racial tensions continued to increase and the lynching of African Americans in the South continued. Racial tensions between lower-status blacks and whites were exacerbated by a new wave of European—mostly eastern European—immigrants. Poverty, overcrowding, and crime increased in the cities as a result of this rapid population growth and prompted Progressives to campaign for stricter sanctions against immoral behavior as well as sanitation reform at the local and regional levels.

The increase in disease epidemics, overcrowding, and filth in the city streets led many to believe that African Americans and foreign-born immigrants were to blame for social and sanitation problems. That is, African Americans and immigrants were considered carriers of disease because they were viewed as not as evolved as white middle-class Americans. Proponents of Social Darwinism posited that the "inferior races" had no other recourse than to accept their innate condition and hope for improvements only as individuals.

According to Lawrence Friedman in *The White Savage: Racial Fantasies in the Postbellum South* (1970, p. 123), there was also the belief at this time that African Americans were black because the entire race had once been afflicted with leprosy, and that all blacks inherently harbored "venereal [sic] diseases." Because of these afflictions, any contact with African Americans, be it sharing living quarters or occupying a railroad passenger car, could render any white person infected. Hence, white people felt that it was imperative that segregation policies stay in place or be more firmly enforced, and many also believed that foreign immigration had to be stopped, or at least, controlled.

THE TWENTIETH CENTURY

The threat of "racial pollution" and the question of how to control it became the crux of social and political discourse between 1900 and 1910. Progressives and Social Darwinists alike felt that to protect society, the unfit elements of society, namely people of color, the physically and mentally challenged, criminals, and the undeserving poor (i.e., those who did not ascribe to middle-class social norms), needed to be prevented from reproducing. Even more imperative was the need to prevent marriage, and therefore procreation, between the pure, moral race (i.e., whites) and the socially unfit. Only by maintaining the purity of the white race could society be saved and progress be guaranteed. To save the dominant groups' racial purity, some reformers advocated eugenics programs and sterilization laws to prevent breeding by the socially unfit; furthermore, antimiscegenation laws were advocated to control marriage and family life.

The early years of the twentieth century were marked by increasing fears of society's "others," and various articles and books were published demonstrating the inherent savagery of African Americans and the urgent need to protect society from it. In 1900, Charles Carroll published *The Negro a Beast.* Carroll was a devout Christian who questioned the humanity of African Americans by taking Darwin and other evolutionary theorists to task with their ideas that all humans derived from the same evolutionary line. He contrasted the physical characteristics of whites and blacks to prove that in no way could blacks and whites derive from the same origin. Carroll noted differences in skin color, hair, cranial capacity, skull shape, and even brain tissue color, and he argued that African American features were more akin to those of apes than to people of European descent. Hence, to Carroll, African Americans should not be treated as humans. Instead, they should be treated as beasts who exist only for the service of the white man. Protecting the racial purity of the white race was essential, therefore, because, according to Carroll (1900),

> the offspring of man and the negro, if bred continuously to pure whites for ages, could never become pure white; you could never breed the ape out, nor breed the spiritual creation in. Hence, they would remain simply mixed bloods, without reference to what their physical and mental characters might be. These measurements demonstrate that if the offspring of whites and negroes were bred continuously to negroes for ages they would never become negroes, but would remain mixed bloods. (p. 49)

Thomas Ryan Dixon. *Dixon's* The Clansman *attempted to demonstrate the beast-like nature of African Americans, and African-American men in particular.* **PRINT COLLECTION, MIRIAM AND IRA D. WALLACH DIVISION OF ART, PRINTS AND PHOTOGRAPHS, THE NEW YORK PUBLIC LIBRARY, ASTOR, LENOX AND TILDEN FOUNDATIONS.**

The Clansman (1905), written by Thomas Ryan Dixon, was another book published during this time that attempted to demonstrate the inferiority of African Americans, especially African American men. Dixon published this book to highlight the beliefs of the Ku Klux Klan, an organization he felt deserved recognition for their service in preserving the purity of the white race. In *The Clansman,* Dixon discussed how the Klan was developed after the Civil War out of necessity to relieve the South from chaos. As opposed to being a terrorist organization based on hatred, Dixon described the Klan as rising from the ashes of the war to protect white southern women from violence perpetrated by African American men, men who were essentially beasts and subhuman.

Robert W. Shufeldt's *The Negro, a Menace to American Civilization* (1907) discussed the origin of Africans and African Americans in a similar vein to Carroll. Like Carroll, he attempted to demonstrate the ways in which Africans and Europeans were physically and psychologically different. To Shufeldt, it was devastating to the white race to interbreed with blacks and create "diseased" offspring. This fraternization could only increase the danger of interbreeding and potentially plunge the white race into evolutionary regression.

With this line of racial discourse in the public forefront, it was not difficult for eugenicists to posit that through selective breeding, biologically superior white men and women could be produced and inferior breeds would no longer be reproduced. Several forced sterilization programs were introduced to hinder the ability of the less evolved elements of the population to continue bearing offspring.

One of the most vocal proponents of forced sterilization and restrictions on interracial marriage was Madison Grant. To Grant, miscegenation was a social and racial crime that could only lead whites to racial suicide. In his book, *The Passing of the Great Race, or the Racial Basis of European History* (1916), Grant noted that interbreeding could only result in the offspring being relegated to the "lower race," because procreation between a highly evolved white person and a black person would pollute the superior person's "germ plasm."

The effects of these perspectives resulted in a high tide of forced sterilizations and tighter restrictions on interracial marriage after 1910. By stringent testing and observation, some argued, the socially unfit and feebleminded could be identified and sterilized. Many patients in mental hospitals, alcoholics, prison inmates, and epileptics were therefore sterilized without their consent. Forced sterilization was seen as producing a good for all of society.

The focus on sterilization as a means of protecting white racial purity, and therefore white social, economic, and political supremacy, continued unabated in the United States until the 1930s, when the Great Depression and foreign affairs shifted the public's attention to other matters. Jim Crow segregation policies, disenfranchisement, and antimiscegenation laws continued well into the mid-twentieth century, however, and even after the civil rights movement of the 1960s passed, many people of color in the United States continue to struggle for equal rights.

SEE ALSO *Black-White Intermarriage; Dixon, Thomas, Jr.; Forced Sterilization; Irish Americans and Whiteness; Ku Klux Klan; Nott, Josiah; Plessy v. Ferguson; Poverty; Racial Hierarchy; Scientific Racism, History of; Skin Color; Subspecies.*

BIBLIOGRAPHY

Brodkin, Karen. 1998. *How Jews Became White Folks and What That Says about Race in America*. New Brunswick: Rutgers University Press.

Carroll, Charles. 1900. *The Negro a Beast, or In the Image of God*. St. Louis, MO: American Book and Bible House.

Claeys, Gregory. 2000. "The 'Survival of the Fittest' and the Origin of Social Darwinism." *Journal of the History of Ideas* 61 (2): 223–240.

Darwin, Charles. 1859. *On the Origin of Species by Means of Natural Selection, or The Preservation of Favoured Races in the Struggle for Life*. London: John Murray.

———. 1871. *The Descent of Man and Selection in Relation to Sex*. London: John Murray.

Dixon, Thomas Ryan. 1905. *The Clansman: An Historical Romance of the Ku Klux Klan*. New York: Doubleday.

Friedman, Lawrence J. 1970. *The White Savage: Racial Fantasies in the Postbellum South*. Englewood Cliffs, NJ: Prentice-Hall.

Grant, Madison. 1916. *The Passing of the Great Race, or the Racial Basis of European History*. New York: Charles Scribner's Sons.

Humphrey, Seth K. The Menace of the Half Man. *Journal of Heredity* 11: 228–232.

Shufeldt, Robert W. 1907. *The Negro, a Menace to American Civilization*. Boston: Richard G. Badger.

Waitz, Theodor. 1859. *Anthropologie der Naturvölker*. Vol. 1. Leipzig: F. Fleischer.

Wilson, William. 1976. "Class Conflict and Jim Crow Segregation in the Postbellum South." *Pacific Sociological Review* 19 (4): 431–446.

Tanya A. Faberson

RACIAL SLAVE LABOR IN THE AMERICAS

No other people in the history of the world are as identified with the institution of slavery as peoples of African descent. While they were not the original slaves and have not been the only slaves, black people came to occupy that status to such an extent that at certain times and in certain places, to be black was almost by definition to be a slave. For the purposes of this entry, slavery is defined as "basically a system of political economy in which the production process is carried on by slaves, human beings owned as property by other human beings. Slaves work under direct coercion, and the product of their labor is owned entirely by their owner" (Alkalimat 1986, p. 67). Slavery does not by definition have a racial element. But as Orlando Patterson has insisted, "race is not a factor to be ignored in the study of slavery where phenotypic differences exist." When Africans became the main, almost exclusive, source of this labor in the Americas, it became the kind of social system most commonly referred to as "racial slavery." Such systems were motivated by the need for cheap labor and the desire for maximum profit and effectively utilized both socially constructed biological categories of "race" and culturally propagated ideologies of racist animosity.

THE GEOGRAPHY OF RACIAL SLAVERY IN THE NEW WORLD

Patterns of "racial slavery" in the Americas cannot be divorced from historical developments in the broader international arena, especially economic dynamics. A fuller analysis should include a broader and historically deeper context not ordinarily considered: the development of the earth's natural environment and the emergence, migration, and "racialization" of the human species from the place now called Africa. Europe, Africa, and the Americas are situated amid oceans and ocean and wind currents that made transatlantic navigation possible with the invention of new shipping technologies. Different geographical locations and climates were more conducive to growing some crops such as sugar and cotton than others, and even to where some crops are best processed and manufactured, a reality that spurred international trade. Cotton, for example, grows mostly in a belt between latitudes

36° south and 46° north, with most being harvested in the early twenty-first century above 30° north (New Orleans is at 30.2° north). The skin color and other body features of the world's oldest human ancestors, who lived in Africa more than 100,000 years ago, would become the basis on which ideas about human differences and "racist" ideas about superiority and inferiority could later develop.

More recent historical dynamics, however, are the common starting points and these took on added significance as global economic competition started to unfold. In the waning centuries of the "medieval" period—Latin for the "Middle Ages" between antiquity and modern, generally between the fifth century and the fifteenth century—a new international economy had been established involving all the major powers of Europe. They all tapped into the worldwide economic network that the Muslims had established after they completed their capture of the Byzantine Empire in the early 700s. Central to this were the Muslim-led development of sugar production in the Mediterranean, sugar's discovery and subsequent cultivation by Italians during the Crusades after 1099 and its introduction to Europe around 1150, and the eventual transplantation of sugar production to Iberia (modern Spain and Portugal), to the African Atlantic (e.g., the Canaries), and then to "New World" plantations beginning around 1500. The outcome of all of this was the consolidation of an Atlantic economy based on sugar production, which became the vessel for a new global system. The exploitation of this new set of relationships—to which the term *colonialism* is often applied—laid the foundation for the expansion of European economies and furthered the political development and consolidation of its major nation-states, a fact not fully enough explored in many discussions of global economic history.

In 1494 Spain and Portugal agreed to the Treaty of Tordesillas, which established an imaginary line of demarcation that had been drawn by the Catholic pope 1,100 miles west of Africa's Cape Verde Islands. The treaty gave Spain control over much of the Americas to the West but prevented it from direct participation in securing slaves from Africa to the east of the line, a privilege that was granted to the Portuguese. As a result, Spain issued the *asiento*, an agreement that allowed other nations, including Portugal, Britain, and Holland, to sell slaves to the Spanish colonies between 1543 and 1834.

The lives and personal livelihoods of two men intent on serving their Christian God and seeking their fortunes—Prince Henry the Navigator (1394–1460) of Portugal and Admiral Christopher Columbus (1451–1506), an Italian sailing under the flag of Spain—were closely linked to the developing world economy in which racial slavery in the Americas emerged, and prepared the foundation for it. Prince Henry's successful 1415 conquest of Ceuta, the Moroccan trading center in North Africa, initiated his lifelong quest to discover and dominate the Eastern sources of the tremendous wealth accumulated by Muslim merchants he found there, especially extensive holdings of gold. Blocked from a route across the Mediterranean because of Muslim control, he sponsored many voyages that eventually led to the rounding of Africa's Cape of Good Hope in 1488. Two of these voyages—in 1441 and 1444—returned to Portugal with Africans, an event that launched the trade of enslaved Africans into Europe. Prince Henry ordered that sugarcane be taken from Sicily to Madeira in the 1420s. By the 1550s these islands and São Tomé all had booming sugar plantations with enslaved African laborers. Prince Henry thus developed the old world precursor of the form of sugar growing—the plantation—as well as laid a foundation for the recruitment of its principal source of labor—Africans.

From his first voyage in 1492, Columbus was eloquent about the importance of gold in a 1503 letter to King Ferdinand and Queen Isabella on his forth voyage, calling it "the most precious of all commodities. ... He who possesses it has all he needs in this world, as also the means of rescuing souls from purgatory, and restoring them to the enjoyment of paradise." But it was gold *and* sugar that was decisive for the rise of racial slavery in the Americas. In 1493, while looking for gold, Columbus took the first sugarcane from the Spanish Canaries to Hispaniola—now the Dominican Republic and Haiti—and this island became the site of the first sugar industry in the Americas and shipped the first sugar back to Europe in 1516. Three factors combined to create what Alfred W. Crosby Jr. (1972) called "the Columbian exchange," summarizing the global developments of this era: the transplantation of sugar to the Americas, access to vast new lands, and a seemingly unlimited source of labor from Africa. By 1630, sugar had spread from Brazil to Guyana, Surinam, Barbados, St. Christopher, Nevis, Montserrat, Antigua, Dominica, Grenada, St. Vincent, and Tobago. Over the course of the eighteenth century, Jamaica became the leading sugar producer in the British Empire. The Spanish undertook similar promotion in Santo Domingo, Cuba, Puerto Rico, and Jamaica.

The colonizing impulse grew out of the system that would in the future be called mercantilism. Because mercantilism sought a favorable balance of trade—where exports exceeded imports—and because precious metals were a primary measure of wealth, the conquest of foreign territory and the subsequent control of the available mineral resources, especially gold and silver, were prime tactics in the arsenal of mercantilism. The demand for labor was shaped by the need for the large-scale labor systems—plantations—on which sugar cultivation was based. Slavery, however, did not emerge immediately as the first system of choice for supplying labor in the colonial territories of European powers, and the slavery that was transferred to the Americas was not mainly or exclusively the enslavement of Africans. White indentured servants were first used, and attempts to forcefully enslave Native Americans led to a disaster of genocidal proportions, with some scholars estimating that perhaps three-quarters of the entire population of the Americas was wiped out in the 1500s. In 1537 Pope Paul III recognized the humanity of Indians and prohibited their enslavement, a ban not extended to Africans. But millions died in battle with the Spaniards and the Portuguese and in forced labor centers such as the mines of Mexico and Peru, with much greater numbers dying in epidemics. This is what Eric Williams meant in *Capitalism and Slavery* (1944) when he declared: "Slavery in the Caribbean has become too narrowly identified with the Negro. A racial twist has thereby been given to what is basically an economic phenomenon. Slavery was not born of racism: rather, racism was the consequence of slavery. Unfree labor in the New World was brown, white, black, and yellow; Catholic, Protestant, and pagan" (p. 7). It was to meet the demand for labor, to use Williams's even plainer words, that "Negroes therefore were stolen in Africa to work the lands stolen from the Indians in America" (p. 9).

SLAVERY, THE SLAVE TRADE, AND THE NUMBERS GAME

As sugar production and mining spread, so too did slavery and the slave trade. Understanding the dimensions of the trade in enslaved Africans as real commodities, not what Sidney W. Mintz (1985) called "false commodities," is necessary to fully understand the impact of racial slave labor in the Americas. One of the most contentious debates in all of world and U.S. history since the 1950s involves the number of Africans enslaved via the slave trade and the social, cultural, economic, and ideological impact and significance for points of origin, points of destination, and the home ports of the traders. This issue was central to one of the two main propositions in Williams's *Capitalism and Slavery*, and it was addressed provocatively in Walter Rodney's classic *How Europe Underdeveloped Africa* (1972), which challenged prevailing paradigms by asserting that the development of the West and the underdevelopment of Africa and the Third World were flip sides of the same coin.

A recent estimate of the total numbers involved in the slave trade was based on detailed compilations resulting from a project organized by David Eltis and a team of scholars at Harvard University's W. E. B. Du Bois Institute for African and African American Research. Published in 1999 as *The Trans-Atlantic Slave Trade* (*TSTD*), this database initially covered 27,227 voyages. That was increased in a 2007 update by 7,000 new voyages and additional information for more than 10,000 already included voyages that Philip D. Curtin had provided in an earlier estimate of the slave trade in his 1969 book, *The Atlantic Slave Trade: A Census*. His figure was challenged and revised upward by Joseph E. Inikori and other scholars, leading to the assertion that roughly 9,566,100 slaves were imported into the Americans between 1451 and 1870. Neither this estimate nor the relative shares of its various national participants were substantially altered by the findings of the Du Bois Institute team, which concluded that some 11,062,000 slaves were transported from Africa between 1519—their date for the first transatlantic voyage from Africa to Puerto Rico—and 1864, the year of the last recorded voyages. Additionally, TSTD estimated that 55.1 percent were transported during the eighteenth century and that 29.5 percent were imported during the first half of the nineteenth century. They also found comparatively minor participation by U.S. merchants, a figure shaped more by their small size and not by moral and ethnical considerations. Only about 2.5 percent of slaves were imported into the United States—some 280,000—and almost 48 percent of these Africans were imported after the American Revolution in 1776. The Du Bois Institute database did cast new light on where the enslaved Africans originated and where they were taken and by whom, information that is important for the study of the cultural dynamics of the African "diaspora"—a Greek word meaning "a scattering or sowing of seeds."

Comparing the growth of the African population in the Americas with the population of European ancestry yields important insights. In 1650 there were approximately 100,000 European colonists in British America and only about 16,200 African slaves, with 15,000 in the British West Indies. The mainland British colonies were 97 percent white, and the British Caribbean islands were 75 percent white. One century later, the mainland was 80 percent white, and the islands were only 16 percent white. In most decades between 1650 and 1750, the percentage increase was greater for blacks than for Europeans. During this period more African people than European people entered the Americas. Up to 1820, among those people who were transported across the Atlantic, Africans outnumbered Europeans by a ratio of more than three to one: almost 8.4 million Africans and 2.4 million Europeans. Between 1820 and 1840, the number of Africans imported as slaves totaled 1,165,900, whereas the number of free migrants totaled only 824,500. The result was the firm establishment of the Atlantic economy based on slave labor from Africa—the demographic revolution long labeled as "the Africanization of the Americas." Scholars who study this issue often ignore the fact that the Americas were already "peopled"—Columbus in 1493 described Native Americans as "a population of incalculable number." They also ignore or slight the role of Africans in the process of "re-peopling" British North America after the genocidal impact on the population of Native Americans, the original inhabitants who were mislabeled by Columbus as "Indians."

ROOTS OF GLOBALIZATION AND THE CAPITALIST WORLD ECONOMY

When comparing the history and geographical distributions of African slaves in the Americas with other economic activity, one is led to the same conclusion reached by Williams (1944): "Negro slavery, thus, had nothing to do with climate. Its origin can be expressed in three words: in the Caribbean, Sugar; on the mainland, Tobacco and Cotton" (p. 23). In fact, it had everything to do with climate, specifically a climate—and geographical regions—that offered competitive advantages in the growth and shipment of sugar, tobacco, and cotton for plantation slave economies. Williams, by contrast, was battling against a climate-based theory that suggested Africans were more fit to work in tropical regions than Europeans.

Some scholars continue to misconstrue the argument in *Capitalism and Slavery* by asserting that Williams emphasized *only* the slave trade rather than slavery as an integral part of a broader global economic dynamic called "the triangular trade" or "the slave(ry) trade" (Bailey 1992, 1990). Inikori's *Africans and the Industrial Revolution in England: A Study in International Trade and Economic Development* (2002) is a powerful contribution to this discussion. His analysis includes the role and impact of African labor in several sectors: commodity production and the growth of Atlantic commerce; the growth of shipping; the development of financial institutions; the mining and production of raw materials and industrial production; expansion of markets; and the rise of manufacturing. Discussions of slave labor in the Americas should not be considered complete without such breadth of coverage.

Inikori concludes that the share of export commodities produced by Africans in the Americas can be summarized as follows: 1501–1550, 54 percent; 1601–1650, 69 percent; 1711–1760, 80.6 percent; 1781–1800, 79.9 percent; and 1848–1850, 68.8 percent. Overall, during this same span, the average annual value of export commodities increased from almost £1.3 million to more than £61 million. These trends can be seen in the big three of British exports: tobacco, sugar, and cotton. Between 1752–1754 and 1854–1856, they comprised between 69 and 77 percent of the value of all exports. Over this same period, the value of tobacco exports increased 2.2 times, that of sugar 2.5 times, and that of cotton an astounding 329 times. The link between these crops and slave labor is clear.

Sugar, for example, shaped the Atlantic slave trade in the early period. "It was Europe's sweet tooth, rather than its addiction to tobacco or its infatuation with cotton cloth, that determined the extent of the Atlantic slave trade," according to Robert William Fogel and Stanley L. Engerman (1974). "Sugar was the greatest of the slave crops. Between 60 and 70 percent of all the Africans who survived the Atlantic voyages ended up in one or the other of Europe's sugar colonies" (p. 16). And most of the world's sugar supply was produced by enslaved African labor in the Americas.

Overall, the significance of commodities produced by enslaved African labor has been vastly underestimated, an important issue in economics theory when the "multiplier effect"—when spending or economic activity in one sector stimulates activity and expansion in other sectors—is ignored by historical and static approaches. Combined, two African-produced commodities—cotton and sugar—accounted for 63 percent of all imports into England in the 1854–1856 period.

Cotton is by far the best example of how the processing of African-produced raw materials undergirded England's Industrial Revolution and highlights the impact of racial slavery first in America and later in the United States. As a share of the total value added in manufacturing, cotton increased its share from 2.9 percent in 1770 to 29.2 percent in 1831. Raw cotton consumption grew from £312,000 in 1770 to £13 million in 1831. The source of this raw cotton is key in understanding slave labor in the Americas. In the 1854–1856 period, raw materials from Africa and the Americas accounted for 43.3 percent of total imports into England. In this same period, raw cotton from the United Sates and produced by enslaved African labor contributed 91.1 percent of this total. Further, Africa and slave-dominated economies in the Americas were important as "vents" or markets for British manufactures and helped in their expansion, consuming almost all of a British cloth called "checks" in 1769. The need for credit in the Atlantic slave economy had a major impact on the development of financial institutions that arose primarily to deal with bills of exchange originating in overseas trade centered in the Atlantic basin (Inikori 2002).

Because of the demand for cotton, the slave population in the United States grew from 697,124 in 1790 to almost four million in 1860 owned by 393,967 slave owners. Forty-five percent of these owners held six or more slaves. It is no accident that the leading cotton-producing state in the United States in 1860—Mississippi—was the state with the largest population of slaves, and it remained a majority-black state until 1940 when cotton was still the largest earner of export dollars for the U.S. economy. But slavery in the United States was a national institution. Slavery in the U.S. North is so often neglected that many people express surprise that owning slaves was an established practice in all of the original thirteen colonies,

Slaves Working on a Cotton Plantation. *Slavery began in America as an answer to the need for cheap labor and the desire for greater profits.* GENERAL RESEARCH & REFERENCE DIVISION, SCHOMBURG CENTER FOR RESEARCH IN BLACK CULTURE, THE NEW YORK PUBLIC LIBRARY, ASTOR, LENOX AND TILDEN FOUNDATIONS.

with almost 50,000 above the Mason-Dixon Line in 1790. Slaves in the North were mainly concentrated along the seacoast, in major cities, and in the few regions such as southern Rhode Island and Connecticut where plantation-style agriculture was conducted (Greene 1942, Melish 1998).

But it was not the numerical presence of slaves and slave labor in the North that was most significant, but rather the North's dependence on the raw materials produced by the labor of enslaved Africans in the southern United States, especially cotton. This provided the platform from which industrial capitalism was launched, a case that parallels the story in England. Between 1787 and 1825, three groups concerned about the economic independence of the new nation used wealth largely accumulated in the slave(ry) trade—buying and selling slaves, manufacturing commodities using slave-produced raw materials, selling to slave-based economies, and so on—to finance and expand the industrial revolution in the United States (Bailey 1990, 1992) the first was the Beverly Cotton Manufactory of Beverly, Massachusetts, launched in 1787 by the Cabot family (brothers John, George, and Andrew, and sister Deborah) and other prominent investors. It lasted for more than a decade and was influential in several ways. It pioneered the use of public credit for private capitalist ventures, employed forty workers, invented new equipment, produced as much as 10,000 yards of cloth of increasing quality per year, and educated and inspired the next generation of industrial innovators.

The second was Moses Brown, a member of the founding family of Brown University in Providence, Rhode Island, in 1791. With the help of Samuel Slater, a young mechanic who violated British laws against the emigration of textile specialists, Brown built the first U.S. mill to use British technology and waterpower to spin raw cotton into yarn. The third and most decisive was

Francis Cabot Lowell and a group that came to be known as the Boston Associates, which founded the Boston Manufacturing Company in Waltham, Massachusetts, in 1813. Eli Whitney's cotton gin solved the bottleneck in the supply of raw cotton by mechanically removing its seed, and this laid the basis for the explosion of cotton production and slavery in the South and of cotton textile manufacturing in the North. Between 1815 and 1860, the consumption of raw cotton in the United States increased from 31.5 million pounds to 470 million pounds, mainly as a result of demand in New England. The contribution of slave-produced cotton did not stop there. In emphasizing that the extension of the domestic market was the key influence on manufacturing development in the United States and that this resulted from regional specialization, Douglass C. North (1961) puts the cotton trade at the very center of this process of regional specialization, concluding that "the growth of cotton income in the 1830s was the most important proximate influence upon the spurt of manufacturing growth of that decade" (pp. 166–167). Karl Marx had already extended this line of thinking on a global scale: "Direct slavery is as much the pivot upon which our present-day industrialism turns as are machinery, credit, etc. Without slavery there would be no cotton, without cotton there would be no modern industry. It is slavery which has given value to the colonies, it is the colonies which have created world trade, and world trade is the necessary condition for large-scale machine industry" (quoted in Bailey 1986, p.10).

Finally, one can also see the impact of slave labor in the Americas not only on nations but also on corporations and their owners that developed through historical ties to the slave trade and slavery and their exploitation of African labor. The controversy sparked by the call for reparations is based in part on such evidence. Among British financial institutions with links to the slave(ry) trade are the Bank of England; Barclays Bank, the third largest in Great Britain in the early twenty-first century; and the insurance underwriter Lloyd's. The Anglo-French financial firm Rothschild is also reported to have such links. In the United States, Wachovia Bank contracted with a historical research firm to explore the role of its predecessors in slavery, and its research revealed that two of its predecessor institutions—the Georgia Railroad and Banking Co. and the Bank of Charleston—owned slaves. The former FleetBoston—once Bank of Boston and subsequently owned by Bank of America—has acknowledged that one of its predecessors was Providence Bank, owned by the slave trader John Brown. Aetna issued an apology in 2000 because it had once issued insurance on slaves.

The State of California and the City of Chicago are among the governmental units that currently require corporations desiring to do business with them to specify any historical relations with slavery, and it was such a law that prompted Wachovia's disclosure. President Bill Clinton came close to an apology for U.S. complicity in slavery on his Africa tour in March 1998, and in November 2006 Tony Blair, then the British prime minister, issued "a public statement of sorrow" over Great Britain's role in slavery and the slave trade. Virginia's 2007 apology was rare among states, and others have followed suit. Even institutions of higher education have engaged this aspect of their legacies, among them Brown University's self-study initiated in 2003 by Ruth Simmons, its first African-American president. Whether the demands for reparations are historically justifiable and exactly how such reparations are to be realized—through payments to individuals, through funding expanded educational opportunities, or through statements of apologies—are the focal points of spirited discussion and debate.

SLAVE LABOR AND THE NONAGRICULTURAL SECTOR

Much scholarly research and debate has centered on slavery in the rise of commercial, manufacturing, and industrial capitalism, and the production of agricultural products. Ironically, the roles enslaved Africans played outside the agricultural and industrial sectors as domestic and personal aides have been more important both historically and currently in shaping the public mind-set of slaves as a subservient class. This fact, for example, was dramatized both by the role of Mammy in the 1939 movie *Gone with the Wind* and by the controversy that this portrayal sparked. For that portrayal, Hattie McDaniel won the first Academy Award presented to an African American. Slaves were essential as maids, cooks, tailors, seamstresses, butlers, and barbers. Traditional economic theorists have been as reluctant to include the important contribution of unpaid slave labor to national productivity—especially the unpaid labor of enslaved service workers—as they have been to include a full accounting of the importance of unpaid labor of women's household work, a point of considerable controversy.

It is in this economic sector where the particular experiences of black women in the slave labor force must be highlighted, a condition described by many scholars as "triple oppression" on the basis of race, class, and gender. "As blacks, slave women were exploited for their skills and physical strength in the production of staple crops," writes Jacqueline Jones in *Labor of Love, Labor of Sorrow* (1985); "as women, they performed a reproductive function vital to the individual slaveholders' financial interests and to the inherently expansive system of slavery in general" (p. 12). In the "Valley of the Shadow" database, a powerful database of Civil War information, one can glimpse service occupations for enslaved women of Augusta County, Virginia—housekeeper, house servant, maid, seamstress, and washerwoman. Men worked in such unskilled jobs as attendants, carriage drivers, gatekeepers, shoeblacks, stage drivers, and waiters. These roles can be confirmed by firsthand testimony in such works as the slave narratives compiled by the Works Progress Administration (WPA) and, especially for black women, in such literary works as Zora Neale Hurston's *Their Eyes Were Watching God* (1937) and Margaret Walker's *Jubilee* (1966).

It is also important to highlight the role of slavery outside the agricultural section in the section of the United States that one scholar called "North of Slavery." In *The Negro in Colonial New England* (1942), Lorenzo Johnston Greene concludes that "to meet the demands of New England's diversified economy, the slave had to be more skilled and more versatile than the average plantation Negro accustomed to ... a single crop. The New England slave had to be equally at home in the cabbage patch and in the cornfield; he must be prepared ... not only to care for stock, to act as servant, repair a fence, serve on board ship, shoe a horse, print a newspaper, but even to manage his master's business" (p. 101).

CONCLUSION: RACIAL SLAVERY, THEN AND NOW

Widespread commemorations and celebrations were planned for 2007 and 2008 to mark the two-hundredth anniversary of the abolition of the slave trade. In the minds of some observers, such celebrations are misplaced. Despite Great Britain's slave trade abolition in 1808 and the Congressional mandate to end the slave trade to the United States that same year, slavery continued in Great Britain until 1833 and in the United States until the Civil War, which cost the lives of more than 620,000 people between 1861 and the abolition of slavery in 1865 with the passage of the Thirteenth Amendment. The fact that more slaves were imported into the United States after the 1808 decree than before demonstrates that racial slavery in the Americas flourished rather than subsided.

The significance of slavery and its legacy continue to echo in the history of the Americas, and in world history, and the debates will continue. Some argue that putting too much emphasis on race and ethnicity—and on racial slavery—hampers progress in achieving racial unity and a color-blind society. Others argue that a focus on racial slavery distorts one's grasp of the economic or class component of slavery in the Americas, and the dynamics and impact of capitalism that should unite working people across racial lines. Still others argue that such historical considerations have little bearing on the current conditions of black people in the United States or around the world, and should be discouraged because they divert the search for solutions to such pressing problems as poverty.

Regardless of what position is taken, one should grasp that the abolition of the slave trade and racial slavery in America and the recognition of the progress since is no substitute for fully understanding the phenomenal contribution that slave labor made to the rise of Europe and the United States. While the debate over profitability may continue, there is too much evidence to dispute that slave labor in the Americas produced an enormous economic surplus or profit that financed many new economic ventures and social and political initiatives. But E. J. Hobsbawm (1968) reminds his readers that the real contribution of the slave(ry) trade was well beyond profits collected by any individual and resides in structural transformation during the period called the "general crisis" that marked the last stage of transition from feudalism to capitalism. It involved the expansion of the consumer market in Europe, the rise of overseas colonies tied to supplying Europe's needs, and the spread of colonial enterprises to provide more consumer goods for Europe and more markets to consume what Europe produced. Racialized slave labor in the Americas was an inextricable component of the very foundation for these developments.

What is needed most is a theoretical paradigm or framework that can be used as a guide to considering how an array of factors—color, class, culture, and consciousness—all interacted (and still interact) simultaneously and across all periods of history to shape the complexity of the black experience in the Americas and, in fact, the experiences of all the peoples who lived and live in what is now popularly called "the Atlantic world." With such a framework, it would be easier to understand that the historical issues connected to racial slavery in the Americas go well beyond academic debate. Worsening race relations amid a deepening crisis of the U.S. and global capitalist economy is one of the dynamics of general interest. The deepening poverty and the spread of AIDS are also disturbing. And the sharpening debates about reparations and the Supreme Court's leanings to revisit and revise affirmative action rulings in the United States, including its June 2007 ruling, are examples of things to come.

If it is true that "the significance of race in the American past can scarcely be exaggerated," as Leon F. Litwack asserts (1987, p. 317), it is even more powerfully the case that the significant contributions that flowed from the confluence of race and color with class and wealth that is the essence of racial slave labor have shaped the history of the Americas in ways that have eluded all but the most perceptive observers. As people seek to understand the realities of a post-9/11 world, the dangerous rise of terrorism, and the appropriate relationship between the developed and underdeveloped sectors of the globe, it would help to have an accurate view of the economic contributions of racial slave labor in the Americas and its broader social and political impact in order to properly grasp the contemporary significance of this bygone era, and to choose the most appropriate road forward for the future.

SEE ALSO *Plantations; Poverty; Slavery, Racial; Slavery and Race.*

BIBLIOGRAPHY

Alkalimat, Abdul. 1986. *Introduction to Afro American Studies: A Peoples College Primer*, 6th ed. Chicago: Twenty-first Century Books and Publications. Available from http://eblackstudies.org/intro/.

Bailey, Ronald. 1986. "Africa, the Slave Trade, and Industrial Capitalism in Europe and the United States: A Historiographic Review." In *American History: A Bibliographic Review*, edited by Carol B. Fitzgerald, 1–91. Westport, CT: Meckler.

———. 1990. "The Slave(ry) Trade and the Development of Capitalism in the United States: The Textile Industry in New England." *Social Science History* 14 (3): 373–414. Reprinted in *The Atlantic Slave Trade: Effects on Economies, Societies, and Peoples in Africa, the Americas, and Europe*, edited by Joseph E. Inikori and Stanley L. Engerman, 205–246. Durham, NC: Duke University Press, 1992.

Blackburn, Robin. 1997. *The Making of New World Slavery: From the Baroque to the Modern, 1492–1800*. London: Verso.

"Born in Slavery: Slave Narratives from the Federal Writers' Project, 1936–1938." Library of Congress. Available from http://memory.loc.gov/ammem/snhtml/snhome.html.

"Complicity: How Connecticut Chained Itself to Slavery." Special issue of *Northeast Magazine. Hartford Courant.* Available from http://www.courant.com/news/local/northeast/hc-slavery,0,3581810.special.

Crosby, Alfred W., Jr. 1972. *The Columbian Exchange: Biological and Cultural Consequences of 1492*. Westport, CT: Greenwood.

Curtin, Philip D. 1969. *The Atlantic Slave Trade: A Census*. Madison: University of Wisconsin Press.

Davis, David Brion. 2006. *Inhuman Bondage: The Rise and Fall of Slavery in the New World*. Oxford, U.K.: Oxford University Press.

Drake, St. Clair. 1987–1990. *Black Folk Here and There: An Essay in History and Anthropology*. 2 vols. Los Angeles: Center for Afro-American Studies, University of California.

Eltis, David, Stephen D. Behrendt, David Richardson, and Herbert S. Klein, eds. 1999. *The Trans-Atlantic Slave Trade: A Database on CD-ROM*. Cambridge, U.K.: Cambridge University Press. Revised February 2007. Available from http://www.data-archive.ac.uk.

Fogel, Robert William, and Stanley L. Engerman. 1974. *Time on the Cross: The Economics of American Negro Slavery*. Boston: Little, Brown.

Greene, Lorenzo Johnston. 1942. *The Negro in Colonial New England, 1620–1776*. New York: Columbia University Press.

Hobsbawm, Eric J. 1968. *Industry and Empire: The Making of Modern English Society, 1750 to the Present Day*. New York: Pantheon.

Hurston, Zora Neale. 1937. *Their Eyes Were Watching God*. Philadelphia: J.B. Lippincott.

Inikori, Joseph E. 2002. *Africans and the Industrial Revolution in England: A Study in International Trade and Economic Development*. New York: Cambridge University Press.

Jones, Jacqueline. 1985. *Labor of Love, Labor of Sorrow: Black Women, Work, and the Family, from Slavery to the Present*. New York: Basic Books.

Litwack, Leon. 1987. "Trouble in Mind: The Bicentennial and the Afro-American Experience." *The Journal of American History* 74 (2): 315–337.

Meinig, Donald W. 1986. *The Shaping of America: A Geographical Perspective on 500 Years of History*, Vol. 1: *Atlantic America, 1492–1800*. New Haven, CT: Yale University Press.

Melish, Joanne Pope. 1998. *Disowning Slavery: Gradual Emancipation and "Race" in New England, 1780–1860*. Ithaca, NY: Cornell University Press.

Mintz, Sidney W. 1985. *Sweetness and Power: The Place of Sugar in Modern History*. New York: Viking.

Morgan, Philip D., and David Eltis, eds. 2001. "New Perspectives on the Transatlantic Slave Trade." Special issue, *William and Mary Quarterly* 58 (1).

North, Douglass C. 1961. *The Economic Growth of the United States, 1790–1860*. Englewood Cliffs, NJ: Prentice-Hall.

Patterson, Orlando. 1982. *Slavery and Social Death: A Comparative Study*. Cambridge, MA: Harvard University Press.

Rodney, Walter. 1972. *How Europe Underdeveloped Africa*. London: Bogle-L'Ouverture Publications.

"Slavery in New York." New York Historical Society. Available from http://www.slaveryinnewyork.org.

Solow, Barbara L., ed. 1991. *Slavery and the Rise of the Atlantic System*. Cambridge, U.K.: Cambridge University Press and Cambridge, MA: W. E. B. Du Bois Institute for Afro-American Research, Harvard University.

Thomas, Hugh. 1997. *The Slave Trade: The Story of the Atlantic Slave Trade, 1440–1870*. New York: Simon and Schuster.

"Valley of the Shadow." Virginia Center for Digital History, University of Virginia. Available from http://valley.vcdh.virginia.edu.

Verlinden, Charles. 1970. "Medieval Slavery in Europe and Colonial Slavery in America." In *The Beginnings of Modern Colonization*, 33–51. Translated by Yvonne Freccero. Ithaca, NY: Cornell University Press.

Walker, Margaret. 1966. *Jubilee*. Boston: Houghton Mifflin.

Williams, Eric. 1944. *Capitalism and Slavery*. Chapel Hill: University of North Carolina Press.

Winsor, Justin. 1891. *Christopher Columbus and How He Received and Imparted the Spirit of Discovery*. Boston: Houghton, Mifflin & Co.

Ronald Bailey

RACISM

SEE *Aversive Racism; Color-Blind Racism; Cultural Racism; Everyday Racism; Implicit Racism; Institutional Racism; Medical Racism; Racism, China; Scientific Racism, History of; Social Psychology of Racism; Symbolic and Modern Racism.*

RACISM, CHINA

The Chinese people have plural origins. They commonly believe that they are "descendents of Yan and Huang" (*Yan Huang zisun*). By all accounts, Yan Di (literally Emperor of Fire) and Huang Di (literally Yellow Emperor) were chiefs of two large tribal unions living in the middle and lower reaches of the Yellow River during the legendary Sage King period (c. 3rd to 2nd millennium BCE). Conflicts between the tribal unions culminated in the War of Banquan, in which Huang Di thoroughly defeated Yan Di and annexed all his tribes. The unified conglomeration of tribes formed the kernel of a growing body of people that would become the Chinese nation. Although Huang Di and Yan Di were hostile opponents, they have been equally remembered as the apical ancestors of the Chinese. Huang Di and his people rose to dominate the drainage areas of the Yellow River known as Zhongyuan, or the "Central Land." The concepts of "Zhongyuan people" and " Zhongyuan culture" became categories to distinguish "self " from "others": "Zhongyuan people" were "us"; "Zhongyuan culture" was "ours." Those who were non-Zhongyuan were "others."

During the so-called Spring and Autumn period (770 BCE–476 BCE) of the Zhou dynasty (c. eleventh century BCE–256 BCE), while the power of the king dwindled, that of the dukes and marquises grew stronger. They were engaged in constant wars of annexation, and by the end of that period, seven of the most powerful states survived. In 221 BCE, the Qin State finally wiped out the last of the other six states and unified China. With the establishment of the Qin dynasty (221 BCE–206 BCE), the Chinese nation took a definitive shape, which has perpetuated and enlarged itself into the early twenty-first century. The term *China*, and its equivalents in the other Western languages, derive from the Chinese word *Qin* (pronounced "chin").

CONCEPTUALIZATION OF HUMAN DIFFERENCES IN EARLY CHINESE HISTORY

Ethnographic literature reveals that ethnocentrism seems to be a cultural universal by default. The ancient Chinese were no exception. They took pride in their sophisticated forms of writings, rituals, and music, while looking down upon those of all others. In early Chinese history, however, human differences were understood as cultural attributes that were individually acquired through enculturation. They were therefore changeable rather than innate and fixed biological features. Moreover, the early Chinese understood that cultural attributes of a certain group were not inherent to that group. Rather, they could be adopted by members of different groups. For the early Chinese, while members of barbarian groups could be civilized, members of civilized groups could also become barbarians. It all depended on what one chose to believe and how one chose to behave. All cultures and practices, of course, were judged against the standard of Zhongyuan culture.

The ancient Chinese summarized their ethnic environment into the conception of *wufang*, or the "five regions"—namely, the Central, East, South, West, and North. The region occupied by the people of Huang Di was called the Central Region, also known as *Zhongyuan* (Central Land) or *Zhongguo* (Central State, also the same term for "China" in contemporary Chinese). The people of Zhongyuan or Zhongguo called themselves Xia or Huaxia, with "Xia" meaning "big" or "great" and "Hua" meaning "beautiful" or "glorious." The Xia called their neighbors to the east Yi, those to the south Man, those to the west Rong, and those to the north Di. The concept of the "five regions" was the Xia's ethnocentric conceptualization of their ethnic environment. The names of the others were general terms referring to the numerous peoples who lived in those regions, rather than names of any peoples in their own languages.

From the second century BCE up to the early twentieth century, Confucianism was upheld as the orthodox ideology by each and every imperial dynasty of China, regardless of the ethnic origins of the rulers. In Confucian classics, there is a coherent and comprehensive theory regarding human differences. According to Confucianism, all human beings are born undifferentiated. Differences in human ways of thinking and behavior, as well as kinds and levels of ability, are results of differences in education. In Confucius's own words: "Disregarding origin, everyone has the capacity to be educated. When the Yi-Di come to Zhongguo, they become (the people of) Zhongguo; when (the people of) Zhongguo go to (the regions of) Yi-Di, they become the Yi-Di. If the Yi-Di practice the rituals of the Huaxia, they are the Huaxia; if the Huaxia practice the rituals of the Yi-Di, they are the Yi-Di."

This open, culturalistic approach to human differences made it possible for the later non-Huaxia rulers of the Chinese Empire to claim to be the legitimate inheritors of the orthodox Chinese tradition. It also enabled members of countless smaller groups to mingle into the ever-growing body of the Chinese nation.

PREJUDICE AND DISCRIMINATION IN IMPERIAL CHINA

Ethnic differences, however, often entail profound political and economic differences that cannot be easily settled by cultural attraction and voluntary assimilation. Records about conflict and culture-based prejudice and discrimination are replete in Chinese historical materials since earliest antiquity.

The Huaxia feared the Man-Yi or Yi-Di peoples even more for their uncivilized culture than for their brutal force.

For the ancient Chinese, if the Man-Yi were unwilling to convert to Huaxia culture, they had to be kept away from the realm of the Huaxia. Confucius pointed out that "the Yi should never covet (the territory of) the Xia and disturb (the culture of) the Hua" and that "(Huaxia culture was so superior that) even a Yi-Di society with a king was lesser than a Xia society without a king." During the Spring and Autumn period, Duke Huan of the Qi State established his hegemony among the competing aristocrats by touting the slogan "Revere the king and expel the Yi" (*zun wang rang yi*). After that, alarming cries, such as "those who are not of my group must have a different mind" (*fei wo zulei, qixin biyi*) and "keep a clear distinction between the Yi and the Xia" (*yan Yi-Xia zhi fang*), became a recurrent theme.

Chinese history entered a prolonged period of fragmentation in the third century CE, after more than four hundred years of unity. Whereas nomads of various ethnic backgrounds invaded from the north, successors to the Han dynasty (206 BCE–220 CE) were driven to the south. It was during this period of great cultural conflict and cross-fertilization that the agriculturalists who had been subjects of the former Han dynasty were generically called "Han" by the nomads. This label has since become the name of the dominant ethnic group in China.

During the period of split between the third and sixth centuries, suspicion and prejudice between the Han and non-Hans ran deep on each side. In a famous essay titled "On the Emigration of the Rong" (*Xi rong lun*), Jiang Tong (?–310) of the West Jin dynasty (265–317) forcefully states that the threat of the non-Hans is due to their ultimate cultural incompatibility with the Han, and he suggests the expulsion of the non-Hans from the Han-controlled areas. About the same time, several non-Han regimes in the north instituted segregation systems to rule their own people and the conquered Han separately.

In late imperial China, two of the nomad groups from the north, the Mongols and the Manchus, succeeded in establishing rule over the entire empire. Both the Yuan Dynasty (1271–1368) established by the Mongols and the Qing Dynasty (1644–1911) by the Manchus claimed their legitimacy based on the Confucian tradition and ruled their empires mainly with the Chinese bureaucratic institutions. At the same time, however, both also took draconian measures of discrimination against the Han in order to safeguard their rule of the minority. People with different ethnic origins had different access to social and political resources. They were also charged taxes and corvee at different rates, and they were subjected to differential criminal codes. Conversely, the Confucian open approach to ethnic differences notwithstanding, both the Yuan and Qing dynasties were overthrown by campaigns of the Han under exactly the same rallying cry: "Drive out the Tartar devils and recover China (*quzhu dalu, huifu Zhonghua*)!"

RACE AND RACISM IN CHINA

The Chinese enjoyed an assured sense of cultural superiority for thousands of years, until it was shattered by the British in the Opium War of 1840–1842. With painful humiliation, the Chinese were forced to assess the causes for the triumph of the Westerners, as well as for their own fiasco. With an urgent sense of desperation, a large number of Chinese intellectuals turned their attention away from the traditional single subject of Confucian classics to the diversified studies of the Western world. Among other Western theories, especially influential were Darwin's evolutionism (popularized in China at the time mostly through a loose translation of part of Thomas H. Huxley's *Evolution and Ethics*) and Johann F. Blumenbach's fivefold division of human races. In the course of reorienting their world by means of the newly borrowed ideas, the Chinese elites replaced "culture" with "race" as the determinant in their conceptualization of human differences.

Kang Youwei (1858–1927) was the most influential Chinese reformist and thinker by the end of the Qing dynasty (1644–1911). Based on a deeply rooted hierarchical conception of culture, and inspired by Blumenbach's racial classification, Kang determined that the "yellow race" should be strengthened through intermarriage with the "white race." In his book expounding the philosophy of the "great unity" (*Da Tong* or *Ta T'ung*), Kang acknowledged the strength and prevalence of the white race. From there he proceeded to suggest that because the yellow race was both populous and wise, an indestructible new race could be produced by intermarriage between the white and the yellow. In addition, the children of this union should be raised in the Western way. According to Kang, while the yellow could be directly whitened, the darker-colored races (except the black) had to first be yellowed, through intermarriage with the yellow race, before they could be whitened. As to the "black race," Kang thought they were so inferior that they had to first be sent to northern regions, such as North America and Scandinavia, to improve their breed before they could be yellowed and then whitened. According to Kang, the "great unity" of the world could be reached when all races were eventually whitened.

The utopian suggestion to reinvigorate China's competitiveness by means of intermarriage with the white race was embraced by a considerable number of vanguard elites, and eugenics started to catch people's imaginations. More and more social and cultural differences were subjected to examination through the prism of racism. In an attempt to understand the world anew, the intellectuals did not hesitate to reinterpret established categories with their newly acquired perspectives. Zhang Binglin (1868–1936), an early nationalist revolutionary and accomplished linguist, went so far as to suggest that while most humans, including the white, had derived from the yellow race, the Di descended from dogs and the Qiang descended from goats. He also reinterpreted culture in terms of consanguinity by proposing that "common culture derives from common blood lineage."

As the racist perspective became the talk of the nation, the usage of the term *race* (*zhongzu*) also spilled out of Blumenbach's five categories. The Han came to be referred to as the "Han race," and the Manchu the "Manchu race." Indeed, the revolution that overthrew the last Chinese imperial dynasty was characterized by the revolutionary leader, Dr. Sun Yat-sen, as a "racial revolution" against the Manchus.

Kang's suggestion for the yellow to intermarry the white, of course, could be nothing but an unrequited wish. As much as he discriminated against the darker-colored "races," the Chinese were discriminated against by the white. An epitome of such discrimination was a sign at the entrance of a park in the British concession in Shanghai reading "No Chinese or dogs are permitted to enter." This sign became one of the best-known materials for patriotic education in China. Becoming victims of racial discrimination, however, did not prompt the Chinese to categorically condemn racism. The notion of the biology-based and hierarchically differentiated races came to China under the rubric of science, and science was a newly found path to modernization. As a proud nation that had just lost its long-standing cultural confidence, the Chinese were too preoccupied with the desire for revival to circumspectly reflect upon the notion of racism. To the Chinese at the turn of the twentieth century, discrimination and oppression by Westerners were simply understood as due to differences in wealth, technology, and military prowess. They believed that if China could strengthen itself in those areas, the nation could rid itself of the humiliation and recover its freedom and glory. Thus, with a strong sense of loss and perplexity, and in a hasty reaction to the adverse reality, the Chinese internalized the concept of racism and justified both the racism of others against themselves and their racism against others.

More than a hundred years later, despite much progress in the social sciences and many changes in official discourse, this racist legacy still lingers among the average Chinese. In a press conference held immediately after the men's 110-meter hurdles in the 2004 Athens Olympic Games, the Chinese gold medalist Liu Xiang remarked: "I did not think of many things (to be possible). I did not think I could possibly win the gold medal. … Now that I finished within 13 seconds, it is proven that the yellow-skinned Chinese can also do well in short distance track games. I thought it was a miracle. It was unbelievable" (Hao et al 2004, Internet site). In dispelling the myth of racial inferiority of the yellow-skinned Chinese, Liu also testified to the tenacious presence of racism in China.

SEE ALSO *Language.*

BIBLIOGRAPHY

Dikötter, Frank. 1992. *The Discourse of Race in Modern China.* Stanford, CA: Stanford University Press.

Fairbank, John King, ed. 1968. *The Chinese World Order: Traditional China's Foreign Relations.* Cambridge, MA: Harvard University Press.

———. 2006. *China: A New History,* 2nd ed. Cambridge, MA: Belknap Press of Harvard University Press.

Hsiao Kung-chuan (Xiao, Gongquan). 1975. *A Modern China and a New World: K'ang You-wei, Reformer and Utopian, 1858–1927.* Seattle: University of Washington Press.

Kang Youwei. 1958. *Ta T'ung Shu: The One-World Philosophy of K'ang You-wei.* London: Allen and Unwin.

Lien-sheng, Yang. 1968. "Historical Notes on the Chinese Order." In *The Chinese World Order: Traditional China's Foreign Relations,* edited by John King Fairbank, 20–34. Cambridge, MA: Harvard University Press.

Nylan, Michael. 2001. *The Five "Confucian" Classics.* New Haven, CT: Yale University Press.

Qiang, Hao, Cao Yong, and Li Yiming. 2004. "Asia has me; China has me: A detailed account on the press conference about Liu Xiang's Championship." Available from http://2004.sina.com.cn/cn/at/2004-08-28/051 1104838.html.

Shimada, Kenji. 1990. *Pioneer of the Chinese Revolution: Zhang Binglin and Confucianism,* translated from Japanese by Joshua Fogel. Stanford, CA: Stanford University Press.

Chuan-kang Shih

RAP MUSIC

In his 1976 book *Roots,* Alex Haley wrote about his extraordinary journey to excavate the narratives of his African ancestry, including his encounter with a griot (an oral historian) in a West African village. This seventy-three-year-old griot recited an extensive history of the tribe, recounting its origins and establishing connections between Alex Haley and his mythological ancestor, Kunta Kinte. Haley was overcome with weeping as members of the tribal community worked together to bring his long-lost African relatives to him.

Amid the powerful energy of ancestral reconnection and historical continuity, one might gloss over a key element in this story: How is it that the griot is able to retain centuries of genealogical information, and perform it basically on demand? He can do this because he performs history in verse. The griot is, in this instance, the ancestral progenitor of the modern-day rapper. Griots retain tremendous amounts of cultural information for spontaneous performances in verse for tribal communities. Of course, years of repetition help to instantiate these tribal histories in the collective memories of the griot as well as his audience, but Alex Haley's experiences, and the powerful narrative that emerged from these experiences, suggest tremendous connections between ancient African griots and rappers of the twentieth and twenty-first centuries.

In no small way, the history and political economy of rap music is reflected in this *Roots* moment. First, the power and political potential of rhymed verse is readily apparent in Haley's interaction with the West African griot. Second, rap music, notwithstanding its modern-day origins as pure entertainment, has always been challenged to shoulder the social responsibilities of the communities from which it emerged. In 1979, rap music exploded onto the popular music landscape with the enormous success of a single by the Sugarhill Gang entitled *Rapper's Delight*. After its release in October 1979, *Rapper's Delight*, with its complete sample of the group CHIC's disco hit *Good Times*, was a mainstay on the Billboard Pop charts for twelve weeks. Although it was not the first rap record—Fatback Band's *King Tim III (Personality Jock)*, released earlier in 1979, is considered to be the first "modern" rap record—*Rapper's Delight* is still considered the popular point of departure for rap music.

RAP INFLUENCES

The griot is only one of several African or African American progenitors of the rapper. In fact, there is a continuous trajectory from griot to rapper that underscores the ever-present relationship between the oral poet and the community within the African and African-American traditions. Other oratorical precedents to rappers and rap music that emerge after the griot but before *Rapper's Delight*, include Jamaican-style "toasts" (a form of poetic narrative performed to instrumental music); various Blues songs (especially where conversational talking styles are present); prison toasts; "playing the dozens" (a game of verbal insults); disc-jockey announcer styles, such as that of Douglas "Jocko" Henderson; the Black Power poetry of Amiri Baraka; the street-inflected sermons of Malcolm X; and the oratorical prowess of nearly all of the prominent black poets of the early 70s, such as Gil Scott Heron, Nikki Giovanni, Sonia Sanchez, the Watts Poets, and the Last Poets.

In addition, rap music might not exist without the powerful influence of James Brown. Known as the "Godfather of Soul," Brown was also the preeminent forefather of rap music. His call-and-response, conversational vocal style; his incredible interaction with his band and audience; and his ear for the most contagious break-down arrangements in the history of black music position him at the genesis of hip-hop culture, from which rap music was derived. Listening to a Brown classic, such as "Funky Drummer" or "Funky President," will immediately make his impact on rap music apparent. Indeed, Brown was rapping before rap music became reified as a popular phenomenon. It is no mistake that Brown's music is still the most sampled and copied sound in rap music.

TYPES OF RAP MUSIC

When all of the historical and influential touchstones for rap music are considered, the fact that rap has become the premier element of hip-hop culture, a culture that has spread all over the world, should be fairly clear. Since 1979, hundreds of rappers have made thousands of records, and many of these have found a wide audience. In order to develop a definitive sense of rap music—especially its connections to race and African-American culture and its relationship to inner-city populations and American popular culture—various subcategories of the genre bear elucidation. The following taxonomy divides rap music into four categories: mainstream, underground, conscious, and gangsta.

Mainstream rap music is the category most widely listened to by the majority population. It is a fairly fluid category. At one point (during the "old school" and "golden age" eras of hip-hop, from about 1975 to 1990), mainstream rap was consciously and consistently political. For example, during their heyday (c. 1988–1989), Public Enemy, whose music was very political, was the most popular rap group on the most popular recording label, Def Jam. By the mid-1990s, mainstream rap's content had completed a dramatic shift toward more violent and misogynistic narratives, allegedly designed to report on the horrific conditions of American inner cities. By the late 1990s and through the first half of the first decade of the 2000s, the content of mainstream rap shifted yet again, this time toward the celebration of conspicuous consumption. Some scholars and fans refer to this current mainstream moment of rap as the "bling bling era" (the term "bling bling" was coined by the New Orleans rapper B.G., short for "Baby Gangsta," in reference to the glistening radiance of his diamond-encrusted platinum jewelry).

Underground rap music is even more difficult to define because it generally takes its cues from mainstream rap and often does not (and by definition cannot) enjoy the popular distribution, exposure, and financial attention and rewards of mainstream music. Underground rap tends to be predicated on regional or local development and support, although with the advent of the Internet

Members of Public Enemy, 1995. *Public Enemy helped to introduce the hip-hop world to overtly political messages through albums such as* It Takes a Nation of Millions to Hold Us Back. © S.I.N./CORBIS.

and imminently transferable mp3 music files, underground networks have developed across local, regional, and even international barriers. Underground rap must also, in both content and form, distinguish itself from popular mainstream rap. Thus, when mainstream rap is about being a gangster, underground rap tends to be more politically conscious, and vice versa. When mainstream rap production is sample-heavy with beats per minute (BPM) hovering in the mid-90s, underground rap will dispense with samples and sport BPM well into the 100s. This symbiotic relationship between the mainstream and the underground is far too complex to fully detail, but inevitably one defines itself against the other in various ways. All mainstream styles of rap were at one time or another considered underground. Some of the most talented underground rappers and rap groups are: The Living Legends, MF Doom, Immortal Technique, The V. I. Kings, The Last Emperor, Medusa, Chillin Villain Empire, Aceyalone, and Murs.

Conscious rap music came into popular prominence in 1982 with the release of Grandmaster Flash and the Furious Five's *The Message*. Conscious, in this case, refers to an artist's lyrical realization of the social forces at play in the poor and working-class environments from which many rappers hail, and in which the music and culture of hip-hop originally developed. *The Message* was a powerful response to postindustrial inner-city conditions in America. Since then, the subgenre of conscious rap music has continued to produce some of the most important songs for the enlightenment and uplift of black and brown people. Run-DMC's "Proud to Be Black," KRS-One's "Self-Destruction," "Why Is That?" and "Black Cop," and Public Enemy's "Can't Truss It," "Shut Em Down," and "9-1-1 Is a Joke" are examples. Conscious rap thrives in the shadows of both underground rap and mainstream rap, even as it innovates and informs a genre that most people associate with violence and consumerism.

Gangsta rap is a subgenre that originates from a complex set of cultural and sociological circumstances. Gangsta rap is a media term partially borrowed from the African-American vernacular form of the word *gangster*. (African American Vernacular English [AAVE], sometimes referred to as Ebonics, employs many systemic rules and features. One of these features is "r-lessness," meaning that speakers drop or significantly reduce the "r" in various linguistic situations.) When the popularity of rap music shifted from New York City and the East Coast to Los Angeles and the West Coast (between 1988 and 1992), this geographic reorientation was accompanied by distinct stylistic shifts and striking differences in the contents and sound of the music. This shift took place in the late 1980s through the early 1990s and is most readily represented in the career peak of the late-1980s conscious group Public Enemy (PE), as well as the subsequent, meteoric rise of NWA (Niggaz With Attitude), a group from Compton, California. Just as the marketing and retail potential of rap music was coming into prominence (both PE and NWA were early beneficiaries of rap music's now legendary platinum-selling potential), the music-industry media clamored to find terminology with which to report on this new, powerful, and vulgar phenomenon. Since the challenges of gang warfare in Los Angeles (and gangster narratives in general—consider *The Godfather Saga, Goodfellas,* and *Scarface,* in particular) were already journalistic (and cinematic) legend, the term "gangsta rap" was coined, and it stuck.

Yet even at its inception, gangsta rap forced scholars, journalists, and critics to deal with the cruel realities of inner-city living (initially in the South Bronx and Philadelphia with KRS-One and Schoolly D, and almost simultaneously with Ice-T and NWA on the West Coast). Still, only the very general realities of poverty, police brutality, gang violence, and brutally truncated opportunity have been subject to any real investigation or comprehension. The whole point of a rapper rapping is to exaggerate, through narrative, in order to "represent" one's community and one's culture in the face of violent social invisibility (consider the collective shock at the rampant poverty in New Orleans unveiled after the devastation caused by Hurricane Katrina). It is not surprising then that gangsta rap was a radical wake-up call, highlighting the aforementioned social ills. Its popularity, however, is more a reflection of mainstream audience's insatiable appetite for violent narratives than it is a reflection of any one individual's particular reality. That is to say, in all forms of rap music, the relationships between author and narrative are not necessarily autobiographical. However, these narratives, in their most authentic forms, tend to be representative of certain post-industrial, inner-city African-American realities.

SEE ALSO *Black Popular Culture; Hip-Hop Culture.*

BIBLIOGRAPHY

Dyson, Michael Eric. 2001. *Holler If You Hear Me: Searching for Tupac Shakur.* New York: Basic Civitas Books.

Miyakawa, Felicia M. 2005. *Five Percenter Rap: God Hop's Music, Message, and Black Muslim Mission.* Bloomington: Indiana University Press.

Toop, David. 2000. *Rap Attack 3: African Rap to Global Hip Hop.* London: Serpent's Tail.

James Peterson

RAPE

Rape is an act of sexual violence, typically perpetrated by males against females or other males. The concept of rape suggests some degree of force in that the sexual encounter is not consensual. Rape is an act of brutality and terror; the rapist is primarily motivated by the need to dominate and control the victim. In the United States, the relationship of rape to race and racism lies in myths created and perpetuated by Europeans about black sexuality that fueled racial violence for centuries. From the slavery era until the mid-twentieth century, myths surrounding black sexuality perpetuated the notion of the hypersexual black woman and the criminally sexual black man. Grounded in the belief that black people were inherently primitive and sexually deviant, these myths served as justifications for various forms of racialized violence by whites toward black men and women. Rape is also a racially significant concept because historically, white women were viewed as chaste and in need of protection; black women were considered unchaste and responsible for any violence directed at them. Well into the twentieth century and beyond, studies show that the experiences of black rape victims are very different from those of white rape victims and that in general, white women's charges of rape are given more credence than similar accusations made by black women or other women of color.

THE HISTORICAL CONTEXT

Myths surrounding black women's hypersexuality developed during Europeans' initial contacts with Africans. Strongly influenced by Victorian values of purity and chastity, Europeans misinterpreted various forms of African culture, particularly African dress and body movements. Europeans often assigned sensual meanings to common African practices that were related to the climate and geography of the continent, such as partial nudity. As historian Deborah Gray White (1985) argues, "the travel accounts of Europeans contained superficial analyses of African life and spurious conclusions about the character of black women" (p. 29). These spurious conclusions gave Europeans license to act out their sexual fantasies and frustrations through brutal and degrading interactions with black women.

For example, in 1810, a young black South African woman named Sara Bartmann was taken to England, where she was put on display for five years as the "Hottentot Venus." Europeans were particularly curious about

Lynching. *A mob surrounds the body of a lynched black man in Ruston, Louisiana. Ida B. Wells's activism directly resulted in a decline in lynchings in the American south.* © BETTMANN/CORBIS.

African genitalia and were fascinated with the size and shape of Bartmann's buttocks, which were shown publicly in various venues. Upon her death at age twenty-five, Sara Bartmann's genitalia were autopsied by George Cuvier, a leading scientist of the time, who compared her sexual organs to those of an orangutan. Her sexual organs were displayed in a Paris museum until 1974. Thus, two very powerful forces influenced European attitudes toward Africans and affected race relations for centuries: obsessive sexual curiosity about the black body and the belief in black licentiousness. These two forces would form the basis of what some feminist scholars call a rape ideology, which frames rape as an act of uncontrollable male lust and holds women accountable for any forceful behavior directed at them. Rape ideology is strongly intertwined with racism in that sexual violence has often been used as a tool of racial oppression.

For centuries in America, rape was largely defined and conceptualized as a sexual act perpetrated by a black man against a white woman. In fact, any accusation against a black man by a white woman would lead to severe punishment or death of a black man. America's legal system provided black men with no protection against false accusations of rape and no justice to any black woman raped by a white man.

THE SLAVE ERA AND BEYOND

From the slave era until the mid-twentieth century, interactions between blacks and whites were colored by a complex racial and sexual ideology that contributed to complicated attitudes, beliefs, and behaviors surrounding rape. For example, during the slave era, some black women consented to sexual relations with white men in order to lessen the inherent brutality of slavery. As they sexually exploited black women, slaveholders also utilized rape as a tool for increasing the slave labor force. Some black women consented to sexual relations with black men at their master's command. Thus, sexual assault—in various forms—was a part of the political economy of American slavery. The sexual exploitation of black women workers remained a persistent practice, challenging black women's sense of respectability for centuries. For example, black domestic workers, who worked in northern cities during the Great Migration in the early twentieth century, experienced rampant unwanted sexual advances while employed in white households. These women—who had fled the South in search of economic opportunities and freedom from legal racism—often had to make choices that compromised their images in the black community.

In the documentary *Freedom Bags*, a film recounting the hardships of black domestic workers in the 1920s, one woman indicates that many black women "had babies by their employers." Thus the complexities of interracial rape were further problematized by what appeared to be black women's willingness to be complicit in their own sexual exploitation. However, black women who consented to unwanted sexual relationships did so because they lacked the power to refuse. These women unwittingly perpetuated the notion of the promiscuous black woman by prioritizing survival over morality.

In 1892 Ida B. Wells turned her attention to the institutionalization of racial violence, particularly in the American South. Deeply angered by the lynching of three black store owners in Memphis, Tennessee, Wells began to reconsider the beliefs that she and most other southerners had about lynching. One was that black men were justifiably lynched for raping white women. Realizing that the three store owners had not committed rape, Wells concluded that lynching was a racist strategy to prevent black economic and political progress. She realized that in the post-Reconstruction South, whites could no longer claim blacks as property, but they could still control blacks by threatening violence. Using her newspaper as a platform, Wells stated unequivocally that many sexual encounters between black men and white women were consensual and that charges of rape against black men were often false. Wells also indicated that rape by white men was far more prevalent, yet white men's sexual brutality went unpunished. Although Wells was forced to flee the South because of her anti-lynching activism, she continued her campaign in New York and eventually brought international attention to her cause.

THE MODERN ERA

Lynchings decreased in the American South as a direct result of Wells's activism. Through her campaign she also underscored the sexual victimization of black women by white men. However, it was not until the 1970s that rape—as a form of patriarchal oppression—became a part of the public consciousness, primarily through the activism of white feminists. Although these activists reconceptualized rape as an act of violence specifically directed at women, most ignored the complex racist underpinnings of rape in America. In 1977 the Combahee River Collective, a black feminist group, identified rape as a black feminist issue and championed the need for rape crisis centers in black neighborhoods. Understanding the historical vulnerability of black women, these activists spoke out against sexual violence perpetrated by both white and black men.

Despite antirape activism that has led to more substantive legal protection for women, race-based inequities in arrests, prosecution, and in attitudes toward rape victims are difficult to eliminate. Studies show that black women are less likely to report rape than white women. Some scholars suggest that this reluctance to report rape is related to black women's acceptance of certain rape myths. Aaronette White (1999) refers to these myths as "mythical gutter wisdom," a rape ideology that dominates and distorts the discourse on violence against women in the black community. White argues, "When Black-on-Black crime is mentioned, rarely do we discuss the sexual brutalization of Black women" (p. 211). When black women do report rape, they are less likely to be believed than white women in similar situations. In court, jurors are more likely to believe that the assailants of white women are guilty than they are to believe a black woman has been sexually assaulted. Across every aspect of the criminal justice process, racial bias can play an influential role.

Throughout America's history, black people have lived with two sources of racist shame: black women's humiliation through rape and various forms of public violence targeting mostly black men. This legacy ripped through the very core of black America when Anita Hill accused U.S. Supreme Court nominee Clarence Thomas of sexual harassment before a congressional committee in 1991. Sexual harassment is a form of institutionalized rape in that it implies an element of sexual exploitation, particularly in the workplace. Many African Americans were more appalled at Hill's public accusations against a prominent black man than they were at the possibility that the accusations could be true. Referring to the congressional hearing as a high-tech lynching, Thomas unearthed shallowly buried racial skeletons and secured his seat on the U.S. Supreme Court. However, both Hill and Thomas could be viewed as victims of a rape ideology that simply assumes new forms from one century to another.

SEE ALSO *Body Politics; Feminism and Race; Sex Work; Sexuality; Violence against Women and Girls.*

BIBLIOGRAPHY

Combahee River Collective. 1982. "A Black Feminist Statement." In *All the Women Are White, All the Blacks Are Men, but Some of Us Are Brave: Black Women's Studies,* edited by Gloria T. Hull, Patricia Bell Scott, and Barbara Smith, 13–22. New York: Feminist Press.

Kennedy, Elizabeth. "Victim Race and Rape." The Feminist Sexual Ethics Project. Available from http://www.brandeis.edu/projects/fse/Pages/victimraceandrape.html

Nelson, Stanley, and Elizabeth Clark-Lewis. 1990. *Freedom Bags.* New York: Filmakers Library. Film.

White, Aaronette M. 1999. "Talking Black Talking Feminist: Gendered Micromobilization Processes in a Collective Protest against Rape." In *Still Lifting Still Climbing,* edited by Kimberly Springer, 189–218. New York: New York University Press.

White, Deborah Gray. 1985. *Ar'n't I a Woman? Female Slaves in the Plantation South.* New York: Norton.

Cheryl R. Rodriguez

RASSENHYGIENE

The German turn toward the subject of *Rassenhygiene* (racial hygiene), or "cleansing of the races," in the middle and late nineteenth century mirrored the international interest in two ideas: (1) the perfectibility of humankind, and (2) the danger of rapid population growth among the lower socioeconomic classes. For many, the improvement of the genetic basis of a nation through the selective breeding of those embodying "ideal" physical characteristics seemed within reach.

Arthur Comte de Gobineau's *Essai sur l'inégalité des races humaines* (Essay on the inequality of the human race) (1853–1855) placed race in the forefront of causation for the rise and decline of nation-states, giving the concept of race both immediacy and a practical application. In a similar vein, Charles Darwin's theory of evolution, explained in *Origin of Species* (1859), brought about an interest in the concept of "survival of the fittest," which was inappropriately adapted to the realm of humans by social Darwinists. Thus, individuals such as Stuart Chamberlain, Francis Galton, and Charles Davenport took leading roles in turning social Darwinism from a theory into a program of practical action called *eugenics.*

In 1905 Alfred Ploetz founded the German Society for Racial Hygiene (*Deutsche Gesellschaft für Rassenhygiene*), which later was subsumed by the International Society for Racial Hygiene. Among its members were some of the most prominent scientists and business people in the United States.

The notion of race gained momentum among the scientific community in the context of making the population stronger, healthier, and more uniform. The term *race* was generally used without a definition, and it could thus be manipulated to fit any circumstance. There was no agreement among scientists on how many races there were in the world, nor even how many races might be found in Germany. There was even less agreement on the identity of the races. Several national studies were undertaken in Germany between 1900 and 1930 by biological and social scientists to determine the answers to those dilemmas, but no determination was made.

German biologists and anthropologists began to move from theoretical involvement with the topic of race to a more practical approach in racial hygiene. Eugen Fischer, Fritz Lenz, and Erwin Baur joined forces to write *Grundriss der menschlichen Erblichkeitslehre und Rassenhygiene* (*Human Hereditary Teaching and Racial Hygiene*), a widely used textbook, in 1921. A revised second edition appeared in 1923. Their goal was to use Mendelian genetics and social Darwinist principals to explain the process of inheritance of desired, as well as degenerate, characteristics within populations. It was in this publication that the first use of the term "Nordic Ideal" was used to refer to Ploetz's earlier claim of Nordic supremacy.

Eugen Fischer, who was named the first director of the prestigious Kaiser Wilhelm Institute for Anthropology, Human Genetics, and Eugenics in 1927, was soon in a position to put a major effort into mapping the racial characteristics of the German nation. With funding from the Rockefeller Foundation, he mobilized a team of leading anthropologists and biological scientists to investigate numerous communities throughout the nation to establish the number and variety of racial groups. The results were disappointing, but the ideas they engendered endured.

With the advent of Hitler's regime in 1933, racial hygiene suddenly had immense political backing. As laws came into effect restricting Jews in all areas of employment and social life, many were forced to seek certificates (*Gutachten*) to prove their Aryan, or non-Jewish, genealogy. Fischer's institute, as well as universities, hospitals, and other institutions, set up experts in the certifying process. To do this job, more than 1,100 doctors were trained in racial hygiene to assist in the process of sorting the country into racial groups. As World War II started, the idea of sorting people in order to maintain and advance "racial quality" continued in Poland, where Germans certified non-Jewish Poles.

Implementation of racial hygiene at first urged the "positive selection" of genetic characteristics valued by the predominantly white male proponents. People with "good characteristics" were to marry and have many children, and to provide a healthy, safe, and nurturing environment for these children. "Negative selection" began with discouraging marriage and procreation, but it soon evolved into the sterilization of those considered unworthy to contribute to the genetic mix.

As the Nazi era continued, negative selection came to mean euthanasia and the elimination of "life unworthy of life." Children were the first to be selected for euthanasia, followed by the mentally ill and eventually those working in concentration camps and as slave laborers who could no longer work due to injury, starvation, or illness. Racial hygiene, which began as a theory of improving the genetic stock of a nation, had evolved into wanton murder and, ultimately, genocide.

SEE ALSO *Ethnic Cleansing; Eugenics, History of; Genocide; Genocide and Ethnocide.*

BIBLIOGRAPHY

Aly, Götyz, Peter Chroust, and Christian Pross. 1994. *Cleansing the Fatherland: Nazi Medicine and Racial Hygiene.* Baltimore and London: Johns Hopkins University Press.

Friedlander, Henry. 1995. *The Origins of Nazi Genocide: From Euthanasia to the Final Solution.* Chapel Hill: University of North Carolina Press.

Kühl, Stefan. 1994. *The Nazi Connection: Eugenics, American Racism, and German National Socialism.* New York: Oxford University Press.

Proctor, Robert. 1988. *Racial Hygiene: Medicine under the Nazis.* Cambridge, MA: Harvard University Press.

Schafft, Gretchen E. 2003. *From Racism to Genocide: Anthropology in the Third Reich.* Urbana: University of Illinois Press.

Gretchen E. Schafft

REMOND, CHARLES LENOX
1810–1873

Charles Lenox Remond, born in Salem, Massachusetts, on February 1, 1810, was the second child of free blacks, John and Nancy (Lenox) Remond. His father was a descendant of French West Indian immigrants, and his maternal grandfather had fought in the American Revolution.

As free blacks, Charles and his sisters, Sarah Parker Remond and Caroline Remond Putnam, grew up middle class, well educated, and very involved in the abolition movement. Sarah was active in the Salem Female Antislavery Society and the Massachusetts Antislavery Society. In 1856, she became an agent for the American Antislavery Society. Caroline served on the executive committee of the American Antislavery Society.

Remond began his abolitionist career in 1838 as a lecturer for the Massachusetts Antislavery Society. As the first black professional antislavery lecturer, he devoted his life to lecturing against prejudice and slavery and advocating equal rights for free blacks. He believed that when the world realized that mind determines the man, that goodness, moral worth, and integrity of soul are the true measures of character, then prejudice against caste and color would disappear.

Remond became one of the original seventeen members of the American Antislavery Society, the first nationwide society. Later, he served as secretary of the American Antislavery Society and vice president of the New England Antislavery Society, as well as president of his county abolition unit. For several years, Remond was the most distinguished black abolitionist in America, eclipsed only in 1841 by Frederick A. Douglass (with whom he often clashed in the 1840s and 1850s because of Douglass's popularity in the movement). He received recognition as a reformer and an advocate of equality for all people. He advised white abolitionists to employ blacks in decent jobs, and he criticized black businessmen whose fear of alienating their customers kept them from publicly supporting the abolition of slavery. He encouraged black youths to join the antislavery movement. Through his encouragement, the Negro National Convention adopted a resolution advising blacks to leave any church discriminating against them in any capacity, including at the communion table.

Remond spoke at public meetings in Massachusetts, Rhode Island, Maine, New York, and Pennsylvania. While a lecturer for the Massachusetts Antislavery Society, he supported leading white abolitionist William Lloyd Garrison, founder of the American Antislavery Society, concerning the principles of nonviolence and nonvoting. He believed, along with Garrison, in the creation of a totally color-blind society, one in which race had no influence at all. Some years later, Remond opposed the appointment of an African American as ambassador to Haiti because he believed a white man would have been the best candidate.

Remond's popularity and social status grew as he continued his quest for equality and freedom. He criticized the foreign slave trade and the domestic slave trade in America, accusing both of supporting slavery because of the profitability of cotton generated from the use of slave labor. He basically believed it was morally wrong to treat black slaves as property and then to abuse them for the sake of the economy, to treat them without humanity.

In 1840, Remond traveled with Garrison on a European tour for nineteen months as a representative at the World's Anti-Slavery Convention in London to gain support for the abolitionist cause and to speak against America's mistreatment of African Americans. While in Great Britain, he appealed to British abolitionist organizations, where his lectures against slavery received high acclaim. He encouraged British religious denominations to refuse to participate in communion services that discriminated against African Americans and to avoid fellowship with proslavery American Protestants.

In 1841, Remond traveled to Ireland to gain antislavery support and reduce the influence of Irish proslavery sentiment in America. In his lectures, he described America's slave system and the oppression of free blacks. "The nominally free ... still suffer all the pains incident to a degraded race," he told a Dublin audience (Osofsky 1975, p. 897). He helped compose "An Address of the People of Ireland to Their Countrymen and Countrywomen in America." Members of the Hibernian Antislavery Society and other interested volunteers distributed it until it had 60,000 signatures, and 70,000 had signed by the final count in 1842. In 1843, he spoke at the national antislavery convention in Buffalo, New York, and criticized black abolitionist Henry Highland Garnet's address at the convention advising slaves to liberate themselves through violence.

By 1847, Remond began to abandon his nonviolence stance to end slavery. He advised slaves to take matters in their own hands against their masters to overthrow slavery. As time progressed, Remond also grew increasingly frustrated over the injustices of racial discrimination and segregation. Thereafter, he protested segregated travel in Massachusetts. He spoke against the *Dred Scott* Supreme Court decision (1857), which ruled that the Constitution did not include rights for blacks, thus depriving them of citizenship and due process of law. He was so disturbed by the decision that he felt he could not remain loyal to a country that treated blacks like dogs.

By 1857, Remond had lost hope for the success of nonresistance in the antislavery movement. At the State Convention of Massachusetts Negroes in New Bedford in 1858, he encouraged convention delegates to support an insurrection among the slaves, declaring that he would rather have them die than live in slavery. He remained vigilant against slavery and supported the upcoming war to end it. During the Civil War, he was active in recruiting black troops for the 54th Massachusetts Infantry, the first northern all-black regiment in the United States Colored

Troops (USCT) unit. He was also active in supporting the United States Colored Troops. After the war, he worked as a clerk in the Boston Customs House and as a street lamp inspector until his death on December 22, 1873.

BIBLIOGRAPHY

Allen, William G., M. R. Delaney, C. Lenox Remond, and Thomas Cole. 1925. "Letters to Antislavery Workers and Agencies [Part 6]." *Journal of Negro History* 10 (3): 468–493.

Daniels, John. 1968. *In Freedom's Birthplace: A Study of the Boston Negroes*. New York: Negro Universities Press. (Orig. pub. 1914.)

Leeman, Richard W., ed. 1996. *African American Orators: A Bio-Critical Sourcebook*. Westport, CT: Greenwood Press.

Osofsky, Gilbert. 1975. "Abolitionists, Irish Immigrants and the Dilemmas of Romantic Nationalism." *American Historical Review* 80 (4): 889–912.

Robinson, Wilhelmena S. 1968. *Historical Negro Biographies*. New York: Publishers Company.

Sokolow, Jayme A. 1984. "The Emancipation of Black Abolitionists." *Reviews in American History* 12 (1): 45–50.

LaVonne Jackson Leslie

REPARATIONS FOR RACIAL ATROCITIES

When a government commits an atrocity such as slavery or genocide, many believe it has, at the very least, a moral duty to make amends to the surviving victims or their descendants in the form of "reparations." The government officials who engineered the atrocity in the name of the government may face individual, criminal prosecution, and they may be subsequently sentenced to death or incarceration, as in the case of some high-ranking Nazi officials after World War II. It has been argued, however, that the government itself has an independent moral or legal responsibility to the victims of the atrocity and that it should provide reparations to the victims in the form of cash payments, community assets, scholarships, educational programs, museums, monuments, or other forms of redress.

REPARATIONS FROM VERSAILLES TO THE HOLOCAUST

The idea that a government should provide reparations to the victims of its past atrocities is a fairly modern notion. Between World Wars I and II, reparations acquired a bad name. The Treaty of Versailles, which ended World War I, imposed reparations on Germany and other members of the Central Powers for atrocities committed during the war. Many in the international community, including the British general Henry Wilson and the economist John Maynard Keynes, believed that reparations authorized under the treaty were excessively punitive, stripped Germany of its dignity, and were therefore a mistake. These and other international figures came to believe that the treaty's draconian reparations program created geopolitical conditions that helped Hitler come to power in postwar Germany. More recently, revisionist scholars have argued that this indictment is overstated and that the Third Reich would have arisen even without the burden of war reparations.

Following World War II, however, the beliefs and opinions regarding reparations were reconsidered within the international community. The concept of reparations was now considered in light of the horrific but well-documented "crimes against humanity" committed against the Jews, the Gypsies, and other victims of Nazi persecution that came to be known as the Holocaust. In this case, Allied Forces recorded the Holocaust on film for the entire world to see. German civilians, many of whom claimed to have had no prior knowledge of Hitler's genocidal operations, were walked through the liberated death camps so that they could witness firsthand the atrocities committed in the name of their government. Although there was no way Germany's new government could adequately compensate the surviving victims or the families of victims of the Holocaust, political leaders of the new German republic felt impelled (some argue they were compelled) to do something. Speaking for the German government and its people, Konrad Adenauer, the first chancellor of the Federal Republic of Germany, announced: "In our name, unspeakable crimes have been committed and demand compensation and restitution, both moral and material, for the persons and properties of the Jews who have been so seriously harmed." With these words, the first modern reparations program was born.

Following Germany's lead, other governments have created reparations programs to redress past atrocities within their individual histories. Many of these reparation programs were a response to racial atrocities. For example, the South African government created a reparations program in the late 1990s for the victims of apartheid. As another example, in 1988, the U.S. government provided $20,000 to Japanese Americans who had been transferred to relocation centers after the Japanese attack on Pearl Harbor on December 7, 1941. The payout, enforced by the Civil Liberties Act, was the culmination of efforts to redress the injustice of discrimination toward Japanese Americans who were variously subject to curfew, restricted from traveling in the Pacific Coast states, and interned during World War II because it was thought that they posed a threat to other American citizens. The signing of the act was the culmination of efforts in the courts and later by individuals and organizations, including the Japanese American Citizens League (JACL), to redress discrimination toward Japanese citizens in wartime America.

Rather than providing reparations, some governments have simply issued apologies. For example, Queen Elizabeth issued a formal apology on behalf of the British government in 1993 for the bloody race wars that stripped New Zealand's Maoris of their tribal lands in 1863. Likewise, in 1996 the Vatican apologized for helping to engineer the removal of Australia's aboriginal children from their families between 1850 and 1967.

Although the U.S. government has issued both apologies and reparations for some of its racial atrocities—including an apology in 1993 for the overthrow of the Sovereign Kingdom of Hawaii 100 years earlier, as well as reparations for Japanese Americans—it has as of 2007 not issued either an apology or reparations to Native Americans for essentially stealing their country, massacring their people, and demolishing their culture. Nor has the United States government apologized or provided reparations to African Americans for racial oppression in general.

Some states have responded apologetically to slavery and other past racial injustices. In 2006 and 2007 four southern states—Alabama, Maryland, North Carolina, and Virginia—passed resolutions apologizing for slavery. In each instance, the governor of the state issued a formal apology, following a vote by the state legislature. For example, in May of 2007 Alabama's governor Bob Riley signed a resolution approved by the Democrat-controlled legislature expressing "profound regret" for Alabama's role in slavery and apologizing for slavery's wrongs and lingering effects. Although it did not issue an apology, the Florida legislature in 1994 provided scholarships to the descendants of a racially motivated massacre that took place in Rosewood, Florida, in 1923. The absence of an apology caused some members of Florida's black community to criticize the legislation. Additionally, the Oklahoma legislature passed the Tulsa Race Riot Reconciliation Act of 2001, which purported to provided redress for the survivors of the 1921 Tulsa race riot. Unfortunately, the redress was never funded by the legislature or the governor, which resulted in the filing of a lawsuit against the state by the survivors. A federal judge eventually dismissed the lawsuit.

The movement for black reparations in the United States, also known as the "black redress movement," seeks to obtain redress, mainly from the federal government, for slavery and Jim Crow, or government-sanctioned racial segregation and discrimination. This American movement is but part of a worldwide effort to gain reparations for African people for the ravages of slavery and colonialism.

Although chattel slavery, or human bondage, has a long and ubiquitous history in Western civilization—extending from ancient Mesopotamia to 1888, the year Brazil freed its last slave, and appearing in virtually every Western society, even among the pacifist Quakers—the Atlantic slave trade was uniquely evil. As one scholar points out, "The trans-Atlantic slave trade vastly devalued human life compared to what existed virtually anywhere on the continent before.... For centuries in Africa, ethical conventions had governed the taking and use of slaves, who in most cases resembled the serfs of Europe more than the chattel of the Americas" (French 1999, p. 357).

Lasting more than two centuries (c. 1638 to 1865), slavery in America not only denied basic liberties to an innocent people, it also visited capital deficiencies upon African Americans—particularly financial capital deficiencies (property and investments), human capital deficiencies (formal education and skills), and social capital deficiencies (social respect and the ability to get things done). These deficiencies and the racist rhetoric used to justify "the peculiar institution," as slavery in America was sometimes called, have survived slavery. They have been handed down to each succeeding generation of African Americans, beginning with the postbellum generation.

When slavery ended in 1865, four million African Americans were set free. Slavery did not, however, fold into a system of racial equality. Instead, after a brief period of Reconstruction in which federal troops were sent to the South to protect civil rights, the southern states imposed a system of racial apartheid on the former slaves. In his retirement years, former president Ulysses Grant wrote about the objectives of southern whites: "by force and terror [southern whites intended] to... deprive colored citizens of the right to... a free ballot; to suppress schools in which colored children were taught, and to reduce the colored people to a condition closely akin to that of slavery" (Kunhardt et al. 1999, p. 28). While the South created a regime of racially repressive laws, the North fashioned an elaborate scheme of racially repressive customs. "The concept of white supremacy had been exalted in the South in defense of slavery, but it was by no means confined to the region" (Ashmore 1982, p. 138). Jim Crow, in short, was not relegated to the South.

The death of Jim Crow came with the passage of federal civil rights laws in the 1960s and early 1970s. African Americans are, however, still at or near the bottom of almost every measure of socioeconomic success in American society, including educational attainment, income level, employment status, and infant mortality. The effects of slavery and Jim Crow can still be felt in the twenty-first century, and reparations are seen as a way to redress these lingering effects.

POSTWAR APPROACHES TO REPARATIONS

Two competing approaches to redressing past atrocities have developed since the Holocaust. These approaches, or models, apply not only to the black redress movement

Pro-Reparations Demonstration, 2002. *African Americans gather to voice their disappointment in the U.S. government for not offering reparations as of 2002.* AP IMAGES.

but also to all redress movements around the world. One model is called the "tort model," and the other the "atonement model."

Although it can be used in the context of legislation, the tort model focuses mainly on litigation as a strategy for achieving redress for slavery or Jim Crow. The tort model's central aim is victim compensation. While a few proponents of the tort model seek to punish the perpetrator government for the atrocity, most "would be satisfied if the government . . . were simply to write a check for X amount of dollars to every slave descendant" (Brooks 2004, p. 98). Since 1917, numerous lawsuits have been brought to achieve this objective. Some have been filed against the federal government, at least one against a state government, and, more recently, many have been directed against private corporations that supported or benefited financially from slavery in the past (some corporations can trace their lineage as far back as the antebellum period).

Whether litigation is brought against a government or a corporation, the claim for compensation is based on a variety of legal theories, including unjust enrichment and international law. Not only in the United States, but in other countries as well, the courts have been unmistakably indisposed toward lawsuits that seek redress for past atrocities. None of these lawsuits has gotten very far, therefore. "In the absence of special legislation or settlement, these lawsuits have been dismissed before the judge has had an opportunity to consider the merits of the claims at trial. Procedural barriers—including questionable subject-matter jurisdiction due to problems of sovereign immunity or the 'political question doctrine,' the lack of a clear right of action, and violations of applicable statutes of limitations—have resulted in pretrial dismissals of every unsettled case" (Brooks 2004, p. 99).

In contrast to the tort model, the atonement model focuses less on the victim than on the perpetrator. It seeks to establish conditions necessary for moral clarity and the prospect of repairing a broken relationship between the perpetrator and victims of an atrocity. Under the atonement model, the victim first and foremost seeks a genuine apology from the perpetrator. The victim then calculates the sincerity of the apology by the weight of the reparations. If the reparations are sufficient, the perpetrator reclaims its moral character in the aftermath of an atrocity, and the victim forgives and moves forward with the perpetrator into a new, healthier relationship. But if the reparations are insufficient to make the apology believable, there is no redemption, no forgiveness, and, consequently, no repair of a broken relationship.

Perhaps the most significant example of the atonement model is the reparations program implemented by the South African government after the dismantling of apartheid in the 1990s. The South African parliament established its Truth and Reconciliation Commission (TRC) in 1995. This body was charged with the task of investigating apartheid-era human-rights violations and recommending ways to mend the cultural and racial divides that remained. The TRC was divided into three committees: the Human Rights Committee was responsible for investigating human rights violations that occurred from 1960 to 1994; the Amnesty Committee considered applications for amnesty from those persons who cooperated in the TRC's investigations; and the Reparation and Rehabilitation Committee was charged with "the taking of measures aimed at the granting of reparation to, and the rehabilitation and the restoration of the human and civil dignity of, victims of violations of human rights."

Reparations recommended by the TRC included individual payments and symbolic gestures, such as renaming of streets and building memorials. Individual payments were limited to those individuals who appeared or were mentioned in testimony before the TRC and were formally designated as victims of apartheid. Although the TRC recommended that these persons receive pensions of up to R23,000 a year for a six-year period, ultimately victims of apartheid only received a one-time payment of R30,000 (approximately $4,500). This relatively low amount, along with the fact that victims of apartheid were prevented from suing directly for damages, led some to claim the reparations paid under the TRC process were insufficient to allow for proper reconciliation.

More broadly, the atonement model, unlike the tort model, attempts to position the black redress movement within the larger international redress movement that has evolved since the end of World War II. Proponents of the atonement model believe there is a fundamental nexus between, on the one hand, a government that would exterminate millions of Jews or permit the sexual enslavement of thousands of teenage girls (the so-called "Comfort Women" who were sexually enslaved by the Japanese Imperial Army during World War II) and, on the other hand, a government that would enslave millions of blacks over two-and-a-quarter centuries and then spend another 100 years persecuting these innocent people. In each case, the perpetrator does not identify with the victim. In each case, the perpetrator sees the victim as something other than a person of equal moral standing.

This absence of identity is the essential mechanism that gives rise to any atrocity, and it is the essential factor that underpins each claim for redress. Proponents of the atonement model ask, "How is it that a Nazi officer (Otto Ohlendorf), a man with degrees in engineering and law, a father of six, a deacon in his church, an outstanding member of his community can be responsible for the murder of more than a thousand Jews. How is it that Japanese soldiers can march into Nanjing, the capital of China prior to World War II, and within the space of a few months kill more people than the number of people that died in Hiroshima, tossing babies in the air and catching them on their bayonets? It is because in each case *the perpetrator does not identify with the victim*" (Brooks 2005, pp. 8–9).

In summary, the tort model is backward-looking, victim-focused, and compensatory, while the atonement model is forward-looking, perpetrator-focused, and racially conciliatory. Although the atonement model is becoming the dominant model in the American black redress movement, as it is worldwide, it has yet to yield any tangible benefits in redressing slavery or Jim Crow. As of 2007 a bill calling for a study of the redress question has been languishing in the U.S. Congress since it was first introduced in 1989 by Representative John Conyers (D-Mich.). Yet the struggle for reparations continues.

SEE ALSO *Apartheid; Holocaust.*

BIBLIOGRAPHY

Ashmore, Harry S. 1982. *Hearts and Minds: The Anatomy of Racism from Roosevelt to Reagan.* New York: McGraw-Hill.

Brooks, Roy L. 2004. *Atonement and Forgiveness: A New Model for Black Reparations.* Berkeley: University of California Press.

———. 2005. "Institutional Atonement for Slavery: Colleges and Corporations." Paper presented at the Seventh Annual Gilder Lehman Center International Conference—*Repairing the Past: Confronting the Legacies of Slavery Genocide, and Caste, October 27–29, 2005,* at Yale University. Available from http://www.yale.edu/glc/justice/brooks.pdf.

Chang, Iris. 1997. *The Rape of Nanking: The Forgotten Holocaust of World War II.* New York: Basic Books.

French, Howard W. 1999. "The Atlantic Slave Trade: On Both Sides, Reason for Remorse." In *When Sorry Isn't Enough: The Controversy over Apologies and Reparations for Human Injustice,* edited by Roy L. Brooks. New York: New York University Press.

Kunhardt, Philip B., Jr., Philip B. Kunhardt III, and Peter W. Kunhardt. 1999. *The American President.* New York: Riverhead Books.

Salzberger, Ronald P., and Mary C. Turck, eds. 2004. *Reparations for Slavery: A Reader.* Lanham, MD: Rowman & Littlefield.

Roy L. Brooks

REPATRIATION OF NATIVE AMERICANS

SEE *Native American Graves Protection and Repatriation Act (NAGPRA).*

REPRODUCTIVE RIGHTS

Reproductive rights are usually defined as "pro-choice," meaning abortion should be legal, safe, and affordable for any woman who desires it. As it relates to sexual reproduction, reproductive rights advocates believe that women should have the right to control their reproductive functions, decide whether to have children or not, and have access to contraception, family planning, and medical coverage. Advocates believe that such rights are human rights encompassing education about birth control and sexually transmitted infections and freedom from forced sterilization and contraception. They also believe that such rights fall within the realm of the right to privacy where women have freedom from government interference in their lives.

Groups and individuals who oppose abortion have been critical of the use of the terminology "reproductive rights" or "reproductive choice" as being ambiguous and vague. It is their belief that once fertilization occurs, reproduction has been completed and abortion is the killing of a human being. Because of these varying opinions on reproductive rights, two self-proclaimed groups have emerged as part of the national and international dialogue: pro-choice versus pro-life.

EARLY BIRTH CONTROL AND EUGENICS MOVEMENT

From the beginning of time, women found ways to prevent or terminate unwanted pregnancies. The *Kahun Papyrus*, a 4,000-year-old document cited as the oldest written document on birth control, mentions vaginal pessaries made of crocodile dung and fermented dough. Early condoms were made from linen and from the skins of sheep, goats, or snakes and were used in many early societies. Dilators and curettes similar to those used in modern-day abortion were found in the ruins of Pompeii, the Italian city that was destroyed by a volcanic eruption more than 2,000 years ago. Other forms of birth control have included herbs and chemicals, dried fish, glass or metal diaphragms, and bloodletting.

The modern birth control movement is said to have originated with Margaret Sanger in the early twentieth century. Sanger was a feminist socialist from New York City and coined the term "birth control." She viewed birth control as a means by which women could be freed from the "tyranny of pregnancy and birth." She championed a woman's right to contraception in the face of early-twentieth-century laws that prohibited it. She felt that women's ability to control their own reproduction was essential to their freedom and equal participation in society. Sanger was founder of the Birth Control Federation of America (BCFA), forerunner to the Planned Parenthood Federation of America. She took the birth control movement a step further by incorporating a eugenics agenda that sought to regulate the reproduction rights of the poor, immigrants, and African Americans.

Thomas Malthus, an eighteenth-century British clergyman and economist, published data that became the basis of the population control movement. Malthus argued that the world's population was growing faster than the Earth's capacity for food production. If measures were not taken to curtail the overpopulation trend, then the world would be faced with poverty, famine, pestilence, and war. He felt that population growth should be restricted to certain groups of people to maintain Western civilization. Specifically, unfit, poor, diseased, racially inferior, and mentally incompetent individuals had to be isolated, suppressed, or eliminated.

Margaret Sanger became a disciple of Malthusian philosophy. She also followed the lead of Emma Goldman, a famous anarchist who had been arrested for distributing a pamphlet titled "Why and How the Poor Should Not Have Many Children." These beliefs ultimately evolved into the eugenics movement in the United States. Eugenics embraced the notion that intelligence and personality traits were genetically determined and inherited.

The eugenics movement gained momentum because of the large numbers of immigrants coming into the United States at the turn of the twentieth century. Because of the fear of "race suicide," native whites were encouraged at the highest levels to have more children for the good of the nation. In his 1903 State of the Union speech, President Theodore Roosevelt stated that willful sterility was a sin for which there was no atonement. This thinking, along with the established belief that there were biological distinctions between whites and African Americans, with one group being superior to the other, underscored the appeal of eugenics in America. The targets were immigrants from southern and eastern Europe, Asians, Jews, and African Americans.

Many states began to enact laws forbidding marriage between people considered to be genetically defective, including drunks, criminals, and paupers. Southern states created publicly funded birth control clinics to lower the black birth rate. Politicians supported eugenic sterilization laws. Minority women were considered incompetent to make decisions about their reproductive lives. In 1924 Congress passed the National Origins Act, which established a quota for immigrants from southern and eastern Europe. Eugenicists opposed social programs designed to improve the living conditions of the poor. They argued that the minimum wage, good medical care, and better working conditions were not good for society because they only prolonged the life of inferior people who would continue to have children. Socially undesirable people were prevented from having children because eugenicists advocated compulsory sterilization as the way to improve society.

Sanger created the "Negro Project" in the 1930s. This project led to the placing of experimental birth control clinics in African American communities. She convinced African American civic groups, prominent black newspapers, churches, and leaders that these clinics would be beneficial to the welfare of "colored people." Such leaders as Adam Clayton Powell Sr. invited her to his Harlem church to speak on the issue. Other leaders such as Charles Johnson, the president of Fisk University, argued that "eugenic discrimination" was necessary. Sanger also recruited such prominent African Americans as Mary McLeod Bethune, Adam Clayton Powell Jr., and Arthur Spingarn to serve on the board of the BCFA. As a result, she and her supporters were able to push birth control and ethnic cleansing as the panacea for societal problems rather than address the role of racism in infant mortality, poverty, and unemployment rates.

POST–WORLD WAR II TO THE 1960S

After World War II and the horrors of Adolf Hitler's eugenics experiments, support for eugenics waned. Efforts at population control shifted from Western countries to the developing world, where populations were growing rapidly. Both India and China devised plans to control population growth. Millions of women in many parts of the developing world were sterilized as a result of mass campaigns to control burgeoning populations. In South Africa, the apartheid government withheld basic health care for African women and promoted population control in its experiment with social engineering. In many African countries, female genital mutilation became a cultural practice. In such countries as Peru women in poor communities were faced with coercion and nonconsensual tubal ligations. In the United States, Native American women had long had foreign values, beliefs, and practices forced upon them, especially decisions regarding reproductive health. Decisions were imposed at the expense of individual rights.

In the 1950s experimentation with oral birth control was tested first on Puerto Rican and Haitian women before being "perfected." The "Pill" was launched in the 1960s as the safest method of birth control. This coincided with the new wave of feminism and the women's movement.

Many women's groups took up the cause of reproductive rights. Support for these rights ran the gamut from abortion to discussions on menopause. Women's groups supported the concept of family planning and were strong advocates of the U.S. Supreme Court interpreting abortion and contraceptive rights within the realm of the Ninth Amendment's statement of the enumeration of certain rights are not to be construed to deny or disparage others returned by the people. The Supreme Court legalized the use of contraception by married people in *Griswold v. Connecticut* (1965) and abortion on the federal level in *Roe v. Wade* (1973). The mainstream movement equated reproductive rights with contraception and access to a safe and legal abortion. Because of this, poor and minority women felt excluded and felt the need to define reproductive rights within their realm of reality.

REPRODUCTIVE RIGHTS FOR WOMEN OF COLOR

Women of color ultimately moved the discussion of reproductive rights beyond contraception and abortion as discussed by the mainstream women's movement. They began to focus on women's access to reproductive health care and the costs associated with such care. They also advocated reproductive justice as a component of reproductive rights, claiming that it was not enough for contraception and abortion to be legal if choices were limited to those with resources. Women of color argued that what happened to women's bodies derived from their circumstances, whether poverty, racism, injustice. Thus, the definition of reproductive rights was grounded by the experiences of their communities and by oppression. For women of color, economic and institutional constraints restricted their choices. Women of color also fully understood the difference between population control and voluntary birth control. The mainstream women's movement failed to connect sterilization abuse to abortion rights. Thus, women of color forged their own movements to broaden the definition of reproductive rights.

The National Black Women's Health Project, formed in 1984, was the first minority women's reproductive health organization. This group and others formed later addressed state-imposed policies designed to control minority women's fertility and focused on issues of reproductive justice. Minority women's organizations felt that the women's movement needed to incorporate "bread and butter" issues (health care, forced sterilization, welfare rights) into discussions about reproductive rights. The movement needed to include minority women, working women, and poor women, not just white women of means; thus, they pushed for the movement to become more inclusive, especially acknowledging the role of racism.

RACISM AND REPRODUCTION ISSUES

The control of African American women's reproductive rights has its origins in slavery. Procreation helped maintain involuntary servitude through the slave owners' ability to control African American women's reproductive lives for economic gain. African American women were used to breed children who would be especially suited for labor or sale, and they had no control over what happened to their children. Oftentimes, slave owners rented physically fit males to serve as studs for their female slaves. Historian Catherine Clinton points out that males considered "runty" were often castrated "so dat dey can't have no little runty chilluns." The rape and exploitation of African American women both before and immediately following emancipation was not considered a crime.

Racism is also credited with birth control becoming a means of solving social problems. Birth control and racial injustice split the African American community. On the one hand were those activists who viewed birth control as a means of racial betterment, whereas on the other hand were those who saw it as racial genocide. The duality of birth control was whether poor and minority women had reproductive freedom through access to contraception and abortion juxtaposed with birth control being imposed on them as a means of reducing fertility. Public policy was forged around this duality.

In 1989 Charleston, South Carolina, instituted a policy of incarcerating pregnant women whose prenatal tests showed crack cocaine use. Local police tracked down pregnant women in the poorest neighborhoods of the city, handcuffed them, and took them to jail. Pregnant women who were already jailed and began labor were taken to the hospital in chains and remained shackled during delivery. Of the more than forty women arrested for prenatal crimes, only one was white. This policy was an example of the rhetoric that degraded and penalized African American women.

On December 12, 1990, the *Philadelphia Inquirer* ran an editorial entitled "Poverty and Norplant: Can Contraception Reduce the Underclass?" suggesting forced contraception as the solution for eliminating the African American underclass. The article indicated that those who were least able to afford and support children were having them and contributing to the poverty level. The article called for the implantation of the long-lasting contraceptive Norplant as the solution. This argument was supported by such books as Richard J. Herrnstein and Charles Murray's *The Bell Curve* (1994), which argued that the higher rate of fertility among "genetically less intelligent groups, including Blacks" was the cause of social disparities. As a result of such arguments, reproductive regulations such as the mandatory insertion of Norplant as a condition of receiving welfare assistance were initiated. The argument made was that if America's social problems were to be solved, then the birth rates of African American women had to be curtailed. As a result, African American organizations and women's groups argued that denying African American women reproductive autonomy served the interests of white supremacy and subscribed to what Dorothy Roberts, in *Killing the Black Body* (1997), argues is a belief that "reproductive politics in America inevitably involves racial politics."

For women in the developing world, reproductive rights cover a broad range of issues, including unsafe abortion, genital mutilation, rape, lack of available contraception, reproductive health policies, and comprehensive sex education. In May 2007 women throughout Africa came together in Accra, Ghana, to march for women's reproductive health rights and issues pertinent to control of those rights.

For women of color, reproductive rights go beyond simply the right to choose. There must also be options from which to choose and the ability to actualize choices made. They have been left out of reproductive rights discussions that had an inherent racist tenor. Thus, for women of color, reproductive rights parallel the quest for justice and equality, broadening the scope of reproductive freedom.

SEE ALSO *Eugenics, History of; Feminism and Race; Forced Sterilization; Forced Sterilization of Native Americans; Motherhood; Poverty; Powell, Adam Clayton, Jr.; Rape; Reproductive Technologies; Social Problems.*

BIBLIOGRAPHY

Clinton, Catherine. 1985. "Caught in the Web of the Big House: Women and Slavery." In *The Web of Southern Social Relations: Women, Family and Education*, edited by Walter Raser, R. Frank Saunders, and John L. Wakelyn. Athens: University of Georgia Press.

Green, Tanya L. "The Negro Project: Margaret Sanger's Eugenic Plan for Black Americans." Available from http://www.blackgenocide.org/negro.html

Herrnstein, Richard J., and Charles Murray. 1994. *The Bell Curve: Intelligence and Class Structure in American Life*. New York: Free Press.

Indigenous Women's Reproductive Rights and Pro-Choice Page. Available from http://www.nativeshop.org/pro-choice.html

Kimelman, Don. 1990. "Poverty and Norplant: Can Contraception Reduce the Underclass?" *Philadelphia Inquirer*, December 12: A18.

Nelson, Jennifer. 2003. *Women of Color and the Reproductive Rights Movement*. New York: New York University Press.

North, Lorna. 2007. "Ghana: March for Women's Reproductive Rights." *Ghanaian Chronicle*, May 18. Available from http://allafrica.com/stories/200705180605/html

Roberts, Dorothy. 1997. *Killing the Black Body: Race, Reproduction, and the Meaning of Liberty*. New York: Pantheon.

Silliman, Jael, Marlene Gerber Fried, Loretta Ross, and Elena R. Gutiérrez, eds. 2004. *Undivided Rights: Women of Color Organize for Reproductive Justice*. Cambridge, MA: South End Press.

Springer, Kimberly, ed. 1999. *Still Lifting, Still Climbing: Contemporary African American Women's Activism*. New York: New York University Press.

Mamie E. Locke

REPRODUCTIVE TECHNOLOGIES

Reproductive technologies involve the techniques and knowledge used to either produce or reduce a woman's fertility. Like other technologies, reproductive technology became increasingly interdependent with science during the twentieth century. As a result, reproductive technologies are becoming more sophisticated. It is ideology, however, that drives reproductive technology development and use. The ideas of white supremacy and patriarchy weave through each of the various ideologies that have informed reproductive technology use, including those centered on constructs of choice and autonomy. These ideologies, in turn, link reproductive technology use with other racist and patriarchal practices.

The ideologies that shape contraceptive use have accumulated and intertwined over time. In the late nineteenth century, social reformers cast contraceptive use as a means of achieving "voluntary motherhood," a concept that, in a limited sense, foretold the late twentieth-century reproductive choice framework for reproductive technology use. The campaign called for women to decide on family size, but it did so to improve women's ability to fulfill their roles as wives and mothers. During the same period, eugenicists campaigned for contraceptive use by members of the lower class and racial minority groups to achieve negative eugenic goals—that is, to prevent births by those deemed genetically unfit by virtue of their poverty or nonwhiteness. They also labeled declining birth rates among wealthy whites as "race suicide," thus undermining the potential gender equality approach to contraceptive use embedded in the voluntary motherhood campaign. Instead, eugenicists' support for contraceptive use made explicit the assumption that ideal motherhood, whether voluntary or not, was white.

Permutations of each of these concerns persist in population policy, where contraceptive technology is critical. Some population experts and programs take a human development approach, which posits that empowering individuals with reproductive autonomy and other human rights is the best way to address the lack of resources in developing nations and impoverished communities. In the human development approach, contraceptives and other birth-control methods are available, but their use is not the immediate goal. Population-control advocates see overpopulation as the primary cause of poverty and other problems. Contraceptive use, sterilization, and immigration restrictions, particularly in developing nations and low-income communities, are their immediate goals.

The ideological conflicts in population policy and contraceptive use play out in debates over specific contraceptive technologies. Efforts by population-control advocates led to the first birth-control pill and other highly reliable contraceptives. Feminists acknowledge that effective contraceptives enhance the ability of women to control opportunities for parenthood, education, and work. However, some also point to problems. The vast majority of contraceptives developed since the 1960s are for use by women, who therefore disproportionately bear the responsibility, cost, and medical risks of contraceptive use. Most of these contraceptives are expensive and therefore inaccessible to low-income women, who are disproportionately women of color. They also require a prescription or implantation by a physician, thus undermining the goal of reproductive autonomy. Most are hormonal or implantable, and while they are more effective than most barrier methods, they also create more medical risk than do barrier methods. The inability of nonbarrier methods to prevent infection by the human immunodeficiency virus (HIV) and other sexually transmissible diseases only adds to the risk factors that women bear.

The development of long-term contraceptives that take control away from the woman have heightened concerns that doctors and officials will abuse these technologies in the pursuit of population control or other goals. Use of the injectable hormonal contraceptive Depo-Provera on low-income black women, Native American women, mentally retarded women, incarcerated women, and drug-addicted women, with little or no explanation of its potentially serious side effects, seems to substantiate this concern. Depo Provera's side effects include loss of bone density and irregular bleeding, as well as the inability to stop the symptoms for the twelve to fourteen weeks it takes for the shot to wear off. Because target populations in both developed and developing nations are disproportionately nonwhite, the goal of reducing population size, paired with concerns about removing control from women raises questions about the eugenic effects, if not the goals, of some population-control efforts.

Eugenics has shaped reproductive technologies other than contraceptives. While nineteenth-century concerns about "race suicide" or the low birth rate among wealthy whites led to pronatalism aimed at wealthy white women, negative eugenic methods included surgical sterilization, segregation, and under the Nazi regime, genocide. By the 1930s, a majority of western nations had enacted laws authorizing involuntary sterilization of those perceived to carry specific hereditary forms of unfitness, including the "feeble-minded" and mentally retarded, those of Asian and African descent, and perpetrators of certain types of crimes. In the United States, during the same period, eugenics merged with racist nativism and produced racially targeted immigration restrictions that overlapped with eugenic sterilization laws. The Page Law of 1875, for example, all but prohibited immigration by Chinese women. This had the effect of inhibiting family formation and birth rates among Chinese immigrants. Since then, other immigration restrictions aimed at racial and ethnic minorities have sought to preserve the whiteness of U.S. national identity by restricting immigration from racialized nations or inhibiting birth rates among immigrants of color.

Abortion may be the most ideology-laden reproductive technology. During the twentieth century, abortion went from being a widely used but socially undiscussed form of birth control to a highly regulated procedure subject to vigorous public debate. The two prevailing ideological frameworks have formed in opposition to each other. The dominant approach of those who support legalized abortion uses a liberal rights-based analysis. This approach casts abortion as the key to gender equality. From this perspective, self-determination for women must include the right to decide whether or not to terminate a pregnancy. Without rights of bodily integrity and decisional autonomy, women cannot fully participate in the political economy or counter norms that define women primarily in terms of their reproductive capacity. The dominant approach of those who oppose abortion and who would restrict access to abortion focuses on the moral status of the fetus. This approach characterizes

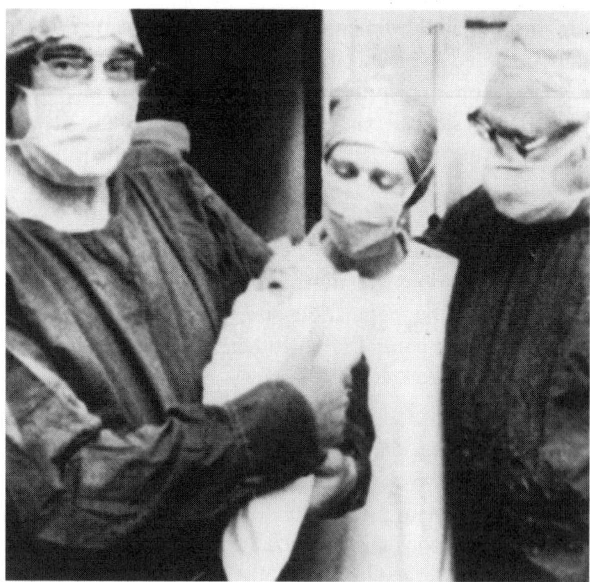

First Test Tube Baby, 1978. *In the 1970s and 1980s, assisted reproductive technologies changed the understanding of infertility from a social disability to a potentially treatable condition.* AP IMAGES.

abortion as the killing of a human. From this perspective, society's primary duty is to protect the fetus, even at the expense of the woman who is pregnant.

While the U.S. Supreme Court recognized in *Roe v. Wade* (1973) that the Constitution protects a woman's right to decide whether or not to terminate a pregnancy, the Court's analysis also permits some regulation of abortion. Abortion restrictions can have a cumulative effect with the greater barriers to health care access that women of color generally face. For example, women of color and low-income women are less likely to have employment-based health insurance or other means of paying for health care. They are more likely, therefore, to depend on government funding, and thus on political will and social policy for access. As a result, the 1976 Hyde Amendment's prohibition of federal funding for nearly all abortions made abortion financially impossible and the right to decide ineffective for many low-income women and women of color in the United States.

The level of conflict over abortion and the interlocking nature of the dominant ideological frameworks make abortion seem unique among reproductive technologies. The level of conflict also reflects the time and effort that both sides of the debate have invested in the issue. To some extent, the focus on abortion has confined the understanding of reproductive liberty to abortion rights. Yet eugenic pronatalism, eugenic population control, and racist nativism so thoroughly inform reproductive technology use that women of color often experience it differently than white women. They have been, for example, more vulnerable to contraceptive and sterilization abuse. The prevailing understanding of reproductive liberty, therefore, fails the needs of minority women.

In the 1970s and 1980s, assisted reproductive technologies changed the understanding of infertility from a social disability to a potentially treatable condition. Physicians, embryologists, and other experts created a fertility industry, premised on the use of assisted reproductive technology, which has been marketed primarily to middle-class, and often professional, women. The juxtaposition of these infertile women with those deemed by social policy as too fertile (low-income women and immigrants of color) created an ideology of infertility that echoed late nineteenth-century eugenic pronatalism. One result is that, despite higher infertility rates, infertility among persons of color has not been recognized as a problem. On the other hand, many have used assisted reproductive technology to create parent-child relationships that challenge heterosexist, marriage-based notions of family. The deliberate use of assisted reproductive technologies to form families with one parent, or with two unmarried parents, often in gay or lesbian unions, undercuts the strength of norms often used to criticize parents of color for failure to use birth-preventing technologies.

Preconception and prenatal testing produces choices for individuals regarding conception, pregnancy, and, to some extent, the health of their potential children. As with abortion, for many women of color the ability to choose depends on the interplay of health-care barriers and the vagaries of government funding. The more subtle issue is that these technologies normalize genetic selection, the core premise of eugenics. Individuals, not government officials, make the selections. But individual selections are subject to the ideological pressures that shape other reproductive technology use.

SEE ALSO *Forced Sterilization; Motherhood; Reproductive Rights.*

BIBLIOGRAPHY

Bunkle, Phillida. 1993. "Calling the Shots? The International Politics of Depo-Provera." In *The "Racial" Economy of Science: Toward a Democratic Future*, edited by Sandra Harding, 287–302. Bloomington: Indiana University Press.

Hartmann, Betsy. 1995. *Reproductive Rights and Wrongs: The Global Politics of Population Control,* rev. ed. Boston: South End Press.

Harvard School of Public Health, Global Reproductive Health Forum. "Reproductive Technologies Web: RT21." Available from http://www.hsph.harvard.edu/rt21/.

Kline, Wendy. 2001. *Building a Better Race: Gender, Sexuality, and Eugenics from the Turn of the Century to the Baby Boom.* Berkeley: University of California Press.

Native American Women's Health Education Resource Center. 2003. *Indigenous Women's Health Book, Within the Sacred*

Circle, edited by Charon Asetoyer, Katharine Cronk, and Samanthi Hewakapuge. Lake Andes, SD: Indigenous Women's Press.

Nsiah-Jefferson, Laurie, and Elaine J. Hall, 1989. "Reproductive Technology: Perspectives and Implications for Low-Income Women and Women of Color." In *Healing Technology: Feminist Perspectives,* edited by Kathryn Strother Ratcliff et al. 93–118. Ann Arbor: University of Michigan Press.

Powderly, Kathleen E. 1995. "Contraceptive Policy and Ethics: Illustrations from American History." *Hastings Center Report* 25 (1): S9–S11.

Raymond, Janice. 1993. *Women as Wombs: Reproductive Technologies and the Battle over Women's Freedom.* San Francisco: HarperSanFrancisco.

Roberts, Dorothy. 1997. *Killing the Black Body: Race, Reproduction, and the Meaning of Liberty.* New York: Pantheon Books.

Silliman, Jael, Marlene Gerber Fried, Loretta Ross, and Elena R. Gutierrez. 2004. *Undivided Rights: Women of Color Organize for Reproductive Justice.* Cambridge, MA: South End Press.

Lisa C. Ikemoto

RESERVATION SYSTEM

Colonial and imperial governments tend to view subordinate populations as problems to be solved, and they design political, legal, and administrative instruments to manage such populations. The Native American reservation system in the United States is one such instrument. The reservation system grew out of earlier colonial policies dealing with land acquisition, access to resources, and the forced relocation of Native American groups. The reservation system is not a necessary or evolutionary stage in the management of Native American peoples, however, but rather a contingent historical development that grew out of prior policies, practices, and ideological formations. In order to understand the reservation system as it exists in the early twenty-first century, one must trace the political and legal antecedents that produced it.

COLONIAL ADMINISTRATION

The colonial roots of the reservation system can be traced to Elizabethan England's expansionist ventures into Ireland and the administration of colonial government there in the sixteenth and seventeenth centuries. One of the key objectives of the colonial apparatus was the "civilizing mission," which sought to bring subordinate populations into conformity with English norms of economy, political and legal standards, social organization, and religion. Civility was held to be coextensive with an agricultural lifeway, democratic governance, common law, and Anglican Christianity. The forced capitulation of the native populations of colonized regions to these criteria was a mandate adhered to by English colonizers. Indigenous populations were uniformly presumed to be inferior races in need of the civilizing institutions and values of Anglo society.

Colonial experiments also sought to develop new mechanisms for dealing with domestic problems, including criminality; population growth and urbanization; changes in political, economic, and social structures that resulted from industrialization; and the transition from mercantilism to capitalism. The colony provided seemingly appropriate avenues for the resolution of both domestic and external political problems. Colonial initiatives fostered an emphasis on the profit motive and competition, which were key ideological frames for colonization and the expropriation of land and resources in colonized areas. These motives provided the basis for expansion, opened new avenues of thought for resolving political problems, and structured interactions between English colonizers in Ireland and North America (and between English colonizers and their European colonial adversaries, including France, Spain, the Netherlands, and Russia).

The invention of reservations must be understood against a background of political economy. Under mercantilism, London merchants engaged in long-distance trade, opened markets, and supplied patronage for the development of fleets and the recruitment of labor. These efforts allowed for the effective penetration of trade sites abroad. The market structures that were created were subsequently fulfilled through the enterprises of trading companies, chartered companies, joint stock companies, and various public-private alliances tasked with the extraction and export of resources and reimportation and sale of manufactured goods. This political economy was designed to shift English dependence away from European competitors and toward the supply of its own raw materials through colonial extraction and exchange. The patterns established in Ireland and exported to North America resulted in the system of population management recognized today as the reservation system.

THE ENGLISH IN IRELAND

The ideology of difference that prevailed in Elizabethan England maintained that the Irish were a savage and inferior race, and the colony was developed to civilize the native population and extract resources for investors and the Crown. Colonial administrators, such as the poet and novelist Edmund Spenser, were assiduous in propagating racial ideas of Irish inferiority and savagery, as well as the absolute necessity of introducing the institutions of civilization to the island. To achieve their objectives, the architects of colonial policy relied upon several instruments of control, including warfare, slaughter, and terror; the confiscation of land and plantations; and forced capitulation to English rule.

In order to accomplish these goals, colonial administrators perpetrated extreme violence against the Irish and transplanted English and Scotish populations to confiscated lands. The English justified these activities by invoking Roman law and Roman and Renaissance precedents. According to precedent, colonization was a normative and civilized mode of governing for putatively superior peoples. In addition, the natural law doctrines that underwrote colonization were sufficient to enable England's invasion and occupation of Ireland and to defend the brutality committed against its inhabitants. Conquest and *res nullius* (empty things) were key principles by which English conquerors subsequently justified their practices in Ireland.

The colonized world was thus designed to create situated replicas of model English settlements. Much of the early colonial effort in Ireland in the late sixteenth century was sanctioned by the Crown, though without its financial support. These were primarily private military and economic adventures, many of which failed. This created the perceived need to improve the colonial project and make the Crown more responsible for oversight and investment. It was under these circumstances that larger-scale plantations were undertaken. Early movements toward centralization were ad hoc and inchoate, however, and it was not until much later, in North America, that the effort became systematic and consequential.

THE ENGLISH IN NATIVE NORTH AMERICA

In North America, the English imported the principles of conquest, *res nullius*, and the just war. Colonists continued to instrumentalize these principles to legitimize the theft of indigenous lands and resources. The English drew heavily upon their experience in Ireland, continuing with successful elements and improving upon the unsuccessful. They were also required to innovate in their interactions with and management of Native American populations. One of these important innovations was the creation of reserves.

Reserves as such had not been created or implemented in Ireland, although the native Irish had been subject to forcible relocation and exclusion from previously held lands. Reserves emerged quickly in North America, however, and they were often established as terms of peace negotiations. Reserves were created for the explicit purpose of bounding populations of Native Americans, of compelling them to remain in designated geographical spaces where their behavior could be supervised. In North America, the English encountered peoples who practiced fundamentally different economic forms and required large land areas to support those forms. To the English mind, this was the apex of the racial concept of savagery, and the civilizing mission in North America necessitated a more intensive approach. It required settlement and domestication of the indigenous populations, the introduction of row agriculture instead of horticulture, and Christianization. The result was the development of the reserve, or, increasingly, the "reservation," and this element was routinely included in treaty terms by the seventeenth century.

Treaty making was a common and enduring instrument for negotiating relations. Typically, treaties stipulated that reserves would be protected from encroachments by the English, but agreed-upon boundaries and other terms were rarely observed by the English, and they were even more rarely enforced by the Crown or colonial governments. Aggressive encroachment thus became constitutive of English settlers' practice. This fostered frequent hostilities, and conquest and just war came to be claimed as the rationale for virtually every conflict over land. The extent of such hostilities increased in frequency and intensity over the course of the seventeenth and early eighteenth centuries, and by the mid-eighteenth century relations with Native Americans were so fractious that their administration was removed from colonial management and centralized under the Crown. This placed the management of Native American relations in royal departments vested with full royal authority, and it also introduced new requirements regarding the acquisition of lands from Native Americans. In particular, colonial governments and individuals could no longer write treaties with Native people, nor could they acquire title directly from Native nations.

Regardless of the Crown's mandate, the colonies refused to comply, and by 1764 it had become obvious that a new policy to regulate commercial and political relations with the Indians was needed. The Crown's key concerns were warfare, the fur trade, land speculation, land encroachments, the frontier, and the boundary negotiations that would permanently separate Native American lands from settler lands along the watershed of the Appalachians. Once formalized, this line was not to be transgressed, but it was constantly moved westward as new treaties, settlements, and purchases were concluded. Thus, the settler frontier moved steadily westward. This policy and the boundary concept were abandoned in 1768 because the costs to the imperial government were too high. Individual colonies, therefore, continued to establish and maintain relationships with Native Americans within their borders, and some of these relationships persisted after the conclusion of the American Revolution. These persisting relationships were codified in the recognition of certain Native American nations by state governments. Many of these state-recognized tribes have state reservations, although these contain significantly fewer inhabitants than federal reservations.

THE U.S. FEDERAL GOVERNMENT AND NATIVE AMERICANS

The formal relationships between England and Native Americans were carried forward into the purview of the United States, and the new nation continued the practice of negotiating treaties with Native Americans as the frontier moved west. Following English precedent, these treaties were primarily land cession arrangements in which Native Americans acquiesced to remain on reserved lands or relocate to new reservations. These cessions were usually purchase agreements, in which the United States committed to annuity payments and maintained control of the funds through a trust arrangement. Most reservations were created through treaties, but Congress has created several by statute, while some were negotiated through executive order. Presidential power to create reservations was eliminated by Congress in 1919, and the secretary of the interior received the capacity to create, expand, or restore reservations. Native American tribes must be recognized by the federal government in order to qualify for federal benefits, but there is no direct correlation between recognition and reservation status, and state recognition does not of itself qualify a tribe for federal benefits.

The U.S. Constitution situated the responsibility for the management of Native American relations with the Congress. The initial constitutional relationship with Native Americans was structured around the idea that indigenous polities were independent sovereign nations, equal in political weight to the United States. Formal relations were centered on trade and intercourse. As the American desire for land and resources increased, however, and as this desire was fulfilled at the expense of Native American peoples, the federal government altered its recognition of Native American sovereignty. After Supreme Court chief justice John Marshall's decision in the 1831 *Cherokee Nation v. Georgia* case, Native Americans came to be seen as "domestic dependent nations" in a trust relationship with the United States government. This political and ideological reorganization enabled the practice of wholesale expropriation of Native American lands, the destruction and forcible relocation of their peoples to suit U.S. needs, and the consolidation of the reservation system. The political and ideological shifts were accompanied by new legal understandings of Native Americans and new initiatives for the management of their populations.

The earliest of these initiatives was called "removal." This idea was promulgated by Thomas Jefferson as an alternative to failed efforts to assimilate and civilize Native American peoples. Removal became federal policy under Andrew Jackson with the Indian Removal Act of 1830, and thereafter it resulted in extreme hardship for many Native Americans. Many groups were either conduced to sign treaties to relinquish land claims east of the Mississippi or compelled by military threat to abandon their lands. The justification for removal and subsequent U.S. policies vis-à-vis Native Americans built upon the ideas imported to colonial America by the English; namely conquest, discovery, and *terra nullius* (empty land). The English, and subsequently the United States, maintained the juridical fiction that they had discovered and conquered a land inhabited by peoples who they believed did not cultivate it, and therefore had no claim to ownership of the land on which they resided. This observation ignored the reality and extent of precontact indigenous agriculture, as well as the fact that Native Americans had domesticated more than half the cultigens then in existence. The putative "civilizing mission" was brought fully forward as well. Native Americans were explicitly described as an inferior race, and only those who would accede to an agricultural and Christian lifeway were considered civilizable (if not quite civilized). Those who would not do so were an obstacle to the success of the fledgling American nation, and such obstacles required elimination. Whether through assimilation or destruction, the goal was the same: the eradication of the difference embodied by Native American individuals and nations.

Removal was replaced in the nineteenth century with reservation policy. Early U.S. reservation theory preferred consolidated reservations and envisioned two large areas (north and south) on which all Native Americans were to reside. The rationale was to eliminate multiple agencies and reduce military obligations, thus shrinking government costs. There was also a desire to create a system in which Indians could be more easily surveilled and controlled. Advocates believed that fewer reservations would reduce tensions between Native Americans and encroaching settlers; facilitate control of the illicit trade in liquor, arms, and ammunition; and make it easier to impose agriculture and education. Reservation theory was deeply influenced by the idea that education and agriculture were the most effective means of civilizing, and it was assumed that, once civilized, Native Americans would no longer want to live as tribal members on reservations. They would instead leave the reservations and assimilate, and their former reservation lands would revert to federal title, to be opened to resale and reentry.

As the frontier was pushed westward and aggressive settler encroachment intensified, U.S. policymakers began to favor a scattered approach. By the mid-nineteenth century, the United States had embarked upon a policy of concentrating Native Americans onto fixed reservations with lands deemed sufficient for actual occupancy. The

Reservation System. *Native Americans pose on the porch on an Apache Indian Mission in Arizona around 1910. The reservation system was established for the settlement and domestication of the indigenous populations, the introduction of agriculture, and Christianization.* THE LIBRARY OF CONGRESS.

federal government also decided at this time to discontinue money annuities in favor of goods, including stock animals, plows, and tools, as well as facilities for schools to teach industrial and manual labor skills. It was also during this period, in 1871, that the federal government ended the practice of treaty making and instead relied upon treaty substitutes, such as statute and executive orders, to govern the formal relations between the federal government and Native American groups.

By the 1880s, the civilizing and assimilationist mission of the reservation agenda was modified to mandate the allocation of lands in severalty (individual ownership), thus encouraging private property ownership and discouraging tribal relations. The Dawes Act (1887) and the Curtis Act (1898) were the primary legislative documents that implemented the terms of individual ownership. These acts provided for the allotment of small, specific parcels of land to Native American families and individuals, and they provided for non-allotted lands to be opened to non-Indian settlement. The net result was the loss of approximately 90 percent of Native-controlled lands to non-Native ownership.

Since the end of the treaty era, federal Indian policy has vacillated between assimilationist and eradicationist alternatives. Some measure of autonomy and self-government was attained following the passage of the Indian Reorganization Act in 1934, but these small successes were soon lost. Following House Concurrent Resolution 108, passed in 1953, the federal government embarked on the termination and relocation policy, according to which Congress sought to terminate the federal relationship with Native Americans and compel their relocation to urban centers. In addition, Public Law 280 (also 1953) conferred on the governments of five states (Minnesota, Wisconsin, California, Nebraska, and Oregon, with Alaska added by amendment in 1958) full criminal and limited civil jurisdiction over reservations. Termination and relocation were catastrophic for Native peoples in the United States, and their effects continue to be felt.

Termination and relocation were followed by the development of self-determination policy. Initially proposed by President Lyndon Johnson in 1968, self-determination was fostered by sovereignty initiatives and Indian activism and resulted in the recognition by the federal government of the unique status of Indian tribes and individuals. President Richard Nixon arrogated to his administration the development of self-determination policy, and it was enacted as law under President Gerald Ford as the Indian Self-Determination and Educational Assistance Act in 1975. It was amended in 1988, 1994, and 2000, and there are still problems with its implementation, but it continues to garner political support within the federal government and among many Native Americans. Sovereignty and autonomy on the reservation are critical and contentious issues, and the management of reservation resources and populations is fundamental to the concept and practice of self-determination. The ambivalent histories and the multifarious relationships between the United States and Native Americans continue to center on the reservation system and the unequal burdens and benefits that accrue to the differential power positions occupied by each group.

INTERNATIONAL IMPLICATIONS OF THE U.S. RESERVATION SYSTEM

The reservation system had unforeseen effects outside of the United States. For example, Adolf Hitler's efforts to contain and eliminate unwanted groups in Nazi Germany required the importation of American technologies, including punch card technology (developed by IBM), the application and instrumentalization of data systems, and the machinery for creating and implementing systems of containment and eradication, such as the reservation system. Nazi administrators, academics, and scientists studied the reservation system and other procedures and mechanisms for managing unwanted populations, including eugenics, euthanasia, and forced sterilization. American theory and practice were well known in Germany by the 1920s, so much so that many appeared in Hitler's manifesto, *Mein Kampf*, including containment, incarceration, isolation, monitoring and surveillance, antimiscegenation, and identifying, circumscribing, and eliminating populations according to race criteria.

BIBLIOGRAPHY

Canny, Nicholas. 2001. *Making Ireland British, 1580–1650.* Oxford: Oxford University Press.

Castile, George Pierre. 2006. *Taking Charge: Native American Self-Determination and Federal Indian Policy, 1975–1993.* Tucson: University of Arizona Press.

———, and Robert L. Bee, eds. 1992. *State and Reservation: New Perspectives on Federal Indian Policy.* Tucson: University of Arizona Press.

Cohen, Felix. 2005. *Cohen's Handbook of Federal Indian Law.* Newark, NJ: LexisNexis.

Philp, Kenneth, ed. 1995. *Indian Self-Rule: First-Hand Accounts of Indian-White Relations from Roosevelt to Reagan*, 2nd ed. Logan, UT: Utah State University Press.

Prucha, Francis Paul. 1984. *The Great Father: The United States Government and the American Indians.* Lincoln: University of Nebraska Press.

Wilkins, David. 2002. *American Indian Politics and the American Political System.* Boston: Rowman and Littlefield.

Wilkinson, Charles. 1987. *American Indians, Time, and the Law: Native Societies in a Modern Constitutional Democracy.* New Haven, CT: Yale University Press.

A. Scott Catey

ROCKWELL, GEORGE LINCOLN
1918–1967

In the middle of the twentieth century, George Lincoln Rockwell, a disgraced former naval commander and disowned son of a prominent vaudeville comedian, created a bridge between the racial ideology of Adolf Hitler's Third Reich and the racism of postwar America, thus facilitating the emergence of the contemporary white supremacist movement. Few twenty-first-century white supremacists remember Rockwell, and fewer still understand the significance of his contribution to their movement, but he was a significant catalyst in the formation of both the ideology and organization of white supremacist politics in the United States, even after his death in 1967.

George Lincoln Rockwell was born in Bloomington, Illinois, on March 9, 1918, the first child of George Lovejoy "Doc" Rockwell and Claire Schade Rockwell. Doc Rockwell was a rising star on the vaudeville comic circuit and a close friend of fellow performers such as Fred Allen, Groucho Marx, George Burns, and Jack Benny. Rockwell's mother, Claire, was an extraordinarily beautiful woman and a professional dancer, but she gave up her stage career at Doc's insistence once their baby was born. Doc Rockwell soon became a major vaudeville star, headlining throughout the country, appearing in several movies, and earning $3,500 per week by the early 1930s.

George Lincoln, or "Link," as he was called within the family, took after his mother in both looks and temperament. He grew to be a tall, handsome, athletic boy with a shock of black hair, piercing dark eyes, and a winsome smile. Like his mother, he was sensitive and artistic, but he was also often the object of Doc's caustic and hurtful derision, disguised as humorous banter.

Doc and Claire Rockwell divorced when Link was six years old. Doc structured the divorce and his time with his children to his convenience. Link and his younger brother, Bobby, spent every summer with their father at his luxurious oceanfront home in Maine. As Link grew, Doc, a very small man physically, seemed to resent Link's physical attributes and frequently used sarcasm to humiliate his son. But Link never stopped seeking Doc's affection and approval, though he never quite seemed to attain either.

Link Rockwell attended several exclusive boarding schools in New England, but he never quite fit in. He was a capable student, bright and clever, but he seldom applied himself. He excelled at art, but did not seem to value what he did best. His charm and charisma were evident from an early age, however.

He attended Brown University but withdrew before graduation to join the U.S. Navy at the outbreak of World War II. Before leaving Brown, Rockwell courted and married a local socialite, Judith Aultman. He became a fighter pilot, eventually earning the rank of commander and seeing action in the Pacific theater during the war.

After World War II, Rockwell tried his hand at commercial art and advertising, but he failed at several businesses, each time failing just as the business seemed on the brink of success, often because of a falling out with a partner or a disagreement with an important client. His first marriage ended in divorce.

During the Korean War, Rockwell was recalled to active duty. While stationed in Iceland he met and married a statuesque blonde, Thora Hallgrimsson, the daughter of a prominent Icelandic businessman. It was at this time that Rockwell became drawn to the philosophy of Adolf Hitler and was awakened to the racial imperative that Hitler represented. At the conclusion of his Korean service, Rockwell returned to the United States and became active in right-wing politics. Whereas his thinking became increasingly radicalized, he remained within the political mainstream, although he steadily gravitated towards the fringe elements of acceptable politics during the 1950s.

In 1959 Rockwell met Harold Noel Arrowsmith, a wealthy racist and anti-Semite who was seeking a bolder political movement to confront what Arrowsmith saw as a Jewish conspiracy to dominate the United States. In Arrowsmith, Rockwell saw an opportunity to finance his transition to a full-time political operative. He would become the bolder alternative Arrowsmith sought, and that same year he formed the American Nazi Party and became its leader. From that point until his death eight years later, Rockwell was the most vocal anti-Semite and racist hatemonger in American politics, using dramatic confrontation, outrageous language, theatrical demonstrations, and violent provocations to garner publicity and coalesce supporters.

Despite its theatricality and prowess at achieving publicity, the American Nazi Party never achieved success by any conventional measure. Its membership never exceeded 1,000, and its sympathizers, broadly defined, likely never exceeded 25,000 nationwide. It operated in abject poverty and was often the subject of scorn and ridicule. As the leader of a political movement, Rockwell was a total failure. But Rockwell's legacy is felt within the white supremacist movement of the early twenty-first century because of three concepts he developed that were later implemented to broaden the appeal of racism to a degree, and among a constituency, that Rockwell did not reach in his lifetime.

First, Rockwell recognized that in the United States the traditional white Aryan concept of the Hitlerian Nazis presented a natural barrier that doomed any white supremacist movement to failure. Rockwell recognized that there were not enough white people of Northern European stock (e.g., German, English, Irish, Scandinavian) in the United States to sustain a majority movement. So, in 1966, playing off an anticipated backlash to Stokely Carmichael's Black Power movement, Rockwell coined the phrase "White Power," defining "white" as anyone who is not black or a Jew. He thus added great masses of newly "white" people as potential recruits to future white supremacists movements.

By opening the door to the "Master Race" to southern and eastern Europeans (e.g., Italians, Slavs, Poles, Greeks, Russians) Rockwell redefined what it meant to be white in America. Large numbers of ethnic Americans who previously had no common identity began seeing themselves by what they were not: black or a Jew. While white racial identity grew slowly in the 1960s and was primarily still only significant as a force of localized backlash to racial incursion in previously segregated neighborhoods, by the late twentieth century Rockwell's definition of white racial identity was the organizing force behind racialist movements such as David Duke's National Socialist White People's Party, William Pierce's National Alliance, and Matthew Hale's World Church of the Creator (later called the Creativity Movement).

Second, Rockwell was the first movement politician to understand the power of combining religious fervor with racialist politics. As early as 1961, Rockwell and his German mentor, Bruno Ludtke, were exchanging correspondence regarding the advantages of utilizing a pseudo-Christian veneer for a neo-Nazi movement in America. By 1965, Rockwell was infiltrating fringe Christian sects with American Nazi Party operatives. His lieutenant, Ralph Forbes, became an ordained Christian Identity minister in California with the assigned task of merging that fringe group with Rockwell's racialist anti-Semitic politics. Rockwell's death in 1967 denied him the opportunity to reap the poisoned fruit his seeds eventually bore, but by the early twenty-first century, dozens of Christian Identity congregations were flourishing throughout the United States, with a theology infused with racist and anti-Semitic principles. Other so-called neo-Nazi religious denominations, such as the Creativity Movement, exist within the contemporary racialist community based on the Rockwell model.

Third, Rockwell popularized Holocaust denial in the United States as a political strategy. Rockwell recognized that the reality of the Holocaust and the impact of the memory of that tragedy within the human community was an impediment to the resurrection of Nazism as a viable political movement. His strategic response was an assault on historic memory. By altering the historic memory, he reasoned, he would lay the groundwork for the eventual acceptance of Nazism in the future. Rockwell understood that acceptance might not come in his lifetime, but, unlike most politicians, Rockwell was willing to plan and implement a strategy that had far-reaching implications.

Rockwell did not originate Holocaust denial, and he did not introduce the concept to the United States. His role was to bring the "big lie" to a mass audience, initially through an interview he gave to *Playboy* magazine in 1966, an interview conducted by the author Alex Haley and read by more than two million readers. In that forum, for the first time, average Americans were introduced to the outlandish notion that the number of Jews killed by the Nazis during World War II was greatly exaggerated, that the very existence of death camps was a fabrication by the Jews themselves to elicit sympathy for Jews worldwide, and that the State of Israel was behind a worldwide plot to trick the world into paying huge reparations and supporting Israel against its Arab neighbors as a form of guilt response to a genocide that never really happened. Rockwell hammered at this theme consistently whenever he spoke during the last two years of his life, and his Holocaust-denial proselytizing energized anti-Semites worldwide.

Rockwell was a unifying figure in the fractious world of neo-Nazi revival in the decades after World War II. At a time when no one else was willing to openly wear the swastika or openly adhere allegiance to racialist and anti-Semitic beliefs, Rockwell held the tattered banner aloft as a rallying point for the demoralized troops of the defeated Reich and its adherents. In 1961 he organized the World Union of National Socialists (WUNS) and became its first commander.

At a time when neo-Nazi activity was banned throughout most of Europe, Rockwell, with the help of a former Nazi soldier, Bruno Ludke, organized a nascent postwar neo-Nazi party in Germany itself, as well as neo-Nazi cells in France, Austria, Belgium, Holland, Italy, England, Ireland, Iceland, Sweden, Argentina, Brazil, and Canada.

In 1962 Rockwell slipped into Great Britain illegally and attended the first WUNS Grand Council Meeting, held in the Cotswalds, England, and hosted by the English Nazi leader Colin Jordan. The national neo-Nazi leaders greeted Rockwell as their führer and the group signed the Cotswold Agreement, a document that pledged international cooperation in the resurgence of white supremacist, neo-Nazi, and anti-Semitic movements worldwide.

George Lincoln Rockwell was murdered on August 25, 1967, a short distance from his American Nazi Party headquarters (Hatemonger Hill) in Arlington, Virginia, by John Patler, a young captain in his party and his protégé. Although Patler was convicted and went to prison for the killing, he never admitted to the murder and many questions regarding motive remained unanswered. The American Nazi Party did not survive long after Rockwell's death.

SEE ALSO *Christian Identity; Duke, David; Holocaust; National Alliance; Neo-Nazis; White Racial Identity.*

BIBLIOGRAPHY

George, John, and Laird Wilcox. *Nazis, Communists, Klansmen, and Others on the Fringe: Political Extremes in America.* Buffalo, NY: Prometheus Books, 1992.

Schmaltz, William H. 1999. *Hate: George Lincoln Rockwell and the American Nazi Party.* Washington, DC: Brassey's.

Simonelli, Frederick J. 1998. "The World Union of National Socialists and Postwar Transatlantic Nazi Revival." In *Nation and Race: The Developing Euro-American Racist Subculture,* edited by Jeffrey Kaplan and Tore Bjorgo. Boston: Northeastern University Press.

———. 1999. *American Führer: George Lincoln Rockwell and the American Nazi Party.* Urbana: University of Illinois Press.

Zeskind, Leonard. 1986. *The Christian Identity Movement: A Theological Justification for Racist and Anti-Semitic Violence.* Atlanta: Center for Democratic Renewal.

Frederick J. Simonelli

ROMA

Throughout North and South America, Europe, Oceania, Africa, and Asia there are groups of people—both communities and families—who refer to themselves as *Gypsy*, *Roma*, or similar terms (e.g., *Sinti* in Germany and *Travellers* in Ireland). Such groups are also known by many different names by non-Gypsies. Across Europe, for example, the terms *Gitanos, Zigeuner*, and *Cigani* might be heard on the street or in bars and cafes. Such communities, whether nomadic or sedentary, are held together or connected by a culture, tradition, and language (as well as common experiences of racial prejudice and discrimination) that sets them apart from their non-Roma neighbors. Gypsies are a scattered, diasporic people who number some 12 to 15 million persons worldwide, the great majority

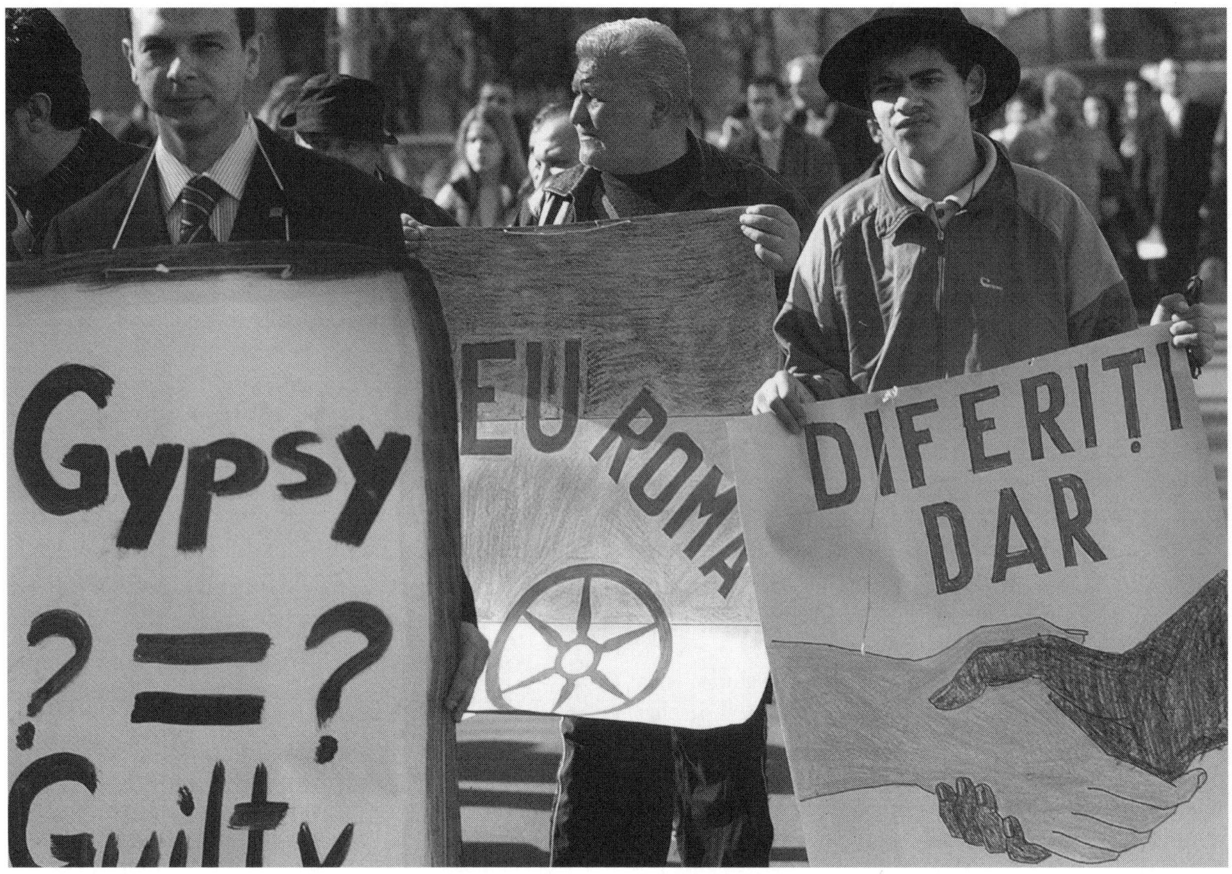

Romanian Gypsy Protest. *Romanian Gypsies carry banners during a march in Bucharest, Romania in February, 2006. Romania's Gypsy community and activists called on the dominant Orthodox church and the government to issue a formal apology for holding them slaves until 1856.* AP IMAGES.

living within the borders of Europe. Accurate demographic data is impossible to gather, largely due to the limitations of census indicators as well as an understandable reluctance on the part of many Gypsies to identify themselves to state officials (for fear of victimization and discrimination).

In addition to heated debates over numbers, there is also much discussion regarding the terms *Gypsy* and *Roma* themselves, along with long-running arguments regarding the early history and migratory movements of these peoples. Some communities reject the term *Gypsy*, finding it both insulting and racist (especially in central and eastern Europe). Other communities, however, attach a historical and political significance to the term and have attempted to, in a sense, reclaim it. The English Romanichal Gypsies in the United Kingdom are in this category. Central to such debates, as the Roma academic Ian Hancock has consistently argued, is a fundamental concern with (ethnic) identity, and with the struggle for Gypsies and Roma themselves to take control of their identity and challenge the largely negative stereotypes that have served to fuel anti-Gypsyism over the years.

The term *Gypsy* itself (sometimes spelled *Gipsy*) derives from the word *Egyptian*. Gypsies were thought to have traveled from Egypt in order to reach Europe in the thirteenth and fourteenth centuries. However, this assumption of an Egyptian origin is inaccurate, and much scholarly work has been conducted on demystifying the early history of Gypsies, with the majority opinion in the early twenty-first century being that such people started to arrive in Europe from about the thirteenth century onward, largely as a result of the Muslim Ottoman Turks taking over the Christian Byzantine Empire. Although an earlier presence in Europe is likely, it is difficult to be certain about this without written records. Confusion also often resulted from Gypsies and Roma being taken as local peripatetic groups. Further academic enquiries (in the eighteenth century, for example) started to suggest a strong connection between the Roma people and India, with close similarities between Romanes (the Romani language) and Indian languages such as Sanskrit and Hindi (among others) being noted and written about. The linguistic evidence appeared to confirm an Indian origin hypothesis. More recently, genetic work analyzing slow-evolving polymorphisms has been conducted at places such as the Centre for Human Genetics at Edith Cowan University, Australia, and this work appears to confirm a direct lineage link between the Roma and certain areas of India.

At the cultural level, especially on the part of scholars and Roma activists, a focus has been placed on deconstructing the fictional Gypsy of literature, film, and music. Due to these efforts, the term *Gypsy* has slowly been replaced in many countries with the *Roma*. The emphasis here has been on trying to humanize a population that throughout history has been subjected to some of the worst examples of state-sanctioned harassment, discrimination, and genocide. It has been estimated, for example, that during World War II up to one and a half million Roma were systematically killed by the Nazis during the Holocaust. Such treatment is not confined to the vaults of history, however. Even in the early twenty-first century, across central and eastern Europe, as well as other countries, neo-Nazi and fascist activity regularly targets the Roma as a "subhuman" population to be attacked and subjected to racialized forms of violence. In the Siberian town of Iskitim, for example, hundreds of Roma were forced from their homes in 2005, and an arson attack that same year left an eight year-old girl dead.

However, such activities are not just the actions of nationalists and extremists. For example, it has become evident from subsequent enquiries that a general anti-Roma attitude among local people, as well as state officials and the police, led to the pogrom that unfolded in the village of Hadareni, Romania, on the night of September 20, 1993. Three Roma people were killed and eighteen houses were destroyed in this attack.

Organizations such as the European Roma Rights Centre (based in Hungary) and Human Rights Watch (based in the United States) monitor anti-Roma episodes across the world and support Roma communities in their efforts to combat the effects of poverty, discrimination, and racism. Much faith has been placed in the "Decade of Roma Inclusion" (2005–2015) project, an initiative largely driven and financed by the World Bank and the Open Society Institute. The aim of this project is to address the deep structural roots of Roma inequality and exclusion across a number of policy areas including major areas of social policy such as education, employment, health, and housing.

For Gypsy and Roma activists it is not enough to leave it to various international bodies and nongovernmental organizations to talk for them. Gypsy and Roma agency and self-organization has been essential to their cultural, economic, and political survival as diasporic groups over the years. They have always relied on their adaptability and flexibility in all aspects of life. A transnational politics of "unity in diversity" has emerged, as evidenced by the various World Romani Congresses that have been held since 1971, that allow different Roma groups to witness and understand their common experiences and not simply focus on cultural and linguistic differences.

BIBLIOGRAPHY

Fraser, Angus M. 1995. *The Gypsies*, 2nd ed. Oxford: Blackwell.

Guy, Will, ed. 2001. *Between Past and Future: The Roma of Central and Eastern Europe*. Hatfield: University of Hertfordshire Press.

Hancock, Ian. 2002. *We Are the Romani People (Ame sam e Rromane dzene)*. Hatfield, U.K.: University of Hertfordshire Press.

Kenrick, Donald, and Grattan Puxon. 1972. *The Destiny of Europe's Gypsies*. London: Heinemann.

Mayall, David. 2003. *Gypsy Identities 1500–2000: From Egipcyans and Moon-men to the Ethnic Romany*. London: Routledge.

Nemeth, David. 2002. *The Gypsy-American: An Ethnographic Study*. Lewiston, NY: Edwin Mellon Press.

Okely, Judith. 1983. *The Traveller-Gypsies*. Cambridge, U.K.: Cambridge University Press.

Colin Clark

RURAL WHITE STEREOTYPING

Certain poor rural southern people who are seen as white, yet well apart from mainstream white America, are often referred to by several stereotyping terms, most notably *hillbilly*. The term has been applied primarily to people living in mountainous or otherwise marginalized locations, particularly in the Appalachians and the Ozarks. Their geographical situation has been presumed to have kept them genetically and culturally isolated, a presumption that at times has been the basis for defining them as a biological category separate from mainstream white America. The term, when used by those in the mainstream, is generally strikingly derogatory. However, the term has been embraced by some rural southerners who apply it to themselves, and to their families and communities, as a form of ethnic identity or to emphasize their social distance from what they consider to be corporate-controlled, northern-dominated, oppressive, mainstream white culture. In the early twenty-first century *hillbilly* is used in mainstream culture to refer to white people of rural origins who continue to resist assimilation into mainstream middle-class culture, maintaining what is seen by the mainstream as an insufficient respect for the values of consumerism, an insufficient respect for authority and for getting ahead, a closed-minded or antagonistic attitude toward the values of a multicultural society, and an irrational resistance to education and "progress."

THE RACIALIZATION OF HILLBILLIES

The mountain people who are seen as the original hillbillies lived on land that was unsuited for intensive cash cropping in areas in the rural South that historically were dominated by slave-holding elites, and later by land-owning elites who managed sharecropping and segregation. Inaccurate ideas of American history perpetuate the belief that, unlike "white trash," who lived among the elites, they were a rural people isolated and independent of the larger stratified society. This version of history implies the existence of a male-centered all-white classless society of small-scale self-sufficient homesteaders, hunters, moonshiners, and craftsmen, hidden away and protected from the outside world by the inaccessibility of their deep mountain valleys and rugged mountain tops. The term *hillbilly* implies that this isolation has produced people who are different from other white people and that this difference lives on in their descendants who have migrated out into the larger, stratified society. The belief in the reality of this genetically or culturally separate race has taken on almost mythic proportions both among outsiders and among some who have embraced the term in reference to themselves.

Supposedly scientific work has lent itself directly or indirectly to the belief that cultural characteristics such as poverty and resistance to what is presumed to be progress are in fact genetic and thus potentially racial. Examples of such "scientific" findings have been frequent over the past two centuries. They include such work as that of Sir Francis Galton in the 1880s and the ensuing four decades of eugenic family studies, purporting to show that traits such as lack of intelligence, criminality, and poverty are biological and inheritable, and also prevalent among mountain families. At the end of the twentieth century, Richard Herrnstein and Charles Murray claimed in *The Bell Curve* (1994) that economic failure results from bad genes, most often passed on by overly fertile mothers of low IQ. Such racialization is common when the political and economic power of elite groups depends on legitimizing the creation of a new category of people available for serious exploitation. Like other groups that have been racialized, mountain people and, more generally, marginalized rural white southerners, have been defined as "Other," so inferior that their very humanity can be called into question. The exploitation of hillbillies is then defined as "benevolence" to the very people being exploited—as providing a civilizing influence, teaching the value of hard work, and protecting women and girls from the violent sexual proclivities of their male relatives.

The belief in the existence of hillbillies has been critical to the definition of whiteness in the United States. At times they were seen as white, and therefore a genetic pool worth mining to offset the pernicious influence of immigration from southern and eastern Europe in the late 1800s and early 1900s, as in Berea College president William Frost's 1899 description of mountain people as "our [Anglo-Saxon] contemporary ancestors." At other times they have served to prove the superiority of "civilized" Americans, as when the historian Arnold Toynbee (in *A Study of History* [1934]) said that Appalachian people were no better than the "white barbarians of the Old-World, the Rifis and Kurds and the Hairy Ainu" (p. 149). Like the Irish and the Jews, the "white barbarians" he listed were regarded as not-quite-white in the eyes of mainstream white America. By turns comic, pathetic, or frightening, but straddling the boundary of whiteness, the hillbilly stereotype, like a number of other race-related stereotypes, helped delineate what "real" whites should be and should not be. Hillbillies were an "Other" close enough to mainstream whites themselves to make comparison meaningful, allowing them to fine-tune their measurements of their own superiority.

HISTORICAL BACKGROUND

Appalachia, contrary to popular belief, never was home to an isolated, classless, all-white society. Even the most rugged mountains of eastern Kentucky were socially stratified from the earliest days of European settlement. Large landowners, both white and, in some areas, Cherokee, owned slaves. Many poor white families were tenants, not independent landowners and hunters. They bore the brunt of the dangers of the conquest of Native American land, and were evicted by their elite landlords as soon as the land they cleared was safe for plantation agriculture. They became the instruments of Thomas Jefferson's strategy for depriving Native Americans of their land. They were equally involved in the partial fulfillment of Jefferson's plan for the construction of a society of small white landowners who would accept elite control of the economic and political system. Wilma Dunaway has shown—in *The First American Frontier* (1996)—that by the mid-1800s large sections of Appalachia were engaged in commercial agriculture, and that large-scale industry, mainly coal mining, lumbering, and textiles, shaped the destiny of much of the area. Despite historical reality, the belief in rugged, independent settlers has persisted, spurred on by both elementary school mythology and a popular culture that claims, for instance, that Davy Crockett (according to a well-known song) was born in the "land of the free," implying that

Destitute Ozarks Resident, 1935. *Certain poor rural southern people who are seen as white, yet well apart from mainstream white America, are often referred to by several stereotyping terms, most notably hillbilly.* THE LIBRARY OF CONGRESS.

the "mountaintops of Tennessee" housed a free people within a slave society, or even that slavery did not exist and that Native Americans had never been driven out.

The origins of the term hillbilly are obscure, but several theories link it to a Scottish background; according to Anthony Harkins (2003, p. 48), one likely explanation is that *billie* refers to a "fellow" or "companion." The term apparently was in use by the end of the 1800s, and it became common in print during the first decades of the twentieth century. This was a time of intense class strife between rural people of European descent and the large national corporations that were coming to dominate more localized southern economies. The People's Party, the Farmers' Alliance, and the Tobacco Wars (or Black Patch War) in Kentucky and Tennessee all signaled an uprising of farmers against the major corporations that controlled the conditions of their lives. Miners' revolts in the Appalachians likewise underlined the exploitation carried out by corporations and the wealthy elites associated with them.

It was during this time (the decades around the end of the nineteenth and early twentieth century) that two already existing stereotypes, one about "mountaineers" and another about poor white people more generally, came together and blossomed into the hillbilly—the lazy, feuding, drunken, bearded, bare-footed, overalls-clad, incest-prone, independent, patriarchal male equipped with an overdose of testosterone and a hair-trigger temper in defense of his honor, and the hard-working, child-producing, brow-beaten woman. A shortage of intelligence and rationality supposedly left them bound helplessly to despicable cultural traditions. The national press largely assumed that the stereotypes represented reality. Such stereotypes served effectively to explain to the rest of the country why these irrational hillbillies would resist the supposedly obvious benefits of dependent development or internal colonialism brought to them by corporations that took away their land. They were converted from diversified subsistence farming into a male labor force dependent for their livelihood on inadequate wages, often in the form of scrip paid by coal companies, under conditions where their lives were dependent upon the inadequate safety measures in the mines. Similar reporting in the national press during the Tobacco Wars, in the early years of the twentieth century, made irrationality and backwardness seem to be the real explanation of why tobacco farmers rose up against the monopolistic American Tobacco Company and the starvation prices it paid for tobacco. The stereotypes, then, did double duty in the local press by explaining why many of the poorer tobacco farmers did not follow the lead of their betters, the big planters who headed the boycott against the company. They were called hillbillies and portrayed as irrational and improvident, obscuring the fact that many were so poor they could not afford to withhold their crop from the market. The stereotype then did triple duty, explaining why it was necessary for the state militia to put down the violence-prone boycotters by force of arms to protect American Tobacco Company property.

Parts of the hillbilly stereotype merged with aspects of the "poor white trash" stereotype in national press reports on the Tobacco Wars. The poor white trash category was clearly part of the South's stratified society—and it was itself, to some degree, racialized. Their poverty was seen as a result of genetic inferiority or sometimes of racial mixing—by the 1920s the Ku Klux Klan was claiming that such people, like Catholics and Eastern European immigrants, were not "100% Americans." One of the defining characteristics of the poor white trash stereotype was a supposedly inherent malevolent racism that led to racist violence in the segregated South. This violence was believed to contrast with the supposed benevolent attitude of racial superiority of their more genteel betters, who claimed to take seriously their duty to care for their supposedly child-like black servants and sharecroppers.

Middle- and upper-class readers and writers of reports on the Tobacco Wars in Kentucky and Tennessee associated the violence of "feuding, gun-happy hillbillies" resisting progress in the mountains with the violence of "white trash" resisting progress as represented by the American Tobacco Company. Consequently, the hillbilly stereotype, when used by the middle and upper classes, now often included racism. In fact, vicious racism did play a part in the Tobacco Wars. Nightriders eventually targeted black farmers for violent attacks and lynchings, driving hundreds of black families from the region in an attempt to reduce the supply of tobacco and thus raise the price American Tobacco would pay the remaining white farmers. Many nightriders probably were poor people. However, this racist violence was not specific to poor whites or to hillbillies; most of the leaders, and apparently many of the masked nightriders themselves, were members of the local elite. And the actual "hillbillies" in the region were targets of violence themselves for refusing to participate in the boycott.

These stereotypes quickly became generic, whether or not the term hillbilly was used. This was the lens through which outsiders perceived the poorer Euro-Americans in Kentucky and throughout Appalachia. That lens applied also to the Ozarks, always part of the hillbilly stereotype, but later gaining greater prominence, particularly with the advent of the television show *The Beverly Hillbillies* (1962–1971).

THE CONTINUING RELEVANCE OF HILLBILLY IDEOLOGY

Hillbilly jokes, movies such as *Deliverance,* television programs such as *The Beverly Hillbillies*, cartoons such as *L'il Abner*, the comedy of performers such as Minnie Pearl and Jeff Foxworthy, tales about the Hatfields and the McCoys, historical and sociological analyses such as Harry Caudill's *Night Comes to the Cumberlands* (1963), experiences related by missionaries to Appalachia, documentaries such as *American Hollow* (1999) and the proposed reality show *The Real Beverly Hillbillies*, all demonstrate the continuing relevance of the supposed existence of people who fit the hillbilly stereotype. They feature, in varying combinations and in varying tones of voice, implications of hillbilly backwardness, stupidity, slovenliness, barbarism, a propensity for addiction, the mistreatment of women, genetic deficiencies, and inbreeding. The inaccuracies of this portrayal of people living in the Appalachian mountains or the Ozarks have been completely irrelevant to the continuing production of the stereotypes. It is important to note that these stereotyping movies, jokes, TV programs, documentaries, and missionary expeditions are produced by people in the mainstream, often with the backing of corporations and of people wielding considerable power; they depict people with very little power who nevertheless seem to refuse to buy into the values of corporate America.

These warped versions of history and of the reality of the lives of poor rural southerners carry a heavy ideological freight. Upper-class exploiters have used them to justify their own use of child labor and the poor wages and lack of safe work environments of miners and textile workers. They use them to explain the continuing high unemployment and low wages of southern workers generally and to justify paying low wages when southerners go north looking for better jobs. This same warped vision keeps the middle class from recognizing this exploitation and, therefore, from questioning the legitimacy of the elite.

For the country in general, racialization of the hillbilly, whether by the new cultural or the old biological version of racism, has played a critical role at various points in the legitimation of the continuously evolving system of race, class, ethnic, gender, and sexual-identity inequalities in the United States. It has been an important ingredient in the racial wedge used to divide and rule the working class, causing black and white members to define each other as the enemy. Equally important, the racialization of hillbillies has been an ingredient in the smokescreen that disguises class in the United States. Hillbilly identity, rather than class, can be invoked to explain ongoing poverty wages for those who are employed, high levels of unemployment, and inequities in health and educational opportunities in Appalachia and the Ozarks among people of European descent. The myth that the United States provides a level playing field, at least for whites, is thus left intact.

The hillbilly stereotype continues to provide white America with both a mirror in which to judge itself and a scapegoat for its failings. Along with stereotypes about rednecks and white trash, it allows middle-class people (through comparison) to perpetuate an inaccurate perception of themselves as free of racism, sexism, and homophobia, as people who are open-minded, progressive, and civilized. If the country continues to have problems with racism, for instance, those problems can often be laid at the door of poor southern whites whose culture or genetics supposedly predisposes them to intolerance and violence. The violence committed or orchestrated by elites can thus be ignored. Presumably, "civilized" elites would not use race to justify the disproportionate jailing of black, Latino, and Native American people, nor would they use a racialized version of religion to justify war. Neither would they beat their wives or discriminate against women in hiring. The persistence of the production of the hillbilly stereotype, and the willingness of the reading and television- and movie-viewing public to consume that stereotype, indicates that it continues to fulfill an ideological need in the lives of people dealing with the inequalities of life in the United States.

SEE ALSO *Galton, Francis.*

BIBLIOGRAPHY

Appalshop Films. *Strangers and Kin: A History of the Hillbilly Image.* 1984. Produced by Dee Alvin Davis III and directed by Herb Smith. Videocassette.

Buck, Pem Davidson. 2001. *Worked to the Bone: Race, Class, Power, and Privilege in Kentucky*. New York: Monthly Review Press.

Campbell, Tracy. 1993. *The Politics of Despair: Power and Resistance in the Tobacco Wars*. Lexington: University of Kentucky Press.

Caudill, Harry M. 1962. *Night Comes to the Cumberlands: A Biography of a Depressed Area*. Boston: Little, Brown.

Corbin, David. 1981. *Life, Work, and Rebellion in the Coal Fields: The Southern West Virginia Miners 1880–1922*. Urbana: University of Illinois Press.

Dunaway, Wilma. 1996. *The First American Frontier: Transition to Capitalism in Southern Appalachia, 1700–1860*. Chapel Hill: University of North Carolina Press.

Frost, William. 1899. "Our Contemporary Ancestors in the Southern Mountains." *Atlantic Monthly* 83 (March): 311–319.

Harkins, Anthony. 2003. *Hillbilly: A Cultural History of an American Icon*. New York: Oxford University Press.

Hartigan, John Jr. 1999. *Racial Situations: Class Predicaments of Whiteness in Detroit*. Princeton, NJ: Princeton University Press.

Herrnstein, Richard A., and Charles Murray. 1994. *The Bell Curve: Intelligence and Class Structure in American Life*. New York: The Free Press.

Newitz, Annalee, and Matt Wray. 1997. "Introduction." In *White Trash: Race and Class in America,* edited by Matt Wray and Annalee Newitz, 1–12. New York: Routledge.

Obermiller, Phillip, and Michael Maloney, eds. 2002. *Appalachia: Social Context Past and Present,* 4th ed. Dubuque, Iowa: Kendall/Hunt.

Pudup, Mary Beth, Dwight Billings, and Altina Waller, eds. 1995. *Appalachia in the Making: The Mountain South in the Nineteenth Century*. Chapel Hill: University of North Carolina Press.

Shapiro, Henry. 1978. *Appalachia on Our Mind: The Southern Mountains and Mountaineers in the American Consciousness, 1870–1920*. Chapel Hill: University of North Carolina Press.

Toynbee, Arnold. 1947 (1934). *A Study of History*. New York: Oxford University Press.

Waller, Altina. 1988. *Feud: Hatfields, McCoys, and Social Change in Appalachia, 1860–1900*. Chapel Hill: University of North Carolina Press.

Williamson, Jerry W. 1995. *Hillbillyland: What the Movies Did to the Mountains and What the Mountains Did to the Movies*. Chapel Hill: University of North Carolina Press.

Pem Davidson Buck

RUSTIN, BAYARD

1912–1987

Bayard Rustin (1912–1987) was a civil rights strategist and humanitarian who shaped the course of social protest in the twentieth century. Born in West Chester, Pennsylvania, on March 17, 1912, Rustin served as Martin Luther King Jr.'s political adviser and as the organizer of the 1963 March on Washington. Although he was best known for his influence on the course of the black protest agenda, Rustin's political engagements extended to organized labor and world affairs. However, Rustin remained an outsider in black civil-rights circles because, unlike most of his peers, he was gay. Throughout much of his career, Rustin tried to control the potential negative impact his sexuality could have on the causes for which he worked.

After a youth grounded in his grandmother's Quaker teachings, Rustin began college in 1932 at Wilberforce University, but he transferred to Cheney State Teachers' College two years later. Finally, in 1937, Rustin moved to New York to enroll in City College. However, rather than immerse himself in academics, Rustin plunged into the cultural and political circles of New York and Harlem. He began his pursuit of social justice by joining the Young Communists League. Then, in 1941, he joined Abraham Johannes (A .J.) Muste's Fellowship of Reconciliation (FOR), an organization guided by the Gandhian principles of nonviolent protest that would later be deployed by civil rights leaders. Rustin became Muste's chief acolyte, but his rise to leadership left him politically vulnerable, and in 1943 he was sentenced to three years in prison for refusing to register for selective service. After leading several civil-disobedience campaigns, Rustin fell under the scrutiny of prison officials, and when inmates complained about Rustin's sexual relationships with other men, he was placed in isolation. He worried that his actions would detract from FOR's cause, and his conduct earned a swift reprimand from Muste.

Rustin began the most productive period of his career upon his release from prison in March 1947. Working with the Congress of Racial Equality (CORE), Rustin orchestrated the Journey of Reconciliation, which involved sixteen CORE members traveling by bus between southern cities in order to test a recent Supreme Court ruling that banned racial discrimination in interstate travel. In the late 1940s, Rustin also traveled abroad as a representative of the pacifist movement. These travels brought him to Africa, where he discovered a sense of kinship that kept him committed to African politics and decolonization efforts. To finance a return trip to Africa, Rustin commenced a speaking tour of the United States. However, in 1953, following one of his speaking engagements in Pasadena, Rustin was charged with lewd conduct for engaging in gay sex. Outraged by actions that he believed jeopardized FOR's mission, Muste asked Rustin to leave the organization.

After resigning from FOR, Rustin became a key player in the civil rights movement. On the recommendation of A. Philip Randolph, a leader in both the trade union and civil rights movements, Rustin went to Montgomery in 1956 to advise King during the bus boycott. Rustin intentionally remained in the background, advising colleagues that his presence in Montgomery should remain clandestine. However, when Montgomery commissioners charged civil rights leaders for illegal organizing, it was Rustin who proposed that the accused turn themselves in to authorities before arrest warrants were issued. Later, on Rustin's advice, King banished firearms from his household, marking a turn in the moral temper of the civil rights movement. However, Rustin's presence eventually drew attention, and he was extracted from Montgomery after a local newspaper alleged that he was wanted for inciting a riot.

Unable to participate directly in the boycott, Rustin did so by proxy from New York. He formed an organization called In Friendship in March 1956, and he publishing King's writings in the journal *Liberation*. In January 1957, Rustin and other In Friendship cofounders Ella Baker and Stanley Levison presented King with a series of working papers that served as the basis for the Southern Christian Leadership Conference (SCLC). The papers, authored by Rustin and Levison, situated the events and provided a political and structural framework for the organization, emphasizing the need for a federation of southern civil rights leaders that would coordinate mass direct action, voter education, and outreach against racial oppression. In the late 1950s, Rustin helped draft King's speeches and articles, and he coordinated his public appearances. Nonetheless, Rustin was again forced to leave his work because of his sexuality. Adam Clayton Powell Jr., an African-American congressman, threatened to announce to the press a fabricated gay coupling between Rustin and King unless they halted plans for a march at the Democratic National Convention. Rustin again put the interests of the movement before his own, voluntarily stepping down from the SCLC.

This did not end Rustin's civil rights career, however. He was once again tapped by Randolph, this time to help orchestrate the 1963 March on Washington. Originally conceived as a militant demonstration against employment discrimination, the march assumed greater breadth with the participation of major civil rights leaders. But with this participation came a number of political conflicts that Rustin and Randolph compelled to deal with. King advised the march organizers that the SCLC's primary concern was civil rights, not unemployment. Roy Wilkins of the NAACP and Whitney Young of the National Urban League sought to de-emphasize civil disobedience and militancy in fear that such action would threaten President Kennedy's proposed civil rights legislation. As a result, Rustin's conception of the march was moderated. Because of focal changes effected by Randolph's efforts to cement the participation of King and other leaders, President Kennedy publicly endorsed the March in July. Still, some leaders questioned whether Rustin, a known gay man, was an appropriate choice as the march's director. As a compromise, Randolph was named director, and, in a show of unqualified support, he named Rustin his deputy.

Randolph's support was well founded. Under Rustin's direction, the March on Washington proved to be a turning point in American history. For the first time, civil rights leaders peacefully coalesced to articulate demands for economic empowerment and civil rights. Again, Rustin's diplomatic ability to smooth over conflicts among march leaders was key. At Rustin's urging, John Lewis of the SNCC modified his speech to eliminate what Wilkins perceived as inflammatory comments. Further, when the SCLC complained that Rustin had purposely marginalized King by placing him last in the program, he explained that each of the other speakers had asked not to follow King. Rustin's instinct was correct: King's "I Have a Dream" speech was the pinnacle of the march, if not a symbolic culmination of the entire movement.

The march was equally a personal triumph for Rustin, who in seven weeks had orchestrated the largest public protest in American history. In addition to providing behind-the-scenes diplomacy, Rustin drafted multiple manuals to guide march organizers, engaged in group training sessions, and recruited a troop of plainclothes black police officers to ensure peace during the march. This work required Rustin to engage in multiple negotiations not only with the march organizers, but also with federal and municipal agencies.

Following the march, Rustin spent the last twenty years of his career with the A. Philip Randolph Institute, engaged in a broad campaign to end discrimination in labor and employment. Increasingly, this work led Rustin away from a strict focus on civil rights and toward international human rights issues. During this period of active outreach, Rustin also became publicly vocal about his gay identity, challenging the civil rights establishment to adopt an agenda more inclusive of black gay men and lesbians and urging community leaders to respond to the ravages of the HIV/AIDS epidemic. Following a humanitarian trip to Haiti, Rustin died from cardiac arrest on August 24, 1987, at the age of seventy-five.

SEE ALSO *Civil Rights Movement; Heterosexism and Homophobia; Powell, Adam Clayton, Jr.*

BIBLIOGRAPHY

Anderson, Jervis, and Bayard Rustin. 1997. *Troubles I've Seen, a Biography*. New York: Harper Collins.

Carbado, Devon W., and Donald Weise, eds. 2003. *Time on Two Crosses: The Collected Writings of Bayard Rustin*. San Francisco: Cleis Press.

D'emilio, John. 2003. *Lost Prophet: The Life and Times of Bayard Rustin*. New York: Free Press.

Levine, Daniel. 2000. *Bayard Rustin and the Civil Rights Movement*. New Brunswick, NJ: Rutgers University Press.

Rustin, Bayard. 2006. *Strategies for Freedom: The Changing Patterns of Black Protest*. New York: Columbia University Press.

———, Ed Edwin, and Walter Neagle. 1988. *The Reminiscences of Bayard Rustin*. New York: Columbia University Oral History Research Office.

Woodward, C. Vann, ed. 1971. *Down the Line: The Collected Writings of Bayard Rustin*. Chicago: Quadrangle Books.

Devon W. Carbado

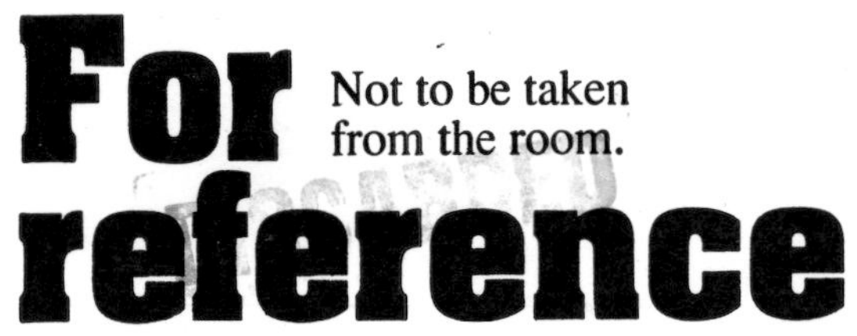
For
Not to be taken
from the room.
reference